THE NATCHEZ COURT RECORDS, 1767-1805
ABSTRACTS OF EARLY RECORDS

Compiled by

MAY WILSON McBEE

CLEARFIELD

Reprinted for
Clearfield Company, Inc. by
Genealogical Publishing Co., Inc.
Baltimore, Maryland
1994, 2003

International Standard Book Number: 0-8063-1452-4

Originally published: Greenwood, Mississippi, 1953
Reprinted: Genealogical Publishing Co., Inc.
Baltimore, 1979

Reprinted from a volume in the Franklin Parish Library,
Winnsboro, Louisiana
Library of Congress Catalogue Card Number 79-88259
Made in the United States of America

PREFACE

The Natchez District consisted of territory that now forms five Mississippi counties, Wilkinson, Adams, Jefferson, Clairborne and Warren, as well as Franklin and part of Amite, which were taken from Adams and Wilkinson in 1809. However, only the western fringes of the last two counties were settled before the American occupation.

Being one of a number of Districts in the Province of West Florida, Natchez was ruled by the British from Pensacola, the Capital of the Province. In the Province of Louisiana, of which the District became a part when taken by the Spanish in 1779, Natchez was apparently also governed directly from its Capital, New Orleans, for more than a year. But after the short-lived insurrection at Natchez in 1781, a Commandant was placed in the district to govern the affairs of the inhabitants and to record all transactions, arbitrations and matters that come before a tribunal. Thus the court records of the Natchez District during the Spanish regime are all available from 1781 to 1798. Whereas, although the Manuscript Division of the Library of Congress has procured from the Public Records Office, of London, photostats of the records of the Province of West Florida, seventy volumes in all, material on one district is difficult to segregate. The Secretary's Account Books were the most helpful. Among the Mississippi Provincial Archives at the Department of Archives and History, Jackson, Miss., is a one-volume transcription from the Public Records Office, of London, of all the British West Florida land grants in the State. This was procured by Dr. Dunbar Rowland when he was Archivist and he included the list of these grants in Volume One of his History of Mississippi. Practically all of these British land grants in the Natchez District, as well as transfers of them, appear in the Spanish records and in the abstracts of title submitted to the United States for confirmation of land in the District, under the title of Written Evidences. The above records are given in entirety in this volume, hence no separate section is devoted to the period of British rule.

The Natchez Records comprise seven volumes, lettered A, B, C, D, E, F and G. They were arranged chronologically, translated, abstracted and transcribed by "David Turner, Keeper and Translator of the Spanish Records of the Mississippi Territory, at Washington, the Capital of the Mississippi Territory." The first was completed 31 March 1817 and the others at intervals of a few months, the last ending September 1818. The original papers from which these translations were made are in three languages, French, Spanish and English, and are now bound in forty volumes. These are invaluable in identification by signatures, etc. Both sets of the records are in the office of the Chancery Clerk of Adams County, at Natchez, Mississippi, in a modern one-story Records Building, adjoining the Court House.

To a dear little lady, of fine Virginia lineage, who enjoyed acquiring books about her ancestors, a friend mentioned the publication of the Court Records of a certain Virginia County where a branch of her family had lived. "Court Records!" exclaimed the lady, aghast, "Why, my ancestors were nice people! They didn't get into Court Records!"

May Wilson McBee

Greenwood, Mississippi,
November 9, 1953.

TABLE OF CONTENTS

NOTE: The alphabetical sequence of family names in the index is sometimes interrupted, especially in names beginning with the letters Ca, Co, Ga, Har, Hut, McCo, McCr, McCu, and Wal. Since some names are therefore out of order, the reader is advised to check the index carefully.

NATCHEZ COURT RECORDS, 1781-1798

BOOK A

Page 1 Appointment of Guardian.

29 July 1781. On information received on the death of Elizabeth Alston, late wife of John Alston, a fugitive Rebel of this District of Natchez, at present with the'nation of Indians, called "Chits" [Chittimaches], where he has taken refuge with most of his property, consisting of slaves, cattle and money, leaving his wife and children in this District, with a part of his slaves for their support, as also cattle, horses, hogs and sheep and a few articles of furniture of little value, thereupon, we, Charles de Grandpre, Lt. Col. of the Regiment of Louisiana, Civil and Military Commandant of the Post and District of Natchez, have appointed Alexander McIntosh, a resident of this Post of long standing, Curator and Guardian to the six children present, (the other being with his father), now considered orphans, knowing no person more worthy to fulfil that charge with probity and disinterestness. p. 2. The six children, minors, are Anne, aged 14; William 12; Jacob 11; Solomon 6; Lucy 7 and Henry 5. As respects the eldest son, Louis, he is not considered as coming within the curator's charge. Said Alexander McIntosh has accepted the same, Wm. Pounteney as surety, who has signed with said curator in the presence of Luis Perez de Bellegarde and Don Joaquim Ossorno, Lt. and Sub. Lt. of Regiment of Louisiana. // 29 July 1781. In order to proceed with inventory, appraisers are named: Isaac Johnson and William Ferguson, residents of this Post, who sign with the same witnesses and Charles de Grandpre. // 13 July 1781. Inventory of Alston Estate.

Slaves: Ranter, native of N. C., aged 35, $350
Jane, his wife, nat. of Va., aged 22, $300
Sarah, their dau., aged 11, $280
Cruce, their son, aged 20 mos., $165
(3) Joseph, nat. of Jamaica, aged 28, $350
Diana, nat. of Guinea, aged 35, $250
Sam, their son, aged 7, $140
Susanna, their dau., aged 5, $130
Anne, nat. of Va., aged 25, $300
Rose, her dau., aged 7, $140
David, her son, aged 4, $130
Phillip, her son, aged, 20 mos., $75

p. 3 (cont.) It being noon, we have adjourned for two hours and said curator and guardian, appraisers and witnesses have signed with us, the Commandant, Grandpre. // The two hours of adjournment having expired, the inventory continued:

Patsey, nat. of Va., aged 22, $300
Stephen, her son, aged 7, $135
Magdalen, nat. of nation called "Nard", aged 29, $280
Mary, nat. of Senegal Nation, aged 37, $250

p. 4. Moveables. // 31 July 1781. Inventory continued. Horned cattle, etc. // p. 5. Lands and Buildings. Tract in the District of Natchez, 4 leagues from the Fort; 150 square arpents cleared and tillable, 650 arpents not cleared; 35 acres in corn; on which land a Dwelling House, 24 feet long by 16 feet, bounded by land of Daniel Perry on one side and on Widow Holmes on the other; with Tobacco House and 15 negro cabbins, parks and enclosures, appraised at $1000. // Titles and Papers: The children have declared that the trunk in the above inventory was filled with effects and sealed, at the house of William McIntosh, as also the papers delivered to said McIntosh, by their deceased mother. // p. 6. 1 Aug 1781. In continuation of above inventory, have proceeded to the examination of trunk. Alexander McIntosh, assisted by Richard Harrison, John Ellis and the Sub. Lt. of Reg. Joaquim Ossorno, and the appraisers Wm. Ferguson and Francis Farrell. First: Sheets, underclothes and other linens. Memo: The whole left for the use of the children. // Titles and Papers: An account book, delivered to curator to examine and ascertain the balance, (marked A); bill of sale from John George to John Alston, dated 20 Feb. 1770, (marked B); two letters from William Alston, dated 29 Aug. 1775 and

4 May 1775, (marked C); an account between Jacob and John Alston, his son, no date, (marked D); will of (7) John Jordain, dated 28 Oct. 1757, (marked E); letter from William Lemos, dated 28 Oct. 1773, (marked G); letter from William Alston, dated 6 Oct. 1775, (marked H); bill of sale of slave from John Samuel to John Alston, dated 7 Sept. 1777, (marked I); bill of sale of 6 slaves from the Sieur Valens to Stephen Comins, dated 26 June 1777, (marked L); bill of sale of negro from Jacob John to John Alston, dated 10 Sept. 1768, (marked M), letter from William Alston, 20 Aug. 1773, (marked F); account between Anthony Hutchins and John Alston, by which a ballance of 978 pounds of tobacco appears owing said Hutchins by Alston, (marked N); a bundle of receipts and settled accounts, (marked O). // p. 8. 11 Aug. 1781. Inventory continued. Cattle, horses and hogs. // p.9. Debts outstanding from account book: John Turner, absconded, $81; Philip Alston, absconded, $41; James Truly $28; Daniel Bush $74; William O'Neal $4; William Smith $4. // Aug. 11 1781. Above inventory approved by Alexander McIntosh and Grandpre. // p. 10. To the Civil and Military Commandant of the Post of Natchez, Alexander McIntosh, Curator and Guardian, has the honor to represent that his duties oblige him to take suitable means for the security of the property of his wards and asks for authority to transport as soon as possible the slaves to New Orleans where they may be legally sold or hired out for the benefit of the minors, being daily exposed to public Robbers who retreat into Indian Nations where sd John Alston, their master, has taken refuge with 11 others of his best slaves, suspicion having arisen that they have been enticed to rejoin said Alston. It being impossible to sell cattle and tools here at this time for want of specie, and, the inhabitants being poor, if sold on credit, these people, being without faith, would later abscond to the Nation, or to one of the Provinces to the Northeast, or to the Belle-Riviere (Ohio) and never heard of again. Your petitioner knows of no better expedient than to keep the cattle until Autumn and then have them driven to New Orleans to be sold. Said p. 11. petitioner cannot be answerable for cattle and other effects since they are killed daily by brigands . . . The five children, his wards, are continually in company with evil disposed persons, receiving from them bad advice. Your petitioner wishes authority by you to send them also to New Orleans where he proposes to place the two girls in the Convent and to put the boys to a trade. Until it can be practical to convert the property to specie, Daniel Perry will take care of it, particularly the cattle, for $15.00 per month. Aug. 11, 1781. // Approved by Grand-Pre. // p. 12. Personnaly appeared Daniel Perry and Alexander McIntosh who declared that on 3 Aug., last, Henry Alston, one of the minor heirs died, and on the 2nd day of same Month died a negro boy, named "Stephen", aged 7 yrs., belonging to sd estate. 11 Aug. 1781. // p. 13. 31 July 1781. Petition of Alexander McIntosh that his wards are destitute of necessities and cloathing; that the cattle are without salt and sufficient corn, asks that a female slave be sold and that Daniel Perry be appointed to manage the plantation. // Notice of sale of negro girl to be advertised to take place 1 August. Grandpre. p. 14. 1 Aug. 1781. At the Hall of our Court, in the presence of Alexander McIntosh, curator and guardian, and of Francois Farrell, surgeon and resident of this place, Richard Bacon, William Hurlbert, Richard Harrison, John Ellis and Joaquim Ossorno, negro Girl, Sarah, aged 12, sold to Don Joaquim Ossorno, the highest bidder, for $250. Signed by all above.

Fees of the Commandant and others:	Rials		
1 sitting at the sale	22		
1 signature in full	4		
Proces Verbal	12		
Petition	5		
Order	2		
Advertisement	8		
Crying Sale	8		
Copies			
4 pages of writing	8		
4 Initials	8		
1 Signature in full	4		
Equalization	8	Dolls.	Rials
	89	11	1

---

p. 15. 30 July 1781. Petition of William Ferguson, one of the principal creditors of William Vousdan, and he, being sent from here, Monsieur De la Villebeurre had put the management of his affairs under my direction and as the estate is still considerably indebted to me, asks to be invested with the authority to manage estate, as the wife, in his opinion, is not capable of settling the accounts of her husband. // Natchez, 1 Aug. 1781. Confirmed by Grandpre. // p. 16. William Pounteny, a resident of Natchez, security for William Ferguson.

---

12 Sept. 1781. Petition of Alexander McIntosh, curator and guardian of minor heirs of Alston, perceiving loss from epidemic of a great number of cattle daily, asks for sale of all those belonging to said minors, payable in one year from day of adjudication, with good and sufficient security. // An advertisement shall be posted giving notice to the Public that a sale of the cattle mentioned will take place on Saturday, morning the 15th inst. Grandpre. 12 Sept. 1781. // p. 17. On morning of 15 Sept. 1781, proceedings of the above mentioned sale in the presence of curator and guardian and others assisting. Buyers: Sieur St. Germain, surety Francois Farrell; Wm. Brocus, surety Abraham Germain; Alexander McIntosh, surety Francois Farrell, Sieur —— Cadet, surety Alexander McIntosh; Richard Swayze, surety Justus King; John Griffin, surety Justus King; Anthony Hutchins, surety Alexander McIntosh; Alexander McIntosh, surety George Rapalje; Sieur Baker, surety David Mitchell; Elijah Swayze, surety Richard Swayze; Francis Spain, surety James Truly; Wm. Brocus, surety Winsor Pipes; George Rapalje, surety Anthony Hutchins; several to Alexander McIntosh for cash. Total sale $964 and 6 rials. Witnesses: Alexander McIntosh, Francis Farrell, Richard Bacon, Henry Roach, St. Germain, William Hulbert, Daniel Ogden, John Townshend, Josanna S-----l. Charles de Grandpre. // p. 20. 29 Sept. 1781. Charles de Grandpre, Commandant of the Post and District of Natchez, at request of Alexander McIntosh, curator and guardian to the children of late Elizabeth Alston and John Alston, absconded, have proceeded to the sale of the remainder of cattle belonging to the estate and some furniture and tools, the purchasers to pay cash. Buyers: Alexander McIntosh, Daniel Perry, John Row, John Peralto, John Heartly and Anthony Hutchins. Total $1518. // p. 22. 29 March 1782. Exposed to sale by Chas. de Grandpre one old broken desk belonging to Rebel, John Alston, found in possession of William Brocus, which having been cried at public sale in presence of Francois Farrell; Don Estevan Minor, Silas Crane and other assistants, to Sergeant of this garrison, Manuel Gutterez for five dollars. Observation: The amount of all the articles sold for cash was received by the guardian, at that time, who was the late Alexander McIntosh, to whom I also paid the sums that I had received which are marked with letter "P" opposite each article and he was directed by me when he went down to New Orleans with the slaves belonging to the estate to deliver to the Supreior Government of this Province a copy of this sale, also a part of the proceeds thereof, namely the whole amount that he had received as above mentioned and for which Anne McIntosh, his widow is now accountable. (p. 23) Every article opposite to which appears a "P" in this form in the margin, with date, are the sums I have received and which I have paid to Lt. Col. Don Pedro Piernas, Commandant of this Post. Total $320.

---

p. 23. 17 Sept. 1781. James Truly and Peter Hawkins, sureties for Henry Roach, for the safety of the property of the children of the late Campbell, who are at present in Georgia, in America, claimed by Henry Roach out of the estate of Philip Alston, a fugitive Rebel, who was executor of the will of the late John Campbell and who, as such, was in possession of the whole property. Creditors are now claiming the amount of their debts. Wit: Francois Farrell, Alexander McIntosh, Anthony Hutchins.

---

p. 24. 21 Sept. 1781. We, Charles de Grandpre, Civil and Military Commandant of the Post and District of Natchez, acting as Notary Public (there being none in the Province), proceeded to the description and inventory of the effects of John Blommart, Chief of the Rebels of this District, contained in four old trunks or chests, which we have sent for from the house of Sieur Ellis, at the White Cliffs, by the Sergeant of this Garrison, accompanied by Sieur Kennedy, late clerk to said John Blommart, which said trunks we found open, the locks broken and the seals torn, which had been put on them by Mr. de la Morandiere, without having taken an inventory of their contents which we have sent for at the request of Anthony Hutchins and Ellis who represent that the contents are exposed to being stolen. Wherefore, having caused them to be conveyed to the Fort of this Post, we have proceeded to open said chests and take an inventory in presence of Don Luis Perez de Bellegarde, Don Joaquim Ossorno, Alexander McIntosh and the Sergeant, Manuel Guttierez. And for the appraisement thereof we have appointed and do hereby appoint Richard Bacon and Pierre Nitard.

Inventory

13 silver spoons, much worn and very light; 8 teaspoons; one small powder box, one pair of small pincers and a pair of buckles, all silver; one small wooden box containing two other tea boxes, two small scales with their weights, for gold, another small toilet box with a string of beads; 1 large writing

box of Russian leather, empty, one tin tea-board with 4 small plates of the same. 1 brass graphometer, not complete, . . . two plated flambeaux with their sockets and two others without sockets and a brass candle stick, . . . a calico mosquito bar; two looking glasses, six inches broad and near an ell in length; ten books in folio and seven in quarto, of divers English authors, three account books . . . one small tin box containing four oil and vinegar cruets; two medallions, one gold of the Freemasons Society and the other silver, one Christal Cylinder. All above found in one large trunk. In another old trunk were found one hundred and twenty-eight books in quarto and six in folio, of divers English authors. In another old trunk: a quantity of Papers and one iron-mounted sabre and one silver-mounted small sword, the blade broken . . . p. 26 . . . kitchen and farm utensils and tools . . . which were all the effects found in the Fort belonging to John Blommart. // p. 27. 30 Oct. 1781. In virtue of the order of the Superior Government of this Province, we, Charles de Grandpre, etc., have seized and confiscated, at the dwelling of William Ferguson, in the hands of the son of the said John Blommart, the effects hereinafter mentioned . . . in the presence of Don Juan de la Villebeuvre, Don Luis Perez de Bellegarde, Don Marcos de Villiers, Capt., Lt., and Sub. Lt. of the Regiment of Louisiana and the sergeant of this Garrison, Manuel Guttierez, Keeper of the King's Store at this Post, all witnesses to the said inventory and appraisement. Four books of accounts, in English, of which an examination will be made when an interpreter shall be procured, four books of different authors, one saddle and bridle. // Effects found at the dwelling of Sieur Ellis at the White Cliffs: Three woman's robes, one of green damask, one linen and the other black and white striped silk; one old black robe, a calico Bedspread, an old muslin apron, one linen handkerchief, one old Powder-bag, (p. 28) two gauze head-dresses, a linen pillow case, . . . two pair of Ruffles, two of Gauze, One green cotton velvet coat, . . . two woman's fans, two pair of Pigeon-coloured Breeches, another vest, three pair of silk stockings and three pair of cotton ditto. One yellow silk bed-spread . . . // Found at one of Sieur Blommart's plantations: Three pictures . . . one Lanthorn . . . One Cypress table; an andiron and pair of tongs . . . (farm tools, cattle, horses, hogs). Plantation near St. Catherine's Creek, 44 arpents of cleared land in cultivation and 56 arpents not cleared, bounded on one side by the land of John Farquhar, on the other by that of William Smith, on which a dwelling house (p. 29) 40 ft. in length by 18 ft. in breadth, with doors, windows, locks, glasses, etc., an indifferent barn, 30 ft. in length by 15 ft. in breadth, and three old cabins, not enclosed. (Note in margin: This settlement, is on land belonging to the King and he never obtained permission to settle on it, the same being within the limits reserved by His Majesty. B. T.) At the dwelling of Patrick Foley: Two mares and one filley, one ass, one broken round table. Effects found in a house belonging to Sieur Blommart in the Town of Natchez, on the river: Two large pictures, one small ditto; one small press or corner cupboard with glazed doors; one broken chest of drawers . . . one pair large scales hung with chains with seven English 56-lb weights, one 14-lb. and one 28-lb. Lot of ground, 100 ft in front, the same in depth, on which stands a framed house, 40 ft in length and 20 ft in breadth, with floored galleries front and back, containing one parlour, two chambers and two cabinets on the back gallery, with doors, windows, locks, hooks, etc. An old store house, 18 ft in length by 16 ft in breadth with a loft and a cabinet and having one door and one window. An old Cabbin 14 ft by 12 ft, planked and roofed with boards, with one door, locks, and hinges. p. 30. On same ground an unfinished frame storehouse . . . The moveable effects have been deposited in the Store at this Fort and delivered in charge of the sergeant, Manuel Guttierez. At the same time, was confiscated a negro man, named "Francis", aged 60, appraised at $150; a woman name "Eleanora", a native of Guinea, aged 18, with her dau. "Betty", aged one year, $300. (Note: The negro man, woman and her dau. have been sent to New Orleans to the Acting Governor, Don Pedro Piernas. Grandpre.) 26 Oct. 1781. Proceeded to seizure and confiscation to the use of the King, sundry effect belonging to John Blommart, Chief of the Rebels in this District, found at the dwelling house of John Smith, Lieutenant of said Rebels, in presence of Messrs. Estevan Minor and St. Germain, and for appraisment thereof appointed Messrs. Pierre Nitard and Michel Lopez. One still, capactiy 160 gallons, with its cap and worm; another, capacity 60 gallons, with its cap and worm. Which was all found at the dwelling of said Smith. p. 31. We have seized and confiscated to the use of the King, a tract of land at the place called "Bayou Creek", 650 arpents, bounded on north by lands of Widow Truly, nw by land of Lum, ne by land of Abraham Adams, and by land not granted, upon which tract there is no settlement. One tract, 100 arpents, on "Bayou Cr."* bounded on all sides by vacant land, on other by Samuel Osborn. [*"Bayou Creek" is apparently Cole's Creek, which was at that time called "Boyd's Creek".] // Another tract of land on the River Mississippi, one quarter of a league above "Bayou Creek", 200 arpents, bounded on two sides by lands not granted, on 3rd by the River, and on the other by lands of the heirs of Alexander Boyd, being a Cypress Swamp and without settlement. Another tract not settled, at the place called "Red Cliffs" (Ecors Rouge) on Bayou aux Boeufs, on (p. 32) the right side and back from the River, 500 arpents of prarie land, bounded on all sides by vacant land. A tract of land, situate at the same place as the preceding, belonging to the late Mary Duyer, wife of John Blommart, 200 arpents, bounded on three sides by vacant lands and on the other by those of the said John Blommart. A tract of land, on East River which falls into Mobile Bay, 119 arpents, bounded by land of Robert Russell and Israel Borthmar. A lot in the Town of Pensacola, No. 102. A tract of 15 arpents in West Florida, at "Roebuck Bay", near Pensacola.

Debts Outstanding to John Blommart

Notes:

Silas Crane, $16, 5 June 1778
Henry Bradley, of Opelousas, $15, 20 Dec. 1777
Wm. Bush, of the Illinois, $19, 5 Aug. 1772
Chas. Larche, of Pointe Coupee, $8, 8 July, 1774
Anthony Baker, of Opelousas, $12, 16 Aug. 1780
Christian Bingaman, absconded, $18, 7 March 1778
Isaac Johnson, of Natchez, $7, 3 May 1780
Samuel Heady, of Natchez, $30, 7 May 1774
p. 33.
Thos. Oakes, a soldier, dec'd. at the Illinois, $64. (n. d.)
L. Charleville, of the Illinois, $11, 1 April 1776
Daniel Lewis, $3, 11 Oct. 1777. (decd. and his widow residing at Baton Rouge, m. to ______________ Carpenter.)
James Strother, the King's blacksmith, at the Arkansas, $116, 3 Aug. 1774
George Bailey, of Natchez, $18, 22 Oct. 1780
Wm. Brown, of the Illinois, $30, 13 March 1776
John Smith, $50, 18 Dec. 1780. (Sd Smith a Prisoner at N. O.)
Israel Mathis, absconded, $13, 8 Dec. 1780
Alphonso Roy, of Pointe Coupee, $64, 25 July 1775
Wm. Brown, of the Illinois, $21, 11 March 1776
Samuel Miller, of Opelousas, $26, 7 March 1778
Thos. Yarrow, of Natchez, $30, 28 Dec. 1780
Anthony Brabason, of Natchez, $12, 10 Sept. 1780
Jacob Darsk. of Arkansas, $25, 13 Feb. 1774
Andrew Nott, of Natchez, $25, 20 Jan. 1780
Sarah Smith, of Natchez, $30, 5 Dec. 1781
p. 34.
Samuel Henry, of Natchez, $15, 14 Feb. 1780
Michael Jackson, Pensacola, $158, 1 Sept. 1779
Robert Smart, (believed to be dead), $52, 16 Sept. 1780
Earl Douglass, $45, 15 Apr. 1780. (he is at Natchez)
Jeremiah Routh, $150, 12 Feb. 1780, at Natchez.
William Bush, of the Illinois, $24, 25 Mch. 1773
James Gillason, decd. in the District, $612, 18 May 1780
(Note: The land on which Wm. Brocus dwells belongs to him.)
William Joyner, on Mobile River, $13, 15 March 1773
James Cole, of Opelousas, on William Vousdan, in favor of
John Blommart, for $9, 26 Feb. 1780, an order.
Order James Cole on Wm. Ferguson, $13, 26 Sept. 1780
" James Cole on James Carter, $115, 26 Feb. 1780
Note Christian Bingaman, absconded, 170 bu. of corn, 6 Dec. 1777
" William Hulbert, 200 bu. corn, 6 Dec. 1777. (He is at Natchez.)

p. 35. Acc't against Samuel Swayze passed to the order of John Blommart by Charles Persey (Percy) and Timothy Turney, $3. Order by Earl Douglass on Anthony Brabazon, in favor of John Blommart for $8, 6 April 1780.

Note on John Conty, $8, 21 Aug. 1774

Note by Cephas Kinnard, of Natchez, $14, 12 Feb. 1774

Receipt by Sieur Mesnard of Arkansas for a note drawn by Cousat, for $65, to be recovered for Blommart, dated 16 Feb. 1778. Receipt by Sieur Mesnard for four strouds rec'd. from Blommart to be delivered to Don Balthazar de Villiers, Commandant at Arkansas. Receipt from Don Balthazar de Villiers, in favor of John Blommart, for sundry notes entrusted to him for collection, dated 15 Feb. 1778.

Note by L'Etable for $46. Note by Tomelet for $120.
Receipt by Mr. Mesnard for a note by L'Esperance and Paquin.
Receipt by Mr. Mesnard for note drawn by La Jeunesse for $12.
Order by Etienne Bartholome on Pierre Borde, soldier, for $15. (n. d.)
Note by Francis Cousat $35. Being all the notes in possession of Mr. De Villiers as appears by his receipt.
p. 36. Obligation of John Louis Pochet, called "St. Germain", Interpreter to the Choctaws at Natchez, owes a balance of $1002, 27 Apr. 1774.
Note by St. Germain and George Kaiser, $1306, 21 Dec. 1774.
Note by George ______, endorsed by St. Germain, 30 Aug. 1772.
Note by Louis Sarbonneau and George Kaiser, $80, 22 Jany. 1777.

A third book containing debits and credits, witnessed by Don Estevan Minor, Aid Major of this Post and acting as Interpreter, as follows:

Silas Crane, of Natchez,
John Lum, of Natchez
p. 37.
Richard Ellis and his ch.
Earl Douglass
Christian Bingaman, absconded
Philip Alston, absconded
John Ogg
John Alston, prisoner at N. O.
John Hosteler, res. unknown
John Tally
James Truly
Luke Collins, of Opelousas
Richard Duvall
John Smith, prisoner at New Orleans
Wm. Eason, prisoner at New Orleans
Caleb Hansborough, absconded
Samuel Osborn
p. 38. William Hulbert
Thaddeus Lyman
p. 39. Benjamin Rogers, of Natchez
Philip Mulkey, absconded
James Truly, of Natchez
Henry Roach, of Natchez
William Reed, Opelousas
Edward Carol, Opelousas
Sterling Spell, of Natchez

John Watkins, absconded
Richard Bacon
George Rapalje
Zebulon Mathis, of Arkansas
Anthony Hutchins
William Case, absconded
Thomas Yarrow
John Turner, absconded
Peter Hawkins, of Natchez
Stephen Holston, of Natchez
Wm. Poultney, of Natchez
Sarah Truly, of Natchez
p. 39. Francis Spain, of Natchez
Patrick Foley, of Natchez
Jeremiah Routh, of Natchez
Elizabeth Boyd, her estate
Thomas James
Daniel Baker
Anthony Baker, of Opelousas
Ebenezer Gossett, absconded
Parker Caradine, prisoner at N. O.
Samuel Wells, Opelousas
Thompson Lyman, absconded
William Oglesby, of Natchez
Andrew Knapp, of Natchez
Nathaniel Johnson, absconded
Samuel Gibson, of Natchez

p. 40. Lists of many bundles of notes, letters and accounts; no names or other data. A bundle of papers belonging to the American Captain James Willing.
p. 41. Note by Anthony Perie, $16, 25 March 1775.
Note by Roger Ross, 29 Nov. 1777. (Deceased without property).
Note by John Farly, 29 Nov. 1777. (Res. unknown.)
Note by Nicholas Smith, $83, 11 June 1776. (Deceased at the Illinois)
Note by John Coleman, 26 March 1777. (Deceased at the Illinois.)
Note by George Rosburg, $44, 6 June 1777. (Deceased at the Illinois)
Note by Francis Rowles, 14 Oct. 1773. Res. unknown
Note by Mathias Frily, 19 Aug. 1777. Decd. Widow and prop. at Natchez.
p. 42. Note by John Armstrong, 25 Mar. 1778. (died without property)
Note by Peter Bruntoux, 24 May 1777.
Note by Jean Thommelette, 31 May 1779.
Note by John Tonny, 4 Feb. 1779.

Note by Baptiste LeMay, 19 Aug. 1775
Inventory taken in the presence of Don Estevan Minor and John Kennedy. Grandpre.
p. 43. 10 Dec. 1781, seizure and confiscation to the use of the King of effects of John Blommart found at the Bayou of Cole's Cr., consisting of the iron work of a water grist mill, with two mill stones, and for the appraisement we have appointed Richard Duvall and Pierre Nitard, witnessed by Francois Farrell and Silas Crane.

Original papers transmitted to New Orleans to Governor of this Province. This is a true copy. Natchez, 15 April 1782. Charles de Grandpre.

---

p. 44. Before me, Charles de Grandpre, Commandant of this District, and Notary Public, there being none in this Province, in the presence of Joaquim Ossorno and Luis Perez de Bellegarde, appeared Isaac Johnson, a resident of the same, who acknowledged to be indebted to Alexander McIntosh, during more than one year for $376, money lent, time of payment long since expired and having obtained from sd McIntosh a delay of two months and a half, for the payment of the sum. The sd Isaac Johnson and Mary, his wife, each for the whole and for each other, hereby promise to pay sd McIntosh at expiration of the term and give as surety a mortgage on two slaves, namely "Stephen," nat. of Carolina, aged abt. 30 and "Mary", a Hibo negro wench, aged abt 25, and generally all the property and estate of which they are now possessed. Signed by both. Wit: Joaquim Ossorno, Luis Perez de Bellegarde.

Charles de Grandpre.

Will of Robert Robinson

Robert Robinson, of the District of Natchez, in the Province of West Florida. All my moveable estate to be sold to pay (p.45) just debts and funeral charges. All my land in aforesaid district to my eight children: Robert, Rhoda, Phebe, Mary, Briant, Caleb, Joseph and John, but if any should not live to an age of 21 years land to be divided between surviving ones. Each to pay equal part of all my just debts that remain after moveables are gone. My good friends, Justus King and Richard Swayze, Jr., to take care of my estate until my children shall come to this Province either themselves or by their attorneys and until they are of age to act for themselves. The profits of the land to be used by executors at their discretion to pay debts or for the benefit of my children. 10 Oct. 1777. Signed with a mark. Wit: Silas Crane, Caleb King, Gabriel Swayze. // 27 Sept. 1778. We, Charles de Grandpre, etc., having caused the witnesses to the foregoing instrument to be cited, they have declåred the signatures thereto to be their own. In consideration of the decease of the testator, notwithstanding the number of witnesses thereto are not competent for the validity (p.46) thereof had the will been made at a period posterior, have homologated and confirmed the same, to the end that it may have full and entire effect. Charles de Grandpre.

Before Grandpre, etc., personally appeared Samuel Swayze, a resident of this District, who has sold and sells to John Heartly a negro man, named "Romeo", native of the Island of St. Christopher's in America, aged 20 yrs., whom he had of William Vousdan; for $300 to him in hand paid by Heartly in our presence., 1 Oct. 1781. Witnesses: William Ferguson and Francois Farrell who have signed with said seller and purchaser and we, the Commandant, aforesaid.

---

p. 47. Before the Commandant, etc., personally appeared David Odom, a resident of Natchez District, who sells to Parker Carradine a tract of land in this District not yet surveyed, with all the buildings and establishments thereon consisting of a house, cabins, parks and enclosures; for $100 paid, the land being bounded by Dibdal Hoth (Holt) and Mr. Stampley, on Cole's Cr. 19 Oct. 1781; witnesses Alexander McIntosh and Francis Farrell, who signed with the above, being first read according to law.

---

p. 48. Personally appeared Alexander McIntosh, a res. of Natchez, and acknowledged that he has received from Isaac Johnson and Mary Johnson the amount of their bond, dated 29 Sept. 1781, released and holding for null and void the said bond, also mortgage of two slaves. 22 Oct. 1781. Wit: Luis Perez de Bellegarde, Joaquim Ossorno.

24 Oct. 1781. On notice received of death of John Holloway, killed by the Indians, have apptd. as guardian to the children, minors, namely George 14, William 13, John 12, Robert 7, Mary 4, James 2 and Elizabeth, widow of sd John, has declared that she is seven months pregnant and has besides another daughter Elizabeth, married to Cady Rabey, and the guardianship falling naturally to the said widow, Elizabeth, we have appointed her guardian of the six children born and to the child yet to be born, which charge she willingly accepted in the presence of Isaac Johnson, Francis Farrell and William Vousdan who have signed with sd widow and Commandant. // p. 49. 24 Oct. 1781. Isaac Johnson and Daniel Perry apptd. appraisers of inventory of estate of John Holloway in presence of Elizabeth Holloway, the widow, Cady Rabey, her son-in-law, Francis Farrell and Silas Crane. Following the inventory of household goods, carpenter tools, plantation tools, animals and slaves, the widow declares that there are two cows and two calves and one heifer belonging to her eldest son given to him by James Grugg (or Gragg); p. 50. also two cows and two calves belonging to her eldest daughter, Elizabeth, given to her on her marriage to Cadey Rabey. And as respects the plantation it belong to Joshua Howard, who is absent from this District.

---

p. 51. 16 Nov. 1781. Seizure and confiscation to the use of the King of animals, cattle, horses and hogs belonging to Jacob Winfry, Capt. of the Rebels in Dist. of Natchez, now in prison in N. O., found in possession of William Haussy in virtue of a bill of sale to him for same by sd Jacob Winfree and in payment whereof the sd William Haussy had given sd Winfree a negro man named "Benjamin", aged about 35 yrs., nat. of Maryland, together with a gold watch, the sd sale having been executed at the time when the rebels were in possession of the Fort of this Post, whereby the said is rendered invalid and whereupon, in pursuance of orders of the Superior Government of this Province, we have proceeded to the seizure, conficsation and sale of sd animals found in possession of sd Haussy, to the use of the King. Upon seizure of other effects of sd Jacob Winfree was found the (p. 52) negro man and the watch before mentioned, belonging to sd Haussy and by him given to Jacob Winfree in payment of the animals. These were delivered to Wm. Haussey and he receipted for them in the presence of Francois Farrell and Richard Harrison, 20 Nov. 1781.

---

p. 53. 16 Nov. 1781. Petition of Mary Carradine that she was a widow with three children when she married Parker Carradine and had possession of 4 negroes and much other property belonging to her three children and is big with another and in much distress, not having wherewith to subsist herself and her children. She asks for help. Signed Mary Carradine. // To Francois Farrell, Attorney for the District of Natchez. Your petitioner, Mary Carradine, according to your orders presents the several persons who have knowledge that she was married to Parker Carradine. David Odom declares he was present at the time when Mary Carradine was married to Parker Carradine and he was the person sent for the minister who married them. Nov. 16, 1781. // Wm. Brocus declared that he was present when Mary Carradine was married to Parker Carradine and that sd Mary had 4 slaves of her own, as likewise hogs, horned cattle, horses etc. (p. 54) Signed with a mark. // 16 Nov. 1781. Wm. Brocus and David Odom declared on oath that Mary Carradine, otherwise Mary Abraham Odum, is verily the wife of Parker Carradine, the Rebel arrested and sent to N. O. and his property confiscated to the use of the King, they having been at the marriage by James Smert (Smart or Smith) in South Carolina where they at that time resided; and which sd Mary Abraham Odam has also declared on oath that she was married to sd Carradine, being then the widow of John Collins (or Collier) by whom she had issue: three children, now living, namely: John, aged 15, Joshua, aged 13 and William, aged 12 years six months. When she was married the second time her property was: 4 slaves, "Peter" aged 30, nat. of Guinea, "Raphael" aged 16, nat. of S. C., "Anny" aged 30, nat. of Va., the fourth was a negro boy who was exchanged for cattle during her community with sd Parker Carradine. She lost vouchers in her emigration from South Carolina to the Dist. of Natchez. Wit: Estevan Minor, Francis Farrell, William Vousdan. // p. 55. 16 Nov. 1781 In consequence of the foregoing declarations of William Brocus and David Odom which appear to verify the property of Mary Carradine and upon the representation by her made, have left in her possession 3 slaves (named as above) and other property until the determination of the Superior Government may be known, William Brocus and John Lusk being securety for the safe keeping of sd slaves and cattle.

---

p. 56. Petition of Widow Coleman, now the wife of Emanuel Madden, begs leave to present a statement of the property of her late husband, dec'd. They were married 12 May 1762. When they married they began the world poor. Her husband was killed by the Indians on 15 May 1781 and at his death left the following property: 5 negroes (named, two natives of S. C., the rest of Africa.), horses, cattle, hogs and 100 arpents on Second Cr., 4 miles from Fort Panmur, near lands of Jacob Winfree and William Case. An agreement respecting the land made with the owner, Robert Robertson, was that, if the Country should remain in possession of Spain, they were to give a horse and two half Johannes; but if the country should revert to the English, they should pay $300. The debts of the estate at the time of the death of Mr. Coleman: $100 to Mr. Farquhar; $39 to Richard Ellis, Sr.; $20 to William Case; $10 to Abraham Horton; $2 to Ebenezer Pipes, $4 to John Bisland; and $2 to Daniel Mygett. The children are: John 15, William 12, Judah 10, Mary 5, James 2. She declares that the above is a true inventory of the estate of John Coleman, her late husband, decd. Natchez, 28 Oct. 1781. Signed Patience Coleman, now Patience Madden. Wit: Francois Farrell, Atty. for the Dist. of Natchez. // (p. 57) Petition of Patience Madden that since the death of her husband she has married Emanuel Madden and has a certificate of same from the minister. As she married before giving an inv. of estate of first husband, she is forbidden by law to be guardian of her children and asks that her present husband be apptd guardian of the minors. Natchez. 28 Oct. 1781. // 22 Nov. 1781, on above petition, Emanuel Madden apptd guardian to his wife's children by her 1st marriage, as named above, likewise the child of wh. she declares herself pregnant. Wit: Francis Farrell, Silas Crane. // Inventory of est. of John Coleman. Appraisers: William Ferguson and Stephen Mayes. pp. 58-59.

---

p. 60. 24 Nov. 1781. Notice received of death of Elizabeth Boyd, late wife of Alexander Boyd, also dec'd, Isaac Johnson is appointed curator and guardian of children, minors, namely: Alexander 16, Hannah and Anne, twins, 6. Wit: Philip Pleasant Turpin, Josiah Flower. (p. 61). Isaac Johnson asks for an inventory as the estate is going to wreck. 24 Nov. 1781. Earl Douglass and James Simmons appointed appraisers. Inventory: household goods, tools, utensils and animals. (p. 62) Lands and buildings. One tract of 77 arpents on Cole's Cr, two small log houses, parks, fences and orchard, ten arpents ready for cultivation. Titles and Papers: Bond of Philip Alston, absconded, in favor of Alexander Boyd, deposited in the Register's Office of this Province; Note by John Blommart for $250; Note by Louis Bingaman $47; Note by William Collerston $21; Note by Jeremiah Routh $5; Note by Philip Alston $66. (p. 63) Surety of Isaac Johnson as guardian and curator of estate of minors of Alexander and Elizabeth Boyd, Earl Douglas. Wit: Don Estevan Minor, Don Marcos de Villiers, Don Juan de Villebeuvre. (p. 64). Natchez 24 Nov. 1781, Advertisements shall be posted at the usual places in this District giving notice that a sale of the estate of Boyd will take place 12 Dec. Grandpre. // 12 Dec. 1781. Result of sale, in presence of Isaac Johnson, gdn., Francois Farrell, Saml. Heady, Wm. Curtis, Earl Douglass, Silas Crane, Samuel Henry, and James Truly. Buyers and sureties; (p. 65) Jeremiah Bryan, surety James Truly; Isaac Johnson, surety Francois Farrell, Robert Ford, surety Samuel Heady, Samuel Heady, surety John Terry, Widow Jane Osborn, surety Jeremiah Bryan, James Truly, surety Francis Farrell. (p. 66) 72 arpents of land on Cole's Creek, with an orchard of 5 arpents and a dwelling house, bounded on one side by land of Alexander McIntosh, and on another by that of estate of Samuel Osborn, other sides vacant, to Jeremiah Bryan, the highest bidder for $101, with surety James Truly. Sold for cash: Isaac Johnson: 50 bu corn for $20, cattle for $70 and hogs for $30; Widow Osborn, a spinning wheel for $1 and 4 rials; Silas Crane . . . for $4.

---

p. 67. 24 Nov. 1781. On notice received of the death of Samuel Osborn, residing in this District on Cole's Creek, Commandant apptd. Jane Osborn, his widow, as guardian of their four children: Samuel 11, "Bud"*8, Sarah 6 and "Buldah" 4, and of the child yet to be born. Wit: Isaac Johnson, Josiah Flower, Philip Pleasant Turpin. (p. 68) Earl Douglass and James Simmons apptd appraisers. Inventory; Household goods, tools and utensils, slaves (2), animals. (p. 69) Tract of 300 arpents at Cole's Cr., bounded by land of Jeremiah Routh on one side and by Jeremiah Bryan, four houses, with parks and enclosures, orchard and garden $300. [Note*: The second son is called "Boyd".] // Debts outstanding: The said widow declares that there is an account in favor of the estate against Thaddeus Lyman in the hand of Don Juan de Villebeuvre of which she does not recollect the amount; an account of $50 against James Ellison, which he acknowledges; acc't of $43 agst. Thomas James; $19 against John Blommart. Total appraisal $2123. // p. 70. 19 Jany. 1782. Widow Jane Osborn requested that the whole of the estate of her late husband, Samuel Osborn, as contained and described in inventory may be allowed and adjudged to her for the amount of the appraisement, which was allowed and she to give good and sufficient security for such part as may be inherited by the children from their late father. Isaac Johnson and

James Truly voluntarily offered themselves as joint sureties of the widow Jane Osborn for the whole estate, not only for any losses or damage occurring to the said estate of the children but also if the same should be destroyed or carried off by the Indians.

---

p. 71. 26 Nov. 1781. In pursuance of the memorial of Mary Smith, wife of John Smith who acted as Lt. during the Rebellion in this Province, and since sent to N. O., have left in power and possession of said Mary Smith the plantation, one negro named "Solomon" aged 40 years, of the Mandingo nation, 29 head of cattle, 4 horses, 24 hogs, besides those running in the woods, of which the number is unknown, all the utensils and furniture for the safety of all which she has given Alexander McIntosh for surety, the said animals and other property to be forth coming when required by law. Wit: Richard Harrison, Francois Farrell. Signed by all of the above.

---

p. 72. 1 Dec. 1781. Personally appeared George Rapalje who sells to James Wilson, here present, 100 square arpents of land on St. Catherine's Creek, on which a dwelling and two negro cabins, bounded by lands of Samuel Gibson, Widow Goodney, Justus King and Francois Farrell, for $100 paid in cash. Done (p. 73) at Fort Panmur at Natchez in the presence of Francois Farrell and Silas Crane. Signed by all the above and Grandpre.

Inventory of the estate of Richard Thompson late of Natchez, deceased. (Endorsed: Dec. 21, 1781) Among items: One plantation on St. Catherine's Cr., 500 arpents . . . $500; another on Cole's Cr. of 100 arpents . . . $100. Total inventory $1889. (p. 74) Appraisement by Silas Crane and James Harman. Names of children and their ages:

Mary Thompson b. Oct. 20, 1765
John Thompson b. Jany. 23, 1767
Sarah Thompson b. Aug. 27, 1769
Nathan Thompson b. Jany. 3, 1771
Thomas Thompson b. Aug. 27, 1773
Matthew Thompson b. June 27, 1775 [This should be Martha.]
Richard Thompson b. Jany. 2, 1775

William Smith married the Widow Thompson, 16 Nov.,1778; when he married he had nothing, and after sd marriage obtained letters of administration from Government of Pensacola which were deposited . . . (obliterated) . . . William Heson and Capt. Philip Barbour were sureties, but Capt. Barbour having emigrated, the matter remained in Statu quo. Signed William Smith.

---

p. 74. 21 Dec. 1781. Having attended the dwelling of Samuel Swayze to proceed to the seizure of the whole estate of Bennet Bellu, an inhabitant of this District, being bankrupt and having a few days since, with five or six other inhabitants, withdrawn to the Indian Nation calles "Chitz" have, for the Appraisement, apptd. James Harman and Winsor Pipes who have accepted same. Wit: Francois Farrell, Don Estevan Minor. (p. 75) Inventory totals $90. 25 Dec. 1781. Appointed to appraise the land of Bennet Bellu, John Hartley and James Harman. Wit: Francois Farrell and Wm. Hulbert. Appraised land bounded on one side by land of Samuel Swayze and on another by James Paul, 3 or 4 arpents . . . $15. Signed by all of the above signed. Charles de Grandpre. // p. 76. 22 Dec. 1781. Sale of estate of Bennet Bellu, to the use of his creditors, in presence of Francois Farrell, Silas Crane, Don Estevan Minor, Nathaniel Tomlinson, James Harman and other assistants. Purchasers: Nathaniel Tomlinson, Winsor Pipes, Silas Crane, Adam Lanhart, Daniel Ogden. (p. 77) 11 Jany. 1782. Sale and adjudication to highest bidder of a piece of land belonging to Bennet Bellu, to the use of his creditors, sold to Cader Rabey for $20. Names of creditors of Bennet Bellu: Samuel Henry, Samuel Swayze, Daniel Ogden, William West, Nannette Brucher, Benjamin Rogers, David Wattman, Roswell Megget, Charles Adams, Jeremiah Bryan, Caleb King. Total due $433. $100 for repartition. (p. 78) 18 March 1782. Appointment of John Lusk and James (?) Heartley to appraise a horse belonging to Bennet Bellu which was delivered to us by an Indian. 20 March 1782, the above horse put up and exposed to sale and having been cried was adjudged to John Row for $20. (p. 79) Assistants: John Kennedy, William Ferguson, Francois Farrell. Charles de Grandpre. Amount of sale $20; expenses $9 -4 rials; net proceeds $10 -4, which has been paid to Alexander Callender, creditor of Bennet Bellu, absconded, on account of $19 due to him, as appeared by his petition annexed. Grandpre. (no petition.)

Enfranchisement. Be it known, etc. that I, Jeannette, a free woman of colour, residing at present in the Dist. of Natchez., having purchased from Don Charles de Grandpre, then Commandant of the Post of Pointe Coupee, a mulatto boy named "Narcisse", my natural son, now aged 8 years, for which I paid him in cash as will more fully appear in the bill of sale, executed at Pointe Coupee afsd. on 7 June 1781, with the intent to enfranchise and set free from all service whatever the said boy. In virtue of my right and privilege, I do hereby renounce all title to sd mulatto boy, my natural son named "Narcisse," and by these presents do enfranchise him from all slavery and subjection whatsoever from henceforward and forever, etc., for surety of which I bind all my estate and means. At Post of Natchez before Charles de Grandpre, Commandant of sd Post. 17 Jan. 1782, to all of which full faith and credit is due, the sd Jeannette, a free woman of colour being well known to me Commandant aforesaid and the sd Jeannette declaring that she cannot write, signed by Don Estevan Minor, Don Juan de la Villebeuvre and Don Joaquim Ossorno, 1st Lt and Aid-Major, 2nd Captain and 3rd Sub. Lt. in Reg. of Infantry of Louisiana, as witnesses and Chas. de Grandpre, Commandant.

---

p. 81. Personally appeared Peter Hawkins, res. of this Dist., who sells to Widow Jane Osborn a negro woman named "Mary", of the Senegal Nation, and a dau., named "Emelia", aged about 5 months, for $450, which the sd widow has engaged to pay at two terms, 2500 pounds of pork at this time and as the 2nd payment, 1 Jany. 1783, the balance in pork and tobacco in equal quantities, at the current prices thereof, for such is the agreement of the parties. Wit: Isaac Johnson and James Truly. Charles de Grandpre. Recept of Peter Hawkins for $250 acct of sale of negro woman and child, for which sum he fully releases the Widow Osborn, 28 Jany. 1783, before Grandpre.

---

p. 82. Appeared David Mitchell and Reuben Alexander and voluntarily offer themselves sureties of the person and conduct of Joseph Smith, now confined in the Fort for having formed a criminal plan of escaping, with Anthony Hutchins, to nation of Indians, called "Chits", and from thence to the Province of Georgia, without any passport or motive save that of a spirit of subordination and sedition; and to ensure a more regular conduct hereafter and more conformable to that of a good citizen who ought to respect the laws of a mild Government. The said Mitchell and Reuben Alexander have bound themselves and their estates, in the presence of Don Estevan Minor, Richard Harrison and William McIntosh. 6 Feb. 1782. Signed, all of above.

Petition of Jeremiah Bryan states that he is a creditor of Wm. Rogers, formerly a resident of this District, to amount of $106, after deducting the amount your petitioner has received, and having waited a long time for payment, petitioner prays for an order that he may be paid out of estate or that land may be sold at public auction for the payment. (no date.) p. 83. 15 Feb. 1782. On petition of Jeremiah Bryan, for appraisal of land belonging to William Rogers, absent, William Vousdan and Richard Harrison appointed; said land (8 arpents cleared), bounded by Sterling Spell on one side and John Lum on another, on St. Catherine's Cr., on which are two old cabins, such as they may be, appraised at $70. // 16 Feb. 1782, above land put up for sale (p. 84) to highest bidder (notice first being posted in the usual places and cried at the Hall of our Court) adjudged to Jeremiah Bryan for $40. // 18 Feb. 1782. Appeared Jeremiah Bryan who sells the above plantation on St. Catherine's Creek to Richard Harrison for $60 ($15 cash, which seller acknowledges, and remainder in month of December ensuring.) Wit: Don Estevan Minor and Don Marcos de Villiers. Chas. de Grandpre.

---

p. 85. 14 Feb. 1782. Personally appeared Stephen Holston, a resident of the District, who sells to Nathaniel Tomlinson, present and accepting, a negro woman names "Rose", a Creole, about 30 years, for $400, of which sum $125 have been paid down and which seller acknowledges to have recd. and remaining $275 to be paid at the end of December, present year. (p. 86) Wit: Estevan Minor and Manuel Guttierez. Chas. de Grandpre.

p. 86. March 23, 1782. Pursuant to orders from the Acting Governor of this Province, Lt. Col. Don Pedro Piernas, we Charles de Grandpre, etc., have left Mistress Hutchins in possession of all her estate with the exception of twelve of her slaves sent to New Orleans, for the safety of which said estate she had given for sureties Isaac Johnson and William Vousdan, in presence of Don Estevan Minor, Francis Farrell, and James Harman, hereby binding themselves that the sd estate consisting of slaves, cattle, and lands shall be forth coming when required by law and for the surety of all which they bind their whole estate, present and to come. Chas. de Grandpre.

---

p. 87. 9 April 1782. Appeared William West and Keaih West, his wife, both residents of this District, sell to Francois Mesnard, resident of Arkansas, here present and accepting, a negro woman, named "Edith", a Creole, aged 16 years, with a negro child, her son, aged one year, named "Thomas", for $400 and one barrel of flour, which sd William West and Keiah, his wife, ack. to have recd. Wit: Don Estevan Minor, Manuel Guttierez. Chas. de Grandpre.

---

13 April, 1782. Personally appeared Samuel Swayzey, a resident of this Post, who by these presents has constituted and appointed for his attorneys, general and special, Messrs. Ephraim Goble, resident of this District, Elijah Horton, of the Province of Georgia, and Nathaniel Coleman, of Virginia, residing near Pitt, each one (p. 88) for the Province in which they respectively resided to recover all sums that may, to said constituent, be due and owing. Wit: Estevan Minor, Patrick Foley, Manuel Guttierez.

---

16 May 1782, appeared Wm. Brocus, a res. of this District, who sells to Francois Valle, sub lieut. of Militia, residing in Illinois, here present and accepting, a negro man named "Jacob", ages 25, nat. of Carolina, for $700, to which sum was appraised a negro man belonging to sd Valle taken by the Rebels in this District, and at public sale which they made thereof (p. 89) adjudged to Wm. Brocus and which he declares not to have paid, the said negro having been stolen and carried off by the Rebel, Bennet Truly, the said negro man, named "Leander" and aged abt. 18, native of Illinois. And it is agreed between the parties that if sd negro "Leander" shall be recovered there shall be a mutual re-delivery and exchange, that is to say, that said Francois Valle shall re-deliver to Wm. Brocus, his negro man, "Jacob" and the said Wm. Brocus shall re-deliver to Francois Valle, the negro man "Leander" without any damages whatsoever. It has also been agreed between the parties that if the said negro Leander shall be found in a distant and foreign country and a journey thither should be difficult and expensive that then the said Wm. Brocus shall remain possessed of sd negro Leander in consequence whereof Francois Valle, in such case, cedes, etc. to Wm. Brocus the said negro, acknowledging to have received the man "Jacob", valued at $700, in payment thereof. Wit: Don Juan de la Villebeuvre, Don Estevan Minor.

p. 90. 22 Apr. 1782. Personally appeared Benjamin Rogers, resident of the District, who sells to Thomas Constock, resident of Post of Arkansas, here present and accepting, the whole of his crop in the ground, planted on 14 acres of cleared land (sd land belonging to the King), bounded by John Heartly, Samuel Lewis, John Row and lands not granted, selling only the crop, horned cattle, little and great, two horses, one mule, and 24 hogs, for $350, which seller acknowledges to have received from purchaser. Wit: Estevan Minor, Samuel Lewis. Charles de Grandpre.

---

p. 91. Appointment of appraisers. Proceeding to the inventory and appraisment of the whole estate of James Gillason, decd., unmarried, about two years ago, with intent of making sale of same for payment of his debts, Wm. Brocus and Daniel Megget appointed appraisers and accept same. Wit: Richard Adams and Francois Farrell. Inventory: Rifle-barrel with mounting; silver shoe buckles; two vests and one shirt; two cows and calves; one box of cypresswood; tract of land at St. Catherine's Creek, one mile from Fort, bounded by lands of James Truly, Wm. Hulbert and Daniel Megget, on which a dwelling house (p. 92) 8 x 18 ft, one small corn house, one kitchen, a fowl-house, a well, parks and enclosures, $60. // 20 May 1782. Public Notice having been given of the sale of the estate of James Gillison, have proceeded to make sale in presence of Francois Farrell, Richard Adams, William Brocus, Danial Megget, James Harman and others assisting, on condition that purchasers pay cash, for furniture and cattle, the land to be paid for the 1st of Nov. this year. (p. 93) Richard Adams bought all of personal estate for $72. Wm. Brocus bought plantation for $40. Charles de Grandpre.

4 May 1782, appeared William Brocus, resident of this District, who appoints Don Estevan Minor, attorney, General and Special, at New Orleans, Lt. and Aid-Major of this Post, with full power to represent him in said city to do, act and transact all preceedings in law necessary in the suit pending between said constituent and the Widow Truly referred by the Commandant of this Post to the Superior Tribunal of this Province, (the suit relative to the carrying -off the negro man "Leander", belonging to Francois Valle, by Bennet Truly, son of Widow Sarah Truly). Wit: Juan de la Villebeuvre, Capt. of the Infantry, St. Germain and Manuel Guttierez.

---

p. 94. 12 May 1782, in the afternoon, appeared Widow Anne McIntosh, who hereby sells to Thomas Green, here present and accepting, a tract of land on St. Catherine's Cr., 500 arpents, as appears by the grant, bounded on one side by sd Creek, on another by John Smith, and on another by lands not granted, upon which a dwelling-house, barn, negro cabins, milk house and sundry other buildings. This sale includes (p. 95) also 133 acres on same creek between first mentioned plantation and sd creek, bounded on one sidy by John Smith, and on the other sides by lands not granted, with no buildings, also sells two horses and one plough, for $1000, on account of which, the purchaser has paid to seller the sum of $280 in a negro man, named "James", aged 12, native of Carolina, which seller acknowledges, the remainder, $720, the purchaser binds himself to pay 1st of December of present year. It has also been agreed that the widow Anne McIntosh shall deliver to said Thomas Green the Titles for said lands when full payment has been paid. (p. 95) And it is further agreed that the above seller shall be free to keep some person or persons on the first mentioned plantation as well as reside there herself, at times, until the whole of the cattle can be gathered; the said widow also reserves that portion of said land planted by persons hired in her service, as likewise that which has been planted by her slaves for their own use; but all that which has been planted for her use shall remain in full property to the purchaser. The said widow has also reserved use of the park in common with the said purchaser to shut up her cattle as the same may be gathered . . . Done and executed at Natchez aforesaid, 12 May 1782, in presence (p. 96) of Don John Girault and Manuel Guttierez, who signed with the parties and we, the Commandant aforesaid. Signed by all the above.

Before me, Charles de Grandpre, etc., appeared John Farquhar, who by these presents, and with the consent of John Bisland, Syndic of and attorney for the creditors of the said Farquhar, has sold to Cato West, 130 acres distant about one league from the Fort of the Post, bounded by lands of Widow Anne McIntosh, John Blommart, and Foley, and land not granted, on which a small house of about 20 feet, with other cabins and buildings. The sd John Farquhar also sells, with the consent of sd John Bisland, to the sd Cato West 6 chairs, one table, 3 pots, one case containing 9 bottles, one skillet, two ploughs, one candlestick, four cups and saucers, two horses, four cows and their calves, one augur, two hoes, two sows, 15 bu. of corn, 40 lbs. of bacon and ten gallons of rum. The sd plantation and other effects sold for $1050 (including two-thirds of the product of the crop in the ground, to be paid at the expiration of the month of December of present year to John Farquhar and John Bisland jointly. Witness: George Rapalje, Dibdell Holt. (p. 97) Signed by John Farquahr, John Bisland and Cato West. // At Natchez, 7 March 1798. Before Don Estevan Minor appeared John Bisland who declared that he received for above a note from Cato West which has been paid in full.

Before Charles de Grandpre appeared Richard Gooding who sells to Widow Anne McIntosh, here present and accepting, a negro man named "Antoine Ellis" aged about (p. 98) forty years, native of Curacoa. Done at Natchez, 17 May 1782, in the presence of Don Estevan Minor and Manuel Guttierez. Consideration $305, which the seller has received from purchaser. Signed Richard Gooding.

Before Charles de Grandpre, etc., appeared David Smith, who sells to Widow Anne McIntosh, here present and accepting, a negro boy named "Luke", aged about ten years, consideration $300, 17 May 1782, witnessed by Don Estevan Minor and Manuel Guttierez, who have signed with the seller. Signed D. Smith.

---

p. 99. Before Charles de Grandpre, etc., appeared John White, who sells to Widow Anne McIntosh, here present and accepting, a negro woman named Jane, aged 18, native of Virginia, for $440 which seller acknowledges to have received in cattle from purchaser, in the presence of David Smith and Richard Gooding, who signed with seller. 17 May 1782.

---

p. 99. 29 May 1782. Before me, Charles de Grandpre, etc., appeared Jeremiah Brian and Patience Brian, his wife, both residents of this District, who by mutual consent and accord both sold to Wm. Dueit (Dewitt), here present and accepting, 20 arpents in said District, one league and a quarter from the Fort, bounded by lands of Justus King, (p. 100) William Duett, Nathan Swayze and John Griffin, also 20 horned cattle, 23 hogs, two horses, two plows, two hoes and two axes and the harness of the horses, for $1000 which sd purchaser binds himself to pay, $200 Nov. 1st and the remaining $800 Jany. 1, next ensuing. Signed by William Duett and Jere Brian. Wit: Francis Farrell, J(ohn) Lusk. Charles de Grandpre.

---

13 May 1782. Before Charles de Grandpre, etc., appeared Francois Farrell, a resident of this Post, who sells to the Lt. of Infantry and Aid Major of said Post, Don Estevan Minor, here present and accepting, a plantation on St. Catherine's (p. 101) Creek, 44 acres of cleared land and 56 acres not cleared, bounded on the lands of John Farquhar and William Smith, on which a dwelling house 40 x 18 ft, with doors, windows, locks, etc., a barn 30 x 15 ft, in bad condition, with negro cabins, parks and enclosures, said plantation being purchased at public sale of estate of John Blommart, seized and confiscated and sold to the use of the King, Consideration $120 in cash. Witnesses: Joseph Duncan, Keder Abie (cannot sign). Signed Francois Farrell.

---

1 June 1782, before Charles de Grandpre, appeared James White who sold to Widow Anne McIntosh, resident of this Post, a negro woman, "Bertha", native of Barbadoes, aged 40; consideration $300, which sd purchaser has paid (p. 102) in cows and horses. Witnesses: Francois Farrell and Silas Crane. Signed James White.

Will of James Perry, of the Natchez District, planter. To my beloved nephew, Barnabas Perry 3 cows and calves, a young bay horse, and for the great affection he hath always shown unto me, all my real estate in this District; to niece, Rebecca Perry, for the great affection I have always had for her, cattle and a horse; to nephew Daniel Perry the same; to nieces, Ann and Lydia, cattle; to brother, Daniel Perry the residue of my est. and he to be exor. 19 March 1782. He signed with a mark. (p. 103) Wit: Isaac Johnson, Benj. Holmes, Michael Hooter. // June 1, 1782, before Charles de Grandpre, etc., appeared Daniel Perry, resident of this District, who has exhibited the will of James Perry, his brother, deceased on 21st of March last, which was executed 19 of said March. (Will proved in detail by witnesses in presence of John Joseph Duforest and Estevan Minor.)

---

p. 104. Received from Don Charles de Grandpre, three negro men, two negro woman and one mulatto child, delivered him by George Rapalje by His Excellency Don Estevan Miro's orders; likewise two negro men, two negro women and three young children, delivered by Carradine and Smith, as aforesaid. At Natchez, June 1, 1782. Wit: Isaac Johnson. (signed) Ann Hutchins.

---

15 June 1782, before Charles de Grandpre appeared Thomas Comstock, resident of Arkansas, who sold to Wm. Ferguson, (p. 105) here present and accepting, 150 square arpents of land in the Natchez District, 8 miles from the Fort of this Post, (the titles saying 13 miles being an error), bounded by lands of Herbert Menester, John Bowls and Benjamin Gower and land that has not been granted, transferring titles thereof, a grant, dated Aug. 6, 1778, by Peter Chester, English Governor of Pensacola, and survey by Eli Durnford, dated 4 Aug. 1778. Consideration: $44 in cash paid. Witnesses: Manuel Guttierez, Francois Farrell. Signed by both seller and buyer and Charles de Grandpre, Commandant.

---

19 June 1782. Before Chas. de Grandpre, etc., appeared Joseph Duncan, who sells to (p. 106) William Dueit, here present and accepting, tract on St. Catherine's Creek, six arpents enclosed and in cultivation,

bounded by Samuel Swayze, Samuel Lewis and Daniel Ogden, which the sd seller purchased from Jacob Paul. Consideration: $150 cash to be paid in October next ensuing. Wit: John Lovelace, Jacob Paul. Signed by both parties and Chas. de Grandpre, Com.

---

25 June 1782, before noon. Before Chas. de Grandpre, appeared Jeremiah Brian, who sells to Robt. Dunbar, here present and accepting, (p. 107) two and one-half arpents on St. Catherine's Cr. enclosed and with a cabin thereon, bounded John Lum, and Richard Curtis and vacant lands. Consideration: $100, to be paid in December next ensuing, which said land having been acquired by said seller in virtue of a private sale made to him by William Smith in manner and form in common use among the English inhabitants of this District. Wit: Estevan Minor, Francois Farrell. Signed by both parties and Chas. de Grandpre.

---

p. 107. 28 June 1782. Before Chas. de Grandpre, etc., appeared Francois Farrell, res. of this Dist., who sells to Abraham Mayes, here present and accepting, 100 arpents, about three-fourths of a league from the Fort, bounded by lands of Widow Sarah Truly, Richard Swayze, Gibson, Stower and Swayze, on which is a log house and cabin, parks and enclosures. Consid: $408, which (p. 108) said purchaser promises to pay to the seller in December next ensuing. Wit: John Girault, Thos. M. Green. Signed by both parties and Charles de Grandpre, Commandant.

---

29 Juen 1782. Before Chas. de Grandpre, appeared Richard Devall, res. of the Dist., who sells to William Pickle, Captain in the service of the U. S. at present in New Orleans in the Province of La., represented by his attorney, Capt. Richard Harrison, here present and accepting, 1200 arpents at Little Gulph, through which runs a creek not named, bounded on one side by land late of Philip Alston, and on other sides by land not granted. (p. 109) Also two stills with their caps and worms, delivered to said Harrison for the said Pickle. Consid: $1000 which sd Richard Harrison promises to pay on demand to sd seller. Wit: Estevan Minor, Will. Ferguson. Signed by Richard Devall and Rd. Harrison, Attorney, and Chas. de Grandpre, Commandant.

---

27 Aug. 1782. Before Chas. de Grandpre, appeared Isaac Johnson, res. of Dist., who sells to Nathaniel Tomlinson, here present and accepting, 200 arpents at Little Gulph, on which is a half-finished house, cabins and barn, bounded on one side by land late of Richard Devall, now of William Pickle, and on the other side by land of Sieur Barbe, and otherwise by lands not granted, the said land having been acquired by seller at the Public Sale made thereof, to the use of the King, having been confiscated as belonging to the fugitive Rebel, John Turner. Consid: $187 which purchaser has paid in cash. Wit: Thomas Green, John Burnet. Signed by both parties and Chas. de Grandpre.

---

p. 110. 11 Sept. 1782. Before Don Estevan Miro, Col. of the Reg. of Inf. of La., Governor of this Province ad interim, acting as Notary Public at Natchez, there being none in this District, in the presence of witnesses, appeared Thomas Marston Green, of sd Dist., who sells to Don Charles de Grandpre, Lt. Col. and Capt. of Reg. of La., here present and accepting, a negro wench, named "Diana", native of Carolina, aged abt. 15 yrs. Consid: $400, paid in cash and acknowledged. Wit: Estevan Minor, Lt. of Infantry and Aid-Major, Sub-lieut. Joseph Campana. Signed by Thomas Marston Green and Estevan Miro.

---

12 Sept. 1782. Before Chas. de Grandpre, etc. appeared William Pontney, a res. of the Post of Natchez, who acknowledges to have (p. 111) received from Richard Harrison the sum of $407, on account of Messrs. Bradley and Harrison, partners, being the amount charged by the said William Pontney in his account agst said partners, delivered to said Richard Harrison, their atty., and for which sum of $407, an order of the court was obtained in favor of sd Pontney. Wit: Franco Manuel de las Carigos and Estevan Minor. Signed by William Pontney. Chas. de Grandpre.

14 Sept. 1782. Before Don Estevan Miro, Col. of the Reg. of Inf. of La. and Gov. ad interim of this Province, personally appeared Richard Harrison, res. of the Dist. of Natchez, who sells to Thos. Green, here present and accepting, a lot of ground in the Town of Natchez, being 102 feet in front with the whole depth from the river to the foot of the hill, bounded on one side by a lot of Richard Bacon and on the other by a lot of Richard Bacon and on the other by the street, on which is a dwelling house; for $6,000, to be paid 1 April 1784; lot and house mortgaged for said payment. Signed by both parties, Estevan Miro and Chas. de Grandpre. // p. 112. Natchez, Feb. 13, 1784. By agreement in the settlement of private accounts, Richard Harrison, Capt. of Mil. in this Dist., has transferred and assigned the foregoing obligation to Alexander Moore, merchant of the Dist. Signed by both with Wit: Estevan Minor, Michael Estava. Trevino (Commandant)

---

p. 112. Before me, Estevan Miro, etc., appeared Richard Harrison, res. of Natchez, who sells to Joseph Forester, here present and accepting, lot in Town of Natchez, 50 ft. in front by 200 ft. in depth, bounded on all sides by lots not granted; for $50, received. 14 Sept. 1782. Wit: Charles de Grandpre, Estevan Minor. Signed by Rd. Harrison and Miro.

---

p. 113. Natchez, Sept. 7, 1782. Petition of Silas Crane to the Governor. A certain James Wilson, by order of Col. de Grandpre, being about to leave this District, having some debts unpaid also some property in possession, found it necessary to appoint some one to settle his affairs in his absence and having, with the approbation of Col. de Grandpre, appointed your petitioner and, having produced to your petitioner an inventory of horned cattle, hogs and debts due to him, the said Wilson, by divers persons, your petitioner consented to act as his attorney and promised, in presence of Col. Grandpre and others to do his endeavors to collect the said horned cattle, horses, etc., as well as the debts due to the sd Wilson, and informing the creditors of said Wilson that your petitioner would pay the debts due by him so far as the proceeds of the property of the sd Wilson would extend and no further. Signed Silas Crane. (p. 114) Natchez, 10 Sept. 1782. The attorney of James Wilson will give notice to the Public, by advertisement, that a sale of the land and cattle in his charge will take place; the proceeds thereof to the use of the creditors. Signed Miro. 16 Sept. 1782. Appointment of appraisers for the above: John Heartly and Cato West. Appraisal follows. (p. 115) 16 Sept. 1782. Sale of above. Witnesses: Silas Crane, Francois Farrell, Thomas Green, Cato West, John Heartley and others assisting. Sales: Horse to Thomas Marston Green, Thomas Green, his father, surety, $80; one mare to Jeremiah Brian, Wm. Brocus, surety, $22; one mare to Roswell Megget, James Harman, surety, $33; one cow and calf, one heifer, to Thomas Marston Green, Thos. Green, his father, surety, $30.4 (p. 116) 100 arpents of land, bounded by Manuel (Samuel?) Gibson, John Hartly, John Ross and Justus King, sold to George Rapalje for $99, Thomas Green surety.

---

p. 116. 18 Sept. 1782, before noon. Appeared Richard Harrison, before Don Estevan Miro, who sells to Don Estevan Minor, here present and accepting, a negro wench, called "Molly", aged 40, native of Virginia, for $400, to be paid on Jany. 1st ensuing. Wit: John Smith, David Mitchell. Signed by both. Estevan Miro.

---

p. 117. To Don Estevan Miro: Petition of James Heayes, who is appointed attorney of Thomas Comstock, a res. of Arkansas, and is gone to Illinois, who authorizes him to sell his property for $1000 and the said Comstock being indebted to the Commandant for horses bought at Public Sale. Natchez 3 Oct. 1782. Signed with a mark. In virtue of the annexed letter from Thomas Comstock, res. of the Post of Arkansas, authorising his partner, James Heayes, to sell all and every his estate in this District, I do hereby permit and authorize sd Heayes to sell the same in the presence of a Notary Public, in the manner most expedient. Signed Miro. // Letter. Ozark, Aug. 14, 1782. Mr. Hayes: In hope that you are in good health, I take this opportunity to inform you that I intend going to Illinois as soon as possible and propose to return in the month of May next if living. I beg that you will take care to put my stamp on all my horses and cows and my mark on my hogs, and, if possible, keep them together; as likewise to pay the Commandant for the five horses that I bought a publick sale, out of the proceeds of my crop; and take up my note and (p. 118) if you have not the means as I believe that you have not, you can have recourse to my friend, Daniel Meggett. N. B. This is to inform you that I can give you no account of your effects mentioned in your order, except the colt which I will keep for you. If you should find the opportunity to sell the plantation and cattle for $1000, do so, or if you can wait until my return, please do the best until my return. I have nothing to say of your friends, of whom I shall always be one, except that I have been robbed by the Arkansas. My compliments to all my friends. (signed) Thomas Comstock. I pray you to write me by the first conveyance and send me an order for your effects. // Oct. 4, 1782. Before me, Don Estevan Miro, etc., personally appeared James Heayes, a res. of the District, who in virtue of annexed letter from his partner, Thomas Constock, authorising him to sell his estate to best advantage, sale made, in conformity to our (p. 119) decree, to Keb. Rabey, here present and accepting, 15 arpents, bounded by lands of Samuel Lewis, John Row and John Hartly, with some hogs for $135, $100 in cash and $35 to be paid Jany. 1783. Wit: Francois Farrell, Silas Crane. Parties contracting have declared they cannot sign. Miro.

---

p. 119. 14 Oct. 1782. Before Don Estevan Miro, appeared Joseph Labrie, physician and practicing at Natchez, who sells to Miguel Eslava, the King's Store-Keeper at this Post, here present and accepting, a negro wench "Modiste", nat. of Cape Francois, aged abt. 25, for $450, paid and acknowledged. Signed by both parties. Wit: Jose Campana, Franco. Manuel de las Cavigos.

---

p. 120. 9 Nov. 1782. Before me, Don Pedro Piernas, Lt. Col. of Reg. of La., Civil and Military Commandant of this Post and District of Natchez, acting as Notary Public, there being none in this Province, appeared Thomas Green who sells to Adam Bingaman, here present and accepting, 500 arpents, according to titles, bounded on one side by lands of John Smith, on another by lands not granted and on the other by said creek, on which a frame dwelling house, barn, negro cabins, milk-house, and other building useful to the plantation, and further 133 acres on same creek, bounded on one side by John Smith and 1st plantation and others not granted, also two horses and one plough for $1000, plantation to be delivered after one month, titles received by him from the Widow McIntosh, now wife of said Bingaman. Wit: Don Miguel Eslava, John Girault. Both parties sign. Pedro Piernas.

---

p. 121. Nov. 15, 1782. Before Don Pedro Piernas, etc., appeared Cato West, res. of the Post and Dist. of Natchez, who sells to Adam Bingaman, 100 English acres one league from Fort, bounded by plantation purchased from Thomas Green by sd. Bingaman, and on the other side by lands of Messrs. Minor and Gooding and lands not granted, on which a house and sundry other cabins and other buildings; also one-half of the potatoes (p. 122) and two stack of corn fodder: for $400, one-half to be paid Dec. next and one-half in May 1783. Wit: Zenon Trudeau, Estevan Minor. Both parties sign. Pedro Piernas.

---

p. 122. 22 Nov. 1782. Before Don Pedro Piernas, personally appeared St. Germain, King's Interpreter of Indian languages, who of his own accord has promised and engaged to be surety of Francois James, detained for debt in the Prison of this Fort for the sum of $160, to be divided in case of insolvency of the sd. James among his creditors, namely: (p. 123) Messrs: Choise, Harrison, Alexander McIntosh, Hutchins, Ponteney, Davenport, . . . Cadien, St. Martin and Antoine Hoa; the sum to be paid in six months, and the said Francois James being and remaining responsible and bound to satisfy said creditors. Fort Panmure at Natchez, signed St. Germain. Wit: Estevan Minor, Zenon Trudeau. Pedro Piernas.

---

p. 123. Dec. 5, 1782. Before me, Don Pedro Piernas, etc., appeared Nathaniel Tomlinson, res. of this Dist., who acknowledges to be indebted to Laurent Darbonne in the sum of $2056, for the purchase of a number of horses which he has in his possession, said sum payable at end of year ensuing 1783, mortgages his whole estate, present and to come. Signed by Tomlinson. Wit: Zenon Trudeau, Franco de las Carigos. Pedro Piernas. The above obligation is null and void, the party having appeared before me and declared that Mr. Tomlinson had satisfied the same at Attacapas. Natchez, 13 Feb. 1784. Trevino.

---

p. 124. 9 Jany. 1783. Before me, Don Pedro Piernas, etc., appeared William Smith and Ann Thompson, his wife, who sell to Thomas Green, here present and accepting, 100 arpents, on a place vulgarly called "Boy's" Creek, by grant thereof, with all buildings and fences thereon; for $300 paid in cash. Wit:

Estevan Minor, Zenon Trudeau. Signed by William Smith, Ann Smith signs with a mark. Piernas.

---

p. 125. 4 Feb. 1789. Be it known to all, etc., that I, William Vousdan, have sold to Joseph Darlington, 500 arpents on Bayou Pierre and bounded as set forth by Title and Plan; for $500 ack. to have received, Joseph Darlington, being here and accepting, before Charles de Grandpre.

---

p. 126. 11 Feb. 1783, afternoon. Before Don Pedro Piernas, appeared Widow Sarah Truly, who sells to Adam Bingaman, a negro named "Duncan", native of Jamaica, aged abt. 25; for $480, which seller ack. to have received in cash. Wit: Jose Campana, Estevan Minor. Signed Sarah Truly. Pedro Pierna.

---

21 Feb. 1783. Before Piernas, appeared John Morris, a res. of the Dist., sells to David Mitchell, a negro man named "Samuel" aged 30, nat. of Senegal, for $320 which seller ack. to have received in cash. Wit: Cato West, Peter Nelson, Estevan Minor. Signed by John Morris. Pedro Piernas.

---

p. 127. 6 March 1783. Before Piernas appeared Richard Bacon, a res. of this Post, who sells to Don Miguel Eslava. store-keeper of this Fort, here present and accepting, a lot in the Town of Natchez, 101 ft. in front by the whole depth from the River to the foot of the hill, bounded on one side by a Lot of Thos. Green, and on the other by the street, on which are 2 dwelling houses, two storehouses, and a kitchen, including a Billiard Table and all its appurtenances; for $800, $400 of which the seller acknowledges to have recd. in cash, and the purchaser binds himself to pay the remaining $400, all in (p. 128) month of Sept. of the present year, and mortgages the sd lots as well as all his other estate and estates, present and to come. Both sign. Witnesses: Jose Campana, Estevan Minor.

---

p. 128. 8 March 1783. Before Piernas, appeared Cato West, a resident of the District, who sells to William Barland, a lot in the Town of Natchez, being 39 ft in front by 102 ft in depth, bounded on one side by Thos. Green and on the other side by the street, on which is erected a dwelling house of squared timber, about 20 ft square; for $100, which seller acknowledges to have received. Signed Cato West. Wit: Richard Devall, Estevan Minor. Pedro Piernas.

---

p. 129. 27 Apr. 1783. Before Piernas, appeared Cato West, who sells to John Bisland, here present and accepting, a negro boy, named John, aged 14, native of Va.; for $400. Signed Cato West. Wit: Francisco Collell, Estevan Minor. Pedro Piernas.

---

p. 129. 27 April 1783. Before Piernas: appeared Henry Richardson, who sells to Sieur St. Germain, here present and accepting, a negro man named "Friday", aged 30, of the Hibo Nation; for $300, (p. 130) which seller acknowledges to have recd. in cattle from the purchaser. Signed Henry Richardson. Wit: Francis Collell, Capt. in Regiment of La., Estevan Minor. Pedro Piernas.

---

p. 130. 4 May before noon, 1783. Before Don Pedro Piernas, appeared Joseph Holden, of this place, who sells to Henry Manadue, here present and accepting, a tract of land in the Dist. three leagues from the Fort, ten arpents in front by forty in depth, bounded by lands of St. Germain and James Spice and by lands not granted; for $140 which seller acknowledges to have recd. in cash and a further sum of $60 which sd purchaser obliges himself to pay all in December next ensuing. Signed H. Manadue. Joseph Holden signs with a mark. Wit: Estevan Minor, Jacob Paul. Pedro Piernas. p. 131. Out of the sum mentioned in foregoing conveyance, there shall be paid to George Castles $42 and one rial for value recd of sd Castles. Joseph (X) Holden. Rec'd the sum of $60 in full, 1 Jany. 1784. signed George Castles. Wit: Cato West.

---

p. 131. 20 May 1783. Before Piernas, appeared Samuel Lewis, who sells to John Lusk, here present and accepting, 200 arpents on Second Creek, ten of which are cleared, on which a log house, bounded on one side by land of Dickson, on another by Jacob Winfree, on another by John Lusk, on the other by sd creek; as set forth in titles thereof; for $400, which seller acknowledges to have recd. Signed Samuel Lewis. Wit: Estevan Minor, Jacob Paul. Pedro Piernas.

---

p. 131. Bond. At the Fort of Natchez, 6 June, 1783. Before Don Pedro Piernas appeared Sieur St. Germain, Interpreter of Indian Languages in this District, who promises to pay to Lt. Col. Don Carlos de Grand Pre or his attorney, $937 and 5 rials, being the amount of sundry merchandise, including costs and charges delivered to him for the purpose of trading with the Indian Nation on the Yazoo River, and which sum he obliges himself to pay in December, 1783, in articles following namely: Bear's oil, tallow, deer, bear and other skins, or otherwise in cash being at his risk and account until delivered to sd Don Carlos de Grand Pre at New Orleans, who on his part shall (p. 132) receive and dispose of the same at the prices current at that time and carry the proceeds thereof to the credit of the foregoing obligation and liquidation thereof. Signed St. Germain. Wit: Don Manuel de las Carigos, Don Antonio Soler. Pedro Piernas. p. 132. Acct received from St. Germain, in April and May 1783. By Skipper Estevan Bissonnet: 17 Oil in bags of deer or bear skins; 6 barrels of ditto; 125 pounds of tallow; 1365 deer and bear skins; 230 pasados; 19 otter skins. (other shipments similar by skippers, Mariano Fernandez, ____Boyer, LaCoste, Guttierez.) p. 133. Note: of the 17 bags, 15 were found two-thirds empty, and of the barrels none were full, wanting from 6 to 11 inches, and none which came from the country contained 120 pts. Many of the skins damaged and others wet, etc. New Orleans, 15 May 1783. Carlos de Grand Pre.

---

p. 133. 25 June 1783. Before Don Francisco Collell, Capt. of Reg. of La., acting Civil and Military Commandant of the Post and Dist. of Natchez, appeared Samuel Lewis and Sarah Lewis, his wife, who sell to John Lusk, a plantation of 100 arpents on Second Creek, bounded by sd Creek and land not granted; for $200 which sellers acknowledge to have recd. Signed Samuel Lewis, Sarah Lewis signed with a mark. Wit: Jacob Paul, Estevan Minor. Francisco Collell.

---

p. 134. June 1, 1783. I, Don Pedro Piernas, on notice received of death of William McIntosh, formerly an officer in the service of His Brittanic Majesty and late resident of this district, have attended at the plantation and dwelling of sd deceased, accompanied by Francisco Collell, Capt. of the Reg. of La. and Don Estevan Minor, aid-major of this Post and having entered sd dwelling found said deceased extended on a bed, the body cold, and appearing to have died a natural death after a long sickness. Signed by Piernas and witnesses. In continuation, in the presence of the abovementioned witnesses have proceeded to collect such keys as appeared most important, and with one have locked a trunk in which deceased kept cloathing, with another a chest which contained table and other linens and the third belonging to a writing desk containing books, accounts and other important papers of the deceased, having for security affixed the seal of my arms, have withdrawn with sd keys in my possession, leaving the aforesaid in care of William Weeks, a resident of this District, to produce when required. Signed as above. // p. 134. 3 June 1783. In consequence of death of Wm. McIntosh, verified June 1, and said dec'd. having left 3 children, two sons and one dau., issue of his lawful marriage with Eunice (p. 135) Hawley, his wife, still living, said sons being William, aged 18, James aged 16, and dau. Mariana aged 19. Alexander Moore appointed curator to said minors to defend their rights, he a merchant of this District, his probity, disinteredness and good faith known to me. He accepts. Signed by Alexander Moore. Wit: Franco. Collell, Estevan Minor. Pedro Piernas. //

p. 135. 4 June 1783. To proceed with inventory of estate and papers left by decd. William McIntosh, an interpreter of the English language being necessary, appointed Don Estevan Minor, adjt. of this Fort. He accepted. Signed Estevan Minor, apptd. by Pedro Piernas. Wit: Franco. Collell. //
5 June 1783. Appraisers of above estate: George Rapalje and William Ferguson. They accepted and signed. //

p. 136. 7 June 1783. William Weeks delivered effects left in his charge and the seals were found to be unbroken. In trunk was the will of William McIntosh, written by Alexander Moore at the request of Wm. McIntosh, who was in too much pain to write it. pp. 137-139 depositions proving the will and a very large inventory. 170 arpents of land on which dwelling house of squared timber, a mill, stable and nine negro cabins, 10 slaves, horses, cattle, hogs, sheep; 3 beds, each with two mattresses, two sheets and one coverlet appraised at $150. Total appraisal $3398. // p. 140. The above estate left in charge of

Eunice McIntosh to keep possession until children shall be of age. Will of Wm. McIntosh, Jany. 12, 1783. Beloved wife, one-third of estate; sons, William and James and dau. Mary two thirds, share and share alike. Signed. Wit: Alexander Moore, Joseph Holmes and Benjamin Holmes.

---

p. 141. Before Franco. Collell, appeared Louis Charbono, res. of the Dist., to George Rapalje, here present and accepting, 100 arpents on St. Catherine's Cr. bounded by lands granted to myself (Charbono) and the purchaser, which I had from Hardy Ellis; for 400 bu. of shelled corn to be paid to me in present year of 1783. Charbono signed with a mark. George Rapalje signed. Wit: Antonio Soler, Joaquim Ossorno. Francisco Collell.

---

p. 141. 3 July 1783, appeared Louis Charbono, res. of Dist., ceded, exchanged and conveyed to George Rapalje, 400 arpents granted by Gov. Miro, on St. Catherine's Cr., b. by lands of Messrs. St. Germain, Laflor and George Rapalje, afsd. and the last named has given in exchange for the same 100 arpents with a house thereon, with 400 rails to enclose same, to be delivered on the land, on St. Catherine's Cr. adj. John Stowes, Samuel Gibson, and Justus King, which sd land was purchased by him at sale of estate of Alexander Hilston, and sd Rapalje binds himself also to pay to the sd Louis Charbono, over and above, $100 in April 1784. Rapalje signed and Miguel Eslava signed for Louis Charbono. Wit: Joaquim Ossorno, Antonio Soler. Franco. Collell.

---

p. 142. Before Collell appeared Jacob Coburn, a res. of the Post, who sells to Joseph Duncan, here present and accepting, 150 arpents on St. Catherine's Cr., with dwelling house, some negro cabins, 17 arpents in corn and some arpents of potatoes and pumpkins, b. on Samuel Swayze, Gabriel Griffin, Samuel (p. 143) Gibson and John Martin: for $600, of which $200 the seller ack. to have recd; $200 to be pd. in Feb. 1784; $200 in Dec. 1784. For surety, purchaser binds his whole estate, present and to come. Both sign. Wit: Miguel Eslava, Antonio Soler. Franco. Collell.

---

p. 143. Before Collell, appeared Windsor Pipes, who sells to Richard Trevillian, 150 arpents on St. Catherine's Cr, with dwelling house, some cabins, one horse mill, with one horse, one cow and two hogs, for $675, which seller ack. to have recd. Signed by both. Wit: Francis Farrell, Richard Bacon.
6 Aug. 1783. Windsor Pipes transfers his whole right and title to above (p. 144) amounting to $275 to Adam Bingaman for value recd. from sd Bingaman in merchandise. 18 Aug. 1783. Signed by Windsor Pipes. Wit: Estevan Minor. Francisco Collell. //
p. 144. 25 June 1796. Richard Trevillian sells the above plantation to Nathaniel Tomlinson for $400, which the seller ack. to have recd. Signed by Trevillian. Wit: Maurice Stackpoole, Juan Girault.

---

p. 145. Before Collell appeared Richard Trevillian, res of the Dist. who sells to Windsor Pipes, here present and accepting, a negro boy named Sam, aged 10, nat. of Va.; for $400 which seller ack to have recd. Signed by Trevillian. Wit: Francois Farrell, Richard Bacon. Franco. Collell.

---

p. 146. July 15, 1783. Before Collell, appeared Louis Charbono, res. of Dist., who declared himself indebted to Louis Chachere for $175, money lent, and obliges himself to pay 1st Oct. 1783, mortgaging 100 arpents on St. Catherine's Cr. b. by lands of John Stowers, Samuel Gibson, Justus King, which plantation he had from George Rapalje in exchange for another. Signed with a mark. Wit: Antonio Soler, Miguel Eslava. Franco. Collell. // July 15, 1783. Luis Charbono really sells to Luis Chachere the above plantation for $375. Same witnesses.

---

p. 147. Aug. 1, 1783. Appeared Estevan Minor, Aid-Major of Post, and sells to John Woods, present and accepting, 185 arpents on St. Catherine's Cr., with dwelling and some cabins, b. by Widow Coleman, now Madden, William Smith and Adam Bingaman, which land was bought by Francois Farrell at the public sale of John Blommart, seized (p. 148) and confiscated to the use of the King; for $300 which sd purchaser binds himself to pay December next ensuing. Signed by both. Wit: Francois Farrell, Antonio Solar. Franco Collell.

p. 148. 15 Aug. 1783. Before Collell appeared William Dueit, res. of Dist., who declares he has recd. from Don Miguel Eslave $1100, which he promises to pay in three months from date, for surety he mortgages three negroes, his property, "Esop" 14 yrs., "Collo" 12 yrs. and "Airy" 12 yrs. Signed. Wit: Francisco Carigas, Antonio Solar. Francisco Collell. The foregoing obligation having been satified, the same is null. Trevino.

---

p. 149. 3 Aug. 1783. William Dueitt, res. of Dist., sold to Benjamin Rogers, also of Dist., 150 arpents with fence thereon, on St. Catherine's Cr., one and a quarter leagues from Fort, b. by lands of Justus King, Nathan Swayze and John Griffin, which sd land he had from Jeremiah Brian; for 300 bu. of shelled corn, 150 bu. at end of this year and the remaining in 1784, said land being mortgaged for same. William Dueitt signed. Rogers with a mark. Wit: Antonio Soler, Miguel Eslava. Phillippe Trevino.

---

p. 150. 8 Nov. 1783. Personally appeared Patrick Foley, res. of District, and acting atty. for Patrick Conroy, Ebenezer Brown and Peter Beason, for purpose of selling and conveying, in their names, to Alexander McIntosh, his heirs and assigns, a tract of land belonging to them, 300 arpents. In pursuance whereof sd Foley sells to Adam Bingaman, lawful heir of the (p. 151) late Alexander McIntosh, here present and accepting, 300 arpents described in annexed plat by Surveyor Gen., bounded by James Lovel, Patrick Stuart, for $300 which seller ack. to have recd. Signed by Foley. Wit: Antonio Solar, Estevan Minor. Before me, Phillippe Trevino.

---

p. 151. 10 Dec. 1783. At the request of Sarah Canhard, widow of the late Sieur Canhard, we, Phillippe Trevino, have attended the plantation and dwelling of sd late Canhard, in presence of undersigned witnesses, to proceed to an inventory of the est. of decd. William Vousdan and John Ellis appointed appraisers, both residents of Dist. Inventory; Plantation on Second Cr., 150 arpènts, established by first husband of widow, the decd. having obtained title for same, which title is at Pensacola. p. 152. Inventory follows. p. 153. The widow declares that whereas at the time of her marriage with the decd. Canhard, she was the widow of Frederick William Shink, decd., of this Dist. about 1771 and no inventory being taken at the time nor marriage contract existing between herself and decd Canhard, her second husband, she declares that the following effects belong to the issue of her first marriage, namely: 28 head of horned cattle belonging to two children of her first marriage, share and share alike, also one mare and three colts, also one mare and three colts belonging to one of her ch. by 1st marriage, named Mary Ann, being a gift from Colin Woods, and another colt and three head of cattle belonging to her daughter named "Nancy" being the gift of Samuel Wells. These animals are included in the present inventory. Signed by William Vousdan and John Ellis, appraisers. Wit: Cachere. Before me, Phillippe Trevino.

---

p. 153. Francois Farrell petitions, wishing to sell six negro men and one negro wench at public sale, to have a day appointed. Natchez, 1 Dec. 1783. Notice will be given at usual places that a sale of the above will take place on 15th instant at the Hall of our Court. Trevino. //p. 154. 15 Dec. 1783. Report of above sale, payable Dec. next ensuing. Negro woman "Victoire" to Sieur St. Germain, for $500; negro man to George Rapalje $446; same to Sieur St. Germain $450; same to Stephen Jordan $500; same to Wm. Vousdan $612; Same to Richard Harrison $671; same to Daniel Burnet $700. Witnesses and assistants who signed with the Commandant, John Burnet, Justus King, George Rapalje, Geo. Castles, Estevan Minor, D. Smith, Cato West, Francois Farrell, Before me Phillippe Trevino.

---

p. 154. 20 Dec. 1783. William Dueitt, res. of Dist., sells negro boy "Airy" aged ten, for $300 to Don Miguel Eslava, present and accepting, payment acknowledged by seller. (p. 155) Signed by Dueitt. Wit: Antonio Soler, Francisco Collell, Russell Jones. Before Trevino.

---

p. 155. 1 Jany. 1784. William Dueitt declared to have recd. from Don Miguel Eslava, Commissary of the Post, the sum of $2000, money lent, and which sd sum he promises to repay in December of this year, for which he mortgages all his negroes and other estate, present and to come. Signed. Wit: Antonio Soler, Francois Farrell, Pedro Azevedo. Before me: Trevino. p. 156. Natchez. 20 March 1784.

Various creditors of the above named William Dueitt having appeared and opposed the foregoing mortgage on the ground that their claims are payable at the end of the present year, and the said mortgage having been granted and allowed on the supposition that no third person was interested thereon, in consequence thereof the mortgage aforesaid is void unless sd creditors shall be paid. Trevino.

---

p. 156. Joseph Forester, inhabitant of this dist., sells to Don Manuel Texada, also a res. of same, a house in town of Natchez, situated between lots of Sieurs Harrison and Tomlinson, (which sd lot I had from the said Harrison and have paid him therefor): for $200, which seller ack, to have recd. Signed by Forester and Texada. Wit: Don Miguel Eslava, Antonio Soler, Estevan Minor. Philippe Trevino.

---

p. 157. Cato West and Thomas Marston Green, jointly declare themselves surety for the safety of the crop of tobacco belonging to Thomas Green (who on his terms has consented that the same shall be carried to New Orleans), the same as if the tobacco was a property to us belonging. 3 Jany. 1784. Signed by Cato West and Thos. M. Green. Wit: Franco. Collell, Es Minor. Before me, Philippe Trevino. The above instrument has become void, the said Green having safely arrived at New Orleans with his tobacco. Trevino.

---

p. 157. John Wood, a res. of dist., sells to Richard Harrison a negro boy named "Jack" for $275, paid. 7 Jany. 1784. Signed by both. Wit: Francois Farrell, Miguel Eslava. Before Trevino.

---

p. 158. 8 Jany. 1784. George Rapalje bought negro at public sale of Francois Farrell, 15 Dec. 1783, not having given surety, does hereby mortgage sd negro as well as other slaves of which he is possessed and whole est. present and to come, to be paid 15 Dec. 1784. Signed. Wit: Antonio Soler, Estevan Minor, Miguel Eslava. Before me Philippe Trevino.

---

p. 159. George Rapalje, of this district to Don Luis Chachere, Merchant, of this Post, a lot 82 ft in depth by 64 ft in width, fronting on the main street of this town of Natchez and b. on the other side by Abner Green, which said ground I purchased at a public sale made by Col. Don Carlos de Grand Pre, of the property of a resident of this District named Thomas Green; for $80, the receipt of which is acknowledged; Luis Chachere, present and accepting. 24 Jany. 1784. Signed by both. Wit: Miguel Eslava, E. Minor. Before Trevino.

---

p. 160. Petition of Peter Hawkins to have public sale of a plantation, credit one year, (one-half cash at sale). Natchez 28 Jany. 1784. Let it be done as is required; notice be given that sale take place on 9 day of month ensuing. Trevino. 9 Feb. 1784. Sale of the above. Plantation adjudged to Miguel Eslava for $225. Trevino.

---

p. 161. Feb. 6, 1784. Estevan Minor to John Woods, resident of this Dist., 94 arpents between lands of Beltre and Baker and Messrs. Bickman and Madden; for $125, receipt of wh. acknowledged. Signed by both. Wit: Miguel Eslava. Before: Trevino.

---

p. 161. William Penrice, res. of the Dist., to Zachariah Smith, of sd Dist., 240 arpents, with two houses and 15 arpents enclosed on St. Catherine's Creek,2 leagues from the Fort, b. on one sidy by Widow Foster; on the other by land of Miller, which land I had from Benjamin Cavel, (p. 162) absconded; for $350, payable at the gathering of the ensuing crop at the end of December of present year, in tobacco at the current price of same in New Orleans. 6 Feb. 1784. Signed by both. Wit: Miguel Eslava, Rd. Harrison, Will. Ferguson. Before me, Philippe Trevino.

---

p. 162. 17 Feb. 1784. Silas Crane, res. of Dist., to John Woods, 325 arpents on Cole's Cr., 11 league from Fort; for $200 payable May 1785; land b. by Dibdal Holt. John Woods, present and accepting. Signed by both. Wit: Es Minor, Francois Farrell, Miguel Eslava. Before me: Philippe Trevino.

---

p. 163. 17 Feb. 1784. Silas Crane, res. of this Dist., to John Woods, 650 arpents on Bayou Pierre, b. by Thomas James and vacant lands, 20 leagues from this Fort, which land I purchased at the Public Sale of the confiscated estate of John Alston in the time of Lt. Col. Don Carlos de Grand Pre, Com. of this Fort and Post; for $400, payable in May 1785. John Woods, present and accepting. Both sign. Same witnesses as above. Before: Trevino.

---

p. 164. 22 Feb. 1784. David Smith, res. of this Dist., to John Burnet, the part which I held in the saw mill in partnership with him and Richard Gooding and which we erected in the Cypress Swamp belonging to the aforesaid Burnet, distant two leagues from the Fort; for $500 payable out of the profits of the said mill (p. 165) as the same may accrue. Signed D. Smith, John Burnet. Wit: Estevan Minor, Antonio Soler. Before me Philippe Trevino.

---

p. 165. 23 Feb. 1784. Richard Devall to George Rapalje, a lot in Natchez between the houses of Messrs. Bingaman and Miguel de Eslava, Military Storekeeper of this Fort, which sd lot I bought at public sale made by Don Carlos de Grand Pre, then belonging to Caleb Hansborough, absconded; for $300, which he has paid to me and a negro named "Levellier" which sd negro I have also recd. (p. 166) The sd, George Rapalje being present and accepting. Signed by Richard Devall. Wit: Estevan Minor, Antonio. Philippe Trevino.

---

p. 166. 24 Feb. 1784. Richard Bacon to Francisco Labisper, an unimproved lot in the town of Natchez, b. by ground of Bigman (Bingaman) on one side and Cato West on other; 57 ft in front by usual depth; for $250 wh. I have recd. Signed Richard Bacon, F. Labisper. Wit: Alexander Moore, Estevan Minor, John Bisland. Philippe Trevino.

---

p. 167. Adam Bingaman, res. of Dist., to Alexander Moore, merchant, of same, a house in town of Natchez, between ground of George Rapalje and Francisco Labisper, which sd house I bought at public sale of estate of John Blommart; for $600 cash which I have recd. Signed A. Bingaman, Alexander Moore. Wit: John Ellis, Francois Farrell, Estevan Minor. Philippe Trevino.

---

p. 167. 26 Feb. 1784. Daniel Baker, who declared to have recd. from Nathaniel Tomlinson of this Dist. $480, money lent, which (p. 168) he promised to pay at the end of two years from date with lawful interest thereon, and for surety, mortgages a plantation, three negroes and fifty hogs, with all moveables belonging to said plantation. Daniel Baker signed with a mark. Wit: Miguel Eslava, Antonio Soler. Philippe Trevino. p. 168. At Fort of Natchez, 11 Jany. 1788. Nathaniel Tomlinson acknowledges that he has received the $480 above mentioned, the said sum included in $600 amount of plantation sold to him by said Baker, annulling mortgage. Signed Nathaniel Tomlinson. Witnesses: Estevan Minor, Juan Careras. Carlos de Grand Pre.

---

p. 169. 27 Feb. 1784. Gibson Clark, res. of Dist., sold to Adam Bingaman, of Dist., negro boy aged 14 nat. of Carolina, $400 recd. Wit: Antonio Soler, Estevan Minor. Gibson Clark signed with a mark. Before Philippe Trevino.

---

p. 169. 5 March 1784. William Deuitt, res. of Dist. of own free will and accord, becomes surety for Russell Jones for the payment for sum or sums of money due and owing by sd Russell Jones in this District at this time and until the signing hereof . . . binding himself and estates present and to come. Signed. Wit: Estevan Minor, Pedro Azevedo. Before: Philippe Trevino.

---

p. 170. James Frazer to Don Miguel Eslava a negro man aged 22, for $300 recd. 15 March 1784. Signed by both. Wit: Estevan Minor, Pedro Azevedo, Antonio Soler. Before Trevino.

p. 171. 15 March 1784. Same as above.

---

p. 172. 15 March 1784. William Carney to Don Philippe Trevino, Commandant of Fort and Dist. of Natchez, negro woman, aged 19, named "Sally", for $375. Signed. Wit: same as above.

---

p. 173. William Carney to Don Miguel Eslava, negro man, "Charles" aged 24; $365. 15 March 1784. Signed by both: Wit: Estevan Minor, Antonio Soler, Pedro Azevedo. Before Trevino.

---

p. 174. Same to same, a mulatto fellow, named "Jacob", aged 20, for $250, 15 March 1784. Signed by both. Same wit. Before Trevino.

---

p. 175. 15 March 1784. William Carney to Don Miguel Eslava, negro men, aged 20, for $300 recd. Signed by both. Same wit. Before Trevino.

---

p. 176. 15 March 1784. James Frazer to Don Miguel Eslava, negro woman, "Sally", aged 20, with her two children, aged 2 and 8 mos. for $400. Signed by both. Same Wit. Bef. Trevino.

---

p. 176. 15 March 1784. Gavin Gowdy, to Don Miguel Eslava, slave aged 24, for $300 recd. Both sign. Same Wit. Before Trevino.

---

p. 177. 15 March 1784. James Mcgillivray to Miguel Eslava, negro fellow, aged 20, for $300. Signed by both. Same wit. Trevino.

---

p. 178. 20 March 1784. Petition of Abraham Mayes to sell at public sale to pay debts: quantity of tobacco, one horse-mill and 140 arpents, 8 of which cleared and well enclosed; b. by Wid. Truly, Richard Swayzey and Stowers, for cash. Natchez, Mch. 21, 1784, Let it be registered; and public notice given of the sale, on the twentieth(?) March 1784. Trevino. Report of Sale: Buyers of personal property, Alexander Moore and William Smith, of plantation 147 arpents on St. Catherine's Cr. Russell Jones for $71. Signed by witnesses: Estevan Minor, Antonio Soler, Wm. (X) Brocus, Chachere, Wm. Smith. Philippe Trevino.

---

p. 179. 3 Apr. 1784. Appraisement. In pursuance of the seizure of a plantation belonging to John Woods, absconded, at the demand of his creditors, Trevino appointed Appraisers, George Rapalje and David Smith, who have promised on oath to faithfully to do same. Wit: Estevan Minor, Francois Farrell. Plantation $400, negro and child $500, total $900. Signed by D. Smith and George Rapalje. Wit: Estevan Minor and Osborn Sprigg. Sale. 3 Apr. 1784, on demand of creditors of John Woods, have proceeded with sale (p. 180); adjudication to highest bidder of plantation, 290 arpents, to Adam Bingaman, for $155 payable Dec. 1784, surety Alexander Moore; of negro woman and child to Estevan Minor, for $561 payable as above, surety Daniel Mygatt, in presence of David Smith, Francois Farrell, George Rapalje and others assisting. Philippe Trevino.

---

p. 180. 2 May 1784. Inventory and appraisement of estate of George Rapalje to oblige him to pay creditors. Richard Harrison and Isaac Johnson appointed appraisers. Wit: Don Antonio Solar, Adam Bingaman. Estevan Minor acting as interpreter. (p. 181) Lands 750 arpents on Buffalo Creek from est. of John Blommart. (p. 182) 600 arpents on St. Catherine's Cr. gr. by Don Estevan Miro; 100 arps. on St. Catherine's Cr. purchased fr. Louis Charboneau; 400 arpents from same; 100 arpents from William Smith, tract granted by Estevan Miro on Bayou Boeuf; house in Natchez by Richard Devall; same from Thomas Green, lot 70 X 80 ft; lot of personal property. Total $9,017. (p. 183) Sale 3 May 1784.

Buyers: Personal property: Estevan Minor, Osborn Sprigg, Russell Jones, Santiago Horton, p. 183. John Dennison, John Arley, Richard Trevillian, Roswell Magget, (p. 184) William Hulbert, Santiago (James) Harman, Samuel Moore, John Row, Lewis Alston, Justis Humphreys. Lot in Natchez 102 ft in front by usual depth, good house and small kitchen, b. by Alex. Moore. and Don Miguel Eslava, to Antonio Soler for $200; (p. 185) Another with well-built house, b. by Miguel Eslava and the street, to Richard Harrison . . . Personal property: buyers, Nath'l. Tomlinson, Don Manuel Texada, Marcus White, Francisco Baso, John Burnet, Jeremiah Bryan. Lot in Natchez, b. by Richard Harrison and Louis Chachere, adjudged to Chachere; land on St. Catherine's Creek to George Casers; personal prop. to John Buhler. p. 186. Sale suspended for lack of bidders. // 3 Sept. 1784. In pursuance of the decree of Don Estevan Miro, 13 Aug. 1784, the estate and effects of sd Rapalje not having been sold for full amount of appraisal thereof, the sale should be annulled and the properties restored to owner with the exception of such effects as may have been consumed, the creditors having granted further delay. Philippe Trevino. // p. 186. 7 Feb. 1784. I, Don Philippe Trevino, having been constrained to arrest and confine in the Fort, the person of George Rapalue, charged with the crime of attempting to promote a general Rebellion in this District against the Spanish Government, which arrest was effected in the night between the 6th and 7th. p. 187-8. Inventory of effects taken. // p. 189. George Rapalje petitions that Richard Harrison, Estevan Minor, Nathaniel Tomlinson (for Estevan Minor), John Buhler, Manuel Texada, Marcus White, Francisco Baso and Lewis Chachere who purchased property at the Public Sale which said sale His Excellency Don Philippe Trevino was pleased to annul, for the benefit of his creditors, respectfully requests that the persons above named conform to this decree and also to pay for the use of the property which they have detained since Sept. 1784, to be put in the hands of Alexander Moore and Abraham Ellis. New Orleans, 1 Feb. 1786. // Order that the execution given by us in Sept. 1784 annulling sale be put in execution, etc. New Orleans, Mch. 30, 1786. Estevan Miro.

---

p. 190. 8 April 1784. Thos. Green, resident of this Dist., to George Rapalje, of same, lot in Natchez, 102 ft in front by whole depth from the street to the foot of the hill, b. by ground of Richard Bacon on one side on the other by the River, or landing of this Post, which I purchased of Capt. Richard Harrison; for $500, recd. Signed by both. Wit: Estevan Minor, Antonio Soler. Before Philippe Trevino. Note: it is understood by both parties to the foregoing sale that the seller has reserved a certain portion of ground ceded to his son, Abner Green, the number of feet not yet determined, b. on all sides by the street. Signed by both.

---

p. 191. John Farquhar, res. of Dist., petitions that, being indebted to James Mather and others, of New Orleans, to whom his whole estate is mortgaged and time of payment expired and George Fitzgerald and John Bisland, attorneys to recover the amount, have determined to sell estate at public sale. An inevitable and considerable loss would be sustained by petitioner and creditors because of scarcity of specie in the District. Prays to direct attorneys to take estate at the appraisment by two respectable persons, one of whom to be named by petitioner and other by attorneys. Natchez, 25 Feb. 1784. (p. 192) Natchez, 25 Feb. 1784. Communicated to the attorneys aforesaid. Trevino. Feb. 27, 1784. Agreed by attys. John Lum and Samuel Gibson appointed appraisers. Total $1380.50

---

p. 193. 25 May 1784. Emanuel Madden and Patience Coleman, residents of Dist., by mutual consent and accord have sold to John Lusk, also of Dist., 100 arpents, 5 leagues from Fort on Homochitto River; for $500 cash. Both sign with a mark. Wit: Estevan Minor, Pedro Azevedo, John Coleman. Trevino.

---

p. 194. 1 June 1784. William Ferguson, of the Dist., to Matthew White, 163 arpents on St. Catherine's Creek, one-half league from Fort, b. on south by lands of Silas Crane, west by Benj. Belk, north by Widow Hutchins, Jacob Cable and William McIntosh: for $300 received. Signed by both. Wit: Estevan Minor, Antonio Soler. Before Trevino.

---

p. 195. 5 June 1784. Abner Green, res. of Dist., to Richard Harrison, a negro man, aged 50, and a negro woman, same age, for $490. Both sign. Same wit as above. Trevino.

p. 196. 12 June 1784. Arthur Cobb, of Dist., to Don Estevan Minor, negro man "George", 18, nat. of Carolina, for $450 paid. Both sign. Wit: Antonio Soler, Josef Capetillo. Trevino.

---

p. 197. 12 June 1784. John Tennison, res. of Dist., to Don Estevan Minor, negro man "Sam", aged 24, nat. of Carolina, for $350, cash. Tennison signs with mark. Wit: same as above. Trevino.

---

p. 197. 12 June 1784. Estevan Minor to Francisco Menar, merchant, of Arcas (Arkansas. Translator), negro man named "Sam", for $500, payable December of this year. Signed by both. Wit: same as above. Trevino.

---

p. 198. 12 June 1874. Richard Harrison, Capt. of Militia and res. of Dist., to Don Estevan Minor, 282 arpents, distant 100 toises from sd Fort; for $564, received. Both sign. Same wit. Trevino.

---

p. 199. 15 June 1784. Estevan Minor to Francisco Menar, negro named "George", 18 yrs old, nat. of Carolina, for $500, payable in Dec. this year. Both sign. Same wit. Trevino.

---

p. 200. 16 June 1784. Silas Crane, of Dist., to William Ferguson, 325 arpents on Cole's Cr., b. on west by Emanuel Lum, on north by David Odam, on south vacant land, on east by Wid. Sarah Truly; for $300 recd., Both sign. Wit: Estevan Minor, Antonio Soler. Trevino.

---

p. 201. 5 June 1784. Stephen Mayes and Abraham Mayes, of Dist., to John Lusk, 100 arpents on Second Creek; for $200 recd. Signed by Stephen Mayes. Same wit. Trevino.

---

p. 201. 1 July 1784. John Stampley, of Dist., to John Hartley, 100 arpents, b. by John Row, Don Pedro Piernas, Don Ventura Collell and Francisco Espen; for $125 recd. Signed John Stampley, John Hartley (in German). Same wit. Trevino.

---

p. 202. 19 July 1784. Stephen Jourdan to my son, Thomas Jourdan, one-half of the property and estate of which I am possessed; 2 plantations, one on Cole's Creek, two negroes, cattle, horses, etc. Son to conduct and work the place as my overseer and manager, as well as the place I reserve for myself, the expenses to be equally divided, during my natural life. Stephen (X) Jourdan, Thomas Jourdan (signed). Same wit: Trevino.

---

p. 203. 27 July 1784. William Vousdan, of District, to Adam Bingaman, negro man "James Terry", aged 28, for $350 cash. Signed by both. Same wit. Philippe Trevino.

---

p. 204. 21 Aug. 1784. In consequence of the meditated flight of Russell Jones without passport and with intent to avoid the payment of debts, have proceeded to an inventory and appraisement of his whole estate for the security of his creditors. Appraisers: William Henderson and John Lum appointed. Inventory: Plantation, 140 arpents, 15 cleared and well-enclosed, b. by Wid. Sarah Truly. Plantation, 100 arpents, on St. Catherine's Cr., b. by Samuel Gibson and Louis Charboneau. Tract on St. Catherine's Cr., 450 arpents, b. by Stephen Holston and lands not granted. (p. 205) 23 Dec. 1784. Sale of Russel Jones' estate. Plantation adjudged to Mr. Chachere $121; horse to Don Juan Rodriguez, $78; same to Francisco Baso/ $36, and Estevan Minor $50; negro to Richard Swayze $260. Total $546. Debts $515, expense of sale $31. Creditors paid sum due them. 17 April 1787. Carlos de Grand Pre.

---

p. 207-8. 31 Aug. 1784. In consequence of the meditated flight of William Dueitt, for security of creditors, an inventory and appraisement of whole estate. Wm. Henderson and John Lum appointed appraisers. Total inventory $4,319. // p. 209. 23 Dec. 1784. On accusation and conviction of William Dueitt of intention to leave this District without passport to evade payment of just debts and in pursuance of order for public sale. Plantation, 600 arpents on St. Catherine's Cr, b. by vacant lands, with a clearing of 15 arpents, well fenced and some negro cabins. Plantation, 400 arpents, on Miss River, b. by Francois Farrell, Stephen Jordan and vacant lands, dwelling house and cabins to Richard Harrison, payable at end of year. Slaves: Negro Man "Ben" to Estevan Minor; "Jupiter", ae 22 to John Row; "Cuff", ae 40, to James Elliott, "June", ae 40, to Matthew White; "Clementon", ae 46, to Nathan Swayzey, woman "Phillis, ae 38 to William Smith, "Dolly", ae 19, to William Smith, girl "Tiney", ae 10, to Margaretta Smith, girl "Tibby", ae 13, to William Smith, child "Mary" ae 7 to same. (p. 211) Statement of the repartition pro rata of the proceeds of sale of above estate and effects, by order of Government. Fees to constable and cries $66-1, Seizure, sale, etc. $191, Rations furnished by King's Store-keeper while in prison, $33. Total $290. To the creditors; Pro-rata: Alexr. Moore $224-4; George Castles $136-3; David Smith $240-4; David Smith $221; Russel (Roswell) Magget $ 4-2; John Burnet $ 402; Gibson Clark $203; Josiah Flower $11 ; Justis King $1 ; p. 211 James Smith $4; Richard Bacon $14-5; William Barland $9-2; William B. Smith $4-5; Samuel Gibson $3-7; Jacob Coburn $3-2; William Brocus $22-4; James Harman $7-4; William Smith $276-2; Estevan Minor $65-4; Miguell Eslava $1483-6; Mathew White $38-1; Chachere $47; Joseph Capetillo $16-2; Carpenter $41-6; Daniel Muguet $82; Estevan Minor $99-3; Natchez, 20 Feb. 1786. Philippe Trevino.

---

p. 212. 10 Sept. 1784. David Smith, of District, to Cato West. 100 arpents near Cole's Creek, b. on one side by land of Samuel Osborn, on other sides vacant; for $150 in cash paid at time of sale. Signed D. Smith. Cato West. Wit: St. Germain, Antonio Soler. Es Minor (Interpreter and witness.) Philippe Trevino.

---

p. 212. 27 Sept. 1784. Jacob Cable, of District, to Polser Shilling, merchant, of same, 74 arpents, a part thereof unclosed, with dwelling, one league from Fort, b. by Stephen Mayes, William Ferguson, George Ralapje and St. Catherine's Cr., which I hold by grant; for $100 cash in hand. Cable signs with a mark. Shilling signs. Wit: Es Minor, Antonio Soler. Philippe Trevino.

---

p. 213. 27 Sept. 1784. Francisco Spain, of District, to Polser Shilling, merchant, of same, 235 arpents, a part enclosed with dwelling, one-half league from Fort, b. as in preceding and also by Wid. Sarah Truly, which I hold by grant; for $160 cash in hand. Acknowledged by Spain before witnesses, the same as above. Philippe Trevino.

---

p. 214. 1 Oct. 1784. Don Miguel Eslava, of District, to Richard Bacon, a house in Natchez, bet. houses of Messrs. Harrison and Rapalje, which said house I had from the same and have paid him for; for $700, payable Dec. 1785. Signed by both. Wit: Antonio Soler, John Jph. Rodriguez, Manuel Garcia de Texada. Philippe Trevino.

---

p. 215. 11 Oct. 1784. Benjamin Rogers, of District, to Richard Bacon, of same, slave, aged 40, for $500 cash in hand. Rogers signed with initials. Antonio Soler, Estevan Minor. Trevino.

---

p. 215. 16 Oct. 1784. Joseph Dyson, of District, to Abner Green, 400 arpents near Cole's Cr. b. land of Charles Howard and lands not granted; for $180 cash in hand. Dyson signed with his mark. Wit; as above. Minor also interpreter. Trevino.

---

p. 216. 16 Oct. 1784. Jeremiah Brian, of District, to Elijah Routh, 72 arpents, at Cole's Cr., by land of Alexander McIntosh, on one side; those of Samuel Osborn on the other, otherwise by vacant land, which I purchased at public sale fo est. of Alexander Boyd and Isabel Boyd, *his wife, both deceased,

Dec. 1781; for $450, (on terms). Signed by both. Same wit. as above with Abner Green. Trevino.
* "Isabel" is used by Spanish for "Elizabeth".

---

p. 217. 5 Oct. 1784. On demand of James Kelly, creditor of Abraham Mayes, for $70, have proceeded to sale and adjudication of a horse mill seized as property of sd Mayes, for sd payment, in presence of Chachere, David Smith, William Barland, John Burnet and others. Horse mill adjudged to Adam Bingaman for $80. Signed A. Bingaman. Wit: Es Minor, Richd. Bacon, Antonio Soler, Chachere. Philippe Trevino.

---

p. 217. 23 Oct. 1784. Estevan Minor to William Weeks, negro woman, "Catherine", aged 18, nat. of Carolina, with her child, ten months, for $700 cash. Signed. Wit: Antonio Soler, Chachere. Philippe Trevino.

---

p. 218. 23 Oct. 1784. Michel Pierre Nitard, merchant, of Arkansas, declared he owed Don Antonio Ramis, a merchant of N. O. or his attorney, $4900, moneylent to assist him in trade, and obliging himself to pay in May 1785, mortgages whole of merchandises of which he is possessed at the afsd. Post as well as all debts outstanding due and owing to him. Same wit.

---

p. 219. 29 Oct. 1784. Richard Devall, of District, declared that he binds himself to deliver on or before Dec. 24 at City of N. O. to Don Antonio Ramis, merchant, or his order, all the plank 10X12 ft long that he may have sawed in his mill at Cole's Creek during said time, to be paid for by Ramis at 35 cents per plank, such being the agreement of parties and the party failing therein shall pay to the other $300. Signed by both. Wit: Estevan Minor, Jno. Joseph Rodriguez, Antonio Soler.

---

p. 220. Will of Sterling Spell, of the District of Natchez, Prov. of West Florida, planter. To my loving wife, Susannah, all my estate during her life or widowhood and at her death to my children, Martha Spell and Benjamin Spell, or to the survivor of them; in case of her remarrying the whole estate to be placed in hands of George Rapalje and Samuel Gibson for the benefit of my ch. and I hereby enjoin them as guardians of my family and exors. of my estate. 12 Nov. 1784. Signed with his mark. Wit: John Shunk and Richard Ellis. (Shunk signed in German.) p. 220. 19 Nov. 1784. In order to proceed with an inventory of estate of Sterling Spell, decd. we have notified Samuel Gibson and George Rapalje of their appointment as executors of will and guardians of the minors, which they have willingly accepted and sworn legally to discharge. // p. 221. 26 Nov. 1784. Inventory $1906. Estate and effects left in charge of Susy Spell, lawful wife and widow and mother of minors, to be kept until her ch. are of lawful age. Signed by executors. Wit: Antonio Soler. Es Minor, Jno. Joph. Rodriguez. Philippe Trevino.

---

p. 222. 10 Nov. 1784. Nathan Swazey, of District, to John Lusk of same, 250 arpents on Homochitto, b. by Alex. Dawson, William Case and sd river; for $250, in hand paid. Signed by both. Wit: Estevan Minor, Chachere, and A. Bingaman. Trevino.

---

p. 222. 27 Nov. 1784. Joseph Forester, of District, to Richard Swayze, of same, 450 arpents for $250, $100 paid and remaining March next. Both sign. Wit: Antonio Soler, Chachere. Trevino.

---

p. 223. 28 Nov. 1784. Major Luke Collins, of Opelousas, sold to John Ellis, of Natchez, 113 arpents on Second Cr., adj Samuel Wells, Wm. Joiner, the creek and James Barbut; for $400 in hand paid. Signed Thomas Collins for Luke Collins. Wit: Est. Minor, Luke Collins, Jr., Antonio Soler. Trevino.

---

p. 224. 28 Nov. 1784. Luke Collins, Jr., of Opelousas to John Bowls, of Natchez, 100 arpents three leagues from Fort, b. by Melor Egleton, Herbert Munster, _____ Stephenson, and land not granted; for $100 recd. Signed. Wit: Estevan Minor, John Ellis, Antonio Soler. Before Trevino.

p. 224. 28 Nov. 1784. Richard Ellis, of this District, to Major Luke Collins, here present and accepting, two tracts on Bayou Teche, in Dist. of Opelousas, one 12 arpents front of Bayou Canon by 40 arpents in depth, running parallel with Bayou Teche; the other 25 X 40 arpents on the coast east of Bayou Teche, (p. 225) joining the other; for $400 in hand paid. John Ellis, attorney for Richard Ellis.

---

p. 225. 4 Dec. 1784. Isaac Johnson, of District, to Thomas M. Green, 200 arpents at Cole's Cr., b. by James Cole; other lands not granted; for $700 in hand paid. Signed by both.

---

p. 226. 9 Dec. 1784. Abel Baker, of District, declared he had made William Foster his atty. to recover and receive from William Hunt $150 at New Orleans as well as other debts owing him. Abel Baker signs with mark, A. B. Trevino.

---

p. 227. 20 Dec. 1784. In order to proceed with public sale of estate and effects of George Castles, decd., notified Don Luis Chachere, merchant, charged with settlement of the accounts of sd estate.

---

p. 228. 28 Dec. 1784. Notice received of the death of Joanna Osborn, widow of late Samuel Osborn and since wife of Elijah Routh, said Joanna died at Cole's Creek and left 4 children, 2 sons and 2 daus. lawful issue by her 1st marriage, the boys Samuel and Boyd, one 14 and the other 11; the daus. Sarah and Buldah. Curators appointed; Isaac Johnson and James Truly, of District, who accepted the charge.
p. 229. 28 Dec. 1784. Appraisers of above estate Richard Harrison and John Burnet, both residents and planters of sd District, who accepted. (p. 230) Jany. 1, 1785. Inventory and appraised $2435. Nothing more being found on account of Elijah Routh, last husband of the deceased Joanna Osborn, having absconded on 26 of last month, taking two children, Samuel and Boyd, three slaves and seven horses and sundry other effects, belonging to the four minors. Signed James Truly and Isaac Johnson. Wit: John Burnet, Jno. Joseph Rodriguez. Trevino. // p. 230. 3 Jany. 1785. Curators ask that estate be sold at public sale (p. 231). Bond of Curators; Richard Harrison for James Truly; Thos. Green, Jr. for Isaac Johnson. (p. 232). Report of Sale of estate of Samuel Osborn, 11 Jany. 1785. Plantation to James Elliot, Thos. M. Green, surety. Other buyers: Gibson Clark, surety John Burnet; James Armstrong; James Elliott; Thomas Calvet; George Killion - surety John Stille, Abner Green- Thos. M. Green;: Thos. M. Green- Abner Green; James Armstrong- John Burnet; William Ferguson- Richard Devall; Jeremiah Brian- James Elliott; James Truly- Jeremiah Brian; Manuel Texada - Estevan Minor; Estevan Minor -James Elliot; William Ferbens- Richd. Devall; John Terry . . . Total $3003

---

p. 234. 26 Dec. 1784. Notice recd. of death of Richard Curtis, res. of this District. (p. 234) Don Estevan Minor, acting as interpreter, declared that the will contained in substance that the said Richard Curtis bequeathed the whole of his estate and effects to his two children, namely a son named Jonathan Curtis, aged 17, and a daughter named Jemimah Curtis, aged 20, appointing as curator to said minors William Curtis and Justus Humphreys to take charge of same. // p. 236. Appraisers for estate: Richard Harrison and John Lum. Inventory and appraisal total $575.

---

p. 237. 3 Jany. 1785. Gibson Clark, of District, to Lewis Fontenot, of Opelousas, a negro woman named "Judy", aged 25, and child, aged 1, nat. of Carolina for $660 rec'd. Gibson signs with mark. Wit: John Buhler, Antonio Soler. Trevino.

---

p. 237. Thomas Calvet, of District, to Louis Fontenot, of Opelousas, negro girl, "Fanny", aged 12, nat. of Carolina, for $340, recd. Calvet signs with his mark. Wit. as above. Trevino.

---

p. 238. 5 Jany. 1785. David Odam to Cato West 200 arpents b. by Dibdal Holt, Henry Stampley, Cole's Cr. and land not granted; for $325, paid in hand. Both sign. Wit: Antonio Soler, Chachere. Trevino.

p. 238. 11 Jany. 1785. Manuel Madden, of District, to Adam Bingaman, 100 arpents on St. Catherine's Cr. b. by land of Silas Crane, Adam Bingaman, Benj. Belk, Daniel Baker; for $125 paid. Signed by both. Same wit. Trevino.

---

p. 239. 15 Jany. 1785. William Ferguson, of District, to Parker Carradine, negro man "Jack", aged 25, for $600 paid in hand. Both sign. Same wit. Trevino.

---

p. 240. 18 Jany. 1785. Lewis Chachere, res. and merchant of Dist., to Richard Carpenter, merchant, of same, house and lot in Natchez purchased at private sale to me by George Rapalje and the other part from Richard Harrison, b. on one side by George Castles, decd., on another by Harrison, and on the street; for $800 in hand paid, reserving for myself a room in sd house until Febuary 1786, without paying rent for same. Both sign. Wit: Est. Minor, Antonio Soler. Trevino.

---

p. 240. 25 Jany. 1785. David Smith, of District, sells to Mary Foster, of same, 500 arpents on St. Catherine's Cr. b. on one side by Richard Ellis, on another by John Oxberry, on another by said Mary Foster and on another by sd creek; for $500 in hand paid. Signed D. Smith, Mary Foster. Wit: Antonio Soler, Chachere. Trevino.

---

p. 241. Stephen Hobson (Holston), of District, to Richard Carpenter, 250 arpents on St. Catherine's Creek, b. by Benj. Belk, John Tally, Russell Jones; for $350 paid. Signed Stephen Holston, Richard Carpenter. Wit: John McFarlan, William Brown, King Holston. Before Philippe Trevino.

---

p. 242. 13 Feb. 1785. In pursuance of a seizure of plantation of Joseph Ford, on demand of Richard Smith, creditor of sd. Ford for $75, we have appointed Messrs. Gibson Clark and Arthur Cobb, both of District, appraisers, who have sworn to acquit themselves of sd charge. // On 19 Feb. 1785. Public notice having been given, proceeded to the sale and adjudication of plantation of Joseph Ford, on demand of Richard Smith, his creditor. Plantation on Miss. River, b. by John Burnet, Gibson Clark and land not granted, _____ arpents, sold to Benjamin Monsanto for $50. Estevan Minor signed for Monsanto. James Armstrong, witness.

---

p. 243. 14 Feb. 1784. In pursuance of a seizure of a horse, the property of William Ryan, on demand of Louis Chachere, Atty. for the estate of George Castles, appraisement of the horse by Wm. Brocus and John Burnet, of District, in presence of Adam Bingaman and Estevan Minor. Value given $30. // 20 Feb. 1785. Sale and adjudication of above, in presence of David Smith, John Burnet, Richard Harrison and others assisting, to Francisco Baso for $34-4 rials. Es. Minor signed for Francisco Baso. The horse was black and 12 years old.

---

p. 244. 27 Feb. 1785. Appeared Carlos Enrique Bachellot, merchant, of District, who declared himself bound to pay Benjamin Monsanto, of same, $500 money lent, in May 1785, mortgages two slaves, "Apollo", ages 24, and "Marie Mart" aged 14. Wit: Chachere, Antonio Soler.

---

p. 245. Mary Higdon, of District, for natural love and affection for my son, Jeptha Higdon, of sd District, and also other causes, etc., have given unto him, the sd Jeptha, upon express conditions hereinafter mentioned, all my goods, chattels and property, real and personal, consisting of four negroes, called "Old Tom", "Young Tom", "Dick" and "Limrick", horned cattle, horses, hogs and every article, thing of whatsoever nature, to have and hold in trust during his natural life but not to sell, dispose of in any way, nor shall it or any part of it, be subject to his engagements, contracts or debts, now or to be hereafter contracted, but at his death to be equally divided among the lawfully begotten heirs of him, my son Jeptha Higdon, who never-the-less is to use enjoy and dispose of all the revenue and profit to be made by using and employing said negroes and stock. If he die without heirs, one negro to go to his wife and the remainder of the estate to revert to me. 1 March 1785. Both sign with their marks. Wit: Stephen Minor, D. Smith.

---

p. 246. 13 March 1785. Nehemiah Albertson, of this district, to Nehemiah Baso, merchant, of same, negro named "Mary" aged 28, for $435 cash. Albertson signed. Wit: William Gilbert, Josef Capetillo.

---

p. 246. 6 April 1785. Goerge Fitzgerald, merchant, of this District, as atty. for James Mather, of New Orleans, sell in his name to Richard Devall, of District, slave named "Lindor" aged 16, which he purchased of Mr. Bellill, planter, at the German Coast; for 450 pounds of indigo to be delivered in December of this year (p. 247) at current value thereof at N. O. at the time afsd. Signed by George Fitzgerald, atty for Mather. Wit: Antonio Soler, Chachere. Before Philippe Trevino.

---

p. 248. Same to same for a negro named "Baptiste", aged 30, being the same purchased of William Vousdan; for $600 payable Dec. of this year. 6 April 1785. Same signatures and witnesses. Before Trevino.

---

p. 249. 16 April 1785. Richard Harrison, of this district, to Polser Shilling, merchant, of same, a house and lot at the landing at Natchez, b. by lots of Francisco Baso, Richard Carpenter, the street and the hill; for $330 cash. Both signed. Same wit. Before Trevino.

---

p. 249. 20 Apr. 1785. Joseph Capetillo, soldier in the garrison of this Fort, at Natchez, with permission of Don Philippe Trevino, Commandant, sold to Alexander Moore, merchant, of this District, a house and lot in Natchez, b. by house of the purchaser, Miguel _________ and the hill, which I had from Charles Henry (p. 250) Bachellot; for 285 paid. Both sign. Same wit.

---

p. 250. 4 May 1785. Richard Deval, of this District, to Francisco Menar, merchant, of same, a negro named "Leville" aged more than 50 years; for $300. Signed by both. Same wit.

---

p. 251. 2 June 1785. Richard Harris, res. of New Orleans, in pursuance of a sale made to him and Caleb Owens, by John White, of this District of 200 arpents on east side of St. Catherine's Cr., b. by land of Daniel Wattman which was made before Don Raphael Perdono, Notary Public of the City of N. O., a copy whereof is herewith presented, which he prays may be transferred and deposited in the Archives of this Province for better surety thereof and as it respects his said partner, it being notorious that the said John White has absconded. (A copy of the deed follows with details (p. 252) about as above.)

---

p. 253. 12 June 1785. On demand of Adam Bingaman, an order of seizure of two tracts of land, the property of Henry Stuart. Appraisement by William Brocus and Richard Harrison, in presence of Stephen Haward. First tract: 500 arpents on St. Catherine's Cr., one league from Fort, b. by William Smith, Bradley, Harrison and Co., and lands formerly of late Christian Bingaman, now belonging to afsd. Stuart. 2nd tract: 200 arpents on St. Catherine's Cr., b. by lands of William Smith, Adam Bingaman, (on two sides) and Daniel Baker. The 1st valued at $1000 and the 2nd at $400. Same date: Notice having been given both lots adjudged to Adam Bingaman at $670. Wit: Es. Minor, Stephen Haward. Before Philippe Trevino.

---

p. 254. Francisco Menar to Don Estevan Minor negro named "Sam", aged 21, nat. of Carolina, which negro I purchased from said Don Estevan Minor;.for $500 payable March 1786. 11 July 1785. Both sign. Wit: Antonio Soler, Chachere. Before Trevino.

p. 255. Don Phelipe Trevino to Lewis Chacere, merchant of this Post, a negro woman "Dolly" aged 20, with child, Joseph aged 2; for $800, payable January 1786. Aug. 6, 1786.

---

p. 256. 6 Aug. 1785. Don Phelipe Trevino to Don Estevan Minor, a negro girl "Mary", aged 10, for $400, payable Jany. 1786.

---

p. 257. 15 October 1785. Margaret Stampley, duly authorized by her husband, Henry Stampley, planter of the District, sells to Thomas M. Green, 100 arpents as by patent of the British Government, 1 Sept. 1777, 30 miles northwest of Natchez, on a branch of Boyd's Creek, b. on the east by sd creek and otherwise vacant lands; for $300 in hand paid. She signs with her mark. Wit: Antonio Soler, Joaquim Ossorno. Franco. Bouligny.

p. 258. 15 October, 1785. John Row, planter of District, to William Vousdan, 250 arpents on Second Creek, 14 miles south of Natchez, as by Royal patent of His Brittanic Majesty, dated 25 May 1779, b. on west by Anthony Hutchins, north by Cephas Kinnard, and otherwise vacant lands; for $580, paid in full. Both sign. Wit: Louis Perez de Bellegarde, Joaquim Ossorno. Before Franco. Bouligny.

p. 258. 20 Oct. 1785. Sarah Truly, to Alexander Moore, merchant, both of the District, 160 arpents, superficial measurement of City of Paris. (footnote by translator: 225 toises set forth on plot of Surveyor Genl. of the Prov., Don Carlos Trudeau, dated 14 Dec. 1782.) granted to me by Don Estevan Miro, 31 Jany, 1785, 2 miles from Fort, b. (n) by Abraham Mayes, (e) by Wm. Hulbert, (s) Francisco Spain, (w) John Stampley; for $250, paid. Both sign. Wit: Joaquim Ossorno, Juan Joseph Duforest. Franco. Bouligny.

p. 259. Joseph Forester, res. of District, to Richard Swayzey, 260 arpents, b. by lands of Samuel Gibson and Stephen Watkins, for $260, paid. Nov. 16, 1785. Both sign. Official witnesses. Before Bouligny.

p. 260. 10 Dec. 1785. Estevan Minor, Adjt. of Fort, to Thomas Haspower, three brute negroes for $1050 paid in full. Both sign. Off. wit. Bouligny.

p. 261. 23 Jany. 1786. Pedro Camus, merchant, of the District, to James Truly, a negro named "Samba", aged 22, belonging to John Charbono, planter, of the German Coast ; for $600 payable Dec. 1786, Richard Harrison being surety therefor, binding himself to produce proof of his authority to make this conveyance and that there is no mortgage on said negro. Both sign. Off. wit. Bouligny.

---

p. 262. 31 Jany. 1786. Stephen Holston to Joseph Holmes, a negro woman, named "Susy", aged ____, and a negro boy, "Isaac", aged 8; $500 paid in hand. Both sign. Off. wit. Bouligny.

---

p. 263. 31 Jany. 1786. Francisco Baso, to Robt. Dunbar, a negro woman of the Macoa Nation, without name, not having been baptized, free from mortgage, (proven by instrument of sale at New Orleans, which I have produced); for $500, of which $400 paid, the other $100 due Dec. of this year. Acknowledged before witnesses: Juan Carreras and Antonio Gras. Robt. Dunbar signs. Bouligny.

---

p. 264. Feb. 2, 1786. Henry Bachelot Deshubles, indebted to Don Francisco de Longuest, for $775, payable 1786, for security mortages two negroes, "Apollo" aged 25, and "Mary Martha", aged 15, which sd negroes were mortgaged to Benj. Monsanto, 27 Feb. 1785, for $500 which has been paid and the mortgage annulled. Signed. Off. wit. Bouligny.

---

p.264. 3 Feb. 1786. Richard Bacon, of this District, to Don Pedro Azevedo, house in Town of Natchez, near the descent of the hill, on the right hand, which said house was erected by sd Bacon. Off. Wit. Both sign. Bouligny.

---

p. 265. 4 March 1786. Don Estevan Minor to Don Daniel Ogden, both of this District, two negroes, "James", aged 35, and "June", aged 40, natives of Guinea; 1st for $500; 2nd for $250, in hand paid.

Both sign. Wit: James Harman, Juan Carreras. Carlos de Grand Pre.

---

p. 266. 16 March 1786. John Lusk, planter, of District, to Anne Gaillard, 250 acres, British pat., dated 13 Oct. 1777, to Nathan Swayze ; on Homochitto River, b. by Wm. Case and Col. Dixon; for $351 paid. Both sign. Wit: Antonio Soler, Estevan Minor.

---

p. 268. 1 April 1786. Don Phelipe Trevino to Don Estevan Minor, negro girl "Mary", aged 12, nat. of Carolina; for $400, paid. Both sign. Wit: James McIntosh, Chachere. Carlos de Grand-Pre.

---

p. 269. April 1, 1786. Don Phelipe Trevino to Don Estevan Minor, 225 arpents on St. Catherine's Creek, b. by Samuel Gibson, Philip Turpin and purchaser; for $300 paid. Both sign. Carlos de Grand-Pre

---

p. 269. 6 Apr. 1786. Don Phelipe Trevino to Don Carlos de Grand Pre, Lt. Col. of Royal Armies and Com. of this Post and District, 140 arpents, 15 arpents cleared, the rest wood land with an old fence, b. on one side by Mistress Truly, late of Alexander Moore, on other by Swayze; for $138 paid. Both sign. Off. wit.

---

p. 270. 22 Apr. 1787. John Bisland to Waterman Crane and Hiburd (Crane), negro "Jupiter" of Senegal nation, aged 30, for $300, "in a note". Signed by Bisland and Waterman Crane. Wit: James McIntosh, Juan Carreras. Carlos de Grand-Pre.

---

p. 271. 20 May 1786. Don Samuel Flower, of District, owes to David Williams, of Dist. of Baton Rouge, $1450, which was lent him in the following manner: $600 paid for him to Mr. Devald (Devall); $400 to Pablo Sharp; $250 to George Profitt, and to which is to be added $200 for interest of two years; for surety mortgages negro boy "Juba", of the Mandengo nation, aged 12; negro woman 'Sukey", a Creole of Jamaica, and a plantation of 400 arpents on St. Catherine's Cr., (p. 272) b. by Messrs. Fort (Ford) and Richard Harrison. Wit: Wm. Pontney, Richard Devall. Carlos de Grand-Pre

---

p. 272. 22 May 1786. James McIntosh to Don Carlos de Grand-Pre, etc., a negro man "Baker", aged 30, which I purchased at the public sale of estate of deceased John St. Germain; for $500 paid. Both sign. Wit: Joseph Rodriguez, Antonio Soler. Before Jno. Jph. Rodriguez.

---

p. 273. 8 May 1786. In pursuance of information received of the accidental death of Juan St. Germain, occasioned by a fall from the top of a tree in the Cypress Swamp, from which his death ensued in two hours, having repaired to the plantation of _______ Burnet*, 2-1/2 leagues from the Fort, where meeting with the King's Surgeon, of this District, Don Louis Faure, who had repaired there immediately on being informed of the accident and found him in the said house (p. 274) already dead half an hour before his arrival; . . . we found the body cold and wantingone leg . . . Signed by Louis Faure, Antonio Soler, Jn. Jph. Rodriguez. Carlos de Grand-Pre. [* Note: John Burnet, A-164.]

p. 274. 9 May 1786. In consequence of the death of Juan St. Germain, verified the 8th instant, the sd deceased having never contracted matrimony nor left legitimate heirs or relations . . . inventory ordered. Don Juan Vauchere, merchant, of this Post, to take charge of estate; appraisers appointed Don Estevan Minor and Richard Bacon. The two appraisers, with witnesses Don Antonio Soler and Jeremiah Brian, with with Commandant, proceed to plantation and late dwelling of the deceased Juan St. Germain, distant abt. 5 miles, to examine papers whether will containing disposition of the estate but found nothing so concluded sitting for today. Signed by all. // p. 275. May 9, 1786. Inventory and appraisement of estate of the deceased Juan St. Germain, native of Paris, France, by appraisers Don Juan Vauchere and witnesses begun. [Several days given to this. Inventory long.] p. 277. Lands: Plantation 1000 arpents on bank of the Miss. River, 5 leagues from Fort, with wooden house built in the English manner and sundry other outhouses, about 40 acres planted in corn, b. by River, land of Benedum [?] land of deceased and vacant land. $500. Another plantation, 600 arpents, similar dwelling, a saw mill of one saw, with appurtenances thereto belonging; b. on one side by above plantation, the Miss. River, and land of Lapuente. $1000. Another plantation, not settled, lately granted near the Yazoo River on West bank of the Miss. (Marginal note: Resumed by His Majesty.) p. 278. Inventory of papers: Note by Francisco Martin, 21 Apr. 1783, $25.; Note by Groves Morris, in favor of Don Louis Chachere (proved to have been paid); Note by Joseph Duncan, 4 Apr. 1783; Note by Peter Nelson, (paid); Note by Jeremiah Routh, 22 July, 1784; Note by George Rapalje, 15 Jany. 1782. (Recovered when estate sold); Note by Joseph Newton, 25 July 1783. (Absconded.); Joseph Olden [Holden], 9 Sept. 1783. (Died without property); Order by Gibson Clarke in favor of deceased. (Declared paid 27 Jany. 1786.); Order by John Holden in favor of Polser Shilling, 12 May 1783. (Died without property); Order by Thomas Reader, in favor of Richard Bacon, 24 Oct. 1783. (Absconded); Order by Abner Grayson, 14 Sept. 1782. (d. no property. Executed.); Note by William Smith, 14 Sept. 1782; an order by Richard Devall to deliver to John Coleman his note for $16, dated 26 Sept. 1784; Note by William Roling, 9 June 1783. (Unknown); Note by Adam Bingaman, 14 May 1783, "for the value of four gallons of spirits."; Note by Charles Royer, 27 Apr. 1785. (Unknown.); Note Patrick McClary, 1 Oct. 1783, (Res. unknown.); Note by John Peters, 5 July 1783. (Not known.); a receipt by Mr. Lachance for a bill of exchange for $4416, 12 May 1786, in favor of deceased. (Marked "at the Illinois"); Note Chas. Howard, 28 March 1786. (Paid by his bond and surety); Note by Robert Cid, in favor of Jeremiah Routh, 22 Apr. 1784. (Proved to have been paid); Note by Benjamin Rogers on Carpenter, 23 Nov. 1784. (Not known.); Many notes for brandy; An order by Moses Bonner for rum, not dated; An order by Mr. Villebeuve, in favor of an Indian, for one bottle of rum and a note by deceased at bottom stating that he had delivered 10 more bottles to the Chief; Note by William Atchinson in favor of McCaul, 4 Feb. 1782; (p. 282) Bill of sale from Peter Acquine, 1 Oct. 1784, for negro woman; same from Denison for negro man; same from Richard Gooding of 600 arpents. Appraisal total $ 6, 766-6-1/2.

---

p. 283. 9 June 1786. John Ferguson, planter, is indebted to Don Juan Vaucheret and John Stilly, for $260, for surety, mortgages 200 acres of land on which he lives, 10 miles from Fort, b. by Messrs Carpenter and Reuben White, also year's crop.

---

p. 285. 4 July 1786. Appeared William and James McIntosh, brothers, of this Dist., who declared that early this morning Philip Alston and Drum Gold*, fugitives, formerly of this district, have stolen a negro man named "King" which sd negro formerly belonged to the "robber" Philip Alston, and purchased by the father of the deponents, at the Public Sale of the estate of the late rebel Alston confiscated to the use of the king. Signed by both. Wit: Estevan Minor, Antonio Soler. Before Grand-Pre. [* James Drumgoole, son-in-law of Philip Alston.]

---

p. 285. 19 July 1786. Appeared John Bisland, res. of Dist., who of his own free will and accord transferred to Susanna Butcher, a negro woman named "Polly" or "Maria", aged 16, to enjoy and possess but not to sell, the said negro and her children, if any, after her death to revert to her brother John. Sd John Bisland also gives to sd Susanna two cows and their calves to be hers until her brother John shall have attained the age of 18, at which time the cows and their increase shall be divided. The above mentioned (p. 296) brother of Susanna is named Alexander and not John. Signed. Wit: George Fitzgerald, John Farquhar. De Grand-Pre.

---

p. 286. July 19, 1786. John Bisland sells to John Farquhar and William Barland 525 arpents, one league from Fort, b. by John Fitzgerald, Stephen Jordan, Stephen Minor, Daniel Grasse and John Lum; for $1000 . . . $500 1 Jany. 1788, $500 Jany. 1, 1789; plantation to be delivered Dec. 1, 1786, the seller reserving for himself all building except two houses until May 15, 1787. Signed Wit: George Fitzgerald, Juan Carreras. De Grand-Pre.

---

p. 287. 7 Aug. 1786. John Burnet sells to William Henderson a negro man named "Butnor", aged 30, and a negro woman "Katy", aged 25, with her two children, aged 3 and two months, all natives of America; for $1000, paid in notes. Both sign. Wit: Surget, Juan Carreras. De Grand-Pre.

p. 288. 24 Aug. 1786. In pursuance of information from John Vaucheret, of the Town of Natchez, of the death of Lorenzo Faverge, have proceeded to an inventory of his estate and effects. He died unmarried without leaving any known heirs in this District. Don Juan Vaucheret appointed to make full disclosure of the effects in his house belonging to dec'd. Lorenzo Faverge. Don Pedro Azeveda and Antonio Gras appointed appraisers. (p. 289) 24 Aug. 1786. Inventory and appraisal. pp. 290-1. Account left in a trunk. 15 prs. of shoes furnished to the family of Mr. Vaucheret, both women's and men's, from 4 May 1786 to Jun 15, 1786, $35; 3 prs. shoes to Lewis Fort, (pd); 1 pr. to Mr. Moore; 1 pr. to Mr. Dupon; 1 pr. to Mr. Jordan ($4); 1 pr. to Don Estevan Minor ($3-4); 1 pr. to "Rosalie". A letter from a brother of deceased Lorenzo Laverge written from Marseilles 6 Jany. 1785, giving information of the death of the wife of the deceased Lorenzo, who we didn't know before was married; 14 letters from dead wife and letters from others. Deceased must have had property in New Orleans. Mr. Bourgeois can give information. Added to inventory: Lot in Natchez (Under-the Hill), 80 ft. front by 120 ft. depth, $80. pp. 293-6. Sept. 2, 1786. It being necessary to appoint someone to represent the heirs, if there be any, of the est. of Lorenzo Faverge, dec'd, and to assist at the sale, Don Luis Faure appointed. (Sale extended over a number of "sittings".) Buyers: Mr. Boucheres, Mr. Stilly, Antonio Gras, Alonzo Segovia, Joaquim De Ossorno, Pedro Azevedo, Don Luis Faure, (one waistcoat and breeches of black satin for $16), one ruffled shirt to Pedro Azevedo for $12, one sett of silver "Hevillas" to Don Luis Faure $12; Jeremiah Bryan, Thomas Green, Wm. Brocus, Estevan Minor, Caleb King, Richard Bell, Gabriel Swazey, Don Antonio Soler. 24 Sept. 1786. The lot in Natchez 80X120 ft, adjudged twice to Alexander Moore at $25 and the third time to Don Luis Chacheret for $81. Total $376-3.

---

p. 292. David William and Francisco Baso exchange slaves. 1 Sept. 1786.

---

p. 297. 12 Sept. 1786. Estevan Minor to Joseph Bernard, 500 arpents, one league from Fort, b. by John Farquhar and vacant lands; for $500 paid. Signed. Off. wit. De Grand-Pre.

---

p. 298. 6 Oct. 1786. Carlos De Grand-Pre, etc., with interpreter of this Fort, Louis Chacheret, have repaired to Bayou Pierre, about 15 leagues from the Fort, to the dwelling place of the deceased James Armstrong with intent to proceed with an inventory of his estate and effects, which are as follows; A plantation for which there is no grant with a small house thereon, in which the deceased Armstrong dwelt and in which were found the following papers: Note of John Folerd (Follard) $200; Order on Craig $102; Note of Wm. Raen (Ryan) $100; ack. of John Stillee abt plantation; Order by John Wood on John White. Inventory of cattle, Oct. 7, 1786. Witness to both inventories Cato West, Manuel Texada, Thomas M. Green, Luis Faure, J. Vauchere, Antonio Soler. (p. 299) Oct. 8, 1786. Repair to one of the branches of St. Catherine's Creek, 1-1/2 leagues from Fort. // (p. 300) 18 Apr. 1787. Sale of estate of James Armstrong, dec'd.; appraisers Cato West and Thos. Green. Total (personal) $802. (p. 301) Sale: 28 April 1787. Buyers: Roswell Megget, Manuel Texada, Caleb King, Abraham Lodell (Lobdell), William Fairbanks, John Smith (Cato West surety), Arthur Cobb, Richard Carpenter, John Girault, Jeremiah Brian. Amount of sale: $884. Fees: To Commandant $81, Sheriff $18, Interpreter $39; Jeremiah Brian and his hands for driving cattle and their care $42, Juan Joseph Rodriguez, King's Storekeeper, for provisions for family $33; Balance $671. List of creditors of estate and prorata recd. Justus King $75-$20; John Short $174-46; Barney Isinhood $20-$5; Josiah Flower $53-$14; Pedro Azevedo $26-$6; Matthew White $74-$19; Richard Carpenter $140-$36; Jeremiah Bryan $175-$46; David Smith $293-$76; (p. 304) George Fitzgerald $150-40; Christian Harman $31-$8; Roswell Megget $10-$2-5; William Barland $12-$3; William Fairbanks $15-$3; William Hurlbert $2-5r; James Harman $4-7r; John Vauchere $328-$87; Lewis Chachere $343-$89; C. Bingaman $67-$17; Wm. Ryan $83-$22; Gibson Clark $35-$9; Polser Shilling $117-$31; Alexr. Moore $84-$22; Thos. Daniels $37-$9; William Smith $12-$3; White and King $42-$10; James Cole $114-$3.

p. 304. 26 Oct. 1786. Bernard Lintot, atty. duly apptd. for James Mather, to whom Richard Devall and Elizabeth, his wife, have mortgaged 1050 arpents with saw-mill thereon and other buildings and tools belonging, for surety of $3900 due and owing since Jany. 1, last past, to be paid on January 1st ensuing. Signed by both men. Off. wit. De Grand-Pre.

---

p. 305. 30 Oct. 1786. John Bisland sells to Nathan Swazey, both of Dist., 3 slaves for $1900, on terms. Both sign. Off. Wit. De Grand-Pre.

---

p. 305-8. 8 Nov. 1786. Information rec'd. of death of Tacitus Gaillard, Commandant repaired to plantation 5 leagues from Fort, on which deceased had dwelt and where his body was found and examined in presence of Don Estevan Minor, Don Joaquim Ossorno, Don Luis Chacheret, interpreter, and inhabitants John Ellis and Abraham Ellis. (p. 307) Will of Tacitus Gaillard, of Dist. of Natchez, Whereas I have advanced portions of my est. to my son, Isaac Gaillard, and to my two daughters, Anne Savage and Elizabeth Farar; to son Isaac $30; to dau. Anne Savage $30 and children of my dau. Elizabeth Farar $30; to dau. Margaret ten negro slaves to the value of one-fifth of my slaves; to my grand-niece, Elizabeth Gaillard, one young negro wench; the rest of estate of every kind to my wife, Ann Gaillard. Wife, (p. 308) eldest daughter Ann Savage, and dau. Margaret and son Isaac Gaillard executors. July 29, 1786. Wit: Jesse Carter, Richard Ellis, John Eldergill, N(ehemiah) Carter, Archibald Palmer, John Ellis. Benjamin Farar, son-in-law, Anne Savage 42 yrs. old; Margaret (Peggy) 25 years. Bill of sale of 14 slaves in favor of Widow Gaillard by the deceased for 480 acres in S. C. belonging to her: South Carolina, 25 Nov. 1752. Whereas Ann Gaillard, wife of Tacitus Gaillard, formerly Ann LeGrand, having by inheritance 480 acres of land, being her one-third part of 1406 acres at Trambor near Santee River in Craven Co. in the Prov. of S. C. and whereas her husband, Tacitus Gaillard, proposed that he would convey to her 14 good negro slaves and settle same in some Trustee for use of her and her children, in case she would join with him in selling her inheritance of said 480 acres and he could have the produce of said sale, to which she agreed, as per certain deeds of lease and release, dated 1 and 2 June 1749, conveying the land to John Mayrant, of Santee, Esq. and John Gendron, Jr. Tacitus Gaillard, Esq. of Charleston, to John Gendron Jr. of Santee, Gentleman, transfers the 14 slaves in trust.

---

p. 313. 28 Nov. 1786. Richard Harrison to Joseph Miller, 100 arpents, for $50 pd., on St. Catherine's Creek, b. by vacant lands. Richard Harrison signed, Joseph Miller signed "J. M.", his mark. Off. wit. De Grand-Pre.

---

p. 314. 5 Dec. 1786. William Brocus to Gerard Brandon, 100 arpents on a br. of St. Catherine's Cr., 3 leagues from Fort; for $400 paid. Gerard Brandon signed; Wm. Brocus with his mark. Wit. official. De Grand-Pre.

---

p. 315. 16 Dec. 1786. William Vousdan to Archibald Palmer, res. of Dist., negro "Jack", nat. of America, aged 16; for $450, to be paid January 1788. Both sign. Off. wit. Carlos de Grand-Pre.

---

p. 316. 16 Dec. 1786. William Vousdan to William Wicks, negro man and woman, natives of Guinea, and their 3 ch., nat. of Natchez; for $1350, payable Jan. 1788. Vousdan signs; Wicks signs with mark. Off. wit.

---

p. 317. 16 Dec. 1786 William Vousdan to Samuel Gibson, two slaves, for $1200, payable Jan. 1788. Both sign. Off. wit.

---

p. 317-8. 20 Dec. 1786. William Vousdan to Abner Green 250 arpents on west side of Second Creek, 14 mi. south of Natchez, b. by Anthony Hutchins, land gr. Cephas Kinnard, and vacant lands; for $600 payable in New Orleans Jany. next ensuing. Both sign. Off. wit.

---

p. 318. John Bisland to Randall and David Gibson, two negroes, natives of Guinea, named Jacob and Alexander, aged 23 and 18; for 4744 pounds of tobacco in hand paid. All sign. Off. wit.

---

p. 319. 23 Dec. 1786. David Tanner to Abraham Horton negro born in Va., aged 32, for $600 paid. Tanner signed; Horton signed with mark. Off. wit.

---

p. 320. Oct. 1, 1786. On demand of Alexander Moore, Syndic of estate of George Rapalje, late planter of this dist., appraisers appointed: Don Juan Vauchere and Adam Bingaman to appraise the house to be sold at Public Sale for debts. Appraisement: $350. (p. 321) Sale. Oct. 1, 1786. House belonging to George Rapalje, in Town of Natchez, b. by ground of Alexander Moore and on other side by Francisco Baso. Adjudged three times to Don Luis Faure for $375. Feb. 1, 1787. On demand of Alexander Moore, merchant of the Dist., and Syndic of est. of George Rapalje to sell plantation on St. Catherine's Cr., also a tract not settled, 750 arpents, on Buffalo Creek; and some cattle and horses, appraisers appointed: William Gilbert and David Smith. Signed by William Gilbert and D. Smith. Wit: Roswell Megget, Alexander Moore, John Henderson. Cattle adjudged to John Ellis, with Estevan Minor surety. Tract on Buffalo Cr., 700 arpents, adjudged, 1st, to Alexander Moore for $250. (All signed). 15 Feb. 1787, land adjudged 2nd time to John Orts at $450. William Smith, a witness. (p. 323) 22 Feb. 1787, sale of land adjudged to Zachariah Smith for $510. John Lusk surety. Signed by Zachariah Smith, Matthew White, Wm. Gilbert, Alexander Moore, J. Henderson, J. Lusk, Antonio Soler. De Grand-Pre. 15 Nov. 1787. 787 acres on St. Catherine's Cr. adjudged (1) (2) and (3) to Alexander Moore for $300, which was appraised at $350, by Matthew White and William Pontney.

---

p. 325. 2nd Jany. 1787. William Henderson sells to Richard King a mulatto named Luis and a negro woman, for $1200 paid. Both sign. Off. wit. De Grand-Pre.

---

p. 326. 5 Jany. 1787. Stephen Holston sells to Mary Higdon, negro woman named Rosa, nat. of America, aged 35; for $400 paid. Holston signs. Mary Higdon makes her mark. Off. wit.

---

p. 327. 5 Jany. 1787. Mary Higdon, widow, res. of this Dist., puts herself in the place of Stephen Holston for payment of $735, due and owing to Don Juan Vauchere, merchant of this Post, and binds herself to pay in 8 days from date hereof, mortgaging her whole estate. (Mary declares she cannot write.) Wit: Estevan Minor, Don Joaquim Ossorno. De Grand-Pre. // Natchez, in Fort Panmur, 10 March 1787. Don Juan Vauchere acknowledges to have rec'd. the above mentioned. Signed J. Vauchere. Wit: Joseph Calvit, Louis Chachere. Carlos de Grand-Pre.

---

p. 327. 15 Jany. 1787. John Stillee to Polser Shilling, negro girl "Phoebe", nat. of Carolina, 11 yrs. old; for $300 paid. Both sign. Wit: J. Vauchere, Isaac Gaillard. De Grand-Pre.

---

p. 328. 15 Jany. 1787. Dibdal Holt to Cato West 600 arpents at Cole's Creek, b. by lands of James Truly and David Holt; for $2000 paid. Both sign. Off. wit.

---

p. 329. 15 Jany. 1787. James Truly sells to Francis Brezina 100 arpents, on Cole's Creek, as shown in plot; for $400 paid. Both sign. Off. wit. Carlos de Grand-Pre.

---

p. 329-330. 15 Jany. 1787. Richard Harrison sells to Polser Shilling tract on the river, containing number of arpents as set forth in the sale made thereof by Don Philip Trevino, being part of estate of Wm. Dueitt, at which sale I purchased the same; for $300, paid. Both sign. Off. wit. De Grand-Pre.

---

p. 330-1. 17 Feb. 1787. Francis Brezina, of this Dist., indebted to Alexander Moore for $210, as surety mortgages 100 arpents on Cole's Cr., bounded as in plot thereof. The sd sum of $210 payable in New Orlenas in one month from date hereof. Grand-Pre.

p. 331. 16 Jany. 1787. Francis Brezina to Alexander Moore a negro lad "Prince", native of Africa, aged 14 yrs.; for $500 paid. Both sign. Wit: Es Minor, Richard Harrison. De Grand-Pre.

---

p. 332. 16 Jany. 1787. John Lusk sells to Isaac Gaillard 650 acres, a British grant to five persons, to seller John Luck 150 arpents, to Sarah Lewis 100 arpents, to Jacob Paul, Sr. and to Jacob Paul, his son, each 100 arpents, and to Samuel Lewis 200 arpents, bounded as set forth in the titles; for $1300 paid. Both sign. Off. wit. Carlos De Grand-Pre.

---

p. 332. 23 Jany. 1787. Richard King sells to John Girault negro man, nat. of Gaurico, aged 30, and a negro woman, nat. of Africa, aged 22; for $1221, $821 of which paid in hand, the remaining $400 payable Jan 1788. Both sign. Off. wit. Grand-Pre.

---

p. 333. 23 Jany. 1787. Benjamin Balk sells to Gabriel Griffing a negro boy named Bob, nat. of Africa, aged 30; for $500 paid. Both sign. Off. wit.

---

p. 334. Antonio Gras sells to Don Juan Vaucheret 1000 arpents on Miss. River, 5 leagues from Fort, b. on one side by John Burnet and on other by lands not granted; for $411 and a pair of oxen at $75, both in hand paid. Both sign. Off. wit.

---

p. 335. Natchez, 11 Jany. 1787. Matthew White and Justus King represent that Stephen Holston owes to them $182 and solicits payment thereof. // Let the defendant be notified to make payment immediately. Grand-Pre. // Jan. 18, defendant notified by Caleb King. // Jany. 18, Stephen Holston's plantation, farming tools and all horses and hogs taken in execution by Caleb King, and one Rifle Gun, in presence of Ben. Carrol. p. 335. Natchez, 13 Jany. 1787. Robert Abrams petitions to receive his share of proceeds of est. of Stephen Holston who is indebted to him in sum of $19. Natchez, 16 March 1787. Let petitioner be included with other creditors. Grand-Pre. p. 336-8. In Fort Panmur in Natchez 9 Feb. 1787, in pursuance of the seizure of the estate and effects of Stephen Holston, at the suit of Justus King; sale . . . Creditors: Mathew White, Richard Carpenter, Pedro, Azevedo, Juan Vauchere, Robert Abrams, David Smith, Lewis Chachere, Alexander Moore. Signed receipt of each for payment received.

---

p. 339. John Stowers to Henry Manadue, negro woman, "Sally", nat. of Africa; for $350 paid. 10 Feb. 1787. Both sign. Wit: J. Girault, Juan Carreras. Carlos De Grand-Pre.

---

p. 340. Louis Chachere represents that Earl Douglas owes him $118 and he cannot obtain payment. Asks for seizure of his estate. Natchez. 15 Jany. 1787. Let there be seizure for amount of debt. Grand-Pre. Natchez 17 Jan. 1787. Thomas Green also asks for same, Aug. 8; Polser Shilling, 27 July 1787; John Short, Dec. 18, 1786. (p. 341) Feb. 1787. Appraisement of plantation on Cole's Creek. Not enough people present to name appraisers or to bid. Apr. 17, 1787. Thomas Green and Cato West apptd. appraisers. Plantation, 150 arpents, $200; hogs $50. p. 342. Roswell Meggett adjudged plantation for $101, Jeremiah Brian surety.

---

p. 343. 14 Feb. 1787. William Brocus acknowledges to be indebted in the value of a negro named "Peter" now in the possession of "Wilson", according to the appraisement or sale thereof made to Joven Folson (Translation: "Folson, a minor"), in case negro shall be proven not to belong to sd Wilson, which proof must be made within the term of one year from date hereof by Tutor or Curator of said Folson, and in default thereof, at the expiration of the time aforesaid, no recourse shall be had against me, as likewise if the said negro shall be proven to be the lawful property of Wilson, this present obligation shall be null and void. Signed with a mark. Off. wit. De Grand-Pre.

---

p. 344. 22 Feb. 1787. Notice from Alexander Manadue of the death of James Brown, deceased, at his house, intestate; repaired to plantation of sd Manadue to make inventory. Small inventory . . . a pair of silver "Evillas" . . . a plantation on Fairchild's Creek, number of arpents not known; (p. 345) Papers: Receipt by Alex. Moore; receipt for money paid by Manadue for deceased to Julian Balen, Storch (?), Hawkins and Bachellot, an account in favor of Samuel Flower for $22. Inventory signed by J. Vauchere, Joseph Holmes, Roswell Meggett, Philander Smith, John Henderson, J. Pickens. 28 Feb. 1787, appraisers apptd; Henry Manadue and David Tanner. Total $270. 6 March 1787, sale of above estate at Fort. Buyers: Henry Bachelot, "Manadue", and Jeremiah Brian. p. 346-7. 4 May 1787. The plantation adjudged at final session to Polser shilling for $65, the highest bid, Isaac Dueitt surety. Creditors: Richard Carpenter, Samuel Flower, Henry Manadue, Justus and Richard King, White and King, Chachere, Pedro Azevedo. Receipt of each for pro rata share.

---

p. 348. 29 Feb. 1787. David Tanner sells to Alexander Moore negro wench "Hester", aged 19, nat. of N. C., for $630 paid. Signed by David Tanner and Samuel P. Moore. Wit: Sutton Banks, Juan Carreras. Grand-Pre.

---

p. 349. 5 March 1787. Rebecca Calvit hereby delivers to William Brocus, here present and accepting, a negro boy named Dick, nat. of Va., 14 yrs. old, receiving in exchange a negro girl named Nan, nat. of this Province, aged 9 years, and $100 cash. William (X) Brocus, Rebecca Calvit. Off. wit. Carlos De Grand-Pre.

---

p. 349. 20 March 1787. John Lusk to William Case, 300 arpents on Second Cr., b. as set forth in plot thereof, which land I purchased at Public Sale of the est. of William Case, confiscated to the use of His Majesty, and which I now sell for $400, paid. Both sign. Off. wit. De Grand-Pre.

---

p. 350. 20 March 1787. Matthew White, planter of Dist., mortgages to James Mather and Arthur Strother, represented by Anthony Hutchins, the following slaves: a negro fellow named Barra, nat. of Guinea, aged 30, a negro wench named Shelah, nat. of same, aged 28, and two negro girls, her children, aged 6 and 4. (Amount of mortgage not given.) Signed by White and Hutchins. Off. wit.

---

p. 351. 23 March 1787. Richard Carpenter to Isaac Johnson, a negro woman named Lucy, with a negro girl, her dau., named Sarah, aged two, being the same I purchased at Public Sale of estate of James Barfield; for $570 paid. Both sign. Off. wit. De Grand-Pre.

---

p. 352. 24 March 1787. William Case to Isaac Gaillard, 300 arpents on Second Cr., b. by sd creek, John Lusk, Myer Dickson and land not granted, which land is a British grant; for $600 paid. Signed by both. Off. wit. Grand-Pre.

---

p. 352. New Orleans, 27 March 1787. Jacob Monsanto, of this City, grants to Estevan Minor, planter, of the Dist. of Natchez, power of attorney to sell for cash, in sd District, property described in Titles thereof, delivered to him March of present year. Before me, Fernando Rodriguez, Notary Public.

---

p. 353. 20 April 1787. Anthony Hutchins, planter of this Dist., mortgages to James Mather and Arthur Strother, of the City of New Orleans, represented by George Fitzgerald, four slaves, all natives of Guinea, as follows: a negro man "Sampson", aged 25; another named "Jacob", aged 18; a negro wench, named "Catherine", aged 20, and another named "Patty", aged 20, which 4 slaves being surety of such sum as shall be paid by said Mather and Strother to Samuel Steer, of Baton Rouge, on acc't. of a Definite Sentence pronounced by the Superior Government in the suit pending in that Tribunal between myself and Samuel Steer. Off. wit. Signed. // Natchez, 24 Dec. 1792. I, James Mather, do hereby declare that Anthony Hutchins has fulfilled the conditions in the foregoing mortgage. Signed.

---

p. 354. 26 April 1787. William Vousdan sells to Reuben Dunham and John Wood a negro named "Boatswain", aged 27, for 6000 pounds of good tobacco to be delivered to the King's Store in New Orleans in month of January 1788 to the order of Don Maurice Cauve and for security the purchasers bind their whole estates present and to come. Wm. Vousdan and John Wood sign. Reuben Dunham signs with "D", his mark. Wit: Antonio Soler, James McIntosh. De Grand-Pre.

---

p. 355. 26 April 1787. William Vousdan to Samuel Flower a negro man named "Essex", aged 25; for $400 payable Jany. 1788. Both sign. Off. witnesses. De Grand-Pre.

---

p. 355. 2 May 1787. On demand of David Ross, merchant of District, have proceeded to the sale of sundry negroes, on credit until Dec. of this year; payable in good merchantable tobacco. First, one negro woman adjudged to Don Juan Vauchere for 2150 pounds of tobacco. Not wishing to sell more on this day we have concluded present sitting. Witnesses: Louis Faure, Richard Harrison, Antonio Soler, Samuel Flower, Antonio Cerrera. Carlos De Grand-Pre.

---

p. 356. 7 May 1787. Juan Vauchere grants full and ample power to Don Solomon Malline, of New Orleans, in my name to sell two slaves, a mulatto named "Frank", aged 17, and another named "Bright", which slaves I purchased at the Public Sale of estate of John Stillee.

---

p. 356. 10 May 1787. George Weigle to John Joseph Rodriguez, Military Store keeper of this Post, 500 arpents on a branch of St. Catherine's Cr. 3 leagues from Fort, as described in the grant from His Excellency, the Gov. Gen. of this Province; for $110 paid. Signed by both. Off. wit. De Grand-Pre.

---

p. 357. 12 May 1787. David Ross sells to Anthony Hutchins a negro named Ben, nat. of Africa, aged 20, for $480, payable Jany. 1788. Both sign. Off. wit. Carlos De Grand-Pre.

---

p. 358. 12 May 1787. David Ross to Don Estevan Minor, negro named "Tom Daniel", aged 30, native of Mount Serratt; for $465, payable Jan. 1788. Both sign. Off. wit. De Grand-Pre.

---

p. 359. 13 May 1787. David Ross to John Bisland, two slaves, one named "Winter", aged 26, and a negro wench named "Nan", aged 15, both natives of Africa; for $675, payable Jan. 1788. Both sign. Off. wit. Grand-Pre.

---

p. 360. 13 May 1787. David Ross to John Farquhar, negro wench named "Cuba", aged 18, nat. of Africa, for $400, payable Dec. 1, of this present year. Both sign. Off. wit. De Grand-Pre.

---

p. 360. 13 May 1787. David Ross to William Barland, a negro named William, aged 30, nat. of Jamaica; for $525, $250 payable Jany. 1788, $275 Jany. 1789. Both sign. Off. wit. Grand-Pre.

---

p. 361. 13 May 1787. David Ross to George Fitzgerald, negro named Betty, aged 30, nat. of Africa, with her two ch. named Grace, aged 10, and Betty, aged 6; for $850, payable Dec. of present year. Both sign. Off. wit. Grand-Pre.

---

p. 362. 9 May 1786. Juan Vauchere, being appointed attorney for creditors of the deceased Saint Germain, considers it indispensably necessary that, without loss of time, the estate, negroes, cattle and furniture should be collected and sold. The cattle in particular, although an inventory has not yet been taken, on account of the plantation and house being filled with Indians disposed to plunder the same and who consider the said effects as their own, the said St. Germain, during his life, having been their interpreter, and having connected himself with an Indian woman, still in the house, by whom he has three children, and who is exciting said Indians to claim said property as their own. Whereupon for security of the creditors, who are many, he prays as above stated. Natchez. Signed J. Vauchere. "Let it be done immediately" Signed Grand-Pre. (p. 362). 13 May 1786. Sale as follows: Buyers: "Soto", Landon Davis, Christian Harman, Antonio Gras, Ezekiel Dueitt, Moore, Moses Boner (Bonner), Jordan, Chachere, Franco. Baso, Alonzo Segovia, Jeremiah Bryan, John Coleman, Louis Chachere, Hartley, Estevan Minor, Juan Vauchere, Wilson, McIntosh, Polser Shilling, Louis Fort, Caleb King, Louis Foster, Abraham Horton, Justus King. Plantation to Antonio Gras for $411, Juan Vauchere surety. First bids on slaves not accepted as they were far from appraisals; determined to send slaves to New Orleans for better sale thereof. Two small houses in Natchez to "Obrian" on third sale for $130. Total from sale $2390.

---

p. 371. 13 May 1787. Thomas Green to Jacob Monsanto, a lot at the Landing of Natchez, granted to William Barland, 102 by 52 ft, b. by River and street; for $100, paid.

---

p. 372. Reuben Alexander to William Cooper a negro woman, Rose, aged 18, and her mulatto child, Dick, aged 2, nat. of the Province; for $500; $250 in hand paid and remainder Feb. 1788. Both sign. Wit: James Truly, Justus King. De Grand-Pre.

---

p. 373. 14 May 1787. David Ross to Antonio Gras and Francisco Baso, two negroes, David, aged 25, and Joseph, same age, nat. of Africa; for $800 payable Jany. 1788. Ross and Gras sign. Baso makes his mark. Off. wit. Carlos De Grand-Pre.

---

p. 374. 14 May 1787. David Ross to Robert Dunbar, a negro, "Romeo", aged 18, of Africa, and a negro wench, "Dinah", 18, of Jamaica, for $850, payable Dec. of this year. Both sign. Off. wit. Grand-Pre.

---

p. 375. David Ross to William Smith, a negro man, named Ishmael, aged 25, for $500, payable January 1788, the said negro remaining mortgaged until full payment; David Smith, his brother, being surety for same. Signed by David Ross, David Smith and William Smith. Off. wit. Grand-Pre.

---

p. 376. 15 May 1787. Richard Bacon, of Dist., mortgages to Don John Joseph Rodriguez plantation on the Miss. River, one-fourth league from Natchez, 250 arpents, to secure $250 due Mr. Moore, for which sum Rodriguez is security; payable Dec. next. Carlos De Grand-Pre. At Natchez, 9 Jany. 1790. Benj. Monsanto having paid amount owing by Richard Bacon to Juan J. Rodriguez, mortgage transferred to him. Signed J. J. Rodriguez.

---

p. 377. May 14, 1787. Richard Harrison sells to Wm. Barland a lot in Natchez, 102 sq. ft. b. on two sides by street, on another by ground of seller, on other by Louis Chachere; for $80, paid. May 18, 1787.

---

p. 378. James McIntosh to Polser Shilling negro, "Peter", aged 28, nat. of Africa, for $375, payable Jany. 1788, to remain mortgaged. 18 May 1787.

---

p. 379. 30 May 1787. James and Elizabeth Truly to Alexander Moore owe $250, to be paid December of this year, and mortgage 5 slaves.

---

p. 379. 30 May 1787. Gibson Clark sells to Henry Manadue 600 arpents, 3 leagues from Fort, 15 arpents in front, following the course of the River, b. on north by La Pointe (Porte); s. by Louis Chachere and Monsanto; for $450 paid. Gibson (X) Clark, H. Manadue.

p. 380. 15 June 1787. James Elliot to Thomas Foster, a negro named "Jesse", nat. of America, aged 14, for $400, one-half to be paid in cash; the remaining $200 Jany. 1788.

---

p. 381. 15 June 1787. John Girault to Lt. Col. Carlos De Grand-Pre, negro "Sam" aged 17, nat. of America, bought at Pub. Sale of est. of James Armstrong, decd.: for $500, in hand paid. Both signed.

---

p. 382. 18 June 1787. Margaretta LaFleur to Jacob Monsanto, represented by Don Estevan Minor, 10 arpents in front by 40 arpents in depth, b. by St. Catherine's Cr., lands of Peter Nelson, and Charles Truss, other sides vacant. Peter Nelson, Tutor to the minors LaFleur, consenting to said sale; for $400 paid. Peter Nelson signs; Margretta LaFleur makes her mark.

---

p. 283. 9 July 1787. Don Estevan Minor, aid-major of Fort, to Arthur Cobb, a negro man "Peter", aged 21, native of N. C.: $600 paid. Both sign.

---

p. 383. 9 July 1787. Don Estevan Minor to Jacob Liephart, a negro woman "Molly", aged 50, native of Va., for $400 paid. Both signed.

---

p. 384. 12 July 1787. James McIntosh, of Dist., to James Sanders, negro "Tom", of Nago nation, aged 25; for $400 payable this year in December. Signed by both.

---

p. 385. 23 July 1787. John Joseph Rodriguez to Edward McCabe, 500 arpents b. as set forth in grant by Gov. Gen. of this Province, for $320 payable December 1788. Wit: Edwardo Castell, Joseph Holmes, D. Smith, Antonio Soler. Carlos De Grand-Pre. // 15 Feb. 1789. Don Juan Joseph Rodriguez declared that have recd. $320 mentioned in the foregoing obligation.

---

p. 386. 4 July 1787. William Falconer, of Dist., to James Kirk, lot 51 ft. in front by 102 ft depth, on Main Street in Natchez, b. on one side by other ground of Wm. Falconer, on another by ground of David Smith, and on the other sides by the two streets forming the Town of Natchez; for $100, $50 of which paid, the remaining fifty payable December next ensuing. Signed by both.

---

p. 387. 26 July 1787. Alexander Moore, merchant of Dist., to John Stampley of same, negro "James" aged 21, nat. of Guinea; for $500, of which $200 payable Jany. next ensuing, the remaining $300 Jany. 1789. Signed by both.

---

p. 388. 3 Aug. 1787. Alexander Moore, merchant of the Dist., to Jesse Carter, of same, 2 negro slaves "Perry", aged 23 and "Peter", aged 13, both native of Africa, for $960, $480 of which to be paid Jany. 1788, and the remaining $480 Jany. 1789. Both sign.

---

p. 388-89. Lucy Crane, of Natchez District, in low state of health, wills to my two sons, Waterman and Hibberd, plantation I live now on to be equally divided between them, also personal property; to granddaughter, Sallomy Lyman personal property. Son Waterman Crane and Justus King executors. 25 June 1787. Wit: Moore Cilon, Jonas Cilon, Christopher Miller, Esther Bradshaw. Signed with a mark. Natchez, 26 Aug. 1787. In pursuance of notice of the death of Lucy Crane, widow of Silas Crane, empower each executor to name an appraiser. Waterman Crane named Caleb King; Justus King named Philetus Smith and they accepted. All signed. p. 390. Inventory: Plantation 110 arpents, 25 arpents enclosed, with an old house thereon; on St. Catherine's Creek, about 3 miles from Fort. 650 arpents on Stone's Creek, 18 leagues from Fort. 325 arpents on Cole's Creek. 10 arpents on Homochitto. Personal property. Total $1486. Signed by appraisers and executors.

p. 390-1. 30 Aug. 1787. Don Juan Vaucheret, of Natchez, merchant, to Jeremiah Bryan, negro "Titus", aged 20, nat. of Guinea; for 2500 pounds of good tobacco in carrots, payable 1st Feb. 1788. Both sign.

---

p. 391-2. 7 Sept. 1787. Wm. Vousdan, planter of Dist., to Isaac and Philander Smith, two negroes "Jacob" and "Jim", both aged 20, nat. of Africa, for $900, $200 payable Jany. 1788, $700 Jany. 1789; said sums payable in silver money. Signed by all.

---

p. 392. 8 Sept. 1787. William Vousdan, of Dist., to David Lambert, a negro named "Yerlan", aged 25, nat. of Africa; for $600 payable January 1789, Elijah Swazey being surety for same, which sd negro I sell for a slave and bound to serve and warranted free from any incurable disease. The three above sign.

---

p. 393. 8 Sept. 1787. William Vousdan, of Dist., to Isaac Johnson, a negro man, "Chilo", aged 14, and a negro woman, "Patience", aged 25, for $900 in silver, $200 payable Jany. 1788, not to be sold or otherwise alienated until payment of sd sum of $900. Both sign.

---

p. 394. 26 April 1787. William Vousdan to David Mitchell, a negro man, "Harry", aged 34, for 5500 pounds of good tobacco, to be delivered to Don Maurice Canoe in New Orleans, 5000 pounds in Jany. 1788, 500 pounds in same place Jany. 1789. Don Carlos de Grand-Pre. certifies that the contracting parties signed and ack. the foregoing.

---

p. 395. 21 April 1787. Sarah Swazey, widow, sells to Martha Cory negro girl "Amy" aged 5, nat. of Dist., for $300 paid. Sarah Swazey could not sign. Signed by Martha Cory, Gabriel Swazey. Wit: Antonio Soler.

---

p. 396. 8 Sept. 1787. William Vousdan, of Dist., to Isaac Alexander, negro "John", aged 35, and negro woman, aged 25, both nat. of Africa, for $900, $300 payable Jany. 1788, $600 Jany. 1789. Both sign.

---

p. 397. 8 Sept. 1787. William Vousdan sells to Samuel Swazey, negro "Willis", aged 13, nat. of Jamaica, for $450, of which $150 Jany. 1788, $300 Jany. 1789. Both sign.

---

p. 398. 11 Apr. 1787. Peter Surget, merchant of Dist., to Justus King, 2 negroes, "Festus", aged 25, "Amos", aged 20, nat. of Africa; for 10,000 pounds of good tobacco in carrots payable and delivered at the landing of Natchez Dec. 1788.

---

p. 399. 15 Sept. 1787. John Burnet, planter, sells to David Smith, negro "Stephen", aged 30, nat. of New England, for $700 payable Dec. of present year.

---

p. 400. 18 Sept. 1787. William Gilbert, of Dist., merchant, to Josiah Flower, negro wench "Kate", aged 14, nat. of Guinea. Signed by both.

---

p. 401. 23 June 1787. Wm. Barland to William Falconer, lot at the landing of Natchez, 102 ft square, b. on two sides by street, on another by Richard Harrison and finally by lot of Don Luis Chachere; for $150 to be paid Dec. present year. Both sign.

---

p. 402. 26 July 1787. Alexander Moore, merchant of Dist., sells to Daniel Grafton a negro "Jack", aged 30, nat. of Jamaica; for $450, payable Dec. of this year. Signed by Moore. De Grand-Pre.

p. 403. 22 Sept. 1787. John Bisland, of Dist. sells to Gabriel Griffing negro wench, aged 20, nat. of Guinea; for 5800 pounds of good tobacco in carrots, delivered at the landing of Natchez, 2000 pounds Dec. 1787, remainder November 1788. Both sign.

---

p. 404. 25 Sept. 1787. Francisco Menard, of the Post of Arkansas, acknowledges to have recd. from Don Estevan Minor $500, price of negro "Sam" sold to him about 2 years past. Signed.

---

p. 405. 28 Sept. 1787. Samuel Flower, planter of Dist., sells to John Griffing negro "Essex", aged 25, nat. of Hibon nation; for $400, payable Dec. 1787. Both sign.

---

p. 406. 29 Sept. 1787. Pedro Surget, merchant of Dist., to Joseph Booner, a negro "Sara", aged 28, nat. of Africa, for $450 pay. Dec. 1788. Signed by both.

---

p. 407. 2 Oct. 1787. Daniel Clark sells to David Smith following negroes; negro man "Bob", aged 24, negro wench "Betty", aged 22, both nat. of Africa, and negro boy "Joseph", aged 14, nat. of Jamaica, for $1150, payable $250 at end of present year, remaining $900 at end of 1788, slaves remaining mortgaged. Signed Daniel Clark, D. Smith, p. 408. At Town of Natchez, 21 Feb. 1789, Ebenezer Rees, attorney for Daniel Clark, declares to have rec'd. satisfaction of the foregoing mortgage of slaves therein mentioned and same is null and void. Signed by Ebenezer Rees.

---

p. 408. 2 Oct. 1787. Daniel Clark sells to James Baker, negro "Quasky", nat. of Jamaica; for $650, payable at end of year 1788, negro remaining mortgaged and Mistress Baker, mother of purchaser, being surety therefor. Signed by James Baker, Elizabeth Baker and Daniel Clark. Before Carlos De Grand-Pre. p. 409. 26 Feb. 1789, Ebenezer Rees, as partner of Daniel Clark, ack. receipt of the negro in above sale from Widow Sally Baker; obligation null and void.

---

p. 409. 2 Oct. 1787. Daniel Clark to Jeremiah Coleman, planter, two negroes, "Judel" and "Industry", nat. of Africa, for $1100, payable at end of 1788, negroes to remain mortgaged. Both sign. Natchez, 2 Oct. 1791. Receipt by "Clark and Rees".

---

p. 410. 2 Oct. 1787. Daniel Clark to two brothers, Thomas and Abner Green, of Dist., 11 slaves (9 men and 2 women), Big Robin, Quaskee, Robin, Quamen, Jack, Luck, Chance and Billy, natives of Africa, Bob, nat. of Jamaica, Patience and Agara, nat. of Africa, for $6,050, payable at end of 1788, or retain $2000 and pay at end of 1789 with 8% interest. The three sign. p. 412. Thos. Wilkins, atty. for Daniel Clark, receipts to Thomas M. Green for $3935 in Mexican silver, at Natchez 29 Aug. 1789. Clark and Rees receipt same for $950, no date. Natchez, 3 June 1795. Ebenezer Rees ack. receipt in sundry payments from Thomas M. and Abner Green for entire payment. Signed. Wit: Estevan Minor, Samuel Flower.

---

p. 412. 2 Oct. 1787. Daniel Clark sells to Elizabeth Baker negro "Ned" and negro woman "Winchester", nat. of Jamaica, for $1100, due end of year 1788. Natchez, 16 May 1795. Ebenezer Rees, vested with full power by Daniel Clark, ack. receipt from Eliz. Baker of full payment. Signed. Off. wit. De Grand Pre.

---

p. 414. 2 Oct. 1787. Daniel Clark sells to John Montgomery, negro boy "Ben", nat. of N. O., aged 12, for $500 in silver, $100 at end of 1787, $400 at end of 1788. Both sign.

---

p. 415. 2 Oct. 1787. Daniel Clark sells to Obadia Brown, negro "Sophia" and boy "Ben", natives of Africa, for $1000, $200 at end of this year, $800 at end of 1788. Both sign.

---

p. 416. 2 Oct. 1787. Daniel Clark sells to Adam Bingaman six slaves; Cumberland, nat. of Jamaica, Mantle, Quamana, Jack, Judy and Callie Bollou, all natives of Africa; for $3350, payable at end of 1788. Both sign.

---

p. 417. 2 Oct. 1787. Daniel Clark sells to George Killian, planter, negro "Trouble", nat. of Jamaica, aged 25, and "Joanna", nat. of Africa, aged 26, for $900 in silver, payable $200 at end of year and $700 at end of 1788, slaves to remain mortgaged. Both sign.

---

p. 418. Daniel Clark sells to Richard King, negroes "Coffee" and "Smart" and negro wench "Diana", all natives of Africa; for $1700. $300 Jany. 1788, $1400 end of year 1788. Both sign. I ack. that I recd. of Mr. Richard King the full amt. of above mortgage. 24 June 1800. (signed) Eben. Rees. Wit: Peter Walker.

---

p. 419. 3 Oct. 1787. Daniel Clark sells to Don Carlos de Grand-Pre negro man "Azor", nat. of America, aged 18, for $700 in silver, $100 in hand paid, $600 payable Jany. 1789. Signed by both. Feb. 12, 1789, Eben Rees, partner of Daniel Clark, receipts for $600 due as above.

---

p. 420. 4 Oct. 1787. Daniel Clark to Squire Boone, two slaves, man "Davy", woman "Kizzy", 1st aged 23, 2nd aged 28, both nat. of Africa, for $1000 in silver at end of 1788. Signed by both.

---

p. 421. 5 Oct. 1787. Daniel Clark sells to Peter Walker and John Henderson negro "Henry", aged 20, nat. of Africa, $600 in silver, payable 1788. Signed by John Henderson for self and Peter Walker, and by Daniel Clark. Eben Rees receipts in full, 25 Jany. 1803.

---

p. 422. 4 Oct. 1787. Daniel Clark sells to Richard Adams, planter, and his son, Jacob Adams, negroes "Angola", aged 22 and "Catherine", aged 18, both nat. of Africa; for $900, $200 at end of present year, rest at end of 1788. Richard Adams signs with "R. A.", his mark, Jacob Adams with "A", his mark. Daniel Clark signs. Wit: Wm. B. Smith.

---

p. 423. 4 Oct. 1787. Daniel Smith sells to James Stoddard, planter, two negro boys, "Cuffy", aged 14, nat. of Jamaica, "William", aged 13, nat. of Africa, for $1000, in silver, pay. end of 1788. Both sign. Natchez, 5 Dec. 1789. Rec'd. of James Stoddard the sum of $1000, amount of foregoing sale.

---

p. 423. 4 Oct. 1787. Daniel Clark sells to Samuel Culberson, two negroes, "Duke", aged 28, "Pompey", aged 30, both nat. of Africa, for $900 in silver, at end of 1788. Surety Squire Boone.

---

p. 424. 6 Oct. 1787. Alexander Moore sells to Richard Harrison negro woman "Charlotte", aged 22, nat. of Africa, and her son, aged 2, for $600 in silver, $300 in Jany ensuing, $300 Jany. 1789. Both sign.

---

p. 425. 8 Oct. 1787. David Williams sells to Samuel Steer, of Baton Rouge, and Benj. Curtis, of this Dist. negro "Hector", of the Mandingo nation, for $480 in silver, $100 in Jany. 1788 and $380 in Jany. 1789. Signed. // Natchez, 26 Apr. 1797. James McIntosh, executor of last will of David Williams, Esq., receipts for above in full. Signed.

p. 426. 10 Oct. 1787. George Forney to Marcus Tyler, 140 arpents purchased from John Row, near Fort, b. by lands of John Hartley, John Lusk and Saint Germain; for $400, $200 at end of present year; $100 at end of 1788; $100 at end of 1789. Both signed.

---

p. 427. 17 Oct. 1787. William Falconer to James Kirk, a lot, 51 ft. in front by 102 ft in depth, at the landing of Natchez, b. by land of purchaser on one side and on other by that of David Smith, and otherwise by the two streets, for $125, payable Jany. 1788. Both sign.

---

p. 428. 20 Oct. 1787. Don Pedro Surget sells to Isaac Tabor, of this Dist. negro "William," aged 20, nat. of Jamaica, for $475 in silver, payable Jany. 1788. Signed Surget, William Taber.

---

p. 429. 24 Oct. 1787. Henry Manadue to Tacy Barcellot, 600 arpents, 3 leagues from Fort, b. (n) John Baptiste LaPorte, (s) Don Luis Chachere and Benj. Monsanto, (w) Miss. River, (e) lands of His Majesty; for $450 in hand paid. (signed) H. Manadue, Joseph Duverge for Mistress Barchellot.

---

p. 430. 27 Oct. 1787. John Bisland sells to Daniel Ogden a negro "Neptune", aged 16, nat. of Jamaica, for $500 in silver, payable 700 carrots of tobacco to be delivered by purchaser Dec. of this year, and also 21 fat hogs, sd tobacco and hogs to be sold by sd Bisland and the proceeds carried to the credit of said Ogden, remainder paid Dec. 1788. Both sign.

---

p. 431. 26 Oct. 1787. Patience Coleman, widow, now wife of Madden, sells to Richard Carpenter negro woman "Amis", aged 19, nat. of Carolina; for $750 in hand paid. Patience signs with mark.

---

p. 432. 6 Nov. 1787. James Elliot sells to Windsor Pipes negro girl "Hannah," aged 12, nat. of America; for $450 in silver, payable $225 at end of December ensuing, $225 Dec. 1788. Both sign.

---

p. 433. 7 Nov. 1787. Jacob Monsanto sells to Waterman Crane negro woman "Betsey", aged 20, nat. of Guinea, for $425 in silver, payable end of Dec. 1788. Josiah Flower, planter, surety. Signed by Monsanto, Frere (brother), Waterman Crane.

---

p. 433. 7 Nov. 1787. Manuel Jacob Monsanto sells to Bennet Truly negro "Bob", aged 25; negro "Sally", aged 20, both nat. of Guinea, $850, payable end of 1788, John Lum being surety therefor. Signed Monsanto, Frere, Bennet Truly.

---

p. 434. 7 Nov. 1787. Manuel Jacob Monsanto sells to James Saunders negro woman "Lucy", aged 26, negro man "Polidor", aged 25, both nat. of Guinea; for $850 in silver, payable end of Dec. 1788, John Lum, planter, surety therefor. Signed Monsanto, frere, James Saunders.

---

p. 435. 7 Nov. 1787. David Holt sells to Richard Carradine negro "Jack", aged 20, nat. of Africa, for $400 in silver, in hand paid. Signed David Holt, Parker Carradine for his son, Richard.

I, David Harper, Keeper and Translator of the Spanish Records of the Mississippi Territory, certify that the foregoing contained in four hundred and thirty-six pages are faithful translations from the Records aforesaid, by me carefully collated and compared and found to agree therewith. In testimony whereof I have hereunto set my hand and seal at the Town of Washington, in the Territory aforesaid, this 31st day of March, one thousand eight hundred and seventeen. Signed D. Harper. (Seal)

BOOK B

p. 1. 8 Nov. 1787. Tacy Barchelot sells to Joseph Laforce, planter, of Dist., 600 arpents, 3 leagues from the Fort, for $400 payable Dec. 25, 1788. Joseph Duverge signed for Madame Barchellot (with a mark).

p. 2. 8 Nov. 1787. Carlos De Grand-Pre, Commandant of the Post and District of Natchez, sells to Samuel Culberson, resident and planter, 140 arpents, 15 arpents cleared, b. by land late of the Widow Truly, now belonging to Alexander Moore, and by lands of Swazey, being the lands sold to me by Lt. Col. Philippe Trevino, for $250 in silver, payable Dec. 1788. Squire Boone, planter of the Dist., surety. Both signed. Wit: John Montgomery.

p. 3. Carlos De Grand-Pre sells to Moses Bonner, of sd Dist., planter, negro man, aged 32, nat. of Africa, which I purchased at public sale of estate of late Juan St. Germain, for 7000 pounds of tobacco in carrots to be delivered at his own charge and risk in King's Store at New Orleans at current price paid by Treasurer, at end of December 1788. Signed M. Bonner, Jr. Receipt of 7000 pounds of tobacco by Don Carlos De Grand-Pre, 12 Feb. 1789.

p. 4. Wm. Brocus sells to Squire Boone 200 arpents, one league from Fort, b. by lands of Daniel Maggett, Alex. Moore, Justus King, and Schilling, gr. by Gov. ; for $500 in specie in hand paid. Squire Boone signs, Wm. Brocus makes his mark.

p. 5. 9 Nov. 1787. Alexander Moore sells to George Killian negro "Jack" native of Africa, aged 40, for $250, paid. Signed by both.

p. 5. 10 Nov. 1787. James McIntosh sells to Christian Bingaman, the younger, a negro man "Pablo", nat. of Africa, aged 25, for $520, payable $200 Dec. 1787, $320 Dec. 1788. Signed by both.

p. 7. Will of Charles Barchelot de Dubles (Hubles), native of the Parish of Voissay in Saint Ange, in France, son of Charles and Anne Draonet. That grant of land which I hold on the Island called "Lapom" [Apple Island] shall serve to replace another grant of land which I sold, belonging to my wife. Debts to be paid from proceeds of money that is owing to him. To my lawful wife, Tacy, all the residue of my estate. 8 Nov. 1787. Wit: Honore Duon, Antonio Soler. Signed Barchellot Des Hubles. (p. 8) At Natchez, 18 Nov. 1787. Information received of death of Henry Barchelot Des Hubles at his plantation. (p.9) Inventory; Island Lapom, without buildings, fences or clearing, hogs running at large. Large merchandise. A long list of debtors.

p. 25. 24 Nov. 1788. James McIntosh sells to Don Estevan Minor a negro "Guilford", aged 28, nat. of Guinea, for $525, payable Dec. 1788. Both sign.

p. 26. Nov. 24, 1787. Same, as above, to same, negro "Sam", aged 25, nat. of Guinea, for $525, payable Dec. 1788.

p. 26. 7 Dec. 1787. Don Pedro Azevedo sells to Thomas Hoffpaver house and store in Town of Natchez, lot 70ft in width to the hill and 180 ft in depth on the two extremes of the river, on the right hand descending the hill; for $650 in hand paid. Both sign.

p. 27. 12 Dec. 1787. John Baptiste Glassion, Jr., by Pierre Camus, his atty. sells to Don Estevan Minor a negro "John" aged 25, for 6000 pounds of tobacco in carrots to be delivered end of 1788. Signed by Camus and Minor. I, Jean Gasseon, junior, give full power to Mr. Peter Camus to sell a negro man "John," aged 25, to best advantage. German Coast, 9 Nov. 1787. (p. 28) At Natchez, 11 March 1789, before Don Carlos De Grand-Pre, Don Pedro Camus, atty as above, ack receipt of tobacco and annulled mortgage. Wit: Eben Rees and Juan Carreras.

p. 28. 14 Dec. 1787. Don Pedro Surget sells to John Martin negro boy "Azor", aged 13, for $450 which sd sum Benjamin Balk, here present, binds himself to pay seller Dec. 1787. All three sign. Natchez, 15 July 1795. Don Pedro Surget receipts for above payment from Balk.

p. 29. 14 Dec. 1787. Ezekiel Dueitt sells to Benj. Balk negro "Maria", aged 26, nat. of Jamaica, with her dau. 12 months, $600 paid. Balk signs, Duet makes his mark.

p. 30. 19 Dec. 1787. William Calvit sells to Samuel Regner negro boy "Hayson", aged 10, nat. of S. C., for $350. paid. Both signed.

p. 31. 21 Dec. 1787. John Farquhar sells to Wm. Barland that part of the plantation that I bought from

John Bisland, b. by John Fitzgerald, Stephen Jordan, Daniel Grafton, and John Lum, and Estevan Minor; for $400 paid. Both signed.

p. 32. 21 December, 1787. James Elliot sells to George Rapalje Carradine, represented by his father, Parker Carradine, negro "Dick", aged 26, a negro "Violet", aged 18, nat. of Africa. Signed James Elliot and Parker Carradine for his son, George Rapalje Carradine.

p. 32. 2 Dec. 1787. Parker Carradine sells to William Collins negro boy named "Joseph", native of Natchez, for the amount due him from the estate of his deceased father, hereby releasing sd Parker from all responsibility relative to the estate and any claim against him. The sd Collins, present and accepting sd negro boy in full discharge. Both sign.

p. 33. 23 Jany. 1788. David Ross to Samuel Flower, negro "Pharoah", aged 21, native of Jamaica, for $412, payable 1 Jany. 1789. Both sign.

p. 34. 23 Jany. 1788. Isaac Johnson to William Vousdan, two slaves "Stephen", aged 38, and "Lucy", aged 26, nat. of America, $240 in specie, $300 in paper money, payable Jany. 1, 1789. Both sign.

p. 35. 3 Jany. 1788. Wm. Vousdan to Anthony Hutchins, negro lad "Ned", aged 24, nat. of Africa, $600 payable Jany. 1789. Both sign.

p. 36. 3 Jany. 1788. John Montgomery sells to Frederick Calvit a negro lad "Dick", aged 14, nat. of Va. for $400 paid. Both sign.

p. 37. John Bisland sells to William Gilbert negro "Thomas", nat. of Guinea, aged 20, for $500 in specie, of which $200 payable in hand and $300 Jany. 1, 1789.

p. 37. 7 Jany. 1788. David Mitchell sells to Nathaniel Tomlinson 159 arpents b. by lands of St. Germain, Daniel Baker, Benj. Balk, and John Coleman, for $400, paid. Both sign.

p. 38. 9 Feb. 1788. Wm. Calvit sells to Alexander negro girl "Hannah", aged 6, for $260. Both sign.

p. 39. 11 Jany. 1788. Daniel Baker sells to Nath'l Tomlinson, 200 arpents, b. by lands of David Mitchell, John Coleman, St. Germain and by lands of His Majesty, for $600, $480 of which I ack. to have received in a bond made by me Feb. 26, 1784, which consequently has become null and void as well as the mortgage therein, and the remaining $220 in specie paid in hand. Signed by Tomlinson. Baker signed with his mark.

p. 40. 11 Jany. 1788. Notice from Alexander Moore of the death of William Pountney at the house of Thomas Wilkins, from a long illnes. He had left note that he had a small trunk at Mrs. Baker's. Commandant with Don Antonio Soler, Nathaniel Tomlinson and Juan Carreras went to plantation of Mrs. Baker and following inventory made: Small personal inventory. Notes due him by Thomas Rull, [Rule], Wm. Wilson, David Williams, Richard Devall, Henry Bradley, Richard Smith, James Willing, Michael Hooper, H. Pounteney, Thos. Wilkins, John Joseph Rodriguez, Don Luis Chachere. Appraisers apptd. Alex. Moore and Peter Walker who accepted. Wm. Pounteny, decd. left no heirs, or anyone charged with their Powers in this Province, Alex. Moore apptd. syndic of estate. Richard Harrison and Matthew White appraisers of horses. Samuel Moore a witness.

p. 43. 17 Nov. 1787. Before Don Micholas Forstall, Commandant of Fort of Opelousas, appeared Symphorieu Caillavet, who appoints as his attorney Stephen Minor to sell 1000 arpents, part of the estate of John Waugh, deceased, 8 miles southeast of the Fort of Natchez, b. by land granted Wm. Johnson, and land of Francis Hutchinson, and, after deducting expenses, to remit to constituent or to Breton D'Orgenoy, at New Orleans. // Land ordered to be put up for sale. // Same sold for the 3rd time to Isaac Johnson, highest bidder with $215. Wm. B. Smith, William McIntosh wit. 26 Jany. 1788.

p. 44. 12 Jany. 1788. William Ferguson, of Dist., appoints David Hoge of New Orleans, atty. to take all legal steps in Superior Tribunal, relative of appeal from judgment given by Commandant at Natchez in favor of Adam Bingaman, respecting a negro girl, binding my whole estate, present and to come.

p. 45. 12 Jany. 1788. Jacob Monsanto to David Smith negro "Cesar", aged 30, native of Guinea, for $500 specie, $200 in hand, $300 Dec. 1788. Both signed.

p. 46. 15 Jany. 1788. Wm. Calvit to Don Peter Surget negro "Hector", 35 to 40 years, nat. of Africa, $400 paid. Both sign.

p. 46. 15 Jany. 1788. Notice of death of Miguel Lopez, of N. O.; appraisers apptd. Peter Walker and

George Fitgerald, merchants of this Dist.. Both accepted. List of accounts due estate: Robert Abrams, David Smith, Edward Stradley, John Coleman, William McFarland, Bingaman Carrol, Pedro Deforde, Henry Bradley, Louis Charbonneau, Alexander McKinney, Peter Hawkins. Receipt of William Allen Smith.

p. 48. 16 Jany. 1788. John Gilbert sells to William Calvit negro "Prince", aged 20, nat. of America, for $450, in hand paid. Both sign.

p. 48. 16 Jany. 1788. John Wood and Reuben Dunham sell to Anthony Hutchins negro "Boatswain", purchased from Wm. Vousdan, representing Mr. Conway, to whom sd negro belonged; for $400 paid.

p. 49. Will of Stephen Jordan, of Natchez District, planter. Legatees: Grandson, William Jordan, my plantation whereon I now live, ploughs, geers, also John Carmack's bond for 140 pounds Va. currency, also an agreement between Evan Shelby and myself for 140 pounds Va. currency, left in the hands of William Cock, atty-at-law in Virginia, also my sled and double trees; to my son Thomas Jordan my cart and gears, hames, breast-bands and saddle; to granddaughter, Peggy Jordan, bed, etc.; to Molly Grafton, my largest table and the best half of my pewter, and the remainder I give to her daughter Elizabeth Grafton; to Thomas Granfton my brown mare and small plough; freedom to my negro "Dick" immediately; executors, John Bisland and Daniel Grafton, planters of said district. Jany. 18, 1788. Signed with a mark. Witnesses: John Short, John Welton, Jacob Seeplear, Wm. Foster, Alex. Moore, Jr., Henry Holston, Moses Bonner, Sr.

p. 50. 20 Jany. 1788. John Burnet sells to Richard Harrison negro "Jenny", aged 25, and "Coboy" aged 25, both nat. of Carolina, with two children, nat. of Natchez; for $800 paid. Both sign.

p. 51. 21 Jany. 1788. David Smith, acknowledges being indebted to Alexander Moore in sum of $600, specie, due Dec. 1788, and mortgages two slaves "Hannibal", aged "30", and wench "Judy", aged 32, both natives of Africa. Both sign.

p. 51. 21 Jany. 1788. David Munro, of Town of Natchez, sells to Don Luis Faure, King's Physician of the Hospital, negro wench "Catherine", nat. of Jamaica, aged 25, for $500, $250 in present month at New Orleans, remainder July next at N. O. Both sign. p. 52. David Munro receipts for the above $500 at Natchez, 9 Aug. 1788.

p. 52. 21 Jany. 1788. David Smith to Don Estevan Minor sells mulatto "Stephen", aged 25, nat. of Carolina, for $700 paid. Signed D. Smith, Estevan Minor.

p. 53. 21 Jany. 1788. Richard Harrison sells to Polser Shilling lot in Town of Natchez, 102 ft. front by 50 ft. depth, cornering on Main Street and b. in rear on vacant ground, for $50, in hand paid. Both sign.

p. 54. 21 Jany. 1788. Richard Harrison to David Smith a lot in Town of Natchez, 102 ft. in front by 50 ft. depth, b. by Main st., a lot of sd David Smith, another lot of Polser Shilling and the Miss. River; for $50 in hand paid. Both sign.

p. 55. 23 Jany. 1788. Don Pedro Surget, of Natchez, to Wm. Erwing, negro "Franky", aged 24, nat. of Africa, for $400, payable Feb. 1789. Ack. receipt in full, 16 Oct. 1799. Chas. Surget.

p. 55. 23 Jany. 1788. Polser Shilling sells to David Smith a lot of ground 102 ft front by 50 ft. depth, b. by Main Street, a lot of sd David Smith and the Miss. River, for $200 paid. Both sign.

p. 56. 23 Jany. 1788. John Lum sells to Ezekiel Dueit negro "Sam", aged 20, nat. of Africa, for $100 paid. Lum signs, Dueit (Dewitt) makes mark.

p. 57. 4 Jany. 1788. Richard Carpenter sells to Robt. Ford negro "Dick", aged 35, nat. of Africa, for $400 paid in notes. Signed by Richard Carpenter.

p. 57. 24 Jany. 1788. David Smith sells to Peter Walker and John Henderson, lot 202 ft. front by 100 ft. depth, with all tenements and buildings, b. by the main street, the cross street and the Miss. River, for $1050, in hand paid. Signed by all.

p. 58. 30 Jany. 1788. James Elliot sells to Wm. Smith two slaves, "Fortune", aged 25, nat. of Jamaica, and "Catherine", nat. of Africa, for $900 paid. Both sign.

p. 59. James Elliot to John Smith two slaves, "Coffee", aged 45, nat. of America, and a negro wench "Phillis", aged 20, nat. of Africa, for $1000 in hand paid. Both sign.

p. 60. Jany. 30, 1788. John Terry sells to James Elliot negro "Anna", aged 17, nat. of America, for $400, paid. Elliot signs; Terry with "T", his mark.

p. 60. 1 Feb. 1788. Isaac Fyffe sells to Isaac Alexander negro "Bob", aged 26, nat. of Africa, for $200 in specie, paid.

p. 61. 4 Feb. 1788. Don Pedro Surget sells to Richard Swazey three slaves: "George", aged 20, nat. of Africa, "Dick", aged 18, "Kandes" (translator's note says "Kindness"), aged 18, for 15,000 pounds of good tobacco or $1500 in specie payable Dec. 1788. Both sign.

p. 62. 9 Feb. 1788. At the house of Alexander Moore, intrusted with the estate and papers of William Pounteney, the sale of above estate: Buyers: Don Luis Faure, John Stower, Frederick Calvit, William Gibson, John Patterson, Alexander Moore, Sutton Banks. Witnesses: James Kirk, Alex. Moore, William Wilson, Wm. Lintot, Caleb King, Carlos de Grand-Pre. Negro boy bought by Sutton Banks for $200, surety Nath'l Tomlinson; horses bought by: Sutton Banks, Chas. Riverden, Christian Harman, Chas. Reben, John Baker, Richard Washen. Net proceeds $448-2. Bill of Mrs. Baker: to Mr. William Pounteney, 3 months and 20 days board at $20 per month $73-3; one month's wages to my son, $14; 1787, May 14, To butter furnished (15 lbs.); to one shift for negro wench $2-6; to 34 bu. corn furnished at different times $34; 1788, January, to cart here $4.

p. 63. 11 Feb. 1788. David Smith sells to James Kirk, 3 lots in Town of Natchez, (1) b. by grounds of Nath'l Tomlinson, Louis Chacheret, purchaser and street that passes at the foot of the hill; (2) b. by grounds of Don Juan Rodriguez, purchaser, Don Louis Chacheret and Royal Street; (3) by purchaser, Don Luis Chachere, River and aforesaid street; for $365 current money cash in hand. Signed by both.

p. 64. 15 Feb. 1788. David Smith sells to Don Rodriguez lot in Town of Natchez, 78 ft. front by 92 ft. depth, b. by grounds of Nathaniel Tomlinson, the purchaser, and James Kirk, with house, 68X16 ft. erected thereon, for $450 payable Dec. present year. Signed by both. At Natchez, 4 Feb. 1789, David Smith ack. to have recd. $450,amount of the sale of his house and lot.

p. 65. 16 Feb. 1788. Daniel Ogden to Samuel Flower negro "Jack", aged 35, nat. of Guinea, for $300, payable Jany. 1789 and $230 Jany. 1790.

p. 66. 16 Feb. 1788. Henry Manadue sells to Mistress Maria Spain a negro wench "Sally", aged 21, nat. of Africa, for $400 paid.

p. 66. 18 Feb. 1788. Sarah Truly to Richard Harrison 600 arpents, on Cole's Cr., 20 miles from Fort, b. by lands of purchaser, His Majesty's land, Waterman Green [Crane], William Ferguson and William Hickson; for $1200 paid.

p. 67. 18 Feb. 1788. Zachariah Smith sells to James Foster 240 arpents on St. Catherine's Cr., b. by Joseph Miller, land of purchaser, creek and vacant land; for $500, $200 in hand paid and $300 in note.

p. 68. 22 Feb. 1788. Don Estevan Minor sells to Arthur Cobb negro "Thomas" aged 30, nat. of Africa, for $600 paid.

p. 68. 23 Feb. 1788. Sale of estate of Henry Bachellot, also on May 3, 1788, 19 July 1788, 26 July 1788, 2 Aug. 1788, and on 4 Oct. 1788, the Island of La Pomme, again exposed to sale and adjudged to Don Luis Faure. p. 73. 6 July 1785. Henry Barchelot, of New Orleans, is indebted to Don Francisco Menard in sum $1550, payable a year from date, mortgages slaves. 1788. Menard takes slaves, the surety for payment. (True copy).

p. 74. 28 Feb. 1789. Don Pedro Camus, res. of District, to Don Nicholas Vergois lot, 267 ft. by 170 ft. in depth, b. by King's Road and ground of Don Luis Vaucheret, a negro, mare, colt etc. mortgaged to Don Pedro Belly, for $2500 to be paid Dec. 1788. 3 Jany. 1789. Don Pedro Belly ack. to have recd. payment of above.

p. 74. 8 Feb. 1788. Parker Carradine, for my son Richard Carradine, to Jacob Cable negro "Jack", aged 18, nat. of Africa, for $400 specie, paid.

p. 75. Don Pedro Belly, of Dist., leases to Sutton Banks, for 3 years ending 25 Dec. 1790, 5 full grown negro men, 7 negro women, 3 negro boys, 1 negro girl and the negro children following their mothers, four in number, for $1000 in specie, at the end of 1788, $1000 at the end of 1789 and $1200 at the end of 1790. Feb. 8, 1788.

p. 76. 1 Mch. 1788. John Lusk sells to Richard Carpenter 294 arpents for $200 in hand paid.

p. 77. 2 Mch. 1788. Francisco Baso and Antonio Gras, merchants and planters of District, and partners for many years, being at present joint owners of the following property: A plantation on St. Catherine's Creek, 200 arpents; another on Second Creek, 200 arps.; a lot in Town of Natchez, with sundry buildings thereon; 11 slaves, horses, cattle, etc. We do covenant and agree that in the case of the death of either party the other survivor shall be testamentary executor of the party deceased and the property above mentioned shall be equally divided. Both sign.

p. 77. 11 March 1788. Thomas Jordan sells to Don Estevan Minor, 389 arpents, b. by lands of John Bisland, Daniel Grafton, Francois Farrell, Peter Watkins and the purchaser; for $400 in hand paid. Both sign.

p. 78. 15 March 1788. Joseph LaForce mortgages to John Girault of this Post, merchant, his estate for $565, payable $33 in hand, remaining $532 at end of present year. (p. 79) 27 March 1793. Joseph LaForce and Louisa Sangerman, wife of sd LaForce, who mutually covenanted and agreed they owed John Girault $709, with interest accrued, sell to sd John Girault two tracts of land in this district, (1) 1000 arpents on the Miss. River, near the mouth of the Yazoo, granted to the father of the wife of said LaForce 16 Dec. 1785; (2) 600 arpents on Bayou Farmer, near Walnut Hills, a little below the lands of John Watkins, granted 22 March 1785, both belonging to wife of sd LaForce as having inherited same from her father.

p. 79. 17 March 1788. Richard Harrison sells to Don Estevan Minor, all the low lands and improvements included between the high lands belonging to sd purchaser and the Miss. River from the line dividing said lands from those belonging to this Fort, said line running North 31 East; for $150 in hand paid.

p. 80. 17 March 1788. Power of attorney from Estevan Minor to Richard Carpenter to sell to the King, the land belonging to me, 300 arpents, b. by lands of this Fort, land of Wm. Barland, by the King's Road, by lands of His Majesty, and by a line running N31 E, passing on top of the hills and dividing the land which I now sell from other land belonging to me adjoining, for $2000 which sd attorney will receive.

p. 81. 28 March 1788. Honore Duon sells to Pedro Camus lot of ground immediately adjoining the Fort of Natchez, 80 ft. in front by 20 ft. in depth, b. by lands of Don Louis Chacheret, for $100 in hand paid, including some timber lying on it.

p. 81. 7 April 1788. John Farquhar, of this Dist., planter, sells to John Fare a negro wench "Hannah", aged 17 yrs. native of Guinea, for $410 paid.

p. 82. 15 March 1788. In City of New Orleans, appeared Nathaniel Tomlinson and ack. to be indebted to Evan and James Jones for $689 due Jany. 1789. For surety, he mortgages 1000 arpents belonging to him in the District of Natchez, on which he resides, b. by Thomas Hutchins on one side and by Anthony Hutchins on the other. Recorded 11 Apr. 1788.

p. 82. 11 April 1788. Squire Boon mortgages to Ezekiel Deitt four slaves belonging to him, "Richard", "Bill", "Patty" and "Lydia", for $982 paper money and fifty dollars in specie, payable before the end of the year.

p. 83. 24 Apr. 1788. Jacques Fournier of New Orleans to Don Estevan Minor a negro girl, "Maria Josepha", aged 12, native of Havanah.

p. 84. 24 Apr. 1788. Jacques Fournier to Maris Spain a negro woman, "Prudence", and her child, "Poll", native of Africa, for $770, payable at the end of the present year. Signed Jacques Fournier, Polly Spain. (p. 85) Natchez, 26 Jany. 1789, Jacques Fournier annuls mortgage as he ack.. to have received full payment of the above.

p. 85. 26 April 1788. Matthew White and Elizabeth Hampton, his wife, mortgage to James Mathews, for $4133, our whole estate or estates and especially a plantation on St. Catherine's Creek, 2 miles from Fort, b. by lands of McIntosh, Polser Shilling, Benj. Belk and Thomas [?] Crane, also 13 slaves. [The last named may be Thomas Green.]

p. 86. 29 April 1788. Christian Bingaman, of Dist., to Adam Bingaman 450 arpents with dwelling house thereon, on St. Catherine's Creek, 3 miles from Fort, for $500, paper money, receipt whereof acknowledged. Both sign.

p. 86. 3 May 1788. Peter Hawkins sells to James Elliot 600 arpents, 200 arpents of which were sold to me by Henry Roach, and the other was granted to Joseph Dawes, b. (n and w) by lands of Alex. Boyd and land settled by Jeremiah Brian, on s. by vacant land, on east and ne by William Ferguson and Ebenezer Gossett, n. by land of purchaser. Signed by both.

p. 87. 4 May 1788. Peter Hawkins sells to John Girault 200 arpents, b. on n. James Elliot; w and s by same, east by William Ferguson, sd. land granted to Ebenezer Gossett from whom I purchased it; for $200 payable end of 1788.

p. 88. 4 May 1788. Bernard Lintot, atty. for James Mather, of New Orleans, sells to Anthony Hutchins, of District of Natchez, five negroes, aged 20 to 35, for $2500, payable $1250 Jany. 1789; $1250 Jany. 1790.

p. 89. 10 May 1788. James Elliott sells to Cato West negro "Anthony", native of Africa, aged 14, for $350 paid.

p. 89. 10 May 1788. William Vousdan sells to Ezekiel Dueitt a negro "Ismael", nat. of Philadelphia, aged 30, for $400, silver Mexican, payable Feb. 1789.

p. 90. 20 May 1788. John Baptiste Perret sells to William Calvit negro "Marinetta", aged 25, nat. of Guinea, for $500 payable $250 at end of this year; $250 at end of 1789.

p. 91. 20 May 1788. Alexander Moore sells to David Mitchell negro "Ben" aged 15, nat. of Carolina, for $510, payable $250 in Jany. 1789; $260 Jany. 1790.

p. 91-2. 23 May 1788. David Holt renounces right and title to a negro named "Bristol" given me by my father Debdal Holt, to be, after his death, held and enjoyed by me, the same having been replaced by a negro wench "Katy" aged 17; given to me by Richard Harrison in lieu thereof, in full compensation.

p. 92. 21 May 1788. Alexander Moore sells to David Holt a negro woman "Kitty" for $530, payable $200 Dec. 1788; $330 Dec. 1789.

p. 92-3. 24 May 1788. Dibdall Holt to Richard Harrison negro "Bristol" aged 30, nat. of Va.; for $600 in specie, in hand paid.

p. 92. 26 May 1788. Alexander sells to Joshua Collins negro "Dick" nat. of Africa, aged 24, for $550, payable $300 Dec. next, $250 Dec. 1789.

p. 94. 5 June 1788. Barney Isenwood, of Natchez Dist., mortgages estate generally to pay Don Luis Cacheret, for $193, before Nov. 1st of the present year, especially 110 arpents on St. Catherine's Creek, b. by land of Montgomery, creek and land of Swazeys, including crop.

p. 94. 10 June 1788. Joseph Capetillo, native of Guadalajara in Kingdom of Mexico, legitimate son of Joseph Garcia Gusman and Maria Martinez Capetillo, his father and mother, and Rosalia, native of New Orleans, natural daughter of Don Carlos de Grand-Pre, marriage agreement.

p. 95. 11 June 1788. William Henderson sells to Sutton Banks negro "Buckner" and his wife "Catherine", with their three children, for $2100, payable $1000 at end of present year; $1100 end of 1789, a mortgage. Rec'd $1000 from Sutton Banks on acc't of $2100 he owes me. Natchez, 12 June 1789 // Letter: Mr. Chas. Norwood, New Orleans. Sir: As you are present holder of a note jointly made and granted by David Smith and myself for $900 silver Mexican dollars due since 18 Aug. last, I promise as soon as I return to Natchez I will send you as further security a mortgage which I have of Mr. Sutton Banks for 5 slaves which mortgage will be transferred according to law. N. O. April 11, 1789. (p. 96) 13 Sept. 1791. William Henderson to James Carrick, for a certain sum due Carrick for negroes which he sold me, I authorize him to receive in my name $1100 due me by Sutton Banks for 5 slaves I sold him. J. Carrick acknowledges to have rec'd from Sutton Banks the 5 slaves purchased from William Henderson, for $1100 together with a negro girl aged 5 as payment of interest thereon. Signed J. Carrick. Wit: Wm. Dunbar, John Ellis.

p. 97. 11 June 1788. Nicholas Verbois, Commandant of Iberville, represented by Bernard Lintot, res. of this Dist., to William Henderson negro "William", aged 30, native of Africa; for $300 payable end of 1789.

p. 97. 11 June 1788. William Barland sells to George Fitzgerald of this Dist., merchant, lot in Natchez on the bank of the River, 102 ft. front by 39 ft. in depth, b. by two streets and by lot and house of Jacob Monsanto; $250 in hand paid.

p. 98. Don Louis Chacheret, of Post. of Natchez, being indebted to Lt. Col. Phelippe Trevino for $753, mortages his estate, present and to come, in favor of sd. Chacheret and promises to deliver to him in payment all the tobacco which he may purchase at the current price of same, to be paid before 1st Nov. of this year. 12 June 1788.

p. 99. 14 June 1788. David Mulkey to Philip Turpin mortgages, for $255, his estate, present and to come, to be paid Dec. 1789. Signed by Mulkey.

p. 99. 14 June 1788. Jeremiah Bryan sells to John Bisland 600 arpents, between St. Catherine's and Fairchild's Creeks, b. by lands of Moses Bonner, William Vousdan, Marie Foster and Madden. Which land I sell with consent of Don Juan Vaucheret to whom the same is mortgaged; for $450, payable Jany. 1789. 14 Feb. 1789, Jeremiah Bryan ack. receipt from John Bisland of $450 for above.

p. 100. 14 June 1788. Don Luis Chacheret given power of attorney to Don Pedro Cenas in the case between myself and creditors.

p. 101. Francisco Menar, Post of Arkansas, merchant, to Don Louis Faure negro "Anthony", aged 18, of Congo Nation. 21 June 1788.

p. 101. 25 June 1788. George Proffit and David Ross sell to Antonio Gras and Francisco Bazo, partners, a negro man named "Francisco" aged 12 and "Catherine" aged 20, natives of Nango in Guinea; for $800, $400 end of 1788; $400 end of 1789.

p. 102. 25 June 1788. George Proffit and David Ross sell to Charles Adams and George Killian a brute negro for $425, one-half at end of present year; the other half at end of 1789.

p. 103. George Proffit and David Ross sell to Joseph Calvit and John Lum a negro man and a negro boy, both brutes, for $850, payable one-half end of this year, other end of 1789.

p. 103. 25 June 1788. George Proffit and David Ross to John Lovelace two negro men and one negro woman, all brutes, natives of Africa, for $1200, the men aged 30, the woman 25, payable $600 Dec. 1788, $600 Dec. 1789.

p. 104. George Proffit and David Ross sell to Robert Ford a brute negro, aged 30, for $425, one-half Dec. 1788, one-half end of 1789. 25 June 1788.

p. 105. 25 June 1788. George Proffit sells to Christian Harman a negro woman, with her child, for $420, $200 Dec. 1788; $200 Dec. 1789. Signed by both.

p. 105. 27 June 1788. Manuel Madden sells to William Ratcliff 100 arpents 10 miles from Fort, b. on Second Creek and as set forth in plot thereof; for $150, paid. Both sign.

p. 106. George Proffit to David Ross and Co., negro "John", aged 12, nat. of Africa, for $360 (Mexican milled dollars). $100 end of 1788; $260 end of 1789. Proffit signed.

p. 107. 4 July 1788. George Proffit and David Ross to John Bolls two brute negroes, natives of Africa, for $800, payable Dec. 1789. Signed. Natchez, 21 Feb. 1796. George Fitzgerald, empowered by David Ross, ack. that Ross had rec'd. payment of the foregoing mortgage.

p. 108. 4 July 1788. George Proffit and David Ross sell to John Henderson negro "Sally," aged 30, for $400 (milled Mexican dollars), $100 at end of 1788, $300 at end of 1789. Geo. Proffit and John Henderson signed.

p. 108. Will of Ursula Simmons, of the Dist., to my son, James Simmons, negro "Aberdeen" and one-half of cattle, etc., which were the property of my dec'd. husband, James Simmons; to son Jacob the plantation I live on and one-half of cattle etc. Son, Charles Simmons, sole executor. 10 July 1788. 22 Aug. 1788, Charles (S) Simmons executor, sureties Wm. Curtis and Joseph Bonner.

p. 109. 11 July, 1788. Pedro Camus sells to Don Louis Chacheret, lot purchased of Honorato Duon, 25 ft. by 120 ft; for $50, paid.

p. 110. 11 July 1788. Pedro Camus sells to Miguel Solibellas lot 55 ft. by 125 ft. for $60 paid.

p. 111. 14 July 1788. George Proffit and David Ross sell to John Bisland negro boy "Tobin", native of Guinea, for $380 (Mexican dollars), one-half at end of 1788, other end of 1789.

p. 111. 21 July 1788. John Marney to Joseph Calvit a stud horse, named "Ranger", which I purchased of Thos. and George Blackmore, for an obligation given by Daniel Broadhead for four negroes, 12 Dec. 1785 which Calvit has delivered to me in payment, the said Marney to deliver to Calvit 8000 pounds of good tobacco at Natchez the next March ensuing; but in case Marney shall not be able to recover the four negroes above mentioned by proceedings at law for that purpose, the said obligation shall be returned to said Calvit who shall in like manner return the horse, if living, and if the horse shall have died in the meantime to account for same.

p. 112. Will of Richard Carpenter, of Natchez, merchant, weak in body: The 800 acres lately granted to me by this government, about 8 miles from the Fort, to my son, James, and my will is that a house, 30 ft. long by 16 ft. wide, be built thereon for the reception of my wife and family as soon as it can be conveniently done. To beloved wife, Mary Carpenter, negro man "Boston", negro woman "Anny", and all the furniture of my house. To son James, girl "Kitty"; to dau. Mary Flowers, negro girl "Rose"; to dau. Elizabeth Boardman, negro named "Jack". To wife, Mary Carpenter, 12 cows and calves and my white horse. My wearing apparel to be sold and proceeds divided equally between my wife, son, my daus. and my sons-in-law. My house and lot at Natchez landing to be sold, also tract of 300 acres which I bought from John Lusk. And whereas there is remaining in my hands some articles of merchandise, the property of Mr. Brown, of Rhode Island, and myself, my executors to get an exact knowledge thereof from Mr. William Ferguson, who is acquainted thereof and they to be disposed of to best advantage together with my other estate for (1) payment of all debts and funeral charges, (2) $500 to build house above described; and the residue to be divided equally between my wife, son James and three daughters, Elizabeth, Mary and Sarah. Exrs; Wife, Mary, daughter Mary Flowers, son-in-law Samuel Flowers and son-in-law, Charles Boardman, with my friends, Mr. David Williams and Bernard Lintot. The above request that 12 cows and calves go to my wife, to be changed; 4 cows and calves to wife and the remaining 8 cows and calves to my youngest children, James and Sarah. (Signed) 14 July 1788. Wit: Geo. Fitzgerald, Alexander Henderson, Geo. Proffit, Wm. Vousdan, Peter Walker, Pierre Bessandon, J. Henderson. 24 July 1788, notice of death of Richard Carpenter at plantation of Samuel Flowers to which he had been removed on night of July 22; Commandant, with Antonio Soler and Don Estevan Minor, repaired to the dwelling house of the deceased in the Town of Natchez and caused the most important keys to be delivered to Commandant, five in number, (1) key to writing desk, (2) key to a trunk, (3) key to the store, (4) key to another trunk, (5) key to cellar; seal of Commandant's arms affixed to said places and things for security, leaving said property in charge of Bernard Lintot, of this District. Signed Bernard Lintot, Antonio Soler, Alexander Moore, Mary Carpenter, David Williams, Carlos de Grand-Pre. // p. 114. 28 July 1788, Samuel Flower appointed, ad interim, until the will is read, curator and guardian of the minors of Richard Carpenter, deceased, namely James and Sarah, 1st aged 8 years and the last 11 months, lawful issue of his marriage with Mary Fairchild, his surviving wife, having also issue by his 1st marriage, two daughters, namely, Elizabeth, wife of Charles Boardman, dwelling in the Parish of Iberville, and Mary, wife of Samuel Flower, of this District, here present. Signed David Williams, Alexander Moore, Bernard Lintot, Sam Flower, Antonio Soler, George Fitzgerald, Mary Carpenter and Carlos de Grand-Pre. Alexander Moore appointed to represent heirs absent, Charles Boardman, representing his wife, Elizabeth Carpenter. James Kirk and George Fitzgerald appointed appraisers. Inventory . . . A house, late dwelling of deceased, in Town of Natchez at the landing, with a kitchen, store and lots belonging, b. by grounds of Polser Shilling and Francisco Bazo and the street, $1500. 300 arpents bought from John Lusk, b. by Benj. Belk, Matthew White, Hailer and Hartley. $250. p. 123-127. Aug. 7, 1788. Estate of Richard Carpenter. Debts outstanding:

Samuel Gibson
Jacob Cobin [Cobun]
Joel Weed
Ephraim Bates
Thomas Nash
Charles Cason
John Holland
Thomas Griffin
Stephen Mayes
Joseph Mills
Richard Gooding
David Tanner
Richard Lord
James White
Wm. Owens
Wm. Wicks
Jesse Hamilton
Clement Dyson
John Jones
James Simons
David Mulkey
John Alexander
John Lum
Robert Kidd
Gabriel Swazey
Wm. Thomas
Joseph Foster
Isaac Fife
Henry Richardson
John Allen
Jas. Richardson
Jas. Baker
Henry Lovick
Gabriel Griffin
Thomas Joice
Robert Campbell
Elijah Phipps
James Truly
Philander Smith
Philetus Smith
William Gilbert
Thomas Dyson
Windsor Pipes
Robert Walter
Joseph Dunker
David Wasman
John Patterson
L. Chacheret

David Smith (for note)
John Adams
Wm. Hamberlan
Saml. Culberson
John Ellis
John Farquhar
John Lovelace
Joel Bird
Archibald Rea
Moses Bonner, Jr.
Wm. Erwin
Benj. Curtis
Joseph Smith
William West
James Hayes
William Vousdan
Geo. Richardson
Hardwick Brown
Polser Shilling
Elijah Swazey
Adam Bingaman
Charles Carter
Robert Farel
Josiah Flower
Abram Horton
Wm. Boyd
Jno. McFarlan
Isaac Ashbel
Wm. Ryan
John Hampley [Stampley]
Manuel Texada
John Welton
John Coleman
Joseph Dyson
Zachariah Smith
Wm. B. Smith
Charles Simmons
William Brown
John Bullen
Thos. Smiley
Bennet Truly
Andrew Andale
James Ervin
Jona. Curtis
John Vaughan
Daniel Berry Jr.
S. Andrews
George Bailey
Milla Ellis
James McGill
Louis Charbono
James Stoddard
Susannah Spell
John Jack
James Brown (dead)
John Foster
Richard Mayes
John Donovan

John Baker
Wm. Barland
Jno. Calvit
Robert Rea
Joseph Calvit
Reuben Prowler
(p. 124) James Heady
Isaac Taylor
Rebecca Dow
Henry Manadue
Wm. Curtis
James Cullen
John Lusk
Archibald Palmer
John Richie
Richard Harrison
James Cooper
Benj. Bullock
Wm. Henderson
Nathaniel Carter
Richard Adams
Waterman Crane
Wm. Ferguson
Arthur Cobb
Justus King
Jesse Walker
Richard Ellis
Robert Gibson
Abrm. Lobdale
Wm. Case
James Lobdale
Daniel Ogden
Jeremiah Bryan
John Harley
Wm. Seldridge
John Townsend
Jas. Wilson
Caspar Sinclair
Thos. Rule
Isaac Johnson
Chas. Adams
Adam Lambert
Mayes Barfield
James Spain (p. 125)
Sutton Bankes
Earl Douglas
Philip Turpin
Jeptha Higdon
John Fowler
Reuben Gibson
Mark Cole
Madame Gaillard
Mrs. Savage
Mr. Barchellot
Michael Gue
Daniel Miller
John Griffin
John Montgomery

D. Flower
Michael Sipes
Benjamin Belk
Nathan Swazey
Joseph Miller
William Calvit
James Armstrong
Jno. Staybreaker
Thos. Freeman
Abram Taylor
John Follard
Alexander Callender
Fred. Calvit
James Swazey
Peter Hawkins
Jacob Paul
Cadey Raby
John Ferguson
John Sinclair
Wm. Brocus
Job Curry
Stephen Holston
Honore Holston [Henry]
Isaac Tabor
Matt. Prock
Harry Phips
Reuben Alexander
Richard Crop
Raphael Jones
John Holston
David Choak [Choat]
Rd. Devall
Wm. Fairbanks
Jas. Cooper
Nehemiah Albertson
Robert Caswell
Stephen Tell
Jno. and M. Woods
Geo. Rapalie
Thos. Joiner
Thos. Trimble
Mark Isler
Edward Murray
Richard Harris
Alexander Farrar
Talbot Carrol
Francis Meeker
William Hulbert
(126) John Whitman
Jona. Hackett
Mary Cole
James Kirk
John Brown
Hubbard Crane
Holmes' "Peter"
Wm. Daniel
Elisha Flower
Wm. Glascock

John Burnet
Abraham Mayes
James Phips
Benj. Botham
John Terry
Wm. Morne
Rd. Miller
Jona. Rucker
Jno. Mackelhenny
Jean Donet
Henry Wilson
Wm. Ellis
Martin Marr
Joseph Ware
George Wesler
James Kelly
Ezekiel Dueitt
Matthew Jones
James Smith
Asael Lewis
Jona. Smith
Jas. McIntire
Wm. Ratcliff
Oswald Yarborough
James Garland
John Skunk
Wm. Lea
Stephen Minor
Nath'l. Tomlinson
Thos. Calvit
Robt. Miller
Wm. Wilson
Joseph Ford
William Jack
John Newton
Geo. Foreman
Bernard Lintot
Wm. Atchinson
Jacob Worley
John Steel
James Saunders
James Bonner
John Dyson
Thomas Daniel
Richard Curtis
John Blondell
Jas. McIntosh
Samuel Beal
Mr. Armstrong
Thos. Nichols
James Oxberry
Chas. Boardman
Philip Urban
John Wilson
Henry Young
James Finn
James Layton
Calatano
Stephen Cole
Jacob Stampley
Alex. Leonard
Reuben Brown
James Elliot
McIntosh's negroes
Reuben Dunham
John Lavall
John Rad
Spete (Carpenter)
Capetillo
Swazey's "Will"
Ansel Bass
Jno. Thompson
Peter Surget
Jno. Holloway
Peter Ferguson
George Killian
Peter Smith
Franco Bercino
Parker Caradine
Wm. Lewis
Thos. Johnson
Wm. Tabor
Squire Boon
Wm. Bell
Daniel Chambers
D. McCabe
Jonas Scoggans
James Cole, Jr.
Beasley Prock
Dibdall Holt
Gibson Clark
Walker and Henderson
Daniel Megget
Thos. Jordan
Randal Gibson
David Gibson
Thomas Farrel
Stephen Johnson
Uriah Smith
Barnet Isenwood
McIntosh's "Peter"
Perry's "Joe"
Franco Garcia
George Stampley
John Rapalje
Jno. Saunders
Martin Trentham
King Holston
Jas. Walker
John Ratley
Joshua Collins
John Swazey
Richard Curry
Sidney Fulton
Solomon Cole
Wm. McColwell
Alexr. Henderson
Wm. Dewit (dead)
Nicholas Brabason
Peter Cahoon
Henry Stampley
Wm. Fowler
Henry Jacobs
Robert Abrams
Jared Brandon
Solare
Edwd. Patterson
George Riggs
Jacob Adams
Wm. Henry
John Spires
Edmund Quirk
Nero Ellis
David Gleason
Abrams
Mary Donelly
Joseph Dodge
A. Cattleman
Thos. Bowers
Bailey Price
Jesse Edwards
Joseph Barnard
Mr. Drawn
Alex. Moore
Henry Jones
John Girault
Alex Boyd
James Davis
Wm. Coleman
Christian Harman
Joseph LaForce
Christopher Butler
Martin Smith
John Martin
Anthony Buckster
Estevan DeAlba
Wm. Hootsell
Wm. Collins
Belk and Jones
Thos. Cummins
John Row
R. Pack
Seth Lewis
Pallidor Ash
Benja. Drake
Wm. David
Brian Perry
Thos. Warren
Wm. Fletcher
James Wade
Joseph Statley
Thos. Vail
Simon Burney
Johnson

John Gilbert	Wm. Black	Thomas Davis
Daniel Clark	David Munro	Wm. Nowland
David Hodge	Job Routh	

---

p. 127. 3 Aug. 1788. Louis Faure sells to David Munro negro named "Anthony, aged 20, nat. of Guinea, for $500 (Spanish milled dollars) in hand paid. Both sign.

p. 128. 4 Aug. 1788. William Vousdan and John Lum sell to Alexander Moore negro man "Jack" aged 22, native of Guinea, for 400 Mexican dollars paid. All sign.

p. 129. Will of Gabriel Fusilier de la Clere, native of Lyons, in France, legitimate son of Don Pedro Fusilier and Ludevina Choreau, deceased. I declare that I have a son and daughter by my first wife, Joanna Roman, namely "Agricola" and Ludevina. I am now the husband, by 2nd marriage, of Helena Soileau by whom I have issue, nine children, namely Gabriel, Estevan and Honorato, sons, and Helena, Brizida, Josephina, Efeine, Amelia and Eugenia, daughters. Beloved wife Helena Soileau, guardian and curator of whole estate, that which I hold in this Province of Louisiana as well as in the City of Lyons, in care of my brother, Don Pedro Fusilier, as likewise all debts due and owing to me. Don ____ Livandais, of New Orleans, my executor. Aug. 5, 1788.

p. 130. 11 Aug. 1788. John Hartley, of the District of Natchez, planter, makes deed gift to my son, Jacob Hartley, of 1000 arpents of land, part of 10,000 arpents which I held at Bayou Pierre, the sd 1000 arpents bounded by another thousand arpents ceded Christiana Hartley and by others ceded to Lizzie Hartley as set forth in the plan of sd 10,000 arpents. p. 131. Same date. Gift deed from same to daughter Catherine Harman of 1,000 arpents part of 10,000 which I held at Bayou Pierre. p. 131. Same date. Gift deed to Christina Hartley of 1,000 arpents, b. by 1000 arpents given to John Hartley and another given to Jacob Hartley. p. 132. Same date. Gift deed to Peter Hartley, of 1,000 arpents, part of 10,000 on Bayou Pierre. p. 132. Same date. Gift deed to Lizzie Hartley of 1,000 arpents, part of 10,000 arpents on Bayou Pierre, as above. p. 133. Same date. Gift deed by John Hartley to son John, of 1,000 arpents as described above. All of the above six gift deeds were signed by John Hartley, in German.

p. 134. Continued sale of estate of Richard Carpenter. Among other things, a spirited auction of the house and lot in Natchez, the property going to Stephen Minor, for $3100, the highest bid, with Ebenezer Gossett surety. 4 Oct. 1788. p. 149 Plantation for sale, 3rd time, to Stephen Minor, for $300, Polser Shilling surety, same date. p. 150. Papers of Richard Carpenter given to William Foster for collecting debts due estate. 19 Oct. 1788.

p. 150. 18 Aut. 1788. Thomas Irwin to Jeptha Higdon a new negro, for $500, $100 Jany. 1789, $400 Jany. 1790. Signed Thos. Irwin, Jeptha (X) Higdon.

p. 151. 18 Aug. 1788. Thomas Irwin to Thomas Foster two new negroes, for the sum of $930, $150 in hand paid; $250 Jany. next, $530 Jany. 1790; William Gilbert surety. (p. 152) 7 Nov. 1790, Thos. Irwin receipts for payment of above in full.

p. 152. 18 Aug. 1788. Thomas Irwin to Frederick Calvit a new negro, for $500, $100 in Jany. next; $400 Jany. 1790. Both sign. Natchez, 14 _______ 1797, William Vousdan, atty. for Thomas Irwin ack. to have rec'd. full amount.

p. 153. 18 Aug. 1788. Thomas Irwin to William Calvit two new negroes, for $1,000, payable $200 Jany. next, $800 Jany. 1790, negroes to be mortgaged, likewise two others, "Sam" and "Matthew". Both signed. (p. 154) 12 May 1795. William Vousdan, atty. for Oliver Pollock, charged with the recovery of debts due to Thos. Irwin, ack. to have rec'd. from Joseph Calvit, brother of above William Calvit, full payment of above.

p. 154. 19 Aug. 1788. David Williams to Benjamin Curtis and William Bell two negroes, "Coffee", aged 35, nat. of Guinea, and "Chance", aged 18, nat. of Africa, for $650 in Mexican silver, $325 end of 1789; $325 end of 1790. (p. 155) Natchez, 26 Apr. 1797. James McIntosh, exr. of estate of David Williams, Esq., certifies that the amount of this bond is fully paid. Signed.

p. 155. 26 Aug. 1788. Thomas Irwin to Frederick Calvit negro aged 25, negro boy, aged 12, both newly arrived, for $933; $200 Jany. next; $733 Jany. 1790. (p. 156.) William Vousdan, atty. for Thos. Irwin, ack. to have recd. from Frederick Calvit, the total amount in the foregoing sale. 14 Aug. 1797.

p. 156. 26 Aug. 1788. Richard Harrison to William Gilbert 398 arpents square, on St. Catherine's Creek, b. on west by Wm. Lum; on north by land of His Majesty, on east by Benj. Belk, on south by Creek and a branch called Sandy Fork. Both sign.

p. 157. 29 Aug. 1788. Thos. Irwin to Nehemiah Carter a new negro wench, aged 20, for $475 (Mex. dollars) payable Jany. 1790, negro mortgaged, likewise a negro of purchaser named "Bob" and two cows marked "N. C.". Jesse Carter surety for Nehemiah Carter. (p. 158.) The undersigned, having full power from Thos. Irwin, have transferred the mortgage in the foregoing to John Mapother for the amt. due from N. Carter, in pursuance of an agreement between the three parties. 14 Apr. 1792, Clark and Rees, by express orders, 13 April 1792. Signed Juan Malpother, N. Carter. Before Manuel Gayoso de Lemos.

p. 158. 30 Aug. 1788. Thomas Irwin to John Lum a negro boy, newly arrived, for $475, $150 Jany. 1789, $325 Jany. 1790, Don Estevan Minor surety. 23 Aug. 1791. As holder of the obligation in the foregoing sale, declare I have to take back from the purchaser the negro therein mentioned and consequently the debt and mortgage are cancelled. Signed William Vousdan, atty. for O. Pollock.

p. 159. Will of James Buchanan, son of John Buchanan and Mary Patton, native of Virginia in the States of America, I am married to Phoebe Hildreth by whom I have no children whatever, bequeath my whole estate to wife, including 1300 arpents of land in the settlements of Kentucky, Province of Virginia. I have hereunto set my hand at the plantation on which I dwell in the District of Natchez, 5 Sept. 1788. Signed J. Buchanan. Wit: Reuben Gibson, Reuben Proctor, Antonio Soler. Jno. Girault, interpreter. Carlos De Grand-Pre.

p. 159. 11 March 1788. Dibdall Holt to Richard Harrison a negro named "May" aged 35, nat. of Africa; for $450 paid. Both sign.

p. 160. 10 Sept. 1788. George Fitzgerald, representing David Ross, sells to James Kirk a negro, "Jack", aged 30, native of Jamaica, for $700, payable Dec. 1789. Both sign.

p. 161. 18 Sept. 1788. Thos. Irwin to Richard Harrison two new negroes for $900, payable 1790. At Natchez, 20 Sept. 1788. Thos. Irwin declares that he had rec'd. from Richard Harrison $900 amount of the two negroes in foregoing sale.

p. 161. 18 Sept. 1788. Thomas Irwin to Don Juan Joseph Rodriguez an African negro wench for $450, payable one-half Jany. next; the other July 1789, the purchaser mortgaging an English negro of his own named "Pablo". Both sign.

p. 162. 18 Sept. 1788. Thomas Irwin to John Lum a new negro, for $462, payable Jany. 1790. p. 163. 23 Aug. 1791. William Vousdan, atty. for O. Pollock, holder of obligation in above sale, agrees to take negro from purchaser cancelling debt and mortgage.

p. 163. 20 Sept. 1788. Wm. Barland to Juan Girault the tract ceded to him in 1782 near the Fort, adj. land of Mr. Minor and that of Don Pedro Piernas, for $70, in hand paid. Both signed.

p. 164. 20 Sept. 1788. Thos. Irwin to Marcus Tyler a new negro, for $175, payable 1790. Wm. Gilbert surety.

p. 164. 20 Sept. 1788. Don Pedro Surget to Charles King negro "Louis" aged 13, nat. of Guinea, for $500, payable Dec. 1789. Both sign.

p. 165. 27 Sept. 1788. Thos. Irwin to Don Estevan Minor a new negro, for $400 in hand paid.

p. 166. Thos. Irwin to Samuel Flower three new negroes, for $1400, payable $200 Jany. 1789; $1200 Jany. 1790.

p. 167. 2 Oct. 1788. Paul Bouet Lafitte, of District of Nachitoches, now in Dist. of Natchez, atty. of Louis Lambre, sells to Estevan Minor negro "Peter", nat. of Carolina, for $500, N. O. end of 1789. Power of atty from Louis Lambre to Paul Bouet Lafitte, 11 Sept. 1788, Dist. of Natchitoches.

p. 167. 10 Oct. 1788. Melling Woolley to Winsor Pipes a negro wench, aged 20, named "Maria", nat. of America; for 5,000 pounds of tobacco and two cows with their calves, for which buyer has given his note. Both sign.

p. 168. 11 Oct. 1788. Windsor Pipes to John Stowers negro wench "Anna", nat. of America, aged 13, for 5000 pounds of tobacco, payable one-half at end of present year and one-half the year next ensuing.

p. 169. 18 Oct. 1788. Sam'l Flower to Benj. Curtis, of this Dist., negro woman, "Charlotte", aged 24, native of Pensacola, for $500, payable in Jany. 1790, for which he has given his note. Both sign.

p. 170. 21 Oct. 1788. Samuel Flower to Daniel Ogden negro wench, "Chloe", aged 20, nat. of Guinea, for $500, in hand paid. Both sign.

p. 171. 25 Oct. 1788. Thomas Wilkins to James Cob a Guinea negro, aged 25, for $500, payable Jany. 1790. Samuel Flower surety. Both sign.

p. 171. 27 Oct. 1788. Ebenezer Rees, of Dist., merchant, to Gabriel Martin negro named "Diego", aged 13, nat. of Guinea, for $600, payable Jany. 1790. Both sign.

p. 172. Daniel Clark and Ebenezer Rees, of Dist., merchants, to Bennet Truly negro "Aaron", aged 30, nat. of Guinea, for $500, due Jany. 1790. John Lum surety therefor. Signed by Rees and Truly.

p. 173. 29 Oct. 1788. Jacob Monsanto to Bennet Truly two negreos, nat. of Africa, for $950, payable Dec. 1789. John Lum surety.

p. 174. 31 Oct. 1788. Jacob Monsanto to Ebenezer Smith, of this Dist., negro "Paul", nat. of Virginia, for $450, due Dec. 1789. Both sign.

p. 174. Will of Anne Gaillard, sick and weak; legatees: daughter Anne Savage; niece Betsey Gaillard, daughter Margaret Gaillard, this plantation of three tracts. All my lands in South Carolina to be sold unless my children choose to settle on them. Estate to be divided: one-fourth to son Isaac; one-fourth to dau. Anne Savage; one-fourth to dau. Margaret Gaillard, and one-fourth to my three grand-children, viz: Benj. Farrar, Anne Frances Farrar and Peggy Farrar. Also $60 a year for five years to be paid annually for education of two boys of Mrs. Phoebe Calvit, and $20 to Phoebe Calvit; also $60 a year for five years, paid annually, for education of two boys, sons of Mr. John Lusk. Son Isaac, daus. Anne Savage and Margaret Gaillard exrs and trustees for my three grand-children, Benj., Anne Frances and Peggy Farrar. Nov. 3, 1788. Signed Anne Gaillard. Wit: Sutton Banks, Margaret Tyler, Charlotte Surgett, William Case, David Mitchell, and Henry Roach. A copy of the original transmitted to the Capital to the Superior Tribunal of this Province. Chas. De Grand-Pre.

p. 175. 5 Nov. 1788. Ebenezer Rees, of this Dist., merchant, to Benj. Balk two negroes, nat. of Guinea, for $1790, payable Jany. 1790. Jeptha Higdon surety for same.

p. 176. 5 Nov. 1788. Ebenezer Rees to Jeptha Higdon negro "Jesse", nat. of Va., and a negro wench "Day", age 9, nat. of Africa, for $650, payable Jany. 1790. Benj. Balk surety. 8th April 1794, Ebenezer Rees takes the above two negroes back and cancels mortgage.

p. 177. 5 Nov. 1788. Ebenezer Rees to Anthony Hutchins negro "Philip", aged 11, nat. of Africa, and girl "Joanna", same age, from same; for $1000 due Jany. 1790.

p. 178. Don Manuel Jacob Monsanto to John Row negro wench "Kate", aged 20, nat. of Guinea, for $425, due end of Dec. 1788.

p. 179. 6 Nov. 1788. Richard Swazey to Daniel Callaghan two negroes "Sam" and "Dick", aged 30 and 18, nat. of Guinea and Jamaica, for $900 in hand paid. Both sign.

p. 179. 8 Nov. 1788. John Hartley to John Ratcliff negro named "Romeo", aged 25, nat. of America, for $500 due in ensuing year.

p. 180. 8 Nov. 1788. Don Estevan Minor to Daniel Clark, of New Orleans, and Ebenezer Rees, of this District, partners, a house and lot in Natchez, b. by lots of Francisco Bazo and Polser Shilling and by two streets, for $3100 (on terms), same as sold at public sale of estate of Richard Carpenter, deceased.

p. 181. 9 Nov. 1788. Alexander Moore to William Collins negro "Jack".

p. 182. 12 Nov. 1788. Jacob Monsanto to Henry K. Cooper, of Dist., negro. William Cooper, his brother, surety.

p. 182. Jacob Monsanto to William Cooper negro. Henry K. Cooper surety.

p. 183. 13 Nov. 1788. William Ferguson to James Kirk two arpents of land on Cole's Cr., 7 leagues from Fort, b. by Thomas Green and said Ferguson, purchased from John Lum.

p. 184. Richard Harrison to John and Alexander Henderson 602 arpents, two leagues from Fort, on St. Catherine's Creek, b. by lands of Alex. Anderson, Gideon Gibson. 14 Nov. 1788.

p. 185. 16 Nov. 1788. John Rumsey, of the Post of Natchez, to Moses Bonner wench "Cecelia", aged 16, nat. of Guinea, for $450.

p. 186. 3 Dec. 1788. Oliver Pollock to Thomas Irwin fifty slaves of the cargo brought by me to this Port from Martinico in vessel "Felix", commanded by Alexander Baudin, for $14,500, paid in bonds for slaves sold by sd Irwin.

p. 188. 11 Dec. 1788. John Buhler to Nathan Swazey "Ceasar", a native of Guinea, for $500 (on time).

p. 189. John Kelly to Juan Girault mortgages estate to cover a loan of $225. 12 Dec. 1788.

p. 89. 15 Dec. 1788. Don Pedro Camus to Don Augustine Solano lot in Town of Natchez, 160 ft. front by depth to the foot of the hill, b. by ground of seller and that of His Majesty, for $170 cash.

p. 190. 15 Dec. 1788. John Rumsey to William Wikoff a negro wench "Mary", for $793 in hand paid.

p. 191. 15 Dec. 1788. William Henderson to Hetman McGlaughlan two negroes, for $1400, on terms.

p. 191. 16 Dec. 1788. Francisco Bazo and Antonio Gras sell to James Truly a negro.

p. 192. 16 Dec. 1788. Filipina Truflo to Jacob Monsanto tract of 100 square arpents on St. Catherine's Creek, for $100 cash.

p. 193. Moses Bonner to Melling Woolley 400 arpents on which I now live, for $1000 (on terms), 17 Dec. 1788.

p. 194. 17 Dec. 1788. Moses Bonner to Charles Boardman tract (no acreage given) 3 leagues behind Fort, b. by lands of my father, Moses Bonner, Manuel Madden, Jeremiah Brian and lands of His Majesty, for $600 (terms). Both sign.

p. 195. 17 Dec. 1788. Phoebe Goodwin to Henry Manadue 600 arpents on Cypress Swamp, b. by St. Germain and John Baptiste Lapuente, 3 leagues from Fort, on which are erected a saw-mill and other buildings, for $1100, in hand paid. Phoebe (X) Goodwin. Wit: Bry. Bruin, Daniel Burnet, Ezekiel Hoskinson.

p. 195. 18 Dec. 1788. George C. Cook to Arthur Carney negro "John", aged 25, nat. of Va., for $500, in hand paid.

p. 196. 18 Dec. 1788. David Ross to George Fitzpatrick negro, for $200 (terms).

p. 197. 18 Dec. 1788. David Ross to William Foster negro.

p. 198. 18 Dec. 1788. David Ross to William Wilson negro "Dublin", nat. of Bahama, for $450 (terms).

p. 199. 18 Dec. 1788. David Ross to Joseph Perkins negro "January", nat. of Guinea, for $200 (terms)

p. 199. 18 Dec. 1788. David Ross to Philip Turpin negro "Tim", nat. of Guinea, for $320 (terms).

p. 200. 18 Dec. 1788. David Ross to Ephraim Bates negro "Dunce", aged 25, nat. of Guinea, for $450 (terms).

p. 200. 22 Dec. 1788. David Williams to James Fournier 120 arpents, 10 or 12 arpents by 40 arpents, part of 1000 arpents granted to Stephen Watts, one mile from Baton Rouge, also negroes, etc.

p. 201. 22 Dec. 1788. Don Estevan Minor to Don Carlos de Grand-Pre 290 arpents, b. by lands of Benj. Balk, Matthew White, Hailer, and John Harley, for $300 (terms). Receipt of Minor for payment.

p. 202. 24 Dec. 1788. John Louis La Croix to Don Louis Faure negro, nat. of Jamaica; for $200 (terms).

p. 203. 27 Dec. 1788. Francis Raymond to Thomas Hoffpaver negro, nat. of Guinea, for $250, paid. Francis (X) Raymond, T. Hoffpaver.

p. 203. Jacques Fournier to Gabriel Fusilier de Claire tract of 12 arpents by 40 arpents, purchased from David Williams, another contiguous tract of 125 arpents, part of land of Stephen Watts, one mile from Baton Rouge. 22 Jany. 1789.

p. 204. 7 Jany. 1789. Melling Woolley to David Holt negro, nat. of Va., for $550 (terms).

p. 205. 7 Jany. 1789. Ebenezer Rees to Thomas Wilkins negro, nat. of Guinea, for $540 (terms).

p. 206. 9 Jany. 1788. Thomas Irwin to Melling Woolley negro boy, newly imported for $450 (terms).

p. 206. 10 Jany. 1789. Job Cory to Matthew White, mortgage of horses, cattle, plantation (100 arpents), b. by lands of Dueitt and Brown, to secure $386.

p. 207. William Vousdan to Richard Dow a mulatto lad, "Jamaica", for $400 (terms). Richard (X) Dow, Wm. Vousdan. 9 Jany. 1789.

p. 208. Thos. Irwin to Thos. Wilkins negro "James", nat. of Guinea, for $450 on terms. Both sign. p. 209. Natchez, 23 Oct. 1790, $450 received on above sale and mortgaged cancelled, it being the said sum paid to Oliver Pollock on account. Signed Thos. Irwin. Wit: G. Cochran, Joseph Vidal.

p. 209. 10 Jany. 1789. Jeremiah Brian to Charles Boardman 400 arpents on St. Catherine's Creek, b. on all sides by lands of His Majesty; for $400 paid. Signed by both. Wit: Sam'l Flower and Soler and Carreras.

p. 209. 10 Jany. 1789. Thomas Irwin to Jesse Carter and Sarah Carter, his lawful wife, four negro boys and two negro wenches, for $2760, Mexican silver, (terms) together with plantation, horses, cattle mortgaged for payment. Signed Jesse Carter, Sarah Carter, Thos. Irwin.

p. 211. 10 Jany. 1789. Thomas Irwin to Nathaniel Ivy two negroes, lately imported, for $7000 (terms). Signed by both. Wit: John Lum, Antonio Soler.

p. 211. 10 Jany. 1789. Thos. Irwin to Arthur Cobb four negroes, for $1750 (terms). Both sign.

p. 211. 10 Jany. 1789. Isaac Johnson to Melling Woolley 1000 arpents on Second Creek (no description), for $650 (terms). Signed by both.

p. 212. Will of Henry Stampley, of Natchez District, planter, very sick; Son Jacob, to take care of William, my youngest son, till he comes of age of 21, that he should see and take care that my son William be brought in the fear of God, and as soon as he is fit, send him to school and let him continue there until he has learning sufficient; my wife, Margaret Stampley, should live and continue on my plantation as long as she should see fit. To my son Jacob Stampley my plantation, adjoining Mr. Dibdall Holt, containing 300 acres. also one cow and her increase and all the hogs on the plantation except one sow; to my son Peter Stampley two cows and their increase and one small rifle gun. 10 Oct. 1780. Signed Henry Stampley. Wit: Samuel Henry, David Holt. I, Jacob Stampley, do hereby promise and engage to take care of my father and maintain him during his life as well as I am able. Oct. 19, 1780. Signed Jacob Stampley. Wit: Samuel Henry. // 10 Jany. 1789. Don Carlos de Grand-Pre, Commandant, etc., received notice from Jacob Stampley of the death of his father, Henry Stampley, and repaired to his plantation on Cole's Creek, abt. 8 miles from this Fort, for inventory and appraisement of estate. Francisco Pavana and James Truly appointed appraisers and accepted. Both signed with Antonio Soler, Margaret (X) Stampley, Jacob Stampley, Carlos De Grand-Pre. Inventory small, signed by the above.

p. 214. Jacob Monsanto to Moses Bonner a negro, native of Jamaica, for $475 (terms). 10 Jany. 1789.

p. 214. 10 Jany. 1789. Thos. Irwin to John Henderson two negroes newly imported, for $1000, in hand paid. Both signed.

p. 215. 11 Jany. 1789. Clark and Rees to William Collins negro woman, lately imported, for $550 (terms). Wit: Soler, Jose Daing. Both sign. (p. 216) Juan Mapother has agreed to take the negro woman back from purchaser on payment of $59, which I have received from Alexander Moore, to be repaid to him by sd Collins, and for security have transferred the mortgage in the conveyance. 2 Aug. 1791. Signed by Collins and Mapother.

p. 216. 12 Jany. 1789. John Bisland to Adam Lanhart a negro man "Cago", nat. of Guinea, for $150 paid and $275 due Dec. 1789. Signed John Bisland, Adam (L) Lanhart.

p. 216. 12 Jany. 1789. Estevan Minor to Arthur Cobb negro "Peter", aged 28, nat. of Va., for $500 paid. Both sign.

p. 217. 12 Jany. 1789. Eben Rees to John Hartley two new negroes, for $950 (terms). John Hartley signed in German. p. 218. Ebenezer Rees ack. receipt of negro from John Hartley and $5 for time he was in his service, also a negro woman and child in place of the other negro in foregoing instrument. Signed by Rees. (Not dated.)

p. 218. 15 Jany. 1789. Ebenezer Rees to Joseph Bonner a Guinea negro named "Swift", for $600 (terms). Signed Ebenezer Rees, Joseph (X) Bonner.

p. 219. 15 Jany. 1789. Thomas Irwin to Wm. Vousdan a negro woman, lately imported, for $400, paid. Both sign.

p. 219. 16 Jany. 1789. Thos. Irwin to Ralph Humphreys a negro man and a negro woman, lately imported, for $950, in Mexican silver, due Jany. 1790. Peter Bryan Bruin surety. Signed by the three.
p. 220. Rec'd. $129.50 on account of the above, at the same time. Thos. Irwin. Wit: Juan Carreras. Natchez, 27 Apr. 1797. Don Francisco Claudio Girod declare to have rec'd. from George Humphreys full and entire payment of foregoing obligation in virtue of transfer thereof made to me by Thomas Irwin. Signed F. Girod.

p. 220. 17 Jany. 1789. John Ferguson to Gideon Gibson 500 arpents on St. Catherine's Cr., b. by lands of Pipes, Samuel Reynolds and Jeremiah Bryan, which sd plantation is exchanged for negro named "Will", aged 25, nat. of America, with consent of Don Juan Vaucheret to whom sd plantation was mortaged and who agrees to accept on said negro in the same form in lieu thereof. Signed Gideon (X) Gibson, John Ferguson. 21 Jany. 1789. Mortgage on negro cancelled by Don Juan Vaucheret, having recd. amount due him from John Ferguson.

p. 221. 17 Jany. 1789. Ezekiel Dueitt to Gabriel Griffin negro for $425. Gabriel Griffing, Ezekiel (X) Dueitt.

p. 222. 18 Feb. 1789. Alexander Moore ack. to have received from my father, Alexander Moore, $1000 in specie and a negro man named "Sampson", in full payment of all claim or claims of mine on the estate of my mother from henceforth, renouncing all right and transferring same to my said Father for $1000 and sd negro before mentioned. Signed.

p. 222. 21 Jany. 1789. Thomas Marston Green to Margaret Stampley negro woman "Sukey", aged 16, nat. of Guinea, $300 in hand paid. Signed Thos. M. Green, Margaret (X) Stampley.

p. 223. 21 Jany. 1789. Hamilton Pollock to Melling Woolley a negro man "James", aged 40, nat. of Guinea, for $350 (terms). Both sign.

p. 224. 21 Jany. 1789. John Ferguson to Samuel Flower a man named "Will", aged 25, nat. of America, for $400 paid. Both sign. Wit: Stephen Minor, Juan Carreras.

p. 224. 21 Jany. 1789. Tacy Barchellot, widow of Chas. Barchellott, to Henry Manadue, power of attorney to take possession of my plantation now in the possession of Joseph LaForce who has not made payment for it and likewise to make a sale of sd plantation to satisfy a debt due to him, the said Henry Manadue, by me. Tacy (X) Barchellott. Wit: John Girault, Juan Carreras.

p. 225. 22 Jany. 1789. Jacob Monsanto to William Ratcliff negro lad "Lindor", aged 14, nat. of Guinea, for 6000 pounds of tobacco in hand paid. Both sign.

p. 225-6. 22 Jany. 1789. John Vaucheret to James Fournier negro woman "Marianne", nat. of Guinea, for $250 in hand paid, purchased at public sale made by David Ross. Both sign.

p. 226. 22 Jany. 1789. Ebenezer Rees to William McIntosh negro "Dick", aged 30, nat. of Guinea, for $500 (terms). Both sign.

p. 227. 23 Jany. 1789. Antonio Gras and Co. to Jonathan Parker a plantation of 5 arpents front by 40 arpents depth with buildings thereon, about 3 miles from the Fort, on St. Catherine's Creek, which land I purchased from Peter Nelson, for $300 (terms). Both sign.

p. 228. 23 Jany. 1789. John Henderson to Isaac Gaillard 452 arpents on Homochitto, 12 miles from this Fort, b. by lands of James Kirk, Joseph Woother [Worthen?] , Donna Rosalia and Nicholas Cob. Plat delivered. Both sign.

p. 228-9. 23 Jany. 1789. Thos. Irwin to Melling Woolley a new negro, for $450 (terms) Both sign.

p. 229. 23 Jany. 1789. Thos. Irwin to Robert Dunbar two new negroes and a negro boy, for $1200 (terms). Both sign.

p. 230. 23 Jany. 1789. Estevan de Alba to Manuel Texada 400 arpents, on Cole's Creek, b. by lands of purchaser, Henry Platner, and by vacant land, for $150 in hand paid. Signed Manuel Garcia Texada, Estevan (X) Alba.

p. 230-1. 26 Jany. 1789. William Henderson to Peter Smith a new negro, for $400 paid. Both sign.

p. 231. 26 Jany. 1789. James Elliott to William Henderson negro "Peter", aged 40, nat. of Senegal, for $300 paid. Both sign.

p. 232. Manuel Texada to William Murray two adjoining plantations, 800 arpents on Cole's Creek, one granted to me by this Govt., 400 arpents, and the other purhcased from Estevan De Alba, for $475, paid. Both sign.

p. 233. 27 Jany. 1789. Manuel Texada to Richard Trevillian a negro lad "Bob", aged 16, and a wench "Sylvia", aged 15, for $1000 (terms). Both sign. Natchez 15 Feb. 1790. Purchase price was not paid, the negroes in foregoing sale restored to the seller. (Signed) Manuel Texada

p. 233. 30 Jany. 1789. Ezekiel Dueitt to Abraham Horton, a negro woman "Patty", aged 24, with dau. aged 1, and negro boy, aged 8, all nat. of Va., for $900 in hand paid. Both sign with mark.

p. 234. 31 Jany. 1789. Don Louis Faure to Thos. Wilkins lot in Town of Natchez, 100 ft. wide and 200 ft. deep,b. by lots of Francisco Bazo and Alexander Moore, for $400 in hand paid.

p. 235. 31 Jany. 1789. Don Juan Girault to James Elliott 200 arpents, b. (n) land of purchaser, (s and w) by land of same, (e) by Wm. Ferguson, for $200, being same sum for which I purchased land from Peter Hawkins, payable end of 1788, and which payment present purchaser binds himself to make, sd. Hawkins being indebted to him. Both sign. p. 236. Bill of Mr. Peter Hawkins to James Elliott, debtor, 29 Apr. 1787. Balance due Elliott after payment of land.. $98.

p. 237. 28 Jany. 1789. John Hartley to Samuel Flower 1000 arps. on Second Creek, b. by lands of William Cooper, Stevan Stevenson, Isaac Johnson, and Christian Harman, with a mill erected thereon, for $1000 in hand paid. Both sign.

p. 237-8. Thomas Irwin to Gibson Clark a negro boy, lately imported, aged 12, for 4000 pounds of tobacco to be delivered to King's Store in New Orleans at end of present year. Signed Thomas Irwin, Gibson (X) Clark. Wit: John Burnet. 3 Feb. 1789.

p. 238. Feb. 3, 1789. Thomas Irwin to John Burnet two new negroes, $1000 (terms), negroes mortgaged, also a bond of Brian Bruin in favor of purchaser for $1000. Both sign.

p. 239. 3 Feb. 1789. William Vousdan to Samuel Gibson negro "Rita", aged 28, nat. of the Isalnd of St Kitt's (Christopher), with her three daughters, nat. of La., for $1000 paid. Both sign.

p. 240. 9 Feb. 1789. Thos. Irwin to John Martin a negro boy, lately imported, for 2100 pounds of good tobacco, to be delivered in New Orleans January 1790. Both sign.

p. 241. 10 Feb. 1789. David Waltmann mortgages to Thomas Wilkins for $200, plantation of 315 arpents, 2 leagues from Fort, b. by lands of John Hartley, Richard Harris, Richard Miller and vacant lands. Signed by David Waltman. Wit: Samuel Moore.

p. 241-2. 10 Feb. 1789. Thomas Jordan mortgages to Alexander Moore, for $275, 600 arpents on Fairchild's Creek, 9 miles from this Fort, b. by Jacob Copperthwait, James Bonner, and lands of His Majesty. Signed Thomas Jordan. At Natchez, 15 Deb. 1797, James Moore, testamentary executor of his deceased father, Alexander Moore, ack. to have received of Thomas Jordan full payment of the foregoing obligation. Signed James Moore. Wit: Juan Girault, Nath'l Tomlinson, Estevan Minor.

p. 242. 10 Feb. 1789. Edward McCabe to Alexander Moore for $470, mortgages plantation, 175 arpents, on a branch of St. Catherine's Creek, b. by lands of Winsor Pipes, John Foster and Alexander Henderson, also some horses. Signed Edward McCabe.

p. 243. 10 Feb. 1789. Cato West to Henry Green negro "Jane", aged 20, nat. of America, for $550 (terms). Both sign.

p. 243. 12 Feb. 1789. Daniel Burnet to Don Estevan Minor negro man "Baptiste", aged 30, nat. of Guinea, for $700, paid, which sd negro I bought at public sale made by Don Phelippe Trevino. Both sign.

p. 244. 12 Feb. 1789. John Burnet to Jacob Monsanto for $1000, mortgages plantation on which he now dwells with all the land and buildings, horses, etc. Signed John Burnet. Natchez, 10 May 1800. I, John Short, attorney-in-fact, for David Ross, trustee for creditors of the late Jacob Monsanto, Manuel Monsanto and Benjamin Monsanto, to collect the debts to the sd Messrs Monsanto in this territory, do hereby certify that I have received the full amount of the consideration money expressed in the foregoing mortgage. Signed John Short.

p. 245. 13 Feb. 1789. James Elliott to Don Carlos De Grand-Pre 800 arpents on Cole's Creek, 400 arpents whereof formerly granted to Dawes and by him sold to Hawkins and the other 400 arpents part of a grant made to me by Gov. of this Province, 20 Oct. 1788, the last b. by the 400 arpents which I bought of Peter Hawkins and lands of Ebenezer Gossett, Adam Bingaman, William Ferguson and by land to me belonging; for $1038 paid. Both signed.

p. 245. 18 Feb. 1789. Justus King to Don Pedro Surget for $1000 in Mexican silver, being for two negroes which I purchased of him and being unable to make payment I do renew my obligation for said sum and my two sons, Richard and Prosper, are sureties for sd sum. Signed by the three Kings.

p. 246. At Natchez, 21 February 1789, at the request of Richard Harrison have exposed at publick sale a plantation belonging to him, 450 arpents, dwelling house etc., at St. Catherine's Creek, 4 miles from Fort, the said Harrison reserving to himself ten square feet in which his daughter is interred. After three sittings in which the bidding did not reach the sum at which Harrison proposed selling the said plantation, it was withdrawn. Wit: John Foster, Francisco Pavana, J. Henderson, Wm. Bacon. De Grand-Pre.

p. 247. 14 March 1789. Ebenezer Rees, partner of Daniel Clark, to Don Joseph Rodriguez four Guinea negroes, for $2225 (on terms). Both sign.

p. 248. 19 March 1789. Having received notice from Jonas Hailer, of the death of his father, Marcus Hailer, commandant and others repaired to his plantation, 1 mile from Fort, to take an inventory of the deceased Marcus Hailer who died intestate, whereupon Jonas Hailer was interrogated and he made declaration that his father had no children but the deponent and that he left no wife, that no one had any claim on the estate as could be testified by William Barland, Joseph Fort and James Stoddard. William Barland testified that during the time he had known the deceased he never knew or heard say that he had any children but the one present nor that he was married, signed William Barland. Deposition of Joseph Fort that he came to this country with the deceased about 14 years ago and he did not know him to be married nor that he had other children than the one present whose mother died in America and was the only wife he had in all the time that he knew him. Joseph (X) Fort. James Stoddard had known the deceased 8 years and he knew his wife died in America and that he never heard that he had any other children. Signed James Stoddard. Jonas Hailer, being the sole heir to estate and effects left by his deceased father, may enter upon and take possession thereof without other formality being required. Carlos De Grand-Pre.

p. 248. 20 March 1789. James Elliot to William Smith three tracts of land, one of which I purchased of Hawkins, 200 arpents, another from Juan Girault 200 arpents and the third I bought from Jeremiah Bryan 200 arpents.

p. 249. 21 March 1789. Jonas Hailer to Don Carlos De Grand-Pre land formerly belonging to John Row, and afterward to John Forney from whom my deceased father, Marcus Hailer, purchased the same, the said land is between the line dividing the land of the said Don Carlos De Grand-Pre which he purchased at Public Sale of the estate of Richard Harrison, deceased, (and which the last-named had from John Lusk), and the line dividing my land from that of John Hartley, which he bought of John Stampley and sold by said Hartley to my deceased father, now belonging to me, the said land being all comprehended between the said dividing line east and west; for $100 paid. Signed Jonas Hailer.

p. 250. 23 March 1789. Robert Carter, sells to Joseph Perkins 170 arpents b. by Charles Adams, John Stille and purchaser, on St. Catherine's Creek, for $300 paid. Signed by both.

p. 251. 2 April 1789. Wm. McIntosh to James Saunders negro, John, aged 30, nat. of Guinea, for $570 specie, payable Dec. 1789.

p. 251. 18 Apr. 1789. Samuel Gibson to James Patten 380 arpents on St. Catherine's Creek, b. by lands of His Majesty and by Creek, for $380 in hand paid. Signed by both.

p. 252. Natchez, Apr. 4, 1789. To Commandant: Henry Manadue, Atty. for Mistress Duon, wid. of Barchellot, represents that Joseph La Force, being insolvent, etc., and unable to pay for plantation she sold him and have abandoned same and absconded, petitions that he may be allowed to enter into possession of same and expose same to sale or otherwise as may need be. (Signed) H. Manadue. Granted as above requested. Natchez 4 Apr. 1789. Grand-Pre. p. 253. Henry Manadue, being fully empowered by widow Tacy Barchellot now married to Honorata Duon, sells to John Baptiste LaPuente, the plantation belonging to said widow, 584 arpents, 3 leagues from Fort, b. north by lands of purchaser, south Don Luis

Chacheret and Benj. Monsanto, west by Miss. River, east by lands of His Majesty. $350 payable December next. Signed H. Manadue, Juan Baptiste (X) La Puerte.

p. 253. 18 April 1789. James Patten sells to Robert Cashol negro woman "Kate", aged 30, nat. of Va., with dau. "Rachel", aged 6, for $500 paid. Both sign.

p. 254. 4 Apr. 1789. Ebenezer Rees to Matthew McCulloch negro girl "Betsey", nat. of Africa, for $450 on terms, girl remaining mortgaged. Both sign.

p. 255. 8 Apr. 1789. Before Jacque Masicot, Judge and Commandant of the Parish of St. Charles on the German Coast, appeared Alexander La Branche, of sd Parish, planter, who gives power of atty. to Peter Walker, of Natchez, to sell to Henry Manadue, for him, negro lad of the Congo Nation, named "William", aged 18, for $450, due Dec. 1790, (said negro being in possession of purchaser since Dec. last past) and to execute a conveyance before Mr. De Grand-Pre, Commandant at Natchez. Signed Jacque Masicot.

p. 255-6 Natchez, 2 May. 1789. Bernard Lintot, atty. of James Mather, in pursuance of request in letter annexed to annul mortgage in favor of sd Mather, by Matthew White and Elizabeth Hampton, dated 26 April 1788, do hereby ack. said mortgage null and void, the said White having paid sum mentioned. Said mortgage was given on a plantation on St. Catherine's Cr., 2 miles from Fort, b. by lands of McIntosh, Polser Shilling, Benj. Balk and Thos. Green, with 12 slaves, (names and ages listed). Signed. Letter from Mather to Mr. Bernard Lintot given, dated N. O., 22 Apr. 1789.

p. 256. Mortgage. 3 May 1789. Matthew White to Alexander Moore, $2964 (Spanish dollars) and $500 current money, to pay Moore March 1790, twelve slaves which were formerly mortgaged to James Mather. Signed. Natchez, 27 Apr. 1796. Before De Grand-Pre, appeared Jane Moore, widow of Alexander Moore, and Robert Scott, exors. of will of said deceased, who delcared the sums in the foregoing obligation had been faithfully paid in indigo seed as per the tenor of the agreement and same was null and void. Signed. Wit: Thos. Wilkins, John Girault.

p. 257. Natchez, 4 May 1789. Andrew Hare sells to Don Carlos de Grand-Pre, Lt. Col. of the Royal Armies, Commandant, Civil and Military of the City and District of Natchez, negro lad "James", aged 13, nat. of Va., for $300 (Spanish). Signed.

p. 257. 7 May 1789. Ebenezer Rees, partner of Daniel Clark, sells to Adam Bingaman a negro man "Carey", aged 30, nat. of Guinea, for $275, on terms. Signed by both.

p. 258. 10 May 1789. Charles Proffit to Melling Woolley negro boy "Thomas", aged 13, nat. of Guinea, for $195 and 200 bu. of corn, payable Jany. 1790. Both sign.

p. 259. 10 May 1789. Antonio Soler, Lt. of Royal Artillery, to Carlos de Grand-Pre 2 negroes, "Davy", aged 22, and "John", aged 12, both nat. of Guinea, $650 current money, on terms, the purchaser putting himself in my place in respect to purchase made by me of said negroes at public sale of estate of deceased Francisco Bazo. Signed by both. Wit: Ebenezer Rees.

p. 260. 19 May 1789. John Calvit to John Girault, for debt of $168 currency, to be paid Dec. next, mortgages 240 arpents on a branch of Homochitto, called "Pretty Creek", with two horses. Signed.

p. 260. 22 May 1789. Charles Proffit to William Ratcliff negro girl "Patty", aged 9, nat. of Guinea, on terms. Both sign.

p. 261. 22 May 1789. Chas. Proffit to Edward McCabe negro girl, aged 10, nat. of Guinea, for $460 specie, (terms). p. 262. 18 Jany. 1790. George Proffit, for Chas. Proffit, declared above sale null and void, payment not having been made, the wench had been taken back.

p. 262. 3 May 1789. Wm. Barland to John Bisland negro man "William", aged 25, nat. of Jamaica, for $450 (Spanish). Both signed. Natchez, 12 May 1789, In January 1789 I promised to pay David Ross or order 275 silver milled dollars of Mexico, for value of a negro man to my satisfaction. William Barland. Wit: James McIntosh. N. O. 23 Feb. 1789. Received of Mr. John Bisland $185 of the within in a tobacco certificate. Signed David Ross. N. O. 9 Apr. 1789. Received of Mr. John Bisland the within balance. D. Ross.

p. 263. 26 May 1789. George Fitzgerald to Reuben Gibson negro "John", aged 35, nat. of Jamaica, for $500 (Spanish) on terms. Both signed.

p. 263. 26 May 1789. Charles Proffit to Daniel Megget 4 slaves, 3 boys, aged 10 to 12, negro girl aged 10, nat. of Guinea, for $1050 (Spanish) on terms. Richard Swazey present surety. The three sign.

p. 264. 26 May 1789. Isaac Johnson, with consent of William Vousdan, here present, to Charles Adams negro woman "Patience", aged 26, nat. of Africa, for $500 (Mexican milled) payable Jany. 1790, at which time purchaser binds himself to pay to sd Wm. Vousdan the sd sum, the sd negro remaining mortgaged to Vousdan. The three sign.

p. 265. 14 Sept. 1789. In consequence of the death of Francisco Bazo, of Natchez, merchant, have attended the dwelling of the deceased, accompanied by Don Antonio Soler, Don Pedro Azevedo, Francisco Pavana and Juan Carreras to affix seals and take possession of the key of sd deceased and Antonio Gras, his partner, res. in this city, and none of the family of the deceased or of Antonio Gras being present, after having affixed the seals on a trunk in the store, then on the front door of sd store, on other door opening into an entry, on door of granary and on two doors of a small cabinet on the gallery of the dwelling house, delivered the seals and care of the house into the charge of Juan Gali, who accepted the charge and signed with the officials. (p. 265) 16 Sept. 1789. The Commandant aforesaid and witnesses repaired to same dwelling with intent to take an inventory of the property of the deceased and no one interested being present, Juan Gali appeared to represent Antonio Gras, partner of deceased. (p. 266) Inventory of the effects found in the shop, (long list covering a number of pages). (p. 275) Bartholomew Bosque arrived in Natchez with copy of the will of deceased. 18 April 1789. (pp. 275-8) Book of accounts:

Cadet Adam Bingaman
Pedro Dolfinde
Mr. Bingaman
John Smith
Mrs. Andrews
Mrs. Rows
Mrs. Lum,
Mr. McIntosh
(William Smith, to be paid by
(Joseph, the Portuguese
Wm. Dunbar
Joseph Martinez
Sutton Banks
Foley, the carpenter
Mrs. Swazey
Wm. Brocus
Mr. Henderson
Daniel Megget
Jeremaih Bryan
Charles King
John Short
Jno. Baptiste Perez
John Welton
Roswell Megget
Wm. Cooper
Joseph Calvit
Nicholas Abram
James Kelty
Jeptha Higdon
Don Luis Faure
Nathan Tomlinson
Moses Bonner
James Truly
John Foster
Isaac Tabor
Benj. Balk
Charles Carter
Franco Pavana
Edw. Patterson

Receipts
John Montogomery
Robert Dunbar
Jonathan Perkins
James Lobdell
Caleb King
John Diana
Jas. Truly
Richard Adams
Nicholas Laberry
R. and Abram Mayes
Jeremiah Routh
John Farquhar
Jacob Paul
Russel Jones
Joseph Capetillo
John Ferguson
Francis Martin
Carol Royal
Manuel Diaz
John Williams
(Henry Holston on
(Richard Brashears
Louis Charbonneau
Bartholomew Perez
John Coleman
Henry Wilson
Barnett Callaghan
Squire Boon (bond)
Adam Bingaman (note)
Luis Chacheret (receipt)
Profit and Ross
Philip Trevino
John Roche
Joseph Moreno

Wm. Henderson
Franco Fourcheau

(The above were small accounts)

p. 279. In pursuance of the demand of Bartholomew Bosque that he be put in possession of estate of testator, as executor, the will is read: Will of Francisco Bazo. New Orleans, 29 July 1788. I, Francisco Bazo, native of La Palma in Majorca, legitimate son of Bartholomew Bazo, deceased, and Catherine Greseto, his wife, of whose existence I am ignorant; being grievously sick but of sound mind and memory; in the City of Majorca, 100 masses to be said for my soul, for an alms of 2 rials for each, according to the custom of the country. I am legally married to Juana Maria Morales, native of the same city of Palma; we have only a son, Bartholomew, aged 19 years, and at time of marriage had only our clothes. As part of my estate, $651 put into partnership with Antonio Gras, of Natchez, as will appear by articles of agreement, my partner put $100 and his industry, the proceeds to be divided equally, etc. To my wife, in gratitude for the great love and tenderness manifested by her during our marriage, one-fifth of estate, after debts are paid, and she to be Tutress and Guardian of our son, my sole heir. Bartholomew Bosque, executor. In case of the death of my wife and my son, estate to be divided between my brothers and other relations, the said division to be made by the oldest and most reputable among them. (p. 282) Letter from Antonio Gras to Bartholomew Bosque, . . . I arrived here 28th April, and received notice of the death of my partner, Baso, which took place April 14 . . . (p. 283.) 25 Apr. 1789. Petition of exr. that effects in the house, the house itself, may be sold at public sale for cash, the cattle and plantation tools payable at end of present year, the negroes and plantation, (on terms) with security. Buyers: Bartholomew Bosque, Manuel Texada, Ephraim Bates, Antonio Soler, Antonio Gras, Joseph Flower, Richard Swazey, Isaac Williams, Richard Harris, Estevan Minor, Isaac Lothrip, John Foster, Francisco Pavana, Ebenezer Dayton and Juan Carreras. House b. by lots of Daniel Clark and Eben Rees, Thos. Wilkins and two streets, adjudged to Antonio Gras. Tract of 800 arpents at Rock á Davion b. by Thos. Douglas and Leberton, adjudged to John Bisland; tract of 200 acres on St. Catherine's Creek, purchased at sale of estate of John Ferguson, adj. Ezekiel Duett adjudged to Bartholomew Bosque. Purchasers: Alonzo Segovia, Juan Gali, Francisco Paulo Gonzales, Bennet Truly, Wm. Weeks, Edward McCabe, William McIntosh, Ebenezer Rees, Gibson Pipes, Jesse Hamilton, William Cooper (surety Wm. Henderson), Anne Swazey, John Wailer, Reuben Gibson, James Kelly, Robert Miller and John Roach.

p. 294. 4 June 1789. John Buhler to Don Carlos de Grand-Pre negro "Lorenzo", aged 20, nat. of Martinique, for $400 in specie, paid. Signed.

p. 295. 5 June 1789. James Elliott mortgages to Thos. Wilkins 350 arpents on Cole's Creek, b. by lands of Adam Bingaman, William Smith, Cato West and Wm. Ford Banks, with another tract of 300 arpents on same creek b. by lands of William Smith, Isaac Johnson, and Cato West; another 846 arpents on Cole's Creek b. by lands of Don Carlos de Grand-Pre, Nevitt Green West, Daniel Clark, William Ferguson and vacant lands, also personal property, including 3 cows mith mark of Cato West, one cow which he had from John Terry and one pair of oxen which he had from Earl Douglass. Signed. Natchez. 13 Nov. 1789. Thomas Wilkins, of Miss. Territory, relinquishes all claim to tract containing 846 arpents, mentioned in foregoing mortgage. Signed. Wit: John Heth, Aaron Heth, John Girault.

p. 296. 5 June 1789. John Brown bargains and sells to Jeptha Higdon three slaves, "Nancy", girl "Jenny", and boy "Pyramus", for $500 (Spanish). Wit: Leonard Wollf. We the subscribers certify that the above mentioned negroes are the property of John Brown. William (X) Colbert, James Colbert, Leonard Wollf. (Note: The signatures of the foregoing were evidently written by the same hand. Translator.)

p. 296. New Orleans, 25 April 1789. Letter to Don Charles de Grand-Pre, Esq., etc. from Mather and Strother. Mr. Anthony Hutchins, having executed a mortgage as security for what might result against him in his lawsuit with Mr. Samuel Steer, and the said Mr. Hutchins having long since terminated the said suit and paid the balance that appeared against him, this is to request you will please to give him full and complete acquittance for same and release his negroes so mortgaged. // Legal release of above by Don Bernard Lintot for Messrs. James Mather and Anthony Strother.

p. 297. 9 July 1789. John Wall, representing Don Francisco Pousset, to Melling Woolley a Guinea negro "Hamlet", of Hibo nation, aged 20, for $500 in specie, on terms. Signed.

p. 297. 20 June 1789. James Patten to John Williams 380 arpents on St. Catherine's Creek, bounded by land of Joseph Foster, sd Bayou and lands of His Majesty, for $530, paid. Signed.

p. 298. 21 June 1789. Charles Proffit, of Baton Rouge, to Maurice Stackpoole, of Post of Natchez, merchant, negro lad, aged 12, native of Guinea, for $400 specie on terms. Signed.

p. 299. 22 June 1789. Chas. Proffitt, of Dist. of Baton Rouge, to Moses Bonner, of Dist. of Natchez, planter, two negro boys and a negro girl, lately imported, aged 12 and 13, for $1070 in specie, on terms. Signed.

p. 300. 25 June 1789. Don Louis Chacheret, of the Dist. of Natchez, power of atty. to Don Zenon Trudeau, Capt. of the Regiment of Infantry of La., to sell negro woman, "Victoria", aged 30, of Congo nation, to me belonging, referring to the public records of New Orleans, relative to the sale of the estate of Saint Germain. Signed.

p. 300. 27 June 1789. James Wilkinson to Jacob Phillis, of this District, a negro man "Benjamin", aged 23, nat. of North America, for $460 in hand paid.

p. 301. 27 June 1789. John Duncan to Alexander Moore, Jr., of this District, negro man "Thomas", aged 30, nat. of Jamaica, for $400 specie which sd sum he binds himself shall be paid to me through his agent, James Johns, in New Orleans, immediately on my arrival there. Signed.

p. 301. 30 June 1789. James Wilkinson to Richard Ellis, of Dist., 7 negroes, (named), native of the U. S. for $3500 specie, terms.

p. 302. 30 June 1789. Richard Scott Blackburn to Richard Ellis, of Dist., planter, 13 negroes, (named) natives of the U. S., for $3000 (Mexican), terms. Signed.

p. 303. 2 July 1789. William Pauling to John Williams, of Dist., planter, negro man "Peter", nat. of Va., aged 21, for $400 specie (terms). Signed.

p. 304. 8 June 1789. Arthur Cobb and son, William, sell to Theophilus Phillips two tracts of land on Second Creek, one granted to Arthur Cobb, 400 arpents, b. by lands of Don Estevan Minor, Daniel Clark, Peter Surget, and sd bayou; the other granted in name of my son, William Cobb, 600 arpents, b. by Louis Bingaman, Daniel Clark, Don Peter Surget and vacant lands, for $1250 in specie, on terms. Signed by the three.

p. 305. 6 June 1789. In consequence of the news from Rebe Quedo of the death of Richard Harris, without having made a will, I, Don Manuel Gayoso de Lemos, have repaired to his plantation to take an inventory of the estate and effects left by sd deceased, and examine papers left in his name by divers inhabitants of this District, which were found as follows: 240 arpents of land which deceased held in common with Caleb Owen, residing in New Orleans. About 10 arpents of this land cleared, a good fence and a small house, in bad condition; a bedstead of English make, a garden, etc. Papers: not so many. Wit: Jeremiah Bryan, George Killian. Appraisers appointed: Jeremiah Bryan and Francisco Pavana. Wit: Maurice Stackpoole, Samuel Ph. Moore, Jeremiah Bryan. (p. 306) Sale. 11 July 1789. Purchasers: Joseph Vidal (Antonio Soler surety), James Wilson (Thos. Balleu surety), Jeremiah Bryan, Antonio Gras, John Green, John Foster, Henry Manadue, Bertrand Lebreau, Antonio Molina.

p. 307. Wm. Lee to Thomas Balleu negro wench "Maria" aged 18, nat of Guinea, which I bought at sale of estate of Bazo and Co.; for $375, which he binds himself to pay said estate. Signed.

p. 308. 20 July 1789. Joseph Miller to Nathaniel Ivy 100 arpents, b. on one side by St. Catherine's Creek, other land of James Foster; for $220 in specie (terms). Both signed with mark.

p. 309. 22 July 1781. John Montgomery mortgages to John Girault for debt of $181, whole estate to be paid December this year. Signed.

p. 309. 27 July 1789. John Hartley to Henry Richardson negro woman "Patti", aged 35, and negro man "Bristoe" for $900 in specie, (terms) John Hartley signs in German. Richardson signs. (p. 310) 19 May 1794, Jesse Hamilton, exr. of will of John Hartley, annuls the foregoing sale, said slaves having been restored to sd estate by conveyance thereof, bearing equal date herewith. Signed Jesse Hamilton, exr.

p. 310. 8 Aug. 1789. Peter Walker, of Post of Natchez, to Henry Manadue, in virtue of letter of attorney from Alexander Labitinchez, (owner thereof) a negro lad of the Congo Nation, aged 18, for $450 (Mexican) Signed. p. 311. Benjamin Monsanto, fully empowered by Alexander Labitenchez, who, in his name, ack. to have received from Henry Manadue the sum mentioned in foregoing sale and granted full discharge thereof. 6 Apr. 1793. Signed.

p. 311. 12 Aug. 1789. Will of Samuel Marshall, of Pennsylvania, in North America, son of James Marshall and Jane Marshall, deceased, (Catholic); appoints Don Francisco Pavana exor; owns 70 acres not in cultivation in Pa. and one mare; a house and household furniture in Pa. I have in the house a mulatto woman, dec'd., named "Nelly", a forge and all tools necessary for the trade of a blacksmith; four shirts in use, one jacket, vest and breeches of cloth, one new hat. David Temple is indebted to me in sum of $30 specie, being the price of a saddle he bought from me; a bond drawn up by Mr. Duett in favor of Alex. Wells for 52 pounds which does not belong to me but was entrusted to me to recover from Dewitt. I owe nothing but the expenses incurred in the house in which I have dwelt during my sickness and that I do not know the amount. I also owe the attendance and medecine furnished by Doctor Flower. After the above mentioned has been satisfied, it is my will that the remainder be divided between my brother, Thomas Marshall and my sister, Margaret Marshall, residing in Pa. Wit: by Gayoso, Don Juan Joseph Rodriguez, Don Joseph Vidal, Samuel Murdock and Joseph Ralston.

p. 312. Aug. 16, 1789. Will of Juan Domingo Tevezola, nat. of the City of Genoa, natural son of Joseph Tevezola by Camilla now living; weak but of sound mind; appoint Alonzo Segovia exor; as guardian to my son, issue of my lawful marriage with Marianna Lambert, dwelling in New Orleans, Andres Fernandez, to educate and take care of him, as also the child of which my wife is now pregnant. I have a house on Bourbon Street in City of N. O., 60 ft. front by 120 ft. depth, b. one side by Mr. Auricoste, and other side by ground of Lorenze Babry, which said property I have acquired since my marriage with Marianna Lambert; negro woman, "Maria", English by birth, now in the possession of my wife and likewise acquired since my marriage; nine covers of silver and one spoon of same. In Natchez, which I brought from the City, merchandise to the amt. of $759, as set forth in the inventory, deducting the amount therefrom which which I have sold, as will appear on my account of sales, stating the names of the persons who are indebted to me. I leave a list of persons living as Fausse Riviere who are indebted to me. Wife to have her part of that acquired since their marriage and the best of the furniture, for the education and care of the children. Signed. Witnessed and signed by Gayoso and Spanish officials.

p. 314. 17 Aut. 1789. Joseph Small, to Thos. Balleu negro "Catherine", aged 27, nat. of Va., for 450 Mexican dollars, on terms. Both sign. Wit: Wm. Henderson and Sp. off.

p. 315. 11 Sept. 1789. Thos. Wilkins, atty. for Daniel Clark, of N. O., to Richard Harrison a Guinea negro, for 450 Mexican dollars, on terms. Bennet Truly surety for same. Signed by the three. Natchez, 19 Feb. 1790. Thos. Wilkins annuls above obligation, having taken back the ngero.

p. 316. 11 Sept. 1789. Thos. Wilkins, atty. for Daniel Clark, Esq., of N. O., to Alonzo Segovia a Guinea negro, aged 20 to 22, for 463 Mexican dollars, on terms. Don Juan Rodriguez surety. Off. wit. signed 3 Aug. 1793. I, John Mapother have received from Catherine Segovia the sum of $473 in specie for above obligation, the same has become null and void.

p. 317. 11 Sept. 1789. Thos. Wilkins, atty. for Daniel Clark, Esq., of N. O., to Justus King, Richard King and Prosper King two negro women and one negro man, natives of Guinea, lately imported, for 1630 Mexican dollars, on terms. Receipt for above amount, Natchez July 26, 1791.

p. 318. 11 Sept. 1789. Thos. Wilkins, atty. for Daniel Clark, Esq., of N. O., to Gabriel Griffing, "Baptist", a native of Jamaica, aged 30, for 600 Mexican dollars, on terms, Elijah Swazey surety therefor. Signed by the three.

p. 319. 11 Sept. 1789. Thos. Wilkins, atty. for Daniel Clark, Esq., to G. Griffing negro man, aged 25, nat. of Jamaica, for 531 Mexican dollars, payable Dec. 1790, Elijah Swazey surety. All three sign.

p. 319. 11 Sept. 1789. Thos. Wilkins, atty. for Daniel Clark, Esq., of N. O., to Daniel Grafton 3 negroes, two of which lately imported, for 657 Mexican dollars, on terms. Signed by both.

p. 320. 12 Sept. 1789. Thos. Wilkins, atty. for Daniel Clark, Esq., of N. O., to James Truly a Guinea negro wench, with her son, for 585 Mexican dollars, on terms, David Holt surety. Signed. July 22, 1791, the undersigned agreed to take back the negro and her son and the purchaser is discharged.

p. 321. 13 Sept. 1789. Thos. Wilkins, atty. for Daniel Clark, Esq., of N. O., to Richard Harrison a new negro for 585 Mexican dollars, payable Dec. 1790. Bennet Truly surety. Signed.

p. 322. 14 Sept. 1789. John Bisland to Beasley Pruett negro, for 500 Mexican dollars, on terms. Signed by both. p. 323. John Bisland cancels bond and mortgage, having received amount, May 3, 1794.

p. 323. 16 Sept. 1789. Thos. Wilkins, of the District, to Don Josef Vidal negro lad "Michael", aged

15, nat. of Jamaica, for $390 (Mex. silver), Don Juan Jose Rodriguez surety. Signed. Note: Thos. Wilkins took back negro in foregoing, sd negro proving useless.

p. 323-4. 18 Sept. 1789. James Elliot to Don Manuel Gayoso de Lemos 350 arpents on Cole's Creek, b. by lands of Adam Bingaman, William Smith, Cato West and William Ford Banks, which sd land was mortgaged to Thos. Wilkins with whose consent I now sell the same, for $2000 (Mexican) paid in an order on the Royal Treasury; said tract having been purchased at the public sale of estate of Samuel Osborn. Signed.

p. 325. 20 Sept. 1789. Abraham Thickston, power (of atty.) to Wm. Thickston, of Ky., to recover in my name, from Adam Blueford, a negro named "Joseph", with certain sums owing and due me, from same. Signed.

p. 325-6. 20 Sept. 1789. Thos. Wilkins, atty. for Daniel Clark, to William Smith a Guinea negro wench for 536 Mexican dollars, payable Dec. 1790; sd wench being mortgaged until final payment and David Smith, brother of William, being surety for same. Signed by William Smith and D. Smith.

p. 326. 20 Sept. 1789. Thos. Wilkins, atty. for Daniel Clark, to Robert Miller negro wench, lately imported, for $536, Mexican silver, payable 1790. Joseph (Jese) Hamilton surety. Both signed.

p. 327. 20 Sept. 1789. Thos. Wilkins, atty. for Daniel Clark, to Thomas Morgan a Guinea negro, for $536, Mexican silver, on terms. Signed. Aug. 8, 1791. I, the undersigned, by power of attorney, have agreed to take back the negro in foregoing sale. Juan Mapother.

p. 327-8. 20 Sept. 1789. Thos. Wilkins, atty. for Daniel Clark, to Richard Curtis a Guinea negro, for $546, Mexican Silver, on terms, John Stampley surety. Signed. Negro taken back by Juan Mapother, by power of attorney. (n. d.)

p. 328-9. 20 Sept. 1789. Thos. Wilkins, atty. of Daniel Clark, to John Hetherington a negro wench, for $536 (Mexican), James Saunders surety.

p. 329. 20 Sept. 1789. Thos. Wilkins, atty. for Daniel Clark, to John Stampley a new negro wench, for $536, Mexican silver, on terms. Jonathan Curtis surety. p. 330. Eben Rees, Esq. ack. to have received full payment in foregoing and mortgage cancelled. 15 March 1808.

p. 330. 20 Sept. 1789. Thos. Wilkins, atty. for Daniel Clark, to James Cole, Jr. a Guinea negro, for 560 Mexican collars, Richard Curtis surety. Negro taken back by Juan Mapother, 23 July 1791.

p. 331. 20 Sept. 1789. Thos. Wilkins, atty. of Daniel Clark, to David Mitchell 2 negro men and one negro woman, for $1608 Mexican silver, mortgaging other negroes. Taken back by Juan Mapother. 17 Apr. 1792.

p. 332. 20 Sept. 1789. Thos. Wilkins, atty. for Daniel Clark, to John Ford negro 'Sappet", for $560, Mexican silver, on terms. Taken back by Juan Mapother, 2 Apr. 1792.

p. 332-3. 21 Sept. 1789. John Bisland to Alexander McCoy a new negro, for $450 (Mexican). on terms. Alex (X) McCoy, John (X) McCoy.

p. 333. 21 Sept. 1789. John Bisland to Michael Guise negro "James", for $350 (Mexican). Signed.

p. 334. 2 Oct. 1789. Thomas Irwin to Stephen Mayes negro wench, for 460 silver dollars, surety Bennet Truly. 26 Aug. 1791, Joseph Vidal agrees to take back negro, being fully empowered to do so.

p. 335. 2 Oct. 1789. Thomas Irwin to William Vardaman an African negro girl, for $500 (Mexican) on terms, William Calvit surety. Signed. 6 Sept. 1791. Jno. Hervy, atty. for the estate of E. G. Gallande agrees to take back above negro.

p. 335-6. 2 Oct. 1789. John Joseph Rodriguez, has appraisement of his house; at $4857; mortgages same to the Royal Treasury for $2000. Signed by him and the officials. A true copy sent, by order, to Capital of Province.

p. 337. 2 Oct. 1789. George Fitzgerald, for Francisco Pousset, sells to Jeremiah Coleman negro wench, "Fanny", for 400 Mexican dollars, on terms. Signed. // 19 Sept. 1792. Natchez. Receipt by George Fitzgerald.

p. 337. 3 Oct. 1789. Thomas Irwin to Nehemiah Carter two negro boys for $760, Mexican silver, payable in tobacco which has been inspected in King's Store at New Orleans, at rate of $8.00 per hundred pounds. Signed.

p. 338. 3 Oct. 1789. Thomas Irwin to Richard Swazey two Ginuea negroes, for $920 (Mexican), on terms.

p. 339. 3 Oct. 1789. Thos. Irwin to Bennet Truly negro man, aged 20 to 25, and 3 negro boys, 12 to 14, for $1670 (Mexican), on terms. Signed.

p. 339. 3 Oct. 1789. Thos. Wilkins, atty. for Daniel Clark, of N. O., to John Courtney negro from 20 to 25, for $580 (Mexican), Mark Cole surety. Mark (X) Cole, John Courtney. // Natchez, 21 July 1791. Receipt for above amount by Juan Mapother, Atty.

p. 340 6 Oct. 1789. Thos. Wilkins, atty. for Daniel Clark, to James Young an African negro, for$560 (Mexican). Thomas Keith and Richard Swazey sureties.'

p. 341. 6 Oct. 1789. George Fitzgerald, atty. for David Ross, to Philip Pleasant Turpin negro "Blizard", for $450 (Mexican), terms. Signed.

p. 342. 7 Oct. 1789. Petition of Benj. Farrar that Lachlan McNeil, of the Island of Jamaica, owes him $90 per attached account; there is in the hands of the exrs. of the late Mr. Carpenter a negro woman, the property of sd McNeil; he prays for an order that the exrs. sell the negro woman to pay said debt. // 8 Oct. 1789. Order for above. (p. 343) Said negro woman appraised at $60 by Sutton Banks and Peter Surget. Sold to John O'Connor for $91.00; cost of sale $11-6; paid to Dr. Benj. Farrar $79-2.

p. 344. 22 Oct. 1789. In response to notice from Isaac Gaillard of the death of Dr. Abner West, which took place at his house 23 Sept. last past, and being informed at the same time that West's property and effects were at the house of William Anderson where sd West had a long time resided, Don Carlos de Grand-Pre went to said house to take an inventory. (This consisted of medical supplies and equipment, including "one saw for legs and arms", clothing, several horses and colts, and some papers.)

p. 344. 22 Oct. 1789. Will of Alonzo Segovia, legitimate son of John Antonio Segovia and Theresa Bayena; married 13 years ago to Catherine Lambert; five children, Dorothy aged 10 or 11, Antonio 9 years, Rosalia 7, Isabella 4 and the youngest* 1 year. Estate to wife and children. John Galy exor. [*Youngest child named Ellen.] Debtors mostly Spaniards.

p. 349. 26 Oct. 1789. James Rapalie, of Natchez, to Joseph Andrews, Opelousas, for $625, mortgage on negro Jacob, native of Boston. Natchez. Jany. 21, 1792. William Wicks, with power of attorney from Joseph Andrews, to recover from Jacques Rapalie; negro security sold and mortgage satisfied. William (X) Wicks.

p. 350. 26 Oct. 1789. William Cooper to Uriah Wiggins a negro wench, "Alice', aged 20, nat. of Va., for $500 specie, for which he gave a note by Richard Swazey. Signed.

p. 350. 26 Oct. 1789. Eunice McIntosh, widow, to Ithamar Andrews a negro named "King", aged 23, nat. of Va., for $550 (Mexican), terms. Signed. Wit: James McIntosh for Mrs. McIntosh, Jose Saing for Andrews.

p. 351. 29 Oct. 1789. Melling Woolley to Samuel Murphy negro boy, "James", aged 12, for $480, Mexican silver. Signed.

p. 352. 31 Oct. 1789. Maurice Stackpoole to John Lum a negro, aged 12, nat. of Guinea, named "James", for $450 Mexican. Signed.

p. 353. 7 Nov. 1789. James Cole to William Henry King, son of Justus King, and Wm. King, son of Richard King, tract of 800 aprents on a branch of Cole's Creek, b. as per plat, for $300 in hand paid. Signed.

p. 354. 9 Nov. 1789. Bennet Truly to Benj. Andrews a negro boy, "Louis", aged 11, nat. of America, for $500 (Mexican), terms. Benj. (X) Andrews, Bennet Truly,

p. 354-5. 9 Nov. 1789. Melling Woolley to Winsor Pipes and William Collins, 400 arpents on Miss. River, 3 leagues from Fort, b. by James Bonner and lands of His Majesty, for 14700 pounds of good tobacco. // Receipt, 17 Oct. 1792, by Melling Woolley to Winsor Pipes. Receipts from Ebenr. Rees to Pipes 1791, to William Collins Mch. 27, 1794.

p. 355. 10 Nov. 1789. Asahel Lewis to Melling Woolley 4 negroes, for $2100 (Mexican), terms. Signed. // 14 Mch. 1790. Lewis and Woolley agree that Lewis shall take back the negroes.

p. 357. 14 Nov. 1789. Charles Percy to Robert Cochran 300 arpents, one league from Bayou Pierre, b. as shown in the plat and grant from the British Government, for $250, Mexican silver. Both sign.

p. 358. 11 Nov. 1789. Pedro Camus, indebted to Don Joaquim Ossorno for $150, mortgages negro, "Sambo", aged 30. Signed.

p. 359. 11 Nov. 1789. Thomas Ballew to John Ratcliff negro woman, "Mary", aged 20, for $400, Mexican silver. Thomas Ballew, John (X) Ratcliff.

p. 359-60. 5 Dec. 1789. James Stoddard to William Henderson two negroes for $1000, Mexican silver, which I bought from Daniel Clark. Signed by both.

p. 360. 7 Dec. 1789. Thomas Wilkins, atty. for Daniel Clark, to Daniel Whittaker a Guinea negro, aged 19, for $536 Mexican silver; without warrantee whatsoever. Joseph Harrison surety. Daniel Whitaker. Joseph (X) Harrison. // Negro taken back by Juan Mapother. (no date).

p. 361. 7 Dec. 1789. Ebenezer Rees to George Killian 3 negro men, one woman, natives of Guinea, for $2100, Mexican silver, terms.

p. 362. 8 Dec. 1789. Ebenezer Rees to Anthony Hutchins 2 Guinea negroes for $926, in specie. Signed.

p. 362. 9 Dec. 1789. Henry Manadue to Bennet Truly, 600 arpents on which is erected a mill, with two pair of oxen, on Fairchild's Creek, b. by lands of Juan Vaucheret, Juan Baptist LaPuente, Moses Bonner and Miss. River, for $1000, on terms. Signed by both.

p. 363. 9 Dec. 1789. Thos. Wilkins, atty. for Daniel Clark, to Abner Green a Guinea negro, for $463, Mexican silver. Signed.

p. 364. 14 Dec. 1789. Don Estevan Minor owes Don Pedro Petit $1246; mortgages negroes "Baptist" and "Stephen". Signed.

p. 365. 19 Dec. 1789. John Burnet to Daniel Burnet two African slaves; for $1000 specie, payable at end of year, negroes to be mortgaged, also a bond of Brian Bruin for $1000 until full payment made. Both sign.

p. 365. 19 Dec. 1789. Richard King to Robert Dunbar 600 arpents between St. Catherine's and Fairchild's Creeks. Signed.

p. 366. 21 Dec. 1789. Samuel Phips, of District, owes Thos. Wilkins and Co. $150 Mexican money, mortgages estate present and to come.

p. 367. 21 Dec. 1789. Benjamin Balk to Don Carlos de Grand-Pre, 191 acres b. on south by Adam Bingaman, north by purchaser, formerly John Lusk's, west Nathaniel Tomlinson, east Silas Crane and Matthew White; for $400 specie. Signed. (p. 367). Benj. Balk transfers above payment to Clark and Rees, part of a payment of a large sum due them by me. 17 April 1790. Receipt to Don Carlos de Grand-Pre for same by Ebenezer Rees. (n. d.)

p. 368. 21 Dec. 1789. Thos. Wilkins and Co. to John Jose Carradine 2 African negroes for $1025, Mexican silver, terms. Parker Carradine surety. Signed by the three. (p. 369) As atty. for Henry O'Neil to whom the negroes belonged, Thos. Wilkins agrees to take back the negroes. 22 July 1791. Juan Mapother.

p. 369. 22 Dec. 1789. Thos. Wilkins to Henry Nicholson negro, aged 20, nat. of Jamaica, named "Wesnesday", for $536 Mexican silver. Signed.

p. 370. 23 Dec. 1789. Joshua Collins to Parker Carradine, the younger, a negro, "Dick", for $525, Mex. silver. Signed Parker Carradine for his son, Parker Carradine.

p. 371. 23 Dec. 1789. James Truly to Richard Carradine negro woman and negro boy. Signed Parker Carradine for his son Richard.

p. 371. 23 Dec. 1789. William West to Thos. Hughes, 190 arpents, on St. Catherine's Creek, b. by lands of Perkins, Doctor Meeker, John Astley and sd creek; for $500 in Mexican silver, Edward McCabe surety. Wm. (X) West.

p. 372. 23 Dec. 1789. Wm. Brown to Peter Walker, power of attorney, during my absence, to sell two tracts of land to me belonging, one to Melling Woolley and one to Ralph Humphreys. Signed.

p. 373. 23 Dec. 1789. Thomas Wilkins, res. of District, to Joshua Collins a Guinea negro, aged 20, for $511 Mexican, terms. Signed. Negro taken back to Juan Mapother.

p. 374. Ebenezer Rees and Daniel Clark, to Daniel Ogden and Alexander Montgomery negro "Will", aged 25, nat. of Guinea, without warrantee, for 500 Mexican dollars, terms. Signed. 25, _____1790. Ebenezer Rees annuls mortgage in foregoing sale, having been paid.

p. 375. 7 Jany. 1790. Thos. Wilkins, atty., to Joseph Harrison an African negro for sum of 487 Mexican dollars. 6 Aug. 1791. Juan Mapother takes back negro. Sale void.

p. 375. 7 Jany. 1790. Thos. Wilkins, atty. for Daniel Clark, sells to Tarpley Bayley an African negro man and woman, for $993.

p. 376. 7 Jany. 1790. Thos. Wilkins, atty. for Daniel Clark, to John Odam an African wench for 487 Mexican dollars, other slaves mortgaged, terms. John (X) Odam.

p. 377. 8 Jany. 1790. George Proffit to Frederick Calvit negro girl, aged 10, for $500 Mexican silver, to be paid Jany. 1791. p. 378. Mary Higdon petitions that in Jany. 1790, she empowered her son, Frederick Calvit to purchase a negro girl for her use from George Proffit. By reason of the death of her son Frederick, she is unable to prove by his testimony that sd slave was thus purchased for her account and is actually her property. Being informed that David Ross is now in this District, petitioner prays that he be cited to declare as to sale. Apr. 5, 1793. Ordered that David Ross appear before me to answer on oath to the interrogation in above petition. Gayoso. 6 Apr. 1793. David Ross appeared and says that he, as exr. of will of sd George Proffit, received from Mary Higdon $460 for a negro girl the same sold by sd George Proffit to Fred. Calvit who has not paid any sum on account thereof and it is known to deponent that Frederick Calvit purchased sd negro for his mother, Mary Higdon.

p. 379. Clark and Rees to Nehemiah Carter two negroes, for 625 Mex. dollars on time, also mortgaged 200 acres on Second Creek, b. by John Ellis and Don Philip Trevino. Signed. One-third of sd plantation transferred to Ebenezer Rees, for a debt of Nehemiah Carter to sd Rees, 13 Apr. 1792. One negro died and was replaced by Rees and one taken back. (Translator says this instrument is unintelligible.)

p. 380. 11 Jany. 1790. Clark and Rees sell to Jesse Carter an African negro, for $525, Mexican silver, on terms, mortgages also another negro and 800 arpents of land on Homochitto, b. by Richard Ellis, Archibald Palmer and lands of His Majesty. Signed. 17 Dec. 1794. Negro taken back and sale null and void. Signed: Ebenezer Rees.

p. 382. 2 Sept. 1787. Peter Surget to Richard Cory a negro man, nat. of Guinea, fór $500 specie. Signed. // p. 382. 2 Sept. 1787. Peter Surget to Richard Cory, a negro man, "Coffee" and a negro woman "Fedelia", native of Guinea, for $1000 in specie or 10,000 lbs. of tobacco in carrots, due Dec. 1788. Signed. // p. 383. 19 Jany. 1789. Job Cory and Richard, his son, do bind themselves to pay to Don Pedro Surget $1421 Dec. 1789, being the amount of slaves in foregoing sales. Signed. // p. 384. 11 Jany. 1790. Pedro Surget transfers to Gabriel Swazey the mortgage I hold on the three slaves in the two foregoing sales. Signed.

p. 384. 11 Jany. 1790. Don Joaquim De Ossorno to Don Juan Jose Rodriguez negro named "Joseph", aged 10-12, nat. of Guinea, for $300 current money. Signed.

p. 385. 14 Jany. 1790. Clark and Rees to Francisco Paris and Gaspar Sinclair two negro men, "Cato" and "Kingston", for 1100 Mexican dollars, on time, negroes and 400 arpents on Cole's Creek mortgaged, the land bounded by John Cable and land of His Majesty.

p. 386. 15 Jany. 1790. Clark and Rees to John Ormesby and David Swazey two Guinea negroes, for $950, Mexican silver, on terms. Signed.

p. 386. 15 Jany. 1790. Arthur Cobb to Don Estevan Minor a negro "Peter", aged 25, nat. of Carolina; for $500 in hand paid, Mexican money. Signed.

p. 387. 24 Dec. 1789. Ebenezer Rees and Daniel Clark to Daniel Ogden a negro "Thomas", aged 25, for $500 milled money. Signed // p. 388. 25 April 1794. Ebenezer Rees annulled the above mortgage, same having been paid.

p. 388. 5 Feb. 1790. In pursuance of notice received of the death of Anna Shields, wife of Adam Bingaman, dec'd. 18 Jany. last past, without leaving any children or relations in this Province, the whole of her kindred being in Ireland, the native country of deceased. Will. 7 March 1786. I give and bequeath to Adam Bingaman, my dearly beloved husband, whom I likewise constitute my sole executor of my last will and testament, all my lands and properties of every kind. Wit: Patrick Foley, Samuel Gibson, Jacob Cobun. (Signed) Ann Bingaman. (Another paper) Deed of gift from Adam Bingaman, of same date, for 300 pounds to be divided between Duncan McIntosh, brother of the deceased Alexander McIntosh, the first husband of the deceased Ann Sheilds, and William McIntosh, son of the sister of aforesaid Alexander McIntosh, all residing in the Parish Inverness in the North of Great Britain. Adam Bingaman mentioned the will he had made in favor of his deceased wife in case she survived him.

p. 390. 8 Feb. 1790. Don Carlos de Grand-Pre to Ebenezer Dayton, 140 arpents of land, 2 miles from Fort, b. by Alexander Moore, Gabriel Swazey and Samuel Swazey and land of His Majesty, for $280, specie, $140 in two pairs of draught oxen, remaining $140 in Dec. of present year. Both signed.

p. 391. 15 Feb. 1790. David Smith, of District, planter, to James Resy, lot of ground, 110 ft. front by the same in depth, from the hill down to the river, in the Town of Natchez, b. on one side by lot of John O'Connor and Don Juan Rodriguez, on another by that of Peter Walker, on another by ground of "Demas" and otherwise by the River, for $100 in hand paid. Signed D. Smith, James Resy.

p. 392. 18 Feb. 1790. Patrick Foley, of this Dist., to William Bassett a negro named "Cocoroco", aged 30, nat. of Guinea, for 6000 pounds of good tobacco in hogsheads, to be delivered at N. O. Dec. of present year. Signed.

p. 393. 19 Feb. 1790. Richard Harrison is indebted to Thomas Wilkins in sum of $400, mortgages negro "Valet", to be paid Dec. 1790. Signed.

p. 393. 19 Feb. 1790. Richard Harrison to Don Louis Faure a negro named "Sancho", aged 14, nat. of Guinea, for $300 in hand paid. Signed.

p. 394. 19 Feb. 1790. Benjamin Monsanto to Henry Manadue a negro wench "Judy", aged 18, nat. of Guinea, for $450 specie, terms. Signed.

p. 395. 21 Feb. 1790. James McIntyre to John Bisland, 500 arpents on Fairchild's Cr., about 2 miles from Fort, b. as per plot. p. 396. Receipt for above by James McIntyre 10 Dec. 1794.

p. 396. 21 Feb. 1790. Nathaniel Tomlinson to David Hodge and John O'Connor, lot 80 ft. front by 102 ft. depth, in the lower town of Natchez, on the street that leads from the hill to the river, b. on west by said street, east by land of David Smith, northwest by river, on south by hill, for $767 in hand paid. Signed.

p. 397. 22 Feb. 1790. Christian Harman, atty. for Thomas Hoffpaver, to Don Pedro Walker tract at the landing with an old house thereon, ___ft in width, from the River to the Hill and b. on other two sides by ground of David Smith and vacant ground, for $200, terms. Signed.

p. 398. 22 Feb. 1790. Taply Bayley to David Smith a negro man "Amos", aged 35, nat. of Virginia, for $575, paid. Signed Taply Bayley, D. Smith.

p. 398. 22 Feb. 1790. William Bracoff to James Glasscock 208 arpents on St. Catherine's Creek, b. as per plat, for $500, on terms. Signed.

p. 399. 23 Feb. 1790. Thos. Wilkins, atty. for Daniel Clark, to Bennet Truly two Guinea negroes, for $1023, on terms, same to remain mortgaged also one named "Jupiter" and one named "Sal". Both sign.

p. 400. 21 Feb. 1790. Ebenezer Rees sells to James Stoddard negro man "Coche", aged 25, nat. of Guinea, for $550, on terms. Signed.

p. 401. 22 Feb. 1790. Waterman Crane to William Gooding 110 arpents, with an old house thereon, b. by land of Widow McIntosh, Adam Bingaman and Matthew White, for $100 paid. Both sign.

p. 401. 21 Feb. 1790. John Williams to John O'Connor a negro woman "Sally" with her daughter of same name, mother a nat. of Guinea, for $400 paid. Both signed.

p. 402. 22 Feb. 1790. David Smith is indebted to Thomas Wilkins for $200, to pay Dec. 1790, mortgages negro man "Amos". Signed D. Smith.

p. 403. 23 Feb. 1790. Jonas Eiler to Christian Harman 400 arpents on St. Catherine's Cr., as per plot, for $200 terms. Signed.

p. 403. 22 Feb. 1790. Richard Harrison to John O'Connor 500 arpents, two miles from Cole's Cr., about 3 miles below little Gulph, b. on west by Nath'l. Tomlinson, north by highlands, south and east by

Miss. River, for $1300 current money, on terms. Both signed.

p. 404. 23 Feb. 1790. David Lambert owes Christian Harman $277 to be paid Jany. 1791, mortgages whole estate. // Nov. 1790. Receipt of Christian Harman for above amount from David Lambert. Signed.

p. 405. 23 Feb. 1790. Thos. Wilkins, atty. for Daniel Clark, to John Lum a Guinea negro, for $536, terms with 10% int., mortgages also negro of purchaser, "Nancy". Signed. // 22 March 1791. Negro wench taken back. Juan Mapother.

p. 405-6. 24 Feb. 1790. William Barland owes to John Bisland $500, mortgages 500 arpents, 3 miles from Fort, at a place called Douglass, with dwelling house and other buildings. Signed.

p. 406. 25 Feb. 1790. Nathaniel Ivy to James Foster 100 arpents on St. Catherine's Creek, b..by lands of sd Foster, Wm. Gilbert and vacant lands. Signed James Foster, Nathaniel (X) Ivy.

p. 407. 24 Feb. 1790. William Dunbar to Richard Bell a negro man, "Sampson", aged 23, nat. of Guinea, for 8600 pounds of tobacco, Wm. Weeks surety. Signed Richard Bell, Wm (X) Weeks. p. 408. 3 Sept. 1796. Wm. Dunbar ack. to have received from Wm. Wicks full payment of above obligation, Richard Bell having satisfied sd Wm. Wicks for the same before his death.

p. 408. 26 Feb. 1790. Henry (X) Phips owes Thos. Wilkins $250, specie, to secure which he mortgages all estate present and to come. // 31 Aug. 1797. Thos. Wilkins ack. receipt of above from Henry Phips.

p. 409. 26 Feb. 1790. Robt. Withers indebted to Thos. Wilkins in sum of $200 specie, mortgages all estate. Signed. // Thos. Wilkins ack. receipt of amount due him from above.

p. 409. 27 Feb. 1790. Rees and Clark to Lt. Col. Don Carlos de Grand-Pre, 254 arpents on Cole's Creek, b. by lands of Adam Bingaman, Thos. Irwin, the seller and land of His Majesty; for $120 in hand paid. Signed.

p. 410. 27 Feb. 1790. James Elliot to Lt. Col. Don Carlos de Grand-Pre, 254 arpents on Cole's Creek, b. by Adam Bingaman on south, Thomas Irwin on east, land of His Majesty on north, by seller on west; for $120 in hand paid.

p. 411. 27 Feb. 1790. Joshua Howard to Christopher Whipple negro, nat. of U. S., for $400, specie. Signed by Howard.

p. 411-12. 3 March 1790. Thomas Irwin to James Stoddard negro man and woman, nat. of Africa, for $900, Mexican money. Both sign.

p. 412-13. 5 March 1790. Richard Harrison to Alexander Moore is indebted for $1500, mortgages 3 negroes and crop made this year. Signed by Harrison.

p. 413. 6 March 1790. Don Estevan Minor, Adjt. Major of this Post of Natchez, to Ezekiel Dueitt two negroes "Bedford", nat. of Jamaica, and "Jack", nat. of Maryland, for $800 Mexican money, on terms. Ezekiel Dueitt signed with mark. "E. D."

p. 414. 6 Mar. 1790. Produced before de Grand-Pre, the will of Daniel Perry, dec'd., in English, informing of the death of sd Perry on 24th March last past, by Daniel Perry, one of the sons of sd Perry, dec'd. [For will of Daniel Perry, see "Written Evidences" A-188.] (p. 415) Wit. to will of Daniel Perry: Jac. Funk, Jr., Dennis Collins, John Martin, Stuart Higginson, Sebastien Derr, Andrew Scanlan, Isaac Johnson.

p. 415-6. 6 March 1790. Richard Harrison to Maurice Stackpoole a negro "Jack", aged 40, for $500 payable in casks, on terms. Signed. p. 416. 9 July 1791. Richard Harrison receipts to Maurice Stackpoole for the amount in the above obligation.

p. 417-8. 8 March 1790. James Hillen to John O'Connor negro wench, "Catherine", for $600, terms. Signed: James Hillen, John (X) O'Connor. // p. 418. 4 Oct. 1790. Receipt of payment by James Hillen.

p. 418. 8 March 1790. James Hillen, of the Dist. of Baton Rouge, to John Cole two slaves, "John", aged 20, nat. of Guinea, and "Anna"; for $900, payable in tobacco. Both sign.

p. 419. 9 March 1790. James Barfield owes Melling Woolley $180, mortgages wench, belonging to me, a nat. of Guinea. // Natchez, 22 Aug. 1795. Melling Woolley declares that he has transferred the above mortgage to George Cochran as security for $220 which he ack. to owe sd Cochran with 10% int. to

25 Dec. 1796. Signed. p. 420. Miss. Territory, Southern Dist., 22 Oct. 1798. George Cochran ack. to have received satisfaction for the within assignment, in consequence the property of the within mortgage reverts to Mr. Melling Woolley.

p. 420. 10 March 1790. Asahel Lewis is indebted to Juan O'Connor for $243, mortgages two negroes "Jack" and "Hubbard". Signed by Lewis. Receipt of Juan O'Connor. (n. d.)

p. 421. 10 March 1790. James Hillen, of Dist. of Baton Rouge, to Jacob Stampley three slaves, for $1050, terms. // 2 Nov. 1791. James Hillen agrees to take back above slaves, whereby the obligation becomes null and void. Signed by both as above.

p. 422. 13 March 1790. Will of Juan O'Connor, formerly of Philadelphia, merchant, and now of Post of Natchez, weak in health, married Ann O'Connor, issue a son, John Francis O'Connor aged 6 or 7, Margarita, aged 2; wife one-third; two thirds divided equally between children; wife, Tutress of children; David Ross, of N. O., John Joseph Patrick, of Manchae, Don Pedro Walker and John Bisland exrs. Natchez. 12 March 1790.

p. 422. 20 March 1790. George Flynn to John Williams two tracts of land, 505 arpents I hold in the Province of North Carolina, in the District of Cumberland*, of which 185 acres are bounded by the _____ of Mr. Bledsoe and by the public _____, being one-half of 370 acres I hold in partnership with James Harper, and the remaining 320 acres bounded by land of Patrick Quigley and 640 arpents I hold in common with James Shaw, for $200 in hand paid. Wit: Presting Tinsley, John Whipple. Signed. [*Note: This is now Middle Tennessee.]

p. 423. 8 April 1790. Jacob Funk to James Hess mulatto man "Jerry", aged 38, nat. of Maryland, for 5000 pounds of good tobacco, to be paid in Dec. of this year. Signed Jacob Funk,Jr., James (X) Hess.

p. 424. 16 Apr. 1790. Daniel Clark and Rees to Reuben Brown and William Cock negro boy "Juba", aged 12, nat. of Guinea, for $500, specie. Signed by all.

p. 425. 16 Apr. 1790. Bennet Truly to Charles Boardman and Asahel Lewis, 600 arpents, with saw-mill thereon, and pair of oxen and all tools and utensils belonging, for $3000, on terms. Signed by all. // Natchez 18 Apr. 1792. The undersigned ack. receipt from Charles Boardman and Asahel Lewis, $660, on account of the sum of $2000 due me from Bennet Truly, sd sum deducted from amount of the bond drawn in my favor. Thomas Wells for Samuel Wells. // May 8, 1793. I, Bennet Truly, ack. $1000 from Charles Boardman and Asahel Lewis on account of the foregoing. Signed. // p. 426. 25 May 1794. Levi Samuel Wells ack. to have rec'd. from Charles Boardman and Asahel Lewis the full amount of the foregoing obligation.

p. 426. 5 April 1790. Robert Conelly, recently from Kentucky, to Lt. Col. Don Carlos de Grand-Pre negro woman, nat. of Va., aged 24, with mulatto child, aged 2, which slaves I had from an inhabitant of Kentucky, Hugh Shannon; for $320, specie, in hand paid. Signed.

p. 427. Will of Ralph Humphreys, District of Natchez and settlement of Bayou Pierre, very sick and weak. After paying Margaret McKenna a legacy of $100 when she is sixteen and my beloved brother shall be decently clothed and maintained during his natural life, wife, Agnes, and sons, George and Ralph, to have all his estate and exrs. of same. Wit: Mathew Terney, B. Bruin, John Burnet, Ezekiel Hoskinson, Joseph Darlington, Lewellyn Price. Proscript. 29 ___ 1790. In consideration of the dowry which I received by my wife Agnes, she shall have the negroes, Cyrus, Sally and their children as her sole property, exclusive of her dividend, also the household furniture and stock of her own, purchased prior to my arrival in this country. In presence of Mathew Terney, Nicholas Grubb, Benj. Grubb, Patrick McDermot, George Wilson Humphreys.

p. 427-8. On April 25, 1790, in consequence of the notice received of the death of Ralph Humphreys, have repaired to the plantation of said deceased at Bayou Pierre, distant about 60 miles from this Fort, accompanied by Don Antonio Soler, Lieut. of Royal Artillery, Don Estevan Minor, Aid-Major of this Fort and Don Francisco Pavana to take an inventory. The estate to be held and enjoyed by his beloved wife, Agnes and his sons, George Humphreys, aged 21, and Ralph, aged 16, and his brother to be maintained. p. 428. Inventory 1000 arpents at Bayou Pierre, known as Grindstone Ford, with saw-mill thereon, tools, implements, with a small house. One saddle horse, a yoke of oxen, one cow and calf, two cows, 2 years old, a number of hogs running in the woods, slaves: Ezekiel, aged 40, Cook, aged 30, Sukey, aged 20, boy, Tom, aged 9. Signed by Agnes Humphreys and above witnesses. De Grand-Pre. // p. 430. 27 April 1790. Samuel Moore and Don Pedro Walker appointed appraisers and accepted. Signed. From account book. List of debts to estate.

John Burnet
John Hartley
Marcus Flower
Edward McCabe
William Bassett
Daniel Burnet
Abram Lobdell
Jarmes Harman
Joel Bird
James Lobdell
Thos. Smith
Manuel Murphy
Estevan Minor
Carlos de Grand-Pre
Mr. Boyer
James Luton
Tarply Bayly
Rosa Bellmiguet
Moses Armstrong
Erastus Harman
David Smith
Francis Brozinas
Ezekiel Hoskinson
Selas Chambers
Wm. Brocus
James Carr
Jacob Cobun
Harry Perry
Benjamin Newman
Roger Dickson
Mr. Matthew
Elias Banatson
William House
John Potter
Wm. Ogilvie,
Gibson Clark
Ephraim Storey
Margaret Gaillard
Wm. Swazey
Wm. McKenna
James Rapalie
Buckner Pitman
Gilbert Younger
Patrick McDermott
Benj. Ivy
Patrick Connelly
Lorezo McNam
John Peters
Thos. Golden
John Humble
Wm. Booth
Thos. Beams
Mr. Wiley
Joseph Butler
John Murphy
Mr. Miller
Mr. Downey
Garret Rapalie
Doctor Terney
Benjamin Grubb
Mr. Flowers
Mr. Hubbard
John Montgomery
Reuben Proctor
Thomas Jones
Christian Winskey

An order to surveyor, William Vousdan, to survey for the deceased 600 arpents of land, to be held during his lifetime. Agnes Humphreys declares that the account against Don Carlos de Grand-Pre had been paid and had been left on the list by negligence. Negroes appraised at $1700.

p. 436. 12 Nov. 1790. Agnes Humphreys states that her deceased husband, Ralph Humphreys, bought from William Brown a tract of land on credit, and she is already embarrassed with debts contracted by her sd husband and asks that, as no formal sale was passed for said tract of land and that she is unable to to make a payment for the same, asks that Brown take back sd land. p. 437. Agnes Humphreys, widow of Ralph and Tutress of children and executrix of sd estate, asks that the papers and accounts be turned over to her that she may collect money due the estate and satisfy claims against the estate.

p. 437. 28 Apr. 1790. Matthew White to Lt. Col. Don Carlos de Grand-Pre 52 arpents of land about 1 miles from Fórt, b. by lands of the purchaser and the seller, for $50. Signed.

p. 438. 26 Apr. 1790. John Williams to Mordecai Throckmorton, negro lad, aged 15, nat. of America, for $390, on terms. Signed John Williams, Jr. Mordecai Throckmorton. // 7 Sept. 1791. John Williams, Jr. to take back the negro in foregoing sale and obligation becomes null and void.

p. 439. 2 May 1790. Richard Harrison to Ezekiel Forman, 450 arpents on St. Catherine's Creek, 3 mi. from Fort, b. by Bennet Truly, John Lum, the creek and Mistress Spell. Signed by both.

p. 440. 4 May 1790. Joseph Page, of the District of Illinois, at present at Natchez, being possessed of a girl child of the age of four or five years, whom I bought from Bisal Bobe of Illinois aforesaid, for a certain sum in hand paid, as per deed of sale in my favor, sd girl being now actually my slave, so hereby declare that in virtue of this instrument, I do grant full and free liberty to the said slave so that she may be held and considered a free person. Signed.

p. 441. 4 May 1790. John Cobun to George Cochran negro lad named "Gib", aged 15, nat. of Va., for $300, paid in notes. Signed by both.

p. 442. 5 May 1790. Ebenezer Rees to Thomas Wilkins 5 negro men and one woman, nat. of Africa, for $1200, terms. Signed Clark and Rees, Thomas Wilkins.

p. 443. 6 May 1790. Thos. Green, of this Dist., do make a free gift and donation to Henry Green, Filmer Wells Green, Abraham Green and Everard Green, my four sons, of 17 slaves (named), with 50 cows, little and great, 6 oxen, 30 horses and mares, small and great, about 100 hogs and 100 arpents of land on Cole's Creek, b. by lands of John Smith and Bingaman, which said land I give to my son Everard solely, and other property to be divided between my four sons as by deed of gift hereunto annexed, 13 Jany. 1785. Signed Thos. Green. // Deed attached: State of Georgia. Thos. Green, now of this State to my beloved sons, Henry Green, Filmer Wells Green, Abraham Green and Everard Green, the following slaves and all the rest of my property now at the Natchez on the River Mississippi, (names slaves), equally divided into lots, giving preference to the eldest according to the ages. Savannah, Ga. 13 Feb. 1785. Wit: N. Long, Wm. Call. Thos. Green.

p. 444. 7 May 1790. John Cowan to Alexander Moore negro lad, aged 16, nat. of Va., for $250 in specie, in hand paid. Both sign.

p. 445. 7 May 1790. John Ormsby, of this District, owes Ebenezer Rees $500 and in security whereof have mortgaged to David Swazey, who has become surety and responsible to Ebenezer Rees for the sum, negro "Frank". Signed.

p. 446. 17 May 1790. Jonas Eiler to William Barland a mulatto woman "Elizabeth", aged 25, nat. of America, with her four children, for $700 specie, paid. Both sign.

p. 446. 14 May 1790. Richard Brough to Don Joaquim De Ossorno, Lt. of the Reg. of Infantry of La., negro "Nell" aged 15, native of America; $190 paid. Signed.

p. 447. 17 May 1790. George Marshall to Don Joaquim De Ossorno negro and her daughter, natives of America, for $250 paid. Both sign.

p. 447. 27 May 1790. Don Joaquim De Ossorno to Don Luis Faure, Surgeon of the Royal Hospital at this Post of Natchez, 3 slaves, a negro man and a negro woman with her mulatto child, all natives of America, for $600 paid. Both sign.

p. 448. 2 June 1790. Silas McBee, citizen of America to Turner Williams negro man, Peter, aged 27, nat. of Va., for $400 paid. Both sign.

p. 449. 2 June 1790. William Smith, to Thos. Wilkins, being indebted to him in sum of $1416, mortgages negro "Fortune", aged 35, woman "Catherine", aged 35, 11 horses marked "W. S.", 25 cattle marked the same, 60 hogs marked with my usual mark; 600 arpents on Bayou Pierre, as set forth in the plot from His Brittanic Majesty, together with all my household furniture, to be paid December 1790, being this present year.

p. 449. 5 June 1790. Jeptha Higdon owes to Clark and Rees $1200 mortgages 600 arpents with house and sundry buildings on a branch of St. Catherine's Creek, ca 10 miles from Fort, b. by Frederick Calvit, Gabriel Griffing and Benjamin Curtis. // 8 Aug. 1794. Ebenezer Rees ack. that Jeptha Higdon had paid him $651 in two slaves which he has delivered and the balance due is $548.

p. 450. 5 June 1790. David Odam is indebted to Aid-Major Don Estevan Minor, in sum $250, mortgages to sd Minor negro named "Stephen", aged 12, to be paid on demand. Signed // p. 451. Natchez, 1 Sept. 1792. Received $8.00 on account and ack the foregoing mortgage cancelled by purchase of the negro boy therein mentioned. Signed. Minor.

p. 451. 10 June 1790. Matthew White to Alexander Moore 430 arpents with dwelling house and other buildings, 2 mi from Post, b. as set forth in plats, for $450 paid. Both sign.

p. 452. 20 June 1790. Walter Beall to Don Carlos de Grand-Pre a mulatto boy, aged 13, nat. of Maryland, for $200 paid. Signed.

p. 452. 27 May 1790. Walter Beall to Don Juan Joseph Rodriguez negro lad "Jacob", aged 19, nat. of Maryland, and a mulatto lad, "Jeremiah", aged 18, nat. of same, for $850, terms. Signed.

p. 453. 27 May 1790. Walter Beall to Antonio Gras negro woman, "Sarah", aged 30, nat. of Virginia, for $185 paid. Signed.

p. 454. 27 June 1790. Walter Beall to Nathaniel Tomlinson six negroes, all nat. of Maryland, for $1300, terms. Signed.

p. 455. 29 June 1790. John Williams, of District, planter, to John O'Connor is indebted in the sum of $350, mortgages 150 acres, 3 mi. from Fort, on St. Catherine's Cr., b. by Wm. Vousdan, Mr. Pavana and another of 380 acres, on which I live, b. by Stephen Minor and Richard Swayze. // Mch. 22, 1792. Mortgage on 150 arpents, above, cancelled and the owner may dispose of same. Signed: John O'Connor.

p. 456. 10 July 1790. James Cole, Jr. to Tarpley Bayley, on branch of St. Catherine's Cr., 200 arpents, b. by John Clark, Samuel Davis, and John Stampley, for $400 on terms. Signed.

p. 456-7. 12 July 1790. Don Louis Faure to William Foster a negro woman, nat. of Ky., with one-year old child, for $450, terms. Both sign. 11 Aug. 1792. Louis Faure received above mentioned sum of $450 and obligation has become void. Signed.

p. 457. 12 July 1790. Robert Abrams to Samuel Martin 262 arpents on Second Creek, b. by Dr. Cambelson, Michael Vore, Isaac Alexander and vacant land, which I had from Reuben Alexander and now sell with all implements and tools, with a house, kitchen and sundry negro cabins and tobacco house, the crop in the ground, 25 head of cattle, 93 hogs, for $1250 on terms, one payment of $334 to be paid to Michael Lopez to whom he was indebted in that sum. Both signed. // p. 458. In pursuance of a petition presented to His Excellency, the Governor, I have agreed and do hereby take back the plantation by foregoing instrument conveyed to Samuel Martin, reserving to myself the claim for such damage as have by arbitrators been awarded in my favor. Signed Robert Abrams, Elizabeth (X) Martin. // Pet. of Robert Abrams. Samuel Martin purchased of him a plantation, part of payment was $300 to be paid to a certain estate. Martin has since gone to the Indian Nation; and according to John Baker he does not intend to return. Abrams asks for possession of plantation. July 30, 1791. // Order: Let Baker be cited to appear and give testimony in this case. July 30, 1791. Notified Baker. Jere Bryan. // p. 459. Deposition of Baker, 1 Aug. 1791. He was at the Chickasaw Nation of Indians and was the bearer of a letter of the wife of Samuel Martin which she had given him to deliver to her husband, which sd letter he delivered into his own hands and Martin, having read same, said "There is nothing to prevent my wife from marrying again for I will not return to live with her again. It may be that I shall return in the course of the winter to see my children but never will I live with my wife again. I am settled here and intend to remain. Tell my wife that she may manage my concerns as if they were her own. I cannot pay for the plantation I bought from Robt. Abrams and he may take it back. I have not much property in that country and, as to my debts there, they may be paid out of the tobacco which I have in Town." Signed by Baker. // p. 460. Inventory by order of the Governor of buildings, etc. by Isaac Johnson, Isaac Alexander and Robert Ford. Aug. 26, 1791. Damage appraised at $158 by Isaac Alexander and Robert Ford.

p. 460. 20 July 1790. William Collins to Richard Ellis, 1600 arpents on Buffalo Creek, b. by John Ellis, Sr., Daniel Clark, Comer Chabaud, for $2000, to be paid in transfer of 4 negroes belonging to purchaser, "Phil", "Cuffy", and "Ben", and negro girl "Peggy", to be delivered December next. Both signed.

p. 461. 1 July 1790. Turner Williams to John Foster negro man "Peter", aged 27, nat. of Va., for $250 paid. Both sign.

p. 462. 30 July 1790. Joseph Ballinger to Don Estevan Minor negro man "Charles", aged 22, nat. of Va., for $350. Both sign.

p. 463. 30 July 1790. Joseph Ballinger to Don Joseph Vidal negro lad "Jumper", aged 19, nat. of Va., for $350 current money. Both sign. p. 463. Joseph Ballinger, by agreement, takes back the negro lad, in satisfaction of above sale, cancelling same.

p. 463. 9 Aug. 1790. John Ratcliff indebted to Alexander Moore for $383, to be paid Jany. 1791, mortgages negro "Romeo" and negro wench "Maria" and her child, aged 6 mos. // 19 Apr. 1790. James Moore, exec. of will of father, decd., ack full payment.

p. 464. 10 Aug. 1790. Wm. Ryan to Alexander Moore plantation of 160 arpents of land situate in this District, 9 miles east of Fort, b.by land of Stephen Stephenson, Charles Carson and Christian Harman, for $160, specie, paid. Both sign.

p. 465. 18 Aug. 1790. Presting Tinsley to Terney Gologer a negro girl, "Esther", aged 8, nat. of S. C. for $74, specie, paid.

p. 465. 4 Sept. 1790. John Newton is indebted to Hugh Rea Slater, for $500, mortgages to sd Slater 5 oxen, 2 cows, 2 steers, one bay horse, one iron grey horse, one colt, 30 hogs, with plantation, 100 arpents, which I now live.

p. 466. 9 Sept. 1790. Joseph Calvit to Thomas Calvit negro wench, "Jane", aged 15, and negro boy, "Harry", aged 12, for $800 paid. Signed Joseph Calvit.

p. 467. 7 Sept. 1790. Benj. Balk to Thos. Wilkins is indebted in sum $1105, mortgages 800 arpents on St. Catherine's Creek, b. by Joseph Calvit, Richard Harrison, Richard Ellis and Gerard Brandon, with tools, etc. Signed. // 9 Sept. 1800. Miss. Territory, Adams Co., Thomas Wilkins, Esq. ack to have recd. full payment of sum mentioned in foregoing mortgage.

p. 467. 9 Sept. 1790. Exchange of slaves by Mary Carpenter and Asahel Lewis. A negro woman owned by Mary Carpenter, "Emma", aged 25, nat. of South Carolina, in exchange for a negro man, "Jameson", aged 25, nat. of Guinea, owned by Lewis.

p. 468. 11 Sept. 1790. Bennet Truly, indebted to Thos. Wilkins in sum of $1055, payable Jany. 1791, mortgages plantation, 100 arpents, on which I now dwell, with crop in ground, tools, a negro man, "Robert", aged 25, and another, "Peter", aged 22, both nat. of Africa. Signed.

p. 469. 11 Sept. 1790. William Henderson to Henry Manadue negro "Peter", aged 22, for $500 paid. Both sign.

p. 469. 30 Sept. 1790. Polser Shilling to Peter Camus a house which I had from Richard Harrison, at landing place, b. by ground of Thos. Wilkins, on other sidy by that of Antonio Gras and otherwise by hill and road leading to the Fort, for $1065, payable in 30 cows with their calves, 20 heifers and 15 steers of 3 years to be delivered to me in November of this present year. Both signed. After signed it was agreed that the house remain mortgaged until Peter Camus shall have made payment.

p. 470. 17 Sept. 1790. Presting Tinsely to David Carradine negro woman, aged 20, nat. of S. C., with her two children, for $500 (Mexican) in hand paid. Signed by Tinsley and Parker Carradine for his son, David Carradine.

p. 471. 25 Sept. 1790. William Ferguson to Thomas Marston Green 348 arpents, b. by John Smith, James Cole, Benj. Stampley, Benj. Roberts, for $350 paid. Wit: Eben Rees. Signed by both.

p. 472. 25 Sept. 1790. Robert Casbol to Richard King, as agent for Samuel Wells, negro girl, "Rachel", nat. of Va., aged 10, for $200 specie, paid. Both sign.

p. 473. 4 Oct. 1790. Andrew Beall, atty. for Walter Beall, to William Weeks two negro women, for $400 current money, paid. Both sign.

p. 474. 6 Oct. 1790. Robt. Casbol to James Kirk 650 arpents on Homochitto, b. by Samuel Phipps, Nicholas Rabb, Messrs Kirk, Henderson, Savage, Lusk and Hutchins, for $1300 paid. Signed.

p. 474-5. 8 Oct. 1790. Ephraim Hubbard to George Cochran 3 negroes, for $450, paid. Signed.

p. 475. 12 Oct. 1790. Daniel Clark and Ebenezer Rees to Jesse Greenfield seven Guinea negroes, for $2400 (terms). Signed. // 21 Apr. 1792. Negro in above taken back by Juan Mapother.

p. 476. 15 Oct. 1790. William Calvit to Don Peter Surget is indebted in sum $1303, payable yearly, mortgages plantation on Homochitto, b. on all sides by vacant lands, also plantation on which I now dwell, 800 acres, b. by lands of John Ford, William Fletcher and vacant lands. Signed. // 31 Oct. 1797. Receipt for $750 on account of foregoing; obligation of 750 acres of land is null and void. Chas. Surget.

p. 477. 19 Oct. 1790. Daniel Clark to Thos. Wilkins five Guinea negro men and one woman, (named) for $1750, terms. // p. 478. Receipt for Daniel Clark, from Thos. Wilkins, for $400 on account of foregoing sale. Eben. Rees, atty. for Clark.

p. 478. 20 Oct. 1790. William Curtis to Memy Lewis a plantation on the high hills of the Miss., at Cole's Creek, 394 arpents, b. by land of John Strawbreaker, the River Miss. and vacant lands, for $500, on terms. Signed: William Curtis, Memy (X) Lewis. [Jemima Lewis.]

p. 479. 20 Oct. 1790. David Lambert to John D. Bredy 400 arpents at the head of St. Catherine's Creek, b. by lands of Adams, George Killian, William Ryan and Charles Cason, for $400, terms. Both sign.

p. 480. 25 Oct. 1790. Don Estevan Minor, Aid-Major of this Post, is indebted to Don Joaquim Ossorno for $900 due this present year, mortgages four negroes. Both sign.

p. 480. 10 Nov. 1790. John Stampley indebted to Alexander Moore for $450 for negro wench he sold me, July 1787, mortgages said negro girl until payment. Signed.

p. 481. 20 Nov. 1790. Andrew Beall, atty. for Walter Beall, sells to William Vousdan negro boy "Abram", aged 13, for $200 paid. Both sign.

p. 481-2. 20 Nov. 1790. Andrew Beall, atty. for Walter Beall, to John Irwin negro boy, "John", aged 11, for $200, paid. Signed.

p. 482. 22 Nov. 1790. Richard Swazey indebted to Don Pedro Surget, for $1200, specie, mortgages five negroes (named). Signed.

p. 483. 24 Nov. 1790. Presting Tinsley to Joshua Collins negro lad "Phil", aged 14, nat. of S. C., for $200,terms. Both sign.

p. 483. 24 Nov. 1790. Presting Tinsley to Catherine Pavana negro girl, "Mariana", aged 8, nat. of S. C., for $120, of which $20 is paid and $100 due in December of this year. Signed by Presting Tinsley, Francisco Pavana.

p. 484. 24 Nov. 1790. Anthony Hutchins to Parker Carradine 242 arpents on Cole's Creek, on which sd Carradine now dwells, for $500 (Mexican), on terms. Both sign.

p. 485. 25 Nov. 1790. Jeremiah Routh is indebted to the estate of Richard Carpenter, decd., in sum $250, due March 1791; mortgages the plantation on which I now dwell, 250 arpents, on Cole's Creek, with yoke of oxen. Signed.

p. 485-6. Presting Tinsley to Parker Carradine negro man, "Peter", aged 20, for four hogsheads of good tobacco, delivered and inspected at King's Store, in course of this present year, together with a horse which I have received. Signed by both.

p. 486. 4 Dec. 1790. Job Cory and Richard Cory to Samuel Wells two negro men and one negro woman, nat. of Jamaica, for $1150 paid. The three sign.

p. 487. 12 Dec. 1790. Samuel Wells to Bennet Truly 240 head of cattle, 163 thereof 4 years old, the remainder 3 years old, for $2000 which I have received in a bond of Charles Boardman and Asahel Lewis.

p. 488. 17 Jany. 1791. John Joseph Rodriguez is indebted to Don Manuel Texada, for $1800 specie, which he has at various times advanced to me, as security, mortgages a number of negroes and a plantation of 400 arpents on St. Catherine's Cr., b. by lands of Mr. Banks and Alexander Moore, oxen, carts, horses. Signed.

p. 488-9. 16 Jany. 1791. Last will and testament of Frederick Calvit opened. Wit: John Short, Henry Green, Filmer W. Green, Gerard Brandon, Gabriel Griffing, Lewis Alston. The Will: Natchez, 22 Sept. 1790. Frederick Calvit, of said District, last will and testament. After paying all my just debts, to my beloved wife, Mary, one-third of what property I may possess, to enjoy the same as long as she lives; but if she should marry then she and her husband shall give my exrs. good and sufficient security that her one-third and likewise what other property she may have possessed at her marriage, shall descend to my children at her decease. To my dear children: Elizabeth, William, Lucrecia, Mumford, Alexander, and Joseph, the remainder of what property I may have at my death (still reserving to my dear wife, one-third). Should wife be pregnant and delivered of a child in nine months, the child shall have his or her share as my children mentioned above. To Rachel Spikes, a poor orphan girl whom I have brought up, a mare, two cows and calves when she comes of age from my estate. My wife, John Bisland, Thomas Marston Green and my brother, Thos. Calvit, of this District, my exors. My dear wife shall not contract any matters of consequence without consulting someone of the exrs. Signed. Wit: John Short, Filmer Green, Henry Green, Gerard Brandon, Gabriel Griffin. // p. 490. Inventory of estate of Frederick Calvitt, decd. Accounts, Doctor McCabe, John O'Connor, Joseph Calvit, Mary Higdon, Parker Carradine, Arthur Cobb, Thos. Darrah, Benj. Belk, Gov. Gayoso, Jesse Hamilton, Isaac Tabor, John Ford, Jeptha Higdon, Caudle Gibson, Doctor Todd, John Riggs, Thos. Dawes, Stephen Minor, D. Rodriguez. // Plantation, 600 arps.; 5 negro fellows, 2 negro wenches, 2 negro children, 3 yoke oxen, about 250 head of cattle, 4 work horses, 16 mares and colts, about 100 hogs, etc. Jany. 18, 1891. Signed John Bisland, Thos. Calvit.

p. 490. 3 Feb. 1791. Don Pedro Surget to Samuel Wells negro man "Jack", aged 22, nat. of Jamaica, for $450 paid. Signed: Pedro Surget, John Wells for Samuel Wells.

p. 491. 15 Feb. 1791. Bennet Truly to John Holt negro man, aged 30, negro woman, aged 35, both nat. of Guinea, for $500, terms. Both sign.

p. 492. 15 Feb. 1791. John Lusk to Anne Savage 100 arpents on Second Creek, b. by Thos. Hutchins and James Kirk, Mrs. Savage and Creek, for $275 in hand paid. Both sign.

p. 493. 3 March 1791. Matthew White, atty. for Christopher Whipple, to David Williams and Bernard Lintot, as exrs. of estate of Richard Carpenter, deceased, a negro man, "Nace", and a negro woman "Aimy", for use of children of deceased, named James and Mary Carpenter, for $600 paid. All sign.

p. 494. 2 March 1791. Robert Stark to Filmer Wells* negro, aged 21, for $200 paid. Both signed.
*[Filmer Wells Green]

p. 495. 2 March 1791. Anthony Hutchins to Abner Green plantation on Second Creek, 434 arpents, a British grant, for $200 paid. Both sign. No description.

p. 495-6. 2 March 1791. Robert Stark to Henry Green two negroes, both aged 20, for $400, paid. Both sign.

p. 496. 9 March 1791. William Groding to Adam Bingaman 100 arpents, b. by lands of Mrs. McIntosh and Alexander Moore, for $200, in hand paid. Both sign.

p. 497. 9 March 1791. William Groding to Adam Bingaman 96 arpents, b. by land of sd Bingaman, for $192 paid. Both sign.

p. 497. Will of Ezekiel DeWitt, March 21, 1791. All property to my beloved wife, Mary, until her decease. At her decease, one-half to the Catholic Church, the other half to Stephen Brashiers, with this reservation, that my negro girl, Margaret, shall have her full freedom and manumission as soon as she becomes of age. Stephen Minor and Sutton Banks executors. Signed with his mark "E. D." Wit: John Potter, Thos. Jordan, John Foster, Jere. Bryan.

p. 498. 27 March 1791. Thomas Jordan, of the District, to John Bisland negro man, "Dick", aged 30, nat. of Guinea.

p. 498. 26 March 1791. Maurice Stackpoole to Samuel Wells negro boy, aged 15, nat. of North America, for $500, terms. Signed Mce. Stackpoole, James Wells.

p. 499. 24 Mch. 1791. John Williams to William Vousdan negro woman, "Dinah", aged 26, nat. of Carolina, and her two dau., "Daphne" and "Patsy", for $500, paid. Both signed.

p. 500. 20 Apr. 1791. Richard Bell to Mordecai Throckmorton, plantation on Cole's Creek, b. by Adam Bingaman, James Cole and Benjamin Curtis, for $800 on terms. Wit: Robert Throckmorton. Both sign. // p. 501. 7 Oct. 1794. Whereas Samuel Bell, late owner of the plantation sold by his brother, Richard Bell, who declared he transferred to Don Estevan Minor the sum of $800 owing to him on account of the said sale, hereby renounces all title and claim to same, having received from said Minor an equal amount. Signed by Samuel Bell and official witnesses. Natchez, Sept. 23, 1797. Don Stephen Minor ack. to have received from Messrs. Throckmorton the different payments on the foregoing obligation as expressed in the annexed account; so that the note of Mr. Cochran and the note of Jas. Hyland, being paid, the balance due will be $236, 6 reals. S. Minor. Wit: Edward McCabe, J. Girault. Account: 1791. Bond of Messrs. Throckmorton, payable one-half Jany. 1792, one-half Jany. 1793, to S. Minor for $800, with interest for five years $1016. Credits: Jany. 1792. Paid by Mr. Alex. Moore $45; Oct. 94 by same $41-6; Mar. 95 by oxen $50, by Robert Throckmorton $230, Sept. by James Hyland $150, Dec. 96, int. of above payments $61-7; balance due $436-6; Dec. 96 by George Cochran $100, Feb. 1796 Mordecai Throckmorton $100. 1797 balance due $236-6, errors excepted. Feb. 23, 1791.

p. 501. 24 May 1791. Benjamin Monsanto, of District, merchant, to Don Luis Faure, lot at the landing of this place, b. by Miss. River, the street and lot of George Fitzgerald, 102 ft front by 52 ft. depth, with house, store and two other buildings, in exchange for negro "Nat". Both sign.

p. 502. 20 May 1791. Daniel Clark, before Gayoso, etc. declared that he had received from Don Arthur O'Neill, Brigadier of the Royal Armies and Governor of Pensacola, $18,000, the sum having been remitted by Don Henry O'Neill to said Brigidier, for the purpose that, with the same, Clark should purchase negroes at Jamaica, to be sold in this Province for account of sd Don Henry O'Neill, at his expense and risk; with the aforesaid $18,000, Clark imported 83 slaves in the Schooner Governor Miro, and which were sold and disposed of as follows: 4 to Don Manuel Gayoso for $1800, 3 to Justus King and sons for $1633; 1 to Gabriel Griffing for $521; 3 to Daniel Grafton for $1557; 1 to Alonzo Segovia for $463; 1 to William Smith for $536; 1 to Robert Miller to $536; 1 to Richard Curtis for $546; 1 to Thos. Morgan for $636; 2 to Richard Harrison for $1035; 1 to James Truly for $585; 1 to John Ford for $560; 3 to David Mitchell for $1608; 1 to John Courtney for $580; 1 to Thos. Reed for $560; 1 to James Cole, Jr., for ___; 2 to Anthony Hutchins for $926; 1 to Abner Green for $463; 1 to Jocina Locoder for $450; all foregoing payable at the end of 1790; 2 to Parker Carradine for $1025; 1 to Henry Nichols for $536;1 to Joseph Harrison for $487; 2 to Tarply Baily for $993; 1 to John Lum for $536; 3 to Nehemiah Carter for $1625; 2 to Francisco Perez and Gaspar Sinclair for $1100; 2 to David Swazey and John Ormsby for $950; 4 to Don Carlos de Grand-Pre for $1600; 1 to William Collins for $550; 4 to George Killian for $2160; 1 to Reuben Brown and Wm. Cock for $500; 7 to Jesse Greenfield for $2400; 6 to Thos. Wilkins for $1750; 1 to Joseph Vidal for $390; 7 to Thos. Wilkins for $1200; these last mentioned sales being payable one-half at end of 1790 and one-half at end of this year, 1791, which said slaves sold, together with four who died at New Orleans, one at Clarkville and one at Natchez, making total of 83 slaves, amounting to $34,511-6r. Clark had no other interest in transaction other than his commission. Here transfers to O'Neill all instruments and sales of slaves by him.

p. 504. Will of John O'Lavery, son of Peter O'Lavery and Maria Juana De Fuentes, of the Kingdom of Navarre; sick in body; own a house in the town of this Post in common with Pedro Ancide, who is likewise owner of the goods and effects therein, being partners in sd house and in trade, and to whom I bequeath my share of same on condition that if he should return to Spain and find my parents living, or my brothers Juan Estevan, Juan Lorenzo, my sister Teresa, he shall pay the value to my said relations and if not to be found then to dispose of same at his pleasure. Juan Perez exor. 30 May 1791. wit: Juan Gali, Manuel Diaz, Don Jose Sainz. // Notice of the death 1 June 1791. His partner being absent at New Orleans, Gayosa repaired to dwelling, accompanied by Charles Todd and Benj. Monsanto. Inventory made.

p. 508. Inventory of Estate of Jere. Routh, decd. Plantation 250 acres, 2 horses and ploughs, 4 iron pots, 1 Dutch oven, 1 frying pan, 1 tea kettle, 1 pot rack, 4 plates, 9 spoons, 2 pewter dishes, 2 milk pans, 2 candlesticks, 2 tin quarts, 4 chairs, 2 chests, 1 trunk, 2 beds, 1 looking glass, 2 axes, 4 hoes, 2 chisels, 1 hand saw, 1 augur, 1 drawing knife, 1 plane, 1 churn and 3 piggins, 1 coffee mill, 1 yoke oxen, a frame of timber for a house. // Cole's Creek, 3 June 1791. Personally appeared before me Elijah and Jeremiah Routh, sons of Jeremiah Routh, deceased, who deposed that the foregoing is a just and true inventory of their deceased father's estate, both real and personal, to the best of their knowledge and belief, exclusive of a certain list of debts supposed to be due from certain persons to the said deceased, amounting to $1333, herewith produced. Before J. Murray. // A duplicate of debts taken from his books and papers: //

Capt. Barbour, $263 and 11 years' interest, total $553

John Armstead
James Cole
Chas. and James Simmons
Wm. Nowland
Josiah Flower
Abram Taylor
Wm. Wilson
John Staybreaker
David Smith, a canoe
Henry Manadue
Thos. Dyson
Richard Trevillian
Henry Platner,
James Armstrong
Barnett Isinhoot
Francis Spain
John Stampley
Geo. Blair, a note
J. Escott, a note
Wm. Tabor
John Stower,
John Burke's note
Capt. Burnet
Hesekiah Harman
Ball
David Odam
Wm. Ferguson
Parker Carradine

The foregoing list of debts referred to in affidavit of Elijah and Jeremiah Routh, as supposed to be due to their father, witness my hand 3 June 1791. J. Murray. // p. 509. Natchez. 7 June 1791. Don Manuel Gayoso de Lemos in pursuance of foregoing inventory taken by my order, have adminsitered oath to Elijah and Jeremiah Routh, sons of deceased, relative to the same, who have declared that said inventory is just and true and that their deceased father had no other property, to their knowledge than what is exhibited therein, and now in possession of his widow.* In witness whereof they have signed this declaration with me and Don Antonio Soler and Don Joseph Vidal, witnesses present. [*Note: 1792 Spanish Census shows Margarita Routh, Jeremiah Routh and Elias Routh in District of Villa Gayoso.]

p. 509. Francisco Menar, of the Post of Arkansas, gives power of atty. to Don Estevan Minor, to claim, recover and receive negro man "Robert", and woman "Mariana" and her children, belonging to me, which slaves have absconded and are now in the Choctaw Nation. Natchez. 16 June 1791. Signed.

p. 509. 25 June 1791. Andrew Hare, of City of Philadelphia, to Alexander Moore a negro woman, "Nancy", aged 26, nat. of America, for $180 paid. Signed.

p. 510. Petition. Natchez. June 28, 1791. John Scott, as one of the executors of the last will of Alexander Turnbull, dec'd., the only exr. in the country, asks for an order to sell negro boy, "Sterling", in his possession, belonging to estate of deceased. // Order that all persons indebted to the estate of Alexander Turnbull, dec'd., make payment to John Scott and that negro will be sold at public sale, at first audience, 2nd July 1791. Gayoso. Joseph Ford and Joseph Harrison appointed appraisers of negro, which appraisal was $300. // At final sale adjudged to William Barland at $210, highest bid. Signed: John Scott, Wm. Barland, Augustus Macarty, Valentin Rincon, Antonio Soler. p. 511. 2 July 1791. Wm. Barland sells above-mentioned negro, "Sterling", to John Scott, for $210, in hand paid.

p. 512. On 6 June 1789. Roger Dixon arrived in the Dist. of Natchez, from Virginia to settle in said District, and brought with him 15 negro slaves, 5 of which the property of his mother, Lucy Dixon, namely: "Billy", "Gloster", "Peter", a blacksmith, _______________; four are the slaves of Lucy Dixon, Jr., his sister, wench "Fanny", girl "Jenny", and two boys, "George" and "Lewis"; two of sd slaves the property of Robert Throckmorton, his brother-in-law, who hath since arrived in sd District and taken them into his own possession; the remaining four, namely "Major", a blacksmith, a wench "Patience", a girl "Rose", and one small boy, "Gloster", are the property of said Roger Dixon, with power to sell on account of the said owners or to settle them on plantations as he should find most suitable. Having the said slaves, except Robert Throckmorton's, still in my possession, and being about to make a journey to Virginia on business, and leaving them settled on a plantation on Cole's Creek, think it proper to have the foregoing account of them recorded in Governor's office that said owners may receive and dispose of their property as they may think proper if any accident happen to myself. May 14, 1791. Signed: Roger Dixon. Acknowledged before Gayoso 6 July 1791.

p. 512. 6 July 1791. Ezekiel Dueitt to Abraham Horton negro "Dick", for another negro to him belonging, "Henry", exchange without recourse against each other. Both sign with a mark.

p. 513. 9 July 1791. Constantine McKenna, in virtue of power from Don Juan Stafford, Capt. in Regiment of Cuba, have received from Ebenezer Rees a negro whom he had in possession, the property of sd Stafford, and to the end that Rees shall be released from all further charge on account thereof. Signed.

p. 513. 19 July 1791. Ebenezer Rees and Juan Mapother have mutually agreed that the claim which Rees, as partner of Daniel Clark, has against Don Henry O'Neill, for whom the sd Mapother is agent, for expenses and commission accrued on account of the negroes belonging to said Henry O'Neill, shall be settled here if Daniel Clark, nephew of aforesaid Daniel Clark, should arrive at this Post before the departure of Mapother for N. O.; but if the said nephew of Daniel Clark shall not arrive here before that time, then the claim and accounts shall be finally adjusted at New Orleans; in virtue of conveyance of sales made by sd Clark and Rees to said Mapother, the whole concern shall be managed by him; and security of sd Clark and Rees, the sum owing by Don Thos. Wilkins shall remain pledged, the sd Clark and Rees becoming security for sd Wilkins and Jesse Greenfield on account of negroes bought by them belonging to sd Henry McNeill, and, lastly, that the aforesaid settlement shall finally be made within the term of two months form date hereof.

p. 514. 20 July 1791. Tarply Bailey sells to Joseph Ballinger a negro lad "Will", aged 18, for $320 on terms, said sum to be held at disposal of Messrs. Thos. Wilkins, John Mapother and George Cochran, to whom I have given my obligation for monies owing them. Signed by all the above. David Ferguson witness.

p. 514. 23 July 1791. James Kirk sells to Don Pedro Ancide a lot of ground at the landing of this Post, 121 ft. front by same in depth, b. by ground of Don Juan Rodriguez. Kirk signed with a mark.

p. 515. 29 July 1791. Don Estevan Minor to Job Routh negro man "Charles", nat. of Virginia, aged 22, for $400 paid. Both signed.

p. 516. 1 Aug. 1791. John Mapother to George Miller, for the use of Baptist Stille, for whom Miller is agent, a negro woman, "Abigail", aged 18, for $350 Mexican silver, on terms. Both signed.

p. 517. Antonio Gras to Patrick Foley, of this District, negro girl "Sally", aged 15, nat. of Va., for 300 Mexican dollars, on terms. Both signed. // Post of Natchez, 21 Dec. 1796. Antonio Gras declared he had received full payment of the foregoing obligation. Wit: Edward McCabe, Jean Girault.

p. 518. 5 Aug. 1791. Don Carlos de Grand-Pre gives power of attorney to Don Carlos Beauvais, of District of Pointe Coupee, planter, to sell five slaves belonging to him. Signed.

p. 518. Natchez. 23 _____, 1791. Ebenezer Rees petitions that whereas during the year last past he sold to James Strother a negro, "Quashee", Don Estevan Minor, security, and said Strother having gone to the U. S. without the permission from the Government, he wishes, with the approbation of Your Excellency, to take possession of said negro and sell same at publick sale, reserving his recourse against the surety for any deficiency in the proceeds of same. Signed. // p. 519. Natchez 23 ____ 1791. Before granting the prayer of the foregoing petitioner, it is necessary to know who has possession of the negro, at what time James Strother left the country. (signed) Gayoso. On 8th Nov. last, I made application to the Commandant to have the negro sold as will appear by a petition of the 7th, and about the beginning of the present year I mentioned the sale to the security, Mr. Minor, and we agreed it should be deferred for some time. Natchez 23 July 1791. // Natchez, 23 July 1791. A memorial in this case having been presented to my predecessor, Lt. Col. Don Carlos de Grand-Pre, and nothing having been done about it, I do hereby permit that notice be given that the negro be sold at public sale to the highest bidder. // p. 519. 6 Aug. 1791. Ezekiel Dueitt and Nehemiah Carter appointed appraisers; value placed at $190, payable one-half cash, one-half at end of present year. Adjudged to Francisco Pavana for $130, he being the highest bidder.

p. 519-20. 7 Aug. 1791. Philip Nolan to Joseph Ballinger negro "Charles", aged 20, for $300, paid. Both signed.

p. 520-522. 23 July 1791. At request of Don Pedro Camus, agent for Don Luis Chacheret, have exposed at public sale a house and lot belonging to said Chacheret, 120 ft. front by 135 ft. depth, at the landing, b. by Miguel Solibellas, on north, Don Pedro Surgett on west, public road on south and Main Street on east, and sold on credit, by consent of agent, and the said house being cried was adjudged, for 1st time, to Francisco Pavana, for $150, he being highest bidder. Wit: Pierre Camus, Franco. Pavana, John Girault, Valentin Rincon, Jeremiah Bryan, Antonio Soler, Manuel Gayoso. // p. 521. 30 July 1791. For 2nd time, above house and lot exposed to sale and adjudged to Francisco Pavana for $161. Same Witnesses. // 6 Aug. 1791. Third and last time, exposed the aforesaid house and lot of ground to public sale, when Valentine Dalton bid $162 for same, a spirited bidding by Pavana and Dalton ending in Valentine Dalton being the highest bidder at $250, it being understood that he purchased the house for Margaret Bobe, widow of Thomas Boutelet, Valentine Dalton being surety for the payment. Cost of sale $21-2.

p. 522. 9 Aug. 1791. Robert Miller to Baptist Stilly is indebted in sum $600, mortgages 250 arpents on Wells Creek, b. by lands of His Majesty. Signed. // 16 May 1798. By agreement of parties, the foregoing mortgage cancelled as follows: Robert Miller gave up to the attorney of Baptist Stilly the tract of land mortgaged, for a certain sum agreed upon, which I believe was $450, to be deducted from the whole debt, and after a settlement made between the parties by Mr. John Eldergill, Miller gave his note for the balance and the attorney of Stilly agreed to receive of Hezekiah Williams (of whom Miller had bought the land) his obligation for the title. May 16, 1798. Signed Jean Girault, Keeper of the Records. // 20 March 1806. Personally appeared Mr. Job Routh, the lawful agent of John Baptist Stilly, the mortgagee mentioned in foregoing deed, who did acknowledge in behalf of J. B. Stilly that the foregoing mortgage is fully closed and cancelled by the mortgager having paid sd Stilly $200 and conveyed to his direction the aforesaid tract of land. Signed by Job Routh and J. Girault

p. 523. 20 Aug. 1791. Don Pedro Surget to George Cochran and David Ferguson house and lot, 80 ft front by 120 ft. depth with all buildings thereon, at the landing, b. on east by house and lot of Widow Boutelet, on west by land of His Majesty, for $300, on terms. Signed by G. Cochran.

p. 524. 10 Sept. 1791. Patrick Foley to James Carrick is indebted for $340 Mexican money, to be paid Jany. 1792, mortgages negro "Sampson", aged 26, nat. of Guinea, five feet high and warranted sound. Signed.

p. 524. 10 Sept. 1791. John Williams to David Williams a negro woman, "Sukey", aged 26, nat. of North America, with her 3 children, for $500 paid. Signed John Williams, Jr. and David Williams. // After signing the foregoing instrument it was agreed that the seller should give to the purhcaser a security who should be liable in case the slaves thus sold should be claimed by another person, and in the meanwhile the purhcaser should in such case have recourse against such other slaves belonging to John Williams for the reimbursement of the sum of $500, paid as above mentioned. Signed John Williams, Jr. // Natchez, 6 Sept. 1793. Before Gayoso, appeared Maria, widow of David Williams, and declared that the above John Williams, having proved that the slaves sold to her late husband, the said David Williams, were really his own at the time of said sale, she, the said widow, hereby annuls the mortgage given by John Williams as security therefor.

p. 526. 12 Sept. 1791. Andrew Beall, atty. for Walter Beall, to Mary Higdon 4 negroes, natives of North America, for $500, $200 of which paid and $300 due June 1792. Mary (X) Higdon.

p. 527. 14 Sept. 1791. Margaret Gaskin to Job Routh negro "Bob", aged 12, nat. of North America, for price of 15 cows and 5 year-old calves, in hand paid. Both sign.

p. 528. 6 Oct. 1791. Winsor Pipes, to John Bullen 225 arpents of land on a branch of St. Catherine's Creek, b. by lands of Joseph Calvit, Jeremiah Bryan and Doctor McCabe, for 25,000 pounds of good tobacco, to be inspected and approved by two planters of the District, delivered Dec. 1791 and Dec. 1792. Both signed.

p. 528. 2 Oct. 1791. William Collins to John Stowers 200 arpents of land, 10 miles from Post, 2 miles from River Miss., which I bought, with other land, in partnership with Winsor Pipes, my father-in-law, and which I now sell for the price and quantity of 4,000 pounds of tobacco to be delivered at the landing of this Post, in good order and inspected by planters in this District. Both sign. // p. 529. 1 Sept. 1792. Wm. Collins acknowledges receipt of 3334 pounds of tobacco from John Stowers on above account. // 9 May 1796. Wm. Collins ack. full payment of foregoing obligation.

p. 529. 5 Oct. 1791. Peter B. Bruin to David McFarlan 13 acres of land, English measure, at the place called "Little Trough" on Bayou Pierre, for a certain consideration in hand paid to my full satisfaction. Both sign.

p. 530. 6 Oct. 1791. James Truly to Wm. Dortch 101 arpents on Cole's Creek, b. by lands of Francisco Spain and William Ferguson, for $200 in hand paid. Both signed.

p. 530. 6 Oct. 1791. William Dortch to George Overaker negro wench "Fanny", aged 17, nat. of Va., for $300 paid. Both signed.

p. 531. Natchez, 11 Oct. 1791. In pursuance of notice of death of Eliphalet Richards which took place on the 10th instant, at his plantation two leagues distant from Fort, Grand-Pre repaired thither to take inventory of said estate in presence of Charles King, Jacob Percy, Joseph Strong. Inventory..(small estate). The said estate to be sold at auction, the deceased having no known heirs in this country, having died a bachelor. // p. 535. List of debts due Eliphalet Richards, taken from his books:

Aaron Adams
Thomas Foster
Nathaniel Tomlinson
David Kenedy
Elizabeth Carr
John Cravan
Daniel Mygat
Cady Raby
Thomas Daroch
Charles Colins
Widow Oliphant
Frederick Man
Rachel Thomas
Benjamin Monsanto
David Mitchell
Hugh Coil
Samuel Moore
John Calvit
John Lum
p. 536 John O'Connor
Wm. Owens
Matthew Williams
James Cole, Jr.
Richard Adams
John Hartley
Wm. West
Richard Miller
Thomas Adams

p. 536.
Nehemiah Carter
Peter Nelson
Robert Abrams
Samuel Phips
Anthy Kean
Wm. Lum
James Kelly
John Ford
Jacob Huffman
Jonas Scoggan
Daniel Harrigal
James Irvine
Major Williams
Edward Patterson
James Spalding
Abraham Clawson
John Gerard
Margaret Rab
Frederick Calvit
Justus King
Richard Trevillian
Isaac Johnson
Jacob Miller
John Adams
(p. 537)
Doctor McCabe
Stephen Mayes
Tarply Baily
Denis Neuville
Benjamin Newman
John Bullen
Cinthia Gibson
Joseph Duncan
Mrs. Foster
Adam Bingaman
Thomas Lord
John Shunk
Ebenezer Dayton
Sutton Banks
Wm. Adams
Wm. Glascock
James Stoddard
Wm. Fletcher
Samuel Kenedy
John Newton
Jeremiah Bryan
Josiah Flowers
John Alston
John Spires
John Debredy
Wm. Alston
Martin Ramsen
Isaac Tabor
John Short
Elijah Swazey
Patrick Tool
Ephraim Bates
Wm. Gillespie
Benjamin Holmes
Jesse Withers
Thomas Rule
Reuben Gibson
James Wiley
David Mulkey
Stephen Minor
Jeremiah Routh
John Ratcliff
Richard Swazey
David Lambert
Bernard Isinhoot
Maurice Custard
Martin Carney
John Warren
Jeptha Higdon
Geo. Baily
Henry Milburn
Joseph LaForce
Louis Charbonneau
W. Martin
Jesse Hamilton
John Lusk
Rachel Newman
David Miller
Robert Withers
John Cole
Job Cory
Wm. Barland
Wm. Short
Christian Harman
Chr. Fulsom
Windsor Pipes
Jacob Airheart
Caleb King
Robt. Dunbar
Mary Pickens
Wm. Vousdan
Thomas Freeman
Wm. Gilbert
Obediah Brown
John Odam
Wm. Thomas
Charles King
Louis Valeret
Nathan Swazey
John Girault
Andrew Scandling
Roswell Mygat
Richard King
Thomas Nichols
Philander Smith
Wm. Vardiman
Calvin Smith
George Clare
George Stampley
Maurice Stackpoole

Wm. Lee
Archibald Douglass
Alex. Farrar
Richard Bacon
Thomas Lampheer
Abraham Mayes
Robert Miller
Jesse Carter
Moses Bonner
John Lay
James Bonner
Martin Smith's wife
George Killian
James Foster
Patterson Taylor
Benjamin Lanier
Jonas Iler

Jacob Files
Jeremiah Coleman
James Sanders
Benj. Bullock
Thos. Jordan
Ezekiel Forman
Isaac Alexander
James McIntyre
Ebenezer Potter
Henry Cooper
________ Sullivan
Mr. Hays
Step. Stephenson
Wm. Winn
________ Strong
Richard Roddy
Theophilus Armor

Total $1023

List of those to whom debts are due by the deceased.

Samuel Swazey
Archibald Ray
Samuel Flower
Alexander Callender
Adam Lanhart
Joseph Ford
David Pickens
Wm. Selking
Henry Richardson
Henry Manadue
George Richardson
David Ferguson
Doctor Todd
Patrick Foley
______ Dumas

Col. Hutchins
Abner Green
Thos. Hughes
Jarus Wilks (N. O.)
Joseph Murray
Wm. Calvit
Wid. Gallager
Jesse Greenfield
Wm. Wicks
Buckner Pitman
Stephen Richards
Benet Truly
Benj. Belk

Accounts unsettled
Jacob Adams, James Glascock,
Israel Leonard, James Rose
Joseph Calvit, John Foster,
John Lindsay.

---

p. 538. 19 Oct. 1791. Sale of estate of Eliphalet Richards. Buyers: Israel Leonard, Jeremiah Bryan, Josiah Flower, John Shipman, Charles King, Sutton Banks, Daniel Sullivan, John Girault, Mr. Forman, Richard Swazey, Augustin Macarty, Hugh Coyle, Samuel Swazey, Wm. Weeks, William Hutsell.

p. 542. 21 Oct. 1791. Garret Rapalje mortgages to Alexander Mayneham two negro women, "Poll", aged 18, and "Sophy", aged 36, security for debt to Mayneham and in particular to estate of Edward Gallandet and other slaves to Robert Dunbar, exor. of will of decd. Gallandet. Signed.

p. 542. Inventory of estate of Wm. Case, decd.
A note between Mr. Case and John Wood, for 3 cows and calves, paid.
A note of John Steel for $15. An account for laying off the Orleans Road, $60. A note of Job Cory for $25. An account agst. Wm. McIntosh for $42. 300 acres, 2 horses, one rifle-gun, 1 belt. Taken from the information of John Lusk. Wit: Matthew McCulloch, James Nicholson, Henry Nicholson. Oct. 21, 1791.

p. 543. 31 Oct. 1791. Juan Vaucheret to Simon de Arze, sergeant of artillery, a lot of ground, with a small house theron, near the Fort of Natchez, b. by the King's Road, his own house and ground of Don Pedro Camus, 192 ft. deep; for $150 for which Simon de Arze binds himself to pay Capt. Don Carlos de Grand-Pre 25 Dec. this present year and mortgages sd lot until final payment and the expense of survey to be paid by purchaser. Signed. // Received for above. April 1792. J. Vauchere.

End of Book B

David Harper, Keeper and Translator of the Spanish Records of the Mississippi Territory. 15 Aug. 1817.

BOOK C

On fly leaf: Thomas Wren, Woodson Wren

p. 1 Post of Natchez, 6 Nov. 1791. David Kennedy, being unable to make payment for a plantation which he bought from James Perry and John Gardeley, in the District of Manchac, of 440 arpents, for $500, do hereby return said plantation to said sellers, in pursuance of an agreement to that effect. He resigns all claim, right, etc. The said James Perry, present and accepting the conveyance for himself and for John Gardely. Signed by both.

p. 1. 8 Nov. 1791. David Ross sells to John Foster a negro man, "Dublin", aged 25, for 5000 pounds of tobacco in hand paid. Wit: Jere: Bryan. Both sign.

p. 2. Natchez, 12 Nov. 1791. Don Juan O'Connor, merchant of this Dist., being authorized to settle the estate of Presting Tinsley, dec'd., requests permission to sell at public sale a negro girl and a horse belonging to said estate. // Granted, same date, by Grand-Pre. // Nov. 16, 1791. Doctor McCabe and Don Manuel Texada appointed to appraise the above. Girl, named "Marianna", aged 9, valued at $100; the horse $30. Edward McCabe being absent, appraised by Manuel Texada and Patrick Foley. // Exposed to sale, the girl was adjudged to Wm. Vousdan for $100; the horse to Augustin Macarty for $28, highest bidders. Wit: Benj. Monsanto, J. Carrick, Antonio Soler.

p. 3. 28 Nov. 1791. Don Luis Faure, Surgeon, etc., to James Carrick a negro man aged 25, nat. of Guinea, for $260 paid.

p. 3. 29 Nov. 1791. John Griffing to James McNulty a negro woman, "Kate", aged 23, native of Carolina, for $620, payable in cattle; for each cow and calf $16; each steer $10; each mare and colt $20; said cattle to be delivered Sept. 1792. // p. 4. 18 Aug. 1792. John Griffing transfers to his brother, Gabriel Griffing, the amount due and owing by James McNulty for the purchase of the negro girl which said slave was the property of his said brother to whom he transfers his interest and claim.

p. 4. Natchez 1 Dec. 1791. Thos. Wilkins, agent for James Carrick, duly empowered, in his name, sells to David Williams, of this Dist., a negro "Buckner", aged 40, a negro woman "Kate", same age, a negro boy "Ben", aged 7, negro girl "Lizzy", aged 4, a child "Rosalind", aged 5 months, for $850, payable Feb. 1792. // Receipt for $600 on account of the above sale, Natchez, 2 Nov. 1792. Thos. Wilkins.

p. 5. 17 Dec. 1791. Will of John Shannon, formerly of Ireland but now an inhabitant of Natchez, Province of La., in the Kingdom of Spain, carpenter and joiner, by trade, very sick and weak; after debts are paid, if there be any left to be divided amongst those who have attended and assisted me in my last sickness, as they may agree, George Cochran, John Scott, and Robert Patten, all of Natchez my exors. Wit: Ebenezer Dayton, Solomon Swayze, John Carroll, Valentine Thomas Dalton, Samuel Swezey, John Scott, Robert Patten, John Thomas, Hiram Swesey. "His property consisted of clothes, tools, books, bonds, notes and book accounts and other property," excerpt from will. // p. 6. On 20 Dec. 1791, John Scott, a resident of said Post, Carpenter in the service of the King, who, in the presence of Geo. Cochran, merchant, Samuel Moore, Valentine Thomas Dalton, Robert Patton, John Carroll, Ebenezer Dayton, Hiram Swezey, John Thomas and Samuel Swazey, delivered to the Commandant a sealed paper endorsed the last will of John Shannon, dec'd., as declared by witnesses on the 19 December, being yesterday. When asked all who had sealed the paper, Valentine Thomas Dalton acknowledged that he had done so. Solomon Swazey, the only witness not present. All testified separately as to signature of Shannon and his own.

p. 7. Miguel Solibellas, Sergt. of the Grenadiers of Reg. of Inf. of La., to Lewis Evans a house and lot adjoining the Fort, 55 ft in front by 20 ft in depth, for the price and quantity of 3000 ft. of plank, 600 pickets, 9 ft long, and $20 in specie, all in hand paid and $100 due Jany. 1793. 29 Dec. 1791. Signed by both.

p. 7. 10 Jany. 1791. Power of attorney from James McIntosh to David Ross, of New Orleans, merchant to recover and receive from Don Estevan Minor, a sum of money due and owing me for negro man "Gilford" as per deed of sale. Signed.

p. 8. Natchez, Jany. 18, 1792. Anne Savage and Mary Savage, executrixes of Anne Willis, deceased, dau. of said Anne, and sister of Mary Savage, give bond to deliver to Henry Willis, husband of sd Anne Willis or his executors all property and effects belonging to said deceased, in this Province, consisting of negroes, horses and cattle. Both signed.

p. 8. Natchez, 31 Jany. 1792. Don Carlos de Grand-Pre, power to Alexander Moore, to sell and dispose of a negro man "Lorenzo", aged 32, native of this Province, for $500 on credit or $400 cash, with security and mortgage on said negro. Wit. Joseph Page.

p. 8. Power of atty. Don Carlos de Grand-Pre to Don Miguel Cantrell, of the German Coast, with power to appoint an atty. under him to represent me and dispose of a negro to me belonging, the same as in the foregoing.

p. 9. William Henderson, an inhabitant of this District, intending to proceed to the U. S. of America on my private business and having contracted several debts in this Province and desiring to secure my estate to my creditors, I leave one of them, namely Mr. John O'Connor, (to whom I owe $5010), the titles of my property, as follows: Patent for 250 arpents on Big Black River in the name of Squire Boon, dated 18 Oct. 1788; one other of 200 arpents at same place granted to sd Boon and one of 250 acres at same place, gr. to said Boon; same 100 arpents on Bayou Pierre to same, etc., Feb. 1792.

p. 10. Natchez 4 Feb. 1792. William Collins to Henry Willis, 1600 arpents, on Buffalo Creek, b. by Daniel Clark, Wm. Chabot and Mary Ellis, for 10,000 pounds of tobacco to be inspected in the King's Store of N. O., to be delivered March 1794, together with a like quantity of tobacco, one-half to be delivered March 1792, the other one-half March 1793. Signed by both.

p. 10. 4 Feb. 1792. George Cochran to Richard Lord 3 negroes, to him belonging, for $500 paid. Natchez 4 Feb. 1792. Both sign.

p. 11. Natchez, 11 Feb. 1792. James McIntosh has received of Israel Leonard and Ithanar Andrews, a negro man, aged 32, which said negro he sold them in year 1789 and which he now accepts in full satisfaction for the amount due and owing on said sale. Wit: John Eldergill and Joseph Vidal. Signed by all.

p. 11. Natchez, 14 Feb. 1792. Alexander Moore to Joseph Murray house and lot at the landing of Natchez, b. by lot belonging to said Moore and by adjoining Bayou, 60 ft front, for $150, terms. Wit: S. P. Moore, Vidal. Signed by Joseph Murray.

p. 12. 20 July 1791. Will of David Munro, of Natchez District. To my nephew George Gun Munro, Esq., in Parish of Bremore in County of Caithness, North Britain, my two negro men named "George" and "Anthony" and my negro wench, "Hannah", also whatever other property I may be possessed of at my decease. Mr. David Ross, Mr. John Bisland and Mr. George Cochran executors. Signed D. Munro. Wit: Alexander Grant, John Short, Wm. Barland, Bennet Truly, Thomas Freeman, Jacob Liephart, William Hamilton. // p.13. The above witnesses proved will at Post of Natchez, 15 Jany. 1792. // 12 Jany., having received notice from Wm. Barland of the decease of David Munro at his plantation 4 miles from Fort, De Grand-Pre accompanied by Joseph Vidal and Valentin Rincon, repaired to said plantation, where they found the body of said Munro whose death appeared to have proceeded from a long sickness. Seals affixed to three trunks containing sundry clothing and papers belonging to sd deceased until an inventory can be taken. // Inventory consisted of the slaves named in his will, two horses, gun, saddle, watch, silver buckles, clothing, several lots of linen, a silver-mounted sword, several books, including a dictionary, and a few other personal belongings. // At the sale of the above property: John Short, John O'Connor, John Bisland, Antonio Soler, Samuel Moore, Valentin Rincon, Jeremiah Bryan, Wm. Barland, George Fitzgerald, Don Joseph Vidal. Sales ending 22 Feb. 1792. An English-Latin dictionary not sold.

p. 18. Post of Natchez, 8 Mch. 1792. William Webb to James Nicholson 600 arpents on the Homochitto, bounded by land of Matthew Davis, the Homochitto and vacant land; for $480 paid. Both sign.

p. 18. Natchez, 9 Mch. 1792. Ebenezer Rees to George Cochran a negro wench "Sally", aged 13, nat. of America, for $230 paid. Wit: David Urquhart. Signed.

p. 19. Mch. 15, 1792. Will of Sarah Truly, of District of Natchez, Province of La., infirm and weak. Be it known, previous to my divising what property I have, Hector Truly, my late husband, made his will in Virginia in America, and soon after died, leaving me executrix and certain property to be equally divided between his children; of which property sundry negroes made a part sufficient for each child to have one. Agreeable to the will of sd Hector Truly, I delivered to all the children aforesaid, each a negro, except to my youngest child, Bennet Truly, who had not at that time or since a negro delivered to him agreeable to the will of his father, Hector, or anything in lieu therefor, and now being desirous to do equal justice to sd Bennet Truly as has already been done to all the other children of the aforesaid Hector Truly, my late husband, it is my will and desire that my executors deliver to said Bennet Truly, my son, immediately after my death a negro wench "Annico" with her two small children, Sarah and Lucy, with all other children that may hereafter be born to her. I give to my beloved son, Bennet Truly, before-named, one large looking-glass. To my daughter Eleanor Spain my feather bed and furniture after Mr. Dibdal Holt breaks up housekeeping, also my wearing apparel, to be divided between her, the said Eleanor and my gr-dau. Sarah Spain. To my beloved daughter, Martha Harrison one pr. of scissors and a thimble to the value of two dollars. All residue of my estate to be divided after my funeral expenses and just debts are paid, to be equally divided between my three children, James Truly, Bennet Truly and Eleanor Spain. I appoint Parker Carradine, James Truly, Bennet Truly and Francis Spain my exors. Wit: Ezek Forman, Wm. O'Connor, Ebenr. Potter, William Hamilton, Bena. Osmin, John Lum. // Whereas a controversy has arisen between the heirs of the late Sarah Truly, concerning the division of her estate, it is mutually agreed between the parties who are James Truly, Bennet Truly, Eleanor Spain and Martha Harrison that the whole of the estate be divided as ordered by the will, dated 15 March 1792, with the exception only that two cows and calves shall be the property of Eleanor Spain and the remainder of the horned cattle shall be and remain the property of the aforesaid Martha Harrison. Signed before Gayoso by James Truly, Bennet Truly, Francis Spain and Richard Harrison. 7 May 1793.

p. 20-1. 22 Mch. 1792. Samuel Gibson to William Vousdan 150 arpents, 3 miles east of Fort of this Post, b. by Wm. Vousdan and Obadiah Brown; for $150 paid. Signed by both.

p. 21. 6 Mch. 1792. Jacob Stampley to Filmer Wells Green, Abraham Green, Everard Green, 350 arpents, b. by David Odam, Thos. Marston Green and Cato West, on Cole's Creek, for $575 paid. Signed by Jacob Stampley and Thomas Green in behalf of his children.

p. 22. Samuel Moore to Gabriel Griffing a negro woman named "Nancy", aged 25, nat. of American in exchange for two horses, which sd horses he has received. Mch. 29, 1792. Both signed. // Gabriel Griffing declared that he had transferred the negro woman in foregoing sale to Hannah Marble who was the owner of the horses given in payment of the said negro woman, which she acknowledges to have received in full satisfaction. Signed Hannah Marble, Gabriel Griffing. Post of Natchez, 31 March 1792. (One horse had two white feet and the other four white feet.)

p. 23. 29 March 1792. George Cochran to Richard Lord a slave named "Gib" aged 18, for $850 paid. Wit: David Urquhart. Both signed.

p. 23. Garret Rapalie to Joseph Andrews a negro wench, "Folly", aged 14, nat. of Guinea, for $400 paid. Signed: Garret Rapalie, Jsh. Wells for Joseph Andrews

p. 24. 4 April 1792. Donna Augustina Solano to Juan Gali lot at the landing, 60 ft front by 80 ft. depth, b. by John O'Connor, Pedro Ancide and seller, for $200 paid. Wit: David Urquhart. Both signed.

p. 24. 16 April 1792. David Williams to Don Manuel Gayoso de Lemos, Gov. of this Post, a negro man "August", aged 22, nat. of Guinea, for $500 in hand paid. Both signed.

p. 25. Francisco Pavana to Policarpo Regillo and Domingo Loredo, soldiers in the Regiment of La., 95 arpents on St. Catherine's Cr., b. by William Vousdan, for $80 paid, including all the hogs on the plantation bearing his mark. Signed by all.

p. 26. 8 May 1792. Benjamin Lanier to Henry Cooper a negro woman "Grace", for $400 in cattle paid. Signed: Benjamin Lanier, Henry (X) Cooper. Wit: David Urquhart.

p. 26. 6 June 1792. Don Juan Girault to Alexander Moore two negroes "Hannibal" and "Judith", nat. of Jamaica, for $380 paid. Signed: Jean Girault, James Moore for Alexander Moore.

p. 27. 27 June 1792. Don Carlos de Grand-Pre to Ebenezer Dayton a negro woman "Anne", aged 27, nat. of Virginia, with a female mulatto child, aged 6 mos., for 260 pairs of shoes, made of good leather and delivered in 13 weeks from date, 20 pairs each week. Wit: James Moore. Signed by both. // p. 28. 15 Apr. 1895. De Grand-Pre ack. to have received amount of the foregoing mortgage and annuls same.

p. 28. 8 July 1792. Henry Roach to Daniel Ogden 250 arpents on Buffalo Creek, b. by John Blommart and Lejeune, for $250 paid. Both signed.

p. 28. 9 July 1792. David Odam to Roger Dixon 225 arpents at forks of Cole's Creek, b. by John Holt and vacant lands, for $782, on terms. Signed by both. // p. 29. 28 January 1797. Roger Dixon being unable to pay the sum in the foregoing obligation, the tract of land shall revert to said David Odam, including all buildings and other improvements made by sd Dixon, agreed to by both parties. Wit: Juan de Mier y Feran, Pedro Walker. Signed by both.

p. 29. 31 July 1792. Estevan Minor to Job Routh a negro "Ned", native of Jamaica, for $400 paid. Both signed.

p. 30. 31 July 1792. George Cochran to William Stevens of N. O., a negro wench, "Sally", aged 16, nat. of North America, to sell for me for the price and on such terms as may be most to my advantage. Signed by Cochran.

p. 31. 4 Aug. 1792. Tarpley Bailey to George Cochran negro lad "George", nat. of U. S. A., aged 14, for $250 paid. Both signed.

p. 31. 9 Aug. 1792. Peter Bryan Bruin to Richard Lord a negro man named "Jim", aged 22, nat. of America, for $400, in hand paid. Both sign.

p. 32. 18 Aug. 1792. George Fitzgerald, atty. for Francisco Pousset, sells to Gabriel Griffing a negro "Phoebe", aged 25, nat. of Guinea, belonging to Pousset, which sd negro was mortgaged by him to Daniel Clark, July 1789, for $500. Signed by G. Fitzgerald, Gabriel Griffing.

p. 33. 21 Aug. 1792. David Ferguson to Frederick Myers a negro woman, "Sally", aged 23, nat. of America, for $375 paid. Signed David Ferguson, Fredèrick (X) Myers.

p. 33. 22 Aug. 1792. John Griffing gives to his brother, Gabriel Griffing 150 arpents of land in exchange for 340 arpents of land, said lands being on Fresh Creek. Both signed.

p. 34. 22 Aug. 1792. John Bolls and John Griffing, both of the Dist., agree as follows: John Bolls gives to John Griffing a negro man "Dick", aged 25, nat. of Guinea, and John Griffing gives to John Bolls, a negro woman "Phoebe", aged 22, nat. of Guinea, in exchange for the negro man. Both sign.

p. 34. 18 Aug. 1792. Gabriel Griffing to my brother, John Griffing a negro woman I purchased from George Fitzgerald, agent for Francisco Pousset, named "Phoebe" and sold by permission of Daniel Clark for same sum and terms as made in above sale. Signed by both. // p. 35. 3 Sept. 1794. Gabriel Griffing ack. to have received full payment of $500 from his brother, John Griffing, in foregoing sale. Signed before Gayoso.

p. 35. 1 Sept. 1792. David Odam to Don Estevan Minor negro lad "Stephen", aged 14, nat. of Opelousas, for $350, paid. Both sign.

p. 36. Don Carlos de Grand-Pre to Don Simon de Arze negro wench "Maria", aged 15, nat. of this Province, for $400. Both sign. // p. 37. 12 Nov. 1792. Receipt of $400 for foregoing sale; Mortgage null and void. Signed Carlos de Grand-Pre.

p. 12. Sept. 1792. Jacob Pyeatt has received notice to evacuate the tract of land on which he now dwells, by order of His Excellency, the Gov. of this Post, which he promises to do at the end of October next, at which time he is to inform said Governor at what place he intends to settle, for his approbation and decision. Signed.

p. 37. Agreeably to the order of His Excellency Don Manuel Gayoso de Lemos, Esq., we, Henry Manadue and Roswell Mygatt, have taken the following inventory of the estate of Daniel Mygatt, dec'd.: One plantation, 150 acres on St. Catherine's Creek; 150 acres on Cole's Creek, bought at the vendue of the estate of Earl Douglass; one plough horse, one yoke of oxen, 13 cows and calves, etc., etc., books of blacksmith's accounts, marked "Books of accounts of Daniel Myggatt and Aron Adams, in partnership; the book of accts. of Daniel Mygatt and James Smith. Signed by both. Wit: Matthew McCulloch, Charles King, William Selkrig. // p. 38. List of notes due Daniel Mygatt, dec'd.: John D. Bredy's note to Wm. Selrig, endorsed; Azavado, Thomas Hubbard, Christobal Gart, Benjamin Hovan, Buckner Pittman, Luis Valaret, Richard Bacon, Josiah Flower, Thomas Comstock's order on William Smith in favor of Daniel Mygatt, William Erwin, Alexander Moore, Henry Quirk, Thomas James, Archibald Rea, Thomas Reed, Isaac Johnson, Esq., James McIntosh, Mr. Peter Walker, Alexander Farrow, Aron Adams, Emanuel Madden. Signed by H. Manadue. // p. 38. List of notes in the hands of Mr. Peter Walker in New Orleans, the property of Daniel Mygatt, dec'd.; John Boles, Mark Isler to Matthew White, Job Cory, Benj. Holmes, Waterman Crane, Reuben Gibson, James Whyley, Obadiah Brown, Phillip Turpin, William Lum, Joseph

Calvet, Matthew McCulloch, Bennet Truly, Cady Raby, John Ethrington, Jeptha Higdon, Robt. Miller, Philander Smith, Isaac Alexander, Benj. Bullock, Henry Cooper, Hugh Slater, John Ratcliff. Total $1243-6. Certified by H. Manadue.

p. 39. 2 Oct. 1792. Polser Shilling, of District, planter, to Don Francisco Gutierrez De Arroyo, of same, house and lot at landing of Natchez, b. on one side by Antonio Gras, Ebenezer Rees, Royal St. and the hill, for $500 paid. Both sign.

p. 40. 15 Oct. 1792. John Terry to James Bonner a negro man named "Samuel" aged 30, nat. of Jamaica, for $300 paid. Both signed.

p. 40. 18 Oct. 1792. Pedro Ancid, of District of Natchez, to Don Luis Faure lot 60 ft. front by 70 ft. depth, with an old house thereon and a quantity of timber, b. by Juan O'Connor, the seller and Royal Street, for $190. Signed Luis Faure, Pedro (X) Anzid.

p. 41. 20 Oct. 1792. Samuel Swazey mortgages to Isaac Gaillard negro "Wilkes", aged 17, nat. of Guinea, for $200, negro to remain mortgaged. Both sign. // p. 42. Post of Natchez, 10 Oct. 1795. Isaac Gaillard declares to have rec'd. of Samuel Swazey full payment of sum in foregoing instrument. Wit: J. Murdock. Signed.

p. 42. 9 Nov. 1792. Francisco Larrosa indebted to Don Antonio Vermello, of this District, for $500, money lent to me by him to pay for house sold me by Polser Shilling, mortgages sd house to him until final payment shall have been made. Francisco (X) Larrosa

p. 43. Natchez, 12 Nov. 1792. Valentine Thomas Dalton promises and engages to dwell in the house of His Excellency, Don Carlos de Grand-Pre, for three years, and during that time to teach all his children to speak and write the English language; De Grand-Pre to pay Dalton $100 per annum and his board, to take effect from the day on which His Excellency and family shall arrive at N. O., it being understood that said De Grand-Pre also gives Dalton for the services, 250 arpents of land on Cole's Creek, purchased by him from James Elliot, b. by land of Thomas Erwin, Adam Bingaman, James Elliot and vacant land, of which said land I have received possession. Both sign. // Natchez, 9 Dec. 1795. Valentine Thomas Dalton declares that he has not fulfilled his part of the foregoing agreement, whereby the same has become null and void and the sd tract of land reverted to Don Carlos de Grand-Pre to whom he has restored the plat and other papers relative thereto and he renounces all claim to same. Both sign.

p. 44. Gideon Gibson to his son, Reuben Gibson, all cattle and horses belonging to me marked "B. B." for $100 in hand paid. 12 Nov. 1792. Both signed.

p. 44. 15 Feb. 1786. Charles Howard, of Natchez, for $100, in hand paid by James Brown, one improvement or plantation on the waters of Fairchild's Creek, near John Stower's plantation whereon he now lives and near to lands of sd Brown. Wit: H. Manadue, Thos. (X) Griffing. Charles (X) Howard. // The foregoing instrument having been filed with suits-in-law, could not be recorded in the proper place.

p. 45. 12 Nov. 1792. Gideon Gibson to my son, Randal Gibson, 335 arpents, 6 miles from this Post, b. by Richard Harrison, Doctor McCabe and John Foster, for $400 in hand paid. Gideon (X) Gibson, (signed) Randal Gibson.

p. 45. 12 Nov. 1792. Gideon Gibson to son, David Gibson, a negro lad named "Neil", aged 16, nat. of Natchez, for $150, paid. Gideon (X) Gibson. (signed) David Gibson.

p. 46. 12 Nov. 1792. Gideon Gibson to my son, Randal Gibson, negro boy, "Harry", aged 8, for $150, in hand paid. Gideon (X) Gibson, Randal Gibson.

p. 47. 12 Nov. 1792. Gideon Gibson to his daughter, Cynthia Gibson a negro woman, "Sylvia", aged 4, nat. of Natchez, for $100 paid. Gideon (X) Gibson, Cynthia Gibson.

p. 47. 12 Nov. 1792. Gideon Gibson to son, David Gibson, 500 arpents on a branch of St. Catherine's Creek, b. by lands of George Killian, Jeremiah Bryan and vacant lands, for $500 paid. Gideon (X) Gibson, David Gibson.

p. 48. 20 Nov. 1792. Alexander Moore to John Scott a negro man "Crony" aged 20, nat. of Jamaica, for $400 paid. Both signed.

p. 49. 5 Dec. 1792. Don Carlos de Grand-Pre to John Smith, Capt. of the Militia and Alcalde of Villa Gayosa, three negroes, Joseph, Philip and James, two first nat. of Guinea, third, nat. of Va., aged 16 to 17, for $1200 Mexican money, terms. Wit: Valentine Thomas Dalton, Joseph Page. Both signed. //

19 Dec. 1792. Don Carlos de Grand-Pre, complying to a decree of His Excellency the Gov., of this date, relative to an offer made by me to Antonio Gras, exor. of the will of Francisco Bazo, has transferred to his order an obligation of John Smith in his favor for $1200, payable in N. O. 1st March next, which said obligation he transfers for $700 only which with $7-2 reals that I have already paid to said Antonio Gras makes $707-2, the whole sum said Grand-Pre owes the estate of Francisco Bazo, the remainder of the obligation, $500, remaining the property of sd Don Carlos de Grand-Pre. Signed Don Carlos de Grand-Pre. // Post of Natchez, 5 Feb. 1795. Don Carlos de Grand-Pre annuls the foregoing obligation of Antonio Gras, the said Gras not having recovered the debt owing by John Smith in consequence he is released from all responsibility respecting $500 therein mentioned. Signed.

p. 50. 15 Dec. 1792. John Calvet to his brother, Anthony Calvet, 300 arpents on the Homochitto, as expressed in plat and titles, for $160 paid. Both sign.

p. 51. 17 Dec. 1792. Ebenezer Dayton to Samuel Wells a negro woman, "Anne", aged 28, nat. of Va., with her mulatto dau. "Lucy", aged 8, payable in cattle, viz: 23 steers, 2 bulls, 42 cows and 20 yearlings in hand delivered and acknowledged. Both signed.

p. 52. Don Carlos de Grand-Pre to Alexander Moore a negro man "Congo", aged 30, native of Guinea, for $325, paid. Both sign. 20 Dec. 1792.

p. 53. 6 Jany. 1793. Don Estevan Minor to Eliza Whittle 1000 arpents, 5 miles from the Fort, b. by Adam Bingaman, John McIntosh and Wm. Dunbar, in payment whereof the said Eliza Whittle gives him another tract, 800 arpents on Bayou Pierre, b. by lands of Joseph Page and John Minor. Both sign.

p. 54. 13 Jany. 1793. William Barland to David Ferguson 8 arpents of land in this town between the house of Hugh Coyle and that of Wm. Barland, for $80, paid. Both sign.

p. 54. 16 Jany. 1793. Joseph Andrews, power of atty. to William Weeks, of the Dist., planter, to assist at the sale of a negro to be sold at publick sale at the house of the Government, belonging to Garret Rapalie, for the payment of a certain sum due to me by said Rapalje, which sd negro is mortgaged in my favor, and to receive the proceeds of the sale therof to be delivered to me on demand. Signed Joseph Andrews. // p. 55. Post of Natchez. 19 Jany. 1793. Patrick Foley and James Truly appointed to appraise the negro to be sold in public sale mentioned in the foregoing. Valued the sd negro at $275. Appraisers sign. // Said negro being immediately exposed to sale for cash, was adjudged to William Weeks for $306. Signed.

p. 56. Eliza Whittle to Don Estevan Minor 800 arpents at Bayou Pierre b. by John Minor, John Page, and vacant lands, in payment whereof the said Don Estevan Minor gives her 1000 arpents, 5 miles from this Fort, b. by Adam Bingaman, John McIntosh, Wm. Dunbar and Charles White. Both signed. 26 Jany. 1793.

p. 56. 8 Feb. 1793. Don Carlos de Grand-Pre to Don Pedro Favrot a negro lad "Sam", nat. of North America, aged 19, for $460, paid. Both signed.

p. 57. 12 Feb. 1793. Edward McCabe to Don Francisco Arroyo a house and lot near the Parish Church for $1000, $500 in goods in hand paid, the remaining in one year or sooner on condition the kitchen shall be repaired, a partition made therein and a room built on the gallery. Both signed. // p. 58. At Post of Natchez, 21 May 1794. Edward McCabe ack. that Francisco Arroyo has satisfied the sum of $500, receipt of which acknowledged. Signed.

p. 58. 4 Mch. 1793. Don Pedro Favrot, Capt. of the Regiment in this Province and Commandant of the troops in Garrison at this Post, to Don Francisco Miranda, assistant military Store-Keeper of said Post, a negro girl "Rose", of the Congo Nation, aged 13, for $300 paid. Both signed.

p. 59. 16 March 1793. Don Luis Piernas, Lt. of the Inf. of La., gives power of attorney to his mother, Felisitas Portneuf, in his name to mortgage a negro man belonging to him, named "Theodore", aged 30, for a certain sum owing by his mother to a certain person in New Orleans. Signed.

p. 59. 18 March 1793. Doctor John Bredy to Nicholas Rab 800 arpents, on St. Catherine' Creek, b. by Charles Cason, John Hartley, George Killian, David Lambert and Isaac Johnson, for $800 payable to the creditors of the seller. Signed John D. Bredy, Nicholas Rabb.

p. 60. 23 March 1793. Thomas Rule to Isaac Gaillard 230 arpents, 9 miles southwest of this Fort, b. by Don Pedro Surget and David Mitchell, and John Henderson, for $100 paid. Signed by Gaillard.

p. 61. Post of Natchez, 26 Mch. 1793. George Fitzgerald declared that at the end of 1789, Don Francisco Pousset sold for account of Daniel Clark and Rees to Thomas Ballew a negro wench, "Sophia", nat. of Guinea, short and thick and spoke English, about 20 years of age when she was taken out of this district by said Ballew; at the time he knew that his tobacco had been refused and sd Ballew escaped on the same day on which it had been determined to pass the sale of the negro wench aforesaid. Signed.

p. 61. 27 March 1793. Patrick Sullivan to Stephen Miller 400 arpents in the District of Villa Gayoso, b. by John Bolls and lands of His Majesty, for $230. Patrick (X) Sullivan, Stephen Miller. // Natchez, 19 April 1793. Patrick Sullivan represents that he wished to dispose of a tract of land on Cole's Creek. I have no demands against him in my hands nor do I know of any. Signed Peter Walker.

p. 62. 4 April, 1793. Antonio Gras, of this Post, merchant, to Caleb Weeks a negro man, "Anthony", aged 39, nat. of Guinea, for $345, paid; said negro having been held in partnership with the late Francisco Bazo, dec'd., for which sd. consideration I do hereby resign all right and title. Caleb Wicks signed with his mark.

p. 63. 2 April 1793. John Barclay to Samuel Levi Wells a negro man, "Jim", aged 20, nat. of Va., for $300 paid. Signed John Barclay. Note: The seller having purchased the negro before mentioned in this district but having no formal sale thereof, has for the security of the purchaser mortgaged another negro to him belonging, "Charles", aged 30, nat. of the Bahama Islands. Signed.

p. 63. 11 Apr. 1793. Don Manuel Texada to Catherine Caldwell a negro woman, "Sylvia", aged 20, nat. of Guinea, for $400 paid. Both sign, Catherine Caldwell with a mark.

p. 64. 4 Apr. 1793. John O'Connor, merchant of said Post, as exor. of deceased David Hodge, appointed by Thomas Durnford, atty., offered at public sale a house at the landing of this Post, one-half thereof belonging to the estate of David Hodge, dec'd.; the same not having been bid two-thirds of appraised value thereof, petitioner asked that other appraisers be appointed to value said house. Signed John O'Connor. // Apr. 8, 1793. Samuel Forman and William Cook, appointed appraisers and accepted. Same date: house and lot appraised at $1100. The house at three public sales adjudged to John O'Connor at $850, he being the highest bidder each time. 17 Apr. 1793.

p. 64. Don Pedro Rousseau, Capt. of the Royal Armies and Commandant of the Gallies, to Don Antonio Marmillion, a negro boy, "Thomas", aged 13, nat. of Guinea, for $260, Mexican, cash and terms. Both sign.

p. 65. 25 April 1793. Power of Atty. from John Barclay to James Steward, to sell to John Coleman a lot of ground belonging to him in this District, which "I cannot sell myself being on departure for America". Signed.

p. 66-7. 27 April 1793. David Ross to John O'Connor a negro man, "Stephen", aged 22, nat. of Guinea, for $400 on terms. Signed.

p. 67. 2 May 1793. James Kirk of this District, planter, is indebted to Wm. Panton and Co. for $2234 which he promises to pay with 8% interest, for security mortgages two negroes to him belonging. [He names ten]. Signed.

p. 68. 2 May 1793. James Kirk sells to John O'Connor a lot at the landing of this Post, 92 feet front by 78 feet depth, b. by Nathaniel Tomlinson, Louis Chachere, the purchaser and the street that runs by the foot of the hill, for $35 in hand paid. Both sign.

p. 68. 5 May 1793. Juan Gali to 1793. Juan Gali to Pierre Gueno a house and lot at the landing, 50 ft front by 70 ft depth, b. by John O'Connor and Pedro Ancid, for $830, on terms. Both signed.

p. 69. Post of Natchez, 8 May 1793. William Ferguson declared that he had purchased from Thomas Durnford, attorney for David Hodge, a negro woman, "Betty", the sale whereof was not executed in the office of this Government. The said Durnford having claimed payment for the said negro woman, he, the said Ferguson, being unable to pay for the same, offered to return the said negro woman which the sd Durnford refused to receive, wherefore the sd Ferguson hereby protests against the sd Durnford for all damages, losses, etc. that may accrue therefrom. Signed.

p. 69. 18 May 1793. Richard Harrison to George Cochran a negro woman, "Catherine", aged 33, nat. of Va., with her dau. aged 10, for $600 paid. Both signed.

p. 70. 23 May 1793. Bridget Roberts to Joseph Murray, merchant, house and lot. 150 ft front by same depth, in New City, Lot No. 2, Sq. No. 4, for $160 paid. B (X) Roberts, Joseph Murray.

p. 71. George Cochran to Richard Lord three negroes, "George", aged 15, "Kate", aged 33, "Sal", aged 10, all natives of America, for $850, paid. 28 May 1793. Both signed.

p. 71-2. 14 June 1793. John Hartley to Ebenezer Rees negro woman "February", aged 23, nat. of Va., with dau. aged 2, for $475, in hand paid. Both sign. Hartley signs in German.

p. 72. Ebenezer Rees to Mary Higdon negro man, "Jesse", aged 35, nat. of Va., for $450, on terms. Mary (A) Higdon, Ebenezer Rees.

p. 73. Big Black, March 3, 1790. This is to certify that in the year 1774 I sent my son Jacques Rapalie, the eldest, to West Florida, with a number of settlers on land I purchased at Homochitto, or where he should like; he then returned with a reserve of 25,000 acres; and then went out on the second voyage with settlers again and purchased in his own name a place at Baton Rouge, and settled the same with negroes from New York; and I sent out a vessel to Guinea for slaves and ordered my son, Jacques, to take out twenty-five of the best for his own use as a gift; and now on my return find my second son Garret has sold five of Jacques' slaves and purchased only three for less than he sold for. I wrote a certain letter to my second son to secure my eldest son's property, to call it his own on account of the war, as he could not come or get permission to come over as he was a prisoner a long time among the British on Long Island; all the property that my son Garret claims is my eldest son Jacques', which I am willing at any time to make appear. Mch. 3, 1790. Signed Garret Rapalie. // I certify that the foregoing is a true copy of the original remaining in the Archives of this Government. Natchez, 20 Aug. 1793. (Signed) Manuel Gayoso de Lemos.

p. 73. Post of Natchez, 27 Aug. 1793. John Houghland and George Stroope declare, on oath, that they were present when William Collins sold to Jacob Stroope a tract of land which seller declared contained more than 200 arpents.

p. 73-4. 6 Sept. 1793. Don Pedro Favrot to Joseph Lambert a mulatto woman, "Margaret", aged 40, for $400, paid. Both signed.

p. 74. 13 Sept. 1793. Pierre Gueno to Juan Perez house and lot, 50 ft front by 100 ft depth, with sundry pieces of timber for building lying thereon, in the town of Natchez, b. by land of Don Pedro Ancid and John O'Connor, for $300, paid. Signed by Pierre Gueno.

p. 75. Will of Anne Savage, widow of John Savage, weak in body. I am the widow of John Savage, by whom I have one daughter, lawfully begotten, aged 23, which said daughter is my lawful heiress. I do bequeath to my grand-daughter, Margaret Ellis, a mulatto girl, aged 10, named "Louisa", dau. of a negro woman, named "Phoebe". I do hereby bequeath sd negro "Phoebe" to Margaret Gaillard, wife of Abraham Ellis, with one son and three daughters of sd negro, on condition, however, that the said five slaves shall be solely for the use and service of the said Margaret during her life and at her death the said slaves shall descend to the children of the said Margaret and which slaves shall not be sold or otherwise alienated by sd Margaret Gaillard, on any pretext whatsoever, nor by her husband, Abraham Ellis. I do hereby bequeath for the education of the two daughters of David Mitchell $100 and for the education of Rebecca Lusk, dau. of John Lusk, $50; and for the education of the son of Tacitus Calvit $50; to my niece Eliz. Sarah Gaillard $200. The residue of my estate, real and personal of every description, whatsoever and wheresoever, be delivered to my daughter, Mary Savage, on condition that my said daughter shall hereafter marry, her husband shall not on any pretext whatsoever dispose of said estate nor any part of it, without the consent of my said daughter. Exr. my brother Isaac Gaillard and Mary Savage, my daughter. At my dwelling in the District of Homochitto. 12 Sept. 1793. Signed Anne Savage. At the time of signing testatrix declared it to be her will that in case of the death of the children of Mrs. Abraham Ellis, the five slaves shall revert to Mary Savage after the death of Abraham Ellis.

p. 76. 25 Sept. 1793. Don Joseph Vidal to Thomas Wilkins and Don Estevan Minor, planters, a plantation lately belonging to William Henderson which he bought at public sale, 800 arpents, 6 miles from this Post, with dwelling house and other buildings, for $950 paid. Signed by all.

p. 76. Will of Henry Manadue, Sr. of Natchez District, very weak and low. After just debts are paid, the remainder of my estate to my beloved wife, Phoebe, for the benefit of raising my two small children, William and Polly, during her life and then the property is to be given to the two children, to be equally divided between them, under the direction of my son, Henry. I give to my son Henry all the tools belonging to the joiner and turner business which I possess and all my wearing apparel. The plantation tools I give to the widow for the benefit of raising necessities for the orphans. There are eight head of horned cattle, 6 heifers and two red steers which belong to my son Henry; he also has some horse creatures of his own property and purchase. I give my daughter Sally the red heifers known as hers; my daughter, Betsy Bonner has two heads of cattle among my stock, a cow and yearly called hers; my dau. Rosy Bonner 6 years past recieved a certain heifer with which she is contented for her part. My well-beloved son, Henry Manadue, Jr., Gabriel Benoist and John Bolls my sole exrs. 5 Sept. 1793. Signed Henry Manadue, senior. Wit: John Reid, Daniel Douglass, Winsor Pipes, David Greenleaf, Nathaniel Holcomb, Abner Pipes, Francis Henderson, Samuel Flower, P. Marshall. // p. 77. 5 Oct. 1793. Post of Natchez. Phoebe Manadue, wid. of Henry Manadue, presented the will of her deceased husband, in present of seven witnesses, who certified to same.

p. 77. Natchez 21 Sept. 1793. Messrs. Benjamin Monsanto and Ebenezer Rees are appointed to make an inventory and estimation of all the property left in this Government by the deceased Mrs. Anne Savage. // pp. 78-9. 65 negroes, names and ages given, value $9,600. Six other negroes, horned cattle, horses, mares, colts, hogs, sheep, oxen, and farm tools. 1100 acres on Second Creek, Mansion house, kitchen, barn, cribs, negro cabins, etc. Total appraisal: $12,218.00. // pp. 80-1. South Carolina. Indenture, 4 June 1776, between Tacitus Gaillard, of Berkley County, afsd. Province, and Benj. Farrar and Isaac Gaillard of same; Whereas the sd Tacitus Gaillard from motives of friendship, love and kindness that he beareth for John Savage of the same place, and his family, and divers other good, just and valuable causes, that the said slaves may be worked, the stock of cattle and household furniture may be and shall be worked and employed and the profit to arise from their work and labour used and improved for the benefit of said John Savage and his family during his life, but so as not to be subject to his debts, the one-third part thereof to be delivered to his wife and the remainder equally divided amongst his children in manner hereinafter mentioned. Tacitus Gaillard deeds all the property to Isaac Gaillard and Benj. Farrar, on condition it be left for John Savage to use but not as his own and immediately after his death, one-third is to be given his wife, Anne Savage and the rest to his children, lawfully begotten. Signed Tacitus Gaillard. Wit: Francis Baker, Wm. Savage. Sworn to by Francis Baker before John Troup. 23 April 1777.

p. 82. Oct. 23, 1793. Benjamin Monsanto to David Kennedy a tract in the cypress swamp, 6 miles from this Post, containing the number of arpents expressed in the plot thereof, in exchange for the timber necessary to build a house 13 ft long by 20 ft broad with four galleries 10 ft wide and shingles to cover the same, all of which to be delivered at the landing of Natchez in the month of May next. Signed by both.

p. 83. Wm. Vousdan to Don Joseph Vidal, Sec'y. of this Government of Natchez, a negro named "Dick", aged 18-20, nat. of Bermuda, a little ruptured, for $220 paid. Signed by both. 5 Nov. 1793.

p. 84. Natchez. 22 Nov. 1793. Joseph Lambert, King's Armourer at said Post, declared having purchased a mulatto woman, "Margaret", aged 40, nat. of La., from Capt. of the Regiment of Infantry of La., on condition that the sd woman should be set at liberty, and desiring to comply with the expressed obligation in the sale, do hereby give liberty to sd mulatto woman from thenceforth and forever. Signed with a mark.

p. 84. 18 Nov. 1793. Charles Boardman, of this District, planter, to Asahel Lewis part of the mill I purchased in the cypress swamp, about 12 miles from this Post, for $1500, payable in plank. Both sign.

p. 85. 19 Dec. 1793. Thos. Wilkins, of this Post, merchant, to Joseph Murray, of same, merchant, lot 30 ft front and in depth to foot of the hill, at the landing of Natchez, b. by land of purchaser and Antonio Gras, the seller reserving to himself a piece of ground nearly in the center of lot, 3 ft by 14 ft, for $133. Signed by both.

p. 86. John Mackie, of this City, to Abraham Thickston, of Dist. of Natchez, negro slave, "Francis", aged 30, being the same I purchased of Marianna Durocher, 6 June 1787, for $300 Mexican money, 16 Feb. 1788. Signed by both. // p. 87. 8 Jany. 1794. Jemima Lewis, wid. of Abraham Thickston, to Peter Walker, the negro man mentioned in foregoing sale for a note in hand given by my deceased husband, Thomas Hoffpaver, for $325. Jemima (X) Lewis.

p. 87. 11 January 1794. Will of John Hartley, of Bayou Pierre, District of Natchez, weak in body. To beloved wife, 1000 acres, being one-fourth of the survey I now live on, to be laid off adj. my daughter Catherine's survey, also a gray mare, etc.; to son John, a slave; to son Jacob, a slave; to dau. Christine, a slave; to dau. Elizabeth one female slave and a horse and colt; son Peter, a female slave, and wife is to support him until he is 18 years old; he is to have a bay mare and colt at my death. I still possess 3000 acres in this survey on Bayou Pierre, exclusive of what I have already bequeathed, to be divided equally amongst all my children, my son Peter's share shall contain the improved part of it where I now live; remainder to be divided equally among children. Mr. Samuel Gibson, Mr. Jesse Hambleton and Christian Harman executors. Signed in German. Wit: Melling Woolley, G. W. Humphreys, William Howe, John Coleman, Hezekiah Harman, Erastus Harman, Ebenezer Smith, Daniel Chambers, Samuel Gibson. // Post of Natchez, 6 Feb. 1794. Ebenezer Smith, who having examined his signature and those of the other witnesses declared the same to be his and their own. // Came Hesekiah Harman, Erastus Harman, G. W. Humphreys, Daniel Chambers, Samuel Gibson, John Coleman and Wm. Howe and made oath as to the will of John Hartley, of Bayou Pierre, 11 Jany. 1794, and ack. their signatures. // p. 90. 30 April 1794. Executors ask for a copy of said will. // 31 April, a copy of will shall be granted executors and they will cause an inventory of the estate to be taken before witnesses and the same lodged in the Public Office of this Government with the will and if no objection is made to the will by the heirs, the executors are authorized hereby to execute its contents. Signed Manuel Gayoso de Lemos. // Bayou Pierre, in the Natchez District, May 5, 1794. The subscribers, heirs of the estate of John Hartley, late deceased, do manifest our approbation of the last will and testament of sd Mr. Hartley and acknowledge we are fully satisfied of contents. Catherine Hartley, John Hartley, Catherine Harman, Christiana Hartley, Elizabeth Hartley. All signed with a mark. Wit: James Harman, Ebenezer Smith, Daniel Chambers, Elijah Smith, Hezekiah Harman, Francis Nailor, William (X) Basset. // p. 90 Inventory of estate of late John Hartley. p. 91. Treasury bills due estate: Beauregard $300, $50, etc. Notes: Isaac Fooy, Philip P. Turpin, Wm. Ratcliff, Andrew Bell, John Ratcliff, George Humphreys, Wm. West, Wm. Atchinson, Samuel Phelps, Wm. Ryan, Henry Richardson. Bayou Pierre, 5 May 1794. // Natchez, 10 May, 1794. Having seen the foregoing approbation of the heirs of the estate of the late John Hartley to the will of the sd deceased, I do hereby authorize the executors to said will to put its contents into execution. Gayoso.

p. 92. George Fitzgerald and John Bisland represent that, being appointed by David Munro, dec'd., executors to his will and being in possession of two negro men and one negro woman and her child and 1000 arpents of land, your petitioners pray that they be allowed to sell the same at public sale, the proceeds subject to the order of the heirs. Natchez, 21 Jany. 1794. // Natchez Post. 24 Jany, 1794, John Girault, William Dunbar, and Polser Shilling, appointed appraisers of the foregoing properties and accepted same. Appraisal: negro man "Anthony", $400; negro man "George", $400, negro woman "Anne", and her children $400; 1000 arpents on Bayou Sara $500. // p. 93. 25 Jany. 1794. Sale: Negro "Anthony" to Thos. Wilkins for $325, Estevan Minor surety; negro "George" to same for $426; negro woman and children to Wm. Dunbar for $555; plantation to Gerard Brandon for $800, John Bisland surety. // George Fitzgerald, exr. of last will of David Munor, dec'd., certifies that Gerard Brandon has paid the full amount of the within obligation, including interest thereon. Signed. Natchez, 11 March 1801.

p. 93. 24 Jany. 1794. Christopher Whipple to Elias Burnett, 361 arpents, on Second Creek, b. by Mathew White, Abner Green and Richard Ellis, for $600 specie, paid. Elias (X) Burnett, C. Whipple.

p. 94. 26 Jany. 1794. William Gillespie exchanges with John Girault, tract of 363 arpents on Cole's Creek, b. by lands of John Holt, Estevan De Alba and His Majesty, for a tract at same place, b. by lands of John Stille, John Artherby, Josiah Flower, Chas. King and Mary Spain, wife of John Girault. Signed by William Gillespie, John Girault, Mary Girault.

p. 95. His Excellency Don Manuel Gayoso de Lemos, Governor of Natchez. Sir: I received yesterday morning Your Excellency's dispatches at the moment I was ready to mount my horse. I immediately dispersed advertisements for a general meeting of the inhabitants on Sunday next and proceeded to pay a visit to poor Mr. Percy, whom I had lately seen in very low spirits. I had received intelligence with Your Excellency's letters, of news that the expedition planning above had been disconcerted. I thought this would clear his mind but behold, Sir, I was too late. I met an express coming to me on the road with the calamitous news which Your Excellency will find in the Inquest enclosed. I have acted only by desire and in concurrence with the friends of the family and Daniel Clark, Esq. Mr. Percy's desk was duly sealed and this morning opened and the will read, which appears agreeable with the new ordinance. Your Majesty will excuse my trembling hand as my heart is deeply affected with this melancholy catastrophe and with the sight of a large afflicted family. Your devoted servant, Francisco Pousset. Mr. Percy's Plantation, 31 Jany. 1794. This letter will be accompanied by letters from the afflicted family. // p. 95. Buffaloe District, Government of Natchez. Inquest taken by Francisco Pousset, Esq., Alcalde of Bayou Sara, on the body of C. Percy, Esq., deceased, at the request of his family and neighbors, on the plantation of the late said Percy, Jany. 3, 1794. Present: Thos. Lovelace, Edward Lovelace, Daniel Ogden, Lewis Alston, James Alston, Hamilton Pollock, David Lejeune, David Jones, Daniel Clark, James Todd, James McNulty and James Robinson. On a view of the body of the said C. Percy and having asked such questions of the witnesses as we thought necessary for proper information, we are unanimously of opinion that the cause of the death of the deceased was owing to insanity of mind. Signed by all of the above, and by Francisco Pousset, Alcalde. // Feb. 1, 1794. I do certify that on my arrival at Mr. Percy's plantation the morning of his exit, I did seal up his bureau which contained his papers, and that the next day after the Inquest, I did open same and take out the will and broke the seal before everyone present. It was publicly read by Daniel Clark, Esq., which said will I declare to be the one annexed hereunto. Francisco Poussett, Alcalde. // p. 96. Whereas Don Manuel Gayoso de Lemos did by his letter to Daniel Clark, Esq., of the district of Buffalo, 5 June 1794, request said Clark to convene at the house of the late Charles Percy, Esq., dec'd. three of the neighbors and in their presence read to Susanna Collins, the widow of the sd Charles Percy and their children (namely, Sarah, aged 13, in August next, Susanna 11 years 25 Sept. next, Thomas aged 8, Catherine aged 6 May 5 last, Luke aged 2 June 24, William 2 years old 5 May last past) the last will and testament of said Charles Percy, deceased, and the said Clark pursuant to His Excellency's direction, set forth in his letter, did enquire whether the deceased Chas. Percy had or has any children by a former marriage; we did therefore enquire of Susanna, the widow, if she knew of any and she declared she does not; and we also made further enquiry and we cannot discover that he had or has any lawful children but those he had by said Susanna. He has a son, Robert, but he, the deceased Charles Percy always denied that he had been married to Robert's mother. Our last enquiry was if the rights of the children of the said Charles Percy and Susanna, his wife, are sufficiently secured to them by the will of their father, and it appears to us, they are not. Signed John Lovelace, Daniel Ogden, David Lejeune. 11 June 1794. Daniel Clark. // pp. 96-7. Letter from Daniel Clark to Gayoso. Clarkville, June 11, 1794. Enclosing the foregoing paper ... The neighbors I called upon to attend me at Mr. Percy's are as respectable as our District affords. How far their conceptions may be right on the points Your Excellency referred to their enquiry is submitted to you. They are of the opinion that Justice is not done the children in the will which lodges a power in the widow replete with possible evils to the orphans, altho Mrs. Percy is a most estimable lady, etc. ... The gentlemen were of the opinoin that the law, the surest and best protector of the rights of the orphans should supercede the will. The legitimacy of Mr. Robert Percy's nativity is a subject which abounds with uncertainty and legal niceties; the deceased frequently declared that he was not married to Robert's mother. Here interest and honor rolls the onus probandi on Robert and if he should succeed in proving the marriage of his father and mother and that he was born in wedlock, I shudder for the consequences to the family here. If Mr. Robert Percy is not a bastard, the children of Charles and Susanna must inevitable be, as our laws admit not of a plurality of wives. Robert's mother is not long dead; and I am persuaded that Charles and Susanna have not remarried since her death. I have not mentioned this to Mrs. Percy ... I have preemptorily refused to act as guardian to her children though I shall always render them every disinterested service in my power. Signed. // p. 98. Reply to above: Requesting that Daniel Clark convene again the same gentlemen that were present on the former occasion, informing them that the legitimacy of Mr. Robert Percy is problematic and regarding their objection in respect to the Justice done the children, he has resolved to consult the Auditor on the matter and in the meanwhile as a precaution, perhaps not necessary, he requests them to appoint a proper person to be depository of the estate of sd Percy, or leave it as a deposit in the hands of Mrs. Percy, if she gives a security to your satisfaction. The three gentlemen are asked to consider themselves guardians of the children to represent them; Mrs. Percy will act for herself and he apoints Mr. Clark for act for him (Gayoso). When he receives an answer from the Auditor, he will send instructions. Signed Gayoso. (no date). // p. 99. Will of Charles Percy, sound in health and memory, beloved wife to have sole care and management of my children as well as of all my worldly property as long as she lives, at her death property to be divided among our then living children or their heirs; when a child marries, she will give to said child his or her share as she thinks she or he may deserve. Wife any my brothers-in-law, Theophilus Collins and John Collins, and Mr. Wm. Vousdan, of Natchez, executors. Jany. 22, 1794. C. Percy. Wit: Samuel Flowers, Daniel Lejeune, Daniel Ogden, John Newton, William Collins. // p. 100. These witnesses, 22 Jany. 1794, were at the plantation of Chas. Percy, Esq., deceased, and did see sd Percy sign, etc. foregoing to his last will and testament and each signed the same as witness in presence of each other. Signed by all on oath. Signed Francis Pousset, Alcalde. // Feb. 20, 1794. Inventory of the property and effects of Chas. Percy, Esq., dec'd., taken by Francis Pousset in presence of Mr. David Lejeune and Daniel Ogden, nominated appraisers, and John Newton and Eusebius Bushnell, witnesses: 55 slaves, young and old, name, age and value; notes and obligations, Henry

Hageroder and Henry Roder, a number, amounting to several thousand dollars, but none past due, Wm. Stephens, Maurice Stackpoole, James Cochran, Lewis Alston, Stephen Minor's order on John Ellis, Francis Doloney, Patrick Foley; among personal effects -- 50 books of different authors and the History of England, a silver coffee pot, 1 large silver cup, 2 small silver cups. Total $22,400. Plantation on Buffalo Creek, 600 arpents, with dwelling house, 10 out houses, kitchen, paled garden, negro cabins, two barns, in one of which a horse-mill, four pairs of indigo vatts and 150 acres under fence.

p. 102. 24 Feb. 1794. Don Estevan Minor to Ann Swezey, wife of Richard Swezey, 225 arpents which was granted to Peter Hawkins, b. by St. Catherine's Creek and lands granted to Samuel Gibson, Stephen Jordan, Joseph Forrester and the seller, as likewise 100 arpents b. by aforesaid tract of 225 arpents and by land of John Bisland and the seller, for $500 paid. Signed by both.

p. 103. 24 Feb. 1794. Richard Swezey to Don Manuel Gayoso de Lemos 260 arpents with buildings, gates and fences thereon, 1-1/2 miles from Fort, b. by lands of Hiram Swezey, Samuel Gibson, Peter Hawkins and lands of His Majesty, in exchange for 325 arpents sold by him [?] to my wife. Both signed. Wit: Estevan Minor, R. King.

p. 103-4. 26 Feb. 1794. John Williams to James Bonner negro girl, "Judy" aged 14, nat. of U. S., for $300. Signed by both.

p. 104. 27 Feb. 1794. James Bonner to Robert Withers, 50 arpents at Pine Ridge, being part of the tract granted him and on which he lives, for $50 paid. Both sign.

p. 105. 1 March 1794. William Thomas and Thomas Van Swearingen to Joseph Vidal negro man "Peter" aged 20, nat. of U. S., and a negro woman, aged 18 and her female child, the mother a nat. of U. S., the child of the Province. These negroes we bought in the U. S. and sell for $650 paid. Both signed.

p. 106. 3 March 1794. Luis Vilaret to Esther, wife of Richard King, Capt. of Militia, 350 arpents on St. Catherine's Creek, b. (west) by Ebenezer Dayton, (south) James Glascock, (east) John Girault, (north) Samuel Swezey; for $400 which I have received in cattle and other effects. Both signed.

p. 106. Will of Henry Vidal, of this Post, merchant, son of John Vidal and Blasia de la Cruz, natives of the City of Auvergne in France, being sick and weak. I have never married. I am in partnership with Manuel Gonzales, but no articles of agreement have ever existed between us. We are indebted to Domingo Lorero for $100; to Antonio Ramon, of N. O. for $132; there is due on sundry notes $100; Milian Carreras owes me $64. We have in specie $292 and we have merchandize and effects which amount to $220 belonging to us both. All of which together with what property I have I give to Manuel Gonzales whom I constitute my sole heir. Post of Natchez, 6 March 1794. Signed. Wit: Don Simon de Arze, Domingo Lorero, Antoine Mouget.

p. 108. John Williams sells to Gerard Brandon, two negroes, both aged 17, "Buck" and "Forlas", nat. of U. S., for $800 paid. Signed John Williams Jr., Gerard Brandon.

p. 108. Benjamin Steel and Hannah Steel to William Collins, a negro woman "Mary", aged 25, nat. of U. S., 14 March 1794. Signed by the three.

p. 109. 15 March 1794. John Williams to Gabriel Benoist, a negro woman "Flora", a negro man "Charles", both nat. of U. S., with a female child "Betsy", aged 3, and a male child "Billy", aged 1, children of the woman, for $1000. Signed John Williams, Jr., Gabriel Benoist.

p. 110. 20 March 1794. John Williams to Robert Scott, a mulatto lad "Natt", nat. of Carolina, aged 15, for $300 paid. Both sign.

p. 110. 26 March 1794. Moses Bonner to Thos. Wilkins, a negro man "Baker", aged 35, purchased by me of Don Carlos de Grand-Pre, for $450 paid. Both sign.

p. 111. 26 March 1794. John Williams to Franco. Gutierrez de Arrozo, a negro woman "Lydia", aged 19, with her son "Ned", aged 4, and dau. "Sally", aged 10, for $850 paid. Both signed.

p. 112. 27 March 1794. William Collins to Ebenezer Rees, a negro woman "Nancy" aged 24, nat. of Va., for $300 paid. Both signed.

p. 112. 29 March 1794. Richard Harrison to David Holt, a negro man "Bristol", aged 38, nat. of Va., for $570 Mexican money, paid. Both sign. // Natchez, 29 March 1794. I do approve of a sale made by Capt. Richard Harrison to David Holt of a negro named "Bristol". (Signed) Alexander Moore. To John Girault, Esq.

p. 113. Post of Natchez, 30 March 1794. Mary Savage gives power of atty. to Isaac Gaillard for me and in my name to sell a tract of land I hold at Pointe Coupee on False River, b. by land of Benjamin Farar and Isaac Gaillard aforesaid, 1000 arpents, as set forth in plan and grant thereof. Signed.

p. 114. 7 Arp. 1794. Peter Bryan Bruin and Elizabeth Edmond, his wife, sell to Thomas Calvet, of this District, a negro boy "Toney", aged 15, nat. of Va., in payment for which he delivered to us 16 cows with their calves and two oxen in full satisfaction for the same. Signed: P. Bry. Bruin, Elizabeth Bruin. Wit: Bryan Bruin, Thomas Calvet, George W. Humphreys. // Sir: I have no objection to Colonel Bruin's exchanging a negro with Mr. Thomas Calvet for cattle. June 27, 1794. Signed Alexander Moore. To Capt. John Girault.

p. 115. 15 April 1794. William Barland to Christopher Miller a lot in the new town of this Post, Lot No. 2, Sq. No. 21, part of the ground granted to me by Don Estevan Miro, Gov. Gen'l, said lot 150 feet square, for $30 paid. Both sign.

p. 115. 15 April 1794. William Barland to Abraham Galtney lot No. 1, Sq. No. 22, in the new town of this Post, 150 ft. square, for $30 paid. Both signed.

p. 116. Benjamin Monsanto to Francisco Caudel, Military Store-keeper of this Post of Natchez, a negro woman "Babet", aged 30, not warranted in any manner, for 325 Mexican dollars. Both signed. 19 Apr. 1794.

p. 117. 22 Apr. 1794. Abraham Horton to Daniel Ogden two African negroes, which I purchased from Don Francisco Mayrone, for $1020, paid. Abraham (X) Horton, Daniel Ogden.

p. 118. 22 Arp., 1794. Daniel Ogden to Gerard Brandon negro man, "Neptune", aged 25, for $500 paid. Both signed.

p. 118. 23 April 1794. Robert Stark to Thos. Foster, of this District, four slaves, nat. of U. S., "Isabella", aged 25, "Jacob", aged 10, "Anaky", aged 5, and "Limerick", aged 2, for $700. Both signed.

p. 119. 23 Apr. 1794. Robert Stark to Samuel Flowers, of this District, physician, three negroes, for $800 on terms. Both signed.

p. 120. 25 Apr. 1794. William Colbert and John Brown, both of the Chickasaw Nation, ack. to have received of Mr. Arthur Cobb, two horses, for the full balance of payment for a negro wench "Nancy", boy "Abraham" and girl "Emma", which they sold to William Cobb for the account of his father, Arthur Cobb, and received of him a negro wench of the said Arthur Cobb. Both signed with a mark.

p. 121. 25 Apr. 1794. Don Martin Palso gives power of Atty. to Benjamin Monsanto, of Dist., to recover and receive from Zenon Balis, the sum of $80 on his note of hand due to the estate of my deceased parents for the purchase of a house. Signed.

p. 122. 8 Apr. 1794. James Hayes to Gabriel Griffing a mulatto man "Henry Jones", who is bound to serve as a slave until Aug. 1801; for $200 in hand paid. Both signed with a mark. // Moorhall, 28 Arp. 1794. Sir: I have no objection to Mr. James Hayes transferring his right to a mulatto man named "Jones" to Mr. Gabriel Griffin. Signed Alexander Moore. To Captain John Girault.

p. 122. 28 Aug. 1794. Juan Girault to Catharine Caudel, wife of Francisco Caudel, military store-keeper of this post, a lot in this town, being lot No. 3, Square No. 8, for $35, paid. Signed: Juan Girault, for Catharine Caudel, Anto. Marmillion. Approved by Francisco Caudel.

p. 123. 28 'pr. 1794. William Colbert, of the Chickasaw Nation, bearer of a note of hand of Jeptha Higdon, for $153, which he lost in the Chickasaw Nation and never did negotiate to any person whomsoever but now has received of sd Higdon full satisfaction and payment of same, and does hereby acquit him of it and makes said note void. The said note was given for the balance due by sd Higdon for price of a negro named "Cesar". William (X) Colbert. // p. 123. William Colbert, native of the Chickasaw Nation, bearer of a note of Charles Lucas to Benj. Belk for $100 with 7 years interest which note he received from Jeptha Higdon in payment for a debt, but having lost it in the Nation, he never received the payment or any part of it from said Lucas or any other person except the said Higdon who paid and gave full satisfaction to said Colbert for the said note; which amount is still due by sd Lucas to said Higdon. 28 April 1794. William (X) Colbert.

p. 124. 30 Apr. 1794. Mary Higdon makes a free gift to Daniel and Gideon Higdon of a negro girl named "Jenny", aged 7, and a boy, "Prince", aged 5, which said negroes and product to be divided equally between sd Daniel and Gideon. Mary (X) Higdon.

p. 124. 5 May 1794. Stephen Minor, of the Natchez, to Comfort Ivy, of the State of Georgia, bond to make proper and sufficient titles to the said Ivy on or before March next, of 2000 arpents on Second Creek, adj. Authur Cobb and Mrs. Sarah Holmes, with all improvements, 100 head of horned cattle with due proportion of cows and calves, two and three years old, 500 bu. of corn, 50 bu. of oats, also a quantity of rye to be sown in due season on the said plantation, and Comfort Ivy obligates himself to receive possession of the said plantation on 1st March next and then pay said Stephen Minor in likely negro slaves, not under 12 years nor over 25 years old, being the price of the plantation and $700 in cash, or negroes, as above, for the price of the cattle, corn and oats as also any quantity of rye sown to be valued per acre for the trouble of sowing. Respecting the price of the negroes, they agree to choose two men of their liking to determine same and agree by their judgment. For true performance of every article herein the parties bind themselves in the penal sum of $500 to be paid by the party failing to the other. Both sign.

p. 126. 17 May 1794. John Williams to Alexander Moore 4 negroes, for $600. Signed: John Williams, Jr., Alexander Moore.

p. 126. Articles of an Agreement. 10 May 1794. At Natchez, Daniel Callaghan, of Opelousas, Prov. of La., to Adam Shepherd and Richard Prather, of Nelson County, State of Kentucky, two settlements and preemption rights in State of Kentucky, one of said Callaghan on the north side of the South Fork of Licking Creek, near Riddle's Station in Hinkstons settlement, taken up April 1775, and the other his brother, Patrick Callaghan's, joining the same on the lower end, which last fell to said Daniel by the death of said Patrick; the said Shepherd and Prather agree to pay the sd. Daniel $1-1/2 per acre for same, if it should not exceed 2000 acres, and if the said entries exceed 2000 acres after deducting all reasonable expenses, they are to pay $1 per acre for such overplus, in the following articles: tobacco, flour, and whiskey; tobacco at $4 per hundred; flour at $7 per barrel, and whiskey at six bitts per gallon; the whiskey and flour to be of good quality and delivered at Mr. Thomas Archer's at Plaquemine on the Mississippi, and the tobacco to be delivered at New Orleans. Signed Adam Shepherd, Daniel Callaghan, R. Prather. Wit: John Girault, Wm. Foster. // Above acknowledged 10 May 1794 before Gayoso at the Government House.

p. 128. 10 May 1794. Jesse Withers to Isaac Gaillard 300 arpents near Second Creek, b. by John Henderson as set forth by plat, for $400.

p. 128. Post of Natchez, 10 May 1794. Don Juan Vaucheret ack. receipt from Antonio Gras of full payment of all sums due to him for land and effects purchased at the sale of estate of Juan St. Germain, dec'd. Signed. Before Gayoso.

p. 129. 10 May 1794. Don Antonio Gras ack. to have received from John Bisland $210 in payment for tract of land belonging to estate of Francisco Bazo and Co. and a horse at the price of $55, which sd land and horse were sold at public sale of sd estate and Antonio Gras was authorised to recover the amount thereof. Signed. Before Gayoso.

p. 129. 12 May 1794. John Williams sells to Samuel Raner a negro girl "Nan", aged 14, nat. of Carolina. Signed John Williams, Jr., Samuel Raner.

p. 130. 28 May 1794. Don Carlos de Grand-Pre to Ebenezer Rees 625 acres of land about one-half league from this Fort, b. by lands of John Stampley, Francis Spain, George Rapalie, William Ferguson, Adam Bingaman, David Mitchell, Juan St. Germain and John Row, for $2500, on terms, Bennet Truly surety. Both sign. // Rec'd of Mr. Ebenezer Rees $1250, 1st payment on sale of my plantation, 1 July 1795. // Rec'd of Ebenezer Rees $1250 in full payment for my plantation and for which a formal receipt is given him. Natchez, 4 ____, 1796.

p. 131. 8 May 1794. Don Carlos de Grand-Pre to Ebenezer Rees a negro man "Andrew", aged 22, nat. of Guinea, for 200 pounds of good indigo to be examined by two capable persons and to be delivered at end of month of November, present year. Both signed. // p. 132. Received of Mr. Ebenezer Rees 200 lbs. of indigo in payment of a negro named "Andrew", which I sold him. Natchez, 4 July 1796. Grand-Pre.

p. 132. Will of Lewis Davis of the Province of West Florida, very sick and weak, to my well-beloved son, Robert Davis, two negro boys, "Jack and Simon"; to my daughter Susannah Davis, two negroes, "Tom and Catharine"; to my son, Lewis Davis, two negroes "Abraham and Adam"; to daughter Martha Davis, two negroes, "Step and Serena", to Martha Davis, my well-beloved wife, three negroes, "Tom, Kate and

Celia"; the rest of my estate, real and personal after paying all my just debts, except one cow and calf apiece to my four children, to remain in the hands of my wife and children as a principal, each child to have an equal share as it comes of age, likewise my wife to draw an equal share with my children. Exors: Landon Davis, Hugh Davis, Wm. Webb, Jr. 3 Feb. 1784. Wit: Amos Fairchild, Wm. Webb.

p. 133. 14 May 1794. Ebenezer Rees to Samuel Levi Wells a negro woman, "Nancy", aged 25, nat. of U. S., for $400 paid. Both signed. // Payment of $400 in foregoing sale was paid in notes of Bennet Truly and Lewis Alston, which the seller has recieved on his own account, without any recourse against purchaser. Signed by both.

p. 133. Inventory of the estate of the late James Cole, dec'd., as declared upon oath by Mary Cole, the widow of deceased, John Cole, the eldest son, Jacob Stampley and Capt. Richard King, of this District, planter; 450 acres of land, one negro, etc. (not a large estate). District of Villa Gayoso, 19 May 1794. Inventory made by J. Murray and J. Smith. Signed.

p. 134. 19 May 1794. Henry Richardson to the heirs of John Hartley, decd., represented by Jesse Hamilton, executor of the will of sd deceased, a negro man named "Bristol", aged 45, and four other negroes, for $650 paid. Both signed.

p. 135. 19 May 1794. Joshua Collins to Norsworthy Hunter, Capt. of Militia in this Dist., 200 arpents of land granted seller 15 March 1789, b. by lands of Rees and Carradine, for $200 paid. Both signed. // p. 136. Sir: I have known Mr. Joshua Collins a long time and believe he is not indebted to any person. I have no objection to his transferring his land or part to Capt. Hunter. Your obedient servant, Alexander Moore. 19 May 1794. To Capt. John Girault.

p. 136. 21 May 1794. Alexander Henderson to William Foster 100 arps. on St. Catherine's Creek, b. by sd creek and lands of Richard Harrison and Samuel Flower, for $100 paid. Both signed.

p. 137. 21 May 1794. Mary Williams to David Ross power of attorney to recover and receive from the estate of Juan Antoine Boidere of the District of Opelousas, planter, deceased, a certain sum due on a negro sold by my deceased husband, David Mitchell, to said Juan Antoine Boidere, which sd negro was mortgaged until final payment. Signed.

p. 137. 22 May 1794. John Williams to Sarah Perkins, wife of Joseph Perkins, four slaves, for $500. Sarah (X) Perkins, John Williams, Jr.

p. 138. State of South Carolina, Laurens County, Mary Williams, of State and Co. aforesaid, for 220 pounds sterling, in hand paid, to John Williams, Jr., sundry negroes, a man "Charles", a woman "Habey", boy "Buck", girl "Nan, child "Ellick". Signed. Witnesses: James Tinsley, Richard Groom. // Clerk's Office 2nd Feb. 1792. I do certify that a bill of sale similar to the within was recorded in my office in order book, page 236 and recorded in Book B, page 360, 26 June 1788. Lewis Saxon, Clerk.

p. 138. State of S. C., Laurens Co. Oct. 26, 1789. Joseph Griffin, of sd county and state, for 100 pounds sterling, in hand paid, by John Williams, Jr., sells sundry negroes, viz: one negro woman "Sukey" and her three children, "Amelia, Lewis and Sue". Signed Joseph Griffin Wit: James Tinsley, Richard Groom. Ack by Groom, one of the witnesses before Thos. Wadsworth, Esq., one of the Judges of county afsd. // 25 Jany. 1792. The within bill of sale rec., in Bk. D. pp. 99-100 and examined by Lewis Saxon, Clerk.

p. 139. State of S. C., Laurens County. James Attwood Williams, of sd county and State, for 90 pounds sterling, in hand paid by John Williams, Jr., for sundry slaves, namely: Old negro woman "Sarah", with male child "John", negro woman "Flora". 6 Dec. 1789. Wit: John Owen, Richard Groom. Signed James A. Williams. Before Thos. Wadsworth, Esq., one of the Judges of sd county, Richard Groom deposeth that he saw James A. Williams assign the within instrument and John Owen as witness. 25 Jany. 1792. // State of S. C., Laurens Co. Clerk's Office. 2 Feb. 1792. The within bill of sale is recorded in Book D. pp. 100-101, and examined by Lewis Saxon, Clk.

p. 140. State of S. C., Laurens County. 25 Oct. 1789. James and Washington Williams, of afsd co. and state, for 300 pounds paid, to John Williams, Jr., sundry slaves: One negro man "Frank", one negro girl "Jude", one negro woman "Linda", and three male children, "Mingo, Simon and Billy", one negro woman "Dina", and two female children "Patty" and "Daphne", one negro woman "Liddy", with a young male child, "Ned". Signed by both. Wit: James Goodman, Jonathan Mote. // Proved by James Goodman before Thos. Wadsworth, Esq., one of the Judges of sd Co. 25 Jany. 1792. Recorded Bk. pp. 101-2 and examined by Lewis Saxon, 2nd Feb. 1792.

p. 140. State of S. C., Laurens County. 26 Oct. 1789. John and Sarah Griffing, of afsd co. and state, for 100 pounds, sterling, paid, to John Williams, Jr., sundry slaves: two negro boys, named "Filas" and "Cato", one mulatto boy "Nat". Wit: Richard Griffin, William Watson. // Wm. Watson proved above before Thomas Wadsworth, Esq., one of Judges of this county and state. // South Carolina, Laurens Co. Clerk's Office, 2 Feb. 1792. The within bill recorded Bk. D. p. 99. Examined by Lewis Saxon, Clk.

p. 142. Inventory of estate of William Curtis delivered by widow of deceased upon her oath. District of Villa Gayoso, 4 June 1794. E. V. Murray, John Smith.

p. 142. 11 June 1794. James Phips to David Mitchell, of this Dist., planter, 400 square arpents, on Second Creek, b. by lands of Nicholas Rab, Don Philip Trevino and land of the purchaser and His Majesty, for $400, paid. James (X) Phips, David Mitchell. // I do certify that Mr. David Mitchell has a good right to purchase land wherever he chooses, 11 June 1794. Alexander Moore. // I have no objection to Samuel Phips selling his land to Mr. David Mitchell, Natchez, 11 June 1794. Alexr. Moore.

p. 144. 4 July 1794. Gabriel Griffin to George Selser a plantation lying on the road leading to the District of Villa Gayoso, b. by lands of Jeptha Higdon, Jeremiah Coleman, John Griffing, John Read, William Fletcher, 600 arpents, for $300, to be paid July 1796. Both signed. // Moore Hall, 4 July 1794. Sir: I have no objection to Mr. Gabriel Griffing disposing of his land. Signed Alexander Moore. To Capt. John Girault, Esq.

p. 144. 9 July 1794. Thomas Jordan to Jesse Withers 100 arpents, part of 600 arpents made to seller in settlemênt of Fairchild's Cr., b. by James Bonner, James McIntyre and lands of seller. Both signed. // Sir: I have given Mr. Thos. Jordan my consent to dispose of to Mr. Jesse Withers 100 arpents of his land that is under mortgage to me, for which he has paid me $100 in part of my debt by a note of Mr. Isaac Gaillard due Feb. next. Alexander Moore. Natchez, 18 Aug. 1794.

p. 145. Ebenezer Rees to Antonio Novella, Artillerist, a house situate at the landing place, built on the corner of my lot with another small building lately occupied by Augustin MaCarty, dec'd., for $270, on terms. 9 July 1794. Signed.

p. 146-7. 29 July 1794. William Dunbar, attorney for Robert Dow, of N. O., physician, to James Montgomery and Dennis Neville, both of Natchez, planters, 1000 square arpents on Cole's Creek, granted to Robert Dow, for $265 on terms, tract remaining mortgaged, also a negro "Alexander", aged 26. Signed by William Dunbar, James Montgomery. Dennis Nevill signed with his mark.

p. 147-8. 21 Aug. 1794. Don Pedro Rosseau to Juan Barno Ferrusola, commandant of Galley "Active", a negro named "Lewis", nat. of Guinea, for $330, paid in a note for same. Both signed.

p. 148. 6 Aug. 1794. Richard Lord to Patrick McDermott a negro lad, "George" aged 16, which I purchased of George Cochran, for $300 in hand paid. Both sign.

p. 149. 9 Aug. 1794. Richard Lord being indebted to George Cochran for $450, promises to pay 1 Aug. 1795, and for security mortgages three negroes, a negro man "Gibb", aged 20, a woman "Sarah", aged 48, and a girl "Jenny", aged 4. Signed. // 13 Dec. 1798. George Cochran, of Natchez, Miss. Ter., merchant, for $450 and interest since it became due, in hand paid by Richard Lord, releases to Richard Lord, the above-named three negroes which were mortgaged as security for payment of said sum. Signed. Wit: John Girault.

p. 150. 9 Aug. 1794. Richard Lord, being justly indebted to William Vousdan, in sum of $667, which he promises to pay 1 Aug. 1795 and for security mortgages negro man "Tim", aged 22, and negro woman "Kate", aged 35 and her daughter "Sally". Richard Lord is also indebted to William Vousdan in sum of $120 and mortgages the product of his sawmill until full pay is made.

p. 150. 16 Aug. 1794. Antonio Gras to Gabriel Ruffat part of lot at the landing of Natchez, 43 ft in front by 46 ft in depth, b. by the hill, on which lot two houses are erected with a kitchen between, for $500, terms. Signed by Antonio Gras. Ruffat made his mark.

p. 151. 6 Sept. 1794. John Stampley to Job Routh 158 arpents near Fort, b. by John Ross, Don Pedro Piernas and lands of His Majesty, granted to Stampley in 1785, for $80 paid. Both sign.

p. 152. 10 Sept. 1794. Ithamar Andrews to Israel Leonard 100 arps. on St. Catherine's Creek, b. as per grant in 1789, for $200 paid.

p. 152-3. 10 Sept. 1794. Don Manuel Gayoso de Lemos to Elias Beauregard, Capt. of the Reg. of La., a negro man "August", aged 30, not warranted from any defects whatsoever. Both sign.

p. 153. Sandy Creek, 19 Sept. 1794. Sir: Agreeably to your Excellency's orders, I have taken the inventory of the property of James Erwin, decd., and enclosed it. The stock is chiefly claimed by the heirs. I have made a true return of all that came to my knowledge. Your obedient servant, William Cooper (signed.) To His Excellency, Don Manuel Gayoso de Lemos. // p. 154. Inventory of James Ervin, deceased: 625 acres of land with crop of corn on same, household furniture, live stock and farm equipment, (not large). 19 Sept. // Petition of Jennet Erwin, who has been married to her deceased husband 27 years and had done her endeavor toward getting a living during my husband's lifetime. Since his death, it seems that he is considerable indebted; asks that she be allowed part of his estate for maintenance. Signed Jennet Erwin. 25 Sept. 1794.

p. 154. 3 Oct. 1794. Don Estevan Minor to Rebecca Perry, wife of Samuel Bell, of Attacapas, planter, a negro man "Peter", aged 25, nat. of Va., negro woman "Phillis", aged 22, nat. of Maryland, with her son "George", aged 2, for $1000, paid. Signed by Estevan Minor and Samuel Bell.

p. 155. 6 Oct. 1794. Parker Carradine to Joshua Collins a negro named "London", aged 35, nat. of Guinea, for $400, payable as expressed in a written agreement between us. Both signed.

p. 155. 18 Oct. 1794. Abraham Ellis and Margaret Gaillard, his wife, to the heirs of Benjamin Farrar 1000 arpents on False River, b. by lands of Isaac Gaillard and Bayou Cattonier, in payment we have received three negroes, "Ismael, Prince and David", as expressed in a deed of even date. Signed by Margaret Ellis and W. Dunbar, exr. of Farrar estate. // p. 156. 18 Oct. 1794. Benjamin Farrar, jun., and William Dunbar, executors of the will of Benjamin Farrar, decd., and guardians to his daughters, Anne and Margaret Farrar, to Margaret Gaillard, wife of Abraham Ellis, three negroes, "Ismael, Prince and David", in payment of which we have received 1000 arpents on False River. Signed by William Dunbar, Benjamin Farrar, and Margaret Ellis.

p. 157. Natchez, 27 Oct. 1794. To His Excellency: Jeptha Higdon represents that some time in the year 1785, his mother, Mary Higdon, did give to him under certain conditions some negro slaves and other property, the document concerning which was recorded in the Archives of this Government, by Commandant Philip Trevino; wherefore the petitioner begs Your Excellency will be pleased to order a copy of said document to be made out for him. Jeptha Higdon.

p. 157-8. 2 Nov. 1794. Joseph Bonner, of this District of Natchez, planter, to the heirs of Henry Manadue, deceased, represented by Gabriel Benoist, John Bolls and Henry Manadue, Jr., exors. of the will of Henry Manadue, decd., a tract of 600 arpents about 8 miles from this Fort, for $300 received from said deceased. All sign.

p. 159. 5 November 1794. George Killian to Andrew Gil a negro man "Smith", aged 20, for $400, paid. Both sign.

p. 160. 5 Nov. 1794. Susannah Spell and John Cole to Samuel Flower 200 arpents on St. Catherine's Creek, b. by Richard Harrison and Moses Bonner, Jr., for $200 paid. All sign.

p. 160. 5 Nov. 1794. George Killian to Thomas Wilkins negro man "Ben", aged 26, nat. of Jamaica, for $400 paid. Both sign.

p. 161. 8 Nov. 1794. James McIntyre to Willis Bonner 150 arpents b. by lands of Willis Bonner and seller, being part of 500 arpents granted said Bonner, for $100 paid. Signed: J. McIntyre, Willis (X) Bonner.

p. 162. Natchez, 12 Nov. 1794. I do hereby acknowledge to have received $50, this day, which with $50 more I had already received, is in full satisfaction for all my claim to the land and improvement I formerly lived on. Jemima (X) Cochran. Wit: Wm. Dunbar, J. Eldergill. Before me, Gayoso.

p. 162. 15 Nov. 1794. Abraham Taylor and Thomas Morgan agree to make an exchange of lands, as follows: Abraham Taylor delivers to the said Thomas Morgan a plantation of 250 arpents on Second Creek, adj. James Oglesby, in exchange for which he receives 250 arpents on Wells Creek, binding themselves to transfer the titles to said lands. Both sign with a mark.

p. 162-3. 29 Nov. 1794. Henry Richardson and Joshua Howard have agreed to make an exchange of land as follows: said Richardson delivers to said Howard 400 arpents on Second Creek, for which he receives a plantation in the District of Homochitto. Both sign.

p. 163. 29 Nov. 1794. Charles King to Isaac Newman 375 arpents in the District of Villa Gayoso, for $500 paid. Both sign.

p. 164. 4 Dec. 1794. Peter Brian Bruin, Lt. Col. in Militia in this Government, is indebted to Ebenezer Rees for $1519 and to George Cochran for $2062, which he promises to pay within four years from date, with 6% interest, and for security mortgages the plantation on which he now lives and the land on which he is going to build a saw-mill, as likewise all such lands I may hereafter purchase for the use of said mill which the said Ebenezer Rees and George Cochran have agreed to assist me in building. All signed. // Memorandum of an agreement made at Natchez, 4 Dec. 1794, between Peter Bryan Bruin and Ebenezer Rees and George Cochran. Details of arrangement. All sign.

p. 165. Bayou Pierre, 12 Dec. 1794. The annexed article having been read and fully explained to me, I do hereby give my full and entire consent and that the four men slaves shall be at all times employed in this business when necessary, viz: "Stephen, Ben, Ben (mulatto), and Peter", and I shall not, under any pretense, employ them otherwise than in support of said new mill, during the hours when they can be usefully employed there. And I do further promise to furnish a wench to cook for the workmen and wash for Mr. McDermott (the person employed to erect mill) and his apprentices. (Signed) Elizabeth Bruin. // Memo. of an agreement between Col. Peter B. Bruin and Patrick McDermott, both of the Government of Natchez. McDermot engages to build and completely finish in a workmanlike manner a saw-mill, calculated to saw plank and scantlin fo 27 feet long, with necessary building, to finish in the best possible manner the dam and all things necessary thereto on waters of Bayou Pierre, and to commence at or before 25 Dec. next, the whole to be completed without delay, provided always that he shall not be interrupted by invasion of the Indians or any foreign enemy. Col. Bruin is to pay him from first sale of plank prepared by said Mr. MacDermot as said mill and delivered at Natchez landing to Messrs. Ebenezer Rees and George Cochran, or either of them, $600 as soon after as funds may be in their hands. Bruin to furnish such assistance as may be required by sd McDermot when force employed by said McDermot is insufficient. Both sign. Wit: Joseph Murray, J. Murdock. // Natchez, 5 Dec. 1794. Peter B. Bruin and Patrick McDermot ack. the above before Gayoso.

p. 167. 6 Dec. 1794. Joseph Calvet to John Foster 138 arpents at St. Catherine's Creek, b. by a branch of sd creek and lands of Winsor Pipes and Gideon Gibson, for $100 paid. Both sign.

p. 168. Inventory of the estate of John Terry, decd., District of Villa Gayoso, as delivered by Sarah, the widow of sd deceased, upon oath, 9 Dec. 1794: plantation of 400 arpents, another tract, 300 arpents, 11 slaves, 15 horses, 80 horned cattle, calves included, 10 sheep, 15 hogs, household furniture, plantation tools. Signed V. Murray, John Smith. // p. 169. Will of John Terry, of District of Villa Gayoso, sick and weak. I appoint Sarah Terry, my beloved wife, and Samuel Davis, executor and executrix, jointly. To Sarah, my beloved wife, all my property that the law appoints to every widow and to keep possession of all my estate for maintneance of herself and all her children. Stephen Terry, my oldest son, when he becomes of age, a negro, to Rhody Terry, my eldest daughter, one negro when of age; same for Jeremiah, my second son; John my 3rd son; Susannah Terry, my 2nd daughter; James and William Terry, my two youngest sons, as much cattle as may be sufficient to make the value of a grown negro equal to any given the other children, the rest of estate to be divided equally. 29 Nov. 1794. John (X) Terry. Wit: Roger Dixon, David Phelps, Wm. Fairbanks, George (X) Stampley, John Holt, Nath'l. Brown, George Dumange, Clement Dyson. // p. 196. District of Villa Gayoso, 9 Dec. 1794. The above witnesses ack. their signatures and that sd John Terry was in his senses. V. Murray, John Smith.

p. 170. 6 Dec. 1794. William Wicks to William Vousdan, 277 arpents at St. Catherine' Creek, b. by Abraham Horton, Gideon Gibson, Ezekiel Dewit and Vousdan for $250 paid. Wm. (X) Wicks, Wm. Vousdan.

p. 170. Natchez, Nov. 5, 1794. Clara Monsanto, wid. of Benjamin Monsanto, decd., represented that sundry persons have claimed from the estate of her husband payment of certain privileged debts, among others, the salary of the overseer of the plantation and the freight of sundry provisions for the use of the said plantation, which may amount to $300 and having no means, she asks that she be allowed to sell a certain lot granted to her deceased husband which would enable her to meet these demands. // John Scott and Frederick Man appointed appraisers of the lot and building thereon and when so appraised the said lot may be sold by the petitioner. Gayoso.

p. 171. Appraisal of lot and building above, $350. Signed Scott and Man. // At Post of Natchez, 10 Dec. 1794. At sale of foregoing lot and building and timber lying thereon, said lot being No. 1, Sq. No. 3, cried for three hours and adjudged to Antonio Gras at $300, he being the highest bidder.

p. 171. 11 Dec. 1794. William Barland to Don Antonio Gras a lot, 200 ft front by 200 ft depth, No. 2, Sq. No. 17, of this town of Natchez, part of 105 arpents granted to him in 1782, for $80 paid. Signed.

p. 172. Don Estevan Minor to William Carney, of this District, 1000 arpents, in District of Bayou Pierre, which he bought of Edward Murray, b. by Samuel Gibson and lands of His Majesty, for $500, on terms. Both sign. // p. 173. Post of Natchez, 4 July 1795, Don Estevan Minor declares to have recieved full payment of foregoing obligation. Signed.

p. 173. William Barland to William Rucker lot 150 ft. square, No. 2, Square No. 31, in this town of Natchez, part of grant to him in 1782, for $50. Both sign.

p. 173-4. Mary Foster, of District of Natchez, to Wm. Foster 400 arpents of land on St. Catherine's Creek, b. by Moses Bonner, and land belonging to her, which plantation she purchased of David Smith, to whom same was granted in 1788, for $400 Mexican coin, 19 Dec. 1794. Mary (X) Foster, Will: Foster.

p. 174. 22 Dec. 1794. Don Juan Vaucheret to Don Carlos de Grand-Pre, 450 arpents on St. Catherine's Creek, b. by Mary Girault, Ezekiel DeWit, Jeremiah Bryan and John Hartley, being part of a larger tract he purchased at public sale of John Still Lee, for $225, paid. Both signed.

p. 175. Post of Natchez, 20 Dec. 1794. Don Carlos de Grand-Pre and Don Juan Vaucheret appeared to settle all matters pending between them resulting from the partnership between them during the last six years, which has ceased. The parties have experienced various difficulties in settling their accounts respecting the share claimed by Don Carlos de Grand-Pre of the whole amount of the sales in consequence whereof divers Judicial proceedings have been had. They, the said parties, in order finally to determine the same have agreed as follows: Don Juan Vaucheret is to remain in possession of all book accounts, notes, bonds and other papers belonging to the partnership, as his own, Don Carlos de Grand-Pre renouncing all claim thereto, on condition that Don Juan Vaucheret shall be responsible for all debts contracted by and for account of said partnership, and pay same, personally, (p. 176) this condition being only a precaution as all debts contracted during the partnership being paid. In consideration whereof, Vaucheret transfers to de Grand-Pre 450 arpents on one of the branches of St. Catherine's Creek, as described in foregoing deed. Partnership began 7 May 1786. Both sign. Wit: Wm. Dunbar, John Ellis.

p. 176. Alexander Moore's Will. Of Natchez District, in perfect health; beloved wife, Jane, extrix, with sons Samuel Philip and James Moore executors; to son William, now in North America, $1000, Spanish milled; to son Alexander two negroes on demand and a clear discharge of his book account; to my dearly beloved wife one-fifth of all I die possessed of during her life and to leave as she thinks proper to our children, hereafter mentioned; to my three sons and daughter, all or the other four-fifths to be divided equally between them at the end of three years, Samuel Philip Moore, James Moore, Sarah Moore and Robert Moore, those are my heirs after the above sums are paid. My two sons, Samuel Philip and James to carry on the business for above term of three years, for the advantage of the whole and are to receive $200 yearly for the same and no more. 9 Feb. 1788. Signed. Wit: William Barland, Archibald Rea, William Collins, John Farquhar, Will: Foster, Samuel Culberson, George Fitzgerald.

p. 177. Will of David Williams, in perfect health; my beloved wife one-third of my estate, real and personal, after her death to be divided amongst our children,that shall be then living; she shall choose her place of residence, the plantation Pine Grove, Belmont, or any other we possess. I also give her all the household furniture to dispose of as she thinks proper; the remaining two-thirds of my estate to be equally divided amongst my beloved children, David, Mary, Gayoso, James Cadwallader and Anna Williams. My beloved wife executrix, my dear brother, James McIntosh, and my (torn), William Williams, executors and guardians of my children. In order to prevent my said estate being injured by precipitate sale or partition, I will and order that all my negroes, stock, and every property whatsoever remain in possession of my beloved wife to be employed by her as she may judge most advantageous upon the plantation for the benefit of her and the children. I do recommend that she spare no expense and pains for the education of our children; to my beloved brother all my wearing apparel and $100 and not more than $200 per year, his board, washing and lodging in my family as long as he lives, horses to ride and to enjoy every other comfort of life, the same as he did in my lifetime. And whereas the plantation named Pine Grove we now live upon is granted to my beloved brother John and beloved sisters, Mary and Anna Williams, I do order that $2000 be paid to them in the City of London, England, agreeable to my promise, for 800 acres belonging to them of the said tract, as soon as possible, they sending full power to my nephew, William Williams, to convey sd land to my son David Williams. I recommend my nephew, William Williams, to the care and protection of my dear wife and that she allow him a generous salary for conducting the business of the plantation and when he shall have earned a few negroes by his industry and should think himself in a situation to settle a plantation for himself. I order that a sum of money be lent to him to purchase four or six negroes in addition to his own, etc. To my mulatto boy, "Bob", his freedom at the age of 21. 7 April 1792. Signed. Wit: Benjamin Monsanto, David Urquhart, Lewis Faure, John Lintot, Wm. McIntosh. // p. 178. On receipt of news of the death of David Williams, Gayoso repaired to the plantation on which he dwells and on inquiry was presented the will which he opened and read before witnesses: Don Joseph Vidal, Benjamin Monsanto, William Williams, John Williams and James McIntosh. 7 day _____ 1793. Signed by all the above.

p. 178. Inventory of the plantation called Spring Grove on Bayou Sarah; negroes, cattle, buildings, tools and implements, belonging to John O'Connor, in the care and management of Mr. William Collins: plantation, 1850 acres, etc. total value $8008. (p. 179) The above is all the property belonging to me at Bayou Sarah, which I declare to be just and true to the best of my knowledge. Natchez, 27 Feb. 1794. Signed: John O'Connor. // A list of the negroes at the beforementioned plantation not paid for and consequently the property of the original owners, Viz: Negroes: Joe, Jim and Dick belong to Mr. Durnford; Lucretia, Scipio and Hercules to Mr. Labateau; Stephen to Mr. David Ross. The above must be paid hire for. Natchez. Feb. 27, 1794. Signed as above. // p. 179. Post of Natchez, 27 Feb. 1794. William Collins, on oath, declared he is in charge at the plantation of John O'Connor of all the property in the foregoing list, which he binds himself to hold subject to the order of the Government and will not suffer any part thereof to be removed without an order from the Government. Signed William Collins. Before Gayoso.

p. 179. List of sundries in possession of Manuel Garcia de Texada belonging to John O'Connor, left with him for sale, on condition. [two and one-half pages of listed merchandise, valued at $1577.] Natchez, 17 March 1794. Signed by Texada. // p. 182. Natchez, 17 March 1794. Manuel Texada charged on commission with some effects belonging to John O'Connor, has been instructed to retain in his possession the said goods and effects, subject to the order of the Government which he has promised to do, unavoidable accidents excepted. Signed by Texada, before Gayoso. Wit: John Girault. // p. 182-3. Natchez, Feb. 24, 1794. In consequence of an agreement made between John O'Connor and Charles McKiernan, wherein it is, among other things, stipulated that the latter shall receive in payment from the former the goods deposited by him in the hands of Don Manuel Texada, in pursuance of the seizure thereof, the said Texada will deliver the said goods to his order whereby his obligation thereto will be discharged. Signed Gayoso. // p. 183. Acknowledgement that he was satisfied for the goods which were in the hands of Manuel Texada. 2nd March 1795. Signed Chas. McKiernan. Wit: Joseph Vidal, Juan Girault.

p. 183. In the matter of the Estate of Scott. Petition: To Governor: Gerard Brandon represents that in 1782 Mr. Wm. Scott, formerly of this place, having obtained a passport from Your Excellency to go to South Carolina to settle his affairs there, left in your petitioner's care three children whom your petitioner has since supported, the time said Wm. Scott intended returning being long elapsed and hearing nothing from him, the petitioner has fears of his safety. Previous to his departure, he made a will and left Mr. Percy, Mr. Gaillard and your petitioner executors of the said will, being now in your petitioner's possession. A few days before Mr. Scott left this country he entered into an agreement with Barney Higgins to take charge of his plantation, stock and other property as by reference to the agreement will more fully appear; the time for which agreement was made being elapsed and no hopes or expectations of Mr. Scott's speedy arrival in this country, your petitioner prays that two persons in the neighborhood be appointed to inspect and report to Your Excellency if sd Higgins has complied with the condition of his agreement with Mr. Scott, and give security that no part of sd Higgins property be removed until it appears that he has fully complied with his engagement; petitioner further prays that an attorney be appointed for the estate of said Scott until his return and the proceeds thereof be applied for the support and education of the children. Natchez, 31 Dec. 1794. Signed, Gerard Brandon. // p. 184. Decree: Natchez, Jany. 14, 1795. Messrs. Gerard Brandon and Isaac Gaillard appointed executors of will of William Scott and authorized to settle all affairs for the benefit of the orphans, and settle accounts with Bernard Higgins. Manuel Gayoso de Lemos.

p. 184. 20 Jany. 1795. William Barland, master taylor, of this District, to Francisco Gutierrez de Arroyo, of same, 2 lots in this town, Nos. 3 and 4, Sq. 23, being part of a grant to him in 1782, for $40. Both sign.

p. 184. Nov. 18, 1794. Messrs. Gabriel Benoist, Charles Boardman, Samuel Marshall and myself, being on a treaty for the plantation belonging to James McIntyre, have agreed to fix a price on it. James McIntyre has voluntarily consented to dispose of it for the benefit of his creditors. Signed Peter Walker.

// In consequence of the above, value of $350 placed on the 350 acres, the whole with improvements $430 and a year's credit; for part payment now a discount of 10%. Pine Ridge, Nov. 22, 1794. // p. 185. Approved by Gayoso, Dec. 20, 1794. // 20 Jany. 1795. James McIntyre, with the approbation of Peter Walker, agent for the creditors of this District, to Samuel Marshall 350 arpents with buildings etc., b. by Thomas Jordan, James Bonner, Henry Manadue and James Jones, granted to him by this Government, for $430, payable in one year. Both sign. // p. 186. Post of Natchez, 8 Nov. 1797. Receipt of Peter Walker to Samuel Walker for $430 full amount in foregoing sale; obligation cancelled. Signed by Walker. Wit: James Spain.

p. 186. 22 Jany. 1795. Isaac Johnson to Thomas Wilkins for $392 mortgages, as security, mulatto girl "Jane", aged 4, another named "Harriet", aged 2, and 800 arpents on Second Creek, b. by Ezekiel Forman, William Ratcliffe and Isaac Alexander, granted to him by this Government. Signed. // Natchez, Nov. 27, 1800. Thos. Wilkins certifies to have received the within consideration in full and the mortgagee, Isaac Johnston, Esq., acquitted therefrom. Signed. Wit: Peter Walker.

p. 187. 23 Jany. 1795. Joseph Flower, of the District of Bayou Pierre, to Don Pedro Walker, of this Post, 200 arpents on St. Catherine's Creek, b. by Chas. King and Richard Adams; for $200, Mexican milled, paid. Both sign.

p. 188. 26 Jany. 1795. Joseph Calvit to Thomas Foster 380 arpents on St. Catherine's Creek, b. by Joseph Forrester and lands of His Majesty, having acquired the land from Samuel Gibson, to whom same was granted, for $450 paid. Both sign.

p. 189. 31 Jany. 1795. Charles McKiernan to Don Pedro Ancid and Domingo Lorero part of lot bought from O'Connor, 78 ft front by 71 ft. depth, for $400. Signed by McKiernan.

p. 189. 4 Feb. 1795. Mary Bonner, wife of Martin Owens, to Willis Bonner negro woman "Cecilia" aged 20, nat. of Africa, which said slave fell to her in the division of the estate between her brother and herself, for $300 in hand paid. Signed Mary Owens, Willis (X) Bonner.

p. 191. 6 February 1795. Joseph Murray to Thomas Tyler lot at the landing of this town, 33 ft by 200 ft, with all buildings thereon, for $450 paid. Both sign. // p. 192. Thos. Tyler to Gabriel Ruffat, a lot at the landing of this town, 33 ft by 200 ft, which lot he purchased of Joseph Murray, for $260, paid, Feb. 7, 1795. Thos. Tyler, signed. Gabriel (X) Ruffat.

p. 192. Whereas Daniel Clark and Ebenezer Rees, late of the City of New Orleans, merchants, in the course of their transactions together, did fall in debt to John Barclay, of Philadelphia, merchant, in the sum of $15,000, rating each dollar at seven shillings and sixpence current and lawful money of the State of Pennsylvania; and whereas John Barclay did, by letter of attorney to Hon Francis Rendon, Esq., intendant of the Province of La., impower him to sue and recover the same, Daniel Clark, considering the indulgence granted the debtors of Louisiana by the Government, and the uncertainty of his life and wishing to secure his friend and creditor, John Barclay, mortgages of his own free will and accord 1000 arpents on Cole's Creek, and 2650 arpents adj. Col. Anthony Hutchins near Ellis's Cliffs on the Miss., now occupied by said Clark. Natchez, 10 Feb., 1795. Signed by Clark. Wit: Edward McCabe, John Girault. Before Gayoso.

p. 193. 12 Feb. 1795. Jonas Scoggins to David Kennedy 4 arpents in front by 40 arpents in depth in Cypress swamp, b. by David Kennedy and Gibson Clark, granted to him 3rd Apr. 1795. Signed by both.

p. 194. 12 Feb. 1795. Polser Shilling, for himself and in name of his sons, sells to John Girault 250 arpents near this Fort, b. by Job Routh, Ebenezer Rees, Don Juan Joseph Rodriguez, Benjamin Monsanto and John Girault aforesaid, which he purchased from Don Juan St. Germain, for $150, on terms. Both signed. // p. 195. Rec'd. of John Girault $100 on account of the present sale, 14 March 1797. Both signed.

p. 195. Inventory: of effects of the late dec'd. John Fowler, taken Feb. 10, 1795. Signed by John Tear, Philip McHugh. // Natchez, 12 Feb. 1795. Patrick Fowler, eldest son of above-mentioned John Fowler, have received into my care the above property. Signed.

p. 195. Natchez, 12 Feb. 1795. Daniel Clark, of District of Buffalo, having received information that Ebenezer Rees, his late partner, had executed an agreement with Col. Peter Bryan Bruin and received from him a mortgage as security of the debt owing by sd Bruin to Clark and Rees, which sd agreement and mortgage were made without Clark's knowledge and participation. He protests against same as he is not named. Rees was only an acting partner and the direction and government was done by Clark, etc. Signed.

p. 196. 14 Feb. 1795. Samuel Flower to Ezekiel Forman land on St. Catherine's Creek, b. as per plat, part of the land which I purchased of Susannah Spell, for $100 paid. Signed.

p. 197. Bernard Lintot to Isaac Caverly a mulatto named "Fortune" aged 25, for $600, on terms. Receipt of full amount, Natchez, May 31, 1800, wit. John Steel.

p. 199. 14 Feb. 1795. Norsworthy Hunter to Thos. M. Green two negroes, natives of Va., for 922 pounds of indigo of 1st quality. Both sign.

p. 199. List of negroes belonging to estate of Richard Ellis at White Cliffs, 31, at Homochitto 115. // p. 200. Will of Richard Ellis, of District of Natchez, planter, weak in body. It is my will that my whole estate be kept together in the same manner as it is now, under the direction of my son John, until all my debts are paid, as well as those contracted by my son John, in his name, as also contracted by my son Richard before his decease, then to be divided as follows: to my dear and beloved wife, Mary, during her life, the use of the plantation whereon I now live at the White Cliffs, containing 1000 acres, also the use of 34 negroes (named), with their increase, four working horses, two plows with gears complete, all my household and kitchen furniture, with all the hogs and cattle belonging to me on said plantation that are not mentioned hereafter, for and during her life then divided as specified; to my son John and his heirs the plantation on Buffalo Creek, granted to Guillermo Chabot, 1600 acres, also 800 acres granted to John Ellis, senior, also 800 acres granted to Wm. Cocke Ellis, on condition that my son John do make good and sufficient titles to my daughter Jane, of 800 acres as near as possible to the settlement that shall be suitable for making indigo; also my tract near the Homochitto, granted to John Hocombe, 667 acres, on condition that he make good and sufficient titles for that half of the tract granted my son John, joining to the tract whereon my son Abram now lives; also 32 negroes (named) with their increase; to my son Abram a tract of land on Cole's Creek, granted to me; also 200 acres gr. to Stephen Jordan that lies within the above tract of 1950 acres, also 20 negroes (named), with their increase; to daughter, Jane, 25 negroes (named) with their increase, during her natural lifetime and my daughter Jane to divide said slaves as she thinks proper between her children in her last will and testament; provided my daughter Jane die without heirs then the abovementioned negroes to be divided between children, John, Abram, Mary and two gr-children, Mary and Martha, daus. of my daughter, Martha, these two drawing one share. To my daughter Mary and her heirs, my plantation at the White Cliffs, 1000 acres, after the decease of my beloved wife, also 150 acres granted to me on the west side of the Mississippi, also 600 acres granted John William Rucker, at the mouth of St. Catherine's Creek, also 11 negroes (named) with their furure increase; to my grand-daughters, Mary and Martha, daus. of my daughter, Martha, 21 negroes (named). If one should die or marry, the other shall be heir to the deceased, if they both should die before they come of age, said negroes and future increase shall be equally divided between my son John, son Abram, dau. Jane and dau. Mary. To Mary, my dau.-in-law, wife of my son William Cocke, deceased, the balance of all debts due me in Virginia, after paying what I owe there, also all the negroes my son, William Cocke, held of mine in his possession in Virginia at the time of his decease. All residue of my estate to be equally divided among my four children, John, Abram, Jane and Mary, in five shares, my grandchildren, Mary and Martha to have one share. 17 Oct. 1792. Signed. Wit: Thos. Burling, John H. White, Sam Davenport, Richard Devall, John Ellis, senior, John Duesbrey. // p. 203. 6 Nov. 1792, the above witnesses ack. their signatures to above will and declared they had not previously been informed of the contents of the will but they had seen Richard Ellis sign same. John Ellis, the eldest, being sick was not present and Richard Devall being out of the District. // p.203-252. Settlement of Estate of Richard Ellis. Large inventory. Description of plantations; 800 arpents on Buffalo Creek, b. by lands of Mr. Chabot, Homochitto River and said creek, with small house, four cabins and a barn 16 ft. square; 1050 arpents at White Cliffs, 5 leagues from Natchez, b. by Daniel Clark, Anthony Hutchins and Don Philip Trevino; 1600 arpents b. by Daniel Clark, and vacant lands; 800 arpents at Buffalo Creek, b. by Jesse Carter and Mrs. Farar; 600 arpents at St. Catherine's Creek b. by Abner Green and vacant lands, 900 arpents in Villa Gayoso District, b. by Daniel Perry; 200 arpents in Villa Gayoso, b. by said Richard Ellis, deceased. // p. 218. Don Estevan Minor, representing that, desiring to settle amicably the affairs of the estate of his father-in-law, Richard Ellis, dec'd., to whom two of the daughters of the petitioner are heiresses, one of whom is lately deceased, petitioner prays that a meeting of all the heirs and executors of said estate may take place as soon as possible to deliberate on all matters concerning same; and in case of a disagreement of parties, that Your Excellency will determine as justice may require. Signed Estevan Minor. Natchez, January 8, 1794. // p. 218. Post of Natchez, 14 January, 1794. In pursuance of foregoing petition, appeared Don Estevan Minor, Abraham Ellis, Jane Rapalje, Benj. Farar representing Mary Ellis, his wife, and John Ellis for himself and Mary Ellis, his mother, heirs of estate of Richard Ellis, deceased, and having conferred relative to the will of said deceased, it was agreed that another meeting should take place. All signed before Gayoso. // p. 218-9. 22 January 1794. Whereas the heirs of the late Richard Ellis did assemble in consequence of the foregoing agreement and determined to leave and refer the settlement of the differences between them concerning the estate of the late Richard Ellis to the decision of Messrs. Anthony Hutchins, Thomas Burling, Ebenezer Rees, Adam Bingaman and Gabriel Benoist. Same authorized to act. And whereas by the decease of one of Major Minor's daughters, he has become a party himself, it is therefore proper that his surviving daughter should be represented by a disinterested person. Wm. Dunbar appointed to represent the said surviving daughter of Major Minor at the arbitration. Signed by all. // June 9, 1794. Natchez. Mr. Rees and Mr. Bingaman obliged to go to New Orleans, Messrs. George Fitzgerald and Joseph Bernard appointed in their places. // p. 221. Letter to Governor Gayoso: Sir: We have again attended to our appointment on the business of the estate of Richard Ellis, decd. to little purpose, nor had we much expected to be useful, from their opposite ideas and different opinions. Our interference therein, we feel would be useless yet we hold ourselves in readiness to obey your future command. Signed by A. Hutchins, Thos. Burling, G. Benoist, Geo. Fitzgerald, Joseph Bernard. 21 June 1794. // 7 July 1794. Another petition of Don Estevan Minor about lack of progress in settling above estate. // Aug. 4, 1794. In reply, John and Abraham Ellis, entrusted with the estate, stated they could not make the settlement required, the said John being very sick. Minor reports that John Ellis crossed the Homochitto 8 days ago and since his return has visited Thos. Burling and William Dunbar, etc. Gayoso orders John and Abraham Ellis to appear on the 8th inst. (August), at the Government House to give a satisfactory answer to the just demand of Major Minor. // Natchez, 13 Aug. 1794. John Ellis appeared and declared that because of illness he could not appear at the time mentioned in the decree and that on Monday, Aug. 18, will produce a faithful account of the whole property. // Inventory follows. Accounts for 135 slaves, 8 having died since death of Richard Ellis, decd., names given. // p. 246. 24 January 1795. May it please Your Majesty: Mrs. Mary Ellis, widow of the deceased Richard Ellis, Esq. and the heirs of Richard Ellis viz: John Ellis, Abraham Ellis, Jane Ellis, wife of George Rapalje, and Mary Ellis, wife of Benjamin Farar, all children of said Richard and Mary Ellis, also Stephen Minor, husband of the deceased Martha Ellis, daughter of said Richard and Mary Ellis and guardian to this surviving daughter, Mary, by the said Martha Ellis, have the honor to represent that an agreement has taken place between the said Mrs. Mary Ellis and the above-mentioned heirs to the estate of Richard Ellis by virtue of which agreement the said Mary Ellis consents to deliver up all property bequeathed to her by the will of her late husband for her use and subsistence during her natural life unto such heirs as are by will appointed to enjoy the same at her decease, under the following conditions; the heirs are to pay said Mrs. Mary Ellis on 1st of March, annually during her natural life, to commence 1st March ensuing, $750 of the coin of Mexico, she shall keep possession of the plantation and house where she now lives, with all the furniture, also five slaves (named), which shall come into the hands of the heirs at her decease, also 10 cows and calves, one pair of oxen, 9 steers, which shall be at her disposal; also cart and furniture, two horses, one mare, 30 sheep, the whole stock of hogs, excepting the part which falls to Jane, now Mrs. Rapalje, shall be given up to Benjamin Farar, who in return obliges himself to furnish the said Mrs. Mary Ellis with pork and bacon for the use of her family. The heirs above-mentioned acknowledge that the said Jane, now Mrs. Rapalje has sole and undisputed right of disposing of her part of the estate. In like manner, the same power is acknowledged to subsist in Stephen Minor with regard to the property left his daughters, in case of the death of the present surviving daughter, Mary, by his deceased wife, Martha Ellis; the said Stephen Minor to have sole right of tutorship of sd dau. Mary, being the natural guardian to his own child, notwithstanding to the contrary contained in the will of testator. Signed by all. // Various settlements and accounts continue to page 252.

p. 252. 16 Feb. 1795. Robert Percy, Lt. of Marines, in the Service of His Brittannic Majesty, having been informed of the death of my father, the late Charles Percy, alcalde of this Government, have repaired hither to settle the account of the estate of my said father, deceased, which I have done with his widow, the other heirs and executors to the will and have received from them the sum of $2000 in full of all claims and demands, renouncing all rights in my favor whatsoever. Signed and acknowledged before Gayoso.

p. 252. 13 March 1795. Daniel Clark and Ebenezer Rees sell to Rebecca McCabe a lot at the landing b. by the principal street, ground of Antonio Gras and Don Francisco de Arroyo, with all buildings, fences, belonging thereto, for $500, on terms. Signed by Rebecca McCabe, Edward McCabe, Ebenezer Rees. // p. 253. Natchez, 7 March 1799. In settlement of accounts with Mrs. Rebecca McCabe, I acknowledge to have received from Mr. William Lintot, $500 in full, for within mentioned house and lot. Signed Ebenezer Rees. Wit. George Ruffer.

p. 253. 4 March 1795. Don Estevan Minor to Thomas Wilkins half of plantation I bought from Don Joseph Vidal in partnership with said Wilkins, dated 2 Oct. last, for $1000 paid. Both sign.

p. 254. 5 March 1795. Thos. Wilkins indebted to Don Estevan Minor for $6000 which sum he lent me without interest, binds himself to pay, mortgaging as security four negroes, George, Anthony, Baker and Ben, 65 head of cattle, 200 hogs, 4 horses, 5 pr. of oxen, 27 sheep and 800 arpents of land 2 leagues from Fort, b. by Joseph Bernard, Charles Norwood and Dorothea Henderson, which said plantation he bought in partnership with said Minor from Don Joseph Vidal. Both sign.

p. 255. 13 March 1795. Don Lewis Faure to Don Francisco Gutierez de Arroyo, lot in this town with dwelling house 35 ft. long by 40 ft. deep with all other buildings, gates and fences, for $1600 (terms.) Both sign.

p. 256. 14 March, 1795. Don Antonio Marmillion to Don Manuel Lopez, merchant, lot at the landing, b. by ground of Don Antonio Gras, Edward McCabe and the two streets, which lot he bought from Polser Shilling, for $575. Both sign.

p. 257. Inventory of Asahel Lewis. Natchez, 17 March 1795. In presence of Don Estevan Minor and Ebenezer Rees, Don Manuel Gayoso de Lemos opened a cypress box which had a good lock and key, and found the following: Receipt from James Willey for a negro belonging to Hugh McGary; note drawn by William Collins for an ox and a hog; receipt from Garret Rapalye senior to his son Garret Rapalye for $12; a sale of a negro from Jacob Nash; a receipt from Mary Carpenter; sale of a horse by William Collins; a draft of Archibald Robertson on Edward McCabe; account against James Rose, deceased, for $18; a bond drawn by Charles Profit; a draft of Mrs. Sybil Nash on the deceased; a memo of payment to Mr. Wells; a draft by Wm. Bacon on his brother, John Bacon, for 5 bu. of corn; freedom of a negro woman "Emma" and her son "Henry", not witnessed. Inventory also included some wearing apparel and the whole was delivered to Joseph Barnard, agent for the estate. // p. 258. Joseph Murray petitioned that the late Asahel Lewis was indebted to him for $43 which was to have been paid in plank; therefore he prays that Your Excellency be pleased to order him the amount in plank so that the petitioner may be able to finish the house he is building. Natchez, 13 March 1795. Signed. // Wm. Kirkwood made oath that the acct. of $23 against the estate of Asahel Lewis is correct. 27 Mch. 1795. Before Ezekiel Forman.

p. 259. Natchez, 23 March 1795. Norsworthy Hunter and Stephen Scriber agree to exchange lands as follows: Hunter delivers to sd Scriber 200 arpents in District of Villa Gayoso, b. by Eben Rees and Parker Carradine, which said land he bought of Joshua Collins, which he now delivers to the aforesaid Scriber, together with six cows, in exchange for 350 arpents on the north branch of Cole's Creek b. by lands of James Elliot, granted to said Scriber by Gov. Genl. Both signed.

p. 259. 3 March 1795. Gerard Brandon indebted to George Fitzgerald for $550, Mexican milled, binds himself to pay within a year, mortgaging two negroes, "Buck" and "Phylis". Signed. // Note: George Fitzgerald agrees that he will wait some months before he puts this mortgage in force in case Brandon should not return from the U. S. at the expiration of the term mentioned. Both sign. // 29 April 1799. Receipt of George Fitzgerald, of Adams County, Miss. Ter., to Gerard Brandon, of same place, for the full and entire payment of the within bond and mortgage which he hereby makes null and void. Wit: George Selser. // March 6, 1795. George Fitzgerald, exor. of the will and agent for the estate of David Munro, decd., has received from Gerard Brandon, also of this Government, planter, the sum of $400, being part payment of a tract of land bought by sd Brandon at public sale of the property of sd estate for $800, the remaining $400 whereof to be paid January next, as will appear by the sale.

p. 261. 9 April 1795. John Welton gives power of atty. to Don Juan Girault to recover and receive from Manuel Madden such sums of money due and owing from him to me in virtue of an award by arbitration in this district. Post of Natchez. Signed.

p. 261. Apr. 11, 1795. Don Joseph Vidal to Capt. Elias Beauregarde, representing widow of the late Don Juan Bienvenue, Capt. of the militia, 1000 arpents, 3 leagues below Red River on east bank of River Mississippi, granted 22 January 1793 by Gov. Genl., for $500 paid. Both signed.

p. 262. 14 Apr. 1795. Samuel Levi Wells, of Opelousas, now at this Post of Natchez, to John Scott, Master Carpenter at this Post, a negro woman "Nina", aged 35, and a mulatto girl "Lucy", aged 10, which I bought from Ebenezer Dayton, for $647 paid. Both sign.

p. 263. 15 Apr. 1795. Don Juan O'Connor to Charles McKiernan 500 arpents at the Little Gulf, for $346, which he has received. Both sign.

p. 264. 15 Apr. 1795. Don Juan Connor to Charles McKiernan two lots at the landing of this Post, with all buildings, gates, fences, etc., one of which he purchased from Nathaniel Tomlinson and the other from James Kirk, for $525, being the appraisal in pursuance of the agreement made by him and McKiernan at N. O. Both sign.

p. 265. 18 Apr. 1795. Eustace Humphreys sells to Henry Milburn 300 arpents b. by Adam Bingaman and Daniel Clark, for $300. Wit: John Still Lee. Both sign.

p. 265. 18 Apr. 1795. John Foster to William Selkrig and George Furney part of a tract he bought from Joseph Calvit, beginning at southeast corner, etc., on a branch of St. Catherine's Creek. All sign. Wit: John Still Lee.

p. 266. 12 Nov. 1794. Caleb Owings to Mr. John Girault, of the Government of Natchez, power of atty. to sell, rent or otherwise dispose of my property lying on the waters of St. Catherine's Creek. Also to recover 90 bu. of corn, rent due by Cady Raby. Signed: Caleb Owings. Wit: J. Eldergill, Eben Rees. // p. 267. Natchez, 20 Apr. 1795. By authority of the foregoing, Juan Girault sells to Andrew Beall all right of aforesaid Owings to 200 arpents bought by said Caleb Owings from John White, 11 Feb. 1785, by sale executed before Raphael Perdonio, notary public, for $200, received in note of said Beall. Signed Juan Girault.

p. 267. Don Joseph Vidal to Antonio Novella a lot b. by ground of Miguel Solibellas, Andres Gil and two streets, for $100, paid. 22 April 1794. Before Grand-Pre.

p. 268. 22 Apr. 1795. Jacob Phillis, of this District, planter, to Don Joseph Vidal, a negro man "Ben", aged 26, nat. of Pa., for $375 paid. Both sign. Before Grand-Pre.

p. 268. 23 Apr. 1795. James Truly to Catharine Caudel negro "Jesta", aged 40, nat. of Guinea, for $300, on terms, said payment to be made to Antonio Gras, agent for the estate of Francisco Bazo and Co. to whom sd negro formerly belonged, the present seller being unable to pay for him. Francisco Caudel signed. His wife does not know how to write. Signed: James Truly.

p. 269. 10 May 1795. Thomas Calvit, of this District, planter, of his own free will and accord, out of the great love which I bear to John and James Calvit, sons of my brother, Joseph Calvit, minors, a gift of a negro wench, "Sene", aged 21, with her son "Isham", aged 4, and a negro lad "Harry" aged 8, which said slaves with all their children, male and female, to be divided between said John and James Calvit when they shall be of age to manage their property. Signed. // Joseph Calvit, father of said minors being present accept the foregoing gift of my brother in their favor, receiving said slaves in my possession and binding myself for their care.

p. 270. 2 May 1795. Thos. Calvit, of this District, planter, of my own free will and accord, and account of great love to Patsy Calvit, dau. of Joseph Calvit, gift of negro girl "Phillis", aged 3, Joseph Calvit, father of said Patsy being present, accepts the foregoing gift of his brother, Thomas Calvit, in her favor, receiving the said slave into his possession, binding himself to the care of same for his daughter, Patsy Calvit.

p. 271. Natchez, Mch. 2, 1795. Petitioners, having been indulged by their creditors with the term of two years to pay their debts in and being apprehensive from the loss of crops, etc. of failing in their engagement, ask permission to dispose of their plantation at public sale Saturday the 7th inst. on terms proposed. Signed John and Alexander Henderson. // Granted, same date, by Gayoso. // p. 271-2. Natchez, March 7, 1795. Sale of above plantation, 1200 arpents, on St. Catherine's Creek, b. by Sam'l. Flowers, Reuben Gibson, William Vousdan, Gideon Gibson and the said creek, with all buildings, payable one-fourth cash, the rest in indigo, clean cotton and cash; cried until noon; adjudged to Don Estevan Minor at $200, he being the highest bidder. // p. 272. Same, 11 March 1795. Same result. // Same, 23 March 1795. Adjudged to John Henderson for account of himself and his brother, Alexander Henderson, for $500. Wit: Estevan Minor, Juan Girault, W. D. Baker, Philip P. Turpin, John Farquhar. Before De Grand-Pre.

p. 272. 24 May 1795. Don Francisco De Arroyo, of this Post of Natchez, planter, to Joseph Lambert a negro woman "Lydia", aged 20, which he bought from John Williams 21 March 1794, for $425. Signed. // p. 273. 20 June 1796. Estevan Minor and Don Joseph Vidal, attys. for Don Francisco de Arroyo, ack. to have recd. from Joseph Lambert full payment for the negro woman in the foregoing sale. Both sign. Wit: J. Murdoch.

p. 273. Post of Natchez, 7 May 1795. Rachael Carter, wife of Nehemiah Carter, of Second Creek, out of great love I bear to my three sons, Nehemiah, Parsons and Isaac, do of my free will and accord make them a gift of 500 arpents in this District, b. by John Bolls, Henry Phips, Samuel Phips and Osborn Sprigg, granted to me by the Gov. Gen'l. of this Province 16 May 1791, with all buildings, gates and fences. Signed Rachel Carter, with the approbation of Caudel.

p. 274. 10 May 1795. Don Pedro Camus to Phillip Engel a lot near the Fort of Natchez, 84 ft. front by the usual depth, with a house thereon, in exchange for a barge to him belonging, with which Camus is satisfied. Both sign.

p. 275. 19 May 1795. James Cole, of this Govt. of Natchez, planter, to James Stuart, of same, sadler, a negro boy "Jack", aged 6, raised in my own family, for $100 paid. Both sign.

p. 276. Will of Samuel Rainer, infirm in body; to son Jesse negro man "Joseph" and negro wench "Suky"; to son Daniel negro "Hiram", negro girl "Nanny"; also to sons Jesse and Daniel, to own jointly, Nanny's child "Joseph"; to dau. Elizabeth Mathews and her heirs negro wench "Nancy"; and to my sons, Jesse and Daniel, and my dau. Elizabeth, all my cattle and horses, hogs and plantation utensils, to be equally divided; if my daughter, Elizabeth, has no issue her part to go at her decease to my sons, Jesse and Daniel. If my beloved wife, Mary, survive me then my will to be of no force until her decease. William Gilbert and James Foster, executors. Wit: Joseph Calvit, Jesse Harper, John Bullin, David Gibson, Daniel Whitaker, Moses Lewis, William Lewis. 14 Jany. 1795. // p. 277-8. Natchez, 10 June 1795. Will above produced before Grand-Pre by William Gilbert and proved by witnesses who signed. James Foster and William Gilbert accepted appointment as exors. // p. 278. 11 March 1795. Jesse Rainer, of the District of Prairie de Rocher in the County of St. Clair, Territory of the United States Northwest of River Ohio, farmer, sends greetings: Whereas Samuel Rainer, father of sd Jesse Rainer, now lives in the District of Natchez in the dominion of His Most Catholic Majesty and is now in advanced years and whereas by reason of the great distance between the County of St. Clair and Natchez, where sd Samuel Rainer now resides, it will be very inconvenient if not impossible for said Jesse to arrive at Natchez aforesaid whenever sd Samuel Rainer shall depart this life (which God prolong), the said Jesse appoints his dear brother, Daniel Rainer, his true and lawful atty. to recover and receive all such sums, bequests, etc., his share of said estate of his father. Jesse (X) Rainer. Before John Edgar, Judge of the Court of Common Pleas of said County of St. Clair. Ter. of U. S. N. W. of Ohio River. // p. 279. Natchez, 13 June 1795. The heirs of Samuel Rainer, being informed of the contents of the will, (1) the widow of the deceased Samuel Rainer renounces the clause in said will authorizing her to keep in her possession the part of the estate pertaining to her daughter, Elizabeth Rainer, wife of James Matthews, the said widow obliging herself to deliver to her said daughter immediately the whole left her by sd will, (2) Daniel Rainer obliges himself to pay to his sister, Elizabeth Rainer, May next $100, for which sum he has given his sister his note; (3) Elizabeth Rainer, wife of James Mathews, shall have full right to dispose of her property; in other respects the will shall remain in full force. Maria (X) Rainer, Daniel (X) Rainer, Elizabeth Mathews, William Gilbert, James Foster. De Grand-Pre.

p. 280-1. 3 June 1795. Daniel Douglass, master saddler, at this Post of Natchez, to David Ferguson and John Murdoch two lots in this town, each 175 ft front by 150 ft depth, Nos. 1 and 2, Sq. 11, granted 3 March, present year. All sign.

p. 281-2. 11 June 1795. Daniel Clark to Daniel Ogden, of Bayou Sarah, planter, three slaves, for $1000, paid. Both sign.

p. 282-3. Will of Ezekiel Forman, of Dist. of Natchez, planter, weak in body. After my just debts discharged by my executor, all my estate which may remain be divided agreeably to law, hereby reserving to myself one-third and one-fifth of same, my beloved wife, Margaret Forman executrix and well-beloved friends, Wm. Dunbar, Ebenezer Rees and Banajah Osman executors and the faithful guardians of my dear children. Mr. Joseph Barnard to take an inventory. 7 May 1795. Signed: E. Forman. Wit: C. West, Theodore Stark, John Lum, Jr., John Lum, Thos. Lanphur. // p. 283. 6 June 1795. Post of Natchez. Ebenr. Rees presented will of Ezekiel Forman, Esq. who died in Dist. of St. Catherine's Cr. on his own plantation on 29 May 1795. // Proved by witnesses present. Executors accepted appointment. // Natchez, 12 June 1795. Will of Ezekiel Forman hereby approved. Grand-Pre.

p. 285. Natchez, 17 June 1795. Elizabeth Whittle exchanges 46 arpents in settlement of Second Creek, b. by Arthur Cobb, Daniel Clark, Pedro Surget and other land belonging to her, to Pedro Surget for 46 arpents b. by lands of said Elizabeth Whittle and other lands of Pedro Surget. Both sign. Wit: William Gillespie.

p. 286. 18 June 1795. William Vousdan, Capt. of 1st Co. of Mounted Volunteers of Natchez, to David Ross, of New Orleans, merchant, power-of-atty. to take and use all lawful means in the Superior Ecclesiastical Tribunal of this Province necessary to the settlement and confirmation of proceedings in a certain suit between myself and Mrs. Hannah Lum, of this District. Documents were ordered to be transmitted to the sd Tribunal for examination and such other ends as may be necessary finally to determine the case; hereby granting authority to the Justices of His Majesty to compel me to the performance of the same as if Judgment had already been given therein. Signed.

p. 286. Natchez, 25 June 1795. Daniel Clark declares whereas on Feb. last past, he gave special power of atty. to Ebenezer Rees to recover his debts and debts due the house of Clark and Rees from inhabitants of this Government, he has now, for sundry causes, revoked such power, without meaning to impeach the good faith and reputation of the said Rees. Wit: Bryan Bruin. Signed.

p. 287. 26 June 1795. Daniel Clark to Anthony Hutchins full power to recover and collect the debts due and owing to the late house of Clark and Rees and all sums owing to me. Wit: Bryan Bruin. Signed.

p. 287. Natchez 6 July 1795. Sally West and Isaac Tabor mutually covenant and agree as follows: The said Tabor declares to have sold and delivered to Sally West 75 arpents, being part of a plantation which was surveyed for him in virtue of a decree of Governor Genl. of the Province, dated Feb. 15, 1788, which said land shall be taken from the southeast corner of said tract, according to plot and to be between the line of George Weigle and a brook that crosses the line of Thomas Green and if this corner between the brook and the lines of Thomas Green should not contain 75 arpents, the line of Weigle shall be followed towards the land of Mr. Dunbar, so as to complete the sd quantity and binds himself to procure for the said Sally West good and sufficient titles within 3 months from date for which Sally West binds herself to pay aforesaid Isaac Tabor $100. Both sign. // p. 288. Natchez 17 Dec. 1797. Isaac Tabor acknowledges to have received from Sally West $100 in full and final payment of the foregoing obligation. Signed. Wit: John Foster.

p. 288. 9 July 1795. Ebenezer Rees declares that 12 March 1787, he formed a partnership with Daniel Clark as instrument in his possession will show, which instrument although the same expired in year 1790, still tacitly exists with respect to payment and recovery of debts owing the said partnership. Protests against Clark giving power of attorney to Anthony Hutchins to collect debts of partnership which may occasion much prejudice and damage to Rees. Signed.

p. 289. 18 July, 1795. John Scott, master builder, to Don John Joseph Vidal lot joining the Fort, No. 3, Sq. No. 1, in this town, with two dwelling houses, kitchens, stables and other buildings thereon, for $700 paid. Both signed.

p. 290. Will of Mathew White, of Natchez upon the Mississippi River, in Province of West Florida, planter, in perfect health. To my dear and loving wife, Elizabeth White, all my estate, real and personal, for her use and the bringing up my sons, Charles and John Hampton White, to hold as my widow but in case she remarries before my youngest son attains the age of 21 years, she is to have one-third equal part which at her death is to revert to my estate; the other two-thirds to be applied to support and maintenance of my said sons. My respected friends, Bernard Lintot and Alexander Moore executors. Oct. 1788. Signed. Wit: William Savage, Constantine MacKenna, Sam'l. Flower, Geroge Fitzgerald, Peter Walker, J. Henderson, W. Murray. // p. 292. Natchez, 13 Feb. 1795. Elizabeth White asks that, in order to reduce the expense of managing the estate of her deceased husband, Matthew White, that she be sole executrix as she has two sons both capable of assisting her. Signed. // p. 293. 17 May 1795. Not granted. Sig. Grand-Pre. Decree that the will of Matthew White be approved without delay. Testimony of witnesses to prove will. p. 294. Elizabeth White, Bernard Lintot and Alexander Moore appointed as executors of foregoing will and make oaths to perform same faithfully and legally. Robert Scott, attorney for Alexander Moore. p. 195. Inventory: plantation 1050 arpents; crop of 50 arpents of corn and indigo; 16 negroes; 15 cows with calves; 22 cattle, 2 yoke of oxen; 3 horses. Signed Elizabeth White, widow, and Charles and John Hampton White, sons. Wm. Dunbar and Thomas Burling appointed appraisers. Total $6565. // p. 198. Villa Gayoso, 14 July 1795, at plantation, William Murray, Esq., Alcalde of this Dist., in presence of Roger Dixon and Lacy Rumsey, testifies as to signing the will of Matthew White. He was sick so had not acknowledged before.

p. 299. Inventory of late Ezekiel Forman, by Joseph Barnard. Exrs. Mrs. Margaret Forman, Wm. Dunbar, Ebenezer Rees and Benajah Osmun. Mr. George Fitzgerald and Gabriel Benoist appraisers. Thomas Lanphier and Robert Penery assistant witnesses. A long list, (to p. 314). $31.431.

p. 314. Natchez, 1 Aug. 1795. Information by means of Jacob Piercy of the death of Joseph Murray, of this Post, merchant, which took place at New Orleans, said Piercy declaring that he attended the funeral; seals placed at his late dwelling house and store in the new town of this Post to secure his property for the benefit of whom it may concern. Maurice Stackpoole was there entrusted by said deceased with his house and store; was informed by him that a shipment of goods had lately arrived belonging to sd deceased which were in a separate store. . . . In the dwelling on the back of the lot, inhabited by the sister-in-law of the deceased, nothing but her wardrobe and some trifles in daily use. The shop was left in charge of John Murdoch and Robert Scott.

p. 315. Natchez, 10 Oct. 1794. Death of Benjamin Monsanto, planter, took place at New Orleans. Property placed in care and charge of Mr. James McIntosh, until some person properly authorized shall appear to whom same may be delivered. Inventory to be made by Don Joseph Vidal and Don Antonio Cruzat. At plantation of Benjamin Monsanto, 3 mi from Post, Mrs. Maria Williams was there; said she had been left in charge of plantation, etc., by Monsanto and his wife when they went to New Orleans. Whereupon she was requested to declare on oath the property and effects in her care belonging, which she did. (p. 316) Inventory: 500 arpents on St. Catherine's Creek, b. by David Williams, decd., and Don Juan Rodriguez, where Monsanto resided. // 14 Oct. 1794. Inventory follows; All important papers in New Orleans. Signed by widow Clair Monsanto. // p. 317-8. Appraisement by Sutton Banks and Don Juan Girault. Total $1901. (Property only.) 3 July 1795. // p. 319. Petition of Don Manuel Monsanto and Company for delay of three years for payment of their debts. His brother, Benj. Monsanto, a partner in trade. Contested by Donna Clara Mota, widow of deceased Benjamin Monsanto. (No date.) p. 326. Benjamin Monsanto's will. Weak; debts to be paid; $2500, milled coin, to be paid to beloved wife immediately, being the sum she brought me in marriage, as will appear by our marriage contract deposited in Perdonno's office, the first year after the fire at New Orleans; negro boy "Hazard" does by right belong to my wife, he being her sole property and paid for with money of her own saving. If it embarrasses my brother to pay wife, he is to give good and undoubted security for same, and pay her regularly interest on same for maintenance; household goods belong to wife; one half of the residue to my beloved wife and one-half to my brother. Wife and brother and friends, Bernard Lintot, Wm. Dunbar and David Williams, exrs. 25 Jany. 1792. Wit: Jane Rapalje, Elizabeth Whittle, Eliza Watts, William (X) Thompson, William Bacon, Daniel Strickland, Samuel Flower and Stephen Mayes. Proved by witnesses and recorded, 5 Nov. 1794. // p. 327-8. List of debts owing Messrs. Monsanto and Company:

William Alston
Robert Abrams
Isaac Alexander
Christian Bingaman, Sr.
Christian Beingaman, Jr.
William Brocus
William Barland
Jeremiah Bryan
Wm. Bonner
Joseph Bonner
Benjamin Belk
John Baker
John and Daniel Burnet
Francis Brezini
Sutton Banks
John Boles
James Cole, Sr.
John Cole
Charles Carter
Job and Richard Cory
Wm. and John Coleman
George Cochran
Jesse Carter
Jacob Shilling
John Staybraker
Thomas Smiley
John Sweazey
Nathaniel Tomlinson
Moses Armstrong
William Cooper
Henry Cooper
William West
Walker and Henderson
Joel Weed
Robert Weathers
John Wiley
John Calvit
William Curtis
John Carroll
William Crane
William Calvit
Jacob Cobun
Nemehiah Carter
Arthur Cobb
Daniel Chambers
Charles Cason
Robert Carter
George Cook
Dueit
David Smith
Wm. Benj. Smith
James Kelly
Wm. Kirkwood
Richard King
Caleb King
Justus King

Philip Turpin
Bennet Truly
Isaac Tabor
James Truly
Mathew White
Cato West
Wm. Murray
Henry Manadue
Alex. McRay
Matthew McCulloch
Wm. Liles
Melling Wood [Woolley]
Jesse Hamilton
Joel Byrd
Thomas Burling
Richard Bacon
(with mortgage of tract)
James Glascock
Daniel Calaghan
Abner Green
Samuel Gibson
John Girault
Randal Gibson
Samuel Heady
Widow Wm. Henderson
David Mitchell
Thomas Hubbard
Joseph Holmes
John Hartley
Jeptha Higdon
James Hayes
Dibdal Holt
Alex. Henderson
Isaac Johnson
Thomas Jordan
Jonas Ilor
Nathan Swazey
Mathew Jones
Madame Livandeau
Lauriaic
Richard Roddy
Wm. Wilson
James Harman for Proctor
Samuel Cooper
Rocheblanc
Madame Charbonet
Dunbar
Mr. Villeret
John Lum
William Lee
John Lusk
David Lambert
David Gleeson
Thomas Green
Robert Weathers
Richard Harrison
Jonathan Parker
John McFarland
Abram Mayes
Stephen Mayes
Roswell Mygatt
Joseph Miller
James Nicholson
Henry Nicholson
Peter Nelson
William Owens
Samuel and Harry Phips
Barnabas and Daniel Perry
Frances Province
Mr. Row
Cader Raby
Daniel Rainer
Thomas Reed
Archibald Rhea
Israel and Phil. Smith
Francis Spain
Ebenezer Smith
Ebenezer Dayton
Thomas Daroch
Richard Dunn
John Ellis
William Erwin
Thomas Essex
Richard Ellis
Hardy Ellis
James Elliott
Joseph Flowers
James Fordric
Isaac Fyffe
John Odam
John Foster
Wm. Ferguson
Thomas Freeman
Ignacio Babin
Brosur
Joseph Hooter

Lists of debts due in the City (N. O.) and Posts follow.

p. 329. Act. of Dower. N. O. 24 July 1789. Benjamin Monsanto, of this Province, legitimate son of David Rodriguez Montsanto and Esther Levy, natives of Hague, in the Republic of Holland, declared that Feb. 1787 he contracted marriage with Clara Mota, legitimate daughter of Solomon la Mota and Rica Coen, natives of Curracoa, who brought him $1500 in Mexican silver and deponent proffered her $1000 of same, in compensation for her just right of one-tenth of estate and she acknowledges same as her dower. Signed: Benjamin Rodriguez Monsanto, Claire Motte. // p. 331. 6 Feb. 1795. Manuel Monsanto gives Power of Atty. to William Gilbert, of Post of Natchez.

p. 332. Natchez, 21 Aug. 1795. Pierre Picard desired to put himself with William Benjamin Smith, Master Shoemaker of known ability, as apprentice, for two years, ending Aug. 21, 1797, etc. Pierre (X) Picard, Wm. B. Smith. Wit: Wm. Dunbar, Ebenezer Rees.

p. 333. David Phelps is indebted to Robert Scott, for $180, which he advanced him for his journey to the Fort of St. Fernando de las Barrancas, and gives him full power to receive his pay as Surgeon of the said Fort until he is fully paid. Natchez, 22 Aug. 1795. Signed.

p. 334. 26 Aug. 1795. Don Estevan Minor to Alexander Ross, of this Government, planter, a plantation on waters of Second Creek, b. by lands of the Widow Sarah Holmes, William McIntosh, Arthur Cobb, Abraham Ellis and Don Pedro Surget, of these Provinces, 1500 arpents, having sold the other 160 arpents to Solomon Wisdom: for $1040, paid. Signed.

p. 335. Petition of Letitia Culberson, as Tutress of her daughter, Nancy Linn has in her possession a negro boy, aged 7, named "Tony", which slave having been sickly, she has determined with the approbation of her said daughter, to sell said slave for her account and with the proceeds thereof to purchase something else not liable to same risk. 24 Aug. 1795. // Same date. Granted, on giving security for the value of negro boy. Signed: Grand-Pre. // 26 Aug. 1795. Sale of same to George Cochran, of Post of Natchez; negro is the son of a negro woman left to her daughter by her father, William Linn; sells for $80, in hand paid. David Phelps, appointed Surgeon of the Post of Fernandez, security. Wit: Robert Scott, Francis Nailor. Signed: Phelps, Letitia Culberson, Nancy Linn.

p. 336. 29 Aug. 1795. Widow Sarah Swezy, of her own free will, makes gift deed to her daughter, Deborah Swezy, wife of Israel Luse, of this Government, a negro girl "Peggy", aged 15, nat. of Natchez. Signed: Sarah (X) Swezey, Deborah (X) Swezey. Wit: James McGill, David Swazey. Before Grand-Pre.

p. 337. 3 Sept. 1795. John Scott, Master Builder of this Fort, to Don Joseph Vaucheret, of this Government, a negro fellow "Cromwell", aged 35, nat. of Africa, which I purchased of Alexander Moore; for $400, on terms. Signed. Wit: Juan Vaucheret, Edward McCabe. Grand-Pre. // p. 338. May 5, 1797. Receipt for full payment.

p. 338. 22 Aug. 1795. Gabriel Swazey, with most profound respect, represents that his brother, Elijah Swazey, died some years ago, having made a will, which from the ignorance of your petitioner has not been presented until now. // Aug. 1795. Let witnesses to will appear. Grand-Pre. // Will of Elisha Swazey, weak; after debts are paid all estate to my brother, Gabriel, who is made sole executor. 5 Oct. 1789. Wit: Nathan Swayze, Caleb King, Henry (H) Lucas, John Ormsby. // 9 Sept. 1795. Will proved by all witnesses except John Ormsby who is absent in the U. S.

p. 340. 12 Sept. 1795. Don Estevan Minor to John Minor, of this Government, planter, a negro lad named "Sango", nat. of Africa, aged 18, for $400, paid. Signed.

p. 341. Exchange. 16 Sept. 1795. Ebenezer Rees, res. of this Govt., to Don Manuel Garcia de Texada negro "Baptist" in exchange for a negro "Robert", which said Texada has delivered to me, with $140, in hand paid. Signed. // 27 Apr. 1797. Ebenezer Rees declares the above made by him as atty. for Daniel Clark and on account of partnership of Clark and Rees. // May 10, 1797. Wm. Dunbar, Esq., atty. for Daniel Clark, confirms the foregoing exchange. Wit: Don Pedro Walker, Joshua Howard.

p. 342. Will of Charles West, of District of Natchez, low state of health; to wife, Sarah West, whole estate during her life or widowhood, in either case, estate to my three children, Thomas West, Cato West, Mary West or as many as may be living. Extrs. loving wife; Messrs. James Truly, David Odam, and brother, Cato West, appraisers. Sept. 1, 1795. Signed. Wit: James Truly, David Odam, Billy Chaney, Everard Green, Parker Carradine, James E. Winn. // Proved by above witnesses, 17 Sept. 1795.

p. 343. 28 Sept. 1795. Agreement; Leonard Kepley and Charles Peack agreed as follows. Kepley to sell Peack his plantation, 350 arpents, in the settlement of Big Black, including the Block-house, in full payment Kepley ack. receipt of $25; Peack to have the land the 1st November next, also a boat to ferry passengers, which is included in the sale. Leonard (X) Kepley, Charles Peack. Wit: Wm. Thomas.
p. 344. Said Kepley gives power of atty. to Wm. Thomas, Dep. surveyor, to transfer land as soon as titles arrive from New Orleans, 28 Sept. 1795.

p. 344. Nov. 21, 1787. Division of property. The heirs of Richard and Samuel Swazey, late planters of this District, represent that the said Richard and Samuel bought of the late Capt. Amos Ogden 19,800 arpents of land north of the Homochitto, being part of a grant of 25,000 arpents by the King of England. The heirs ask for a division. Signed: Sarah Swazey, Samuel Swazey, Nathan Swazey, Elijah Swazey,

Hannah Curtis, William Weeks, Stephen Swazey, Rachel Swazey, David Lambert, Rhoda Lambert, Richard Swayze, Elisha Swazey, Gabriel Swazey, Sarah King, Lydia Cory, Mary King. // Plan of Division wit. by Isaac Johnson, Joseph Barnard, Ebenezer Dayton, 22 Sept. 1795, and signed by: Hannah (H) Curtis, Obediah Brown, Elijah Swazey, Hannah Chambers, David Lambert for wife, Rhoda, Elijah for Stephen Swazey and Rachel Bell, Reuben Brown, Samuel, Nathan and Elijah.

p. 346. Oct. 1, 1795. Helena Adams, to son, William Adams a negro boy, "Harry", aged 7, nat. of Natchez. Eleanor (E. A.) Adams. Wit: John Williams.

p. 346. 2 Oct. 1795. Joseph Vidal to Estevan Minor 800 arpents, 2 leagues from Post, b. by Joseph Barnard, Charles Norwood and Dorothea Henderson which said plantation I bought at public sale of the estate of William Henderson, decd.; for $1000 paid. Both sign. Wit: Thos. Wilkins.

p. 347. 7 Oct. 1795. John Stampley to Hugh Matthews and Richard Roddy 400 arpents, part of plantation on which said Roddy now dwells, to be equally divided between them; for $50 from Richard Roddy received and from Mathews a horse at $20 and $60 in silver and a note for $40 and from both a good title to 300 arpents of land in this Government. Signed by John Stampley and Richard Roddy.

p. 348. 7 Oct. 1795. John Courtney to Jonathan Jones, both of this Government, 400 arpents in the District of Villa Gayosa, at the place called "the Bluffs", b. by Wm. Curtis and His Majesty's lands, gr. to me in 1789; for 8 cows with their calves, received in payment. Both signed. Wit: Mce. Stacpoole, Ebenr. Rees.

p. 349. 10 Oct. 1795. Samuel Flower, physician, has received of Bernard Lintot, exor. of estate of Richard Carpenter and guardian of James and Sarah Carpenter, children and heirs of sd Richard Carpenter, decd., $100 (Mexican) which he binds himself to pay with interest on demand of sd Lintot, at 6%. Signed. Wit: John Potter.

p. 349. 11 Oct. 1795. Thomas Wilkins makes bond to pay Bernard Lintot, exor. of estate of Richard Carpenter and guardian of the minor children for $500 to him lent by Lintot, 14 Feb. last past. Signed. Wit: Maurice Stacpoole. // Natchez, 31 May 1800. Lintot's receipt for the above and interest.

p. 350. 19 Oct. 1795. William Dunbar, Dep. Surv. and exor. of will and estate of Benj. Farar, decd., late of South Carolina, planter, and Benjamin Farar, only son and heir of all lands of sd deceased in State of S. C., give power-of-atty. to Ebenezer Potter, of same place, to direct, manage, etc. all affairs relating to said estate of said Benj. Farar, decd. in S. C. Both signed. Wit: Benajah Osmun, Ebenezer Rees.

p. 350. 21 Oct. 1795. In consequence of the death of James Irwin, who died intestate, leaving several children, minors, Joshua Howard appointed tutor and curator to said minors, namely: James, aged 24, Joseph, aged 22, Isaac, 20, Margaret 16, William 14; appointment accepted.

p. 351. 21 Oct. 1795. William Barland, of Natchez, taylor, to Thomas Tyler, of same, Lots 2 and 4, Sq. 16, part of the land granted me in 1782; for $140. Wit: Bennet Truly.

p. 352. 5 Nov. 1795. Anne Frances Farar, wife of Samuel Charles Young, of the District of Pointe Coupee, power of atty. to said husband to manage and conduct her affairs of all kinds. Signed. Wit: Abram Ellis, Nathan Dix.

p. 352. Inventory of property and effects of Alexander Moore, deceased, 10 Nov. 1795. 450 arpents near St. Catherine's Creek, 2-1/2 miles from Fort, bought from Matthew White, deceased, $2500; 160 arpents, 2 miles from Fort, bou. from Mrs. Sarah Truly; 700 arpents, 3 miles from Fort, bought at George Rapalje's sale; 160 arpents, 9 miles from Fort, bought of Wm. Ryan; 1000 arpents, on Bayou Pierre, about 30 miles from Mississippi River, granted to Alexander Moore, junior, deceased, being the same tract bequeathed to William Moore by his deceased father's will; 2364 arpents, near Walnut Hills, about 60 miles from Fort Panmur. // A number of slaves, indigo, etc. appraised at $15,163, Nov. 10, 1795. Signed Samuel P. Moore, Robert Scott, Jane Moore. // p. 354. Division, by agreement, of slaves: Mrs. Jane Moore, $600; Mr. Robert Moore $300, Mr. Robert Scott, on account of his wife, Mrs. Sarah Scott $600; Mr. Samuel P. Moore for himself and brother, James Moore jointly $800. Nov. 10, 1795. Signed by all.

p. 355. 14 Nov. 1795. William Barland to Louis de Lat Lot 4, Sq. 16, between lot of Antonio Gras and that of Don Francisco de Arroyo, being part of land granted to him 1782; for $80 paid. Wit: James Truly.

p. 356. 25 Nov. 1795. Alexander and John Henderson, brothers and partners, of the German Coast, to James Foster, of the Government of Natchez, 100 arpents at St. Catherine's Creek, beg. at a "Post Oak", which serves as a boundary between Alexander Henderson and the land we bought from Richard Harrison, following creek to a rivulet called "Henderson's Spring Branch", etc. for $100 paid. Signed by John Henderson for self and Alexander Henderson. Wit: Edward McCabe.

p. 356. 28 Nov. 1795. John Savage and Peter Riley, both of this Government, an agreement: John Savage permits Peter Riley and wife to live and dwell on his plantation during their natural lives, and Riley, a tanner by trade, and Savage shall erect a tannery where both shall work and equally divide profits. During the time that Savage is unmarried, wife of Riley shall make, mend and wash his clothes. Both sign. Wit: John Ferguson.

p. 357. 27 Nov. 1795. Inventory and appraisement of effects belonging to estate of Doctor Charles West, dec'd. Total $1604. Done at Cole's Creek, and signed by James Truly, David Odam and Cato West. Wit: Will. Ferguson.

p. 358. 28 Nov. 1795. Margaret Dosa, wife of John Williams, with consent of husband, sells to Thos. Martin Lot 4, Sq. 25. for $350, on terms. Wit: Thomas Hughes.

p. 358. From Carondelet, etc., to Manuel Gayoso de Lemos: Decree in consequence of Joseph Murray's death. In pursuance of the petition of Maurice Stacpoole and Juliana Robinson, his wife, praying whereas said Juliana is sole heiress of Joseph Murray, dec'd., named as such in his will, the whole of the estate be delivered to them; granted if said Stacpoole and wife give bond to satisfy and pay all debts and legacies bequeathed by testator. 14 Nov. 1795. // p. 360. Natchez, 9 Dec. 1795. To the Governor: Maurice Stacpoole for himself and wife, Juliana Robinson, presents herewith the order in their favor from the Superior Tribunal of these Provinces for the property and estate inherited by sd. Juliana from her deceased brother-in-law, Joseph Murray. // 9 Dec. 1795. p. 361. G. Cochran, John Scott, Robt. Scott, exors. of will of Joseph Murray, dec'd., do not require security and ask that estate be released to Stacpoole and wife. // p. 361. 9 Dec. 1795. Same done at the late dwelling and store of Joseph Murray, dec'd. in presence of John Murdoch and Juan Girault. Signed by Maurice Stacpoole and Juliana Robinson.

p. 362. Nov. 12, 1794. Thos. Wilkins represents that Widow Henderson is in possession of two slaves which are mortgaged to James Carrick for whom the petitioner is agent, which slaves were left with the widow merely to assist in getting her crop, which, being done, the petitioner asks for appraisement and sale of slaves. Granted. Gayoso. // 22 Nov. 1794. Wm. Dunbar and Wm. Cooper appointed appraisers of above slaves and accepted. // After several offerings and small bids the two slaves were bid in for Carrick by Thomas Wilkins at $150. The appraisement was $350.

p. 363. 12 Dec. 1795. Samuel Flower to Thos. Foster, both of the District of Natchez, 310 arpents on St. Catherine's Creek, same which he purchased of Moses Bonner, with 80 arpents more of a grant of 95 arpents, 21 Apr. 1789, reserving 15 arpents on the line of Reuben Gibson, and also 200 arpents which he purchased of Susannah Spell, b. by land of Moses Bonner, Mistress Cochran and land he sold to Ezekiel Forman, dec'd., for $800 paid in full. Both sign.

p. 364. 12 Dec. 1795. Samuel Flower to Moses Bonner negro "Juba", Creole, aged 19, for $400, paid.

p. 365. 12 Dec. 1795. Thomas Foster to Samuel Flower both of the Natchez District, 380 arpents on St. Catherine's Creek, as per plat, being land I purchased from Joseph Calvit; for $500. Signed.

p. 366. 12 Dec. 1795. George Killian to King Holstein, both of this Government of Natchez, negro man, aged 28, for $400, $200 paid in hand. Both signed.

p. 366. 12 Dec. 1795. Moses Bonner to Samuel Flower 310 arpents on St. Catherine's Creek, b. by lands of Mistress Foster and Mistress Spell, granted 1 Apr. 1789, for $400 paid. Both sign.

p. 367. Will of William Murray of Villa Gayoso District, in Govt. of Natchez, very sick and weak. All property in the Province of Louisiana to remain unsold during the life of my wife, Martha Murray, with the express priviso that her son, James McIntyre, do not live with her, knowing that he would waste and expend any property in his hands. But if he lives with her, property to be sold and divided as the law directs; to Anna Maria Rumsey one-fifth to be paid to her at said Martha Murray's death. All other estate in this or any other country to my beloved son, Wm. Murray, reserving to his mother all her rights provided for by the respective laws of the countries wherein my estate shall be, also to Anna Maria Rumsey the said one-fifth; also to son William a gold watch in hands of Mr. Oliver Pollock, also a ring and stock buckle now in my possession and my seal bearing my arms. Executors: my friends,

William Dunbar, of Second Creek and John Smith, of Villa Gayoso, Esquires, respecting and belonging to this country. I appoint my son, Wm. Murray sole exor. of all and every other part of this my last will. Signed W. Murray. 7 Sept. 1795. Wit: Thos. M. Green, Everard Green, Roger Dixon, Bernard Isenhoot, Jacob (X) Cable, William Smith, Frederick Cable. // 19 Dec. 1795. Proved by witnesses // 3 Dec. 1795. Exors. accepted. p. 371. Inventory and appraisal of above estate. Plantation in District of Villa Gayoso, b. by lands of Jeremiah Routh and William Gillespie, $800, and dwelling house, etc. Total $2862. Sundry papers in possession of Oliver Pollock in the U. S. and sundry drafts and warrants on State of Virginia. 9 Jany. 1796.

p. 372. 14 Jany. 1796. Alexander Ross to Luther Smith, both of Natchez Dist., mulatto lad "Daniel", aged 19, nat. of West Indes, for $500 specie, paid.

p. 372. 20 Jany. 1796. GrandPre having summoned Alexander Ross asked if he had any claim against the estate of John Gali, decd., he answered that he had not, that he had been paid the $1000 owing him from said estate and the mortgage on the sundry slaves had been satisfied. Signed. Wit: Wm. Dunbar.

p. 373. 15 Feb. 1796. Daniel Ogden, of the District of Buffalo, to Alexander Montgomery, of same, a negro woman "Phoebe", aged 23, with child aged 6 mos., for $200 specie. Both sign. Wit: Abram Ellis.

p. 373. Don Estevan Minor to Don Francisco Guttierez de Arroyo negro man "Baptist", aged 35, for $400, on terms. Both sign. 16 Feb. 1796.

p. 374. 16 Feb. 1796. Power from Don Francisco Guttierez de Arroyo to Don Estevan Minor to represent me in every way in this District.

p. 375. 20 Feb. 1796. Mary Higdon, of this Government, to John Calvit and James Calvit, both sons of Joseph Calvit, my son, gift deed of negro man "Jesse", aged 35, to belong to said two children equally. Joseph Calvit accepts same. Signed: Joseph Calvit. Mary (X) Higdon.

p. 375. 24 Feb. 1796. Abram Ellis to Alexander Montgomery negro "Isaac", aged 19, for $500 paid. Both sign. Wit: John Bolls.

p. 376. 24 Feb. 1796. John Bolls, to Joseph Calvit, both of Natchez Dist., negro man "Ned", aged 20, nat. of Guinea, bought from Messrs. Ross and Proffit in 1788, for $400. Both signed. Wit: Abram Ellis.

p. 377. 27 Feb. 1796. Gertrude Solibellas, with permission of her mother, her father being absent, sells to George Overaker, Lot 4, Sq. 2, with house thereon, for $150. Samuel Flower signed at request of Mistress Solibellas, G. Cochran signed at request of Miss Maria Gertrude Solibellas.

p. 377. 28 Feb. 1796. Joshua Howard to James Moore, exor. of estate of his decd. father, Alexander Moore, 500 arpents I purchased of Joshua Stockstill, in the year last past, b. by Chachere, LaFleur, Beesley Pruett and vacant land, for $400 paid. Both signed. Wit: George Cochran.

p. 378. 5 March 1796. Estevan Watts, dwelling at Post of Natchez, power of atty. to Don Christoval de Armas, dwelling in the City of N. O., to prove the distinction of my birth and that of my lawful wife, Frances Asheton Watts, and for that purpose to present writings, witnesses, proofs, etc., necessary thereto. Signed. Wit: John Ellis.

p. 379. 9 March 1796. Thomas M. Green to Louisa Wylie, dau. of John and Louisa Wylie, 100 arpents, being 4 arpents in front on west line, running east along south line to include 100 arpents, part of 800 arpents granted to me; for $100 paid. Signed by Thos. M. Green and John Wylie.

p. 379. 19 March 1796. Mary Savage, legitimate dau. of John Savage and Anne, his lawful wife, declared she is of full age of 25 years and lawfully married to Robert Johnson, and her deceased mother having appointed her brother, Isaac Gaillard, exor. to her will and guardian of said Mary who is sole heiress of her mother, decd., asks receipt and possession of all the property, estate, rents, effects, etc., of the estate of her deceased mother, and does release her said uncle, Isaac Gaillard, from the charge of guardian and executor. Signed Mary Johnson. Wit: Ranaleigh Hogan, James Spain.

p. 380. 19 March 1796. Robert Johnson and Mary Savage, his lawful wife, sell to Mary Foster, negro woman "Flora", aged 36, and her dau. "Lucy", aged ___, and son "Elisha" aged 5, for $800 specie, in hand paid. Signed by Robert and Mary Johnson. Mary (M) Foster. Wit: Raneleigh Hogan, James Spain.

p. 381. 2 April, 1796. Don Juan Girault to Don Simon de Arze, Sergeant of Royal Artillery lot near Fort, part of land which he bought of Wm. Barland; for $42, paid. Both signed.

p. 381. 19 March 1796. Joseph Lambert, cutler, of this Government, to Daniel Grafton, Lt. Militia of same, negro woman "Liddy", aged 22, for $300 paid. Joseph (X) Lambert. Wit: George Cochran.

p. 382. 6 April 1796. David Ferguson and John Murdock, in the name of Reed and Forde, sell to Abner Green, of this Government, planter, two lots in this town, Nos. 3 and 4, in Sq. 15, for $100, paid. Signed Ferguson and Murdock. Wit: John Wilson. // p. 383. Miss. Ter., County of Adams, 21 Nov. 1804. David Ferguson, late agent for Messrs. Reed and Forde, of Philadelphia, and Abner Green, correct error in above deed, which should be Lots 2 and 4 of Sq. 15, and not Lots 3 and 4. Both signed. Wit: J. Girault, Keeper of Records.

p. 383. 9 April 1796, Joshua Stockstill, of this Government, to Joshua Howard 500 arpents near Cole's Creek, as in plat, gr. to him in 1789; for $250, paid. Joshua (X) Stockstill, Joshua Howard. Wit: Roger Dixon.

p. 384. Inventory of estate of Joseph Scofle, decd. $252. Given in by Sarah and John Roberts. Signed Sarah (X) Fake, John (X) Roberts, Wit: William Smith, Solomon Cole. Appraised by Michael Fake and Jacob Holt, appointed. Signed Jacob Krumbholt, Michael (X) Fake. Inventory taken by me, 14 April 1796. John Smith.

p. 384. Benjamin Farar to William Dunbar, both of this Government, full power and authority to represent him in all matters pending between him and his brothers, co-heirs to the estate of their decd. father, Benj. Farar. Signed. 20 Apr. 1796.

p. 385. 20 Apr. 1796. Philip Lewis Alston to John Baptiste Nicolet, of Pointe Coupee, power to represent me in all matters pending between me and Don Lorenzo Sigue and likewise claim a land belonging to me, which, it is said, Penrice has given to Ramier or to some one of his family. Signed. Wit: James McNulty.

p. 385. 22 Apr. 1796. Appraisers of estate of James Erwin, decd., Henry Cooper and Benjamin Holmes, appointed by William Cooper, Esq., report value, $1370. // p. 388. May 27, 1796. Petition of Jennet Erwin, widow of James Erwin, decd. for support in her old age from estate. // Sept. 3, 1796. Order by Gayoso: one-fourth of said estate to be set aside for her.

p. 390. 8 April 1796. Robert Stark to Mary Balk negro woman "Lucy", aged 40, for $300, paid. Thos. Calvit signs for Mary Balk. Wit: Thos. Wood, George Cochran.

p. 391. 28 Apr. 1796. Robert Stark to Benjamin Farar negro "Simon", aged 18, for $500, paid. Both signed. Wit: Richard King, Abram Ellis.

p. 392. 28 Apr. 1796. Robert Stark to Thomas Calvit, both of this District, negro "Juby", aged 21, for $500, paid. Both paid. Wit: Thos. Woods, Geo. Cochran.

p. 392. 22 Sept. 1793. Will of Gabriel Griffing, of Province of La., Dist. of Natchez, in bad health. Exrs. my loving and faithful friends: Cato West, Jeremiah Coleman, Elijah Sweazy. Wife, Hannah, shall hold and enjoy all of my estate during the minority of my beloved children, Jeremiah, Archibald, Eunice, Huldy, and the child my beloved wife is now pregnant with, for the use of raising and educating them; after children come of age if my dear wife remain in widowhood, she to enjoy one-half of my estate during widowhood or natural life when my youngest child arrives to age, other one-half to be equally divided among my children. If wife remarry, whole of estate to be divided among children. Signed. Wit: Job. Cory, Abel Eastman, Daniel Douglass, Samuel Flower, Jacob Cobun, John Orr, John Arden. // 13 Apr. 1796. Above will, sealed, delivered to Grand-Pre. // 7 May 1796. Witnesses Abel Eastman and Job Cory proved will and signatures of the other witnesses who were absent. // p. 395-6. 9 May 1796. Inventory of estate of Gabriel Griffing, by Elijah Swayze, Jeremiah Coleman and Cato West. Wit: Abel Eastman, Alexander Callender.

p. 396. 19 May 1796. David Mitchell to Christian Gilbert 200 arpents in Second Creek District, adj. Isaac Gaillard and land Mitchell exchanged with Israel Smith, being the eastern part of land granted to Samuel Phips, which Mitchell purchased from him, for $300. Wit: Jas. McNulty.

p. 397. 19 May 1796. David Mitchell to Israel Smith, of this Government, a portion of land in the Dist. of Second Creek, the western half of the tract which I purchased of Samuel Phips and ought to contain 200 arpents, adj. Don Philip Trevino and Nicholas Rab; in payment, I have received another tract, 500 arpents on Bayou Sara, granted said Smith in 1790. Both sign. Wit: Jas. McNulty.

p. 397. 28 May 1796. Receipt of George Fitzgerald to Thos. Wilkins for $650, entire payment for two negroes which Fitzgerald bought at public sale of estate of late David Munro, 25 Jany. 1794, the said Wilkins having paid a further sum of $200 and the obligation is void. Both sign. Wit: James Spain.

p. 398. 30 May 1796. Jesse Terry, nat. of the U. S., to Joseph Vidal, Secy. of this Government, a negro wench "Betsy", aged 20, which I had from my wife, Mary Freeman, deceased, to whom same belonged, for $300 paid. Signed. Wit: Edward McCabe, Capt. of Militia. // I, the undersigned certify that the negro woman above-mentioned has been proved to be the property of the above-mentioned Jesse Terry and his wife. (Not dated). Signed H. W. T. Bastrop.

p. 399. 30 June 1796. Henry Richardson to Jesse Ratcliff, both of this Government, 600 arpents in District of Homochitto, which I received from Joshua Howard in exchanged for another tract, for $100 paid. Both sign. Wit: Roger Dixon.

p. 399. 13 June 1796. Francisco Pousset, attorney for David Lejeune, of Bayou Sara, to Robert Collins, of same, 400 arpents on Bayou Buffalo, a grant to him in 1789, for $400, paid. Signed by Pousset, Robert (X) Collins. Wit: John Wall, H. Hunter. // p. 400 12 May 1796. Bayou Sarah, Government of Natchez. Power of David Lejeune, late of the District of Bayou Buffalo, now in Dist. of New Feliciana, to Francisco Pousset, Esq., of Dist. of Bayou Sarah, planter, to accept a deed of conveyance from John O'Reilly of 600 arpents, purchased of him in Dist. of Bayou Sarah. // p. 440-401. 13 June 1796. John O'Reilly to David Lejeune 600 arpents at Bayou Sarah, as granted sd O'Reilly 30 March 1795; for $600 paid. Francisco Pousset, being present and holding a special power to receive said land, accepts this instrument. Signed. Wit: Hugh Coyle.

p. 401. 15 June 1796. Simon de Arze, Sergt. of Royal Artillery, to Luther Smith, of Government of Natchez, planter, lot 100 ft front by 125 ft depth, with a half-finished house and fences thereon, which I purchased from Don Juan Girault; for $275 paid. Signed.

p. 402. Maurice Stacpoole petitions that he be allowed to sell lands, houses and effects belonging to estate of Joseph Murray, decd. June 4th, 1796. Signed. // Granted, same date, by Gayoso. Don Antonio Gras appointed Commissioner for above sale. June 18, 1796.

p. 402. 25 July 1796. John McDowell to George Cochran in the name of and acct. of Frederick Zerbin, physician, in New Orleans, a negro woman "Pleasant", aged 20, with her mulatto dau. aged 8 mos., for $350 paid. Both signed.

p. 403. 8 Oct. 1792. Articles of agreement between Daniel Burnet and Richard Lord; for $2500, Mexican, to be paid by Lord, (on terms), Daniel Burnet agrees to make legal right to one-half of a saw-mill at Grindstone Ford, on Bayou Pierre, and to one moiety of 1000 acres of land adjoining thereto, being the tract whereon Daniel Burnet now lives, to be divided as follows: Lord to have all land on the west side of the Main Road to the center of the Mill on the south side of Bayou Pierre; and shall be permitted to erect a grist-mill below the saw-mill on Lord's part of land, etc. Signed by both. Witness: P. Brian Bruin, William Dunbar. // p. 404. 27 June 1796. Mrs. Tomasin Lord, atty. for her husband, Richard Lord, resigns her claim and her husband's to land to George Humphreys and is released from any obligation upon them on account thereof. Signed: Tomsey Lord, Dan'l. Burnet. p. 404. 8 June 1796. Tripartite agreement between Mrs. Tomasin Lord, John and Daniel Burnet of other part and George Humphreys in behalf of himself and his mother, Agnes Humphreys, of 3rd part. Said Humphreys in possession of a bond of John and Daniel Burnet, on which a balance is due, the sd bond dated 17 July 1790, drawn in favor of Agnes, George and Ralph Humphreys, and the said John Burnet and Daniel Burnet are in possession of a bond of Richard Lord's on which an unsettled balance is also due, both of which bonds were given for a tract of land and mill formerly on Bayou Pierre. It is agreed that Mrs. Tomason Lord shall give up her husband's right to said mill seat unto aforesaid Agnes and George Humphreys, also deliver them a negro named "Jack", a four-year old steer, a two-year old heifer, two breeding sows, all the mill irons that are Mr. Lord's, etc., including James Lobdal's obligation for making 94 pairs of shoes, Abram Lobdall's note for $10, one pair of plough irons and 2000 cypress pickets to be delivered at the Natchez landing, in consequence thereof the said Humphreys obliges himself to give her full acquittance upon her husband's obligation to John and Daniel Burnet, which acquittance John Burnet does hereby oblige himself to give to said Humphreys on receiving a full discharge upon the bond given by him and his son Daniel to Agnes, George and Ralph Humphries. Signed John Burnet, G. W. Humphreys, J. Girault for Mrs. Lord. Wit: Roger Dixon, George Overaker. // p. 405. 27 June 1796. Daniel Burnet to George Humphreys, both of this Government, a portion of land on Bayou Pierre, being the same I had sold to Richard Lord, one-half of a grant of 1000 acres granted Burnet 31 Aug. 1790, to be divided as expressed in agreement made with sd Richard Lord, for $800 in hand paid. Both sign.

p. 406. 2 July 1796. Don Carlos de Grand-Pre, of Natchez, to James Kirk, planter, power to represent him and take charge of all lands he holds in this Government. Signed. Wit: Eben Rees.

p. 406. 16 July 1796. Jemima Lewis, wife of James Lewis, of Villa Gayoso, in the Government of Natchez, for love and affection for my children: William Hutsell, John Hutsell, Joseph Hutsell, Catharine Hutsell and Abraham Hyler, my estate, goods, chattels, property, real and personal, of every kind, consisting of 600 acres in the forks of Fairchild's Creek, say Cole's Creek, 400 acres on Bluffs near Villa Gayoso, cattle, furniture, etc., out of which to son Abram Hyler one bed, bedstead and furniture, one mare and colt, one cow and calf, the remainder to be divided equally, each to have one-fifth, to take effect after her death. Signed with a mark. Wit: John Bisland, George Overaker. Ack. before Gayoso, July 16, 1796.

p. 407. 21 July 1796. Agreement, Wm. Tabor and Thos. Harrington. Wm. Tabor agrees to complete title to a grant of 300 acres surveyed in his favor many years ago, on Stoney Creek, b. by Wm. Brocus, Gibson Clark, Roswell Mygett and Lucius Smith, within two months; and Harrington is to pay for same $113, payment to be made in horses and cows. Both sign. Wit: John Still Lee.

p. 407. 21 July 1796. Wm. Brocus, planter, manumits slave "Nanette", aged 19, Creole, of New Orleans which he purchased some years past from James Elliott, as the father of said slave is a free negro and has applied for her freedom and paid by his attorney the amount of her appraisement, $460. Wm. (X) Brocus. Wit: Roger Dixon.

p. 408. 17 June 1792. Benjamin Monsanto, of New Orleans, receipt to David Williams, of same, $1000 (silver), being money lent me without interest or premium, mortgages several negroes and estate. // Copy of the original obligation presented by Don Manuel Monsanto against the widow of Don Benjamin Monsanto. 22 July, 1796.

p. 409. 27 July 1796. Charles Boardman to Thomas Freeman, both of the Government of Natchez, 200 arpents, part of a grant on St. Catherine's Creek, b. by Richard Carpenter, being 8 arpents in front on the Sandy Branch of sd creek, for $200 paid. Both sign.

p. 410. New Orleans, 28 Nov. 1795. Will of Thomas Wood, practitioner of physic, all his estate, wearing apparel, medecines, etc., to be turned over to Jarvis Wilcox, after my lawful debts have been discharged; if any balance remains worth consideration, that is above twenty pounds, he may acquaint my father whose name is James Wood, factor, Stenton, North Britain, nigh Dunbar, who will have true and legal claim, provided he allows to said Jarvis Wilcox a proper allowance for his trouble and expense. Signed. Wit: Caleb Owings, Frederick Albright, George Burns, Richard Bailey, John Harrison, J. D. Woodward, John Kotts. // 26 July 1796. Inventory. At Mr. Lewis Evans, medical books, medecines, wearing apparel. At Mr. Philip Engle's, 1 pr. saddle bags, bridle and saddle. In the woods, one bay horse. // 13 Aug. 1796. Appraisement and sale. Total $269. Wit: Eben Rees, Wm. Gillespie, V. T. Dalton, Joseph Vidal.

p. 418. 18 Aug. 1796. Henry Milburn to John Dyson, both of the Government of Natchez, 100 arpents, part of 300 arpents granted Eustace Humphreys, on a branch of Fairchild's Creek, for $80, in hand paid. Both signed. Wit: Lewis Throckmorton.

p. 418. 18 Aug. 1796. Henry Milburn to States Trevillian, represented by his father, Richard Trevillian, 100 arpents on a branch of Fairchild's Creek which I purchased of Eustace Humphreys, said 100 arpents to be taken from south part of said grant, for $80, paid. Both sign. Wit: Lewis Throckmorton.

p. 419. 20 Aug. 1796. John Girault to Sebastian Estradas, lot of ground I purchased of William Garland, 100 ft by 150 ft depth, b. on west by lot which I sold to Joseph Martinez, for $45. Signed. // p. 420. 26 Aug. 1796. Sebastian Estrada assigns above to Job and Jeremiah Routh, for $100. Sebastian (X) Estrada.

p. 420. Manuel Garcia de Texada to John Fake, of Dist. of Gayoso, 264 arpents gr. to Richard Trevillian from whom I purchased the same, for $312 (terms). 31 Aug. 1796. Both signed. Wit: Bennet Truly. // Natchez, 7 March 1798. John Fake, not being able to pay the amount mentioned in above sale, restores plantation to Texada who receives same. Both sign. Wit: Ebenezer Rees.

p. 421. Will of Pierre Surget. 1 April 1791. It is my will that my wife enjoy the use of all my property, having several children who are unable to provide for themselves and must needs be brought up, neither sons nor daughters, when of age, shall be entitled to claim anything from her, it being understood that she shall pay such debts as I may have and I request of the officers of Justice who are authorized to watch over the interests of minors, will allow her to transact and undertake whatsoever she may judge to be for the benefit of her family, without interruption. Signed. // Natchez, 4 Apr. 1791. Wit: Geo. Fitzgerald, Benj. Monsanto, Ezek. Forman, Joseph Murray, J. Eldergill, George Cochran, Sam'l. J. Forman, Patrick Foley. // p. 422. Second Creek, 27 July 1796. By virtue of authority from His Excellency Don Manuel Gayoso de Lemos, Gov. of Natchez, I, William Dunbar, in the presence of the five subscribing witnesses open the will of the late Peter Surget, which he received from Mrs. Surget. Wit: Geo. Rapalje, Jesse Greenfield, John Ellis, Thos. Burling, N. Carter. // Proven by witnesses, Natchez, 28 July 1796.

p. 423. 4 Sept. 1796. Don Simon Arze to George Overaker a negro woman "Lucy", aged 35, nat. of Africa, which I purchased at public sale; for $150, paid. Both sign. Wit. James Stuart.

p. 423. 7 Sept. 1796. David Lambert and Rhoda Lambert to William Weeks, all our right and title to 500 arpents in Homochitto District, being part 1026 arpents inherited by sd Rhoda Lambert from her parents, which sd land is to be taken from the south part; for $250, paid. William Weeks and David Lambert Sign. Rhoda (X) Lambert.

p. 424. 17 Sept. 1796. Parker Carradine to Peter Hill, both of this Government, 200 arpents at Fairchild's Creek, part of 600 arpents granted to me in 1789, which I transfer in consideration of the said Hill having settled the said grant and living thereon during three years. Both sign. Wit: William Gillespie.

p. 425. 26 Sept. 1796. John Scott, Master Builder of this Post of Natchez, to Antonio Molina, of the King's Schooner, Vigilant, a half of Lot 4, Square 1, adjoining Lot 3 of said square, which said lot was granted me; for $40, paid. Signed.

p. 425. 30 Sept. 1796. Joseph Pannill, of District of Bayou Sarah, to Francis Pousset, Esq., of same, nine slaves (named), all natives of America, for $2900, paid. Both sign. Wit: John Wall, Wm. White. // p. 426. This is to certify that the negro "Hercules" mentioned in the foregoing bill of sale, has been returned to his master, Col. Joseph Pannill, and makes no part of the sale, which is hereby cancelled with respect to said negro. Signed by all. [n. d.]

p. 426. 30 Sept. 1796. Francisco Pousset, of the District of Bayou Sara, sells to Joseph Pannell, of same place, 1500 arpents, for $3000 in hand paid, described in plat and grants delivered to purchaser. Both sign. Wit: John Wall, Wm. White.

p. 427. 30 Sept. 1796. John Wall, of Bayou Sara, to Joseph Pannill, of same, 500 arpents which I purchased of Francis Pousset, as will appear by deed passed before Commandant of Baton Rouge; for $1000, paid. Both sign. Wit: Francis Pousset, Esq., Wm. White.

p. 428. 6 Oct. 1796. Sarah Sweazey, wife of Justus King, of this Government of Natchez, and Villa Gayoso Dist., to Richard King, Prosper King, Elizabeth King, Catherine King and William Henry King, the following property: two young negroes and 729 arpents which I hold at "Ogden's Mandamus", which I inherited from my deceased father, Richard Swazey, as will appear in the partition of his estate, for $800 in hand paid. Signed: Sarah King, Justus King, Richard King, Prosper King, Eliz. King, Catharine King, Wm. Henry King. Wit: John Stephens, Cyrus Hamilton. Gayoso.

p. 428. 8 Oct. 1796. William Dunbar and Ebenezer Rees, as Syndics for the creditors of Melling Woolley, sell to Patrick McDermot negro "Louis", sold to said Woolley by Francisco Merone, of N. O., on mortgage, which said mortgage is here cancelled by Wm. Dunbar, atty. for F. Merone; for $500 paid. Both sign. Wit: John Arden, Geo. Cochran.

p. 429. 11 Oct. 1796. Jacob Adams, of this Government, to Wm. Atchinson, of same, surveyor, 313 arpents in the settlement of St. Catherine's Creek, b. by John Hartley, Josiah Flowers and land granted to said Adams, for $250 paid. Signed: J. Girault for Jacob Adams, William Atchinson. Wit: Thos. Wilkins, Ebenr. Rees.

p. 430. 17 Oct. 1796. Wm. Atchinson sells to Wm. Gillespie, both of this Government, 50 arpents of above tract, for $50, paid. Both sign. Wit: John Wylie.

p. 431. Natchez. 17 Oct. 1796. Manuel Lopez, Lt. in co. of Artillery of the Militia of this Fort, is surety for Margaret Beauvais, widow of Thomas Bentley, who desired to take with her to N. O. a mulatto woman named "Celeste", seized and deposited in charge of Antonio Gras, and it being necessary to give security for the safety of sd woman in case her said mistress be allowed the use of her. Signed.

p. 431. 20 Oct. 1796. John Henderson, of this Government, is indebted to Joseph Andrews, of Dist. of Opelousas, for $463, specie, mortgages slave "Sampson", nat. of Guinea, aged 28. John Henderson signed for self and Alexander Henderson. Joseph Andrews. Wit: J. Eldergill. // p. 432. Natchez, 8 Oct.. 1799. Received of Alexander and John Henderson sum mentioned in within mortgage with interest. Signed Joseph Andrews. Test: John Steel.

p. 433. 19 Aug. 1796. Will of Robert Scott. I leave as exors. my beloved wife, my brother, William Scott, my brothers-in-law, William and James Moore and the Rev. McLennan, full power to act and take inventories themselves without assistance from the officers of the Government. To my brother, William Scott Lot 3, Sq. 5 with house I intend to put upon it and $1000 to enable him to make a livelihood in a strange country or assist him to leave it as he thinks proper. The entire remainder to my wife but if she is pregnant, one-half to the child and one-half to her. Signed. Wit: Ebenr. Rees, Benj. Osmun, Job Routh, John Ellis, Gilbert Mills, Andrew Scandlan, Daniel Swazey. // p. 434. Natchez, Oct. 21, 1796. The undersigned respectfully represent that the sealed paper herewith presented contains the last will of Robert Scott, lately deceased at N. O. Signed J. Moore, William Moore, Wm. Scott. // Same date. Witnesses proved will of Robert Scott and it was ordered recorded.

p. 435. John Ellis, planter, of this district, and one of the exors. of estate of late Richard Ellis, decd., deposited in the Archives of this Government, sundry documents belonging to said estate and prays for an order that said papers be delivered to petitioner. Natchez, Oct. 29, 1796. Signed: Ellis. // Grants of land that are in the office, belonging to the estate of Richard Ellis, decd. are to be delivered to the petitioner under his receipt. Natchez, 29 Oct. 1796. Manuel Gayoso de Lemos.

(1)	Letters Patent	for	1000	arps.	at White Cliffs	to Richard Ellis
(2)	" "	"	1850	"		to Richard Ellis
(3)	" "	"	667	"		to John Hocombe
(4)	Lease.........	"	"	fr " "		to Richard Ellis
(5)	Release.......	"	"	" " "		" " "
(6)	Grant	"	150	"	at Natchez	" " "
(7)	"	"	1600	"	" "	" Wm. Chabot
(8)	"	"	800	"	" "	" Wm. Cocke Ellis
(9)	"	"	800	"	" "	" John Ellis, Sr.
(10)	"	"	600	"	" "	" Wm. Butler

29 Oct. 1796. Received above grants, etc. Signed: John Ellis.

p. 435. 3 Nov. 1796. Solomon Hopkins, of this Government, to Hannah Brown, wife of John Chambers, with approbation of her husband, a negro woman named Margaret, aged 16, nat. of Guinea, for $400, paid. Signed: Solomon Hopkins, John Chambers. Wit: John Bell.

p. 436. 3 Nov. 1796. John Chambers and Hannah Brown, his wife, to Solomon Hopkins, 455 arpents, being one-half of a tract bequeathed to Reuben Brown and his sister, Hannah Brown, in the grant called "Ogden's Manadamus", which we inherited from our parents, for $450, paid. Signed by the three. Wit: John Bell.

p. 437. 9 Nov. 1796. Andrew Scanlan, of this Dist., to estate of Robert Scott, Lot No. 1, Sq. 26, granted him, with house and other buildings, for $300, paid. Signed: Andrew Scandlan, William Moore. Wit: Edward McCabe.

p. 437. 11 Nov. 1796. Don Estevan Minor to Don Juan de Castanedo, of N. O., power of authority to settle a suit instituted against me by Charlotte Fayende, wid. of Don Philip Trevino, and one brought by me against Panthon, Lesly and Co. Signed. Wit: Charles Surget.

p. 438. 19 Nov. 1796. Adam Bingaman gives power and authority to George Garland, Esq., of New Orleans, to release and take from prison of said city a negro named "Romeo", belonging to him, and sell said slave for his account. Signed.

p. 438. 19 Nov. 1796. Don Estevan Minor to Jesse Rainer a negro boy "Stephen", a Creole, aged 17, for $400, paid. Jesse (X) Rainer, Estevan Minor. Wit: Adam Bingaman.

p. 439. 19 Nov. 1796. Jesse Rainer to Job and Jeremiah Routh, both of this District, negro "Joe", aged 35, negro woman "Sukey", aged 34, both natives of Guinea, boy "Joe", Creole, aged 2, for $700, paid. Jesse Rainer, Job Routh. Wit: A. Bingaman.

p. 440. 19 Nov. 1796. Samuel Flower, by his attorneys, Wm. Dunbar and John Eldergill, sells to Henry Stevens, of this District, planter, 380 arpents on St. Catherine's Creek, which was formerly granted to Samuel Gibson and purchased by Flower from Thomas Foster; for $500 (terms), David Ferguson security. Henry (H. S.) Stephens, William Dunbar, J. Eldergill. // p. 441. Receipt of Wm. Dunbar and John Eldergill, attorneys for Samuel Flower, to Henry Stevens for full amount and release David Ferguson from his security.

p. 441. Will of William Gilbert, in low health; to son, William, all that part of stock of cattle under care of James Hayes, at Homochitto, branded "W. G.", all the rest of my estate to my wife, Nancy, and her five children, namely, James, William, Mary, Elizabeth, and Thomas. Exrs. James Foster, Joseph Bernard and William Foster. In the Fork of St. Catherine in District of Natchez, 12 Nov. 1796. Wit: John Henderson, J. Eldergill, Thomas Foster, Ambrose Foster, Pre. Camus, Wm. Lum, Gideon Foster. // p. 442. Natchez, 22 Nov. 1796. William Foster, in the name of the widow, Nancy Gilbert, widow of William Gilbert, decd., presented to me this paper, sealed and endorsed "the will of William Gilbert, deceased, to be opened after my death." // Proved by witnesses, 29 Nov. 1796. // Inventory, May 1797, by Mr. Wm. Foster, one of the exrs.

p. 442. 4 Dec. 1796. Thos. Tyler, indebted to Gabriel Cerre, of St. Louis, in the Illinois, merchant, in sum of $1027, being for purchase of slaves in 1786, mortgages "Maria Louisa", a negro woman. Signed. John Murdoch, witness.

p. 443. 14 March 1796. James Ogilsby, of this District, planter, to Anthony Hoggatt, of same, 500 arpents in District of St. Catherine, b. by Peter Nelson, Charles Percy and John Wagh, as set forth on plat thereof, made by Wm. Vousdan on 14 Aug. 1787; for $400, terms. James (X) Ogelsby, Anthony Hoggatt.

p. 444. 23 Dec. 1796. Peter Walker, atty. for Don Juan Joseph Duforest, of N. O., to Richard Harrison, of this District, a piece of land on a branch of Cole's Cr., commonly called "Holt's Fork", being part of 1000 arpents belonging to Don Juan Joseph Duforest, and granted to William Hiorn by the British Government; for $250 (terms). Signed by both. Wit: John Burnet.

p. 445. 24 Dec. 1796. John Henderson ack. to have purchased in partnership with his brother, Alexander from Richard Harrison, 602 arpents on which purchase there remains due $372 for which they gave their note due Jany. 1791 and said note having passed into the hands of Messrs. Robert and George Cochran, John Henderson makes bond for same, mortgaging the tract of land on which he now dwells, except a small piece of land sold to James Foster which does not exceed 100 arpents nor include any of the buildings or improvements. Signed: John Henderson for self and Alexander Henderson. Wit: Edward McCabe. // p. 445. Miss. Ter., Adams Co., 14 Jany. 1802. Receipt of George Cochran in the name of Robert and George Cochran to Alexander and John Henderson for full satisfaction of foregoing debt. Witness: Peter Walker.

p. 446. Natchez, Jany. 18, 1797. Petition of Buckner Pittman, of this Government, that on 31 Aug. 1792, his papers were seized by Capt. Richard King as your petitioner was informed by order of Your Excellency; petitions that they be returned to him, enclosing a list of same. // p. 447. Natchez, 18 Jany. 1797. Received papers mentioned in this inventory. Signed Buckner Pittman.

p. 447. Jany. 23, 1797. Don Manuel Gayoso de Lemos certifies that, by the records of the Govenrment, it appears that in 1790 a suit by Alexander Moore, of this Post, merchant, against Edward McCabe, for money due on a mortgage of a plantation about 2 leages from this Post on the King's Road leading to the District of Villa Gayoso, said plantation containing 150 arpents, houses and improvements, adj. John Foster, Thomas Hughes and others, the same being exposed to public sale, was adjudged to David Ferguson, of this Post, merchant, the 4th day of ____, the same year, 1790, for $460. Signed. // p. 447. 23 Jany. 1797. David Ferguson sold to Thomas Martin, the plantation in the foregoing certificate, for $500, on terms. Signed: David Ferguson. Thomas (X) Martin. Wit: Richard King.

p. 448. 28 Jany. 1797. Roger Dixon, of District of Villa Gayoso, planter, and David Odam, agreement, on the return of land Roger Dixon bought of Odam, 9 July 1792. Both sign. Wit: Edward McCabe.

p. 449. Will of John Kendrick, poor health. 26 Jany. 1797. Debts to be paid: John Savage, a young cow, with 300 pounds of cotton, a young heifer that runs at Mr. Belt's (Belk?), with my corn and half of my hogs; the other half of the hogs I leave to Cornelius Crawley, with my wearing apparel, for his care of me in my sickness. Mr. Eben. Rees and Mr. Gabriel Benoist are to divide the rest of the horned cattle, that is to say, my share of them I bequeath to Mr. Gabriel Benoist and Mr. Ebenezer Rees is to have his part of them. My bay mare and dun colt with the remainder of my cotton I bequeath to Mr. Gabriel Benoist, whom I appoint my sole exor, to see that this my will shall be punctually and justly performed. I bequeath to John Savage my right and claim to 200 acres of land for which Mr. Peter Walker will make him a true title. John (X) Hendrick. Wit: Jno. Reilly, Wm. Shaw, John (X) Dun, Richard (X) Riland, James (X) O'Neal. // 6 Feb. 1797. 6 Feb. 1797. The above will presented and proved by witnesses. Gabriel Benoist accepted executorship.

p. 450. n. d. Don Louis Faure, Surgeon, to Don Estevan Minor a piece of ground, 62 feet wide and 34 perches long, in the environs of this town, in exchange whereof I received a piece of ground, between my grant and the cliff, running the length of my land. Both sign.

p. 451. Will of Obediah Brown, of the District of Natchez; land I bought of Samuel Swazey, decd., 250 acres, to my daughter Hannah Chambers, also negro wench "Sophia"; to my dau-in-law, Susannah Brown, negro girl "Sukey", my brother-in-law, Elijah Swazey, and beloved friend, Caleb King, my executors. Jany. 30, 1797. Signed: Obadiah Brown. Wit: Israel Luce, Gideon Hopkins, George Crawford, Justus King, Samuel Swazey, Francis Luce, Richard (X) Luce, Joseph McMahan, David Lambert. // 9 Feb. 1797. Caleb King delivered to Gayoso the above will. Witnesses prove same. // p. 452-3. Inventory of estate and effects of Obadiah Brown, decd. 14 March 1797. Total $2036. Signed Caleb King, Elijah Swazey, Nathan Swazey and Isaac Johnson.

p. 454. 9 Feb. 1797. Henry Milburn, of this District, planter, to John Courtney, of same, 100 arpents on a branch of Fairchild's Creek, being part of 300 arpents purchased of Eustace Humphreys, for $300 (terms). Both sign. Wit: Ebenezer Rees, Charles Surget.

p. 455. 13 Feb. 1797. Joseph Duncan to David Ferguson, merchant, 100 arpents on St. Catherine's Creek, b. by lands of Samuel Gibson, Samuel Swazey and His Excellency Don Manuel Gayoso and said creek, for $220 (terms). Both sign. Wit: Ebenezer Rees, Lewis Evans.

p. 455. 16 Feb. 1797. William Rucker, of Town of Natchez, to Luther Smith, of same, Lot No. 2, Sq. 31, which I bought of Wm. Barland, for $350, with house. Both sign. Wit: J. Burnet.

p. 456. 8 Feb. 1797. Before John Smith, Syndic for the District of Villa Gayoso, David and Susanny Odam, who have been duly sworn, declare that a negro woman named "Rachall", the mother of ten children, now in possession of Mary Carradine and is her property, given to the said Mary Carradine by her father, Abraham Odam, senior, decd. Susany (X) Odam, David Odam. Wit: John Smith, John Brooks. // 17 Feb. 1797. Before Don Manuel Gayoso de Lemos appeared Parker Carradine, an inhabitant of this Government, and declared that the within declaration is true and acknowledged to have in his possession the said slaves lawfully belonging to his said wife, Mary Carradine. Signed. Wit: R. King, Peter Walker. Gayoso.

p. 456. 18 Feb. 1797. Abraham Villaret to John Murdoch, cattle, for $140 and other property. Signed. Wit: J. Eldergill, John Girault.

p. 457. 25 Feb. 1797. Louis Delat to Don Antonio Gras, Lot 4, Sq. 17, being part of land granted to William Barland in 1782, for $100. Both sign.

p. 457. 26 Feb. 1797. Catherine Vilaret, lawful wife of Louis Vilaret, of New Orleans, power and authority to Abraham Vilaret, our son, for me and my husband, representing us, etc. Signed with mark. Witness: George Cochran.

p. 458. Natchez, Feb. 20, 1797. John Ellis promises to give all right and title I have or had to two certain tracts of land on Second Creek, one granted to Wm. Joiner, by the British Government, for 500 acres, the other 113 acres granted by same to Seth Doud, unto Mrs. Jane Rapalie, in consideration and in consequence of a final adjustment of all affairs relating to estate of the late, Richard Ellis, Esq., which when terminated I agree to perform when I receive her power to invest me with 800 acres she was entitled to by the will of her late father. Signed John Ellis. Wit: Abram Ellis, Benjamin Farar. // Natchez, 27 Feb. 1797. At the request of Mr. George Rapalie I certify the within to be a true copy of a document presented to me and signed as in this copy. (signed) Manuel Gayoso de Lemos. // Natchez,

20 Feb. 1797. Being this day appointed by the heirs of the late Richard Ellis, Esq., deceased, to collect all demands against said estate and being executor of said estate, we hereby acknowledge to have received from Mrs. Jane Rapalie an acct. of $1268, fully prov. by her and to be settled as toward settling her share of the estate's debts. Signed: John Ellis. Wit: S. Minor, Benj. Farar. The above is a true copy of a document presented to me by Mr. George Rapalje certified at Natchez, 23 Feb. 1797. Signed: Gayoso.

p. 459. 8 March 1797. John Tally to William Vousdan, Captain in the Militia of this Government, a negro named "Little Peter" which I purchased of John Turnbull, for $507, being the amount owing by me to Messrs. Morgan and Mather, as will appear by my note. John (X) Tally, William Vousdan. Wit: Ebenezer Rees.

p. 460. Will of William Carney, of Government of Natchez. Just debts paid and residue to my two nephews, Arthur Carney, of the Choctaw Nation, and William Carney of the State of Georgia. Exors: the aforesaid heirs and my friends, Samuel Gibson, and Wm. Brocus, both of the District of Bayou Pierre in this Government. Jany. 2, 1795. Wit: John Girault, Richard King, Prosper King, Thomas Dunby, Samuel Gibson, Ephraim Storey, Samuel Cobun. // Natchez, 24 Feb. 1797. Samuel Gibson presented the above will. William Carney died at his plantation on Bayou Pierre some days ago. // Feb. 27, 1797. Will proved by witnesses. // p. 463. 10 Apr. 1797. Inventory. Ebenezer Smith and George Humphreys appointed appraisers. [Total not given but it would have been quite large.]

p. 465. 13 March 1797. John Savage, of District of Natchez, planter, to Don Francisco Lenan, curate of the Parochial Church of this Post, 1000 square arpents in the District of Bayou Pierre in this Govt., on south branch of James Creek, b. by lands of Melling Woolley and Patrick Cogan, for $500 (Mexican), paid. Both signed.

p. 466. 20 March 1797. Inventory of estate of Jemima Lewis, as given by Joseph Hutsell, authorized by William Hutsell; witnessed by Harry Green, Roger Dixon.

p. 466. 24 March 1797. Philip Engle, of this Post of Natchez, planter, to Don Estevan Minor, piece of ground at the landing, b. by the street dividing my ground from that of Rebecca McCabe, part of 16 arpents granted me 15 June 1795, 60 ft front on the road leading up the hill and same in depth to the river by two parallel lines running north 26 degrees west. Signed.

p. 467. 24 March 1797. Don Simon de Arze to Don Francisco Caudel a lot of ground adjoining this town, with two dwellings and other buildings, in exchange whereof I have received a lot of ground in the City of N. O. with buildings thereon, for $150 paid. Both sign.

p. 468. 25 March 1797. Philip Engle to Bernard Lintot, of this Government, planter, a piece of ground between the cliff and the river, bounded by a piece I sold Don Estevan Minor, 432 ft in front on the road leading up the hill and running north from said hill and road 432 ft to the river, for $600 paid. Both sign.

p. 469. 5 April 1797. Samuel Flower to Charles Boardman 1900 arpents which I hold in this Government, 900 arpents on southeast branch of Cole's Cr. granted to me 21 Apr. 1788, 800 arpents on Second Cr. which I bought from John Hartley, to whom same was granted 25 Feb. 1788, and 200 acres granted by British Government, for $1900 in hand paid. Both sign.

p. 469. 12 Apr. 1797. Sebastian Bosque, atty. and admr. of estate of Francisco Bazo, to Antonio Gras, late partner with the deceased, 200 arpents near St. Catherine's Cr., for $200, payable on settlement of the account of said estate. Both sign.

p. 470. 12 Apr. 1797. Peter Nelson, of this Government, to James Hoggatt, of this Post, merchant, 300 arpents b. by lands of James Oglesby and of His Majesty, which said land was granted me 15 Mch. 1788, for $300 paid. Both sign. Wit: John Wilson. // p. 471. At time of signing seller declared that he had obtained 100 arpents of said land from the British Government and 150 arpents from Henry Bradley, to whom it was granted by said government, and having lost titles at the time of the Revolution in this country he obtained titles of same from this Government later as above. Both sign.

p. 472. 14 April. George Humphreys, of this Government, to Claudius F. Girod, of N. O., merchant, now present, two slaves, negro man "Cook", aged 36, and negro woman "Sukey", aged 26, both nat. of Africa, which said slaves were bought by my deceased father from Thomas Irwin, for $1000, (Mexican dollars) in hand paid. Signed: C. F. Girod, G. W. Humphreys.

p. 471. 22 Apr. 1797. John Bisland, of this Government, to James Hoggatt, of same, merchant, 750 arpents on waters of Cole's and Second Creeks, granted to me 6 Mch. 1788, b. by Peter Camus and Louis Chachere, and lands of His Majesty, for $750, (note). Both sign.

p. 472. 25 Apr. 1797. Edward McCabe to James Moore, exor. of his decd. father's estate, 500 arpents at Bayou Pierre, in District of Natchez, granted to me 4 March 1795. Both sign. Wit: Richard King, Lacey Rumsey.

p. 437. Inventory of property of William Scott, decd. Plantation of 400 acres on Homochitto, adj. Ruffin Gray, negro aged 50, etc. Natchez, 26 Apr. 1797. Signed Gerard Brandon.

p. 473. 4 May 1797. Joseph Vauchere, of Govt. of Natchez, to Lewis Wells, of the Post of Rapides, negro "Cromwell", aged 37, native of Africa, which I bought from John Scott; for $400 (terms). Both sign.

p. 474. Natchez, 3 May 1797. Petition of James Sanders, whose father died 20 April, leaving a small estate. The petitioner's mother, wid. of deceased, is living and 3 other children who are lawful heirs of the estate. Being the only one of the legal heirs present, asks that he be put in legal possession for the benefit of the co-heirs and the creditors of deceased father. His mother, brother and two sisters are now in S. C. His deceased father had a woman living with him who now claims some of the stock. Signed. // Same date. Isaac Gaillard, Esq. will take steps to procure will of deceased James Sanders, if any there be and other proof, etc. When that is done, you will send the papers to me. Signed by Gayoso, // p. 475. Will of James Sanders, of Dist. of Natchez, Province of La. Debts to be paid; to beloved wife, Mary Dumas, one-half of tract whereon I now live and one-half of all the property I shall have in this country; to son James the remaining half of the land and one-half of the property. My wife, Mary Dumas, of the Dist. of Natchez; and George Dumas, of same, exors. Ruffin Gray, of this District, to make inventorn and appraisement. 5 Apr. 1796. Signed: James Sanders. Wit: John Ellis, Justus Andrews, Joseph (X) Miller, Timothy Edwards, Giles Edwards // John Ellis, Justus Andrews, Joseph (X) Miller and Giles Andrews make oath that they saw James Sanders sign above will. Sworn before Isaac Gaillard.

p. 475. 9 March 1797. Don Francisco Lennan, Curate of the Parish Church, to David Ferguson, of sd Post, merchant, 5 arpents in the environs of this town, b. by land of Joseph Vidal, Lewis Villaret, and by the King's Road, granted me 6 Feb. 1795, for $275 payable in 3 months. Both sign.

p. 476. 9 May 1797. Don Francisco Lennan, as above, to Charles Watrous, Esq., Surgeon in the American Army, 5 arpents in the environs of this town, b. by land of Don Manuel Gayoso de Lemos, William Vousdan, Don Juan Girault and Anne Dunbar, granted me 6 Feb. 1795, for $150 paid. Both sign.

p. 477. 19 May 1797. Sale of the effects of late Obadiah Brown by order of the Governor: Purchasers: Joseph Erwin, Elijah Swazey, Daniel Swazey, Simon Presler, Peter Presler, Zadoc Barrow, Isaac Johnson, Solomon Hopkins, Samuel Coens, Gideon Hopkins, Samuel Heady, Stephen Stephenson, John Mitchell, Samuel Swazey, Jr. Total $614.

p. 478. 29 May 1797. Pedro Walker, as atty. for Don Juan Joseph Duforest, Capt. of Militia and Interpreter for His Majesty, in City of N. O., to James Moore, exor. of estate of his deceased father, Alexander Moore, and for estate, piece of land (no acreage given) in Villa Gayoso District, on a branch of Cole's Cr. called "Holt's Fork", part of 1000 arpents granted to sd Don Juan Joseph Duforest, of which he sold a part to Richard Harrison, the remainder he now sells, b. by sd Harrison, Richard Ellis and Alexander Callender, for $250, paid. Both sign.

p. 478. 7 June 1797. Ebenezer Rees, exor. of estate of Jacob Copperthwait, decd. to Robert and Isaac Taylor, sons of Isaac Taylor, of this District, 200 arpents in the settlement of Fairchild's Cr. b. by James McIntyre, James Wade, John Bisland and seller, part of a larger grant, for having cleared a part of the tract and made roads and bridges as required by law to ensure said grant. Signed by Ebenezer Rees, and by Isaac Taylor, Sr. for sons. Wit: Wm. Dunbar. // p. 479. Power and authority given by Charlotte Bryan, widow of Jacob Copperthwait and Tutress to the minors, and Don Juan Francis Merieult, exor. of the will, both of New Orleans, to Ebenezer Rees, of Natchez Post, to transact all business of the estate. Signed by Charlotte Copperthwait, J. F. Merieult. N. O. 26 June 1793.

p. 480. 14 March 1797. John Girault for himself, his children and heirs, to Polser Shilling 125 arpents near the Fort of this Post, b. by Richard Bacon, Don Juan Joseph Rodriguez and other land, being half of 250 arpents which I purchased of sd Shilling, who had the same from Juan St. Germain, for $150 paid. Both sign.

p. 481. 13 June 1797. Polser Shilling to Charles Watrous, Physician in said Government, the above 125 arpents.

p. 481. Natchez, 27 June 1797. Petition of Samuel Flower sheweth that in 1777 he married the daughter of Mr. Richard Carpenter, who died at Natchez in 1788. In the will of Richard Carpenter, he bequeaths to his daughter, Mary Flower, negro girl "Rose" and one-fifth of all his property after all debts and legacies were paid, your petitioner appointed one of the executors. He has received at several times on account of his wife, Mary Flower, the sum of $2718 and signed a receipt for $2603 and did receive as his wife's property, in 1780, 6 cows and 7 calves, the increase being now 110 head of cattle. Petitioner asks that the above account of his wife's property be registered in the Archives of this Government. Signed. // Gayoso orders that copy of will showing above mentioned legacy and certificates from exors showing sums paid. // p. 482. Bernard Lintot, one of the exors. of will of Richard Carpenter, which was dated 14 July 1788, certifies the above statements. June 28, 1797.

p. 482. 1 June 1797. Peter Walker declares that by an instrument, dated New Orleans, 15 Sept. 1795, Don Juan Baptist Durel sold to this deponent and his mother-in-law, Maria Catherine La Roche, a house in said city at corner of Bienville and Chartre Streets, on a lot 60 ft front by 100 ft deep and whereas said house was paid for by said Maria Catherine Leroche, without any assistance from deponent, he doth hereby declare that he has no right and title in aforesaid house and lot, renouncing same for himself and heirs. Signed. Wit: Don Juan Murdoch, Job Routh.

p. 483. Natchez, 21 June 1798. Elenor Adams declares that her son, Thomas Adams, decd. left some property in the hands of several different persons; as he died intestate, his property devolves to the petitioner who asks for order to take such property. Eleanor (E. A.) Adams. // Same date. Upon condition of the petitioner being answerable for the debts due by the late Thomas Adams, her son, she is hereby authorized to receive and take possession of all property she may find belonging to her said son. Gayoso.

p. 483. 5 July 1797. Elizabeth Mathews to Job and Jeremiah Routh, of this District, planters, a negro woman, Nancy, aged 25, native of Africa, $300, paid. Signed: Elizabeth Mathews, J. Allen Mathews, Job Routh.

p. 484. Will of Manuel Gonzales, lawful son of Louis Gonzales and Maria Martinez, natives of the Town of Castro Marin in Portugal, and that I am not married, my parents being dead, I have no lawful heirs. I hereby constitute Julian Delgado my sole heir by reason of the sincere friendship he has always shown for me and the assistence he has given to me on all occasions, he to be my principal exor. and after him Antonio Molina. 10 July 1797. Signed for the testator, Domingo Lorero. Wit: Simon de Arze, Juan Mier y Feran, Manuel de Lemos.

p. 485. 13 July 1797. Wm. Cooper to Manuel Garcia, of Town of Natchez, negro woman, "Maria", native of Jamaica, aged 30, for $500 paid. Both sign. Wit: Hugh Mulhalen.

p. 485. 2 Aug. 1797. Rebecca McCabe to Christopher Miller part of Lot #4, Sq. #3, that lies southeast of a rivulet that runs across the square, for $250, paid. Both sign. Wit: James Nelson, Jos. H. Hoell.

p. 486. 3 Aug. 1797. Christian Bingaman, of Government of Natchez, to William Ratcliff 550 arpents in District of Feliciana, 2 miles northeast of River Miss. granted to me 20 Apr. 1791, for $800 paid. Both sign. Wit: Thos. Vause.

p. 487. 4 Aug. 1797. Maria Pasqualy Sovillas, of neighborhood of Natchez, in virtue of full powers from my husband, Don Miguel Sovillas, here present, sell to Don Manuel Texada a negro named "Queen", to me belonging, aged 35, which sd slave my husband had from John Forbes; for $350, which the sd Manuel Texada paid to my husband in divers effects. Joseph Vidal signs for Maria Pasqual.

p. 487. 9 Aug. 1797. Don Joseph Vidal to Winsor Pipes, of this Government, planter, a negro "Dick", aged 19, for $450 and a pair of oxen, on terms. Both sign. Wit: John Minor.

p. 488. Natchez, 18 Nov. 1796. Agreement between Col. Peter Bryan Bruin, George Cochran and Ebenezer Rees and Patrick McDermott, which was to be completed agreeable to an instrument of writing now in the Secy's office, which work was not been done; said McDermott to receive for services and work of every description $400 full payment on his part; said P. B. Bruin also agrees to a full discharge for what he has delivered and paid to said McDermott. The $400 aforesaid to be paid from the proceeds of a quantity of plank now lying at Bayou Pierre, which said Bruin agrees to have sent down and sold with all possible dispatch. Both sign. Wit: Wm. E. Hulings, Wm. Lintot, // Natchez, 14 Aug. 1791. Received from Col. Peter Bryan Bruin by hands of George Cochran $400, in payment of obligation to me in full. Signed Patrick McDermott. Wit: Alexr. Murdoch, Wm. Miller, Dennis Collins.

p. 489. 12 Nov. 1796. Samuel Flowers, of District of Bayou Sarah, to Eugene Gomez negro woman, "Sarah" who has to serve until 7 Oct. 1798, which said negro I bought at public sale of estate of Adam Cloud; for $72 paid.

p. 489. 16 Aug. 1797. Eugene Gomez transfers the time of the above negro woman to Antonio Novellas, for $60. Signed. Wit: Pedro Walker.

p. 490. 17 Aug. 1797. Jesse Ratcliff, of District, to Isaac Tabor, of same, 600 arpents in District of Homochitto, granted to Joshua Howard 1794; for $150 in a note. Both sign. Wit: M. Stacpoole.

p. 490. 19 Aug. 1797. Waterman Crane, of District of Natchez, to George Cochran, of this Post, merchant, one-half of 600 arpents, granted me Aug. 30, 1793, for $300 paid. Both sign. Wit: James Spain.

p. 491. 21 Aug. 1797. John Chambers and Hannah Brown, his wife, to Solomon Hopkins 154 acres, part of a greater grant which Hannah Brown inherited from her parents, on Sandy Creek, b. by Elijah Swazey and lands sold by us to Samuel Carnes, for $231, Mexican Money, on terms. Signed by John Chambers and Solomon Hopkins. Wit: Gideon Hopkins.

p. 492. 21 Aug. 1797. John Chambers and Hannah Brown, his wife, of this Govt., to Samuel Carnes, 154 acres, (as described above), b. by land of Daniel Hickey and Gabriel Swazey and land we sold Solomon Hopkins, for $231, Mexican money, on terms. All three signed. Wit: Gideon Hopkins.

p. 492. 23 Aug. 1797. Memorandum of agreement between William Smith, of Bayou Pierre, Thomas Wilkins and George Cochran, merchants, who promise to advance said William Smith from time to time a sum not exceeding $600 to enable him to complete a saw-mill which he has begun to erect on lands granted to him in the District of Bayou Pierre, 26 Dec. 1795, as will appear by the grant No. 827, containing 800 acres, and for surety of payment of the said advances, as also the sums severally due to Thomas Wilkins and George Cochran, respectively, and interest; note due Wilkins, dated 31 Dec. 1790 and Aug. 1791, for $1609, note to Robert Cochran, 1 Dec. 1790, for $283, on which endorsed $141 in hand of George Cochran; William Smith mortgages all the lands he possesses in the District of Bayou Pierre, with the stay of execution, granted on the condition that the whole proceeds of the mill be applied toward discharging and paying the advances and when the same completed to discharge debts still due. Signed by William Smith, Thomas Wilkins and George Cochran.

p. 493. 6 Sept. 1797. Lidia Swezey, wife of Job Cory, for love and affection to my children, Richard Jeremiah, David, Martha, Sarah, Lidia, Mary, Prudence and Elizabeth, lands I inherited from my parents at the Ogden Grant on Homochitto, to be equally divided among them; (description of what part each to get, also gift of slaves); to take effect after her death. Signed: Lidia Cory, Job Cory. Wit: Benjamin Holmes, Isaac Erwin.

p. 494. 13 Sept. 1797. Reuben Dunham, of Bayou Sarah, to Thomas Dawson, of same, 500 arpents, adj. Caezer Archinard, Patrick Foley, Samuel Young and Bayou Sara, grant No. 727, for $400, terms. Reuben (X) Dunham, Elizabeth (X) Dunham, Thomas Dawson. H. Hunter, Alcalde.

p. 495. Will of Christopher Butler, of Natchez District, 8 July 1791. Debts to be paid from money due him. To James Bolls, my well-beloved friend all money that remains, if any, with all personal property, lands, horses, gun and wearing apparel. John Bolls sole exor. Christopher (X) Butler. Wit: Charles (X) Carter, Robert (X) Carter, Benjamin Newman, John Boggs, Wm. Shaw, Thomas Reed. // Sept. 30, 1797, above will proven by witnesses. John Bolls accepts executorship.

p. 496. 14 Sept. 1797. Solomon Swazey, of this Government, to James Moore, exor. of estate of Robert Scott, decd., and for said estate lot #1, sq. #18, granted me 5 Oct. 1795, for $325 paid. Solomon (X) Swazey. Wit: Ebenezer Rees.

p. 497. 14 Sept. 1797. Wm. Atchinson to Charles Dowlin 550 arpents on waters of St. Catherine's Creek, b. by lands of David Smith, Jeremiah Bryan, John Bisland, Zachariah Smith and James Foster, according to plat and grant made to me in 1791, for $300 on terms. Both sign. Charles King.

p. 497. 15 Sept. 1797. Peter Walker to Charles King, both of Dist. of Natchez, 200 arpents on a branch of St. Catherine's Cr., b. by lands of Jacob Adams and Richard Adams, as per grant to Joshua Flowers, which sd land I bought from sd Flowers, $369 paid. Both sign. Wit: James White.

p. 498. Richard Graves to Polser Shilling, both of Government of Natchez, negro "Michael, aged 15, for $382, paid. Both sign.

p. 499. 7 Sept. 1797. Will of J. Vauchere. As guardian of my minor children, Margaret L'Estages, my wife, and to her I give all her right and pretensions which she brought in marriage and moreover one-half of all my property after my death. As there are sums of consequence due me in America as well by Congress as by individuals, I nominate my eldest son, Joseph Vauchere, to collect same, to whom I give one-third of such collections as he shall make for his trouble and care, also his right to a part with my other children, according to law; after my debts are paid they are to share equally. Executor, with Margaret L'Estages, my wife, Mr. Armont Duplantier, of Baton Rouge. Signed: J. Vauchere. Wit: P. Camus, Juan Perez, Christopher Milier, John Overaker, George Overaker, Lewis Evans. // 23 Sept. 1797 above will proved by witnesses. Wit: Gerard Brandon.

p. 499. 28 Aug. 1792. Will of William Scott, of Dist. of Natchez, Prov. of La. After debts paid, estate to dearly beloved children, exors who are to be guardians, Isaac Gaillard, Charles Percy and Gerard Brandon, who are to see about education of children. Signed. Wit: Christopher Bolling, Jo Dick, Adam Cloud, John Bolls, Thomas Reed, William Johnston, Ephraim Coleman. // 23 Sept. 1797. Above will proved by witnesses.

p. 501. 23 Sept. 1797. Isaac Tabor to John Foster, both of this Government, 600 arpents in District Homochitto, as set forth in grant to Joseph Howard in 1794; for $150 in hand paid. Both sign. Wit: Gerard Brandon.

p. 501. 25 Sept. 1797. Parker Carradine to Manuel Monteguardo negro "John", aged 11, for $300 paid. Both sign.

p. 502. Will of Joseph Barnard, of this District. Dear wife, Jane, is entitled to some property now in her mother's hand which justly belongs to her, from her late father's estate, the same when recovered is, of right, absolutely and solely hers. My wife, Jane Barnard, the natural guardian of our five children, Louisa, William, Joseph, Edmund and one unborn; it is my wish that my property remain in her hadns for her and their support and maintenance during her widowhood, etc. 21 Sept. 1797. Robert Dunbar and Gabriel Benoist executors. Signed. Wit: Charles Watrous, John Sullivan, James Scott, Charles Anderson, William Moore, Hugh Davis, David Ferguson and Christopher Miller. // Natchez 27 Sept. 1797. Witnesses prove above will. Executors: Gabriel Benoist, Wm. Dunbar, Robert Dunbar and Joanna O'Brien, widow of the deceased, accepted as executors.

p. 502. 27 Sept. 1797. John Barclay to John Raford Coleman and William Coleman, of Bayou Sara, tract on west branch of Bayou Sara, b. by lands of John Welton and lands of His Majesty, as is grant No. 497 to me, in exchange for 300 arpents on Willing's Creek. Signed by the three. Wit: Lewis Alston.

p. 504. 27 Sept. 1797. John Raford Coleman and William Coleman, of Bayou Sara, planters, to John Barclay, of same, 300 arpents on Willing Creek, b. by land of Louis Alston and land of His Majesty, as appears in grants thereof to John Coleman, and to William Coleman, No. 144; for 500 arpents of land which we have received. Signed: John Raford Coleman, John Barclay, William Coleman. Witness: Louis Alston.

p. 505. 28 Sept. 1797. Gideon Hopkins to Isaac Johnson, 500 arpents in District of New Feliciana, bounded as in grant No. 641; for $500 paid. Both sign. Wit: George Overaker, John Ferguson.

p. 505. 30 Sept. 1797. Manuel Lopez indebted to Gregorio Bergel, both of this Post, for $3,000 specie, resulting from our partnership, bond to pay. Signed. Wit: J. Moore. // p. 506. Receipt of Gregorio Bergel for full payment of above obligation from Manuel Lopez. Natchez, 14, March 1797. [?]

p. 506. 13 Sept. 1797. John Tear, of this Government, to William Moore, of this Post, merchant, 700 arpents in District of St. Catherine, b. as in grant in my favor No. 734; for $500 paid. Both sign. Wit: J. Ferguson, George Overaker.

p. 507. 22 Sept. 1797. Don Joseph Vidal, of this Post, to Gregorio Bergel Lot No. 3, Sq. No. 1, which I purchased of John Scott, with buildings, for $1000 paid. Gregorio (X) Bergel. Wit: Melling Woolley. // p. 508. Gregorio Bergel transfers lot and buildings in foregoing instrument, to Don Manuel Lopez, for $750, paid. 30 Sept. 1797. Juan Girault signs at request of Gregorio Bergel, Manuel Lopez.

p. 508. Natchez, 9 Oct. 1797. Executors of Joseph Barnard, decd., all except Wm. Dunbar who was prevented from being present by illness, met and appointed Thos. Wilkins and George Fitzgerald as appraisers. Wit: Simon Boland, Darius Anderson. /Rather large estate but not totaled./

p. 510. 4 Oct. 1797. John Barclay, planter, to Ebenezer Rees, merchant, both of this District, 320 arpents on Willing Creek b. by William Alston, Lewis Alston, and lands of His Majesty, with 50 arpents reserved for myself in sale of land to said Rees. 9 March last; for $600 paid. Both sign. // p. 511. 9 March 1797. John Barclay to Ebenezer Rees, both of District of Bayou Sara, 1200 arpents on said Bayou, b. by other land belonging to me, land of William Brown, 400 arpents of which granted to Bartholomew Bestoso, 400 arpents to William Collins, 400 arpents to William Brown, together 1000 arpents on Willing Creek contained in 4 separate grants, also hogs, cattle, feed, etc., for $4070, payable next June. Both sign. Wit: Nathan Dix, Luis Faure, Wm. Lewis. // p. 512. Natchez, 14 Oct. 1797. John Barclay acknowledges to have received full payment for the foregoing and the mortgage cancelled. Signed: John Barclay. Wit. Estevan Minor.

p. 512. 14 Oct. 1797. Daniel Clark, of the Dist. of Natchez, gives full power and authority to Daniel Clark, Jr. to represent me in suit I have pending with Stephen Watts and Mrs. Frances Asheton Watts, for recovery of certain monies. Signed: Daniel Clark.

p. 513. 23 Oct. 1797. John Newton to Samuel Watson, both of the District of Natchez, 200 arpents in Dist. of Sandy Creek, b. as grant in my favor, No. 974, for $150 paid. John (X) Newton. Wit: Isaac Alexander, John Burney, Isaac Johnson.

p. 513. 23 Oct. 1797. Margaret Coleman, widow of John Row and exrx. of his will, with approbation of my son, John Row, Jr., to Job and Jeremiah Routh, 170 arpents, one-half league from the Fort, b. by lands of John Stampley, Francis Spain, George Rapalye, John Lusk, and John St. Germain and was granted to my deceased husband, 15 May 1795, for $300 in hand paid. Margaret (M) Coleman. Wit: William Gillespie.

p. 514. 24 Oct. 1797. Adam Schnyder, planter, to George Cochran, merchant, both of Govt. of Natchez, 600 arpents in District of Cole's Creek, 25 miles north of the Fort, b. by lands of William Richey, George Cochran and William Moore, as in form No. 460, 30th Aug. 1793; for $135 paid. Both signed. Wit: William Collins.

p. 515. 28 Oct. 1797. William Bell, planter, to William Cheney, both of the Govt. of Natchez, 120 arpents in District of Cole's Creek, part of grant of 400 arpents gr. to me; for $200, paid. Both sign. Wit: Wm. Ratcliff, George Forman.

p. 515. Petition of heirs of estate of late Asahel Lewis, because of death of Mr. Barnard, the estate is left without a trustee, and may suffer for want of a person to take charge of affairs before the wishes of the absent heirs can be known, they pray that Mr. Ebenezer Rees, be appointed jointly with Wm. Lewis to take charge of the business in the meanwhile, and that they be authorized to receive the papers of the estate from G. Benoist, Esq. Natchez, Oct. 25, 1797. Signed; Sarah Lewis, Moses Lewis, Wm. Lewis. // p. 516. 31 Oct. 1797. Ebenezer Rees and Wm. Lewis accepted the charge of trustees to the estate of Asahel Lewis, deceased. Both signed. Wit: Charles Surget.

p. 516. 31 Oct. 1797. William Calvit to Don Carlos Surget, both of the District of Natchez, 750 arpents at the fork of Homochitto River, and b. as in grant to Calvit, dated 27 Feb. 1789; for $750 paid. Signed: William Calvit, Chas. Surget. Wit: Eben. Rees, Wm. Lewis.

p. 517. Natchez, 28 Oct. 1797. William Ratcliff deposes on oath that he did purchase from Mr. William Hayes 200 acres on Second Creek, joining land of Emanuel Madden, part of 400 acres gr. said Wm. Hayes by British Government, 14 Nov. 1776, which patent was brought from the Land Office at Pensacola by Col. Hutchins and was in deponent's possession a considerable time and by him delivered to William Hayes who declares that he lost it; deponent declares the 200 acres remaining are to the best of his knowledge still the property of said Hayes. Signed: Emanuel Madden.

p. 517. 6 Nov. 1797. William Hayes to Reuben Baxter, of Dist. ot Natchez, planter, 200 acres hereinbefore mentioned; for $150, paid. Both sign. Wit: Juan Girault, Estevan Minor.

p. 518. 6 Nov. 1797. Maria Foster to Thomas Foster, both of the Dist. of Natchez, 444 arpents in Dist. of St. Catherine, and b. as in grant to me, 6 Mch. 1788; for $400 paid. Mary (X) Foster, Thomas Foster. Wit: Hugh Stevenson, John Foster.

p. 519. 6 Nov.1797. William Foster to my brother, Thomas Foster, 100 arpents on St. Catherine's Creek, b. by lands of Richard Harrison, and Samuel Flowers and sd creek, which I purchased of Alexander Henderson, for $200 paid. Both sign. Wit: Samuel Marshall, Peter Walker. Before Estevan Minor.

End of Book C

"I, David Harper, Keeper and Translator of the Spanish Records of the State of Mississippi, certify that the foregoing contained in 519 pages are faithful Translations from the said Records, by me carefully compared and found to agree therewith. In testimony whereof I have hereunto set my hand at Washington in the State aforesaid 30 April 1818." (signed) D. Harper (Seal)

Book D

p. 1. 27 April 1784. John Farquhar, of District, planter, to John Bisland a certain quantity of cattle, (listed), for $310, on terms. Both sign.

p. 1. 27 Apr. 1784. John Farquhar to George Fitzgerald, of N. O., merchant, tract of 400 arpents, a part under fence and a house thereon, about 1 league from Fort, b. by Stephen Minor, John Bisland and vacant lands, gr. me by this Government; for $500 specie, on terms. Both sign.

p. 2. 15 May 1784. Nathaniel Tomlinson and John Lusk, of this Dist., of our own free will and accord, from motives of friendship for Richard Trevillian, also of the District, planter, become liable and responsible for the person of said Richard to his Excellency the Commandant of the Post, Don Philip Trevino, to the end that he may be liberated from the Fort of this Post, where he now is in confinement, and attend freely to his affairs, until the final conclusion of the Process against a certain Henry Car, a soldier also confined in the said Fort, in which process the sd Richard Trevillian is implicated, binding ourselves, etc. Both signed. // Natchez Nov. 20, 1784. The foregoing bond given by Nathaniel Tomlinson and John Lusk has become satisfied and void, the affair which gave occasion to it having been finally settled. Signed Trevino.

p. 3. 26 May 1784. Richard Swayzey, Stephen Jordan, Thomas Jordan, all of this District, planters, of own free will and accord, make bond for the person and conduct of Emanuel Madden, to His Excellency, Don Philip Trevino, as respects his conduct in this District during the time the same may be commanded by His said Excellency, binding ourselves, our estates, etc. Signed by the three.

p. 3. June 6, 1784, Thomas Green, of District, appoints my loving sons, Thomas Marston Green, Cato West, and Abner Green, my true and lawful attornies to ask, demand, and recover, etc., all debts due me in this country. . . . as I might or could do were I personally present, etc. Signed. Wit: John Eldergill, Joseph Stanley, John Smith.

p. 3. 5 July 1784. Philip Trevino, on information of death of Mr. Henry LaFleur at St. Catherine's Creek, have appointed Margaret Lafleur, now his widow, Tutress of children by this marriage, Margaret aged 17, Mary 14, Hannah 11, Sarah 8, Magdalen 6. // Inventory. . . . Debts due him by: Jacob Babe, Patrick Clemens, James Cannon, Donald McPherson, Leonard Webb, Mr. Lemaire, Edward Careless, Jno. Bradley, James Willing, Sterling Spell, Anth. Barbazon, John Bolls, Silas Crane, Wm. Hurlbert, Geo. Castles, James Kelly, John Shoate. Signed: Margaret (X) Lafleur, William Calvit, Sutton Banks, // 5 July 1784. Margaret Lafleur, widow of Henry, petitions that whole of estate held in common between herself and her late husband be allowed and adjudged to her at the valuation that has been made thereof, on giving good security for the part that belonged to her children. This was granted. Peter Nelson, of this District, voluntarily offered to be surety for widow, Margaret Lafleur.

p. 6. Agreement. 10 Sept.1784. Osborn Sprigg, of District of Natchez and Province of La., and James Cole, Jr., of same, agree that James Cole take into his possession all the stock of mares and colts that said Sprigg may have and take such care of them as to increase and benefit said stock, . . . for two years, at the end of which James Cole to take one-fourth of the increase as his own. James (X) Cole, Osborn Sprigg ack. before Trevino.

p. 7. Dec. 1, 1784. Information of death of Bazil Dubois, watchmaker by trade, who died on the other side of the river on board the barge belonging to Don Marcus Joseph Yregollen, lately arrived from America, by natural causes occasioned by a long illness. // 3 Dec. 1784. In pursuance of death of Basil Dubois who left a son aged 3 mos. and 3 days, not yet baptised, lawful issue of his marriage with Maria Isabella Bernardeau yet living, who is not settled in this district but purposes to return to the French part of the Island of St. Domingo, of which she is a native, who was made guardian of the child; Henry Barchellot and Francisco Sabisper were made appraisers of estate of said Dubois. // p. 8. 5 Dec. 1785. On board the barge where her husband, Basil Dubois died, in the presence of the witness, Maria Isabella Bernardeau, his widow, declared that she desired to renounce in due form of law, both for herself and for her son, all claim to the estate of her deceased husband, claiming only her right and that of her son as established by law and according to the contract of marriage, and requiring the depositions of Don Marcus Joseph Yregollen, owner of the barge and Don Juan Monge, surgeon of the said vessel, who heard the declaration of her husband before his death. // p. 9. Deposition of the above: Dubois called both to his bedside when in full possession of his memory and senses, and declared that he had deceived and defrauded Maria Isabella Bernardeau, his present wife, in their contract of marriage, executed before a Notary at Cape Francois, in which he appears to have had at that time 70,000 livres currency of that Island, and 10,000 livres which he stated to have paid the creditors of her deceased parents, all of which he declared was false, on the contrary he had no money and had also received several further sums belonging to his wife. Both signed. // Inventory. 6 Dec. 1784. In a trunk: $3120 in Dubloons, $280 Spanish money; $32, $35 and $86 in small coins; $100 in 23 Louis D'or of France; total $3549; 7 complete suits of clothes, 12 pairs of silk stockings, worn; 1 pr silver buckles; 1 pr. of gold buckles; 1 pr pistols; 12 shirts; 6 cravats; $3,905; which was left in possession of the widow. // Marriage Contract. Cape Francois in the Island of St. Domingo, appeared Basil Baclin Dubois, watchmaker of this City, dwelling in the street called St. Mary, in this city, native of the Town of Foucine in Franche Conte, of full age, son of Vincent Baclin Dubois and Mary Rene Gaux, his wife, being a widower by the decease of Maria Angelica Grazil, of the sd Town of Foucine; of the one part, and Elizabeth Claudine Bernardeau, native of the City of St. Marck in this Island, of full age and daughter of Joseph Bernardeau and Mary Genevieve Jolly, both deceased, dwelling in the Street called St. Mary in this city, of the other part. Which said parties mutually contracted and agreed to celebrate the rites of marriage between them; they shall be tenants in common in all property of which they are now possessed and may acquire, according to the custom of Paris, which governs this Colony; not liable for debts contracted by either party previous to their marriage. The estate of the future wife consists principally in the lots, lands and houses inherited from her deceased father and mother, to whom she is the sole heir by the death of her brother, (descriptions); also the sum of 40,000 livres owed to her by Sieur LaFargue of the City of St. Mark, balance of purchase money of a plantation and ten negroes sold by her to said LaFargue, which two items amount to 65,000 livres, from which is deducted 10,000 livres owing by her to her future husband and paid by him to discharge sundry debts owing by the parents and brother of said future wife, which reduces her share in the common fund to 55,000 livres. His estate 60,000 livres in gold and silver, proceeds from his trade and from sale of his stock and 10,000 livres due to him by his future wife. . . . They declare that the regard which they mutually entertain for each induced them to live together with the intention always of marrying, and from their cohabitation they have two children, a boy born Aug. 1, 1780 and a girl born 9 April 1782, which said children they call to their inheritance as such children as may or shall issue from their present marriage. Sept. 5, 1782.

p. 12. 6 Dec. 1784. Inventory of estate of Israel Folsom, of Cole's Creek, by Cato West and Thomas Murdock. Wit: Jacob Stampley, George Stampley, Will (W. H.) Hamberling, Alexander Boyd. // The estate of Folsom to E. Murdock, Dr. 1785. To one mare $40; Pd Mr. Hamberling $35-5; Pd to the Catalonian $17; Pd to S. Dealve $4; For sd est. and decd. $10; Pd Wilson for Coffin $3. By Cow and calf $20; 280 lbs of live pork $17-2; same $17-2; by 50 fowls $12-4; by 10 fowls $3-6; balance due E. Murdock $38-7. // I approve the above account presented by Mrs. Murdock and the balance due on said acct. will be paid by James Elliot, trustee of said account. Trevino. // p. 13. Mch. 4, 1789. This is to certify that Ebenezer Folsom hath received from Edmund Fulsom 3 mares and one horse and saddle; as also one fusee, of the estate of Fulsom. Wm. Hamberling, George Clare. // Natchez 5 Sept. 1788. About 3 years ago I was charged by Mr. Trevino to endeavor to settle the affairs of an estate belonging to the orphans of a certain Folsom, decd. at Cole's Creek; in consequence Mr. Cato West (in behalf of Mrs. Murdoch) and myself did settle the accounts between Mrs. Murdoch and the estate; that I did several times ask Edmund Folsom, the eldest of the orphans, to recollect any and every property belonging to the estate that had been consumed while it had been in possession of Mrs. Murdoch or her husband who was appointed executor but was then dead; that Edmund answered that everything he recollected had been mentioned in the settlement; within a day or so I sent Edmund, with a negro to assist, with two horses and a slide to bring the property belonging to the said estate to my house; he brought some property and delivered it to me and did not mention having left any property of said estate behind at Mrs. Murdoch's; some short time after, at the request of said orphans and Mr. Jeremiah Bryan, their affairs were given into Mr. Bryan's hands. Signed James Elliot. // Mch. 6, 1789. By order of Mr. Trevino who was then Commandant of this Place, I took inventory of the estate of Israel Folsom, decd., and to the best of my remembrance the cattle were not all present but were taken as the children described them. Signed Cato West.

p. 13. 16 Feb. 1785. In Fort Panmur at Natchez, Margaret Lafleur, being indebted to Benjamin Monsanto, of Pointe Coupee, in sum of $1701, to be paid in specie Dec. this year, mortgages plantation on which she now dwells, until final payment shall have been made. Her attorney, Peter Nelson, signed for her.

p. 14. 30 Jany. 1785. In consequence of death of Joseph [Jesse] Carter, who died unmarried and without lawful heirs, William (X) Brocus and James Stoddard appointed appraisers of his estate. Amount $147 // 6 Feb. 1785. Sale of same: Buyers: John Bisland (most of items); William Smith, 2 blankets, "of two points" for $5.00, and one horse; horse by Joaquim de Ossorno. Total $151-17. // p. 15. Natchez, Sept. 28, 1780, I promise to pay bearer $6.00 1 Nov. next, for value received. Signed Jesse Carter. // 4 Nov. 1784. Be it remembered Jesse Carter, son of Thomas Carter, has sold all merchantable tobacco which comes to his share, to Mr. John Bisland for $9.00 per hundred-weight (french) and to allow Mr. John Bisland $20 for finishing the crop, said Jesse Carter being ailing and not able to do it himself, agreeable to his original contract as overseer. Jesse Carter. // p. 16. 21 Jany. 1784. Agreement between John Bisland and Jesse Carter, both of Dist. The said Bisland to give Jesse Carter one share of all that shall be raised on said John Bisland's plantation this year, excepting pumpkins and pease, and also victuals and washing, with liberty to use pumpkins for one horse or mare during the time they may lay open in the field. Said Jesse Carter, on his part to work honestly and faithfully until the crop is finished, that is to say until the corn is housed and the tobacco prized and to do during that time what said Bisland may think proper with regard to raising the crop, etc. Both signed. Wit: John Farquhar, Geo. Fitzgerald. // Detailed settlement of the account of Jesse Carter and John Bisland.

p. 17. 5 Feb. 1785. William Morning, uncle of the five orphans left by his sister, wife of David Golsin* requests to have the said orphans put under his care, as well as their property, (small inventory), promising to take good care of said orphans and their property. He signed with a mark. *[Gholson?]

p. 17. 23 March 1785. John Burnet to St. Germain, for $800 (Spanish money), payable January next, two/thirds of a certain saw mill now occupied and on or near the land of Richard Goodwin, with the same part in a yoke of oxen at the Mill and the wheels and chain and everything belonging to said mill; one/third part belonging to Richard Goodwin, also my right to said mill and all that belongs to same and to the timber now standing which belongs to same. Signed John Burnet. Wit: H. Manadue.

p. 18. 9 April 1785. John Bisland to George Fitzgerald ten cows with their calves and six heifers with increase of same since March 1784 to present time; for $282 in hand paid. Signed.

p. 18. 7 May 1785. In pursuance of information of the death of Isaac Lewis, who left no lawful heirs nor any known relatives in this country; inventory and appraisal made, Wm (X) Brocus and Arthur Cobb appraisers. Total $365-4. // p. 19. Public sale of above estate. May 7, 1785, after public notice, on demand of creditors. Buyers: Wm. Brocus, Jacob Paul, Laurence McMin, Abraham Roberts, John Coleman, Sutton Banks, Charles Adams, Chas. Jones, James Armstrong, Joseph Ford, Francisco Baso, Samuel Bell, Wm. Bacon, William Smith, James Cole. Total $482-2. // p. 20. Will of Isaac Lewis. 31 Jany. 1785. After funeral expences and debts are paid, the remainder of my estate to my beloved brother, Abel Lewis, . . . including horses and cattle, some of which are in the hands of Stephen Stephenson and there to remain by contract, as also my plantation, of which he hath possession until January next. The remaining part of my horses are in Opelousas, that is to say, one mare and colt and one two-year old, together with my cattle, goods and chattels, which are at Natchez. I desire that Mr. James Cole, Sr., may have the management of same, whom I appoint executor until my brother shall arrive. Wit: Will Bell, Abraham (x) Roberts, Stephen (X) Stephenson.

p. 21. Natchez, 27 Aug. 1785. Inventory of property of Melchoir Donoso, who died on the above date in the house of Don Manuel Texada, of this Post, merchant, death preceded apparently by a long sickness. He left no lawful heirs nor relations in this country who may lay claim to his estate. Appraisers appointed, John Gordon and George Fitzgerald. // p. 22. Appraisement; total $252.

p. 23. Bond. 30 April 1785. Jeptha Higdon, of own free will and accord, security of Benj. Carroll in sum of $211 due and owing by him to sundry merchants, binds himself and estate.

p. 24. Bond. Natchez, 20 Dec. 1785. Josiah Flowers and William Hurlbert, both of the District, of free will and accord, become sureties in persons and property for John Burrell, George Burrell and Nathan Little, persons who came here with William Davenport, although not making a part of his force, for which reason they have been detained in this Fort and are now liberated under the present security, on condition that they appear when required and be of good behavior until permitted to be a subject. Signed by all except the Burrells who made their marks.

p. 24. Bond. 20 Dec. 1785. James Cole, of own free will and accord, becomes surety for John Coleman who came here with William Davenport and could not return with him, for which reason he was detained at the Fort and is liberated now to demean himself as a good and faithful subject until his Excellency, Don Estevan Miro's pleasure shall be known relative to his being admitted as a subject of His Catholic Majesty. Both sign.

p. 25. Bond. 21 Dec. 1785. Isaac Johnson become security for Samuel Culbertson who came here with Wm. Davenport and could not depart with him, etc. Both sign.

p. 25. Bond. 7 Jany. 1786. Matthew White and Bennet Smith surety for said Smith in bond given by the latter to estate of George Castles to satisfy any debts he may owe estate. Both sign. Wit: Jas. McIntosh. // p. 25. 16 Feb. 1796. Bennet Smith and Matthew White (Wm. Pounteny acting as interpreter), declare that the security given by the said Matthew White, extended only to the property in money and effects received by the sd Bennet Smith for account of the estate of George Castles, and that all such property and effects shall be applied to the payments of lawful debts of said estate and in case such receipts shall not be sufficient to discharge the said debts of said estate; that said appearants do not contemplate being liable in their own private property. Signed by both. // p. 26. Bond. 14 Jany. 1786. Bennet Smith made verbal demand against Lewis Charbono and St. Germain, for amount of a note which said Charbono drew 22 Jany. 1784 in favor of George Castles for $188, the said St. Germain also being surety. Both being present, acknowledged themselves unable to make immediate payment. Charbono offered to make over wages and profits that may derive from a trading voyage he is about to make to the Indian Nations, in which the said St. Germain has assisted him with the means. Signed by Bennet Smith and St. Germain. Charbono made his mark.

p. 26. 3 March 1786. Power of attorney from Don Juan Joseph Rodriguez, Military Store Keeper of the Post of Natchez, to Don Francisco de Castro, of the Treasury of the Province of Louisiana, to act for him as he might do if present.

p. 27. 15 March 1786. George Fitzgerald, of the Post of Natchez, merchant, to John Farquhar, of the District, planter, 6 cows with their calves and 6 heifers 18 months old, with increase since 1st Mch. 1784, for $282, in hand paid. Both sign.

p. 28. In pursuance of the order of Don Estevan Miro, Gov. Genl. of the Province, to deliver and pay to David Tanner $136, proceeds of his boat sold at public sale by order of Commandant Francisco Bouligny, I, the present Civil and Military Commandant of this Fort and District, have paid, on 5 April 1786, to Don Juis Chacheret, atty. for sd David Tanner the aforesaid sum of $136, the receipt whereof he doth acknowledge. Signed Carlos de Grand Pre, Chacheret. Wit: St. Minor, James McIntosh.

p. 28. William Pountney becomes surety for the person of Simon Burny, who is permitted to remain, said Pountney binding himself to produce him if required. Signed by Pountney.

p. 28. Bond. [n. d.] Joseph Forester binds himself to pay to Mr. Dupont $35, value of a mare sold to him and $20-1/2 value of another mare, both of which are in dispute between the parties, on condition that Dupont shall in four months from date appear with sufficient proof that the said mares belong to him, then if he does not appear the said Forester shall be free to dispose of said mares at his pleasure. Both sign. Off. witnesses. De Grand Pre.

p. 29. 8 June 1786. William Vousdan was security for John Tally to Messrs Morgan and Mather, merchants, of N. O. in $280 (hard dollars) being the price of a negro woman and child which Tally bought of George Mather, brother of the afsd Mather; in Nov. 1779, David Williams came to Natchez, commissioned by sd Morgan and Mather and presented Vousdan the obligation of said Tally and documents proving sufficiently that the demand of sd Tally agst Col. McGilvray who resided at Pensacola would not be allowed, no such condition being contained in the obligation given for the negroes. Whereupon Vousdan repaired immediately to the house of sd Tally, assuring him that he was ignorant of the contents [of the papers] ; and that the sd Tally without regard to his reputation, absconded with all sd papers and the value of sd negroes, leaving deponent to pay the money, which he was compelled, by law, to do and had received no compensation. Signed William Vousdan.

p. 29. Agreement. 31 Oct. 1786. Juan Joseph Martino obliges himself to deliver to John Ellis on his plantation at White Cliffs, in Oct. 1787, 107 horned cattle (description) and said Ellis binds himself on receipt thereof to pay sd Juan Martino at the end of the year 1787, sum of $900 and a further $900 at end of 1788. Signed Juan Joseph Martineaux, John Ellis.

p. 30. Bond. 5 Jany. 1787. Mary Higdon, widow, puts herself in place of Stephen Holstein to pay sum of $735 owing by Stephen Holstein to Don Juan Vaucheret, of this Post, merchant, to pay same in eight days from date and mortgages her whole estate. Said Mary declared she could not write. Ack. before Carlos de Grand Pre.

p. 30. Agreement, 18 Jany. 1787, between John Farquhar and David Smith to divide equally between them the loss or gain that might result to them from proceeds of 48 heads of hogs which were on a raft built on two perougues and sunk near White Cliffs and which said hogs are to be collected in the woods at the expense of the parties contracting and to be embarked and conducted by sd John Farquhar to New Orleans and sold on joint account of said John Farquhar and David Smith; the said parties binding their estate present and to come for the performance thereof and renouncing all laws in their favor. Both signed. Wit: George Fitzgerald, Isaac Gaillard. The said parties have agreed to employ some other person to assist in conducting hogs.

p. 31. Agreement. Stephen Jordan, John Welton, John Coleman, William Coleman. Jordan to let to above-mentioned the plantation that he now lives on for one or three years from 5 Jany. 1787, with 2 horses, 2 ploughs, 2 setts of gears, 7 breading sows, 35 pigs and 100 bu. of corn for use of the horses and hogs and also one negro man for six weeks only, such time as he may take to feed and water Jordan's hogs. John Welton, John Coleman and Wm. Coleman, for their part, to put six sufficient hands on above-mentioned plantation to make sufficient fence from house to creek and to give Stephen Jordan one/third of corn, tobacco and oats, with one/half of increase of animals, and return all equipment and animals, the one-third of crop and one/half of increase of hogs to be delivered yearly to said Jordan. Stephen (X) Jordan, John Welton, William Coleman. Wit: William Cooper, D. Smith. // Natchez, 15 Feb. 1787. The foregoing agreement shall be valid unless the said plantation, horses or effects shall be mortgaged for debt and creditors should require that the whole or a part be sold in payment. Grand Pre.

p. 31. 23 March 1787. Isaac Johnson is indebted to Richard Carpenter and promises to pay on or before Jany. 1, 1788, the quantity of 5030 lbs of tobacco and for security mortgage two negroes "Stephen" and "Lucy", both aged 26. Signed by both. // p. 32. 22 Jany. 1788. Richard Carpenter acknowledges to have received from Isaac Johnson the quantity of 5030 lbs. of tobacco and the foregoing mortgage is null and void.

p. 32. Power of Atty. Eunice McIntosh to David Ross, to purchase sundry slaves, binding her estate present and to come. Signed.

p. 32. Will of Joseph Forester, native of Ireland, resident of the District of Natchez, weak in body. I bequeath to the daughter of Patty McKee, formerly living at Jacob's Creek near the crossing place, within about 42 miles of Fort Pitt, her child, aged about 15 years, all my property both real and personal, after debts and burial expenses are paid. My trusty friends, Caleb and Justus King, to receive and sell and affirm all debts, property or properties belonging to me. New Orleans, 10 July 1787. Signed. Wit: Wm. Smith, Robert Scazey, Wm. Coxon.

p. 33. Natchez, 5 Sept. 1787. Paul Lafitte, of Post of Nachitoches, bind myself to deliver to Don Estevan Minor, adjt. of Fort of Natchez, in October next, 1788, 300 head of cattle, (description), on the right bank of the river Mississippi, directly opposite to the Town of Natchez, for $4293, which Minor binds himself to pay, (on terms). Both bind their estates. Both sign.

p. 34. Bond. 25 Sept. 1787. William Henderson and John Lum bind themselves in person and property for John Burnet, confined in this Fort, to the end that said Burnet may, on our security, be set at liberty, until the case against him may be finally determined. Both sign. Carlos de Grand Pre.

p. 34. 31 Jany. 1788. Power of Atty. William Cooper of this Dist., planter, to William Benjamin Smith, for me, to appear before the Superior Tribunal of this province, to claim two slaves belonging to me, now in prison of New Orleans, a negro man "Peter" and a woman "Mary", which said slaves ran away from this Post of Natchez about five months since. Signed. Before Carlos de Grand Pre.

p. 34. May 1, 1788. Exchange. John Montgomery has exchanged with Thomas Wilkins a red (or bay) horse 8 years old with one white foot, named "Doctor", not branded, for a horse to sd Thos. Wilkins belonging, 7 years old, branded "W. S." and "A. M." and $70 to boot, which sd Wilkins has paid to me, binding ourselves that said horses were our own property. Both sign.

p. 35. Bond and mortgage. 4 May 1788. Don Juan Girault, of Post and District of Natchez, merchant, binds himself and estate to Lt. Col. Don Carlos de Grand Pre for security of payment of sundry sums he owes to divers merchants in New Orleans, as will appear by documents in his possession and in possession of Don Carlos de Grand Pre who has become security for these debts. To secure him for the payment of which and also for the sum of $905, specie, which he lent from motives of kindness and without interest, he mortgages to Grand Pre his plantation near the mouth of St. Catherine's Creek, 361 arpents, with house thereon, b. by Don Philip Trevino, Richard Ellis and Mary Green, also house on lot of ground lately bought from Don Estevan Minor, b. by the King's Road near this fort, and lands of Barland and of Mr. Peyroux, and 200 arps. at Cole's Creek, b. by James Elliot and William Ferguson, as also some cattle (described). Signed by both before official witnesses. // Natchez, July 1, 1796. The foregoing mortgage is annulled and void. Signed Carlos de Grand Pre.

p. 36. 7 May 1788. Bond. John Burrell is indebted to Don Juan Vaucheret for $105, to be paid 25 Dec. this year; mortgages two mares. John (X) Burrel.

p. 36. 8 May 1788. Peter Cenas, of N. O., gives power of attorney to Don Juan Vaucheret, merchant, to settle accounts I have pending with Peter Camus and Honorato Duon and to receive sums owing by them to me. Signed.

p. 36-7. 26 May 1788. Agreement between John Ford and John Baptiste Ferrall. The said John Ford to work on and conduct plantation to said Ferrall belonging, for two years; to commence at end of December next and ending last of Dec. 1790, the said Ford engaging to build dwelling house and negro cabbins on sd land; and Farrel engaging to put on the sd plantation six or more slaves and to furnish all tools necessary for the plantation, 4 horses, 1 pr oxen, and sufficient provision for the use of the slaves and the family of sd John Ford, and at the end of the crop the same to be divided, supposing 6 slaves are put on the plantation, the crop shall be divided into 8 shares, John Ford to get 2 shares and in like proportion he is to get 2 out of 8 shares. Both sign.

p. 37. Don Carlos de Grand Pre, now Civil and Military Commandant of the Post and Dist. of Natchez, husband of Helena Page and guardian of her rights, give full power to Don Augustus Choteau to represent my proper person, rights and actions to recover and receive from the Executor to the Will of Mr. Viviat the property bequeathed by him to my said wife in the possession of Mr. Cerre. 29 May 1788.

p. 38. 14 June 1788. Don Carlos de Grand Pre, Commandant, etc., in order to carry into effect a former decree, have proceeded to the appraisement and sale of a horse belonging to John Wood, appoints as appraisers Nathaniel Tomlinson and Josiah Flowers. Wit: James Garland, Robert Miller. Appraisal, $55.00. At sale of horse, it was adjudged to James Garland, the highest bidder for $38. Expense of sale $18; to creditor, James Erwin, $20.

p. 39. 10 Aug. 1788. Maria Page to Don Solomon Maline, power, for me and in my name in the City of New Orleans, to receive from Don Marcos de Villiers the sum of $229 owing to me on his note, with interest thereon. Signed.

p. 39. 16 Aug. 1788. Sale. Don Carlos de Grand Pre has proceeded to the sale and appraisement of a cow and calf seized as the property of John Carr, to satisfy his debt to John Montgomery. Robert Ford and Winsor Pipes appraisers; appraisal $20. At sale, same adjudged to Juan Carreras for $25. Net to creditor $14-4.

p. 40. 22 Aug. 1788. Bond of Charles Simons, holder of the property of the two minors, James and Jacob Simons, delivered to him by their mother, Ursula Simons, as being inherited from their father, which consists of: plantation, 400 arpents, near Cole's Cr. on bank of Mississippi, one negro named "Aberdeen", 28 horned cattle, 34 hogs, 9 horses, household furniture (listed). Security for Charles Simons, William Curtis and Joseph Bonner. Charles (X) Simons. The bondsmen sign. [The name is Simmons]

p. 40. 13 Nov. 1788. Don Carlos de Grand Pre, on information of the death of Christopher Thompson, at the plantation of William Barland, and that all his property and effects are at the house of Alexander Moore, repaired thither to take inventory. // 15 Nov. 1788, Jacob Monsanto and Pedro Azevedo appointed appraisers. // p. 42. Personal appraisement $895. Papers of Christian Thompson: Letters from Archie Thompson, brother of deceased, Andrew Thompson, James Haler, William Thompson, David Thompson, Thomas Thompson, George Sharer, William Caldwell. A grant of land to Pedro Pepino; a certificate of his birth and conduct; an obligation of Robert Patton for £ 56; an order on Daniel Clark for $44; receipts of James Springer for $45, Robert McKay and James McNulty. // p. 44. 6 Dec. 1788. Sale of property and effects of Christopher Thompson. Buyers: Benj. Monsanto, Alex. Moore, Daniel Thompson, Pedro Azevedo, Antonio Soler, Wm. Selkrig, Mr. Monro, Jacob Monsanto, Thos. Perkins,

Thos. Hoffpaver, Juan Carreras, John Burnet, Louis Faure, Juan Joseph Rodriguez, Jeremiah Brian, Stephen Minor, Mr. Burrel, Philip Turpin, J. Fournier, Justus Andrus.

p. 49. 14 Oct. 1785. Messrs Matthew Elliott and William Caldwell, Detroit, power of atty. to William Pauling, also of Detroit.

p. 49-50. 18 Nov. 1788. Helen Humphries Pruet, power of atty to James Richardson for me and in my name, etc. to recover and receive the estate left me by my deceased father, being the only child living. Helen (X) Humphries Pruet. Before Grand Pre.

p. 50. 26 Dec. 1788. At the request of John Pickens, Don Carlos de Grand Pre repaired to the plantation of Josiah Flowers to make sale of sundry mares and horses to Pickens belonging, payable on terms with security. Buyers: Cader Raby, surety Prosper King; Samuel Head, surety Henry Kirk; Ryan Chisholm, surety David Smith; John Calvit, surety Joseph Higdon*; Henry Kirk, surety Samuel Head; Stephen Richards, surety James Kirk; Waterman Crane, surety Abraham Casamore; James Wilson, surety Thomas Bellew; John Calvit, surety Jeptha Higdon; William Glasscock, surety William Lewis; Alexander Moore, surety Daniel Maguet; Henry Kirk, surety John Calvit. * [Jeptha]

p. 51. 12 Dec. 1788. Sale of horses, etc. belonging to John Pickens and Richard King. Buyers: Thomas Loyd, surety Prosper King; Robert Miller, surety John Pickens; John Ford, surety Robert Miller; Alexr. Moore, surety David Maguet; Juan Carreras ______; Richard Harris, surety Abraham Calsaman [Castleman]; John Whiteman, surety Letman McGlaughlin; John Helen, surety Francisco Pavana; Wm. Selkrig, surety David Haltman; Charles Carter, surety Daniel Megget; Joseph Dobbs, surety Nathaniel Abel; Robert Miller, surety John Pickens; Richard Adams, surety Archibald Martin; Thomas Brown, surety James Garland; Wm. Henderson, surety Arthur Cooper. Witnesses during the sessions: Richard Harris, Edward McCabe, Joseph Flowers, Andrew Walker, John Farquhar, Franco. Pavana, Hugh Magowne, Jere Bryan, Daniel Megget and Wm. Henderson.

p. 52. 24 Dec. 1788. Thomas Hoffpaver power of atty to Christian Harman to receive all debts owing and due to me and to take charge of house and lot which I hold in Town of Natchez. Signed.

p. 53. [n. d.] Thos. Irwin, of Natchez, merchant, indebted to Juan Baptiste Legret, for $4804, has delivered to sd Legret four obligations of divers inhabitants of this district amounting to the sum of $4583 in coin of Mexico, which said Legret engages to recover and reduce into paper, being accountable to me for the surplus after decuting the sum due him; on condition however that if he shall not be able to recover the amount of said obligations I am bound to pay him the sum I have acknowledged. The obligations being (1) Raphael (Ralph) Humphreys for $950, (2) Thos. Burnet for $1000, (3) Melling Woolley $400, and Joseph (Jesse) Carter $2232. Both sign.

p. 54. Jany. 3, 1789. Maria Page to Victoria Deneufville, dwelling in New Orleans, power for me and in my name to receive from Marcos Coulon de Villiers, sum of $229 due me on his note, with interest. Signed.

p. 54. 27 Jany. 1789. Manuel Texada to Don Juan Joseph Rodriguez power to manage all my concerns and business in Natchez. Signed.

p. 54. [n. d.] Power from Don Carlos Boucher de Grand Pre to Don Solomon Maline of the City of New Orelans, merchant, to appear before Superior Tribunal of this Province to defend suit instigated by my mother, Lady Theresa Galord de Grand Pre, relative to my house which she occupies, to take all lawful means to defend my rights in conformity with my exposition to said suit, dated 35 Dec. last past. Signed.

p. 55. Will of John Pickens. 18 Jany. 1789. Weak in body; after debts are paid, the remainder to be divided into three equal parts, one-third to my beloved wife, Mary, one-third to the child that my wife is now pregnant with, the remaining one-third to my brother, David Pickens; my friends Robert Miller and Charles Collins exrs. Signed. Wit: Richard King, John Griffing, John Bell, Justus King, Prosper King, Oswell (X) Yarborough. // At Natchez 22 Jany. 1789. Richard Miller appeared to inform of death of John Pickens who died the 18th of the present month at the house of Justus King, to which he had removed by reason of sickness, intending to make a journey to the Choctaw Town and the sd Richard thereupon delivered the sealed will of sd Pickens and the witnesses who signed with him being present, Don Carlos de Grand Pre immediately opened the will in their presence. // p. 56. 26 Jany. 1789. De Grand Pre and assistants repaired to house of Richard Adams in which the widow of sd deceased John Pickens lived in order to take inventory. // p. 57. Same date, the Commandant repaired to plantation of Richard King who has in his charge sundry horses and mares belonging to him and the deceased John Pickens in partnership, also sundry notes given by individuals for horses sold, and proceeded with inventory. Notes by the following

Richard King
John Gilbert
Nathaniel Fulsom
Hetman Kirk
Joseph Moore
Barney Isenwood
Samuel Bell
Lewis Bennet
James Wilson
Joseph Ford
Geo. Fitzgerald
William Brocus
John Young
Samuel Cooper
Richard Adams
John Adams
Alexr. Moore
Jonathan Curtis
Thomas Brown
Joseph Martinez Rubio
Juan Carreras

p. 57. inventory of notes due John Pickens, deceased.

Jeremiah Carter
John Murdoch
George Selden
Samuel Gibson
Wm. Silvester
David Waterman
Jacob Cobun
William Young
Arch. Rea
James Smith
Jeremiah Bryan
John Whiteman
Thomas Lloyd
John Bond
Alexander Farrow
John Calvit
Oswell Yarborough
Charles King
Francisco Pavana
Henry Kirk
Jonathan Rocart
Richard Adams
Waterman Crane
William Glascock
James Sanders
Elijah Phipps
Richard Kenes
Job Cory
Josiah Flowers
John Carr
Wm. Wilson
Roda McPech
Nehemiah Carter
Samuel Gibson
Stephen Minor
Richard Swayze
Joseph Dunkin
Chas. Bishop
Jame McIntyre

---

p. 60. 28 Jany. 1789. David Munro to Clark and Rees power to settle all my business in New Orleans.

p. 60. 26 Jany. 1789. Manuel Texada to William Hamberling 9 saddle horses for 3700 lbs of tobacco, French weight, to be delivered Dec. 1789 on bank of Miss. River at Cole's Creek, Henry Platner surety for same. Signed by the three. // 27 March 1798. The foregoing instrument is cancelled, the party having paid part of the amount therein mentioned and given his obligation in cotton at the end of the present year, in the presence of Cato West, Esq., alcalde of the District of Villa Gayoso.

p. 61. Anthony Bowkes to Isaac Johnson power to claim and receive the papers left by me in the office of Raphael Perdonno, relative to the estates of my brothers, Thomas and Raphael Bowkes. 4 Feb. 1789. Signed.

p. 62. 5 Feb. 1789. Agreement. Simon Peter Daigret binds himself to work for Mr. Hardy Ellis during 10 months from date hereof in payment of $100 which I owe said Ellis and in case I find it convenient to pay said sum this obligation will be void. Both sign.

p. 62. 11 Feb. 1789. Hardy Ellis owes Louis Badisin $750 to be paid by Nov. 15 of this year, mortgages horses and cattle, hereby ack. by Don Estevan Minor, atty. for Badison. Signed.

p. 63. 7 Apr. 1789. Judith Coleman, widow of James Baker, acknowledges to have received from her mother, Patience Welton, holding the estate of my deceased father as admx. thereof, $35 in full. The estate of Mr. William Coleman to Patience Coleman. Dec. 31, 1787. To sundry debts paid as follows to Mr. Chachere $18; Caleb King $3; Winson Pipes $10; Patrick Foley $39; John Short $25; George Fitzgerald $212; John Alston $83; Stephen Minor $13; Jas. McIntosh $2; Jeremiah Bryan $3; John Girault $4; Mr. De Grand Pre $20; Col. Hutchins $175. Total Inventory $1126 Mrs. Patience Welton's one-half $702. Due each child $35.

p. 63. Sale. 14 Feb. 1789. Sale of sundry horses belonging to the partnership of Richard King and John Pickens, deceased, on terms with security. // p. 64. Buyers and sureties:

Buyers	Sureties
Cady Raby	Joseph Ford
Francisco Pavana	Antonio Soler
Sutton Bankes	Justus King
Henry Johns	Sebastian Dar

Moses Bonner	James Bonner
Prosper King	Justus King
Michael St. John	J. J. Rodriguez
_______ West	Peter Steer
John Hascover	Joseph Bonner
James Wells	Henry Kirk
Thomas Brown	Hugh Magowan
Jesse Hamilton	Ebenezer Dayton
David Lambert	Chas. King
John Foster	Prosper King
William Bacon	Francisco Pavana
Ebenezer Dayton	Jesse Hamilton
John Patterson	John Adams
Charles King	James Hess
Juan Carreras	Franco Pavana
Jacob Adams	John Adams
John Adams	Jacob Adams
Richard King	Justus King
Mrs. Adams	John Adams
Jesse Hamilton	Jeptha Higdon
Jacob Monsanto	Wm. Gilbert
Prosper King	Justus King
Philip Turpin.	Francisco Pavana

Wit: Prosper King, Franco. Pavana, Antonio Soler, Jos. Duncan, Gerard Brandon, James Patton. De Grand Pre.

p. 65. 20 May 1789. Bartholomew Bosque to Antonio Soler, power to recover amount of sales made for cash or credit due to estate of Francisco Bazo, deceased. Signed.

p. 66. 23 May 1789. Samuel Heady indebted to Don Juan Girault for $108, mortgages horses. Signed.

p. 66. 14 May 1789. Thomas Nash indebted to Don Juan Girault for $10.00, Robert Miller security. Thos. (X) Nash, Robert Miller.

p. 67. 23 May 1789. James Hayes indebted to Juan Girault, for $8.00, John Stampley security. James (X) Hayes, John Stampley.

p. 67. David Mulkey indebted to Don Juan Girault mortgages his estate, etc. 6 June 1789.

p. 67. Samuel Ewing, of District of Natchez, to James Morrison, power to receive from sundry debtors of Pointe Coupee, the sum of $290, owing to me on notes which I have delivered to said attorney. 30 June 1789. Signed.

p. 68. 7 July 1789. John Lum indebted to Juan Girault for $172, binding person and estate. Signed.

p. 68. 14 July 1789. Thomas Ford indebted to Juan Girault for $47, binding self and estate. Thomas (X) Ford.

p. 69. July 18, 1789. Don Estevan Minor, Adjt. of this Fort of Natchez, to Don Carlos de Grand Pre, power to look after my affairs and receive amount of my pay as adjutant since July of the year last past. Signed.

p. 69. Agreement. 20 July 1789. Daniel Callaghan, of Opelousas, contracts to deliver at the Post of Natchez, on the other side of River Mississippi, from 80 to 140 head of horned cattle (described), which I sell to Don Juan Joseph Rodriguez, Military Store Keeper of this Post of Natchez, at price of $16 Mexican dollars per head, on or before September of this present year, provided the roads are practicable and if not this obligation is void. Signed by both. // p. 68. 11 Sept. 1789. Receipt of Daniel Callagham for $317 on account of 140 head of horned cattle as per annexed obligation, by Don Juan Joseph Rodriguez. Signed.

p. 70. 18 Sept. 1789. John Turnbull to Maurice Stackpoole power to act for me and in my name and to manage all my concerns of business as if the same were his property. Signed.

p. 70. 9 Oct. 1789. Antoine Bienvenu, of Illinois, to John Macarty, of N. O., power for me and in my name to recover and receive and settle my affairs with all my debtors. Antoine (X) Bienvenu.

p. 71. 10 Oct. 1789. Thomas Vause to Nathaniel Tomlinson, for me and in my name, power to claim a gray horse and colt in possession of Dinsmore who resides in the Choctaw Nation. Signed.

p. 71. 16 Oct. 1789. Thomas Creighton to John Hailer, for me and in my name to settle all debts due to or by me as if the same was his own property. Signed.

p. 71. Natchez, Nov. 13, 1789. John Bolls, of this District, petitions that he has been detained prisoner in the Fort for 8 days on account of a matter that he is persuaded he can prove he is wholly ignorant of; the petitioner has a large family and a great part of his crop is on the eve of being lost by his absence. Signed. // Natchez, Nov. 13, 1789. Let the bail offered by petitioner be given and he may then be set at liberty. Grand Pre.

p. 72. 13 Nov. 1789. Israel [Ezekiel] Dewit, of Dist., planter, gives bond for the person of John Bolls that he may released from prison and return home to attend to his crop and remain there or any part of District. Signed with his mark "E. D.".

p. 72. 18 Dec. 1789. John Baptiste Legret to Peter Walker, power to recover and receive all sums of money owing to me personally and make necessary quittances in my name. Signed.

p. 72. 23 Dec. 1789. Thos. Hughes to John McGery power to recover and receive for me and in my name the inheritance belonging to my wife, now in the possession of Mrs. Bitsell, widow of Henry Bitsell, and appear before all competent Tribunals. Signed.

p. 73. Dec. 31, 1789. Robert Cochran to George Cochran, my brother, power for me and in my name to receive sums of money due me and settle and improve a tract of land in said district granted to me by His Catholic Majesty, on the Homochitto. Signed.

p. 73. 20 January 1790. Melling Wooley, being lawfully possessed of a bond drawn by Winsor Pipes and William Collins in my favor, for 14700 lbs. of tobacco, hereby assigns and transfers to Thos. Irwin 7000 lbs. of same to pay for value which I have received of sd Thomas Irwin. Signed.

p. 74. 25 January 1790. Jesse Withers is indebted to Thomas Wilkins for $152, mortgages horned cattle. Signed.

p. 74. 8 Feb. 1790. Catharine Lambert, widow of Alonzo Segovia, in consequence of a debt owing by my deceased husband to Don Andrew Fernandez for $446, mortgages estate. Signed with a mark.

p. 74-5. 22 Feb. 1790. Robert Miller is indebted to Thomas Wilkins for $500, James Sanders surety for same, also mortgages cattle. Signed.

p. 75. 23 Feb. 1790. David Lambert is indebted to Christian Harman in sum of $277; mortgages estate Signed. // 7 Nov. 1790. Received of David Lambert $277; mortgage satisfied and void. Signed Christian Harman. Wit: John D. Brady.

p. 75. 1 March 1790. Nehemiah Carter indebted to Thomas Irwin $760; mortgages estate. Signed.

p. 76. 10 March 1790. Thomas Dyson indebted to James Elliot, for $126; mortgages two horses. Thomas (X) Dyson.

p. 77. 12 March 1790. Samuel Heady, indebted to Don Juan Girault, merchant, for $108, and to Don Estevan Minor, Adjt., for $150, to be paid to them or their order, in N. O., out of the proceeds of my raft of timber which I am now about to descend with to that City. Signed.

p. 77. 16 March 1790. Assignment: Melling Wooley, having transferred to me, Thomas Irwin, an obligation for 7000 pounds of tobacco to be paid by Winsor Pipes and William Collins, now transfer the said obligation to Messrs Clark and Rees. Signed.

p. 77. 20 March 1790. William West indebted to Thomas Wilkins and Co. mortgages horses and cattle. William (X) West.

p. 78. 21 May 1790. Jonas Isler is indebted to Thos. Wilkins and Co. for $93, mortgages cows and calves. Signed.

p. 78-9. 5 June 1790. William Wilson, indebted to Thomas Wilkins for $300, mortgages cattle. Signed.

p. 79. 5 June 1790. James Truly and William Ferguson are indebted to Don Estevan Minor for $136; mortgage cattle. Both signed.

p. 79. 5 June 1790. James Kelly, indebted to Thomas Wilkins and Co., for $207, mortgages horses.

p. 80. 23 June 1790. Joel Bird, indebted to Thos. Wilkins and Co. for $20, mortgages cow and calf. Joel (X) Bird.

p. 80. 23 June 1790. Joseph Green to Thomas Wilkins indebted for $80, mortgages two cows and calves. Signed.

p. 81. 23 June 1790. Robert Miller, indebted to Thos. Wilkins and Co. for $680, mortgages 15 cows and calves. Signed.

p. 81. 23 Juen 1790. John Williams acknowledges to owe Thomas Wilkins and Co. $234, for which he mortgages horses and cows. Signed.

p. 81. 27 June 1790. Walter Beall gives power to Andrew Beall to buy, sell, alienate and appear at law against my debtors. Signed.

p. 82. 19 July 1790. John Strabreaker, indebted to Thomas Wilkins for $148; mortgages cattle. Signed.

p. 83. 22 July 1790.. Robert Abrams owes to Thos. Wilkins $59; mortgages one horse. Signed.

p. 83. 22 July 1790. Thomas Rule, indebted to Thos. Wilkins for $49; mortgages horse and cattle. Thomas (X) Rule.

p. 83. 25 July 1790. Matrimonial contract to be celebrated between Robert Miller and Miss Sarah Cole and she being desirous to ascertain the property she possesses in case of need at a future day, this is an inventory thereof, taken in presence of witnesses. Two good mares, 4 cows and calves, 3 3-yr-old heifers, one 4-yr old steer, 5 hogs, a good bed and furniture, some household furniture, and one good side saddle. Wit: John Searcy, Jacob Stampley, Solomon Cole. // I acknowledge receipt of the above property into my possession. Signed Robert Miller.

p. 83. 3 Aug. 1790. Antonio Gras, Louis Vilaret and Samuel Swayze agree to a partnership for making bricks in a kiln to contain 70,000 on following conditions: Antonio Gras shall put two negroes to work, provision for the said negroes to be furnished by Louis Vilaret, the said Gras paying him $6 per month for their provisions and no more; and Samuel Swazey shall furnish horses and oxen to haul sand, wood and water and his sons to assist in the work, the wood to be cut at the expence of the concern, the said Vilaret to oversee the work and in case he is ill he shall put some other person in his place, etc., the bricks to be divided equally. All sign.

p. 84. Natchez, 9 Aug. 1790. George Overaker declared that on the 8th instant in road leading from plantation of Mr. Girault to that of Mr. Cooper, he lost a pocket-book containing sundry notes and papers. which declaration he thinks necessary to make to the end that the drawers of said notes may not pay the amount thereof to any person or persons other than himself, who is the lawful owner thereof. Signed.

p. 84. 2nd Sept. 1790. Thomas Irwin to James Kennedy, merchant, of New Orleans, power to recover and receive from Joseph Francisco Vento, of the City of Havana, $5640, Mexican coin, to me owing, which said sum ought to be in the hands of Mr. Berenquel, of said City, to the intent and purpose of paying the debts which said Irwin and James Patterson contracted in Philadelphia in 1786, the balance after paying said debts to be refunded to me the said Irwin or to my son John. And if Mr. Thomas Plunket should by virtue of a former power given to him for the same purpose have received the before mentioned sum, he will immediately pay over the same to said Kennedy or his order in virtue of this present power. Signed.

p. 85. 13 Sept. 1790. Dennis Carey declared that one day in July present year he being at the landing of this Town, he lost an obligation for $25 which Hugh Coyle gave him to take care of an which had been already paid and to the end that the person who may have found the said obligation shall not claim the amount thereof from said Coyle, he has made the present declaration. Signed.

p. 85. Natchez, 15 Sept. 1790. Petition of Ezekiel Forman, states that a young woman, Elizabeth Church, on about the 9th of August last past, died in petitioner's house without making any will, as you petitioner believes. Your petitioner has been informed that very strange accounts have been circulated, since the death of the sd Elizabeth, relative to property that she had in this country; that your petitioner doesn't know, at present, of any person so competent to give information about the said deceased and her property as a certain William Chambers, who, as your petitioner is informed, is in daily expectation of leaving this country; and whereas your petitioner conceives himself materially interested in making every possible enquiry respecting the property of said deceased, he presumes to pray that examination of William Chambers aforesaid may be taken at large upon this business before he leave the country, etc.

p. 85-6. Oct. 6, 1790. William Henderson and Joseph Holmes become responsible for the person of Charles Lucas that he the said Lucas shall deliver to Ebenezer Folsom a horse he has now in the Nation, to be delivered on the first order of Folsom and the expense of bringing said horse from thence to be borne equally by Lucas and Folsom. Wit: Wm. Gilbert. Signed by Henderson and Holmes.

p. 86. 7 Oct. 1790. Ezekiel Dewitt becomes surety for Solomon Glegen in sum of $112 to be paid to Ebenezer Folsom for 5 cows belonging to him which were killed by mistake. Folsom acknowledges to be satisfied. Ezekiel (X) Dewitt, Ebenezer (X) Folsom.

p. 86. 11 Oct. 1790. Robert Collins sells to Ebenezer Folsom 4 cows and one mare for $128, value of 5 cows which were killed by mistake, belonging to said Folsom. Robert (x) Collins, Ebenezer (x) Folsom.

p. 87. 11 Oct. 1790. Archibald Rea and Daniel Harragill, sureties for the person of Jacob Adams so that Adams may be released from this Fort where he is now a prisoner and return to his house, the sd sureties being unanswerable for any insult sd Adams may offer to Elias Richards or to any person in this Dist. Signed by Rea.

p. 87. Oct. 18, 1790. Manuel Diaz to Antonio Sosada, dwelling in New Orleans, power to represent me, receive moneys, etc., owing to me. Signed.

p. 87. 23 Oct. 1790. Bond by Estevan Minor to Thomas Wilkins and Company in sum of $2031, to be paid Jany. 1791 in 25 hogsheads of good tobacco inspected at King's Store. Signed. // Natchez, 30 Aug. 1797, Thos. Wilkins acknowledges to have received from said Estevan Minor full payment of foregoing obligation.

p. 88. 3 Nov. 1790. Jacob Cable, indebted to Estevan Minor in sum of $280, specie, promises 2000 lbs of tobacco in New Orleans. Jacob (x) Cable.

p. 88. 12 Aug. 1790. Having received notice of the death of Joseph Small at plantation of William Henderson, 7 miles from Fort, repaired to said place to take inventory. Witnesses assisting; James Morrison, Francisco Pavana, Antonio Soler, Wm. Henderson. De Grand Pre. // p. 89. 13 Aug. 1790. Having heard that sundry effects of Joseph Small, decd., were at the house of Antonio Gras, have repaired thither and administered the oath to said Gras. Took inventory. // James Morrison also had some effects of deceased which he had taken care of by request, as follows: (mostly goods, by the yard.) // p. 90. David Ferguson and Maurice Stackpoole appointed appraisers. At sale buyers: John Foster, Mathew Diaz, Dr. Todd, David Williams, Mr. Scott, Solomon Link, Antonio Gras, David Ferguson, Juan O'Connor, Francisco Pavana, James Ross. // p. 92. 4 days taken to examine papers in said estate. p. 93. List of papers: . . . a bundle of accts. between deceased and Andrew Beall; an award by Peter Walker and Juan O'Connor; a receipt of Andrew Beall for sundry notes received from deceased; accounts agst Abner Green and Maurice Stackpoole.

---

p. 94. 21 Nov. 1790. Luis Chachere, formerly of the Post of Natchez but now of the Post of Opelousas, gives power of atty. to Pierre Camus, of Natchez, to manage and transact all his affairs. // Copy certified March 8, 1791, to Opelousas.

p. 95. 22 March 1790. Robert Abrams, indebted to Don Pedro Surget in sum $161, being amount of a joint note drawn by George Cook and myself to pay Dec. 1790 out of money I am to receive from Samuel Martin for a plantation which I sold said Martin, who is surety for said sum. Signed.

p. 95. David Ross to William Stephens, Esq., of N. O., merchant, for me and in my name to appear before the Superior Tribunal and take all means and ways to recover debts due to me by sundry individuals. 25 Nov. 1790.

p. 96. Copy of original account produced by Thomas Irwin, Esq. and requested to be filed in office of Secy. of Government. 10 Dec. 1790. Signed: Grand Pre. // 1786. Messrs. Irwin and Patterson in acct. with Daniel Clark as atty. for Peter Whitesides and Co. and Andrew Petit and Thomas Burns. N. O. March 19, 1789.

p. 96. Natchez, March 16, 1790. From Mr. Thomas Irwin, the following obligations as deposits on account of Messrs. Miller and Abercrombie.

Nathl. Ivy $683 Jordan and Withers $35
Roger Dixon $282 James Elliot $41
Andrew Jackson $150 Cory and Cobun $78
Christopher Bowling $52.4 Pipes and Collins $560
Isaac Tabor $27.6 Total $1939.3

A true copy taken at the request of Thomas Irwin to remain in Records of the Government of Natchez. Dec. 10, 1790. Carlos De Grand Pre.

p. 97. Natchez 11 Dec. 1791. Having received information from the officer on guard at the landing that a dead body was found lying in the Gallery of the house belonging to Juan O'Connor, have repaired thither accompanied by James Ross and Don Louis Faure, surgeon; found a body of a man lying on his side with arms crossed, and, having enquired of the bystanders if they knew the deceased, was answered in the affirmative that his name was Jacob Holmes. Surgeon reported there were no marks of violence on the body and to all appearance his death had proceeded from intoxication and being exposed to the cold all night. Signed: James Ross, Louis Faure, Antonio Soler, Edward McCabe, Carlos de GrandPre.

p. 97. 29 March 1791. Thos. Irwin, of this Post, merchant, gives power of atty. to Adam Bingaman and John O'Connor to settle my affairs, etc. in this Post. Signed.

p. 97. 4 April 1791. Martha Davis, wife of Patrick Foley, power of attorney to my husband, Patrick Foley, to recover and receive from Juan Constance $150 due me from said Constance by instrument on record in New Orleans. Signed Martha Foley.

p. 98. 4 May 1791. William Murray, executor of will of Joseph Chalon, deceased, power to Isabella Rousseau, widow of said deceased, to receive all papers, documents necessary to liquidate estate of deceased from the dower of said Isabella as wife of decd, which said papers ought to be in possession of Catherine Murray, Oliver Pollock or John Buckley, dwelling in the U. S. Signed W. Murray.

p. 98-9. Natchez, 21 June 1791. Don Juan Joseph Rodriguez, of Natchez, gives power of atty. to Don Manuel Texada, of same, to manage my property and estate as I could or might if present. Signed.

p. 99. Natchez, 26 July 1791. Manuel Diaz gives power of atty. to Antonio Molina, both of Natchez Post, to collect sundry horses and mares which I have running in this District and to sell same at a fair value. Signed.

p. 99. Natchez, 3 Aug. 1791. Don Joseph Vidal to Don Joseph Sainz, of the Regiment of La., power to settle and adjust in New Orleans accounts which I have with the Accountant of the Army of this Province from Jany. 1, 1788 to last Jany. 1789, when I held the office of Storekeeper of the Post of St. Mark of Apulacha, which sd accounts have not been settled. Signed.

p. 100. Power of atty. from Richard Harrison to Alexander Moore to do with my affairs as I could or might do if present. 8 Aug. 1791. Signed: Richard Harrison.

p. 101. 11 Aug. 1791. Maurice Stackpoole to George Cochran and David Ferguson, power of attorney. Signed.

p. 101. Aug. 31, 1791. Tarpley Bayley to George Cochran two hogsheads of tobacco, to me belonging, now in the hands of Stephen Cole, for value received of Cochran. Signed.

p. 102. 6 Sept. 1791. Bennet Truly to Daniel Clark, Jr., merchant of N. O., power of atty. to perform and transact in N. O. all my affairs. Signed.

p. 103. 2 Oct. 1791. Geo. Cochran sells to Barney Isenhoot one pair of mill-stones for seven cows with their calves. Signed.

p. 103. 4 Oct. 1791. John Williams power of atty. to Thos. Green and Cato West.

p. 103. 12 Oct. 1791. Francisco Gonzales, private in 8th Co. of 2nd Batallion of Reg. of Inf. of La., power of atty. to Don Manuel Almirez, of Dept. of War in this Province, for me and in my name to receive a sum of money due to me from Rev. William Savage. Signed: Francisco (x) Gonzales.

p. 103. 20 Oct. 1791. Agreement: Joseph Ballinger, of Kentucky, U. S. A. (now in the District) and David Ferguson, of the District, Whereas Jos. Ballinger did lately sell in Opelousas County three negro slaves and other property, part his own and part belonging to said Ferguson, the proceeds of which are now in his possession in this District, in cash and different kind of horse creatures, that is, horses, mares, geldings and mules, as will appear by the schedule of said property hereunto annexed, which property it was their intention to take into Kentucky under the supervision of said Ballinger, and there dispose of for tobacco and other produce. In order to more fully promote their joint interest they enter into a partnership. (Details recited.) Signed by both. Wit: G. Cochran.

p. 104. Natchez, 9 Dec. 1791. Notice of the death of William Kelsey, of District, settled on a plantation 40 miles from Fort, on the other side of Buffalo River; said river not at this time fordable and road impracticable, Don Carlos de GrandPre directs Charles Percy, Esq., dwelling near said plantation, to take an inventory, in the presence of two witnesses, of effects left by said Wm. Kelsey, including all papers of said deceased. // p. 104. 18 Dec. 1791. Don Carlos de Grand Pre, having received information from His Excellency Don Manuel Gayoso de Lemos, Col. of the Royal Armies and Governor of these Provinces, directing me to compel payment of the sum of 3133 rials owing by William Kelsey to the Royal Treasury for damaged produce delivered by sd Kelsey, have seised a Barge lying at the landing with all therein contained belonging to sd William Kelsey. In the barge were found: First, a barge 43 ft. long and 7-1/2 ft broad, 6 old oars, one rudder and tifler, without cable, mast or sails, which sd barge I have delivered in charge of Don Juan Castanedo, Military Storekeeper. // Letter from Charles Percy, enclosing inv. $99.

p. 105. Don Juan de Castanedo, Military Storekeeper of Post, in pursuance of the leave I have obtained to descend to the Capital of the Province to render accts. of my office, give power of atty. to Don Joseph de Castanedo, my brother, to exercise the duties of my employment until my return. Natchez 31 Dec. 1791. Wit: Valentin Rincon. Signed.

p. 106. Henry Willis to Anne Savage and William Garland power to manage my concerns. Natchez, 4 Feb. 1792. Signed.

p. 106. 23 Feb. 1792. Joseph Murray, merchant, of Natchez, power of attorney to John Reed. Signed.

p. 107. 23 Feb. 1792. John O'Connor, of Natchez, merchant, to Thomas Durnford, merchant, of N. O., power to recover debts in that District or any part of this Province, to pay debts, and in a special manner settle matters pending with the estate of Patrick Foley, decd. a short time since in New Orleans, in whose charge I had placed sundry merchandise for sale on my account, and merchandise to Wm. McFaden belonging, placed with me for sale and by me confided to said Foley, decd., as will appear by his papers. Post of Natchez.

p. 107. Post of Natchez, 2 May 1792. In consequence of there being near this Fort on the ground of the King an old house standing within range and impeding the play of the Artillery, contrary to all rules of fortification, Don Manuel Gayoso de Lemos, has determined to demolish said house and to the end the owner thereof may not at any time hereafter claim more than the value, appoints the Master Carpenter who conducts the buildings and works of this Fort and assisted by another Master Carpenter, named Bertrand Febreau, to appraise the same, who value said house at $25. Signed John Scott, Bertrand (x) Febreau.

p. 108. 4 May 1792. Arthur Cobb and John Foster, appointed to appraise a yoke of oxen belonging to the estate of John Pickens in order to make sale thereof, value same at $50. Signed by both. // Same date. Oxen exposed to public sale and adjudged to Samuel Flowers for $40, being the highest bidder, payable in specie in two months.

p. 108. 31 May 1792. Bond of John Ivers to produce the person of Thomas Beams before the Government of this Post in pursuance of an order, in the suit of Ebenezer Folsom claiming certain moneys due him by said Beams. Signed by both. Wit: David Urquhart.

p. 108. Natchez, 26 June 1792. The undersigned, dwelling in the Town of Natchez, acknowledge to have received notice not to allow prohibited games of any kind in our houses neither by troops nor by inhabitants, that we shall not open our houses before the rising of sun to sell any kind of liquors nor after eight o'clock in the evening in the winter and nine o'clock in the summer, and that during the hours allowed no excesses shall be permitted, or, if we cannot prevent such, we oblige ourselves to give immediate notice to the nearest guard, and finally that we shall not buy or sell to or from any slave unless such slave shall have a written permission from his or her master or mistress, under penalty of $25 and 8 days imprisonment for 1st offence, double for the second and in case of a third offence a treble fine and banishment from the District. Signed Juan Gali, Manuel Lopez, Simon de Arze, Peter Camus, Manuel Garcia de Texada, Juan Carreras, Pedro Hamer, James Willey, David Ferguson, Edward McCabe, Joseph Murray, George Overaker.

p. 109. Natchez Post, 19 June 1792. Isaac Telfair informs Don Manuel Gayoso of loss of one of seven flat boats in his care and that he wishes to protest against the same to release himself from all responsibility towards those concerned. Don Estevan Minor interpreter for witnesses: Account by said Telfair: The boat lost named "Nancy" belonged to Mr. Andrew Holmes, left Frankfort under his charge May 1st 1792, her cargo tobacco in hogsheads which are still aboard, nothing having been moved since she was loaded. Last night, between 9 and 10, said boat being fastened to the shore at the landing of this Town, he perceived accidently that the said boat made water, whereupon he called up the hands belonging to said boat, also those belonging to the other boats under his command, who all came immediately to assist in stopping the leak and bailing out the water but all their efforts were unavailing, as one of the side studs was broken off and the planks burst loose; the said boat sank before any of her cargo could be gotten off. Said Telfair is 24 years old. Signed by Telfair. // p. 110. Next appeared James Martin, master of said boat named "Nancy" and the hands belonging to same: Thomas Elmore, John Grimes, Thos. Lynch and Robert Potter who declared the same as above. Signed by all.

p. 110. Natchez, 27 June 1792. Inventory of papers belonging to Adam Ware, decd., late a Constable, and delivered to William Collins, his executor, to enable him to settle the affairs of the estate, - - - Obligations of Nehemiah Carter, Hugh and Thomas Ross, and Stephen Richards. // 1st Sept. 1792. William Collins asks for a sale of a horse and saddle belonging to estate of Adam Weir, decd. Appraisers: Geo. Forman and David Odam; Horse $50, saddle $6. // Public sale: saddle adjudged to William Short for $15, surety Wm. Collins; horse to Valentine Rincon for $26.

p. 111. 11 Aug. 1792. John Rhea, owner and master of a flat boat and a barge, bound from Kentucky, loaded with tobacco and peltry and other effects of that country, presented the annexed Proces-Verbal made by himself and crew 23 June last and signed by five witnesses who were present, by which it appears that on 22nd of that month another flat boat belonging to him was wrecked, also loaded with tobacco, in descending the creek called Beachy, a branch of the Kentucky River, prays that the witnesses he had might be examined and a copy of the examination be delivered to him. // Interpreter, Don Juan Girault. Joseph Hammond's testimony: He is a hand on board the flat boat now at this place and came from Kentucky in company with another flat boat not here, descending Beach Fork, the current being very swift, in turning a point, the other flat boat struck on a rock, being carried against it by the force of the current and split immediately and filled with water; notwithstanding the united exertions of the boat's crew and those of the two boats in company, they could save nothing of the cargo but some bear skins and a small quantity of cheese; does not know the amount of the cargo but the boat was as large as the one now here, and as deeply loaded; that she had her full complement of hands on board and besides a Guard of men from Kentucky to defend her against the Indians; he considers the loss unavoidable. He is 27 years old. Signed. David Urquhart witness. // Testimony: Edward Cowan, a Catholic, nothing more than contained in the declaration of Joseph Hammond, the two being together at the time. He is 27 years old. // Test: Michael Schneider, one of the hands of the flat boat now here. The same as told by Joseph Hammond. 29 years old. // p. 113. Testimony: Henry Stevens, a passenger on board of one of the two boats arrived from Kentucky on 11th inst.; left the settlements in Kentucky with his family as passengers in a flat boat belonging to John Rhea in company with a barge and another flat boat now here and in which he came to this place after the loss of the boat in which he set out from Kentucky. The said loss took place in the precise manner as declared by foregoing witnesses, but that he and another followed the fragments of said boat 3 miles from the place and could save nothing but a part of his clothes and his bed. He is 50 years old. // Testimony: John Rhea. Flatboat called "Experience" in rear of other two boats; accident 4 o'clock P. M.; 50 bear skins saved but they were much damaged; next day caught a barrel of whiskey, mixed with water from the river; loss unavoidable; recourse against insurers for cargo. He is 26 years old. Signed. // Testimony of the boatmen to boat "Experience" belonging to Mr. John Rhea, of Bardstown, Ky., lost 22 June 1792; last they saw of the boat was 200 miles down the river. She was then driven ashore and had only 2 hogshead of tobacco left in her, the remainder having floated out. It was not possible for Mr. Rhea to take the tobacco on board his other boat, she being full loaded and no means of getting it in. The Beach Fork was in what is generally allowed a good state to go down with safety and the boat was sufficiently manned. After the loss we entered on board the other boat called "Success".

---

p. 114. 6 Sept. 1792. Juan Perez, Assistant in the King's Hospital at this Post of Natchez, appoints Don Miguel Saint John, of N. O., to defend the suit brought against John O'Lavery. Signed.

p. 115. 19 Sept. 1792. Mary Higdon, of the Dist., agreed from motives of charity to take home Theophilus and Isaac Marble, orphans and about 12 years old, to give them an education suitable to their station in life and to keep them until they shall attain the age of 21 years; they are bound to serve me like a mother; at the end of time I am to give each a complete suit of clothes and a horse and saddle. // p. 115. 24 Sept. 1792. John Arden does the same as above for orphan girl Louisa Marble, aged about 7 years, to educate as I would my daughter and to treat her as such until she is 18, at which time to give her a complete suit of clothes. // p. 116. 24 Sept. 1792. David Douglass binds himself to take under his care a boy, Stephen Marble, and to give him all the things necessary and to learn him the Carpenter's trade on condition that he stay with him until he is 21 years old, being now 14; at expiration, he is to have a complete suit of clothes and the tools necessary to commence working for himself.

p. 116. William Bishop engages to take under his care a girl named Nancy Kidd, aged 2 years, to whom I promise a regular education and to maintain her decently until she is 16, during which time she is to obey me as a daughter; at the end she is to receive a complete suit of clothes. 24 Sept. 1792.

p. 117. 18 Oct. 1792. Inventory of property of James Smith, decd., by H. Manadue, Jos. Duncan, Chas. Jones, Thos. Hughes. A list of accounts on the books of James Smith, deceased, for blacksmith work:

William Brocus
Samuel Gibson
Garret Ralapje
Ephraim Storey
Benjamin Fry
Gibson Clark
James Harman
Jeremiah Brian
Daniel Chambers
Yankey Smith
Joseph Calvit
Moses Armstrong
John Odam
Christian Harman
George Coborn, merchant
David Ferguson
Thomas Daragh
Abner Pipes
George Killian
Cader Raby
Widow Calvit
William Owens
Winsor Pipes
John Girault
John Craven
Jacob Cable (p. 118)
Alexander Moore
Adam Weir
Lewis Evans
James Hayes
Wm. Collins
William Baker
James Hylands
Doctor Henderson
Capt. Richard King
Doctor Flower
Charles Jones
Christian Harman
William Fletcher
Nehemiah Carter
William D. Smith
Doctor Edward McCabe
Jonas Iler
William Liles
Luis Valeret
Randol Gibson
John Clark
Benjamin Balk
John Griffin
Joseph Duncan
Patrick McDermot
Capt. Dick
William Chance
Justus King
John Foster
Samuel Cooper.
James Mullen's note

Total $580-3-1/2
(Signed) H. Manadue.

p. 118. 26 Oct. 1792. Don Carlos de Grand-Pre, Lt. Col. of Royal Armies and Civil and Military Commandant of Post and District of Natchez, in the absence of the Governor, to Capt. Estevan Miro power to represent my person, rights, etc. with estate of Solomon Malline, late of New Orleans, who was indebted to me in a certain sum of money, and likewise to demand a copy of the partition of the deceased Mrs. Francisco Dufresne, who died in the District under the command of Don Miguel Cantrell, Lt. in the Royal Armies, which said partition was made about 6 years ago and the documents relating thereto are in the office of Don Pedro Pedescleau, which demand is made in the right of my wife, Elinor Price Page, heiress-in-law. (Signed) Carlos de Grand-Pre.

p. 118. n Oct. 17, 1792. Don Carlos de Grand-Pre to Don Francisco Collell, Capt., to defend the right of my mulatto slave, "Isaac", in the suit brought against him at this place and to be tried at the Capital. Natchez.

p. 119. Natchez, 6 Nov. 1792. Juan Garcia, soldier in the Regiment of Inf. of La., in Garrison at the Post of Natchez, to Don Joseph de Ocon, of the City of N. O., to receive money due me as prize money, arising from a vessel captured having contraband goods, named "St. John the Baptist", taken about 8 leagues from the City, my share therein amounting, as I have heard, to $118, which I have understood is in the hands of Don Joseph de Ebia, Capt. of the Port of New Orleans. Signed.

p. 119. 13 Dec. 1792. Power of attorney by Frances Asheton Watts, dwelling in this District, to her husband, Stephen Watts, and Evan Jones, to act for her as she could or might do if present. Signed.

p. 120. Jany. 11, 1793. Bond. William Gorman, indebted to Don Gabriel Cerre, of the Post of St. Louis, in the Illinois, merchant, in the sum of $561 since 1786, which I promise to pay to Cerre or his order. Signed.

p. 120. Post of Natchez, 28 Feb. 1793. Don Carlos de Grand-Pre to Don Juan Girault to settle all matters of business pending with Don Juan Vaucheret, in conformity with the instructions given by me the 25th of this present month. Signed.

p. 121. Post of Natchez, 26 March 1793. Don Lucas Alvarez, Capt. in the Royal Armies and Lt. in the Company of Light Troops of the Havannah, now on duty at this Post of Natchez, Prov. of La., in consequence of the death of the curate, Don Joseph Timenes de Mendoza, who left a house in the suburb of the City of Vigo in Gallicia and other property in said city, and myself and my brothers, being lawful heirs of my said uncle, do hereby empower my sister Donna Ignacia Alvarez Timenes to take possession of my share of the estate left by my uncle, Don Joseph Alvarez de Mendoza and enjoy the same during her life, for such is my will. Signed.

p. 121. Post of Natchez, 11 Apr. 1793. Power of Atty. from Ebenezer Dayton to Robert Cochran, to recover from James Smith, now in N. O., having absconded from this District, the sum of $59, owing me by said Smith. Signed.

p. 121. 17 Apr. 1793. Sale by William Rucker to Jonas Scoggins, one black horse, about 13 hands high and branded on left counter ƎME Signed. Wit: Asahel Lewis.

p. 122. Post of Natchez, 6 May 1793. Power of Atty. from Mary McIntosh, widow of David Williams, decd., to Charles Norwood, dwelling in New Orleans, to recover and receive sundry debts owing me by several persons in that place, also from _____ Boisdore, planter, in Opelousas. James McIntosh for Mrs. Williams.

p. 122. Jonas Iler, of this Dist., to Job Routh, of same, in and during my absence to attend to and manage my business, etc. Natchez, 12 June 1793. Signed.

p. 122. Natchez. 24 July 1793. Bond. Joseph Lambert, Master Armourer of this Fort, indebted to Millan Carreras, Sergt. of Reg. of La. and now in Garrison at this Post, for $300, being money lent, to pay April 1794; in case of accident, Catherine Lambert, my sister, who will also sign, becomes surety for same. Joseph (X) Lambert, Catherine Lambert.

p. 123. Post of Natchez. 5 Aug. 1793. James Hillen, Patroon of a Barge bound from N. O. to this Port, with merchandise belonging to divers individuals of the same, declared that on the 27 July 1793, at about 3 P. M. the current being very strong compelled him to tow the Barge and having ascended some distance in that manner, the towline broke and the said barge struck against a snag about 2 feet under water, which made a hole in her bottom, through which accident the cargo became wet and some part lost, the articles saved being contained in the schedule annexed; said barge was rotten and had no cable that was sufficient to hold her. Signed. // p. 124. Next appeared Juan De La Crux, one of the hired hands belonging to the Barge, who testified: (same as above). He is 28 years old. Signed with a mark. // Next appeared Manuel Camilla, one of the hands of sd Barge. Accident occurred about 15 leagues from this place . . . 37 years of age. Signed with a mark. // Next: Manuel Rabarez, another hand to sd barge . . . 37 yrs. old. // p. 124. Inventory of sundry articles saved from wreck of James Rose's Boat, stove near Loftus Cliffs, and transported to this place: Philip Barbour's, 2 cases sugar, 2 tierces rum, 1 case liquors, 2 trunks, 5 demijohns, 8 bottles wine, 5 kegs raisins, 1 portmanteau, 1 barrel coffee, 1 saddle, 1 barrel salt, 1 case wine. . . . Robert and George Cochran: 1 demijohn, a small anchor vinegar, 1 Pipe rum, 3 hogshead same, 1 same wine, 1 barrel coffee, 2 tierces of same, 4 barrels of Porter, 1 same of Linen, 1 barrel of lump sugar, 22 bars of iron, 3 kegs nails, 1 mattress and bolster. . . . James Murray, 1 guaging rod. . . . James Fowler 1 trunk, 6 chairs, 2 bars of iron, 2 reams of paper. Natchez, 6 Aug. 1793. Signed: James Hillen, Patroon. Wit: A. Bingaman, Archibald Robertson, William Daniel, Wm. Kirkland, John Potter.

p. 125. Samuel Steer, of District of Baton Rouge, now in this place, makes a free gift of $2000 of coin of Mexico, to Maria Lintot, legitimate daughter of Bernard Lintot and Catherine, his wife, with whom I have contracted matrimony, which said sum it is my will that she hold and enjoy in case she shall survive me, to be paid out of my estate, present and to come, after my decease and not before. Natchez, 19 Aug. 1793. Signed.

p. 125. Don Francisco Caudel, Military Storekeeper General at this Post of Natchez, to Don Andrew Armesto, power to receive from the Treasurer of the War Dept. the salary due me since the 1st of January this present year to the amount of $400 and no more, being the price of a negro I bought from him. Aug. 14, 1793.

p. 126. 9 Sept. 1793. Aaron Adams to William Selkrig, both of this District, power of Atty. until my return from the U. S. for which I am about to depart. Signed.

p. 126. 31 Oct. 1793. Inventory of William Wilson's property, taken at Mr. Christian Bingaman's plantation where the sd Wilson now resides. Horned cattle which Mr. Wilson expects on the division of the stock between him and Mr. Bingaman, and other cattle and horses. 9 horses and mares, 3 colts, 1 rifle gun, one smooth gun, one old saddle. The horned cattle are in the swamp and not to be got out until next spring at high water. Wit: Lewis Alston, William Coleman. Signed John Wall, Dep. Alcalde.

p. 127. Post of Natchez, 15 May 1794. Protest. Appeared Joseph Antonio Campos, soldier in the 7th Co., 1st Battalion, Reg. of Inf. of La., who declared he left N. O. in command of a Perogue bound for this place, having on board a lad put in his care by Simon Labarta, aged about 8 years, to be delivered to "Charles, the Maltese", who acted the part of a father to him, being married to his mother. On the 24th day of the voyage, in crossing the river they encountered a large raft of drift wood and the deponent went forward to clear the Perogue from said raft and encourage the men at the oars when turning his face toward the stern he perceived the said boy in the river, about 10 or 12 fathoms from the boat; the deponant immediately sprang into the river to save him but before he could reach him the said boy disappeared. Signed with a mark. // Depo. from Joseph Ruissenior, private 2nd Co. 2nd Bat. same regiment; same account; aged 24. // Andrew Bertrand, a private, same account, aged 21 // Joseph Rinz; the same; aged 24.

p. 128. Natchez, 8 Jany. 1794. Peter Walker, power of atty, to George Cochran, to attend to business in District.

p. 129. Agreement. 27 March 1794. Caleb Biggs, of Dist., obliges himself to work for his Excellency, Don Manuel Gayoso de Lemos, for 6 months, from 15 Apr. next, as carpenter and wheelright, for which he is to be paid $90 and furnished with lodging and board during said six months. Signed.

p. 129. Affidavit. Natchez, 3 June 1794. Catherine Smith declared that a certain John Sutton having robbed her of certain articles, was ordered to be apprehended; he was accordingly taken by George Bailey and Israel Leonard and conducted to this Fort, where he made his escape, and thereupon the said Bailey appeared with the following articles found with him, a hat and a bed quilt, belonging to said Catharine Smith.

p. 129. Bond. 7 June 1794. Samuel Davis of Natchez Dist., of free will and accord, becomes responsible for person and conduct of Jesse Miller, also of this Dist., now confined in Prison of this Fort, binding himself to produce the person of said Miller whenever required. Signed.

p. 130. Natchez June 9, 1794. Agreement. Benjamin Adams, Doctor of Physic and Polser Shilling. Said Adams covenants and agrees to take Mr. Shilling under care, who is now deprived of the use of one of his thighs, from this date and promises to pay close attention and use the utmost ability to cure and make sound and well the complaint the said Shilling labors under in his thighs, that is to say, Doctor Adams engages to make a perfect cure of said Shilling in term of three months, so as to be able to walk without the help of a staff. In Consideration, Polser Shilling promised to pay $100 in specie. Signed by both. Wit: V. T. Dalton.

p. 130. Post of Natchez, 2 June 1794. Indenture. Michael Helingher, of this District, aged 21, declared he had put himself apprentice to Robert Patton, Master Tanner and Currier, of known ability, who doth hereby agree to learn him the trade of Tanner in three years, ending 3 June 1797, not concealing from him any part of the theory or practice thereof, . . . to keep apprentice in his house and give him good and wholesome provisions, clothes, washing and sufficient clothes as if he were his son and the said apprentice is not bound to work at the trade but at any decent employment which will not impede him in acquiring the said trade. At the end, he shall have a good horse, saddle and bridle free.

p. 131. Inventory of estate of Jesse Dewitt, 21 July 1794. Thomas Lamphier's note for $100; wearing apparel and clothes, $38, total $138. Appraisers, Israel Leonard, Chas. King. Natchez, July 23, 1794. Rec'd the above-mentioned property into my care for the benefit of the creditors. Signed: Archibald Rea. Wit: John Girault.

p. 131. Antonio Gras, of this Post, merchant, Power of Atty. to Louis Delate, to recover and receive at the Post of Baton Rouge, the inheritance of my wife, Genevieve Delate, also all debts, etc. due me personally from sd estate. 14 Aug. 1794. Signed.

p. 131. Mortgage. Natchez, 16 Aug. 1794. David Phelps, of Natchez, to Robert and George Cochran, all right, etc. in one-half of a billiard-table and the appurtenances thereof, being the same now in use and occupied by me at the Natchez Landing, as also the amounts (p. 132) due me by book accounts, the estate of John Hartley, Sr., deceased, and John Hartley, Jun. $100; Gibson Clark of Bayou Pierre $50, Nathaniel Tomlinson abt. $60. Signed. Wit: J. Eldergill.

p. 132. Post of Natchez, 18 Aug. 1794. Richard Lord presents full power of atty. to his wife, Thomasina Lord. Signed.

p. 133. Inventory of sundries, late property of Elijah Routh, decd., now in possession of Margaret Routh, his mother, delivered on oath: 4 cows and calves, 2 yearling heifers and 1 yearling bull or steer, a pair of oxen at Isaac Johnson's, Esq. Dist. of Gayoso. Margaret (M) Routh. The above inventory was taken by me as delivered on oath of Margaret Routh this 18 Aug. 1794. Signed: W. Murray.

p. 133. Samuel Bell, of Attacapas, planter, as attorney for my wife, Rebecca Perry, sells to Don Estevan Minor, Capt. in the Royal Armies and Adj. Major of this Post of Natchez, all horned cattle belonging to my sd wife in this District to the number of 80 head more or less, all branded "R. P.", for $500 in hand paid. Natchez Oct. 3, 1794. Signed.

p. 134. Post of Natchez, 25 Oct. 1794, John Farhqhar declared that in Feb. 1789, he received a note drawn by Frederick Calvit, payable to bearer for $60; after some time he passed said note to Gabriel Griffing, without having recovered any part of said sum. Signed.

p. 134. Will of William Falconer, Storekeeper on Cole's Creek, Dist. of Natchez, Prov. of La., in perfect health. To dispose of my worldly affairs I depend on the discretion of my friends, Mr. George Fitzgerald and Mr. David Ross, merchants of this District, to act as my executors, along with my lawful brother, Cosmo Falconer, writer, in the City of Edinburg in the Kingdom of Great Britain. (1) Debts to be paid, (2) remainder to be remitted as collected to aforesd Cosmo Falconer by my executors in this country, which shall be divided among my brothers and sisters equally. My effects consist chiefly in notes and accounts to be seen in my ledger for 1790; also one-half of the debts in company with Mr. James Kirk to be seen in a small ledger in my possession. If my father, who I trust is alive, shall be in need of any part of my estate for his present sustenance, my brothers and sisters shall allow it to him and pay him 5 per-cent a year on whatever they shall receive during his life. I am the lawful son of Sylvester Falconer, born in the Parish of Logi, County of Aberdeen, Kingdom of Great Britain. 25 Feb. 1791. Wit: Wm. Barland, Richard Harrison, Parker Carradine, David Odam, James Truly, Ebenezer Dayton, William Curtis. // p. 135. 8 Nov. 1794. George Fitzgerald presented to Gayoso the above will of William Falconer, who died in the Dist. of New Feliciana. Prove by Parker Carradine and David Odam. // Nov. 17, 1794, James Truly, Richard Harrison, Wm. Barland and Ebenezer Dayton testified as to signing above will. // George Fitzgerald asks that the books of the late William Falconer be put in his possession. Nov. 15, 1794. Order for above.

p. 136. Natchez, 3 Dec. 1794. Jeremiah Miller, dwelling in this Dist., 19 years old, apprentices himself to Patrick McDermot, carpenter and millwright, who consents to receive him as apprentice and to teach him said trade of millwright, on condition that he remain with him to end of July 1796. Usual terms. Jeremiah (X) Miller, McDermot.

p. 137. List of sums I have paid for account of Mr. James McIntyre to his creditors: James Kirk, Mr. Chas. Bishop, John O'Connor, Peter Surget, Maurice Stackpoole, Peter Walker, George Fitzgerald, Daniel Clark, Messrs. Monsanto, Alexander Moore. Total $125. Natchez, Dec. 10, 1794. John Bisland declares before witnesses the above payments were made for Mr. James McIntyre and he hereby indemnifies him against the lawful claim of any of the above. Signed: John Bisland.

p. 137. Clara Monsanto, wid. of Benj. Monsanto, decd., of this Government of Natchez, to Don Antonio Argote, of N. O., power to attend and adjust all matters I have pending in relation to the estate of my deceased husband. Natchez, 10 Dec. 1794. (Not signed.) Wit: Jean Girault, Agepeto Corchado.

p. 138. Messrs. James Todd and Archibald Rea. Gentlemen: Having by accident heard of the death of Etienne Ferland, Storekeeper, and being unable to attend immediately in person, you are directed and empowered to take an inventory. Signed: Francisco Poussett, Alcalde. Bayou Sara, Dec. 3, 1794. // Inventory of Etienne Ferland. 97 items. Value $260. Books, notes, etc. sealed up and retained by us. Signed: James Todd, Archibald Rea, and ack. before Poussett, Alcalde, 5 Dec. 1794. // p. 139. Memo of notes and obligations examined, 11 Dec. 1794. Wit: Lewis Alston, James Todd, and John Baptiste Daste. James Rose, Natchez; William Collins, Raphael Ramo, Opelousas; Joseph . . . , Claude Delat, . . . Mahier, Baton Rouge; John Bansanto, N. O.; Nicolas Sazage (gone to Ill.); Francis LaValeur, Thompson's Cr.; Robert Collins; Mr. Livaudais, near New Orleans; Vahamonde's order on Madame Dauphine, bartered to Etienne Ferland; Joseph Morcau (1777); Pierre Bouze to Pierre Manuel (the last two notes left with Etienne Ferland by Blancard, since drowned; Joseph Duforge; Wm. Alston; Wm. Thompson; James Todd; John Rafford Coleman; Reuben Jelks; Wm. Alston's assumption for Wm. White; paid by White; Benjamin Burnet, Moses Johnson; John Coil's note. Wit: James Todd. // p. 140. Dec. 12, 1794. To His Excellency, the Gov., from Francisco Poussett, Alcalde, informing him of death of Etienne Ferland, who kept a small store at Mr. Barclay's. He wrote Mr. Rea and joined him in a letter to Mr. Todd who lives with Mr. Barclay, authorizing an inventory. No will found. From inventory, it may be enough to pay debts but little more. He left a young woman who bears his name, but, as she said, only under contract of marriage. She has two infants, twins, at breast, and is in a miserable condition. I had the store closed and left key with Mr. Todd, directing him to allow the poor woman such necessaries as may be expedient. He owes Messrs. Laberthe and Barriere, in N. O., $519 and Mr. David Ross $19. If Your Excellency should order the sale of the effects, the sooner it could be done would be the most advantageous, as some things are wanted immediately, salt for instance, and the inhabitants would supply themselves with little necessaries that otherwise they will purchase in New Orleans, this being the time of going down. The bearer is a young man, Jean Baptist Daste, who was hired by the deceased at 12 per month. // p. 141-5. Sale of the above effects, at the house of Mr. Barclay, 27 Dec. 1794. Buyers: John Alston, John Wall, F. Poussett, James Todd, Wm. Alston, J. B. Daste, Solomon Alston, J. Grady. A. Rea, H. Hunter, B. Bestos, J. Baker, J. Coleman, W. Coleman. Total $233. Numbers of articles given to the woman before the sale. Letters to Mr. Vahamonde, Commandant at Baton Rouge, and Anslem Blancard, Esq., Commandant at Thompson's Creek, dated Bayou Sara, 30 Dec. 1794, from Poussett asking that the notes due the estate in those districts be collected; also a letter to Mr. Duparc, at Pointe Coupee, Jany. 7, 1794; and to Mr. John Girault, Notary Public at Natchez, same date, with accts of James Rose and John Coile; to Messrs. La Berthe and Barriere was sent the N. O. notes. All come to $763.

p. 145. 6 Jany. 1794. David Holt and David Odam, in the District of Natchez, to Parker Carradine, of same, power to settle all matters we have pending against Alexander Moore in New Orleans. Both sign.

p. 145. Advertisement. Whereas partnership of Clark and Rees has long since expired and there still remain large sums of money due to them it is requested that their debtors will use every exertion to pay them in the course of the present year, and that all those who have any demands against them bring in their accounts. Natchez, Feb. 7, 1795. This is a true copy of advertisement fixed at the Govt. House, 7 Feb. 1795.

p. 146. Thos. Murray to Philip Gray, power to settle all accounts I have pending at the German Coast. 3 March 1795. Signed.

p. 146. Hannah Vousdan gives power to my son William Lum to manage and conduct the suit I have instituted to prove my marriage with William Vousdan and to claim from Wm. Vousdan the property belonging to my first husband, William Lum. Natchez, 17 March 1795. Signed.

p. 147. Inventory of estate of John Newton, decd., who departed this life Apr. 3, 1795. Wearing apparel and bed clothes. He owed Mr. Labrie, Mr. Wylie, Mr. Williams, Mr. Valleret, Mr. Jackson, Mrs. Hamilton, Mr. Coyle, the barber, the washerwoman, the merchants, the Doctor, and funeral expenses. Total $125. Signed: Valentine Thomas Dalton.

p. 147. Natchez, 13 Apr. 1795. William Sharbert apprentices himself to Simon Grimber, hatter, who agrees to receive him as such and teach him the trade in couse of 6 years; keep him in his house; give him diet, washing and lodging as if he were his own son; at the end of time he is to have a horse, bridle and saddle free. Both signed.

p. 148. 20 April 1795. Charles Quin apprentices himself to William Benjamin Smith for 3 years to learn the trade of shoemaker; usual terms. Signed by both.

p. 148. John O'Connor, of Natchez, gives power of atty. to Don Pedro Walker, Natchez, 7 May 1795.

p. 149. Natchez, 16 June 1795. John Williams, of this Post, apprentices his son, Joseph Williams, aged 8 years, with Robert Patton, master tanner and currier, who consents to teach him the trades; the boy to live in the house and under the care of said Patton until 21 which will be Aug. 1, 1807, when he will receive a complete suit of clothes and a good horse, saddle and bridle. John Williams surety for his son, Wm. Benja. Smith surety for Robt. Patton.

p. 150. Natchez, 6 Nov. 1797. Mary Foster, of this Government, of her own free will and accord and for love and affection for her cousin, Levi Foster, son of Thomas Foster, of the same place, makes him a gift of 200 arpents of land, being part of a grant to her of 640 arps. Mch. 6, 1788, to be taken and measured in the middle of said grant in parallel lines. Signed with a mark. Wit: John Foster, Hugh Stephenson.

p. 151. Jacintha Gallagher and Joseph Vidal, living in this Town, to John Minor, Lot No. 2, behind the Church, in Square #34, for $100, in hand paid. Natchez, 8 Nov. 1797. Signed: Jacinta Gallagher, Joseph Vidal.

p. 151. Natchez, 8 Nov. 1797. Dennis Collins, of Natchez, to Philip McHugh, of same, tract of 248 arpents, near Cole's Creek, b. by John Fowler, Benj. Newman, Christian Bingaman, Alexander McIntosh, as set forth in the titles in my favor, Sept. 1, 1795. Both sign. Wit: Nathaniel Tomlinson, Thomas Foster.

p. 152. 8 Nov. 1797. Domingo Lorrero, of this Town, to John Minor, two lots behind the Church, lots 3 and 4, Sq. 34, for $280 in hand paid. Signed. Wit: Peter Walker.

p. 153. Isaac Johnson, of the Dist. of Natchez, planter and Alcalde of Second Creek, to his son, John Hunter Johnson, of same place, 600 arpents in District of New Feliciana on Alexander's Creek, b. by lands of Alexander Sterling and Alexander Fulton, as set forth in titles in my favor, dated 5 Dec. 1795. Both signed. Wit: John Eldergill, Russel Bean.

p. 153. Oct. 20, 1797. Antonio Novella, power of atty., to Maria Francisca Borses, my lawful wife. Signed. // Maria Francisca Borses, wife of Antonio Novellas, in virtue of foregoing power, sell to Don Lorrero and Pedro Ancid, partners, a house and lot in this Town, No. one, sq. two, belonging to my husband who purchased from Don Joseph Vidal, for $700. Signed with a mark. Wit: Juan Girault, William Gillespie.

p. 154. Natchez, Nov. 1797. Chas. King sells to Benajah Osmin, both of Natchez, 115 arpents, on a branch of St. Catherine's Cr., b. by lands of John Hartley, Jacob Adams, Willian Atcheson and other land of the seller. Both signed. Wit: Wm. Atcheson, Andrew White.

p. 155. 17 Nov. 1797. Arthur Cobb, to Charles Surget, both of Natchez, a plantation in District of Second Creek, b. by lands of William Cobb, Peter Surget, Estevan Minor, Daniel Clark and Elizabeth Whittle, 500 arpents, 400 arpents surveyed in my name and 100 arpents were included in 600 arpents surveyed in the name of my son, William Cobb, for $1000, in hand paid. Both signed. Wit: Waterman Crane.

p. 156. Natchez, 17 Nov. 1797. Daniel Clark to William Dunbar, Esq., surveyor, power to recover and receive all debts owing in this district to the late partnership of Clark and Rees. Signed.

p. 156. 20 Nov. 1797. Hugh Coyle to John Bisland, both of Natchez Dist., 240 acres b. by lands of Richard King, John Foster, Benj. Balk and Richard Harrison, as set forth in titles in my favor, No. 690, dated 30 Aug. 1795; for $130 paid. Both signed. Wit: Thos. Foster.

p. 157. To His Excellency, the Gov., pro tem. Daniel Fowler, of this Govt. represents that by the loss of his brother, he is become sole heir of his late father's estate and whereas he is yet a minor, he prays that a guardian for him be nominated; having full conficence in friendship and integrity of Mr. Gerard Brandon, he begs leave to recommend him for the purpose. Signed. Natchez, Nov. 20, 1797. // Nov. 22, 1797. The Alcalde of the District of the residence of the deceased John and Patrick Fowler, will furnish a just inventory in order that measure may be taken to secure said property to petitioner, who is the son, and a minor, of above-mentioned John Fowler. Signed: Stephen Minor. // p. 158. Inventory of estate on oath of Mr. Philip McHugh in whose custody I found it, valued by Major John Williams and William O'Connor, on oath. Plantation 240 acres ($240). Total $783, including small balances on notes of James Highlands, George Smith and Jonathan Selser. St. Catherine's District. William Vousdan, Alcalde. Mr. Gerard Brandon made guardian and accepts charge. 2 Dec. 1797. Wit: Dennis Collins, Patrick Garnett (or Gurnett).

p. 158. Patrick Gurnett to John Arden, 240 arpents on St. Catherine's Creek, b. by lands of Alexander McIntosh and Pedro Camus, as set forth in titles 28 Feb. 1795. Natchez, 12 Dec. 1797. Both sign. Wit: Caleb King, Nathaniel Tomlinson.

p. 159. [n. d.] Isaac Johnson, of Govt. of Natchez and Alcalde of Dist. of Second Creek, to Benj. Farar, of same place, 1400 arpents of land of Second Creek which he acquired as follows: from Michael Hooter, 8 Mch. 1776, 450 arpents, a Br. gr. to sd Hooter 21 Sept. 1772; 150 arpents bou. of Evan Cameron by deed dated 3 Sept. 1777, Br. gr. to sd Cameron 22 July 1776; the remaining 800 arpents gr. him by the Govr. Genl. of Province 6 March 1789; for $4200 in hand paid. Both signed. Wit: John Minor, Peter Walker.

p. 160. 12 Dec. 1797. Thomas Jordan, of Dist. of Natchez, to William Collins and Abner Pipes, Jr. jointly, 400 arps. being the south part of grant in my favor of 600 arpents, 12 Mch. 1788, for $221 and 10,000 pounds of cotton, which I have received from Wm. Collins and 10,000 pounds of cotton, 2500 pounds of which I have received from Abner Pipes, the remaining 7500 pounds of cotton to be delivered by him, one-half next crop, and one-half the crop following. Signed by the three above. Wit: James Spain.

p. 161. Wm. Atchinson, of Natchez, to Ephraim Blackburn, 263 arpents of land, being part of grant in my favor No. 350, of which I sold 50 arpents to Wm. Gillespie, for $526 (on terms). Both signed. Wit: Geo. Cochran, Post of Natchez, 30 Dec. 1797.

p. 161. 30 Dec. 1797. Mortgage. Peter Bruin, Lt. Col. in the Militia of this Govt., dwelling in Dist. of Bayou Pierre, indebted to George Cochran, merchant of this Post, in $4193 ; to Ebenezer Rees, also merchant of this Post, $3281, which sums he expects to pay in course of two years with 6% interest; for security he mortgages all plantations & land he holds in the District of Bayou Pierre, namely 1800 arpents granted by this Govt. 20 July 1796, No. 836; another tract, 800 arps. granted the same date, No. 838, together with buildings, mills, improvements thereon, including especially the plantation on which he resides and on which he has erected a saw-mill. Signed: P. Bryan Bruin, Eben Rees, Geo Cochran.

p. 162. 30 Dec. 1797. Don Joseph Vidal, Capt. of Artillery in Militia of this Post and Dist., to Don Estevan Minor, Capt. in the Royal Armies, 19 arpents and 57 perches of land, part of 29 arpents and 7 perches granted to him by His Maj. which are in front of the house in which I now dwell, b. on north by land of Estevan Minor, south by Francisco Lenan and otherwise public roads, for $460 in hand paid and with express condition that he shall sell him 30 arps. of his land, b. on northeast by 10 arpents remaining to me of aforesd 29 arpents and that he shall leave open 30 ft in width for a road in front of Vidal's house until the said road shall meet the public road. Signed by both. Wit: Peter Walker, John Minor.

p. 163. 8 Jany. 1797. Sale. Drury Ledbetter to Samuel Cooper, of this Dist., a negro man, "Ned", aged 30, nat. of America, for $500 in hand paid. Both sign. Wit: James Spain.

p. 164. 10 Jany. 1798. William West, of this Govt., to Thomas Hughes, of same, 190 arpents in Dist. of St. Catherine's, as in titles in my favor, No. 424, for $500 in hand paid. Wm. (X) West, Thos. Hughes. Wit: Maurice Stacpoole.

p. 164. 10 Jany. 1798. Sale. Richard King to James Boles and John Roberts, 103 arpents, b. lands of John Bolls, Frederick Calvit, Jeptha Higdon and other land belonging to the sd King, being part of grant No. 499 in favor of King in Dist. of St. Catherine, for $2.00 per acre in hand paid. Signed by the three above. Wit: Wm. McIntosh, Waterman Crane. // Whereas a deficiency of 42 acres is found in survey sold by King, in consequence of which a deed for 59 acres only under the same has been accepted by James Bolls and hereby the forgoing contract rendered null and void. 13 Aug. 1800. Richard King on his part agrees the foregoing contract remain null and void and every part thereof shall for nothing be, having by and with the consent of the said James Bolls and John Roberts, given a deed to another person for the above-mentioned 59 acres. Signed. // p. 165. Richard King sells to John Bolls the 59 arpents in the above deed, part of grant No. 499 for $2.00 per arpent. Both sign. Same witnesses.

p. 167. Jany. 1798. Henry Stevens, of the Dist. of Natchez, to Wm. Vousdan, of the Dist. of St. Catherine, a plantation, b. by Joseph Forrester, Joseph Duncan and other land as per plat and grant to Samuel Gibson 5 Dec. 1782, 380 arpents which he purchased of Samuel Flower, for $1000 in hand paid. Henry (X) Stevens, Wm. Vousdan. Wit: Chas. Adams.

p. 167. 16 Jany. 1798. Joseph Martinez, of Post of Natchez, to Calvin and Luther Smith, of same, lot 100 ft front by 155 ft depth, being the same he bought from Don Juan Girault, for $140 in hand paid. Signed by Martinez and Calvin Smith. Wit: Wm. B. Smith.

p. 167. 22 Jany. 1798. George Overaker to Patrick McDermott a negro woman "Lucy" which I bought of Simon de Arze, for $250. Signed. Wit: D. Mitchell, David Ferguson.

p. 168. 25 Jany. 1798. Clement Dyson, of this Govt., to John Courtney, of same, 160 arpents, b. as per grant to him, No. 548, 26 Nov. 1793. Clement (X) Dyson, John Courtney. Wit: Wm. Owens.

p. 168. 20 Jany. 1798. Wm. Owens to Eustace Humphreys, both of Govt. of Natchez, 100 arps in southeast corner of my grant No. 738, adj. John Bisland and James McIntyre, for $200 paid. Both sign. Witness: Wm. McIntosh.

p. 171. 30 Jany. 1798. Thos. Morgan to Abraham Taylor 250 arpents in this District, b. by James Oglesby, as per grant to him 10 Mch. 1789, in exchange for another tract described by deed of even date. // p. 171. 30 Jany. 1798. Abraham Taylor to Thos. Morgan tract in this Govt. as described in grant to him, No. 822, 20 Dec. 1794, in exchange for another tract conveyed to Taylor by deed. Both sign with mark. Witness to both deeds: Cato West.

p. 171. 3 Jany. 1798. Thos. Morgan, of Dist. of Natchez, to James Moore, as executor of the will of his dec'd. father, Alexander Moore, and for acct of the sd estate, 250 arpents in this Dist., on Well's Cr, being the same which I had from Abraham Taylor and b. as per grant No. 822 to sd Taylor, for $200 paid. Thos. (X) Morgan, Jas. Moore. Witness: Cato West.

p. 172 Elias Bonnell to John Foster 400 arpents on the Homochitto granted to him by the Gov. Genl. of this Province together with an island in same river as per grant No. 284, which land he sells in exchange for a negro woman. Feb. 2, 1798. Elias (X) Bonnell, John Foster.

p. 173. 3 Feb. 1798. David Ferguson, merchant, sold to George Cochran lot #4, Sq. #9 in this Town, part of the ground he bought of William Barland, for $12 in hand paid. Signed.

p. 173. 12 Feb. 1798. Stephen Cole, of this Dist., planter, to his brother, Solomon Cole, 300 arpents on Cole's Creek, between two branches thereof, and b. as per grant to him No. 421, for $150 paid. Both signed with a mark. Wit: Isaac Foster, Josiah Crane.

p. 174. Hugh Mathews to John Stampley, 300 arps granted to him, No. 609, which I sell in part payment of a plantation which I have this day bought of said purchaser. 12 Feb. 1798. Both sign. Wit: Isaac Foster, Ebenezer Petty.

p. 174. 12 Feb. 1798. John Stampley to Hugh Matthews, of this Dist., 350 arpents in Dist. of Cole's Creek, b. by Richard Roddy, and by other land to him belonging, being part of a grant to him, No. 567, of 800 arpents, to be taken from the middle of the said grant, reserving on the east 50 arpents for said Roddy and 400 arpents on the west to said Stampley, for $120 and 300 acres of land at Big Black. Both signed. Wit: Isaac Foster, Ebenezer Petty.

p. 175. 13 Jany. 1798. John Stampley to John Minor, both of this Govt., 400 arpents part of grant to Stampley No. 567, to be taken from west end thereof, leaving on the east end 50 arpents sold to Richard Roddy and 350 arpents which he sold to Hugh Matthews, for $200 in hand paid. Signed. Wit: Josiah Crane, Ebenezer Petty.

p. 176. 14 Feb. 1798. William McIntosh, to John Cammack 100 arpents b. by Robt. Ford, Daniel Perry and other land belonging to McIntosh, being part of a grant to him for 800 arpents, for $200 in hand paid. Both signed. Wit: Eben Rees.

p. 176. 17 Feb. 1798. John Cammack, of this Govt., planter, to Thos. Tyler, of this Post, merchant, a house and lot, No. 3, Sq. 32, for $500, on terms. Both signed. Wit: Drury Ledbetter. // 14 Jany. 1799, John Cammack ack. to have received full payment for the house and lot conveyed in foregoing deed. // To Mr. John Girault. Sir: Please to take off the mortgage on the house and lot which I sold to Mr. Thomas Tyler, as he has settled with me for it. You will oblige your humble servant, John Cammack. Oct. 29, 1798. Wit: Reuben Baxter, Thos. Reed.

p. 178. 22 Feb. 1798. John Ellis, of Dist. of St. Catherine, to John Ellis Jr., of Dist. of Homochitto, 800 arpents between Homochitto and Buffalo Creeks, b. by William Cocke Ellis, which land was granted to said John Ellis by Gov. Gen. of Province, in exchange for 500 arpents in two grants to Richard Ellis, deceased, which he has received to his full satisfaction. Both signed. Wit: Wm. Connor, Abram Ellis, John Blackburn.

p. 178. 22 Feb. 1798. John Ellis and Abram Ellis, executors of the estate of our deceased father, Richard Ellis, to John Ellis, of this Dist. of St. Catherine, two tracts of land, one of 320 arpents, other of 180 arpents, which said lands were granted to Richard Ellis, 31 Jany. 1788, which said lands we sell in exchange for 800 arpents granted aforesaid John Ellis, wherewith we are fully satisfied. Signed, John Ellis, Sr., John Ellis, Jr., Abram Ellis.

p. 179. 28 Feb. 1798. William Barland to John Bisland, both of Dist. of Natchez, Lot. No. 1, Sq. No. 17, 200 ft in front by 150 ft in depth, for $70. Both sign. Wit: J. Eldergill.

p. 180. 3 March 1798. Daniel Clark, of Dist. of Buffalo and Alcalde of the same place, power of Atty. to Daniel Clark, Jr., of the City of N. O., merchant, to recover and receive all sums due me in sd city. Signed.

p. 180. 5 March 1798. Frederick Kimball, of the Dist. of Bayou Sara in the Govt. of Natchez, to Don ____ Guignon, dwelling in N. O., power of Atty. to appear before the Superior Tribunal of this Province in suit I have instigated against William Weeks, of Dist. of Bayou Sara, to compel him to fulfill his agreement in relation to a plantation he sold me, as will appear by the accompagnying, dated 2 Feb. 1796. Signed. Wit: Josiah Crane, Isaac Foster.

p. 181. 7 March 1798. Don Manuel Garcia de Texada, of Natchez, merchant, to Cato West, Alcalde of Villa Gayoso, 264 arpents as per grant to Richard Trevillion, No. 723, for $300 paid. Both signed. Wit: Eben Rees, Lacy Rumsey.

p. 181. 10 Mch. 1798. Maurice Stacpoole, of this Post, to Don Manuel Garcia de Texada, of same, lot in Town, with all buildings thereon consisting of a dwelling house, a kitchen and some other tenements, being adjudged to me at public sale of estate of Don Miguel Solivellas, 14 Feb. last past, for $1000. Both signed. Wit: Jean Girault, Joseph Vidal.

p. 182. 14 March 1798. Solomon Cole, of Natchez, to William Thomas, 300 arpents, granted my brother Stephen, as per grant to him No. 421, which he conveyed to me as of record, for $600 paid. Solomon (X) Cole, William Thomas. Wit: Drury Ledbetter.

p. 183. 9 Mch. 1798. Don Pedro Camus, of Dist. of Natchez, to Andrew A. Elliott and John Walker, of same, 200 arpents on Second Creek, b. by John Hartley and John Newton, as per grant to Camus, No. 814, for $230 in hand paid. Both sign. Wit: Isaac Foster, Lewis Shelton, Joseph Vidal.

p. 183. 21 Mch. 1798. Antonio Molina, Commanding His Majesty's Galley, "The Vigilant", now at this Post of Natchez, to Antonio Reynes, of same place, the half of a lot of ground in this Town, being lot No. 4, Sq. No. 1, and is the half which joins No. 3 in the same square, which I purchased from John Scott, Carpenter, and which I now sell with the buildings thereon, for $395 (on terms). Both sign. // p. 184. Natchez 1st May 1798. In virtue of Power of Atty. from Antonio Molina for that purpose, I have annulled the foregoing obligation, the same having been satisfied and fully paid. Signed Manuel Garcia de Texada.

p. 184. 1st April 1799. Antonio Molina, Commanding "the Vigilant" lying near this city, to Don Manuel Garcia de Texada, of Post of Natchez, power of atty. to annul and grant a formal receipt in favor of the estate of Antonio Reynes, decd. for sum of $350, price of house and lot I sold and which sum I have received from exors. of said Reynes. Antonio Molina. New Orleans, Copy signed by Carlos Ximenes.

p. 185. 22 Mch. 1798. Thomas Thompson, of Dist. of Natchez, to John Minor 800 acres on east bank of the Mississippi, opposite the first island in the Big Black River, b. on all sides by lands of His Majesty, of which land I took possession on 25 Feb. 1795, as per certificate of Surveyor Gen. 15 Feb. 1795, for $800 paid. Both sign.

p. 186. 23 March 1798. David Mitchell to Calvin Smith 400 arpents on Second Creek, b. by lands of Philander Smith, Stephen Minor, Abram Ellis and Amos Ogden, as per grant to him, No. 435, for $400 paid. Both signed. Wit: Samuel Hutchins.

p. 186. 24 Mch. 1798. Don Luis Faure, Surgeon of the Royal Hospital at this Post, to David Ferguson lot of ground near Natchez, b. by lands of Stephen Minor and Philip Engle, 16 arpents as per grant to him, for $1200, $200 in hand paid; remaining 1st June 1798. Both signed. Wit: Jas. Moore.

p. 187. 24 March 1798. Margaret Gallagher, of Post of Natchez, to John Minor, of same, 1000 arpents on the north branch of Cole's Creek, b. by Jacintha Gallagher, on south by Wm. Daniel, west Job Routh, as per grant to her 15 Feb. 1795, for $1200 in hand paid. Both sign.

p. 188. 26 March 1798. Agreement. John Vidal, dwelling at the landing place at this Town, who covenanted and agreed as follows in respect to the partnership which had existed between said Vidal and the deceased Estrades viz: the said Vidal shall pay to the Arcangle Rouillet $180 in full for the part her deceased husband had in the partnership, wherewith she is satisfied to renounce all further claim; and the said Vidal for his part shall remain owner of all the effects and outstanding debts due and belonging to the Firm, and shall pay all debts owing by the same, out of his own proper means. Both sign.

p. 188. 26 March 1798. Don Luis Faure, Surgeon of the Royal Hospital, at this Post, to Thomas Freemen and John McKee, 1000 arpents on a branch of Cole's Creek, b. by Nathaniel Kennison, Joseph Ford, Capt. Perret and John Ford, as per grant to him No. 770, for $350. Both sign. Wit: Jas Moore.

p. 189. 27 March 1798. Before Don Joseph Vidal, Capt. of Artillery, and Secretary for His Majesty, charged with the command of said Post. Andrew Gill, Surgeon in the Post, is lawfully possessed of a negro woman from Jamaica, named "Jennet", valued at $375, and John Scott, master carpenter said Post, lawfully possessed of a negro woman from America, named "Nanny", valued at $400; they exchanged said slaves and said Andrew Gill has paid said John Scott $25 in hand to make up difference. Both signed. Wit: Patrick McDermot.

p. 189. Ezekiel Dewitt to Pedro Walker, both of the Dist., 300 arpents on Bayou Sara, b. south on lands of sd Walker, north vacant, as per plat, for $400 specie paid. 28 March 1798. Ezekiel Dewitt makes his mark, Pedro Walker signs. Wit: Maurice Stacpoole, Domingo Lorrero.

p. 190. Jacintha Gallagher, of Town of Natchez, to John Minor, of same, 1000 acres between north branches of Cole's Creek, abt. 35 miles northeast of Fort Panmur, b. on south by Margaret Gallagher and otherwise vacant, gr. to her by Carondelet 25 Mch. 1794, surveyor's certf. 25 May 1795, for $1100 paid. 29 Mch. 1798. Both sign.

p. 190. 28 Feb. 1797. Edmund Johnson, of Dist. of Natchez, planter, is indebted to George Cochran for $152 with int. from 1st of present month, and sd Cochran, having engaged to make him other advances, not to exceed $400 in the whole, said Johnson promises to pay said Cochran Feb. 1st 1798 and as security mortgages a negro woman, "Let", nat. of U. S. Both sign. Wit: Will. Ferguson. // (The foregoing mortgage being filed with the suits at law could not be inserted in the proper place. Translator.)

p. 191. Natchez, 12 July 1797. Don Estevan Minor to Philip Engle, a piece of land between land gr. sd Philip Engle and the top of the cliff, b. below by land Minor sold Don Luis Faure, above by Minor's land, in front by brow of the cliff and behind by land of buyer; for $600 paid. Both sign.

p. 192. 17 Mch. 1798. Rebecca McCabe to Andrew Scandlan, a small house at the foot of the road leading down the hill together with half of the lot, being the lower half, for $300 paid. Signed Rebecca McCabe, Alexander Scandlan. Wit: Eben Rees.

p. 193. 19 Mch. 1798. Peter Camus, of Natchez, for myself and children and heirs, to Andrew Augustus Ellicott and Peter Walker, of same place, a plantation of 400 arpents, on the Homochitto River, b. by Samuel Swayze, Vaucheret, Bouille and by lands of His Majesty, as per grant to him No. 759, for $300 in hand paid. Signed by both. Wit: D. Gillespie, Chas. Anderson.

End of Book D

Translated by David Harper and so certified, Sept. 1, 1818.

BOOK E

pp. 1- Petition of John Row. (n.d.) Mr. William Vousdan, at his own house, bargained for my plantation, Mr. John Lum being present. He agreed to pay 585 Spanish-milled dollars, out of which sum, I have received $360, the balance remaining due to me, besides a private account of $66. I sued him before Mr. De La Villebeuvre and from him making so many excuses, the suit was delayed. // Bond of William Vousdan, of the Natchez District, West Florida, to John Row, in the full sum of 1200 Spanish-milled dollars, for the payment of $585. 3 Feb. 1778. Signed, William Vousdan. Wit: John Lum, Jacob Winfree, Jacob Cobun. // Bond of John Row for same amount, same date, for the transfer of his plantation to said Vousdan, 255 acres. Same witnesses. // p. 3. 14 Aug. 1781. // Before Don Carlos de Grand-Pre, Commandant, etc., came Anthony Hutchins, who declared that sometime in the year 1778, it was said that William Vousdan and John Row had bargained concerning a plantation of John Row's on Second Creek, that William Vousdan confessed to have purchased the said plantation which, at that time was not secured by patent, and that he, Vousdan, was to be at expense of doing the needful in every particular toward procuring a patent for the said land and Row was to sign him a good and sufficient deed for the same. Signed, Anthony Hutchins. // The verdict. We have condemned and do hereby condemn William Vousdan to make payment of $66 being the account of the plaintiff, John Row, and as respects the sum remaining unpaid of the land sold to Vousdan same shall not be paid to plaintiff until he shall have procured titles in form, which are in the archives of Pensacola, and the said land shall remain mortgaged as surety for the aforesaid sum, due to Row. 24 Aug. 1781. Signed, Charles de Grand-Pre.

p. 4. Petition of William Ferguson in behalf of William Vousdan, who sold to Samuel Swayze, Sr. sometime in the summer of 1777 a negro fellow called "Romeo", for which Swayze gave his bond for $325 payable in the summer following, which said bond Vousdan transmitted to Pennsacola to Mr. John Miller, as per receipt, to be recovered for his account. The bond is still unpaid in the hands of Mr. Miller. Signed, William Ferguson, acting for Vousdan, Natchez, Aug. 30, 1781. N.B. Your petitioner is willing to guarantee said bond by giving sufficient security. // Natchez, 5 Sept. 1781. Parties have been heard, and I do hereby condemn Samuel Swayze to the payment of $325, being the value of the negro named "Romeo", sold to him by Wm. Vousdan, within two months from this day or in default thereof to restore the negro with all the damages for the time that he has had him in his service. Signed. Charles de Grand-Pre. // p. 5. Natchez District. Oct. 1, 1781. William Ferguson petitions that he understands that Mr. Swayze has sold the negro that was in dispute between him and your petitioner in behalf of Mr. Vousdan, and he proposes to give the money he receives (p. 5) for the negro to Mr. David Ross, his lawful attorney. Petitioner begs that you will make good the judgment. // Natchez. 1 Oct. 1781. Let seizure be made of the sum of $300 in the hands of John Hartley, being the amount of the sale of the negro "Romeo", sold to him by Samuel Swayze, said sum to be made to Wm. Ferguson, lawful attorney of Wm. Vousdan, to whom said sum was due by said Samuel Swayze.

p. 5. Oct. 28, 1781. Pet. of Patrick Foley, that he has an acct. agst Stephen Holstein, of this District, for $54, for merchandise. etc. // Natchez, 28 Oct. 1781. Let Holstein be notified. Chas. de Grand-Pre.

p. 6. The petition of Barbour and Harrison represents that they hold a note of Stephen Holstein, of this District, planter, for $195, which is due long since. Natchez 21 Oct. 1781. // Same date. Let the party be notified. Grand-Pre. // Pet. of Stephen Holstein states that he was a short since at the point of death and sent his daughter to settle with Richard Harrison. Since that time, being at Natchez, he was called by said Harrison to settle his account, and asked said Harrison for his account and he said it amounted to $300, to which your petitioner replied "Your account is very large". Your petitioner told him he would pay him when his hogs were fat and he replied "Very well. I could sue you if I would." Now here is a poor, sick old man and miserable in his family and the promise of a gentleman, like Mr. Harrison, is forgotten. I have reason to think that the intention of that gentleman is to deprive me of my slaves, for the want of which myself and my poor children would suffer, for two negroes raise our provisions. But I hope that your honor will allow me time until my hogs are fat. Signed Stephen Holstein. N.B. At that time I had confidence in Mr. Harrison. I hope that you will site that the said Harrison appear with the book and my account before you. Oct. 24, 1781. // Same date. The party declares he needs the money and prays for a seizure. Let it be done as required. Signed Grand-Pre.

p. 7. Petition of Wm. Ferguson in behalf of William Vousdan lays before Commandant an account against Stephen Holstein for $17. Oct. 1, 1781. // 7 Sept. 1781, we, Charles de Grand-Pre, etc. in virtue of a decree in favor of Messrs. Barbour and Harrison, William Ferguson for Wm. Vousdan, and Patrick Foley, ordering seizure to be made of the property of S. Holstein, debtor to the persons aforesaid, have proceeded to the appraisement of a negro boy named "Duke", aged 11, and for which purpose we have appointed Messrs. Holt and Kelly, and the said negro boy was, by the appraisers, valued at $300 and the said appraisers and Francis Farrell and Silas Crane, witnesses have signed with us. Signed Dibdal Holt, James Kelly and others. // 7 Nov. 1781. At the demand of Messrs. Barbour and Harrison, and others, we have proceeded with this sale and adjudication of a negro boy seized as belonging to Stephen Holstein, debtors to the persons above named, and the said negro boy having been put up for sale to the highest bidder, was adjudged to Nathaniel Tomlinson for $248. [The creditors received the full amount of their debts.]

p. 8. Pet. of Wm. Ferguson that Silas Crane owes him $435 and not having made a title for land according to his bond, petitioner, having waited three years, prays for an order for payment. Nov. 27, 1781. // Bond of Silas Crane. [Charges and counter-charges follow, in which is shown that Silas Crane was in West Florida as early as 1774. Also, a firm of Lum, Williams and Company and a Jesse Lum were in the district at that time.] In same suit in Natchez Dec. 7, 1789, Silas Crane states: The grants made by the British to settlers in this province were as follows: (1) to the head of a family 100 arpents gratis, (2) to each child or servant 50 arpents, which were called the head rights and which we bought and sold among ourselves, as our own property, and he who bought the most was the best man and we gave bonds to make title as soon as the land should be surveyed and the papers delivered from the office of the Governor. That is the nature of the bond I gave to Messrs. Williams and Wm. Ferguson. Signed, Silas Crane. // Pet. dated 8 Dec. 1781, the said Ferguson had permission to choose the land where he might find it convenient, for two years. He told me he had located the lands on the Tombigbee, and I never knew that he had not until today. I was always ready to make him a title for the same, which he never asked for. // Natchez, 14 June 1782. The parties having been heard and their allegations examined, we have condemned Silas to deliver to Wm. Fergusón 300 acres of land at any place in the district within six weeks.

p. 15. Richard Harrison and Phillip Barbour, creditors of the estate of Daniel Lewis for $500 as manifested by the agreement annexed, and the widow of said deceased, having contracted matrimony with Richard Carpenter, of the Post of Baton Rouge, your petitioner prays for an order of payment, etc. 23 July 1782. Signed Richard Harrison. // Bond: I, Daniel Lewis, of Manchac, West Florida, to convey to Messrs. Barbour and Harrison, 500 arpents of land on the Big Black or in the neighborhood thereof in this Province. 11 May 1777. Signed, Daniel Lewis. Wit: Wm. Vousdan, Abel Lewis. // New Orleans, 29 May 1777. Sir: I pray you to deliver to the bearer, Mr. Lewis, $500 in negroes (p. 18) which you will take from the Brig of Capt. Taylor. Barbour and Harrison to Mr. John Campbell. // Received two negroes in consequence of the said order from Mr. John Campbell, 23 Aug. 1777, appraised at $477. Signed Nathaniel Lewis. // Let payment of the aforesaid $500 be made out of the estate of the widow and minors of Daniel Lewis, and the guardian and administrator be furnished with copies of the said proceedings for his justification and discharge when a division shall be made amongst the parties interested. Estevan Miro.

p. 20. Est. of Nehemiah Albertson. E. Minor to Mr. Trevino. Sir: On my arrival at Mr. Johnson's I found Albertson very ill and in an hour he died. Thinking it expedient that Mr. Howard should continue his journey, I appointed Mr. Chacheret and Mr. Johnson to appraise the two horses belonging to him and likewise requested those gentlemen to take an inventory of his clothing. // List of effects found with the deceased Albertson, at the time of his death, and left in the care of Mr. Isaac Johnson: One small bundle containing 18 lbs. of gunpowder, another with 18 lbs. of bullets, one bear skin, one deer skin, one waistcoat of green cloth, one saddle and one pack-saddle, one bridle, being all that was found and delivered as aforesaid. (signed) Isaac Johnson. Note: The saddle and bridle were delivered to Mr. Howard. At the request of Mr. Howard, who was stopped in his journey by the death of the late Albertson, and being in public service, [adcaldes], we appraised the two horses and the saddle, which he (Howard) had barrowed from the said Albertson, and which was valued as follows, one horse, $40, and another 35, and bridle and saddle $15, which was all that Mr. Howard took with him. 17 July 1785. (signed) Chacheret and Isaac Johnson. // Papers: Chickasaw Nation, 18 Oct. 1783. On or before 1st Dec. I promise to pay Camp Welly, a half-breed living in Flackthidon the sum of $350. (signed) Nehemiah Albertson. // An Article of Agreement between Nehemiah Albertson and Saint Germain. // The account of partnership with Mr. St. Germain and Mr. Nehemiah Albertson, of this Province. Two pages of articles, no names. // Articles which Mr. Charbonneau received of Mr. Albertson in payment of account of $172 owed by Albertson to Antonio Gras . . . . powder, lead and gun flints. // Chickasaw Nation. Robert Braswell to Henry Duke, two kegs of rum, Oct. 16, 1783. // Acct with Alexander Moore, 26 May 1785. // Antonio Gras and Co. hold Albertson's note for $102, signed 15 July 1785 // John Roche of the Town of Natchez, pet. that,having furnished Nehemiah Albertson with sundry articles to amt. of $426, as security for which Albertson, before his death, had delivered to Roche a negro now in his possession, which sd negro he asks that he be allowed to sell at public auction to obtain payment for the debt. Natchez, 24 Aug. 1785. // Inventory and effects found to belong to Nehemiah Albertson at his death and appraisement thereof by Alexander Moore and Don Carlos Barchellot. 22 Oct. 1785. Total $700. A slave, powder, bridle and the like. // At sale of above by Don Francisco Bouligny, Civil and Military Commandant of Fort Panmure and the Dist. of Natchez, at the landing of the Town of Natchez, the negro "Hector" for $600, 50 lbs. of gun-powder to David Smith for $45, 150 lbs. of bullets and 200 gun flints to David Smith for $42, one saddle and bridle to Charles King for $15, 5 pack-saddles to Joseph Faure for $3, one horse and one mare to Jeremiah Bryan for $70, another horse for $76, to same. Total $852. // In pursuance of a notice the Commandant had posted,the creditors of the deceased appeared: a half-breed named Campbelton, Francisco Bazo, Jeremiah Bryan, Mr. Faure and Mr. Minor. [Jeremiah Bryan a cred. in sum of $175.]

p. 28. Claim by Jacob Elliott, of N. O. who sold to George Rapalje, of Dist. of Natchez, planter, now in the City, five slaves, [names and ages given] also a barge with four oars, etc., which said negroes I bought out of a cargo brought to this port by Don Juan Maysar, from Jamaica, by permission from the Superior Government, about a year since, and which said slaves together with the barge I did sell free from mortgage for $1480, payable with a bill of exchange for $500 payable 27 July of the present year, drawn on Garret Rapalje at 30 day sight, dwelling in New Jersey, and a bond drawn on George Rapalje for $490 and another bond in my favor on terms, secured by mortgage of slaves and Rapalje's plantation on St. Catherine's Creek, on which he dwelt, of 400 arpents, 6 Aug. 1784. Certified by Rafael Perdonno, Notary Public. // New Orleans, 17 June 1785. James Elliot petitions as to the above sale, that he has not been paid anything except the bill that George Rapalje had drawn on his father at New York. The negro woman has died and he petitions that since the loss of the negro woman and the use of the other negroes cancells the money he has received, asks that the seizure of the plantation be made to satisfy the mortgage. // In pursuance thereof seizure of the slaves and plantation for $1480 and for $250 for use of negroes as contract provided, ordered by Estevan Miro, N. O. June 1st 1785. Richard Duvall was surety for James Elliot, of Cole's Creek. // The sale, 3 Dec. 1785, before Don Francisco Bouligny, etc. James Elliot bought the negro man "Pitcher" for $600, also "Dick" for $500, and the two children for $420. The plantation, on the third and last bidding was adjudged to John Joseph Rodriguez for $535, the highest bidder. Fort Panmur at Natchez, 7th March 1785. James Elliot receipted for $1750. // George Rapalje, being in N. O., asks that the land sold be the part that his old house was on and not that on which he has built, since the contract was made, a new house, and the Commandant so ordered, 30 March 1786. Signed by Estevan Miro.

p. 33. Alexander Moore, merchant of Natchez, represents that the creditors of Mr. George Rapalje being very pressing for their dividends, asks that an order be given that Mr. Abraham Ellis who was to serve with him, either act or resign, so there may be some settlement. Natchez, 28 April 1787. Signed Alexander Moore. // Natchez, 29 April, Mr. Abraham Ellis replies that the distance of his dwelling, as well as the care of his plantation, prevents him from attending to any business other than his own. He resigns. 4 May 1787. // Alexander Moore made the sole agent of Rapalje, to sell and recover all money coming to said estate, // The land bought by Don Rodriguez will remain in his possession and notice will be given of the day of the sale of the other properties. 16 July 1789. Grand-Pre.

p. 36. Catherine Dewitt, of the Dist. of Natchez, lawful wife of William Dewitt, begs leave to represent that the Commandant of said District having sequestered the whole estate of her husband, for the payment of pretended creditors, as can be proved when needful, asks for a passport to proceed to the Capital to obtain justice from Your Excellency, which was denied her there, a rumor having been spread that her husband was on the point of absconding and in consequence of that report, he was confined in the Fort and the Commandant not only sequestered his property but mine also and that of my children whose estate was secured by the instrument hereunto annexed; that sometime after he was set at liberty, but a part of the property was detained in the Fort and a part delivered in charge of Don Estevan Minor and the men who worked on his plantation. Wherefore your petitioner asks that our property be restored to us and a term allowed for the payment of the debt owing by her husband. // The Commandant will enquire in what manner William Dewitt became indebted to Don Estevan Minor, David Smith, John Burnet, Gibson Clark, and Arthur Cobb in the sum of $1700 and for security whereof sold conditionally to Adam Bingaman five slaves, namely "Stephanie, Mingo, Monday, James, Felix" and a child, the said five slaves to be restored to said Dewitt and obliging the said creditors to return to the said Bingaman the sums that they have respectively received from him until the results of the said enquiry shall have been made known in this Tribunal. And in any case, reserving the property of Catherine Dewitt as expressed in the deed of gift executed by said Dewitt in North Carolina on 2 Jany. 1781. Signed Estevan Miro. *Notation: Catherine signed her name "Catherine White Dewitt" to the above petition. // North Carolina. Know all men by these presents that I, William Dewitt, of Burke County, in the Province aforesaid, for and in consideration of one pound of lawful money to me paid, etc. do hereby grant to Catherine White the following negroes, namely, Ben, Phillis, Jenny and Mary and I do likewise grant to Catherine Dewitt, my daughter, the following negroes, Phoebe, Sambo and Juno, and I do likewise give and grant to my son, Jesse Dewitt, negroes, Coffee, Stephany, Judo, Monday, James, Dodd and Simeon and to my daughter, Martha I give and grant negroes named Phillis, and her child and Jupiter, and by these presents etc. confirming the above. Jany. 1st 1781. Signed William Dewitt, in the presence of John White, Benj. White, Joseph White, Thomas White. Before me John Sumter, J.P., appeared personally Benj. White who made oath that he saw William sign the within instrument and that he saw Joseph White and Thomas White sign their names thereto with himself. 2nd Jany. 1781. John Sumter, Benj. White. // p. 38. To Don Philipe Trevino, Commandant, the undersigned respectfully represent that for many reasons they are induced to believe that Mr. Leaperat [Leaphart] is the author of the false deed of gift made by William Dewitt in favor of his wife and children and pray that you will order him to appear before you and declare the truth on oath. Natchez, 14 Feb. 1785. Gibson Clark, John Burnet and D. Smith. // The declaration of Reuben White and Mrs. White, his mother, sayeth that in the latter part of the year 1781, John White was living in Washington, North Carolina, and that he went to Kentucky to buy salt and when said White set off for salt the deceased wife of Mr. William Dewitt was alive and when the said John White returned William Dewitt's wife was dead and Mr. Dewitt had gone to Burke County near about 100 miles the contrary way to be married to the woman that he now has got, and to the certain knowledge of Reuben White, John White never saw Mr. William Dewitt nor his present wife from the time he set off to Kentucky till after Mr. Dewitt was married to this woman and had returned back to Washington County, nor does he believe that Mr. Dewitt ever made this present wife any right to one negro till they came to this country and if he has since he believes it to be a forgery and from very good circumstances. They are as follows: James White, deceased, father of Reuben White, and husband to Mrs. White, told them in his lifetime that Mr. Dewitt wanted him to be a witness to a deed of gift to his wife and children since they came to Natchez and got into debt and, to defraud their creditors, and James White, now deceased, said to Mr. Dewitt and to his brother John White, that he would do no such thing for every negro Mr. Dewitt had and persuaded his brother, John White, not to witness it; told him if he did that he could not answer for it at a future day. 31 Jany. 1785. Signed in the presence of William Smith, Joel Byrd, Tarusha White and Reuben White. // p. 39. Deposition of Elizabeth Stillee. I do hereby certify that I heard Mr. William Dewitt say sometime in the year 1783 that he had not as yet given anything to his wife nor children, notwithstanding his wife had said that part of the property her husband had was hers. I also heard James White say sometime before his death that Mr. Dewitt asked him to sign as a witness to a deed gift he had made to his wife and children of all his property and said James White told Mr. Dewitt that he would not sign any such writing, that it was wrong, that he was trying to cheat his creditors of their just dues. I certify upon oath this to be the truth and nothing but the truth. 4 Feb. 1785. Elizabeth Stillee signs with a mark. Wit: John Burnet. // Deposition of Elizabeth Raby. I do hereby certify that I was personally present and heard Mr. Dewitt say sometime after he came to this country that he had never given anything to his wife and children. Natchez, 4 Feb. 1785. Signed Elizabeth Raby. Wit: John Burnet. // North Carolina, Burke County. I, William Dewitt, do give and grant unto Catherine White the following negroes, Ben, Phillis, Jenny and Mary. 1st Jany. 1781. Signed William DeWitt (No witnesses). // Deposition of John Lovelace. I, the subscriber, having been called in before the commandant of the Post, and taken my oath, confess and declare that in the month of September last past I was sent for by Mr. Wm. Dewitt and, having arrived at his house, he begged me to make him a deed of gift of all his negroes in favor of his wife and children, giving me form how it was to be laid out and the name of the Justice of the Peace which was John Sumpter, and desiring me to antedate the said writing the 1st of Jany. 1781, the which I complied with without any difficulty to oblige him, which I have made known, not thinking it would prejudice any person unless it was attended by bad consequences, which I sign for the truth and nothing but the truth. Signed John Lovelace. Wit: William Smith, James Armstrong and Estevan Minor. Signed Philip Trevino. // Here follows again a copy of the forged deed from Dewitt. // p. 41. Deposition of John Still Lee. I do hereby certify that Mr. John White was asked by Mr. William Dewitt to go with his wife to New Orleans to testify that a deed of gift he had made to his wife and children was just and, in consequence of which, said White had applied to the Commandant for a passport and the Commandant told said White that he should go if he would pay his debts. At the same time, the said White came to me and asked me if I would be his security for a sum of money he owed Mr. Alexander Moore and on his return from Town he was to pay me again as he told me he was to receive from Wm. Dewitt $100 for his trouble in going to Town to declare his said deed of gift to be good, saying at the same time that he could not earn money so fast any other way. I do declare the above to be true. Natchez 5 Feb. 1785. Signed John Still Lee. Wit: William McIntosh, J. Bingaman. // p.41. To Don Philipe Trevino, Commandant, etc. the undersigned have the honour to represent that the deed of gift made by William Dewitt and in virtue whereof his wife has obtained an order from the Government by which the said purchasers of said property of said Dewitt are required to restore the same: to us who are well-acquainted with Dewitt and whose doubts in this respect amount to certainty, we have no hesitation in saying that the deed of gift in question is forged. What probability can there be that Dewitt would in the month of January 1781 make a deed to his second wife when his first wife was living and more than one year before his second marriage took place. By the documents hereunto annexed, it will appear that his pretended deed was forged and his own bad conduct made it necessary for him to frustrate and defraud his creditors for having trusted him. We feel that it would be difficult to force him to make this confession more especially since he has had the good fortune to impose on the Government and knows that the punishment that would follow detection could not be greater than the offence. But would it be possible to persuade us that Dewitt, if such a deed had really existed, would have suffered the property to be seized and sold, not only without availing himself of such deed but even without saying that it existed. No, his whole conduct shows that he left this place in haste to avoid discovery which he thought more likely to be made here than at New Orleans. We flatter ourselves that the forgery being proven we shall experience no difficulty in obtaining revocation of the judgment which he has obtained by fraud. May it please you to suspend execution of the judgment of the Superior Government until the foregoing documents and reasons in support of them may be examined and the said judgment reversed or confirmed. Natchez 25 Feb. 1785. Signed John Burnet, Gibson (X) Clark, A. Bingaman. The petition is granted. The papers will be sent for His Excellency's perusal and determination therein. Signed Trevino. // The documents, being examined, the contract of marriage of Catherine Dewitt is declared to be illegal and she is deprived of the benefit claimed in the virtue thereof. Signed Estevan Miro and Leonardo Poinz. The Commandant of the Post of Natchez will pay the debts contracted by William Dewitt or such of them as shall be proven from the proceeds of the sale of the negroes, and it appearing that said debts have arisen in part from bets made by him in horse-racing, they will be determined according to the customs of the country of which he is a native. But in the future, the Commandant of the said Post will not permit similar practices under such penalties as the nature of the case may require. Estevan Miro, Leonardo Poinz.

p. 43. Petition of Margaret Woods that, on viewing the miserable situation to which she is reduced, she prays an order that a certain negro wench, named "Rebecca", with her children, be restored to her, which said wench was given to her by her husband, John Woods, at the time of her marriage, about eleven years ago, and in all their difficulties was never taken from her, as she had a property in said wench, her husband having sufficient property to satisfy his creditors without taking hers. Margaret Woods, Natchez, 16 January 1784. // Same date. The prayer of the petitioner appearing just, the same is granted. Signed Trevino. // Permission is granted to the wife of John Woods, absconded, to go to New Orleans on business. Natchez, 13 Nov. 1784. // I do hereby certify that I set off from the Natchez landing to go to New Orleans, having my passport on board. I was stopped to speak to Mr. Trevino who forbid me taking Mrs. Woods into my boat, except that she went on board at that place. She had a passport and I told her that I could take her in at the Cliff. This was on the 13th of November, 1784, Mr. Minor. being the interpreter. Signed Daniel (D) Perry. // I do here certify that I heard the above-mentioned words spoken by Mr. Minor to Mr. Perry. Signed Jessè Hamilton. Natchez, 23 Feb. 1786. // To His Excellency, Don Estevan Miro, Gov. Genl. of the Province of La., Margaret Woods, of the Dist. of Natchez, has the honour to represent that her husband, John Woods, being a simple man and somewhat addicted to liquor, concluded a bargain with a certain Stephen Minor for a tract of land in the said District of Natchez, containing about 200 arpents, together with 3 horses, 3 cows and 2 plows, and being intoxicated at the time, agreed to pay the said Minor for the same the enormous sum of $1500, a sum far beyond the real value thereof, and much more than the husband of your petitioner was able to pay without a total ruin of himself and family, as the event has proved. When the sum became due, being unable to make payment, execution was issued against the husband of your petitioner and not only the land, plows, horses and cows were sold but also five slaves. Will your Excellency be pleased to consider the case. Signed Margaret Woods. New Orleans, 16 March 1786. // p. 44. The Commandant of the Post of Natchez will make enquiry for what sum the said plantation was sold by Mr. Estevan Minor to John Woods. He will signify why Margaret Woods was prevented from descending to the City in 1784 in November, and at whose instance she was detained, and transmit this information to this Government.

New Orleans 30 March 1786. // Before me Francisco Collell, Commandant of the Dist. and Post of Natchez, appeared Don Estevan Minor who has sold, ceded and transferred to John Woods, here present, a tract of land on St. Catherine's Creek of 185 arpents on which are erected a dwelling house and some negro cabins, b. by lands of Widow Coleman, Widow Smith, Adam Bingaman and C. Bingaman, said land being part of the estate of John Blommart, sold to Francois Farrell at public sale to the use of the King, for the sum of $300 payable in the month of December next, and for security, the said purchaser binds his whole estate and estates, granting authority to compel him to the performance of the same, as if the judgment had been already given. Natchez. August 1st, in the morning, 1783, in the presence of Franciois Farrell, and Antonio Soler, who have signed with the said parties contracting and I the Commandant. Copied from and compared with the original records in the Archives in my charge. Natchez, July 4th, 1786 Signed Carlos de Grand-Pre. // p. 45. I do hereby certify that I was at Mr. Minor's plantation both before and after he sold it to John Woods and from the exceedingly good order it was in and the crop had so good an appearance at the time it was sold, for there were 15 acres of corn, near 3 acres of oats, potatoes of both kinds and pumpkins, likewise a good garden, all in the best of order imaginable, agreeable to the rules of planting and the production of the land here, if taken proper care of, there would have been at the harvesting 35 bushels to the acre. Further I heard Mr. Woods say that he expected to make more on the plantation than would pay his purchase from Mr. Minor, that he had a great bargain, for, by the purchase of the plantation, he had a home with everything about him, the same as though he had been settled a number of years and further I heard said Woods say he had with the plantation 3 horses, 3 cows and calves, 2 plows and gears, rum, sugar, coffee and other things, and further, he, the said Woods, sold the three horses to the best of my remembrance for upwards of $300, as witness my hand, 3 July 1786. Signed Stephen Haywood. // I do certify that we were on Mr. Minor's plantation both before and after he sold it to Mr. John Woods and from the exceedingly good order the plantation and crop were in, at the time it was sold to the said Woods, it appeared to us that there were 15 acres of corn in good order which agreeable to the produce of corn in this part of the country is from 30 to 35 bushels to the acre and that the said Woods told me that he expected to make enough from this crop as would nearly pay Mr. Minor for the plantation and he was satisfied and he should not have made anything with his negroes if he had not the purchase as it was too late to make a crop elsewhere. Besides the corn there was several acres of potatoes and oats and a very good garden. Signed by John Ellis and Richard Harrison. // I do certify that I was sent for by Mr. Stephen Minor to go and assist him in taking a negro fellow he had lost and he told me he was hid in a cane-brake by Mrs. Woods. According to his request, I went with him in company with several others where we found in possession of Mrs. Woods a negro wench, Mr. Minor told me he had consented one Mrs. Owens should take away. I also declare that the said negro that Mr. Minor had lost was caught that same night on Mrs. Woods' plantation about one o'clock. Natchez, 3 July 1786. Signed: Daniel Mygatt // p. 46. Deposition. I do hereby declare upon oath that a few days before Mr. John Woods let Mr. Stephen Minor have the negroes for the money he was in debt to him, Margaret Woods, wife of said John Woods, came to me and said that ever since she had been married she was used to have negroes to wait upon her and that it would go very hard with her to be without a negro to do her business but she feared that it would take all her husband's negroes to pay the debts. I asked her if she could not lay in a petition to the Commandant claiming the country-born negro wench, called "Beck". She said it was doubtful it would do as she brought but five guineas in gold to Mr. Woods when she was married which she lent to pay a part of the purchase of the wench called "Kate". And further I do declare that some short time after, Mr. Minor having in his possession two negroes that he had bought of the said Woods, one Mrs. Owens came to me and told me that Mrs. Woods had been several times to beg her to steal a negro wench her husband had sold Mr. Minor. I asked her if she knew what Mrs. Woods intended to do with the wench. Mrs. Owens said that Mrs. Woods told her that she had the negro fellow of Mr. Minor hid out in the cane-brake, and if she could get the wench, she would immediately go the the Choctaw Nation after her husband, as he was to wait there for her on the path. I then told her that she ought to go and inform Mr. Minor of Mrs. Woods' intention and proceedings, which she agreed to and we went together and made the matter known to Mr. Minor. Signed Patience Welton with her mark. Wit: John Welton, Stephen Haywood. // I do hereby certify that I have been often at Mr. Minor's plantation, both before and after he sold it to John Woods and from the very good order the corn was in and other things there were on the said place when he sold the place to said Woods, he told me he expected to make nearly as much off the plantation to pay Mr. Minor for all he had bought of him. Furthermore he said that he was satisfied with the bargain, etc. Natchez, 9 July 1786. Signed A. Bingaman. // I do hereby certify upon oath that the time Mr. Minor lost his negro fellow, named "London", that he bought of John Woods, the said negro was harbored by Mrs. Margaret Woods, wife of John Woods, in a cane-brake. This she, herself, told me. (p.47) Moreover, I saw the wench with victuals for the said negro. She sent a man to me to buy a horse from me to send the negro away to the Choctaw Nation, and likewise begged of me and my wife to steal a wench, named "Kate", that Mr. Minor had bought of her husband. We both agreed that we would, in order to satisfy her until we could acquaint Mr. Minor of her intentions, which we did. Also, I further declare that at the time when he let Mr. Minor have the negroes for the money he owed, his wife Margaret came to me and told me she was afraid her husband would not be able to pay his debts without selling all his negroes and asked me if I did not think she should not get one of the negroes if she told the Commandant it was hers. I told her that she knew very well that she had no claim to any. She told me she preferred a wench named "Kate" but she wanted to carry away a fellow named "London" or send him to the Nation, so she thought it would be better to claim the fellow's wife, "Beck", as the fellow would be much easier to take away with his wife than without her. I further declare that I live a near neighbor to Mr. Woods both in Carolina and in this country and I never heard from him or his wife or any other person that any of the negroes was his wife's before it was said that Mr. Trevino had given her one. Sometime after said Woods had purchased the plantation from Mr. Minor, he had some stock and I heard him say he was well satisfied with his bargain. 7 July 1786. Signed William Owens. Wit: James Elliot, Stephen Haywood. // p. 47. Natchez, 28 June 1785. I do here certify that some short time after John Woods sold Stephen Minor a couple of negroes, Margaret Woods came to me and told me that she had a negro fellow harbored out in a cane-brake, named "London", said negro her husband had sold to Mr. Minor, and begged me to go to Mr. Minor's and carry away a negro wench, named "Kate", and she would make me satisfied for doing so; that her husband was going to the Choctaw Nation and that she wanted to send them, that is "London" and "Kate" immediately after him to the Nation. I told her that I would do it, that I might have an opportunity to acquaint Mr. Minor of her proceedings and intentions as I thought it my duty to do so, which I did the next day, and after consulting Mr. Minor, he agreed that I should take the wench, "Kate", and he would follow me with a guard, saying, by that means, he would get this fellow, "London", who had been lost some time. I took the wench and left her in the woods near a half a mile from Mrs. Woods' house, at the place she appointed, saying she would come in the night and take away the wench, and also I do declare that I heard Mrs. Woods say that she had no claim to her husband's negroes, not bringing anything with her but five guineas and that in gold which she lent her husband to pay a part of the wench, "Kate", neither did I ever hear Mr. Woods say that his wife brought with her when he married her any negroes and I am sure that her father never gave her a negro. Signed Susannah Owen. Wit: Stephen Haywood. // p. 48. I do certify upon oath that I was sent for by Mr. Stephen Minor to assist him in taking a negro fellow which he had lost and as he told me the said negro was harbored out in a cane-brake by Mrs. Woods. At his request, I went with him about one o'clock at night and caught said negro near the crossing place of the bayou, being the place he expected him, where I was sent to make watch by Mr. Minor. It was on Mrs. Woods' plantation that I caught said negro. Mrs. Woods, the wench and the child of this fellow were caught by the same party that Mr. Minor had sent out watching, as Mrs. Woods was bringing the said wench and child to the said father, as the fellow confessed to me when I caught him, and the distance between was so very short that when I took the fellow I could distinctly hear the men speak who took the wench and child. The fellow told me that Mrs. Woods had persuaded him to run away and told him Mr. Minor intended selling him to the Spaniards, that if he would lie out a while when Mr. Woods returned he would carry away the negro and his wife and child. Mrs. Woods finding herself detected in stealing the negro, endeavored in some way to satisfy herself by following the party and giving leave to her tongue, which for a space of time dealt out scurrility in the greatest abundance. Cole's Creek, 7 July 1786. Signed Abraham Moyes. // Natchez, July 3, 1785. Deposition of William B. Smith. I do hereby certify that we live adjacent to the plantation Mr. Stephen Minor sold to John Woods and that when he delivered said plantation to Woods it was in good order as it is possible to be and as good appearance for a crop as any in the country (same description as in other depositions), also horses, cows, dishes, 10 bushels of corn, etc. The horses were sold, one for $140, another for $100, and the 3rd about $80, this we are knowing to, and we never heard Woods say he was dissatisfied with his bargain until the time of payment, but that he always seemed contented. Signed William B. Smith, Philetus Smith. // Deposition of Jeremiah Bryan. Mr. Minor sent for him and told him that he had lost a negro named "London" and he had been informed that Margaret Woods had him hidden in a cane-brake and Mrs, Woods has sent Mrs. Owens to steal one of his wenches away, called "Kate", and that Mrs. Owens had given him information of it. He told Mrs. Owens to take her away in order to catch the fellow. He asked me to go with him to assist in taking the negro . . . We immediately set off . . . . . (same account as given in other depositions) . . . . . Signed Jeremiah Bryan, witness, Stephen Haywood. // To the Civil and Military Commandant at Natchez, Stephen Minor presents a list of the property sold to John Wood and it totals $500. // Natchez 26 April 1783 Memorandum of what he had spent on the plantation, $37 for a well, etc. $74 fences made by his negroes, total $988. This by Woods. // Deposition by Stephen Jett that he heard Woods say that he had offered Minor all sorts of propositions to keep him from foreclosing. // p. 53. Fort Panmur, Natchez, 1st July 1786. Daniel Perry was called to appear. James McIntosh acting as interpreter, he was asked why he had not taken Margaret Woods on board his barge for New Orleans, in the month of December, she having a passport. He had agreed to do so but before getting under way, Don Estevan Minor appeared to deliver an order to the deponent forbidding him to embark the said Margaret Woods at any other place than Natchez, the said Margaret being present when said order was delivered observed that the order was unnecessary as she had declined going to New Orleans and thus voluntarily remained at Natchez. Signed in the presence of John Ellis and Juan Carreras before Grand-Pre. // On the same day appeared Jesse Hamilton who declared that to his knowledge she did intend to go to New Orleans on the barge of Daniel Perry but just before Perry left the Commandant Trevino and Don Estevan Minor appeared at the landing, as above, except he does not know why said Margaret did not go as intended. Wit: John Bisland, Daniel Mygatt. Before Grand-Pre. // Natchez. This is to certify that I heard John Wood say that a certain negro woman named "Rebecca" was the property of his wife, Margaret, that he gave her to his wife at the time of their marriage. 4 Oct. 1784. Signed Stephen Jett. // Deposition by Archibald Rea, 1 Oct. 1784. He had heard Capt. John Woods say that the negro woman named "Kate" was the property of his wife, who was given to his wife as a legacy by her father, Matthew Thompson, at her marriage to said Woods. // This to certify that I heard Capt. John Woods, twelve years ago or upwards make a free gift to his wife, Margaret Wood, of a negro girl name "Rebecca" then aged 8 years, and the said John Woods did then divest himself of any right and title to her. Signed John Pickens. Oct. 1, 1784. // Petition of Margaret Woods, about three years since she arrived in this district, possessed of 5 slaves, three of which belonged to her husband and a negro woman and child belonged to herself, in proof of which certificates Nos. 1 and 2 are added. Her husband, John Woods, imprudently purchased a plantation, etc. (as recited before) . . . Signed Margaret Wood. // The Commandant of the Post called those making depositions to appear. John Pickens ack. his statement and changed it in no way; Archibald Rea the same; the affidavit of Stephen Jett could not be taken, Jett being absent from the District. // In pursuance of this, order was given that the negro woman and child be given to Margaret Woods. // p. 57. Esteven Minor represented that he had been notified of this decree of the Gov. Genl. of the Province, and he requested suspension of the execution until he could present further evidence, having proof of the falsehood of the accusations made against him by the said Margaret. 29 June 1786. // 31 Aug. 1786. In order to comply with the order of the Tribunal to ascertain the value of the aforesaid plantation, witnesses were summoned. John Bisland appeared, and declared that he thought that the price of the plantation for $300 was perfectly correct and also of the other things except the price of an axe and corn $4 too much; William Brocus thought the plantation, cattle, etc. was priced justly; William Henderson had agreed as to prices being right except axe and corn; Benjamin Balk, same opinion // Fort Panmur, 1st Aug. 1786, to carry into effect the order of the Superior Tribunal before me (p.61) John Ellis appeared, confirmed certificate before Margaret Woods, etc. ; also Daniel Mygatt the same; Patience Welton, confirmed deposition; Adam Bingaman confirmed deposition; William Owen confirmed statement; Jeremiah Bryan; William B. Smith and Philetus Smith confirmed certificates; Abraham Mayes same. // 30 Sept. 1786. Appeared Susanna Owens confirmed statement; Richard Harrison confirmed statement; // In pursuance of the affidavits given in this case on oath, the sale of the plantation and other effects from Don Estevan Minor to John Woods is confirmed and the proceedings are hereby returned to the Commandant at Natchez. New Orleans, 16 Dec. 1786. Signed Estevan Miro. // I, Don Philipe Trevino, Lt. Col. etc. certify that at the public sale of the property of John Woods, absconded, which took place on 3 April of this year, Don Estevan Minor, adjutant of this Post, purchased a negro woman, aged 20 years, with a child, the said woman and child having been appraised at $500, for $561. 10 June, 1784. Signed Philipe Trevino. // Examined. Margaret Woods is excluded from all claim to the woman "Rebecca" and the proceedings to be transmitted to the Commandant at Natchez. Natchez, 16 Dec. 1786. //

p. 66. To His Excellency, the Governor, William Dortch says that some time ago he made an exchange with George Overaker to whom he delivered a negro woman for a plantation and some cattle and that he came to the office to receive a reciprocal title to the property exchange, giving his bill of sale of slave to Mr. Overaker and receiving a sale for the plantation from Mr. James Truly who had sold the plantation to Mr. Overaker, petitioner not suspecting any deception in the matter, thought himself safe but to his great surprise was informed by a friend that the land that he had bought was the property of Mr. William Ferguson, to whom he applied to know the truth of the matter and found that it was claimed by Mr. Ferguson and he would not pass title for it. Petitioner asks for the return of his slave and his bond.

Signed W. Dortch. Natchez, 15 June 1792. // Same date. Mr. George Overaker will appear before me at the Government House on Wednesday next. Signed: Gayoso.

p. 67. Indenture made 20 Nov. 1797 between Charles Adams, of the Natchez District, Province of West Florida, planter, to John Bullen, of same, for payment hereinafter mentioned, 425 acres on the waters of St. Catherine's Creek, granted to Charles Adams by the Spanish Govt. 15 Mch. 1789, in consideration of $600 payable:$298 towards the discharge of the following debts of sd Adams; to William Stevens, N.O. $38; to Thomas Irvine $28; to William Foster $99; to George Fitzgerald $96; David Ross $27; the balance on certain terms, with reference to part of land being in litigation with Mrs. Juliana Thomas, in promise made by Adams to sell to her husband, William Thomas. Signed, Charles Adams, John Bullen. Before Estevan Minor. Wit: John Foster, Thos. Foster, John Girault.

p. 69. Indenture, 12 March 1799 between Randall Gibson, of Southern District of Miss. Ter., and Charles Adams, of same, whereas John Bullen, 20 Nov. 1797 purchased of Charles Adams a certain tract on St. Catherine's Cr., part of land being in litigation with Mrs. Juliana Thomas, whereas John Bullen has not complied with any part of the conditions and is now absent from this Territory, the said Randall Gibson, as the representative of the said John Bullen, takes upon himself, and at his own risk and peril for himself, to relinquish all claim of the said Bullen to the said 425 acres. Signed by Randall Gibson, Charles Adams, in the presence of Leonard D. Shaw, John Girault. // p. 70. Charles Adams, for and in consideration for $450 to me in hand paid, by Capt. William Thomas, sells part of the above tract, to include the improvements made by Thomas and his family, beg. tree in line of John Killian to Harris's line and to the corner of Robert Carr, etc. Signed by Chas. Adams, Natchez, 24 March 1795. Wit: John Girault, Chas. Spain. Before Manuel Gayosa de Lemos. // William Thomas and Charles appear and bind themselves by this agreement. Adams to receive negroes to amout of $400. p. 72. Charles Adams petitons that he had not the least expectation of recovering any satisfaction from Mr. Thomas for the land and plantation sold him as from every account he was cast away on his passage to the U.S. The petitioner having laid out of his pay considerable time and no expectation for ever getting anything for it, asks that the plantation be returned to him. Charles Adams, Sept. 20, 1796. // Sept. 22 Juliana Thomas appeared before the Court asks for three days delay so that she may prepare her defense. // Her answer to above petition: Her husband had paid for the land but when he took the commission to buy slaves with $400 of the money for Charles Adams, he made it understood that he would not take any of the risk. Signed: Juliana Thomas, Natchez, 28 Sept. 1796. // p. 73. Charles Adams, in reply, states that he can prove that Mr. Thomas did not pay him anything for the plantation but that he was to bring him negroes for him to the amount as it appears by his obligation, which he has not complied with, he thinks he should have his plantation and, in order not to distress the family, he offers Mrs. Thomas a dwelling and a piece of cleared land where he now lives until she can secure a better accommodation, upon condition that she would peacefully give up the plantation. Natchez, 1st Oct. 1796. // Juliana Thomas petitions that an order be issued that Adams make her a good and sufficient title to the land he sold her husband, in order that she may begin planting a crop for her large family dependent upon her. Natchez, 9 Jany. 1797. // Charles Adams again summoned to live up to the tenor of his obligation or produce his objections, according to his bond on record. Natchez 9 Jany. 1797. // Charles Adams petitions that he had never received any payment. It is true that he acknowledges to have received value but the value was the obligation of Mr. Thomas and not money. This can be proved by the witnesses to the transaction. The petitioner was to run the risk of the negroes or other property to be bought but as the negroes were in the United States where the said Thomas never reached, no loss was sustained and the petitioner can prove by the evidence of Major Minor that Mr. Thomas had no money to carry with him, therefore he could have lost none on his way. Petitioner asks that Major Minor be called as a witness to the bond to declare whether I received value for the said land except the obligations and then order Mrs. Thomas to comply immediately with the tenor of same. 17 Jany. 1797. Charles Adams. // Declaration of Capt. Stephen Minor will be taken and notice to Juliana Thomas. Signed Gayoso // Minor's deposition: 10 Feb. 1797. Stephen Minor appeared and on oath declared that in a conversation that he had with William Thomas a few days before his departure for the U.S. he told me he was to bring a negro or negroes for Charles Adams from America for the payment of a plantation he had purchased of him and although said Adams had acknowledged the receipt of the money for the payment of the land it was only a matter of form but that the negroes were to be Charles Adams risk after purchase. The said Capt. Thomas had no money with him for he requested the deponent to lend him wherewith to pay his passage to America. This the deponent refused doing. Signed Stephen Minor. Before J. Vidal, Jean Girault, and Gayoso. // p. 72. Juliana Thomas petitions, replying to that of Charles Adams, that William Thomas, her husband, might have asked Mr. Minor to lend him money to defray the journey to the U.S. but that does not prove that he had not then in his hands money which he had paid to Adams for the said land and which Adams had deposited with him to buy slaves, etc. (a long petition, denying tenor of Minor's deposition, etc.) Signed: Juliana Thomas, 10 Jany. 1797. // To the Governor: Charles Adams represents that he claims from Juliana Thomas a plantation which he sold to her husband (recounting the case as already stated). Natchez, July 11, 1797. Charles Adams. // July 11, 1797. Juliana Thomas is ordered to appear at the Govt. House, tomorrow at 10 o'clock. Signed Gayoso. // The parties have appeared in public audience, and the proceedings read, William Selkrig representing Juliana Thomas, who declared that Charles Adams stopped at his mill a day or so before Thomas left for the U.S. and told him that he was sending the money paid for the plantation by Thomas to buy negroes, and the deponent asked if he ran the risk of sending the said money and he answered that he did. The deponent answered that it was a great risk to run. 26 Aug. 1797. Signed William Selkrig. Wit: Estevan Minor, John Girault.

p. 78. Bill of sale from Alexander Moore to David Odam of a negro girl, named "Betty", 15 years old, native of Africa, for $530, (on terms), the said girl being mortgaged until final payment. Said David Odam, being present, accepted. 22 May 1788. Official witnesses. // David Odam petitions that the negro woman in above sale was ill at the time but Mr. Moore claimed the illness was of no consequence. She died in 18 days and he gave immediate notice to Mr. Moore who said little but the petitioner has been told that he went to the Office and ordered a sale to be made which he signed himself without the knowledge or participation of the petitioner. Natchez, 11 Oct. 1794. Presented this to Mr. Moore. Signed John Ferguson. // Alexander Moore in answer to above petition: 19 May 1788, I sold to David Odam a negro wench, named "Betty", about 14 years old, to David Holt a wench about 15 years and to David Mitchell a negro boy about 14 years old and took their separate notes for the amounts. I delivered them the negroes in good health which they all took away and sent my son, Sam, to the Office to have the sales marked out, it being impossible to have got them that day, I called in a few days and signed them, which they were to do when they came to town. Odam and Holt called the 17 June and I told them the sales were ready. Odam replied that his wench was dead, occasioned by her menses and two or three days illness. Since the day of sale until a few days ago I never heard Mr. Odam complain. In Jany. 1790 I made a demand upon him for the account being $966. Mr. Carradine came to my house and offered me 20% to wait upon him and I said I would wait at 10% and took their joint note, payable in a year which is proof of what I mention. Signed Alexander Moore, Natchez Oct. 22, 1794. // Communicated the foregoing to David Odam. J. Girault. // David Odam represents that he understands that Alexander Moore is under arrest and not knowing if the arrest may prevent the suit, asks for a decision. Natchez. 8 Nov. 1794. David Odam. // Same date. Mr. Alexander will answer foregoing petition either himself or by attorney, to relieve him of any difficulties that his arrest may cause him. Signed Gayoso. Notified the above 11 Nov. 1794. // I have no other answer to give to the annexed petition but that which I have already given to his former petition. Natchez, 12 Nov. 1794. Signed Alexander Moore. On same day notified Odam.

p. 82. To His Excellency, the Governor. Petition of "Molly", a negro woman, the property of the late Jacob Leaphart, says that the said Mr. Leaphart purchased her near seven years ago and that for many reasons and her great attention to him during his long illness, her great industry, she having by it and her own management within a few years paid the great part of his debts, and, above all, for her advanced age, being near seventy years old, it was his intention to give the petitioner her freedom, which he communicated on his death bed to different persons but more particularly to Mr. William Barland whom he desired to procure a person to draw up a testament but, his time being shorter than expected, before anyone could, it pleased Almighty to withdraw him from hence, by which accident, the petitioner, contrary to her late master's will, is left a slave. The principal creditors of her said late master, being sensible that she had been the means of their receiving the part they have got out of his debts, being also assured that it was his wish that she should be free, are willing to give their consent that she be set at liberty. Natchez, 20 Sept. 1793. Signed Molly. // Natchez, 23 Sept. 1793 (p. 82) The petitioner will express who are the other persons besides Mr. William Barland who were acquainted with her late master's intentions, when on his death bed, regarding granting her her freedom and when all these persons are mentioned, Ezekiel Forman is commissioned to receive their declarations on the subject, as likewise is Mr. Fitzgerald as the greatest creditor of said Jacob Leaphart and make me a return of the proceedings. Signed Gayoso. // p. 82. Philip Hart. Respecting a negro wench called Molly, on Tuesday next before Jacob Leaphart died, the said Jacob called to him, the said Philip, and asked him if he would do a piece of business for him. Philip answered that he would do anything for him that he could. Then said Jacob "Take my horse and go and look for old Mr. Short. I want him to settle my affairs, for I shall die soon, and I want to give Molly her freedom. I promised Mr. Minor I would, when I bought her, and she has been very faithful to my interests and tender and careful of me in my long illness." Philip, in consequence took Jacob's horse and went to look for Mr. Short but could not find him and Jacob died the next Friday morning. Philip (X) Hart. Oct. 21, 1793. Signed Ezekiel Forman. // The declaration of William Barland respecting the negro wench called "Molly", the property of the late Jacob Leaphart. William Barland says that a day or two before the death of Jacob Leaphart the said Jacob sent for him and told him that he wished to settle his affairs, that he was very low. William told him that John Short would be a very suitable man and that he had better send for him. Jacob said No, that he did not apprehend any immediate danger but if William should see Short to send him to him. Wm. said that seeing Short was very uncertain and he had better send for Mr. Bernard. Jacob said he did not like to trouble him and the same day he did send for Short but could not find him. William advised him to make a will but Jacob said the Government and his creditors would do what they pleased afterward, that all he wished was that his debts be paid and that Molly should have her freedom and said that with Molly given her freedom she would soon pay his debts. Signed William Barland. 20 Oct. 1793. Signed Ezekiel Forman. // p. 83. Declaration of Mr. George Fitzgerald, supposed to be the largest creditor of the late Jacob Leaphart, who said that he had a good opinion of the negro wench "Molly" who has for some time past had the care and management of Jacob Leaphart's place and property and so well is he convinced of her industry and integrity that he is willing so far as to his respects that Molly should retain the property in her hands and he will look to her only for payment. Signed George Fitzgerald. Taken by order of His Excellency. Oct. 20, 1793 by Ezekiel Forman. // I have no demand against Jacob Leaphart as Molly paid me in full. 20 Dec. 1793. Alexander Moore.

p. 83. To His Excellency, the Governor, John Savage petitions that he has had some difficulty with Peter Riley, his partner in a tanyard, and whereas the parties have agreed to refer the decision of their contest to the arbitration of Messrs. John Boles and O'Brien, both of the District of Villa Gayoso, they, the said arbitrators, wish to be authorized by Your Excellency for the purpose. Natchez, 1st Oct. 1796. Signed John Savage. // Pine Ridge, Oct. 8, 1796. Mr. O'Brien being now absent, the parties are willing to substitute for him Mr. William Thomas, and do hereby bind themselves under the penalty of $500 to abide by the decision and award of Messrs. John Boles and William Thomas, who in case of a disagreement between them will chose an unpire. Peter O'Reilly, John Savage. Before Gabriel Benoist. // p. 84. Both inhabitants of the Govt., who agreed as follows: John Savage is to permit Peter O'Reilly and his wife to live upon his plantation during their natural life and they are to erect a tannery to be under the direction of said O'Reilly who is a tanner by trade and they, the said Savage and Riley, are both to work at the said tannery and also to tend the plantation and they are to divide equally, each one-half the benefits of the work, both leather and crops of any kind whatsoever, being equal partners in everything, share and share alike. In case either or the other be sick so as to be unable to work, he is to hire a hand in his place at his own expense. All hirelings or other charges in common in the partnership shall be paid out of the proceeds of their work, before dividing the profit. If the wife of Riely should survive her husband, she has the privilege of continuing the partnership with Savage under the condition of finding at her expense a hireling to work in her husband's place. All the time that Savage remains single the wife of Riley is to make, mend and wash his clothes and do the work of the house for both indifferently and for the true performance of this obligation they bind themselves. Peter Riley, John Savage. Wit: Jno. Girault, John Ferguson. // Charges and counter charges, refusals to accept the award of the arbiters who were ordered to try again with great effort to dissolve the partnership which Riley absolutely refused to do. Depositions by Daniel Lowery, Alexander Terrill, John Minor, William Shaw, John Reed, Philip Sixe, James Hyland, James Terry and Jeptha Higdon. // p. 96. Natchez, 12 Dec. 1796, Messrs. Bryan and Bolls [Arbiters] and the two parties are ordered to appear at the Govt. House next court day. // Agreeable to your order we (p. 96) have reconsidered the award in the matter of Peter Riley and John Savage and herewith hand you our decision: We observed Your Excellency's instructions that John Savage cannot be deprived or dispossessed of his land or any part of it regardless of his will or inclination unless receiving adequate compensation for the same, and we examined the tanyard with the works appertaining thereto which from our valuation is worth $128 and Riley has established himself there, relying on the correctness of Mr. Savage, his partner, who consented not reluctantly for the said Riley to live there during his life. The agreement was in good faith to be adhered to by both parties, otherwise the bond of $500 was recoverable. Neither does it appear that Riley has broken the agreement . . . Riley is as indigent as is possible and would be utterly ruined without the tan-yard, while to Savage it would be of trifling value. Several neighbors had contributed to Riley in the erection of the tanyard. The land Savage gave is a small pittance. Signed John Bolls, William Bryan. Apr. 1797. // The award is: that Riley shall continue on the premises, having the liberty to carry on the tannery business independent of Mr. Savage, allowing him 4 acres of ground to cultivate and he shall not by any means destroy the timber on the said land unnecessarily, taking bark from such trees as Mr. Savage shall point out; in case the said Riley should chose at a future date to remove from the premises, the works and the tools shall devolve to Savage. John Bolls and William Bryan. // The above approved by Gayoso 19 April 1797. // (More repititious depositions in this case which antedate the above award. The case ends at the bottom of p. 99))

p. 100. Before Don Carlos de Grand-Pre, appeared Henry Barchellot des Hubles who presents his opposition to the sale of a negro woman of Mr. David Tanner. Your Excellency was pleased to allow him but six days to produce the titles and proof of property in favor of the person for whom your petitioner is acting, this time being too short to procure said documents, and he prays that your order that said David Tanner and his wife and James Wilson appear before you to declare on oath what they know respecting the right and claim of the wife of your petitioner to the said negro woman. Natchez, 22 Feb. 1787. // Persons mentioned are to appear before me to declare on oath what they know respecting the negro woman in question. Signed Grand-Pre. // p. 100. Fort Panmur at Natchez, 24 Feb. 1787. Pursuance of the foregoing decree appeared David Tanner, of the Dist. of Natchez, planter, and his wife, Mary Barnes, and at the request of Don Henry Barchellot des Hubles, in answer to the interrogation respecting the negro woman, "Esther", brought by them from North Carolina and now about to be sold for payment of his debts, declare that, at the time of his marriage, his father gave him six slaves, among which was the negro woman, "Esther", and he believes his father did say that, considering that he was about to emigrate from North Carolina to a foreign country the said negro woman might serve his wife and then descend to his oldest daughter, but that his memory is not sufficient to enable him to affirm this as an absolute fact which is all that he can say. To the same question, put to his wife, Mary Barnes, she replied the same. Signed by David Tanner, Mary Tanner, Louis Chachere, before Grand-Pre.

p. 101. 23 March 1787. Fort Panmur at Natchez. Before me Don Carlos de Grand-Pre, appeared Arthur Cobb, of the District, planter, who of his own free will and accord, has become surety for two negro women and one negro girl, named "Belinda" and "Dorinda", belonging to John Stillee who are seized and confined at the seat of Don Juan Vauchere for a large sum and which slaves in consequence of the security given by said Cobb, both in person and estate, are delivered to the said Stillee, the said security being held to produce them when required and obliged to pay the value thereof without any other form or protest. Signed by all. Wit: Estevan Minor, Isaac Gaillard. Before Carlos de Grand-Pre. // To Don Carlos de Grand-Pre; Petition that having been pleased to grant to him the seizure of the whole estate of John Stillee, your petitioner prays that an estimation may be made of the same with the view of making sale thereof. Signed J. Vaucheret, Natchez, March 26, 1787. // The parties will appoint appraisers to value the property seized. Signed Grand-Pre. Same date. // Fort Panmur at Natchez, 27 March 1787, Jeremiah Bryan, sheriff of the property of John Stillee, by virtue of the above decree states that, as appraisers, Vaucheret names Richard Harrison and Stillee names Arthur Cobb, who appeared and accepted the appointment. Wit: Thos. Wilkins, Samuel Flowers, and John Henderson. // Vaucheret, of Natchez, (p.102) merchant, asks that the slaves be confined in the Fort, March 22, 1787 // Order for same and rest of the estate be put in the hands of some person so that it will be forthcoming when required. Signed Grand-Pre. (Note: These two items should have been entered at the beginning of the report on this suit.) Fort aforesaid, March 28, 1787. I, the Commandant, accompanied by officials, have repaired to the plantation of John Stillee, for the appraisement of the slaves, etc. . . . . . . Total appraisement $4210 (p.103) // At Fort Panmur at Natchez, the sale of the estate of John Stillee for the payment of debt. (This covers pages 100-111).

p. 112. Manuel Texada petitions that Richard Mayes is indebted to him for $125, in satisfaction whereof Mayes gave him an obligation to deliver him five cows through January last past and the delivery not having been made, although frequently requested, petitioner prays Mayes should be made to deliver said cows or in default thereof to make a payment of the sum. Manuel Texada, Natchez, Feb. 23, 1787. // Order by Grand-Pre. // 13 Mch. 1787. Manuel Texada petitions that Mayes has absconded and asks that when a sale of his property is made that the petitioner may be included among the number of creditors, and entitled to a dividend of the proceeds. Annexed is the document, dated 2 Jany 1787, showing the obligation.

p. 113. The fugitive Mayes was indebted to Stephen Minor for $286; to Peter Surget for $72; and to Vaucheret for $89, who ask to be included in the list of creditors. Natchez, 31 March, 1787. // Alexander Moore, merchant, also a creditor of the fugitive, Richard Mayes, for $127; (much of which is for rum); Richard Carpenter creditor to amount of $478, dated 18 Nov. 1786. // At Fort Panmur, 27 March 1787. In pursuance of an order have proceeded to the appraisement of a negro confined in this Fort, belonging to the said Mayes, have named Justus King and John Girault to act, who have accepted . . . Negro valued at $500. At the Fort, the same date, at the sale of said negro, he was adjudged to

Don Pedro Surget for $461, he being the highest bidder. Those present signing with official witnesses. James McIntosh, Surget, Peter Camus, J. Vaucheret, Manuel Texada, Richard King. Before Grand-Pre. There being no other property belonging to the said Richard Mayes, the sale was closed. Net proceeds $436. This was prorated among the creditors, each giving his receipt.

p. 116. Richard Carpenter represents that Richard Mayes, James Barfield, and Michael Asbrama, the one being the other, are indebted to him in the sum of $503; asks that said debtors be condemned to make payment thereof. Signed: Richard Carpenter, Jan. 29, 1787. // Notify the partners to pay immediately or appear immediately before me. // Richard Carpenter petitions that Messrs. Barfield and Asbrama have been pillaged by the Indians and prays that you will issued an execution against all the said persons, or one of them, they being jointly and severally bound. Feb. 26, 1787. // Let seizure be made of the property of the three persons named above. Grand-Pre. Feb. 28, 1787. // Seized the property of James Barfield, a negro wench and two children for the within debt. Signed: Caleb King. // The estate of James Barfield to Isaac Johnson, debtor: Boarding, schooling and clothing his daughter from Nov. 1st 1785 to 1st March 1787, 16 months at $6 per month. $96. For boarding and clothing two negro children for 3 months. For 3 months of a negro woman's time lost in attending her young child. $25. For the work of a negro woman at $100 per year, (credit), reducing the debit to $61. Wit: Sutton Banks and A. Bingaman. Another account of Isaac Johnson, mostly cash paid out for Barfield. // William Brocus petitions that James Barfield was indebted to him for $43, being unaware until today that the property had been sold, asks that although he is late in filing his claim, he be allowed his share. Natchez, 23 March 1787. // Isaac Johnson petitions that James Barfield at his departure hence left with the petitioner his daughter together with a negro woman and two children, on condition that if the work of the said negro woman did not be worth the education, clothing and maintenance of his daughter, as also the clothing of the said negro woman and maintenance of the two negro children, that the said Barfield should be accountable for the balance to your petitioner. Moreover, your said petitioner has paid for sd Barfield the sum of $81 as will be appear by the receipt thereof. Mr. Richard Carpenter by virtue of the execution obtained the fees on the said slaves and the petitioner prays that no more of the property of the said Barfield may be sold than will be necessary for the payment of his debts. The eldest child of the negro woman belongs to the daughter of the said Barfield by gift executed many years ago. Petitioner hopes that the bill of the food, clothing and money advanced will warrant a preference in payment to him. Natchez 17 March 1787. // Adam Bingaman and Sutton Banks appointed to appear at the place of Isaac Johnson to appraise the work of the negro woman and the education of Barfield's daughter together with the maintenance of the two negro children, and report thereof. The seizure of the negro girl, "Lucretia" is void until further orders. Grand-Pre. // Dec. 1785. James Barfield to Cato West, Debtor. For one large hog $25. Petition of Cato West that this be included in accounts owed by James Barfield. // A long itemized account of what James Barfield owes to William Brocus. // p. 119. At the Fort Panmur at Natchez, 21 March 1787. Don Carlos de Grand-Pre, in order to carry into effect the decrees for the foregoing petitions, have appointed Don Juan Vaucheret and Justus King to appraise negro woman. She was valued at $500 and the said negro woman being immediately thereafter exposed to sale, was adjudged to Richard Carpenter for $565, he being the highest bidder. Whereupon we have closed this present sitting and signed with the assistants and witnesses. Creditors: Richard Carpenter, Isaac Johnson, William Brocus, Cato West; their receipts given for their shares.

p. 121. Peter Hawkins versus George Rapalje. Peter Hawkins represents that in January last past, he sold to Mr. Rapalje a tract on Cole's Creek for $300, payable, $150 in hand and the remainder all in the present month as will appear by his obligation to that effect. When the imprisonment of said Rapale took place, after the bargain was made, the petitioner had received but a small part of the money that was to be paid in hand, and having sold his land entirely for the purpose of paying his creditors, he prays that you will grant him permission to sell the said land again for the use of the said creditor, on condition of refunding to the said Rapalje the sum which he received from him, in as much as he was not bound to make a title until final payment. Natchez, 27 Jany. 1786. Signed: Peter Hawkins. // Jany. 28, 1786. Petitioner will produce the witnesses to the sale of this land to George Rapalje together with the notes and bonds delivered by the latter in payment for the same. And will, himself, appear before me on Tuesday next, to declare on oath the amount he has received from said Rapalje. Signed: Bouligny. // Note of George Ralapje, Jan. 8, 1785, to pay Peter Hawkins $65 on demand and in the month of January next ensuing I promise to pay Mr. Peter Hawkins or his order, on account of Garret Rapalje, the sum of $150 for value received. Signed: George Rapalje. // Manchac. 10 Nov. 1785. Sir: the letter you gave Mr. William Smith on Mr. George Rapalje, 8th of last January, for $11, being the balance due on Joseph Dawes' note, was never accepted and consequence thereof your forthcoming for the same, if you wrote it off from Mr. Rapalje's note, you must debit him for the same again. Your order, as it was delivered to me by Mr. Smith, with the endorsement on the same, I have sent up to Mr. Bingaman to present to you, and to whom I request that you will pay the same, without permitting it to go before your Commandant, which will only be attended with further expense. Your very humble servant. J.R. Fitzpatrick. To Mr. Peter Hawkins. // At Fort Panmur, Natchez, 4 Feb. 1786, appeared Mr. Peter Hawkins who produced Mr. Sutton Banks as witness to sale made of his land to George Rapalje, who, on oath, said he was a witness to the sale of the land by Hawkins to Rapalje, and the said Rapalje paid Hawkins a note for $50 and that was all he knew. Also was produced a note for $150 due in one year and another for $65 due on the account of $150 to be paid in hand. He, the said Hawkins had received a further sum of $23 in addition to the $50 as testified to by Sutton Banks, making together $73, leaving Rapalje debtor for one-half of the sum together with his note of $65 and the $11 the amount of the draft given him in favor of Fitzpatrick. Signed Peter Hawkins and Sutton Banks. Before Bouligny. // Fort of Natchez, Feb. 4, 1787. The plaintiff in this suit will refund the $73 which he has received from George Rapalje and this sum will be included in the estate of Rapalje, the said Peter Hawkins then being at liberty to dispose at pleasure of the land at Cole's Creek, which he had sold to said Rapalje, without having to be exposed to complaint which might be hereinafter made by Rapalje. Signed Francisco Bouligny.

p. 123. Peter Hawkins versus Ebenezer Gossett. Peter Hawkins petitions that Ebenezer Gossett, late of this District, was indebted to him in the sum of $123 and he is informed that he died lately in the Prov. of Georgia. At the time of his departure, he had been in possession of a small tract on Cole's Creek which was all the property he possessed in this District, and your petitioner, having no means of obtaining payment from said Gossett, prays that he will be permitted to settle on the said land. Natchez, Feb. 17, 1784. Signed Peter Hawkins. // Petitioner, having produced documents proving the debt to the amount stated, he is hereby allowed to take possession of the land belonging to Gossett. Signed Trevino. // I, Peter Hawkins, of the District of Natchez, on 8th Jany. 1785, do hereby warrant, defend and give possession of 200 acres about 4 miles from the mouth of Cole's Creek, granted by letters patent and now delivered to George Rapalje which was granted to Jacob Paul and 200 acres granted to Ebenezer Gossett, to all which he hereby renounces all claim to the said George Rapalje on account of Garret Rapalje, for $300 by his obligation and acquittance. Signed Peter Hawkins. Wit: Parker Carradine, Wm. Gilbert.

p. 123. Bennet Smith versus Luis Chacheret, Fort Panmur at Natchez, 24 Feb. 1786. Bennet Smith, of his own free will and accord, desiring to terminate finally this suit pending between them and the estate of George Castles, he and Chacheret have mutually convenanted and agreed as follows: Don Luis Chacheret shall pay to said Bennet Smith in full the sum of $1400, for which sum he has, in my presence, given three notes, $600, payable ten days from date, $266 payable one month after date and $534 payable January 1787, amounting to $1400, being the full account against Chacheret, as administrator of the estate of George Castles. The said Bennet Smith being fully satisfied for his interest in the same. Signed: Chacheret, Bennet Smith. Wit: A. Bingaman, James McIntosh, Juan Careras, before Francisco Bouligny.

p. 124. Jane Rapalje versus creditors of George Rapalje. Jane Rapalje petitions, in relation to the negro named "Robin", detained in prison in this City, as the property of her husband, that the said negro was purchased by her husband with the sum given to her by her brother, Abraham Ellis, who may be interrogated on the subject, as will appear by a note on the back of the deed of sale from William Calvit, which said deed will be found among the papers seized by the Commandant of Natchez when the husband of the petitioner was arrested, and your petitioner represents further that Daniel Clark, of this District, merchant, was securety for the value of the said negro, in case the facts thereinstated are not available at the time fixed by Your Excellency, for the necessary inquiry to be made by the Commandant of the Dist. of Natchez. Petitioner asks that the enquiry be made and the said negro delivered to your petitioner. Signed: Jenny Rapalje. // The Commandant of the Post of Natchez will make the enquiry necessary to ascertain whether the negro named Robin be the property of Jane Rapalje as proceeding from a gift made to her by her brother, Abraham Ellis, and Daniel Clark will be accepted as security for the negro, which is hereby fixed as $400, at which said negro is appraised. New Orleans, 4 Dec. 1785. Signed: Estevan Miro. // At Fort Panmur at Natchez, 16 March 1786. In pursuance of the foregoing decree of His Excellency, Don Estevan Miro, Gov. Genl. of this Province, I, Don Carlos de Grand-Pre, (p. 125) have caused Abram Ellis to appear before me, who, being duly sworn, declared that he did really make a present to his sister a short time after her marriage with George Rapalje, consisting of a horse, saddle and bridle, valued at $120, and twelve head of cattle, that he did not know how they had been disposed of or to whom they were sold but he remembered to have heard that George Rapalje and his sister had bought a negro from William Calvit, named Bob or Robin, and paid for him in cash, which is all that he knows of the matter, except that William Calvit and Don Estevan Minor could give better information in the case. Signed: Abram Ellis. Before Carlos de Grand-Pre. // On the same day, appeared William Calvit, who, on oath, declared that he had sold a negro to George Rapalje and his wife. Q. How was the negro called and what payment made? A. He sold to George Rapalje a negro named "Robin", who paid the greater part of the purchase in cattle and the balance in specie, and at the time of the delivery of the said cattle, the said Rapalje declared that the said cattle belonged to his wife, who was present and reserved one milk cow out of the number, for her own use. Signed with the witness and interpreter, James Harman, James McIntosh, with the Commandant. At the same time, appeared Estevan Minor, who declared on his word of honor, it is true that Abraham did give his sister a horse, which the deponent afterwards bought for $80. He signed as above. // Having examined the papers, negro "Robin" is confirmed to Jane Rapalje, as proceeding from the present made to her by Abraham Ellis. New Orleans, June 9, 1786. Signed Estevan Miro.

p. 126. To the Governor General. Bennet Smith versus the estate of John Holly. Bennet Smith petitions that $846 as stated in the accounts, herewith presented, is due him from the estate of John Holly, being the amount of principal and interest, and there being an amount in the hand of Richard Carpenter and other executors, asks for an order that the said debt be satisfied by the said executors. On the affidavit of Isaac Johnson made before His Excellency, the Commandant of Natchez, that he did actually pay the aforesaid sum to the said Holly for the account of the petitioner. Signed Bennet Smith. // The Commandant of the Post of Natchez will call Isaac Johnson to appear before him. // If the said estate is indebted to said Bennet Smith in the sum of $846 then the Commandant will oblige Richard Carpenter to pay that amount to the said Smith, he giving the necessary receipt for same. New Orleans. 19 Nov. 1785. Signed Estevan Miro. // The estate of John Holly to Ben Smith. . . . . 1773. This sum paid to said Holly by Isaac Johnson by order of Jacob Blackwell to be delivered to me at Jamaica, being the proceeds of two negroes sold to Jerome LaChapelle and elven years interest on the said sum according to the custom of the English merchants in this country, $396. Signed Bennet Smith. p. 127. Isaac Johnson will appear and give testimony. // Fort of Natchez, 17 Dec. 1785. Appeared Isaac Johnson, in pursuance of the decree of His Excellency, Don Estevan Miro, and proved by documents that the estate of John Holly was indebted to Bennet Smith in the sum $424 and the interest on the said sum for 11 years, amounting in the whole to $787, made on oath, but he could not swear that the sum had not been paid in the meanwhile. Signed: Isaac Johnson. // Mr. Carpenter, executor of the estate of John Holly will satisfy Bennet Smith to the amount of $787, which appears to be owing to him by said estate. Signed: Francisco Bouligny. // To His Excellency, Richard Carpenter, exr. of the estate of John Holly petition in behalf of Elizabeth Holly, only daughter and heiress of John Holly, decd., residing at Baton Rouge, in defense of the heiress and in reply to the claim made by Bennet Smith against the estate brought before His Excellency Miro at N.O., that Mr. Smith, in his memorials, state that a certain sum, which appears only by the account which he has presented and demands that the sum be paid to him on the affidavit of Mr. Isaac Johnson, that the said Johnson paid that sum to Holly for Smith's account. In the opinion of the petitioner, nothing appears in Johnson's declaration but that the said sum was sent to Holly but he knows not if the sum was kept by Holly and consequently he cannot know if the estate is indebted to Smith for that sum. Smith who arrived in this country a few months since knew not of this shipment of money, until told by Mr. Johnson. Capt. Holly was owner of a sloop which he had chartered at Jamaica to a certain Jacob Blackwell to bring him and his goods thence to this River, and from hence to carry goods back again, at a certain rate per month. He arrived here in the summer of 1773 and departed again in Dec. or Jany. following. In 1774, Capt Holly was in partnership with some Jews of Jamaica in a voyage to this river. He arrived here in the summer of the year in the vessel called "The London Packet" and departed hence in Jany. 1775. It is to be noted that Mr. Blackwell was here the whole time mentioned and if he had shipped money to be delivered to Mr. Smith and he had received advices of no payment having been made, he would certainly have suspected Mr. Holly and would have made every enquiry of him and written letter after letter until the matter was ascertained. In the year 1775, Capt. Holly returned here in the schooner "Bennett" in partnership with Mr. Bennet Smith. They both arrived and departed together in the year 1776. If Capt. Holly had committed the crime attributed to him, Mr. Smith had then favorable time to learn about it and to recover his money. In the summer of 1776, Capt Holly returned to the river with a sloop belonging to him and became a planter at Baton Rouge, where he bore the character of an honest man until his death in 1780. The undersigned has taken the defense in this matter only because he because he believes it. He knew Capt. Holly a long time. First, when he left Long Island, master of a vessel and, afterwards, the whole time that he traded on this river, and never the least suspicion that he was capable of an action so base as that he was charged with. Natchez, Jany. 1786. Richard Carpenter. // 9 Jany. 1786. The foregoing will be annexed to the documents presented by Bennet Smith and he will be notified thereof that he may answer. Signed Bouligny. // Bennet Smith's reply. Captain Holly (p. 129) was captain of the vessel in which the money was shipped and it was paid to him and to him the letter of advice enclosing the receipt was entrusted as stated by Mr. Isaac Johnson who paid the money in conformity with the order of Jacob Blackwell, etc. (nothing new). signed Bennet Smith. Jany. 19, 1786. // Jany. 20th. Isaac Johnson having made a declaration the money had been paid Holly for Smith, the estate will reimburse said Smith, no proof having been made of the payment of same to Smith. Signed: Francisco Bouligny. // Richard Harrison asks that he may have copy of the proceedings in the case. Apr. 3, 1786. // The party will be informed that the papers will be transmitted to His Excellency, the Governor, of this province. Grand-Pre. // Judgement confirmed by Estevan Miro, N.O., 9 June 1786.

p. 131. Stephen Jordan versus Thomas Jordan. Petition of Stephen Jordan, of Natchez Dist., planter, declares that some time since he made an agreement with his son, Thomas, by which his said son agreed to furnish to your petitioner such provision as he might have need of, lodging, etc., as will appear by the contract hereunto annexed. His son so far from having complied with his contract had not given him enough to eat and that he cannot live in his own house by reason of the ill-treatment he receives from the wife of the said son and his children, who abuse him at all times, so much so that he cannot remain unless his son be compelled to fulfill his contract and oblige his wife and children conduct themselves as they ought toward the petitioner. Natchez Aug. 5, 1786. Stephen Jordan. // Thomas Jordan will comply in tenor with the contract made with his father furnishing him with such provisions as he is bound to do, both by his agreement and by the ties of nature and will compel his wife and children to treat his father with the respect that is due him. Signed Grand-Pre. // Stephen Jordan declares that the foregoing order has been notified to his son and he has not complied therewith in any manner. Pet. asks that son be summoned before you to make such arrangements as to Your Honor may seem just and mete, in relation to the contract made with him by petitioner. Oct. 14, 1786. Signed. // Parties will appear before me on the first day of audience. Grand-Pre. // Contract. Stephen Jordan gives, etc. to son, Thomas Jordan, his whole property, real and personal, excepting two cows and calves, two sows and their litters of pigs, one young iron-gray mare, his own chestnut, bald-faced riding horse, one grubbing and one weeding hoe, one axe, one set of gear and one plow. It is agreed between the parties that the horse shall be kept on the plantation as the other horses. Should Stephen leave the house he now lives in, Thomas Jordan agrees to build him another house on any part of the woodland that he, Stephen Jordan, may choose. Thomas Jordan promises to furnish Stephen with board, lodging, washing, mending and making of linen, and to pay Stephen Jordan $200 yearly as long as Stephen Jordan lives, also 600 pounds of meat yearly as long as he lives, namely, 200 lbs. of beef, 200 lbs pork and 200 lbs of bacon, also 60 bushels of corn yearly, and to pay all of Stephen Jordan's debts as they come due. Thomas to have the crop in the ground and he is not to sell any of the property or convey it away on any pretense whatever except to pay the debts above mentioned. Stephen to have one-half of the household furniture. Natchez, Sept. 15, 1785. Stephen Jordan signs with a mark. Wit: Daniel Grafton, Robert Dunbar. Before Bouligny. // p. 133. We, the subscribers chosen by Mr. Stephen Jordan and Thomas Jordan, do award to avoid any further trouble between them, that Thomas Jordan give up everything on the plantation without reserve, his own household furniture and clothes excepted, to the said Stephen Jordan and the said Stephen Jordan to pay him $500, one-half shall be paid on or before 1 Jany next and the remainder the year following. The said Stephen Jordan shall pay all the debts contained in the above schedule. Natchez, 21 Oct. 1786. Signed: Sutton Banks and Caleb King // This arbitration approved. Signed Carlos de Grand-Pre. // Stephen Jordan, feeling aggrieved by the award, prays that the matter be referred to the Tribunal of Don Estevan Miro, the Gov. Genl. 17 Feb. 1787. // To His Excellency Don Estevan Miro, Thomas Jordan declares whatever injury he might have sustained from his father, his filial respect will induce him to overlook it, if he did not subject himself, his wife and children to the necessity of receiving assistance from strangers to enable them to exist . . . . . . He has fulfilled the contract to best of his ability . . . . . but I owe to my family for their assistance in improving the plantation for a term of three years . . . . . he allowed me after the award but twenty-four hours to remove my family, then sick, and would not suffer me to take even a measure of corn to make bread. A stranger assisted me and gave us bread and succor. My father has complied in part by paying the debts as they fell due. Feb. 26, 1787. Signed // The award of the Commandant at Natchez in the above case confirmed by Estevan Miro.

p. 135. Louis Chacheret versus his creditors. Fort Panmur at Natchez, 7 March 1788. A meeting of the creditors of Don Louis Chacheret, convoked at his request, consisting of Don Pedro Camus,

Don Pedro Azevedo, for himself and for Lt. Col. Philip Trevino, Don Luis Faure as atty. for Juan Perrete, Honore Duon for himself and for Don Pedro Camus, Don Juan Vaucheret, Don Pedro Walker and Co., and Don Juan Girault, appointed to represent the absent creditors, to deliberate on the measures necessary to be taken, etc. Don Pedro Walker unanimously appointed Syndic and the books and other papers be delivered to him. The whole estate and effects of said Chacheret to be exposed to public sale for the payment of debts, on credit until the end of the year on account of scarcity of specie at this time. Signed by all before Carlos de Grand-Pre.

p. 136. John Ellis versus Mrs. Gaillard. On 27 May 1788, at the request of John Ellis appeared before me, Don Carlos de Grand-Pre, Anthony Hutchins who declared that about 14 years since Gov. Chester, in the name of His Brittanic Majesty, issued a proclamation in this district that the lands that were cleared and in cultivation should be granted in preference to those who had made such improvements and that thenceforward such persons might consider such lands as their own, that, in virtue of this proclamation, John Ellis made the clearing on the land now in dispute between him and Mrs. Gaillard. Sometime afterward, Lt. Col. Dixon applied for a grant and, judging that this tract would suit him, made application for the same, and notwithstanding opposition was made by Ellis, the said Dixon obtained the land, contrary to all right, from the Government at Pensacola. But, making no improvements or settlements thereon, John Ellis maintained possession of the land until the arrival of Tacitus Gaillard with (p. 137) his family, in this District, to whom he lent the use of it, until he could suit himself elsewhere and which the widow of said Tacitus wishes to appropriate to herself. Wit: Isaac Johnson, Don Estevan Minor. Signed Anthony Hutchins. Before Carlos de Grand-Pre.

p. 137. Adam Bingaman versus William Ferguson. Adam Bingaman petitions that since he was in a treaty with Wm. Ferguson for a tract of land on condition that said land was watered and that good titles should be made for same, but notwithstanding repeated demands from your petitioner, the said Ferguson has never complied with his agreement to make the necessary titles, several years having elapsed since the parties were in treaty, your petitioner considers the same to be void as if it never did exist, whereupon your petitioner prays that you order the said William Ferguson to restore to your petitioner the negro girl lent to him long since to take care of his child and which said Ferguson refuses to return, alleging that he bought her and that the land in question was in part payment, which is denied by your petitioner. Nov. 3, 1787. Signed. // 20 Nov. 1787. William Ferguson will restore to Adam Bingaman his negro girl unless he has reasons to adduce to the contrary, in which case the parties will be heard at the first audience. Grand-Pre. // William Ferguson represents that in Aug. 1785, Mr. and Mrs. Bingaman lent him a young negro girl, aged at that time about 4 1/2 or 5 years, that in the month of February, following, he purchased the said negro girl from Adam Bingaman for a tract of land, containing 550 arpents, for which said Bingaman paid him a further sum of $200, that is to say, your petitioner owed him at that time $100 and the balance was paid to the petitioner in the presence of Mr. Car.-penter. He had before that time delivered to Mr. Bingaman the plat and patent to the land, which he has kept ever since and, wishing to have the sale of the land drawn in the English manner, petitioner complied with his wish, the said instrument he has yet also in his possession. That, afterwards deciding that the sale should be executed before the former Commandant and recorded in the archives of the Post, your petitioner likewise consented and so soon as he was to have the document ready your petitioner and his wife were to attend at the Fort and Bingaman promised to go for that purpose and sign and the deed. 10 Jany. 1788. Signed. // p. 139. The parties having appeared and Adam Bingaman having proved that he did not at any time sell the negro girl to Wm. Ferguson, the said Wm. Ferguson is condemned to restore to Adam Bingaman the negro girl in question. Signed Grand-Pre. // 10 Jany. 1788. Before Grand-Pre, Wm. Ferguson appeared and declared that he appealed to the Superior Tribunal for judgment. // N.O. Judgment rendered at the Post of Natchez by the Commandant, is hereby confirmed. Estevan Miro. Feb. 29, 1788.

p. 140. John Vaucheret, of Post of Natchez, merchant, petitions that John Ferguson is indebted to him in sum of $231 secured by his land, crop and other properties. Since then he has endeavored to sell the said land to others and has delivered to your petitioner no part of the crop. Prays for payment or execution agst the property. 20 Dec. 1786. // Order that John Ferguson pay without delay. Dec. 22. // Notified John Ferguson. Caleb King. // By order of the Commandant have seized the property of John Ferguson, 200 arpents, of which 9 arpents are enclosed, adj. Rayner, Jeremiah Bryan, Richard Carpenter, and other land of Ferguson. Appraisers appointed: Peter Walker and Thos. Wilkins. Value placed at $135. // p. 141. 4 Feb. the sale of the plantation, which having been repeatedly cried was adjudged to (1) to Peter Camus for $30; 6th Feb. (2) to Peter Camus for $30; 14th Feb. (3) not being bid to two-third of value, the plantation was not sold. Signed by witnesses, et al. // Petition of Juan Vaucheret asks that the plantation be re-appraised at a lower value. 27 Apr. 1787. // p. 142. 28 Apr. 1787. Justus King and John Hartley appointed to reappraise said plantation. Valued same at $100. Grand-Pre. // Same date. Sale of plantation; was adjudged to Francisco Bazo for $93, the highest bid, net proceeds $65 which was paid to Don Juan Vaucheret, plaintiff and creditor. Grand-Pre.

p. 142. Anne Gaillard versus John Ellis. Anne Gaillard of Dist. of Natchez, represents that in the year last past that she presented a petition to the Commandant praying for a grant of 1000 arpents on the Homochitto River, bounded by lands of Richard Ellis, William Case, John Lusk and Nathaniel Tomlinson, the same having been granted by the Spanish Government to Col. Dixon, and your petitioner obtained from Your Excellency an order of survey for the said land, which she had settled and cultivated for many years, which order of survey your petitioner could not prevail upon the surveyor, William Vousdan, to execute, but on the contrary gave order to John Ellis to survey said land. Asks that the land be granted to her. Anne Gaillard. // The Commandant at Natchez will make the enquiry necessary concerning the foregoing. Signed Miro. // p. 143. In answer to Mrs. Gaillard's petition, he states that Mrs. Gaillard declared that she obtained a piece of land now in dispute, and that she had cultivated it for many years. This was with your petitioner's permission as he hopes has been proved by the depositions of Messrs. Sanders and Vousdan. (a repetition of the case.) May 20, 1788. John Ellis. // Depositions of Isaac Gaillard, James Barfield, John Pickens, David Mitchell, for Mrs. Gaillard; and at the request of John Ellis, came James Saunders who declared that he had heard Mr. Tacitus Gaillard say that the land he lived on was lent to him by John Ellis but he intended to do everything he could to get a grant in his own favor, the said land is the same land now in dispute. // 21 May 1788, appeared William Vousdan, who declared in his duties as a surveyor for the District he learned that the land in question was and now is the property of John Ellis who lent Tacitus Gaillard the use of it to make a crop to assist him on his first arrival in this colony. It was not surveyed until 1786, at which time, Ellis had an order of survey from the Superior Tribunal. Being certain the land did not belong to any other person, he surveyed the land and having fixed the bounds gave Ellis the plot and description of same. Signed. Wit: Estevan Minor, Philip Trevino. Before Grand-Pre. // Same day, appeared Stephen Mayes who declared that about 14 or 15 years since he came to settle in this district and at the time of his arrival, he was employed as overseer by John Ellis who put him on the land now in dispute and that with ten negroes he cleared 72 arpents which he put in cultivation and until then no person had a claim to said land but sd Ellis. // July 1788. It appears that John Ellis has long been in possession of the land in question, ... and it would appear that Mr. Ellis is entitled to the land claimed by Mrs. Gaillard. Signed Carlos de Grand-Pre. // Order that proof be furnished in writing by both sides, etc. New Orleans. Estevan Miro.

p. 147. Nelly Price and others versus the estate of M. Lopez. Nelly Price, free woman of color, petitions that she lived six years with Miguel Lopez, deceased, on wages, at the rate of $10 per month, besides other sums which the petitioner paid to divers person for the said Lopez, as will appear by the account hereunto annexed. The petitioner represents that Your Excellency having granted a lot at the landing at Natchez to the said Lopez and your petitioner, at her own expense, built a house on part of this lot, given to her by said Lopez for that purpose. She prays that you will permit her to take possession of said house, having no place to dwell, and likewise to order that your petitioner be reimbursed to the amount of her account from the state. Your pet. can prove the facts set forth above. Signed Nelly Price. 20 Feb. 1788. The account follows: Cash paid to William Barland, Christian Harman, Mr. King, Mr. White, Francisco Bazo, Mr. Gilbert, to wages for six years. Total $967. // p. 148. 2 Aug. 1788. At the request of a free mulatress, Nelly Price, appeared before me, Don Carlos de Grand-Pre, William Irwin, who declared, on oath, that one day, at the house of Miguel Lopez, the said Lopez told him that a part of the house belonged to the mulatress, Nelly Price, whom he had in his service. Signed Wm. Irwin. Wit: J. Vaucheret. // 9 Aug. 1788, appeared Luis Charboneau, who, on oath, declared that in the month of June, 1782, Miguel Lopez and the said Nelly Price having quarreled, the latter left him and lived in another house in this District, and the said Lopez, having solicited her to return, she refused to do so unless he should allow her $10 per month, to which the said Lopez agreed and she returned to work for him. Signs with a mark. Wit. Adam Bingaman. Before Grand-Pre. // p. 149. At the same time appeared Patrick Murphy, an invalid soldier, who on oath, declared that in June 1782, being at the house of Miguel Lopez, he observed the mulatress, Nelly Price, crying and enquiring the cause, was informed that the said Lopez had beaten her, whereupon she left, etc. (the same account as above). Signed. Wit. A. Bingaman. // 28 Aug. 1788, appeared Joseph King, who, on oath, declared that in the year 1782, being hurt by a fall, he stayed at the house of Miguel Lopez and that during that time Lopez said, in his presence, that he had hired the mulatto woman, Nelly Price, at $10 per month. Signed before Estevan Minor and D. Smith. // At the same time appeared David Smith, who, on oath, declared that he heard Miguel Lopez say that he paid wages to the said Nelly but he could not say how much, Lopez not having said the amount. Signed D. Smith. Wit. Juan Carreras, Don Estevan Minor. Before Carlos de Grand-Pre. // Examined. If the mulatress, Nelly Price, can prove by competent witnesses that the sum she claims is owing her, the Commandant will cause the amount to be paid to her from the estate of the deceased. New Orleans. June 12, 1788. Signed: Estevan Miro. // Pensacola. Pedro Bingas makes known to the Commandant that the estate of Miguel Lopez is indebted to him for $66, being the amount of two casks of rum sold to Lopez. // Decreed. New Orleans, 17 June 1788. Order to be transmitted to the Commandant of the Post of Natchez, to pay Pedro Bingas out of the estate of Miguel Lopez the sum of $66, owing him. Signed Estevan Miro. // p. 150. Natchez, 10 Sept. 1788. Sale of house of Miguel Lopez, deceased; said house having been cried and no bids made, proceedings closed. Wit: Juan Carreras, Thos. Wilkins, Sutton Banks, J.B. Perret, Pedro Walker, Antonio Soler. Before Grand-Pre. // 17 Sept. House again exposed and no one having bid, sale was closed; 24 Sept., for the third time, the house exposed to sale which was bid to the sum of $200, that sum being less than two-thirds of the appraisal, the said house was not sold. Same witnesses. // 14 Feb. 1789. For the last time, the house was exposed to sale, which was bid this day bid to $300 by Robert Abrams; to $301 by Nelly Price; finally to $335 by Nelly Price to whom the same was adjudged. She offered William Brocus for surety. Said purchaser made her mark, before witnesses. // 13 June 1789, the mulatress, Nelly Price, not having been able to pay for the house purchased by her, belonging to the estate of Miguel Lopez, deceased, and sold at public sale, and she having no property, Robert Abrams, being present, accepted the house for $334 payable as before-mentioned.

p. 152. The minors of Coleman versus Manuel Madden. Petition: Richard Carpenter, of Natchez Dist., petitions that Manuel Madden owes him $49, prays that said Madden be compelled to make payment thereof. 20 Jany. 1786. // Let the party be notified to pay or give his reasons to the contrary. Bouligny. 21 Jany. 1786. // Notified by James Harman, Constable. // John Lusk petitions that Manuel Madden owes him for $22 and asks payment. 18 May 1786. // Let the party be notified, etc. Grand-Pre. 25 May 1786. // Notified Madden. Signed Jeremiah Bryan. // To Don Carlos de Grand-Pre, Commandant, Natchez, the widow Coleman, now Welton, represents that, owing to the indifferent conduct of Manuel Madden, her children, as well as herself, are apprehensive of the safety of their property now in the hands of said Madden, wherefore she prays that you order Madden to render an account of his administration and confide the care of the property to Mr. Welton, my present husband. The said Welton binding himself out of the proceeds thereof to pay all of the just debts due on account of same. March 15 1786. // March 21, 1786. The petitioner, according reports, being married to Welton, her lawful husband, named Madden, now in the District, and charged with the estate of the minors, and the petitioner denying the legality of her former marriage, I have appointed Messrs. Anthony Hutchins and Isaac Johnson, both Justices of Peace during the time of the English Government, and being versed in the custom and manners of that country to determine what should be done in the case and declare the forms necessary in marriage according to the rights of their religion, to the end that justice may be done. Signed: Grand-Pre. // We, Anthony Hutchins and Isaac Johnson, having maturely taken the premises mentioned in consideration, say that the marriage solemnized by Samuel Swazey, deceased, between Manuel Madden and widow Coleman, relict of William Coleman, deceased, was and is legal and lawful, and the said Patience, is, in our opinion, at this time, the lawful wife of the said Madden. Natchez, 3 Apr. 1786. Signed: Anthony Hutchins, Isaac Johnson. // p. 154. The minors Coleman, named, John, William, and Judith, all being of sufficient age to choose a curator, represent that the conduct of their present tutor, Manuel Madden, in their opinion, being such as to endanger the safety of their estate, asks that John Welton be their curator, and to authorize said Welton to compel said Madden to give an account of the property left by William Coleman, their deceased father. 24 May 1786. Signed by Chacheret for John, William and Judith Coleman. // 26 May 1786. Let John Welton be informed that (p. 154) he has been chosen by the minors of Coleman to be their curator, and in case he shall accept thereof to produce security for the property to be entrusted to his care. Grand-Pre. // p. 154 Emanuel Madden represents that in pursuance of the decree of the Commandant, of the 3rd, he is ready to deliver to the Colemans the whole of the property belonging to him in his possession, at the same time, your petitioner asks that a part of said property be assigned to him, sufficient to satisfy the debts contracted by him for the use of said Colemans, and which debts were indeed contracted by their mother before she left Natchez to go to Cumberland. Pet. also requested that he be assigned a portion of the crop which he made last year in payment of his work, and that the accounts be allowed by arbitration. June 6, 1786. Signed: Emanuel Madden. // Natchez. June 7, 1786. Petitioner will present the account of the debts and expenses of the curator as repects to the crops he is allowed to dispose one-half thereof. // p. 155. 3 June 1786. In pursuance of the foregoing petition and order thereon, before me, Don Carlos de Grand-Pre, appeared John Welton, of this District, planter, appointed curators of the minors, John, William and

Judith Coleman, which said charge he has accepted and has presented William Brocus and Robert Abrams as sureties in their persons and estates, which said persons having been informed of the extent of the obligations they were about to contract, have voluntarily undertaken the same and have signed with the interpreter, James McIntosh, and Don Estevan Minor and Juan Carreras, as witnesses. All sign. Grand-Pre. // The est. of Wm. Coleman, decd. to Manuel Madden, debtor, . . . To Mr. Grand-Pre and others shortly after my solemn marriage to the widow of said Coleman, payments, to St. Germain, Alexander Moore, William Smith, William Cocke Ellis, George Castles; tobacco sold in town, five cows killed for the family at $30 each, 4 oxen killed for family $40 each, to Stephen Holstein for meat, amount owing to Anthony Hutchins, with int.; to Geo. Fitzgerald, Mr. Lusk, William Vousdan. My charge for taking care of the family for 22 months $550; cash paid to Mrs. Bingaman for treating a sick negro. (Not totalled.) Inventory of the minors: negro man "Sampson", ae 50, same "Adams" ae 20; negro woman, ae 30, negro girl, ae 14, negro boy ae 12; 3 horses, 14 hogs, plantation, 100 arps. on Second Cr., one cow and two heifers, debts outstanding as declared by Patience Coleman: Wm. Case $10; Abraham Horton, Ebenezer Pipes, John Bisland, D. Mygatt, Madden, Patience Coleman. Signed with a mark. Witnesses. // p. 156. James McIntosh represents that Manuel Madden owes Bennet Smith $84, the greater part thereof was contracted by his wife who is now the wife of John Welton, before her departure from Natchez for Cumberland. Asks for immediate payment for Smith. Signed: James McIntosh. // Manuel Madden represents that in reply to above petition of James McIntosh, agent for the est. of Geo. Castles, that the demand is just and ought to have been paid long since. // p. 158. John Welton, charged with the management of the estate of William Coleman, decd., asks that the two responsible person be appointed to examine the account presented by said Madden as also that produced by your petitioner, that we may be able to recover sum due by said Madden owing to said estate. Oct. 28, 1786. // We have named Jean Girault and Peter Walker to examine the accounts between said Welton and Madden. Grand-Pre. // We are of the opinion that we should follow the report of an examination of the accounts as made by Anthony Hutchins and George Fitzgerald by order of Mr. Bouligny which is in possession of said Madden. 27 Jany. 1786. (Several items which should have been charged to Madden and not to the estate, including a horse.) Signed John Girault and Peter Walker. Oct. 17, 1788. // John Welton represents that the arbitrators for the Coleman estate agst Manuel Madden have condemned the said Madden to pay to the sd estate $125 and asks that the said Madden be compelled to pay said sum without delay and also to deliver to the petitioner a negro named "Peter" who was by said Madden put into possession of Alexander Moore and was sold by said Moore, although said Madden and sd Moore had no right to sell said negro belonging to the estate before-mentioned. John Welton. Oct. 25, 1788. // Oct. 25, 1788. Manuel Madden will pay the petitioner as charged with the estate of Coleman the sum of $150 the award of the arbitrators. Signed Grand-Pre. As respect the negro Peter, he will reply to the claim made, exhibiting the documents authorizing him to sell the negro and his motive for so doing. // Emanuel Madden appeared on 29 Oct. 1887, and in answer to the interrogation relative to the negro Peter belonging to the said estate, declared, on oath that he hired the said negro to Alexander Moore, merchant, by order of Don Francisco Bouligny, then Commandant, and sd Moore took sd negro to New Orleans as a hireling and during his stay there the said Moore sold the said negro of his own accord without any order from this deponent. On return of said Moore to Natchez, he merely informed the deponent that he had sold the said negro and gave credit for the amount of the sale in account of sundry merchandize bought by deponent at his store. Wit: Francis Parbens, James Garland. // John Welton, of sd Post, pet. in pursuance of the declaration of Madden that he had never authorized Alexander Moore to sell the negro Peter, belonging to the heirs of Coleman, asks the order that said Moore restore the said negro without delay and to pay the hire thereof from the time the said negro was hired to him by said Madden. Nov. 8 1788. John Welton. // Alexander Moore represents, that in reply to suit by Messrs Welton and Madden, that about three years since he advanced Emanuel Madden and his wife merchandize and money for the use of their family to amount of more than $500 and the said Madden gave him, as security for the debt, the possession of a young negro aged about 15 yrs. and wishing to take said negro with him to N.O. caused the said negro to be valued by Messrs. Harrison and Fitzgerald who appraised the negro at $500. While your petitioner was at N.O. he received a letter from his wife and son saying that Mr. Madden had requested them to write to me to sell the said negro if possible but not to bring him back to Natchez as his wife was coming back with another husband. It being the petitioner's power to prove this, he asks that you appoint a date to determine the matter. // Alexander Moore will pay to John Welton $500 which he received for the sale of the negro in question. Grand-Pre. // 8 July 1789. Before Gayoso. In pursuance of the foregoing decree appeared Alexander Moore who, in his presence, paid to John Welton $500 for the negro mentioned in the foregoing proceedings. In receipt whereof John Welton has signed before Don Estevan Minor, and Joseph Vidal, witnesses.

p. 160. Peter Walker and J. Henderson versus Squire Boon. Peter Walker and John Henderson petition that a certain Squire Boon owes them by note and account $179. The said Boon answers that he could not pay the debt without selling a negro woman. The petitioners ask that you will be pleased to order the sale of the woman. Dec. 23, 1789. // p. 161. Ebenezer Rees declaring that Clark and Rees had been paid by Boon for the said negro woman, the seizure is granted. Signed Grand-Pre. // Petition from Peter Surget that Squire Boon owes him various accounts and debts amounting to $103 and asks that the sum may be paid to him out of the proceeds from the sale of the negro woman seized by Walker and Henderson. // The petitioner is entitled to be paid out of the sale of the negro woman seized by Walker and Henderson. Grand-Pre. 31 Dec. 1788. // Dec. 30, I, Squire Boon, for value received do promise to pay Peter Surget the sum of $40. Signed. // One week after date, I, Squire Boone, promise to pay to Peter Walker the sum of $13. Signed. // Squire Boone ack. before me that he owed the foregoing sum. Grand-Pre. // Statement with Walker and Henderson. (Very long) // Messrs John Girault and William Henderson appointed to appraise the negro woman and accepted. Value $250. Signed with witnesses. Proceeded with sale of the negro woman. Cried and adjudged to Peter Surget for the sum of $125. Present: Peter Surget, Jeremiah Bryan, Antonio Soler, Peter Walker, Philip P. Turpin, and Charles de Grand-Pre.

p. 164. Louis Chacheret versus Ryan and Isenwood. Luis Chacheret pet. that by order of the Constable, he has seized the plantation of William Ryan and Barnet Isenwood, wherefore he prays that you order an appraisement of same, and sale whereof on the first day of audience thereafter. // 12 Feb. 1789. An appraisement and sale of said plantation will be made. Grand-Pre. // 13 Feb. George Eason and Joseph Ford appointed appraisers, and accepted. The said land consisting of two tracts, each valued at $100. Signed, both with a mark, before witnesses. // 21 Feb. 1789, Sale of land. (1) One tract b. by John Ford, Charles Cason and George Killian. Other b. by Justus King, Richard Swayze and St. Catherine's Creek. (2) 28th Feb. 1789, 200 arpents adjudged to Luis Chacheret for $10. (3) 7th March 1789, no offers. Proceedings closed.

p. 165. Alexander Moore versus Jonas Iler. Alexander Moore, merchant, petitions that Mark Isler, deceased, was indebted to him for $476 and his son, Jonas Isler, being appointed to settle the affairs of his deceased father, prays that he orders Jonas Isler to pay him the said amount. 11 July 1789. // Same day. Jonas Isler will settle the account owing by his late father to Alexander Moore. Gayoso. // 15 July 1789. Notified according to order and he confessed the debt to be just. John Foster, Constable. // Alexander Moore asks seizure of so much property as will be sufficient to pay the sum owing him. Aug. 6, 1789. // Order for same. // In pursuance of the demand against Mark Isler, decd. or his estate, seizure has been made of the property in the possession of his son, Jonas Isler, asks for an appraisal and sale of same. // 5 Dec. 1789. Polser Shilling and William Henderson appointed appraisers. // p. 167. 200 arpents of land, with dwelling house, one-half mile from the Fort valued $200; the negro boy, aged 7, named John, value $200, nothing more to appraise. Sale of plantation, adjudged to Alexander Moore at $100 (1); negro boy adjudged to Jonas Isler for $205, current money, surety, William Barland, to be paid in 15 days. (Further proceedings in this case appeared to have been lost. Signed: Translator.)

p. 168. Benjamin Farrar versus estate of Tacitus Gaillard. In pursuance of the decree of His Excellency, Governor of the Province, in proceeding before the Superior Tribunal, at New Orelans in the case of Benj. Farrar versus the Exr. of Tacitus Gaillard and Anne Gaillard, deceased, which said exr. is Isaac Gaillard, and to the end that said decree may be carried fully into effect, they, the said parties, have mutually agreed to chose for arbitrators, two to be chosen by each party, to examine and settle the accounts pending between the said parties, the same shall be taken from a list of 16 persons, named by His Excellency, Don Manuel Gayoso de Lemos. Post of Natchez, 19 June, appeared Bernard Lintot, appointed by Isaac Gaillard, to be one of the arbitrators, and Lintot accepted thereof. Bernard Lintot, Alexander Moore, chosen by Isaac Gaillard. The arbitrators have agreed to meet at the house of John Ellis, as the most convenient place to all. Alexander Moore, Sutton Banks, George Fitzgerald, Thomas Kirk, Thomas Green, Abner Green, James McIntosh, Isaac Johnson, John O'Connor , Peter Walker, Cato West, David Williams, Benjamin Monsanto, Col. Peter Bryan Bruin, Bernard Lintot, Melling Woolley, all residents of the Dist. of Natchez, make up the list from which the arbitors are to be chosen. Col. Peter Bryan Bruin and Isaac Johnson chosen by Farrar. Col. Bruin could not serve on account of illness of his wife, and Sutton Banks was chosen in his place. [The settlement covers pages and pages. Besides accounts of the income from crops, etc. the will of both Tacitus Gaillard and his wife, Anne, are given, also documents from South Carolina, given in other parts of these records, covering pp. 168-219.]

p. 220. Col. Williams petitions that, pursuance to a decree of the Gov. Gen. of the Province, permitting him to make a search through the Province for slaves which have been stolen from divers inhabitants of the U.S., for which persons he was attorney, taking declarations and transmitting same to the Superior Tribunal. He found in the possession of Richard Harrison a negro woman, named "Jane" with her children; in the possession of John Bisland a man named "John"; and in possession of William Calvit a negro woman named "Alice" and her daughter. Therefore he asks that these men be ordered to appear before the Commandant, as well as Henry Manadue, William Henderson, Mrs. Henderson and Jesse Wheeler, as witnesses. June 12, 1790. Signed: Turner Williams. // Grand-Pre orders that these men appear before him on the 16th. // Notified by John Foster, Constable. // Williams was empowered by Peter Walker and John Tear to seek and restore slaves for them. Said slaves were in Kentucky and he found them in possession of Andrew Beall in this District, and he asks that James Harrod, William Tinsley, Francis Williams and Dewitt be summoned as witnesses. Witnesses appeared; Jas. Harrod testified that he knew the negro Isaac in Kentucky and he was in possession of James McFadden who brought him from North Carolina to Henry French, who later told deponent that he wanted to take his slaves to another country or he would lose them. The deponent was preparing to make a voyage and French arranged to come along with him and brought four slaves. He left on a flat boat and French, who had come down the river in a pirogue, got on his flat boat. When we came to Great Falls, our only stop, Henry French hid the negroes. French could not be questioned as he was not in the District. // William Henderson declared that about ten years ago, together with a certain Burnet and others Americans were under command of Gen. Clark in S.C. and the said Gen. having given orders to plunder that part of the country, then in possession of His Brittanic Majesty, permitting them to appropriate to their own use whatsoever (p. 222) they might find, they got hold of sundry negroes who said they belong to Scott and King, who had joined the British, and they believed the said Burnet sold said slaves to Richard Harrison and William Calvit, planters of this District, which he had gotten possession of like many others, but he cannot say positively that the said slaves were sold to Calvit and Harrison. Signed William Henderson. // Turner Williams reports that he had not been able to locate the slaves that he was looking for, and that he would have to go back to Kentucky and get more evidence to support his claim. He would return later.

p. 223. William Collins versus Ebenezer Rees. William Collins bought a negro woman "Mary" from Ebenezer Rees and paid part of the purchase price. She was not well at the time and Rees said she had had fever and hadn't quite recovered but that she was all right. She was not able to work and they say she is leprous. He asks that Rees take the negro back and return his payment. // Commandant ordered the King's physician, Don Luis Faure, to examine the negro. He reported that she had a certain disease and was lame in one leg and a venereal disease of long standing. // Rees claimed the disease was not one that was classed as justifying the cancellation of a sale and the Commandant ruled with him.

p. 224. Sutton Banks versus the estate of William Hiorn, deceased. When he came to this country, Sutton Banks was empowered by John Noble Taylor to settle his commercial affairs with the said Hiorn, from whom he was instructed to claim sundry sums of money he had received on account of said Taylor. On his arrival, he was informed that Hiorn had departed for Europe. A short time after that, he perished at sea, and in consequence Banks addressed himself to William Pounteney who was Hiorn's agent and asked for a settlement, but he was always put off on account of the absence of the agent, Mr. James Mather. Finally Banks went to New Orleans to consult Mather but he couldn't get any satisfaction and when he returned Pounteney died. The estate was indebted to the petitioner for $836, and the firm of Mather and Morgan also sued the Hiorn estate before Sutton Banks could file a claim. In consequence, the plantation, called "Belmont" was put up for sale at their request. At that time, Bernard Lintot was representing Mather and Morgan. At the sale, the bidding was very active, and the plantation was adjudged to James McIntosh for $1625. The other bidders were William Vousdan, Bernard Lintot, James McIntosh, Sutton Banks and David Williams. p. 229. Henry Manadue versus John Baptist LaPuenta. LaPuenta was indebted to Henry Manadue, who on Feb. 12, 1790, petitions land be sold to pay the obligation. Appraisers: Polser Shilling for Manadue, and John Foster for LaPuenta. At 3rd and final sale, Henry Manadue and James Bonner were bidding against each other and the land was adjudged to Manadue for $300. All sign. Before Grand-Pre.

p. 232. Alexander Moore versus Edward McCabe. Edward McCabe owed Moore $470, by mortgage on record, which Moore petitions to be paid. 25 Feb. 1790. // Order for same by Grand-Pre. // McCabe notified by Roswell Mygatt. // Petition by Moore that the property be seized, appraised and sold, with the mortgage annexed, the plantation of 150 arpents on a branch of St. Catherine's Creek, bounded by the lands of Winson Pipes, West, John Foster and Alexander Henderson, also horses, 10 Feb. 1789.

Plantation valued at $600 by Ezekiel Dewitt and Joseph Perkins, appraisers. At the 3rd and last sale, the bidders were John O'Connor $400, David Ferguson $405, Samuel Moore $450, Ferguson $460 to whom it was adjudged. Witnesses: John Foster, John Ferguson, William Chambers, William Gilbert, William Henderson, Joseph Vidal, before Grand-Pre. Plantation sold on time, O'Connor surety for David Ferguson. // James Moore, acting for his father, acknowledged to have received from David Ferguson the sum of $460 the amount of the foregoing sale.

p. 235. Anthony Hutchins versus William Gorman. Petitioner understood that William Gorman intended to withdraw to the Indian Nation and he asks that said Gorman and Samuel Wells be summoned to appear immediately. Gorman had a bond of Hutchins, who had fulfilled the contract for which the bond had been given but he not gotten the bond from Gorman. 10 Nov. 1790. // John Foster, the Constable, will notify Gorman and Samuel Wells positively to appear the first day of audience, the 13th. Signed: Grand-Pre. // Anthony Hutchins declared: 16 or 17 years ago I bought a tract of land from Wm. Gorman, giving him my bond in payment. Sometimes afterwards he was about to depart on a hunting party and being indebted to several persons, we met, the said Gorman, Samuel Wells and myself, at the landing to settle our affairs, at which time I paid him a small sum of which he had need and gave him some notes payable to the order of several creditors, the whole making the exact amount for which I had given him my bond. I have punctually paid the above-mentioned notes. On demanding my bond from said Gorman, he told me that he had left it at the house of Mr. Wells, but after many efforts to get the note he had been unable to do so. 6 Nov. 1790. // Nov. 12, John Foster reported that he had notified Wm. Gorman according to the order and on the 15th had notified Samuel Wells. On the 13th William Gorman appeared and said that he had never had any such note from Hutchins but that he had a memorandum for $130 belonging to the estate of Jacob Winfree given by said Hutchins, dated 6 March 1775. Signed by Gorman before official witness and the Commandant.

p. 237. Martha Foley versus Landon Davis and Hugh Davis. Martha Foley, widow of Lewis Davis, represents that the deceased father of her said late husband, Lewis Davis, by his will left to his three sons, Landon, Lewis and Hugh a certain number of slaves to be equally divided among them after the death of his wife and the said Lewis Davis, husband of the petitioner, having died a short time before his mother, his two brothers, Landon and Hugh, have appropriated to themselves the whole of the said slaves without allowing any part thereof to the children and lawful heirs of her deceased husband, Lewis Davis, but had kept possession of the slaves ever since the death of her late mother-in-law, deceased in the year 1784. 5 Feb. 1791. Signed: Martha Foley. // Same day. Gayoso ordered that Landon and Hugh Davis appear before him on Saturday the 12th, with the will made by their deceased father. // Galvestown, June 12, 1790. This is to certify that Lewis, Landon and Hugh Davis have made a settlement of the estate of Robert Davis, deceased, and that Lewis Davis has got a negro woman, named "Kate", in full for a debt due to him from the said estate, and that the other two equal parts are two negro boys, "Jack" and "Simon". Signed Lewis Davis. Witness: Hugh Davis. // The will of Robert Davis, p. 238 "Being sick and weak but of perfect memory, I, Robert Davis, of the Province of Georgia, planter, to my beloved son, Lewis Davis, two negro slaves, "Bolling" and "Phoebe", with a feather bed and furniture; to my beloved son, Landon Davis, two negro slaves, "Samson" and "Sarah", with feather bed and furniture; to my beloved son Hugh Davis, three negro slaves, "Roger", "Joe" and "Cochena", with a feather bed and furniture; to my well-beloved wife, Grace Davis, one negro girl, "Hannah" forever, with a feather bed and furniture, and I lend to my said wife, Grace Davis, four negro slaves, with their increase, "Charles", "Jug" during her widowhood and out of the income of the four negroes to maintain, clothe and bring up my son, Hugh Davis, until he comes to the age of 20 years. If the said Grace Davis should marry or die then the said negroes with their increase shall be equally divided between Lewis Davis, Landon Davis and Hugh Davis, share and share alike. To my well-beloved son, Nathaniel Davis, 20 shillings lawful money of Great Britain, likewise, to my beloved son, Isom Davis, 20 shillings, to my beloved son, Robert Davis, 20 shillings, to my beloved daughter, Obediah Floyd, 20 shillings, to my beloved daughter, Sarah Burks, 20 shillings, to my beloved daughter, Elizabeth Sexton, 20 shillings. I give to my three sons, Lewis, Landon and Hugh Davis the remaining part of my estate, real and personal, to be equally divided among them I nominate my two sons, Lewis and Landon Davis or the survivor of them executors of my last will and testament. 5 Sept. 1771. Signed Robert Davis. Wit: Thomas Spell, Mager Spell, Sterling Spell. // p. 239. Landon and Hugh Davis, brothers and executors of the will of Lewis Davis, represent that we have ever since the death of our said brother left in possession of the widow the slaves and other property belonging to the estate of the said Lewis Davis, to work and use the same for the benefit of the heirs of the said estate, but some time since, the said widow married a certain Patrick Foley who has some new negroes of little value whom he has put to work with the slaves belonging to the heirs on joint account, intending to draw one-half of the proceeds. The said Foley also keeps his store and has given clothes to the children without our knowledge or consulting with us. Ask that the Commandant take whatever measures he thinks best to prevent the heirs from being defrauded of the proceeds of the labor of their slaves. 2nd Feb. 1791. Signed: Landon Davis, Hugh Davis. // Hugh Davis represents that the time when his brother, Lewis Davis, was unmarried he had a daughter by a woman in Georgia who applied to the law and obtained a judgment against said Lewis by which he was condemned to maintain the said child, which he did for some time, but, having married, he put the child with his mother but since 1774 the said child has been lamed and has not been able to do anything and her father has made no provision for her in his will but his mother having bequeathed the children of said Lewis a negro girl notwithstanding by his father's will, it will appear that his mother had no right to dispose of the said negro girl, your petitioner prays that in consideration of the unhappy situation of the child that you will leave to her the said negro girl for her support. 2 Feb. 1791. Signed: Landon Davis, Hugh Davis. // p. 240. I do hereby declare that Lewis Davis did acknowledge to me that a girl named "Nelly" now living at Mr. Davis's was his child and further that Mrs. Davis, the mother of Lewis Davis, did frequently tell me that he did own to her that the child was his. Rebecca Ambrose. Feb. 13, 1791. // Deposition of Reuben Gray. I do hereby certify that a girl named "Nelly" living at the house of Hugh and Landon Davis, has always passed as the bastard child of Lewis Davis; that she was believed to be such by the said Lewis Davis, by the said Davises and Mrs. Davis who took the said girl when a child, and she has continued with them ever since. Having always lived near and intimate in Mr. Davis's family, this has come within my knowledge. Ruffin Gray. 15 Feb. 1791. // Deposition of William Scott, (same as other deposition, naming 1776 as the year in which the girl began living with the Davis family.) Feb. 11, 1791.

p. 240. Maurice Stacpoole versus the estate of John Proffit. To His Excellency, the acting Governor, Maurice Stacpoole represents that George Proffit, deceased, did accept from your petitioner before his death an obligation given to him by said petitioner for $450 drawn by John Lum in payment of $400 owing by said petitioner to said Proffit and for which the petitioner had previously given him his own obligation which was returned to him by said Proffit at the time of the aforesaid acceptance and the executor of the will not being present in this district, your petitioner asks that Patrick Foley and the aforesaid John Lum be called to appear before him, being well-informed of the agreement made between the petitioner and the said George Proffit, to the end that the pet. may be enabled to take such measures as acceptable to the executor of the estate, David Ross. 29 March 1791. Signed: Maurice Stacpoole. // p. 241. 29 March 1791. Patrick Foley and John Lum will appear and declare what they know in the matter of the foregoing petition. Signed: Grand-Pre. // On 30 March 1791 appeared John Lum, who being sworn, replied that about a year since, being at the landing of this place, he met George Proffit and asked him if he would accept the obligation of this deponent, which he the deponent had purchased from Maurice Stacpoole in payment of the sum of $400, owing by the said Stacpoole to the said Proffit for a negro purchased from him, to which the said Proffit replied that it was indifferent to him whether the sum was owing to him by the deponent or by Stacpoole, and thereupon agreed to receive the obligation of this deponent in payment of what was owing to him by Stacpoole and discharge the latter from the debt. Signed: John Lum. // At the same time appeared Patrick Foley, who, being sworn, said he was well-acquainted with the matter in question which was as follows: Maurice Stacpoole bought from George Proffit in May 1789 a negro for $400 which said negro he sold again to John Lum for $450 and being talking together in the presence of the deponent respecting said negro, he, the deponent, heard said Stacpoole tell said Proffit that he had sold the negro to John Lum for $450 and asked said Proffit if he would take the obligation of said Lum which was payable at the same time and was drawn for $50 more than the obligation which Stacpoole had given for the said negro but he would be willing to lose the said profit if Proffit would accept the obligation of Lum and give him up his own, with the proviso that the said Proffit would never have recourse against said Stacpoole for the said debt. George Proffit said he was satisfied with the proposal and would accept, which was done in the presence of the deponent. He, Stacpoole, endorsing and transferring the obligation of Lum to the said Proffit, and the latter by the same act, giving up to Stacpoole the obligation that he had previously received from him. Signed: Patrick Foley. Before Grand-Pre. // Stacpoole asks for copies of the above to present the executors of Proffit. // Granted by Grand-Pre. p. 243. John Hervey versus William Waterman. John Hervey, exor to the will of Edgar Gallaudet, decd., represents that in Sept. 1789, Thomas Irwin, then charged with the corcerns of Gallaudet, sold a negro woman to William Waterman for $500, payable in Dec. 1790, and, not having received any part thereof, he was desirous of taking back the said negro woman but found that since she had been in possession of said Waterman she had contracted diseases from bad usage as to be nearly useless, wherefore your pet. asks that said negro woman be appraised and sold at public sale, the said

Waterman giving securety for the difference in the value of the slave now and when she was sold to him. 31 Aug. 1791. Signed: John Hervey, exr. of estate of Edgar Gallaudet. // Sept. 1, 1791. Wm. Waterman appeared and proved by the affidavit of Ebenezer Fulton and Sarah Fulton, his wife, that immediately after sd Waterman bought the negro woman in question from Thomas Irwin, he the said Waterman, sold the slave to the said Fulton in exchange for cattle and said Fulton, having kept her a short time, found that she was infirm and incapable of work and in consequence whereof he returned the said slave to sd Waterman, who also presented Beasley Pruit who confirmed the foregoing statement and said that the said negro woman had continued in the same state ever since, being entirely useless to the owner. In consequence whereof, it is ordered that John Hervey, exr. of the estate of Edgar Gallaudet, to which est. the said slave belonged, to take back the said negro woman at the same price for which she was sold, hereby annulling the sd sale. As respects the wages allowed for the hire of the said negroes the parties will chose arbitrators who have a knowledge of the said slave to determine the same. // p. 244. In pursuance of the foregoing decree, John Hervey asks that the Commandant choose the arbitrators to determine the hire of the woman for the two years Waterman kept her in his service. Signed: John Hervey, exr. of Est of Gallaudet. 1 Sept. 1791. // In pursuance of the foregoing petition, I do appoint Beasley Truitt and Ebenezer Fulton, being nearest neighbors and knowledge of the said negro woman. 3 Sept. Appeared Beasley Pruitt and Ebenezer Fulton who declared that from the knowledge they have, as near neighbors of Wm. Waterman, of the negro sold by Thomas Irwin to Waterman, it appears to them that no wages should be paid for said slave whose trifling services could not be equivalent to her maintenance. Wherefore it is ordered that said Hervey do receive the said woman from the purchaser. Signed: Manuel Gayoso de Lemos.

p. 244. To His Excellency, the Acting Governor, Alexander Moore represents that Wm. Henderson owes him for $300, together with int., security whereof he mortgaged two slaves, of which debt sd Henderson has paid nothing; asks for payment. 28 Sept. 1791. Signed Alexander Moore. // Sept. 30, William Henderson will appear at the first audience, with the slaves mortgaged. Petitioner will also attend, Signed: Grand-Pre. // Natchez, Oct. 2, 1791. Went to house of Henderson, who was not at home but left word that he appear. Jere Bryan. // Oct. 8, 1791. The parties have agreed that the two slaves mortgaged shall remain three months longer in possession of the debtor to facilitate him in satisfying the amount of mortgage and if the same be not paid at the end of that time, the said slaves shall be taken possession of by Alexander Moore to be appraised and sold to satisfy the debt of the above. Signed: Grand-Pre. // The time the slaves were to be left in possession of William Henderson being expired, and the said Henderson still being unable to pay the said debt, Robert Cochran and David Ferguson chosen appraisers and accepted. Negro man valued $350 and the negro woman the same. Signed by Robert Cochran, David Ferguson. Charles de Grand-Pre. The slaves were offered three time and no one bid two-thirds of the appraisal value thereof. Sitting was closed. // 17 March 1792. Alexander Moore petitions that the two slaves were mortgaged by David Smith and transferred by him to William Henderson and were by Henderson in the presence of the then Commandant, Carlos de Grand-Pre, delivered to the petitioner to be sold at public sale to satisfy the sum of $300, with interest and cost due by said Henderson, and being part of the sum of $600 for which the slaves were first mortgaged, we, the said parties, appoint other appraisers. // In compliance with the foregoing petition, Ezekiel Forman, William Vousdan and John O'Connor appointed. For good reasons I have appointed John Mapother in the place of John O'Connor. Signed: Gayoso. // Valued by the appraisers: Both worth $450. 2nd March, 1792. Signed by the three appraisers. // 24 March 1792. Two slaves above-mentioned exposed at public sale adjudged to Don Juan Girault for $380, he being the highest bidder. Witnesses: Joseph Vidal, Augustine Macarty, Francisco Pavana, Robert Ford, David Holt, John Girault. Before Manuel Gayoso de Lemos.

p. 248. James Kirk, of this District, planter, petitions that he sold a lot at the landing at Natchez to Pedro Ancid, for $160, of which sum he received $60 and the term of the remaining being expired, the petitioner demands payment but was answered by said Ancid that his whole property was seized whereupon your petitioner prays that in case the house built on the said lot be sold that he may receive payment of the said sum of $100 from the proceeds. Signed: James Kirk. 29 March 1792. // Not withstanding the seizure of the estate of Pedro Ancid and claim of the petitioner is valid and will be attended to. Signed: Gayoso.

p. 248. Daniel Clark and Ebenezer Rees, of the District, traders, represent that they were lately connected with Thos. Wilkins in commerce; that their said connection was, by mutual consent dissolved, and that, on a settlement of their accounts, falls indebted to the said Clark and Rees about $6,000, and said Wilkins being rendered inactive by illness, the petitioners ask that debtors pay their indebtnesses to Clark and Rees, and to none else until the said Thos. Wilkins pays off the debt which he owes said Clark and Rees. Signed by both. 14 Nov. 1792. // To be communicated to Thos. Wilkins. // Petition of Thomas Wilkins. In answer, he asks that said Clark and Rees make known the reasons they have not settled with him, ageeable to the terms proposed by themselves. // Order that Daniel Clark, Daniel Rees and Thomas Wilkins appear 3rd Dec. Signed: Gayoso. // 3rd Dec. The parties having appeared before me, I have determined with their consent to appoint William Dunbar and Barnard Lintot Arbitrators, and in case of disagreement they are (p. 249) to choose an umpire. Signed by all before Gayoso de Lemos. // In obedience to the command, we have examined with due attention the sundry points in this dispute and are of the opinion that Mr. Wilkins ought not to be charged with interest until after the term stipulated, second, that Mr. Wilkins is entitled to his half-share of 5% of all negroes sent to the Natchez for sale by Clark and Rees and should be so credited. 29 Dec. 1792. Signed: Bernard Lintot, William Bunbar. // Award of arbitrators approved and confirmed by Manuel Gauoso de Lemos. 9 Jany. 1793.

p. 250. Petition of Melling Woolley, submits the following true statement of his case with Mr. Moses Bonner relative to a slave. In the month of May 1788, your petitioner purchased a slave from Mr. Wall for $500, the property of Mr. Francis Pousset under mortgage to Mr. David Ross, $250 of this your pet. paid when it became due. Sometime before this your petitioner became indebted to Mr. Moses Bonner for some corn and a tract of land to $600 and did enter into an agreement of the sale of the above slave in part payment of the land and corn. Mr. Bonner was not unacquainted that such mortgage existed but was by your petitioner especially informed of it, which the cause no title was ever demanded. Previous to the negro being taken into custody by Mr. Vousdan, the attorney for Mr. Ross, your petitioner stated the arrangement he had made for the payment of the balance which was by the tobacco which Mr. Bonner took at Your Excellency's order. Asks that Bonner pay for the hire of the negro which he has given up and taken some tobacco (to pay for the corn probably). 15 Oct. 1792. // Messrs. Gabriel Benoist and Winsor Pipes are appointed to give their opinion concerning the hire of the negro requested. // We, Gabriel Benoist and Winsor Pipes, it appears to us that at the time that Mr. Bonner had the slave in his possession, he did very reasonably look upon him as his own, since he was paid for, consequently no hire can be reasonably demanded by Mr. Woolley for which he had received the payment. If he were to pay for the hire of the negro, he would be entitled to interest on the money he had paid for him. There was no choice of his keeping the negro or the tobacco. Mr. Bonner is entitled to received interest on his debt to Mr. Woolley until it was paid, after he returned the negro, which was four months. Dec. 23, 1792. Signed by both arbitrators. [Note. The above was Moses Bonner, Jr.]

p. 252. Jacob Phillis versus Maurice Stacpoole. Jacob Phillis, being indebted to Maurice Stacpoole, in the sum of $142 for having been security for John Ormsby, who owed the sum to said Stacpoole, the petitioner went on a journey from this district to Mobile and during his absence, the said Stacpoole maliciously represented that the petitioner had absconded to avoid paying the said debt, and transmitted two notes of your petitioner for the said amount to John Joice, living on the Tombignee, to recover the amount thereof, and the Commandant there directed the seizure of the negro belonging to the petitioner, which was freed only on the security of Freeland on condition that your petitioner would return to the district and pay the full amount to Maurice Stacpoole. Whereupon your petitioner returned here on 20 Nov. last and offered said payment in horses according to the tenor of his notes but the said (p.252) Stacpoole declined receiving the same and your pet. at length appeared before Your Excellency who, in pursuance to the documents produced, ordered the said Stacpoole to appoint an appraiser to value the said horses, with which Stacpoole has not complied. Pet. asks if Stacpoole refuses the payment that Your Excellency will interpose your authority. Jacob Phillis. 31 Oct. 1792. // Maurice Stacpoole will go immediately to the house of Nathaniel Tomlinson with such persons as he may choose to appraise the horses which he will receive in payment of the petitioner's notes. Same date. Signed: Grand-Pre. // Notified Maurice Stacpoole of your order to which he makes frivolous answers. Signed Joseph Vidal. // Jacob Phillis represents that Maurice Stacpoole has refused payment of his notes and ignored your orders wherefore he prays that Your Excellency will grant a certificate which he may present at the Posts of Mobile and Tombigbee for the information of the Commandants thereof and to ask that the said Commandant to command John Joice to deliver to the petitioner which he has done all in his power to satisfy. Nov. 2, 1792. Signed: Jacob Phillis. // Maurice Stacpoole having declined to appoint an appraiser and another to be chosen on the part of the debtor, Jacob Phillis, as to the value of the horses to be taken in payment of $142, amount of his notes, and the expense of keeping said horses at this place being heavy, falling on the debtor by the unwillingness of the creditor to receive them, I hereby appoint on the part of

Stacpoole, Nathaniel Tomlinson who with James Sanders, chosen by Jacob Phillis, will make the appraisement of said horses. // Said appraisers have accepted and signed. // 3 Nov. 1792. Before Don Carlos de Grand-Pre, appeared Jacob Phillis with sundry horses in payment of a debt contracted with Maurice Stacpoole and appraisers, James Saunders and Nathaniel Tomlinson, who appraised the said horses, on oath, as follows: One for $45, one for $40, one for $20 and a mare 12 years old with a colt for $37, total $142, which being sufficient for the said debt we have closed same and signed with the appraisers. Wm. Gorman, Don Joseph Vidal, witnesses. Maurice Stacpoole will be informed of the judicial appraisement of the four horses presented by Jacob Phillis to satisfy a debt to Stacpoole of $142, for which he gave his notes payable in horses and said horses are left, by my order, at the house of Nathaniel Tomlinson and if on this day the said Stacpoole shall not appear to take charge of them, the damages and expenses accruing from his disobedience shall be and remain on his account, and the said Stacpoole will be informed that from this moment, the said Jacob Phillis is released from the debt, his notes being considered satisfied. Signed: Grand-Pre. // New Orleans, April 25, 1792. Mr. John Joyce. Sir: I beg leave to enclose Jacob Phillis's note for $142 and John Ormsby's for $126. I believe that Phillis is the only one on whom to depend. He is a young man, about 5 feet, 10 inches high, with a good complexion, dark hair about 25 years old and rather slender. He has a remarkably stout fellow, his man "Ben", with him and two likely horses. Ormsby is about the same age, taller and stouter. They may attempt to go to the States. Signed Maurice Stacpoole. The following is a copy in my possession. Signed: J. Stephens. 28 Aug. 1792. // Nov. 7, 1792. Pet. of Maurice Stacpoole. (Very long.) // To be carried into execution notwithstanding. Signed: Gayoso.

p. 258. Joseph Calvit versus John Williams. Joseph Calvit declares that he has a mortgage on the plantation on which Major Williams resides for $400 besides interest. The said Mr. Williams makes no use of the plantation that can turn to advantage and it has greatly depreciated since he had it in possession for want of repairs to the buildings and having permitted Mr. Dayton to cut a vast quantity of timber and take a great quantity of bark off the said plantation. He prays that he have the plantation valued and sold. Signed: Joseph Calvit. Dec. 19, 1792. // In consideration that the petitioner has a mortgage on the plantation, Ezekiel Dewitt and William Wicks [Weeks] are appointed appraisers. 380 arpents, 2 houses of little value, b. by St. Catherine's Cr., land of Joseph Duncan, Richard Swayze and Don Estevan Minor, appraised at $300 cash. [Not signed] Notice of sale in February at three different times to the highest bidder. // 6th Feb. 1793. Don Manuel Gayoso. At third sale adjudged to Joseph Calvit for $300, cash, the highest bidder. Signed by Joseph Calvit, and witnesses, H. Manadue, John Arden, Joseph Vidal. Before Blas de Bouchet.

p. 260. Juan Girault versus John Montgomery. Petitions that part of the effects mortgaged to him by the late John Montgomery were sold to Buckner Pittman and others by James Finn and the widow Montgomery, wherefore the pet. prays that Mr. George Cochran, of Bayou Pierre, be authorized to claim the property wherever it may be found and that it may be estimated at cash price and delivered to the said George Cochran for the account of the petitioner for the payment of this mortgage, amounting to $260. 16 Oct. 1792. Signed: John Girault. // Same date. Granted. Gayoso. // To Col. Bryan Bruin, Alcalde of the Bayou Pierre District, John Girault petitions that, in pursuance of the foregoing petition, he will cause the plantation, settled by the late John Montgomery, to be appraised in cash and delivered to the petitioner in settlement of his claim. Nov. 24, 1792. // In compliance to the above request, have caused Messrs. Melling Woolley and Capt. Richard King to appraise this land at cash and report. Bayou Pierre. Nov. 28, 1792. Signed: P. Bryan Bruin. // The land situated near the south branch of Bayou Pierre, b. by lands of John Gibson, Fordyce, Abner Green, Elijah Smith, Elisha Flowers and Thos. Hubbard, containing 597 acres, on which a small house, a well, a field and an orchard, all decayed and in very bad repair. Appraised the same to be worth $250 cash, from which sum the cost of obtaining a title is to be deducted. Dec. 3, 1792. Both sign. // Petitioner confirmed in possession of the said land, in virtue whereof the mortgage is to be considered foreclosed, and the land will be surveyed in favor of the said John Girault to possess the same as his own right and property. Signed: Manuel Gayoso de Lemos.

p. 262. Manuel Garcia de Texada represents that Richard Trevillian, of this District, owes him $303, for the hire of negroes, as will appear by his notes, asks that Trevillian be ordered to make payment. 29 Aug. 1792. Signed: Manuel Texada. // Ordered that Trevillian be notified to make payment immediately or appear before Gayoso on next day of audience. Same date. // Texada petitions that, Trevillian having acknowledged the debt, order for the seizure of the property of sd Trevillian be made to the amount of the said debt and cost. 1 Oct. 1792. // 13 Oct. 1792. Mr. Richard King is required to send a party to conduct Mr. Richard Trevillain here. Signed: Gayoso. // p. 263. Your petitioner, Richard Trevillian, having been twice summoned before Your Excellency to answer the debt due Manuel Texada, asks that an allowance be made to the petitioner for the inconvenience of having maintained and taken care of the said Manuel Texada's family, being an expense and trouble that few in your petitioner's circumstances could bear without compensation, especially as his whole family has been, for days and weeks together, prevented from attending to their own business by attending to Manuel Texada's wife in a long fit of illness when left at your petitioner's house by the said Texada and taken care of by his desire. // Let the foregoing be communicated to Manuel Texada and Trevillian be notified not to leave this Post until the matter be determined. // Manuel Texada states that the allegations of Richard Trevillian are frivolous and unfounded, intended merely to gain time. The said petitioner does not know that the said party has had any family for the last two years upward. If the said Trevillian has any account to present, he may do it afterwards. The debt being acknowledged by said Trevillian, consideration is asked in the seizure of the property. // Having agreed to allow Trevillian until Saturday next to appear to settle accounts, I have confirmed same. // Richard Trevillian, not having made any arrangement for paying the debt, it is ordered that his property to be seized to the amount thereof. // Petition of Manuel Texada, res. of this Post, that Richard Trevillian not having given up sufficient property to cover the debt and execution, thereby increasing both trouble and expense, prays an order that said Trevillian appear before you and declare the property in his possession, and that the same may be the amount of the said debt and cost. Nov. 3, 1792. Signed: Manuel Garcia de Texada. // Granted and Trevillian will be notified. // 10 Nov. 1792, appeared Richard Trevillian, who being sworn, declared his property to be as follows: Negro, "Gloster", aged 13, 4 cows and 2 calves, one horse, two pairs of oxen, 7 hogs, 5 young hogs, about 80 bushels of corn, and a plantation containing 260 arpents, being the whole of his property, to the best of his knowledge. Signed before Don Joseph Vidal, Valentine Rincon, witnesses. Before Manuel Gayoso. // Appraisers of above property appointed: Thomas Green, Thomas Calvit. Total value; about $600. Other creditors of Trevillian, Alexander Moore and others, asks for a preference. // In answer, we are not charged with the recovery of any other debts owing by the aforesaid Trevillian. // 3rd sale. The plantation was adjudged to Texada for $150. Other property sold for $281, Texada also the purchaser. This was before Blas de Bouchet.

p. 268. The petition of Elizabeth Brantley, late of the United States of America, represents that in 1789 she was owner of a slave, called "Solomon", which slave was under the condemnation of crime, for murder, but, finding means to make his escape, he got on board a canoe and came down the river, as your petitioner received information, intending for some part of the Mississippi. Being informed that Mr. Thomas Martin was coming to this country, she entered into an agreement for the said slave, for 250 silver dollars, no part of which has been paid. She came to this country, and Mr. Martin said he would return slave or pay her for him, neither of which he has done. Your petitioner understands that the negro has been sold several times and is now in possession of Melling Woolley. At an application to Melling Woolley to give him up, he is willing to do, provided he receive Your Excellency's orders for that purpose. She signs with a mark. 23 April 1793. // Same date, Thomas Martin is hereby ordered to appear before me on the 25th instant. Signed Gayoso. // 4 May 1793. In pursuance of the petition of Elizabeth Brantley, caused to appear before me, Joseph Howard, Melling Woolley and Thomas Martin who were successively masters of the negro in said memorial, and have mutually considered the circumstances of this case, having determined that Melling Woolley, who is now in possession of said slave, shall return the same to Joseph Howard, who shall refund to him the amount received in payment, and that said Howard do the same with Thomas Martin, who shall return the said slave to Elizabeth Brantley, who is bound to receive and convey the said slave, immediately out of this District, since she has stated in her memorial that the said slave had, in the United States, committed murder, and by the laws such can neither be sold nor suffered to remain in this country. Which decree the said Woolley, Howard and Martin, are hereby informed and required to obey. Signed in the presence of Vidal and Rincon. Melling Woolley, Joseph Howard, Thomas (T) Martin. Before Manuel Gayoso de Lemos.

p. 269. 30 Sept. 1793. Don Antonio Soler, to carry into effect the orders of Don Pedro Favrot, acting commandant of the Post and District of Natchez, in the absence of the Governor, have repaired to Stoney Creek, and sending for the Constable for the said District, ordered him to go to the house of Jacob Coven [Cobun] and to arrest the sd Jacob Coven and Samuel Coben, his son, and the said Constable having returned that he had arrested the aforesaid Jacob Coben but that the son, Samuel, was gone to Opelousas, whereupon I gave orders to the said constable to convey the said Coben to Natchez to be delivered to the acting-governor, Don Pedro Favrot. Signed: Antonio Soler. // Immediately afterwards, I proceeded to take an inventory of the property of the said Jacob and Samuel Coben, as follows: plantation of 800 arpents of land, on Stoney Creek, with sundry old buildings thereon, negro man, "James", aged 30, negro woman, abt. same age, negro girl "Sophia", aged 7, 11 hogs, 5 horses, one set of plow irons, complete, 8 arpents of corn in the field, ready to gather, being all that was found belonging to said Jacob Coben, and which I have left in charge of Samuel Gibson, who promised to take care of and deliver same when required. Stoney Creek. Oct. 1, 1793. Signed: Samuel Gibson, Agapito Carchado. Antonio Soler. // Stoney Creek. 3rd Oct. 1793. Before Antonio Soler, appeared the constable of this district, who declared that it was impossible to conduct Jacob Coben to the Post of Natchez, at this moment, he, the said Jacob, being dangerously sick in his bed, but that he will bring him on so soon as he may be in condition to bear the journey. Signed: Antonio Soler. // 7th Nov. 1793. The constable of the District of Stoney Creek declares that the son of Jacob Coben, having returned from Opelousas the same night of his arrival, escaped with his father, and that notwithstanding the most diligence search, we could not find either of them. Therefore he concludes that they have gone to the Indian Nation. Signed: Antonio Soler.

p. 269. Benjamin Monsanto versus James Sanders. Benj. Monsanto represents that in November 1787 his brother, in the course of trade in which they were partners, sold to James Sanders a negro woman named "Louisa" for which the said Sanders is still indebted in the sum of $90 for not having completed the payment. In December 1788, the said woman having been seized in the suit of John Whipple, who claims a certain sum due him out of the sale of said slave, wherefore your petitioner asks that the sale of said negro woman be prevented until he shall have been for her. Signed: Benj. Monsanto. 4 Oct. 1793. // 4 Nov. 1793. The usages of restoring slaves to the sellers thereby when not paid for being established in this Government, we do hereby direct that the negro woman shall be sold and from the proceeds thereof Benjamin Monsanto be paid the sum due him, and that the remainder be applied to the debt owing to John Whipple, in obedience to the order of the Superior Tribunal. Signed: Gayoso. // A copy of the bill of sale from Monsanto to James Saunders for the negro, dated 7 Nov. 1787. Witnesses by John Lum, Antonio Soler, Juan Carreras. Before Carlos de Grand-Pre.

p. 271. Christopher Whipple, of the Dist. of Natchez, petitions that, for four years, he lent money to Thomas Rule and Matthew White, who in consequence of the indulgence granted by the Government to the inhabitants of the district, have always refused to pay him although able to make payment. Being, himself, indebted to sundry persons, he prays that he be authorized to instruct his attorney, George Cochran, to recover said debt. Signed: C. Whipple. // N.O. 10 July 1793, the Governor of the Post of Natchez, will do justice to the petitioner, allowing his attorney to collect the debts due him, being money lent. Signed: Baron de Carondelet. // The persons named in the foregoing petitions will immediately pay the sums owing by them and making payments to George Cochran, who is authorized to that effect, and in default of which their property will be seized. Signed: Gayoso. // Sept. 23. Notified Thos. Rule. Sept. 28, notified James Saunders. // George Cochran represents that, in pursuance of the foregoing decree, the persons names Thomas Rule and James Saunders and Matthew White of this District, planters, have been notified to pay the sums owing by them, respectively, and petitions that the property may be appraised and sold. 8 Oct. 1793. // Order for same by Favrot. Same date. // Appraisers appointed: Thos. Wilkins and Antonio Gras. Negro "Louisa" and her son "Henry" $340. At public sale, both adjudged to Don Francisco Guettierez de Arroyo for $290. Negro woman adjudged to Don Simon de Arze for $290. From the above sales Benjamin Monsanto was paid $199, and Christopher Whipple $150, for which both receipted.

p. 273. Petition of James Elliot, of the Natchez District, planter, that he purchased of Sutton Banks a negro for $450, last spring, notwithstanding that the negro was not sound at the time of the said purchase. He hesitated to buy him, unless said Banks would engage to refund the purchase money in case his suspicions should be well founded. To which the seller agreed as will appear by the bill of sale hereunto annexed. Certificate is also annexed, which will serve to prove that the said negro has always been of little value, if not a burden, having but short intervals of apparent good health. Being anxious to cure him, the petitioner has used (p. 273) every means for this purpose, as well as medecine and rest. Notwithstanding, his disorder increased and toward the close of autumn, he died. Asks that Banks be compelled to refund the amount paid for said slave. Signed: James Elliott. 2nd March 1786. // 3rd March 1786. To be communicated: Grand-Pre. // Know all men by these presents that I, Sutton Banks, have sold to James Elliot a negro man, named "True-blue", said negro warranted against all claims, and for payment of whom I do hereby acknowledge to have received $450 and I do agree to take back the said negro at the said price at the expiration of one year provided he is not sound. March 12, 1785. Signed: Sutton Banks. Wit: Wm. Gilbert. // I do certify that I was overseer of James Elliot's plantation and slaves at Cole's Creek this year past and sometime last winter he brought home a negro named "true-blue" who was sick when he came and continued a short space of time sickly. He had a lameness in one side which unabled him very much. In the fall of the year he was ill for a long time and died. Signed James Jackson. 12 Dec. 1785.

p. 275. Bennet Truly versus Thomas Irwin. Bennet Truly, of the District, planter, represents that he gave sundry notes in obligations of various planters, inhabitants of the district, to Thomas Irwin in pay for some negroes purchased from him but the said Thomas Irwin, having left said obligations in the hands of other persons, who have not proceeded against said debtors, the said notes and obligations remain unpaid and your petitioner cannot compel payment, for want of the papers, he asks that Irwin be ordered to give an acquittance for the same, they amounting to $1100. 6 Feb. 1791. Signed: Bennet Truly. // Thomas Irwin will deliver to the petitioner the papers in the foregoing petition, that he may be enabled to recover the amounts thereof, otherwise the amount will be charged to him as cash received. If he has anything to acknowledge to the contrary let it be stated. Signed: Gayoso. // In answer to Mr. Truly's memorial of the 6th, Thomas Irwin states that Truly bought 4 negroes from him at 12 months' credit, for which he gave John Lum for security and mortgaged the negroes until paid. Last year when I learned that Mr. Lum was not able to pay his own debts, and Mr. Truly having sold one or more of the negroes, who were mortgaged, and sent them to Opelousas without my knowledge, rather than expose him for this action, I asked him for counter security and he gave me several obligations for tobacco, payable this year. Permit me to say that I do not think that any of those persons are ready to comply with their obligations as John and Richard Harrison are a part of these securities to be paid in Kentucky tobacco, to be brought down the river this year by John Harrison who has not yet arrived. If any of the others are ready to pay the amount of their security, I have to request that Your Excellency order them to deposit their tobacco in such place as you think proper, and if required I will give any security that their papers will be sent up from New Orleans by the first conveyance after my letter reached that place, which I shall write by Mr. Macarty's boat which goes next Saturday. I request that you will not exonerate Mr. Truly for his just debt for those negroes through the excuse of the papers of the counter security being in New Orleans as I am very near certain that the papers can be had here before any of the debtors are ready to pay. Signed: Thomas Irwin. 9th Feb. 1791.

p. 276. Richard King represents that in the time of the very unhappy revolution in this country, my father and uncle, Justus and Caleb King, were driven by the savages from their habitations and came to settle near the Fort; that Mr. De La Villebeuvre, who was then Commandant, placed them on land about 3 miles of said Fort, commonly called King's Ridge, where they settled under the immediate eye and protection of the Government and upon which they erected much and considerable improvement; that in the year 1789 Louis Valleret came to the country and after much importunity did pervail on the petitioner's uncle and father to sell him the said improvement, which they did as they thought it lawful to do so, having before their eyes many precedents, not only by the inhabitants but even of the Government having sold many improvements at public vendue. From which they could not conceive that they were doing wrong as it was the practice of the country and the Government. They sold it for $300 which the said Valleret agreed to pay, one-half in six months with property which he said was to be sent to him from the Illinois; the other half was to be paid in bricks a year afterwards, but no property has ever come from the Illinois and the bricks he made have been otherwise used, so petitioner's uncle and father have never received anything although four years have ellapsed since the said Valleret has had the place in his possession. During which time, he has suffered the buildings and fences to go to ruin for want of repair and has destroyed a great part of the timber, and finding he could not cultivate it or put it in repair, he has now abandonned it and in all probability it will be all in waste in a short time as he has no hands to put on it. Also when he bought the plantation, it was to remain mortgaged for payment, and if it were not paid for, it should revert to the sellers. Ask that Valleret pay for the use of the property and for the damage he has done to it. 25 June, 1793. Signed: Richard King. // That Valleret be notified to pay the petitioner or return the plantation to him, but the petitioner cannot take possession thereof until the crop has been gathered. He may, however, work, the land that is not in cultivation. Signed: Gayoso.

p. 277. Peter Walker versus Jemima Lewis. Jemima Lewis, widow of Abraham Thickston,* deceased, represents that her said husband at the time of his decease was indebted to different persons considerable sums of money, which she has paid and discharged, both in money and her own obligations, as will appear by the list of vouchers, handed herewith; that she has, at considerable expense and risk, performed a journey through the Wilderness to Kentucky in order to receive some property of her said husband, to enable her to discharge his debts, without being able to obtain anything whatever. Whereupon, she asks that her share of his estate and the debts that she has discharged, whether in cash or by her own assumption, as also a reasonable and sufficient allowance for her expenses may be secured to her as her part, and that the remainder may be divided among her said husband's creditors. Signed: Jemima Lewis. 18 June 1793. // Messrs. Moore and Walker will examine the memorial of Jemima Lewis and make me a report thereof, this being one that lies within their inspection as agents of the recovery of debts in this district. // In consequence of a decree pending on a petition presented by Jemima Lewis, dated 18th instant, Peter Walker, as one of greatest creditors of Abraham Thickston, called on Jemima Lewis in order that she, as possessor of the effects of the late Thickston, her deceased husband, should give a statement thereof, which she refused unless the creditors would agree to reimburse her a sum of upward of $500 which she pretends to have advanced to her late husband and paid on his accounts since his decease . . . . . . Her late husband was considered a man of property. She demands also a reasonable allowance for her expenses in going to Kentucky . . . . . . Petitioner requests that Jemima Lewis be obliged without delay to give up negro man named Francois, belonging to the estate and acknowledged as such by herself, and that William Curtis who sold the plantation to said Thickston be obliged to appear and declare on oath by whom and in what manner he was paid for the said plantation. Signed: Peter Walker. 20 June 1793. // Jemima Lewis answers Mr. Walker's charges that she possessed no property before her marriage to Abraham Thickston, she offers as proof that she did possess some stock and a good crop of her own, the certificate hereto annexed, they being the papers marked 1 and 7. In Paper 8, to a gift deed to her children Abraham Thickston was a witness, and he also signed a certificate that she had a right to make the said gift deed. The property was hers before her marriage to Thickston. This deed of gift was to answer the purpose of a will. The property was and is not yet delivered but reserved by the petitioner for her children, she conceding herself, in this case, as their natural guardian. It would be very hard if her and her children's property be applied to said Thickston's debts, when it was acquired by herself through industry and frugality, particularly when the said Thickston left property of his own in Kentucky sufficient to pay his debts if his creditors will apply for it. The negro mentioned by Mr. Walker was bought in partnership between said Thickston and petitioner, etc. In regard to the tract of land which the petitioner did purchase and pay for herself, it is her own property except a small balance due to William Curtis as will appear by the said credits. She has proof of these. Signed: Jemima Lewis. 5 Sept. 1793. // p. 281. Jemima Lewis's evidences: (1) Natchez, 31 Aug. 1793. I do hereby certify that the widow Hutsel bought of me in the year 1786 4 cows and calves, for which I received cash in hand paid from her. Signed: Minor. // I hereby certify that the Widow Hutsel had horses, cows and hogs in the year 1784, of her own property. Signed: Samuel Heady. // (2) This will certify that some time in the fall 1786, I sold and delivered to Jemima Hutsel two cows and old calves for which she paid me. Aug. 27, 1793. Signed: John Girault. // (3) This is to certify that Widow Hutsel bought two cows and calves and a heifer and paid me for same in the year 1785, and one that she received of me the same year on James Wilson's account. Signed: Christian Bingaman. Aug. 27, 1793. // (4) This is to certify that about five years ago I bargained and sold to Mrs. Hutsel two cows and calves, branded, for which she paid me in sewing. Signed: Adam Bingaman. 30 Aug. 1793. // (5) We do hereby certify that this woman before she married Thickston had a good crop of corn and tobacco through her own industry, besides other properties. We believe she had 500 bu. of corn. Signed: Simpson Holmes, William Glasscock, Jere Hooper, and Stern Steuben. // (6) This is to certify that in the year 1787, (I bought) seven heads of hogs, at $3 per hog, for which I gave my note to Thickston and when that note became due I found it in the hands of William Henderson. I asked him how he got it and he told me that he got it from William Curtis which said note I paid to the said Henderson. Aug. 26, 1793. Signed: Arthur Cobb. // (7) I, William Glasscock, do certify that in the year 1787, I knew Mr. Thickston to have 12 heads of horses in his possession, which horses were called hers and I knew not of any person claiming them. Signed William Glasscock. // I certify that seven years ago I knew Mrs. Hutsel to have a considerable number of cattle and hogs and three or four horses, which was before I ever knew Abraham Thickston. Aug. 27, 1793. Signed: William Cooper. // I do hereby certify that Mrs. Lewis had horses, cows and hogs of her own before she married Mr. Fickston and I never knew any other person to have claim to them afterward. Signed: Stephen Stephenson. // This may certify to all whom it may concern that I, Samuel Swayze, did about the latter end of the summer in 1784 cart two loads of household furniture for Mrs. Hutsel, now Mrs. Lewis, from the Natchez landing to Second Creek. Signed: Samuel Swayze. // (8) West Florida, Dist. of Natchez. I, Jemima Hutsel, do given grant and bestow to my son, Absolem Hutsel, five cows and one mare, together with their increase, to my daughter, Catherine Hutsel, five cows and one mare. I, Abraham Thickston, do hereby acknowledge that the stock she has given to her children was her own property before I married her. I also do quit claim any title to the same. Oct. 8, 1788. Signed: Abraham Thickston. Wit: Paul Glasscock. // Statement of the monies paid by Jemima Lewis to the creditors of the estate of Abraham Thickston, her former husband. To money paid Stephen Minor, Henderson and Short, etc. Total $505.

p. 283. Roger Dixon versus his creditors. Roger Dixon petitions that he finds it very difficult to settle with Mr. Odam although he has done everything in his power to effect it, and has waited upon him so long to come to a decision. The petitioner knows no other action than that of offering the whole of his property to be disposed of for the payments of his debts. 24 March 1794. Signed: Roger Dixon. // A meeting of all the creditors will take place at Mr. Wilkins' who shall preside at it. Signed: Gayoso. // 4th April 1794. Meeting of the creditors. A suggestion by Mr. Dixon, that he mortgage his plantation on which he is now living, also his negroes, which he lists, all natives of Virginia, twelve in all. His principal object in making this proposition is to allow him to sell his property to the best advantage, to satisfy the whole of his obligations, that at the expiration of the present year, on the 31st of January, provided a satisfactory arrangement has not been previously made, he asks that the same may be brought to public sale. The plantation on which he now lives is under mortgage to David Odam, for security of his immediate demand, but he has agreed to the plan. Natchez. 4 Apr. 1794. Signed Roger Dixon, David Odam, Clark and Rees, Thomas Wilkins, David Ferguson for Reed and Ford, and R. and G. Cochran. // 5 Apr. 1794. I do approve of the foregoing agreement of Roger Dixon with his creditors and the mortgage will accordingly be drawn, by which he gives to his creditors in foregoing agreement to be paid in January next ensuing, with interest. Signed: David Odam, Clark and Rees, John O'Connor, Reed and Ford, Thos. Irwin, Maurice Stacpoole, Melling Woolley, Stephen Minor, Thos. Wilkins, Robert and Geo. Cochran. Statement of what Dixon owes and what he has. His plantation is in the Dist. of Villa Gayoso, b. by John Terry and John Holt. Signed: Roger Dixon.

p. 286. Parker Carradine versus John Williams. Complaint of Parker Carradine against John Williams. The defense by John Williams. We do not find that any suit has been instituted nor exists for the recovery of certain negroes from Parker Carradine, but he, Parker Carradine, apprehends from reports circulated from an order issued by Your Excellency respecting payment to be made for them, a claim for certain negroes which he, Parker Carradine, purchased from Preston Tinsley wherefore said Parker Carradine alleges that he made these purchases in consequence of the insurance from John Williams that the property thereof was in said Preston Tinsley; that John Williams is going to leave the country and Parker Carradine views are to compel Williams to secure to him the property of said negroes before he leaves the country. // The undersigned received testimony on oath that, previous to the purchase of the negroes by Parker Carradine from Preston Tinsley, that John Williams did advise the said Carradine to make the purchases, that the property was in Tinsley and he might with safety make it, but we do not find that Parker Carradine did or at any time intended to make any use of this declaration, except to quiet his fears and apprehensions . . . . . We do find in the possession of Parker Carradine several letters from Williams to Preston Tinsley, from which letters, it does appear that John Williams did actually consider the property of those negroes to be in Preston Tinsley, etc. Questions and answers. Q. Do you know anything regarding the sale of certain negroes by Tinsley to Parker Carradine? A. I do not know anything. But I received from Preston Tinsley, that he had purchased the negroes from his brother, part of the purchase he had paid in land and a part was yet owing. Q. Did you know anything of this sale of negroes from James Tinsley to Preston Tinsley before you came to this country? A. Nothing more than answered to the first query. Q. Do you know both or either of the witnesses to this bill of sale and did you see it signed? A. I do know persons of those names but do not recollect seeing these names written to the bill of sale. (This interrogation was of John Williams.) Have you ever had any private conversations with Preston Tinsley about the nature and extent of power to sell or dispose of the slaves. A. Tinsley informed me that he had an opportunity of buying to advantage and could pay his brother the sum that remained due and keep a handsome profit for his own use. Q. Did you know, before you came to this country, of the design of Preston Tinsley coming to this country with these negroes? A. Preston Tinsley's intention, I understood from himself, was to settle in Cumberland but do not recollect a word that ever passed between James Tinsley and myself on the subject of letting his brother have the negroes. Q. Did Tinsley, at that time, communicate to you his intention of intrusting this property to his brother, Preston? Do you know James Tinsley's handwriting? A. I have in my possession James Tinsley's attested handwriting and would produce but I would not swear to his handwriting. Q. When Parker Carradine applied to you for information respecting Preston Tinsley's right to sell the negroes, did you expect that any future demand would be made by James Tinsley? A. I did not expect that any demand would ever be made. Q. Do you judge the name of James Tinsley on the bill now before you to be the handwriting of said Tinsley? A. From the comparison, I am inclined to believe that it is not his handwriting. // Upon the whole, the undersigned are of the opinion that there was a length of time sufficient between Tinsley's coming to this country with those negroes and his making a sale of them to Parker Carradine to have effected any fraud by the said Preston Tinsley, free communication having at all times been open between this country and America and as Parker Carradine's purchase was fair, open and for a valuable consideration, he ought to hold the negroes in question. It does not appear, to the undersigned that John Williams had absolute complicity. Signed G. Cochran, Thomas Wilkins and Ezekiel Forman. // Having examined the foregoing award and all the papers thereto, I do declare that Mr. John Williams should not be answerable for the sale of the negroes from Preston Tinsley to Parker Carradine but that James Tinsley, having left the said negroes in the peaceful possession of his brother, Preston Tinsley, for a long state of time, for which they were universally looked upon as his own property, the sale by him to Mr. Parker Carradine shall be valid and in full force, and should James Tinsley make appear in due time a lawful claim against the estate of Preston Tinsley, he shall have appropriate dividend with the other creditors of said Preston Tinsley. 7 Apr. 1794, at Govt. House at Natchez. Manuel Gayoso de Lemos.

p. 289. Paulina Ferguson versus Elizabeth Truly. Petition of Paulina Ferguson that the heirs of the estate of Samuel Burch, deceased, had the honor of petitioning on the 28th, that they had previously presented one on the same subject, in May 1792, setting forth their claim to said estate in possession of James Truly and their mother, the admx., pointing out men by whom the property in question might be fully proved to belong to the said estate when Your Excellency was pleased to say that it was a matter of some moment and would require some time to consider and that you would give particular attention to it and they might rely on justice being done. Your pet. represents that this estate has been in their possession for near fifteen years and not accounted for as detailed by the sketch already given Your Excellency; asks for a partition, especially as your petitioner, who has been married eleven years and has five small children and can never stand in more need of her part than at present; that Mr. Truly and her mother have often said, especially lately when the negroes are likely to be sold, they would give up a certain wench, named "Sal", and her children to the heirs after the affair of Mr. Moore was settled, but as that matter is in a manner satisfied and the negroes not to be sold they are for keeping everything by bringing charges against the heirs. But when he is pushed for money, he will then say the property belongs to the estate. Your petitioners think that it is hard that he should have sole enjoyment of it any longer when he has told Your Excellency that it belongs to the estate, and the heirs have great want of it, myself in particular. Signed: Paulina Ferguson. Feb. 24, 1794. // I do hereby commission Mr. William Murray to examine into the matter represented in this petition, and the parties are hereby ordered to produce any documents or information that sd Wm. Murray may require. Signed Manuel Gayoso de Lemos. // p. 290. In obedience to Your Excellency's order, in the petition of William Ferguson, I have the parties concerned before me. The most essential document, namely an authenticated inventory of the property left by the deceased Burch is not obtainable, having been lodged in the records of Pensacola, and is now God knows where. I have carefully considered such papers as were reproduced and as far as I am capable of judging on them, I am of the opinion that the agreement herewith transmitted to Your Excellency is amply just and equitable on the part of the administrators and is agreeable to the petitioner as well as the other heirs of sd Burch, if present. The parties have signed mutual receipts and acquittances, herewith also. If this amicable settlement meets with your approbation, the parties wish the same to be entered of record. I have heard that James Truly always treated the children of said Burch with paternal care and regard. Signed: J.W. Murray. // Memorandum of an agreement made 15th April 1794, between Elizabeth Truly, administratrix of the estate of Samuel Burch, deceased, and heirs of said estate, in manner following: The administratrix, by this agreement, does put the said heirs in quiet and peaceful possession of the following negro children, belonging to said estate, namely, to Paulina Ferguson, dau. of said Samuel Burch, one negro boy, named "George", abt. 5 years old, to John Burch, a mulatto girl, named "Juliet", aged abt 7, to William Burch, one negro by the name of "Lewis", abt. 3 years, to Washington Burch, one mulatto girl, "Daphne", abt. 1 year old, to Samuel Burch, the youngest heir, the first child that a certain wench named "Sal" may have, and after then the said wench to remain with Mrs. Truly until her natural death, belonging to her said heirs, and what increase the said wench may have in the meanwhile, to be given up to the said heirs when demanded, clear of all charges for raising such increase, but if anyone of the said heirs be going out of this said government, the said wench should be valued and such part or parts paid by Mr. Truly or the said Elizabeth Truly or in case of default the said wench to be sold for the purpose. But as John Burch, son of the said Elizabeth Truly, is gone to America, it is thought that he will bring with him a certain negro wench, named "Maria", left by the said Samuel Burch in South Carolina. In that case, the said Maria and her increase will be divided equally among the said heirs and the said Elizabeth Truly's children by her last marriage. Signed: Elizabeth Truly, James Truly, and ack. before me, 30 April 1794, J.W. Murray. // At the Post of Natchez, 16 May 1794. I, Manuel Gayoso de Lemos, having read and examined the foregoing agreement, do hereby approve the same and order that the same be deposited in the Archives with other documents in the case. Signed. // 15 April 1794. Received of Paulina Ferguson, John Burch, William Burch, Washington Burch and Samuel Burch, heirs of the estate of Samuel Burch, deceased, the full satisfaction for their raising, clothing, etc., since their father's death, and for all other accounts. Signed: Elizabeth Truly, James Truly. Dist. of Villa Gayoso. // Above receipt ack. before W. Murray 30 Apr. 1794. // Received of Mrs. Elizabeth Truly, admx. of the estate of Samuel Burch, decd., full satisfaction for our respective shares of said estate agreeable to the agreement made by the said Elizabeth Truly with the heirs of the estate, which when complied with will be in full for same. Signed: Paulina Ferguson, William Ferguson, William Burch, Washington Burch. Ack. before me, 30 Apr. 1794. Signed: W. Murray. // Received from Paulina Ferguson, full satisfaction for a negro girl named "Zilpha", bought from us in 1790, then belonging to the estate of Samuel Burch, decd., which property we warrant and ever defend, etc. Signed: Elizabeth Truly, James Truly. Apr. 15, 1794.

p. 293. Patrick McDermot versus Daniel Burnet and Richard Lord. Pet. of Richard Lord showeth that your petitioner, an inhabitant of the Government of Natchez, residing in Bayou Pierre, pursuant to an order of the 5th inst., is persuaded that your order and decree disrespects the rights of any individual and that a true representation of the case between your pet. and Mr. Patrick McDermot would be acceptable to Your Excellency. The demand that McDermot made on your petitioner is for services the said McDermot made at the saw-mill a considerable length of time before your petitioner made the purchase thereof; that as this is a charge made before the property came into your petitioner's hands, and that he never did directly or indirectly employ the said McDermot in any service of the kind, for which he makes the demand, he hopes Your Excellency will not consider him at all responsible to McDermot, etc. July 15, 1794. Signed: Richard Lord. // p. 294. Natchez, July 23, 1794. Mr. George Cochran will appear at Govt. House tomorrow, the 24th, to give evidence required in the foregoing petition. Col. Bryan's letter of July 18th, giving evidence, will be hereunto annexed. Signed: Gayoso. // Personally appeared George Cochran, who being duly sworn, said that previous to the time Richard Lord purchased from Daniel Burnet half of the saw-mill and plantation, on Bayou Pierre, the latter expressed to the deponent that he would not give to the said Lord any advice that might prevent the purchase that he then contemplated, to which the deponent replied that he should not unless applied to for that purpose, in which case he would give it. A short time subsequent to this, Lord did apply to deponent for his advice and then informed the deponent that one of the conditions on which he expected to make the purchase was that he would have the right of returning the said saw-mill and plantation in case he could not make the payment, forfeiting only the improvement he should make, etc. Later, he heard John Burnet say that Mr. Lord had made the purchase for $2500 without any reservation or condition. Signed: G. Cochran. Wit: Estevan Minor, John Girault. Before Gayoso de Lemos. // p. 296. 18 July 1794. I have the honor to acknowledge the recipt of Your Excellency's favor, of the 16th inst., and in answer, do confidentially assure you that no objections by either Lord or Burnet were made in my hearing, at the time of signing, and there is no studied ambiguity of expression in that agreement. It is couched in terms as familiar as any in the English language and which the merest capacity might readily understand. I remember perfectly well that each article of the agreement was distinctly read to the parties and when finsihed the question was asked if it fully expressed their meaning and their assent was given before I proceeded to another. After it was finished and they both agreed that there was nothing more to be added, I read it over agin. I then left it with them and desired that they would examine it with attention as it was an affair of considerable consequence, which they did and executed it without any reserve whatever. I am persuaded that Mr. Lord did not, at that time, have the slightest intention of returning the property but that he thought that he had made an advantageous bargain. I protest to Your Excellency that I never made use of any argument of any kind to induce Mr. Lord to sign the agreement, that I felt myself in no way interested in the event, nor shall I be in any manner affected by Your Excellency's final determination in this business. When I charged Lord with having misrepresented my agency in this business, he declared himself nowise positive that I had made use of such language. I have returned the papers. Signed: P. Bryan Bruin. // A copy of the contract to be added to the proceedings and then a decree will be issued. // Patrick McDermot represents that he has done a great deal of work to the mill on Bayou Pierre, now the property of Daniel Burnet and Richard Lord, that he has presented several petitions soliciting the payment for said work, not being able to receive any but evasive answers from both parties, etc. Signed: Patrick McDermot, 23 July 1794. // The claim of Mr. McDermot being just, the proprietors of the mill will immediately pay him, in default of which sufficient property will be executed to pay the debt. Let parties be notified by John Ferguson, constable, who will make to me a return of the proceedings. // Aug. 1, 1794. Bayou Pierre. Presented the within decree to Messrs. Lord and Burnet, proprietors of the mill, who say it is not in their power to pay immediately. Then executed a negro wench, the property of Mr. Daniel Burnet, aged about 21 years, named "Betty", also executed a negro boy, abt. 16, named "George", the property of Richard Lord, for the debt of McDermot. // Articles of agreement entered into the 8th Oct. 1792 between Daniel Burnet and Richard Lord. Daniel Burnet, for and in consideration, previously recorded. // Natchez, July 24, 1794. Richard Lord will comply with the tenor of his agreement, which is expressed in the plainest terms and he makes no objection to them, jointly with Daniel Burnet, which articles were sent me to be approved and recorded. By depositions of P. Bryan Bruin and George Cochran there papers there was no fraud. Signed: Manuel Gayoso de Lemos.

p. 299. Sarah Smith versus James Smith. Sarah Phips, the wife of James Smith, of Bayou Sara, sets forth that her husband without any reason or provocation has driven her from him with two helpless children, and has taken every means of support from her and the children, although she has greatly contributed by her industry to acquire what little property they have. He has taken everything from her and left her and the children in want and misery. After having driven her away, he has destroyed the property greatly and ran away himself. During his absence, Your Excellency was pleased to permit the petitioner to take what property that was left into her possession which she did and took care of it and was using her endeavors to bring up the children to be good members of society, but at his return, he has again banished the petitioner with the two youngest children, one of which is sick, etc. 3rd June 1792. // Francis Poussett will examine into the premises and act according to justice. Gayoso de Lemos. // Articles of agreement between James Smith, of the Dist. of Natchez, and Sarah, his wife. For divers causes and mutual consent, we, from this time forward, are to remain and live apart and separate each from the other, having no dependence on each other for livelihood or things of this world. We mutually agree that the said James Smith shall have henceforward solely the care and direction of their two eldest children, Prestwood and John, and it is also mutually agreed that the youngest child, named "Nancy", shall remain with her mother, the said Sarah Smith, until she attains the age of 6 years, with this promise that said Sarah give sufficient security that the child shall not be removed to any part out of this district. It is further agreed that if sd James Smith is not satisfied with the way the child is brought up by the mother after six years he shall be at full liberty to take the said child under his own care. As to their worldly affairs, the said Sarah shall receive one horse and saddle, three cows and calves, 25 bu. of corn, and 500 lbs. of pork, and she, having received this and being fully satisfied, all other property shall remain entirely to James Smith, without any claim whatsoever on her part. Signed: James Smith, Sarah (X) Smith. Wit: David Mitchell, Philetus Smith, Jacob Earhart. // p. 301. This to certify that about a year ago, James Smith came to my house and said he and his wife had parted and asked me to witness an article of agreement, concluded by them. When his wife came to sign it, it seemed very much against her will and she said it was to satisfy him that she did so. Natchez. June 14, 1794. Signed David Mitchell. // I certify that about 18 months ago James Smith told me that he and his wife, by mutual consent, had agreed to part and desired me to witness an article of agreement, which article his wife appeared very unwilling to sign and said that she did it only to satisfy him. Signed: Jacob Earhart. // This is to certify that I, Samuel Phips, of Natchez, do bind myself in the penal sum of $100 to James Smith, of same place, to see that his child, Nancy, shall not be removed out of this district until she shall attain six years of age, also that if he is not satisfied with the manner of its bringing up, I bind myself to deliver her when she shall so attain that age, to the said Smith or his order. 2? Sept. 1792. Signed: Samuel (X) Phips. Wit: Jacob Earhart, Philetus Smith. // To Francis Poussett, Esq. Alcalde of the Dist. of Bayou Sara. The petition which was sent in by Sarah Phips, to whom I was married, to His Excellency, asking to be separated from me, and to be allowed a portion of the property with which God blessed me, being referred to you, I beg leave to detail to you the circumstances which render the separation a blessing, the better to enable you to decide. Sarah Phips was an orphan brought up by Mrs. Hutchins from the age of 8 or 9 years until she was 12 or 13. She then went to her brother, Samuel Phips, where she lived until the time I placed my affection on her and addressed and married her. For my part it was a marriage of love, she being without friends, without money, even destitute of clothing and indebted for $31. To manifest my affection for this woman I made my wife, I purchased for her a suit of clothes and afterwards paid the above sum to her creditors, with as much cheerfulness as if I had contracted the debt myself. My sole study was to improve by every act, attention and indulgence the love of my wife, and we lived near three years as happy as any couple in the country, no bickerings, nor suspicions of infidelity disturbed our conjugal happiness. Then my wife grew sullen and abusive and on the most trifling occasions called me dirty names. This change in my unfortunate wife's conduct distressed me beyond conception until at last I discovered that she had engaged in an intrigue with a neighbor who had seduced her and to whom I believe she had prostituted herself, etc. Eventually I resolved with pain to exercise my authority and leave her, etc. Whatever be the decision as to the division of my property between us, I shall fully submit. [Gives an inventory of what he has. One of the items he gave her on separation was 400 lbs of cotton owing him by her brother, Elijah.] Signed: James Smith. 19 June 1794. // Bayou Sara. p. 305. Dist. of Natchez. Sarah Smith, wife of James Smith attended by her two brothers, Samuel Phipps and Elijah Phipps, who gave the following answers to the questions put to them. She did not see the petition to His Excellency before it was presented. She wrote to Mr. Girault containing the substance of it, which her brother, Samuel, took to Natchez. Petition was read to her and she acknowledged it to be what she wished to say. She has been married about nine years. . . . . (details of what he had when they were married) . . . For two or three years they were only tolerably happy. Their tempers did not suit. She worked in the field when he went abroad. She did not separate from him willingly, although they lived in great dispute. She remains with her two children at the house of her brother-in-law, William Joyner, wholly dependent. Signed: Sarah Smith, Elijah Phipps, Samuel (P) Phips, John Wall. Before Francisco Poussett, alcalde. // Jan. 18th. James Smith attended and desired me to summons Henry Phipps and Samuel Phipps, also Joseph Miller, to be examined. // p. 306. June 23. Mr. James Smith attended with Henry Phipps and Joseph Miller. Henry Phipps made answer to the sundry questions put to him by James Smith, on oath, as follows; He did not know his sister, Sarah Smith, was in debt when she married. He knows his sister to be of a very hasty temper. He may have said he did not think they would live long together. He cannot say that his sister parted freely from her husband. She cried and was very loathe to part with her children. He acknowledged that Mr. James Smith did always treat him and their whole family as a friend. He did say that Mrs. Smith, Mr. James Smith's mother, would be a very proper person to bring up his 3rd child, Nancy, about 4 years old. He signed with a mark before Poussett. . . . Declaration of Joseph Miller. He is sorry to be called upon this occasion. He actually did memtion without intention that he does not think that Mr. William Collins was sober at the time. Joseph (X) Miller. // Mr. Poussett, Sir: This is to inform you that Mr. William Collins and myself were talking together and among other things he told me that James Smith's wife told him that she would leave her husband and children and go with him over the world. This I am willing to swear if I am called on. Joseph Miller. Wit: Justus Andrews. // List of sales of cattle, hogs and tools made by Sarah Smith the eight days of James Smith's absence, among items " a 2-yr old heifer for Anna Killian's spinning wheel". // 27 June 1794. Having examined the foregoing documents by which I find it impossible for them to live together in peace, and I do hereby commission Francis Poussett to take an inventory of all their property, real and personal. From the mass, James Smith is to have the value of what he had when he married, the remainder to be equally divided between the husband and wife. Guardians are to be appointed for the children, who will be heirs of both their father and mother. They are to decide among themselves with whom the children shall live. A regular article of separation is to be signed by the parties. The whole of the proceedings to be lodged in the office of this government. Signed: Manuel Gayoso. // July 1st 1794. Came a constable with a letter to Mrs. Smith at Natchez to acquaint her with the decree. Mrs. Smith and her brother, William Joyner, to attend. // William Smith, brother of James Smith, attended in behalf of his brother, who says he is very ill and cannot attend and requested me to act for him in virtue of a power of attorney. // Granted. Francis Poussett. Mr. Daniel Ogden and Eusebius Bushnell were appointed to go to the plantation of James Smith and there survey the stock and utensils and appraise the same, which they did accordingly and made the annexed return thereof. // July 1st. William Smith, Sarah Smith and Mr. Joyner, attended, as Mr. Bushnell, John Lovelace and John Wall also, as assisting witnesses. Mr. Lejeune being sick, Mr. Smith proves his brother's power of attorney, annexed. Proceeded to the appraisements of James Smith's property before and at the time of his marriage, a negro not included as he disposed of him in the Indian Nation and produced nothing in his place. William Smith had a letter from his brother annexed. The appraisement of the plantation and crop was made by Mr. Wall and Mr. Lovelace and added to the general appraisement. The articles of separation were then read and signed by Sarah Smith and sent to James Smith to be signed before a witness. William Smith is presented by his brother to His Excellency as guardian for the two eldest children and security for his property. // James Smith, of the Dist. of Buffalo, for divers good causes, have ordained my loving brother, William Smith, of this Government, to be my true and lawful attorney for me and in my name, etc. Signed in presence of John Lovelace and Eusebius Bushnell. // Bayou Sara, July 9, 1794. Personally appeared John Lovelace and Eusebius Bushnell, witnesses to above power and proved same. // Power of attorney accepted. Signed: William Smith same witnesses. Before Francis Poussett, alcalde. // Dear Sir: I understand that you want to know what property I left at Tombigbee. I left a small horse, my clothes and some small implements for the work of my trade. That is all. I have no assurance that I my ever get them again. As I could not immediately meet with employment, I was at some expense for my sustenance and was forced to sell my negro boy. I have since the inventory recollected that I was possessed of before I was married a negro not in the inventory of what I had at that time. Signed James Smith. // The inventory of his possessions before marriage amounts to $747. // Inventory of property of James Smith, of Buffalo Creek. Amounts to $866. // Mrs. Smith says there are three horses not accounted for, etc. etc. // From our instructions, we did not consider that we had anything to do with the land and crop. Signed Daniel Ogden,

Eusebius Bushnell, appraisers. // Articles of separation bet. James Smith and Sarah Smith. [Long. . . . . as to their children, the two oldest boys, Prestwood, aged 7, and John, aged 5, remain with their father, and the two youngest, Nancy, a girl of 3, and James, aged 18 months, are to remain with their mother, subject to the Governor's decree, with guardian and security of property.] James Smith signed, Sarah (X) Smith. Same witnesses. Before Francis Poussett, alcalde. July 9, 1794. William Smith security for his brother, James Smith. // James Smith apprentices his son Prestwood Smith, being 7 years oldMarch 1st, 1794, to his brother, Wm. Smith, until he is 21 years old, to learn the art of silversmith, during which time his master's secrets he shall keep. Matrimony he shall not contract neither shall he absent himself at any time without leave. William Smith to give him two years schooling and teach him the art of his calling. Signed by both. July 9, 1794. // July 8, 1794. Indenture. James Smith of the Dist. of Buffalo, the Government of Natchez, bound his son, John Smith, as an apprentice unto William Smith, of same government, until he is 21 years old, he being 5 years 8 Sept. 1793, to learn the art and mystery of a silversmith, etc. same as above. // Samuel Phipps presented himself and makes bond as security for Sarah Phipps. p. 314. William Joyner appointed guardian of the two youngest children by Sarah Smith, named Nancy and James. 24 July 1794. Signed by William Joyner. Wit: Joseph Vidal and John Girault. Before Manuel Gayoso de Lemos, Commandant. // Division and delivery of property. Receipt and discharge of Samuel Phipps for his sister. Signed Francis Poussett, alcalde.

p. 315. His creditors versus William Henderson. Peter Walker, an agent for the creditors of this district, and John O'Connor, as the greatest creditor of the late William Henderson, planter, represent that, having had certain information of the decease of the above-mentioned William Henderson, we think it our duty to have an inventory of the estate made immediately, in order that it may not be embezzled, of which we are very apprehensive. We ask to be authorized to take the above-mentioned inventory, as agent and greatest creditor. 18 April 1793. Signed: Peter Walker, John O'Connor. // Granted. Same date. The documents to be returned attested by two witnesses to be present at the proceedings. Signed: Manuel Gayoso de Lemos. // In virtue of the foregoing decree, we, Peter Walker and John O'Connor, attended at the dwelling house of the late William Henderson, accompanied by Mr. Joseph Bernard and Mr. George Fitzgerald, as witnesses, and having applied to Dorothy, the widow, for a statement of the property left in her hands by her late husband when he left the country, she gave in the following account: One tract of land situate on the Bluff, about two leagues northeast of Fort Panmure, containing 800 acres, with house and improvements, on which she and her family now dwell, (the above tract mortgaged to Mr. James Carrick, merchant in N.O.); one tract of land on the Homochitto, 500 acres, on which there is a ferry, authorized by the government; one tract on Bayou Pierre, 400 acres, on which there is likewise a ferry; three tracts situate at the Big Black, one, on which there is a ferry, 250 acres; another 250 acres, and another 200 acres; four negroes, horses, cattle, and hogs, and the following notes, numbered as in the margin: Mordecai Richards, William Robinson, Soloman Whitley, William Atchinson, Abraham Mayes, William Kelsey, Edmund Quirk, Samuel Head, William Owens, Samuel Murphy, Stephen Minor, Stephen Minor's order on Nathaniel Tomlinson, other papers, etc., tools, household furniture, kitchen furniture and milk-house untensils. Further, Mr. Burrel Stroud said that when William Henderson died in Kentucky, he had in his possession several obligations and other effects, and that they remained in the hands of Capt. James Morrison, who is expected down very shortly. Above inventory certified by Peter Walker, John O'Connor, Joseph Bernard and George Fitzgerald. 22 Apr. 1793. // Obligations in the hands of John O'Connor where they were lodged by the late William Henderson before his departure from this country where they still remain. These were by Moses Armstrong, Wm. Bassett, Christy Bolling, Samuel Heady, William Barnett, Daniel Burnet, Gibson Clark, George Cochran, Jacob Cobun, Louis Charboneau, William Cheney, Thomas Evans, John Farquhar, John Ferguson, Benjamin Grubb, John Burnet, John Booth, George Bailey, Thomas Beans, Charles Carter, Waterman Crane, Silas Chambers, William Curtis, John Chambers, Isaac Fyffe, John Ford and Robt. Miller, Samuel Gibson, James Glasscock, Ezekiel Hoskinson, Margaret Harman, Thos. Hubbard, Ralph Humphreys, Nathaniel Ivy, Joseph Dove, Thomas Jordan, Joseph King, Justus King, William Kelsey, Thos. Kelly, James Lobdal, James Leyton, Richard Miller, John Montgomery, Roswell Mygatt, Thos. Nash, Francis Nailor, John Nailor, John Newton, John Ormsby, William Oglesby, William Owens, Ebenezer Potter, Reuben Proctor, John Peters, Llewellen Price, John Proctor, Mordecai Richards, Jeremiah Routh, Martin Ramsey, Stephen Richards, Archibald Rea, Cornelius Shaw, Lucius Smith, Elijah Smith, Ebenezer Smith, Ephraim Story, James Smith, Michael Squire, William Smith, William Tabor, William Vaucheret, Melling Woolley, John Williams. I certify that the above obligations are those sent to me at New Orleans in 1791 by the late William Henderson. May 19, 1793. Signed: John O'Connor. // To His Excellency, the Governor, Mr. William Thompkins, present owner of the plantation on which the late William Henderson's family resided, has requested that the stock belonging to the estate, being very troublesome, be disposed of in order that his crop be no longer endangered therefrom; that it be appraised and sold. Signed Peter Walker. July 16, 1794. // Same day. Joseph Bernard and George Fitzgerald, planters of the district, are appointed appraisers of the property of William Henderson, decd., as prayed for in the foregoing petition. // Total value of said stock $600. // Sale ordered of same. // Post of Natchez, 28 July, 1794. At the plantation of the late Wm. Henderson, have proceeded with the sale of the cattle, no bidders appeared. // 8 Aug. 1794. Sale took place. Buyers: Don Pedro Walker, Ezekiel Forman, for $354: Sale continued. Cattle sold for $379. Concluded 10 Aug. 1794.

p. 320. Andrew Beall versus the executors of John Hartley. Petition of Andrew Beall shows that some time last fall John Hartley, decd., being at this place under the doctor's hands, sold to your petitioner a plantation on St. Catherine's Cr. adj. his place, in consideration of which your petitioner was to pay the said Hartley $200 in the spring and the balance which was $200 more in twelve months. One of his executors, Christian Harman, knowing the circumstances, after Hartley's death, requested Mr. Cady Raby to ask the petitioner whether he intended to keep the place, and the petitioner positively told Mr. Raby, in the presence of John Freeland and Robert Holloway, that it was his determination to keep it, of which Mr. Raby informed Mr. Harman, and he appeared well pleased. Some time later, Mr. Harman saw Raby and informed him that he had seen Jesse Hamilton, another executor, and had informed him of the sale and he was well pleased and told him to tell petitioner to take possession as soon as it was convenient to him. In consequence of which, he sent crews on the fields to commence plowing, and Mr. Joseph Perkins ordered his people off, saying that he had purchased the land. Petitioner understood that Mr. Perkins had applied to Harman for the place but was told that it was sold to him. Natchez, 11 March 1794. Signed: Andrew Beall. // Natchez, March 15, 1794. The executives of the estate of Mr. Hartley will fulfill the bargain that was standing between said Hartley and Mr. Andrew Beall, and the constable, Wm. Gorman, will notify Mr. Perkins not to interfere in this business, being by no means authorized to do it. Signed: Gayoso. // The petitioner and the executors of John Hartley will all appear at Govt. House, with all their evidences, on Saturday next, 17th instant, to proceed to a termination of this affair. // Personally appeared Christian Harman, on oath, declares that some time after Mr. Hartley's decease Jesse Hamilton advises the deponent to ask Mr. Beall if he chose to keep Mr. Hartley's plantation and if he did he might take possession of it, on paying $200 down and $200 next fall. Not seeing Mr. Beall, he sent him word by Mr. Raby, who some time afterwards informed him that Mr. Beall said he intended to keep the plantation, of this, the deponent informed Jesse Hamilton. Signed: Christian Harman. // Personally appeared George Freeland, who said he was present as claimed by Mr. Beall when Mr. Raby gave the above message to him. // Alex. Freeland swore that Mr. Beall's negro woman had said that Mr. Perkins' daughter had told her not to come back to the plantation as her father had bought it. Signed. // Jesse Hamilton, exr. of est of John Hartley, asks for the deposition of Polser Shilling to elucidate the contest. Polser Shilling, being ill, he asks that someone be sent to take his deposition. 17th May 1794. . Signed. // Mr. Jean Girault will go to the dwelling of Polser Shilling and take the deposition before two witnesses, and Joseph Perkins will appear on Wednesday next. // Jean Girault, in the present of Archibald Douglas and Christian Braxton, took the deposition of Polser Shilling, who although indisposed was of sound mind. He said that the last time that John Hartley, deceased, was at this place he remained some weeks sick at the deponent's plantation, and during which time he repeatedly requested the deponent to try to sell the plantation he had on St. Catherine's Cr. To this, the deponent asked why he did not sell it to Andrew Beall. He replied that Beall had often talked of buying it but had never come to any conclusion. He also wanted Mr. Cushing to buy it. He said that Hartley went immediately home and shortly afterward died; that Charles Carter desired the deponent to enquire of the said Hartley if he might live on the plantation another year on rent, which the deponent told Hartley, who said that if he did not sell it, Carter might have it one year more. But as a further proof that the said place was not sold by the said Hartley, he told the deponent on the very moment of his going away that if he did not sell the said plantation, he intended moving some of his own family down on it and keep on it a number of beeves to kill for public use. Signed: Polser Shilling. Witnesses above named. p. 324 The deposition of Joseph Perkins: Being duly sworn, he says that the late John Hartley, deceased, on his way home the last time he was at Natchez, did stop at the deponent's house and talking over the plantation the said Hartley had at St. Catherine's, he told the deponent that he intended to come down and live there himself and put his son to school and he would fence in a large part of it for 50 or 60 head of beeves which he would try to place for the use of the troops and the public, and when he had done this and put a cabin on it he would not sell it for $600 and he would never more rent to such people as Beall and Carter who would sooner fetch rails from the half-way hill than maul them. Signed: Joseph Perkins. // To Andrew Beall: The last time I saw you, you wanted my plantation. If you still want it come directly as

I have an offer for it. I am not able to ride else I should come myself. Please let me know. Signed: John Hartley. Jany. 12, 1794. // This is to certify that some time before Mr. Hartley died I was at his house and I wrote a letter to Mr. Andrew Beall. [As given above.] Signed: Isaac Rapalje. Bayou Pierre April 19, 1794. P.S. I am willing to make oath to the above, if required. I.R. // Bayou Pierre, 14 July, 1794. Mr. Isaac Rapalje, being duly sworn said about 4 days before the demise of John Hartley Sr., He asked him to write a letter in the name of said Hartley to Mr. Andrew Beall. [Same as in letter above.] p. 325. Natchez, April 13, Having duly considered the foregoing proceedings, and finding sufficient proof that a bargain really existed between the deceased John Hartley and Andrew Beall for the plantation in question, which nothing but John Hartley's death prevented from confirming and further as the executors, themselves, did confirm verbally said agreement, the exrs. of said estate are ordered, without delay, to confirm the title of said land to Andrew Beall, and exrs. are to pay the cost. Court charges: $45. // Then notified the acting exr. in this suit, Jesse Hamilton. Signed: J. Girault.

p. 326. Jacques Rapalje versus William Dunbar. Jacques Rapalje represents that he is informed that his father did mortgage a certain negro named "Joe" for the payment of a debt of $170 to the estate of Edgar Gallaudet and the execution has issued for the payment of the said mortgage. Petitioner desires to inform Your Excellency that the said negro is the property of the petitioner and that his father has no right or title in him and that the said mortgage was made without the said petitioner's knowledge or participation, for which reasons, he conceives it to be of no value. The petitioner would be willing to come to the assistance of his father but not at the sacrifice of his only negro, without whose service he would not be able to subsist, having already sacrificed four other slaves for his father's use, in this province. Besides he is bound for debt of $250 more for him. But there is a debt of $200 due to his father by Messrs. Perry and Fooy, had he asks that it be applied to the payment of this execution and that the mortgage be annulled. Signed: Jacques Rapalje. 17 Sept. 1793. // 18 Sept. 1793. The petitioner will produce the documents proving his claim to the said negro. Signed: Gayoso. // To the Commandant. Jacques Rapalje, eldest son of Garret Rapalje, represents, having given full power to his father to withdraw from his brother, Garret Rapalje, the property in this district to him belonging, and having been informed that his father has, without his knowledge, mortgaged a negro named "Joe", which said negro he had received from his said brother and to the petitioner belonging. He prays that Your Excellency will order a copy of the petition of his father to the Governor General of the Province and the Governor's decree thereon that he may prove his title to the said negro. Signed: Jacques Rapalje. Baton Rouge, 12 Oct. 1793. // Whereas the petition has been presented by Garret Ralapje against James Rapalje, his son, respecting the delivery of a plantation now in his possession, which said petition and the decree thereon are as follows: Garret Rapalje, of the Big Black in the Dist. of Natchez, now in the City, represents that his eldest son, James Rapalje, bought in his own name in 1775 from Wm. Marshall 500 arpents in the Dist. of Baton Rouge, which he settled with a number of white hands and some negroes which I had given to him and having continued thereon for the space of a year, and your petitioner having arrived in this country with another son, named Garret Rapalje, Jr., the eldest son returned to America on business and with the intent to bring out the whole of his family. Your petitioner also returned to American three or four months afterwards, but, war having taken place between the Americans and the British, could not obtain permission to return. Being sick at the time of my departure from hence, your petitioner left the plantation of his eldest son in the care of his other son, Garret, without making any conveyance to him of the said plantation and negroes, and the said Garret now refuses to restore possession of same. Asks that an order be granted to the Commandant at Baton Rouge compelling him to deliver the whole property, real and personal, belonging to James Rapalje, eldest son of the petitioner. Signed: Garret Rapalje. // A copy of the petition will be transmitted to Don Joseph Vahamonde, Commandant of the Dist. of Baton Rouge, with order that, after examination of said documents presented by the petitioner, he will do justice to the party and if a suit be instituted that he will return the instruments to the Tribunal. Signed: Estevan Miro. 20 Aug. 1790. Rafael Perdonno. Notary. // Same day. Notified Garret Rapalje. Rafael Perdonno. // As Commandant of Fort aforesaid, I certify that on 21 Sept. 1790, Garret Rapalje received from his son, Garret, on the division made of the property which was in his care in this district a negro lad, aged 12, named "Joe", 14 . . . 1793. Signed: Vahamonde. // To His Excellency the Governor Jacques Rapalje represents that he labors under many difficulties in his suit with Robert Dunbar, acting executor of the est. of Edgar Gallaudet, decd., for want of evidences which cannot be procured here and asks permission to have the contest decided at Baton Rouge before Capt. Vahamonde, Commandant of that Post, who was ordered by the Gov. Genl. to settle the division of my estate, then in the hands of my brother, which concerns the property in question. Signed: Jacques Rapalje. Natchez, July 23, 1794. // William Dunbar represents, in reply to Mr. Rapalje's memorial, that this suit has lasted 8 months, in which time he has been to Baton Rouge to procure evidences. If he has not done so, it is not reasonable to suppose that he can procure other proof. Signed Wm. Dunbar. // Considering that Mr. Jacques Rapalje has had sufficient time to collect all his evidences that could be useful and that the certificate of the Commandant of Baton Rouge proves the negro in question to belong to his father, having fallen to him by the division of the property, and he must produce the negro to satisfy the mortgage of Edgar Gallaudet, due by his father. Signed: Manuel Gayoso de Lemos. // Presented the above decree to Mr. Rapalje. He said he means to petition His Excellency for an appeal. // Pet. to Governor Genl. Signed 26 Aug. 1794.

p. 330. George Humphreys versus William Brown. About five years ago, my father purchased a tract of land from William Brown on Bayou Pierre and agreed to give $1000 for it. After my father's death the payment became due and as I could not comply with the obligation, I agreed to make rights to the said Brown of 460 acres of land adjoining said plantation, which were then said to be vacant and persuaded said Brown to take it and give me up my father's obligation, which he did, and now holds my obligation to make him titles above-mentioned. I am informed that Mr. Brown has not only got the land which my father purchased of him but also part, if not all, that I obligated myself to make over to him, as a recompense for giving up my father's obligation, wherefore I cannot comply with my obligation. I have a desire to do justice, therefore humbly ask Your Excellency to direct my conduct. Signed: G.W. Humphreys. Oct. 15, 1794. // It has not been proved that the land sold by William Brown to the late Col. Humphreys did not belong to Silas Crane, who bought it at public sale, as land confiscated and sold by the government, therefore the petitioner is exempted from making title to said Brown and the obligation so to do is to be given up and any money he has advanced will be returned. Signed: Gayoso.

p. 330. Don Simon de Arze versus Don Andres Gil. Don Simon de Arze, Sergeant of the Royal Artillery, represents that, three months since, he sold Don Andres Gil, Surgeon at the King's Hospital, a negro woman and her son, for $400; that at the end of 15 days, the purchaser had represented that the negro boy had a small rupture, the petitioner agreeing to abate $50 from the price which was accepted by a note, of which the following is a copy: "Friend Simon: I will agree to keep the negro woman at the price of $350 and the cure of the boy will be at my risk. Have the writings drawn up and I will sign them." Notwithstanding which, he has this day returned the negro woman with a note, saying that the said negro woman has turned out to be a thief and a drunkard, which said defects were known to the petitioner, who sent the negro woman back with the message that he would not take her back without an express order from Your Excellency. The negro woman returned a second time very ill-used and burned with a sad-iron between the shoulders, the negro boy being exposed on the top of the gallery of his house. Wherefore your petitioner prays that Your Excellency will be pleased to order that the said Andres Gil be compelled to keep the said slaves which he has lawfully purchased by instrument duly executed. Signed: Simon de Arze. Natchez, Aug. 12, 1794. // Don Luis Faure, Surgeon of the Royal Hospital, will examine the negro woman and boy above-mentioned and certify from whence proceeded the bruises and other marks of violence upon them. This being done, Don Andres Gil will be notified to appear before me tomorrow morning and show cause against the prayer of the petition. Signed: Gayoso. // 14 Aug. 1794. Certificate given by Don Louis Faure will be annexed to the proceedings in due time. // Presented the above to Andres Gil by John Ferguson. // Bill of sale from Don Simon de Arze to Don Andres Gil of a negro woman, named "Lucy", native of Guinea, aged abt. 35, with her son "Henry", nat. of Natchez, aged 2, which sd slaves I bought at public sale of James Saunders which I sell free from mortgage for $350 payable as follows, etc. 16 June 1794. Before Gayoso. // p. 333. Don Louis Faure, Surgeon of the Royal Hospital, certifies that, in pursuance of an order from the Governor of the Post, I have examined a negro woman at the house of the Sergeant of Artillery of the Post, and I found her to be burned on the upper and lower part of the right shoulder and other marks on the ribs of the same side. Natchez, 14 Aug. 1794. Signed: Louis Faure. // By order of the Gov. of the Post I have communicated the above to Andres Gil for his answer. // p. 334. Natchez. Aug. 30, 1794. Let Don Andres Gil be notified to make his defense in person, or by attorney within three days, or judgment will be given for contempt. Let him be also informed that if he does not immediately provide a place of departure for the negro woman and boy, a proper place will be found and expenses will be borne by the party against which judgment may be given. Signed: Grand-Pre. // Communicated the foregoing to Don Andres Gil. Signed: J. Girault. // Same to Don Simon de Arze. // To His Excellency. Don Andres Gil, physician practicing in the Royal Hospital in the Post, in answer to the suit instituted against him by Don Simon de Arze, claims that the woman was warranted from any vices and defects, etc. // Ordered to prove that the woman had such as justified him in returning her. // Don Juan Vaucheret proved that he saw the negro woman intoxicated and he, having given her some clothes to wash, missed a waistcoat, etc. // p. 324 [The parties compromised out of court.]

p. 343. William Smith versus P. B. Bruin. Francis Nailor and William Smith, both of Bayou Pierre, represent that some time ago Col. Bruin and memorialists made an agreement for the exchange of a quantity of land on Bayou Pierre for the mutual benefit of both. The land which Col. Bruin was to give your memorialists is a mill seat, on which a grist mill was formerly erected and on which your memorialists intended to erect a saw mill. William Smith, one of the memorialists, was to give the same quantity of land out of a survey on which he now lives, which joins Col. Bruin. Col. Bruin was so eager to obtain this part of your memorialist's plantation and conclude the agreement that a time was appointed when it should be marked out, which was done by Col. Bruin who marked the boundaries he wished to make and cut his name on trees which may now be seen. This part of the land Col. Bruin has now under fence and in cultivation before a full and legal transfer could take place. Your memorialist was obliged to procure the consent of Thos. Wilkins, Esq. who had a mortgage on the land, of your petitioner, as security for monies owing to him. At the request of Col. Bruin, your memorialists waited on that gentleman and obtained his permission. Nothing was now wanting but his presence to effect a transfer. An agreement was made which was to be ratified as the law directed. To this both parties pledged their honor. In virtue of this agreement and in full confidence in Col. Bruin's honor strictly to adhere to it, your memorialists purchased mill irons amounting to upwards of $200, engaged hands to assist them in effecting it in all possible expedition. No sooner had Col. Bruin been informed of the advantage that would arise from it than he violated his honor by flying from his agreement, informing your memorialist, that he should erect a mill there himself. Your memorialist being disappointed by Col. Bruin not complying and having gone to a very considerable expense, determined on finding some other situation, which we did, on vacant land adjoining the Bayou Pierre Swamp, which could not possibly injure any person's property. Your memorialists obtained a certificate from Mr. Dunbar that it was vacant and applying for it by petition from Your Excellency obtained a grant of it, with an order endorsed by Your Excellency: "Commence immediately", which we have done and, with assistance we have already cut down much timber as will make the frame. We propose continuing the labor until the mill is completed, having a number of hands engaged with everything necessary, it will not be much more than three months, if not interrupted, before the mill will be sawing. Your memorialists beg leave further to represent we have good cause and can prove it by the oaths of respectable people that Col. Bruin and Mr. Price have made a private agreement to exchange some land and that the land petitioned for by Mr. Price is to accommodate Col. Bruin, presuming on Your Excellency's approbation. If this proceeding be admitted by Your Excellency, no doubt Col. Bruin would direct Mr. Price to take the swamp in his survey for the benefit of the timber, which your memorialists principally depended on to support the mill which Your Excellency has given them leave to erect. We sue for justice, nothing more. Signed: William Smith and Francis Nailer. Natchez, Nov. 8, 1794. // To be communicated to Col. Peter B. Bruin, who will reply in continuation. // In answer to the various misrepresentations of the above memorialists, William Smith did some time since propose to this memorialist an exchange of a few acres of land which I on certain conditions agreed to, first, the land he wished should not injure my plantation as it was actually within my boundaries, nor encroach on the land claimed by Mr. Price; the other was that Mr. Smith should make me a perfect title to the land. The land he offered me is under mortgage together with all his other property to Mr. Wilkins, and the land which I was to give him was entirely out of my boundary, and was not at my disposal to give him. . . . . And Smith and Nailer have petitioned you for permission to have a mill lower down on Cypress Swamp which, if granted, your petitioner will not only be deprived of all privilege in this form but barred forever from the privilege and advantage of erecting a saw-mill on the land which he has purchased. Signed: P.B. Bruin. //. Before me, Don Manuel Gayoso, appeared Lewellyn Price, an inhabitant of Bayou Pierre, who deposes that he bought six years ago from a certain James and Mark White their claim to a piece of land on Bayou Pierre, which is the same that is now in dispute between Col. Bruin and William Smith and Francis Nailer, for which he paid the sum of $260; that he resided on the same a long time and has since obtained a grant for same; that he has petitioned for it before Nailer petitioned for it. // Before me, Gayoso, appeared Ezekiel Hoskinson and deposes that last Monday week he was at Col. Bruin's house when Mr. William Smith came there and told the Col. that he had heard he had bought Mr. Price's land, to which Col. Bruin answered that he had, provided the Government approved of it and permitted the sale to be confirmed. Mr. Smith said it would be a loss to him of about $300 because he had purchased mill irons with a view of building thereon. To which the Colonel answered that there need be no loss to him as he would buy the irons of him at whatever price was reasonable. Mr. Smith said that he would not sell the irons; that he would rather build upon his own spring branch and that Mr. Price's place was a matter of little consequence to him. Signed: Ezekiel Hoskinson. // To be communicated to Francis Nailer and William Smith. // William Smith and Francis Nailer, represent that Col. Bruin has in no respect represented the true account of the bargain that was made between him and your memorialist for the mill seat in dispute, wherefore, they ask that Col. Bruin may be called before Your Excellency and there declare, on oath, to the following questions: (1) If he did or did not agree to exchange the said mill seat for a piece of land he marked off belonging to William Smith, provided the said mill seat came within his boundaries; to declare his reasons for not complying with said bargain; and if said mill seat fell within his boundaries did he not feel bound to make the exchange. Signed: Wm. Smith, Francis Nailer. // In answer to William Smith and Francis Nailer, in their address of the 11th, I observe that . . . . . [vague and about the same as before.] Signed: J. Bryan Bruin. // On examination of the allegations of the parties, I find that William Smith has no right to contract for the land in question, his own land being mortgaged, and this decree to be communicated to both parties, and acknowledged by Smith. // Both parties notified by Capt. Estevan Minor. All sign.

p. 348. William Nowland versus Charles Carter. Wm. Nowland represents that some time ago, Charles Carter offered to sell him a negro man, which he said he bought of Mr. Ezekiel Dewitt, and from appearances was not worth much. However, he said that he could work at plantation work very well and we agreed that the petitioner should take him home and try him. If he suited, he was to pay $75 for him, on account of which he let Carter have a horse at $60 and paid him $6 more. It was some time before he could have a trail of the negro being lamed by a burned foot. After he got well, the petitioner soon discovered that he was rather a charge than anything else and therefore he sent him home and wrote to the master that he would not suit the petitioner, and he is now at Mr. Dewitt's. The petitioner has written twice to the said Carter to come and settle with him and receive his negro but as he does not come, the petitioner begs that Your Excellency will order him to do so and return the property he has received, and pay the costs of the suit. Signed: Wm. Nowland. // Charles Carter is hereby ordered to appear. Signed: Gayoso. 3rd Nov. 1794. // Notified Carter. Signed: John Ferguson. // Charles Carter, in reply, claims that Nowland has had the negro a year and through his lack of care the negro had become badly burned; that he had not had the papers prepared for signing because he had gone as a volunteer to the Capital in the service of His Majesty, etc. Signed: Charles Carter. 11 Nov. 1794. // To be communicated to the party. // On the same day communicated to Wm. Nowland. Signed: Ferguson.

p. 350. Wilford Hoggatt versus Elizabeth Hoggatt, We, Adam Hollinger and Leonard Marburry, being appointed by Don Juan Antonio Bassett, Commandant of the Post of St. Stephens, to settle the dispute of property between Mr. Wilford Hoggatt and Elizabeth Hoggatt, and having heard the claim of said Elizabeth and the objections made by Wilford, are of the opinion that the said Wilford Hoggatt do immediately deliver to said Elizabeth Hoggatt two negroes, claimed by her, named "Toby" and "Jack", now at work with Mr. Gerald Byrn on the King's work in Pensacola; that in lieu of the negro woman sold to Mr. Kerney she shall be entitled to 21 head of cattle and $40 which she received at Natchez; that he, the said Hoggatte, shall pay to Elizabeth Hoggatt $100 for the compensation of the use of the two negro men, Toby and Jack, since she has been at Natchez. Signed: Adam Hollinger, Leonard Marburry, and Juan Antonio Bassett. 30 Nov. 1794.

p. 350. Joel Weed versus Peter Camus. Joel Weed showeth that he has been living 12 months on a tract of land on Second Creek, for which land Squire Dunbar gave him a certificate as being vacant, and for which your petitioner made application and Your Excellency was pleased to grant it. I gave $7 for my petition and my warrant now lies in the surveyor's hands: I have also made a great improvement besides purchasing the old improvements which were made by a certain John Brand, and now your petitioner, to his great surprise, finds the said land is claimed by a certain Mr. Camus, who, by information has never done anything on the land. Your petitioner is poor and destitute, and asks for relief. Signed Joel Weed. 6 Dec, 1794. // Mr. William Dunbar will furnish information on this subject. // Having examined the documents produced by Mr. Peter Camus, I find the legal transfers of the land in question from the person who made the original improvement down to Peter Camus, who offers to prove by the evidence of Major Williams that he gave permission to a certain Jacob Adams to reside on the place and preserve it for him and the said Adams afterwards sold it to the petitioner for a cow and calf. 6 Dec. 1794. Signed: Wm. Dunbar., dep. surv. // Natchez, 6 Dec. 1794. Jacob Adams has offered to return the petitioner the cow and calf he received from him; and to pay the damages he caused him by inducing him to settle on a place he had no right to, which damages shall be adjudged by the alcalde of the district, and the said Adams is to pay the cost of the same. Signed: Gayoso. // Personally appeared before me Jacob Adams, who being sworn, declareth that he became possessor of the land claimed by Peter Camus from John Brand, who lived on the land and the report is untrue that the deponent had permission to reside on the place from Mr. Camus and declares solemnly under oath that he has never exchanged either with Mr. Camus or Major Williams words on the subject of the land or the improvements. Signed with a mark. Before William Dunbar. Second Creek. 9 Jany. 1795.

p. 351. Phoebe Calvit versus William Calvit. Phoebe Calvit, lawful wife of Wm. Calvit, represents that, by reason of the cruelty and ill-usage of her husband, she has been obliged to leave his house, and finds herself with nothing wherewith to subsist, and although she had property before her marriage, consisting of a negro, a bed and furniture, valuable horse and a saddle, her said husband refuses to restore any part thereof but has sold her negro, without the consent of the petitioner, that Thomas Vause, of Bayou Pierre, is acquainted with the state of the property of your petitioner before her marriage, and she asks that said Thos. Vause be ordered to appear to prove same, and that her husband be ordered to restore to her the bed and other property possessed by her before her marriage, and that she be allowed such support by her husband as Your Excellency deems just, observing that during the twelve years of her marriage she has received nothing from him, not even clothing. Natchez. 19 Dec. 1795. Signed: P. Calvit. // p. 352. Bayou Pierre. May. 20, 1796. Came Thomas Vause before me and declared on oath that, about 13 years ago, he was called in by William Calvit and Phoebe Crawford to write a bill of sale of a negro boy named "Peter", from said William Calvit to sd Phoebe Crawford, which he did and witnessed and saw the said negro boy delivered by Wm. Calvit to Phoebe Crawford. This transation took place in Holstein in North Carolina. He thinks the consideration mentioned in the bill of sale was 80 pounds. He also remembers that Phoebe Crawford did let Wm. Calvit have a horse which he saw Wm. Calvit sell to Capt. Thomas Aimey, but for what sum he does not remember. Signed: Thomas Vause. Before me. P. Bryan Bruin.

p. 352. Melling Woolley versus his creditors. Melling Woolley, an inhabitant of this government, showeth that he advertised requesting the attendance of his creditors at the house of Mr. Lewis Evans on 1st of this month when your petitioner would make proposals for the settlement of his accounts, mutually for the benefit of the whole, even at a sacrifice of all of his property. A part only of his creditors attended, who on examining into the state of your petitioner's affairs and hearing the proposals your petitioner made, unanimously agreed to accept them and give a full discharge. Your petitioner now supplicates Your Excellency to direct the further proceedings that no complaint be made of irregularity and that the whole of his creditors may approve of his conduct. Signed: Melling Woolley. Natchez. July 2nd, 1794. // Melling Woolley's creditors at Natchez: Mr. Bolling, Mr. Surget, Mr. James McIntosh, Mr. S.C. Arroyo, Mr. Wilkins, Messrs. Clark and Rees, Messrs. George and Robert Cochran, David Ferguson, John O'Connor, Archibald Lewis, John Wilson, Hugh Coyle, Mr. Dunbar for Mr. Gallaudet, Mr. Girault, Mr. Girod, Messrs. Mather and Strother, Mr. Miron, Mr. Cavalier, Mr. Copperthwait, Mr. Hyser, Mr. McNulty, Mr. Archibald White, Mr. Wm. Stephens, Mr. George Mather. // Natchez, 16 July 1794. To the creditors of Melling Woolley: . . . . [In his proposal he lists his creditors as above, giving the amount of each debt, total $7,000. He then gives an inventory of what he has and what is owing to him. These men owe him: Matthew White, Alexander Moore, Richard Trevillian, Anthony Booker, John Hartley, James Wilson, John Lum, James Garland, Samuel Culberson, Jacob Leaphart, John Stay- William Thomas, Thos. Smiley, Thomas Lampkin, Thomas Balleu, Eleanor Adams, William Kirkwood, Matthew Jones, Dr. Selden, Jacob Clark, Henry Jones, Thomas Irwin, Sebastian Den, Jacob Wordly, Louis Charboneau, J.B. LaPuente, Richard Bacon, Richard Devall, John Elmore, Mr. King, Sr., John Ford, Roger McPeak, Samuel Heady, Gideon Gibson, John Odam, Ha Shaff, W. L. Caldwell, John Brand, George Bailey, Christian Winsky, Jacob Jarret, Jeremiah Bryan and John Booth. Total $765. Notes bring this amount up to $2770. Three more pages concerning an agreement with the creditors, including those at New Orleans, too.]

p. 358. David Kennedy versus Jonas Scoggins. Natchez. 3 Nov. 1794. In consequence of the representation of David Kennedy, I do hereby order Wm. Dunbar, Esq. to cause the lines of the said David Kennedy's lines to be examined and to make me a report thereof. Signed: Gayoso. // Certificate that I have caused the lines of Jonas Scoggins and the late Benjamin Monsanto to be verified and find the front lines of the late Monsanto to consist of 125 perchs agreeable to the plat furnished by Wm. Vousdan, Esq. and the lands on which said Scoggins has been at work are within his own survey and entirely without the lines of Benj. Monsanto, now the property of David Kennedy. Cost of survey and certificate $8.00. Natchez. 26 Nov. 1794. William Dunbar, dep. surv. // David Kennedy represents that several years ago he bought of Mr. Benj. Monsanto land in the Miss. Swamp, the boundaries thereof clearly and plainly expressed, a copy of which is herewith presented. // Jonas Scoggins declares that Henry Manadue was the person appointed by Mr. Monsanto to direct the surveying of the land and he thought that it was proper to lay the land a little lower down the river than expressed in the sale passed by the Office and it leaves a vacancy of 40 rods between the upper line of Mr. Monsanto's land and the lower line of

Gibson Clark, and all the line he took he had a right to. // Natchez, 7 Feb. 1795. Jonas Scoggins and David Kennedy appeared to pay Scoggins $7 in timber for the disputed land.

p. 360. William Cobb versus Arthur Cobb. William Cobb petitions that some years ago his father, to encourage him, promised to allow him a share in the crop. The petitioner being very industrious and at a time when his father was much indebted and had few or no hands to work in the crops, so that his father paid most of his debts and acquired considerable property. On account of the share that was due to the petitioner, by agreement with his father, he brought him from New Orleans a negro man whom he gave to the petitioner, and said negro has always been called his, with the knowledge of all the neighbors. Petitioner's father never made a title of the said slave to him, but in lieu thereof he now refuses to give him up and also another slave bought of William Carpret and John Brown, of the Chickasaw Nation, which is the petitioner's own property, as will appear by the bill of sale in the records of the Government. The petitioner's father has retained in his possession some horses, the property of the petitioner, who can prove the truth of these assertions by different evidences, and his father has discontinued to allow him the share he has promised, for reasons unknown to the petitioner. Natchez. Jan. 22, 1795. Signed William Cobb. // p. 361. Mr. Cobb and the petitioner will attend at the Govt. House on Wednesday. Signed: Gayoso. Wit: Israel Smith, Landon Smith, David Mitchell and Isaac Caverly // 2nd Feb. 1799, Israel Smith, being sworn, declared that about 5 years ago, he was at the house of Arthur Cobb, immediately after his return from New Orleans and he heard Arthur tell his son, William, that he had purchased three negro fellows, a wench and child, and that as soon as they arrived his son should have his choice of the fellows. He had frequently afterwards heard the said Arthur Cobb as well as the rest of the family call one of those negroes, by the name of Brisco, as "Billy's negro". Signed: Israel Smith. Before Wm. Dunbar. // Second Creek, 2 Feb. 1795. David Mitchell appeared and declared that two or three years ago, being at the plantation of Arthur Cobb discoursing with him about the value of negroes, he remarked that there were then passing two negro fellows, one of which he said belonged to his son "Billy" and the other to himself; and before the above-mentioned time, the said Arthur Cobb told the deponent that he had made the exchange with his son Billy by giving him a certain reddish gray filly, 3 years old, for two other young creatures. Signed: David Mitchell. Before Wm. Dunbar. // Petition of Arthur Cobb shows that his son Billy has lately presented a petition praying certain property which he calls his own to be delivered to him; the petitioner lately in conference with his son offered him all the property he had provided for him which largely exceeds the portion he can give to his other children, on condition that he would not marry or have any connection with a certain Patsy Baker nor follow any kind of gambling and endanger his property. Etc. His objections to the young woman are numerous. Signed: Arthur Cobb. Natchez, 7 Feb. 1795. // Wm. Cobb will attend the Govt. House on Wed. next, with the petitioner. Order by Gayoso. Feb. 7th. 1795. // The parties appeared according to the above decree and after hearing all their representations and evidences, it was agreed and determined that a certain negro named "Bristol", now engaged in working the swamp for Arthur Cobb, immediately when the work now begun is finished shall be delivered to William Cobb and Arthur Cobb shall also allow his son ten dollars per month from this day until he returns the said negro for his hire, the said negro being acknowledged the property of the said Wm. Cobb. as also two horses and some stock of cattle now in the possession of Arthur Cobb, the whole of which is to be delivered to said Wm. Cobb to enjoy the same as his own upon the condition that he shall not sell or otherwise alienate any of the said property until a final division of the estate of the said Arthur Cobb shall take place, the said Wm. Cobb renouncing all claim to all property now in the possession of his father. Both have signed before the undersigned witnesses. It is further agreed that Wm. Cobb may immediately dispose of two cows and calves and also that the whole of the increase of the stock now acknowledged as his shall be at his own disposal and free from the conditions imposed on the rest of the property. Wit: Gabriel Benoist, R. King. Before Manuel Gayoso de Lemos.

p. 363. Charles McKiernan versus John O'Connor. Don Francisco Luis Hector, Baron de Carondelet, of the Order of St. John, Brigadier of the Royal Armies, Governor, Vice Patron and Royal Intendent General of this Province of Louisiana and of West Florida, Inspector of the Regular Troops and Militia of the same, for His Majesty, to His Excellency, Don Gayoso de Lemos. Whereas in pursuance of a certain proceeding in my Tribunal before the present notary, by Charles McKiernen versus John O'Connor, for the recovery of certain moneys mentioned, an agreement was made and executed, of which the following is a copy: Charles McKiernan and John O'Connor, res. in this City, agree that for the entire payment of $5,131, which J. O'Connor owes to sd McKiernan for principal and interest up to the day he presented an account in law, agreed that O'Connor shall deliver to him the merchandise which I have at my house at Natchez and the sd house and lot and all other buildings erected thereon, and the lands I hold at a place called "Little Gulf", all the property at a price to which the same may be appraised by four appraisers to be chosen by us, two by each party, excluding expressly, as we do hereby here exclude, Anthony Hutchins and William Vousdan, and with the proviso that the buildings shall be separately valued by two surveyors, other than those above-mentioned, to be also chosen by us. And O'Connor shall make a bond to the sd McKiernan of $500 payable out of the proceeds of his present crop as soon as he shall receive the same and will deliver the payment of this sum. // The above agreement was examined and approved by Carondelet. 7 July 1794. [The case continued through p. 376, giving, in detail, the different appraisals, with discussions and objections to certain appraisers. Joseph Murray was made umpire of the appraisers, who were Messrs. Ezekiel Forman, Peter Walker, Ebenezer Rees and Antonio Gras.]

p. 377. Bernard Lintot versus James McIntosh. Bernard Lintot, representing Messrs. Mather and Strother, attorneys for the executor of William Hiorn, decd., represent, in reply to the representation of James McIntosh, of the 17th, praying that the petitioner should put him in possession of 1000 acres which he purchased at the public sale of the estate of said deceased, that the said 1000 acres was sold to the deceased by Mr. Daniel Clark for a very considerable sum, being part of a tract of 3,000 acres then belonging to said Clark; that your petitioner has no knowledge of any boundaries to the said land than those mentioned in the sale by the said Daniel Clark, made to the deceased, which refer to the original titles, granted to said Clark by the British Government. From the various revolutions afterwards, it has become impracticable to ascertain the ancient boundaries wherefore your petitioner prays that Your Excellency will order a new survey made. Signed: Bernard Lintot. Natchez. 20 Sept. 1791. // Order by Gayoso, same date: Wm. Dunbar, Esq., assistant surveyor of this Dist., will cause the land mentioned in the foregoing petition to be surveyed and have the bounds fixed and have the same communicated to the parties. // In obedience to the above order, William Dunbar, submits a description of the land, and plot. Natchez. Oct. 6, 1791. Signed: Wm. Dunbar, Dep-Surv. // Natchez, Dec. 1792. Sutton Banks will explain his motives for opposing the execution of the order given by me for surveying and putting James McIntosh in possession of the 1000 acres of land bought by him at the public sale of a place called "Belmont", and proceeding from the estate of the deceased William Hiorn, who purchased the same from Daniel Clark as appeared from the titles as exhibited to me. Signed: Gayoso. // To His Excellency, the Governor: James Mather, for himself and Patrick Morgan, claims that the est. of Wm. Hiorn is indebted to them for $915 since 1778, with interest, and they applied to the Supreme Tribunal, which sd Tribunal, 8 June 1789, ordered that sd debt be paid out of the estate, which held 1000 acres of land in this district. Which land was sold and adjudged to James McIntosh payable at a fixed time, which term expired, which payment sd petitioner claimed and McIntosh refused, who had not been able to get papers and description of the land. Natchez. 23 Dec. 1792. Signed: James Mather. // Sutton Banks answers James Mather, saying that in 1776, the plantation where he now resides was purchased of Daniel Clark, for $4686, Spanish milled, and the tract was to contain 2000 acres of land, being the remainder of a 3000-acre tract granted to said Clark and wife, the other 1000 acres being already sold to Wm. Hiorn, deceased; that the said Hiorn soon after his purchase of the above 1000 acres did employ and assist Mr. William Vousdan to survey and lay off the land. Detailed descrition of boundary lines, etc. Banks claims that the survey was not correct. // Another petition by James McIntosh, 27 Jan. 1795, which was ordered to be annexed to other proceedings. // Note: Documents in support to this claim are (1) grant to Daniel Clark, Esq. from British Govt. for 3000 acres; (2) a lease and release from sd Clark to Wm. Hiorn of 1000 acres which was the Belmont tract; (3) the record of the purchase of said 1000 acres at public vendue. The two first to be found belonging to Mrs. Mary William's at Government House in the hands of Mr. S. Watts.

p. 382. James Hoggatt, for James Bosley, claiming a slave. James Hoggatt petitions that on board on one of the flats lately come down he has found a girl belonging to Mr. James Bosley, of Cumberland, who escaped from the house of her master on the 9th of March last as will appear by two letters from Bosley herewith, asks that the declarations be taken of Elizabeth Martin, Hugh Thompson, John Morris and Archibold Lewis, to prove the property and order said slave to be delivered to the petitioner, who is ready to give his bond and security that he will cause to be tran'smitted from Cumberland sufficient documents to prove the said girl to be a slave. Natchez, 25 April 1795. Signed: James Hoggatt. // Granted by Grand-Pre the same day. The witnesses cited will be summoned to give their testimony. // Here recorded the two letters from Bosley: Near Natchez, Messrs. Anthony and Wilford Hoggatt. Gentlemen: I wrote you a few days ago but lest that should miscarry I now write again informing you that on the 9th instant was stole from me a mulatto girl, names "Cass" about 15 years old. She was taken by an Indian slave, named "John Smith", the property of Gen. Colbert of the Chickasaw Nation. They went down Cumberland in a canoe and it is more than probable that they will make into your country. If so, I entreat you to use your utmost endeavors to have her secured and forwarded by your brother James to whom I have also written by this opportunity respecting her. Your sister and brother William are well and join me in wishes for your welfare, etc. Signed: James Bosley. // Nashville, 25 March 1795. To Mr. James Hoggatt, Esq. Natchez or New Orleans. I have to inform you that your family are all well and everything about your plantation goes on prosperously. But I must inform you that on 9th instant "Cass" was carried off down the river in a canoe by a certain Indian slave, belonging to Gen. Colbert, etc. [same as in the preceding letter.] // Post of Natchez, 7th April, at the instance of James Hoggatt, representing James Bosley, residing in Cumberland, appeared Elizabeth Martin, of this district, who declared, on oath, that the negro girl here present was the property of James Bosley; that she lived a long time in the neighborhood of sd Bosley and knows the girl very well, who was called "Cass" and she knew the mother of Cass, called "Linda", also the slave of Bosley. Signed with a mark before Estevan Minor and John Girault. // At the same time appeared Hugh Thompson and he said that about 5 years ago he lived in the house of James Bosley in Cumberland who had several slaves, very light colored, among them, this girl named Cass and her mother "Linda", but the mother of Linda was black and called "Nelly", all of whom belonged to Bosley. Signed: Same witnesses. Also appeared John Morris who decalred that he left the house of James Bosley on 14 Feb. last and that the girl now present was there at that time and she was called "Cass", and her mother "Linda", and grandmother "Nelly", as above. Signed before same witnesses. // Same day appeared Archibald Lewis who declared that he went aboard the flatboat with Mr. James Hoggatt and when the girl in question came down, who when called by the name of "Cass" answered; and she said that the Indian had taken her behind the corn field near her cabin and carried her to New Madrid from whence she came down in the boat. Signed. Same wit. // At Post, 28 April, Grand-Pre caused to appear before him the girl in the foregoing proceeding. Q. What is your name? A. Cass. Q. To whom did you belong? A. I lived with Capt. Bosley. A. Who is your mother? A. Linda, living also with Capt. Bosley and her grandmother was "Nelly" and belonged to Wm. Cate. Q. Were any of your family free? A. No, except her uncle James who had gone back to Holstein. She signed with a mark.

p. 384. William Vousdan versus Philip P. Turpin. Philip Turpin was indebted to Mr. David Ross, of New Orleans, merchant, for $270, balance due for a negro called "Jimmy" and for the hire of a negro man named "Boatswain". Pet. for payment, 5 March 1795. Signed: Wm. Vousdan. // 20 March. Let Turpin be notified: Signed: Gayoso. // Notified same day by John Girault. // Estevan Minor and John Girault commissioned to settle the accounts between David Ross and Turpin. [Accounts follow. Outcome: The negro "Jimmy", morgaged for the amount due, was sold at public sale and adjudged to Don Joseph Vidal for $302 cash. Receipt of Wm. Vousdan for $352.]

p. 391. Case of Dorothea Henderson versus Henry Manadue. Petition of Dorothy Henderson that her late husband was bearer of a note or bond of Theophilus Thompson for a likely negro which obligation her said husband did negotiate to the said Thompson's brother, for a negro which proved not to be his, and was taken from him, as is testified by the annexed declaration of Burrel Stroud. And whereas there is a negro in possession of Henry Manadue, the property of said Theophilus Thompson, the petitioner asks that the said negro be delivered to said petitioner that she may enjoy his work as interest on the money due his master until the matter be finally determined. Natchez, 24 March 1795. For D. Henderson. // Burrel Stroud appeared before the Commandant, Manuel Gayoso de Lemos, at the request of Dorothy Henderson, and declared that he traveled from Georgia to Kentucky with the late Wm. Henderson in 1793; that a certain Giles Thompson did fall in company with them on the way; that on the way from Hazel Patch to Lexington the said Giles Thompson sold to Henderson two negro slaves, one called "Dick" and a girl called "Nancy". One negro Henderson paid for with an obligation he had of Theophilus Thompson, brother of the said Giles, for a likely negro, and the other he paid for in cash in horses. But some time after the said Giles Thompson had returned, the said negroes were claimed by one John Perry, proved by due course of law, and given up by the aforesaid Henderson, who had no recourse, as Thompson was then gone, but he told the deponent that he should lose but one negro for there was at Natchez, a few miles from his own plantation, a negro the property of the above-mentioned Theophilus Thompson, which he would attach. But the said Henderson died at the Falls of the Ohio and the deponent, only, went on to Natchez, where, after his arrival, he enquired for the property of Theophilus Thompson and found that Mr. Henry Manadue had in his possession a negro belonging to said Thompson. He did inquire of said Manadue if he thought or knew if Theophilus Thompson was indebted to anyone in this country, to which the said Manadue answered that he owed him nothing but he believed that he owed something to William Henderson, of which the deponent thought it his duty to communicate to the widow, also to give notice to the government, and did acquaint Mrs. Henderson and Major Minor of the same.

Natchez, 13 March 1795. Burrel Stroud, signed with a mark. Before Gayoso. Wit: J. Eldergill and John Girault. // Appeared Capt. Stephen Minor, Aide-Major of the Post, who declared that Burrel Stroud above statement is true, to the best of his recollection. Signed: Stephen Minor. // The widow, Dorothy Henderson, petitions that, by the testimony of Burrel Stroud and Stephen Minor, Capt. of the Army, it is proved that Henry Manadue has a slave, belonging to Theophilus Thompson, and prays that said negro be delivered to petitioner. 16 May 1795. Dorothy Henderson. // 16 May 1795. In pursuance of the proceedings, the Commandant issues an order that the said negro be delivered to the widow of said Henderson, in satisfaction of the obligation of the said Thompson. // To the above, Henry Manadue, of the district, planter, answers that the said Theophilus Thompson had contracted a debt to my late father, for board as well as other things furnished to him and likewise some debts paid by your petitioner for him, as will appear by receipts in his possession, and he can prove that said Thompson had said that he owed his father a horse of value, which he was bound to bring him, and for which he left the negro in pledge; asks for a preference to his just claim. Signed: Henry Manadue. 23 May 1795. // 30 May 1795. Gabriel Benoist, Esq. is hereby authorized to take all the information relative to the claims of these parties. // Henry Manadue presents an itemized account against Theophilus Thompson, also one for Phoebe Manadue for board making clothes for him, including furnishing the material for same. The board for 8 months at one time and 10 months at another. Total $143. Witness: John Bacon and Joseph Vaucheret. Phoebe (X) Manadue. // Before Gabriel Benoist appeared Joseph Vaucheret who declared that about the month of December 1791 Theophilus Thompson, then about to depart for the United States of America, was in treaty with the deponent for some animals which said deponent was selling and in payment thereof he was to bring him a negro on his return. The deponent consented to this bargain on condition that Mr. Henry Manadue, Sr., would be surety for the same. When requested, Manadue refused and said that he would not be security as Thompson already owed him money. Before that time, Manadue had told him that Thompson owed him a stud horse of value which he was to bring him on his return from the U.S. Thompson also told the deponent that he owed Mr. Manadue a stud horse and it would be one of the best horses ever brought into this country. Signed: J. Vaucheret. // Before Gabriel Benoist. Pine Ridge. June 15, 1795. Personally appeared Joseph Bonner who declared that Theophilus Thompson was here two different times and he always stayed at Mr. Manadue's house and it could not have been less than 18 months, and that a certain large bay horse, formerly his, did belong to Manadue. // Personally appeared David Greenleaf, who declared that Theophilus Thompson, being in this country not less than 18 months, always stayed at Manadue's house; that when Thompson left this country the last time, he said that if he did not return the property he left behind should be Mr. Manadue's // Manuel Madden also testified that Thompson stayed with Manadue. // Henry Manadue declared that the negro had been in his father's family ever since his master went aways, which was three and a half years ago, and when his master was in this country, he was employed in his service and sometimes hired out. He left no other property with his father. A bay horse which some people think belonged to him. . Very vague. Benoist presents the above depositions to the government. // p. 396 Natchez, July 1, 1795. As, in this case, the claim of the widow Henderson is based on obligations, although not produced is proved to exist, expressly given in payment for a negro, being an object in the favor of the estate of Henderson, on which the decree of the 16th of May was founded, ordering the widow to be put in possession of the negro in question, but not to sell or in any ways alienate the same, but which, however, is not thought sufficient proof in her favor to authorize a decree of final possession. An order, on the other hand, considering the evidence produced in the favor of Manadue against the deceased Thompson, respecting various bargains and affairs between the parties, deceased, but without mortgage on the negro in question for the security for the payment for any such account, said accounts not acknowledged or accepted by Thompson, and no notes or receipts in favor of Manadue. [The Commandant leaves the question in obeyance until the Governor of the District shall determine it.] // Notified the foregoing decree to Henry Manadue. 1 Nov. 1795. Signed Jean Girault.

p. 397. The declaration of Anthony Hutchins, at the Post of Natchez, on this 3rd of May 1795, before Don Carlos de Grand-Pre. At the request of Elizabeth Tomlinson, appeared Anthony Hutchins, who declared that in 1787 or 88, talking with Nehemiah Carter concerning a tract of 100 arpents, which said Carter had bought, he told him as a friend that the buildings were out of the bounds of said land and advised the said Carter to apply for a grant to secure the said buildings but said Carter replied that he would not, observing that these people, meaning the Spainards, would not be long here and he was glad the 100 arpents were bought in the name of his wife, for he would never hold land under a Spanish title. The deponent is near 70 years of age. Signed: Anthony Hutchins. Wit: Jean Girault, Estevan Minor and Daniel Douglas. Before: Carlos de Grand-Pre.

p. 397. Edward McCabe versus Pedro Labarse. McCabe represents that Pedro Labarse was to pay him $150 on account of house and lot sold to Labarse and his brother, Samuel, the time being expired on the payment of which sum he was to make legal titles, and the said Samuel being absent and leaving no money to pay his proportional part and Pedro being unwilling to return said house to the petitioner and annul the contract, he prays that Your Excellency authorize him to that effect. Signed: Edward McCabe. Natchez, 25 May 1795. // As we, the abovenamed Samuel and Peter Laberce, find it impossible to make good the several payments due to Capt. Edward McCabe for part of his lot on which a billiard room stands and which we lately purchased from him, we agree that the bill of sale made to us be cancelled, on condition of receiving the original obligations given him for the same, and being acquitted from all claims of damages, etc. Signed: Peter Lacerce. Wit: Maurice Stacpoole. Natchez. 28 May 1795. // In consideration of the parties being agreed in relation to the retrocession of the house and lot the sale of which was not completed, the annullment prayed for is ordered and the property restored to Edward McCabe and all the obligations for the payment thereof to Peter Laberce.

p. 399. William Dunbar and others versus Melling Woolley. The undersigned agents for the creditors of Melling Woolley, having given notice that a public sale would be made of some slaves belonging to said Woolley, ask for an appraisment thereof and the sale be carried into effect. 13 June 1795. Signed: Wm. Dunbar, Ebenezer Rees and G. Cochran. // Granted, the same day. Samuel Flower and Richard Devall appointed appraisers, and they accepted. [Details of sale extended to page 401.]

p. 402. Executors of Ezekiel Forman versus the estate of Adam Cloud. Said executors petition that the sale of the estate and effects of Adam Cloud, in conformity to public notice already given to that effect, be on Saturday 1st of August, according to the inventory hereunto annexed. Natchez, July 11, 1795. Signed: William Dunbar, Ebenezer Rees, and Banajah Osmun. // Granted as requested. Grand-Pre. Same date. // At the Post of Natchez, 1 Aug. 1795. Peter Walker and Joseph Barnard appointed appraisers. [Appraisal follows.] At the sale, a negro woman and two sons were adjudged to Samuel Flowers; negro boy "Nathan' to Ebenezer Rees; two horses to Alexander Ross; tract of land to Richard King. Appraisers of the live stock were Peter Walker and Richard King. [A long appraisal follows.]

p. 404. Agreement of the heirs of Richard Swayze. The widow and heirs of the late Richard Swayze, deceased, appear before Your Excellency and declare that the division of the estate has been omitted until now, owing to various circumstances, and being desirous to have the same done, they have mutually agreed to appoint and nominate Messrs Joseph Bernard, Isaac Johnson and Ebenezer Dayton to do the same, and have appointed the 22nd day of the present month for the business to be commenced. The parties wishing that the said division be made legally and duly authorized so as to become permanent, they pray Your Excellency to issue a decree to authorize the proceedings of said gentlemen, and when terminated to confirm the same and make it of record. Natchez 8 Sept. 1795. Signed: The widow Swayze, Sarah King, Lydia Cory, Mary King, Richard Swayze, Deborah Lusk, Gabriel Swayze, Gabriel Swayze as heir and executor of Elijah Swayze, deceased. // The request of the parties granted by Grand-Pre. Sept. 18, 1795. [In the agreement which follows Deborah is called "Deborah Luce" and she signs "Deborah Luse", which was her name.] // In obedience to the foregoing order of government, we, Isaac Johnson, Joseph Bernard and Ebenezer Dayton, as arbitrators therein named for making a division of the property, real, personal and moveable, of the late Richard Swayze, deceased, met according to order Sept. 22, 1795, at the dwelling house of widow Sarah Swayze, widow of said deceased, when and where the heirs of the said estate all personally met, excepting Capt. Richard King met as representative of his father and mother, Justus King and Sarah King, who by sickness were unable to attend, and the said heirs having then and there made and agreed upon an inventory containing the whole of the said property and then and there unanimously agreed upon every particular respecting the said wishes for the division of the property, which, agreeing with our judgment of the equity and legality of the business do therefore make and declare our award and definite division of said property in terms conforming with their said unanimous agreement, namely: that each of the said heirs shall hold and enjoy to them respectively, the respective tracts of land in Ogden's Mandamus that are marked for them, respectively, in a plat of said land hereunto annexed, with this difference that the said widow Sarah Swayze shall directly or as soon as may be secure to her daughter Deborah Luce said 600 English acres, marked in the said plat in the name of said widow, who is to make a deed of gift of same to her said daughter, Deborah Luce, and her heirs forever and that the said widow Swayze shall have, hold and enjoy 5/6 part of the horses and cattle and the negro men named "Peter" and "Antoine" and the woman named "Mary"; and to Richard Swayze the negro man called "Titus" and an equal undivided half of a pair of mill stones with the half of the spindle thereto and crowbar and to Gabriel Swayze the other equal undivided half of said mill stones, spindle and crowbar; and to Deborah Luse the negro girl "Margaret" after the death of her mother, Sarah Swayze, and from her brother, Gabriel Swayze, $67 in six months to pay for her and her family's passage from New Jersey and 1/6 part of the whole stock of horses and live cattle, to her and her heirs forever; and to Mary King and her heirs shall be paid as per note of even date $450 on 1st April next by her brother Gabriel Swayze; and to Sarah King the negro boy "Ishmael" and the negro boy "Hope"; and Lydia Cory shall have the negro girl "Judith" and negro boy "Jack"; and each of the said four daughters, Sarah, Lydia, Mary and Deborah, in consequence of preferences in their favor as above, have agreed and we do adjudge and award shall and do quit claim for themselves and their heirs all rights that do or may exist as creditors or heirs to the estate of the said Richard Swayze, their deceased father, or to that of their said mother, Sarah Swayze, after her death, which quit claim they do and shall make in favor of their two brothers, Richard and Gabriel Swayze and their respective heirs. Etc. Ogden Mandamus, 23 Sept. 1795. Signed: Isaac Johnson, Joseph Bernard, Ebenezer Dayton. We, the several heirs named and alluded to in the foregoing award do voluntarily and gladly subscribe our respective names as thereby declaring our mutual consent and unanimous agreement of a division as stated in said award, etc. Signed at Ogden Mandamus in the Dist. of Natchez, 23 Sept. 1795, by Sarah (X) Swayze, Richard King for Sarah King, Lydia Cory, Richard Swayze, Mary King, Deborah Luse, Gabriel Swayze. Wit: Ebenezer Dayton, Isaac Johnson, Joseph Bernard. // Natchez, 26 Sept 1795. Approved and recorded in the Archives. Signed: Carlos de Grand-Pre.

p. 406. Hannah Lum versus William Vousdan. [Case covers pp. 406-425.] Hannah Vousdan petitions that she has some difficulty with her husband, William Vousdan, respecting some property which was her property before her marriage, and the benefits arising therefrom, and in order that the petitioner may be authorized to call on him to account for the same, it is first necessary to prove that your petitioner was lawfully married to said Vousdan, and for that purpose, asks that Your Excellency call Colonel Hutchins, ordering him to certify what he knows respecting the marriage. 4 March 1795. Signed: Hannah Vousdan. // Same day. Anthony Hutchins, Esq. will certify what he knows respecting the petitioners demand. // Deposition of Anthony Hutchins. Some time before the country of the Natchez was conquered by His Most Catholic Majesty's arms, it was the custom of this country, particularly in the absence of clergymen, to celebrate marriages by special licenses from the Governor and that bond and security should be previously given to prevent exceptional persons from joining in holy estate of matrimony and as I was first of the Quorum here and Commissioner of the Supreme Court of Pensacola, such licenses were lodged in my hands to furnish the several magistrates, the whole being exhusted and the distance to Pensacola great, I did venture to marry Mr. Vousdan and Mrs. Lum without a license or bond, as I intended to procure such license afterwards, but it was omitted from some cause or another, yet the ceremony was performed and they were married. Certified 5 March 1795. Signed: Anthony Hutchins. // Hannah Vousdan leaves before Your Excellency the certificate given by Col. Hutchins, respecting the marriage of the petitioner with Wm. Vousdan, agreeably to Your Excellency's order of the 4th instant, which your petitioner prays may be communicated to said Vousdan, with an order for his immediate answer. March 11, 1795. Signed: Hannah Vousdan. // Communicate to William Vousdan for his answer. Signed: Gayoso. Mch. 13, 1795. // Notified Wm. Vousdan. J. Girault. // Wm. Vousdan's answer: He represents he was surprised at the two memorials of a woman calling herself "Hannah Vousdan" and a certificate from Col. Hutchins. His reply is that he was never married to that woman or to any other in his life, and that the matter was and is impossible in nature, he being a Roman Catholic and she being of some unknown profession. The matter is thus: About 18 years ago, she had some difficulty with a company of merchants, called Williams and Ferguson, at which time your memorialist boarded at her house. She requested of him to become her friend and your memorialist continued to settle her affairs with said company and others. But busy tongues began to suspect there was something more than ordinary in this connection and to save appearances, especially with her brother-in-law, she assumed the name of Mrs. Vousdan and it became so familiar that your memorialist did not hesitate to call her by that name until, at length, she was known by that name and no other. She lived with him for some time in that character and he paid a great deal of his own money to extricate the woman from her embarrassment with her creditors and keep her and her children together until they might be able to refund the money. At length, through her getting into a state of insanity, your memorialist placed her and her children in a house to themselves, allowing them a negro wench to attend them and keep them in a state of cleanliness till she recovered tolerably. She then applied to Mrs. Hutchins to get your memorialist to let her go to live with her brother-in-law. He sent for John Lum, said brother-in-law to take her and her children away together with three negroes and everything that they might chose to take. That happened about 13 years. As to the certificate of Col. Hutchins, it is vague and ambiguous, and calculated to save her credit and that of her sons who are grown. Etc. Memorialist has claim to considerable of their property. . . . . . Her son is married, six years past. . . . . .

Ask that Hannah Lum give security for the cost of this mad suit, also for a balance of $2600 due your memorialist, documents for which he is ready to prove. .... Signed: William Vousdan. 14 March 1795. // To be communicated to Hannah Vousdan. As to the security mentioned by Wm. Vousdan, it will be considered at the proper time. Signed: Gayoso. // Notified Hannah Vousdan. Signed: John Girault. // Hannah Vousdan appeared and empowered her son to represent her in this suit. Hannah Vousdan's reply. . . . . . Asks that Col. Hutchins be called and asked if he did or did not, at the request of William Vousdan, marry the petitioner to sd Vousdan; if he did not consider the marriage lawful at that time; if the petitioner was not considered by him and others of this district the lawful wife of said Vousdan for many years. Also asks that the wife of Col. Hutchins be called to declare, on oath, if she was or was not personally present when your petitioner was married to said Vousdan; and if she did or did not visit your petitioner as the lawful wife of sd Vousdan and as such considered her. Asks that he produce, without delay, a just statement of the property and outstanding debts the petitioner was possessed of when married to him, also what property he possessed at that time. 21 March 1795. Signed: William Lum, empowered. // Let Anthony Hutchins be cited to appear before me to make affidavit; as respecting Mrs. Hutchins, commission issued to Isaac Johnson, Esq., to take her declarations in my name in due form. Let Wm. Vousdan be informed of foregoing memorial. // Notified Wm. Vousdan. Sig: John Girault. A. Hutchins was cited to appear. Isaac Johnson commissioned to take depo. of Mrs. Hutchins. // Post of Natchez, 10th Apr. 1795, appeared Anthony Hutchins, Esq., who was interrogated if he had not, at the request of Wm. Vousdan, married him to the widow, Hannah Lum, etc. Answer: It is true that Wm. Vousdan did personally and without any disguise request him to marry him to Hannah Lum and accordingly he did marry them in conformity with the English ritual and the custom in this country; that after said ceremony, the deponent did receive and consider the said Hannah Lum as the lawful wife of William Vousdan; that he never suspected any such difficulty in that respect as has now arisen, to which, he added that he performed the ceremony in the custom of this country and although he was requested that it be private, it was no less binding than if it had been public. As a friend of the family of Lum, he was glad that the widow married Vousdan because he was able to settle the affairs of the estate of Lum, which were involved and intricate. Sg: Anthony Hutchins. Before Manuel Gayoso de Lemos. // Communicated same to William Lum. Sig: John Girault. // Apr. 10, 1795. (p. 412) Natchez District of Second Creek. Personally appeared before me, Isaac Johnson, one of the magistrates assigned to keep the peace in the district aforesaid, Mrs. Ann Hutchins, who says, on oath, that she was personally present when William Vousdan was married to the widow Hannah Lum, and that she did visit her after her marriage as the lawful wife of Mr. Vousdan and always considered her as such. Signed: Ann Hutchins. 28 March 1795. Signed: Isaac Johnson. To be annexed to other papers. // Communicated to Wm. Lum. // Debtor: Hannah Lum, in account current with Wm. Vousdan. Nov. 28, 1777, William Hiorn's note, paid to Messrs. Miller and Co. and John McGilvray's Co. per receipt $500; Samuel Swayze's note $325 to same co.; James Robinson's sworn account to Messrs. Barbour and Harrison, being balance due him for building a house at Natchez, $150; Richard Thompson for same $75; Isaac Johnson for same $40; Feb. 1779 William Ferguson, due Williams and Ferguson, $446; Wm. Swanson's acct. $25; John Farquhar, for sundries you took up under pretense of sending to me but in reality to run off with the famous Philip Alston to Cumberland and actually got as far on your way as Petit Gulf, $700; int. on above $500. [Further interest items, almost equal to the principal. Amount claimed as paid out: $2261. Int. $2059.] Contra; credit: 1777. By house at Natchez sold to John Blommart $500; plantation near Mr. Bingaman, 90 acres, sold to Mr. Farquhar, $300; empty cupboard sold to Mr. Farquhar, $15; by a large table $20 in 1780; int. on $500 for 16 years, at 6%, $48; int. on $300, etc . . . Mrs. Lum may say that the plantation at Mr. Bingaman's sold for $1300, whereas she has credit for only $300, but she must own that I sold Mr. Farquhar 20 cows and calves which at $25 per cow and calf, the usual price, at that time, and 1000 bu. of corn, leaves the plantation . . . . . ; to Mr. John Ellis for negro called "Joe" which was his . . . . As to outstanding debts owing to Mrs. Lum, Miller and Swanson collected them to pay themselves, to whom all such were made over, and receipts for which are in my possession, etc. He begs that William Ferguson who was in partnership with Mrs. Lum's husband, Jesse Lum, at the time he was killed, is better acquainted with her circumstances than any other person in the country and lived chiefly with her before they disputed about her property, and your memorialist asks that he be questioned as follows: whether he thought there was property enough of Hannah Lum to pay the debts of her husband, Jesse Lum, at the time Wm. Vousdan undertook to settle these accounts; did not Wm. Vousdan pay his own money to pay those accounts; did not he, Ferguson, look upon the negroes now in possession of Hannah Lum to be paid for by Wm. Vousdan; did not said Hannah Vousdan run off with Philip Alston, taking not only the said negroes with her but other negroes belonging to said Vousdan; to his, the said Ferguson's, own knowledge did not the said Ferguson endeavor to rescure the said negroes from her, as the property of Vousdan and did not she go as far as Little Gulf on her way, while Wm. Vousdan, through the intrigues of her friends and other enemies, was imprisoned in N.O. Mch. 23, 1795. // Mch. 27, 1795. Let William Ferguson be cited to appear before me the first day of audience, to testify as to several points above-mentioned. // Notified Mr. Wm. Ferguson in writing. Sig: John Girault. // At the Post of Natchez, 9 April 1795, appeared Wm. Ferguson, who being sworn and questioned as to Hannah Vousdan being able to pay the debts of her deceased husband, Jesse Lum, at the time Vousdan undertook the same, replied that it has been so long since that time he cannot be certain but he does believe that with three slaves, Isaac, Jack and Linda and a plantation, stock and furniture, all of which said widow then possessed, she had enough to pay the debts, besides she had a house in Natchez. Q. Did William Vousdan pay the debts of the estate out of his own property. A. He only knows that he paid them part in money and part in government certificates more than a year after he undertook the settlement of the estate, it is probable he may have paid such debts with the proceeds of the estate itself. Q. If he does not think that Wm. Vousdan paid the value of the negroes now in the possession of the widow out of his own proper means? A. The widow bought those slaves at public sale of the estate before Wm. Vousdan took the management into his hands, and he does not think that Wm. Vousdan paid for those slaves, unless he paid monies to the estate for that amount. Q. Does he not know that the widow ran off with Philip Alston and carried away with her not only those but also other slaves of William Vousdan. A. At the time of the revolution in this government, many of the inhabitants went with their property, fearing to lose same, at which time, William Vousdan was prisoner in New Orleans, and the aforesaid Alston persuaded the widow that it was to her interest to escape with her slaves and other property, and that accordingly she went with said Alston, leaving her slaves with a certain Winfree, to bring them on, and the deponent, being then agent for William Vousdan, opposed it and the widow then returned and remained at the house of the deponent until the return of her husband. Q. Did not Ferguson claim such slaves as those of Wm. Vousdan, and did not the widow go as far as Little Gulf during the time sd Vousdan was confined in the City due to the intrigues of the friends of the widow and enemies of sd Vousdan? A. He detained the slaves as property of said Vousdan and wife as being charged with the concerns of said Vousdan then confined, but he did not know that his imprisonment as due to enemies or other causes. It is true that his wife went as far as Little Gulf but took no slaves with her. Sig: Wm. Ferguson. Before Gayoso de Lemos. // Ezekiel Forman, Wm. Dunbar and Gabriel Benoist appointed arbitrators to settle the dispute. The undersigned arbitrators, appointed for the purpose of deciding certain contraverted accounts between Capt. William Vousdan and Hannah Lum, respecting the estate of the late Jesse Lum, in part managed by said Capt. Vousdan. Having duly examined the said accounts and claims of both parties, are of the opinion that Wm. Vousdan has made payments on account of said estate fully equal in value to the sums that have, at times, come into his possession proceeding from said estate, together with such part of estate as may have remained in his possession, the arbitrators are rather of the opinion that the payments made by Capt. Vousdan have exceeded the advantages he has derived from the estate, but finding it impossible to arrive at an exact statement, for want of vouchers, which Capt. Vousdan declares to have been lost during his absence at New Orleans, the arbitrators are therefore of the opinion that the claims of each party are balanced by those of other and do therefore award that, as Capt. Vousdan has been credited for the amount of Samuel Swazey's note for $325 which note does not appear as yet paid to Messrs. Miller and Co., Capt. Vousdan shall become security that this demand shall not at any future period be claimed from the estate of Jesse Lum and that the parties shall interchangeably pass receipts exonerating each the other from all future claims respecting the said estate of the late Jesse Lum. 7 Nov. 1795. Sig: Wm. Dunbar. // Communicated the document to Capt. Wm. Vousdan. Communicated to William Lum.

p. 425. William Collins versus estate of Henry Willis. Isaac Gaillard, executor of the will of Anne Savage, decd., represents that a part of the estate of the said deceased is the property of Henry Willis, who is now absent, and sundry claims appearing which the petitioner cannot pay until a division of the estate shall have been made, prays that Your Excellency order a division of said estate and appoint proper persons to represent the said Willis and take into their possession such part thereof as belongs to him. 16 May 1794. Sig: Isaac Gaillard. // In answer, Wm. Collins represents he sold to Mr. Henry Willis in 1790 a plantation for $1600, which was to have been paid in three payments as will appear by notes and obligations in the petitioner's hands; that the 1st payment of $400 was to have been made in March 1794, for which payment, Mrs. Anne Savage became bound by her acceptance of Mr. Willis's order on her; also no part of the debt has been paid and now the whole sum has become due, and there is no appearance of Willis returning shortly; the delay has been very detrimental to the petitioner; asks for consideration. Sig. Wm. Collins. 3rd June 1794. // William Collins represents that it has now been several years that he has been without his money duing by Mr. Henry Willis for his plantation. Asks again for an immediate division of the estate and a trustee appointed to represent Mr. Willis, who may be empowered to pay the petitioner without delay the balance due him. Miss Savage joins the petitioner in asking an immediate division of the estate, that the part belonging to these parties may be ascertained and dealt with according to law. 20 Oct. 1794. Sig: Wm. Collins // Another petition by Wm. Collins. It has been more than five years since he sold the land to Henry Willis, deceased, at Bayou Sara, which sale he made to pay some debts, prays for immediate division of the estate of Mrs. Savage. 2nd Nov. 1795. // Isaac Gaillard answers Wm. Collins. Denies that Mrs. Ann Savage's estate is in any way responsible for the debt of Henry Willis, her son-in-law. Nov. 9, 1795.

p. 428. William Vousdan versus Richard Lord. Wm. Vousdan, Capt. of the Mounted Militia of this Dist., claims that Richard Lord is justly indebted to him for $787 which said sum was attached and left in said Lord's hands by order of the Governor of the district, and in consequence whereof said Lord executed in favor of the petitioner a mortgage of three slaves as security for the payment, as will appear by the copy of the mortgage filed in the archives of this government. As the time of payment has expired, petitioner prays that an order issue that the representative of the said Lord who is absent from the district, or his wife, do pay the petitioner, or in default of same that said slaves mortgaged to the petitioner be sold, or any of them as may be sufficient. Sig: Wm. Vousdan. 23 Sept. 1795. // It appearing by the annexed obligation, dated 9 Aug. last past, for a certain sum therein mentioned that the time of the payment is expired, let it be notified to the debtor, Richard Lord, his wife, or his attorney, to make payment without further delay than three days of the sum mentioned. Sig: Grand-Pre. // This order was communicated to Mrs. Lord, in the presence of James Glasscock and Mr. Love, by John Ferguson. // William Vousdan, represents that at the request of Mrs. Lord, he had consented to allow a further delay of fifteen days to produce the slaves mortgaged and the time being expired, Mrs. Lord having sent one of the slaves into the Cypress Swamp into a dangerous place, the petitioner prays that Your Excellency order the said slaves produced without delay, that they may be appraised and sold without delay. // Granted. Let notification be made. // Mrs. Lord delivered me the above negroes. Sig: John Savage. Bayou Pierre. 20 Nov. 1795. // The mortgage of the said slaves to Vousdan by Richard Lord is herein given. // Henry Nicholson and Ezekiel Dewitt appointed appraisers. Negro man and his wife and daughter valued $550. Ezekiel Dewitt signed with his mark (D). Nicholson signed. Post of Natchez, 16th Dec. 1795. Sale of slaves and adjudged to William Vousdan for $700 cash, he being the highest bidder. Witnesses: Estevan Minor, Wm. Lewis, Parker Carradine, Wm. Vousdan, Samuel Flowers, Bennet Truly, John Girault.

p. 430. William Vousdan versus Richard Lord. Wm. Vousdan represents that Ebenezer Dayton is indebted to Richard Lord for $100 for the hire of the slaves which were mortgaged to the petitioner and the proceed of the sale of the slaves falling short of the amount of the debt due from said Lord to the petitioner, asks that Dayton keep in his hands the amount of said hire to complete the same, duing and owing by said Lord to the petitioner. // Dayton is notified to retain the hire of the slaves until further order.

p. 431. Mary Carpenter versus the estate of Jeremiah Routh. Mary Carpenter represents that she is empowered to collect the debts owing to her deceased husband, among which is a mortgage on a tract of land belonging to Jeremiah Routh, deceased, for $150 and legal interest and ask that said land may be exposed to public sale and proceeds thereof applied for payment of said mortgage. // Let the heirs have notice and if they consent let them sign their names in testimony thereof. Grand-Pre. // In conformity of the foregoing decree, we inform you that, knowing the debt to be just, we consent to land mortgaged being sold. Signed Margaret Routh, Job Routh. Mch. 27, 1796. p. 431. At the Post of Natchez, 5 March 1796, to carry out the prayer of the foregoing petition, Parker Carradine and William Ferguson are appointed appraisers of plantation, which they valued at $200. Both signed. The present acting Governor has exposed to sale the plantation aforesaid, situated in the district of Villa Gayoso and bounded by the lands of William Murray and David Hodge, being the same that was mortgaged to Richard Carpenter. [Adjudged to Job Routh for $175 at all three slaves, the cost of sale being $25. William Lewis receipted for amount due Mary Carpenter, his Mother.] 12 March 1796.

p. 433. Thomas Wilkins versus Ebenezer Dayton. 18 April 1796, Ebenezer Dayton appeared and binds himself to pay Messrs. George and Robert Cochran $446, coin of Mexico, being the amount of two bonds, one dated 30 Oct. 1794, etc. // Thomas Wilkins petitions that he has been informed that Ebenezer Dayton proposes to execute a mortgage in favor of George Cochran of his real estate, the petitioner, being a creditor of said Dayton, asks consideration. // [Recitation of the law regarding mortgaging property when a previous mortgage is still in effect, dated 18 Oct. 1792.] Post of Natchez, 30 Apr. 1796, appeared Ebenezer Dayton and two notes being shown to him, one in favor of Thos. Wilkins and one in favor of Abel Eastman. He ack. the signatures to be his own.

p. 435. Rachel Hartley versus estate of John Hartley. Pet. of Rachel Hartley, of Bayou Pierre, in the district of Natchez, showeth that she was the lawful wife of Jacob Hartley, who died 14 April, without making a written will or testament, having no children nor other heirs except brothers and sisters, and the petitioner, having been his wife 16 months during which time she bore him a son who died before his father. Some short time before the death of your petitioner's husband, he did verbally speak and declare in the hearing of two witnesses that if he should die, it was his will that your petitioner, calling her his wife, should have all his property and receive his dividend amongst his brothers and sisters, as children and heirs of John Hartley, deceased, who are now trying to deprive your petitioner of all the property of her deceased husband, to which property she conceives she has the fairest claim, for the whole or, at least, as much as will afford her a decent living and comfortable maintenance . . . . Sig: Rachel Hartley, Bayou Pierre. Aug. 15, 1794. // The petitioner will present a document to prove her marriage to the deceased Jacob Hartley. Manuel Gayoso de Lemos. // Natchez, 3rd Sept. 1794. Notified the above decree to the petitioner. // The petitioner presented the annexed authentic document, proving the lawful marriage of the late Jacob Hartley. // The proceedings will be transmitted to Col. Peter Bryan Bruin who will cause the date of the decease of the late Jacob Hartley to be ascertained and an inventory of the property he possessed at his death to be made out and also the depositions of the witnesses the petitioner offered to produce to prove her said husband's will in her favor. The whole to be done in the presence of the said Col. Bruin and witnesses and then returned to me. Sig: Manuel Gayoso. // I do hereby certify that Jacob Hartley and Rachel Bond were joined together in holy bonds of wedlock in the presence of witnesses hereunto subscribing their names. Sig: W. Murray. Wit: Solomon Whitley, Maurice Murray, Lacy Rumsey, Maria Rumsey. p. 436. To His Excellency, the Governor. Catherine Hartley, widow of the late John Hartley, represents that she has been told that a certain Rachel Bond, who lived with the petitioner's son, Jacob, decd., has presented a petition to have the property of your petitioner's son, on the pretense of having been married to him. The petitioner believed that her son had some intention of marrying this woman but from the most notorious bad character which she bears, the deceased's father, the petitioner and all the family oppose the connection, nor does any of them know whether they were married. Her treatment of him during his illness proved that she had no affection for him . . . . Sig. Catherine Hartley. // Inventory of the estate of Jacob Hartley: 1000 acres; [Very little else.] 20 Sept. 1794. Wit: G.W. Humphreys, Solomon Whitley, Francis Nailor. Before P. Bryan Bruin. // Bayou Pierre, 19, 1794, came John Coleman before the alcalde of this district and declared, on oath, that he was present when Jacob Hartley died which happened on 4 April of this year; he, being asked if he had ever heard Jacob Hartley declare his will at any time in regard to the disposal of his property, declared that he hadn't. Questioned by Rachel Hartley: Did you know me to neglect him during his sickness? A. I never saw you refuse to do anything he desired you to do. Sig: John Coleman. // Erastus Harman declared that he was present when Jacob Hartley died and to the best of his remembrance it happened 4 April last. He did not hear Jacob Hartley make any verbal will nor did he hear him say anything after he was with him for the last time before his death. He did not observe that Rachel, his wife, neglected him. . Sig: Erastus Harman. Wit: P. Bryan Bruin and Bryan Bruin. // Peter Sirlott declares that he was present at the time that Jacob Hartley died, which he remembers was in April last but the precise date he does not remember. He never heard him at any time declare how he would wish his property to de disposed. Q. by Rachel Hartley: Did you ever know me to refuse to do anything for my late husband? I do not remember that you refused to do anything for him, nor do I remember that he asked you to do anything. Q. Do you think that he was in his senses before he died? A. I cannot tell for he was speechless for some time before he died. Sig: Peter Sirlott. Same wit. as above. // Castle Bruin. May it please Your Honour to remit to Your Excellency papers relative to the claim of Rachel Hartley, the depositions of the witnesses who were summoned and examined agreeable to Your order and the schedule of the property, which the late Jacob Hartley died possessed of. It does not appear from any evidence which has been brought before me with the view of establishing the fact that the deceased made a nuncupative will in his last moments or that he was capacitated to do it. They all agree that he was speechless for some days before he died. Mr. Catherine Hartley has applied to me to examine some evidences tending to invalid the claim of Rachel Hartley but I have declined doing it, not having Your Excellency's instructions for that purpose. I have this moment received a proclamation from Your Excellency relative to adulterated coin and I shall not fail to make the contents as public as possible, etc. Sig. P. Bryan Bruin. // To His Excellency Governor Gayoso, the petition of Anna Catherine Hartley showeth that whereas she understands that her son's pretended wife is making application to Your Excellency for her son's property and that she understands that the said Rachel has set forth that her son made a will and left what property he had to her, which your petitioner is sure is false. as he made no written will, for about nine days before he died, he said that all that he had in the world should go to his decrepit mother and his soul to God. Her son was not twenty years of age when he joined himself to her in marriage .... [accuses his wife as the means of shortening her son's days and those of others.] Had I not applied to a man on this creek I should have lost two more of my children as this man declared in his opinion that they were poisoned, and by several other circumstances and her threatenings, it appeared evident that she poisoned them. Please direct Col. Bruin to examine this affair, according to evidences and examinations and transmitting their depositions to Your Excellency. Sig: Anna Catherine Hartley. 23 Sept. 1794. // Col. Bruin is hereby authorized to take depositions of certain persons as may be presented by the petitioner, which when done are to be transmitted to me. Sig: Manuel Gayoso de Lemos. // Communications to John Hartley. J. Girault. // Depositions by order of His Excellency, at the request of Ann C. Hartley. Peter Sirlott, being first sworn, declared that he was at Mr. Hartley's to the best of his remembrance about five or six days before the decease of Jacob Hartley and that he heard the said Rachel, his wife, say that he, the said Hartley, smelled so bad that she could not bear to go nigh him. As regards his being poisoned and his death being caused thereby, he knows nothing. // George W. Humphreys declared that he knows no circumstances to induce him to believe that Jacob Hartley was poisoned. Sig: G.W. Humphreys. // Hezekiah Harman declared that he was called in to set up with the late Jacob Hartley about two days before he died and he observed that his wife, Rachel, was not so attentive and tender of him as she ought to have been, but from what cause this neglect proceeded he knows not; he has no reason to believe that he was poisoned; the body both of Jacob and of his sister, Betty, had some extraordinary appearances on them which he had not observed on any other corpse which he remembers to have seen; they both swelled to an extraordinary size and in about four or five hours after his sister Betty died, the blood forced its way out of her mouth and nose and the same effects were produced on the body of Jacob Hartley and about 12 hours after death there were purple spots on both the faces of him and of his sister. Sig: Hezekiah Harman. // Orphah Leonard declared that she was, at the time of the late Mr. John Hartley's death, at the house of Jacob Hartley, and she heard Rachel Hartley say that she had put a bridle of a horse or a halter on John Hartley when he went to Cole's Creek or he would not have come home sick. She knew no circumstances to induce her to believe that the late Jacob Hartley was poisoned, or any of his family. Sig: Orphah (X) Leonard. // Christian Hartley declareth that she heard Rachel Hartley say, after her brother, John Hartley, was taken sick that she, Rachel Hartley, had put her witch-halter on him when he went to Cole's Creek or he would not have returned sick. She knows nothing of any part of the family having been poisoned. Sig: Christian (C.H.) Hartley. // Catherine Miles was at the house of her late father, Mr. John Hartley, about nine days before the death of her brother, Jacob Hartley, and she heard him at that time declare that he willed his property to his mother and his soul to God. Rachel Hartley was present and laughed heartily. She believed that her brothers, Jacob and John, and her sister, Betty, were poisoned. When asked what reason she had for so believing, she answered that she was told so by Mr. Nicholas Sirlott, a neighbor who was called in to administer some relief to her brother John and her sister Christina and who didn't relieve them. Q. What reason had he that Rachel Hartley was responsible? A. I have reason to believe that she did administer it because she threatened to take satisfaction on the family. She said she would have satisfaction if it was seven years afterwards. She declared to the truth of what Hezekiah Harman deposed of the dead bodies of her sister and her brother, Jacob. Catherine Miles, signed with a mark. Bayou Pierre, 8 Oct. 1794. Before P. Bryan Bruin. // Abigail Adams, being sworn, declareth that she remembers to have heard her son, Joseph, say before his death that in the course of last spring he happened to be at the house of the late Jacob Hartley when he breakfasted of milk together with other things that he was very soon affected and in an extraordinary manner, that he set out from the house to the Widow Humphreys and lost the use of his limbs for some time on the road, being obliged to dismount and remain some time on the ground before he could recover the use of himself and with difficulty reached Mrs. Humphreys plantation where he continued sick all night and he never recovered his health but died the month following. She often heard him express great surprise at the effect which the milk produced so suddenly upon him. He died on the ninth day from the time he was taken down and all the extraordinary appearances which were remarked to have taken place on the dead bodies of Jacob and Betty Hartley were visible in his corpse. Abigail Chambers, signed with a mark. Bayou Pierre. Oct. 7, 1794. // Katina Proctor declared to the same effect but with the additional circumstance that Joseph Chambers told her a little before his death that he had crossed the Bayou Pierre on foot the morning after he had breakfasted at Jacob Hartley's as beforementioned and that he attributed his illness in a great measure to a cold caught thereby. Katina (X) Hartley. // Nicholas Sirlott declared that he was called in by Mrs. Hartley's family to administer to the relieve of John and Christina Hartley after they were taken sick; that he refused to take them under his charge while a regular physician attended them; that he was not up to the practice of physics; that on their informing him the second time that their physician had been discharged he would be glad to do what he thought proper to save them; he did prepare and administer to them an antidote against poison which in a short time restored them both to their health. He declared his opinion from the beginning, from symptoms that attended their disorder that those that died in the family as well as those he relieved were actually poisoned but by whom he knows not. Signed Nicholas Sirlott. Before Peter Bryan Bruin. // Natchez 27 Oct. 1794. Issued an order at the request of William Hartley for William Murray, Esq. to send a certificate signed John Hartley, authorizing him to marry Jacob Hartley to Rachel Bond. Signed: Gayoso. // Same date. I issued an order for Dr. David Phelps to appear and give his deposition as required by Rachel Hartley. Signed Gayoso. // Notified the parties. Sig: John Girault. // p. 442. Appeared Dr. David Phelps, who being duly sworn deposeth that some time last spring, perhaps in April, he was called upon to visit Betsy Hartley. When he arrived at Bayou Pierre she had been buried some time, so that he saw her not. Her sister, Christina Hartley was also sick. The family said she had the same ailment as her deceased sister. He stayed there some days and administered medecine to her and he thinks her disorder to have been a bilious nervous fever, of which she recovered. In the month of May following he was called to visit John Hartley, Jr., who was attacked with the same complaint, with the same symtoms as his sister showeth. Only that his nerves were more affected. He treated him and attended him above a week and he is now recovered. Q. Did they display any symptoms of having been poisoned? A. That they did not have any such appearance. 3rd Oct. 1794. Sig: David Phelps. Wit: Jean Girault, Estevan Minor. Before Gayoso de Lemos. // In pursuance of your order to me, I employed several hours searching for John Hartley's certificate signifying in very broken Dutchified English his consent to his son's marriage with the girl he brought, namely Rachel Bond. They were accompanied by Solomon Whitley, the father-in-law of the girl. I questioned the young man why his father did not come with him, to which he answered, and I think Whitley did also, that Hartley had a very sore leg which rendered him unable to ride for some time. He then produced his father's certificate signifying his consent. The very circumstance of its being so very incorrectly worded gave it, in my opinion, the more probability of authenticity. Added to this, I could not suspect that Whitley could run the risk of perjury nor that the son could be so base as to forge his father's name, which might be so easily detected in the old man's lifetime. I heard no surmise of the certificate not being genuine for a considerable time afterwards. I had an opportunity of conversing with Captain Burnet who told me that old Hartley had not written nor signed the certificate but that he had consented to its being written and that while the match was by no means agreeable to him, he had been reconciled to his son and that the son and his wife lived on the old man's plantation. I am not surprised that I paid no attention after this to the scrawl of a certificate questioned. I married the young man by the name of James, not Jacob, as Your Excellency calls him. Sig: W. Murray. District of Villa Gayoso. 30 Oct. 1794. // I do hereby certify that Mrs. Catherine Hartley did at certain times offer me $100 if I would swear that Rachel Hartley had poisoned her family. I told her that I could not swear to that for I did not know who it was who poisoned the family. Sig: Nicholas Sirlott. // To His Excellency, the Acting Governor, Anna Christina Hartley, the widow of the deceased John Hartley, represents she has a suit pending in the Tribunal against Rachel Bond respecting the estate of Jacob Hartley deceased and as a division of the estate of her deceased husband, according to the tenor of his will, cannot be made until the said suit shall be determined, wherefore she prays that the said case be taken into consideration and determine as may be right. Natchez, 9 Dec. 1795. // At the request of Anna Christine Hartley. Granted. Sig: Grand-Pre. // Communicated to Hezekiah Harman, representing the widow Hartley. // Power of atty. from Rachel Hartley to Melling Woolley to represent her, etc. to sue for, recover and receive . . . whatsoever belongs to me from the estate of the decd. John Hartley, Sr . . . etc. Signed with a mark. Nov. 22, 1795. Wit: Ebenezer Smith, Jesse Howard, Ezekiel Miller. Rachel Hartley appeared before me and asked if I would give a sanction to the within instrument by certifying that her consent had been given in my presence that Mr. Melling Woolley should act as her attorney in the business. Something prevented my compliance of her request at the time but, it having been represented to me that my certificate is necessary to enable her attorney to institute a suit in her favor, I have from a regard of justice thought proper to certify that Rachel did apply to me for this purpose. 28 May 1796. // Rachel Hartley, widow of Jacob Hartley, decd., by her attorney, represents that the deceased John Hartley, Sr. did during the lifetime of your petitioner's husband make his last will and testament, dated 11 Jany. 1794, and bequeathed to your petitioner's husband, aforementioned, being one of his sons, considerable property, soon after which said John Hartley died and a short time after, before a division of the property was made, made, your petitioner's husband died . . . . . Mr. Hamilton, one of the executors, who had found means of taking into possession all of the cash, notes, bonds and other properties belonging to the estate and likewise the distribution of the same, dividing the effects how and to whom he pleased without reference to the will and set your petitioner's claim at naught and refused making any division to her, alleging that she was not lawfully married . . . She obtained a certificate of her marriage from William Murray of Cole's Creek whom Your Excellency had authorized to issue same. . . . . Asks for a just division, agreeable to the intent and meaning of the will. Melling Woolley, atty. for Rachel Hartley. 27 May 1796. // 3 June 1796, Whereas it is evidently proved that the petitioner was duly married by William Murray, Esq., who was authorized to do it; she is destitute except what she may derive from her husband; she is therefore entitled to a one-fourth of her said husband's estate, which provision is made for her by the law entitled Quarta Marital and whereas her said husband did survive his father, it is understood she is to be put into possession of a fourth part of the property inherited by her said husband on account of his father's death, as well as a fourth part of the property in his possession, and as the family of Hartley have maintained this suit obstinately without right, they shall pay the cost of the suit. Sig: Manuel Gayoso de Lemos. // Notification of this decree sent to executors of John Hartley in writing. Same date. Sig: Jean Girault. // Same day, I communicated this decree to Mr. Melling Woolley. Sig: Jean Girault.

p. 445. Roger Dixon versus Robert and G. Cochran. Roger Dixon petitions that, having made a conditioned bargain with Mr. George Cochran last February was a year for a negro wench and boy and leaving the said negroes in the possession of the said Cochran who was not performing the conditions agreed upon and the time being elapsed, he asks the said negroes be restored and said Cochran be obliged to pay damages, equivalent to the losses of the services of the said negroes. 2nd Apr. 1796. Sig: Roger Dixon. // Same day. Let it be given. Grand-Pre. // Apr. 2, 1796. Notified George Cochran. Jean Girault. // 9 Apr. 1796. At the Post of Natchez, at public court, appeared before me George Cochran, representing Robert and George Cochran, and Roger Dixon, who produced the agreement in question, written in the English language. Much time being spent in verbal allegations of both parties, the matter was adjourned until next audience, when they will present their allegations and other documents in writing. Sig: Carlos de Grand-Pre. Jean Girault interpreter. // Pet. of George and Robert Cochran, who represent that on 4 Apr. 1794, said Roger Dixon made an agreement with his creditors, of whom your petitioners were among the most considerable, and executed a mortgage recorded in the Archives of this government, of which a part of the second clause is recited, as follows: "that his motive for making this proposal being to have the opportunity of selling his property to the greatest advantage. He reserves the right of selling to his creditors or any of them, or any other person whomsoever such part of said property as may be sufficient to pay the whole or part of his debts, on condition that the proceeds of such sale be directly applied to that purpose and that no preference be given but that the highest bidder have the right of purchase." [This case extends from the bottom of p. 445 to the middle of p. 506. After Cochran explains how they had lived up to the contract, all the accounts of Roger Dixon are given in detail with all of his creditors.] Natchez, 16 June 1796. The allegation of the parties being well grounded, it is declared that the said Roger Dixon is entitled to the benefit of the delay granted by His Majesty on 7th December 1794 so far as it relates to the actual state of his debts and as respects the mortgage made on his property it must be understood that it extends only to such property as lawfully belongs to him and not to that he holds in trust. Signed: Manuel Gayoso de Lemos.

p. 506. Maurice Stacpoole versus Jesse Hamilton. Petition of Maurice Stacpoole that the following persons are indebted to him: Ebenezer Dayton, John Williams, James McIntyre, Jesse Hamilton, Isaac Johnson, Samuel Flower, Andrew Scanlan: asks order for payment without delay. Natchez. March 11, 1796. Sig: Maurice Stacpoole. // March 11, 1796. Such of the debtors as have no objections to the account of Mr. Stacpoole will pay to him within three days from notification hereof the sums they respectively owe or in default they will be compelled by law. Sig: Grand-Pre. // Notified Mr. Jesse Hamilton on his plantation on Cole's Creek, distance 15 miles, also Mr. John Williams. March 16th. Sig: Wm. Gillespie. // Jesse Hamilton having failed to pay debt after being allowed 15 days extension, sufficient property is ordered to be executed for said debt. and cost. Sig: Grand-Pre. [This case covers several pages more, Hamilton petitioning that his corn and tobacco be sold instead of the negro so condemned; John Smith, Esq., of the Dist. of Villa Gayoso, reporting that the said corn and tobacco were unfit for sale; Hamilton, still obdurate, replying that he was not in Judge Smith's district and therefore his ruling was invalid, at which the Commandant ordered that said Smith handle the case regardless of which district Hamilton lived in. Robert Hamilton, now living in New Orleans, was also injected into the case, but Lewis Evans, his attorney, answers that Jesse Hamilton had little or no claim against said

Robert Hamilton except as a small creditor, and that Jesse Hamilton claimed a lot which belonged to the trustees of Cloud's estate. Jesse Hamilton represented that Henry Milburn, the Constable, with William Smith, came to his plantation for property to be sold to pay Stacpoole when it had not been appraised and no notice of sale had been made. Whereupon he was allowed time to give an inventory of his holdings so that they could be appraised.]

p. 510. Protest. At the Post of Natchez, 21 July 1796. Appeared Isaac Gaillard, of this district, planter, who declared that from information received from various sources he has reason to believe Robert Johnson who married the niece of the appearant was married to Margaret Greer, daughter of Andrew Greer, now living at Knoxville, and it is said Mary Savage, daughter of the deceased sister of the appearant, has made a donation inter vivos in favor of the said Robert Johnson under the persuasion that he was her lawful husband. Therefore the said appearant, being of the opinion that the said Robert Johnson has committed a fraud and capital crime in marrying again while his first wife was still living, hereby protests in full form against the said donation and all other writings, public and private, that have been or may be made by his said niece in favor of the said Robert Johnson, all of which to be null and void and of no effect, which said protest he makes as guardian of his said niece and prays that all the property be and remain under the care and possession of this appearant until the matter shall have been examined and ascertained, and that all contracts made by said Johnson be declared null and void. Wit: Edward McCabe, Melling Woolley. Sig: Isaac Gaillard. Before Manuel Gayoso.

p. 511. Agnes Humphreys claiming her marriage portion. Agnes Humphreys represents that she is in possession of two slaves, named Silas and Sally, with their children, which were bequeathed to her by her deceased husband in compensation for the portion which she brought in marriage as will appear by the will of her deceased husband in the archives, as it also appears by a certified extract from the will of her deceased father that the property left to her by her said father was entailed to her and her heirs and therefore cannot be responsible for the debts of her deceased husband. Asks that the annexed documents be examined and the said slaves declared to be her own property, entailed on her, and that the same be recorded in the public archives of this government. Natchez. 21 July 1796. Signed: Agnes Humphreys. // Same date. Let the documents mentioned in the foregoing petition be produced to me for my determination. Signed: Gayoso. // It appearing by the will of Ralph Humphreys that he bequeathed to his wife the slaves beforementioned acknowledging that he had received a portion in marriage with her and also appearing by the certificate duly authenticated by the keeper of the records of the County of Fayette in Pennsylvania that the deceased father of Agnes Humphreys entailed property on her, wherefore it is declared that the negroes, Silas and Sally, are independent property of the said Agnes Humphreys and liable only for her particular contracts and none other. Signed: Manuel Gayoso de Lemos.

p. 511. Bennet Truly versus Neil McKan. Bennet Truly, of this government, petitions that during the course of the winter of 1795, he contracted with and obliged himself with considerable expense to provide timber and build a house for Mr. Neil McKan in the new town, which house when finsihed, it was mutually agreed by the several parties, should be estimated by good workmen indifferently. In order to conform strictly with this agreement, the aforesaid Cornelius McKan and your petitioner entered into an instrument of writing, or arbitrary bond, and named Mr. John Scott and Joseph Duncan and Thomas Thompson to value the same, which they did, as will appear by their writing hereunto annexed, dated 30 June of this year. Your petitioner, from a variety of circumstances equally unfortunate, as well as the great scarcity of cash in the place at present, desires to liquidate some debts and asks that Neil McKan be ordered to pay him the amount of the appraisal which was $319, with another debt of $14 for firewood, iron, etc. Natchez, 20 July 1796. Signed: Bennet Truly. // Same date. The petitioner and Cornelius McKan will appear before me next court day. Signed: Gayoso. // Notified Bennet Truly, signed J. Girault. // We, John Scott, Joseph Duncan and Thomas Thompson have valued the timber and workmanship in the house mentioned in the article of agreement; value the timber at $267 and the carpenter's work at $50. June 30, 1796. Signed by all three. // Neil McKan petitions that the work on the house was poor and that it leaks and the appraisement too high, and asks that the work be re-examined and re-appraised. Sig: Neil McKan. // The same appraisers report, giving the value of material at $217, and work $50, total $267. Sig: John Scott, Joseph Duncan, Thos. Thompson. 27 July 1796. // We approve the appraisement and order it to be recorded and the parties to conform to its tenor. Sig: Gayoso.

p. 513. Ebenezer Dayton versus his creditors. Petition of Ebenezer Dayton to the Natchez Government. 9 May 1796. New debts due for cattle from Mr. Geo. Cochran, Gabriel Griffing, Melling Woolley,

Bryant and Daniel Perry, Nathaniel Ivy, Nathan Swayze, William Lee, Ephraim Bates, William Gilbert, Widow Percy, Ambrose Foster, Francis Henderson. New debts not for cattle: Mr. Geo. Cochran, Samuel Flower, Manuel Lopez, James Garret, Wicoff and Garland, Joseph Castanado, Fernando Alsar, William Stephens, Alexander Boyd, for keeping cattle and butchering them at Nogales, Mr. John Booth, Henry Noble, John Thomas, William Dunbar, as exr. of est. of Mr. Gallaudet, William Foster, James Garret, Thomas Wilkins, Abel Eastman. Creditors: Mr. Wm. Dunbar, representing James Carrick and the est. of Melling Wooley, Ebenezer Rees for himself and for Wicoff and Garland, William Gilbert for himself and William Stephens, Thos. Wilkins, Geo. Cochran, Maurice Stacpoole, for himself and Samuel Flower, Stephen Minor, for himself and for Don Joseph Castanado, Don Antonio for himself and for Manuel Lopez, Mr. Bryan and Daniel Perry, William Lee and Henry Noble. The statement of Ebenezer Rees being read, it was proposed by the creditors to allow him until Saturday, 30th of this month, to send to Nogales for his son to be surety for said Dayton or to join with him if the delay asked for be granted. // p. 527. Post of Natchez, 30 July 1796. The creditors of Ebenezer Dayton amend in his statement, some of them represented by their attorneys, as likewise Nathan Swayze, Elisha Cushing, Cornelius Sealey, and William Collins for Susannah Percy, also creditors. It was resolved that Thos. Wilkins and Ebenezer Rees do immediately proceed to take an inventory of the real and personal property of Ebenezer Dayton. Don Estevan Minor, interpreter; Don Joseph Vidal, Don Juan Girault, witnesses. Signed: Manuel Gayoso de Lemos. // To the several gentlemen who convened at Natchez at the Govt. House, as creditors of Mr. Ebenezer Dayton. Gentlemen: I am informed you have requested that I should be bound as security with my father for the payment of his debts. My several reasons for declining to so bind myself are: I am advised not to be so bound; I am not capable nor qualified to manage so complicated a business as his nor am I rightfully able to understand the thing so as to know whether others do it properly or not. I have in some measure learned the Spanish language and have become both acquainted and pleased with their customs and manners, and, having formed my connections among them, wish to hold myself in constant readiness to remove with them in case any change of government should take place here. This I cannot do if I encumber myself with my father's affairs here, which might require a long time. Etc. Signed: Jonathan Dayton. // John Thomas and Daniel Holstein were witnesses to . . . . Petition of Ebenezer Dayton 17 June 1796.

p. 539. James Simmons versus Solomon Cole. James Simmons represents that he and his brother, two orphan minors, were left with their brother, Charles Simmons, who was older and married, and took charge of their property. But their brother Charles also died and the exors. of their parents being also deceased, the petitioners remained without anyone to do them justice. The widow of their brother and guardian had entered into a second marriage with a certain Solomon Cole, who now endeavors to defraud your petitioners of a part of their property. They pray for an order to protect the rights of your petitioners, an inventory of the property left by their parents being filed in the archives of this government. Natchez. 17 March 1796. Sig: James Simmons for self and brother. // Solomon Cole, of this government, planter, represents that he has married the widow of Charles Simmons who was guardian of his two brothers, James and Jacob Simmons, and was exr. of the estate. The said minors, having, in his absence, called his wife to account for the administration of their property, through fear, his wife made a show of settlement and gave them a note of the balance which appeared in their favor and although the said note has been satisfied and paid to them, with the exception of one cow, they refuse to give credit of the same on the note. They are making out accounts from their memory without any proofs against their sister-in-law. Asks that the minors appear and settle the whole account. There should be no complaint on either side, your petitioner having refused to settle this affair by arbitration of a certain John Smith, knowing he had not been friendly to the deceased, on the contrary had endeavored to take the property out of his power. Natchez. 18 March 1796. // James Simmons debtor to Charles Simmons, 1784. In swap for a horse $15; to the odds between guns $10; cash lent $20; paid schooling, 3 months, $6; Mr. Brown $18; Courtney for board $7; // Granted. Let James Simmons and his brother appear on the first day of court with their papers, and the petitioner will also appear. Natchez, March 19, 1796. // Inventory of the estate of late James Simmons, deceased, left in the possession of Charles Simmons, the son of James, also deceased, was delivered to us, on oath, by John Terry and the widow of Charles Simmons: Plantation 400 acres on the Bluff, a negro man named Aberdeen, abt. 25 yrs. old; 15 head of horses, 20 cows and calves, 56 head of other horned cattle, 10 sows and their pigs, 8 large barrows, 10 shoats, plow, one feather bed and bedding, 9 pots, a wooden chest, 6 pewter plats. Dist. of Villa Gayoso. 4 June 1794. W. Murray, John Smith. Delivered to Charles Simmons with the two children. 23 July 1778. One negro boy named "Aberdeen", 28 head of cattle, 34 hogs, 9 head of horses, household furniture, one bed, 6 pewter plates, one butter dish, two pots. I do declare to have delivered the above to Charles Simmons, being the property of James Simmons, deceased, now taken in full possession by him for the use and benefit of the two youngest children. Signed: Ursual (X) Simmons. Wit: John Dyson, Thomas Dyson. This deed and her will are recorded in the archives. // Will dated 10 July 1788. Chas. Simmons approved as exr. 22 Aug. 1788. // We, the subscribers, do hereby certify that we have received our full portion of the estate of James Simmons, decd., and we have no objections to the will of Ursula Simmons in favor of the two youngest children. 23 July 1788. William Curtis, Chas. (S) Simmons, Clement (X) Dyson, Squire Thos. Smiley, Joseph Bonner. [Note: In James Simmons' petition for a land grant in 1785, he stated that he had eight children. W.E. Bk.B-186.] Pine Ridge. Aug. 6, 1796. Before me, Gabriel Benosit, one of the alcaldes of this government appeared Mr. Nathaniel Brown, who declared that about 1786 he received from Charles Simmons $18 for schooling two children one year, namely James and Jacob Simmons, sons of Ursula Simmons, wife of James Simmons, deceased. Sig: Nathaniel Brown by Gabriel Benoist.

p. 541. Daniel Rainer versus Robert Miller. Daniel Rainer represents that some days ago he exchanged a horse with Mr. Cummins for a note of Robert Miller. Said Cummins assured him before witnesses that the note was just and he had been to the said Miller who acknowledged the note and was going to pay. Miller now denies the note to be just and will not pay. Pet. asks that the note be made just, or have his property returned to him. Sig: Daniel Rainer. St. Catherine's district. Aug. 24, 1796. // Natchez. 24 Aug. 1796. Robert Miller will appear before me on Saturday next, the 27th. Sig: Gayoso. Notified Mr. Robert Miller on his plantation on Cole's Creek. 24 miles distant. He says he will attend. Aug. 25, 1796. Sig: Wm. Gillespie. Fee; $4. // Robert Miller, having appeared and acknowledged the note in foregoing, said he would pay it if he had not given up his property to his creditors. It is ordered that George Cummins return to Daniel Rainer the effects which he has received in exchange for said note, which the said Rainer will return to him. Sig: Manuel Gayoso de Lemos.

p. 542. Winifred Ryan versus William Ryan. Natchez. June 25, 1794, personally appeared before me Winifred Ryan who declared that her present husband has for a long time treated her very ill and that she being advanced in years cannot bear it any longer, etc. She signs with a mark. Mrs. Sarah Purcions makes oath that several years ago she remembers that Winifred Ryan came to her house and from her appearance she thought that her husband had been whipping her and after some time Mrs. Ryan acknowledged that her husband had beat her. 18 June 1794. Before me William Cooper. Sarah Purcions signed with a mark. // Before me, Wm. Cooper, one of the magistrates of the district, appeared Mrs. Elizabeth Raby and declared that about nine years ago she lived on the same plantation with Wm. Ryan and the deponent heard the said Ryan beating his wife and immediately ran over to Ryan's house and there saw a stick about the size of her thumb, both ends worn out, and she took up the stick and found that it was split open which she verily believes was worn out on his wife. She also saw a number of bruises and swelled places on Ryan's wife. She had evidently been severely beaten. She believes he has led his wife a very unhappy life. 18 June 1794. Sig: Elizabeth (X) Raby. Wm. Cooper. Likewise Cady Raby declares the whole above declaration to be true except the marks on the woman which he did not see. Cady (C.R) Raby. Before Wm. Copper. // p. 543. We certify that last Monday Mrs. Ryan sent to Mr. John Wells for some person to come to Wm. Ryan and we went to the house where we found Wm. Ryan very angry and asked if we had come to guard him and we went on with a great deal of unnecessary discourse and, at length, he told Thomas Wells to take away his wife whom he also ordered to go away and accordingly Mrs. Ryan went to Mr. John Wells to stay all night. It appeared that she was afraid to stay at home for fear of her husband. 18 June 1794. Thomas (X) Wells. After Mrs. Ryan went away, Ryan said she should pay for it when she was alone. Sig: John Cason. // Inventory of the property of Wm. Ryan. Signed: Wm. Copper. // Petition of Winifred Ryan that her husband, Wm. Ryan, had absented himself from this government and left her with a family of children to maintain with very little property with which to sustain them; that when she married him she had considerable property which belonged to her and three children by a former husband, the greater part of which the said William Ryan has disposed of and made away with which she was obliged to permit, 16 of the cattle named in the inventory are those she bought with her own money and the household furniture is also hers and one mare and colt, but having three children of her first marriage and six by her second and desiring to do equal justice to them all, she asks that the property may be divided and an inventory made of each one's part, that no confusion may happen in the future. Mr. Ryan owes a great deal, which is a large reason for his going away and it is probable that the creditors will endeavor to secure what is left. She hopes that the situation of the children left behind will be considered. Natchez. 27 July 1794. Sig: Winifred Ryan. // 13 July 1794. Appeared Elizabeth Raby who did depose that she went with her mother, about ten years ago, to the house of William Ryan to purchase a feather bed; that the bargain was made between the deponent's mother and Mrs. Ryan who sold her only bed to this deponent's mother for a cow and calf which she wanted to give milk for her sick children, being reduced to this necessity, having no other means to purchase, and her husband, Wm. Ryan, not having any cattle at that time; that the said Wm. Ryan was present at that time at the whole transaction and said nothing, upon which this deponent's mother asked if he had any objections to the bargain, to which he replied that he had nothing to say to it; and the deponent also recollects that the cow thus exchanged was afterwards called, in the family, the cow of Mrs. Ryan's eldest son. Elizabeth Raby, signed with a mark. Wit: John Girault, John Eldergill. // Be these proceedings handed to Mr. Alexander Moore, the agent of the creditors of this country, to make his answer thereto. // p. 544. Answer thereto: I have made a demand upon the land of the petitioner's husband where she lives of $49 cash paid Mr. Vousdan and the Surveyor General in Jany. and May in 1789, with $6 interest, and I still retain the grant for the payment and although Ryan owes upward of $100 besides, I shall be content to receive the $60 payable at the crop. Sig: Alexander Moore. // Made known the contents to this petition to Mrs. Ryan. J. Girault. // Govt. of Natchez, Sandy Creek Dist. Personally appeared before me, Wm. Cooper, one of His Majesty's alcaldes, Mr. Richard Trevillian and his wife, Patsy Trevillian, and, on oath, declared that about 12 or 13 years ago they knew Winnie Ryan in the State of North Carolina and she owned a tract of land and three cows and young cattle and a likely horse and mare and some hogs, two feather beds and other household furniture. This was before she married Mr. Ryan. The deponents further say that Mrs. Ryan behaved herself like a prudent good woman and bore a good character so far as they knew, 19 July 1794. Wm. Cooper. // William Ryan represents that owing to some difficulty between himself and his wife, he was so weak as to absent himself from this government, hoping that his wife, during his absence, finding the want of his industry, would be brought to reflection and decide to live in peace with him. But on his return he found that she had absented herself from the plantation and taken with her all the family property. Ask that he may not merit your displeasure and that he be allowed to return to his plantation that he may raise a crop for the benefit of his creditors. 7 March 1795. Sig: Wm. Ryan. // Isaac Johnson, Esq. will take cognizance of this affair, and call before him necessary witnesses, the parties and make a report. // Wm. Ryan notified. // We, the undersigned, inhabitants of the Natchez district, do hereby certify that we know Wm. Ryan for several years and to be peaceable, inoffensive, industrious and loyal to this government, and obliging to his neighbors. Minor. I know nothing contrary to the above recommendation. Robert Moore. I know nothing ill of Mr. Wm. Ryan. He paid me for surveying his land. Wm. Vousdan. Charles King, William Clark, Dennis Collins, Joseph Killian, Chas. Cason, Thomas Reed, Joseph Perkins, John Bullen, Randal Gibson, Joseph Harrison, A. Bingaman, Wm. McIntosh, Richard Miller, John Bolls, Robert Hamilton, Ezekiel Dewitt, Robert Carter, Wm. Peel, Henry Holstein, John Odam, Abraham Tyler, David Lambert. Before John Girault. Another petition from Winifred Ryan, giving an account of the property she had before she married Wm. Ryan and asking that she be given her property so that she may raise her fatherless children. Sig: Winifred Ryan. 31 Aug. 1796. // Winifred Ryan having presented proof of stock and other personal property, proceeds of property of which she was possessed before her marriage with Ryan, she therefore shall retain possession of the same for the benefit of herself and all her children, and a tract of land having been granted to Wm. Ryan, it shall be disposed of for the benefit of the creditors as they think most advantageous to them. Be this notified to the parties and creditors. Signed: Manuel Gayoso de Lemos. Natchez, 10 Aug. 1796.

p. 546. Ezra Marble versus David Douglas. Ezra Marble represents that four years ago his father died and petitioner, being the eldest son, took charge of the family. There being several small children, he put some of them as apprentices at different places, by order of His Excellency the Governor, and among them was a boy, named Stephen, apprenticed to David Douglass to learn the trade of carpenter and, by agreement, was to be also taught to read and write, but it appears that the said Douglas has entirely disregarded his obligation, in as much as he kept the said boy about four years without teaching him any part of his trade but on the contrary has used him as a servant, washing dishes and milking cows, nor has he given him any education, as will appear by the annexed certificate of persons dwelling in his immediate neighborhood, wherefore he asks that the said apprentice be taken out of his power that your petitioner, as his eldest brother, may procure him a place where he may learn a trade and, in the end, be useful to society, enabled to make a living for himself in an honest way. Natchez. 17 Aug. 1795. Signed: Ezra Marble. // We, the subscribers, do certify that we live in the neighborhood of David Douglas and are acquainted with him and his apprentice, Stephen Marble, and the said apprentice has been with him nearly four years and we do not think that the said Douglas has taken any steps to learn the said apprentice his trade or given him an education, which, it is said, he was, by agreement, to do; on the contrary he keeps him employed in menial work such as milking cows, washing dishes and other such business, which must be a detriment to him and prevent him from acquiring a trade and he is already advanced in years, this we certify to the best of our knowledge, at the request of the apprentice's brother. 15 Aug. 1795. Jeptha Higdon, John Calvit, Richard Roddy, Benjamin Curtis, Mary Higdon, David Greenleaf, Wm. Calvit and Benj. Newman. // Natchez, 6 Sept. 1795. To be communicated to David Douglas. Signed: Grand-Pre. Presented this to Mr. Douglas who will appear next Saturday. J. Ferguson. Fee: $3. // To His Excellency, the Acting Governor, David Douglas represents that the representation made by Marble as to my conduct toward his brother, my apprentice, is false and in proof, the part where he says I have not given any education to his brother is imaginary I present to your Excellency a specimen of his writing. This boy is very small and it is true that I have not made him work much at the carpenter's trade as Your Excellency knows that in the first place children should be taught to read and write and afterwords put to work; as to my making him a servant, I can prove by those who are really my neighbors, as those who sign the certificate presented by Marble do not live near my dwelling. They are persons who wish to oblige him and the greater part do not know what they have signed, but the truth of the matter is that I have had this boy nearly four years and I have maintained him all this time when he could be of no use to me and now when he begins to be able to make me some return for the cost of his maintenance, they wish to take him from me, to aid them in the work in their swamp where he would learn nothing but to be a vagabond, without a trade, like the others of his family, and the said boy, having been delivered to me by His Excellency the Governor, I trust that Your Excellency will not allow that he should be taken from me by his caprice and that of others, for having taken charge of him as an orphan I wish to keep him and learn him my trade and enable him to maintain himself, and become a good member of society. Signed: D. Douglas. Natchez. 26 Sept. 1795. // Same day. In order definitely to settle the matter between the parties and do justice to them both, David Douglas will be notified to present the boy to John Scott and Frederick Man, master carpenters of this post, and also to Valentine Dalton, schoolmaster, who will examine him both in respect to his progress in the carpenter's trade and in reading and writing and make report to me of the result of said examination. Sig. Carlos de Grand-Pre. // On same day and year, notified the above to David Douglas and Ezra Marble. Sig: Jean Girault. // Notified: Valentine Dalton, Frederick Mann and John Scott. Sig: Jean Girault. // We, the subscribers, have examined the affair between Mr. Douglas and his apprentice and have agreed that the apprentice is to remain with his master and he to fulfill his agreement by having him educated agreeable to his indenture and that he may immediately be put to the trade. Signed: V.G. Dalton, Frederick Man, John Scott. The parties will conform to the opinion of the arbitrators and the apprentice will remain with his master, who, on his part, shall give him the necessary education. On same day notified Ezra Marble. J. Girault. Communicated to David Douglas. Whereas Stephen Marble, apprenticed to David Douglas, has absented himself, without leave, from his master's house and it is evident from various circumstances that he is harbored by his brother, Ezra Marble, therefore the said Ezra will deliver the apprentice to his master within four days or otherwise the said Ezra shall be lodged in the prison of this Fort and there remain until the boy is delivered to his master. Notified at the home of Ezra Marble, he being absent at Big Black. His brother says that at his return he will immediately submit to justice. // p. 548. David Douglas represent that Ezra Marble endeavored in the month of Sept. 1795 to deprive your petitioner of his apprentice and Your Excellency having ordered arbitration of the case, it was determined in favor of your petitioner, as will appear by the documents, but the said Marble having in contravention of decision of the arbitration given by the arbitrators and of the sentence of Your Excellency has received the apprentice into his house, and the same being made known to you, you were pleased to order Marble to prison until said apprentice should return to his duty which order was executed on the 8 Dec. last, and your petitioner knows not for what motives said Marble was same day liberated from the Fort without having delivered up the apprentice. Such was the fact, for one of his brothers was bringing the apprentice home to your petitioner when he learned that Marble was discharged from the fort and in consequence of that information, he did not deliver him but conducted him to Big Black where he now lives, wherefore your petitioner prays that Your Excellency will determine whether your petitioner shall have his apprentice. // Ezra Marble will deliver to David Douglas, without delay, otherwise he will be conducted to the prison of the court and there remain until his order shall be obeyed. Communicated: Order to take the body of Stephen Marble, apprentice of David Douglas and bring him to my presence. The syndics of the different districts are to take the necessary steps to have him apprehended and furnish the constable with means to take him. Ezra Marble being present at the audience at the same time heard the allegations on both sides, permitting Marble to bring the apprentice himself to save the expenses . . . . . Messrs. Dalton and Man are required to examine these proceedings and report whether they think David Douglas has furnished . . . . to the apprentice or not. Their report was that Marble's complaint was without foundation. // John Arden of Cole's Creek, 27 Aug. 1796. I do certify that David Douglas used Stephen Marble more like one of his own children than like a strange child both in the household and in schooling. Signed: John Arden. // Wm. Noble. I do here certify that I have been a neighbor to David Douglas nearly three years and I have been acquainted with the apprentice, Stephen Marble, and do know that he has been well-used, in every respect I think an apprentice ought to be used. I believe that he gave him as much learning as he conveniently could which was as much as the other boys got. // Prosper King certified that I lived a near neighbor of David Douglas the whole time that Stephen Marble lived with them and he was well-used, etc. // Justus King certified the same. I understood that the boy was persuaded away by his brothers and other people. // John Griffin certified the same.

p. 552. Jonas Scoggans versus George Clare. Jonas Scoggans represents that being desirous of paying some debts, he decided to dispose of part of his land on which there was some improvement, in the month of March to Mr. George Clare, an inhabitant of this place. The transaction took place at the dwelling house of your petitioner, at which time the said Clare signed two notes to your petitioner for the value of the said piece of ground in the presence of two witnesses, and in turn your petitioner signed on his part an instrument, the purport of which was to engage himself to make the titles to the land in due form at the office of the government. A short time had elapsed when your petitioner was informed that the two notes were seen in the possession of Mr. Clare. At this intelligence, your petitioner seached among his papers for the above notes, never suspecting that they were not in his custody, but to his disappointment found that they were not there. Still willing to entertain a favorable opinion of Mr. Clare, he went to him to know the certainty of the matter. He acknowledges having the notes in his hand but neither then or since has returned them or ever has been near your petitioner though he has repeatedly promised to come. Whether the notes were taken away by design or inadvertency Your Excellency will be best able to determine. Your petitioner not being able to stir out of doors for several weeks, he asks your consideration of the papers annexed, etc. Signed Jonas Scoggans. Natchez. 23 July 1796. // John Smith, Esq. will cause George Clare to appear at Government House as soon as possible after notification and answer the complaint of Jonas Scoggans. // We, the undersigned, witnessed two notes of hand signed and given by George Clare to Jonas Scoggans for $175 each, that is to say, one note 20 months later, with lawful interest. Daniel Finan and John Shoneuer. [Letter from George Clare stating that he did not know that he had the notes until he was nearly home and he had no intention of taking them nor of not living up to the agreement to pay for the land, etc.] To Mr. Jonas Scoggans: Sir: I think you set your reasons high in sending me such a message, threatening me with the constable, as if I had your property in my hands, which you know I have neither your obligation, right or title for the land and as for your bare word that you have nothing of the obligation, that does not decide the matter. I can testify on oath that I did not fetch them off with me. Etc. [Makes several offers of payment for the land and claims his share of the crop which is on it. Offers as much as $100 worth of hats as part payment.] // They mutually agree to submit to Messrs Joseph Bernard and William Owens, if they cannot agree, they ask that an umpire be appointed. Sig: William Clare, Catherine Scoggans. // I do hereby approve of the persons appointed as arbitrators for the parties and if an umpire should be wanted Gabriel Benoist will appoint him. Sig: Manuel Gayoso de Lemos. // Mr. John Bisland will act as umpire in case Joseph Bernard and William Owen cannot agree, in the above arbitration. // Pine Ridge. Aug. 19, 1796. Joseph Bernard and William Owens, arbitrators to settle the dispute between George Clare and Jonas Scoggans, not concurring in opinion, Mr. John Bisland, being nominated umpire, was called in to decide the difference. After maturely considering from whence the cause of the contest arose between the contending parties, we subscribers do agree that it is evident that Mr. George Clare was not informed how to fulfill his engagement according to bargain with Jonas Scoggans and his failure or omission we must attribute solely and entirely to the folly and imprudence of Mr. Clare, we therefore do award the said George Clare to pay to Jonas Scoggans in the month of January next the sum of $75 or the equivalent in ginned cotton and the cost of this suit shall be defrayed by Mr. Clare. Any obligations signed by the said parties previous to this decision respecting the purchase of said land shall be forever void and of no effect. Nevertheless the said George Clare shall keep quiet possession of the land belonging to the said Scoggans until he has taken the present crop off the land which shall be accomplished in a reasonable time and the said Clare shall quit all claim and restore possession of the land in question to Jonas Scoggans on the first day of January next. Signed: John Bisland, Joseph Bernard. Costs $7.

p. 555. James Stewart versus Gabriel Ruffat. Gabriel Ruffat represents that he was applied to by a certain planter for one or two barrels of salt which sd planter left in his house in his charge. But the petitioner, on oath, declares that in February last that he put the salt into his kitchen and at the end of 3 or 4 days the same planter, or one of his company, came and took away one of the said barrels, paying to the negro who attended in the store two rials for the storage. After two or three days, came another planter, with a boy, and took away the other barrel, paying also two rials for storage. Now, the said planter comes forward claiming one of the two barrels of salt which he said that he has not received and it appears to your petitioner that it is very hard when the same has been delivered. He asks the said planter be questioned. Signed: Gabriel (X) Ruffat. // James Steward, of this government, represents that last year he left in the house of Gabriel Ruffat two barrels of salt in storage until he could get a cart to carry it to his plantation. // Decision: Being proved that Stewart delivered the barrels to the house of Ruffat, the sd Ruffat will prove the delivery of them to Stewart or will pay him the amount thereof or return him a barrel of salt of the same quality within three days. Sig: Manuel Gayoso de Lemos.

p. 557. Henry Bair versus Polser Shilling. Henry Bair represents that he did agree with Polser Shilling some time ago to make some leather into shoes for which he was to receive 6 rials per pair. He agreed to make them at this cheap rate in consequence of Shilling agreeing to find thread, wax and every other material and to pay the amount in cash on the work being delivered. The said Shilling neglected to procure these articles for a long time and represented to Your Excellency that the work was neglected by your petitioner and obtained an order for the petitioner to make the shoes immediately. In order to comply herewith the petitioner was obliged to furnish the aforesaid materials and also some sealed leather. Your petitioner did finish the shoes and delivered them to Shilling and asked for the payment of the work together with the price of the materials he had furnished, the whole amounting to $33, for which the petitioner has received $10 in goods but Mr. Shilling refused to pay the balance. He asks for justice. 24 Oct. 1796. Sig: Henry Bair. // Polser Shilling will attend at Govt. House tomorrow morning. Gayoso. // Nov. 27, 1796. Polser Shilling and Henry Bair having appeared before me and stated their cases, it was mutually agreed between them that Ebenezer Dayton and William Smith would examine the shoes made by Bair, and Shilling bonds himself to pay to the latter such price for the shoes as the said two persons shall award. Sig: Polser Shilling, Henry Bair. Before Manuel Gayoso. // In obedience to the above order Ebenezer Dayton and William Smith have fully heard the parties and examined their accounts and carefully reviewed the shoes and their workmanship and on mature and deliberate consideration are fully agreed in our opinion and judgment that the workmanship of the shoes is so bad that the defendant ought not to be obliged to receive them, therefore we judge that the plaintiff ought to pay for the leather he received $32 or return leather to that value and also to pay the defendant $3 and one bit for the balance between the goods received and the shoes delivered, which two sums amount to $35 and one bit due the defendant with cost of the suit. Sig: W.B. Smith and Ebenezer Dayton. // Natchez, 5th Sept. 1796. I approve the foregoing opinion of the arbitrators. Let it be notified to the parties.

p. 558. The King versus Henry Jones. Post of Natchez, 19 Aug. 1795, appeared Barnabus Perry and informed verbally as follows: that the mulatto, Henry Jones, a slave of Gabriel Griffing, has grievously and dangerously wounded a mulatto woman named Diana, at about 6 o'clock in the morning of this day, the property of the deponent; that the said mulatto has escaped and is secreted somewhere near his plantation. In consequence of all which, I, Don Carlos de Grand-Pre, have issued orders for the apprehension of the mulatto and it has been necessary to repair to the plantation of the said Barnabus Perry to take the declaration of the wounded and that of the surgeon attending. And, being myself indisposed, I have commissioned for that purpose, Don Joseph Vidal, Capt. of the Co. of Artillery, of which appointment he will be notified. // 19 Aug. 1795, Don Joseph Vidal, etc., in pursuance of the foregoing, has set out for the plantation aforesaid, in company of Don Juan Girault, John Ferguson and James Ross, acting as an interpreter. Signed by all. // At the plantation of Barnabus Perry, in the district of Villa Gayoso, distant 18 miles from the Post of Natchez, I, Don Joseph Vidal, have arrived and, it being necessary. administered oath to the witnesses, aforesaid. I entered the room in which was the mulatto woman named Diana and by means of the interpreter asked her name and she answered that she didn't know that she wanted to sleep. She was then asked who had wounded her to which she answered she did not know that her side pained her. In other words, it was noted that she was out of her senses and her master and mistress and others in the house said she had been in that state since the night before . . . . . It being evident that she could not give testimony in a legal manner, I have suspended further questions until her situation might authorize me to resume the inquiry. Signed with the interpreter and witnesses. // At said plantation, same date, Samuel Flower, physician, being present, the following questions were put to him. His name is Samuel Flower and he is married and professes the art of medecine. He declared that yesterday morning he was called to attend the said mulatto woman; that on arrival he proceeded to examine the wounds she had received and found three in the head which had penetrated the skull, and which he does not consider dangerous. Another wound on the right breast which penetrated to a depth of 8 inches between the ribs and the flesh, and 3 inches in breadth, which he considers very dangerous and mortal. Besides this the woman seems to have been struck and kicked in the stomach. She is out of her senses but when he first arrived she was in her senses and told him it was Henry Jones who had wounded her. The deponent is 43 years old. He acknowledged the foregoing deposition. // The proceedings delivered to Lt. Col. Carlos de Grand-Pre, acting as Governor, in six leaves of writing. // 22 Aug. 1795. I, Don Carlos de Grand-Pre, having recovered from my indisposition, have continued the proceedings in the above case. The mulatto, Henry Jones, belonging to Gabriel Griffing, having been apprehended, is lodged in this fort, by Messrs. Henry Stephens and Jonathan Rucker. Have caused the said persons to appear before me and Barnabus Perry, to take their oaths. Henry Stephens, being asked his name, etc., answered that his name was Henry Stephens, he was married, and by trade a carpenter. He knew the mulatto, Henry Jones, and he thought he was imprisoned for having wounded the mulatto woman, named Diana, belonging to Mr. Barnabus Perry. The affair had happened near his house on the 18th of this month, and Barnabus Perry had requested him to search for the mulatto man and he and Jonathan Rucker followed a path in which they perceived the footprints of said mulatto and came to an old cabin in which said mulatto was concealed, washing a bloody handkerchief. As they approached the house, the deponent ordered him to give up the knife with which he had wounded the woman. He immediately did so, and they tied and conducted him to the fort. He presented the knife to the guard on duty at the fort. Stephens, the deponent, is 50 years old. Signed: Henry (H.S.) Stephens. Same day. Barnabus Perry, being sworn, said he was a bachelor and a farmer; being in his own house on the 18th he heard persons crying and inquiring who cried, he was told that his mulatto woman, Diana, was stabbed by the mulatto Henry Jones; the said woman was brought into the house bleeding and she said the mulatto, Henry Jones, stabbed her when she was in the woods looking for the cows to milk them accompanied by her sister, Phillis, and the man came out of the woods and said "Dinah, now I will settle with you." and began to beat her and stab her. Phillis begged him not to kill Dinah and he said if she did not let him alone, he would give her the same. Barnabus Perry, the deponent, is 37 years old. // 2nd Sept. 1795. Appeared Jonathan Rucker testified about the same as others, and was 28 years old, and a bachelor, and a farmer. Next appeared Phillis, sister of the woman Dinah, testified as told by Barnabus Perry. She is 23 years old. // 23rd Sept. 1795. Delay in proceedings caused by illness of Don Carlos de Grand-Pre. It was necessary to go to Perry's plantation to question Dinah, the woman, who has not yet recovered from her wounds. For a long time she considered Henry Jones as her husband. He had run away to the woods and wanted her to go with him; at her refusal, said if he left, he would leave her fit for nothing.

p. 569. Henry Jones deposed that he was married to the woman Dinah and had been married by Mr. John Lovelace, etc. [Several pages of about the same. Jonathan Rucker was a native of Va. Samuel Flowers a native of the U.S. Diana a native of Natchez and slave of Barnabus Perry.] Henry Jones considered of good character until his abuse of Dinah, by Justus King, John Griffing, Reuben Newman, Solomon Alexander, Adam Lanehart, James Perry, Isaac Newman, Jesse Hamilton and William Matthews. Cole's Creek. // Petition of Hannah Griffing that she has received orders to pay $177 costs on account of the criminal attempt by one of her slaves on the person of a wench, belonging to Mr. B. Perry, which slave is out of her possession at present and has been ever since the above affair. She thinks the greatest part of the costs should be on Mr. Perry as he has encouraged the wench to leave her husband and take up with another. Etc. Signed: Hannah Griffing. // Aug. 24, 1796. Having examined the proceedings in this case, I find that the mulatto is guilty of the crime laid to his charge but in consideration of the situation of the widow, I do hereby pardon Henry Jones and permit him to return peacefully to his duty on the express condition that he shall not transgress in the future and that he be kept from the neighborhood of B. Perry, and the widow of the said Griffing shall pay the cost of the suit. Sig: Manuel Gayoso de Lemos. // Jeremiah Coleman, exor. of the est. of Gabriel Griffing, complains that the cost of the suit is nearly $250 and the said Jones has caused the loss of time to his late master, Gabriel Griffing, of about 12 months and other damages have arison to the estate because of it. // The allegation set forth considered, it is ordered that the mulatto Henry Jones, shall serve his master four years more than he was bound.

p. 575. James Kirk versus Samuel Cooper. [A long drawn-out suit.] James Kirk represents that a certain Samuel Cooper in 1788 did, by his negligence or inattention, burn or suffer to be burned a quantity of tobacco amounting in value to $287 as will appear by the account annexed; he prays that Cooper be ordered to pay the said sum without delay, or in default thereof to order his property to be seized for the amount. Signed: James Kirk. Natchez. 14 March 1796. // To be communicated to Samuel Cooper with the account and his letter that he may acknowledge his signature. // By virtue of the foregoing decree, I notified Samuel Cooper at the plantation of Mr. Mitchell, 15 miles, and presented the within writing to him which he read and acknowledged to be the same he sent to Mr. James Kirk after the barn was burned. Fees: $3. March 30, 1796. Signed: Wm. Gillespie. // Debtor, Mr. Samuel Cooper in account with James Kirk. To 200 1/2 hogheads of tobacco, burned by you in a drunken frolic. $220. By your share of 250 pounds of tobacco $33. Balance due James Kirk $187. Sir: Trouble and necessity obliges me to inform you of my great misfortune by accident of fire which has ruined me. By honor of a gentleman, it was not by indolence or neglect. The fire caught on the lower end of the barn, my being in the same. The chief of the negroes were in the far field. We done all in our power but to no purpose. Signed: Samuel Cooper. Sept. 10, 1788. // p. 576. Natchez, 13 April 1796. Messrs. Isaac Johnson and Alexander Ross are appointed to examine the accounts pending between Mr. James Kirk and Samuel Cooper, making me a report of the same. Sig: Grand-Pre. [More than three pages of these accounts follow. Samuel Cooper lists a number of items in James Kirk's statement to which he objects. Depositions as to the quality of cotton and tobacco destroyed. Samuel Cooper's account with James Kirk, Esq. William Dunbar and Ruffin Gray appointed arbitrators to settle the matter. More accounts follow. The article of agreement made Oct. 13, 1787 between James Kirk, planter, and Samuel Cooper, overseer. Cooper to take charge of a plantation and fourteen negroes. This ratified by Grand-Pre.]

p. 594. Extracts from the records of the Orphans Court of Philadelphia, Prov. of Penn. respecting such parts of Ralph Asheton's estate as, by petition, were allotted to Margaret and Frances Asheton. To Margaret Asheton, second daughter of the said Ralph Asheton, decd., were assigned as her one-sixth part of the real estate, the two following tracts of land and their appurtenances, marked M on the draft attached, one of them in Blockley Township, being part of two tracts, one the original purchase of William Powell, the other the original purchase of William Smith, beginning at part of a line of John Warner's land on Lancaster Road, thence along the said road . . . , thence by land hereafter assigned to Frances Asheton, deceased, ... to the middle of the Haverford Road . . . . to a post in the line of Richard Marsh's land, thence by lands of John Warner . . . to the east side of the Schuylkill River, on the west end and north side of Sassafras Street, up said street a certain distance to Schuylkill Front Street; to the said Margaret to be held by her or her heirs and assigns forever, of which one-sixth part, we have assigned to one Susannah, widow of the said Ralph Asheton, decd., one-third part of the 150 acres of land, with one-half part of the saw-mill thereon, beginning at a post in the middle of the Haverford Road, on the east side of the said Mill Creek, thence by a tract hereafter assigned to Frances Asheton to the middle of the Haverford Road, then along same, containing 50 acres of land, we have assigned and delivered as above-said to the said Susannah Asheton to be held by her and her assigns during her life as one-third of the said Margaret's one-sixth part of the said real estate. Unto Frances Asheton, youngest daughter of the said Ralph Asheton, decd., we have assigned and delivered several tracts or lots of land hereinafter mentioned and described with their appurtenances marked in the draft hereunto annexed with the capital letter F; one of them situate in the township of Blockley aforesaid, part of the original purchase of William Powell and part the original purchase of William Smith, beginning at a post in the middle of the Lancaster Road, afsd, to a post in the Haverford Road, to a post in the line of Richard Marsh's land and the corner post of James Coult's and Company's land, to land belonging to the heirs of George Roach, containing 190 acres of land, another situate between the River Schuylkill and the

Schuylkill Front Street, beginning at a post on the east side of Schuylkill and the south side of Sassafras Street; another piece in the said city between Schuylkill Front Street and Second Street; another lot of ground in the said city above said Front and Second Street, containing in breadth 102 feet and in length 396 feet, bounded westward by said Front Street, northward by Mulberry Street, on south by a lot of ground belonging to the heirs of Benjamin East, on other side by a lot of ground formerly granted to Samuel Claridge; an annuity of 10 pounds per annum issuing out of 10 tenements and lots of ground in the said city of Philadelphia, payable to Elizabeth Senny, during her life, we have assigned and delivered to be held by Frances Asheton her heirs and assigns, as her one-sixth part of the real estate above-mentioned. We have assigned and delivered to Susannah, widow of the said Ralph, one-third part of 190 acres, as above described, to be held by Susannah Asheton and her assigns for the term of her life. I do hereby certify that I have compared the within and foregoing writing and do find it to be just and true extract from the records of the Orphans Court, held at Philadelphia for the city and county of Philadelphia, 17th Nov. 1749, before Thomas Lawrence. William Allen, Certimus Robinson, Esquires, Justices of said court. In testimony hereof, etc. and fix the seal of the said court, this 10 May MDCCXCVI (1796). Signed: Joseph Hopkinson, Clerk. Copies of Margaret and Susannah Asheton's wills: In the name of God, Amen: I, Margaret Asheton, of the City of Philadelphia in the Province of Pennsylvania, spinster, in declining state of health, etc. . . I nominate my mother, Susannah Asheton, to be the sole executrix of my last will and testament, to sell my property and give 100 pounds to my brother, Ralph Asheton, 100 pounds to be put at interest and this interest to be given for the use of my aunt, Rebecca Goad, of London, widow, during her natural life, and upon my aunt's decease I give the said principal of 100 pounds to my brother-in-law, James Humphreys, all the residue and over plus money, arriving by the sale thereof, I give unto my honored mother, I also give and devise to my sister, Frances Asheton, her heirs and assigns, all my piece of land on the east side of the Schuylkill River, in or near the said city, containing about 5 acres with the appurtenances, to the Pennsylvania Hospital I give 10 pounds to be paid the treasurer toward promoting their charitable designs, all my plate I give to be equally divided between my said brother Ralph and my sister, Frances, and my niece, Susannah Humphreys, likewise all my wearing apparel to my sister Frances, except such parts thereof my honored mother shall think proper to give to my said niece, Susannah. After my debts are paid, I give unto my said mother, Susannah, the residue of my estate. Aug. 5, 1761. Signed: Margaret Asheton. Wit: James Stephens, John Baldwin, John Riley. // Will of Susannah Asheton: of the City of Philadelphia, etc. being weak and sick, my son, Ralph Asheton, my executor, my body to be interred in a plain mahogany coffin, without a pall, after my just debts and funeral expenses paid, at the discretion of my executrix, hereinafter named. As to my worldy estate, my just debts and funeral expenses to be paid, and my son, Ralph Asheton, shall give my executrix full anf final discharge, under his hand and seal, discharging her from all debts, dues, claims and demands whatsoever touching and concerning my administration of the goods and chattels, rights and credits, which were my husband's, Ralph Asheton, late of the city of Philadelphia, deceased, upon executing and delivering such discharge to my executrix, I do give and bequeath to my said son, Ralph Asheton, the sum of 150 pounds of money of Philadelphia, also one pair of silver candlesticks, whichever he shall make choice of, with the silver snuffers, also my gold watch. I also do hereby discharge my son, Ralph Asheton from all dues and demands whatsoever which I have now against him. I do devise and bequeath to my daughter, Frances Watts, her heirs and assigns, all the rest and residue and remainder of my estate, real and personal, lands, tenements, rents, hereditaments and real estate, whatsoever, lying and being with their appurtenances, to have and hold, etc. and I do nominate my daughter, Frances Watts to be sole executor of my last will and testament, etc. 23 March 1767. Signed: Susannah Asheton. Wit: John Rice, Rebecca Rice, Peter Thompson. This is to certify that the foregoing true copies of the original wills of Margaret Asheton and Susannah Asheton, deceased, remaining of record in the office at Philadelphia. 21 May 1796. John Wampole, the register. Inventory of the estate of Susannah Asheton, late of the city of Philadelphia, deceased, taken by the subscribers, 4th Feb. 1768. Sundry gold and silver to amount of 51 pounds, bill of credit 100 pounds, etc. [four pairs of silver candlestick, two with snuffers and stands, silver coffee pot with stand, one silver tankard, quart, one silver waiter, etc. etc . . . . . . personal belongings many and of best quality. .] // I, Mathew Irwin, Esq., Master of Rolls of the state of Penn. and Recorder of Deeds of the City and County of Philadelphia do certify that on 29 June 1768, Stephen Watts, executor of the last will and testament of Susannah Asheton, entered satisfaction in my office in full for principal and interest of a mortgage dated 23 Dec. 1761, given by Aven Hassert to Susannah Asheton for 300 pounds of lawful money of Pennsylvania, for which sum, the said Aren Hassert mortgaged two certain buildings on the north side of Carroll Hill Street, between Front and Newmarket, at the north end of the city of Philadelphia. // I also certify that on 29 March 1778, Stephen Watts, exr. of the will of Susannah Asheton, deceased, entered satisfaction in my office for the interest of the mortgage from the 18 Oct. 1766, given by John Gibbons and wife to Susannah Asheton, for 150 pounds, for which sum the said John Gibbons and wife, mortgaged a certain piece of land commonly known by the name of Lee Garden, in county of Philadelphia. 20 May 1796. Signed: Matthew Irwin. // Manuel Gayoso de Lemos has recorded the various instruments presented to me. 15 Sept. 1796. Sig: Manuel Gayoso de Lemos. // City of Philadelphia, 23 Sept. 1793, before me, Asheton Humphreys, Notary, in and for the Commonwealth of Pennsylvania, appeared Mathrew Clarkson, Esq. and declared that some time in June 1774, he, at the request of Stephen Watts, then of the said city, did sell and dispose of sundry lots of grounds situated on the River Schuylkill, being the freehold and inheritance of Frances Watts, wife of Stephen Watts, unto sundry persons to the amount of 2502 pounds which sum was paid into the hands of said Stephen Watts. Sig: Mathew Clarkson. In testimony whereof I, the said notary, have set my hand and seal, etc. Sig: Asheton Humphreys. Notary Public. 1793. // I, Frances Watts, of the government of Natchez, do hereby give my full power and authority to Don Manuel Justus, dwelling in the city of New Orleans, for me and in my name representing my person, etc. to appear in law and plead and defend the suits now pending and may hereafter occur in any Tribunal in these provinces, and particularly to claim and recover my patrimonial and hereditary property and any other property to me belonging in any manner whatsoever, etc. Sig: Frances Asheton Watts. Wit: Joseph Vidal, John Girault. Before Manuel Gayoso de Lemos.

p. 605. Dec. 21, 1796. George Rapalje and Jane, his wife, petition that Jane, on her part, during the absence of her husband, did engage Peter Lee to undertake for her the management of a plantation on Second Creek and put under the care of the said Lee, negroes, horses, ploughs, etc. sufficient to make a crop of corn and cotton which he engaged to do for one-fifth of what was made. And he did receive pork, coffee and sugar for his years provision and the use of two milk cows which he had leave to raise and a few hogs. On the arrival of her husband, he inspected the conduct of said Lee and finding it not in any wise proper, did request her to consent to his being dismissed as he had been advised by Col. Anthony Hutchins, Mr. Jones and Mr. James Spain, who were kind enough to visit the fields and were of the opinion that the said Lee did not act properly, from state in which they found the crop. In consequence of the large family of the said Lee, his wife did request that he might probably act with more care and industry. . . . . . but he acted no better, etc. Sig: George Rapalje, Jane Rapalje.

// Peter Lee replies that he was making a good crop until the arrival of Mr. George Rapalje, who had so disturbed him and his operations by employing the hands at work not belonging to the crop. Now the petitioner foresees that he will not make sufficient crop. 26 July 1796. Sig: Peter Lee. // I recommend that William Dunbar, Esq. alcalde of Second Creek, examine into this matter and authorize him, in my name, to take the requisite proceedings and report thereof. // Second Creek. Recommend that David Mitchell and Philander Smith visit the fields of Mrs. Rapalje.

p. 610. Luis Gonzales versus Bennet Truly. Luis Gonzales, of this Post, in the name of Manuel Guillamil, represents that in 1795 Bennet Truly gave his obligation to the said Guillamil for a quantity of timber to be delivered in the course of two months and in default of said delivery at the time mentioned, to pay $100 damages for the injury that might result to same Guillamil for such default, which said obligation is in my possession and is dated 3 Jany. 1795, and delivery was to have been made the 3rd March of same year, which was not done until the month of April and there still remains due 2800 feet of plank not yet delivered; prays that said Truly be ordered to appear and be compelled to make payment penalty. Signed: Luis Gonzales. Natchez, 7 Sept. 1796. // Bennet Truly will appear before me the first day of audience and the plaintiff will also attend. Sig: Gayoso. 10 Sept. 1796. // 17 Sept. 1796. Bennet Truly, having appeared, declared he had allegations to make that he deemed proper. The proceedings were left in his hands to consider. //

p. 612. Ebenezer Rees, of this Post and City, represents that he contracted the above Luis Gonzales and Manuel Guillamil for a quantity of timber and white oak plank to be delivered in said district of Natchez, amounting to several hundred dollars, which said plank was delivered according to contract and part of the money paid as will appear by account settled and signed by one of the contracting parties and by which account a balance of $332 appears clearly due your petitioner, which said account is herewith presented. Your petitioner having appeared before His Excellency, the Governor, to obtain payment, the parties have transferred it to the Superior Tribunal. Asks that Luis Gonzales, who is in this city, acknowledge his signature to said account. Signed: Ebenezer Rees. // p. 614. Natchez, 21 Sept. 1796. It appearing from the settlement made between the parties in the presence of Capt. Estevan Minor in the recourse of Gonzales to the Superior Tribunal and the obligation which he gave to Ebenezer Rees for the sum of $200, resulting from a compromise made in New Orleans with the approbation of His Excellency the Auditor, that Luis Gonzales has no right to the penalty of $300 and shall pay the cost of this suit.

p. 614. William Gilbert represents that, as attorney for the creditors of the late Messrs Monsanto, he requests to expose at public sale a certain negro woman named Betty and her children, Prince and Delia; asks for the necessary orders for the sale. Natchez, 10 Sept. 1796. Sig: William Gilbert. // Natchez, 14 Sept. 1796. Let the negro woman and her two children be appraised by Edward McCabe and Polser Shilling; appraised the slaves at $325 together. At 1st sitting Thos. Martin, the highest bidder at $315; 2nd, James McIntosh for $300; 3rd, James Foster and Mary Williams bidders, the negroes being adjudged to Mary Williams, the highest bidder for $450. Sig: Wm. Gilbert, James McIntosh, for his sister Mary Williams. Thomas Foster, Polser Shilling, Jean Girault, William Gillespie, Wit. Expense of sale $30. Receipt of Wm. Gilbert for the creditors for $423.

p. 616. Rhoda King versus Edward Carrigan. Rhoda King represents that a certain Carrigan has been so daring as to call her and her family very indecent names and in the presence of witnesses, namely Thomas Regan, James Conway, Thomas Knott and Mr. Hardeman. Asks punishment for the offender. 6 Sept. 1796. Sig: Rhoda King. // 9 Sept. 1796. In consequence of the foregoing, appeared Thomas Regan who said that he was at James Wiley's where he heard Edward Carrigan abuse Charles King, calling him a rogue and his wife and daughters indecent names. Thomas (X) Rogan. Wit: Jean Girault, Edward McCabe. Immediately afterward appeared James Conway, who, on oath, sayeth that in a dispute between Charles King and Edward Carrigan, Carrigan abused King very much [in the same words as Hogan's deposition] and when King resented his remarks, Carrigan flew at him and struck him with a stick. Sig: James Conway. Same wit. // Thos. Knott, having appeared, declared the same as the other deponents. Sig: Thomas Knott. Then appeared William Oxberry, that some time last week he fell in company on the road with Charles King and Edward Carrigan and they were disputing, Edward Carrigan calling King and his family indecent names. William (X) Oxberry. Wit: Joseph Vidal, Jean Girault. Before Manuel Gayoso. // At the request of Charles King, personally appeared, Michael Donelly, who being sworn, said the night before last Carrigan stood before his own door and said many insulting things concerning Charles King and his family, ordering the deponent to go and tell King about it. Sig: Mike Donelly. 24 Sept. 1796. // Having examined the depositions taken at the demand of Rhoda King, and the abuse of the said Carrigan being fully proved, it is ordered that the said Carrigan be arrested and imprisoned until he shall prove the truth of the defamatory language he has used against the said Rhoda and her family, or make such satisfaction to the parties injured as to make them withdraw the suit. But at any case, the said Carrigan to pay the cost to be taxed by Don Juan Girault, according to the tariff. // May it please Your Excellency, Carrigan's wife, Mr. Gillespie and James Swift go in this morning to testify in Carringan's behalf. Be assured that Charles King's drunken gang swore to what was never mentioned by Carrigan. Gillespie is an honest man and a neighbor of Carrigan and King. Last night, King's daughter was sent, no doubt by her father and mother, to Mrs. Carrigan's house where she abused this poor little woman and even struck her and was escorted by a fellow by the name of Donelly, exulting over this poor woman, calling her every insulting name, then singing round her cabin all night. I am convinced there is very little truth in what was sworn against this poor stranger. Everyone knows that Charlie King's character is infamous in the neighborhood; that he always has a gang of fellows ready to swear anything he desires, who live in his house. Patrick Conelly, at the Natchez, and James Smith, who were present when what passed declared that King was solely in fault. The poor woman was abused in the night time with two infant children, and her husband in jail. Signed: Wm. Vousdan. // In consequence of the foregoing report, William Vousdan, alcalde of the district of St. Catherine, will proceed to obtain information of what is alleged against Charles King and his family, and the abuse made to Carrigan's wife and likewise concerning the irregularity of said King and his family, calling, for the purpose, the most reputable characters in the neighborhood of the aforesaid persons, taking their oaths and depositions, etc. Capt. Jean Girault will transmit to Capt. Wm. Vousdan the proceedings on the subject. // St. Catherine's district. Sept. 27, 1796. In obedience to the above decree: Patrick Conelly, being sworn, says he was present at the dispute between Carrigan and King at James Riley's Tavern; that King was continually aggravating said Carrigan, telling him among other things that he was cuckolded by his wife, that said King struck Carrigan on the cheek to provoke him, before Carrigan made any defense with a weaver's yard which he had in his hand; that very abusive language passed on both sides but no mention was made against King's wife and daughter. Sig: Patrick Connelly. Major John Williams deposeth that he was at Mr. James Wiley's Tavern when Charles King and Edward Carrigan provoked one another much with abusive language but he declares that there was not a word passed by Carrigan against the character of Mrs. King and her daughters. Sig: John Williams. Mr. James Wiley, the tavern keeper, was next sworn, and said, that hearing very loud language in the room passing between Charles King and Edward Carrigan, he, as master of the house, ordered them both out of the house, but the deponent never heard Carrigan make indecent remarks about King's wife and daughters, nor was there anything of that kind in the abusive language that passed between them. Sig: James Wiley. James Smith, next deposeth that, being present at the time of the dispute between these men at Wiley's Tavern, and abusive language about sd Carrigan's wife, and Carrigan told him that he was a rascal and a rogue; the language became very abusive but he never heard Carrigan say the things about Mrs. King and her daughters, as claimed; that Charles King came to Mrs. Carrigan's and abused her and told her he had had her husband put in jail and he would stay there, and later King's daughter came there and abused and struck Mrs. Carrigan, while Barney Donelly encouraged her. 27 Sept. 1796. Signed: James Smith. Travina Carrigan, wife of Edward Carrigan, being next sworn, declared that last Sunday night Charles King came to her house and gave her very abusive language, etc. and in about a hour his daughter came with Barney Donelly and struck her with a stick crying out that her father should be governor of Halfway Hill, threatening Mrs. Carrigan's children that if she caught them outdoors she would whip them. Signed with a mark. Mr. William Gillespie, being next, deposeth that the other evening he went to Mrs. Carrigan's to tell Mrs. Carrigan that her husband was in jail and coming there, Mr. Charles King was going away and saying very abusive things to Mrs. Carrigan. Further, on looking over the oaths sworn, he declareth that those men were, like Charles King, drunkards, and Conway was a party with King abusing said Carrigan. Sig: Wm. Gillespie. Before Wm. Vousdan, alcalde for St. Catherine's Creek.

p. 622. William Gilbert versus Daniel Callaghan. William Gilbert, attorney for the affairs of Messrs. Montsanto, represents that he is a creditor of Daniel Callaghan for $93, with interest since Dec. 1792. Said Daniel Callaghan is now on his way to the U.S.; he prays that he be ordered to pay his said debts before his departure. Signed: William Gilbert. Natchez. 19th Oct. 1796. // Daniel Callaghan is ordered not to absent himself from the town before he presents himself before me to answer the complaint. // Daniel Callaghan, an inhabitant of Opelousas, in answer to William Gilbert's petition, represents that the obligation was given in New Orleans where the payment was to be made. Your petitioner is an inhabitant of Opelousas where his wife and five children live on his plantation; he has been permitted by the Gov. General to go to America to settle an affair of importance, which may be lost by the death of some of the witnesses who now exist. A short delay at this season might make it impossible for him to go this year. Mr. Gilbert has acted contrary to law to stop him at this place where he is unprovided, when the obligation is to be paid in N.O. where the executors of the late Mr. Montsanto reside. Asks that Mr. Gilbert send said obligation to N.O. to said executors. For his safety, the petitioner offers security. Sig: Daniel Callaghan. Natchez. 21 Oct. 1796. // Considering that this is not the place of residence of Callaghan and the great injury he might sustain by being detained on his journey, which he has commenced, having a passport from His Excellency, the Gov. Genl. of these Provinces, the security which he offers shall be accepted, being sufficient for the safety of the debt. Sig: Manuel Gayoso de Lemos.

p. 624. Landon Davis represents that he paid Ann Carr all that he was ordered to pay from Your Excellency excepting $50 which he tendered to her several times but that the said Ann has refused deliver up his daughter which was one of the conditions observed by Your Excellency, and the said Ann residing at the time at the Nogales, asks that she be ordered to send his daughter without delay and to appoint some person to receive the balance due to her from the petitioner and in default thereof that the said Ann appear before His Excellency, the Commandant of Nogales, there to give a discharge in full to petitioner, expressing therein that she has no further claim against the petitioner whatever; and the said Commandant be authorized to transmit the same to Your Excellency to be deposited among the records of the government. Natchez. Oct. 26, 1796. Sig: Landon Davis. // The Commandant of Nogales will do the needful in this particular and compel the party to accept the proposal of the petitioner, she having agreed to the same. Sig: Manuel Gayoso de Lemos. // At the Fort of Nogales, 26 Oct. 1796. In pursuance of the foregoing decree, before me, Ann Carter appeared and being informed of the petition of Landon Davis, she said that she would not deliver the girl and she discharged the sd Landon Davis from all sums of money duing and owing from him to her, the said Ann, from henceforth forever on condition that he shall never claim the girl before mentioned. The said Ann Carter, not knowing how to write has made the mark of the cross, before myself, Don Rafael Croquer, Don Andrew Gil, witnesses present. All sign. Before Elias Beauregarde. // Pursuant to instructions of 21 Oct. 1796, from the Rev. Dr. Swayze, we have taken under consideration maturely the matter in dispute between Miss Ann Carter and Mr. Landon Davis respecting the character of the said Ann, the maintenance and support of the bastard child and do hereby and determine that the said Davis shall be at the whole expense of maintenance at the discretion of the rector-pastor of this district until she may be fit for the nunnery; that the said Davis shall immediately pay the said Ann $100, also he shall purchase in New Orleans in January next a likely negro to the value of $500 which shall be approved of by Mr. Daniel Clark and Mr. James Mather for the entire permanent use of said Ann until the child shall arrive at the age of 18 years and until she shall afterwards arrive at the state of matrimony and then the possession to be vested in the said child. Natchez, 25 Oct. 1788. Sig: Anthony Hutchins, Bernard Linton, Isaac Johnson, Peter Walker. I oblige myself to comply with the above. Signed Landon Davis. // The foregoing obligation has become null and void, the said Ann Carter cancelling same. Let the same be communicated to Davis. //

p. 625. Simon McCay represents that he is the bearer of a note of John Cocke and James Wiley for $40 which he has not been able to recover, ask that the immediate payment be ordered, with costs. Natchez 6 July, 1796. Signed: Simon McCay. Notify John Cocke and James Wiley to appear and acknowledge their signatures to the note and to pay the amount thereof within three days or in default thereof seizure will be made to the amount of the debt. 6 July, 1796. Sig: Gayoso. // Notified James Wiley. Sig: Jean Girault. // 7 July 1796, appeared James Wiley, who examined the note and acknowledged the signature thereon to be his own, having signed the same as surety for John Cocke. Sig: James Wiley. // Simon McCay petitions for the seizure of property to the amount of the debt and cost. Sig: Simon McCay. James Wiley says he has no property but his house and lot which he gives up freely, it being the same whereon the said Wiley now lives. 14 July 1796. Fee. $1. William Gillespie. [McCoy makes a number of petitions and by Sept. 29 asks that said Wiley, on whom Cocke's debt seems to rest, pay the expense of McCay in waiting in Natchez for payment which he needs urgently.] // Oct. 30, 1796. Let the seizure on the house of James Riley be made and appraised. Notified by the Constable. John Scott and Thomas Thompson appointed appraisers. House appraised at $550. Notice of sale, but no report. Fees. $15.

p. 630. Robert Miller versus creditors. In obedience to Your Excellency's order of 5th instant, at a meeting of my creditors, Thomas Wilkins and Robert Moore, two of his creditors, were appointed agents in behalf of the whole. The petitioner's cattle broke out of their pasture and when they were driven back to the plantation, some of them were lost, and they were so wild that he can never recover them; of the remainder about 30 heads were given to John Jones and Philip Hayes in payment of said beaver fur and 5 heads were sold to Williams for labor, principally clearing land and cultivating tocacco; 6 heads to John Searcy; and 8 sold to John Adams; 2 horses sold to John Searcy, one to Wm. Radcliff, one to James Irwin for boarding before he was married; there remain 3 heads of horses and mares on hand. Natchez 11 Oct. 1796. Sig: Robert Miller. Petitioner's wife was also possessed of some property of her own which she offers to give up in payment of the petitioner's debts on condition that his creditors will grant him a general release so that he may without interruption endeavor to find means of supplying his family, but unless this release is granted she wishes to retain the privileges granted her by the laws of Her Sovereign to save herself and children from becoming objects of misery and a charge to society. Some of the creditors were: Maurice Stacpoole, David Ferguson for Reed and Ford, John Wilson, Baptiste Trenier, Robert Moore, John Martin for David Myat's est., Peter Walker, Thos. Wilkins, Jesse Hamilton. Messrs. Robert Moore and Thos. Wilkins, Syndics were reported to have received from Robert Miller a statement of his affairs. [Case apparently suspended for the time. p. 635.]

p. 635. Petition of Thomas Regan, at Natchez, Oct. 29, 1796, in which he said that he had done carpenter work in the house of Mr. Thomas Martin, and they both wished to have the work worked valued by carpenters. // John Scott and Thomas Thompson appointed to appraise said work. In their opinion, Mr. Martin should pay Mr. Regan $142 for the work. Signed by both. // Regan notified.

p. 636. Samuel Cooper versus James Kirk. [This suit covers pages 636-643. Samuel Cooper, not being the only plaintiff, there is also an award to Isaac Johnson, Esq., and Alexander Ross. These accounts were approved by the Commandant, Gayoso, 13 Sept. 1796. The arbitrators before whom the evidence was submitted were Wm. Dunbar and Ruffin Gray. Charges $23 exclusive of constables fees and arbitrators costs.] The defendant, not being able to pay said costs, the constable was ordered to execute seizure of sufficient property of Mr. James Kirk for the same. Signed: Gayoso. 5 Dec. 1796. Sufficient cotton belonging to said James Kirk, Esq. was delivered by him to pay the above debts and costs. A question of the quality of the indigo that Kirk paid in liquidation of his debts. Christopher Gilbert and Israel Smith were two of the witnesses present when it was opened and it was not good. The report of the arbitrators was the indigo was damaged while in Mr. Kirk's possession consequently they were of the opinion that Mr. Kirk should keep the indigo and Samuel Cooper should be allowed the average price that Mr. Kirk's part of the crop sold for in N.O.; and that Mr. Kirk be allowed till the sale of his present crop to make payment, paying Cooper interest at 6%. Signed by both. Approved by Gayoso.

p. 643. We, the undersigned, having attentively heard the cause of the differences between Winsor Pipes and John Bullen, respecting an agreement between them, feel that $109 is due Mr. Pipes from the said Bullen, and the sum shall be paid on or before Jan. next, being in full consideration of all the demands of said Pipes against John Bullen. 14 Dec. 1796. Sig: John Bisland, Robert Dunbar, Joseph Bernard. // Approved the said settlement. Let the parties be notified. Sig: Gayoso.

p. 643. Post of Natchez, 27 Feb. 1796. Respecting a certain Randolph, supposed to be the owner of a negro, who calls himself free, have caused the negro, named James, to appear before me and when interrogated whether he belonged to the said Randolph, he replied that he was free; that the said Randolph passing by the Falls of the Ohio, had engaged him to go with him to Philadelphia as a servant, whereupon he reminded the said negro that he had said here and other places that he belonged to the said Randolph, and he replied that it was true that he had said so at the request of the said Randolph who promised that if he consented to be sold that he would give him $100 and that he might afterwards escape from his master when both would go by land to America; that Abel Spragg and John Macklin now in this district know him to be free as well as many other persons, in consequence whereof I caused these two persons to appear before me and they being duly sworn, declared that they knew the said negro James, having seen him several times at Fort Washington, and at the Falls of Ohio, that everyone knew him to be free, and moreever the law of that country does not admit of slavery and Abel Spragg added that he, himself, had come down with the aforesaid Randolph at the same time the negro said he was free and it is certain that, at New Madrid, he did, by agreement with the said Randolph, declare that he belonged to him. Both the said deponents said that the said James was free. Wit: Joseph Vidal and Jean Girault. On the same day, Edward Randolph appeared, on oath, declared when asked if the negro James belonged to him, that the said negro is his slave, he having purchased him from a certain William Holmes who won him at cards; that he gave the said Holmes $100 at the Falls of the Ohio, who gave him the bill of sale herewith presented, signed also by Joseph Dunlevy and Philip Riley, witnesses; that it is true that he heard it said at New Madrid that the negro had been free but was sold for a certain time as a punishment for crimes he had committed; and, having communicated to him the declaration that the negro James has made, he declared the same to be false, asking that the Lieut. Gregg now about to go to the U.S. take the negro, with his consent, with him to that country so that the truth may be ascertained to the end the truth be known, and by the same opportunity he will transmit a power to claim from the said William Holmes the sum which he has acknowledged to have received for the said negro from the appearant, in case he cannot prove the property of said negro. Philip Riley then appeared and, being sworn, he was asked if the signature at the foot of the bill of sale from Holmes to Randolph was his, which he acknowledged to be his own, which he had written on a bill of sale for a negro which Holmes had sold to Randolph, which negro Holmes had won at cards, and for which negro Randolph had paid $100 in the presence of the deponent. // In consequence of the request of Edward Randolph, and in pursuance of the affidavits given in this case, I have declared the said negro James to the aforesaid Lieut. Gregg, in proof whereof he has signed with myself and the witnesses. 4 March 1796. Sig: Carlos de Grand-Pre.

p. 645. Anthony Hutchins versus William Miller. Petition of Anthony Hutchins represents that in April last he left N.O. and put his boat in the care of Capt. Wm. Vousdan and Ephraim Marcellus, the patroon, to provide a freight for her, with instructions that if the freight could not be procured that in your petitioner's behalf they should hire her at any price so that she might be taken to the Natchez, and she was therefore hired in the following manner, to Mr. William Miller, that is to say, the boat and all the utensils for three months, to commence from May 1st last at $1 per day and the said Miller was to pay $1 each day afterwards until he should deliver her to your petitioner at the Natchez. But the said Miller hath not paid any part thereof nor delivered her to your petitioner according to agreement; he asks that said Miller may be held to make payment according to his contract. Nov. 14, 1796. Sig: Anthony Hutchins. // Mr. Wm. Miller will appear at Govt. House to answer the petitioner the next court day. // Before me appeared Mr. George Cochran, merchant of this place, who acknowledged himself to be entered as security for Wm. Miller in the suit between Mr. Hutchins and said Miller, which Col. Hutchins accepted and he is to seize the boat of the said Cochran when offered here. Sig: George Cochran, Anthony Hutchins. Wit: Louis Throckmorton, Ebenezer Rees. // Before me appeared Col. Anthony Hutchins who acknowledged to have received the boat, alluded to in these proceedings, agreeable to the above security, which was delivered by George Cochran. Wit: Edward McCabe, Stephen Minor. Before Gayoso. 2 Dec. 1796. // Before me appeared Wm. Farmer, who, on oath, deposed that Mr. Marcellus, the patroon of Col. Hutchins' boat, told this deponent that he had hired the said boat to Mr. Wm. Miller for 3 months at $1 per day and the said boat was to be returned at N.O. at the expiration of the said time. Signed: Wm. Farmer, paid by Mr. Miller 10 rials, before Samuel Flowers and Ebenezer Rees, witnesses. Before Gayoso. // List of the utensils belonging to the barge hired to Mr. Miller, which he received with said barge: 14 oars, 2 tarpaulins, 1 awning, 2 boat hooks, 2 bow fasts, 1 stern fast, 1 pot, 1 dutch oven, 2 drawning knives, 1 axe, 1 hand saw, 1 hammer, 1 calking iron, 1 inch auger, 2 wooden bowls, 1 lock. Certified by Ephraim Marcellus. Deposition of Ephraim Marcellus: Testimony the same as that of Anthony Hutchins regarding details of the barge being hired and to be taken to the Natchez. Nov. 7, 1796. Sig. Ephraim Marcellus. Also a deposition to the same effect from William Vousdan. Signed: Cottonfield, 9th Nov. 1796. William Vousdan, which signature he acknowledged at the Govt. House.

p. 648. Patrick Conelly versus Elizabeth Tomlinson. Patrick Connelly represents that an application has been made by Susannah Galtney, a child of eleven years of age and sister to your petitioner's wife, in consequence of barbarous and cruel treatment she has received from Mrs. Tomlinson. Your petitioner begs liberty to explain to Your Excellency that this child lost her parents by death at a very early period of her life and was taken by Mrs. Tomlinson through profession of humanity and good will. Your petitioner is sorry to observe that almost ever since that time the unfortunate child has been a slave and treated with the most unparalleled cruelty, and notwithstanding that she uses every effort to please the said Mrs. Tomlinson on all occasions and to render herself useful in every kind of labor as could be expected of a child of her years, she passes a painful life and is treated of a footing with a negro. It was yesterday so serious that she was obliged to fly to a neighboring farm and ask for shelter and protection, where she had an opportunity of showing the marks of a horse-whip on her back given by the said Mrs. Tomlinson; asks consideration of this alarming case of this unfortunate orphan in order that she may be removed to some place where she may be humanely treated. Natchez, 8 July 1795. Sig: Patrick Conelly. // To be communicated. Signed Grand-Pre. Same day. // Petition of Elizabeth Tomlinson, in reply to the above, sayeth that about ten years ago, a female child was brought and left in my house who could neither walk nor talk, brought by her sister, Priscilla Galtney. This infant I took and raised in industry, giving her education as my own, and she is now known by the name of Susannah. Some time past, her brother called on me. I offered him the child, on his paying me about half the value of the trouble of raising her and $20 for her schooling, being what I paid. He replied that it was not convenient for him to take her. I then asked him to take her and let his sister Priscilla have her. He replied that he did not like her husband and said that it was best for her to stay where she was as he had no right to think that she was unjustly dealt by. Petitioner now finds that there are people who wish to have her service without giving a reasonable consideration for her raising and schooling and have represented to Your Excellency that this child is barbarously abused by stripes and bruises done lately and for the truth of this, your petitioner asks that this child may be examined by some impartial judges. Your petitioner has no objection to her brother, Abraham Galtney, having the child on his paying $20 per year for six years and $20 for her schooling. Natchez. 11 July 1795. Sig: Elizabeth Tomlinson. // 11 July 1795. Having heard the parties and examined the child, it appears that her relations, being in extreme poverty, wish to have the girl for the benefit of the little work she is able to do. This being manifest ingratitude to Elizabeth Tomlinson by them, to whom the said child was carried by her said relations at a very tender age, who received the said child, fed and clothed her until she reached the age of twelve years, being an act of charity and generosity on the part of said Elizabeth Tomlinson, who also gave the sum of $20 for her schooling. Notwithstanding which, the child complains of cruel treatment and excessive whipping she receives and what she feels still more sensibly the negro wenches are also permitted to treat her in the same manner, she therefore wishes to live with her sister. Two witnesses, namely, Elizabeth Earhart and John McIntyre have declared, on oath, that they were frequently present and were spectators of said bad treatment which was repeated as often as three times in one day, for not having finished work given her to do without regard to her strength. The said cupidity of the said Elizabeth Tomlinson has effaced from the child's memory the benefits she has received. In order to present other extremes which might arise from the present proceedings, be notified to Conelly that he is allowed to take the girl, sister of his wife, on the express condition of paying to the said Elizabeth Tomlinson the full amount of her estimated expenses for the said child, or otherwise she shall remain with the said Elizabeth Tomlinson, who is ordered to treat this orphan with more decency and humanity or on the first notice to the contrary she will be taken from her, with the loss of the whole expenses. Sig: Carlos de Grand-Pre. Natchez. 11 July 1795. Notified to the parties. Signed: J. Girault. // p. 650. Abraham Galtney versus Elizabeth Tomlinson. Abraham Galtney petitions that a most destroying situation of an orphan child, of about 13 years of age, his sister, obliges him as her brother to acquaint Your Excellency that this unfortunate child has for many years suffered great tyranny and affliction. It is well-known that she began to serve well and very early every menial service and the petitioner conceives that this service might be adequate compensation for the trouble she occassioned; and the petitioner will reimburse for any money that might have been paid for her schooling. Dec. 1 1796. Sig: A. Galtney. // Summons has been issued for Mrs. Tomlinson to appear at the Govt. House. // Mr. Girault. Sir: Please destroy the papers belonging to Mr. Galtney, by his Excellency's orders. Sig: Elizabeth Tomlinson. March 17, 1795. // In consequence of the above order I have delivered to Abraham Galtney the obligations concerning this suit. To Mrs. Tomlinson 6 yrs. of maintenance $120; schooling $20; to 3 years labor $90 (credit); balance due Mrs. Tomlinson $50.

p. 652. Job Routh versus Anthony Hutchins. Job Routh represents that he holds a tract of land, the titles whereof are in the possession of Anthony Hutchins who refuses to deliver the same to your petitioner, notwithstanding various applications for same. Sig: Job Routh. Natchez. 13 July 1796. // July 14. Anthony Hutchins will deliver to petitioner the titles that he demands or appear before me on Wed. the 20th. // Anthony Hutchins replies that all the papers and concerns respecting the above petitioner are out of the Dominion and therefore prays for three months to send for them that they may be laid before Your Excellency for your consideration. 12 Nov. 1796. Sig: A. Hutchins. // Granted same day. Let Job Routh be notified. Sig: Gayoso. // Job Routh represents that Col. Hutchins is in possession of the titles to a tract of land originally granted to the petitioner's father by the British Government and whereas many applications have been made to him for several years for the said title he has always put off the delivery of them on vague pretences, and he has, at last, declared the same to be out of the Dominion and required three months for the purpose of procuring them; asks that said Hutchins be ordered to give sufficient security that he will deliver the same within the said term of three months. Sig: Job Routh, Natchez, 12 Nov. 1796. // Anthony Hutchins answers that Job Routh who is said to be heir of Jeremiah Routh, deceased, that nigh about the year 1775 or 1776, it was proposed by the said Jeremiah Routh, who was a very poor man, and scarcely able to maintain his numerous family nor pay the expenses of taking up a piece of land, that if the petitioner would apply to the Governor in Pensacola for 500 acres in the said Routh's name and pay all costs and charges, that he, Routh, would make a deed of conveyance to your petitioner for one-half thereof, to be divided in quantity and quality and that at such time as your petitioner should require it after the said grant shall be obtained and before it should be put into his hands, etc. and that your petitioner did accordingly apply in the said Routh's name and did pay with his own money all costs and charges thereon and did also purchase an improvement on the premises, so that the whole was completed without cost whatsoever to the said Routh, and after the revolution of the country by the arms of Spain, the said Routh refused to make a conveyance agreeable to his contract and obligation, therefore your petitioner naturally refused him the patent, on which he, Routh, petitioned to the Commandant without success, who ordered him to comply with his contract before the grant should be delivered to him, and afterwards in 1781 the patent with other papers were unfortunately lost and previous to that time, in 1777 or 8, the notorious Capt. Willing was taken and he carried away the aforesaid obligation with him with many other effects. Yet notwithstanding such misfortunes, it may be within the power of your petitioner to procure an abstract from the records now in Great Britain or he may hope of regaining his obligation from Philadelphia. Natchez. 25 Nov. 1796. Sig: Anthony Hutchins. // Isaac Johnson will appear at the Govt. House. // 3rd Dec. 1796, appeared Isaac Johnson, alcalde for the district of Second Creek, who, duly sworn, concerning the obligation of the late Mr. Jeremiah Routh to Col. Hutchins, for conveying to him one-half of the land the said Hutchins should obtain in Routh's name from the British Government, he had formerly been several time in company with Col. Hutchins and the late Jeremiah Routh when the conversation turned on the agreement respecting lands and the said Routh acknowledged always having given a bond to said Hutchins to make him a title to one-half of the said grant, and he understood that all expense had been paid by Col. Hutchins and in his last conversation when he was present Col. Hutchins did say to Routh "I will give or take $500." and the said Routh replied that he did not wish to sell but "I will give you $500 for your part." But the said Routh did not live to perform the agreement. Sig: Isaac Johnson. Wit: Lewis Evans, James Wiley.

p. 355. Antonio Gras versus Joseph Duncan. Antonio Grass represents that he had a contract with Joseph Duncan, who was take a house down and put it up in another place in the same manner in which it was before; this was not done well and asks for an appraisal of the work. Natchez Nov. 13, 1796. // Let Duncan be summoned. // Duncan declared he had torn down the house which was at the landing and he should like to have it inspected and his work appraised. Report of appraisers, John Scott, John Tear and Thos. Thomson, while the work was not the best, the roof was of shingles, whereas the former roof had been of pickets, the difference in the work was made up by the extra labor necessary to put on said roof. Dec. 3, 1796. // Approved by Manuel Gayoso de Lemos. // The expense of the suit, $5, was to be shared equally.

p. 656. Job Routh petitions that in 1791 a certificate from William Dunbar that a tract of land, 400 acres on the North Fork of Cole's Creek, joining James Elliot and Wm. Daniels was vacant, and he had applied for it from the government but he had never had any reply and now someone else is claiming the land. Dunbar acknowledged that he had given said Routh a certificate that the said land was vacant. William Daniels was ordered to restore the house he had taken off the land and Job Routh was to put back a cabin he had removed from Daniels' land. Both sign.

End of Book E. [No certificate by the translator, Harper.]

BOOK F

p. 1. William Clark versus Stephen Jordan. Anthony Barbason declared that some time in August 1779, speaking to Mr. Wm. Clark concerning a small yellow cow, with whitish horns, said Barbason asked whose cow she was and he replied that she was once mine but I made a present of her to Mrs. Jordan. Sig: Anthony Barbason. 25th July 1781. Before Isaac Johnson. // Patsy Hawkins declared that in August 1780 William Clark came to the house of her husband, in company with Andrew Whitefield, and drove some cattle there belonging to said Clark; that Clark said: "Well, I have got my cattle from Mr. Jordan, at last."; that a small yellow cow was one of the number, which cow she milked from August until late in the winter. Patsy (X) Hawkins. 25 July 1781. Before me: Sig. Isaac Johnson. // Sarah Holmes declares that her son, Joseph, desired her to get $20 from William Clark; that she went to the Natchez landing at the time that James Willing came down the river in the beginning of the year 1778; that Clark told her that he had not the money and asked her if her son Joseph did not owe money to Stephen Jordan and if Clark took up her son's note to Stephen Jordan would it not answer the purpose; that she told Clark that was as good to her as cash and said Clark went away and returned with said Jordan with him and Jordan said to her that he had not her son's note with him but if Clark's note would do for what she owed him he would return the note to her. She told Jordan that it would and Jordan accordingly send the note for $20 to her a few days afterwards and she knew nothing of any bargain or sale between William Clark and Stephen Jordan. 26 July 1781. Before Isaac Johnson. // We hereby condemn Stephen Jordan to restore to the plaintiff the said cow and her calves claimed by him and to the payment for the costs. Sig: Grand-Pre.

p. 2. Hannah Vousdan versus Emanuel Madden. The petition of Hannah Vousdan showeth that some time last spring she did sell unto William Coleman, who is since dead, a sow with five pigs for 24 bushels of corn. Your petitioner also sold to Emanuel Madden two sows for 41 bushels of corn. The said Madden since the death of the said Coleman seems to have the management of the sd Coleman's affairs and has lived with the family since and for some time before. Of the above 65 bushels of corn, I have received 15 bushels on the account, by their people, there being neither Madden or any of the family at home as they had moved up for fear of the Indians after Mr. De la Villebeuvre had given up the fort. But before I took or ordered any to be taken, I spoke to Mr. Coleman at the landing about what was to be done with the corn and he answered: "It is certain that you cannot do without the corn but it must be measured." Since the fort was given up by Mr. Blommart, I have had 5 bags more of corn, about 12 bushels. Madden now claims that I took the corn from the wrong crib and will not pay the balance owing me. This corn is all the dependence I have for my family until fall. Natchez. 3 July 1781. // To be communicated. Sig: Grand-Pre. // Emanuel Madden answers that he had corn in partnership with William Coleman, who had sold his part of the corn to Mr. Farquhar, and it had not been divided. Mrs. Vousdan left the corn exposed to weather, hogs and horses, etc. // Appeared before Don Carlos de Grand-Pre, William Ferguson who declared that some time after William Vousdan's affairs were put under his direction by Mr. De la Villebeuvre, he saw Emanuel Madden, and in discussion of the exchange of the sows for the corn, he understood that part of the corn would be at Mr. Kinnard's. Sig: Wm. Ferguson. Aug. 10, 1781 // Aug. 15, 1781 Cephas Kinnard testifies denying the damage and waste. Sig: Cephas Kinnard. // Emanuel Madden shall deliver to Hannah Vousdan 35 bu. of corn, only 3 bushels deducted for waste. Said Hannah hereby discharged from all responsibility. Madden to pay the cost. 24 Aug. 1781. Charles de Grand-Pre.

p. 3. William Brocus versus Benjamin Day. Wm. Brocus petitions that one Benjamin Day, late of Natchez, now absconded, in March last past, received 11 good hides from him in order to tan the same, and to deliver your petitioner one-half of the same in good leather, which he has failed to do. 17 Aug. 1781. Wm. (X) Brocus. // Aug. 18, to be notified to Benjamin Day or his attorney, to be answered within three days. Grand-Pre. Notified, Aug. 20, Silas Crane. // Pet. of Wm. Brocus for an execution on the property of said Day 24 Aug. 1781. // Granted. // Aug. 24, 1781. By virtue of the power to me given, I will put up at public sale a horse from the estate of Benj Day, late of the district, to satisfy William Brocus in consequence of the above judgment. Sig: Silas Crane. // Aug. 27. At public sale at the gate of the fort, a horse belonging to Benj. Day offered to satisfy a debt to Wm. Brocus, finally adjudged to Wm. Brocus for $22, out of which he has paid $8 for costs.

p. 6. Richard Bacon versus Hardy Ellis. In June 1778, at the time when Col. McGillvray commanded here, your petitioner purchased a crib of corn, 200 bushels, from Seth Winslow, and received a bill of sale for same; your petitioner departed for New Orleans and left said corn and other affairs in charge of Mr. Wells, who sold said corn to Mr. Bethune and before the said Wells had time to deposit the said corn in the fort, Alexander McIntosh, caused the same to be seized in pursuance of an execution he had against the said Winslow for $25, judgment having been given him before the arrival of James Willing. At the same time your petitioner had obtained judgment against sundry persons but he could not obtain execution, notwithstanding it Mr. McIntosh obtained the same. Since all judgments before the arrival of Willing were made void, the petitioner thinks that that of Mr. McIntosh should be made void also. At the sale the corn was sold to Mrs. Ann McIntosh, for 2 1/2 bits, who was the only bidder at the sale, no other person present having meddled therein, knowing the said sale to be unlawful, without the order of the Justice of the Peace. Etc. As Hardy Ellis paid a part of the corn to Mrs. McIntosh for his own debt, he should pay me for my corn either in money or return to me an equal amount of corn. Sig: Richard Bacon. July 21, 1781. // Hardy Ellis, on oath, stated that he had advertised the sale of the corn on an order obtained by Mrs. McIntosh and authorized by the Magistrate. Mr. Wells objected saying that he had a bill of sale which Richard Bacon had left with him to take care of the corn; at the sale he asked if it was lawful for him to sell the corn and a magistrate present said that it was not and he said he would not sell the corn until he was sure, but Mrs. Anne McIntosh being present said her husband had left her to act in all his business, that she would pay all damages that would befall the sale and he sold the corn at 2 1/2 rials per bushel. Sig: Hardress Ellis. Before me at Natchez, J. Blommart. // West Florida, Natchez Dist., George the Third, by the Grace of God, of Great Britain, France and Ireland, King, Defender of the Faith, etc. to Joseph Holmes Greeting: We command you, of the goods and chattels in your district of Seth Winslow, you make $24-4 rials which Alexander McIntosh before the Justices of our court did recover against him and also $4 for his costs and have that money before our said Justices in Natchez the first Tuesday in Aug. next. Signed: John Blommart, Esquire, one of our Justices of Natchez. 9 June 1778. Mr. and Mrs. McIntosh ask that the proceedings of Bacon against Ellis be put off until Mr. McIntosh is able to appear in his own behalf as it is an affair which concerns him and nothing but his low state of health should prevent his attendance. 24 July 1781. // Be it known that I, Joseph Holmes, do remember to have seized the property of Seth Winslow by a decree of this fort and that I requested Mr. Hardress Ellis to ascertain the quantity of corn, etc. Signed: Joseph Holmes. Wit: Jacob Winfree and Wm. McIntosh. // Messrs. Rapalje and Pounteney appointed arbitrators for Richard Bacon; Anthony Hutchins and Isaac Johnson the same for Ellis. Decree; While Bacon is due damages, Ellis is not the offender, as he acted under orders from the government then in control. Bacon to pay costs but not barred from suit against obtaining judgment from guilty parties. 29 Aug. 1781. Charles de Grand-Pre.

p. 14. Barbour and Harrison versus James Oglesby. The petition of Barbour and Harrison shows that James Oglesby, late of this district, owes them $4 and he has property in this district and they ask that since the petitioners are his oldest creditors that this will be taken in consideration. Aug. 30, 1781. Signed: Richard Harrison for Barbour and Harrison. // Bill. Feb. 6, 1777. Total $6 with credit of $2 paid by Mrs. Sarah Truly. // Order that the wife pay the principal of the debt but no interest, no legal demand ever having been made.

p. 15. William Brocus versus John Alston. John Townsend and Tobias Brashears declared that they were witnesses to a sale made by John Alston to William Brocus of all his cattle, for which William Brocus paid him certain money. Sept. 5, 1781. Signed by both before Luis Perez de Bellegarde and Alexander McIntosh.

p. 15. William Ferguson versus John Turner. In consequence of a judgment obtained by Wm. Vousdan against John Turner, a fugitive from here, begs an order for an execution against the said estate in favor of said Vousdan. Signed: William Ferguson. Francis Farrell, interpreter. // Natchez, Aug. 24, 1781. Let seizure be made to the amount of $70 being the price of the cattle. Sig: Grand-Pre. // At the sale, the cow and calf seized for said debt, they were adjudged to a negro belonging to John Alston, named "Ranter", for the sum of $26 in hand paid. Wit: Robert Rapalje, Francois Farrell, St. Germain, Receipt by William Ferguson of the $26. 25 Sept. 1781.

p. 17. William Brocus versus John Alston. Appeared Nathaniel Tomlinson and Benjamin Balk acknowledged to have received from Wm. Brocus for the account of John Alston, absconded, $18 in silver, leaving a balance of $10 which the said Brocus bound himself to pay and Benj. Balk also ack. to have received from said Brocus $20 for the account of the said Alston, and for which the said Alston and heirs are indebted to the said Brocus. Signed by both.

p. 18. John Hartley versus Andrew Welsh. Petition of John Hartley that he obtained execution against Andrew Welsh, amounting with the costs to $17. He asks that the matter be considered. Natchez. 17

Sept. 1781. Sig: Hartley. // Let the seizure be made of cattle or effects to be brought to the fort for sale. Grand-Pre. // 24 Sept. 1781. John Duncan, in pursuance of an execution in favor of John Hartley, against the property of Andrew Welsh went to his house, about a league and a half from the fort and seized a brass kettle containing about eleven gallons, appraised at $12, six plates and one dish valued at $2, and other household utensils, and one cow and calf appraised at $20, all of which I have conveyed to Natchez, 25 Sept. 1781. // Appraisers: Alexander McIntosh and Nathaniel Tomlinson, who appraised the whole at $37. Proceeded with the sale of same: Brass kettle adjudged to Alexander McIntosh for $10; plates and dishes to Francis Farrell for $4; sundry articles to Luis Perez de Bellegarde for $3; cow and calf to Stephen Mayes for $16; total $34. Signed by wit: Richard Harrison and John Kennedy. Fees $12. $17 to John Hartley and $6 to be refunded to Welsh. Natchez 28 Sept. 1781. Order that the overplus be paid to Patrick Foley, the greatest creditor of Andrew Kennedy. Sig: Grand-Pre.

p. 20. John Stowers and others versus John and Samuel Watkins. Petition of John Stowers represents that he holds a note drawn by John and Samuel Watkins, late of the district, absconded, for $19, asks that an order issue from their estate for same. Natchez. 19 Dec. 1781. Sig: John Stowers. // Let seizure be made to the amount of the same. Sig: Grand-Pre. // 24 March 1781. Joseph Duncan, in consequence of the above execution by Alexander McIntosh, St. Germain, and John Stowers, seized a sundry lot of household utensils, appraised at $32; sale of same on the 25th Sept. 1781, in presence of Nathaniel Tomlinson, Richard Harrison, Francis Farrell, Alexander McIntosh and others assisting. Utensils adjudged to Michael Lopez for $11; total sale $30.

p. 22. Alexander McIntosh versus John Hoge. Sale and adjudication of a cow and calf and a mare seized as the property of John Hoge and appraised by William Pounteney and Richard Devall at $25. Cow and calf adjudged to Hulburt for $12 and the mare sold for $10. Wit: Farrell, Justus King, and Patrick Foley. Same was paid to the above.

p. 22. James Truly versus Philip Mulkey. Truly represents that Philip Mulkey, late of the district, absconded, with $23 owing to petitioner; asks that execution against his property be made. // Let seizure be made of a horse, of his property. John Duncan, Constable. Distance one league. 2 Oct. 1781. Sale and adjudication of same: Said horse was adjudged to Abraham Mayes for $20, cash in hand; Wit: Farrell, David Odam, Silas Crane, Joseph Duncan. Charles de Grand-Pre.

p. 24. Wm. Vousdan versus James Wilson. An account against James Wilson for $189, damages resulting from the villainy of said Wilson as follows: 2 horses $100; 5 cows and a calf at $20; heifers at $10 and 1 mattress, charged by John Blommart, Esq. $34, in payment of which I received three horses from Wilson valued at $180, and of which horses two were stolen and, I have reason to believe, by the companions of said Wilson immediately after they were delivered. Asks that the said Wilson be called before you to render an account of what he has done with my property in my absence. Sig: William Vousdan. // James Wilson is ordered to appear on Monday, the 8th instant. Oct. 6, 1781. // Parties being heard it is ordered that Anthony Hutchins, Isaac Johnson, Samuel Lewis and William Ferguson be notified to appear before us on Wed. 10th, on the demand of James Wilson to give testimony. // Examined, the parties and witnesses being heard, it is decreed that James Wilson pay to William Vousdan the sum of $30 for damages by the sale of cattle in his absence, made by his wife in a state of insanity, and shall restore the mattress belonging to John Blommart, Esq. and the said Wilson shall retain possession of the cattle. Fort Panmur. 10 Oct. 1781. Grand-Pre.

p. 25. William Vousdan versus John Farquhar. Wm. Vousdan petitions that he has an account against John Farquhar, of this dist., for $400. Having been a long time absent, the said Farquhar saw the property of your petitioner sold in open day, although indebted to him, without offering to assist him in his absence. Now that your petitioner has returned to this place, he has reason to believe that the said Farquhar intends to send away his slaves with David Ross who departs this evening or tomorrow morning, intending to evade his debts to your petitioner; he prays that Your Honor take the matter into consideration. Sig: Wm. Vousdan. Natchez, 6th Oct. 1781. // Let it be notified that John Farquhar be forbidden to remove any of his property out of this district until the present affair shall be finally settled, also to make his defence. // John Farquhar represents that he would not have given Mr. Vousdan any trouble about the debt, if it had been in his power to pay it when it became due, the charge that he intended sending his slaves out of the district and defraud Vousdan is entirely false. It is also in the power of the petitioner to prove that he took no advantage of Mrs. Vousdan in the absence of her husband. Oct. 9, 1781. Sig: John Farquhar. // Examined. We do hereby condemn John Farquhar to pay

Wm. Vousdan the amount of his obligation of $500, dated 24 August 1780 and due 30 March of the present year with interest. The said Vousdan deducting from the said obligation the sum of $216, as follows: $54 paid by sd Farquhar to Mr. Strother for the account of plaintiff, $162 for a cow, two horses, one plow, one hat, 5 bu. of corn, etc., leaving a balance $283. Sig: Grand-Pre.

p. 26. Peter Hawkins and others versus Andrew Whitfield. Hawkins represents that he has an account against Andrew Whitfield, late of this district, for $61; asks for an order on Whitfield's property. Sig: Peter Hawkins. Oct. 12, 1781. // Natchez, Oct. 19, 1781. Hawkins again asks for execution against the estate of Whitfield. // Let seizure be made as demanded. Grand-Pre. // Petition of Gideon Gibson that he was employed by Andrew Whitfield as overseer and it was mutually agreed that the work done by your petitioner should be valued by two appraisers and your petitioner has called on three neighbors, namely Robert Dunbar, John Shunck and Richard Curtis, to value his work in the absence of Whitfield, and they have appraised the same at $107 to which he has added 15 bushels of corn delivered to William Ferguson on an order drawn by Whitfield, the petitioner is a poor man with a large family and asks for your consideration. Oct. 16, 1781. Sig: Gideon Gibson. // Petition of John Farquhar represents that he has an account agst Andrew Whitfield for $39 besides a joint note drawn by Whitfield and your petitioner, asks for consideration. Sig: John Farquhar. Oct. 19, 1781. // 20 Oct. 1781. In pursuance of a decree, Silas Crane has seized the property of Andrew Whitfield as follows: one horse, one cow and calf, 15 bu. corn, one horse-plow, one grindstone, one looking-glass, one chest, one old pair of trousers, one old linen jacket, 2 dozen brass buttons, 15 bu. potatoes, 200 pumpkins to be conveyed to the fort at the order of the Commandant. Sig: Silas Crane. // 23 Oct. 1781. Appraisement of the effects seized etc. Total $75. Signed before Silas Crane, James Truly. Charles de Grand-Pre. // Oct. 24, 1781, sale of the above. Witnesses: Alexander McIntosh, Francis Farrell, Isaac Johnson, William Vousdan and others assisting. Buyers: William Vousdan, David Odam, Mr. Hartley, Richard Bacon, Francis Farrell, Silas Crane, William McIntosh, John Farquhar, for $67, deducting costs.

p. 30. Richard Harrison versus John Holstein. Pet. of Richard Harrison, dated Natchez, 21 Oct. 1781, representing that he is the holder of a note drawn by John Holstein for $22, the term of which is long expired and the said John Holstein having some property to satisfy the same, petitioner asks for an order for a payment from said property. Sig: Richard Harrison, for Barbour and Harrison. // 22 Oct. 1781. Let the party be notified to pay or an execution will be issued. Sig: Grand-Pre. // 7th Nov. 1781. Have appointed Dibdal Holt and James Kelly as appraisers of a horse, the property of John Holtstein, seized at the suit of Richard Harrison, which they have appraised at $16. // 7th Nov. 1781, I, Grand-Pre have exposed to public sale the above horse, etc. in presence of Francis Farrell, Silas Crane, and other witnesses assisting. Horse adjudged to Lewis Roberts for $12, he being the highest bidder.

p. 31. William Pounteney versus Bradley and Harrison. Richard Harrison represents that as an attorney for Messrs. Bradley and Harrison, he has been condemned to pay out of their property the amount of an account brought against them by Wm. Pounteney and having no means to satisfy the debt but by selling the cattle which they have in this district; he asks that as many of said cattle as will satisfy the debt be sold. Dec. 2, 1781. Sig: Richard Harrison. // Public notice will be given that the cattle above-mentioned will be sold on Dec. 4th. Sig: Grand-Pre. Isaac Johnson and John Stowers appointed appraisers; 57 head of horned cattle, young and old, appraised at $285. Both sign. Wit: Estevan Minor, Francois Farrell. Grand-Pre. // At plantation of Mr. Bingaman, the sale of the above cattle took place. Wit: Isaac Johnson, Francis Farrell, Silas Crane, Stephen Minor, and others assisting. Richard Harrison bought all for $217. // 10 Dec. 1781. Sale of property of Bradley and Harrison continued. Joseph Duncan and David Odam appraisers, valuing the cattle at $35. Sale of same. All adjudged to Richard Harrison for $40. // 23 Feb. 1782. Another sale of above cattle, appraised by Wm. Pounteny and Wm. Ferguson at $170. In presence of Silas Crane, Nathaniel Tomlinson, John Farquhar, John Burnet and Stephen Minor, and others assisting. All adjudged to Richard Harrison for $179.

p. 35. James Wilson versus Winfred Hoggat. Pet. of James Wilson that he has an account against Winfred Hoggat for $81. Natchez, Oct. 15, 1781. Let the attorney for Winfred Hoggat be notified. GrandPre. Richard Bacon and John Kennedy appointed appraisers, valued the cattle seized at $40. Buyers James Wilson and Alexander McIntosh, for $58. // Nov. 7, 1781. Dibdal Holt and James Kelly appraisers, valued cow and calf seized at $15. Adjudged to Lewis Roberts for $13. // 9th Nov. 1781, two oxen appraised at $37. At sale adjudged to Wm. Vousdan for $43. Silas Crane receipts for $115 amount of sales of above cattle, for the payment of debt to James Wilson which said sum I have paid the said Wilson, after deducting the cost of the sale.

p. 38. James Kelly versus Kilketh King, John Felt and Thompson Lyman. James Kelly petitions that he has a demand agst Thompson Lyman, an absconded rebel, for $28 for a horse for which he gave an order on Justus King for a rifle, who had no rifle from Lyman. Sig: James Kelly. 19 Sept. 1781. // Thompson Lyman will pay the preceding within three days or they will be proceeded against according to law. Grand-Pre. // Natchez, 20 Sept. 1781. Dibdal Holt and John Kelly to appraise 60 bu. of corn seized as the property of Kilketh King and John Felt, killed by the Indians, and Thompson Lyman, absconded, 20 bu. thereof belonging to each; appraised at $60. Sale of above 7th Nov. 1781, for $14 by King, 28 by Lyman due to James Kelly adjudged to Mrs. Alexander McIntosh for $38. Wit: Silas Crane, Richard King, Wm. Ferguson and Wm. Vousdan. Fees: 46 rials. From the sum $10 to be deducted for John Felt, and the balance paid to James Kelly. // 22 Jan. 1782. Isaac Johnson and John Row appraisers of 200 bu. corn belonging to Kilketh King and John Felts, killed by the Indians at Big Black, seized by Jeremiah Routh and Silas Crane, creditors for $55 and $12, respectively, valued at $100. Witnesses: Isaac Johnson, Silas Crane, Richard Harrison, and others assisting; said corn was adjudged to Stephen Minor for $49, $42 for Jeremiah Routh and $7 for Silas Crane. Isaac Johnson signing for his father-in-law, Jeremiah Routh.

p. 46. Petition of Sarah Truly to relate in what manner Bennet Truly has acted since 1773 when your petitioner came to this country. The first year we were all sick and made no crop. Your petitioner was obliged to sell a negro and buy provisions. The next year, he [Bennet] went to the river as a hireling with a certain Lum to row his boat, his wages to be paid in corn for the family use. Instead of returning home, he remained four years hunting. When he returned, your petitioner was planting corn but he remained in the neighborhood until autumn when he went to hunt a second time and in his absence and all those with him were taken prisoners by Capt. Willing and all went down to New Orleans. Some days before the death of Capt. Reuben Harrison he returned to this place and served in the militia during the remainder of the year. The next year he came to my house and finished making the crop with my three slaves and out of the said crop, your petitioner paid $300 owing by him in the neighborhood. Your petitioner then gave him charge of 4 negroes with whom he made 3000 lbs. of tobacco, the whole of which your petitioner received. Your petitioner then sold her plantation with the intention of establishing another, as was customary at that time, but was not allowed by Mr. De la Villebeuvre. Your petitioner waited on him in company with Dr. Farrell and was informed that he would not allow inhabitants to sell one plantation and establish another for he expected some settlers to arrive in the country. Sig: Sarah Truly. Jany. 21, 1782. // Another petition by Sarah Truly, same date, recounts details of property of Bennet Truly. When he returned from hunting up the river, he had little, part due him from Wm. Ferguson, for which he got some cows and calves, the other part consisted of a rifle gun, with which he bought a horse from one Hooper, which horse he has with him now. During the time he was with me, I let him have two horses, a saddle, cloth and money sufficient for his pocket, which horses he parted with, as to the cattle he had, there is not one of them in my possession, as some he killed, others he sold, and the rest died of distemper. I am willing to certify that there is no property of Bennet Truly in my possession, nor yet do I know of any in the district. No doubt, it is thought that this mill is his. It is true that he made the bargain for it, as also for many others for me, but it was by and with my permission and my property paid for it. It seems that he has promised Farney the stones in this mill, but I can prove by Mr. Crane that I told Bennet when I first heard of it that he should not take or meddle with them under any consideration whatever, as Farney is as much bound as Bennet in building the mill they began; [she objects to being called on to pay Bennet's part.] The late troubles have prevented their executing their plans, and many others have met with like disappointments. If I should be ordered to pay Bennet's obligation, I pray that you will order Mr. Farney to wait with me until the ensuing crop as it will be a great damage to me to be obliged to sell a negro which I am sensible will not bring half his value at this time. Besides I have put the negroes under an overseer who will naturally demand the number he has agreed to. Etc. 21 Jan. 1782. // Natchez. 18 March. Let George Farney produce an exact account of all his expenditure for the mill as also what he has received on account thereof in horses etc. And the widow Truly will also furnish what proof she has within three days. // Declaration of Wm. Black that he gave flour several times to George Farney for the use of the other mill which they were then building, being ordered by Bennet Truly to let the said Farney have any quantity of meal he might need; he had also had meat from Truly's mother and once sent a hireling for meat, on which Mrs. Truly cursed Farney and the mill, that they had had too much from her already while she was in New Orleans and that she would give nothing more. 23 Jany. 1782. Sig: Wm. Black. Declaration of James Fleet. Mistress Truly and I came together from New Orleans last year. On the way up, she frequently encouraged the hands to row briskly, saying that we should have plenty of meat when we reached home, but when she reached home there were but two pieces left. She scolded very much and inquired what had become of the said meat, to which the girls answered that their brothers had given meat to Mr. Farney and had killed fresh meat also. I, also, after my arrival gave him bear meat, he came for more meat from Mrs. Truly. Sig: James Fleet. Declaration of Eleanor Spain. All that I know respecting the provisions received by George Farney from Bennet Truly from the mill was when my mother was absent at New Orleans, Bennet Truly killed a hog and as I had need of part of it, I applied to him for the same, but he informed me that he could not, having killed the said hog for the use of George Furney at the mill. As to Bennet Truly he had no property whatever in this district as far as my knowledge. I have heard my mother say that she had no concern with Bennet Truly and George Furney in their mill but, on the contrary did not approve of their connection. Sig: Eleanor Spain. Natchez, 23 March 1782. Declaration of Tabitha Spain. I know that Bennet Truly often gave meat and meal to George Farney, belonging to my grandmother for the use of the mill which they were then building and I have often heard my grandmother scold Bennet Truly on account of the mill also on account of a horse given to a certain Samuel Benjamin, for work done at the mill. March 23, 1782. Sig: Tabitha Spain. Declaration of Patsey Truly. When my mother was in New Orleans, my brother killed hogs several times for George Farney's use at the mill, also gave salted meat and meal, and he also gave a horse to Samuel Benjamin for work done at the mill. I am certain my brother has no property in this district except a horse that was in the possession of a Thomas Rule. Natchez. 23 March 1782. Sig: Patsey Truly.

p. 50. Sterling Spell versus Christian Bingaman. Petition of Sterling Spell that he had a demand against Christain Bingaman, late of this district, the balance of a note for $59 due 9 April 1781, it being money out of his pocket; asks that the attorney of the said Christian Bingaman be ordered. Sterling (X) Spell. // 24 Aug. 1781. After examination of the note, order to atty. to pay. The answer: No property, no attorney. Sig: Silas Crane. // 26 Feb. 1782. John Short and Richard Adams, of this district, to appraise a mare property of Christian Bingaman, absconded, as also a horse, at the suit of Sterling Spell for $59. Above valued at $18. Sale of same, 27 Feb. 1782, which were adjudged to Joseph Coupley for $25.

p. 51. Sterling Spell and others versus Benjamin Carrol. Spell petitions that Carrol is indebted to him for $13, asks for an order of payment. March 14, 1782. Let him be notified to pay. Grand-Pre. 23 March 1782. James Truly petitions that he also has an account against Benjamin Carrol for $13, and asks execution against same. The horse seized was adjudged to Stephen Minor for $14, to be divided between the two plaintiffs. Cost of $4 deducted first.

p. 53. Roswell Mygett versus Jeremiah Routh. Petitioner has a demand against Jeremiah Routh, inhabitant of this district, for $8 due for fees of Justice paid by petitioner for the said Routh. April 6, 1782. Sig: Oswell Mygett. Let him be notified to pay. Sig: Grand-Pre. // Appointed Thomas Farrell and Patrick Foley to appraise the horse of Jeremiah Routh, seized to pay Mygett. Horse valued at $15. Adjudged to Roswell Mygett for $19. Witnesses attending: Francis Farrel, Silas Crane, Patrick Foley, Isaac Johnson, William Hubbard, John Farquhar, Charles Adams, James Harman. Fees $7.

p. 53. Jeremiah Routh versus Thaddeus Lyman. 29 April 1782. Have appointed John Hartley and Patrick Foley as appraisers of two pairs of iron-bound wheels, property of Thadeus Lyman seized for $139. Same valued at $38, including some old iron. At sale same adjudged to Jeremiah Routh for $40. Wit: Francis Farrell, Isaac Johnson, James Harman, John Hartley, Silas Crane, William Hubbard, Christopher Leightholder. Charles de Grand-Pre. Fees: to Judge $5; Constable $1; attorney $1.

p. 55. Sutton Banks versus Richard Harrison. Sutton Banks, atty. of John Stephenson, Esq., of Pensacola, for the estate of Barbour and Harrison, represents that Philip Barbour, late of this district, was formerly appointed attorney for the said John Stephenson to take charge and care of a certain number of cattle left with Samuel Wells to the halves. Three years since, the said Wells, being about to leave the district to reside at Opelousas, the said cattle were divided and it was found that 220 heads belonged to the said estate as well as a sum of several hundred dollars profit, arising from the cattle sold, which sum was received by said Barbour at New Orleans out of the property of said Wells. At the departure of said Wells, William Pounteney was appointed to take care of the said cattle by the said Philip Barbour, which he did until the arrival of Richard Harrison, who presented himself as partner and attorney of the said Philip Barbour and claimed the said cattle which were delivered to him. But William Pounteny having a demand against the said cattle, amounting to $407, to pay which demand, the aforesaid Harrison, exposed said cattle to public sale, and as your petitioner is informed, 50 heads thereof were bought in by said Harrison at $4 to $6 per head, when he might have killed a few of the cattle for the use of the garrison and paid the demand. Asks that said Harrison produce an account of all the sales, etc. Sig: Sutton Banks. 11 Sept. 1782. // Richard Harrison will reply to the above within 3 days. Sig: Miro. // To His Excellency, Don Estevan Miro: Petition of Richard Harrison represents that Mr. Sutton Banks has erred in representing to Your Majesty that Capt. Barbour was appointed attorney to Mr. Thomas Bentley, late of Manchac, now of the State of Virginia, who was always the real agent on the Mississippi for the said Bradley and Harrison. The said Bentley confided the whole of the cattle belonging to Bradley and Harrison to the care of Capt. Philip Barbour in whose charge they remained about ten years, which will appear by the power of atty. given by Mr. Thomas Bentley to Capt. Barbour. Capt. Barbour, having made out his accounts against Messrs. Bradley and Harrison, took them with him to Virginia to settle with Mr. Thomas Bentley. Mr. Sutton Banks has also represented in his petition that Capt. Barbour is indebted to the estate for several hundred dollars, which I cannot believe as I know that Capt. Barbour has considerable accounts agst. the estate and I have no doubt that an amicable settlement has before now taken place between Capt. Barbour and Mr. Bentley, who is the authorized agent. Mr. Banks undertakes to say that I am a partner with Capt. Barbour which I am not, nor have not been during the five years past. Our partnership was dissolved in March 1778 and I have no other property belonging to him in my hands except land, his other property being in the City of N. O. and in the State of Virginia. Mr. Banks complains also that I sold part of the cattle belonging to Bradley and Harrison to satisfy the demand of Mr. Pounteney agst the estate. I was sued by Mr. Pounteney for $406, the amount of his account against the said cattle and they were exposed to public sale by the Court to satisfy the said claim. He asks that the property of Bradley and Harrison remain in the hands of your petitioner in whom it was confided by Mr. Barbour until his return which will be early in the Spring and that everything relative thereto be deferred until his arrival. I am unacquainted with his private affairs and he can better make his arrangements with them himself. Sig: Richard Harrison. 18 Sept. 1782. // Examined. Mr. Harrison will remain in possession of the Bradley and Harrison property until the arrival of Mr. Barbour and, in the meanwhile, shall not dispose of any part without the knowledge and consent of Mr. Sutton Banks, attorney for Mr. Stephenson. Signed: Miro. // West Florida. I, Thomas Bentley, late of London, have been appointed attorney for the curators of Bradley and Harrison, of this Province and of the Illinois, in virtue of the power thus given do authorize Philip Barbour to act for me and in my name as attorney for the curators of Bradley and Harrison and to their use, etc. At Manchac, 7th day June 1772. Signed: Thomas Bentley. Wit: Peter Lyon, Thomas Newman.

p. 58. Benjamin Balk versus Richard Harrison. Benjamin Balk, of the district, planter, represents that James Robertson owed him $36, being for money lent for his board and the said Robertson having died, appointing Richard Harrison his heir. 17 Sept. 1782. Signed: Benjamin Balk. The party will produce proof of his claim against the estate of the said Robertson. // Party having produced a document in his favor and evidence of a witness, Richard Harrison is ordered to appear before me at the first audience. // Sir: I request a favor of you as I do not return back by way of Natchez to settle some little business for me, in particular with Mrs. Sarah Truly who has some property of mine in her hands which is two cows and some increase which she refuses to give up. I applied to the Commandant for a summons which was granted but I never could get her to trial before I left. I therefore beg of you to request the Commandant to have her before him. Should she deny the cows were mine, ask her if she did not receive them from my brother, knowing they were mine. I do hereby declare I have never given or disposed of them in any way. Signed: James Robertson. William Smith's wife was present when the cows were delivered to me by her husband. J. Robertson. p. 59. I do empower Benjamin Balk to act for me in regard to this. Signed John Montgomery. // Natchez, July 9th, 1786. The foregoing being exhibited by Col. John Montgomery, who acknowledged his signature thereto as his own and that the signatures of James Robertson are truly his and such as he usually makes. Sig: John Montgomery. // In virtue of the above, I have ordered Mrs. Sarah Truly to give the cows and increase to Mr. Benjamin Balk. Fort of Natchez, Nov. 10, 1781. Sig: Grand-Pre. // Sir: Please to pay Mr. Benjamin Balk $39, it being my bond for one officer and soldier and charge it to the State of Virginia. Signed: John Montgomery, Lt. Col. Dec. 13, 1780. To Oliver Pollock, agent for the U.S. of America, at New Orleans. // Exhibited same to Mr. John Montgomery, who ack. his signature. Grand-Pre. // Petition of Richard Harrison. He has never acted as agent for James Robertson but only for Capt. Barbour to whom the said Robertson owed a large sum of money, and the petitioner never had in his possession any funds belonging to said Robertson, except a small sum arising from the sale of some cattle, ordered to be sold to pay a debt of Capt. Barbour, which sum was but a small part of the debt owing by said Robertson to said Barbour. The will was of property in Virginia which he expected his relations there to leave to him. Sig: Richard Harrison. 22 July 1786. [The dates are very confusing.]

p. 60. Phoebe Calvit versus William Calvit. Agreement made between William Calvit and Phoebe, his wife, namely: The said Wm. Calvit consents that Phoebe, his wife, shall live separate in a house near to him, which house shall be considered her own and shall not be in any manner subject to his order or commands, nor molested nor troubled by him, or any of his family. The said William Calvit also binds himself to furnish her subsistence separately, that is to say, to furnish her with good and wholesome provisions of the country for herself and two children, sufficient for her housekeeping, also a spinning wheel, cards and cotton, and to allow his negro woman to wash her clothes and that of her children, likewise 4 cows and calves, to milk for her use, a young negro named Sam for her servant and a horse at such times as may be thought needful, and for the full performance of these conditions, he binds himself in the penal sum of $500 to be paid to her and her heirs. Sig: William Calvit. Wit: William Pounteney, William Smith. Certified to be a faithful translation into the English language. Sig: Jean Girault. [No date.]

p. 61. John Ferguson versus Richard Bacon. William Henderson, Patrick Foley and John Joseph Duforrest, arbitrators appointed by the Commandant, Don Francisco Bouligny, to settle an affair between Richard Bacon and John Ferguson, we are of the opinion, after examining witnesses that Mr. Richard Bacon is indebted to Mr. John Ferguson for a balance of $100 which shall be paid to sd Ferguson in November next. Natchez, Oct. 1785. Signed: Wm. Henderson, Patrick Foley and John Joseph Duforrest. // Jany. 26, 1786. Mr. Bacon will pay sum of $100, awarded as above. Sig: Francisco Bouligny. // March 15, 1786. Richard Bacon notified of the within order but he refuses to pay. Sig: John Harman, constable. Fee $2. Executed seizure of the land and improvements of Richard Bacon on the river below Natchez, also a black mare, saddle and bridle, to satisfy the above debt. Sig: John Foster. Debt: $100, int. for 3 yrs. $30. Total $130.

p. 61. Adam Bingaman represents that the estate of Henry Stewart, decd., has for nearly 7 years been indebted to him for $248. Capt. Davis, agent of the estate, declares that he has nothing belonging to the said estate but a tract of land on St. Catherine's Creek; petitioner therefore prays, considering the legality of his debt which is proved, that an order be given that sd land be sold to satisfy the same. New Orleans, Apr. 6, 1785. Sig: A. Bingaman. // Examined. Let the sum of $248, owing by Henry Stewart, be paid out of the proceeds of the sale ordered by the decree of the 11th instant. New Orleans. Apr. 12, 1785. Sig: Estevan Miro.

p. 62. James Hurst versus Stephen Minor. James Hurst represents that Oct. 21, 1784 he left the river Showang where he had bought 32 bundles of deer skins, containing in all 1300 skins and to begin his voyage down the Mississippi River with intent to proceed to New Orleans, but on reaching the Grand Gulf he was informed by a certain Michael Lopez that the Commandant of Natchez would not permit him to go down the river, whereupon he left his boat and people at the Grand Gulf and went down with the said Lopez intent to appear before the Commandant, but, on arriving in Natchez, the said Lopez planted him on a willow point before the fort and told him to remain there until he gave notice to the Commandant. On the day following, in the evening, the said Mr. Minor crossed the river and told him to return to Grand Gulf and bring his boat down to the Natchez, there to remain until the Commandant received orders that he would be allowed to continue down to N. O. Several hours later he received a written order that if he did not return to the place from which he came, his property would be confiscated. Your petitioner then set off with his boat, which was not of the kind proper to ascend the river and at about three leagues from Natchez, Mr. Minor overtook him and told him that he would buy his skins if he would take horses in payment, telling him, at the same time, that he could go through the Choctaw Nation to Georgia in 8 or 10 days. He asked Mr. Minor if he would be allowed to go to New Orleans without his cargo and Mr. Minor said he would not be allowed to go down the river on any account. Your petitioner was then under the necessity of delivering to said Minor his boat and skins, amounting to 1300, for which the said Minor gave your petitioner two horses for which he charged $210 and $100 in money, amounting to $310, the said boat and cargo being worth at the regualr price $1300. The petitioner having delivered his boat and skins, he was told by said Minor to begin his journey through the Choctaw Nation, adding that if the inhabitants furnished me provisions he would be subject to punishment. He then hired an Indian for $30 to conduct him to the Choctaw Nation. After a six day journey, the said Indian left your petitioner in the woods. Not knowing what road to follow or how to subsist and being 200 miles from any settlement, your petitioner wandered about for 34 days and at last arrived at Mobile where he could obtain no more than $50 for the two horses, which the sd Minor had sold to him for $220. The Commandant immediately gave your petitioner a passport to come to this place. Asks that justice be done to him. New Orleans, 8 March 1785. Sig: James Hurst. The Commandant of the Post of Natchez will take cognizance of the complaint of James Hurst against Don Estevan Minor and take all steps necessary to ascertain the truth of the allegations of said Hurst, and return to this tribunal. Sig: Estevan Miro.

p. 65. Isaac Johnson versus William Pounteny. William Pounteny, being charged with the affairs of William Hiorn, and a demand being lately made on said estate by Isaac Johnson, which your petitioner cannot satisfy, the same appearing to him unjust, asks for a hearing and order the said Johnson to appear. Your petitioner also observes that the said estate is indebted to him and he, like others, cannot obtain payment, without your permission to sell the estate. Sig: Wm. Pounteny. Natchez, Nov. 11, 1787. // Fort of Natchez, 23 Nov. 1785, the parties will appear at the first audience and Wm. Pounteny will produce the accounts of the estate with which he is charged. Signed: Bouligny. // Natchez, 25 Nov. 1785. The parties are notified to appear. // Isaac Johnson, of this district of Natchez, represents that your petitioner being at the White Cliffs on 24 Feb. 1778, when Mr. James Willing and a party of men lay preparing to set off for New Orleans and that your petitioner rode a remarkably fine horse which said Willing took a fancy for and asked your petitioner if he would sell it, that he would give $150 for him. The petitioner did agree to let Willing have the horse for $150. Willing called a man by the name of Sergeant Williams. Your petitioner refused to give up the horse unless Willing gave him good security upon the spot. Upon which Mr. Willing told your petitioner to walk up to William Hiorn who stood at about 50 yards distance and Mr. Willing told Mr. Hiorn that he had purchased the petitioner's horse and desired Mr. Hiorn to pay $150 to your petitioner for the said horse and Mr. Hiorn said "I will pay $150 to Mr. Johnson on your account, upon which the petitioner did deliver up his horse to Mr. Willing. That your petitioner did several times make application to Mr. Hiorn previously to his leaving this country for the money; that Mr. Hiorn did for some time make evasive answers and then denied ever promising the payment. Though half the Natchez district either from being present or hearing of it knew that Mr. Hiorn was indebted by assumption on Mr. Willing's account to the petitioner for $150. Sig: Isaac Johnson. New Orleans, 31 Jan. 1785. // This is to certify that I was at White Cliffs on 24 Feb. 1778 when Isaac Johnson did sell to James Willing a bay horse for $150 and that William Hiorn did become responsible for the payment of $150 on James Willing's account to said Isaac Johnson for a bay horse. Natchez, 20 Oct. 1785. Sig: Richard Harrison. // Natchez, personally appeared before John Blommart, of His Brittanic Majesty's Justices of the Peace, Sterling Spell who, on oath, declared that on 24 Feb. 1778, then being at the White Cliffs, was present when James Willing did buy a horse from Isaac Johnson, Esq. for $150 and that said Johnson did refuse to deliver said horse until said Willing would give security for the payment. They went together to William Hiorn, Esq. who stood near and said Willing asked Hiorn to pay the said Johnson $150 for he had bought his horse and Hiorn said he would, and that then Johnson did deliver the horse to the said Willing. Sterling (S. S.) Spell. Before J. Blommart. // I do certify that William Hiorn did tell me one day as well as some other people in Capt. Blommart's house in Natchez, that he was security to Isaac Johnson, Esq. for a horse which James Willing insisted upon having and further that Mr. Willing declared that had not Johnson consented to let him, the said Willing, have him, he would have taken him by force, but said Hiorn rather than have Johnson lose his horse, he should pay it himself, or words to that purpose. 31 Jan. 1784. Sig: William Vousdan. // Personally appeared before me, John Blommart, Esq. one of His Brittanic Majesty's Justices, Ephraim Thornell who being sworn, said that 24 Feb. 1778, being at White Cliffs was present [same as sworn by other deponents.] Sig: Elphraim Thornell. 12 Apr. 1780. // In consideration of the foregoing declarations, the Commandant of this Post, will compel James Willing to pay to Isaac Johnson the sum due him and in case in the absence of said Willing or that he has no property in this district, the said Commandant will compel payment from William Hiorn, his surety, and from the persons charged with his estate. Sig: Estevan Miro. p. 66. Isaac Johnson to the Civil and Military commandant of the Post of Natchez, Isaac Johnson represents that some time past he presented to Your Honor a decree of His Excellency Don Estevan Miro, Gov. Genl. of the Province, in his favor against the estate of William Hiorn for $150; asks that the decree be executed and Wm. Pountney, agent of said estate, be ordered to make payment. Natchez, 13 April 1785. Sig: Isaac Johnson. // Wm. Pountney represents that as Mr. James Mather is also agent, that this matter be settled in New Orleans. He has already sent the papers there. Sig: Wm. Pountney. Granted. And the petition to be transmitted to the Superior Government and Isaac Johnson will be notified to appear before the said tribunal, with the needful documents. Sig: Trevino.

p. 66. John Buhler versus Estevan Minor. Estevan Minor owes John Buhler $97. Payment is asked. Sig: John Buhler. [No date.] New Orleans, Apr. 12, 1785. The Commandant of Natchez will cause to be executed his former decree in favor of John Buhler against Adjt. Don Estevan Minor. Sig. Miro. // Natchez, Nov. 22. Don Estevan Minor, adjt. will certify the sum claimed in the foregoing petition. Francisco Bouligny. // Pet. of John Buhler for order to condemn payment of $97 owing him by Estevan Minor. Natchez, 26 Jan. 1785. Let the debtor be notified to pay immediately or to state his reasons. // Estevan Minor answers John Buhler, acknowledges the debt, of the former decree he was not notified until now, and the said Buhler is indebted to him for $100 which he is ready to prove, asks payment of the overplus by said Buhler due the petitioner with cost of suit. Sig: Estevan Minor. Natchez, Nov. 23, 1785. // Petitioner will produce the document referred to. // George Fitzgerald, Chachere and Richard Carpenter, arbitrators appointed to settle the above dispute are of the opinion that Stephen Minor should be allowed $100 for translating some business last January. 7 June 1786. Signed.

p. 68. Emanuel Madden versus Widow Coleman. Whereas Lt. Gov. Bouligny has referred to our consideration how much of the above accounts ought to be paid by Emanuel Madden and what part thereof by the estate of William Coleman, decd. which we have considered accordingly. We are of the opinion that the said Madden pay $193 and $698 to be paid of the said estate, exclusive of William Mygat's amount against said estate. Natchez, Jan. 27, 1786. Sig: Anthony Hutchins, George Fitzgerald. Madden to pay Carpenter, Mr. Moore and Geo. Fitzgerald. Estate to pay Col. Hutchins with int., est. of Castles, and Geo. Fitzgerald. [Three pages of accounts.]

p. 71. P. Hawkins versus George Rapalje. Pet. of Peter Hawkins that in January last past, he sold George Rapalje a tract on Cole Creek for $300, $150 paid in hand, the remainder this month. Then the said George Rapalje was imprisoned which took place a few days after the bargain was made. Your petitioner had received but a small part of the money to have been paid in hand, and, having sold the said land entirely in view of satisfying his creditors, asks that he be allowed to sell the said land for the said creditors on condition of refunding to Mr. Rapalje what he has received from him on account thereof. Sig: Peter Hawkins. Natchez. 29 Jany. 1786. // Pet. is ordered to make proof of the sale made by him to George Rapalje and to produce the notes and obligations given to him. On Tuesday next when he is ordered to appear before me, etc. Sig: Bouligny. // I promise to pay to Peter Hawkins or his order an account of Garret Rapalje, $150 for value received. 8 Jany. last. for $11, it being the balance due on Joseph Duncan's note was never accepted and you are forthcoming for the same. If you wrote it off Mr. Rapalje's note, you must debit with the same again. Your order as it was delivered to me by Mr. Smith with his endorsement for same I have sent to Mr. Adam Bingaman to present to you and to whom I request that you will pay the same without permitting it to go before the Commandant, which will only be attended with further expense which I do not wish to do if it can be avoided. Sig: John Fitzpatrick.

p. 72. James Brown to John Still Lee. John Still Lee represents that he was condemned by the award of arbitrators to pay a certain Brown whom he had hired as overseer last year, the quantity of 150 bushels of corn and 1600 pounds of tobacco, notwithstanding the said Brown worked only 12 days with your petitioner, having hired himself to work elsewhere. Without refusing altogether to abide by the said award, your petitioner thinks he may observe that the arbitrators have made the same allowance for the said Brown as if he had complied with his agreement, of which a translation is hereunto annexed. If the arbitrators had considered that the petitioner was obliged to hire another person in the place of the said Brown as will appear by the certificate herewith, the award would have been different and your petitioner thinks he should deduct from the allowance made to the said Brown by the arbitrators the amount your petitioner paid to the person whom he employed in his stead while the said was receiving wages elsewhere. Natchez, 8 March 1786. Sig: John Still Lee. // John Still Lee, of said dist., represents that the said Brown did hire himself for nine months in the year to another planter who paid him wages, etc. [Same as in the foregoing.] Natchez, March 15, 1786. Sig: John Still Lee. // Let the plaintiff be notified to appear at the first audience with the original articles of agreement and the award referred to. Sig: Grand-Pre. // Articles of agreement made between John Still Lee and James Brown. Witness: H. Manadue. 9 March 1785. // I do certify that George Holloway told me that he worked with John Still Lee at $1 per day in the crop that James Brown left in order to make it fit for sale. [Not signed.] We, the arbitrators chosen by Mr. Still Lee and Mr. Brown, have measured the tilled ground of the plantation of said Still Lee, which is in good order, containing 21 acres in corn and 7 acres of tobacco, and have allowed the said Brown his part of the crop according to the articles of agreement, [the same award as given.] Sig: Abraham Mayes, William Daniels, 29 May 1785. Before me, Trevino. // It is mutually agreed between the parties that there shall be deducted from the amount of the award against Still Lee in favor of James Brown the sum of $77 in full of all deductions.

Confirmed. Signed Charles de Grand-Pre.

p. 74. Pierre Decou versus Polser Shilling. I take the liberty of informing you that the security given by Monsieur LaCroix of Polser Shilling who has bound himself to pay sum mentioned in the enclosed receipt; asks that Shilling be compelled to pay same. Bearer hereof will receive the sum and transmit to me. Sig: P. Myeux. Pointe Coupee, 27 June 1787. // Please pay to Antonio Gras. // Pointe Coupee, 1 Apr. 1786. Polser Shilling appears and binds himself to pay to Pierre Decou $50 in one month from this date, or restore the boat in which he is now going to New Orleans. A like sum paid by the said Decou with the knowledge and permission of the Commandant for the compensation claimed by the Tunica Indians for saving the said boat which they threatened to cut to pieces for firewood unless the said sum was paid to them. The said Polser Shilling giving as security for the person of Michael LaCroix, and both of them granting authority to the Justices of His Majesty to compel them of same. Signed: Polser Shilling. A true Copy. Nicholas DeLessize. I have received from Monsieur LaCroix the sum of $50 by him for Polser Shilling, whereof I have given this receipt at Pointe Coupee, 1 March 1787. Signed: Pierre Decou Nicolet. Mr. Polser Shilling, Sir: Please pay the amount of the enclosed receipt to Mr. Peter Walker and his receipt shall be in full for the canoe. Sig: Michael LaCroix.

p. 75. James Elliot versus Abner Green. James Eliott represents that some time since he contracted with Abner Green to build a flatboat to carry corn to New Orleans which the said Green did accordingly build. But when your petitioner had put a part of the lading on board, the boat leaked so much that he was compelled to unload for fear of losing the property on board and after a strict examination of said boat, it was found that her bottom was bad; asks that three proper persons be appointed to examine the said boat and the amount of damages your petitioner is likely to suffer, as well by the delay as by the useless expenses already incurred. Natchez, April 8, 1786. Signed: James Elliott. // The parties will appoint, each one, an arbitrator to examine the state of the boat in question, and in case they cannot agree, I do hereby appoint Mr. Richard Devall to act as umpire. Signed: Grand-Pre. Joseph Duncan and Caleb King appointed to examine the boat, as also Earl Douglass, Richard Devall and John Smith to be assisting them. Signed: GrandPre. // Natchez, 13 May 1786. Notified the abovementioned persons according to orders. // Cole's Creek. We find the boat sufficiently finished to take her loading with the greatest safety. Signed John Smith, Earl Douglass. // Natchez, May 27, 1786. In my opinion, on examining a flat said to be the property of Mr. Abner Green that she is not sufficient to carry her burden of corn, and further declare that I took particular notice of her after being repaired and then in my opinion a few days before she was put into the water that she wouldn't bear any burden sufficient to load her by reason I could not see a timber placed in her in any workmanlike manner. Sig: Richard Devall. // I do certify that I was passing and repassing when he was repairing a flat for Mr. Elliott, and in my opinion it was not sufficient to carry a load. Sig: Andrew Randell. // Being a person requested by Mr. James Elliott to give my opinion on oath, it is my opinion that the boat was not done in a manner to be any service whatever. Sig: Peter Couglin. Natchez, May 23, 1786. // p. 77. Deposition of William Geoghegay, Cole's Creek, 26 May 1786. // Statement of an account amounting to $400. // Deposition by Abner Green and answer by James Elliot // Statement by John Smith, alcalde at Villa Gayoso. Natchez, 8 Aug. 1786. John Smith declares being with Abner Green when he was repairing a flat since sold to James Elliot, I was suspicious that she was rotten and, having an intention of shipping some freight in her, as Abner Green, at that time, had an intention of going to New Orleans in her himself, I took a chisel and examined thoroughly every place that had the least appearance of defect and found her perfectly sound and she was more easily examined as every part was at that time very clean and dry. Soon afterward, I heard Mr. Green say he had been to Mr. Elliot to deliver him, according to bargain, the said flat, etc. // Caleb King declared that he considered the flat insufficient, occasioned by her lying dry and the shrinking of her plank, that she might have been more sufficient at the time she was to have been delivered. // William Nowlin declares that after James Elliot was in possession of the flat sold to him by Abner Green, I several times delivered corn on board, etc, etc. William (x) Nowlin. 7 Aug. 1786. // James (X) Edwards' deposition. // Thomas (X) Calvit, Thomas (T) Dyson, depositions. // Cato West, William Richardson depositions. // I do certify that I was a number of times with Abner Green when he was repairing a flat, etc. Nehemiah Martin. // Depo. of William Vousdan. // New Orleans, 20 Oct. 1786. On examination of the foregoing, I revoke the judgment pronounced by Don Carlos de Grand-Pre, Commandant of the Post of Natchez, 6 June, present year, in favor of James Elliot against Abner Green condemning the first named to pay for the flat built by said Green and hereby releasing said Green from all damages and expenses, and do order that Elliot do pay the cost of this suit. Hereby determined and returned to the Commandant of the district. Signed Estevan Miro.

p. 92. The King versus David Smith. In Fort Panmur at Natchez, Aug. 4, 1786, in pursuance of the order of Don Carlos de Grand-Pre, Lt. Col. in the Royal Armies, Capt. of the Grenadiers in the Reg. of Infantry of Louisiana, and Civil and Military Commandant of sd Fort and District, transmitted to David Smith, planter, settled at Bayou Pierre, to appear immediately before me, the said Smith appeared on the day of the date thereof, having been informed that he had written a certain letter to Tacitus Gaillard, found in a path leading to Cole's Creek, and the said Smith being duly sworn by means of Jacob Monsanto acting as interpreter, on the Holy Evangelists according to the rights of his religion, to answer truly to such questions as shall be put to him on the part of the King, the signature of the letter was shown to him and he was asked if he acknowledged the signature to be his own and such as he usually made, to which he answered and swore by all that he holds sacred that the signature was not his own nor written by him, although it is evident that the malfactors who wrote and signed the said letter took great pains to imitate his signature but he can prove by a reference to his writing and by a judicial inquiry which he prays may be immediately instituted that the whole is a forgery and that it will appear by his way of thinking, his general conduct, his fidelity and obedience since he settled in this District, that the favored protection he has received from this Spanish Government has inspired him with the utmost gratitude, which said inquiry he prays may be made by twelve respectable persons among the Planters and Merchants of the District and that, in the meanwhile, Mr. Caleb King and Mr. William Henderson may be accepted as sureties for his person; it being easily proved that he has never at any time had communication or correspondence with Tacitus Gaillard, whom he believes to be wholly ignorant of the existence of this letter, fabricated by his enemies here, at the same time declaring that he had never at any time had communication with Davenport, and that the malice and perfidy of his dispicable enemies will be exposed in this black proceeding, protesting formally against the tenor of the said letter written in a hand different from the signature, declaring the one and the other to be absolutely false. Whereupon, having compared the known signature of the accused with the signature at the foot of the letter in question, an evident difference was perceived, in consideration whereof I, the Commandant, accepted sureties offered and have granted the Official Inquiry prayed for and the said accused has signed with the Interpreter and Antonio Soler, Lt. of Royal Artillery, Don Joaquim Ossorno, Lt. of Grenadiers in the Reg. of Louisiana, witnesses present. Signed: Jacob Monsanto, Antonio Soler, Joaquim de Ossorno, David Smith, Charles de Grand-Pre. // Bond of Caleb King and William Henderson who voluntarily become security, etc. for the person of David Smith to abide result of an accusation against him respecting a seditious letter said to have been written by Smith and addressed to Tacitus Gaillard. // In Fort Panmur, at Natchez, Aug. 5, 1786, before Charles de Grand-Pre, Alexander Moore, Richard Carpenter, George Fitzgerald, Samuel Flower, Mathew White, Richard Harrison, John Bisland, Caleb King, William Henderson, Thomas Green, Richard King, Zachariah Smith who offered to declare their opinion of the conduct, habits, etc., of David Smith. Having examined well and compared with many others of said David Smith in their possession, they unanimously declared neither the seditious letter nor signature thereto was the handwriting of sd Smith, and further that they know him to be a man of honor whose conduct has always been correct and well-known to all the Inhabitants of the District and they hold him incapable of any attempt against the Government of His Majesty. (Signed by all.) // In Fort Panmur, at Natchez, 6 Aug. 1786. The Commandant, with interpreter and other Spanish officials, repaired to the plantation of Tacitus Gaillard, who was confined to his bed. Inquired if he knew a certain David Smith, inhabitant of Bayou Pierre, and what opinion he had of him, "on the Bible" he answered that he knew the person named, having seen him once, but could not form an opinion of him as he had never even heard him spoken of until now. Had he ever had a correspondence with him? No. After some reflection, Tacitus Gaillard observed that his conscience obliged him to declare that he had heard speak of a letter said to have been written by said Smith and that he believed it to be a forgery. Signed Tacitus Gaillard, Jacob Monsanto, Joaquim de Ossorno.

p. 96. Turner Brashears versus James Stoddard. Turner Brashears, lately of the Nation, represents that near three years since, a gray horse was stolen from him, now about six years old in the Choctaw Nation where your petitioner then lived, and having found, two days ago, the said horse near the plantation of a certain James Stoddard, he caught said horse and led him to the house of said Stoddard who told the petitioner that said horse belonged to him and that he bought him from a certain Griffing who he believed had him from Benjamin Rogers, who had him from St. Germain. Your petitioner can readily prove by Joseph Duncan and his father that said horse belongs to him, he prays that James Stoddard be ordered to restore to your petitioner his said horse. Nov. 12, 1786. Sig: Turner Brashears. // Petitioner will produce sufficient proof that the horse which he claims belongs to him. Sig: Grand-Pre. // Natchez, 12 Aug. 1786. The annexed certificate being sufficient proof of property, the horse will be restored to claimant, the present possessor having recourse against the seller, and so on. Sig: Grand-

Pre.

p. 97. The King versus Michel Lopez. In Fort Panmur in Natchez, 6 March 1786, appeared Samuel Smith, of same, and declared that he was lately in the service of Miguel Lopez, planter at Grand Gulf, with whom he went to the Choctaw Nation, from whence he is now returned, being dissatisfied with the wages and treatment he received from the said Miguel Lopez. Whereupon, I have appointed Juan Careras to act as notary and Don Estevan Minor as interpreter. After which Samuel Smith, being duly sworn, declared that he was twenty years old, a Protestant, and was born in Ireland; he was a laborer and he came to this district about four months ago with Mr. Chacheret from Cumberland. He had not taken the oath of fidelity. He was asked why he had not taken said oath when it was well-known that no one could remain in this district without the formality. He answered that it was because Mr. Chacheret told me that it was not necessary as he had already informed the Commandant that he had brought down two hands with him. He was engaged in the employment of the English mulatto woman, named "Nelly", who was housekeeper for Miguel Lopez, and went with her to the plantation at Grand Gulf, where he met with the aforesaid Lopez, with whom he engaged to work on the plantation, where he received $12 a month. While he was working there two persons of this district came to the house of Lopez, named Johnson and Trimble, who were going to hunt on the river, without being provided with passports, and said Lopez lent them a pirogue and a gun, which happened about ten days before Christmas; four days afterwards came Tacitus Gaillard and his son Isaac with three negroes and a white man named Hughes, who said they came from the Choctaw Nation. They remained two days and two nights and they had five horses and three mules. On the third they went and encamped in a woods about a league and a half from the plantation, at Big Black, from whence they came daily to the house of Lopez for provisions. While they stayed at that place Lopez did not visit them until he decided to join them in the village of the Nation where they now are with the said Lopez. Yes, he knew they were fugitives from the district. Being but a poor hireling, he did not think because of his knowledge of these men he would be considered a partaker of their delinquency. The said Gaillard said he left the district because the Spaniards would not allow him to live in that territory. They stopped in the Nation to prepare for their journey to Carolina. He did not know what Gaillard had agreed to pay Lopez for the services he rendered him. When asked why Lopez went to the Indian Nation he replied that a certain Armstrong, of this district, having come there, had a private conversation with Lopez, and he, Samuel Smith, learned that said Armstrong had informed Lopez that he would be apprehended by the order of the Commandant for having received into his house the said Gaillard, which determined him to go to the Nation. The Gaillards were at Big Black when Armstrong gave Lopez the above information and on the same day Isaac Gaillard came to the house and Lopez communicated to him the said information. They decided to immediately set out for the Yazoo Nation. Armstrong informed Lopez of the detachment of troops ordered out under Don Antonio Soler and Don Joaquim de Ossorno and that a party was ordered to apprehend Gaillard and Lopez. He was asked if Armstrong said that he was commissioned by the Commandant to discover the encampment of Gaillard and to serve as a guide to the officers who commanded the party, to which he replied that he had not. He does not know where Armstrong now is. The above being read to him by the interpreter, he acknowledged the same and had nothing to add. He signed with a mark. Before Carlos de Grand-Pre. // p. 100. Fort Panmur. 27 July 1786. Miguel Lopez, having appeared of his own free will and accord, was committed to the prison of this fort. Same notary as above; George Fitzgerald appointed interpreter. The free negro woman named Nelly, called before the Commandant, declared that her name was Nelly Price and she had been in this country twenty years. She deals in merchandise and settled at the Grand Gulf and she cultivates the ground and also trades with the Indians; for three years past she lived and was in partnership with Miguel Lopez. Tacitus Gaillard and his son came there . . [About the same as in the deposition of Samuel Smith, adding that James Armstrong did say that he had been commissioned to find the camp of the Gaillards and be a guide for the party sent out to apprehend them. She is 46 years old.] // Next appeared Thomas Boles, who, on oath, in answer to questions put to him, declared that he had been in the district twenty years, and employed in agriculture, employed by Lopez who gave him $10 per month, and he is 44 years old. [Being at work in the fields most of the time, his testimony is not so full as the two above, but he was at breakfast when James Armstrong appeared and said to Lopez "You here eating breakfast and two pirogues coming up the river to arrest you."] At the Fort aforesaid, 28 July 1786, Miguel Lopez, in the prison of said fort, was notified that it was necessary that he choose a godfather to defend him in his trial, whereupon he made choice of Don Joaquim de Ossorno, whereupon I proceeded to take the confession of the criminal, who, being sworn, declared that he understood the Spanish language sufficiently to understand all questions put to him, that he was a Roman Catholic, that he was born in the town of Mahon, and was 34 years old and had been in this province about 15 years; he settled at the Grand Gulf where he traded with the Indians, having permission from the Governor General of the Province to so trade with the Indians, fugitives from the district, Tacitus Gaillard and his son, Isaac, with another white man named Hughes had been to his house with some negroes belonging to Gaillard, but he had never seen any of them before, etc. [largely what had been deposed before by others .... he called the destination for which he and the Gaillard party set out "the Yazoo Village" .... He denied having offered to procure an Indian chief to serve as guide to Gaillard, at which he was told that it was known that he did make an agreement for Gaillard with a Choctaw chief named Payuma. He replied that Gaillard made the bargain with the chief at his house. Etc., etc.] He signed with a mark. The criminal was withdrawn. All witnesses ratified their testimonies. 29 July 1786.

p. 107. The King versus James Armstrong. Circular addressed to Alexander Fraser, Benjamin James, James McIntosh, residing in the Chickasaw and Choctaw towns. Sirs: It being the custom and interest of all nations to apprehend highway robbers who by force of arms strip travellers and enter the houses of citizens and plunder their most valuable effects, and even the horses which are so necessary for the support of their families, this is to inform you that a troup of these vagabonds have associated in this District to commit atrocities abovementioned and it is expected will shortly take the route of the Indian towns with their ill-gotten plunder to avoid their punishment imposed by the laws of all nations for such offences. Under the impression I point out to your notice James Armstrong, and his two sons and a negro belonging to him, and likewise John and James Lovell, real and pretended brothers, and James Blair, who have lately robbed many inhabitants of the District of their firearms, clothes, goods, saddles, bridles, horses, etc. to the end that should these villians who have committed these outrages against the peace of society and the majesty of the law appear at the Indian settlements you might be pleased to have them arrested and with their booty conveyed under a strong guard to this District to receive the reward. Have just learned that a certain Jeremiah Routh is an accomplice and has left this District with the effects plundered by Armstrong and companions. I have also to request that you will not admit any person into your settlements unless provided with a passport in form. Those to appear without such recommendations to be considered as vagabonds, disturbers of the public tranquility and the welfare of the society in general. May God preserve you many years. Fort Panmur at Natchez, Aug. 16, 1786. P. D. Such persons as may compose the escort of the prisoners and the property plundered will be amply recompensed for their service. ____________ Signed: Carlos de Grand-Pre.

Circular to William Brocus, Samuel Gibson, Roswell Mygatt, William Tabor, Prosper King, Ezekiel DeWitt, John Swayze, James Swayze, William Smith, John Coleman, Samuel Walker, Waterman Crane, Israel Leonard, John Pickens, John Ford, James Stoddard, John Martin, Jeptha Higdon, Richard Adams, John Adams, Edward Lovelace, Adam Lanehart, Jeremiah Coleman, John Lum, John Stampley, William Collins, John Kincaid, Joseph Fort, and Elias Bonnell. The robberies lately committed by rebel James Armstrong, his two sons and negro, together with the vagabonds, named John and James Lovel and George Blair, who forcibly entered the houses of four inhabitants of this District and putting them in fear of their lives, stripped their dwellings of everything most valuable they could carry off, such as clothes, goods, firearms, horses, saddles, bridles and other effects, contrary to the public peace and tranquility, being well-known. In order to promptly and effectively remedy these, to cut short the course of these villians, I do hereby command all inhabitants, without exception to unite immediately and in parties of twenty persons and pursue these public robbers without delay until they are taken dead or alive, the public tranquility in a measure depending on their apprehension, as also on the expedition used, in which every person is interested. It is therefore recommended to the inhabitants to concert among themselves the best means of taking these robbers, each party taking a different route and such as they expect most likely to be used by these villians in placing ambushes for them where they might think needful and where they may intercept them on their return from their nocturnal expeditions. At Fort Panmur at Natchez, 12 Aug. 1786. Signed Carlos de Grand-Pre.

p. 108. A letter from Don Manuel de Texada. Sir: I have to inform you that last night at twelve o'clock, Armstrong and five white men, well-armed, invested my house, robbed me of two horses which they were tying when, hearing a noise, I went out and accosted them mildly, being alone and unarmed, represented to them that it was grievous to see my horses taken before my face, to which Armstrong answered that he had ordered them to be taken and if any person said a word he would take his heart out, and at the same time told his companions to examine the house for a saddle and take it also, as likewise any firearms they might find, and not finding any firearms, they took my saddle and bridle, a great coat, a yard and a half of cloth and a handkerchief, from whence they went to the house of Stephan de Alva, where finding nothing that suited them but one gun, they took that and went away, uttering two thousand bravados, Armstrong saying that it was he who commanded at Cole's Creek and he expected in a fortnight to have men to take the fort. From thence they came to the house of James Cable and finding only his wife at home, they ransacked the house and finding nothing that suited them but a rifle, two blankets and a saddle and bridle, they took these articles and went away, swearing they would have Cable's life. It is my opinion that if Your Excellency should not take some effective means, Armstrong will soon have troops strong enough to ruin all the settlers on this creek. I should have waited on Your Excellency in person but at present am somewhat lame, etc. God Preserve you Many years. Cole's Creek August 10, 1786. Signed, Manuel Texada. To His Excellency, Don Carlos de Grand-Pre.

p. 109. I, the undersigned, Surgeon of the Hospital of Natchez certify that on the 16th day of August, 1786, a certain James Armstrong was brought to the Hospital wounded in the right eye by a ball which penetrated and came out about an inch above the eye-brow, I also found another ball in his head which lodged upon the skull. The wounded man continues to be attended daily by order of His Excellency, Don Carlos de Grand-Pre, Commandant of the Fort and Post. In testimony, whereof, I have given these presents, to serve when need be. Signed, Louis Faure.

At Fort Panmur at Natchez, 17 August 1786, I, Don Carlos de Grand-Pre, in order to take the confession of James Armstrong, who is badly wounded, in Hospital to which he was brought by one of the parties detached to arrest him and in danger from dying from one moment to another, wherefore it is necessary to examine him without loss of time, I have appointed Juan Careras to act as Clerk, which he has accepted and promised faithfully to discharge the same, and has signed with the King's Solicitator, Carlos de GrandPre, Juan Carreras. It being necessary to appoint an Interpreter to translate the confession of the criminal, James Armstrong, and the declarations of the witnesses in the case, all of whom speak the English language, I have appointed Mr. George Fitzgerald, who, being informed of said appointment, has accepted thereof, in witness whereof he has signed, with the King's Attorney and the Clerk. Witnesses also present: Don Antonio Soler, Lieut. of the Artillery, and Don Joaquim de Ossorno, Liet. of the Grenadiers. All of whom have repaired to the Royal Hospital where the said James Armstrong lay wounded and inquired if he would swear before God truly to answer such questions as should be put to him on the part of the King, to which he answered, laying his hand on the Bible according to form and rites of his religion that he would declare the truth. What is your name? James Armstrong. What religion? Protestant. Where were you born? In South Carolina. By whom were you wounded, and with whom? He does not know exactly who shot him but he is certain it was one of the party who came to take him, and he was in the company of his father, his younger brother and John and James Lovel. How long had he been in that company? They joined company about seven days before. What had they been doing? Robbing. State truly how many robberies they committed and on whom. John and James Lovel and his father, himself and his father's negro went to the house of Manuel Texada and by force of arms robbed him of two horses, a saddle, two bridles, and a cloth great coat, and the same night they went to the house of John Cable, whom they robbed of a bag, two blankets, a horse, a saddle and bridle, from whence they went to the house of Jeremiah Routh to supper. Did they commit any violence in these robberies? Threatened that if any resistance was made they would take the property by force and shoot them. Did they go to the houses of any other person? They went to the house of David Odam whom they robbed of a rifle and from thence they were to the house of Jeremiah Routh from whence they took a barrel of whiskey. To whom did the barrel of whiskey belong? It belonged to George Blair. Name all of the other inhabitants whom they robbed. The same night they robbed the house of Stephen de Alva and James Cole, from each of whom they took a rifle, with the same violence as before mentioned. Who furnished them provisions? They concealed themselves in the house of Jeremiah Routh who furnished them provisions. How many persons were in the troup where they first met together and for what purpose? The troup consisted of his father, his father's negro, the brothers Lovel, George Blair and himself, and the manner of their meeting was as follows: The two Lovels and George Blair, hearing his father was about to set out to the Indian Nation, came to the house and dissuaded him from going to the Indian Nation but rather to join with them in robbing in the District, and they accordingly robbed the houses before mentioned, as also those of Douglas and Sinclair, at each of whom they took a rifle. If he has any knowledge of a seditious letter found in the District, bearing the signature of David Smith and addressed to Tacitus Gaillard? That letter was written by George Blair who counterfeited the signature of Smith. If he knows for what purpose the said Blair fabricated the said letter. With the intention of ruining Smith and his family. If he knew any other persons who intended to join the troup. None. If his brother was concerned in their robberies. No, he was too young, and never left home. If they intended to leave the District and at what time and where did they intend to go? They intended to leave the District in two days and go to the State of

Georgia. Where was his brother? When the party appeared he flew to the woods. Where were the rest of the troup? Also in the woods. Where is the negro, before-mentioned? It would appear that next day Lovel stole a horse from Richard Dunn and that the negro followed them. Where was he when he was wounded? And was he armed? He was near the house and had his rifle. Why he did not surrender to the party when ordered to do so? He was not at liberty to do so, being under the orders of his father. And Lovel and his brother threatened to kill him in the house if he did not go out with his rifle and defend himself. If his father stood on the defensive when ordered to surrender? He did. Where was his father killed by the party? In the same tobacco field, distant about an acre from the house. If he had not concerted a project of robbing the stores in Natchez? He never concerted any project, but being under his father's command was bound to obey his orders. He did hear the Lovels one day propose to rob the stores of Natchez but his father objected going so near the Fort. If he has anything more to say and how old is he? At present, he doesn't remember anything more except he heard the Lovels say that they intended to kill Joseph Duncan; and he is eighteen years old. And the foregoing confession being read to him by the interpreter, he acknowledged it to be the same he has made, ratifying and confirming the same on the oath which he has taken, and not knowing how to write has made the mark of a cross, in the presence of the King's Attorney, the Interpreter, the Clerk, and the witnesses assisting. Signed: Carlos de Grand-Pre, George Fitzgerald, Antonio Soler, Joaquim de Ossorno and Juan Carreras.

At the Fort on the same day and year before-written, appeared William Brocus who headed one of the parties detached to take the troup of robbers commanded by James Armstrong in this District and the said Brocus, placing his hand on the Bible according to the custom of his religion and promised to answer truly such questions that should be put to him by the interpreter on the part of the King, to relate circumstantially every occurence that took place from the time the party left the Fort until their return. On the road to the Cole's Creek they joined another party who sat out on the same expedition under command of Samuel Gibson and it was agreed to keep together until they obtained some encouragement of Armstrong but about three leagues from the place of meeting they discovered footsteps and tracks of horses leading towards said Armstrong's plantation which they followed until within 500 paces of the house where they dismounted and left one-half of the company with the horses and the other half proceeded to within 200 paces of the house from whence they perceived the wife of Armstrong in the cowpen, who, seeing them immediately, left off milking, and finding that Armstrong had likewise perceived, they separated a second time, one-half passing through a tobacco field to the rear of the house and the other half approaching in the front, calling to him to surrender to the King, to which he answered that he should surrender with his rifle and at the same time going into the house to get it, where he encouraged the men in the house to stand to their arms and defend themselves, and appearing at a window of the house in front of us, called out to come on and try it, whereupon we approached still calling on him to surrender. When close upon him he determined to go out by a back window, which they effected and perceiving his troop ready to fire upon the party, I ordered one-half of the men to fire, at which charge the said Armstrong fell dead and his son was badly wounded in the forehead, one ball appearing to pass through his head and one lodged therein and likewise a ball in the right side. By the same discharge another of the troop was wounded who however escaped with the others, with whom we found it impracticable to come up with although we followed them by their tracks all day until they crossed Stoney Creek where we lost them. The party under command of Samuel Gibson remained at the house to collect the arms of the dead and the wounded and some horses which they had stolen and took an inventory of everything in the house and on the plantation, which when done, they conveyed hither together with the wounded and the wife and the rest of the family of the deceased, being all that occurred within the knowledge of the deponent, upon the oath which he has taken and, not knowing how to write he has made the mark of the cross, in the presence of those in preceding.

p. 112. Next appeared before me, Samuel Gibson who headed the other party and being sworn by means of the interpreter to answer truly such questions as should be put to him on the part of the King, was required to make a circumstantial relation of all that occurred on the expedition he commanded against the troop of robbers. On the road leading to Cole's Creek they fell in with a party under the command of William Brocus, being on the same expedition and agreed to continue together to Cole's Creek and about the distance of three leagues at a place of junction, they perceived horse tracks leading to the plantation of James Armstrong, which they followed until within 500 paces of his house where they left their horses with half the company and advanced with the other half toward the house. At the distance of 200 paces from the said house they discovered the wife of Armstrong in the cowpen, milking, and Armstrong himself near the pen watching, and perceiving that he had discovered them, they quickened their pace, calling to him to surrender in the name of the King, at the same time dividing to surround the house, to which he answered that he would surrender with his rifle, going into the house and taking it up, at the same time encouraging his troops not to surrender. Whereupon we approached the house and Armstrong, appearing at the window, told the party to come on and try it. Finding the house nearly surrounded, he determined to escape with his men by the back window. We came up with him and again ordered him to surrender to the King, but instead of so doing he prepared to discharge his rifle. Whereupon I gave the word to fire, by which discharge the said Armstrong fell dead and his son, James, fell also, being badly wounded. Another of the troop was wounded but escaped. The rest were pursued by the party headed by William Brocus but I remained in the house to take an inventory and to collect the arms and horses stolen and take measures to relay the wounded Armstrong, his mother and the rest of the family hither. Which being done, I came to render an account of the expedition and further the deponent sayeth not. Signed Samuel Gibson. Witnessed as in the preceding.

At Fort Panmur at Natchez, 19 Aug. 1786, voluntarily appeared Moses Armstrong, bringing with him the negro Sam who had escaped the day of his father's death with the two Lovels and George Blair, and it being necessary to take his confession by the means of an interpreter, Mr. George Fitzgerald being indisposed, I appointed Don Estevan Minor, Adj. Major of the Post, for that purpose, which he accepted. (p. 113) Then I caused the said Moses Armstrong to appear before me, who being duly sworn by the interpreter to answer truly such questions as should be put to him on the part of the King, was asked his name and how old are you? Moses Armstrong. Sixteen years. Where were you born? In South Carolina. What religion? Protestant. From whence came you now? He came from Stoney Creek to the house of Gibson Clark. With what motive did you go to the house of Gibson Clark? Having heard that his mother and the rest of the family had gone to Natchez, he went to the house of Gibson Clark as being the nearest, with the intention of bringing to the Fort his father's negro Sam. Where was he when the detachments of Samuel Gibson and William Brocus surrounded the house of his father? He was in the house carroting tobacco. What other persons were in the house at the time? The whole family were in the house, likewise John and James Lovel and George Blair, who were sitting with his father at the door. Why they did not all surrender when ordered to do so? Having always heard his father say that he would not surrender to any party sent to take him, therefore when the detachment appeared, knowing that his father would not surrender and supposing they would fire on him, he fled to the woods for fear of being killed. Did you take any arms with you? No. In what manner did you join the company who escaped? When they fled they took the same course that he had taken and overtook him. Were they armed? Each one had a rifle. How long did you stay with them and how were they employed? The day following the detachment appeared, he slept with them but early the next morning finding there were several paths leading from the place where they slept, Blair and the Lovels took one path and he and the negro took the path leading to the plantation of Gibson Clark. Did you hear any conversations from which you could infer what resolution they had taken? John Lovel purposed remaining in the District and the other two planned taking refuge in the Nation. Did you accompany your father in any of the robberies? He never left the plantation where he was employed about the crop. What effects and cattle did your father bring to the house which he had stolen with the company before-mentioned? His father and the others had stolen two horses, two saddles, two pair of boots, a great coat, etc. from Manuel Texada and a horse and saddle from Richard Dunn but they left another in its place, but they saw three rifles and a gun which they said they had taken from the houses of Stephen de Alva, James Cole, David Odam and Jacob Cable. Were all the horses and effects they had stolen taken to your father's house? They were all in a camp about 70 yards from the house. Did you know what further plans your father and his companions had concerted? They were making ready to go to Georgia. Your father took his negro with him when he went to rob. Was this negro armed? He always took his negro with him but always unarmed. The last time, however, the negro returned to the house with a small gun. Who furnished your father and his companions with provisions while they were out on these expeditions? He does not know. Have you heard them hold any seditious conversations concerning their mode of life? He did not hear any such conversations but remembered to have heard his father, on the day of his death, say that in two days he would leave the District. Had his father and the rest of the troop quitted the house when he fled? He remembered that his father and one of the Lovels were outside the door but he could not recollect where the others were at that moment. Have you any knowledge of a seditious letter addressed to Tacitus Gaillard bearing the signature of David Smith? He never heard of such a letter. Did you ever hear your father say that he had frequented the house of Jeremiah Routh and obtained provisions there? He remembers to have heard them say that they had taken a horse between Routh's house and that of Jacob Cable. Did the two Lovels and George Blair who had come to your father's house intend to go with him to the Indian Nation? The persons named came to my father's house and as they approached father called to them to halt until he knew their business. They talked apart for a time but he doesn't know on what subject. Do you know of any other persons who intended to join your father's troop? No. Did you from the place where you hid see your father killed and brother wounded? He saw nothing of it but he heard the report of the rifles. Have you anything more to say? No. The foregoing being read to him by the interpreter, he acknowledged it to be the same that he had made, having nothing to add nor diminish thereof, and not knowing how to write has made his mark in the presence of the King's Solicitor, the Interpreter, the Clerk and witnesses assisting. p. 114. Next I caused to be brought before me the negro belonging to the deceased James Armstrong, named Sands, whom I ordered to lay his hand upon the Bible and swear to truly answer all questions which shall be put to him on the part of the King. What is your name? Sands. To whom do you belong? James Armstrong, deceased. Religion? None. How old are you? About fifteen years. Where were you born? Georgia. Did you come to the District with James Armstrong, decd? Yes. How did his master employ him? Tending the crops. Did you outgo lately with your master and for what purpose? He went with his master to take care of the horses. Were you armed when you went out with your master and who went with him? He was armed with a gun and the persons who went with him were two Lovels and George Blair and his master's son James, all of whom were armed with guns. Did his master's other son, Moses, go with the troop? No, he always remained at home, employed about the crop. For what purpose did they go out thus armed? To steal horses, saddles and rifles, which they did at the house of Manuel Texada. [The same details of the robberies as given by the others.] How did your master happen to join the company with Blair and the two Lovels? They came to his master's house to join him. Do you know of any other person attending the troop. No. [Same details of his flight and staying with the Lovels and Blair the first night in the woods and going with Moses Armstrong to Gibson Clark's plantation.] The foregoing being read to him he acknowledged and confirmed same.

Next I caused to appear before me, Sarah Armstrong, widow of James deceased, who laying her hand on the Bible promised before God to answer truly such questions as should be asked on the part of the King. What is your name? Sarah Armstrong. With whom do you live? With her deceased husband, James Armstrong. What employment? Tilling the ground. Do you know the mode of the life your husband lived lately? James and John Lovel and George Blair came to the house with whom her husband had a secret conversation which she did not hear, after which her husband set out with them and took his son James and his negro Sands with him and returned with some horses, saddles, rifles, and other articles which they said they had stolen. How often did they go out? She doesn't know the exact number of horses, etc. that they stole nor from whom. Where did they put these stolen horses, etc? In a camp about 70 paces from the house. She is forty years old. [She knew nothing more.] The declaration was read to her by the interpreter and she ratified the same, not knowing how to write she signed with a cross.

Next appeared Gibson Clark, who being duly sworn, etc. What is your name? Gibson Clark. Where is your plantation situated? On Stoney Creek. Did Moses, the son of James Armstrong, deceased, and his negro Sands come to your plantation? Yes. For what purpose did they come? He asked them the same question and they said they wished to come to the Fort, whereupon he conducted them hither. Did you have any conversations with them on the way? He did not except to ask them the whereabouts of the two Lovels and Blair, and they replied that they had left them on the road to the Choctaw Nation. Have you anything further to declare and what is your age? Nothing further to declare and he is 26 years old . . . . Confirmed the above declaration and signed with a mark.

p. 116. Next I caused to appear Manuel Texada, a Cole's Creek planter, who being sworn, was asked his name. He gave a circumstantial account of what happened on the 9th inst between himself and James Armstrong and his troop, which he wrote to His Excellency the following day. Does he know the names of the five white men mentioned in the letter who accompanied James Armstrong? He knew none of them except Armstrong and his son James. Did he perceive the son of James Armstrong named Moses among them? He was very certain that the son mentioned was not with them. Have you anything further to relate? No. He does confirm the said account. He signed with the officials.

On the 21 of August 1786, appeared James Cole, planter, who being sworn, etc. What is your name? James Cole. Were you robbed by the troop under command of the deceased Armstrong? If so relate what happened on that occasion. On the 11th about midnight, came to his house James Armstrong with the two Lovels and George Blair, all armed. John Lovel and Blair presented their rifles at his breast and the others robbed him of a shirt and two handkerchiefs, and he heard others talking a short distance from the house, but knows not who they were. Did you observe the two sons of Armstrong and his negro? He heard voices but he knew not who they were. Nothing further to declare and he is 24 years old. Declaration confirmed after being read to him.

Next was called Estevan de Alva, planter, who being sworn, etc. asked to relate in what manner he was robbed by the troops of James Armstrong. On the 9th about midnight, James Armstrong, his son James and his negro Sands with two Lovels and George Blair appeared in the yard of his house. He was at that time asleep but was awakened by the barking of the dogs and got up and went toward them. They had already taken two horses from the yard belonging to Manuel Taxada and John Lovel asked him if he had a bridle or a gun, to which he answered that he had no bridle, whereupon the said Lovel went into the house and took his gun.

Did they threaten you with any violence when they robbed you? They said but little to him but threatened Manuel Texada, the owner of the horses, that if he did not hold his peace that they would take his heart out. Was the other son of Armstrong among the troops. He did not see him. Nothing more to declare and he is 36 years old. Confirmed the above declaration and not knowing how to write he made his mark.

Next caused to appear Richard Dunn, being duly sworn, etc. State the effects stolen from you by James Armstrong and his troop and the manner. They came to his house and took his horse on the night of the 9th and in the morning early he went to the plantation of a certain Routh where he found his said horse loaded with the clothes of John Lovell and perceiving that no one saw him he took his horse and rode him into the woods where he remained all day. While he was in the woods his people told him that they returned to his house in the night and took two blankets and a saddle. That same night he went to sleep in the house of David Odam and in the night James Armstrong, his son James, the negro Sands, two Lovels and George Blair came there and took his horse again and Blair left the horse he rode, and inquiring for the deponent was told he was in the house, and putting him out they made him by force hold up his right hand, intending to shoot a ball through it, which being seen by David Odam and his family, they begged John Lovel who was the person going to shoot him to forgive him, which he did and the deponent returned to his plantation. Did he see Moses Armstrong among the troops? No. Nothing more to say and he is 30 years old. He made his mark.

p. 117. Next to appear before me, David Odam, who being sworn, etc. If robbed by the troop under James Armstrong, state the particulars of said robbery. Sometime in the night of the 10th, the said James Armstrong, his son James, and his negro Sands, the two Lovels and George Blair came to his house in search of Richard Dunn whom they declared that they would kill but at the intercession of the deponent and his family they spared his life and went off, taking with them the horse of the said Dunn and the rifle of the deponent, which they took by force, being all well armed. Did he observe Moses, the other son of Armstrong with the troop? No. Nothing more to say. He is 27 years old. Acknowledged and signed.

Next appeared before me, Gaspar Sinclair, who being duly sworn, etc. His account of being robbed by the troop of James Armstrong. On the morning of the 10th, the troop of Armstrong, consisting of himself, his son James, his negro Sands, the two Lovels, and George Blair came to his house where his wife was alone, took his rifle and then coming into the field where he was working, John Lovel showed the rifle and told him to take leave of it for he would never see it again. On the day James Armstrong was killed, John Lovel came again to his house, he not being at home but his wife was there and Lovel took by force a horse, saddle and bridle. Was Moses Armstrong with the troop? He did not see him. Nothing further to relate. He is 27 years old. Acknowledged and signed with his usual mark.

Next appeared before me, Jacob Cable, who being duly sworn, etc. Relate the manner in which you were robbed by the troops under James Armstrong. On the 9th, James Armstrong and son James, his negro Sands, the two Lovels and George Blair came to his house in his absence, his wife only being at home and robbed him of a horse, saddle and bridle, and on returning home he was informed thereof and finding the tracks of his horse he followed the said tracks which led him to the plantation of a certain Routh where he found his horse in the hands of the negro Sands, who being alone the deponent took the said horse from him by force and mounting him rode home. Telling his wife to keep a good lookout for he expected they would come back in search of him. He rode from plantation to plantation spreading the alarm. In the meanwhile the said troops returned to his house and robbed him of two blankets, a pair of buckskin trousers, two bags, all of which he took with threats and violence, as related by his wife. Did his wife see the other son of Armstrong named Moses? No. Nothing more to relate. He is 50 yrs. old. Ack. and ratified above, not knowing how to write he has made his mark.

Next appeared Elias Douglas, who having been sworn, etc. What occurred to him on the night of the ninth instant? James Armstrong, his son James, the two Lovels and George Blair and Armstrong's negro came to his house on horseback. John Lovel rummaged his house and asked for his rifle, to which he replied that he had no rifle in his house, having loaned the only one he had to Abraham Selar. This being heard by Armstrong he said they would go and get it, and they went that night to the house of Selar and took the rifle. He did not see Moses Armstrong among the troops. Nothing further to relate. He is 48 yrs. old. He made his mark.

p. 122. Next appeared before me Susannah Cable, wife of Jacob Cable, who being sworn, etc. [Deposition the same as that of her husband, and she is 30 years old.] Signed with a cross.

Next appeared Margaret Sinclair, who being sworn, etc. [Wife of Gaspar Sinclair and her deposition is just what he had said. She is 40 years old.] She signed with a mark.

At Natchez, 21st August, 1786, the King's Solicitor, in this cause, accompanied by the Clerk, and two assistants, repaired to the Hospital, where I found the body of James Armstrong and directed the Surgeon of said Hospital to give me a certificate of the manner of his death, hereinafter inserted in the proceedings. "I, Louis Faure, King's Surgeon of the Post of Natchez, do certify that a certain James Armstrong died at the Hospital of the said Post, on the 21st day of August of the present year 1786, in consequence of a gunshot wounds he received in the head. Signed by Louis Faure, Antonio Soler, Joaquim de Ossorno, Juan Carreras and Carlos de Grand-Pre.

p. 124. William Selkridge and others versus Emanuel Madden. Selkridge represents that Emanuel Madden is indebted to him for $10; asks that said debtor be condemned to pay. 27 Jany. 1786. // Natchez, Feb. 4, 1786. Let the foregoing be filed with the other demands against Madden. Sig: Bouligny. // Anthony Hutchins showeth that Mrs. Patience Coleman, wid. of Wm. Coleman, late of the Natchez, was indebted to John Farquhar, by note for $138, which, she said, was the greatest part thereof due from the said Coleman's estate. After her marriage to Emanuel Madden, to prevent a suit, the memorialist, at the request of said Patience, paid the said Farquhar the aforesaid sum and took a note for the same from the said Emanuel, since which the said Patience has eloped from Emanuel her said husband and married a man in Kentucky and hath not paid any part of said debt, nor hath Emanuel, her husband, any property whereby the said debt may be discharged, yet hath sufficient assets left by the deceased and from whom the aforesaid debt became due. Asks that the said debt with interest thereon may be paid out of said assets. Oct. 21, 1785. Sig: Anthony Hutchins. // Emanuel Madden promises to pay Anthony Hutchins on order $139. 19 Nov. 1781. Sig: Emanuel Madden. Wit: John Prentice.

p. 125. Polser Shilling versus Thomas Wilkins. Shilling represents that he has rented a house at the landing of Natchez to Mr. Thos. Wilkins for $15 per month until said house should be repaired and then at $20, per month. Now the said Wilkins refuses to pay said rent for the time he occupied the same, asks that he be compelled to make payment. 13 Sept. 1788. // If the said Wilkins has anything to allege against the said claim, he will be pleased to have an arbitrator appointed to settle the matter. Sig: Polser Shilling. Let the parties choose four arbitrators to determine the matter. // We, the arbitrators chosen by the order of the Commandant to decide the above dispute, are of the opinion that Mr. Shilling shall build a chimney to the dwelling house on the end next to the stable before the cold weather sets in and likewise cover, board up and hang a door to the stable before he, Mr. Shilling shall be entitled to $20 per month rent. We also award that Mr. Wilkins shall pay the said Shilling at the rate of $15 per month from 15 April last past until the above-mentioned work be completed, and afterwards at $20. Natchez, 25 Sept. 1788. Geo. Fitzgerald, J. Henderson. // Approved. Sig: Grand-Pre.

p. 125. Arbitration between Jeremiah Bryan and John Ferguson. We, the subscribers, being chosen by the above to settle all disputes and accounts between them, and hearing their pleas etc., do give as our opinion that the said Bryan is to pay the said Ferguson at the rate of 100 hard dollars per year from the time he was in his employ and all the constable fees that are due the said Bryan and Ferguson and all the profits that have arisen while they were in partnership be divided equally between them and that each of them collect his part of what money is due to them in the constable business and that Ferguson pass up all accounts that are not already done. Oct. 2, 1788. Signed Justus King, Samuel Rawn, John Montgomery and Ezekiel Dewitt.

p. 126. Gaillard versus Mayes. Messrs. Fusilier and Langourand appointed arbitrators in the above suit. Natchez. 4 Oct. 1788. Sig: Grand-Pre. Having heard both parties, we find the testimony by both to be insufficient to lead to a certain conclusion, we do hereby determine that the said parties shall bear the loss of the horse equally between them. Sig: Fusilier de la Clair and Langourand.

p. 127. Arbitration between Philip Trevino and Louis Chachere. We, the undersigned, arbitrators appointed by the above to settle a controversy between them, have declared as follows: there shall be allowed to Mr. Trevino $2 per day from the day of his departure; the interest for 14 months be reduced to two months. Signed by both. 6 May 1788.

p. 128. Declaration of James Wilson, Fort Panmur at Natchez, 18 Aug. 1788, appeared Charles Carter who declared that three hogs in dispute between James Wilson and Jeremiah Bryan are the same that Mrs. Still Lee sold to the said James Wilson a few days before she left this district; that one of the hogs has the mark of John Still Lee, another has the mark of his son, and the third is not marked. He, the said deponent, was present when Mrs. Still Lee sold the hogs to the said Wilson; that she had many hogs in a pen that she offered publicly for sale and if Jeremiah Bryan had a right to any of them, he had then an opportunity to make his claim. It is certain and true that the said hogs belonged to said Wilson, who bought them as aforesaid. Charles (C) Carter. Before Grand-Pre.

p. 128. Creditors of Louis Chacheret, after an examination by Peter Walker, Sundic appointed by Mr. De Grand-Pre, 7th of last month, of the books of Mr. Chacheret, show his stock to be $11943 and his debts $10177, and considering the small amount he has been able to recover this year, which has prevented him from fulfilling his engagements, do determine to favor the said Chacheret as much as possible and allow him three years for the payment of the several sums due to us without interest. Sig: Jean Vaucheret, Duon, Camus, Walker and Henderson, and Louis Faure. Apr. 2, 1788.

p. 128. Jane Rapalje versus Anthony Hutchins. Jane Rapalje petitions that a certain Anthony Hutchins has a horse belonging to your petitioner which he refuses to restore, and asks Hutchins be ordered to restore the horse without delay. Natchez 24 Dec. 1787. Sig: Jane Rapalje. // Anthony Hutchins, Esq. will restore to Jane Rapalje the horse claimed by her, or adduce his reasons to the contrary at the first audience. // Appeared Anne Hutchins and declared what she knew relative to the horse in dispute between Jane and her husband, Anthony Hutchins, Esq., and that during her husband's absence from this district in 1782 they lost a mare having a young colt that continued to run with the rest of their horses, that George Rapalje, in collecting his horses, took this colt, already well grown, and marked it with his own brand. Being informed thereof she claimed the said colt from Rapalje as her property, stating that if said colt was not branded before, it was because it had not been caught, but it was well-known to belong to her, to which said Rapalje replied that he would mark all the horses he found unmarked and besides he had a great many in the district. Thereupon the deponent determined to claim the said horse in law and went to Mr. Minor and he told her that she had nothing to do but put her brand on the horse which was known to be her property and the deponent did accordingly cause him to be branded and has kept him since that time, without any demand on the part of present claimant. She solemnly affirms that the said horse is her property and that no person had a right to him. Sig: Anne Hutchins. Wit: Peter Walker, Antonio Soler. // On the same day appeared Samuel Hutchins who declared that the horse claimed by Jane Rapalje is the property of his father and mother; that having from his youth looked after the cattle of his father, he can safely affirm that the said horse belongs to him. Sig: Samuel Hutchins.

p. 129. Arbitration between John Farquhar and Samuel Rainer. Arbitrators, appointed by Carlos de Grand-Pre to settle an affair between John Farquhar and Samuel Rainer respecting a note given some time ago by the former to the latter, we are of the opinion that the said John Farquhar has paid on account in favor of this note $360 which leaves a balance of $16 overpaid and we think the note and the money overpaid should be given by Rainer to said Farquhar. 9 Feb. 1788. Natchez Landing. Sig: Alexander Moore, Peter Walker.

p. 129. Juan Vaucheret versus Andrew Rendell, who is indebted to said Vaucheret, as per note hereunto annexed, asks for payment thereof. Natchez, 30 March 1787. // Let the note be presented to the party and if he acknowledges the signature to be his own, he is ordered to make payment thereof. Grand-Pre. // Note for $21, payable Dec. next. 29 Aug. 1787. Sig: Andrew Randal. // Cole's Cr. Apr. 18, 1787. Notified defendant. Fees $5. Jeremiah Bryan. // Andrew Randall delivered up a horse to satisfy the said debt and the cost, which horse ran away and was found in the possession of John Kincaid. // Jany. 10, 1788. Wm. Henderson and Bennet Truly appraisers of said horse; valued $50. At public sale the horse was adjudged to Jeremiah Bryan for $34. Fees to constable and Commandant $20.

p. 130. John Pickens versus John Woods, who is indebted to him for $8, by note annexed. 25 June

1787. Sig: John Pickens. John Woods notified July 26, Aug. 10, Jany 5, 1788. I then went to the Cliffs and brought Woods to the fort. Roswell Mygett. // John Vaucheret represents that John Woods owes him $47; asks payment thereof. Dec. 27, 1787. // Woods notified twice by constable, Roswell Mygett. // 16 January 1788, appraisers appointed, David Smith and John Bisland; valued horse, saddle and bridle at $55. Signed by both. At sale, same adjudged to Israel Leman for $66. Wit: D. Smith, John Bisland, Peter Walker, Antonio Soler, J. Henderson. Commandant's fee $10, constable $7.

p. 130. Jean Girault represents that a certain John Montgomery owes him $200 and the said Montgomery having set out for Bayou Pierre without any arrangement to pay petitioner; asks that a black horse, belonging to said Montgomery in the hands of Mr. Minor as also some cows running at the plantation of said debtor. Sig: J. Girault. Nov. 12, 1788. [The account was for itemized merchandise for provisions, crockery, etc.] William Vousdan and Isaac Johnson appointed appraisers; valued horse at $60; at sale adjudged to Ebenezer Rees for $52.

p. 133. Declaration of Mark Cole, Fort Panmur at Natchez, 28 Jany. 1789, that he lost on the King's Road an obligation in his favor drawn by William Irwin for $232 which has been satisfied by said Irwin, hereby annulling the said obligation. Signed: Mark Cole, James Irwin.

p. 134. Jeremiah Bryan versus Robert Urie, who owes him $305; asks seizure be made in default of payment. 15 Jan. 1789. Signed. // After adjustment of accounts the sum was altered to $213. // 24 Jany. 1789. Daniel Mygett and Matthew Jones, blacksmiths, appraisers; blacksmith tools which were mortgaged, valued at $150, after three delays at request of debtor, the sale took place and the forge and tools was adjudged to Juan Carreras for $151. Net proceeds $115.

p. 137. Estevan Minor versus Barnet Isenwood, who owes him $50. Asks for payment. Minor requests that Stephen Richards hold the property which he has belonging to said Isenwood until the debt is paid. 28 Jany. 1789. // Granted. // 8 Feb. 1789. Estevan Minor petitions that the horse, plow complete, two bridles, and two collars belonging to the debtor be appraised and sold to satisfy above debt. // 11 Feb. 1789. Henry Manadue and Stephen Mayes appointed to appraise above property, which they value at $47. At sale the property brought $43. Costs $12.

p. 139. Suit of Pedro Azevedo versus John Staybraker, who owes him $60 and asks payment. 28 Dec. 1788. // Cole's Creek. 1 Jany. 1789. Notified Staybraker. Fees $5. Roswell Mygott. // 21 Jany. 1789. Jeremiah Bryan and Henry Manadue appointed to appraise a horse, saddle and bridle, mare and colt and a plantation of John Staybraker. Horse $50, mare and colt $30, saddle and bridle $18. Sale of same, at which Joseph King appeared producing a bill of sale of said horse and mare together with a note for the value thereof, and having proved his right to said animals, they were delivered to him. The saddle and bridle were adjudged to Juan Carreras for $12. The sale equalled the amount of the fees.

p. 140. Joseph Leonard versus James Wade, who owes him for $100, and asks payment thereof. Jany. 10, 1789. // Jean Girault and Sutton Banks, appraisers, value the horse at $80. Parties compromised and the horse withdrawn. Sig: Grand-Pre. [Plaintiff also called Israel Leonard.]

p. 141. Robert Abrams versus John Whitman, who owes him $133; asks payment thereof. // Dec. 15, 1788. Levied execution on a horse and two bolts of linen. Richard Harris. Roswell Mygott and Polser Shilling appointed appraisers. Valued horse at $30. Adjudged at sale to Francisco Pavana.

p. 142. Petition of Betty and Jude, daughters of a free woman in Carolina and were bound as apprentices by Court of Judicature until they should arrive to the age of 21, and they were brought to the Natchez as such, where they were taken by Capt. Willing's party and were sold here as slaves. The petitioners have served the whole time of their indenture and several years more, ask to be liberated. New Orleans, 21 March. Witnesses: Col. Hutchins and lady.

p. 143. This to certify that Mr. Samuel Bell and Mistress Rebecca Perry were this day married by me according the form of the Church of England, by consent of Rev. Mr. Savage. 28 May 1789. Signed: Justus King.

p. 143. Messrs. William Irwin, John Martin and Jesse Hamilton are hereby ordered to examine on their honor whether Henry Jones, mulatto, has worked and sufficiently paid Mr. Daniel Perry with 20 days, he declared to have worked lately, and they will also determine if the negroes that Mr. Perry lent to the said Jones have also done their duty as hirelings. And that they will determine the difference between them concerning the work and put the same in writing. // Cole's Creek, 8 June 1789. It is our opinion that Henry Jones shall pay $8 or make 800 good fence rails on Mr. Perry's plantation or such part of it as Mr. Perry shall choose. Signed: Jesse Hamilton, William Irwin, John Martin.

p. 143-4. His creditors versus the estate of Robert Johnson. Robert Johnson, deceased, to Elizabeth Rainer, for washing and mending his clothes one month; making one coat and 5 yards of linen; for making 5 pairs of britches; for one sheet. Total $21. // The estate of Robt. Johnson to John Finn, debtor. Blanket, to boot in swapping horses, cash paid Wm. Gilbert; for making coffin; for taking an inventory of his property; and taking it for sale to the landing; total $31. Receipt of same. Jesse (J) Finn. Wit: John Ferguson. // At Natchez, 6 May 1789, appeared Jesse Finn with some effects of Robert Johnson, deceased, for public sale to pay some debts of same. John Bisland and Francis Pavana as appraisers. Total $43. [mostly wearing apparel.] 20 June, 1789. Appraisers of horse of said Robt. Johnson, decd., Stephen Mayes and Joseph Smith valued same at $35. Not being able to sell the horse at two-thirds of value, said horse was re-appraised at $20. Buyers at the sale were Daniel Rainer, William Weeks, John Carreras, Don Louis Faure, Alonzo Segovia. Total sale amounted $36. Horse was finally adjudged to Antonio Gras for $14.

p. 145. William Weeks versus Philip Turpin. 21 July, 1789. Next March I promise to deliver to Mr. William Weeks or his order for his stepson, Stephen Swazey, a likely mare and colt, in consideration for a mare I shot belonging to said Swazey, and whatever may be the value of her and the mare I shot as estimated by two impartial men, indifferently chosen that have a knowledge of her, the surplus to be accounted by the party having the most valuable part. Sig: P. P. Turpin. This is to certify that in regard to Mr. Weeks breaking open my house and breaking my gun, it is out of my power to prove it and what I have said is only from what Elijah Swazey told me of said Weeks threatening to prevent me from shooting. Sig: Philip P. Turpin. Same date. Wit: J. Eldergill.

p. 146. Debtor John Brown in account with Richard Carpenter, creditor. To your proportion of freight on 8 barrels of salt from Baton Rouge to Natchez. $16. To loss of remittance of tobacco in 1786-7, $383. Etc. Balance due John Brown from the estate of Richard Carpenter, $2599, being the award of the arbitrators in settling the accounts between John Brown, of Rhode Island, merchant, and the estate of the late Richard Carpenter.

p. 147. The King versus Richard Linchy. Oct. 1, 1789. Post of Natchez. Don Antonio Soler, commissioned by His Excellency, Don Carlos de Grand-Pre, and charged with the military and civil command in the absence of the Governor, to take cognizance of a robbery committed in the house of Benjamin Farrar, in which a man was wounded. Joseph Fainz to be clerk, etc., Don Estevan Minor, Adjutant Major, to be interpreter. Francisco Pavana and Peter Walker to be witnesses in this suit. Appeared, first, Benjamin Farrar, who replied, on oath, when questioned; he does not know Richard Linchy but knows that last night he broke open and entered the house of the deponent, and having stolen sundry effects was caught in the act by the slaves of the deponent who were about to tie him, but he escaped from them and finding they could not come up with him, a slave, named James, shot him and advancing to him, the wounded man knocked the said slave down with his fist; his cries brought the other slaves who secured the man and brought him to the kitchen where the deponent questioned him respecting the effects which he had stolen. These he had hidden in the woods and the next morning they were found there. They were three blankets, three tablecloths, five towels, one silver spoon and a knife. He had broken open the doors of the house and the storeroom. He had also taken clothes belonging to the slaves, a shirt he had on when captured. In the same place were found some ropes which James Kelly declared belonged to him and a bag of meal which Mathew White said belonged to him. He did not know that he had been robbed before until the thief when questioned said that he had stolen other things that he had in the woods. Christian Bingaman and James Kelly found the articles. Farrar has nothing more to declare and is 50 years old. // The same day appeared the negro James, not being of age to be sworn, he declared that the night before being asleep was wakened by a noise and he perceived the other negro bringing the thief into the kitchen and at the same moment, his master came in and told them to tie the said thief and keep him there until morning. The said thief laid down in the kitchen and they covered him with a blanket and the companion having gone out of the kitchen, the thief cut the rope with his teeth and, throwing the blanket over the deponent's head, started to escape, the deponent called to him twice to stop and crying that he would not, still continued running, and the deponent fired at him with small shot which brought him to the ground and when he advanced to secure him, he gave the deponent a blow with his fist which knocked him down. Then the other negro came up and between them they secured him and brought him back to the kitchen. [He tells the same as Farrar about the articles that were stolen.] He was 16 years old. // The other negro named "Hercules" related, on oath, what had passed the night before. He said he met Linchy in the yard and Linchy asked him to go with him and he refused to do so and he then offered him $100 to do so and he consented not knowing what his intentions were, telling him to wait until he got his blanket and his pipe, and going into the kitchen he hid himself to see what the man Linchy would do. Then he saw Linchy go into his master's closet whereupon he left his concealment and met Linchy coming out with an egg and a brass candlestick and the deponent laid hold of him and Linchy struck him several times with the candlestick and the deponent cried out that there were thieves in the house, and the negro James came to his assistance and between them they tied him and carried him to the kitchen and their master came in and told them to take care of him until morning. [the rest of his testimony as stated above.] Deposition of Linchy, taken at the King's Hospital. He declared he was born in Virginia and had been in this district since the month of June last. [Testimony about as told by the others.] He said he was persuaded to steal by two Germans, living near the Bingamans, named William and George. He had no fixed place to sleep. He slept sometimes at one place and then at another. He had no property. He is 22 years old. // Oct. 2, 1789. The solicitor accompanied by the clerk in consequence of the death of the beforementioned Linchy, occasioned by his wounds, went to Hospital attended by witnesses and Don Louis Faure, surgion of said Hospital, who examined the body to give his opinion. He said the death had been occasioned solely by the wounds he had received and the quantity of blood lost. // Appeared William Graeding who, on oath, declared he had seen him for he had been to Graeding's house twice. He denied discussing in any manner robbery with Linchy. // Next appeared George Bevelin, who on oath declared that he had no knowledge of the robbery in the house of Benjamin Farrar. Also denied talking about a robbery with Linchy. He is 35 years old.

p. 152. Fort of Natchez, 14 Nov. 1789. His creditors versus Louis Charbonneau. Joseph Ford and George Shilling appointed to appraise a horse the property of Charbonneau, seized for the payment of debts; valued the horse at $25.

p. 153. Thomas Reed versus Maurice Custard. Arbitrators to settle dispute between Thos. Reed and Maurice Custard concerning a barge, we, William Smith and William Vousdan, chosen by the parties, differing in opinion on same, David Ferguson appointed umpire, and are unanimously agreed that the said barge is the just property of Thomas Reed and that he still owes $70 for the barge, out of which he is to pay the costs of this suit and the remainder to Maurice Custard. 13 Jany. 1791. Sig: William B. Smith, William Vousdan, David Ferguson.

p. 153. Arbitration between Wm. Falconer and John Smith. John O'Connor and Peter Surget chosen as arbitrators. 24 Feb. 1790. George Fitzgerald to be umpire. Sig: Grand-Pre. Award: Mr. John Smith is justly indebted to Mr. Falconer in $102. Sig: John O'Connor, Pierre Surget. George Fitzgerald. Approved: Grand-Pre. 25 Feb. 1790.

p. 154. 7 March 1791. Personally appeared Anthony Hutchins who declared that in November 1783 Capt. James Colbert, of the Choctaws, trader, then at St. Augustine, in the Province of East Florida, to apply to this deponent to write a letter in his name and behalf to John Miller, Esq., formerly of Mobile, West Florida, and then in London, requesting him in case of his, Colbert's, death that he, Miller, would take and keep in his hands, after the deducting the amount of $50, sterling, all such money as he, as his attorney, had received or should receive for him, to be appropriated to the use and benefit of his son, James Colbert, a half-breed, whom he had placed in the counting-house of Messrs. Panton, Leslie & Co., and this deponent sayeth that he doth firmly believe that the annexed paper is the said letter dated St. Augustine, 12 Nov. 1783. And he remembers to have written such a letter at the request of the said James Colbert, deceased, and he is convinced that it was the full intention of the said deceased that the said letter should answer a testamentary purpose in favor of the said son, expressing himself at that time as if he had presaged his approaching death, which happened on the road not many days after. The said Colbert, before the writing of said letter, showed great signs of uneasiness respecting his son but afterwards became better satisfied, having essentially put him under the guardianship and governance of his attorney, by said letter, in whom he said he greatly confided and in whose hands the money he was entitled to from the government would be entirely safe for his said son's use. He appeared to be much disspirited and no less apprehensive, having, as he said, enemies in every quarter, etc. Sig: Anthony Hutchins. Acknowledged by Manuel Gayoso de Lemos to be a true copy. 7 March 1791. // St. Augustine, 12 Nov. 1783. Sir: I came to this place, 5 Nov. last, and have been detained by sickness every since but am now in a recovering way and shall set out for the Choctaw Nation in a few days. I left my home and came here on account of my exertions against His Majesty's enemies, and as peace is concluded, large demands are made by the Spaniards. I don't know how far their influence may extend with the Indians of their party toward seizing on my property in that country. I expect attempts will be made and I hardly know how to act on the subject. I thank you for the trouble you have always taken on my account and am glad to hear that you have been fortunate enough to recover the amount of my bill. I am sorry that I am constrained to draw on you for my part of the sum that is in your hands but, having lost my horses, they being stolen at the time of my illness, have drawn on you for 50 pounds in favor of Messrs. Panton, Leslie and Co. The residue, with such other moneys as you may receive from me, you will please keep in your hands and appropriate it for the best purpose you can for the use and benefit of my son, James Colbert, and as I don't know how the case may happen to be with me yet, being in the greatest danger from exasperated enemies, left and forsaken by the very power that I have strenously endeavored to support and defend, and by looking forward, I expect I may have many difficulties to encounter. Etc. I have left my son in the care of Messrs. Panton, Leslie & Co., closely engaged in the business of their store. I hope he may be teachable, that he may be fit for such business . . . . . I could not prevail on your traders to carry your pelfry to Augustine, both on account of the distance and the fear of some miscarriage on the way but as the Turnbulls are to carry their skins to New Orleans under American protection, I have thought it best for your skins to be delivered to them to be transported in their name so they will be carried by your traders to the Chickasaw Bluffs and then down the Mississippi. Mr. James McGillvray is lately gone to the Nation who will be better able to act in the affair. Etc. Sig: James Colbert.

p. 156. May 22, I, the subscriber, Hayden Wells, as exor. of the estate of Christopher Leightholder, have received of Joseph Calvit, now of Natchez, $800 for the use of said estate, being in payment of a note given by said Calvit to said Leightholder, 8 Sept. 1788, which note was deposited in the hands of William Gilbert in Natchez by said Leightholder. This therefore is a full receipt and discharge. Sig: Hayden Wells. Davidson County. This day Haydon Wells came before David Hay and Lardner Clark, Justices of the Peace, and acknowledged the above receipt for the purpose therein mentioned. Signed by both. Territory of the United States South of the Ohio, Davidson County, I, Andrew Ewing, clerk of the said county, hereby certify that the within David Hay and Lardner Clark are two of the Justices of the Peace in and for the above county, etc. Sig: May 2, 1791.

p. 156. Arbitration between Obadiah Brown and Richard Corey. The award is that the said Cory shall deliver to the said Brown what stock and other properties that was considered as the said Cory's wife's properties and on payment of $45 due from said Corey to Brown, said Brown agrees to give the said Corey a feather bed and bedding, a gray mare and her increase, as full satisfaction for the $45. Natchez. 7 June 1791. Sig: Obadiah Brown, Richard Corey.

p. 157. Shipwreck of a barge. At the Post of Natchez, 4th July 1790. Appeared Greenbury Dorsey, who declared that he left this post with two flatboats loaded with tobacco and other effects for New Orleans which said boats and barges he brought from Kentucky; that about five leagues distance from this post, at a place called White Cliffs, one of the said boats, called the Washington, commanded by Benjamin Taylor, struck on a log which could not be avoided by reason of the velocity of the current, and in consequence whereof the said boat immediately sank. The said misfortune happened on the 3rd instant at 4 p.m., the said boat having on board 54 hogsheads of tobacco, 25 thereof belonging to the deponent, and the remainder belonging to Messrs. Thompson and Co., also 600 pounds of hog lard, 350 feet of walnut plank and a quantity of hemp, belonging to this deponent. Said boat and cargo, being insured in Philadelphia, he declares that he hereby abandons the said boat and cargo to the insurers thereof, and that a person may be appointed by the judge to represent said insurers to the end that the said boat and cargo may be sold at public sale and proceeds thereof may be remitted to the insurers at Philadelphia. Let two intelligent persons go to the place where the said boat now is and examine the situation and he asks that the master of the said boat and some of the hands be examined. Sig: Greenbury Dorsey. // By virtue of an order of Don Carlos de Grand-Pre, we visited the flat called the Washington and finding it made fast to the shore near the White Cliffs foundered, containing 54 hogshead afloat in her and a quantity of hemp. White Cliffs, July 4, 1790. Sig: John Ellis, Thomas Burling. // Same date. Appeared Benjamin Taylor, Capt. of the said flatboat, declared, on oath, that he left this place the 3rd instant with the boat, Washington, under his command, bound for N. O.; at about 5 leagues from this place, at White Cliffs, about 200 yards from a large bar, the said flat got into a strong eddy, from which it was impossible to row her out, and the wind, at the same time blowing hard, made it impossible to avoid the bar; thus in their endeavors to do so they struck against a log and, the waves running high, the water came in both sides of the bow, whereupon they made every exertion to get to shore, which they at length effected, the said boat being then half filled with water and sent a man on shore with a cable sufficiently strong to hold her, but a moment after the strength of the current aided by the quantity of water in the said boat, broke the cable and the boat could not be brought to shore for some time. At length, however, they succeeded in getting her nearer the shore so as to make her fast by the bow and stern, and finding it impracticable to save the cargo they abandoned the said boat. Sig: Benjamin Taylor, before Joseph Vidal and Carlos de Grand-Pre. // Next appeared James Lee, who, on oath, declared that he was a hand on the said boat from Kentucky. // Next appeared Isaac Taylor, also a hand on said flat from Kentucky going to N. O. Same deposition. // At the request of Mr. John O'Connor, have appointed Mr. Fitzgerald and David Ferguson to appraise the flat boat, called the Washington, and cargo, etc. They appraised the same at $150. Signed by both. Whereupon it was exposed to public sale and adjudged to Bernard Lintot for $110. Next appraised was the 19 hogshead, belonging to Messrs. Thompson and Co., valued at $30, exposed to sale and adjudged to Alexander Mills for $30.

p. 160. Elisha Canety, son of William Canety, decd., of his own free will, apprenticed himself to his brother-in-law, John Clark, wheelright, to learn the art, from date to serve for two years and a half, etc. Signed. William Clark, John Clark, Elisha Canety, Richard Roddy. Before Gayoso.

p. 161. Louis Faure versus Maurice Stacpoole. 18 July 1790, arbitrators appointed to settle the suit pending between them, David Williams by Stacpoole and Sutton Banks by Faure, and, in case of a disagreement, an umpire to be named. Stacpoole still indebted to Faure for six hogsheads of tobacco at $25 for each hogshead, which he ought to pay this ensuing crop, because the tobacco delivered to Dr. Faure liable to inspection in N. O. which proved non-merchantable. Arbiters differ and Bernard Lintot, the umpire, agreed with Mr. Banks that Maurice Stacpoole make good the sum to Faure.

p. 163. William Chambers versus William Brenner. Chambers claims that Brenner was arrested at this post on 21 July 1790, at the instance of Chambers, accusing him for having stolen sundry effects from his store. He declared that the said Brenner was hired by him and worked in the store belonging to Mr. Peter Walker, where the deponent kept his tools, of which Mr. Walker kept the key. The said Brenner got the key from Mr. Walker on the pretense of going to work as usual. Mr. Walker's son informed him that the said Brenner had taken an axe from the store and hid it in the grass and Mr. Walker informed the deponent, who immediately applied to Don Antonio Soler, who sent two soldiers of the guard to arrest Brenner, which was done. He is 21 years old. Signed. // William Brenner appeared and admitted stealing two axes from the store and selling them, one to a certain Dumars and the other to Samuel Moore. He was about to take another axe but was prevented by Mr. Walker's son. He is twenty years old and has nothing to say in his defense.

p. 164. Declaration of Lardner Clark and Justinian Cartright. State of N. C., Davidson County, Feb. 14, 1789. The above came before David Hay, a Justice of the Peace, and made oath that they had frequently known hard money to be exchanged at the rate of one hard dollar for five paper, last year 1787 and 1788; he had exchanged some, himself. Certificate that David Hay is one of the Justices of the Peace of Davidson County, etc. Signed: Andrew Ewing, clerk of said county. Feb. 14, 1789. A true copy in the English language taken at the request of George Cook and deposited in the records of this government. Note by George Cook. Good to the bearer, the month of March next for $209 (hard dollars) for value received. Sig: Christopher Leighthölder. Wit: Benjamin Allen. A true copy of the original note presented by George Cook.

p. 165. Declaration of Charles Jones, who appeared at the Post of Natchez, 13 Nov. 1790, at the instance of Polser Shilling, and declared that about five years ago, he found a note near the house of a certain Gras and by the endorsement thereon showed it was drawn for $40 and he took the said note to the house of James Strother, where he then dwelt and the said Strother said he would keep the said note until the owner should claim it, which the deponent could not do himself as he was on the point of leaving for America. Sig: Charles Jones. Wit: Joseph Vidal, Manuel Martinez. Before Gayoso.

p. 165. Before me, Don Manuel Gayoso de Lemos, appeared Mr. Benjamin Grubb, at the request of Mr. James Elliot, and made oath on the Holy Evangelist, to the following statement that he, Benjamin Grubb, lived a near neighbor to Thomas Green, senior, now of this district, on the Congaree river in South Carolina, and about three years before removed to this place. This deponent had perfect knowledge of said Green being arraigned for clandestinely taking both hogs and sheep, and in both cases said Green compromised the matter in the suit and paid the cost. That he, the said Green, also took in the same manner a boar from Charles Quail, for which crime he was a second time arraigned and settled out of court. Natchez, 21 March 1791. Sig: Benjamin Grubb. // p. 166. Dist. of Villa Gayoso. Personally appeared John Donelson, who, on oath, deposed that John Jarrett told him that he had rented from Mr. Thomas Green, senior, his place upon the bluff, at the rent of six chair frames, and the said Jarratt was also to take care of Mr. Green's hogs and stock on sd plantation and other property on the place. The deponent said that to his knowledge that there was left in the loft of the house when Jarrett took possession there one rifle barrel and one shot-gun barrel, but before the house was planked they were carried away, by whom the deponent kneweth not. The yard to the house was fenced in except two gaps of passage made by Mr. Smith for hauling bricks through, etc. 15 June 1793. Sig: John Donelson. Again questioned he said that there were 5 or 6 large barrows which were intended to be put up for fattening but couldn't be got up and the whole amount of hogs belonging to Mr. Green was twenty or more. Sworn before W. Murray. p. 166. Personally appeared John Donelson, of Cole's Creek, who deposeth that when John Jarrett took possession of Col. Thomas Green's house at the bluffs of Villa Gayoso in 1791 there was left in the said house two cables or large ropes for the use of the flat, which were little used, the property of said Thomas Green, which with a variety of other articles given in charge of said John Jarrett, and what was done with them this deponent does not know. Sig: John Donelson. Natchez, Nov. 6, 1793. // Feb. 15, 1791. David Odam, of Cole's Creek, said that after Christmas last his largest hog came up to his house shot, with a bullet in the side of his head and bleeding very fresh but he cannot tell who had done it but he had lost hogs. Sig: David Odam. // Thomas Calvit, of Cole's Creek, when required to tell what he knew of unlawful killing of hogs in the Cole's Creek district, declared that he had lost hogs himself and he does not know who killed them but was confident that there was such a practice carried on for some time. Sig: Thomas Calvit. Wit: Christopher Bolling. // Cole's Creek, 10 Feb. 1791. William Barfield being called on to relate the same as above, declared that he had often heard of James Elliot and William Fairbanks hunting with their dogs in the woods for hogs and on Saturday last he was at Fairbanks' house and to the best of his knowledge he thinks that said Fairbanks had in his smokehouse near a thousand weight of dried bacon and had 11 hogs in his pen. He likewise helped Mr. Richey with his hogs and found a ball shot in one. Signed with a mark. Wit: John Brooks. // Cole's Creek. Feb. 11, 1791. John Richey, on oath, declared that January last he was working at Capt. James Elliot's house and the same Elliot went several times to hunt hogs and killed and brought some home; he said they were his wild hogs which he and William Fairbanks killed in conjunction. He never knew Col. Green or any of his family to hunt after hogs. Sig: John Richey. Wit: Christopher Bolling.

p. 167. Declaration. Be it known that I, Mark Lee, do hereby declare that I sold to Mr. Custard a flat boat to me belonging in November past and being informed that during my absence from home a brother of mine, claiming the said boat, sold the same to a certain Reed, wherefore I do declare, on oath, that the last-mentioned sale is null and void, and the sale made by me remains in full force. Natchez, 16 April, 1791. Signed: Mark Lee. Wit: Manuel Martinez, Joseph Vidal. Before Gayoso.

p. 168. Richard Harrison versus Dibdall Holt. Richard Harrison in account with Dibdall Holt. To a negro man named "May" . . $500; to one named "Bristol" $600; to stock, horse, cattle as per bill of sale $457; to a flat $100; to a note of Cato West $500; to payment of a note received of William Gilbert $400; to Richard Harrison's obligation to maintain Dibdall Holt, the literal performance thereof appearing at this time impracticable $500; balance due Richard Harrison $108. Contra Credit: 1791. By amount of account assumed to pay Richard and Reuben Harrison, sworn to, $88; by Sundries furnished and paid for Mr. Holt as per an account rendered this day and sworn to $875; by sundries/paid to Alexander Moore on account of D. Holt, certified by James Moore $820; by payment to William Gilbert on account of James Truly $20; by note of D. Holt settled in account of Wm. Gilbert $62; by Parker Carradine, paid him $300; by David Holt, paid him $530; by payment to Alexander Moore on account of David Holt and Sarah Truly as per Moore's account $462. The arbitrators in the dispute between Dibdal Holt and Richard Harrison, are of the opinion that the balance of $108 is due to said Richard Harrison, agreeable to the statements here made without estimation of Mr. Harrison's bond which we have made in case it shall meet with concurrence of His Excellency the Governor, but not otherwise. Sig. William Murray, Bernard Lintot. July 14, 1791. Approved and accepted by the parties involved. All sign.

p. 169. Declaration. Personally appeared Jacob Rhodes, who, being sworn, sayeth that some time in October he was at the plantation of John Adams when Maurice Stacpoole called on him to settle their accounts. Nothing was settled but deponent was of the opinion that only $20 difference between their accounts remained; and that there was some mention of beaver hats. Natchez, 2nd Sept. 1791. Sig: Jacob Rhodes. Wit: Jean Girault, Stephen Minor. Before Gayoso de Lemos.

p. 169. Thomas Calvit versus Arthur Cobb. Thomas Calvit, as exor. of the will of his deceased brother, Frederick Calvit, represents that, during the lifetime of his said brother, Arthur Cobb applied to him to let the said Cobb have in his care and keeping a horse belonging to the said Calvit valued at $800 for the purpose of knowing if he could run and with no other view whatever, promising to restore the said horse in the same condition and to pay any damages that said Calvit might suffer in the value of the said horse in his possession. The said Calvit lent him the horse on the conditions proposed. Sometime after, the horse being in bad condition, the said Cobb proposed to return him to Calvit, who, on being informed of his condition, refused to receive the horse, replying that Cobb should restore the horse in good condition, as he was when he received, to which Cobb replied that if the horse died he would pay for him, that if the said Calvit received he would hold himself responsible. On those terms, Calvit received the horse back from Cobb and in the course of a month the horse died. Calvit demanded payment from Cobb who proposed to compromise the matter and give a negro in payment which he valued at $600. Some difficulties took place and the matter remained unsettled and Cobb, to the knowledge of your petitioner, amused Frederick with almost daily propositions respecting the payment and, confiding in his promises, Calvit took no legal steps and, on the promises of Cobb not being realized, Calvit died and his heirs remain unpaid; asks that Cobb be made to pay the aforesaid sum of $600, and default to compel him thereto by the rigor of the law. John Boles, John Smith, Grover Morris can testify to the above. Thomas (X) Calvit. Natchez, 23 Sept. 1791. // Same date. Let the person named in the foregoing petition appear before me. // Personally appeared John Boles, who, being duly sworn, declared that on a certain day, at the landing of this Post, he met Arthur Cobb and asked him the condition of the horse he had in his possession belonging to Calvit, which horse he had heard was sick, to which Cobb replied that the horse was very sick and he expected he would die in which case he would have to pay for him. Boles is 46 years old. Sig: John Boles. // I do certify that I was at the house of Mr. Frederick Calvit at the time Cobb brought and delivered to the said Calvit a stud horse, the property of said Calvit, which horse was dangerously hurt while in the possession of said Cobb and upon Cobb saying he was sure the horse would die the said Cobb said he would agree to pay the whole price of the said horse or a part, which of the two I am not at all clear but believe that he did agree to pay for the said horse. Signed: Groves W. Morris.

p. 171. James Kelly versus Israel Leonard. At the Post of Natchez, 17 Nov. 1791, before me appeared, at the instance of James Kelly, William Baker who, being sworn, being asked what he knew respecting the horse claimed by James Kelly and Israel Leonard, declared that he knows the horse in question to be colt of a mare belonging to said Kelly. He is 18 years old. // Then appeared Daniel Strickland, who, being sworn, declared the horse in question has always followed a mare belonging to James Kelly, as a colt. He is 25 years old. // Appeared Jacob Piercy who, being duly sworn, declared that he formerly lived with Samuel Kennedy who had a mare by which the horse in question is a colt and he assisted him to mark the said colt and some time afterward said Kennedy made over and gave up his property, trading the horse in question to Mr. Eliphalet Richards in payment of debts and said Richards exchanged the said colt, now the horse in question, with Israel Leonard for a horse, to the said Leonard belonging. // Next appeared Samuel Havard, who, on oath, said that the said horse [Same as preceding statement.] He is 22 years old. // Appeared John Lindsay, who, on oath, declared the same as deposed by Strickland and Havard. He is 19 years old and signed with a mark.

p. 173. Nathan Lytle versus William Davenport. At the instance of Nathan Lytle, a native of Hartford, State of Maryland, complaining of a certain treatment of a certain Davenport and his companions, namely John Smith, James Boyd, Alexander McComsey, Joseph Duncan, John Wood, and James Davenport, have summoned Mathew Jones and Letitia Culberson as witnesses. First appeared Matthew Jones, who, being sworn, declared he was a native of London and a Protestant. In 1785 he knew Nathan Lytle on the Ohio where James Davenport and his companions compelled the said Lytle by force to accompany them and on his refusal a certain Captain Smith who was of the company ordered him to be tied and severely beaten, which was done by all those on board and among them he particularly recollects, John Woods, James Boyd, James Davenport, Alexander McComsey and Joseph Duncan, as well as the captain, John Smith, who likewise cruelly beat said Lytle, all of which was done in the presence of the deponent on board the said boat which was in company with the boat to which this deponent belonged. Mathew (X) Jones. Before witnesses. // Next appeared Letitia Culberson, said she was a native of Maryland and a Protestant. In 1785 there was a boat at the Falls of the Ohio under the command of William Davenport in which a number of men were embarked who were said to be coming to this district to take possession of Natchez and the deponent was intending to come to settle in this country and obtained from said Davenport passage on said boat, in which the said Nathan Lytle had also embarked with the intention of leaving said boat at the mouth of the Ohio and going from thence to the Illinois, which he attempted to do accordingly but was detained on board by force. Two of the men who attempted to leave by swimming to the shore were fired upon by the others, etc. Lytle was stripped and beat before the deponent who hurriedly withdrew so she cannot know who gave the blows but she heard them. She was 27 years old. Signed: Letitia Culberson. // Also came Francisco Brezino who was a native of Saxony and a Catholic. He said that having the intention to settle in this country he came to the Falls of the Ohio where he bought a boat which was taken possession of by a certain William Davenport, ... finding there was no remedy, he was compelled to give up his boat and take passage with him. That the said Lytle embarked with the intent to land at the mouth of the Ohio, etc. [Same as the other depositions as to Lytle being severely beaten.] He is 50 years old. Sig: Francis Brezino.

p. 175. Mary Bonner versus Samuel L. Wells. Joseph Bonner, brother of Mary Bonner, in her name represents the ungracious treatment of Samuel Wells towards his said sister, who confiding in the promise made to her by said Wells in the presence of three persons of the family that he would marry her, and, blinded by her passion for him, had the misfortune to bring his son into the world, of which the said Wells is father. The said Wells being now in this place but a few days since called upon to fulfil his promise of marriage which he did not deny but it appears that he has obtained a passport and is about to leave the district with the intent to evade the performance which, being the case of the total ruin of a young creature, may it please Your Excellency to take the matter into consideration and order that the said Wells be arrested. May it please Your Majesty also to stop the said Wells who plans to cross the river early tomorrow morning on his way to Opelousas. Dec. 5, 1791. Sig: Joseph Bonner. // Samuel Wells will appear before me the first court day to answer the foregoing complaint and the commander of the guard at the landing is required to prevent his leaving the district by way of the river until further order. Dec. 6, 1791. // Then went to the house of Mrs. Foster and notified Mr. Wells who promised to appear accordingly. Jany. 6, I then received fresh orders from Mr. Grand-Pre and the said Wells appeared as soon as he received the orders from me, saying he was willing to appear at any time when called upon if he is in the district and promised that he would not leave the district until this is settled. Sig: Jere Bryan. // Post of Natchez, 9 Jany. 1792. At the instance of Samuel Wells, appeared Mary Bonner, who, being duly sworn, was required to relate the nature of her connection with the said Samuel Wells, whereupon she declared she had a particular regard for the said Wells who on several occasions promised to marry her and that she confiding in his honor and blinded by the affection that she had for him had the misfortune to give birth to a son, which she solemnly declares to be the child of the said Samuel Wells and expects the said Samuel Wells to fulfil his promise of marriage which he voluntarily made. She is 19 years old. Signed: Mary Bonner. // Let the foregoing be notified to Samuel Wells for his answer thereto. Signed: Grand-Pre. // To His Excellency, the acting Governor, Samuel Wells in answer to the declaration of Mary Bonner, of the 19th, sayeth that her assertion of his promise of marriage is false; that it is evident that neither she nor her family expected him to marry her since June last when her situation was publicly known the petitioner was here and being about to return to his residence at Opelousas no opposition was made to his departure by any of the family but on the contrary they endeavored to effect a marriage between her and a certain Glassock whom they engaged in work on the plantation with that view and to whom they offered a slave and other advantages, etc. Offers evidences of said Glasscock and William Foster. Signed: S. L. Wells. Jany. 20, 1792. [Mary Bonner answers, saying that the family had confidence in his promise to marry her is the reason he was not approached before; asks that he be not allowed to leave the Post. Jany. 21, 1792.] Samuel Wells is forbidden to leave this district. Jany. 21, 1792. Grand-Pre. // Willis Bonner appears to prove the promise of marriage made by Samuel Wells to his sister, Mary Bonner. He declares that Samuel Wells said that as soon as he could arrange his affairs it was his intention to marry his sister. He is 22 years old. // p. 178. Bond of Samuel Wells. I, Samuel Levi Wells, do bind myself to fulfil the articles of agreement with Mary Bonner who has a natural son whom I acknowledge to be mine, I promise to pay the said Mary Bonner $25 per annum for ten years, to commence on 1st day of December last past to nurse and bring up the said child. I promise to give the said Mary Bonner a complete suit of clothes immediately and that I shall not claim the said child until he shall attain the age of ten years, after which it is agreed that I may take him under my care. Should the said Mary Bonner marry I shall then have the right to claim the said child and the said Mary Bonner shall not send the said child out of this district without my consent on condition I fulfil the foregoing agreement in her favor, William Foster being my security for the performance and granting authority to the Justices of His Majesty to compel me thereto as if judgment had already been given, etc. Post of Natchez, 21 March, 1792. Moses Bonner, brother of the said Mary Bonner, being present and accepting the said agreement in her behalf. Signed by both. Wm. Foster, Augustine MaCarty witnesses. Before Antonio Soler.

p. 179. John Smith versus Gibson Clark. Being chosen an umpire in a matter of controversy between the above, the original arbitrators having disagreed in their opinions, wherein it is alleged by said Smith that he suffered from the abuse of said Clark of the loss of an eye and personal injury, my award is that the said Clark should give the said Smith $200 in any produce he may have, namely cattle, horses, hogs or grain, at the option of said Smith, provided that as ascertaining this fact has chiefly depended on the assertion of Smith, he, the said Smith, does voluntarily and of his own accord wait on His Excellency, the Governor of Natchez, and there give his deposition before him that he is deprived of the use of and the benefit of an eye and thereby incapacitated earning his living by his trade by means of the abuse he has received from said Clark. Natchez, April 9, 1792. Wit: David Ferguson, William B. Smith.

p. 179. Arbitration between Isaac Gaillard and Maurice Custard. Award: Mr. Isaac Gaillard shall deliver to Maurice Custard Job Corey's note of hand for $17 and give him his own certificate that he held in his own possession, Mr. Henry Willis's note for $5, which he is now issuing; and on the part of the said Custard, he shall immediately repair all the blacksmith tools that were in his possession, the property of Mr. Gaillard, which reparation to be judged by John Lusk, that he shall also deliver to the said Gaillard 60 bu. of corn and pay him $13 for balance of all accounts presented to said arbitration. Natchez, 28 Apr. 1792. Signed: Wm. Dunbar, Jean Girault. Approved by Gayoso.

p. 179. Maurice Custard versus Isaac Gaillard. Custard petitions that at the end of crop last year he had 190 bu. of corn put into a crib on the plantation of Mr. Isaac Gaillard where the corn grew, being the part that belonged to your petitioner; that he did owe to Mr. Gaillard 50 bushels of said corn and was always ready to deliver it when demanded, the remainder of the said corn, he sold to Mr. Wm. Dunbar and hath received payment for the same. Mr. Dunbar now demands the corn agreeable to bargain; in your petitioner's absence, Mr. Gaillard has on various pretexts taken away the said corn and your petitioner is unable to perform his engagement with Mr. Dunbar. Asks that this case be taken into consideration. Natchez, 15 May 1792. Signed Morris Custard. // Natchez May 19, 1792. Isaac Gaillard will state reasons for detaining the corn belonging to claimant. // Natchez 2 June 1792. Mr. Isaac Gaillard appeared and proved that he was authorized by Mr. de Grand-Pre, while Commandant in his absence, to withdraw the corn which was owing to him by Maurice Custard not being liable to answer for the remainder as it was not put into his immediate care and that the place where it was was broken open without knowledge of the said Custard and the said Gaillard is not responsible for the quantity that was found in the crib. Custard will pay the cost.

p. 180. Nathaniel Ivy versus William Weeks. One day last week a very valuable mare owned by Nathaniel Ivy, the petitioner, was shot by Mr. Weeks' negro by order of his master, of which she died to the great loss and detriment of the petitioner, being one of the two he has to attend his crop with; he was told by the Weeks that the mare had stamped into Mr. Weeks' enclosure but the petitioner cannot learn that she did any damage and if she had he does not conceive that any person was entitled to kill her before they had sent the petitioner word and taken the accustomed steps. // Ezekiel Forman, Esq. is desired to hear the complaint expressed in this petition and what Mr. Weeks has to say in his defence. // Award: The said William Weeks to deliver to said Ivy one old mare with many brands on the off shoulder and one small bay mare with a sucking colt, white faced, branded on the near shoulder WO, in full compensation of the said Nathaniel's loss. 9 July 1792. Sig: Ezekiel Forman. Receipt of Nathaniel Ivy for the above.

p. 181. Post of Natchez, 5 August 1792. Appeared Adam Lanehart who swore that he had lost a pocketbook containing the following papers, a note of Thomas Brenton for $50, another of same for $23; another drawn by a carpenter, named Hackett, for $50, another by Mr. Vashery for 1 1/2 dollars, and sundry other papers. Signed: Adam (A) Lanehart. Wit: David Earhart, Valentine Rincon.

p. 181. Joseph Calvit versus William Gilbert. Calvit petitions that in 1788 he was compelled to give to Christopher Leighthholder $800, being security in behalf of John Montgomery, which note was deposited here in the hands of Wm. Gilbert and since paid in full proved by annexed document, legalized at Nashville, asks that William Gilbert give up said note to the petitioner. Sig: Joseph Calvit. 28 Apr. 1792. // Mr. William Gilbert will return to Mr. Calvit the note mentioned in the above petition, or appear before me. // Having heard Mr. Wm. Gilbert and viewed a copy of the will of Mr. Christopher Leighthholder, properly authenticated and an acquittance for the note by the exors. of the will, Mr. Gilbert shall give up the said note, after receiving an indemnifying receipt from Mr. Calvit. Sig: Gayoso.

p. 182. Copies of sundry papers deposited in the archives by John Foster. // Oct. 10, 1781. I promise to pay to Benjamin Kerkindal a likely young negro, between 16 and 20, on or before the 10 April next ensuing. Signed: Henry Manadue. Wit: Jacob Brown, Absolem Chrisom. On the back of the same: I do hereby assign all right and title to the within note unto John Foster, Feb. 17, 1786. Signed: Benjamin Kerkindal. // To Mr. Henry Manadue, senior. After my conference with you I would be very glad if you would pay Mr. John Foster a likely young negro which I paid you for in Carolina, as Mr. Foster has paid me for him, and I do hereby empower him to receive the said negro from you. P. S. I shall be in that country this fall, Captain Prince in company with me. We are in good health. Your devoted friend, etc. Feb. 17, 1786. Signed: Benjamin Kerkindal. // Feb. 17, 1783, came before me, James Molden, magistrate of the county, Absolem Chrisom and swore that he saw Henry Manadue give the note to Benj. Kerkindal. Sig: Ab. Chrisom. Before James Moulden. // I promise to pay to John Foster or his order one likely negro, Virginia born, between the ages of 14 and 20 without an impediment to be delivered to the said Foster's dwelling in the district of Natchez, on or before 1st of February next ensuing for value received. 19 Oct. 1789. Wit: James Rhoad, Saml. (S) Jones, Turner Williams. Signed: // May 17, 1792. Received of John Foster $200 in trade for chance of his property on Holstein River, which property he has empowered me to recover and receive and which is in full all demands to this day. John (X) Hunnicut. Wit: Randal Gibson, John Ferguson. The foregoing are copies of papers left in the office of this government by John Foster, the originals of which he carries with him to Cumberland. Natchez. 27 Aug. 1792. Signed: Gayoso.

p. 183. John O'Connor versus Elizabeth Swazey. John O'Connor petitions that he is indebted to Mrs. Swazey for $7 and a certain William Cocke who owed the petitioner $12 offered the petitioner to pay him in Mrs. Swazey's hand, upon which the petitioner went to Mrs. Swazey with the said Cocke and she did then agree to cancel the $7 the petitioner owed her and pay $4 more to the petitioner, the said Cocke having afterwards run away from this place, the petitioner asked Mrs. Swayze for the $4 and she refused it and sued the petitioner for $7 and Mr. de Grand-Pre, then Commandant, after hearing the evidences and finding moreover that the said Mrs. Swazey and her family were privy to the elopement of the said Cocke and their son, did give judgment that she should pay the petitioner the said $4 but she still persists in disobeying the order and claims the $7; asks that she may be condemned to pay the debt and cost. Natchez, 3rd Oct. 1792. Sig: John O'Connor. // Samuel Swazey will without delay pay to John O'Connor $4 or appear before me on Saturday next, to make known his reasons. By order of His Excellency, (signed) Minor. // Account of Elizabeth Swazey agst John O'Connor, deceased. To weaving 24 yards of cloth in 1790 $6, to putting up tobacco, done by my late husband $2. Total $8. Signed: Samuel Swazey, Elizabeth Swazey. Natchez, March 31, 1794.

p. 184. Thomas Calvit versus Arthur Cobb, referred to Ezekiel Forman, Samuel Flower, William Vousdan. In compliance with Your Excellency's order, 14 July 1792, the matter of Thomas Calvit, representing Frederick Calvit, and Arthur Cobb, after several postponement, was heard and the evidences being so contradictory, the decision is rendered very disagreeable to the arbitrators. [Reviews testimony at long length and repititious.] Above arbitrators to meet again and the parties agree to abide their decision, two other arbitrators to be appointed to serve with the three above. Signed: Gayoso.

p. 186. I certify that 1st June I applied to Mr. Bonner for 30 bushels of corn and presented John Short's order for that quantity and was shown a certain quantity which he said was the corn referred to and the said corn was the greater part rotten and otherwise unfit. I certify the corn crib, in which it was, was not sufficiently covered to keep the rain out but appeared to have lain exposed for a considerable time. Signed: F. W. Green.

p. 186. Indulgence granted to the inhabitants of the government. Whereas a memorial has been presented from the inhabitants of the district on which a decree has been issued at N. O. on 13 Feb. 1792, in pursuance of the representation by His Excellency, Don Manuel Gayoso de Lemos, Commandant of the dist. of Natchez, that for the general welfare it is time to temper the authority of the law respecting the collection of debts in the said district, otherwise the benefit of His Majesty's clemency would prove elusive and the debtors would not have the advantage intended, and from this date all executions against all inhabitants in the district thereof be suspended until His Majesty's further pleasure shall be known. At the same time the debtors are thus secured from distress, their creditors should have a guarantee for the ultimate payment of their debts, wherefore the means pointed out by His Excellency, Governor Gayoso, shall be carried into effect, namely that an account shall be taken of estates and effects in possession of the debtors, the inhabitants of this district, which shall be considered mortgaged to the creditors for the amount of their debts to the exclusion of the debts they may hereafter contract, etc. 15 March 1794. Signed: Carondelet, before Pedesclaus, notary.

p. 187. To His Excellency, the Baron de Carondelet. Petition objecting to the above decree. Signed:

Alexander Moore, Daniel Clark, Manuel Monsanto, William Stephens, John O'Connor, David Ross, Thomas Durnford, Charles Norwood, Peter Walker. They also offer a counter solution. // Following person summons to meet: Alexander Moore, Thomas Ford, William Vousdan, George Fitzgerald, Peter Surget, Benj. Monsanto, William Dunbar, John O'Connor being absent and not summoned. [This extends to p. 193.]

p. 193. William Smith versus James Harrow. We, the subscribers, being chosen to examine and compare four different signatures in the name of Thomas Hubbard, by Mr. William Ferguson and the said Hubbard, and being of different opinions, have called in the umpire, Mr. George Castles, who was chosen by the commandant, and after having thoroughly examined the same, we do find that Thomas Hubbard has endorsed a note in question which appears to be the same handwriting as the other three notes and find the balance due to Wm. Ferguson from the said Thos. Hubbard is $80 and the cost of the suit for which he is to give his note due in 12 months and security from the estate. 12 Dec. 1793. William Smith, not agreed. James Harrow agreed. George Castles umpire. Approved by Trevino.

p. 193. I promise to pay or cause to be paid to Mr. John Dyson two young likely cows and calves to be delivered to Cole's Creek on 1st Sept. next for value received. 22 Dec. 1793. Sig: John Carroll, Clement (X) Dyson. I promise to pay or cause to be paid to John Dyson or his order the sum of $25 and two gentle cows to be delivered to Cole's Creek on 1st May next for value received. Sig: John Carroll. 22 Dec. 1793.

p. 194. Job Routh versus Sutton Banks. Sutton Banks appoints as arbitrator of the dispute John O'Connor and Job Routh appoints George Cochran. Cochran declines and Joseph Bernard was appointed and accepted. Award: Mr. Job Routh should deliver to Mr. Sutton Banks nine head of cattle as described in their agreement, 12 Nov. 1792, and as there were 100 heads less than called for, Mr. Banks should pay Mr. Routh 90 Spanish dollars. Signed by both. I approve the arbitration. Manuel Gayoso de Lemos.

p. 195. Louis Vilaret versus Andrew Scandling. Post of Natchez, 30th April 1793, appeared the above parties and declared some differences having arisen respecting a contract between them, they have agreed to leave the determination to James Wiley and Charles King, Wiley chosen by Scandling and King by Vilaret.

p. 195. Benjamin Steel versus Gabriel Griffin. Post of Natchez, 27 May 1793, a dispute having arisen between the above parties, have caused both to appear before me and have informed said Griffin that if it should be proved hereafter that he should go to the house of said Steel and held any communications with the wife of said Steel without his knowledge and consent, he would be severely punished; and the said Steel was at the same time informed that he should not insult the said Griffin under a like penalty, which they both promised to observe. Both signed. Signed: Gayoso.

p. 196. John Mapother in account with Daniel Grafton. To cash paid by Mr. Wilkins in 1791, to Mr. Savage 1791, etc. The foregoing statement is what appears to be just and the manner in which the merchants in general follow in charging interest and recovering in the different states by others than the debtors drawn, and interest on the interest, which he should pay. Signed: John O'Connor.

p. 197. Christopher Miller versus Juan Carreras. In obedience to the order of Your Excellency, Juan Carreras represents that he has delivered to Christopher Miller the saddle which he claimed was stolen from him. This saddle was obtained by your petitioner from the Capt. of Engineers in exchange for another and your petitioner knowing him to be above suspicion did not inquire from him from whom he had it, but on receiving the saddle he had some knowledge of the person who sold it to the Captain of the Engineers but sickness of your petitioner has prevented him from instituting an inquiry and it may be perhaps an instigation of Miller as he has produced no testimony except that of his younger brothers. Natchez, 25 June 1793. // To be notified to Christopher that he may bring witnesses to prove that the saddle delivered by Juan Carreras belongs to him. 26 June. // Appeared before me, Christopher Miller and his witnesses, Thomas Johnson and John Row, who being duly sworn declared that it appeared to them to be the saddle belonging to Christopher Miller, they being at the house of the said Miller when the saddler brought it and had seen Miller riding on it frequently since.

p. 197. John O'Connor versus William Vousdan. John O'Connor petitions that since his residence in this government he had been in the strictest habits of friendship with William Vousdan and until within a short time since and to his utter astonishment he was accosted by said Vousdan in the most opprobrious, calumniating terms, and he propagated reports malignant and false, tending to destroy your petitioner's reputation, etc. He has plundered your petitioner's property, pried into his private concerns, and robbed him of several valuable papers among which was a note of your petitioner to him for $200, etc. Jany. 6, 1793. // William Vousdan blames a lot of disorder on his plantation during his absence on O'Connor. Etc, etc. [Continues to p. 210. Confused and unimportant.]

p. 210. Asahel Lewis versus John O'Connor. Lewis petitions that in 1790 he applied to Mr. John O'-Connor, a merchant of this place, for a loan of $183 on interest for one year; necessity obliged him to comply with the demands Mr. O'Connor chose to impose upon him of $35 being added to the principal and two slaves be mortgaged for security. He understands that O'Connor has begun a suit to recover the money and the petitioner asks that he be granted some time. Signed: Asahel Lewis.

p. 211. Lewis Alston versus Frederick Kimball. District of Baton Rouge, Bayou Sara, Natchez government, 2nd Aug. 1793. Personally appeared before me Francis Pousset, Esq., alcalde for the said district, Lewis Alston, inhabitant and planter at the Tunica, being duly sworn, deposeth before Mr. John Wall and Archibald Rea, who were summoned as witnesses, that yesterday evening, after giving a little entertainment to a few of my friends and neighbors, I intended to take a ride to Mr. Burnet's and I asked some of the company who had dined with me and were going the same road to wait a little and I would go with them. Col. Henry Hunter and Col. Kimball had come to my house after the dinner and were at that time part of the company. I had been informed that Col. Kimball was very much displeased with me and I wished to speak with him and know the reason. When I came up with the company who had set out a little ahead of me, I inquired for Col. Kimball and was informed that he had gone ahead. I set off in a gallop to overtake him. When I came to Mr. Barclay's I was told that he had passed about two minutes before but the person who told me begged that I would not overtake him for he was in a furious passion and threatened me. However, as I did not think Col. Kimball could hurt me and I only wanted to convince him that I did not merit his ill-will, I pushed on and over took him. [This resulted in a fight, in which Col. Kimball was beaten by Lewis Alston. Depositions of John Welton, Patience Welton, his wife; William White, living at Mr. Barclay's plantation; James Alston, brother of Lewis, lame in one hand; Benj. Burnet, appointed to examine Col. Kimball as to his wounds, reported a bruised and scratched nose. (p. 217); Mrs. Juliet Scott Barclay; William Brown; p. 219. Aug. 24, 1793. Col. Henry Hunter; Robert Munson, Col. Kimball; p. 224, Sept. 7, 1793. Mrs. Winifred Munson, wife of said Robert; Reuben Dunham. Robert Munson and his wife, Winifred, were guests at the dinner given by Lewis Alston, Aug. 21, 1793, and Lewis Alston told her, both before and after dinner, that he intended to leave with them and he would get Col. Kimball's eldest daughter, Rebecca, and carry her to his sister's, Mrs. Williams', and thence to Mr. Sterling's and thence to Pointe Coupee and there get married and that she, Mrs. Munson, and Susan Burnet were "allotted" to go to Pointe Coupee to see them married. On the porch as they were leaving the house of Lewis Alston, Mrs. Munson told the above to her husband, Robert Munson, who highly disapproved of it and said he would tell Col. Kimball, as he was a father and had daughters of his own. Kimball had left a few minutes before but Munson rode ahead and caught up with him and told him of Lewis Alston's plans. He thanked him and rode rapidly toward his home, followed in a short while by Lewis Alston. When Col. Hunter and Munson finally caught up with Alston and Kimball, who was also just up from illness and seemed in a bad condition, Col. Hunter started after Alston but Munson said he was a younger man and nearer Alston's age and Col. Kimball was his friend; a fight followed, Col. Hunter finally calling Munson, who had Alston down, to desist.] The Retreat, 12 Sept. 1793. Sir: Just as I had sealed up the package, which accompanies, the bearer brought me a sealed petition which I regard out of my cognizance. Col. Kimball will be at the Natchez in three or four days. I beg leave to lay the petition before you. Lewis Alston first runs off with Col. Kimball's daughter and then desires to know his reasons for withholding his consent. Yours, etc. (signed) Francis Poussett, alcalde of District of Bayou Sara and Tunica. // To Francis Poussett, etc. Lewis Alston begs leave to represent to you that some time ago he applied to Col. Frederick Kimball for permission to pay his addresses to Miss Rebecca Kimball, to give your petitioner leave to make proposals to the young lady and to marry her if she was willing. As soon as he found that the young lady's affections were engaged he thought it proper to refuse to let your petitioner marry her as he had promised, for which reason, your petitioner has taken such measures as he thought necessary to get married without Col. Kimball's consent and for the satisfaction of Mr. Barque, parish priest of Baton Rouge, the petitioner begs that you will call before you the said Col. Kimball and desire him to give his reasons for withdrawing his consent and attempting to prevent our nuptial. Etc. Signed: Lewis Alston. // Natchez, 20 Sept. 1793. To be communicated to Frederick Kimball that he may reply thereto. Signed: Gayoso.

p. 227. Thomas Wilkins versus Joseph Murray. Thos. Wilkins represents that he made a new set of books from Mr. Joseph Murray's entries and books and asks that arbitrators be appointed to settle the question and goods remaining in their hands. 25 Sept. 1793. Sig: Thos. Wilkins. // John O'Connor, Esq. alcalde, and George Fitzgerald appointed arbitrators, it being the agreement that the goods in hand be equally divided in case of a separation. Signed: Gayoso. // Award made and approved by Manuel Gayoso de Lemos.

p. 228. Israel Smith versus Arthur Cobb. Israel Smith petitions that yesterday the 28th, he was assaulted on his return home from the Govt. House by Arthur Cobb in company with his son, William, who rode up to the petitioner and, seizing the bridle of his horse, ordered him to get down and take off his saddle with the intention of robbing him of his horse. The petitioner, perceiving that Mr. Cobb was not armed with an offensive weapon, and with his son, who was less violent than his father, prevailed upon him to desist. It is no new thing for Mr. Cobb to attack your petitioner and his brothers against whom he has unreasonable enmity. They can prove by the evidence of Archibald Sloan that Mr. Cobb declared that he carried a knife for the purpose of using it against Smith, his son-in-law; Elijah Adams told William Glasscock that Mr. Cobb carried a large club to a foot race at Simon Holmes' where he expected to meet the Smiths to be used against them. Homes and Stephen Holstein saw this heavy club in his hand and, at this time, the brothers of your petitioner feared to go abroad alone for fear of being waylaid by this violent man; asks for measure of safety for himself and brothers, etc. Sig: Israel Smith. // Personally appeared before me, Isaac Johnson, one of the magistrates of Second Creek, James Kelly, who, being sworn, sayeth that, being at a race that was to be run near the house of Robert Abrams, at the latter end of August, last year, and seeing a number of people gathered together in a crowd, the deponent went to see what the matter was and he attempted several times to get into the crowd but was prevented but having by force pressed through the throng he saw Arthur Cobb and Luther Smith laying side by side, apparently fighting, on an uneven piece of ground, and Smith had his thumb in Cobb's eye; deponent took Smith's thumb out of Cobb's eye and took Cobb in his arms from Smith. Signed: James Kelly. // Appeared before Isaac Johnson, one of the magistrates of Second Cr., William Baker, doth say, on oath, that he was at the house of Robert Abrams when Arthur Cobb and the Smiths had the difference, which caused Cobb the loss of his eye, that the deponent saw Courtland Smith and Arthur Cobb fighting together at the end of the chimney of Robert Abrams' house, and the blood flowing from Cobb's eye. Signed: W. D. Baker. 4 Sept. // This is to certify that when Mrs. Smith lay on her death bed she bequeathed her riding horse to her husband and desired that he would keep it. Signed: Sarah Carter. [Certificate to the same, signed Sarah Williams.] Second Creek, 3 Sept. 1793. Sir: I received your summons by Mr. Abrams and I am so much indisposed that it is impossible for me to attend today. I judge that it is to give evidence in the suit of Mr. William Cobb and Israel Smith. In conversation with Mr. Smith I asked him what he would do if Mr. Cobb claimed his horse. He said why, the horse is mine, he belonged to my wife, and he shall never have the horse alive. That is all I know. Sig: Isaac Caverly. // William Cobb swears that the horse is his and he lent it to his father four years ago and he informs me he lent it to my sister. Signed: W. Cobb. 3rd Sept. 1783. // Deposition of Jesse Carter that Arthur Cobb attacked Smith (Israel) on the road and Philander Smith came between them, and Cobb used much abusive language. Sept. 2, 1793. Sig: Jesse Carter. // Simpson Holmes deposition that he asked Glasscock why Mr. Cobb carried the heavy club at the race and he replied that he carried it for the Smiths. Sig: Simpson Holmes. 3 Sept. 1793. // Solomon H. Wisdom swears that he saw Mr. Cobb catch the horse by the bridle that Mr. Israel Smith was riding and tell him that it was his son's horse and he must alight. 3 Sept. 1793. Sig: Solomon H. Wisdom. // Sometime since Mr. Arthur Cobb and myself being at the house of Mr. Mann and drinking some grog and conversing of people, who to my best knowledge were the Smiths, Cobb suddenly rose up and seemed in a great passion and swore that he would have revenge and drew a butchers knife from his coat and shook it. I desired Philetus Smith to caution his brothers to take care. Sig: A. Sloan. 3 Sept. 1793. // p. 230. Deposition of John Minor who was close to the fight that Arthur Cobb forced on Smith at the time of the race and he watched closely and while he saw Cobb try repeatedly to gouge Smith who kept his eyes protected as best he could but he never once tried to gouge Cobb, that the injury to Cobb's eye was due a kick. Smith was under Cobb from the first and seemed to act only in defense. Sig: John Minor. 3 Sept. 1793. This is to certify that I was with Mr. John Minor at the time the above took place and what he said is true and I was an eye witness to all that took place, as beforementioned. Natchez, 3 Sept. 1793. Sig: William McIntosh. // This is to certify that I heard Dr. Todd say he called at Arthur Cobb's and had seen his eye and was of the opinion that he would not lose it if any care was taken but that he believed that he wishes to lose it from the neglect he paid to it. Signed: Jesse Greenfield. Sept. 4, 1793. // I do hereby certify that no man interferred in parting Mr. Cobb and Mr. Luther Smith but Henry Holstein and his brother and at the same time of their being parted Mr. Kelly stood by at which I held one of his arms to prevent his interfering. Signed: John Minor. // I do hereby certify that I was present at the plantation of Mr. Robert Abrams on Saturday Aug. 25th when a dispute arose between Mr. Courtland Smith and Mr. Cobb when Mr. Cobb insisted on fighting said Smith and Smith refused to fight him and went out of his way and Mr. Cobb followed him and forcibly fell on him, Smith threw Cobb off him doing him little or no damage, saying that he would not fight an old man, after which he forced a dispute with Luther Smith and Cobb fell on him and endeavored to gouge him. Smith endeavored to defend himself until they were parted. Second Creek, 2nd Sept. 1793. P. Hawkins. // Personally appeared before me, Isaac Johnson, Jeptha Higdon, on oath, did say he met Cobb with a bandage over one eye and he said that he had gotten drunk and had a fight with the Smiths and received a kick in the eye. Jeptha (X) Higdon. 17 Sept. 1793. [Depositions of William Ryan; Henry Holstein who with the aid of his brother, King Holstein, parted Cobb and Smith; King Holstein, who denied that Kelly touched either Cobb or Smith; Simpson Holmes, the same; Abram Ellis; James Kirk;] Before me, Don Manuel Gayoso de Lemos, 5 Sept. 1793, appeared Arthur Cobb who promised in my presence that he would never again molest the person of Israel Smith or any of his family, nor commit any damage to their property and for security whereof he binds his person and estate and promises to bind two persons of property, etc. John Eldergill and Lewis Evans became responsible for the conduct of said Cobb. All sign.

p. 235. I, Jemima Lewis, do give full power and authority to Don Juan Girault in my name, etc. to settle all matters between me and Mr. Peter Walker. 5 Sept. 1793. Jemima (X) Lewis.

p. 236. Francisco de Arroyo, of this Post, petitions that a certain Augustine Macarty has used many expressions injurious to his reputation respecting a draft of 120 rials, etc. Asks that depositions be taken of Francisco Godey and others. Aug. 9, 1793. // Aug. 9, let the passport of Augustine Macarty be detained in the office of the Post and let Don Francisco Godoy, Thos. Wilkins, Esq. and Juan Texada be notified to appear before me. // Same date. Appeared Don Francisco Goday, who, placing his hand on the hilt of his sword, promised to answer truly, etc. and declared that on the 7th instant at John Texada's house, he saw the said Texada hand to Augustine Macarty a certificate which Macarty examined and, smiling, said that the said certificate was false. // Next appeared John Texada, declared, on oath, that he went to the house of said Macarty to deliver a draft of $15 and he refused to receive it unless it was endorsed by Thos. Wilkins. Etc. // Next appeared Thomas Wilkins deposed that his negroes were employed at a public work at the Post, that although he and his negroes were in N. O. he had a negro belonging to Reuben Gibson, who owed him some money, at work at the Post and the said labor being in payment of Gibson's debt. Wilkins was 39 years old. // Same day, appeared Augustine Macarty, who, on oath, denounced the depositions of Francisco Goday and Juan Texada as fabrications as he never intended such expressions against the reputation of Don Francisco De Arroyo nor did he suspect that the certificate in question was false, in proof of which he received it in payment of a debt owing to him by the said Texada, etc. // p. 240. Natchez, Aug. 10, 1793. To be communicated to Don Augustine Macarty. Since the said Macarty has a flat of the King to be transported to the Capital, a passport will be issued to him, the present proceedings suspended until his return and transmitted to the Superior Tribunal if the parties request it. Sig: Gayoso.

p. 240. Jeremiah Routh versus John Olivary. Petition of Jeremiah Routh that about twelve months ago your petitioner did bring to the landing the frame of a house 40 feet square for sale and when the river rose had it piled up near the back part of Mr. O'Connor's lot. The frame consisted of 12 principal pieces, 13 joists, 28 studs, 28 sleepers for the piazza, 14 sills, 13 speelers for the house, 4 cap-plates, 260 light lathes, 8 braces, 6 end-sills, 12 piazza posts, 52 rafters. A few days ago, your petitioner was informed that a certain John Olivary had appropriated the principal pieces of the frame house and was building a house for himself. Upon the application to the said Olivary for payment, he offered to pay me for the pieces of timbers which he had taken, but the petitioner refused as the remaining parts of the frame were useless to him or a purchaser and insisted upon him paying for the whole, but was willing to leave the price to any two men chosen by the parties. But he would not comply to the proposal. Signed: Jeremiah Routh. 8th March 1791. // Let John Olivary be notified that he is answerable for the timber he has in possession. Sig: Gayoso. // John Olivary, in reply, represents that he has 15 pieces of timber in question which were lent to him by the patroon Molina. 9th March 1791. Sig: John Olivary. // Pursuant to a decree, an order was issued for John Short and Robert Creighton to appear as evidences at the request of Job Routh. Signed: John Girault. // Personally appeared Robert Creighton, who deposes that he was employed by Jeremiah to get the frame of a house with him, which was done and rafted down and placed close to Mrs. Baker's lot; that sometime afterwards he saw two main sills and two wall plates, 8 posts and some braces of said frame put in a house at the landing where a long billiard table was kept by a Spaniard, whose name this deponent does not know. Signed by

John Girault at the request of Robert Creighton. 15 Dec. 1794. Appeared Anthony Molina, who, on oath, declared that the timber which he lent to John Olivary were 15 pieces which he found adrift in the presence of divers persons, and the said Olivary gave him in exchange for the timber a mare which he has still in possession. He is 33 years old. Signed: Antonio Molina. In pursuance of request of said Molina, appeared Fernandez when he was asked if he knew of any timber at the landing in 1790 belonging to Jeremiah Routh, replied that in 1790 there was much timber at the landing and high winds and the rise of the water set said timber adrift and he, Antonio Molina, caught some pieces opposite the house of Alexander Moore, and then he lent or sold them to John Olivary. He was 27 years old. Next appeared Gabriel Blanco, carpenter of the Squadron or Galley, declared that Jeremiah Routh had a quantity of timber at the landing in 1790 and the rise of the water set the timber adrift and Antonio Molina caught some pieces with a piroque which he put in the yard of his house and sold or lent it to John Olivary. He was 32 years old. // The declaration of John Short concerning the house frame of timbers, the property of the late Jeremiah Routh, he says that in the year of 1790 the late Jeremiah Routh came to the subscriber with a written order to dispose of the house frame of timber lying piled up above John Olivary's billiard house. Some time after Mr. Daniel Ferguson purchased this timber conditionally but each party was to choose a carpenter to estimate its value and subscriber noticing that some part of the timber was sawed in two and called Mr. Lord to witness thereto who said that the whole frame of timber did not appear to be there, that some of it must be gone. Mr. Routh being sent for came down and on examining his timber observed that several parts of it were wanting. Mr. Olivary was then building an addition to his house and making it wider than it was before. Mr. Routh, well-knowing his timber, that he had sawed and squared himself, found a number of the largest pieces of his timber in Mr. Olivary's possession. // Job Routh petitions that he humbly conceives the foregoing proofs sufficient to establish his claim to the timber of his late father, lost at the landing. The parts that Olivary had made use of made the rest useless and the petitioner asks for the payment of the same from the property of the said Olivary according to the estimate of two intelligent persons appointed by Your Excellency. Natchez, 10 Jan. 1795. Sig: Job Routh.

p. 243. The King versus Zachariah Smith. Petition of Zacheriah Smith, an unfortunate old man, conscious of his own feeling and principle that influenced his conduct before he came to this country and an all-time sense that he has deserved a better fate, who has no charge to bring against any but to exculpate himself by relying on the evidences of the most respectable inhabitants of this country some of whom were acquainted with your petitioner before he came to this country, namely, Col. Hutchins, Dr. Flower, Mr. Alexander Moore, Mr. Robert Dunbar, John Smith, Esq., Mr. John Henderson, Mr. Adam Bingaman, Mr. Daniel Clark, Mr. Lovelace, Mr. LeJeune, Mr. Wm. Collins, Capt. Nicholson, Mr. Ruffin Gray, Mr. Hugh Davis and others. These gentlemen as far as they know will justify your petitioner as an honest man, a fair dealer, and a quiet and peaceful neighbor. Your petitioner has been charged with encouraging his children in evil practices, and he pleads that he is not guilty of the charge and particularly that he was never present at a quarrel his sons were engaged in. Your Excellency has been informed that your petitioner was not only consenting but aiding and assisting his two unhappy sons, James and Zachariah, in making their escape from the justice of this government. The reverse of this was the case, your petitioner was convinced that they were cleared of the charge against them and in proof of this your petitioner refers you to Capt. Nicholson and Mr. Ruffin Gray who were with him at his son James's house and they heard your petitioner make use of every argument in his power not only to dissuade them from leaving the country but from a consciousness of their innocence to persuade them to go immediately down according to the order. James and Zachariah answered to your petitioner that a certain paper which James had signed for the sake of peace had been their ruin and that they could not take his advice in this matter, that they were afraid of the power of Mr. Percy, that they would rather leave the country than be confined in prison. Your petitioner's sons have committed a great fault in not immediately obeying the order of government but your petitioner is very confidant that this is their only crime. Etc. (p. 244). Natchez. 10th Feb. 1794. Sig: Zachariah Smith. // 15 Feb. 1794. I do hereby commission Francis Poussett, Esq. to make exact inquiry as to the character of Zachariah Smith's family and particularly his sons, James and Zachariah, now absent. // Deposition of Capt. Nicholson: The above petitioner did request him to go with him and Ruffin Gray to advise his son, James, to obey the Governor's order to appear before him and by no means to quit the country. The answer that James Smith made to his father, to my recollection, was as set forth in the said petition. My intimacy with the family does not enable me to say more as I only saw them now and then as they called at my house. 18 Feb. 1794. Sig: James Nicholson. // Next appeared David Lajeune who deposed that he had known Zachariah Smith since I came to live in this district about four years since. He has always been a good, obliging neighbor to me. I have no acquaintance with his sons, James and

Zachariah. Buffalo Dist. 20 Feb. 1794. Sig: David Lejeune. // From Mr. Lovelace: I do certify that Mr. Zachariah Smith has lived in this neighborhood five years and has been a quiet and peaceable neighbor and his sons, James and Zachariah, have been often at my house and always behaved civilly and orderly. 27 Feb. 1794. Sig: John Lovelace.

p. 245. Mrs. Elizabeth Roberts made oath that her husband, Jonathan Roberts, was settled on Mr. Mather's plantation at Bayou Sara by agreement but about six weeks ago her husband abandoned her and enlisted as a soldier, and left her big with child and she has two young children by her former husband, Henry Grant, but she has some little property when she married Jonathan Roberts but he has none. Some time before Roberts left her she was invited by Mrs. Green who lived with Moses Johnson to go and stay with her for awhile and she did, with Roberts consent. Johnson was then gone to Orleans with the volunteers. [She detailed the work that she did and the supplies she furnished while at the house of Moses Johnson during two months and a few days she stayed as well as listing her belongings she had taken there from the Mather plantation.] When Moses Johnson returned he exacted a note for $40 from her for board for herself and two children, and is claiming her possessions in payment. [Affidavit of Moses Johnson who denies Mrs. Roberts story; she was not invited to his house, etc.]

p. 246. Sir: I herewith return to Your Excellency the petition of Zachariah Smith with such evidence annexed as I have been able to procure. Mr. Gray was not at home but his wife told me that his testimony would be the same as Capt. Nicholson's. All the other names mentioned are in the vicinity of the government house. The old man seems very much borne down by affliction. His sons, James and Zachariah, must have suffered a great deal and I make no doubt are sorry for their faults and will be careful of their conduct in the future if Your Excellency will extend to them mercy ..... I enclose two depositions, Mrs. Roberts and Moses Johnson. I have ordered that her property be restored to her and she has given security that she shall not part with any of it until I receive Your Excellency's answer. I think the man has overcharged her. Moses Johnson also holds a note of John Green for $67 due ever since July 1791. This Green has left the country some time past and has a tract of land here and his wife who lives with Johnson. Johnson's suit is to have the land sold to pay the debt. Mrs. Roberts has a very worthless husband. Devall married them before the proclamation. She is very poor and has two children and now big with child. Etc. (p. 247) If Roberts has any pay due him, etc. Sig: Francis Poussett, March 11, 1794. // May it please Your Excellency, I have known Mr. Zachariah Smith but four years and have had some dealings with him. I have always found him to be an honest, punctual man, a peaceful, inoffensive, kind neighbor. I have had very little acquaintance with his two sons, James and Zachariah, but I have never heard anything against their moral character until Mr. Percy charged James with burning a hole in Percy's boat which unfitted her for service. This charge I believe was malicious and ungrounded and am firmly of the opinion that the hole burned in the boat was perpetrated by Indians at the time they hunted in the swamps adjacent. Charging James with the crime incited the irritation of an innocent man and an altercation ensued between Mr. Percy and him about the boat which Mr. Percy had borrowed from him. When James came for the return of the boat, it was lost and Mr. Percy replied that he would pay for her. Smith replied that it was his boat that he wanted and his money he might keep to pay his ferriage over the River Styx. For this rude language, the magistrate should have given Smith a night's lodging in the blockhouse. Zachariah also offended Mr. Percy with some like remark. These, sir, are the only crimes that drove those unfortunate brothers from the country and the government they liked and admired and from their aged and affectionate parents and beloved brothers and sisters and numerous connections. Some time after the burning of the boat, the peaceable father waited on Mr. Percy and expostulated with him of the heinous and false report, stygmatizing him and his sons. He succeeded in settling the affair of the boat, but as his sons, James and Zachariah, had behaved with him, Percy demanded that they must make written confession and all would be well. Mr. Percy read to them a paper purporting that they had deported themselves with disrespect toward him, declaring their sorrow in so doing and asking his pardon. This paper they signed without hesitation, believing it to be what had been read to them but, alas, it turned out to be of a very different tenor. Mr. Lejeune, perceptor in Mr. Percy's family, was called upon to sign the confession as a witness. He wanted to read what he was to sign but Mr. Percy would not let him peruse it, though he showed it so soon as the Smiths were gone. As soon as the Smiths had signed and Lejeune had witnessed the surreptitiously obtained confession, Mr. Percy shook hands with the father and the sons and assured them that all things should be forgotten, etc. Notwithstanding which, after showing the inhuman confession to all the neighbors, he, Percy, went to Natchez and I believe to represent the Smiths and their family in a very unfavorable light. On his return, he sent for the father and two sons. The sons he ordered to proceed to the seat of government and to the father he said: "Old man, I am determined to destroy you, your seed, being and generations. I have power to send you where you shall not be seen or heard of by anyone in this district again." I am not an eye-witness to these facts but I believe them all as the truth, and I assure Your Excellency, not to asperse the character of the dead but in honor and justice to the living, to the much injured Zachariah Smith and his two sons, James and Zachariah, that I give this certificate my signature. Loftus Cliffs, March 15, 1794. Daniel Clark.

p. 249. Thomas Beans versus Moses Armstrong. William Bassett declares, on oath, that he had in charge a pacing bay filly, at that time the property of Thomas Beans, marked with a "T.B.", but he knows nothing of the same being sold. 3 Sept. 1794. Before P. Bryan Bruin. // Reuben Proctor declareth that, during the past winter, he and Thomas Beans set out for Natchez with the Bayou Pierre Volunteers with the intention of going with the company to New Orleans but were discharged at Natchez and permitted to return home; that they returned together and on the way they stopped at Cable's; that in conversation, Mrs. Cable expressed her surprise that James Davenport had not furnished her with a mare that he had promised her. The deponent asked what kind of mare he had engaged to furnish her and she answered a bay pacing mare and gave further description, which led Thomas Beans to conclude as we left the house that it must be his mare as he knew no other of the description she gave in the settlement. He added that if he wanted his mare, he should pay well for it. // William Brocus, being sworn, declared that about six weeks ago, when the volunteer company set out for New Orleans, Moses Armstrong called at his house and asked him if he knew anything of a little bay mare that belonged to Thomas Bean running on his range. Brocus answered that he knew her well. Armstrong then told Mr. Brocus that he had bought her and asked him what he thought she was worth. Brocus replied that if Armstrong had bought he thought he knew about her and he asked what he gave for the mare. He replied a fine cow and calf and $10 more in trade. He replied that he had given more than he would have given. A fortnight later he saw Armstrong at Mr. Cobun's in company with James Davenport and he and Davenport were then trading for this mare and two others that were running on the same range; Davenport objected as he had never seen the mares and Armstrong then referred Davenport to the deponent as to the value and Mr. Brocus declined giving his opinion, but promised to point the mares out to Mr. Davenport. The bargain was however closed and Mr. Brocus was called upon to witness the agreement. In March Davenport came for the mares, which Mr. Brocus allowed him to have. 10 Sept. 1794. Before Bruin.

p. 250. Mary Smiley versus Thomas Smiley. Mary Smiley, the wife of Squire Smiley and widow of James Crunkleton, represents that an execution had been levied upon a mare the property of her children of her first marriage for the claimant of a debt of her present husband, Squire Smiley, appointed guardian of the said children; she is ready to make oath that the property seized was the property of my late husband; asks that the property of her children be ascertained. Sig: Mary Smiley. // Pass the petition to John Smith, Esquire, and he will examine into the matter. Sig: Gayoso. // By testimony of Henry Manadue the said mare was bought by Thomas Smiley of Manadue's father and the payment was 75 carrots of tobacco. [Smiley also beat his wife unmercifully. The magistrates advised that Smiley be made to work for the government for the benefit of his creditors. John Crunkleton, son of Mrs. Smiley, had previously made an inventory of his property and the mare in question was not listed.] Signed by William Murray and John Smith. // A quit claim by Thomas Smiley to any and all property his wife, Mary Smiley, had when he married her. 11 Sept. 1785. Signed: Squire Thomas Smiley. Wit: H. Manadue, Thomas (X) Griffin. // Abram Scriber personally appeared 24 Aug. 1794 and declared that he was at Joseph Dyson's and Thomas Smiley came there in a great passion and asked his wife why she was always coming there whenever his back was turned and she replied that she was tired of staying at home and he ordered her not to take his children abroad any more and was rough with his wife. 24 Aug. 1794. Villa Gayoso. Sig: Abram Scriber. // [Mrs. Smiley testified to the same, saying that she went to her mother's. Her description of what occurred being the same as Scriber's indicates that Mary Smiley was a daughter of the Joseph Dysons.] Depositions of Joseph Bonner, John Jones, John Staybraker and Stephen Scriber of Thomas Smiley's cruelty to his present wife. Before John Smith. Aug. 1794.

p. 253. John Williams versus John Smith. Petition of John Williams that John Smith, Esq. was indebted to him for $104, for negro hire, but because of evidences of friendship and hospitality had no written agreement with Mr. Smith and he now says that the bargain was made with Mr. Cato West, 1st Dec. 1793, which Mr. West positively denies. When your petitioner returned from the U.S. he asked for his negroes and Mr. Smith said he had no right to take them at least until the end of the month and no time was set for payment. 18 March, 1794. Sig: John Williams. // John Smith will make his reply at once. Showed the above to John Smith and he said he would attend at government house when convenient to him and not sooner, as he was not obliged to wait on Mr. Williams. Fee $3. Sig: William Gorman. // John Smith will answer to this and appear at the government house, positively, on Friday next. Signed: Gayoso. // John Smith claims he used the negroes when not needed in order to have them to complete raft and to have them taken away when they were at work on it was a hardship, etc.

p. 255. The King versus Robert Stark and Thomas Green. The petition of Robert Stark and Thomas Green shows that your petitioners find themselves very uncomfortable in their confinement from their families and concerns. They were well apprised of Your Excellency's good intentions respecting their honorable acquittal but as Col. Bruin's delay to come down on account of his indisposition may be protracted to a considerable length of time and add greatly to the distress of your petitioners, they beg leave to give reliable security to appear at any time within two months at any place directed. 26 March 1794. Signed: Robert Stark, Thomas Green. // Before me appeared George Cochran and Ebenezer Rees who declared that they become responsible for the persons of Robert Stark and Thomas Green and will produce them whenever required. This security to continue only for two months. Both signed. Before Gayoso.

p. 256. John Gaskin versus Jacob Huffman. John Gaskin, of district of Villa Gayoso, makes oath that the violent threats made against him by Jacob Huffman causes him to think his life as well as his property is in danger and asks that said Huffman may be bound over for the safety of person and property of him, the said John Gaskin. 25 April 1794. Before William Murray. // Personally appeared Jacob Crumholt and John Roberts and made bond for $200 for 12 months from this day that Jacob Huffman shall behave himself peaceable toward John Gaskin and shall not hurt the said Gaskin by any manner or means, nor his property. 25 April 1794. Signed William Murray. [The daughter of the wife of John Gaskins was poisoned accidently at the house of Charles Collins, a neighbor, previous to which a Michael McGinnis had brought into the house a vine and Mrs. Collins said it was poisonous and threw it away. Various depositions that the vine from which tea was made which caused the death of the girl was like that Mrs. Collins threw away, etc. Depositions by Richard Adams, Benj. Fletcher and his wife, Sarah, Cato West, John McDonald.]

p. 259. Margaret Gaskins versus Charles Collins. Margaret Gaskins represents that some time ago a misfortune happened to her, her daughter being poisoned at a neighbor's house, called Charles Collins, and it is said accidently. This accident, as may be expected, has caused a difference between the two families and many disputes, so much that Charles Collins and his wife have contracted a hatred and malice against the petitioner and her husband, which is plainly demonstrated in a variety of circumstances, the last of which is the subject of the present petition and is as follows: Thomas Adams having made a crop of corn jointly with the petitioner's husband stored his share up on the plantation in a crib to which his brothers and relations had frequent access and used a good deal of it when he was in New Orleans. At his return he complained that the crib had been plundered and indirectly accused the petitioner's husband with taking it. This happened long before the accident at Collins' and nothing was said as the accusation was not positive but now since this malice has taken place in the Collins family against the petitioner's, he, the said Collins, has offered to swear that he saw the petitioner take corn out of Adam's crib, which the petitioner declares to be utterly false and dictated by malice. Signed: Margaret Gaskin. // John Smith, Esq. will collect all the information in his power respecting the nature of this petition. Sig: Manuel Gayoso. 1 Aug. 1794. // Edmund Johnson appeared before me 9 Aug. 1794 and deposed that some time in June Mrs. Collins rode to the fence and prevailed on my wife to go with her to Mr. Robertson's and there Mrs. Collins mentioned that she had seen a form of an advertisement along the road and that Mr. Hunt went in pursuit of it and I have also seen it there and it is my opinion that the aforesaid writing was lodged there by Mrs. Collins and Mrs. Fletcher. Sig: Edmund Johnson. Before John Smith. // Same day, appeared Joseph Green and made oath that "some time in May last I was in company with Mrs. Collins and she said that she had been making some candles and she had reserved an inch of candle to grease Mrs. Gaskin's throat and Mrs. Gaskin replied that if she was a prudent woman she would not abuse her in such manner without provocation, at which Mrs. Collins said that she was in no way sorry for what she had done." Sig: Joseph Green. Before John Smith. // Same day Henry Falconer appeared and made oath that some time in July last he passed Mr. Charles Collins' house and he called him in and after being there some time Mrs. Collins told him that they had a song and he asked her if it was a blackguard song that was reported about and she answered that it was. She handed it to her husband and he read it over and she asked him if he had a desire to read it and he told her no. She asked the reason he did not and he told her that he had no desire to learn such songs. He was of the opinion that Mr. Gaskin's family had been the instigation of the above disputes. Sig: Henry Falconer. // John Smith, Esq. Your petitioner showeth that the misfortune which happened on Cole's Creek was laid to the charge of Mr. Charles Collins through which means Mr. Charles Collins has tried out of spite and malice to blast the reputation of the petitioner; that some time ago there was some writing containing some scandal against Mr. Gaskin's family found in the neighborhood which appeared to be written by Charles Collins. Signed John Gaskin.

p. 261. Daniel Rainer versus Ebenezer Rees and Melling Woolley. Daniel Rainer represents that Mr. Melling Woolley being some years ago in possession of the petitioner's note of hand for $24 called upon the petitioner to pay it which he did in work done for him on his plantation as fully appears by the subjoined documents. Notwithstanding Your Excellency's decree obtained two years ago and upwards for the delivery of said note which has been repeatedly notified to Mr. Woolley and Mr. Rees, they still persist in retaining it, exposing the petitioner for payment of same for the second time, etc. Asks for an order that former decree be fulfilled, and condemn Rees and Woolley to pay costs, the suit being caused by Mr. Rees not complying to Mr. Woolley's request which hereunto annexed. 22 July 1796. Daniel Rainer by John Girault. // Same date. Ebenezer Rees will immediately deliver the petitioner the note mentioned in this petition or show just cause for his refusing it, before next court day. Signed: Gayoso. // Ebenezer Rees acknowledges to have received notice; that Clark and Rees sold to Mr. Melling Woolley, 8 Aug. 1788, merchandise to a very considerable amount. They, finding that he did not fulfil his engagements, arrested him in New Orleans for payment of same, and on Feb. 15, 1790 he paid into the hands of Daniel Clark Esq., sundry obligations which he endorsed, among which was the obligations above alluded to. Your petitioner cannot conceive what right Mr. Woolley had to receive payment of a note which had every reason to suppose was paid. In consequence of an order from His Excellency the Governor General in favor of Daniel Clark, Esquire, he was ordered to deliver into his hands all the obligations and papers belonging to co-partners, Clark and Rees, which he complied with. Therefore, your petitioner is not in actual possession of the note mentioned. Sig: Ebenezer Rees. // Communicated to Mr. Rainer. Fee $1. Wm. Gillespie. // Mr. Melling Woolley is ordered to give full satisfaction to the petitioner for his note within three days or produce just cause to the contrary. Notified Mr. Melling Woolley 24 Sept. 1796. Fees $1. Gillespie. [Another petition by Daniel Rainer.] Woolley will immediately return the note to Mr. Rainer and Mr. Rees shall have recourse upon Mr. Woolley. Sig: Gayoso.

p. 263. Frederick Mann versus Stephen Mayes. We, the subscribers, being appointed by Your Excellency to adjust the accounts of Mr. Frederick Mann and Stephen Mayes, find a balance in favor of Frederick Mann of 1 rials in payment of which sum the said Mann will make good and deliver to the said Mayes the following articles, one coffee mill, one teapot, 1 pr. tong and shovels, 1 pr flat irons, etc., due in a barter for a horse. 22 April 1794. Signed: Joseph Murray, G. Cochran. Award approved.

p. 264. Peter Bryan Bruin versus John George. We, the subscribers being appointed by His Excellency's order to arbitrate certain controversies between Col. Peter Bryan Bruin and John George, both of the settlement of Bayou Pierre. Personally appeared before us, William Smith, David McFarland, William Byrd, and Peter Bryan Bruin who made oath to answer the questions concerning their knowledge of the above controversy. Mr. McFarland said that Col. Bruin complied with the agreement as far as he knows; but the said John George had not done so. Mr. William Smith sworn, said that Col. Bruin did furnish the said George with the oxen mentioned and horses, also with the indigo working tools and utensils and the indigo vats were made under John George's inspection and direction, etc. Signed: William Smith. Joel (X) Byrd agreed that Col. Bruin had complied with his agreement. Col. Bruin said that in August 1792 [two pages of the delinquencies of said George as overseer.] Arbitrators: John Smith, Thomas Calvit. Award in favor of Col. Bruin.

p. 268. Lewis Bingaman versus Alexander Boyd. Bingaman states that he has in his possession a bond of the late Alexander Boyd, decd., for $186 with lawful interest, and he went to the vendue of the estate of said Boyd with the intention of purchasing some articles and he bought to the amount of $46 for which the managers made him give his note but did not make it negotiable to the intent that it should be discounted on the petitioner's bond and looked upon it as a matter completed and patiently waited for the balance which he has not received. Mr. Levi Wells asked him for the payment of the note. May 2, 1794. Sig: Lewis Bingaman. // Levi Wells will appear before me next week in answer to this complaint. // Mr. Wells will give up the note of Mr. Bingaman and the amount of Mr. Bingaman's note will be deducted from the bond and the exrs. of Boyd's estate will give their note to Bingaman for the balance. The settlement will take place before Isaac Johnson, Esquire, except the delivery of the note which shall be done immediately.

p. 270 William Gorman versus Anthony Hutchins. Bernard Lintot and Isaac Johnson, arbitrators. It appears to us that the said Gorman is indebted to Mr. Hutchins in the sum of $50, Mr. Gorman having produced no proof of his having paid, but as we suppose it contrary to the common law and the unavoidable uncertainty of long standing in liquidating accounts, we are of the opinion that it ought not to bear interest as also that it may remain unpaid until Mr. Hutchins shall have procured a certain certificate. Signed: Bernard Lintot, Isaac Johnson. 26 March 1791. // Natchez, 7 May 1794. Col. Hutchins having procured the certificate mentioned in the foregoing report and the two gentlemen having given their opinion, I do hereby approve same and order it communicated to the parties. Sig: Manuel Gayoso. Certificate: Please to let Mr. William Gorman have goods to the amount of $50 and I shall accomodate it to you should William Gorman fail in payment. Sig: Anthony Hutchins. I do hereby certify that I delivered to Mr. William Gorman to the amount of the within order, and that Mr. Gorman did fail in the payment thereof. Therefore I demanded the money of Col. Hutchins and he paid me $50. Signed: Isaac Johnson. 11 Dec. 1790. Received from Mr. Gorman of this date his note for $50 in full for the amount. Signed: Anthony Hutchins. Memorandum of $130 left in my hands by William Gorman to settle with and pay to the administrators of Jacob Winfree, deceased, on condition that the said admrs. will acquit and execute a general release to said Gorman. Signed: Anthony Hutchins. Dear Sir: I received a letter from you concerning the dispute between you and Mr. Gorman on account of a certain debt you owed him formerly. I remember perfectly that you gave me credit in my bond for $130 which amount I got from Mrs. Winfree which happened to be in 1776 and from the papers of our settlements I am satisfied that it was in the month of February or nearly that time. I have no news worthy of relating but I am very poor and distressed. I shall be exceedingly glad to see you and your family once more. My wife gives her compliments to Mrs. Hutchins and family. Your real friend and humble servant, Philip Alston. June 17, 1791. South Territory, Tennessee County. This day, Philip Alston appeared before me, a Justice of the Peace, and made oath that in the year 1776, in month of February, agreeable to Mrs. Elizabeth Winfree's wish and request Col. Anthony Hutchins did pay to this deponent $130 which was due from William Gorman to the estate of Jacob Winfree, deceased, which was discounted at that time due from this deponent to the said Hutchins. Signed: Philip Alston. Before John Phillips, J.P. 7 June 1791. [Hutchins had testified that he had fully satisfied his obligation to said Gorman having paid the money by order of Messrs. Winfree to Philip Alston, now in the U. S. but that the receipt and discharge for same with many other papers had been forcibly taken from him by a certain James Willing and his gang. He has further proof thereof sent for to the said Alston by Mr. Green to procure a certificate.]

p. 272. William Mulhollan versus Thomas Landphier. Mulhollan represents that Thomas Landphier did one day this week maim, wound and cripple one of the petitioner's oxen so that the oxen has become useless and his dependence for making his crop was the use of said oxen for the support of his family and payment of his rent. 14 June 1794. Sig: Wm. Mulhollan. Col. Hutchins is authorized to call before him Thomas Landphier and examine into the nature of the complaint of the petitioner and on finding said said Landphier guilty of the charge laid against him without sufficient cause or reason, he will have him brought to this fort. // I hereby commit Thomas Landphier to the fort there to remain until a discharge has been sent him by Mulhollan. // Declaration of David Mitchell that with Samuel Phipps on Friday last he went to view Thomas Lanphier's cornfield fence on the complaint of William Mulhollan against him for wounding and maiming his ox and he heard Lanphier say he was only sorry he had not killed him. Etc. // Declaration of John Kinnard that he saw at Thomas Lanphier's the wounded ox which had been struck in the back with a hatchet, it seems, and Lanphier said he would rather kill the ox than lose his corn. // Lanphier, confined to the fort, was brought before His Excellency, the deposition being read to him, he was reprimanded and ordered to pay the damage for the ox and remain confined for his punishment for his threats. Sig: John Girault. // 20 June 1794. Appeared Ebenezer Rees and said he would be responsible for the conduct of Thomas Lanphier that he may be released. Signed: Ebenezer Rees.

p. 273. Alexander Ross versus Jeremiah Miller and Wm. Newman. We, the subscribers hereto, do engage ourselves to go on board the bateau of Mr. Alexander Ross, at present of New Orleans, commanded by Mr. Wm. Falconer, boatman, and to be diligent and careful and subject to the same regulations as other boatmen employed on the Miss. River and, in consideration whereof, the said Ross engages to provide the customary provisions and drink and pay each of us 12 Spanish milled dollars on the bateau's arrival at Natchez. 1st May 1794. Thomas Twentyman, William Newman, Jerry Miller, [all of whom sign with a mark.] p. 274. Memorandum. I do hereby certify that Jeremiah Miller and William Newman, two hands on board Alexander Ross's barge did leave clandestinely about 19 leagues above New Orleans the 6th day after leaving the harbour. I also certify that Mr. Ross paid each of them

$4 and I gave them four bits of their wages, jointly, and Mr. Newman bought a pair of shoes from Daniel Maletto, belonging to Messrs Cross to be paid out of his wages. [Extra expense caused by their action listed.] Natchez. 2 July 1794. Signed: Wm. Falconer.

p. 275. William Wheeden petitions that in 1791 he applied to and was engaged by Col. Hutchins as overseer to make a crop of tobacco and was to receive one-sixth of proceeds for his services. When the crop was housed and part of it appraised in hogheads, Col. Hutchins found fault with the treatment in handling and ordered your petitioner to leave the plantation, the petitioner thereby defrauded of the value of his labor. June 30, 1794. // Col. Hutchins will put his answer to the petition in writing. Signed: Gayoso. // Objections to William Wheeden's petition: Wm. Wheeden did agree to make a crop of tobacco on my plantation; managed it very badly and my home overseer and hands had to weed and save all he could; even the housing of it was bad and the greater part of the crop was house-burnt. I did not order him from the plantation but urged him to stay and separate the worst from the better that he had mixed, that he might make something of it, assuring him that if he left he would lose his part of it. [Details of the care and treatment of tobacco.] Mr. Jacob Phillis, Mr. William Baker and Mr. George Aldridge having seen the tobacco, can testify to its condition.

p. 276. Jacob Stampley versus Hugh Davis. Jacob Stampley represents that in March last he was in New Orleans prepared to deliver to Hugh Davis some merchandise and a small coil of rope to be brought up to his place freight for which the petitioner paid immediately as will appear by said Davis's receipt, here annexed, and after the petitioner left town the said Davis did put the petitioner's goods on board of Wm. Falconer's boat which was lost, the petitioner's trunk of merchandise was put ashore before the boat sunk and it was seized upon and detained by Mr. Matthews with other effects for the payment of the negro who was lost in diving. His property was saved before the boat was sunk and before the negro was employed to dive. 20 May 1794. Sig: Jacob Stampley. // Received of Mr. Jacob Stampley, one trunk and a small coil of rope in good order which I promise to deliver at the Natchez landing, the danger of the river excepted, the freight paid. Signed: Hugh Davis. New Orleans, 24 March 1794. // At the complaint of Mr. Jacob Stampley, Hugh Davis is ordered to appear at the government house the first court day after notification of this order. // I do hereby obligate myself to produce within a reasonable time the effects mentioned in my receipt to Jacob Stampley for his order at the Natchez landing, or pay him the value thereof. 24 May 1794. The danger of the river for my own boat excepted. Sig: Hugh Davis. Before Gayoso.

p. 278. Joseph Murray versus George Overaker. Joseph Murray, an inhabitant of the town of Natchez, represents that he has lived under your government for years, etc. etc. complains of an outrage and abuse he has received from George Overaker, who, without provocation abused and assaulted him, leaving him in a mangled condition. He requests the testimony of Mr. Daniel Douglass, Mr. Archibald Douglass, John Wilson, James Stuart, Capt. Thomas and Samuel Thomas. Natchez, 25th ____, 1794. [*This continues for several pages. The witnesses above appear, except the two Thomases.*]

p. 282. Peter Presler petitions that he, having administered to the estate of his son-in-law, John O'-Connor, begs leave to gather the stock that is running at large belonging to said estate and also transact every other thing belonging thereto, he being accountable to the creditors for any lawful claim against said estate. Natchez, 24 July 1794. Sig: Peter Presler. // In consequence of Peter Presler becoming responsible for the debts of John O'Connor, he is hereby authorized to take possession of all property whatsoever belonging legally to said O'Connor. Sig: Gayoso.

p. 283. Benjamin Steel versus William Calvit. Steel petitions that William Calvit by false representation made by him, Your Excellency did order John Smith, Esquire to execute property of the petitioner, that William Calvit's claim was erroneous as the petitioner did not receive the number of logs as he alleges, a great difference in the sum owed him can be proved by an agreement in the hands of John Wiley, and the notice of seizure was not delivered to him as he was in the swamp making a raft to go to N. O. and on his return found that his property had been taken from him without his knowledge and without an opportunity of making his defense. 10 June 1794. // Constable will order William Calvit to appear next Wed. with the petitioner and they are to bring with them their articles of proof and necessary witnesses. John Wiley, Samuel Osborn to appear. // Aug. 6, 1794. Mr. John Girault will examine the accounts between the parties and make a statement of it. // The representation of Benj. Steel being just, William Calvit who led myself and John Smith, Esq. into error to obtain the execution of the property of Mr. Benj. Steel is hereby ordered to return the property to him clear of cost and Steel is to deposit into the office of the records the above balance of $22 to be paid to Calvit upon his returning the property executed. Signed: Manuel Gayoso de Lemos. //

p. 285. Daniel Callagan versus Stephen Winter. Daniel Callagan, of Opelousas, represents that he has a note for two likely mares and colts payable by Mr. Stephen Winter, lately of this place but now of New Orleans, who left a horse in the care of Mr. Job Routh, of this place; asks an order that the horse be produced that he may be sold to pay your petitioner. 8 May 1794. Sig: Daniel Callagan. // 9 May 1794. Let Job Routh be summoned, etc. // Job Routh represents that he has a horse in his possession belonging to Stephen Winters and he willing to pay the value thereof brought against said Winters, and asks that appraisers be appointed to value the horse. // Robert Cochran and Joseph Bernard appointed and appraise the horse at $25. Both sign.

p. 286. William Cook versus Andrew Scandlan. William Cook, resident of this place, represents that about the 9th of this month, being in a frolic and drinking party at James Wiley's, did make a sort of bargain with Andrew Scandlan about a horse, proposing to pay Scandlan about $80 for same, for which purpose I was persuaded to give my note. But I was much intoxicated with liquor and did not know what ruinous bargain I was making. The horse, not worth $80, is not intrinsically worth $20, being unsound having had a wound in his shoulder. 17 Aug. 1794. Signed. // Andrew Scandland will appear before me next court.

p. 287. Alexander Moore versus Philip P. Turpin, who is indebted to your petitioner for a note $113 and interest. 12 May 1794. // Philip Turpin will pay Mr. Moore the value of the note. [Statement shown covering nearly two pages, followed by a statement by Philip Turpin.] Philip Turpin answers that he never directly received anything concerning the charge against him, etc. // Arbitrators appointed, George Fitzgerald, John Murdock. Their reply; 9 Aug. 1795, Philip Turpin is justly indebted to Mr. Moore for $110, with 10% int. from 31 Dec. 1790. Both sign. I approve the settlement except the interest which Mr. Moore will reduce to 6%. Signed: Manuel Gayoso de Lemos. // Communicated to Mr. Scott who appeared in behalf of Mr. Moore. Sig: John Girault. [This continues for two more pages.]

p. 296. Edward McCabe versus Peter Surget. Edward McCabe represents that he had with Don Pedro Surget an account in which he had been charged with interest of 15% and the said Surget has received more than was lawfully due to him, accounts annexed. 24 May 1794. Signed: Edward McCabe. [Account follows.] 27 Aug. 1794. Received of Don Pedro Surget his note for $20.

p. 297. Alexander Moore versus Joseph Duncan. Petition that Duncan owes Moore upward of $120 for merchandise. [Account follows, 2 pages. Counter charge by Duncan that Moore owes him $85.] Frederick Mann and John Scott appointed to settle disputes.

p. 300. William Lee versus Daniel Harrigal. Sandy Creek District, William Cooper, J.P. before whom appeared Mrs. Susannah Lee who made oath that Daniel Harrigill told her that he helped Thomas Nash to kill two hogs the property of Alexander Farrar and one Moore, and that he helped Silas McBee catch a horse the property of David Williams, deceased, and the said horse ran about the pond where David Odam now lives and that he piloted the said McBee out of the settlement to the other side of William Calvit's with the said horse and negro man that stayed at said Harrigill's and that the said negro had hired himself from his master to trade for himself and the said negro had come from below and the said Williams had wrote a free pass for the negro. Susannah (S) Lee. 21 July 1794. // Personally appeared before William Cooper, Daniel Harrigill who made oath that about four years ago William Lee came to his house and asked him to go bear hunting with him and they went to the plantation where Thomas Belleu ran away from. As they were going to the place, William Lee proposed to said Harragill to steal a bar for a plow from said plantation but said Harragill did not and they then returned back by the house where stood a spinning wheel, etc. 27 Aug. 1794. // Beesley Pruett made oath that William Lee offered to sell him a spinning wheel which he thought to be the property of Thos. Belleu. 27 Aug. 1794. // Aug. 29, appeared Mary Ratcliff and made oath that on Friday last Daniel Harrigal came to the house of John Ratcliff and carried off a rifle of the said Ratcliff. // John Ratcliff and Joseph Slater, who, being sworn, said that Daniel Harragill hollowed to the deponents as they were working in said Ratcliff's field where they were working and Harragill had the rifle which he had just taken out of Ratcliff's house and was his property.

p. 302. Before me, Manuel Gayoso de Lemos, appeared at the instance of Norsworthy Hunter, Capt. of the Militia in this government, Col. Henry Hunter, a gentleman of good repute, who, being duly sworn, deposes that about the year 1753 or 4, his elder brother, William Hunter, of Nansemond County, in Virginia, was married to a certain Ann Norsworthy by an orthodox minister named Webb, and remarkable for being near-sighted, and the marriage was celebrated in the house of a certain widow Norfleet in the vicinity of the town of Suffolk. The said Norsworthy Hunter is the only issue of this union and was always held as the lawful heir of Thomas Norsworthy, deceased, said to be an only surviving brother of the said Ann Norsworthy; that the said Norsworthy Hunter, at court held for the Isle of Wight County, 6th July 1786, upon his motion, together with William Whitfield, James Young, Francis Young, his security, received a certificate for letters of administration on the estate of Thomas Norsworthy, decd. in due form of law, signed by Francis Young, deputy clerk of court. Natchez, 22nd Oct. 1794. Sig: Henry Hunter. Before Manuel Gayoso, Stephen Minor and Joseph Vidal.

p. 303. William Hamberlin versus Charles Collins. Wm. Hamberlin made oath that in 1791 I was informed that Winlock made his escape out of the country. I went to Mr. Charles Collins and inquired where said Winlock was and Mrs. Collins made answer that he went to his plantation. I told her I had been by his plantation and he was not there, etc. 16 Aug. 1794. Before John Smith at Villa Gayoso. // George Jones appeared, 16 Aug. 1794, and made oath that in 1791 he and Charles Collins were hunting in the woods met with Winlock and Gilbert riding and asked Winlock where he was going and he said he was going to Bayou Pierre and Winlock called Collins aside and when Collins returned from Winlock he told me that Winlock had cleared out. Winlock cautioned Collins not to inform anybody of their escape. // He, Charles Collins, asked me to go down to Hamberlin's with him he told him that Winlock was going away and he had better follow him as he was his security and if the tobacco did not pass he would have to pay him. Sig: John King. // In suit of Wm. Hamerlin versus Charles Collins, having considered the disputes of the parties and perceive by every circumstance that Charles Collins must have been conscious of Winlock making his escape out of the country, I therefore gave judgment against the afsd. Chas. Collins, which is transmitted to Your Excellency. 16 Aug. 1794. Sig: John Smith. // p. 304. Having examined the proceedings and parties, I do commission Capt. Wm. Vousdan to hear the further evidence and make report. // In obedience to Your Excellency's order I have examined the proceedings and think from the evidence that Charles Collins knew that Winlock was leaving the country and was in collusion and he must pay the costs.

p. 304. Complaint of William Owens against John Henderson for having traded him two horses for a gun which horses, Owen represents, were not the property of the said John Henderson. // Henderson summoned to appear, and, at the request of Owens, Barney McLaughlin and Jonas Scoggins also summoned. Parties appeared the 17th, also Henry Manadue. McLaughlin stated that a gray horse ran in the range near Owens and the mare had two colts, one of them was lame and he had considered these creatures to be the property of John Henderson but he was not certain. He was at Owens when Henderson came there and began a conversation about trading for a gun and they did trade. Henderson gave the horse and mare and two colts for the gun. He gave a bill of sale for them. Owen asked what if these horses are not yours and Henderson said if they were not I'll give other creatures of equal value. Sig: Bernard McLaughlin. When Martin Owens, son of Wm., came for the bill of sale to Henderson from Quirk and when he saw it he said he believed they were the same creatures John Henderson had given a bill of sale for and the parties appeared satisfied. Sig: Henry Manadue. Jones Scoggans, at Henderson's request, testified that he was at Mr. Owens when Henderson came and traded two horses he owned that were running out, etc. Signed. Owens to prove the horses belong to other than John Henderson.

p. 306. Elizabeth Baker versus Ebenezer Rees. Eliz. Baker represents that she is indebted to the house of Clark and Rees and the account is incorrect, one item being for the hire of a negro, which negro, she claims, was the property of her deceased son. 29 Sept. 1791. // To be communicated. // This is to certify that I did in 1789 owe Mr. Baker $16 in silver which Mr. Ebenezer Rees assumed on account of Col. Peter Bryan Bruin and have the receipt of Mrs. Baker in lieu of that sum, both dated at Natchez 10 Feb. 1789. Signed Frederick Mann. Wit: John Burnet. // I ack. to have received from Mrs. Baker at the hands of Mr. Tomlinson certificates of tobacco by her delivered amounting to $937, out of which I promise to pay Mr. Jacob Copperthwait $137 as soon as I receive the cash from the certificates. Signed: Daniel Clark. Receipt of Copperthwait. I was present at the dispute of Mrs. Baker and Mr. Rees in Feb. 1789, respecting the hire of a negro man purchased by Mr. James Baker, son of Mrs. Baker, etc. Signed: Jesse Greenfield. [Accounting detailed.] p. 311. Arbitrators: Messrs. Cochran and Woolley. Decision that there was due to Clark and Rees by the late Mrs. Baker, now Mrs. Tomlinson, on 1st July 1793, $260. Sept. 5, 1794. Sig: Joseph Murray. Approved by Manuel Gayoso.

p. 312. William Smith versus Manuel Rice. William Smith, an inhabitant of this government residing at Bayou Pierre, begs leave to represent that sometime in the year 1791 he had engaged Manuel Rice, an inhabitant of Bayou Pierre, to complete a piece of work for your petitioner at the Nogales; needing a yoke of oxen your petitioner let him have them and not long afterward, owing to wanton and cruel abuse of said Rice, they both died. The following circumstance which he can prove, your petitioner submits: A certain warm day being driving the oxen, the said Rice laid down in the woods to sleep during which time, the oxen strayed from the place where they were standing some short distance to the shade. On his awakening and finding them gone, he followed them and tied or chained them with a log to a stump and with a hand spike or piece of wood which he had used to load and unload the timber he was hauling did beat and abuse the oxen at intervals for upward of an hour and did not desist until ordered by the Commandant to do so, as also to let go his oxen. Upon which one of them immediately dropped dead and the other died the ensuing morning. Natchez. Aug. 19, 1794. Signed: William Smith. // The parties being residents of Bayou Pierre, Col. Bruin will examine the case, make me a report and give his opinion. As Mr. Beauregard is actually present in this place, the petitioner will apply to him of what he knows on the subject. // I certify that, being military store-keeper at the Nogales, William Smith had a driver named Rice who beat and abused the oxen he drove very much. 20 Aug. 1794. Sig: Juan Barno Ferrusola. // I certify that being Commandant of the Fort at Nogales, William Smith, master carpenter at the block-house, had a driver named Rice who beat and abused the oxen of the said Smith very much, for which I frequently reprimanded him. Natchez. 20 Aug. 1794. Signed: Elias Beauregard. // We, the undersigned, certify that in the year 1790 we found the carcass of an ox, belonging to William Smith, master-carpenter at the block-house at Nogales, lying near the fort very much beat and bruised which we attribute to the person who had the ox in charge and we were ordered by Don Elias Beauregard, Commandant, to throw the carcass in the river. Nogales. Aug. 25, 1794. Pedro Azevedo, Agnacio Delino. [Testimony of Solomon Whitley, Elizabeth Whitley, William Bassett Robert Campbell, William Chaney, Mathew Fallon, James Wood, Patrick Fallon, Isaac Rapalje, and others, some at the request of Rice saying the oxen died of distemper. Several mentioned Mr. William Beard who was the partner of Smith in his work at Nogales.] Natchez. Whereas it appears from the evidence produced by William Smith that the oxen died of the abuse received from Emanuel Rice, which is not contradicted by said Rice's evidences, therefore the said Smith is entitled to receive the value of them from the said Rice. Signed: Manuel Gayoso de Lemos. Cost: 2 decrees, etc. $11.

p. 318. Groves Morris versus Richard Harrison. Personally appeared 17 Aug. 1794, Groves Morris and, on oath, declared that some time in Oct. last he applied to Capt. Harrison to engage him as an overseer "on which we agreed and I endeavored to do my duty as such. Later there arose a dispute between Capt. Harrison and myself and I was very desirous to leave his employ but was persuaded by Harrison not to do so." When the crop was almost finished he would come into the field to pick quarrels and finally ordered him off the place and had the plank floor taken out of his room. Etc. Before John Smith. // April 1794, I was at Mr. Morris's one evening and Mrs. Morris called Morris in to coffee and Morris replied that he hardly had time to drink it he was so backward in his work by the losing of Bristo from the plow, that he was afraid he would hardly make one share, let lone two. Mr. Morris went to Natchez and got Mr. Mayes to help him plow, etc. Martha (M) Mayes. Before John Smith. [She said she was frequently there as she had her weaving there and she always saw him at work.] 11 Oct. 1794. // Abraham Mayes testifies. Signed. // Richard Harrison's statement, 8 Aug. 1794. Francis Spain's testimony, also James Spain, John Donaldson, Jeremiah Miller. Alexander Callender and Wm. Irwin appointed by the parties to examine the crop and state that it was more the fault of the employer than the overseer. It also appearing that Mr. Harrison drove off the overseer and would not permit him to finish the job. Therefore Mr. Richard Harrison will be accountable to said overseer, Groves Morris, for the whole of his part of the crop, according to their agreement, which appears to have been two shares out of twelve, and the said Mr. Harrison is also to pay the cost of this suit. Communicated the above to Mr. Harrison. Sig: Jean Girault. 11 Dec. 1794. Groves Morris was ordered with his two horses to finish the crop.

p. 324. David Ferguson versus Samuel Forman. David Ferguson represents that he has Samuel Forman's note for the delivery of 2500 pounds of inspected tobacco at some convenient landing place on the Kentucky River by Feb. 1, 1793 but which he has in no wise performed; that he repeatedly applied to sd Forman for settlement in cash on reasonable terms, which he has evaded; asks for an order of settlement. Sig: David Ferguson. Natchez. 14 Aug. 1794. // Aug. 20, Samuel Forman ordered to appear tomorrow. Sig: Gayoso. // 19 Nov. 1794. Samuel Forman appeared and promised to pay Ferguson. Messrs. Murray and Thomas appointed to ascertain the cash price of tobacco in Kentucky. Court charges $6.

p. 325. Estevan Minor versus Ebenezer Dayton. Don Estevan Minor, Capt. of the Royal Armies and

Adjt. Major of the Post of Natchez, represents that Ebenezer Dayton owes him $500 for cattle which he is now killing at the Post of Nogales and appropriating the proceeds thereof to other purposes; asks that since this is a privileged debt the Commandant at said Post be directed to retain the sum in his hands and remit the same to the Secy. of this government. 2 Dec. 1794. Sig: Estevan Minor. // [Dayton claims the cattle was bought from Bisland, etc. Bisland also petitions.]

p. 328. Adam Cloud versus William Vousdan. Your petitioner has been charged of theft by Mr. Vousdan in various places and companies; asks for a hearing and the attendance of all evidences. 11 Nov. 1794. Sig: Adam Cloud. // Vousdan accused Cloud of having two pigs that belonged to his negro "Ben". 17 Nov. // Wit: Ezekiel Dewitt who declared that the negro was unreliable. [Long and repetitious.]

p. 333. Thomas Wilkins versus Ebenezer Dayton who owes him more than $300, most of which for oxen delivered to him at the Post of Nogales long since, etc. 3rd Dec. 1794. Signed. Dayton's reply states that the same he made to Mr. Minor will cover the question, except the amount claimed is not correct. // Dayton promises an obligation of William Brocus in one month and two others in two months.

p. 334. Clement Dyson versus Jeremiah Bryan, for the return of his note to Bryan which he had paid and Bryan had never returned although repeatedly requested to do so. It appears that Dyson is now requested to pay said note. Asks that said note be given up to him. 22 Nov. 1794. // Clement Dyson will produce witnesses before the alcalde where they reside and transmitted to me. Sig: Gayoso. // John Staybraker, of Villa Gayoso, appeared and made oath that he was present and saw Clement Dyson make payment to Jeremiah Bryan for a note of his and heard Dyson demand the note and Bryan said he could not find it. The next day when he came back to Natchez, Dyson asked Bryan for the note again and he said he could not find it. Sig: John Staybraker. // Thomas Dyson, of Villa Gayoso, made oath to the same. Before John Smith. Clement Dyson having made sufficient proof that he has paid the note the holder of it will give it up to the said Dyson or he shall have recourse on the property of Jeremiah Bryan, for what he has paid for it.

p. 335. Robert Davis versus Barnabus Higgins. [Higgins had brought suit agst Davis for taking some of his hogs. Davis has proof to the contrary and wants Higgin's assertion disproved in court. Testimony to be taken before Col. Hutchins.] Witnesses: John Ellis, Abram Ellis, Stephen and Thomas Ambrose, Elijah Phipps, Elijah Ambrose, Mrs. Foley, Hugh Davis, Henry Stroud, Landon Davis, Archibald Palmer, Thos. Cummins, John McKay. [Verdict rather complicated as it was the custom for hogs to run wild "on the island", marked so they could be identified.]

p. 338. James Stuart versus Samuel Davis, who, at the house of George Overaker in Natchez, where he had come, after sleeping some time in a chair, woke and pretended to have lost a sum of money and then and there accused Stuart who was present of having taken it, and Stuart asks that he may be permitted to vindicate his now injured character and the depositions of Mr. John Carmack, Joseph Woodward, John Thompson and Maurice Custard be taken and that upon finding the said Davis guilty, order him punished. Sig: James Stuart. 17 Jan. 1795. [Samuel Davis, "an old man" came into Overaker's drunk and after having another drink went into a back room and fell asleep in a chair. Once during the evening James Stuart and Maurice Custard went in the back room to warm and later Samuel Davis awoke and said he had been robbed and that James Stuart had been robber, but the witness declared that Stuart had not gone near said Davis, John Thompson who was there also declared the same. Character witnesses state that Stuart who came from Georgia had a good name and would not have taken the money: Joshua Howard, Isaac Alexander, William Ratcliff, Robert Abrams and Isaac Johnson. 5 June 1795.]

p. 346. Robert Creighton versus Jeremiah Routh, who owes him $272, as will appeared by a certificate of the widow, asks for payment from estate. Signed: Robert Creighton. Aug. 7, 1792. // William Murray, Esq. will inquire into the said case. Sig: Gayoso. // Sir; I examined Elijah, the elder son of Jeremiah Routh, decd. who wrote the certificate of the widow specifying that the said sum was just, and likewise looked over the inventory and the list of debts supposed to be due the deceased, Jeremiah Routh, I conceive the debt of Robert Creighton to be a privileged debt, being for wages. Your Excellency may think it proper to authorize a sale and some person to collect the debts. Sig: Wm. Murray.

p. 347. Thomas Lovelace versus James McNulty. Bayou Sara, 2 Feb. 1794. Sir: I enclose two letters from Thos. and Edward Lovelace by way of petition against one McNulty, of the Opelousas. A considerable time ago, I wanted an attachment on the horses. No answer. Signed: Francis Poussett. I exchanged horses with Mr. James McNulty for which he gave me over and above the barter his notes for $12, etc. Sig: Thomas Lovelace. David Jones certifies that he was a witness.

p. 349. Articles of agreement, 7 Feb. 1794, between Luis Valeret and Abram Valeret, both of the dist. of Natchez, Prov. of West Florida, for and in consideration of Abram Valeret making and burning a kiln of brick to the amount of 50 or 60 thousand, the profits arising from the sale of which bricks to go wholly to the said Luis Valeret for lawful debts. Abram to furnish his own material. The yoke of oxen and cart to be Abram's lawful property in payment. Both sign. Wit: William (X) Beard.

p. 350. Samuel Cooper versus John Vaucheret, against whom said Cooper has had an account of many years. // Mr. Vaucheret will pay in 8 days. Arbitrators appointed to settle the matter.

p. 351. Richard Harrison versus John and Alexander Henderson, whose note for $372 dated 1791 and received nothing of principal or interest. // Natchez, 20 March 1794. Messrs Henderson will make immediate payment or give their reasons. Signed: Gayoso. // The majority of the creditors of Alexander and John Henderson have agreed to give them time and to receive portions according to the amount of their demands. The demand of Richard Harrison, not being of a privileged nature, must conform to the agreement.

p. 353. Estevan Minor versus James Hyland. Minor represents that Mr. Mordecai Throckmorton is indebted to him for $400 for his half of the price of a plantation bought of Richard Bell which obligation is transferred to the petitioner, and whereas James Hyland is indebted to Throckmorton for the rent of the said plantation and the hire of a negro, therefore your petitioner asks that said James Hyland make payment of the sum of $150, being the sum he owes, into the hands of the petitioner on account of the price of the said plantation, as a privileged debt. 10 Jany. 1795. // The debt being privileged, James Hyland will make payment of same to Capt. Minor in consequence of which this decree shall be notified to Mr. Throckmorton and James Hyland. Agreement between Throckmorton and James Hyland dated 1 Jany. 1794 and witnessed by Isaac Newman and Simon Newman. Throckmorton assigns the above payment of $150 to Stephen Minor.

p. 355. Daniel Douglass versus Patrick Connelly. Douglass has a note in hand of Patrick Connelly to be paid in a horse or mare valued at $40, as by note presented, for which the petitioner gave full value in saddlery, etc. Conner is well able to pay the same, but he has refused to do so. Natchez. 3rd March 1795. Sig. Daniel Douglass. // Connelly appeared and having no just cause not to pay his note he was ordered to pay same and the cost of the suit.

p. 356. Stephen Minor versus Anthony Hutchins, two of whose notes of hand he holds for labor done by his hireling, William Ivery, due since April 1791 and 1792, with a balance due of $112, exclusive of interest. 14 Aug. 1794. Sig: Stephen Minor. [Arguments pro and con and counter claims but settled 3 June 1794.]

p. 356. Negress Amy versus the heirs of Asahel Lewis. Petitioner represents that her former master gave her, in recompense of her service one horse which she has in her possession but finding that the heirs of her sd master intend to deprive her of the said horse, begs that Mr. William Collins and Mr. Abner Phipps give their declaration before Mr. Ezekiel Forman, Esq. of what they know of the right to the said horse, to the end that title to the horse may be confirmed. She signed with a mark. April 23, 1794. // Ezekiel Forman will take declaration on same. // Owing to the illness of Mr. Forman, this is transferred before G. Benoist, Esq. // This is to certify that I went to trade with Mr. Lewis for his black horse but he said I must apply to Amy for him for he had given her the said horse. Sig: Wm. Collins. Pine Ridge, 24 Apr. 1794. Before me, Gabriel Benoist. // Personally appeared Abner Pipes, Jr. who, on oath, declared that he once heard the late Asahel Lewis, speaking to the negro woman, Amy, refer to the black horse as hers. Signed.

p. 363. Nehemiah Carter versus Anthony Hutchins, who has a mare in his possession belonging to the petitioner which he refuses to deliver. Sig: Nehemiah Carter. // The parties to prove the property before Isaac Johnson. [Appeared Samuel Heady, William Mulhollan, Stephen Stephenson, Israel Smith, Elias Bonnell, and make depositions. No decision given.] Anthony Hutchins submits the decision to a further inquiry, 3 June 1795.

p. 364. Ebenezer Dayton versus the inhabitants of Natchez. Agreement made and concluded between John O'Connor, Esq., Lewis Evans, as trustees appointed by the inhabitants of Natchez Township to keep in repair the public roads of the one part and Ebenezer Dayton, of Natchez, of the other: For twelve months, Ebenezer Dayton to be in charge and keep in repair the newly made road from the Church to the Natchez landing, and shall at the end of said term leave the road in good repair, for which he binds himself and heir in the penal sum of $200 and in case of default on his part to be paid to the inhabitants of the said township; and the said O'Connor and Lewis Evans, for themselves and the said inhabitants obligate themselves to pay the said Ebenezer Dayton 130 Spanish milled dollars as follows, $65 at the end of six months and $65 at end of 12 months. All sign. Wit: J. Murdoch. // Dayton itemized the number of days he worked, etc. Petitions claim Dayton failed in his agreement. Sig: Antonio Gras, Joseph Murray, Lewis Evans, Robert Scott, Edward McCabe, John Arden, John Wilson, Daniel Douglass, George Overaker, George Cochran, D. Odum, and Maurice Stacpoole. [Pages of this and accounts of Dayton.] p. 384. John Wilson being called upon to tell what he knows gives a list of inhabitants in the Natchez Township who had to contribute to the upkeep of the road under Dayton's care. Don Francisco de Arroyo, Don Estevan Minor, Benjamin Montsanto, John Bisland, John Scott, John Wilson, William Barland, Louis Valeret, Hugh Coyle, Lewis Evans, Reuben Baxter, Sargeant Sullivan, William Falconer, the Indian interpreter, estate of Don Juan Rodriguez, in the possession of Favrot, the house next to it near the hill, the house inhabited by Don Francis Caudel, Madame Segovia, Madame Bently, Sergeant of the Artillery, Simon de Arze, Mr. Davenport for the house he lives in, Mr. John O'Connor, Mr. Edward McCabe, the house John Gali lived in, Pedro Ancid, Don Manuel Texada, Francisco de Rosa, Mr. Frederick Mann, Messrs Clark and Rees, David Ferguson, Messrs. Robert and George Cochran, Mr. Macarty, Signor Ferado himself and house, Signor Charles Maltez, Mr. Balding, Don Antonio Gras, Mr. Joseph Murray, Mr. Thomas Wilkins, Messrs. Moore and Scott, Alexander Moore for his house, Mr. George Overaker, Mr. Thomas Tyler.

p. 390. John Barclay versus James Todd. Barclay prays redress for an injury received from a certain James Todd which affected his honor and that of his family. The said Todd was the son of an old and intimate friend of your petitioner and being at Bayou Sara in a distressed condition and no subsistence but the product of his daily labor, your petitioner, by reason of friendship for his father, received him into his house free of charge where he remained until the time of your petitioner's departure for the U.S. where he had an affair to settle at this time. He gave the said Todd the charge of his plantation and property and the care of his family, consisting of his wife and four small children. Your petitioner has been married near ten years and during that time lived in the most perfect harmony with his family having always found his wife estimable, affectionate and virtuous, to all of which she joined the advantages of a good education given to her by her parents. But this traitor, in the named of friendship, at once ruined the petitioner and his whole family, having found means by a moment of weakness in the wife of your petitioner to seduce her and was not ashamed to live openly with his wife and had a child by her which he publicly acknowledged to be his own. Your petitioner returning from a long and dangerous journey during which he had met with many misfortunes, asks that you have this imposter arrested immediately and punished according to the wise laws of the kingdom. Signed: John Barclay. // The necessary steps will be taken. Sig: Grand-Pre. // Another petition of John Barclay that the damage done to his property amounts to $300 and asks that this be ordered paid by the perpetrator, James Todd. 22 June 1795. Sig: John Barclay. [A statement of the damages.] // Francis Poussett, Esq. and Mr. Henry Hunter appointed to examine the plantation and value the damages, caused to John Barclay by the neglect of James Todd. Sig: Carlos de Grand-Pre. // Petition of John Barclay showeth that whereas there has been a controversy between the petitioner and James Todd who has been and is confined in this place on the suit and representation of said petitioner, said Todd has made and given your petitioner full satisfaction for all injuries done to his plantation and all injuries directly or indirectly suffered by me from said Todd, and as it is your petitioner's wish that every recollection of that animosity be buried in oblivion; asks that the said Todd be immediately liberated from his confinement, he paying the cost of the present suit. 5 June 1795. Sig. John Barclay.

p. 394. Charles McKiernan versus Ebenezer Dayton, who, being in want of cattle for his butchery at Nogales, solicitated your petitioner to take some cattle from a certain Stephen de Alva who was indebted to your petitioner, the said Dayton promising to pay your petitioner therefore. // Natchez. 4 Jany. 1795. The parties being heard this day and a letter from the creditors of Dayton noted, it is ordered that the said Dayton pay the amount named in said letter to be paid on the 28th and not before, which is one month from the time Mr. McKiernan proposes to depart from this government. Sig: Carlos de Grand-Pre.

p. 395. John Still Lee versus John Vaucheret. John Still Lee, formerly an inhabitant of this government but now residing at Tombigbee, states that years ago, John Vaucheret, being then a merchant, contracted with the petitioner to furnish him with goods to keep a retail store in the country to be a joint account and risk, etc. His property sold and applied wholly to Vaucheret, including a quantity of cattle and a plantation belonging to the orphans of the late James Holliday whose widow the petitioner had lately married and which she made many fruitless attempts to recover for her children. // Messrs. Robert Scott, George Cochran and Joseph Murphy appointed examine witnesses and accounts and make report. At request of Vaucheret, Peter Walker was added to the above committee. [Several pages of accounts.] 12 Feb. 1795 the arbitrators report that George Cochran was obliged to go to N. O. and someone be appointed in his place. Sig: Joseph Murray for the arbitrators. John Murdoch named, who also went to N. O., and John O'Connor apptd. // Decree, April 10, 1795, $470 due from John Vaucheret to John Still Lee. John Vaucheret to pay the cost of the suit. Sig: Gayoso de Lemos. [Several pages of the fees charged in suit.]

p. 422. Charles McKiernan versus Thomas Green who owes him $18, being for medicine due to Samuel Flowers who transferred the acct. to your petitioner. 16 Sept. 1795. // Mr. Green notified and he rpplied that he would not do it until Dr. Flower returned to him the order he gave to him on Mr. Reed or prove that he has not received any part of that account. 22 Sept. 1795. Villa Gayoso. Sig: David McFarland. // Same date. Charles McKiernan asks that an execution be granted on the property of said Green for the amount of the debt. // This being a privileged debt, let an execution be issued against the property of Thomas Green for the amount of the debt and cost unless the said debt be paid immediately. // Green said he had already paid or if he had not he would never pay; that he had no property to be executed upon. Sig: John Ferguson. Fees: $4.

p. 422. Polser Shilling versus Matilda Surlott. Polser Shilling, of this district, represents that he was condemned to pay to Matilda Surlott $10 from which judgment he appeals; asks that Michael Infield and Lawrence Heard give testimony. A few days before the petitioner went to N. O. the father of Matilda Surlott came to his house and requested hospitality which was granted to said Surlott and his family for a few days, the said Surlott being sick. He remained in the house of your petitioner all the time he was gone to New Orleans and on his return your petitioner was compelled to turn them out. The said Matilda Surlott assisted the wife of your petitioner to spin and when the cloth was finished she received her proportion thereof and she now demands payment for same and the alcalde condemned me to pay the $10.

p. 423. Daniel Sullivan versus John Brooks, who owes him 25 gallons of good whiskey as will appear by his note of May 1794. 8 Aug. 1795. The parties appeared and it was agreed that John Brooks should make payment in a horse or cattle to be appraised by two persons named by the parties, at the rate of 12 rials for each gallon of whiskey. And John Brooks shall pay the cost of suit. Both sign.

p. 423. Daniel Griffin versus Mary Calvit. Petitioner represents that he received a note from John Farquhar drawn by Frederick Calvit, deceased, for $70 which note your petitioner lost in 1789, at which time, with the Governor's permission, he gave public notice thereof, and the said note not appearing your petitioner demanded payment from the widow of said Calvit, who refused payment unless your petitioner could produce said note. Sig: Gabriel Griffin. // To be communicated to the widow.

p. 425. Robert and George Cochran versus Mordecai Richards, who owes them $167 by sundry notes. They have been informed that Richards has made bets on a horse race and has lost $100 to Daniel Douglass, Joseph Duncan and others which is immediately to be paid; asks an order to attach sufficient property to discharge the debt owing them, and a final settlement of his account. 25 Nov. 1795. // If foregoing can be proved property will be attached. Sig: Grand-Pre.

p. 426. Jesse Hamilton versus Archibald Douglass. Hamilton petitions that he gave to Archibald and Daniel Douglass various materials to make saddles for your petitioner, of which they made three very badly, and refused to restore the remaining materials and to settle their accounts with him. 16 Sept. 1795. // Archibald Douglass represents that Jesse Hamilton bound himself by the note hereunto annexed, whereby he promised to give Douglass three good cows for three saddles but he refused, etc. // 21 Oct. 1795. Jesse Hamilton will deliver without delay to Archibald Douglass the three cows according to his obligation. // Parties appeared and agreed to leave the examination of cattle to Daniel Perry and Adam Lanehart.

p. 426. John Simpson versus Archibald McDuffy and James Singleton. 17 Nov. 1792. Messrs Nehemiah Carter and Nicholas Rabb hereby appointed to examine the work done by James Singleton on the plantation of Archibald McDuffy. Award: one-half the value for the said Singleton's labor. 19 Nov.

1795. Signed by both.

p. 427. Edward McCabe versus Hugh Thompson, who owes him $20. McCabe asks for payment or work on his house. 17 Nov. 1795. Signed. // Thompson not having replied, let sufficient property be executed for the debt. // Thompson replied that he had nothing but his tools and house furniture.

p. 428. Joseph Slater versus Solomon Wisdom. 1795. To clothing and board of Sarah Wilson at $2 per month for two years $96. // Natchez, 30 May 1795, errors excepted. Solomon Wisdom kept an orphan child in his care, signed: Joseph Vidal. 10 Aug. 1795. Arthur Cobb and Susannah Cobb, his wife, do hereby certify that they do not think that Sarah Wilson, the daughter of James Wilson, deceased, whom Mr. Solomon Wisdom had in his care, was, when she came to him, anywise able to earn her living for she was too small and sickly, neither do they think she is able to earn her living now. May 29, 1795. Signed: Arthur Cobb, Susannah Cobb. // The undersigned doth say that Sarah Wilson, dau. of the late James Wilson did live at his house 12 months before said Sarah did live at Mr. Wisdom's and the opinion of the undersigned is that the said Sarah was able to earn her clothes and victuals at the time she went to live with Mrs. Wisdom. Signed: Robert Abrams. Wit: Isaac Johnson. // Same deposition from Kesiah West. // Philander and Esther Smith declare the same as Arthur and Susana Cobb, concerning the above. // Messrs. Dunbar, Burling, Johnson and Greenfield appointed to determine the just sum to be paid to Joseph Slater* for keeping Sarah Wilson. May 30, 1795. Sig: Grand-Pre. Award: Joseph Slater shall pay to Solomon H. Wisdom, at the rate of $2.50 per month for two years $60 for the whole. Second Creek, 13 Oct. 1795. Signed: Isaac Johnson, Thomas Burling, Jesse Greenfield and William Dunbar. // Approved.

p. 429. The King versus James Cooper. The declaration of Elizabeth Campbell saith that she heard James Cooper tell her father concerning his loading a man's gun at the Walnut Hills, and he heard the report of a gun and the man was not seen any more. 20 Aug. 1795. Before William Cooper. Eleanor Pruett appeared and said that some time past, James Cooper was at her house and was telling her what he had done at Walnut Hills and that he had put powder and mud in a man's gun and rammed it down and the man went away and he had heard the report of the gun and it was like a swivel on a cannon and he never heard of the man any more. 20 Aug. 1795. Before William Cooper.

p. 429. Daniel Douglass versus John Dunn, who owes him $37, and asks an execution against property for the said debt. 7 Jany. 1796. // March 9, 1796. Execution levied on a crib of corn of 150 bushels now in the care of Wm. Baker. Sig: Wm. Gillespie.

p. 430. Negress Emma versus heirs of Asahel Lewis. Emma represents that Asahel Lewis did in his lifetime promise to give her her liberty. // Let the papers of Asahel Lewis be examined to see if there be any document to prove the statement. // In pursuance of the foregoing the annexed paper which appears to have been written by said Lewis was found by which he gives liberty to the negro woman, named Emma, and her son Henry. Messrs George Cochran, John Murdoch, Joseph Bernard and Charles Boardman appointed to examine the same and give their opinion as to its authenticity. Signed: Carlos de Grand-Pre. Nov. 1, 1794. Know all men, etc. it is my wish to set my negro wench, Emma, free. Sig: Asahel Lewis. // John Williams is a native of Maryland and married and 41 years. [Apparently made deposition.]

p. 439. William B. Smith versus Terza Duon. Smith represents that he purchased from James McNulty a horse described in a bill of sale annexed; the said horse now in the possession of Frederick Barrow and asks that said Barrow return horse to petitioner. 10 Oct. 1795. Sig: William B. Smith. // Bill of sale. To James McNulty a sorrell horse branded T. R. with a bald face, two hind feet white and eleven years old, the said horse, being in Mr. Collins' possession at Penrice's old place. Signed Ethrington. Wit: Noel Soileau. // I do hereby authorize Mr. John Hubbard to take my sorrell horse I bought of John Ethrington and was left with Mr. Collins on the plantation where Penrice used to live. I authorize Mr. Hubbard to act as if I were present. Sig: James McNulty. 29 Aug. 1791. // Mr. Collins. Sir: Please let Mr. James McNulty have my sorrell horse I left in your possession. This shall be your receipt for same. I expect to see you in the course of a month. Sig: John Ethrington. // Natchez. 23 March 1792. I certify that I did get a petition wrote to Pointe Coupee for Terza Duon against John Ethrington for some property he had received of her and was always of the opinion that a sorrell horse, the property of John Ethrington, was in consequence of said petition given to said Tursa Duon. I have often heard that no part of the property of Mr. Ethrington belonged to anyone but Turza Duon, except a

* Error: Solomon Wisdom instead of Slater.

plain gold ring and some earrings, from her father, David Tanner. Signed Lewis Alston. // The horse Mr. Smith has demanded from Mr. Barrow is mine. I let Mr. Barrow have the horse for his wife to ride to the Rapides. The same bill of sale Mr. Smith sent to Pointe Coupee by Mr. Cady but the Commandant of that post gave me the horse for a just debt that Ethrington owed to me which revoked the bill of sale. Better than three years ago I saw Mr. McNulty at Mr. Valleret's and he said that he would take the horse from me and I told him that I would go to the government and did so. Mr. McNulty did not appear. I told His Excellency about the bill of sale and how I came by the horse. He told me that if I could prove what I said that I could keep the horse. I applied to Lewis Alston and he got the petition wrote for me which I presented to the Commandant at Pointe Coupee and the Governor told me that I should keep the horse. Oct. 13, 1795. Sig: Tursa Duon. // Oct. 27, 1795, Natchez. Mrs. Duon not having appeared to answer the claim of William Smith respecting the horse, she is ordered to appear without fail on the next day of audience, which will be on Wed. the 28th, and in default she will be barred from having any hearing hereafter. Sig: Grand-Pre. // Oct. 25, 1795. I notified this decree to Madame Duon. She said that she will attend on Wednesday if she can but she does not think it is possible. Fees: $3-4 rials. John Ferguson, constable. // Natchez, 12 March 1796. Whereas the term granted to Mrs. Tersa Duon for producing vouchers for her claim for the horse in dispute between her and Mr. William Benjamin Smith has ellapsed, she is therefore ordered to deliver the said horse immediately to him and pay the cost of suit but if she, in the future produces positive proofs of her right she shall be admitted. Sig: Carlos de Grand-Pre. // Communicated this to Wm. Cooper, Esq. on his plantation on Sandy Creek. Sig: Wm. Gillespie, constable.

p. 440. Estevan Minor versus Ebenezer Dayton, who is indebted to him for $600 and legal interest. 9th Jany. 1796. (Detailed statement follows.)

p. 442. Everard Green versus John Richey, who has cut a quantity of timber in the cypress swamp granted to your petitioner, without his permission, but on the contrary your petitioner did several times order him to desist which he refused, using many injurious expressions against your petitioner and his father; asks that Richey may be ordered to pay petitioner for the timber which he has cut and appoint capable persons to value the same. 30 Sept. 1796. Sig: Everard Green. // Same date. In consequence of the statement made by the petitioner, John Richey is ordered immediately to evacuate the land belonging to petitioner on which he has cut timber for his own personal benefit without consent of the lawful owner and it is further ordered that all the timber cut on said land shall remain the property of the petitioner, the said Richey being expressly forbidden to meddle therewith unless some compromise shall take place between the two. Signed: Grand-Pre. // Communicated this to John Richey and he says that he has cut no timber on the land of Mr. Green and has the government's permission for what he has done but he will appear at the government house immediately. // John Richey represents that the petition of Everard Green as to his cutting timber on his land is without foundation, that the petitioner cut timber, to make a flat-boat to carry logs to N. O., on the land of James Mather, with his permission. Green made a similar complaint to His Excellency the Gov., who, hearing the truth, ordered Green to desist from troubling your petitioner as will appear from the decree herewith presented. 15 Oct. 1796. Sig: John Richey. // Said Green shall pay all costs and damages arising from his unjust complaint. More of same.

p. 445. Henry Noble versus Ebenezer Dayton, who is indebted to him for $155 for labor. 13 April 1796. Sig: Henry Noble. [Details.]

p. 447. Elizabeth White versus the estate of Alexander Moore. Eliz. White represents that there was a contract between her deceased husband, Matthew white, and Alexander Moore, also deceased, dated 28 Dec. 1793, for such quantity of indigo seed as should be found on their plantation at the time of their agreement and such quantities as should be made the two following years, 1794 and 95. [This continues for a number of pages.]

p. 452. Phoebe Calvit versus William Calvit. Phoebe Calvit represents that by agreement between herself and William Calvit, her husband, dated 14 March 1795, her said husband bound himself to allow her a separate maintenance but your petitioner, having received so much ill treatment from him, was compelled to seek her residence elsewhere. She lived a long while with Mr. Gaillard and others until her husband, having made many fair promises to the late William Savage, curate of the parish, who persuaded your petitioner to return and live with her husband again and she did, but in fear. But from ill-treatment, she cannot continue to do so. She had a slave before her marriage, a horse, bed and furniture and a side saddle. The negro belonging to her was sold by her husband without her consent to

Dr. Farrar; asks an order that he deliver her another negro of equal value out of his own stock to be appraised by Thomas Vause and Daniel Miller, both of Bayou Sara, who knew the value of the petitioner's slave and other property. Sig: Phoebe Calvit.

p. 453. Thomas Wilkins versus Ebenezer Dayton. 18 Apr. 1796, appeared Ebenezer Dayton who declared himself bound to pay Messrs. Robert and George Cochran for 460 Mexican dollars and he does hereby mortgage a plantation, to him belonging, b. by Alexander Moore, Richard King, and Margaret Watts, for security of the above sum, etc. Thomas Wilkins represents that, being a creditor of Dayton as will appear by his obligations, etc., asks that the said mortgage shall not be executed. Sig: Thos. Wilkins.

p. 455. Andrew Beall versus Nehemiah Carter, who owes him $32 and interest since 1789 for the hire of negroes to saw plank. Sig: Andrew Beall. // Natchez, 1st Aug. 1795. Nehemiah Carter appeared and promised to pay at the end of Dec. //

p. 456. Bailey Chaney versus Robert Stark, indebted to him for $24; asks that John Smith, Esq., be authorized to take cognizance of the case, etc. 20 April 1796. Sig: Bailey Chaney. // Henry Milburn to execute the property of Col. Robert Stark to amt. of $32, 8 April 1796. // Stark's answer that the account included items dated back to 1779, and Chaney maliciously presented his petition 18 days before petitioner set out on his journey. Petitioner resided on the same plantation with the said Chaney for a number of years, etc.

p. 457. James McNulty versus James Patton and Job Routh. James McNulty, of Avoyelles, complains that he came to this district on or about 1791 and brought a stud horse and two mares with colts, soon after which they all strayed away and that his business obliged him to leave the country before he could collect them; that he publicly advertised them, describing their brands and flesh marks, offering a reward to be paid in leather and shoes, Robert Patton having been engaged to receive the said horses if found and give them salt at proper times and endeavor to accustom them to the range adjoining him. McNulty also said that the afsd horses were found but he has not received any of them or any satisfaction therefore; that immediately after they were found the said Job Routh made application to Patton saying he wanted the horse to ride but Patton said that the mares were accustomed to being with the horse and they would follow him. Routh agreed to take care of them all and return when they were called for. William Smith was a witness to this agreement with Job Routh who now denies the terms, and confirms same on oath. McNulty petitions, 30 April 1796, that William B. Smith, Nathan Thompson and John Shunk have not appeared to be sworn and appraise the horses which were left with Robert Patton and it appears they are combined to delay your petitioner and cause him ruin as he cannot arrive at the Arkansas in time to join his companions who are there waiting for him to proceed together on their business, prays a termination of the business so petitioner may get a just value of his horses. // Appraisers appointed to appear at my dwelling house tomorrow morning or they will be punished for contempt. // They appeared and appraised horses and signed: Wm. B. Smith, Nathan Thompson, John Shunk. Before De Grand-Pre. Natchez 28 April 1796. McNulty was paid the appraisal of the horses and the estate of Robert Patton paid the cost of the suit. 11 May 1796. [Case continued several pages.]

p. 468. Gabriel Ruffat, a resident of this post, petitions that since His Excellency's decree he has endeavored to procure money to make the payment of a note to Francisco Lorero and Co. and offered to pay interest to anyone who would lend it to him but without success; asks for time until he can receive a sum due him from Don Joseph Piernas. Natchez, 27 May 1796. // Order for seizure of property amount of debt.

p. 468. Roger Dixon versus John Richey and others, who owe him $60 being proceeds of sundry articles sold him in N. O. on account of your petitioner, for which he received the cash; that George Humphreys owes him $80 for hire of negroes as will appear by his note and interest. 21 Oct. 1795. Sig: Roger Dixon. // Execution against property of John Richey and Adam Sneider, his surety for the above debt. Sig: Manuel Gayoso de Lemos. 28 May 1796. // Property of George Humphreys executed one dark bay horse and one yoke of oxen.

p. 469. Christian Bingaman versus William Dunbar. Bingaman purchased a negro from Dunbar on account thereof he paid him at various times the proceeds of the petitioner's crops and now the said William Dunbar is indebted to him for $140 and he has refused to pay the same to petitioner. The Governor, hearing the reasons on both sides condemned the said Dunbar to pay the aforesaid amount which he has not done, etc. 2 Nov. 1795. // Wm. Dunbars presents account, 1791, 92, 93 and 94, with a balance due from Bingaman to Dunbar of $55. // Natchez 25 July 1796. Parties to call their accounts and the costs cancelled. All sign.

p. 472. Richard Harrison's petition: In the past year, the first season he ever attempted making a crop of cotton, he erected a gin for the purpose of cleaning it and the three condemned bags were a part of his crop last picked in the fall, after the leaves and snow had fallen and mixed with it; and as my first essay was not sent to the market as prime cotton. Also, he understands that the persons who took it to the landing immediately put it on an open boat where it lay several days exposed to excessive rains. 28 May 1796. Sig: Richard Harrison.

p. 474. Ezekiel Dewitt versus Rees and Gonzales. Dewitt represents that Ebenezer Rees and Luis Gonzales requested your petitioner to sell them some white oak trees which he did not wish to do, having but a small number on his land, but they having declared that they were in want of them to fill a contract with the King, your petitioner consented and agreed that the value of the timber should be estimated by disinterested persons; asks that appraisers be appointed for this. // Ebenezer Rees denied that he bought any trees from Dewitt but acted only as interpreter for Gonzales. // Daniel Grafton and Polser Shilling appointed to appraise the timber. We find 46 white oak trees cut and value them at $46.

p. 475. George Cochran and others versus Bennet Truly. 19 May 1796. I, Manuel Gayoso de Lemos, having received information that the gin for cleaning cotton, belonging to Bennet Truly, is not in good condition, from which a great injury may arise to the planters of this district, have notified sd Bennet Truly to discontinue the use of the said gin until the same be duly examined, etc., and for that purpose I have appointed Don Stephen Minor and William Vousdan, who will examine the same machine and report to me their opinion thereof. // 24 May 1796. [Rather favorable report on machinery but the gin open on all sides and too much cotton crowded into the gin at one time. Instructions sent Bennet Truly as to remedy for defects, showing governmental concern in protecting planters and their produce.] I proceeded to the plantation of Bennet Truly and not finding him there I administered oath to Mary Lum, his wife, and required her to make a true disclosure of the property of her husband, Bennet Truly, which she did as follows: Inventory of his property. Signed by Estevan Minor, Joseph Vidal and Jean Girault. Also account book of plantation and of the mill. A negro woman called "Amity" and her two children, were declared to belong to the sister of Bennet Truly, named Judith Truly and left in said Mary Truly's care, by reason of their mistress being gone to England. // We, the subscribers being appointed to inspect a piece of ginned cotton in the house of Edward McCabe, do hereby report. Owners report [sic.] Christian Bingaman, William Foster, Caleb King, R. and G. Cochran, Ferguson and Murdoch, Capt. Vousdan, Bennet Truly. [Report of cotton in detail and at great length.]

p. 485. William Foster versus Bennet Truly. Foster represents that some time in May last, your petitioner took to the gin of Mr. Rees and Truly some cotton to be ginned on shares; by inspectors appointed by Your Excellency the cotton was found to be wetted in bagging and rotten and afterwards burned by Your Excellency's orders. I was informed that Mr. Rees was ordered to pay for the cotton but has never done so; asks for consideration. // Order to pay by owners of gin. Ebenezer Rees agreed to pay on the arrival of Wm. Lintot's barge from N. O. which was agreed to by Mr. William Foster. 21 July 1796. Signed: Gayoso.

p. 488. George Cochran versus James McIntyre. Cochran represents that on 13 Nov. 1795 your petitioner entered into an agreement with James McIntyre, of this place, to furnish said McIntyre with certain sums of money to enable him to carry into effect a ginning machine, which sum $81 he has refused to pay. Signed Geo. Cochran. // Know all men, etc. that I, James McIntyre, having undertaken to construct a ginning machine conformably to one introduced into the government by John Barclay and not having the means of obtaining materials and supplies for completing the machine, I obligate myself to George Cochran, of Natchez, to fulfill the following engagement, etc. Accounts of the material and produce provided. p. 493. Award of arbitrators: Mr. George Cochran shall allow Mr. James McIntyre for the gin when he delivers it to him $150. 30 July 1796. Sig: Peter Walker, Lewis Evans and John Scott.

p. 493. Ferguson and Murdoch versus Rees and Truly. David Ferguson and John Murdoch represent that out of sundry quantities of cotton in the seed delivered by them to Bennet Truly to clean in the gin on the plantation of Ebenezer Rees they received from the said Truly 17 bales of cotton weighing 4485 pounds which Truly delivered to your petitioners; asks that intelligent persons inspect said cotton to check the fraud. Eleven bales were reported as entirely useless as water and seed have been introduced in these bales to add to weight; asks for pay for said cotton, $976. 8 June 1796. [Etc., etc.]

p. 498. Ebenezer Dayton, being of age, being sworn, deposeth at the request of Jacques Rapalje that he was at Nogales at the time when Jacques Rapalje purchased from Andrew Scandlan a very large pirogue for $20, saying that it was for the purpose of bringing corn from that place to Big Black for the deponent who had agreed for the said corn at 7 bits per bushel but before said Rapalje had any time to make use of the pirogue, the same was taken from him by order of by Capt. Deleno, then Commandant of the Nogales, for the use of the King to pursue a raft of timber which had the night before broke loose from the galley belonging to the King, which raft pursued by the pirogue was overtaken and safely taken to Natchez, which pirogue was soon afterwards stolen said to have been by some deserters from the King's galley and was afterwards said to have been sold on the coast below and came into the hands of Gideon Hopkins and the deponent saw said pirougue in the possession of said Hopkins at Natchez loaded with household goods bound for Bayou Sara. The government demanded said pirougue from said Hopkins but he, on the plea of the necessity to move his family which was then on board was allowed to proceed in her to Bayou Sara, giving his obligation to return and pay for her, depositing $16 in the hands of the government. 6 Oct. 1796. Signed: Ebenezer Dayton. // Appeared Gideon Hopkins who, on oath, deposeth that when he moved from the Natchez landing, the boat in which his effects were loaded was proved by Ebenezer Dayton to have belonged to Jacques Rapalje, an officer in the King's employ, and in consequence was claimed by the government. The deponent was permitted to proceed with his voyage on giving his obligation to return the boat or pay $20, which obligation he delivered to Mr. Girault but paid no money nor left any in deposit or otherwise with said Girault. A statement that he did is false. Sig: Gideon Hopkins. 3 Nov. 1796. [John Arden certifies that Hopkins gave no money to Girault.]

p. 499. George Cochran versus Ebenezer Dayton. Cochran represents that he holds a note of Ebenezer Dayton and Cornelius Ceeley for $122 payable in April Last. 1 Oct. 1796. // The trustees of the affairs of Ebenezer Dayton will acknowledge the above reservation, if such was made, that I may proceed with justice. Signed: Gayoso.

p. 500. James Stewart versus Caldwell Eastridg. James Stewart represents that when he left the U.S. he passed through the Creek Nation and there left his family at the household of Caldwell Eastridge when he returned to Georgia to settle some business. When the petitioner returned, he was accused by said Eastridg of having taken two of his horses from him, which being a malicious and false assertion, alarmed the petitioner much, but, being in Indian country, could have no recourse or redress but offered to prove the contrary by the declaration of the person of whom he bought the horse. Said Eastridg said that would satisfy him and promised to go there with the petitioner but at the moment of going he declined and sent his partner who came with the petitioner and received the certificate from the person whose horse he sat and that he brought no horse there and took none away but the one he sold the petitioner. Petitioner then moved to the settlement of the Tombigbee where he lived for several months in peace but one day, being on his way to the Tensas River where he had some horses, he was surprised by the aforesaid Eastridg and some accomplices he had brought with him who took the petitioner prisoner and carried him away to the Nation and treated him very cruelly, threatening to take his life and forcing him to give them his horse which was a fine one and his note for $40. The said Caldwell Eastridg has arrived in this government which is the first opportunity the petitioner has had to bring him to justice and asks for consideration and redress. 19 Jany. 1795. Sig: James Stewart. // James Stewart will produce the proof of the charge. // Jany 24, appeared Wm. Joiner who said he was with James Stewart going from Tensas to Tombigbee when they stayed at Mr. Cornel's on the Alabama River. The next morning they met on the other side of the river Caldwell Eastridg and a certain Rollins and they seized upon Stewart, telling him he was their prisoner. Stewart asked upon what authority he was taken and Estridg took out his gun and said "This is your authority and for a farthing I'd blow your brains out." They abused Stewart very much and took his horse, a valuable one and gave him another to ride and they mounted and made Stewart go before them and proceed to the Nation. The deponent returned home. Signed William Joiner. // 27th Jany. 1795. Personally appeared John Still Lee who, on oath, said that when James Stewart moved to Tombigbee River settlement he lived near the deponent; and he had a very valuable horse which he took over to Mr. Sinda's. The said Stewart went over to Tensas to bring home his horse and some time afterwards there was a report that Stewart had been waylaid and taken off to the Nation. The deponent happened to be at the Commandant's when Stewart returned and declared that one Caldwell Eastridg and one Rollins and Robert Walton had waylaid him at the Alabama river at Mr. Cornell's and had carried him to the Nation. [Same as above.] Signed: John Still Lee. p. 502. // Natchez, 27 January, 1795. Caldwell Eastridg appeared at Government house and declared that James Stewart had stolen two horses from him and he sent after them and they were found with two persons to whom Stewart sold them and they would not give them up unless

Stewart went in person to prove them. This testimony was sent to Col. McGilvray who advised the deponent not to go to Georgia where he would run risk. He was given an order if he ran upon Stewart to take him and bring him to justice, which he did and carried him to Gen. McGilvray where he was tried and condemned to pay the petitioner for his horses and he, in consequence gave up his horse and 40 pounds sterling for the other horse. He signs with a mark. // p. 505. James Stewart in answer denies Eastridg's charge, saying he was not tried legally but before some people of Eastridg's choosing, no evidences were produced against him, etc. The companions of Eastridg when he took Steward were desperadoes. 30 Jany. 1795. // Eastridg asks that the trial be postponed until he can have time to procure his evidences. // Petitioner is allowed one month from this day to produce his evidences. // Sandy Creek, personally appeared before me, William Cooper, Mrs. Elizabeth Morris and made oath that she was at Caldwell Eastridge's in the Creek Nation and Gen. McGilvray came there and said that it was nearer for Eastridge to go to Tombigbee than to go to Georgia for his horses for he had received papers from Georgia that satisfied him that Stewart had taken Eastridge's horses and in a short time Eastridg went after Stewart and brought him to the Nation and, as she understood carried him before Daniel McGilvray. Elizabeth (X) Morris. 7 March 1795. // I, Frederick Kimball do certify that, to the best of my recollection, in Sept. 1791, on a journey to the Creek nation I met Caldwell Eastridg, Robert Walton and a certain Rollins, all armed, and I asked them where they were travelling. They told me, to Pensacola. I went on my journey. When I arrived near Charles Weatherford's, I met Weatherford, and he asked me if I had met the above-mentioned men and I said I had. He said that Eastridg had accused Stewart of stealing horses from him. "But", said Weatherford, "Stewart has a fine horse which I believe is their principal object, and I have been trying to get an Indian to go and give Stewart notice of their design for I believe Stewart is as clear of stealing the horses as you or I." I went on my journey until I came near the Oconee and met one Crane Gustavus and I told him of the affair and he said Stewart was clear of the horses, for he believed he knew what was gone with Eastridge's horses. 7 Feb. 1795. Signed Frederick Kimball. Before Isaac Johnson. // Caldwell Estridge institutes suit against James Stewart for recovery of the money due on the note for 40 pounds sterling, being the value of a horse which said Stewart stole from him. 20 June 1795. // Robert Walton appeared before me and swears that Caldwell Eastridg had positive orders from Alexander McGilvray, Commander in Chief of the Creek Nation, to take James Stewart and his property to satisfy said Eastridg for the horses he stole. Etc. Signed: Robert Walton. // Charles Weatherford, being sworn, declared that he saw in Alexander McGilvray's possession a letter and other proof against James Stewart for stealing two horses. The letter came from Georgia where Stewart sold them. Etc. Signed: Chas. Weatherford. [Other depositions upholding Eastridge.] // Answer by Stewart that all the above depositions are false, with no witnesses, etc. Moreover all certificates are given by persons interested, one of them being an accomplice. // Deposition of John Holloday who makes oath that in 1791 the deponent was in the State of Georgia when James Stewart came in from the Creek Nation at the same time that Caldwell Eastridg accused said Stewart of having carried his two horses there the deponent said that Stewart brought but one horse; and he knew Eastridge's horses which he said he lost and the horse that Stewart brought down to Georgia was not the horse of Eastridge. He returned to the Creek nation with Stewart. [Etc. etc. rather complicated.] He said Stephen Sullivan gave his certificate that Stewart had bought a horse from him and Eastridge was satisfied with said certificate. Sig: John Holliday. 22 June 1795. Before Wm. Cooper. Etc. [The outcome not given.]

p. 510. James Kelly versus John Lanier. James represents that John Lanier claims that James Kelly killed a beef that was not his own; asks that Lanier be punished for an attempt to hurt the reputation of the petitioner, who luckily had several witnesses present when he killed the said beef, who can testify that it was of the petitioner's brand and no other. Witnesses: Daniel Strickland, John Lockhart, John Reed, James McIlhaney and John Keeting. 14 Sept. 1796. Signed James Kelly. // Isaac Johnson Esq. will take cognizance of this matter and make inquiry. Sig: Gayoso. // Second Creek. Deposition of John Lanier and above-named witnesses, also William Ratcliff, James Irwin, William Alexander, Martha Keeting, Charles Reed, Solomon H. Wisdom. // Whereas the evidences produced were against the petitioner, he is proved guilty of charge and he is to remain in confinement for eight days time, within which he is to produce what he has to allege in his favor. Sig: Gayoso.

p. 518. Benet Truly versus Ezekiel Dewitt who claims that Truly is indebted to him for $1025 with int. for five years, and produced his note, asking for payment of same. // Notified same. Benet Truly claims the signature is not his own. Truly represents that in 1789 Ezekiel Dewitt presented the petitioner a forged obligation for $1025 specie as will appear by the document annexed. 25 Mch. 1795. // In answer, Ezekiel Dewitt declares that he now is ready to declare who wrote the obligation in question, and declares that it was written by the said Bennet Truly. Ezekiel (E. D.) Dewitt. [A long statement by Bennet Truly covering many pages. William Thomas, a native of the United States of America, married, 51 years old; David (X) Patterson, nat. of Ireland, a bachelor and traveler, 24 years old; Ezekiel Dewitt, a nat. of the U.S., farmer, 53 years old; Dorsey Pentecost, Thomas Manley, George Miller, all these were witnesses.]

p. 531. Hardress Ellis versus John Hutchins. Hardress Ellis represents that he had a young mare running in the range of Mr. Farrar's horses and under the care of Mr. Farrar's stock-keeper, and he was surprised to find on sd mare another brand of some of Col. Hutchins' family and soon after discovered that she had been branded by John Hutchins and by him sold to Robert McCoughland, who is now in possession with John Hutchins' bill of sale for said mare.

p. 533. Benjamin Crubb versus James Sullivan. Petitioner left horses in the hands of James Sullivan of Kentucky to the amount of $150 which property was to be disposed of for the benefit of said Crubb and the proceeds remitted to him at this province. He has certain information to lay before Your Majesty that this property has been really sold by the said Sullivan and the value received by him, the said Sullivan has failed to remit to your petitioner; the said James Sullivan has money in the hands of Mr. David Ferguson for the amount he stands indebted to your petitioner; asks that an order be granted to receive same from David Ferguson. // Mr. David Ferguson will retain in his hands the money belonging to James Sullivan until further orders and petitioner will produce the proof he has to support his claim. Sig: Manuel Gayoso de Lemos. 26 Sept. 1796.

p. 534. John Smith and others versus William Kirkwood. 2 Dec. 1796. William Kirkwood is ordered to pay the amount of his notes to John Smith, Esq. and William Barland immediately or to appear before me next Saturday. Sign: Jean Girault.

p. 534. William Ferguson versus Nathaniel Tomlinson. Ferguson represents that Nathaniel Tomlinson about 1787 promise to give your petitioner a likely two-year old filley in place of a young horse he had in a mistake branded one of the petitioner. 15 Aug. 1796. // Nath'l. Tomlinson will deliver to the petitioner the said mare with reasonable increase. //

p. 535. William Ferguson versus Robert Moore. Ferguson represents that some years ago he left with Alexander Moore a patent for 500 acres of land, having no call for it until lately, knowing that it was safe, and desiring to ascertain a particular boundary, he wrote for it, Moore refused to give it up; asks that it be delivered to petitioner immediately. Sig: Wm. Ferguson. // Order as requested.

p. 536. Stephen Minor versus Gabriel Ruffat. Minor represents that Ruffat is indebted to him for $260. // Persons charged with the affairs of Gabriel Ruffat will pay what is legally due from said Ruffat to Stephen Minor. Sig: Gayoso.

This the end of Book F. with the usual certificate of same by David Harper, Keeper and Translator of Records, including 536 pages.

BOOK G

p. 1. James Jellison versus Alexander McIntosh. In the City of New Orleans, 27 May, 1780, appeared John Blommart, Esq., who declared that, by power of attorney given him by James Jellison, executed the 13th instant, which has not since been revoked, and by a special clause therein he does substitute Francisco Broutin to pursue the suit instituted by said Jellison versus Alexander McIntosh. Done in the presence of Don Fernandez Rodriguez, Peter Cowley and Adrian De la Plaza, residents of this city. Signed: Blommart. Before me, Leonard Miranza, notary public. // The undersigned attorney for James Jellison represents that Alexander McIntosh, now in this city, is indebted to the said Jellison for $439, which obligation was signed in the presence of Patrick Foley, then an officer under the said McIntosh, who verified and declared the said signature; asks that this document be translated into the Spanish language and returned to the petitioner. Sig: Francisco Broutin. // Don Juan Joseph Duforest being absent in the country, request that some intelligent person be appointed in his stead as interpreter in this case. // Richard French appointed interpreter in the above case. // N. O. 29 May 1780, appeared Patrick Foley who, on oath, declared that the note shown him was written by him and signed by the said Alexander McIntosh in his presence. Sig: Patrick Foley. Before Richard French and Leonardo Miranza. // N. O. 2 June 1780, appeared Ann Shell [Shield] lawful wife of Alexander McIntosh, who, being duly sworn, declared that the writing on said obligation was the hand-writing of her said husband, and written in his usual manner. Sig: Ann McIntosh. // Received of Mr. James Jellison two sets of certificates on the government for $438 which I promise to be accountable for, the danger of the river, seas and enemy excepted. Natchez. 1st January 1779. Sig: Alexander McIntosh. // Statement: Mr. Alexander McIntosh to James Jellison debtor 1779. To 2 sets of vouchers, Jan. 1, 1779, $438, int. on same $35; to work on barn and wagon $6. Total $479. By note given you at Natchez $40. By balance due James Jellison $439. Wit: J. Blommart. The above balance due me and I have received no part thereof. Sig: James Jellison. 15 May 1780. // Personally appeared before John Blommart, Esq., William Ferguson who, being sworn, declared Mr. Alexander McIntosh, formerly Captain and Commanding Officer of Fort Panmure, some time in September 1778 until 10th Dec. following did receive bills of exchange from the Board of Ordinance in Pensacola for the works done at said fort from the 1st September 1778 to 10 Dec. following, among which was included the building of a blockhouse and the finishing of another which was done by James Jellison, to the sum of $438. Signed: William Ferguson. 8th April 1780. Before me, J. Blommart. // I do certify John McGillvray to act as clerk of the garrison and works. 24 - 26 Sept. 1778 to Dec. 10th following. Alexander McIntosh then commanding. Sig. Will Ferguson. // The undersigned attorney for James Jellison in the suit instigated against Alexander McIntosh for the recovery of $439 has been informed that a certain John Baptiste Macarty has money in hand belonging to said Alexander McIntosh proceeding from the sale of tobacco, and he prays that said Macarty be ordered to declare the exact sum in his possession belonging to said McIntosh and that the said sum be held in his hands subject to the order of the Tribunal. // By order of His Honor Don Pedro Duvergais, alcalde of the City of New Orleans, 3 June 1780, on same day notified Don Francisco Broutin; and on same day, appeared John Baptiste Macarty, who being sworn, declared that he had in his hand the sum of $500 belonging to Mr. Alexander McIntosh, whereby the notary notified him to hold the sum in his possession subject to the order of the Tribunal. // The undersigned attorney for James Ellison in the suit instituted for him for $439 represents that he is ready to produce his witnesses to prove the justice of his demand. // The claim of the party cannot be admitted here, it being necessary that the signature be annexed and acknowledged by the debtor before an execution can issue and this examination should be made before the judge at the place of the debtor's residence, who alone is competent to try the cause before the attachment of the sum in the hands of John Baptiste Macarty is annulled and the plaintiff shall pay the cost.

p. 4. James Harman versus Jacob Cobun. James Harman holds a note by Thomas James drawn on Jacob Cobun for $130, exclusive of interest, asks for an order of payment. Jany. 6, 1781. Francis Farrell, atty. for the district of Natchez. // These parties being heard, we do hereby condemn Jacob Cobun to pay $130 to James Harman. Sig: Grand-Pre. // Jacob Cobun replies that he believes that the above-mentioned note was given to Harman by the said James for the purpose of being restored to the petitioner who prays that Your Excellency will examine the said Harman particularly as to in what manner the said note came into his possession, Thomas James, at this time being indebted to the petitioner. 9 Jany. 1781. Sig: Jacob Cobun.

p. 5. Michael Hooppock versus John Kennedy. Patrick Foley and Wm. Ferguson being chosen by the parties to decide a dispute between Michael Hooppock and John Kennedy, upon seeing Mr. Hooppock's accountable receipt to Mr. Alexander McIntosh for a note of Christian Princle [?] for $96 can but order that Mr. Hooppock make good his receipt and have recourse to the said Kennedy. Signed by both. // Received of Mr. Alexander McIntosh Christian Princle's note of hand for $96. It ought to be received from said Christian or Thomas Price [?] for which I am accountable. Sig: Michael Hooppock.

p. 5. A. McIntosh versus I. Johnson, who owes him $385. Aug. 1, 1781. Isaac Johnson appeared with a negro wench in payment of debt which is not sufficient and your petitioner asks that said Johnson pay before his departure. Sig: Alexander McIntosh. // Another petition by McIntosh, dated Sept. 13, 1781. // Let seizure be made. Sig: Grand-Pre.

p. 6. Peter Hawkins versus Andrew Welsh. Hawkins declared that he lent Andrew Welsh a cow and a calf to supply his family with milk and the said Welsh shot the said cow which died shortly afterwards. Andrew Welsh is famous for shooting his neighbors' cattle and making use of them and he has been publicly tried and condemned to jail for three months. // Andrew Welsh will appear tomorrow and bring some of his neighbors with him.

p. 6. John Townsend versus John Holloway. Townsend has an account against John Holloway for $12; asks for an order of payment. Sept. 8, 1781. Sig: John Townsend. Bill enclosed. // In reply John Holloway states that he has an account against said Townsend for two pirougues, in one of which the petitioner came to this district and left in the care of the negress, Eleanor Price, from whom the said

Townsend took it, the other was blown out into the river, and your petitioner commissioned the said Townsend to recover it for him which he did by paying $4 to a certain Baptiste in the presence of Mr. Gaillard and at the same time exchanged it for a smaller one which would facilitate him on his way to Natchez. Now the said Townsend refuses to make any compensation for the said pirougues. Asks for a judgment for same. // Let this be communicated to the plaintiff. //

p. 7. John Townsend versus Joseph Stanley, who owes him $2. Statement of same.

p. 7. Barbour and Harrison versus John Choat. Petition shows that John Choat, late of this district, is indebted to them for $14, as per account annexed, and said Choat still has property in this district and as the petitioners are the oldest creditors they ask that the amount be paid. Fees for suit $6. Account. 27 May 1776. [Merchandize. The earliest item dated 1771.] By cash from John Horsler $5. by Ellis and Mayes $15. By one horse named "Cloud" $70. By interest on average of four years $28. Balance $14.

p. 8. Roswell Mygatt versus Jeremiah Routh. Mygatt holds a note of Jeremiah Routh, of Cole's Creek, planter, for $17; asks for an execution against his property. 27 Sept. 1781.

p. 8. Jeremiah Bryan versus John Row. I, John Row, have bargained and sold to Abraham Geney, both of the district of Natchez, 8 head of horses, 26 head of horned cattle, 31 hogs and also all my stock and improvements on a plantation on St. Catherine's Creek, with houses, fences, etc., in consideration of 400 Spanish milled dollars in hand paid. 24 Nov. 1779. Sig. John Row. Abraham (X) Geney. Wit: James Peterkin, Caleb Hansborough. The above is void until the obligation is fulfilled, namely the above-named John Row shall deliver to Abraham Geney the articles therein named. Pray that Your Honor will compel John Row to deliver a cow belonging in the stock of the foregoing sale. Sig: Jeremiah Bryan.

p. 12. Eleanor Price versus John Farquhar. She has an account agst Farquhar for $5.00. Sept. 19, 1781. // John Farquhar will pay the $5 or be compelled by law. Eleanor Price will restore to him the four small jars belonging to him. Sig: Grand-Pre.

p. 12. Alexander McIntosh versus Nathaniel Allen, who owes him $12 for the rent of a house belonging to the petitioner. 26 Sept. 1781.

p. 13. William Brocus versus Phillip Mulkey, late of the district, now a fugitive rebel, owes him $48; as said Mulkey left property in this district, he asks that he be included with other creditors. Bill enclosed for $59, with credit of 11 bushels of potatoes.

p. 13. Philip Mulkey to Benjamin Balk, for cash lent . . . . . Joseph Duncan will proceed to execute all the property belonging to the rebel Philip Mulkey, absconded. Signed: Grand-Pre. Natchez. Oct. 8, 1781.

p. 13. John Kennedy versus William Case, now a fugitive rebel owes him $50, being for a mosquito bar which Mr. John Blommart lent to the said Case and it belonged to the petitioner, for which the agent of said Case refuses to make payment. // The agent of Case will pay this claim otherwise the constable will seize the property of said Case. Sig: Grand-Pre. Oct. 3, 1781.

p. 13. Michael Lopez versus Juan Gali. The petitioner claims he has an account against Gali, late of this district, amounting to $9. // Let agent of the said Gali pay the amount, 11 Oct. 1781.

p. 14. John Farquhar versus Peter Hawkins. Farquhar represents that he holds a note of Peter Hawkins for $104; asks for payment. 11 Oct. 1781. Let notice be given. Sig: Grand-Pre. // Reply of Peter Hawkins who represents that the note was given to a certain Whitefield and by him endorsed to Messrs. Green, Farquhar and Co. As soon as these gentlemen received the note, Mr. Green came to the petitioner and inquired if he had any tobacco for sale. He said that he had but he kept it to pay the said note. Thereupon the said Green said "If we take up your note are you willing to deliver us your crop of tobacco?" to which the petitioner answered in the affirmative and gave his obligation to that effect. An agreement was made in writing witnessed by John Bisland and William Ferguson and at the time agreed upon your petitioner delivered the tobacco. Now your petitioner is sued by Mr. Farquhar for the amount of the note and no credit is given for the tobacco. Oct. 12, 1781. // Parties being heard, Hawkins condemned to the payment of $79 to Green and Farquhar and the latter to give up his note for $104.

p. 14. Jeremiah Bryan versus Philip Mulkey. Petition of Bryan that he has an acct. against Philip Mulkey, late of this district but now a fugitive rebel, for $9. Your petitioner subscribed $4 for supporting said Mulkey as a preacher but as he had not fulfilled his engagement, the petitioner thinks the said subscription should be refunded. Sig: Jeremiah Bryan. // Seizure has already been made of the property of Philip Mulkey and when the sale shall have been made the petitioner may appear and prove his demand. Sig: Grand-Pre.

p. 15. Barbour and Harrison versus Andrew Knox, who owes them $46 as per account annexed. // Let the agent be notified and Parker Carradine particularly to pay the demand. [The account is dated Nov. 1777 and the petition Oct. 12, 1781.]

p. 15. Anthony Hutchins versus Richard Bacon. Hutchins petitions that a barrel of flour he purchased in June of Mr. Tomlinson to be put in the store of Mr. McIntosh but James Smith who was employed there with two negroes belonging to Mr. McIntosh put it into the house of Richard Bacon, at whose door the said flour was inspected. When your petitioner applied for the said flour he refused to deliver it and even denied that said flour was ever put into his house. 11 Oct. 1781. // Declaration of James Smith: A short time after Capt. Morander obtained possession of Panmure, he, Smith, was at the door of that part of the house of Mr. Bacon where Mrs. McIntosh then lived he saw two barrels of flour opened, one for use of Mrs. McIntosh and one for Mr. Hutchins' use. The one for Mrs. McIntosh was taken to her own store and the other was rolled part of the way to the same place, but being forbidden to take it there for want of room, it was taken to the house of said Bacon, and Smith rolled it into the same room where other flour was stored but on the opposite side, on the left hand. Sig: James Smith. // The parties' witnesses being heard, it was decreed that Richard Bacon shall not be held for the barrel of flour which, if put in his house, was done without his knowledge. Cost of suit to be paid equally.

p. 16. John Townsend versus David Waltman. Petitioner is holder of a note of John Coleman for $7, and David Waltman promised to pay the said note for Coleman; asks execution against the property of said Waltman. 15 Oct. 1781. Signed John Townsend. // Let seizure be made as required. Sig: Grand-Pre.

p. 16. Anthony Hutchins versus James Smith. [Another suit about the lost barrel of flour.] Since Richard Bacon has cleared himself of the responsibility for the flour, the petitioner is of the opinion that James Smith must have been at fault and Hutchins asks to be reimbursed by Smith. // The parties being heard, James Smith is ordered to deliver to Anthony Hutchins the barrel of flour in question or the value thereof, $28, he, the said Smith, having no orders to move the said flour, and not being able to prove to whom he delivered it.

p. 16. Negro James versus Clement Dyson and John Staybraker. Negro James, formerly belonging to Philip Alston, represents that he sold a quantity of corn to Messrs. Clement Dyson and John Staybraker, for $5, for which they gave their joint note drawn in the name of Philip Alston, the former master of your petitioner, according to the English law, which forbids a negro to claim in his own name. Asks for an order to be paid by John Staybraker, Clement having left the country. Francis Farrell signed for negro James. Natchez, 21 Oct. 1781. // Note: Five months and ten days after date, we, or either of us do promise to pay to Mr. Philip Alston or order five Spanish milled dollars on demand. 26 Dec. 1780. Clement (X) Dyson, John Staybraker. Wit: Thomas Moseley. // Let notice be given to purchasers to pay the amount claimed.

p. 17. William Vousdan versus Richard Bacon. Vousdan petitions that he has a demand against Richard Bacon for a cow and calf for Alexander Graden, a fugitive rebel, since Bacon chooses to purchase the property of the petitioner in his absence, he ought to be responsible to the petitioner. // Let notice be given. Grand-Pre.

p. 18. Silas Crane versus Jeremiah Hill. Crane represents that under the British Government he obtained judgments against Jeremiah Hill for $7 and Hill promised to work for petitioner in payment; asked for an execution against the said Hill. 21 Oct. 1781. Sig: Silas Crane.

p. 18. Silas Crane versus Benjamin Carrol. Crane obtained judgment against Benjamin Carrol for $8 of His Excellency Monsieur Delavillebeuvre; asks execution against said Carrol. 21 Oct. 1781. Signed: Silas Crane. // Let seizure be made as required. Sig: Grand-Pre.

p. 18. William Ferguson versus John Choat. Ferguson has an account against John Choat, late of this district, now in the woods, amounting to $12; as said Choat still has property in this district, asks an order for payment. // Let seizure be made of the fugitive rebel. Sig: Grand-Pre. 23 Oct. 1781.

p. 20. Widow Jane Ogden versus Sterling Spell. Widow Jane Ogden represents that she bought from

Sterling Spell, of this district, planter, two cows and two calves in exchange for a mare and the said Spell promised to deliver the said cattle when demanded. Some time after, Mr. William Canada, who was employed to receive the cattle for her, called on Spell and demanded the cattle as per agreement, but in place of two young cows and calves which said Spell had contracted for, he delivered an old cow of ten years. Signed Jane Ogden. // The parties may appoint arbitrators to settle the matter in dispute. 24 Oct. 1781. Sig: Grand-Pre.

p. 20. William Vousdan versus John Terry, against whom he has an account for $13 being for the surveying of his land. 26 Oct. 1781. Account: John Terry to William Vousdan, for surveying 150 acres land and mileage, $10; interest thereon for two years $2 and 3 rials. // Let John Terry be notified to pay. Grand-Pre.

p. 21. William Brocus versus William Vousdan. William Brocus represents that he arrived with his family in December last past, and the wife of the said William Vousdan came to the petitioner and told him that a certain James Robertson held a bond of her husband for $47 and she was apprehensive of a suit and she asked the petitioner to rake up the said bond and she would pay him cows, which she did. Wm. Ferguson since then has paid $40 on the said bond and there remains $9 but Vousdan refused to pay him. 21 Nov. 1781. // Let notice be given. Sig: Grand-Pre.

p. 21. William McIntosh versus Anthony Hutchins. Wm. McIntosh represents that a note of Anthony Hutchins endorsed to him by James Farley, of Pensacola, for $85, which Hutchins claims was already paid, etc. Sig: Wm. McIntosh. // Answer of Anthony Hutchins: On 5 Nov. 1779, petitioner gave his note for two debts, one due by Parker Carradine, the other from Alexander Boyd, expecting to receive the amount thereof from them; that same day I gave to Mr. Farley a draft for that amount on Messrs. Bay and McCullagh, attys., who accepted it in his and my presence and promised to pay same. Now that my said attorneys have paid said sum as I suppose they have, it will be hard to pay it again. [He desires to have the matter cleared up, etc.] If the note has not been paid, I hope I may be indulged until I have time to collect the money from the estates of Carradine and Boyd who contracted the debt. Nov. 21, 1781. // I am sorry to say that I am indebted in several sums of money to people who would not themselves wish to distress me. Lately I have had several misfortunes; first, from Capt. Willing and his party, second by the unfortunate sloop Catherine in the Mississippi, and by the insurrection in Natchez and I have struggled hard against the banditti who by every art and contrivance sought the ruin of the Natchez. Sig. Anthony Hutchins. Natchez. Nov. 21, 1781. // Anthony Hutchins will produce a receipt or pay the note in the hands of William Brocus.

p. 22. William Vousdan versus Richard Ellis, Sr. Petition that William Vousdan has an account agst Richard Ellis, Sr. of this district for $51. Nov. 15, 1781. // Let notice be given. Grand-Pre.

p. 22. Barbour and Harrison versus Caleb King. Petitioners represent that Caleb King owes them 70 bushels of West Indian corn. Nov. 22, 1781. Signed: Richard Harrison. // In reply, Caleb King petitions that in Oct. 1777 Capt. James Willing made an attack on the Natchez and your petitioner gave his note to Joshua Howard, of this district for 70 bushels of corn, which note was endorsed to Barbour and Harrison and when the note became due the two Harrisons, William Reed and your petitioner were at Natchez in the month of February and your petitioner told Mr. Harrison that the corn was ready, that is to say that it was at the Homochitto where it was to be delivered to Harrison who asked your petitioner if he could not deliver it to the White Cliffs which was three miles from Homochitto. The petitioner replied that he could not that he was bound to deliver the corn to the Homochitto and not at White Cliffs and I had no horses to carry it there. However I told him if he would make a deduction of ten bushels from the 70 bushels, making it 60 bushels, I would deliver the corn at St. Catherine's at the plantation of William Reed to which the said Harrison agreed. Now the petitioner asks that he be allowed to pay Harrison for 60 bushels according to that agreement. // Caleb King condemned to pay 70 bushels of corn due to the tenor of his note.

p. 23. Barbour and Harrison versus Justus King, who owes them $13. Let debtor be notified of same. Sig: Grand-Pre. Nov. 23, 1781.

p. 24. William Vousdan versus John Rowe. Vousdan demands a cow and calf which was in dispute between him and a certain Bryan which was granted to him by an order of court. Witnesses cited: Samuel Lewis and wife, Jacob Paul, Jr. and Jeremiah Bryan. // Parties and witnesses having been heard we do condemn John Rowe to deliver cow and calf to Wm. Vousdan which have been proved to belong to him. Sig: Grand-Pre.

p. 24. Anthony Hutchins versus Richard Bacon. Richard Bacon was ordered to deliver to your petitioner a saddle. Instead of obeying the order, he did lend and hire the said saddle to the same person he had lent and hired it to before, etc. // Let Richard Bacon be notified to immediately conform to a former decree or he will be condemned to pay the value of the said saddle. Sig. Grand-Pre.

p. 25. Silas Crane versus Kilkart King. Silas Crane petitions that he holds a note against the late Kilkart King, who was killed at the Big Black, for $12 and the said King, having a crop of corn before his death, which is to be brought to Natchez for sale, petitioner asks that he be paid out of the proceeds. Nov. 12, 1781. Signed: Silas Crane. // Let the signature to the note be proved. Grand-Pre. "I, the subscriber, promise to pay to Silas Crane or order the just sum of $12, for value received. (Signed) Kilkart King. 21 March 1780." On the above the owner received $6 and 6 rials and the balance is still owing. Natchez, Nov. 12, 1781. Grand-Pre.

p. 25. Stephen Jordan versus Thaddeus Lyman. Stephen Jordan petitions that he has received judgment against a certain Thaddeus Lyman late of this district, for $12 including the cost of suit and the said Lyman having left property in this district, petitioner asks execution against said property. Nov. 30, 1781. Sig: Stephen Jordan. // Let the petitioner be paid in due time. Sig: Grand-Pre. Dec. 1st, 1781.

p. 26. Henry LaFleur versus Henry Bradley, who owes him, by account, $1320, exclusive of interest. Said Bradley, formerly of this district and now in England, is also indebted to the petitioner for taking care of his cattle for two years, which two last items are not charged in the account. Jany. 2, 1782. Sig: Henry LaFleur. [Another petition by same, complaining that Richard Harrison, agent for Bradley delaying settlement unnecessarily. Jan. 14, 1782.] Statement of account, beginning 1768. John Bradley to Henry LaFleur. Trading for Mr. Mills on your account, by leave of the Commandant. $30; merchandize, bear and deer skins, etc. May 1769; 1770; total $1320. // Accounts to be examined but in the meanwhile the petitioner be given security for the balance due to him. Sig: Grand-Pre.

p. 27. George Forney versus Bennet Truly. Forney represents that he has an account against Bennet Truly, late of the district, absconded, for $126 and said Truly having left property in the hands of Sarah Truly, his mother, asks for payment. Jan. 6, 1782. Signed: George Forney. // Petition of Sarah Truly that the account of George Forney against her son Benet Truly for $126 for work done at the mill which said Forney and her son agreed to build and hold in partnership; thus her son can only be liable for one-half of the cost. They obtained permission to erect the mill from Mr. Delavillebeuvre but afterwards learned that the land on which it stood was claimed by Philip Barbour and Capt. Delavillebeuvre forbade them to continue. Signed; Sarah Truly. January 1782. // The agreement made and fully concluded by George Furney, of district of Natchez, West Florida, and Benet Truly of same. Witnesses: Jacob Stampley, John Rowe. Natchez, 24 Nov. 1780. // The witnesses having been heard, we do hereby condemn the widow Truly, being in the possession of property of Benet Truly, to pay George Forney the sum of $126, being money lent and hands' wages. Sig: Grand-Pre. [The account is given.]

p. 30. Peter Hawkins versus John Farquhar. Peter Hawkins represents that a suit brought by John Farquhar against John Short before Your Honor was on account of a contract made with your petitioner who gave his obligation in March last for 8000 staves to be delivered at the place where they should be made which obligation is now in the hands of Farquhar; about ten days since he employed a certain Turpin to examine the said staves and he examined only a part of said staves which he rejected for being less than 4 inches in width which is not usual at this place or at New Orleans where they are received; the standard width is but three inches. Signed: Peter Hawkins. // Mr. John Rowe will repair to the plantation of Mr. Peter Hawkins to examine the staves. // Report by John Row, cooper, chosen by the parties to examine the staves: There appears to be 6620 good and merchantable staves and 1325 for heading amounting to 7995 which we hereby order John Farquhar to receive, 5 staves wanting shall be furnished or paid for and said John Farquhar shall restore the obligation. Sig: Grand-Pre.

p. 32. Jesse Carter versus John Smith. There is a balance due to Jesse Carter by John Smith which we do order to be paid in three months with the costs. Signed: Thomas Green, John (X) Perry. Cole's Creek. Jan. 27, 1782.

p. 32. John Hartley versus Stephen Holstein. Hartley is holder of a note drawn by Stephen Holstein for $60. Francis Farrel attorney. Let him be notified to pay. Sig: Grand-Pre. 28 Jan. 1782.

p. 32. Eleanor Price versus James Barfield, who is indebted to her for $38, being for provisions furnished to him when he was prisoner. Natchez 30 1782. Let notice be given to pay. [Itemized account. one item: For dinner to yourself and wife . . . . For provisions furnished you while in the fort, Oct. 26 to this date, 48 days.] // Mr. and Mrs. Baker both saw Hansborough take James Barfield his gun to pay his and his wife's board for the time that he was in the garrison. // The parties and witnesses being heard, I do hereby condemn Mrs. Barfield to pay to the free mulatto woman, Eleanor Price $38 for provisions furnished to Barfield during his detention in the prison of this fort and the wife shall be paid for the gun delivered to Hansborough out of the property of the latter. Signed: Grand-Pre.

p. 33. William Hurlburt versus John Hogg, who is lately absconded from here, and against whom he has an account for $9, being for fees in the time of Mr. Delavillebeuvre when as constable your petitioner levied execution on the property of said Hogg and the suit was stopped by Mr. Blommart shortly after the revolt took place and prevented the petitioner from obtaining payment. The property of said Hogg is now in the hands of Mistress Osborne and she refuses to pay the petitioner without an order from Your Honor. Signed: William Hurlburt. // Let the property of John Hogg be seized in the hands of Widow Osborne. 2nd Feb. 1782. Sig: Grand-Pre.

p. 33. John Hartley versus Stephen Holstein, against whom he has a judgment for $6, which debt has not been satisfied. Petitioner asks an execution on the property on the property of said Holstein. Sig: John Hartley. 2 Feb. 1782. // Let it be done as required. Grand-Pre.

p. 34. James Truly versus Stephen Holstein, against whom he has an account of $7. Sig: James Truly. // Let him be notified. Sig: Grand-Pre. Feb. 6, 1782.

p. 34. John Hartley versus Reuben Alexander. John Hartley petitions that he has a demand against Reuben Alexander for $48, on account of his negro who has stolen the above sum from him. The said negro was taken and brought before the Justice of the Peace. The next day the judges assembled at the trial of the negro of the said Reuben Alexander but, by some means, the negro escaped to Baton Rouge where he remained and was taken. Your petitioner was robbed by said negro in the following manner: Upon his arrival at White Cliffs, the said Alexander left the boat, and much against my will went home. At my landing at Natchez, I found said Alexander there. We bought a trunk between us to put our clothes in. The said trunk having no key, we were obliged to lock it with a nail. The said Alexander was at trunk to get a packet of letters addressed to Captain Foster and he neglected to fasten the said trunk. The negro on the boat at the time, watched for an opportunity and robbed me of $100 in cash which was occasioned by the neglect of said master. The negro was since with Mr. Holloway and at the death of said Holloway the negro was sold. The said Alexander receiving advice of the sale of the said negro went to Baton Rouge lately to receive payment for said negro. Asks that Alexander be made to pay him. Sig: John Hartley. Jan. 10, 1782. N. B. I found $52 in the possession of the said negro. // Natchez, Jan. 14, 1782. Let the parties be summoned to appear at our audience. Grand-Pre. // The parties will appear before Isaac Johnson, William Pounteney and Richard Harrison and produce their proofs. The award: The negro who stands accused was by his master given up to the English law and he escaped from the officers of justice, without the knowledge or consent of his master, we are of the opinion that his master is not liable on his account, for had the negro not escaped, his life would have in forfeit to the law upon the fact being proved. Also we look upon the master as being most aggrieved by the theft as he has been without the benefit of his negro for three years. Signed by the above. 5 Feb. 1782. // Petition of John Hartley represents that a certain Benjamin Rogers was present when Reuben Alexander requested that the suit might be deferred until the arrival of Mr. Johnson, of Cole's Creek, giving for reason that he wished to have the suit determined by the English laws, petitioner asks that the suit be determined by English laws. Sig: John Hartley. Jany. 29, 1782. // Award: as Alexander has suffered the greater loss, he should not have to pay the sum stolen by said negro. Sig: Grand-Pre.

p. 36. David Odam versus William Clark, against whom he has a note for 550 pounds of pork. Jan. 26, 1782. // Let him be notified to pay.

p. 36. William Hurlburt versus Stephen Jordan, against whom he has an account for $10 and $3 fees to the attorney. // Stephen Jordan condemned to pay William Hurlburt and Francis Farrell, being for fees and cost of suit.

p. 36. John Follard versus Richard Adams, against whom he has a note for $3. Feb, 14, 1782. Sig: John Follard. // Richard Adams replies that John Follard owes him $8; asks for a determination of the matter. Sig: Richard Adams. // Parties summoned to appear Feb. 19th. // 27 May 1782. Richard Adams having appeared six times in our audience on business in question and John Follard, the plaintiff, not having attended, the said Folard notified to appear, in default thereof he will be condemned to the costs of the suit and will be debarred from any further hearing in the case. // The parties being heard, Follard condemned to pay Richard Adams $3 and 4 rials being for corn furnished to him and said Adams shall pay to said John Follard $3 and 5 rials, the amount of his note, and as to the hauling and the account of the rum, the parties shall produce their proofs.

p. 37. Stephen Stephenson versus James Wilson, against whom he has an account of $23. Feb. 14, 1782. Sig: Stephen Stephenson. // James Wilson represents that said Stephenson was engaged to make a crop and petitioner was at great expense repairing fences which were in bad order, which petitioner would not otherwise have done and the said Stephenson worked only two or three half days during a period of three weeks, but was always on hand to get breakfast, dinner and supper; asks that petitioner be paid for these provisions. Stephen Stephenson to James Wilson debtor: $6 and 5 rials. 2 bushels of corn $2; hog lard and tobacco $3. Total $11 and 5 rials.

p. 38. James Wilson versus David Wathman, against whom he has a note for $15. Feb. 21, 1782. Signed: James Wilson. // David Wathman's reply that he can prove that the said note was paid by Stephen Holstein; asks that James Wilson be ordered to give up the said note. // James Wilson shall return to said Wathman the said note and shall pay said Wathman $9 balance. 23 March 1782.

p. 38. James Truly versus Stephen Holstein. Truly petitions that he has obtained before Your Honor judgment against Stephen Holstein for the sum of $7 and asks an execution against said Holstein. // Let it be done as required. Feb. 21, 1782. Sig: Grand-Pre.

p. 39. Poultney and Duvall versus Jacob Paul, against whom they have an account for $14, being for 120 pounds of salt; ask an order for payment. 21 Feb. 1782. // To be communicated. Sig: Grand-Pre.

p. 39. John Farquhar versus Richard Adams, Michael Guise and Nathan Swazey. Petition of John Farquhar represents that he had a crib of corn broken open by Richard Adams, Michael Guise and Nathan Swazey, all of this district and all concerned in same; asks for an order of payment either in corn or money. Sig: John Farquhar. 4 March 1782. // To be communicated.

p. 39. John Farquhar versus Anthony Brabazon, who made an agreement with him as follows: "I do bind myself to make 5000 fence rails for John Farquhar, to be finished by the end of January next and to be approved by Archibald Palmer who is to receive them from me, for which I am to be paid $1 per hundred and receive provisions during the time I am making the said rails and to receive payment on a note now owing to said Farquhar. Dec. 5, 1781. Sig: Anthony Brabazon. Wit: Wm. Ferguson." Now said Brabazon refuses to comply with the agreement; asks that Brabazon be compelled to comply with said agreement. Sig: John Farquhar. // To be communicated. Natchez. 4 March 1782.

p. 40. John Bisland versus Peter Hawkins, against whom he has an account for $12; asks order of payment. Natchez. March 4, 1782. // To be communicated. // Account: For stirrup irons, $12. Sept. 1781.

p. 40. Patrick Foley versus Peter Hawkins, against whom he has an account for $61; asks for order of payment. March 19, 1782. The account, July 29, 1780. To thread, printed linen ($25), and a bottle of rum. April 1781 Coffee, sugar, 2 bottles of rum, etc. // Petition of Peter Hawkins declares that he has an account against Patrick Foley for $67 and asks that Foley be ordered before you so that we may settle our accounts. The account annexed.

p. 41. John Bisland versus Peter Hawkins, against whom he has a judgment for $12 and asks an execution for that amount. Let it be done. Sig: Grand-Pre. Natchez. 14 March 1782.

p. 41. Matthias Prock versus Peter Hawkins, against whom he has an account for $14 and asks for order of payment of same. April 2, 1782. Matthias Prock. Let the notice be given to the party. Grand-Pre.

p. 42. Ephraim Goble versus Peter Hawkins. Petition of Goble that he has a demand against Peter Hawkins for $3 and asks for payment before petitioner leaves for Philadelphia. Apr. 2, 1782. Signed.

p. 42. Peter Hawkins versus Silas Crane. Peter Hawkins represents that Crane has kept his money in his hands thereby causing much expense to him in paying his just debts; asks that Crane be summoned to appear and answer what he has done with the money of your petitioner. March 27, 1782. Sig: Peter Hawkins. // Let Silas Crane immediately produce the money claimed by the petitioner.

p. 43. Mathias Prock versus Stephen Holstein. Prock represents that he was hired by said Holstein to take care of his cattle in the woods and for which Holstein refuses to pay. 28 March 1782. Signed. //

The parties having been heard, we do hereby reject the claim of the plaintiff against Stephen Holstein. April 27, 1782. Grand-Pre.

p. 44. Thomas Rule versus Sarah Truly. Thomas Rule petitions that he had a contract with Bennet Truly for a horse in the manner following: He gave the said Truly a silver watch valued at $30, a rifle valued at $62, and he engaged to dig a well on that part of the plantation of said Truly which should be pointed out by Mr. Bisland to furnish water in four months from the day of the agreement. He was supposed to dig the said well in the autumn and called on the said Truly for the hands which he was to furnish to assist him but the said Truly excused himself by saying that he was engaged with his crop and would be glad if he would defer it until next fall. Unfortunately the revolt took place at Natchez and the widow Truly having built a fort or block-house on her land or the land of Benet Truly and the rebels who took refuge there, fearing they should want water if attacked by the power against them, dug a well. Your petitioner was always ready to comply with his agreement. Sig: Thomas Rule. April 11, 1782. // Petition of Sarah Truly represents that she demanded from Thomas Rule the sum of $60 due from him to her son Bennet Truly for a well, which the said Rule had contracted to dig, which can be proved by George Forney. // Thomas Rule shall dig the well which he contracted for on the plantation of Benet Truly. The said Rule having been paid for it and the well shall be dug in the season customary in this district. Sig: Grand-Pre.

p. 44. John Bisland versus Alexander Grading. John Bisland petitions that during the time of the revolt, Alexander Grading did kill and cause to be killed a number of beeves for the use of himself and company which said beeves were the property of your petitioner for which Mr. Grading had no order from his Commander, Mr. Blommart, as Mr. Blommart afterwards declared upon his word of honor. Mr. Grading then, before setting off for the Chickasaw Nation offered your petitioner a note of hand for a part of the beeves in the presence of Mr. Spell, for which Mr. Grading said he owed your petitioner $80, which he said he would pay as soon as he was able. Since the return of Mr. Grading he refuses to make the promised payment. Some time before Grading returned from the Chickasaws, one Grove Morris being at the house of your petitioner said he had bought a small quantity of tallow from Mr. Grading and when your petitioner said the price was low, Mr. Morris said that the tallow had not cost Mr. Grading money but really belonged to the petitioner. April 18, 1782. // To be communicated. To Alexander Grading debtor to John Bisland. Six beeves which you killed at $20. Contra To what I received in part payment from Groves Morris 3 yards of homespun. Balance $113. // Deposition of Sterling Spell that he was present when Grading killed two of the beeves and also when Grading said he would pay for them. // Parties and witnesses heard, we do condemn Alexander Grading to the payment of $80 in month of December next, being the value of four beeves killed by him belonging to Mr. Bisland, during the revolt. Sig: Grand-Pre.

p. 45. Daniel Mygatt versus Samuel Heady, against whom he has an account for $25, being money lent, rum sold and blacksmith work done at my shop. Signed. May 6, 1782. // Parties being heard, we do condemn Samuel Heady to pay Daniel Mygatt $18 and 2 rials, in full of all accounts. Sig: Grand-Pre.

p. 46. ______ Cadet versus William Pountney. Cadet petitions that last Sunday he was bringing home a young bull. In front of the house of Mr. LaFleur the said bull broke from him and escaped into the woods and the petitioner crossed St. Catherine's creek in search of said bull and on Tuesday morning found him coming out of Mr. Pountney's park with his ears cut and the mark of the said Pounteney. 26 May 1782.

p. 46. John Lusk versus Richard Duvall, against whom he has an account for $33; asks for an order of payment of same. May 13, 1782. Account annexed: April 19, 1782. // Duvall ordered to appear. // John Lusk will return to Richard Duvall all the iron he received from him and the two brothers Mygatt will tax all the work done by him. Sig: Grand-Pre.

p. 47. William Weeks versus Job Cory. We, the subscribers, Silas Crane, William McIntosh and Isaac Johnson, being appointed by the Commandant to settle the dispute between William Weeks and Job Cory concerning an account and articles of agreement delivered 10 Feb. last past are of the opinion that the balance of $30 to be paid to said Weeks by said Cory and that William Weeks and Job Cory should immediately hunt the hogs that were in dispute and that Wm. Weeks should deliver to said Cory one-half of the increase as per said agreement, also the said Cory shall deliver to said Weeks all the stock of cattle that may be alive within two months. Signed by all. April 23, 1782.

p. 47. William McIntosh versus James Truly. Petition of William McIntosh has an account against said Truly for $9 and asks for an order for payment of same. May 18, 1782. // Receipt in full by

McIntosh. Let Crane look for his. [Crane was constable.]

p. 48. Benjamin Roach versus Benjamin Carrol and William Clark. Petition of Benj. Roach that he suffered much damage from Benj. Carrol and Wm. Clark setting their dogs to worry four of his hogs which are likely to die in consequence, exclusive of another hog which is missing. June 15, 1782. Signed. // June 22, 1782. It appears that Benj. Carrol and Wm. Clark left their fences in such bad condition and open and the dogs destroyed the provision of the hogs, said Carrol and Clark shall pay such reasonable damages to the plaintiff as shall be awarded by Messrs. John Bisland and Richard Harrison. After consideration, said arbitrators decided that the defendants should pay Roach $15, as he lost two shoats and 5 pigs and had a great deal of trouble curing others of his stock bitten by the dogs. 27 July 1782. Signed by both.

p. 48. Jeremiah Routh petitions that he has an account against Thaddeus Lyman, late of this district, now an absconded rebel, for $109 for which he has judgment; asks an execution against the property of said Lyman. Sig: Jeremiah Routh. 16 July 1782. The estate of Thaddeus Lyman to Jeremiah Routh. Cannoe, chains, rum, Matthew Phelps by Oliver Lyman $10, wagon, total $109.

p. 48. Pleasant Turpin versus Richard Duvall. Pleasant Turpin represents that Richard Duvall owes him $27, balance for work due as cooper; that he was hired to Devall for $1 per day from the time I left the Natchez till I returned and I was 22 days in his employ, working in his boat. I should have sued him before the Governor then had I not been dissuaded by Mr. Pounteny. Duvall refuses to pay me because I assisted Mr. James to kill his hogs when he had given permission to Mr. Devall to kill them. Mr. James and Mr. Duvall held the boat in partnership but I was hired by Mr. Duvall. Sig: Pleasant Turpin. 15 July 1782.

p. 49. George Bailey versus Samuel Heady. Bailey petitions that Samuel Heady owes him for $26, balance of account. Signed. 28 July 1782. [Statement of account. June 1780.]

p. 49. John Bisland versus Thaddeus Lyman, against whom he has an account of $9, being for a pair of stockings and the hire of a negro, on which he has received $2, leaving a balance of $7; asks to be included with the other creditors of Thaddeus Lyman. Signed. Aug. 16, 1782.

p. 50. Philip Pleasant Turpin versus Josiah Flower. Turpin petitions that on 1st May he brought suit against Josiah Flower who prayed that the matter might be left to the decission of Silas Crane and Justus King, to which your petitioner consented. The award of the said arbitrators was that Josiah Flowers should pay petitioner $33 and 6 bushels of corn in twenty days from the 8th of May, both parties being bound in the penalty of $100 to abide by the said award. Your petitioner has received $19, the said Flowers refusing to pay him more; asks that an order be given that so much the goods of said Flower be sold to cover the balance, the amount being money that said Flowers made use of belonging to said petitioner. Sig: Philip Pleasant Turpin. Aug. 17, 1782. // Silas Crane will compel Josiah Flower to pay the sum of $33 and in default thereof he will seize cattle in the amount of the balance, to sell in payment, also 6 bushels of corn. Sig: Girault. [Copy of the award dated May 8, 1782.]

p. 51. Joseph Usher versus Richard Bacon. Petitioner took the plantation of said Bacon for one crop or two or three years, the said Bacon promising to furnish 15 bushels of corn but petitioner has received but one and one-half bushels and that was rotten. Mr. Bacon was to furnish two cows and a calf besides hogs. Petitioner has not received the cows and calf and but six hogs. Mr. Bacon was also to furnish the hands to work the crop and he has failed in that; asks that Bacon be compelled to comply with his agreement. Sept. 5, 1782. Joseph (X) Usher. Since the petition sold his part, one half, to St. Germain, being indebted to him, and his wife being dead, he wishes to work elsewhere.

p. 51. Jacob Cable versus Ferguson and others. Petition of Jacob Cable represents that he settled on a piece of land on St. Catherine's Creek and has cultivated the same for 7 or 8 years but Mr. Ferguson has now settled on same land. Cable can prove by evidence of William Ferguson and Doctor Farrell that he is the oldest settler and that Forney from whom Dr. Ferguson purchased settled on the land of your petitioner and tried to injure it and that James Truly has settled on the other side of him by purchase from said Forney and also on land of petitioner; he asks that surveyor be ordered to fix the limits of his land, not that he wishes to injure any of his neighbors but that his 100 arpents be secured to him. Oct. 16, 1782. Jacob (X) Cable.

p. 51. John Lusk represents that the plantation of his father-in-law, William Case, being sold at public sale by Col. Grand-Pre, then Commandant, and your petitioner became purchaser thereof for $25 and said Commandant, deeming so small a sum so far short of the real value of said land, caused it to be again sold at public sale, and your petitioner again became the purchaser for $61, which said sum he has paid to the Commandant and your petitioner is well persuaded that Your Excellency will not suffer the surveyor to cut off 25 arpents of land for which he has already paid; the petitioner is persuaded that neither Your Excellency nor the surveyor were informed that he purchased the land from Col. De Grand-Pre, then Commandant, and paid for it which however can be proved by the records. The bounds were fixed in the time of the British Government and sold as containing that quantity. Sig: John Lusk. Oct. 18, 1782.

p. 52. John Lusk versus Benj. Balk. John Lusk represents that a difference has arisen between him and Benj. Balk concèrning a tract of land on which he now lives, which he bought at public sale, and no mention was made of the number of arpents in said tract. The petitioner purchased the tract according to the ancient bounds, which said bounds are still to be seen and the same comprehended all the lands belonging to the father-in-law of the petitioner. A surveyor of the fort came to survey the lands of said petitioner and of the said Benj. Balk, his neighbor, and we agreed to commence the line between us at the corner of my lands as being the oldest settler, and continued the said survey with three corners of my land ascertained, on which my name is still to be seen. I requested Mr. Balk to make enquiry at the fort if the survey was sufficient and he went accordingly but no interpreter being there, the surveyor came with Mr. Balk and told me that one square arpent was to be taken from my land. I informed the King's interpreter, Mr. Duforest, that I had purchased the land at public sale and requested him to ask the Governor for a formal title. He made answer that what land I had purchased at public sale could not be taken from me by any person, that a surveyor was coming from the City to survey my land then I would obtain a title, my claim being the oldest in date. Sig: J. Lusk. Oct. 22, 1782. [In settlement each land holder above gave to the other certain strips of land.]

p. 53. Pierre Nitard versus Sterling Spell, who owes him $50 for pork delivered; asks that Spell be compelled to pay said sum. // Sterling Spell notified to appear at government house. Sig: James Harman, constable.

p. 53. Polser Shilling versus John Short, who has made unreasonable difficulties in settlement of accounts with petitioner. Dec. 12, 1782. Signed. // Richard Bacon and Patrick Foley appointed arbitrators to settle this dispute. Award: John Short is due $9-5 rials. All provisions not used on the voyage to be divided between the parties. Signed by both.

p. 54. St. Germain versus Abraham Mayes, of this dist., owes him $140; asks an order of payment of same. Sig: St. Germain. 28 Dec. 1782. // Abraham Mayes notified by J. Harman, constable

p. 54. St. Germain versus William Dewitt, who owes him $20; asks for an order of payment. 28 Dec. 1782. // Let the party be notified to pay.

p. 54. St. Germain versus Thomas Yarrow, St. Germain represents that he is the holder of a note of said Yarrow for $9; asks for an order of payment. 28 Dec. 1782. // Let the party be notified, etc. Signed: Piernas.

p. 55. St. Germain versus Benjamin Carrol, whose note for $76 the petitioner holds. Order of same requested. 28 Dec. 1782. // Order for same.

p. 55. St. Germain versus George Bailey. St. Germain petitions that he is the holder of two notes drawn by George Bailey for $24, which being due an order to pay requested. // Order to pay. Sig: Piernas. 29 Dec. 1782.

p. 55. St. Germain versus Joseph Green, of Cole's Creek, against whom he has an account for $7; asks an order for payment of same. Signed. 28 Dec. 1782. // Order to pay, etc. Sig: Piernas.

p. 56. St. Germain versus William Clark, who owes him $14; asks for an order of payment. // Let the party be notified to pay. Sig: Piernas. 29 Dec. 1782.

p. 56. St. Germain versus Stephen Holstein, who owes him a note for $68; asks an order for payment. // Let party be notified to pay. Sig: Piernas. Dec. 29, 1782.

p. 56. St. Germain versus James Oglesby, against whom he has an account for $11; asks for an order of payment. // Granted by Piernas. Same date.

p. 56. St. Germain versus David Wathman, against whom he has a demand for $23; asks an order to pay. // Party be notified, etc. Piernas. Same date.

p. 57. Francois Jacques versus William Hurlburt, who owes him $10 for leather; asks for order for payment. 25 Dec. 1782. // Let the party be notified to pay. Sig: Piernas.

p. 57. Articles of agreement between Mr. David Wathman and George Weigle. The said David Wathman conveys and transfers to George Weigle all right, etc. to a certain tract of land on St. Catherine's Creek, b. my lands of Messrs. Mygatt, Adams and Ogden and other lands of sd Wathman, to be delivered 1st Feb. and make a title to same; Weigle to pay Wathman $72, one half immediately in goods, the other half December next. Dec. 30, 1782. Both sign. Wit: Wm. Atchinson, Richard Brashears.

p. 58. Richard Harrison versus Francis Farrell. The affair between Richard Harrison and myself respecting a note of mine: In 1776 I gave my note to Oliver Pollock for . . . . . . , one for $30 and one for $180, and the said Pollock being my friend said in the presence of Mr. Henderson that he would not exact any interest; some years afterwards said Pollock endorsed the said notes to Col. Montgomery, who on his arrival here informed me that he was in possession of the said notes, and he said that Pollock asked to learn if I could pay the said notes but if I could not he could send them to my mother from whom he was certain of receiving payment. As I could not pay the said notes he promised that he would return the said notes by the first opportunity and not finding an opportunity, when he departed a few days later, he left them in the hands of Mr. Blommart to be returned to Mr. Pollock. The next news I had of them was after the rebellion when all the papers of Mr. Blommart were seized and my notes, unfortunately for me in the said papers and in the hands of Don Estevan Minor. I can prove by Mr. George Rapalje that the other day, being at the house of Mr. George Castles I asked Mr. Harrison what he intended to do with my notes, to which he answered that he did not know. I then enquired by what means the notes had come into his hands after the seizure of the fort and by whose order. He replied by the order of Mr. Pollock. I then decided that he had had a written order from Mr. Pollock. He said that he believed he did. Then I desired him to show me the said letter, for I believed that he had no authority whatever to take possession of said notes, which were among the papers of a confiscated estate . . . . I have paid in the presence of Mr. Harman and Mr. Ferguson, on the condition that the note in dispute should then be sent to Mr. Pollock at Philadelphia, and the said Harrison said he had no further demand against me. I like nothing better than to pay my note but not here but in Philadelphia where my property lies and I could pay it without inconvenience, etc. Sig: Francis Farrell. Dec. 31, 1782.

p. 59. Patrick Foley versus Peter Hawkins. Foley petitions that Hawkins bought a barrel of rum from Miguel Lopez for $90 with the said petitioner security for the sum and the time of payment being expired, the petitioner had to pay same and asks that he be paid for same by the sale of a negro belonging to said Hawkins. 7 Jany. 1783. // Let Peter Hawkins pay within 3 days or the negro above-mentioned will be seized. Sig: Piernas.

p. 59. Abraham Mayes versus Peter Hawkins, whose note he holds for 1400 pounds of tobacco; asks for order of payment. Signed 8 Jany. 1783. // Peter Hawkins notified.

p. 59. John Widewilt versus Abraham Mayes, who owes him $14 and by account $2 and for Patrick McLary by account $5; that these men be compelled to make payment of the above sums with costs. Sig: John Widewilt. Feb. 8, 1783. // Although notified Abraham Mayes has made no appearance and Widewilt asks execution against his property. Granted by Piernas.

p. 60. Elizabeth Baker versus Emanuel Madden. Eliz. Baker represents that Emanuel Madden, absconded from the district, stole a horse belonging to her husband, valued at $60. He stole the horse about a year since as can be proved by Benjamin Winfree and Robert Kidd. The husband of your petitioner, by reason of sickness has been a long time unable to attend to his business and if the petition must sustain the loss of her horse she will be reduced to sell her property to procure subsistence for her children. Sig: Elizabeth Baker. Feb. 9, 1783. // The said Madden to appear and petitioner to prove he stole her horse. Sig: Piernas.

p. 61. James Kelly versus Abraham Mayes, owes him a note for $50; asks for an order of payment. 8 Jany. 1783. Sig: James Kelly. Let the party be notified. Piernas. // Mayes notified and not responded. Kelly asks for an execution against his property. /Note annexed, witnesses by William Brashears. 17 Oct. 1782./

p. 61. John Farquhar versus Peter Hawkins, owes him $46; asks an order for payment of same. 8 Jany. 1783. // Notified by Jas. Harman, constable.

p. 61. Stephen Jordan versus George Jeffries, who owes him $7; asks order of payment. Stephen (X) Jordan. Jany. 8, 1783.

p. 62. Stephen Mayes versus Peter Hawkins, who owes him $58; asks an order of payment. Account annexed. 14 Jany. 1783.

p. 62. James Truly versus Joseph Dunham, who owes him $10 on account. 15 Jany. 1783. Signed. // Let party answer in three days. Sig: Piernas.

p. 63. George Rapalje versus John Farquhar, whose note for value received he has in his possession, which said note Farquhar has acknowledged in the presence of several witnesses. Your petitioner being convinced of his evil designs and being irritated by the falsehoods advanced by said Farquhar against the character of the petitioner, in a moment of passion which he confesses to be wrong did chastise the said Farquhar for his insolence; asks that Farquhar prove his accusations or condemn him to the payment of $5000 injury done to the reputation of your petitioner. Sig: George Rapalje. 15 Feb. 1783.

p. 63. Richard Devall versus Richard Harrison. Richard Devall represents that he sold a tract and two stills to Richard Harrison for $1000 which was executed before Mr. De Grand-Pre, said Harrison having drawn on Captain Pickle, of New Orleans, for the whole amount. When order was presented to said Pickle he paid only $500 for the land, refusing to pay $500 for the stills by reason he had only given orders to purchase the land and not the stills, etc. He asks an order for payment from said Harrison. 20 Jany. 1783. Certificate from William Pickle that he had paid for the land but not for the still. 12 Sept. 1782.

p. 64. William Pountney versus Richard Ellis, who owes him $560, being money advanced for him three years since. 15 Jany. 1783. Sig: Wm. Pountney. // Let it be communicated. Sig: Piernas.

p. 64. John Widewilt versus John Coleman, owes him $18; asks that Coleman be compelled to make payment of same. Statement annexed.

p. 64. St. Germain versus Jeremiah Routh, of this district, planter, who detained the barge of the petitioner for two days; asks that said Routh pay $40 for the delay of his barge. 15 Jany. 1783. Sig: Peter Nelson, atty. for St. Germain.

p. 65. St. Germain versus Joseph Holden, who is indebted to him for $180; asks for an order of payment. Natchez. 15 Jany. 1782. // Order that party will pay within three days or state reasons. Sig: Piernas.

p. 65. John Farquhar versus Jeremiah Routh, who owes him $17 by note; asks that he be condemned for payment of same. 21 Jany. 1783. Signed.

p. 66. Francis Lansphier versus Jeremiah Routh, who had a contract with your petitioner to build a bateau of certain dimensions for $80, payable in merchandise, on condition of delivery of sd bateau to your petitioner by the 15th of December 1782 and on the penalty to pay your petitioner $2 per day until delivered; asks for the damage occasioned by his negligence as your petitioner has been forced to delay his voyage, also a note for $48. Sig: F. Lansphier. 23 Jany. 1783.

p. 66. Richard Ellis versus Stephen Mayes. Hardress Ellis declares that the affair between Capt. Richard Ellis and Stephen Mayes is of the nature following; At the death of Richard Ellis, son of Thomas Ellis, he had the bill of sale for some negroes which was of no importance to the said Mayes. The said Hardress Ellis gave the note to the sd Mayes to give to Captain Ellis as belonging to him, which the said Mayes promised to do in two or three days but not having done soon, the said Hardress Ellis desired him a second time to deliver it. Jany. 21, 1783. Signed: Hardress Ellis.

p. 67. John Bisland versus the King. John Bisland represents that he is the owner of a pirogue which he has been informed a certain John Forester has taken by order of the government. The said pirogue cost your petitioner $50 as will appear by the receipt from Thomas Carter when your petitioner lent him said pirogue to bring up Mr. Vousdan for whom said Carter was overseer. Your petitioner still has the receipt which was given for value of the pirogue. He has been deprived of his pirogue for two months and having need of it to make a voyage to the City of New Orleans he will be under the necessity of purchasing another at his own expense. Signed: John Bisland. 29 Jany. 1783.

p. 67. Wm. Vousdan versus Thomas Carter. Petitioner represents that when about to depart from Baton Rouge he appointed an attorney to attend to his affairs and employed Thomas Carter as overseer of his slaves and covenanted to pay said Carter such sum as determined by two persons to be chosen for that purpose. During his absence the said Carter killed six of my beeves, etc. Sig: Wm. Vousdan. 21 Jany. 1783. // Thos. Carter notified to appear. Sig: James Harman, constable.

p. 67. Richard Bacon versus Abraham Mayes. Bacon presented a petition against said Mayes who has not answered thereto. He asks that property of said Mayes be executed on for the sum of $8 by default. 24 Jany. 1783. // Granted. Piernas.

p. 68. Pierre Nitard versus Abraham Mayes, asks that property be condemned for the sum owing him.

p. 68. Richard Bacon versus Richard Adams, who owes him $63; asks an order for payment of said sum. // Let debtor be notified to pay or appear before me within three days. Sig: Piernas. // Bacon petitions that Richard Adams has neither appeared or paid and asks that sd Adams be condemned by default and an execution against his property for sum and costs. March 10, 1783. // Granted. Piernas.

p. 69. Jeremiah Routh versus Sarah Truly, who owes him 6 bushels of corn lent to her by the petitioner; asks that she be compelled to return the corn and pay cost of suit. Sig: Jeremiah Routh. // Let the party be notified to pay or appear before me in three days. Sig: Piernas. 30 Jany. 1783. // I left notice with Mrs. Sarah Truly to attend the within order. Fee. $1.

p. 69. Thomas Green versus his creditors. Green represents that he has done everything to pay and satisfy his debtors without success. The following are indebted to him: Richard Harrison for $447; Adam Bingaman $137, George Rapalje $46, Jeremiah Routh $54, Richard Devall $496, of which he owes his creditors $645. He prays that Your Excellency stop any suits against him until he can obtain payment for said creditors. 8 Feb. 1783. Sig: Thomas Green.

p. 69. Elizabeth Holloway versus Thos. Rule. She represents that Thomas Rule owes her $4 and 4 rials for carpenter's tools lent to him, namely one hand-saw, one chisel; asks for payment. Sig: Eliz. Holloway. // Let Thomas Rule be notified to make satisfaction within three days.

p. 69. William Smith versus Thomas Green. Smith represents that a certain Thomas Green is indebted to him for $250 and the term of payment being expired since Christmas last and the petitioner being about to go to New Orleans for necessities for his family, although Your Excellency has granted the said Green time to pay his debts, your petitioner asks for consideration as the said Green has received value from him and his case is pressing. // Let Green be notified. // William Smith asks that said Green be condemned by default and asks an execution on his property for sum with costs. Feb. 24, 1783. Sig: William Smith.

p. 70. Michael Lopez versus Anthony Barbason, who owes him $47; asks for an order of payment with cost of suit. Feb. 12, 1783. // Let Barbason be notified to pay. Cole's Creek, 18 Feb. 1783. I notified Anthony Barbason. J. Harman, constable. Fees: $5. // [On Feb. 24, 1783, Michael Lopez petitions again, asking an execution by default. Granted by Piernas.] // Anthony Brabason represents that he has been sued by Michael Lopez, Stephen Mayes, William Ferguson and Saint Germain; that Stephen Mayes has already received $25 from petitioner, etc. will pay as soon as possible, having wood and pirogues ready to bring to the landing. Signed. 6 March 1783.

p. 71. Richard Bacon versus Joseph Holden, owes him money and asks that he be condemned to pay same, $17. 13 Feb. 1783.

p. 72. Richard Bacon versus Thomas Green, who owes him $192; asks that said Green be condemned to make payment of same and cost. 13 Feb. 1783. Signed. // Another from same against same. 24 Feb. 1783.

p. 72. John Lusk versus Richard Devall, who owes him $35, for which he had judgment but has never received payment. Lusk is sued by Richard Bacon and asks for payment from Devall with cost of suit. Sig: John Lusk. 17 Feb. 1783.

p. 73. Joseph Calvit versus Benj. Carrol who owes him $3; asks for an execution against sd Carrol.

p. 73. Anne Hutchins versus John Ellis. Ann Hutchins showeth that in 1777 Anthony Hutchins, your petitioner's husband, obtained a warrant out of the office at Pensacola for surveying for him land lying near and adjacent to the Cliffs, commonly called Ellis's Cliffs, which land, pursuant to said order, was surveyed by Wm. Vousdan and returned to the land office. As your petitioner is not certain whether there was any further grant obtained for said land and is now apprehensive that Mr. John Ellis has a design to get it granted to him and thereby deprive your petitioner's children of their rights, to whom it was made over by their father, as may be seen by the papers in your petitioner's hands. Asks that the premises be taken into your consideration. Sig: Ann Hutchins. Feb. 17, 1783.

p. 74. Thomas Green versus Jeremiah Routh, who owes him $30, and Green asks that he be made to pay. 26 Feb. 1783.

p. 75. Eleanor Price versus Thomas Green, who owes her $26, being for rent of the house occupied by him; asks that he be compelled to pay sum with costs of suit. 26 Feb. 1783. // To be communicated to Thomas Green. Statement annexed.

p. 75. Eleanor Price versus John Stowers, who owes her $14; asks that he be made to pay same. 25 Feb. 1783. Statement: To sundries $4, to a plow $2, to attendance on a wench in labor $8.

p. 75. James Cole versus Jeremiah Routh, who owes him $150 by note which your petitioner put in the hands of Mr. Blommart and was lost with his papers. Said Routh acknowledges to have given his note for the sum mentioned but declares he paid the said note. He has no receipt or paper to prove the payment. 29 Feb. 1783. // Let Routh be notified to appear, etc.

p. 75. Josine Marebois versus Jeremiah Routh, who owes him $32 by note; asks that he be made to pay. 26 Feb. 1783. // Let Jeremiah Routh be notified. Sig: Piernas. // Cole's Cr. 27 Feb. 1783. Fee $5. Wit: Jeremiah Bryan.

p. 76. Matthias Prock versus James Hayes who owes him $3; asks that he be made to pay. 28 Feb. 1783.

p. 76. James Kelly versus Abraham Mayes, who owes him $27; asks that he may be made to pay same and costs. 28 Feb. 1783.

p. 76. John Still Lee versus Abraham Mayes, who owes him $23; asks that he be condemned to make payment. 17 March 1783. // Mayes notified by Silas Crane.

p. 76. Daniel Baker represents that he gave to Lieutenant Don Louis de Grand-Pre a joint note drawn by himself and David Mitchell for $52 being for cattle sold at public sale, said note being payable in nine months but said Mitchell declared that he paid the same to Col. De Grand-Pre who promised to return the said note, or give him a receipt against it, and Mr. De Grand-Pre went from hence without returning the said note or giving any receipt. To pay this note again, particularly in his afflicted situation, would be a hardship; and asks the Commandant to write to Mr. De Grand-Pre to know if said note was really paid. 6 March 1783.

p. 77. Peter Nelson versus creditors of Saint Germain. Peter Nelson, atty. for Mr. Saint Germain, represents that a certain James Fleet is in the employ of the said St. Germain and the petitioner has paid all the debts of the said Fleet except $90 owing by him to John Still Lee for which he has offered horses in payment; that he was also willing to pay the creditors of St. Germain as soon as possible, which he cannot do until he recovers the debts due to St. Germain which are considerable. Your petitioner being unwilling to sell the effects of the said St. Germain in his absence; asks that the creditors wait until the arrival of St. Germain which your petitioner expects daily. 6 March 1783. Peter Nelson, atty. of St. Germain.

p. 77. Jeremiah Routh versus his creditors. Routh represents that he has been sued by several persons namely Henry LaFleur, Mr. St. Germain, and others and he understands that an execution is about to issue against his property which he confesses to be just but unfortunately pillage by the Indians is the cause of the petitioner finding himself at the mercy of his creditors. He can prove by his neighbors that although poor he has always maintained a large family of children by the sweet of his brow and paid his debts until now. The Indians have stolen every one of his horses and reduced him to giving his last cow to pay a debt to a certain Thomas Green, his hogs that were not taken by the Indians are running wild in the woods; asks that he be granted until the next crop for the payment of his debts. Sig: Jeremiah Routh. 7 March 1783.

p. 77. Thomas Green versus Jeremiah Routh, who owes him $24 by note asks for payment and cost of suit. [This is a note to Polser Shilling and transferred to Green.]

p. 77. James Cole versus Jeremiah Routh, who owes him $39; asks for an execution. // Granted. // Received of Jeremiah Routh on account of the within execution $25, for which I gave him my receipt. Sig: James Harman, constable.

p. 78. Manuel de Las Carrigas, Lieut. of the Regiment of Infantry of La. of the garrison of this post, represents that, being informed by Louis Betancourt, private in said regiment, that he had seen the horse of your petitioner which was left running in the cane with other horses of the inhabitants in the hands of an Indian who rode him past the plantations of Don Estevan Minor and Mr. Bingaman toward the plantations of LeFleur and Louis Charbonneau, whereupon your petitioner went in search of said horse and passing by the first plantation to a mill commonly called Lafleur's Mill where he found his said horse with some mares, the said horse having a fresh brand on him said to be that of Louis Charbonneau. The petitioner took said horse to the house and the woman of the house declared in the presence of Mr. Bingaman that she knew the horse to belong to Charbonneau, having seen him frequently in his possession. Petitioner asked her who had sold the horse to Mr. Charbonneau for he had purchased the said horse from Don Carlos de Grand-Pre for $35 as can be proved by creditable witnesses and which he had never sold to Charbonneau nor to any other person, the petitioner having refused Don Estevan Minor who offered him $40 for same. 8 March 1783.

p. 79. Jeremiah Bryan versus Thomas Yarrow, who owes him $52; asks that he be made to pay. 22 March 1783. Note: On or before 29 Jany. I promise to pay or cause to be paid to Mr. Jeremiah Bryan or order 70 milled dollars for value received. Signed: Thos. Yarrow. Wit: James Kelly. 12 Nov. 1782. Petitioner asks an execution against the property of Yarrow.

p. 79. Richard Bacon versus James Kelly, who owes him $72; asks that Kelly be condemned to pay. 11 March 1783. Etc. // Execution against property granted by Piernas. May 1, 1783.

p. 79. Richard Bacon versus Anthony Bouker, who owes him $48; asks for payment. 11 March 1783.

p. 80. James Harman versus Abraham Knapp and Ithamar Andrews. Harman represents that he rented a piece of ground from William Ferguson, a part of which he then rented to Knapp and Ithamar Andrews who covenanted to pay the said Wm. Ferguson their equal proportion of the land. Ithamar Andrews having measured the said land found the rent for the land they used to be $70 which they have not yet paid the said Ferguson according to their agreement. 11 March 1783.

p. 80. Abraham Moore versus Polser Shilling. Abraham Moore represents that on 6 Feb. last, the petitioner engaged with a certain Polser Shilling to row from hence to New Orleans and back to Natchez, and the said Polser Shilling in the presence of witnesses agreed to pay each hand four rials per day. 26 Feb. being the time we left Natchez and 31 March when we returned. Said Shilling refuses to pay us according to agreement; asks that he be made to pay. Sig: Abraham Moore. 14 Apr. 1783. Bill for same annexed for $12.

p. 80. William Hurlbert represents that Charles Adams owes him $11 and asks that he be made to pay same. 24 March 1783. Etc.

p. 81. St. Germain versus Anthony Barbason, who owes him $36; asks that he be condemned by default and granted execution agst his property. // Granted by Piernas.

p. 81. St. Germain versus Abraham Mayes. St. Germain asks that Mayes be condemned for payment of 2400 pounds of tobacco and property executed on for that amount. Sig. St. Germain. // Granted. 23 April 1783. // Same versus same for $37. Asks for payment.

p. 81. Reuben Alexander versus Thos. Carter, who owes him $30; asks for payment. 24 March 1783.

p. 82. Daniel Baker versus Robert Kidd, who owes him $30; asks for payment, etc.

p. 82. Sarah Truly versus Judith Holstein. Sarah Truly represents that Judith Holstein is indebted to her for $9 by account; asks that she be condemned to pay of same and cost of suit. Sig: Sarah Truly. 13 March 1783. // Judith Holstein notified according to order. Sig: James Harman, constable. // Bill: July 1782. Paid Foster for your third part of rum and taffia on the voyage; paid Vousdan for your part of beef, 10 pounds; paid Vousdan for your part of the boat $10; paid Vousdan for your half for the negro hire $3. I don't think I have any right to the negro hire as I had a hand of my own on board. Credit: By a hog she let Wm. West have $7. Balance $9.

p. 83. Eleanor Price versus John Stanley, who owes her a cow which Stanley promised to pay her for taking care of a wounded Indian. Petitioner sent a man to Cole's Creek for the cow, and road being too bad to bring her down by land, whereby the cow was killed, the petitioner only received three quarters thereof, which she sold to the garrison; asks that she be paid for the remainder of the said cow and the hire of the man. 27 March 1783. Eleanor (X) Price.

p. 83. Jeremiah Bryan versus George Bailey, who owes him $5 by one note and 120 pounds of lard by another, and also $4, which Thomas Green promised to pay to your petitioner, the said Bailey having sold a cow and calf to a certain Simmons to pay a debt for said Green, wherefore petitioner asks that said Bailey and Green be condemned to pay the sums aforesaid. Sig: Jeremiah Bryan. // Let parties be notified. // Green claimed the payment of two notes and hath not answered in any manner. // Bryan petitions that an execution be made against the property of said Bailey and Green for payment and cost of suit. 14th ____ 1783. // Granted by Piernas.

p. 84. John Farquhar versus John Short. Petition showeth that an order of payment be made but the defendant did not attend and consideration is prayed for.

p. 85. Archie Palmer versus John Farquhar, who owes him $200 by note; asks payment as petitioner is indebted to divers persons. Signed. // Let Farquhar be notified to pay in three days. Sig: Piernas.

p. 85. William Cocke Ellis versus John Farquhar who owes him $39, being balance on his note; asks for payment. 7 July 1783. Signed. // Let Farquhar be notified to pay debt in three days or appear before me. Sig: Collell. 9 July 1783.

p. 86. John Farquhar versus his creditors. Farquhar represents that in 1781 your petitioner was compelled to give up his property to his creditors on account of the failure of his crop of that year. Trustee appointed was John Bisland. He had done everything in his power to do justice to his creditors. Last year he sold his plantation and had much trouble to make a crop this year on the plantation on which he is now settled; he asks that his creditors wait until the end of the present crop when he will divide the whole among his creditors. Sig: John Farquhar. 8 July 1783.

p. 86. William Ferguson versus St. Germain and others. Wm. Ferguson represents that St. Germain and George Hazard are indebted to him on a joint note for $211, asks for payment. 1 April 1783. Signed. // To be communicated to Mr. St. Germain. Sig: Piernas.

p. 87. Miguel Lopez versus Abner Green, who owes him $8. Lopez asks for payment of same. 2 April 1783. Sig: Miguel Lopez. // Let Green be notified to pay. Sig: Piernas.

p. 87. John Short versus Matthias Prock, who owes him $35; asks that he be made to pay same. 2 April 1783. Signed. // Granted by Piernas.

p. 88. William Jones versus Polser Shilling. Jones represents that on 6 Feb. last, he was engaged by a certain Polser Shilling to row from Natchez to New Orleans and back. Polser Shilling agreed to pay each hand 4 rials a day from 6 Feb. to 31 March. Due him $26. Asks for payment.

p. 88. Alexander McComsey versus Richard Bacon, who owes him $6; asks that he be made to pay, 3 April 1783. Signed. // Order to satisfy debt.

p. 88. St. Germain versus Abraham Hayes, who owes him $37 and he has not appeared according to order. He asks an execution against his property. Signed. // Granted. Sig: Piernas. 23 April 1783.

p. 89. St. Germain versus Wm. Ferguson. St. Germain represents that in answer to the notification made to him of the petition of Wm. Ferguson claiming the payment of a note of $1700, of which he is the holder, drawn in favor of Groding, deceased, that a demand of this nature should not have been made by any other person. Petitioner represents that the first debts he contracted with Groding were paid by Mr. Blommart, and your petitioner satisfied the one in question three months afterwards; and in the second instance, your petitioner drew a note to the order of said Groding, being the note in question, the payment of which he is now unjustly demanded with the hope of surprising the diligence of Your Majesty, the same having been paid at the same time with several others given by your petitioner, namely to Mr. Cassel, Messrs. Montsanto and others by execution they obtained from Monsieur Dela Villebeuvre, Commandant of Manchac, where the petitioner then made his residence, in pursuance of which his whole property was seized, amounting at least to $2000, put into the hands of a certain Felix Patrick with orders to satisfy the above debts, in which the note of $211 was included, but since the seizure above-mentioned your petitioner has frequently met with the said Groding, they passed six months together, they saw and conversed together in this post, they met at the Illinois where your petitioner was in possession of near $6000 which he carried always about him in gold and which was well known to the said Groding; if anything was due him he would certainly have profitted by the occasion and demanded his payment of same. Also there is due to your petitioner 8000 deer skins by the Indians settled at the Rapides, of which your petitioner demanded payment accompanied with some threats which he conceived the only measure to obtain the payment, but the Indians made a different interpretation and their chief came to this post and represented to Mr. Miro, Governor of the Province, that the goods sold to them were prohibited and forbade the Indians to pay for them. Whereupon your petitioner represented that the Indians came for those goods themselves and forbidding them to pay for the said goods would prevent the petitioner from satisfying the debts he had contracted for the goods, to which His Excellency replied that your petitioner had nothing to fear. The goods prohibited to Indian were also prohibited to him and consequently no suit could be brought for such. Signed: St. Germain. // Notified Wm. Ferguson to appear.

p. 90. P. Turpin versus Richard Harrison. Philip Turpin was employed by Capt. Harrison to make 10 casks for tobacco which he did, expecting to be paid for same by said Harrison to whom the same were to be delivered. Harrison said he could not pay for same until he had received the money from Peter Hawkins. He asks for payment. 16 April 1783. Signed. // Mr. Harrison notified to answer the foregoing.

p. 90. Philip Turpin versus the estate of McIntosh, which owes him for $8. Turpin asks for payment of same. 16 April 1783. // To be communicated. // I notified Adam Bingaman to pay or appear before the Commandant and make his objections. Sig: Silas Crane, constable.

p. 91. Richard Bacon versus Patrick Foley, who owes him $25; asks that he be made to pay same. 13 March 1783. // Let Patrick Foley be notified. // Bacon petitions that Foley has not appeared in answer to the order and asks that Foley be condemned by default and an execution against his property be granted for the aforesaid sum. 25 April 1783. // 11 May 1783. Granted by Piernas.

p. 91. Richard Bacon versus Richard Adams, now confined in the fort, who owes him $70 and has property sufficient to pay him; asks that said Adams be condemned to pay the aforesaid sum. 31 May 1783.

p. 91. Ann Yarrow versus Thomas Yarrow. Ann Yarrow represents that some time since waited on Your Excellency to inform you that she had left her husband in consequence of the ill treatment she had received from him. She has two children to maintain to which her husband has not in the least contributed. She has no property of her own and is obliged to work incessantly to support them; her husband has sold all the furniture even to her bed leaving her and her children exposed to the world; asks that her said husband be ordered to contribute to the support of the children. Signed: Ann Yarrow. 26 May 1783. // Let Thomas Yarrow be notified to appear before me in three days that justice may be done. Sig: Piernas. // Yarrow notified by Silas Crane, constable.

p. 92. Charles Royer versus Joseph Donne, who owes him $9; asks that he be condemned to pay same. 8 March 1783. // Communicated. Sig: Piernas.

p. 92. Daniel Baker versus Robert Kidd. Robert Kidd represents that he has been sued by Daniel Baker, to whom he has given his note, and he understands that he is ordered to pay half the amount and, being a poor man compelled to earn his bread by the sweet of his brow, asks that he be allowed until the next crop for the payment thereof. Sig: Robert Kidd. 11 May 1783. // Granted for the time mentioned. Sig: Piernas.

p. 93. Michael Lopez versus Sarah Truly, who is indebted to him for $9 for a pirogue stolen by her negro and, having received no satisfaction for the same, asks that she will be condemned to make payment of same with costs. 6 May 1783. // I notified Sarah Truly according to the above order. Sig: James Harman, constable.

p. 93. William Barland versus Alexander McIntyre. Barland represents that Alexander McIntyre indebted to him for $9 for tailor's work; asks that payment be made to him. Sig: Wm. Barland. 17 May 1783. // Notified. // Account: For making a vest $1; seating a pair of britches 4 rials; to storage your effect from Jan. 1st to 1st April $8.

p. 94. Benjamin Carrol versus George Jeffreys who owes him $8; asks that he be made to pay same. 8 May 1783.

p. 94. Alexander McConnel versus the estate of Joseph Dawes. McConnel represents that the estate of Joseph Dawes owes him $734 by account and asks that payment and costs be made him as he is a poor man and in bad health. 8 May 1783. // Let him produce his claim by authentic documents. Sig: Piernas. // Joseph Dawes to Alexander McConnel. To 6 heads of horses $450; to 19 yards of s striped linen at $3 per yard $57; to 36 yards of striped linen $108; to ounces of cotton thread $2; to 10 yards of holland at $3 per yard $30; to one handkerchief $2; to one hammer and cash lent $70; to 1 comb and girt $2; to 8 1/2 yards of linen $8.50; to 1 bu. of salt $4. due to Alexander McConnel.

p. 95. Henry Stampley vs John Short, who is indebted to him for $6, having been hired to row his boat to Baton Rouge two years ago and not yet been paid; asks said Short be condemned to pay same. 11 May 1783. Signed. // Let Short be notified to pay the debt. Sig: Piernas. //

p. 95. George Weigle versus Jeremiah Bryan. Weigle represents that Jeremiah Bryan against decency and humanity has bitten your petitioner and kicked him in the testacles to the great pain of the petitioner and for no other reason but for having said that Bryan had been in your petitioner's cornfield. He had found his corn and pumpkins broken down and he had good reason to believe that it was done by said Bryan. // Jeremiah Bryan ordered to appear before me. Signed: Piernas. //

p. 96. George Craven versus Daniel Grafton. George Craven represents that he is accused by Daniel Grafton of stealing an iron pot. Your petitioner being one day in the woods saw a runaway negro belonging to Dr. Farrell, who on perceiving the petitioner escaped leaving an iron pot in the woods which your petitioner carried to the place where he then dwelt. Your petitioner then gave public notice that he had found the said pot and eleven months elapsed without anyone claiming same and your petitioner lent the said pot to a certain Kelly, informing at the same time the above circumstances. Daniel Grafton went to the house of the said Kelly and took the pot away without the knowledge of your petitioner, at the same time accusing him of having stolen it. Asks that Grafton make satisfaction for the injury done his character. 12 May 1783. Signed: George Craven. // Let both parties be notified to appear before me. Sig: Piernas. 10 June 1783.

p. 96. William Ferguson versus Stephen Mayes. W. Ferguson represents that an affair between him and Stephen Mayes who agreed to make a crop together on said Mayes plantation this season; your petitioner desired Mayes to meet him before Your Excellency in order to make our signed agreement and he has not complied; asks that the said Mayes do appear and comply with his agreement with your petitioner. Signed: Wm. Ferguson. May 12, 1783.

p. 97. Martha Gibson versus John Still Lee, who owes her $10, being for taking care of him in a sickness a long time since, and the sd Lee refusing payment thereof. Signed: Martha Gibson. // Let John Still Lee be notified to pay. Sig: Piernas. // Notified by Silas Crane, constable.

p. 97. Richard Adams versus James Jellison, deceased, who was indebted to him. Col. De Grand-Pre promised your petitioner that he should be paid out of the proceeds of the property of said Jellison pro rata with the other creditors which, however, was not done. Asks that Your Excellency will cause the archives of this post to be examined to ascertain if there is any property of said Jellison out of which the demand of the petitioner may be paid. Sig: 19 May 1783.

p. 97. Adam Bingaman versus Luis Charbonneau. Adam Bingaman asks that Your Excellency compel Luis Charbonneau restore to him a mare which he has possession of for some months and which he says that he got from the Indians. The petitioner, knowing the said mare to belong to him, claimed her from said Carbonneau who refused to deliver her; asks that said Charbonneau be compelled to restore said mare without delay, said mare bearing petitioner's brand which Charbonneau ought to have noticed when he bought the said mare from the Indians or others. Signed: Adam Bingaman. 26 May 1783. // Let Charbonneau be notified to appear before me. Sig: Piernas.

p. 98. Richard Gooding versus Patrick Foley. Richard Gooding represents that a certain Patrick Foley is indebted to him for 15 bushels of corn, being for the hire of his negro for one month, and having frequently demanded payment from sd Foley and received nothing, asks that he be compelled to do so, with costs of suit. 29 May 1783. Sig: Richard Gooding. // Let Patrick Foley be notified to satisfy the debt claimed, or appear with the plaintiff before me. Sig: Piernas. // Notified by Silas Crane, constable. // 31st Aug. 1783. Let the defendant be notified to pay the 15 bushels of corn and cost of suit in three days or in default thereof his property will be seized. Sig: Trevino. 31 Oct. 1783.

p. 98. Adam Bingaman versus John Choat, who owes him $24 by note; asks that said Choat be condemned to pay same with costs of suit. 17 May 1783. Signed. // Let the debtor be notified to pay or appear before me in three days. Sig: Piernas. 4 June 1783. // I notified John Choat 25 June 1783. James Harman, constable.

p. 98. Thomas Green versus Adam Bingaman, who owes him $25; asks that he will be condemned to pay same. Signed. 28 March 1783. // Notified the defendant to appear. Sig: Silas Crane, constable. // Adam Bingaman to Thomas Green. Feb. 26, 1783. To order on you from Mr. Shilling $130; by order on James Truly $88; by cash $7; by hire of a bateau to Cole's Creek $8. Balance $27. [With this statement was a letter from Adam Bingaman stating that the enclosed account shows that the claim against him by Thomas Green is unjust and asks that Green be made to pay the costs of this suit.] 1st May 1783.

p. 98. William Pounteney versus Joseph Copel. William Pounteney represents that it was not his fault that he did not pay the note to Joseph Copel as it was not presented to him, etc. Sig: Wm. Pounteney, 14 June 1783. He asks to be allowed to kill some cattle and pay the proceeds to pay the said note. // Granted as requested.

p. 99. Richard Bacon versus Daniel Baker. Bacon represents that he lost two calves, one of which he found in possession of Daniel Baker. // Notified Daniel Baker according to order. James Harman, constable.

p. 99. Pedro Azevedo versus Wm. Pounteney, who owes him for 57 days attendance and medecine; asks for payment for same. 16 July 1783. Signed.

p. 99. James Willing versus Louis Charbonneau. Willing represents that a bay horse was stolen from him by the Indians and carried by them to the Nation and said horse was purchased by Saint Germain and is now in the hands of Louis Charbonneau. Your petitioner can prove by witnesses that said horse belongs to him and asks that Your Honor will compel Charbonneau to restore the horse to him. 1783. Signed James Willing. // Let the foregoing be communicated to the party. Sig: Collell.

p. 100. Zaccheus Routh versus Sarah Truly. Routh represents that at the time of his departure from hence he left in the hands of Sarah Truly a looking glass and 9 pictures and on his return the said Sarah Truly refused to restore them; asks that she be ordered to restore the said articles. Signed. // Let Sarah Truly be notified to restore the looking glass and pictures within three days or appear before me. // Notified by James Harman.

p. 100. James Willing versus William Hiorn. Willing represents that in Jany. 1777 he was sent here by Governor Galvez with letters to Congress, since when and up to the present time, your petitioner has lost considerably by the unhappy revolution at Natchez. His property was sold as belonging to John Blommart and he was only attorney for your petitioner. Wherefore he asks Your Excellency to expedite his affairs that he may return home. Asks that two persons be appointed by Your Excellency to determine any difficulties that may arise between him and those who are indebted to him. He represents further that William Hiorn the last attorney appointed for your petitioner sold a saddle horse and other effects and he asks that Mr. Pounteney, the exr. of the estate of Mr. Hiorn be ordered to make a settlement with your petitioner. Signed. 20 June 1783. // The petitioner will present his accounts to the exors. of Hiorn, deceased. Signed: Collell. Statement follows.

p. 100. Arthur Cobb versus Russell Jones. Cobb represents that a certain Russell Jones owes him $650 by note; and, having received no satisfaction whatever, asks that Jones be condemned to make payment of the sum with cost of suit. 24 June 1783. Signed: Arthur Cobb. // Let Russell Jones be notified to pay. Signed: Collell.

p. 101. William Calvit versus Stephen Jett. William Calvit represents that a certain Stephen Jett who had made a complaint against your petitioner is a man of bad character; that Jett about the 7th of October last on the Holstein River, without any cause whatever, did conceal himself near the road from whence he fired upon your petitioner with intent to kill him and did break the right palm of your petitioner. Unfortunately your petitioner met with the said Jett at the house of Mr. Brocus and your petitioner being a little in liquor a dispute took place between them and they fought until they were parted. Your petitioner is very sorry for what has passed and asks the clemency of Your Excellency. Signed: William Calvit.

p. 101. Silas Crane versus Saint Germain. Silas Crane represents that a certain Saint Germain is indebted to him for $29 by account and asks that payment be made with cost of court. 8 July 1783. Signed: Silas Crane. // Let Saint Germain be notified to pay the debt, etc. Sig: Collell.

p. 101. Sarah Truly versus James Willing, who owes her $86 by account, having frequently demanded payment thereof, has received nothing but promises; asks that said James Willing be condemned to pay same, with costs of suit. 11 July 1783. Signed. // Let James Willing be notified, etc. Signed Collell.

p. 102. Richard Ellis versus Stephen Mayes, who has sued your petitioner for two slaves on account of the sale made to him by Richard Ellis, my nephew, of 6 slaves, two of whom are yet living, which sale was made to him by Hardress Ellis, brother of said Richard Ellis, to deliver same to uour petitioner. A certificate of same is in the possession of your petitioner signed by said Hardress, stating that the bill-of-sale is of no value, having received a compensation for the same. If this certificate is not sufficient, the petitioner will cause the said Ellis to come from Opelousas where he now dwells. Signed: Richard Ellis. // To be communicated to Stephen Mayes. 3rd July 1783. Sig: Collell.

p. 102. Polser Shilling versus Thomas Baker, who owes him $32; asks that he be condemned to pay same, with cost of suit. Statement annexed, for merchandise. 14 July 1783. // Let Thomas Baker be notified.

p. 102. Elizabeth Lanehart versus Jesse Withers. Elizabeth Lanehart represents that her husband having a design to sell his plantation to Jesse Withers without her permission, she represented to her said husband that it would be more profitable to wait until the crop was gathered and they could better judge what measures to take. Notwithstanding he sold the same for a horse, a ewe, a colt and two iron pots, all of which do not amount to one-half the value of the plantation. Wherefore your petitioner, not having consented to said sale, prays that Your Honor will order the said Jesse Withers to take back the effects beforementioned and return said plantation and crop to your petitioner. Signed: Elizabeth Lanehart. 14 July 1783. // Let Jesse Withers be notified to take back the effects which gave in payment for the plantation of Elizabeth Lanehart. The sale of the plantation without her consent, to whom it belonged being null and void. Signed: Collell.

p. 103. Henry Roach versus David Smith. Henry represents that he has been sued by a certain David Smith and ordered to pay the said Smith 150 bushels of corn, being for the purchase of a water-mill; that since the termination of the said suit, your petitioner called on said Smith and offered to pay him two bushels for one and return the mill to him, provided he would wait for said corn until October next, but the said Smith refused all offers of petitioner. The petitioner is willing to do all in his power to satisfy said Smith but he has no money to do so, and as his corn will soon be ripe he will soon be in a situation to discharge the debt. Asks to be allowed until October next to pay said debt. 14 July 1783. Signed: Henry Roach.

p. 103. Polser Shilling versus mulatto Lewis, who owes him $9; asks that he be condemned to make payment of same with cost of suit. 14 July 1783. Signed. // Let the debtor be notified to satisfy the debt, etc. Signed: Collell. [The bill was for merchandize.]

p. 104. Russell Jones versus Arthur Cobb. Russell Jones represents that the note for $500 for which he was sued by Arthur Cobb was for and in consequence of a horse race between him and petitioner. The said Cobb having also drawn a note for the same sum which notes were lodged in the hands of Richard Brashears and to remain in his possession until both parties should appear before him and delivered to the one who won the race. Your petitioner considers himself as much entitled to claim the race as said Cobb and he has been treated with manifest injustice which he hopes to make fully to appear to Your Honor. The judges who decided the race in favor of said Cobb were William Brocus and Mr. Higdon, both relations of said Cobb, and your petitioner has been informed that said Brocus was interested in said race to the amount of $100 which sum he bet on Cobb's horse and Mr. Higdon is so advanced in years that he could not see the distance of half the course. I trust that Your Honor will not consider these to be proper judges and they adjudged the race to Cobb by eight inches only, which is a very delicate matter. Notwithstanding your petitioner believes the race to have been in his favor, to avoid all dispute, your petitioner offered to run the second time but the said Cobb has always refused, which may convince Your Honor that your petitioner was unjustly treated. The other judges were Henry Holstein and John Terry who are ready to declare that if the race were run a second time they would give it to your petitioner. Asks that the race be run a second time and in the meanwhile the notes held by Mr. Brashears. 7 July 1783. Sig: Russell Jones. // 11 July 1783. Let Jones, Cobb, Brocus, Higson, Holstein, Terry and Brashears and the witnesses each party may have to produce be notified to appear before me at eight o'clock tomorrow morning, that the matter may be examined. Signed: Collell. Natchez, 12 July 1783. // The above named notified by James Harman, constable. // We do hereby certify that the race between Arthur Cobb and Russell Jones for the sum of $500 was to the best of our judgment won by the said Cobb and as judges appointed by mutual consent of the above, we do give it as our opinion, the horse called Redhead, belonging to Arthur Cobb, won the said race by eight or nine inches. 15 July 1783. William (X) Brocus, Henry Holstein, Daniel (X) Higdon. Wit: Richard Brashears. We, Joseph Newton and James Tinsley, do solemnly declare that Richard Brashears, a son-in-law of William Brokus, did bet on Cobb's horse, to which horse William Brokus, one of the judges and father of Richard Brashears, gave the race. 17 July 1783. Joseph (X) Newton, James Tinsley.

p. 105. Elizabeth Baker versus John Hinman, who has ill-treated her, who in company with James Kelly took down the bars of your petitioner's park whereby her horse escaped and has not since been heard of and as the said horse was accustomed to come up every morning to be fed your petitioner is induced to believe that the said Hinman has the horse in his possession. James Kelly who was in company with him says that he heard the dogs bark at the house of your petitioner and shortly after the said Hinman came running behind him out of breath and cursing the family of your petitioner. He said he had thrown down the bars and the horse of your petitioner not having been since found, your petitioner is persuaded that the said Hinman has the horse in his possession or knows where he is. 16 July 1783. Sig: Elizabeth Baker.

p. 105. Daniel Mygatt versus Peter Hawkins, who owes him $13 by note; asks that he be condemned to pay same. Signed. // To be communicated. Sig: Collell. 17 July 1783.

p. 105. Russell Jones versus Arthur Cobb. Russell Jones represents that he is obliged to object to Messrs. Brocus and Higdon as judges of the races between Cobb and your petitioner by reason that they are both interested in favor of said Cobb. John Newton and James Tinsley are ready to declare on honour that they made bets with Brashears who is the son-in-law of Brocus. William Rollins and William Dewitt made bets also with the Calvits who are the sons-in-law of Mr. Higdon, to which may be added that the said Higdon is so blind that he cannot see any distance, etc. 17 July 1783. Signed. // Although it appears that the judges had two sons in law interested in the horse race, circumstances cannot prevent them from deciding on the horse of Cobb as the other two judges declare that the horse called "Redhead" won the race by eight or nine inches and it shall be held that Russell Jones has lost the sum of $500 depending on said horse race. In testimony whereof I have signed. Natchez, 18 July 1783. Signed: Collell.

p. 106. Louis Chachere now of this post versus John Newton, who owes him $23, and the said Newton being about to depart for the Indian nation, your petitioner prays that you will order him to pay same before he shall obtain a passport. Signed. // Let John Newton be notified to pay or appoint some person to pay said debt when it shall become due. Sig: Collell. 29 July 1783. //

p. 106. James Willing versus Sarah Truly, who owes him $313; asks that she be ordered to make payment of the said sum, with costs of suit. July 15, 1783. Signed. // Let Sarah Truly be notified to pay, etc. Sig: Collell.

p. 106. Richard Bacon versus Stephen Minor. Bacon represents that he is considerably indebted to Mr. Campano; that on March last he sent the key of his trunk which was at Mr. Castles, there being sundry government bills to Lt. Minor who counted said bills in the presence of witnesses amounting to $212, of which he took possession, saying at the same time that he had a government bill for $295, which as he was indebted to your petitioner he would pay to Campano the difference of $18, wherefore petitioner gave Minor credit for that sum on his account. But the said Minor has failed in the payment thereof in the sum of $88 which he promised to pay on account of Thomas Green, and $19 on account of James Truly, all of which was to have been paid in the month of March last. Bacon asks that Minor be ordered to make payment according to his agreement. Signed. 25 July 1783. Account of bills: Amount of bills delivered to Mr. Minor $212. Amount assumed by Mr. Minor $18. Amount assumed for Thomas Green $88, and for James Truly $19. // To be communicated to Stephen Minor for his answer. Collell. // John Short will pay to Lieut. Col. Campano the sum of $100, being a difference of accounts between Messrs. Minor and Bacon. Signed: Collell.

p. 107. William Ferguson versus Noah Pittman, as overseer, whose insolence and laziness was so great that petitioner was compelled to dismiss him; asks that Pittman be ordered to pay petitioner the ballance of his account. Signes: Wm. Ferguson, 30 July 1783. // Let the party be notified to pay or give security within three days. Collell. // Notified Noah Pittman. James Harman, constable.

p. 107. John Rowe versus Thomas Rule, who owes him $7; asks that sd Rule be condemned to pay same. Signed. 31 July 1783. // Let Thomas Rule be notified, etc. Signed: Collell.

p. 108. Richard Bacon versus John Short, who owes him a hogshead of tobacco which said Short shipped on board the King's sloop without the knowledge of your petitioner. Mr. George Castles, on his way to New Orleans, called at the house of the petitioner and informed him of said shipment and while conversing about it, the said Short also arrived without mentioning the tobacco until reproached by said Castles for his silence respecting it and he promised to pay your petitioner $52 on the Sunday next ensuing. 30th July 1783. Signed: Richard Bacon.

p. 108. James Willing versus Saint Germain, who owes him $1048 by notes and accounts acknowledged by said Germain; asks that said Germain be condemned to make payment of same. Signed. 28 July 1783.

p. 109. Silas Crane versus John Lusk. John Hartley, being chosen arbitrator in dispute between John Lusk and Silas Crane concerning the brand of a certain cow in possession of John Lusk and claimed by Silas Crane, is of the opinion that a C placed on an L in this manner and further said not. 7 Aug. 1783. Sig: John Hartley.

p. 109. Michael Lopez versus George Rapalje, who owes him $338; asks that he be made to pay the same. // Let George Rapalje be notified. Collell. 6 Aug. 1783.

p. 109. George Rapalje versus Richard Bacon, who owes him $473, exclusive of interest for two years, and Bacon has refused to pay a draft of your petitioner for $30. 4 Aug. 1783. Signed. // Let Richard Bacon be notified to pay or appear, etc. Collell.

p. 109. Louis Chachere versus William Dewitt. Chachere represents that on the 13th instant he made a wager with William Dewitt for $50 and a mare valued in the same sum and although Dewitt acknowledges to have fairly lost the wager, he refuses to pay the money or deliver the mare; asks that Dewitt will be compelled to do justice. 19 August 1783. // Let Dewitt be notified to pay Chachere the $50 and the mare which he lost at the horse race within three days. Signed: Collell.

p. 110. Louis Chachere versus Joseph Duncan, who owes him $84; asks that Duncan be compelled to pay of same. 9th Aug. 1783. // Let Mr. Duncan be notified to pay the debt, etc.

p. 110. Francis Routh versus Richard Bacon. Routh represents that he won from a certain Richard Bacon on a horse race a mule valued at $20 which he can prove by the testimony of Michel Lopez, the same being a debt of honor, petitioner asks that Bacon be compelled to make the payment with cost of suit. Signed: Francis Routh. 20 Aug. 1783. // Richard Bacon shall pay the $20 or deliver the mule within three days. Collell.

p. 110. Eustace Humphreys versus Groves Morris, two of whose notes, drawn for $15 and $3, he holds; asks that Morris be condemned to make payment of same and cost of suit. 25 Aug. 1783. Signed. // Let Groves Morris be notified to pay etc. Collell. // Cole's Cr. I notified Groves Morris. James Harman, constable.

p. 111. Silas Crane versus John Lusk. Crane petitions that if any difficulty should arise respecting the certificate of John Odam and James Wilson, the said Odam and Wilson be summoned to appear before Your Honor to be examined. Sig: Silas Crane. // We, the subscribers do declare that some time in the spring before last we did brand a number of cattle for Silas Crane at the house of John Lusk, said cattle were part of a stock which formerly belonged to William Case and were sold at vendue and we having received a certain young cow now in dispute between Silas Crane and John Lusk do believe said cow to be one to be branded by said Crane as it appears to be branded with the same brand that we branded said Crane's cattle with and on the same part of the body but her natural marks and age we do not remember as we also branded one of that size and color for Richard Deval. John (X) Odam, James Wilson. 4 Oct. 1783. N. B. This may certify that I took the evidence of the above John Odam and that he declared it to be the truth. Signed: Justus King. // We, the subscribers, having been at the house of Mr. John Lusk and received a certain cow in dispute between Silas Crane and said Lusk and heard their disputes about the said cow, after considering their own pleas about the matter, and the evidence produced, it still remains in doubt with us, as the evidences do not seem to be positive, although they are most in Crane's favor. Signed Justus King, Samuel Gibson. //

p. 112. Silas Crane versus John Lusk. Crane represents in relation to a cow in dispute between John Lusk and petitioner, that your petitioner appeared before Messrs. Hartley and Johnson, arbitrators, on the day and place appointed and produced his titles for the said cow but Mr. Hartley refused to examine them, saying that it was not the matter in question but that the point in question with the arbitrators but which of the brands on the cow was the oldest. Your petitioner is ignorant of that matter and Mr. Hartley did not hear anything about the brand by which I claimed the said cow. Mr. Harman informing him that the only matter to determine whether the letter "C" or the letter "L" was the oldest brand. Etc. Oct. 7, 1783. // This is to certify that we, the subscribers were at the house of John Lusk to decide a dispute between John Lusk and Silas Crane. The said cow was branded on the left cushion with "W.C." and on the left shoulder appeared to be the letters "J.L.", but it appeared to us that an "L" had been put upon a "C" or "C" upon an "L" but which was put there first we cannot tell. Mr.

Crane said the brand by which he claimed the cow was a small "C" under the "W.C." and that he knew not how any other brand came on the cow. But Mr. Lusk claimed the cow by the "J.L." but somebody had defaced the "L" with the "C". We then examined Mr. James Wilson, the only evidence present, and he said that he and John Odam branded a number of cattle for Mr. Crane some time ago on the plantation of Mr. Lusk and that they put a small "C" under "W.C." on the left cushion and that the cow in dispute was the same color, etc. Signed. Justus King and Samuel Gibson.

p. 112. Thomas Yarrow versus the mulatto Lewis, who owes him $6, and he asks that he be made to pay the same. // Said mulatto to be notified to pay, etc. Sig: Collell.

p. 113. Thomas Rule versus Samuel Heady, who owes him for $4; asks that he be condemned to pay same. 2 Oct. 1783. Signed. // Let Heady be notified, etc. Collell.

p. 113. Francis Farrell versus Abraham Mayes, who owes him $25 by note which expired Dec. last; asks that Mayes be condemned for payment. 15 Oct. 1783. Signed: Francis Farrell. // Let party be notified. Collell.

p. 113. Joseph Newton versus Louis Chachere, who owes him $15 for taking care of his store for 15 days in his absence; asks an order of payment of same. Oct. 14, 1783. // Let the defendant be notified to pay the debt claimed, etc. Collell.

p. 113. Francis Labispierre versus John Brown and others. Petitioner represents that John Brown and James White are indebted to him for a joint note for $45 and asks that they be condemned to pay same. Oct. 8, 1783. // Let the defendants be notified to satisfy the debt. Collell.

p. 114. Eunice McIntosh versus James Willing. Eunice McIntosh represents that having some accounts to settle with James Willing, they have agreed to leave the settlement thereof to Alexander Moore and Wm. Ferguson; asks that these gentlemen be authorized for that purpose. Signed Eunice McIntosh. 15 Oct. 1783.

p. 114. Richard Harrison versus Jeptha Higdon, who owes him $50 and he asks payment of same. 15 Oct. 1783. // Let Jeptha Higdon be notified, etc. Signed: Trevino.

p. 114. Louis Chachere versus William Dewitt. Chachere petitions that he is the holder of a note drawn by Wm. Dewitt for $50 due on the 12th; asks that said Dewitt be condemned to pay same. Oct. 16, 1783. // Let Wm. Dewitt be notified to pay the sum of $50, claimed, etc. Signed: Trevino.

p. 114. Jesse Hamilton versus Stephen Minor. Hamilton represents that about February last petitioner rented a plantation from Stephen Minor with the building thereto belonging for one year, for which the petitioner agreed to pay said Minor 100 bushels of corn, a part whereof said Minor has already received. About the 8th or 9th of Sept. said Minor sent a large family of people to said plantation, whom your petitioner refused to receive, whereupon the said Minor came in person and despite of your petitioner lodged the said family on the said plantation, at the same time ordering the corn of your petitioner to be thrown out of one of the buildings for the accomodations of said family, to the great loss of your petitioner. Signed: Jesse Hamilton. Oct. 17, 1783. // Defendant will appoint two arbitrators to determine the damage which the plaintiff may have sustained. Signed: Trevino.

p. 115. Robert Carter versus Devilliers. Robert Carter represents that during the time he was in prison, the Commandant DeVilliers sent for from his house a mare, a gun and other articles. On his return the petitioner did receive his gun but his mare was at the Quichata and he has never recovered the other effects; asks that his case, as a poor man, will be taken into consideration. Signed. Oct. 19, 1783. // The Commandant of the Post of Arkansas will take measures to have the property of the petitioner taken from him restored to him. Signed: Miro.

p. 115. George Castles versus Joseph Holden, who owes him $36; asks that said Holden be condemned to make said payment of same. Oct. 18, 1783. Signed. // Let the defendant be notified to pay, etc. Trevino. // Clark's Creek Oct. 20, 1783. I notified Joseph Holden, etc. Jeremiah Bryan. Fee: $5.

p. 116. Francisco Labispere versus William Harrigal who owes him $41, asks that he be condemned to pay same. Oct. 20, 1783. // Let the defendant be notified to pay. Trevino. // Notified by James Harman, constable.

p. 116. Francisco Labispere versus Jeremiah Routh, who owes him $117; asks that he be condemned to pay same and cost of suit. Oct. 24, 1783. Signed. // Let the defendant be notified. Trevino

p. 116. Susannah Maimes versus Patrick Maimes. Petitioner represents that she was lately married to Patrick Maimes; that her said husband had no property of any kind, and having since contracted debts in several places, your petitioner is apprehensive that property belonging to her children by a former marriage may be taken to satisfy the said debts; asks that the property of the orphans may not be liable for said debts, contracted by my said husband. Signed: Susannah Maimes. Oct. 22, 1783. // Let Patrick Maimes be notified to appear before me on Tuesday next that justice may be done in the premises. Trevino.

p. 117. George Castles versus James Willing. George Castles, atty. for John Donoho and as such is holder of a note drawn by James Willing for two cows and calves and a heifer, due since August 1777; asks for Donoho that debtor be condemned to pay for said cattle. Oct. 27, 1783.

p. 117. Daniel and Roswell Mygatt versus Francis Spain and others. Daniel and Roswell Mygatt represent that the undernamed persons owe them several sums; asks that the said debtors make payment. Oct. 28, 1783. Francis Spain $15, James Truly $12, Sarah Truly $18, David Odam $4, David Holt $7, William Dewitt $53.

p. 117. Your Excellency, Richard Bacon represents that your petitioner has a controversy with Mr. Smith of the following nature. The said Smith in February 1778 bought the improvements on a piece of land and a few days afterwards set out for New Orleans but lately returned to this place. In June 1778, Col. McGilvray the British Commandant, at the time, granted permission to a certain Oxbury to settle on the same land and the said Oxbury sold the said improvement in October 1779 for $27, the land itself could not be sold, being reserved to the use of the King and any person settling thereon being liable to be moved by the government and in this situation the place remained for four years. About a year since your petitioner bought the improvement from a certain West who had permission from Mr. Grand-Pre to settle on it. The petitioner had previously in 1782, presented to Governor Miro a plat of this lot of ground drawn by Richard Harrison when His Excellency was pleased to grant the same to your petitioner with 200 arpents of land adjoining; in consequence whereof your petitioner gave up the land granted to him by Mr. Grand-Pre, and removed to the land in question in December last, whereas he has had a great expense in enclosing 60 arpents and cleared about forty arpents and erected buildings. Some days since, being in company with Mr. Smith, he proposed to him to leave the matter to be decided by two disinterested persons and the said Smith agreed and two persons were chosen. Whereupon your petitioner asks that the matter in controversy with said Smith and your petitioner be determined by arbitration. Signed: Richard Bacon. // To be communicated to the other party for his answer.

p. 118. Francis Labispere versus John White, who owes him $68 and $12 by account, the first by note; he asks that payment be made for same. Oct. 28, 1783. // Let John White be notified to pay said claim, etc. within one month or property will be executed. Signed: Trevino.

p. 118. Benjamin Rogers and Richard King versus Samuel Cooper, who owes them $9 by note; asks that he be condemned to pay same. Oct. 29, 1783. Signed by both. // Let Cooper be notified to pay within three days. Trevino.

p. 119. William Vousdan versus Cephas Kinnard, who owes him for $45; asks an order that he pay same. // The plaintiff and defendant will appear before me at the first audience. Messrs Vousdan and Kinnard will abide by the award of Messrs. Castles and Moore, this day appointed arbitrators. Cephás Kinnard to William Vousdan. 1779. 9 pounds of salt, etc. $45. Counter account: June 1779. For drawing timber; for drawing a hogshead of tobacco, etc. $39.

p. 119. Francis Labispere versus James Kelly, who owes him $33; asks that he be made to pay same. Nov. 7, 1783. Kelly will be allowed until the end of the month to pay and in default thereof his property will be executed. Trevino.

p. 120. Louis Chachere versus Thomas Rule, who owes him $16; and asks that he be made to pay. Nov. 11, 1783.

p. 120. Ann Hutchins versus John Short, who is indebted to her for $40; asks that he be made to pay. // Let the defendant be notified to pay, etc. Trevino.

p. 120. Samuel Davis versus Richard Ellis, who owes him $7; asks that said Ellis be condemned to make payment. // To pay within eight days. Trevino.

p. 120. John Short represents that he has been sued by Mrs. Ann Hutchins for a note drawn by a certain Hurlbert Rees, endorsed by David Mitchell to your petitioner, and by him to said Mrs. Hutchins. Hurlbert Rees was at that time an inhabitant of Mobile and Mr. Hutchins promised to send there for the payment, the said note being payable at Mobile and not at this district. I assumed that Mr. Hutchins had sent the note to Mobile and his not having done so is the real reason that he has not received payment. Petitioner, therefore asks that Your Honor will not condemn him to pay the said note, Hutchins having neglected to follow means to collect the same. Signed: John Short. // The petitioner is allowed until the 15th of next month to make payment. Trevino.

p. 121. Negress Betty versus James Willing, who owes her $10 being for washing and mending his clothes, and being informed that he is about to depart from this district, she asks that he be compelled to pay said debt. 27 Nov. 1783. // Capt. Willing will pay the petitioner the sum of $10 the amount of her account. Trevino.

p. 121. Elizabeth Baker versus Robert Kidd, who owes her $60; asks that he be compelled to make the payment thereof. 6 Sept. 1783. Signed. // Let Robert Kidd be notified to pay the claim, etc. Collell.

p. 121. Benjamin Rogers versus David Wattman. Rogers petitions that he suspects that David Wathman has killed his heifer, the said Wathman having carried meat to a friend at the fort and Mrs. Duncan and Mr. Richard King said that they saw Mr. Wathman passing Mr. King's bench twice with meat. Your petitioner went to Wathman and asked to see the hide of the beef he had killed last and he said that the dogs had eaten it; and he then inquired of whom he had bought the said beef and he had bought the heifer with a black cow from the plantation of Mr. Belk and Mr. Samuel Lewis being present said that the black cow must have brought the heifer in her belly. Petitioner asks that Wathman may be ordered to produce the skin of the said beef, two only of the three beeves he killed being known by the neighbors to havė belonged to him. Signed. // Let David Wathman, Richard King, Jacob Paul and Samuel Lewis be notified to appear before me at next court. Signed: Collell.

p. 122. Daniel and Roswell Mygatt versus their debtors. They represent that three years have elapsed since they gave public notice to their debtors to make payments and your petitioners, being indebted to several merchants of this place, asks an order of payment from their debtors in general that they may appear before Your Honor to show to the contrary. Signed by both. Sept. 18, 1783.

p. 122. Ann Hutchins versus Thomas Rule, who owes her $35 by note; asks that debtor be compelled to pay same. Sept. 2, 1783. Signed. // Let Thos. Rule be notified to pay said debt in three days, etc. Collell. // White Apple Village, March 3, 1783. Three days after date I promise to pay Mrs. Ann Hutchins $35 which I have received. Thomas (X) Rule. Wit: John Prentice.

p. 123. Jeremiah Bryan versus Silas Crane, who owes him $9 by note; asks that he may be made to pay same.

p. 123. Stephen Hayward versus the estate of Alexander McIntosh, of which he is a creditor in the sum of $108, which he can prove by his obligation in his possession; asks that the heirs be condemned to make payment. 23 Feb. 1783. Signed. // To be communicated. Piernas.

p. 123. Silas Crane versus John Lusk. Silas Crane represents that judgment having been given against your petitioner respecting a cow in dispute between him and said Lusk, asks that he be allowed him and his witnesses to be heard before your court. Sept. 29, 1783. Signed.

p. 124. Matthias Prock versus Stephen Holstein, who is indebted to him for $10; asks that he be condemned to pay same. 28 Feb. 1783. Signed. // Let Stephen Holstein be notified to pay, etc.

p. 124. Sarah Truly versus Melling Woolley. Sarah Truly represents that Mr. Ferguson has examined the books of Mr. Woolley in connection with Mr. Harrison and he finds nothing charged against your petitioner from 25 August 1776 to the end of the book, therefore she asks that Woolley will be ordered to pay the balance due to _____. Signed: Sarah Truly, Will: Ferguson.

p. 124. Archibald Palmer represents that a certain John Farquhar is indebted to him for $200. 22 December 1783. // Let John Farquhar be notified to appear at the first audience, to satisfy the debt claimed. Trevino.

p. 125. Saint Germain versus Benjamin Rogers, who owes him $28 by account; asks that he be made to pay. Dec. 2, 1783. Signed. // Let the defendant be notified to pay the debt, etc. Trevino.

p. 125. Saint Germain versus Stephen Hayward and Charles Howard, who are indebted to him by a joint note for $880; asks that the debtors be condemned to pay same. 2 Dec. 1783. // Let the defendants be notified to pay within 6 days, etc. Trevino.

p. 125. Louis Chachere versus Richard Bacon, who owes him $91. Being about to depart for the capital, petitioner asks that Bacon be condemned to make payment of same. 9 Dec. 1783. // Let defendant be notified to pay within five days, etc. Trevino.

p. 126. John Hartley represents that John Woods owes him $3 payable on demand; asks that the said debtor be condemned to make payment. Signed. 2 December 1783. // Let the defendant be notified to pay within six days, etc. Trevino.

p. 126. Joseph Duncan versus Joseph Ford, who is indebted to him for $11; asks that the debtor be condemned to pay the same. 4 Dec. 1783. Signed. // Let debtor be notified to pay same, etc. Trevino.

p. 126. Joseph Duncan versus James Wilson, who owes him for $49; asks that Wilson be made to pay same. Dec. 4, 1783. Signed. // Let debtor be notified to pay same, etc. Trevino.

p. 126. Joseph Duncan represents that a certain free mulatto, named Lewis Clare is indebted to him for $20 by note and prays that he be condemned to make payment of same. Dec. 4, 1783. Signed. // Let defendant be notified to pay within three days, etc. Trevino.

p. 127. Joseph Duncan versus Stephen Holstein, who owes him $40 by note; asks that he be condemned to pay the same. 4 Dec. 1783. Signed. // Debtor to pay within three days, etc. Trevino.

p. 127. Benjamin Rogers versus Henry Roach, who owes him $7; asks that debtor be condemned to pay same, with cost of suit. Dec. 5, 1783. Signed. // Let defendant be notified to pay in three days, etc. Trevino.

p. 127. Benjamin Rogers versus David Crow, who owes him $9; asks that Crow be condemned to pay same, with costs of suit. Dec. 5, 1783. Signed. // Let deft. be notified to pay in three days, etc. Trevino.

p. 128. Charles Royau versus Patrick Foley. Charles Royeau represents that Patrick Foley owes him $25; asks that he be condemned to pay same with costs of suit. Dec. 5, 1783. Signed: Charles Royeau. // Let defendant pay in three days etc. Trevino.

p. 128. Benjamin Rogers versus Benjamin Brashears, who owes him $10; asks that debtor be condemned to pay same with cost of suit. Dec. 1, 1783. // Let debtor be notified to pay, etc. Trevino.

p. 128. Benjamin Rogers versus Thomas Rule, who owes him $6; asks that he be made to pay with costs of suit. 5 Dec. 1783. Signed. // Let debtor be notified to pay in three days or, etc. Trevino.

p. 128. Elijah Routh versus George Bailey who owes him 1000 pounds of tobacco by note; asks that he be condemned to pay same and cost of suit. Dec. 5, 1783. Signed. //

p. 129. Benjamin Rogers versus Moses McCann, indebted to him for $5; asks that he be condemned to pay same and cost of suit. 5 Dec. 1783. Signed. // Let the defendant be notified to pay same in three days or, etc. Trevino.

p. 129. Benjamin Rogers versus Thomas Yarrow, indebted to him for $13; asks that he be indebted to pay him same with cost of suit. 5 Dec. 1783. Signed. // Ordered to pay in three days, etc. by Trevino.

p. 129. Joseph Duncan versus John Choat, indebted to him for $20; asks that debtor be condemned to pay with cost of court. 4 Dec. 1783. Signed. // Let defendant be notified to pay within three days or, etc. Trevino.

p. 129. Charles Royeau versus James Kelly, indebted to him for 100 pounds of pork and $2 in money; asks that he be condemned to pay same. Dec. 5, 1783. Signed. // Let deft. be notified to pay etc. Trevino.

p. 130. Benjamin Rogers versus John Lovelace, who owes him $9 by note; asks that said debtor be condemned to pay same and costs of court. Dec. 5, 1783. Signed. // Order to pay in three days or execution will issue. Trevino.

p. 130. Archibald Palmer versus John Farquhar. Palmer represents that he was overseer for John Farquhar in 1782 and during that year said Farquhar went down to New Orleans to give up his property to his creditors by whom the said Farquhar and John Bisland were appointed agents; that on the said Farquhar's return with a letter of license, your petitioner inquired of him and Mr. Bisland if he should continue according to the agreement with him, the said Farquhar, and was told by them to continue. Some time afterwards a certain Cato West arrived from New England, to whom the said Farquhar and Bisland sold the plantation on which your petitioner was making a crop, which he bought from your petitioner for $300 and shortly afterwards paid him $100 on the account, now said Farquhar objects to pay your petitioner the balance due him, saying that his property belongs to his creditors in general. Etc. Dec. 8, 1783. Signed.

p. 131. John Smith versus John Ellis, who is indebted to him for $19. Dec. 10, 1783. // Order to pay by Trevino. Richard Harrison and Wm. Vousdan chosen arbitrators by the plaintiff and defendant do award to the plaintiff no right to bring suit, therefore we acquit the defendant of paying anything. 19 Dec. 1783.

p. 131. Polser Shilling versus William Hurlburt, who owes him $22; asks that he be made to pay same with cost of suit. 10 Dec. 1783. Signed. // Let the defendant be ordered to pay within three days etc. Trevino.

p. 131. Joseph Duncan versus James Willing, who is indebted to him for $70; asks that he be condemned to pay same with cost of suit. 4 Dec. 1783. Signed. // Let the defendant be notified to pay within 3 days or etc. Signed: Trevino.

p. 131. Joseph Duncan versus Philip Shaver, who owes him $63; asks that he condemned to payment of same with cost of suit. Dec. 18, 1783. Signed. // Let the defendant be notified to pay, etc. Trevino.

p. 132. Silas Crane represents that he is certain that he paid money to Col. De Grand-Pre or he is more deceived than he ever was before, but if he should be compelled to pay again, he begs that he will be allowed some time by reason that more is so difficult to procure. He begs that his little property may not be exposed to public sale, having sundry sums due to him. He is satisfied to mortgage his property to the government, that is to say his cattle. By his calculation he owes but $300 and $400 are owing to him. As respect to money owing by Mr. Platereau he intends to recover that debt immediately; as respect to note to Fanchonette, your petitioner believes that it has been paid. 15 Dec. 1783. Silas Crane.

p. 132. William Smith versus Stephen Haywood, indebted to him for two years in the sum of $36. He is holder of an obligation given by Stephen Haywood to John Fitzpatrick amounting, with the interest thereto, to $3035, which was transferred to your petitioner by said Fitzpatrick as security for the sum of $400, with order to recover the amount thereof; asks that the debtor be condemned to make payment and cost of suit. 5 Dec. 1783. Signed.

p. 132. Thomas Rule versus Daniel Baker, who owes him $34, and asks for payment. Thomas (X) Rule. 15 Dec. 1783.

p. 132. Elizabeth Baker versus James Willing. James Willing gave to her son, John Baker, a colt, having found his mare, in the presence of Stephen Haywood, Isaac Johnson and Mr. Buckner, notwithstanding which the said Willing has sold the said colt to Mr. Belk. She asks that he be made to appear with witnesses beforenamed and show cause why he should not restore said colt. Aug. 26, 1783. Signed. // Let Captain Willing be notified according to order to appear tomorrow. Arbitrators will be appointed to determine the matter.

p. 133. Grove Morris versus Benj. Carrol, who owes him $28; asks that he be made to pay. Account follows.

p. 134. Saint Germain versus Silas Crane. St. Germain represents that he has been sued by Silas Crane, a constable of this district, without any previous demand of payment on petitioner, which is contrary to the practive established that the plaintiff should always make a demand before bringing a suit. Your petitioner was appointed by Col. De Grand-Pre to proceed against the estate of Thomas James, an absconded fugitive, which was afterwards confiscated for the use of the King as the King never pays costs, your petitioner does not think himself bound to pay the exorbitant charges of Silas Crane in the matter wherein he was not interested, and besides your petitioner doubts whether Silas Crane was employed in the proceedings. It was Francis Farrell who wrote all the petitions and he has never been paid nor ever demanded payment in consequence of property being confiscated for the use of the King. Signed: St. Germain. Jan. 4, 1784.

p. 134. Sarah Truly versus Sterling Spell, who owes her $70 by note; asks that the same be recovered with cost of suit. Signed. 1st Jany. 1784. // Let defendant be notified and pay within three days or execution will issue. Trevino. [Account follows.] John Lum and Francis Farrel appointed arbitrators and they report after studying the accounts that Sterling Spell is indebted to Sarah Truly for $14.

p. 135. George Weigle versus David Waltman, who owes him $70; asks for payment and cost of court. By testimony of Richard Brashears and Roswell Maxwell same can be proved. Signed. Jany. 3, 1784. // Let the defendant appear before me at first audience. Trevino.

p. 135. St. Germain versus Joseph Duncan, who is indebted to him for $330; asks that he be made to pay same with cost of suit. 7 Jany. 1784. // Let defendant be notified to pay within 8 days or, etc. Trevino.

p. 135. St. Germain versus Jones and Duncan, who owe him $479; asks that they may be made to pay same with cost of suit. 9 Jany. 1784. Signed. // Let the defendants be notified to pay within 8 days, etc. Trevino.

p. 136. Michael Lopez versus Jeremiah Bryan, who owes him $7 since last year and suggested that the petitioner take payment in corn, to which the petitioner replied that he could not do that at that time, his pirogue being fully loaded for GrandGulf, but when he arrived he would send back the pirogue for the said corn. And your petitioner did accordingly send the pirogue and four men with orders to take the corn to the amount of the debt but Mr. Bryan told the men that if they wanted the corn they must shell it, to which they replied that they were hired to work the pirogue and not to shell corn. Finally one of the men finding that nothing else could be done, he consented to shell the corn and did shell 15 bushels and 2 bushels of trash which said Bryan delivered to them, for which your petitioner was compelled to pay the hands for 8 days at $2 per day. // Let the defendant be notified to complete the payment of the debt and the expenses incurred by the petitioner or the default of the debtor. Trevino.

p. 136. George Castles versus Thomas Yarrow, who owes him $55; asks that he be made to pay with cost. Jany. 9, 1784. Signed. // Let defendant be notified to pay in 3 days, etc. Trevino.

p. 137. Samuel Davis versus Peter Hawkins, who owes him $60; asks that he be made to pay with costs of suit. Jany. 9, 1784. Signed. // Let the deft. be notified to pay, etc. Trevino.

p. 137. Sutton Banks versus Stephen Howard, who owes him $126 by note; asks that he be made to pay with cost of suit. Jany. 8, 1784. Signed. // Notify deft. to pay, etc. Trevino.

p. 137. St. Germain versus Joseph Holmes, who is indebted to him for 407 rials; asks that he be condemned to payment thereof with costs of court. Jany. 9, 1784. Signed. // Let Deft. be notified to pay, etc. Trevino.

p. 137. St. Germain versus Josiah Flowers, who owes him $60; asks that he be made to pay with cost of court. Jany. 9, 1784. Signed. // Order that he pay within three days, etc. Trevino.

p. 138. St. Germain versus William Clark, who owes him $25; asks that he be condemned to Payment with costs. Jany. 9, 1784. Signed. // Let Deft. be notified to pay, etc. Trevino.

p. 138. St. Germain versus Wm. Hurlburt, who owes him $24; asks for payment and costs of court. Jany. 19, 1784. Signed. // Order to pay, etc. Trevino.

p. 138. St. Germain versus the estate of Cephas Kinnard, which is indebted to him for $120 on account; asks order for payment and cost of court. Jany. 9, 1784. Signed. // To be communicated to the party or parties for an answer. Trevino. // Roswell Mygatt, constable notified.

p. 139. St. Germain versus Joseph Holden, indebted to him for $257; he being the greatest creditor of said estate, there being anything left after the widow and children are provided for, your petitioner having no intention to distress them, he may be paid a part of said debt. Signed. Jany. 9, 1784. // To be communicated to the parties for their answer.

p. 139. St. Germain versus Charles Howard who owes him $44; asks that he may be made to pay with costs. Jany. 9, 1784. Signed. // Let the deft. be notified to pay, etc. Trevino. // Cole's Cr. Jany. 17, 1785. Notified Chas. Howard. Jeremiah Bryan.

p. 139. John Short versus Mathias Prock. Short petitions that in May last James Holly delivered to him a note drawn by Mathias Prock for $25, for which said note, your petitioner gave him a receipt and your petitioner applied to Dr. Farrell to draw a petition for payment of said note which he delivered with note enclosed to constable James Harman, who said he left the same in the fort to be recorded in the archives, wherefore petitioner asks an order that Harman produce sd note and petition and that you will order the said Mathias Prock to pay the amount on condition of receiving a guarantee of record of same. Jany. 9, 1784. Signed.

p. 139. Nathaniel Tomlinson versus William Mainer, who owes him for $60; asks that debtor be made to pay same and cost of court. Signed. Jany. 11, 1784.

p. 140. William Hurlburt versus John Morris, who owes him $9; asks that he be made to pay same with cost of court. Jany. 13, 1784. Signed. // Order that he pay in three days, etc. Trevino.

p. 140. Richard Bacon versus William Ferguson, who is indebted to him for $107; asks that he be made to pay same with cost of suit. 13 Jany. 1784. Signed. // Notified to pay, etc. Trevino.

p. 140. Richard Bacon versus Charles Adams, indebted to him for $22; asks that he may be made to pay same and cost of suit. Jany. 13, 1784. Signed. // Let the deft. be notified to pay, etc. Trevino.

p. 140. Richard Bacon versus Stephen Mayes, indebted to him for $23; asks that he be condemned to pay with cost of court. Jany. 13, 1784. // Let the debtor be notified to pay the same, etc. Trevino.

p. 141. Wm. Hurlburt versus Joseph Calvit, indebted to him for $26, asks that he be condemned to make payment with cost of suit. Jany. 13, 1784. Signed. // Let the deft. be notified to pay, etc. Trevino.

p. 141. Richard Bacon versus Joseph Duncan, who owes him $29; asks that he be made to pay same with cost of suit. Jany. 13, 1784. Signed. // Let the party be notified to pay, etc. Trevino.

p. 141. Elijah Routh versus Stephen Minor. Routh represents that in January 1782 the petitioner did with the permission of Lt. Gov. Grand-Pre purchase from a certain Peter Hawkins a negro woman and her children for $450 and as soon as the sale was executed before Mr. Grand-Pre, he paid said Peter Hawkins in pork to the amount of $156, the balance remaining $293. Your petitioner having received an order from Mr. Duval on the commissary of the post for $200, which paid for the second payment, the balance remaining was $93 and 6 rials and in Jany. 1783, he paid Mr. Minor in the presence of witnesses $93 and 6 rials, at the same time delivered to him the receipt of Peter Hawkins for $156 and 2 rials, and he tore the receipt of Peter Hawkins and the order and threw them into the fire and when your petitioner desired him to give up his note for $450, the whole amount being then paid, the said Minor answered that the said note must be deposited in the Spanish archives according to the Spanish custom and he would not return it to the petitioner. When the matter became a dispute, your petitioner came before you as did Mr. Deval and Mr. St. Germain as witnesses, but Mr. Minor acted as interpreter and would not present the evidence and Your Honor condemned me to pay $303 twice. Your petitioner prays that Your Honor will grant him another hearing, that he be allowed to produce his witnesses. Signed: Elijah Routh. Natchez, Jany. 13, 1784. // Let the foregoing be communicated to the defendant.

p. 142. John Hartley versus Moses McKan, who owes him $8; asks that he be made to pay same and cost of suit. Natchez, 10 Jany. 1784. Signed. // Let the deft. be notified to pay, etc. Trevino.

p. 142. Reuben Alexander versus Sterling Spell, who owes him $34; asks that he be condemned to make payment of same with cost of suit. Jany. 16, 1784. Signed. // Let the deft. be notified to pay, etc. Trevino. // The parties will nominate an arbitrator within three days and the party failing shall lose his right. Trevino. //

p. 143. Michael Lopez versus Susannah Owen, of the post and dist. of Natchez, who owes him $19 by note; asks that she be condemned for payment and cost of suit. 16 Jany. 1784. // Let the deft be notified in three days, etc. Trevino.

p. 143. Benjamin Rogers versus Groves Morris, who owes him $6; asks that he be made to pay same and cost of suit. 16 Jany. 1784. Signed. // Let the deft. be notified to pay etc. Trevino.

p. 143. Michel Lopez versus Joseph Green, whose note in favor of Christopher Leightholder, he holds and past due; asks that he be condemned to make payment and cost of suit. 16 Jany. 1784. // Let the defendant be notified to pay in 8 days, etc. Trevino. Cole's Creek. Feb. 16, 1784. I notified Joseph Green. Jeremiah Bryan.

p. 144. Michel Lopez versus Jesse Withers, who owes him $31; asks that he be made to pay same and cost of court. 16 Jany. 1784. Signed. // Notify Deft. to pay within three days, etc. Trevino.

p. 144. Michel Lopez versus David Smith, who owes him $4; asks that he be made to pay. Natchez, Jany. 16, 1784. Signed: // Let the party be notified to pay within three days, etc. Trevino. // Notified the defendant, as directed, 17 Jany. 1784. Roswell Mygatt. Fees: 4 rials.

p. 144. Michel Lopez versus Peter Hawkins and Patrick Foley, who are indebted to him on a joint note for $27; asks that they be condemned to pay same with cost of suit. 15 Jany. 1784. Signed. // Order that they pay within three days, etc. Trevino.

p. 145. William Dewitt versus William Brocus and others. Wm. Dewitt represents that he lent William Brocus, Lewis Alston and Joseph Duncan a horse which cost him $90 to go in pursuit of the rebels, wherefore he asks that the said persons be ordered to pay him for the said horse. Jany. 16, 1784. Signed. // Let William Brocus contribute with other inhabitants by agreement among them to satisfy this demand, deducting from the amount the sum of $10 for the proportion of the petitioner therein.

p. 145. George Killion versus John Owens, who owes him $25; asks for payment with cost of suit. Jany. 16, 1784. // Let the defendant be notified to pay in three days, etc. Trevino.

p. 145. George Weigle versus David Wathman, who owes him $47, fees included, and petitioner having judgment against sd Wathman, asks for execution against the property of said Wathman. Jany. 17, 1784. Signed. // Let the defendant be notified to pay immediately, in default thereof an execution will be levied for the amount. Trevino.

p. 145. Wm. Ferguson versus Abraham Horton, who is indebted to him for $26; asks that he be made to pay with costs of suit. Jany. 21, 1784. Signed. // Let defendant be notified to appear before me at the first audience. Trevino.

p. 146. John Hartley versus William Trevillian, who owes him $20; asks that he be made to pay with cost of suit. 20 Jany. 1784. Signed. // The defendant notified to pay within three days, etc. Trevino.

p. 146. William Smith versus George Rapalje, who is indebted to him for $202, being due; asks that the debtor be condemned to pay with cost of suit. Jany. 20, 1784. Signed. // Defendant to pay within 6 days. Signed: Trevino.

p. 146. Polser Shilling versus Richard Brashears, who owes him $94, and he asks that the debtor be made to pay same with cost of suit. 20 Jany. 1784. Signed. // Let the defendant be notified to pay in 5 days, etc. Trevino.

p. 146. George Castles versus Richard Brashears, who owes him $22; asks that he be condemned to pay same with cost of court. 23 Jany. 1784. Signed. // Let the deft. be notified to pay within three days. Trevino.

p. 147. William Hurlburt versus Richard Brashears, who owes him $46; asks for payment with cost of suit, 23 Jany. 1784. Signed. // Three days allowance or execution. Trevino.

p. 147. George Castles versus William Tabor, who owes him $18; asks that he be made to pay with cost of suit. 23 Jany. 1784. Signed. // Let the deft. pay in three days or execution will issue. Trevino.

p. 147. St. Germain versus Peter Hawkins, who owes him $203; asks for payment and costs of suit. Signed. // Peter Hawkins will deliver the negro woman to St. Germain as security for the debt which he owes him.

p. 147. Richard Brashears versus Isaac Fyffe who owes him $50 by note, asks that he be paid, with cost of court. 27 Jany. 1784. Signed. // Let the deft. be notified to pay in three days, etc. Trevino.

p. 148. Richard Brashears versus James White who owes him $19, asks for payment of same with cost of suit. Jany. 27, 1784. Signed. // Let deft. be notified to pay in three days, etc. Trevino.

p. 148. Isaac Tabor versus John Craven, who owes him $19 and asks that he be condemned for payment and costs. Jany. 27, 1784. Signed. // Let the deft. pay in three days or execution by default. Trevino.

p. 148. Louis Chachere versus Stephen Mayes, who owes him $25, asks that he be made to pay same with costs. 27 Jany. 1784. Signed. // Let the defendant be notified to pay, etc. Trevino.

p. 149. Michel Lopez versus John Choat, who owes him $54, asks that he be condemned to pay same and costs. Signed. Jany. 29, 1784. // Let the deft. be notified to pay, etc. Trevino.

p. 149. Charles Royeau versus Joseph Duncan who owes him $27; asks that he pay same and costs. 29 Jany. 1784. Signed. // Let deft. be notified to pay, etc. Trevino.

p. 149. Russell Jones versus Joseph Duncan. Russell Jones represents that Joseph Duncan has treated him very ill in regard to a partnership subsisting between them for sundry horses they bought from the Indians and the said Duncan having put the whole proceeds thereof in his own pocket and has besides made use of the goods of the firm for his wife and family and the notes of the firm have been given for all of the expenses of the said family, all of which can be proved by petitioner, asks that some person be appointed to take care of the notes and affairs of the partnership until the affairs can be settled. Feb. 3, 1784. Signed. // The constable is ordered to bring to this fort the person of Joseph Duncan without delay. Trevino. I executed the above. Sig: James Harman. Fee $1. // p. 150. Russell Jones represents that he entered into partnership [as above stated.] Memorandum of monies paid out by Joseph Duncan: to George Castles $22; to Justus and Richard King $80; to Polser Shilling; Joseph Ford, Mr. Qua___, a horse exchanged with Mr. Ironmonger, an ox bought from John Hartley, to James Cole, to Mr. Cobun, to Wm. Barland, to Mr. Benjamin Rogers, to James White, to William Dewitt a hat bought for Finley, to Adam Bingaman, to Mr. Maines, to Rogers and King, to Stephen Mayes, to A. Moore, to Richard Brashears, a horse sold to Raby, an ox bought from Mr. Still Lee, to Mr. Girault, to Mr. Foster, to Stephen Minor, total $1120.

p. 150. Richard King versus Mathias Prock who is indebted to him for $35, asks for payment and court costs, or that he be compelled to work with him for the amount. 20 Feb. 1784. Signed. // Constable will immediately bring Mathias Prock to the fort. Trevino.

p. 150. John Farquhar versus Justus King, who is indebted to him for $23; asks for payment of same. Signed. Feb. 20, 1784. // Let deft. be notified to pay in three days, etc. Trevino.

p. 151. George Castles versus John Choat, who owes him $41; asks that he be paid with costs of suit. 23 Jany. 1784. Signed. // Let deft. pay within three days, or etc. Trevino. // Notified John Choat according to order. Jany. 26, 1784. James Harman, constable.

p. 151. William Dewitt versus Adam Bingaman. Wm. Dewitt represents that he is indebted to Adam Bingaman for $1100, which he advanced to him in money some time since, and $400 more for goods furnished him, with $100 premium on the advance afsd, of which he gave his bond payable 16 April next. The said Bingaman at the same time took from your petitioner six negroes, little and great, whom he keeps in his possession and service as mentioned in the bond afsd. which he extorted from your petitioner who was under great difficulties at the time and unable to pay the said sum, being old and infirm and in want of said slaves to till the ground to support his numerous family, it being now the season to plant, prays for consideration and for an order for Bingaman to return the said slaves, a bond for same to be executed and recorded in the archives to be payable one year from date, for $1500, paying an int. of 5% allowed by the Spanish laws. Sig: Wm. Dewit. Feb. 24, 1784. // In consequence of the foregoing statement, Adam Bingaman will immediately restore the slaves mentioned and the two parties will appear before me within three days. Signed Trevino. Feb. 27, 1784. Notified Adam Bingaman. James Harman, constable.

p. 152. Richard Bacon versus Nathan Tomlinson. Bacon hired to Nathaniel Tomlinson a flatboat for 30 days for which he was allowed by arbitrators the sum of $25 being the matter of damages sustained by said boat, the said sum to be paid immediately but your petitioner gave Tomlinson until Christmas for payment thereof as well as an account of $2 and 7 rials and $2 and 3 rials for the cost of suit making in all $34 awarded by James Harman and John Ellis, asks that debtor be condemned to make payment. Signed. // Let both parties be notified to appear before me the first audience. Trevino.

p. 152. George Weigle versus Richard Brashears, who owes him $32; asks that he be made to pay same. Jany. 25, 1784. Signed. // Let the deft. be notified to pay in three days, etc. Trevino.

p. 152. Phoebe Calvit versus Stepehn Jett. Phoebe Calvit represents that some time since she lived with a certain Stephen Jett until she had one child by him and was again pregnant when she found that he had deceived her and had another wife, of which she was before ignorant; that on this discovery your petitioner determined to leave the said Jett and it was mutually agreed that they should separate. Your petitioner afterwards married William Calvit who had his arm broken by a ball fired by said Jett with intent to kill and while in that situation the said Jett came to the house swearing that no one but himself should have your petitioner and has since taken her child by stealth for no other purpose but to torment your petitioner, saying that he would carry the child among the savages to be revenged on her, which he will probably do, having no fixed residence and no means to support the child. She prays for consideration and that the said Jett will be compelled to restore her child and such measures may be taken to prevent him from troubling her in the future. Feb. 17, 1784. Signed. // Stephen Jett is ordered to restore to the petitioner the child whom he took from her and then to appear before me. Trevino. // I notified Stephen Jett. James Harman, constable.

p. 153. Christian Myers versus Richard Bacon, who owes him $25 by note for payment whereof your petitioner received an order on John Short but agent of the said Short refuses to pay same although he has property of said Bacon in his hands; asks that he be made to pay. // Let John Short be notified to pay the foregoing amount immediately and in default thereof the constable is ordered to bring him to the fort. Trevino.

p. 153. Wm. Vousdan versus Adam Bingaman. Vousdan represents that he presented certain papers to Lt. Col. Don Philipe Trevino respecting a certain negro sold to Alexander McIntosh and Col. Trevino having heard the defense of Adam Bingaman who is successor or said McIntosh ordered the matter should be determined by arbitrators. The Arbitrators appointed were Alexander Moore and William Smith who condemned the said Bingaman to pay your petitioner $172. Adam Bingaman, although he has nothing to complain of in the award, obtained from Col. Trevino an appeal to the higher tribunal, contrary both to law and equity. March 4, 1784. Signed. // I, Francis Farrell, do declare that all the knowledge that I have of the matter between William Vousdan and Adam Bingaman is that when said Vousdan was in prison that Alexander McIntosh obtained an order from Mr. Jean Delavillebeuvre against the property of said Vousdan and that the constable, Patrick Clemens, seized a negro named James Terry, belonging to said Vousdan, but if the said slave was sold at public sale I am ignorant of it. I know that the wife of said Vousdan was insane and capable of committing any folly and although I was the interpreter appointed by Monsieur Delavillebeuvre and attended in this matter I have no knowledge that the slave in question was sold in virtue of a decree. Signed. March 5, 1784. // Adam Bingaman to Wm. Vousdan. To amount of negro man, Tom Terry, sold by Alexander McIntosh without authority. $500. To cash paid Patrick Clemens at time, etc. Balance $172. by arbitrators, Alexander Moore and William Smith. // Order from Trevino that Adam Bingaman pay Wm. Vousdan $172. March 5, 1784.

p. 155. Judith Holstein versus David Choat. Judith Holstein represents that a certain David Choat has carried off the daughter of your petitioner, the wife of Thomas Holmes, and the child of said Holmes has also been carried away by said Choat and her daughter. Said Choat is a man of infamous conduct in other respects, having stolen horses in the province of Cumberland. She prays that consideration for the mother of a family and order that said Choat desist from having intercourse and all connection with her daughter and that the child of the said daughter may be placed under the care and protection of your petitioner. May 7, 1784. Signed: Judith Holstein. // In consequence of the statement in the foregoing memorial, the constable is ordered to bring David Choat and Mrs. Holmes to the fort and place the child of Mrs. Holmes in the hands of the petitioner. Trevino.

p. 156. John Short versus James Forester, who owes him $28 and a note drawn by James Frazier for $20; asks payment of same with cost of suit. March 1, 1784. Signed. // Let the defendants be notified to pay within three days or, etc. Trevino.

p. 156. Polser Shilling versus Dibdal Holt, who owes him $55, asks that he be made to pay same with costs of suit. March 3, 1784. Signed. // Let the deft. be notified to pay etc. Trevino. Cole's Cr. March 12, 1784. Dibdal notified. Jeremiah Bryan. // Settled this day. 21st April 1784. Jeremiah Bryan.

p. 157. Mary Foster versus Thomas Rule, who owes her $28; asks that he be condemned to pay same with costs of suit. March 9, 1784. Signed. // Let the deft. be notified to pay in three days, etc. Trevino.

p. 157. Barney Isenhoot versus Samuel Cooper, who owes him $25; asks that he be made to pay same with cost of suit. 9 March 1784. Signed. // Let the deft. be notified to pay same in three days etc. Trevino.

p. 157. John Terry versus Thomas Green. Terry represents that he is the holder of two notes drawn by Green, one for $92 and the other for two cows and two calves or $50; said notes being due he asks that the debtor be condemned to pay same and cost of suit. March 9, 1784. // Let the deft. be notified to pay within 15 days or execution will be issued. // Cole's Creek, March 10, 1784. I notified Thomas Green according to order. Jeremiah Bryan. Fees $5.

p. 157. James Wilson versus Stephen Mayes, who owes him $59; asks that he be made to pay with cost of suit. May 11, 1784. Signed. // Defendant to pay in three or execution will issue. Trevino.

p. 157. Polser Shilling versus Henry Richardson, who owes him $117; asks that he be made to pay same with cost of suit. March 27, 1784. Signed. // Deft. to pay in eight days, etc. Trevino.

p. 158. St. Germain versus William Owen. St. Germain is in possession of a note drawn by Owen for $200; asks that he be paid the same. March 27, 1784. // Let deft. be notified to pay etc. Trevino. // Notified by Roswell Mygatt.

p. 158. Samuel Davis versus Cato West. Davis represents that he has been sued by Cato West for $50 on his note; having no money nor means to procure money immediately, he is content to give cattle in payment; asks that the said cattle be appraised by two honest men. 28 March 1784. Signed. // Let the foregoing be notified to Mr. Cato West that he may appoint one appraiser and the debtor another. Trevino.

p. 158. Alexander Moore versus John Burney, who owes him $782; asks that he be condemned to pay with cost of suit. April 1, 1784. Signed. // Let the deft. be notified to pay within six days, etc. Trevino. Notified by Roswell Mygatt, constable.

p. 159. Alexander Moore versus Job Cory, who owes him $20; asks that he be ordered to pay with the cost of court. 1st April 1784. Signed. // Let deft. pay in three days or execution will issue. Trevino.

p. 159. William Smith versus William Pountney. William Smith represents that a certain Wm. Pountney owes him $26; asks that he be made to pay same and cost of suit. April 1, 1784. Signed. // Let deft. be notified to pay, etc. Trevino.

p. 159. Thomas Green versus Richard Harrison, to whom he sold two negroes in the month of August 1782 and the said Harrison was to deliver to your petitioner 22 heifers three years old and two cows and calves immediately. When he applied for the cattle he replied that it was impossible to get them at the moment, they being in the swamp. In short, this is in the year 1784 and there still remain 8 heifers and their increase to be delivered; he asks that the said Harrison be ordered to deliver to petitioner the eight heifers with their increase, having need of same to satisfy his debts. April 17, 1784. Signed. // Let Harrison be notified to deliver the cattle he owes or let him appear before me.

p. 160. Silas Crane versus James Wilson, who owes him $84; asks that he be made to pay. 17 Apr. 1784. Signed. // Let the deft pay in 8 days. Trevino. // In pursuance of the award made by the arbitrators which has been presented to me, it is hereby ordered that James Wilson do pay to the plaintiff $46 within 80 days. 14 June 1784. Signed: Trevino. Notified by Roswell Mygatt.

p. 160. George Weigle versus James Wilson, who owes him $24; asks that he be condemned to pay same with cost of suit. 19 Apr. 1784. // Granted. Trevino.

p. 160. St. Germain versus Pierre Nitard, who owes him $580 remitted to him by Charles Royeau, being the proceeds of goods which your petitioner furnished to said Royeau in partnership but the said petitioner is indebted to Pierre Nitard for a personal account of $119, leaving a balance of $461 of the money remitted by said Royeau, which said balance the petitioner asks Your Honor to stop in the hands of the said Nitard in order for him to pay the same to Don Carlos de Grand-Pre on account of your petitioner. Signed. // Let Pierre Nitard be notified he is ordered to comply with the prayer of the foregoing petition. Trevino.

p. 161. Thomas Reed versus Thomas Green, who owes him for $131; asks that he be made to pay same with cost of suit. 8 July 1784. Signed. // Let deft. pay in 8 days, etc. Trevino. // Notified Green. Jeremiah Bryan. Fee $5.

p. 161. St. Germain versus Wm. Pountney. St. Germain has a complaint to make against Wm. Pountney who has marked with his mark two cows and calves belonging to said St. Germain, also two cows and a bull belonging to Charbonneau. Asks that said Pountney be ordered to appear before Your Honor, etc. 3 June 1784. // Let Wm. Pountney, the petitioner and Charbonneau appear before me at the first audience. Trevino.

p. 161. William Brocus versus William Dewitt. Brocus represents that Wm. Dewitt owes him $100 by note; asks that he be made to pay the same. 19 June 1784. // Let the deft. be notified to pay, etc. Trevino. Notified by James Harman. Fee: $1 and 4 rials.

p. 161. William Calvit versus Daniel Higdon, who owes him $922, on a bond, of which he lately paid $100, and it was agreed that the matter be settled by arbitration, but on the day set Higdon did not attend, wherefore the petitioner asks that the same be settled by Your Honor. June 21, 1784. Signed. // Let Daniel Higdon and petitioner be notified to appear before me at first audience. Trevino.

p. 162. Richard Bacon versus David Pickens, who owes him $30; asks that he be made to pay with cost of suit. 26 June 1784. Signed. // Let the deft. be notified to pay etc. Trevino.

p. 162. Juan Gali versus Pedro Azevedo. Gali represents that he furnished Azevedo in the short time they lived together the articles in the account hereto annexed amounting to $154; asks that Azevedo be condemned to make payment of same. 13 July 1784. Account. Signed.

p. 163. James Simmons versus Earl Douglass. Simmons represents that a certain Earl Douglass told your petitioner about 8 days ago that Your Honor had granted him the land on which your petitioner now dwells and has had in his possession now for four years, having bought the same from Parker Carradine of Cole's Creek. The said Douglass seems to have some right to the land by purchase from John Bell but your petitioner can prove that said Douglass has acknowledged that he never paid for said land and the bargain was of no consequence and the said Douglass being present when your petitioner bought the land and made no objection or claim in the course of four years that said land has been in the possession of your petitioner. August 5, 1784. Signed. // In pursuance of the statement in the foregoing memorial, let Douglass be notified to appear before me with his papers and witnesses at the first audience. The petitioner will also appear with his witnesses. Trevino. // 13 August 1784. Earl Douglass and James Simmons both appeared with the witnesses for both sides, and having maturely considered the documents presented on both sides, I have determined that the said Douglass has no right to the land in possession of the said James Simmons, the same having been proved in my presence to belong lawfully to Simmons, the actual occupant. Signed: Trevino.

p. 163. Stephen Minor versus Thomas Rule, who owes him $55; asks that he be made to pay the same. Natchez, 14 May 1784. Signed. // Let the deft. be notified to pay or the execution will issue. Trevino. Statement follows: Your note in favor of Mr. Hutchins $35, same in favor of Christian Bingaman for $12, to private account with me; saddle of Mr. Hutchins lost $26; Contra: By saddle lost by Christian Bingaman $37, Balance $36.

p. 164. Ambrose Gaines versus John Woods, who owes him $92; asks that he be made to pay the same. 10 Sept. 1784. // Granted as required. Trevino.

p. 164. Their creditors versus Dewitt and Jones. The creditors of William Dewitt and Russell Jones represent that the said Dewitt and Jones being confined in the fort for attempting to leave the country without passports and being informed that Your Honor intended to send their property to New Orleans to be sold to pay their debts, the undersigned, being the majority of their creditors, pray Your Honor to take into consideration the cost and expense of sending the said property to the City and the delay that will thereby be caused in payment. Therefore, we, as also the said Jones and Dewitt pray that the said property may be sold at this place, having determined all to give the full value to the articles exposed to sale. Natchez. Sept. 22, 1784. Signed: Alexander Moore, Estevan Minor, John Burnet, Miguel Esclava, George Castles, William Smith, D. Smith, Gibson Clarke. // In consequence of the reasons in the foregoing memorial contained, the prayer of the petitioners is granted unless the superior government shall otherwise order, in which case, time will be given to them to make their representations. Signed. Trevino.

p. 165. John Hartley versus William Ryan. John Hartley represents that he has been condemned by arbitration to pay Wm. Ryan $25 and cost of suit, and your petitioner having reason to believe that one of the arbitrators was motivated by reason of revenge against him, arising from a former dispute; humbly prays that Your Honor will name six persosn and permit your petitioner and the plaintiff each to choose three of the number to decide the matter impartially. Natchez. 26 Sept. 1784. Signed John Hartley. // Notwithstanding the matter in controversy between John Hartley and William Ryan has been decided by arbitrators chosen by the parties, for the reasons given in the foregoing petition, the matter shall again be considered, for the purpose each party shall chose three arbitrators and for the seventh I do hereby appoint Wm. Henderson, that the dispute be definitely settled and concluded.

Signed: Trevino. // We, the subscribers chosen to settle the dispute between Wm. Ryan and Mr. John Hartley, are of the opinion that the said John Hartley is justly indebted to the said Ryan in the sum of $25, 22 Oct. 1784. Signed: D. Smith, William B. Smith, William Henderson, Richard Curtis, A. Bingaman, and Samuel Gibson.

p. 165. Alexander Moore versus Ambrose Gaines, who owes him $199; asks that he be made to pay or give security for same. Oct. 2, 1784. Signed: // Granted and let notice be given to Gaines.

p. 166. John Woods versus Russell Jones. John Woods represents that about a month since, being at Natchez with Russell Jones confined in the fort, or rather a prisoner on bail, your petitioner having a note of $100 in hand, the said Jones snatched it from him by force and went and changed the said note, of which he kept $23; petitioner prays that he will order Jones to refund to your petitioner the sum aforesaid with the cost of the suit. 3rd Oct. 1784. Signed. // Nov. 7, 1784. Russell Jones is ordered to pay petitioner without delay the $23 he took from him by force and any person who may have received the said money from said Jones is ordered to return it to him, no person being ignorant that his property is under seizure and that he is not allowed to dispose of anything to the damage of his creditors. Signed: Trevino.

p. 166. William Brocus versus Ambrose Gaines, who is indebted to him for $60; asks that he be made to pay with the cost of the suit. Natchez, 5 Oct. 1784. Signed. // To be communicated for his answer. Trevino.

p. 166. Louis Chachere versus Cephas Kinnard, who owes him $35; asks that he be made to pay. Nov. 5, 1784. Signed. // Let the deft. be notified to pay the debt in this memorial. // Done by J. Harman.

p. 166. Alexander Moore Jr., versus David Wathman, who owes him $22, asks for payment of same, with costs of suit. 18 Nov. 1784. Signed. // Granted. Trevino.

p. 167. Alexander Moore versus David Wathman, who owes him $45, asks that he be condemned to pay same with the cost of suit. 19 Nov. 1784. Signed. // Let the deft. be notified to pay. Trevino.

p. 167. James Wilson versus Alexander Callendar, who owes him $85; asks that he be condemned to pay with cost of court. 19 Nov. 1784. // Let the deft. be notified. Trevino.

p. 167. St. Germain versus Russell Jones and Joseph Duncan, who, in partnership, are indebted to him for $479; asks that they be condemned to pay with cost of suit. Dec. 2, 1784. Signed. // Let the defendants be notified to pay in three days, etc. Trevino. Silas Crane, constable notified. Fee. $1.

p. 168. Baso and Gras represent that they bought at the public sale of Jacques Rapalje a number of hogs which were at the time in a very sorry condition, amounting to 21 heads, as will appear by the certificate of two planters of your district. The said hogs have since cost us a considerable sum, being obliged to feed them corn and pumpkins, and the petitioners pray that they be allowed to kill the said hogs and the said Rapalje refund to them the expense they have incurred. Dec. 11, 1784.

p. 168. William Smith versus John Lusk, who is indebted to him for $515; asks that he be made to pay same with cost of suit. 23 Dec. 1784. Signed. // Let the deft. be notified to pay, etc. Trevino.

p. 168. Charles Adams versus David Smith. Charles Adams represents that he had written articles of agreement with a certain David Smith to make a crop for him in a space of two years and that he did accordingly make and finish the said crops and the said Smith turned away your petitioner without giving him his share of the same. The said Smith now refuses to make any arrangements with your petitioner who proposed to submit the matter to arbitration but said Smith refused to make any compensation for the loss and damage sustained by your petitioner who is a poor man and has no other way to subsist but by the sweat of his brow. He prays that you will order the witnesses before to determine the right. 23 Dec. 1784. Signed. // Let parties notified to appear at first audience. Trevino. // Natchez. 12 Jany. 1785. I notified David Smith according to order, and summoned Henry Roach and James Foster, James Harman, constable.

p. 169. William Smith versus Jeremiah Bryan, who owes him $59; asks that he pay without delay. 6 Jany. 1785. Signed.

p. 169. William Smith versus James Wilson and William Hulburt. Smith represents that James Wilson owes him $21 for a saddle bought at vendue. William Hurlburt, his surety. Natchez. Jany. 6, 1785. // Let debtors be notified to pay. Trevino.

p. 169. William Smith versus William Hurlburt, who owes him $43; askś that he be made to pay. Jany. 6, 1785. Signed.

p. 169. Jeremiah Bryan versus George Bailey, who owes him $115; asks that he be made to pay. Jany. 7, 1785. // Let deft. be notified to pay, etc. Trevino.

p. 170. John Lusk versus Stephen Cole, who owes him $23; asks that the debtor be made to pay. 13 Jany. 1785. Signed. // Let the deft. be notified to pay, etc. Trevino.

p. 170. William Hirlburt versus Mrs. McIntosh, who owes him $70; asks that debtor be compelled to pay with cost of suit. 22 Jany. 1785. // Let the deft be notified to pay or show cause to the contrary.

p. 170. David Smith versus James Oxberry, who is indebted to him for $35, same being due, petitioner asks that debtor be ordered to make payment thereof. Natchez, 22 Jany. 1785. Signed: David Smith // 29 Jany. 1785. Let the deft. be notified to pay or show cause etc. Trevino. Natchez, same date. Let seizure be made.

p. 170. Louis Chachere versus Elijah Routh, who owes him $87; asks that he be made to pay with cost of suit. Natchez. 26 Jany. 1785. // Let deft be notified to pay etc. Trevino. // Jany. 28th 1785. Let seizure be made. Trevino.

p. 171. Louis Chachere versus Albertson who owes him $450 as will appear by his note and account acknowledged by him; asks that debtor be compelled to pay same with cost of suit, or detain his property consisting of negroes at the fort as security of the debt. // Let the deft. be notified to pay, etc. and let his negroes be conducted to the fort. Trevino.

p. 171. Louis Chachere versus Jeremiah Bryan. Chachere represents that he is due from Jeremiah Bryan $59 to Chachere, as atty. for George Castles and Bryan has attempted to elude the payment thereof. Payment of same requested. Jany 31, 1785. Signed: Chachere. // Let the deft. be notified to pay or show cause to contrary. Trevino. // Feb. 5, 1785. Let seizure be made. Trevino.

p. 171. Elijah Routh versus the estate of Samuel Osborne. Elijah Routh, of the district, represents that since the death of his wife, who was before the widow of Osborn, the property belonging to your petitioner has been inventoried with the estate of Samuel Osborn, deceased, the husband of your ptitioner's late wife. Asks that a negro wench, two horses, a number of cows and hogs, and household furniture inserted in said inventory belonging to your petitioner and not the said estate. 7 Feb. 1785. Signed. //

p. 172. John Short versus Nehemiah Albertson, who owes him $15; asks that he be made to pay same with cost of suit. Feb. 11, 1785. Signed. // Let the defendant be notified to pay, etc. Trevino.

p. 172. Francis Labispere versus John Farquhar, who owes him $94; asks that he be paid the same with cost of suit. 16 Feb. 1785. // Let the deft. be notified to pay same or show cause etc. Trevino. Notified. James Stoddard, constable.

p. 172. Widow Spell versus Nathaniel Ivy, who owes her $15; asks that he be made to pay with cost of suit. March 29, 1785. // Let deft. be notified to pay, etc. Trevino.

p. 172. Jacob Phillis versus Richard Swayze, who owes him $54; asks that he pay same with costs. 29 March 1785. Signed. // Let the deft. be notified to pay or show the contrary. Trevino.

p. 173. William Selkrig versus James Findley. William Henderson and James Findley are indebted by joint note to petitioner and he asks that they be condemned to pay with costs. 5 April 1785. // Let the deft. be notified etc. Trevino.

p. 173. Henry Roach versus Stephen De Alva and Stephen Holstein. Roach represents that Stephen De Alva owes him $14 and Stephen Holstein owes him $6; asks that they be condemned to pay same with costs. 5 April 1785. Signed. // Let the defts. be notified to pay, etc. Trevino. // Let seizure be made. Natchez. 9 April 1785.

p. 173. David Smith versus David Choat, who is indebted to him in the sum of $25 or 25 bushels of corn and Stephen Holstein in sum of $10 or 10 bushels of corn; asks that they be condemned to pay same with cost of suit. Natchez, 7 April 1785. Signed: D. Smith. // Let the defendants be notified to pay, etc. Trevino. // Natchez, 16 April 1785. Let seizure be made. Trevino. Notified according to order. James Stoddard. David Choat's cost $2 and 5 rials; Stephen Holstein's $2 and 4 rials.

p. 173. James Findley versus Abner Green, who owes him $13; asks that he be made to pay with costs. 18 April 1785. Signed. //

p. 174. Wm. Hurlburt versus John Smith who owes him $16; asks that he be made to pay with costs. 9 May 1785. Signed. // Let the deft. be notified to pay, etc. Trevino. // We, the subscribers, arbitrators between Wm. Hurlburt and John Smith, having heard the parties and examined their account are of the opinion that there is due Wm. Hurlburt from John Smith $8 and 6 rials with costs of the suit. May 14, 1785. Signed: James Harman and Charles Adams.

p. 174. James Mather versus Richard Devall. James Mather, of this City, merchant, represents that Richard Devall, of the post of Natchez, indebted to him in the sum of $6000, as will appear by his obligations in favor of your petitioner, executed before the commandant of said post, with mortgage on all his property, the terms thereof have long expired, etc.; asks that Your Excellency order the Commandant at the Post of Natchez, Don Carlos De Grand-Pre, in virtue of said obligations, being part of the records of said post, do compel said Devall by vigor of law to make payment of the amount in conformity with the said obligations and make sale of all the property belonging to said Devall, especially that part mortgaged to your petitioner. New Orleans. July 14, 1787. Signed: James Mather. // The Commandant of the Post of Natchez, in virtue of the obligations in his power will compel Richard Devall to make payments of the sums in the said obligations expressed, for which purpose he will seize the property of the said Devall and sell same at public sale in the manner prescribed by law. New Orleans. 18 July 1785. Signed: Estevan Miro. // To Lt. Col. De Grand-Pre, Military and Civil Commandant of the post and district of Natchez, by the fate of an execution being levied on all my property in consequence of a mortgage given to Mr. James Mather by me, I will, of my own accord, deliver to the attorney of Mr. James Mather a just inventory according to the said mortgage in every particular and likewise make visible to the appraisers the said articles as they now stand and will deliver the same in public at the time of the sale. This I leave to Your Honor's approbation to prevent any additional expense to the large sum that I am now owing, etc. Natchez, 12 Sept. 1787. // Granted in pursuance of the consent of Mr. Lintot, attorney of James Mather. Both parties will chose appraisers to value the property. // We, the undersigned, have at the request of Richard Devall and Bernard Lintot, attorney for James Mather, have to the best of our judgment appraised the plantation and other properties hereinafter mentioned belonging to sd Devall at the cash prices; 1050 arpents of land in good condition for a mill, with a house thereon, and 20 arpents under fence at $6000; 5 large working oxen with their yokes, one devil complete, etc. $21; almost all the ironwork for a mill and about 50 pounds of broken chains $518; etc,; one negro man named "Linder" $700; one named "Baptiste $600. [not totalled.] Signed: Thomas Green, James Kirk. // At Fort Panmur at Natchez, 8th Oct. 1787, I, Don Carlos De Grand-Pre, in pursuance of the foregoing memorial and decree, have repaired to the plantation of Richard Devall, in company with the two appraisers, James Kirk and Thomas M. Green, chosen by the parties to value the property of said Devall about to be sold for the payment of his debts, who have promised to discharge which appointed, etc. and have signed with me and the witnesses. James Kirk, Thomas M. Green, Roswell Mygatt, Daniel Mygatt, Estevan Minor, John Ferguson, Antonio Soler and Carlos de Grand-Pre. // At the post of Natchez, 13 Oct. 1787, Don Carlos de Grand-Pre have proceeded to make sale of the property of Richard Devall. The plantation of 1050 arpents was adjudged for the 1st time to Don Juan Vaucheret for $2500; 5 work oxen to Bernard Linton, also the mill-work, all the rest to Bernard Lintot. Sale closed for the day. All sign. // At the Post, 1st December; sale for 2nd time of plantation, which was adjudged to Bernard Lintot for $3000, he being the highest bidder. Witnesses: Wm. Boyd, Samuel Flower, Wm. Henderson, John Burnet. // The 3rd time said plantation was adjudged to Bernard Lintot for $4505, the highest bid, but with the express condition that Devall should have the liberty to cut timber thereon to finish the contract he had with Francisco Bouligny. Signed: Bernard Lintot for James Mather, James Kirk, J. Henderson, Pedro Surgęt, Manuel Texada, Jacob Monsanto, and Don Carlos de Grand-Pre. Net proceeds: $5826, remaining in the hands of the creditor and purchaser jointly. Grand-Pre.

p. 178. Sutton Banks versus George Bailey. A controversy between these parties and both having been heard and evidences of James Kelly, we find that Mr. Bailey left the employ of Mr. Banks without any just provocation and are of the opinion that Mr. Banks pay $20 to Bailey which includes some small accounts between them and is agreeable to them both. 26 May 1789. Ezekiel Dewitt and H. Manadue, arbitrators. // I approve the foregoing award of the arbitrators. Signed: Grand-Pre. // The constable Joseph Foster, will seize the horses belonging to George Bailey to be sold as prayed for. Grand-Pre.

he has obtained an execution against the property of George Bailey and the seizure of the horses were specially mortgaged to him for a sum of money which was to be paid to him for his creditor, Richard Carpenter, by arbitration in his favor; asks for the appraisement of said horses and other property. May 23, 1789. Signed. // Granted by Grand-Pre. // Francisco Pavana and Richard Harris were appointed to appraise the horses and other property of George Bailey and they accepted same. // At Natchez, 30 May 1789. Sale of one horse and was tried and sold to Sutton Banks for $34 and said Banks received said horse in full payment of all demands agst said Bailey. Before Carlos de Grand-Pre.

p. 180. Samuel Lusk versus Mordecai Morgan, who came with your petitioner from the American settlement and is indebted to him by note and account for $29, which he promised to pay out of proceeds of some iron which he worked up to sell in this district but the said Mordecai Morgan, being in the boat of Patrick Shirley, was killed by the Indians on the passage and the said Patrick Shirley is in possession of the whole of his property; your petitioner prays that you will order that the property be appraised at cash prices and a part thereof be delivered to your petitioner sufficient to discharge the debt owing to him. Signed. 3 May 1790. // I promise to pay or cause to be paid to Samuel Lusk or his order eleven pounds N. C. currency. Signed Mordecai Morgan. 20 Nov. 1789. // Let an inventory an appraisement be made of the property left by the person abovementioned, killed on his voyage from America, for the payment of his debt. // An Appraisement of $355 and sold for $72 and 62 rials, net. $41 paid to Lusk. $31 to Patrick Shirley.

Page 181. The King versus Robert Stark and others.

At the Post of Natchez on the 18 February 1794, I, Don Pedro Favrot, Capt. of the Reg. of Infantry of La., charged with the Civil and Military Command of said Post, in pursuance of the order of His Excellency, the Governor Don Manuel Gayoso de Lemos, Col. in the Royal Armies, informing me that having been advised of the disloyal expressions of Robert Stark in this District, he commanded the said Stark to be arrested and confined in the said Fort, as likewise a certain Henry Milburn, whereupon and in pursuance thereof, I have proceeded to take the necessary testimony in the absence of said Governor, and it being necessary to appoint two interpreters who understand English and Spanish languages, and the two assistant witnesses, I have for the former office appointed Don Esteven Minor and Don Joseph Vidal and for the latter Don Martin Palao and Don Antonio Crusat, who, informed of said appointments, have accepted thereof and promised on oath to faithfully discharge the same. In testimony whereof we have signed. Estevan Minor, Joseph Vidal, Antonio Crusat, Martin Palao, Pedro Favrot.

At the Post of Natchez at the day, month and year before written, I, the said Don Pedro Favrot, caused to appear before me, the said Henry Milburn, who being duly sworn, on the Holy Evangelist's, by means of the interpreters promised to answer truly to such questions as should be put to him and was thereupon asked his name and country, to which he answered: "Henry Milburn, native of Virginia." Q. If Robert Stark frequented his house and if he had any conversations with him concerning enemies, as it is said, coming to attack this province? A. That about twelve days since, Robert Stark called at his house and among other discourse, of a domestic nature, which he had with said Stark, the following was mentioned: that Mary Higdon told him that Col. Thomas Green mentioned in her presence, at the house of Thomas Calvit, that there were in this District several letters from Gen. Clark purporting that if all the inhabitants of this District would remain quiet in their houses without taking arms against those who were about to come down from the United States against this province, that in such case they would not be molested by the enemy nor suffer injury, and that if the government compelled them to take up arms they should do as little damage as possible consistently with the appearance of being in earnest, and that Stark further said that Col. Bruin had received or was in possession of a letter to that purport, to which said Stark added that it was his opinion that if the enemy did come they would pursue that line of conduct, and such of the inhabitants of this District as took up arms against them would be roughly treated while those who did not would receive no injury. Q. Who were those present when this conversation took place? A. Norsworthy Hunter, Capt. of the Militia, and John Coyle, but he does not remember if Hunter was present at the whole conversation with Stark or only part of it. (p. 182). Q. If he knows whether the said Robert Stark held the same conversations at other places? A. He does not know that he did. There are several persons in the Villa Gayoso acquainted with it and he believed that they had their information from said Stark. Q. Why he did not give notice of this matter to the Government when he knew that in the oath of fidelity which he took on settling in this province, he promised to give notice of any attempt against the peace or interest of said Province that might come to his knowledge. A. As Mr. Hunter, abovementioned, and an officer of the Government, was present, he thought if it was a matter of consequence he would inform the Government; and besides Stark saying that Col. Bruin had letters to the same purport, he presumed that he, Bruin, has already communicated it to the Government. Q. If any of the time he heard said Stark holding any conversation inimical to the Government? A. No. Q. If he has anything more to say and how old he is? A. He has nothing more to say and he is 32 years old. And the forgoing being read and explained to him by the interpreters, Don Estevan Minor and Don Joseph Vidal, in the presence of the witnesses assisting, he acknowledged it to contain the declaration that he made on the oath which he has taken and has signed with myself, the interpreters and witnesses assisting. (All signed).

Next to appear before me, Robert Stark, who being sworn, etc. was asked his name, country and condition, to which he answered: Robert Stark, native of Virginia, married and dwelling in this District. Q. If he knows Henry Milburn and was at his house about twelve days ago and what conversation he had with him concerning the enemies said to be coming to attack this province. A. That he does know Henry Milburn and was at his house at the time mentioned, and that he there mentioned that Mary Higdon told him that she being at table at the house of her son, Thomas Calvit, Col. Thomas Green came there and said he had passed the night at the house of Col. Bruin, which he had left that morning, and then the said Green began to relate, being also seated at table, that there were letters in the Government from the United States purporting their intention of attacking this Province and intimating that they did not expect to be considered as enemies of the inhabitants of this District, but if the said inhabitants should be compelled by the Government to take up arms they must do so and not withstanding they should be well-treated. The said Mary Higdon added that the letters also mentioned, according to the statement of said Green that many persons were coming from the United States with their families and cattle for land in this District, which is all he said of the matter. Q. If he did not give his own opinion on the subject of this conversation at the house of Milburn? A. He does not remember that he did but his opinion is that should the inhabitants of this District take up arms against the enemy they would be treated by them worse than if they did not, and that is an idea which appears to him reasonable. Q. To whom he communicated this information? A. He does not recollect to have mentioned it to any other person except to the Corporal of the Reg. of La., attached to the Villa Gayoso, namely one Romero. Q. Why he did not communicate the information to the Government, etc.? A. He did not communicate it because he took the whole to be a falsehood and because Norsworthy Hunter told him at the time when he mentioned the above report that the whole of it was false. He, the said Hunter, had heard it three months before and that such stories were unworthy of credit. Q. If he has anything more to say and how old is he? A. He has nothing further to say and he is 54 years old. He acknowledged same and signed with myself, the interpreters and witnesses assisting. (All signed.)

p. 183 (cont.) At the Post of Natchez, this 4th day of March, 1794, I, Don Pedro Favrot, etc., caused to appear before me Narsworthy Hunter, Capt. of the Militia, in the presence of the interpreters and witnesses assisting, and the said Hunter, putting his hand on the hilt of his sword, promised on his honor to answer truly to such questions as should be put to him, whereupon he was asked his name and employment, to which he answered: Narsworthy Hunter, a Capt. of the Militia of this District. Q. If he was present at the house of Henry Milburn when Robert Stark was there discoursing on the report current in this District that the enemies were coming to attack this province. He answered that he will make a circumstantial relation of what he heard as follows: That Robert Stark and deponent, going to the house of the said Milburn, Robert Stark said that on the road he heard Mary Higdon relate that there were letters in this District coming from the persons in America who intended to attack this province, stating that, not withstanding their said intention, that they would not injure the inhabitants of this District since their intention was to make a conquest of this country, on which the said Stark observed that he thought it impossible that such letters should have been received in this District since Col. Bruin had received none and he had many friends in America and he believed that if Col. Bruin had received any such he would immediately have communicated the information to His Excellency the Governor of this District, adding that if he, Stark, had received any such letter, he would have given notice thereof immediately. Whereupon the deponent said that whether the reports were true or false, they ought not to be circulated as they would tend to create bad impressions on the inhabitants of the District. At this time the deponent and Stark reached the house of Milburn and Stark enquired of said Milburn if he had heard the report, which he had before related to the deponent, to which the said Milburn answered that he had heard nothing of it and the deponent again observed to Stark that such enquiries were improper and might have bad consequences. Q. Why he did not communicate this to the Governor? A. Because his reasons for not communicating was, first, that the whole appeared to him to be false, and, again, because Stark told him that the report was current at Bayou Pierre and he was persuaded that it had already reached the Governor of the Dist. Q. If he has anything more to relate and how old he is? A. He has nothing further to relate and he is 38 years old. He acknowledged the foregoing declaration and signed with the interpreter, myself, and the witnesses assisting.

p. 184. At the Fort of Natchez, 6 March 1794, before me Don Pedro Favrot, etc., charged with Civil and Military Command in the Post and District, in the absence of the Governor, appeared Mary Higdon, in pursuance of orders given for the purpose, having been duly sworn, etc. being asked her name, country and condition, to which she replied: Mary Higdon, native of Pennsylvania, and widow of Daniel Higdon. Q. To make a circumstantial relation of what she told to Robert Stark concerning the report of an enemy coming to attack this province. A. That, being one day at the house of her son, Thomas Calvit, and sitting at table, Col. Green came in and, seating himself, Calvit enquired of the said Green what news he had heard, to which said Green replied that he had heard at Bayou Pierre from a woman that Gen. Clark had sent word to the inhabitants of the District that his intention was not to rob and murder them, only to make a conquest of the country. And the said Calvit enquired of Green if this was known to Col. Bruin. He answered in the affirmative and added that Col. Bruin appeared to be uneasy and apprehensive that the enemy would rob and murder if they came. This the deponent related to Robert Stark the day following, being all she has to say. She is seventy years old. The foregoing deposition being read to her by the interpreters, she acknowledged it to be the same that she made on oath, and not knowing how to write she has made her mark and I have signed with said interpreters and the witnesses assisting.

Next, I caused to appear before me Thomas Green, confined in the Fort of this Post, and, in the presence of the interpreters and witnesses, being sworn, etc., whereupon he was asked his name, his country and condition, to which he answered that his name was Thomas Green, native of Virginia, and married. Q. To make a natural relation of what he said at the house of Thomas Calvit, concerning enemies intending to attack the province. A. Being sometime since at Bayou Pierre on business, he went to the house of a certain Gooding who enquired of the deponent if he had heard the report current in the District, to which the deponent replied that he had not, on which, said Gooding informed him that she knew that three men who came from America in a flatboat had landed at Bayou Pierre and told several inhabitants, among others William Smith and Stephen Richards, that Gen. Clark was not coming to this country to rob or murder the inhabitants of this district, his intention being only to conquer the country, that immediately after, the deponent went to the house of Col. Bruin, with the express intention of communicating the information to him, as Colonel of the Militia and alcalde of this District, and, having informed him of all that he had heard from Mrs. Gooding Bruin told him that he had been informed of the report two days before and the deponent observed that it was well. He had done his duty in comunicating it, and they conversed concerning the matter for some time but nothing particular was mentioned showing that Col. Bruin was uneasy that the enemy was coming to rob and murder or otherwise injure the inhabitants. From Col. Bruin's, the deponent went to the house of Thomas Calvit and related there the information he had received from Mrs. Gooding and further he knows not in the matter, being 74 years old. He acknowledged the foregoing to be the deposition that he has made under oath. He has signed with the officials.

p. 185. At the Post of Natchez, on the 7th day of March 1794. Before me, Don Pedro Favrot, charged with the Civil and Military Government of said Post and District, in the absence of the Governor, in pursuance of orders given for the purpose, appeared William Smith, who, being sworn on the Holy Evangelist's to answer truly to such questions as should be put to him, was asked his name, country and condition, to which he replied: William Smith, native of North Carolina, and married. Q. Relate what you told to Mrs. Gooding respecting three individuals who came down in a flatboat from North Carolina. A. Being on horseback on his way to Nogales, he met with Stephen Richards and Jacob Piatt and the deponent enquired of the latter if he had any news, who answered that he had been told by three men who came down in a flatboat that the Sans Culottes intended to attack this Province but that as the Congress were opposed they were in want of money for the expedition and it would be difficult for them to get here, or if they did come it would be very late in the season; and that is what the deponent repeated to Mrs. Gooding, and nothing else. Q. If he did not tell Mrs. Gooding that Gen. Clark had sent word to inhabitants of this district that they need not be uneasy since he came only to conquer the country and not to plunder it. A. He told her no such thing, nor anything other than he has already related, being all that he knows in the matter, and he is 35 years old. The foregoing being read to him, he acknowledged it to be the declaration that he made, and has signed with Favrot and other officials.

Immediately thereafter, I caused to appear before me Stephen Richards, who being sworn, etc., was asked his name, country and condition, to which he answered: Stephen Richards, native of Maryland, and married. Q. Make a circumstantial relation of what he told Mrs. Gooding concerning persons arrived from America. A. Col. Bruin having charged him to be on the outlook for boats coming from above and to enquire the news there, he went on board a flatboat and enquired for news of a certain David and others who came down in her, who told him that he had heard that some Frenchmen and Americans intended coming to this country but they were in want of money and as it was said that Congress discountenanced them he did not think that they would come, or if they did it would be very late in the year, their bills of exchange being refused. They also said that some of their principal men, who intended coming to this province, said they did not intend to kill or plunder but came for other purposes, which the deponent communicated to Col. Bruin, as he had been directed in the presence of Captain Burnet, and he also related the same to Mrs. Gooding, being all that he knows in the matter, and that he is 34 years old. He acknowledged the foregoing to be the declaration that he had made, and signed with Favrot and the other officials.

p. 187. At the Post of Natchez, on the 8th day of March, 1794, before me Don Pedro Favrot, etc., in pursuance of orders to that purpose, appeared Phoebe Gooding, who being sworn, etc., was asked her name, country and condition, to which she answered: Phoebe Gooding, native of South Carolina, and a widow. Q. What did she tell Thomas Green concerning the coming of the Americans to this Province? A. That Stephen Richards informed her he had heard from two persons who came down in a flatboat that the Americans would perhaps come down to attack the province, that if they did they would not do damage to the inhabitants of this District, being all that she told the said Thomas Green, and all that she knows in the matter, being 26 years old. She confirmed the foregoing as the declaration that she made and, not knowing how to write, made her usual mark.

At the Post aforesaid, on the 12th of March 1794, before Favrot, in consequence of the foregoing declaration, appeared Peter Bryan Bruin, Col. of the Volunteer Militia, who promised to answer all questions, etc. Q. If he received any information of certain Frenchmen said to be coming down the Ohio River to attack the Provinces, and if so to make circumstantial relations thereof. A. That he received no other information of the matter than that derived from the proclamation made by the Governor of the District, except one day Thomas Green, Senior, enquired of him if he knew anything of letters from America, said to have been received here, to which the deponent replied he knew of no such letters, nor had he heard speak of any. Q. If the said Thomas Green did not tell him the contents or purport of those letters? A. Thomas Green said that the contents or purport of those letters was that if the inhabitants remained quietly in their plantations, no injury would be done to them, to which the deponent replied that he did not believe that any such letters had been received in this District, because the Commandant had ordered that all letters that arrived be stopped and enclosed under cover to the Government of his Post. Q. If the said Green did not tell him from whom he had received the information? A. No. Q. If the said Green did not tell him that he came expressly to give him notice thereof as alcalde of that district and that he thought that it was his duty? A. No. He said no such thing, and told him only what he has related, and that the deponent told him that he did not believe any part of it. And this he said to prevent him from speaking of it in other places, knowing him to be a great talker. Q. If he had heard nothing of this matter from any person before he heard it from Thomas Green. A. He heard it first from Col. Green and some days afterwards was told by Stephen Richards that some person who came down in a flatboat told him their opinion was that if those people came they would not injure the inhabitants, that they were coming only to make a conquest of the country. Q. Why he did not give notice to the Government of this matter at the time he heard it? A. He did not think it to be necessary, looking on the whole of it as a report without foundation and unworthy of notice, from source it was derived. He thought it sufficient to contradict it to the said Green. Q. If two men from America did not go to his house, named Carter and Prince, and what conversation he had with them? A. The two persons named did stop at his house and he asked Carter what was said in America of those people who proposed to come down here, to which the said Carter answered they were well disposed to come but he did not think that they would because the President of the United States had ordered the Governors on the Ohio to publish a proclamation that any American who should engage with those people should be severely punished, according to law, and that the said Governors had executed the order of the President, wherefore those people couldn't carry their design into effect and having inquired of Prince what was said about it in Cumberland, he replied there was no person there who would attempt such a thing against the orders of the Congress except a certain Montgomery who could not obtain credit for four rials in that country who might undertake such an enterprise; and when the said persosn left his house, he charged them on their arrival in Natchez to communicate the same to His Excellency the Governor without fail. Q. Why he did not, himself, communicate this to the Governor by letter and not depend on those men to do it. A. He did not communicate himself with the Governor because one of those men, named Carton, is an inhabitant of New Madrid and told the deponent that he was a bearer of a packet from which he judged that if he were worthy of that mission he may be safely depended. He has nothing further to relate and acknowledged the foregoing declaration to what he had made, and signed with the Commandant, interpreters and witnesses assisting.

page 188. At the Post of Natchez, 28 April 1794. I, Don Pedro Favrot, commissioned by His Excellency, the Governor of this Post, to continue this examination, in consequence of the absence of Don Joseph Vidal, sent on a special commission for the service of the King, who was appointed as one of the interpreters, I have appointed in his stead Don Juan Girault, who being informed of said appointment has accepted thereof, etc. Signed by all the officials. Whereupon, before me and the witnesses assisting, appeared John Burnet, who being duly sworn, etc., was asked if he heard of the reports spread about by two men who came down in a flatboat from the United States of America in the month of February last. A. Stephen Richards told him that those two men who came from America and spread a report among the inhabitants that, in case the French should attack the district, they would not injure such of the inhabitants as did not take arms against them, but such as did take arms would be roughly treated. Q. If he knows that those men were at the house of Col. Bruin and said anything to him on the subject? A. He knows nothing about that. Q. If he has heard any of the inhabitants of Bayou Pierre say anything about this report? A. The deponent being Capt. of the Militia of this District and having received an order from His Excellency, the Governor of this District, to hold his men in readiness for services when required, the deponent accordingly gave orders to the inhabitants to prepare themselves in case of necessity to defend their property and the country, to which several of them replied that they would follow His Excellency, the Governor, to defend the country with much pleasure but as to property they would not defend that with any pleasure because they considered the property in their possession as belonging to the merchants and it seldom happened that men went into the field without some loss of lives, in that case the merchants would take the property left by the deceased, and his widow and children might starve, in consequence of which the deponent went to the house of Col. Peter Bruin to communicate it to him for the information of His Excellency, the Governor; which having been done, the said Bruin told him he should not communicate it to the Governor, it being, in his opinion, a matter of little consequence, whereupon the deponent requested him to write a letter for him to His Excellency and he would sign it, to which he replied that he would not as the Governor was well acquainted with his style in handwriting, whereupon the deponent went to the house of Melling Woolley and requested him to write a letter for him which said Woolley accordingly did, which is all that he knows of the matter, being 52 years old. The foregoing being read to him, he acknowledged the same contained the declaration he has made and signed with the officials.

p. 190. At the Post of Natchez, on the 2nd June 1784, before Don Manuel Gayoso de Lemos, etc., in pursuance of an order given by me, personally appeared at my dwelling Peter Bryan Bruin, Col. of the Militia, and Lt. Col. Carlos de Grand-Pre, and the interpreters in this case, Capt. Don Estevan Minor, Don Joseph Vidal, Secretary of the Government, and Don Juan Girault, present, I read to them the contents of the summary from the first proceeding to the last declaration which was translated into the English language by the said interpreters, in testimony whereof all signed and transmitted this to Peter Bryan Bruin, Col. of the Militia, that he may answer charges against him. Signed Manuel Gayoso de Lemos.

p. 190. Henry Trigg versus Matthew White, who owes him $39; asks that he may be made to pay same. [Trigg dwelling in this City.] New Orleans, 17 Oct. 1789. // The government of Natchez will compel Mr. White to pay Henry Trigg the amount due him. El Baron de Carondelet. // Matthew White is ordered to appear in person or by his attorney to examine his signature and acknowledge or contest the debt claimed. Note: 21st April 1789. I promise to pay Henry Trigg $39. Signed Matthew White. Received from Mr. Moore $2 on account, June 18, 1789. Henry (X) Trigg. // Henry Trigg hereby ack. to have received payment by Don Antonio Soler for the sum of $39, amount of a claim filed in the archives of this post against Matthew White. Wit: Juan Carreras. // Natchez 20 Oct. 1794. I do hereby certify there is in the files of these archives a suit against Matthew White, etc. [certificate of the above] signed Jean Girault.

p. 191. Stephen Minor versus Ebenezer Rees. About two years ago Ebenezer Rees sold to James Strother a negro for $500, payable at the end of the year, and your petitioner being surety for payment. Some time after the sale Strother absconded from the district, leaving the said negro and other property behind. In this event Rees took possession of the said negro carrying him to his plantation where he employed him in his own service, and at the end of 18 months appeared in law and demanded that said negro should be sold which was granted and the negro was sold at public sale to him for $130, which course he took without consulting with petitioner, which, as surety, he ought to have done. Now Rees demands from your petitioner the sum for which the negro was first sold, asks for consideration that Ebenezer Rees should have claimed from the law a seizure of all his property when Strother absconded, that the same should be sold at public sale, and if the proceeds thereof were not sufficient to cover the debt he could have recourse on the petitioner, but instead of taking that course, he kept the negro in his own possession and profited by his labor for 18 months and when he thought proper proceeded to sell him with the idea that the petitioner would be ignorant enough to pay his unjust demands. Etc. 28 July 1792. Signed. // Let it be notified that Ebenezer Rees has no claim on Stephen Minor on account of the debt owing to him by James Mather, since it is necessary to prove that a debtor is insolvent before recourse can be had from surety. Signed Gayoso. // Don Estevan Minor represents that in a difficulty between himself and Ebenezer Rees, concerning the sale by said Rees to James Strother, 21 Feb. 1790, and also by Messrs. Clark and Rees to Jesse Greenfield, 12 Oct. 1790, it is necessary that he should have copies of the said sale, asks that said copies be delivered to him. Signed. // Granted. // Copy of sale of negro man to James Strother for $550, Don Estevan Minor being surety for this payment. All sign. Copy of sale by Clark and Rees to Jesse Greenfield, seven brute negroes, free from mortgage, for $1200. 12 Oct. 1790. All sign. Receipt of $400 on account from Greenfield. [Five of the above were returned as buyer was not able to pay for them; the other remaining in possession of Greenfield. John Mapother.] The above true copies of records. Signed. Manuel Gayoso. [Same suit continues to p. 199.] Last instrument a petition by Minor that the suit be brought before the Superior Tribunal. 29 Aug. 1794.

p. 199. Gabriel Benoist versus Juan Joseph Rodriguez, who owes the estate of Henry Manadue, deceased, for $744, as will appear by the sworn account annexed, signed by sd Rodriguez. Benoist as executor of said estate asks that said Rodriguez be made to appear before Your Honor, etc. [This suit also covers four pages. Henry Manadue had an agreement to furnish some plank for something at the fort and there was a storm which damaged some building.] Deposition of James Cole. He declared that in 1790 he worked at the carpenter's trade in the employ of Don Juan Rodriguez and in that time he saw brought from the mill belonging to Henry Manadue for the said Rodriguez about 3000 feet of plank, more or less, and about 10500 feet of lathes, which is all that he can say. He is 23 years old. // Before John Smith, Esq. one of the alcalde's of this government, appeared son of Henry Manadue, Sr. who declared that the above mentioned plank had been laid at the water side according to Mr. Rodriguez's order and that he never did receive any payment but the credit above given. Sept. 1793.

p. 203. Simon Gonzales versus Robert Withers and John Shunck. Simon Gonzales rppresents that a certain Philip John Negler, sailor in the galley of His Majesty died at the Royal Hospital at this post on the 8th February last past, appointing your petitioner his executor and declaring in his last will that Robt. Withers, planter, owed him $124 and John Shunck $35, your petitioner prays in order to enable him to discharge the demands against the said deceased that Your Excellency will order the said persons to pay the sums described. Simon Gonzales. 3 March 1795. // Robert Withers and John Shunck will appear before me at the first audience to answer the above. // Robert Withers to appear on Saturday next. J. Ferguson, constable. Notified J. Shunck to appear. J. Ferguson. // Fort of Natchez. 21 March 1795. In pursuance of the above, appeared John Shunck who acknowledged the claim on him and prayed for a delay of payment until the return of Mr. Thomas Wilkins from the Capital, which was granted. Also Appeared Jesse Withers who acknowledged the debt and promised to give a horse in part payment and to pay the remained at the next crop. Manuel Gayoso de Lemos.

p. 203. Calvin Smith versus Charles White. Calvin Smith represents he was engaged by Charles White to take charge of his plantation and slaves as overseer, in pursuance he took possession of same and worked until now and the plantation is in good order and the crop in the ground. The brother of said White has lately arrived and thinking they could manage a crop without the assistance of your petitioner, they sought a quarrel with him to turn him off and deprive him of his wages. Your petitioner is unwilling to go without his wages and damages, the season being now so far advanced that he cannot begin another crop. Asks that two capable persons be appointed to examine the plantation and the work done by the petitioner and make report thereof to Your Excellency for further consideration. Calvin Smith. 21 May 1795. // Granted. I do hereby appoint Mr. Greenfield and Carter to visit the plantation of Mrs. White and examine the work done by the petitioner toward making a crop. Grand-Pre. // In consequence of an order from Mr. De Grand-Pre, we, the subscribers, went to the plantation of Mrs. White and carefully examined the same and find it in good order. Signed Jesse Carter, Jesse Greenfield. 23 May 1795. // The parties being heard at three different time, and Charles White having offered none but vague and unfounded assertions upon which it would appear that he did not turn away the overseer, Calvin Smith, on account of any neglect as it is proved by two disinterested planters that the crop is in good order but from some private distrust which moved him to charge the said Smith with bad conduct. I do hereby order the said Charles White to permit the said Smith to continue the crop on the conditions first made between them, otherwise he shall pay him his wages for the time he worked and further indemnification of three months wages as damages, in consideration that the season is too far advanced for him to find employment for himself and shelter for his family on another plantation, and also for breach of contract on the part of White. Grand-Pre. 30 May 1795. // Notified the parties. Jean Girault.

p. 204. Charles Jones versus James Hyland. Charles Jones represents that four years ago his brother-in-law, James Hyland, being without cattle to supply his children with milk, your petitioner lent him nine head of cows without any compensation. At the end of the year, the said Hyland having bought cows for himself and being no longer in need of those cows, offered to return them but your petitioner having no place to put them, left them another year and agreed with the said Hyland that for his trouble in taking care of them, he should received such part of their increase as was customary in the country, which your petitioner believes to be the one-fourth part, but the said Hyland has taken the one-third part, not only for the year lapsed after the agreement but also for the year he had them on loan and now refuses to deliver the cattle to your petitioner. 30 May 1795. Signed. // James Hyland is ordered to return the cattle belonging to petitioner which he shall deliver at his own expense at the dwelling of said petitioner and if he has any cause to show to the contrary, he will appear before me, etc. Signed. Grand-Pre. // In answer, James Hyland represents that the cattle were brought with effects in the hands of the wife of said Jones; that the wife of said Jones died about four years hence leaving three children and praying her brother-in-law, the petitioner, to take them under his care as tutor and curator, which he did, and the said Jones with inhumanity, neglected them entirely, and has not given them the least assistance since the death of their mother or even called to see them but on the contrary is living with the widow Smith, spending all his time and what he can make on the said widow and her children. The cattle being all that the mother left to the said orphans petitioner as their uncle and guardian wishes to keep them; besides Charles Jones has a forge complete which was given to his wife by her brother, with the express condition that it should be employed for the benefit of the said children, and it is well-known that the said Jones is using the forge to pay the expenses of his illicit connection with the said widow Smith, it appears to petitioner that the same ought to be taken out of his power and hired out for the benefit of the said children who are the true owners of it. // Both parties will appear and plead their cause before Gabriel Benoist, Esq. // Charles Jones that the cattle were the property of his children from their uncle is false as can be proved; nor did their uncle ever own the forge and tools. etc. It is true that there was a good property left by their uncle for the maintenance of the children but this property is in the hands of George Overaker and Lewis Evans who are also possessed of some bedding and household furniture belonging to the children; he asks that said Overaker and Evans give good accounting of the property in their hands and an inventory thereof be lodged in the archives of this government of this district, etc. Natchez, 10 June 1795. Signed Charles Jones. // Charles Jones and James Hyland being in dispute over some cattle put into the hands of said Hyland by Jones have agreed as follows; that the cattle shall be put in the care of some good person who shall take care of the three children of the said Jones and his deceased wife, one of which is his, for the benefit of said children. Messrs. George Overaker and Lewis Evans, brothers-in-law of the deceased Mrs. Jones, approve of this arrangement as far as in their power and will join the other two parties to have a person who will take care of the children security for their property and bound to the government according to law. 12 June 1795. Charles Jones, James Hyland, George Overaker, Lewis Evans and Gabriel Benoist.

p. 207. Calvin Smith versus Charles White. Notwithstanding the decree which Your Excellency was pleased to issue against Charles White for the payment of wages to your petitioner for a breach of contract, the said White has not paid any attention to said order and petitioner asks that a portion of his property be seized for the said cause. July 4, 1795. // Let the heirs of the estate of Matthew White be notified again to comply without delay to the decree of this tribunal, dated 30 May last and in default thereof the property will be seized to pay the wages of the petitioner. Grand-Pre. July 10, 1795. // Notified the order to Messrs. Charles and Hampton White. They said that they had not the money but Mr. C. White said he would attend to it tomorrow. J. Ferguson.

p. 207. Daniel Clark versus Ebenezer Rees. Clark represents that in an article of partnership which existed between him and Rees since 1787, it was covenanted that said Rees should be the only acting partner, leaving to the petitioner the management and direction of the concerns of said firm, and as the said Rees had no stock in the said firm it was conditioned that he should have but the third part of the profit after paying expenses. Further, the said partnership has been dissolved since about four years and during that time notwithstanding your petitioner has repeatedly endeavored to obtain from Rees a settlement of accounts pending between them, he has been unable to succeed. The petitioner seeing great delay in recovering debts due the firm, in order to facilitate the recovery, on his arrival at Natchez at the commencement of the present year, he executed a power to said Rees for that purpose and for good reasons determined some time afterwards to revoke the said power and appoint another person in his stead which he accordingly did, at the same time requesting the said Rees to deliver to his attorney all the obligations which said Rees has refused to do and on the contrary has given notice to said debtors to pay him only, wherefore the said Rees must have much property in his possession of which your petitioner knows not whence the same has been derived and especially as he has not settled the accounts of the late firm; he has recourse to the justice of Your Excellency. New Orleans, Oct. 15, 1795. Sig: Daniel Clark. // New Orleans 17 Oct. 1795. Granted in full. The Secretary will issue an order to the Commandant at Natchez to carry the same into effect and advise me of the result. Le Baron De Carondelet. // List of sundry property claimed by Ebenezer Rees, on which there are some mortgages. 1000 acres of land on Fairchild's Creek; 575 acres on Second Creek; negro man "Tobey"; wench "Phoebe"; boy "Harry"; boy "Quash"; boy "Jamaica"; boy "Pompey"; boy "Swift"; 60 head of cattle; 625 acres near the landing (mortgaged); 500 head of hogs; about 12 horses; farming utensils, etc. 17 Nov. 1795. Signed Ebenezer Rees. Examined by Grand-Pre.

p. 208. James Leasure versus Polser Shilling, who owes him $56 in part for wages and part for money deposited in the care of his wife, the receipt of which he has acknowledged but has refused to pay, accusing him of the rupture between him and his wife which is no more than of his own framing to defraud the petitioner of his earnings and labors, it being known to the world that such disturbances between him and his wife were frequent before the petitioner knew them; asks that he may not be deprived of his wages. 10 Jany. 1795. // Polser Shilling and petitioner were ordered to appear at government house tomorrow at ten o'clock. // Personally appeared the parties and Shilling having acknowledged that he had the money deposited by said Leasure, he was ordered to return it in the same specie in which he had received it, etc. Received of Mr. Polser Shilling $55 and 4 rials, being in full of all demands which I have received all in silver. James Lashire. Wit: S. Minor, Jean Girault.

p. 209. Jason Lawrence versus Henry Willis. To Don Manuel Gayoso de Lemos, Gov. of the Post of Natchez. Whereas a petition has been presented before my tribunal in the name of Jason Lawrence by his attorney duly appointed against Henry Willis for the recovery of certain monies together with a certain instrument or deed as follows: that Jason Lawrence of this city sells to Henry Willis a plantation to him belonging on the Homochitto River in the district of Natchez, containing 100 square arpents bounded on both sides by the vacant lands of the Crown, which said plantation was granted to me by His Excellency, Don Estevan Miro, 15 March 1789, which I now sell, etc. for $500 payable in four years from date. Henry Willis, being present at the time and receiving said plantation, etc. Signed at New Orleans, 2nd May 1791, by both and same certified by Pedro Pedesclaus, Notary Public. (p. 210) // At City of New Orleans, 3rd June 1796, appeared Mary Bryan, lawful wife of Jason Lawrence of this city, empowered by her husband, executed before a Notary the 26 June 1795, which has not been since revoked, which said Mary substitutes in her place Don Manuel Dejustus Calvo. // N. O. June 6, 1796, Manuel Dejustus Calvo, etc. represents that Henry Willis is indebted to constituent in the sum of $500, the term of payment whereof is expired since May 2 in the year last; asks that Your Excellency transmit instructions to the Commandant at the district of Natchez to compel said Willis or his executor, in case of his decease, to pay the said sum of $500 and in default thereof to let the execution on the plantation mortgaged to Jason Lawrence. // Let the order prayed for on the part of Jason Lawrence that the debt be paid be immediately issued. Carondelet.

p. 211. Post of Natchez, 17 Jany. 1797. Don Manuel Gayoso de Lemos in order to carry into effect the foregoing decree, caused to appear before me Isaac Gaillard and Abraham Ellis, husband of Margaret Gaillard, heirs to the estate of their parents, and the first named being in possession of the estate of Henry Willis who is said to reside in the United States, to whom, in the presence of Don Estevan Minor and Don Joseph Vidal, witnesses assisting, have caused to be read the foregoing dispatch by Don Juan Girault, interpreter, in testimony, etc. All sign.

p. 212. Lucius Smith versus Roswell Mygatt. Lucius declares, etc. that he did marry an orphan girl, daughter of the late Favel, planter, who in an early period of her age came into the care of Roswell

Mygatt by his marrying her mother, and at that time, about fifteen years ago, the petitioner's wife and her sister possessed each a cow and calf which had been given them in trust by their mother for their sole use and benefit and property of them by their aunt. The aforesaid Mygatt received the said stock into his care and did make it a rule to kill all the male increase of said cattle as compensation for bringing up the two orphans and their heifers and their increase were reserved and always acknowledged by him and known to the neighbors to be the property and right of said orphans, who being now both married, one to the petitioner, the other to Daniel Sullivan, they have applied for the said stock and its increase but have been refused. Etc. To establish their claim, Your Excellency will require Col. Bruin, in whose neighborhood they reside to receive evidences of witnesses residing at Bayou Pierre, and, after collecting evidences from both sides, to submit same for judgment to Your Excellency, etc. If Mygatt should make further charges for the care of the orphans, the petitioner wishes to state that his wife being six years old when she went into his care, she was soon able to do services equal to the trouble she occasioned and she lived with him until she was 20 years old, during which time, she assisted in bringing up the small family of young children, in spinning, washing and every other work, by which she much more than paid him for all cost and trouble she could have caused him. Dec. 20, 1796. Signed. // Col. Peter Bryan is hereby commissioned to take the evidences required by both parties. Gayoso. (p. 213.) Thomas Evans, being duly sworn, declared that he lived in the family of Roswell Mygatt for two or three years, about nine years ago, and that during that time he had frequently heard Mygatt say that he owned no part of the stock in his possession but that it was the joint property of his step-daughters, Ann and Catherine Favel, who then lived with him. He remembered that said Mygatt sold one or two beeves of the stock to the fort and killed one or two for the use of the family. The orphans were then young but were employed in such occupations as suited their years and sex. Signed. Thomas Hubbard also added that he had frequently heard Mygatt say that he had made use of the males of the stock to repay him for the raising of the orphans. // Elisha Flower declared on oath that he had lived some years in the neighborhood of Roswell Mygatt. [Same declaration as that of Thos. Hubbard./ He remembers Ann Favel, the present wife of Lucius Smith, who had lived with Roswell Mygatt until her marriage, and always understood that she was industrious and useful. Signed. Before Col. Bruin. Bayou Pierre, Jany. 4, 1797. // I do here certify that I have often heard Roswell Mygatt say that the stock in his possession was the property of his wife's daughters and he would never convert any part of it to his own use but they should have the whole. Ann, the wife of Lucius Smith had the character of a notable industrious young woman and her clothing while she lived with Mygatt consisted of plain homespun. Signed James Harrison. Jany. 17, 1797. // Deposition of Samuel Swayze. /Same as the preceding in every detail.] // Before me, Manuel Gayoso de Lemos, personally appeared Patience O'Brian, who deposes that in the year of the seige of Baton Rouge she did give into the care of her sister, Ann Favel, one cow, the property of which she did invest in the daughter of Ann, who is now the wife of Mr. Lucius Smith and that Roswell Mygatt did acknowledge the said cow and calf and increase thereof was the property of said Ann, the present wife of Lucius Smith, and she never heard him deny it. He had denied it to others until the decease of his wife. Patience (X) Obrian. Before Jean Girault, Ebenezer Rees. // William Selkrige said that, having an inclination to exchange a heifer with Roswell Mygatt for one in his possession, the said Mygatt replied that he must exchange with Ann for the heifer was hers and applying to Ann she said that Mygatt might do as he pleased and they did make the exchange. He had heard both Mygatt and his deceased wife say that the cattle belonged to the children. // Lucius Smith declares that he has reflected that the suit that he has instituted against Roswell Mygatt might cause him more expense and loss of time than the benefit he would derive from it; also that he might cause some disagreeable dispute in the families, and he is therefore resolved to drop the suit, resting satisfied with what he has already received from said Mygatt at his marriage; asks that the proceedings cease and the petitioner will pay the costs. Lucius Smith. // To be annexed with the proceeding and filed. Manuel Gayoso. Jany. 9, 1797.

p. 214. Joseph Bernard versus James Glasscock. Joseph Bernard declares that he is in possession of documents by which he can prove a demand against Glasscock, of this district, for $135; asks a full or partial payment immediately. Signed. 15 Jany. 1797. // Glasscock will appear before me tomorrow to answer the demand made agst. him. // Parties having appeared before me, Glasscock produced a receipt from Joseph Small by which it appears that Glascock paid him in full and had bound himself to return the bill on which the demand originated, being a fraud on the part of Small who later transferred the obligation of Glascock to Jason Lawrence and the said Lawrence has never presented the said obligation in this district where Glasscock resides which prevented recourse against Small or his prop-

p. 215. Jesse Hooper versus Ebenezer Rees. Hooper represents that having had dealings with John O'Connor in 1789 and having paid off the whole of these dealings with him to Mr. Eldergill, then his clerk, Mr. O'Connor was then in New Orleans and had with him a note of your petitioner which was to be delivered upon his return as hereunto annexed will appear, but O'Connor has never sent it to Mr. Rees to oblige your petitioner to pay it again; asks that Mr. Rees be ordered to deliver up the said note. 27 Jany. 1797. Signed. // Parties appeared and the receipt having been presented, the note was ordered to be given up. Ebenezer Rees to have recourse to Mr. O'Connor or who ever it may appear. Manuel Gayoso de Lemos.

p. 216. John Barton represents that, having entered into matrimony with the widow of the late Daniel Mygatt, who had several small children by her first husband, he conceives necessary for reserving in the family, that justice may be done to all, the creditors and to the petitioner, that estimation of what property belongs to estate be made and recorded but as the estate is very poor and there are a number of orphans it would be too expensive to go through a course of law; he therefore asks that Your Excellency authorize the alcalde of the district have the same done with the assistance of some neighbor so that it may be attended to with less expense. Signed. 23 Jany. 1798. // I do hereby commission and authorize Mr. William Vousdan to do the needful in the business required by the petitioner and return the proceedings to the record office. Manuel Gayoso de Lemos. // St. Catherine's Cr. Jany. 30, 1797. In obedience of order, I have called Mr. Caleb King and Wm. Gillespie and repaired to the plantation of the late Daniel Mygatt and valued the following property with Mr. John Barton. [The property valued at $822. Signed by all.] The following notes were due: For smith work; Jeptha Higdon's note, Job Cory, Richard Bacon, Samuel Heady, Alex. Moore, Jr., Benj. Hoven, Matthew McCullagh, Buckner Pittman, John Cavelry, Thos. Hubbard, Christopher Gart, Robert Miller, James Glasscock, Capt. Matthew White, Henry Cooper, Benj. Bullock, Benj. Truly, Nicholas Rabb.

p. 217. William Kirkwood versus Kennedy and Irwin. Wm. Kirkwood represents that some time ago William Irwin applied to Petitioner to sell him as will make 20000 staves, which petitioner offered to sell for $50; said Irwin complained that the price was too high, to which petitioner observed that his timber was very convenient to the river and of a very good quality. Some time later, Irwin told petitioner that he had purchased what timber he wanted from Kennedy, the petitioner's neighbor. The petitioner then told said Irwin not to cut any timber on his land, that his line ran on the upper side of the Big Bayou and the said Bayou was within the petitioner's line, and also offered if he and Kennedy would procure a compass he would go and show them the line to prevent disputes. But the petitioner hearing no more of the matter for some time, went to see what was doing and found they had cut a vast number of his best trees, most of them in or near the center of the petitioner's land and counted about 8000 hogshead staves on the place, and such staves can be obtained from extraordinary timber. The damage done to the petitioner is considerable and asks restitution. 15 Sept. 1796. Signed. // David Kennedy, Wm. Irwin and petitioner ordered to appear next day. // In obedience of the decree of His Excellency Don Manuel Gayoso I caused the line of demarcation to be run between the lands of William Kirkwood and Kennedy and it is certain that Wm. Irwin has cut a quantity of oak trees on the land of Kirkwood, which I certify. Sig: Wm. Dunbar, Dep. Surv. // William Irwin represents that the staves he made from wood he bought of David Kennedy be detained until the suit between Kennedy and Kirkwood is determined, the said staves being exposed to be floated away by the river which is now rising and an opportunity arising for selling them, he prays that Your Excellency permit him to sell the same on conditions as Your Excellency may deem proper. // The petitioner may sell the staves alluded to and retain the money in his hands until the suit is determined. Permission agreed to by Wm. Kirkwood. All sign.

p. 218. Michel Lopez versus John Ferguson, who owes him $32; asks that he may be made to pay the same. Jany. 21, 1791. // Called at plantation of Mr. Ferguson and he was not at home. Communicated to his wife. // Ferguson to pay at once or property will be executed. // Ferguson represents that he has no way to pay the debt but by getting the fees due to him from the public. For four or five years past he has been wholly employed in that line. [Constable.] // It is agreed that Mr. Lopez allow Ferguson further time, until the end of February next. Signed by both.

p. 219. The heirs of Samuel Lewis versus John Tally. Know all men by these presents that we, Sarah Fulsom, Rebecca Foster, Samuel Lewis and Thomas Foster, Jr., heirs of the late Samuel Lewis, decd., do hereby empower etc. John Ferguson, of the dist. of Natchez, our true and lawful attorney, to sue for and receive a certain negro named "Peter", about 25 yrs. old, the property of the estate of Samuel Lewis, decd., which said negro was left with John Turnbull, Esq. by Ebenezer Fulsom and traded by Mr.

Turnbull to John Tally, who has the said Negro now in his possession. Signed: Rebecca Foster, Sarah (X) Fulsom, James Foster, Jr., Samuel Lewis. Wit: Wm. Selkridg, George Norriss, Ezekiel (D) Dewitt, Joseph (X) Harrison. // John Ferguson, attorney for the heirs of Samuel Lewis, deceased, represents that Ebenezer Fulson, having married the widow of sd deceased, left a slave belonging to said heirs in the hands of John Turnbull who of his own authority without any title whatsoever appropriated the same slave to his own use, in payment of a debt owing to him by sd Fulsom and afterwards sold him to John Tally, who has him now in possession and the said being the property of the said heirs they petition that Your Excellency order said Tally to deliver him up without delay and have his recourse on said John Turnbull. Signed. Feb. 6, 1796. // Let the document proving the property of the negro in question be produced and let John Tally and Ebenezer Fulsom be notified to appear with all the parties concerned on 1st court day. Sig: Grand-Pre. Feb. 13, 1796. Let Messrs. Anthony and Wilford Hoggatt appear as witnesses to prove whether or not the negro was the property of Samuel Lewis, decd. // Sarah Fulsom declared that the negro in question was the property of Samuel Lewis who brought him from Georgia where he got him from his brother or sister. After the death of said Samuel Lewis, deponent married Ebenezer Fulsom, who of his own authority left the negro in the hands of John Turnbull, as security for a debt which he owed him. // Nancy Stewart, who on oath declared: To her knowledge Samuel Lewis brought the negro in question to Cumberland and had him in possession all the time he lived there, having received him from his brother and sister; at his death the negro remained in the possession of his widow, now married to Ebenezer Fulsom. She is 28 years old. Nancy Stewart. 28 Sept. 1796. // Appeared William Joiner, who on oath declared he knows that Samuel Lewis went to Georgia in search of an inheritance and at his return brought with him two negroes, named Big Peter and Little Peter. Etc. Signed. // It being proved by the foregoing that the negro in question really belongs to the orphans of Samuel Lewis and it is ordered that the sd negro be brought here to deliver to their attorney and John Tally will take his recourse on whomsoever it may concern. Manuel Gayoso de Lemos. // John Tally produced the said negro, etc. All sign. Note: See final termination of this suit.

p. 221. John Webster versus Maurice Custard. Webster represents that he worked in the shop of Maurice Custard over 16 months at $15 per month and also furnished Custard with sundry articles as per acct. annexed and has been called upon to settle his affairs with said Custard before William Cooper, Esq., which has been done in some measure but not to the satisfaction of the petitioner, who finds himself obliged to have recourse to Your Excellency for justice and re-examination of the accounts; asks that Custard be ordered to produce his accounts against the petitioner since the commencement of their dealings. Signed. 7 March 1795. // William Cooper will forward to Isaac Johnson, Esq. all the proceedings of the above suit, the petitioner having agreed to submit the matter to his decision. Gayoso. // Personally before me, Isaac Johnson, J.P. of Second Creek, James Todd's deposition of a settlement of accts at the beginning of 1793, the receipts of each were written by said Todd and they were exchanged. 18 Oct. 1796.

p. 222. Heirs of Samuel Lewis versus John Tally. (cont.) I do certify that in 1795, Sarah Fulsom gave a receipt to her husband in full for a negro which I understood had been transferred to Mr. Turnbull and Mr. Joyce in consequence of a bill of sale Fulsom gave for a quantity of cattle to her youngest son although Fulsom said he had no right to pay anything for the negro which was sold to get necessaries for the use of the family, but to avoid disputes he would give the cattle. Signed William Cooper. Sandy Creek, 23 Feb. 1797. // John Turnbull, of Baton Rouge, planter, solemnly makes oath that Mrs. Sarah Fulsom did live at Tombigbee where deponent kept a store in 1788 and she had a large family and he constantly furnished her and her family with their necessities, which was their only support and it was Mr. Fulson that he trusted as she had some property of her own; her then husband had none, nor would the deponent give him any credit; that being much indebted to Fulsom and Joyce, partners, she, herself, did sell to the deponent and his partner the negro named "Peter" and she did herself send him to them in part payment of the said debt. Immediately afterwards, the deponent and said Joyce did dispose of the negro to said Tally. John Tally did then live at Tombigbee and for three years afterwards Mrs. Fulsom did live there at the same time and never made any claim or demur and they have also lived in the Natchez government about three years and no claim was ever made against negro Peter. Signed. 18 Feb. 1797. John Turnbull appeared and swore to the above instrument. // David White appeared and made oath that he lived at the Tombigbee at the time Mrs. Fulsom did who was his sister-in-law, the family were supplied with necessities by Turnbull and Joyce, etc. [Same as told by Turnbull.] Signed: David White. At Post of Baton Rouge appeared David White and ack. the above statement. // The parties in the above suit having appeared before me, etc, it was ordered that the negro Peter should be returned to John Tally and the heirs of Samuel Lewis may apply directly to Mr. John Turnbull for any claim that they may have, or intend to make for the said negro. Gayoso.

p. 225. George Cochran versus George and Thomas Sullivan. Three yrs. ago the petitioner gave his note to George Cochran for $51 for goods then received from Mr. Cochran, at which time Ebenezer Dayton owed to your petitioner a larger amount and said Dayton at the request of your petitioner by his letter and other assumptions became holden to Mr. Cochran as his security of said note, which note at several times, said Dayton endeavored to procure from Mr. Cochran to give to your petitioner in payment by reason that every payment he could and did make was credited to other demands he owed Cochran, and Cochran refused to look to your petitioner and Dayton severally but to them jointly. Your petitioner therefore, for a time was unable to settle with either of them but Mr. Cochran later promised to look to your petitioner only. Since then, contrary to his promise, Cochran now makes his demand for the payment of said note and refuses to receive good merchantable property from your petitioner at its value, which he is ready to give; prays that Mr. Cochran may be ordered to look only to your petitioner and take from him the property in payment. Signed Thomas Sullivan. 10 Feb. 1797. // Your petitioner, George Cochran, represents, referring to the payment by Ebenezer Dayton for the amount of hirelings wages as privileged, etc. asks immediate payment. Signed. 10 Feb. 1797. // Let Thomas Sullivan appear and declare how many horses he has on the other side of the river and give public notice that the same may be sold on Saturday next, the nineteenth. // Thomas Sullivan appeared and declared that he had left in possession of Job Routh on the other side of the river nine heads of horses and one colt. Thomas (X) Sullivan, before Ebenezer Rees and Thos. Barkley. Gayoso. // To His Excellency the Gov. George Cochran represents that he does positively deny that he ever made Thos. Sullivan any declaration that he would only look to him and not to Ebenezer Dayton for the payment of his note, etc. Signed. Feb. 11, 1797.

p. 227. Nathaniel Tomlinson versus Samuel Flower. Tomlinson represents that he received from John Ferguson in 1790 a note of Jesse Finn's for $35, which he delivered to Dr. Samuel Flower for payment of work done by said Finn for the estate of the late Richard Carpenter's crop but the said Dr. Flower hath not returned the said note nor paid any part of it and Ferguson having applied several times that he couldn't get payment from Finn's estate. Lately Dr. Flower alleged to have lost the note. Ferguson declares that he could have recovered the note if he had had it in due time. The petitioner is accountable to him for the value thereof. 21 Feb. 1797. // Be notified that Dr. Flower personally appeared before me, one of the syndics of the district, Samuel Flower, who declared that in 1790, he received from Nathaniel Tomlinson a note signed for Jesse Finn for $30, which said note Samuel Flower endeavored to recover payment from the estate of Richard Carpenter, now Samuel Flower declares that he never received value for the said note but by some accident the said note is mislaid or lost so that it cannot be returned to Tomlinson. Signed. Before Wm. Dunbar. // Dr. Flower shall be accountable for the amount. Gayoso.

p. 228. John Wilson versus Melling Woolley, who owes him $115 for blacksmith work done for the use of his plantation. Woolley having become insolvent, his property was put in the hands of trustees for the use of his creditors and your petitioner being assured that his debt was privileged put sd Wooley's note into the hands of Wm. Dunbar, Esq., one of the trustees, as payment for a debt due by your petitioner due to him. Since which time Mr. Dunbar has called for his money and refused to give your petitioner credit for Woolley's note. Signed. 14 March 1797. // The debt being privileged the trustees of the estate of Melling Woolley will admit and put it as such. Gayoso. // Communicated to George Cochran, Ebenezer Rees and Wm. Dunbar, Esq.

p. 229. Nathan Dix versus the estate of Thomas Woods. In answer to the memorial of P. Engle, Nathan Dix represents that Lewis Evans purchased at the sale of the effects of Dr. T. Woods to the amount of $48 for which he obtained Your Excellency's order that your petitioner should take his receipt for the same and your petitioner acted in obedience thereto; that he was frequently applied to by the said Evans for the remainder of his account which he paid being fully satisfied by the said Evans that he had paid and expended more than $20 in cash for the coffin, grave-digging and necessary linen necessary for the funeral of the deceased, not particularized in his bill, and from your petitioner's own knowledge of the trouble and disagreeableness of the deceased in his illness at the said Evans house, he differs much in opinion with Mr. Engle in regard to his bill for though the charge is in one, in fact it is in several paid by Mr. Evans. Your petitioner has yet in his hands money belonging to the estate and a chest of medecine which if sold at vendue would bring perhaps something considerable but the former he would not disperse without your order as there are fees due to the office or the latter without your instructions lest they should sell under price and the petitioner incur blame from the executors for whom he acts. He is entitled something for the lost of his time and for his trouble and whatever Your Excellency may be pleased to allow him may be retained in his own hands out of the funds in his possession. Signed. 9 March 1797.

p. 229. Alexander Ross versus Henry Nicholson. Alexander Ross represents that he has obtained different executions against Henry Nicholson without being able to obtain any payment and whereas cotton was lodged in possession of Hugh Davis for the purpose of paying this debt; asks that orders be issued for immediate payment of this debt. 4 March 1797. Signed. // Notify Henry Nicholson to pay this debt in three days, or appear at govt. house. // Mr. Henry Nicholson said that he had put his cotton in the hands of Mr. John Ellis to be ginned but he would bring Mr. Ellis's obligation to the amount of the debt, to be paid in New Orleans when the cotton is sold. He will appear at the government house. Sig: Wm. Gillespie. Fees: $4. // To His Excellency the Acting Gov., Alexander Ross represents that Henry Nicholson owes him $40, as will appear by his note dated Oct. 11, 1794, which he has been unable to recover. // I notified the above to Henry Nicholson on his plantation of the Homochitto, 14 April 1796. He ack. his signature at the foot of the note and said it was just. // He is ordered to comply with the tenor of the decree the 15th inst. Signed: Grand-Pre. // By virtue of the foregoing decree I levy execution on all the crop of cotton that Mr. Henry Nicholson has made for the purpose of paying the debt of Mr. Alexander Ross and the cost and the cotton is in the care of Mr. Hugh Davis who promises to keep it in his possession until opportunity offers and cause to be taken to Natchez and place it in the depository's office. Signed: Hugh Davis.

p. 231. William B. Smith versus Louis and Abraham Vilaret, who owe him $102 for provisions and necessaries furnished to his family and hirelings, and whereas the debt is of a privileged kind and Vilaret and his wife have moved from their residence to New Orleans and have empowered their son Abraham to settle and pay their debts; asks judgment agst the said Abraham Vilaret for payment and in default give execution against their property for debt and cost. Signed. // The party will appear to acknowledge debt and make payment without delay. // The balance and costs of the above was settled this day by ________, March 24, 1797. Signed William B. Smith.

p. 232. Peter Lee versus Isaac Gaillard. Peter Lee represents that Isaac Gaillard for Miss Polly Savage owes your petitioner $88 as will appear by the statement of petitioner's account; he understands that Gaillard claims of petitioner payment of a horse he sold when in the employ of Miss Savage by direction of Mr. Willis to one Robert Treat for which the said estate received said Treat's note for $40 and a mare and colt which are now in possession of said estate, so your petitioner has no cercern in the business only as he acted under the direction of said Willis. Signed. 24 Jany. 1797. // Isaac Gaillard represents in answer to Peter Lee's claim for $80 which he received from Wm. Henderson for two valuable mares in virtue of Mr. Henry Willis's order which he was to deliver to Mr. Willis with a complete saddle horse, which he has not done, as trustee of the estate, he thinks he is entitled to retain the sum on account of the price of said mares which he received nearly five years ago. 20 July 1796. Signed. // I do hereby certify that I have often heard Mr. Henry Willis say that in exchange of the saddle horses between him and Peter Lee he gave Peter Lee no difference between them; that Mr. Lee told him that Willis's saddle horse would do him as well to ride through the Wilderness as his own. // To His Excellency the Governor, Peter Lee showeth that the estate of the deceased of Mrs. Ann Savage is justly indebted to your petitioner for $68 during the year '69 as by the account herewith laid before you. Since the death of Mrs. Savage a fictitious demand has been raised against your petitioner by persons acting as agents of the estate for the price of two mares which was delivered to your petitioner by Mr. Wm. Henderson on the order of Capt. Henry Willis who was then in charge of the business of that estate and as the statement by Mr. Gaillard was totally different from what it should be, your petitioner begs permission to lay before Your Excellency the actual account of what occurred. He was employed by Willis as an overseer and he acted from Feb. 15, to 15 Aug. at which time your petitioner went, with said Willis's approbation to the State of Kentucky for his family, with view of returning immediately to this country; that before his departure Mr. Willis requested your petitioner to take through with him two mares for the purpose of purchasing and bringing back with him a horse such as Mr. Willis described for the use of the plantation, he bearing the risk of said and also allowing your petitioner an allowance for any charge he may be at in accomplishing this business. In response to which petitioner carried Mr. Willis's order to Mr. Henderson and received the two mares for the purchase of a horse required of him and also made a purchase of one for his own use, for which he gave Henderson an order on Mr. Willis for $82. On the way to Kentucky, in the nation he lost the two mares sent by Mr. Willis and in consequence of which he could not bring him the horse. After his return he again engaged in the employ of the estate and it was not until lately that the charge for the two mares was brought against your petitioner by Mr. Gaillard and Dr. Johnson. He does not deny having received the two mares but at the time he suggested the possibility of a charge being brought against him or his family but Mr. Willis assured him that no charge was made on the books for them. (p. 235) In obedience to the command of His Excellency, the Governor, we, the subscribed arbitrators, have examined with attention the amounts, documents and evidences produced by the parties and have the opinion that Peter Lee has an unquestionable claim to a balance of $29 due him from the estate of Mrs. Savage and that in regard to other claims we are of the opinion that six months should be allowed to said Lee to bring forward proof of the delivery of the mare and colt and also the same time until the return of Miss Savage to prove the delivery of three pieces of nankeen valued at $8, which articles have to be paid for if proven; also a note of hand of Robert Ford in favor of Peter Lee for $40 now one of the issues of this administration and ought to be restored to Peter Lee. Second Creek. 31 March 1797. Signed William Dunbar, Ruffin Gray. // Natchez, same day, I approve the foregoing arbitration, etc. Jean Girault, recorder of the records, will deliver to Mr. Peter Lee the note mentioned.

p. 236. John Barclay versus Polser Shilling. Barclay represents that he purchased from Polser Shilling 400 acres of land as will appear by consignments, herewith presented, on condition that petitioner should obtain a grant from same from the government in his own name. The petitioner finds to his great surprise that Shilling had a claim and a grant for the very land himself. Petitioner asks that the warrant that was issued to Shilling be delivered to petitioner that he may obtain a patent for the land agreeable to contract, Shilling having sold said land and he can have no lawful use thereof. Jany. 18, 1797. Signed. // Parties are ordered to appear before me. // Received of Mr. William Smith $300 for which I assign, etc. to said William Smith all my right and title to land surveyed in my name, 10 Dec. 1782, by Don Carlos Laveau Trudeau, Surveyor General of the Province of Louisiana, etc. about 3 miles from Fort Panmur on St. Catherine's Cr., 120 acres, b. on north by Wm. Brocus, south Jacob Cable, east by the Creek, and on west by an old tract of Mrs. Sarah Truly and Francis Spain, also my improvements on same. 13 Jany. 1785. Signed: Stephen Mayes. Wit: Wm. King. // I sign over all my right and title to the land mentioned to the within bill of sale to Jacob Hope by his paying to me or my executors $1 for each acre contained in the tract. Signed: Polser Shilling. Wit: John Short, Elisha Cushing, Ebiather Squier. // I do hereby assign all my right and title to within land to Mr. John Barcley who agrees to petition for it in his own name. 25 Feb. 1796. Signed: Polser Shilling. Wit: Jean Girault. // I do hereby assign all my right and title in the foregoing tract to Mr. Ebenezer Rees, for value received in his obligation of this date. 23 July 1797. Signed: John Barclay. // Know all men by these presents that I, Francis Spain for and in consideration of $160 to me in hand paid have bargained and sold to Polser Shilling, of this district, a tract and improvements on or near St. Catherine's Cr. bounded by lands of Capt. Matthew White, those formerly of Mrs. Truly, being 235 acres. Jany. 30, 1786. Wit: Wm. Gilbert, Charles White. Signed: Francis Spain. // Bill of sale for the within land to Elizabeth Yarrow for value received. Signed: Polser Shilling. Wit: John Short, Elisha Cushing, Abiatha Squier. // I do hereby assign all my right, etc. to the within mentioned tract of land to Mr. John Barclay for value received. Signed: Polser Shilling. Wit: Jean Girault. // The parties having been heard, it appeareth that Polser Shilling sold the land to John Barclay and kept the titles in his possession, he is ordered to deliver them to the purchaser, and it appears that the grant to same is in the hands of Wm. Dunbar, Esquire. Let him deliver it to said Barclay that he may obtain a title in form. Signed: Manuel Gayoso de Lemos. // Notified Polser Shilling in the presence of Capt. McCabe and Mr. R. Dixon. Jean Girault. Notified same to Mr. Ebenezer Rees representing J. Barclay. J. Girault.

p. 240. Joseph King versus Stephen Stephenson, of the dist. of Second Creek, who is justly indebted to your petitioner for $99 as it appears by the judgment of Isaac Johnson, Esq. The said Stephen Stephenson not having yet adopted any measures to take down the raft of timber referred to in the said judgment . . . . . .

p. 241. James Ross versus Thomas V. Dalton. James Ross represents that Thos. V. Dalton, his father-in-law, holds in his possession a negro wench named "Sally", aged 20 or 22, which wench the said Dalton gave to the wife of your petitioner when she was a child and as it appears that he now wishes to appropriate the said wench himself, he asks that Your Excellency will order the said Dalton do not under any pretext whatever remove the said wench from this post until your petitioner shall have time to prove that she belongs to his wife. 6 Sept. 1796. May it please Your Excellency to order John Scott and Polser Shilling who were present at New Orleans at a certain transaction relative thereto and and who are well acquainted with the matter to appear here and declare what they know thereof and that their depositions may be transmitted to the superior tribunal. Signed: James Ross. (p. 242). At the post of Natchez, 19 Sept. 1796, appeared Polser Shilling before Don Manuel Gayoso de Lemos, Don Juan Girault appointed interpreter, etc. Shilling was asked to relate what he knew of the above matter and declared that a certain William Hyser in New Orleans told the deponent that Valentine Thomas Dalton had mortgaged the negro wench in question as security for a debt which he owed and when the term was expired the said Hyser claimed that the said wench should be sold which could not be done, the said Dalton producing documents proving that she belonged to his daughter. He is 51 years old. Signed. Next appeared John Scott, master carpenter, who being sworn, etc. When he lived in New Orleans he went frequently to the house of said Dalton and heard Mrs. Dalton say that the negro in question was the property of his daughter who is now married to James Ross and Thomas Dalton also told him several times that the wench belonged to Nancy. He is 36 years old. (p. 243). Natchez. 24 Sept. 1796. James Ross having requested depositions of Andrew Bell and John Williams, appeared Andrew Bell who declared he was a native of the United States and a bachelor and that when Valentin Dalton lived in the swamp with the deponent, he, Dalton, told him several times that the wench in question belonged to his daughter, Nancy, now the wife of James Ross, which is all he knows in the matter. Signed Andrew Beall. Now appeared John Williams who is a native of the U.S. and married; declared that frequently in conversations the said Dalton told him that the said wench was the property of his daughter, Nancy, who is the present wife of James Ross. He is 40 years old. p. 244. I, Don Francisco Lennan, curate of the Parish Church of Saint Salvador in the post of Natchez, do hereby certify that James Ross is married and lives by his salary as attendant of said Church without any property or rents whatsoever, that he maintains himself decently without any cause or complaint, etc. 19 Oct. 1796. Natchez. Signed: Francisco Lennan. // To His Excellency the Gov., Margaretta, dau. of Valentine Thomas Dalton, informs Your Excellency that her sister, Mrs. Ross, lays claim to a negro wench named "Sally" in consequence of a promise her father made to her in her infancy but as my father never made over said wench to my sister, I am of the opinion that I, as one of his heirs, have an equal claim to the property of my father and said wench, therefore, I oppose Mrs. Ross taking said wench from my father and she would rather remain with them and maintain the family he has still under his care. Signed: Margaret Dalton. Nov. 6, 1796. // The petitioner earnestly wishes that the dispute between him and Mrs. Ross might be amicably settled and asks that Your Excellency appoint any number of gentlemen he pleases as arbitrators to examine the affair and their judgment laid before Your Excellency for your final decision. Signed: Valentine Thomas Dalton. // In pursuance the preceding, James Ross appoints Mr. George Cochran on my part to settle the said matter on condition that I be not held liable for the costs as I have no means to pay same, etc. Signed: James Ross. Natchez. 10 Nov. 1796. // Mr. Ebenezer Rees appointed by Valentine Dalton. [This arbitration soon failed, Ebenezer Rees claiming whatever share Valentine Dalton had in the negro and getting permission to keep her until the case was decided, James Ross, often called Rose in the papers, went for her took her away from Rees, using abusive language and encouraging the wench to do the same. Ross then asks for time to get copies of court papers from New Orleans in which Valentine Dalton deposed that the negro belonged to his daughter Ann, which were granted but the superior tribunal required proof of his marriage to said Ann and much space is devoted to such proof in which his wife is called Ann Watson, which marriage took place in a Catholic church in Natxhez "three years ago".] // Deposition of Thomas Valentine Dalton: Sometime in the year 1790 a certain negro girl named Sally belonged to a young woman named Nancy Watson; that his mother gave him money to purchase said negress for the said Ann Watson's use, which woman is now the wife of Mr. James Ross. // New Orleans, May 16, 1797. I do hereby certify that a wench named Sally was in 1790 given for a debt of Mr. Valentine Dalton for a billiard table sold and delivered to him and he, the said Dalton declared that the said negro girl belonged to a young girl named Ann Watson, who was then under the care of said Dalton. The wife of the said Dalton said the same to me, that the wench did belong to the said wife of Mr. Ross. N.O. May 17, 1797. Signed: Mary Fitzgerald. // I, Antonio Gamelin, notary public of Post Vincennes, have recorded a negro girl the property of Ann Watson which was purchased for the aforesaid Ann Watson and for her use and benefit. The said orphan child being raised by Valentine Thomas Dalton. She was born at Fort Pitt in 1779. I acknowledge myself to be accountable to the said Ann Watson for the said negro. Given under my hand at Post Vincennes, Feb. 28, 1789. // Valentine Thomas Dalton, of this City represents that he is in possession of a negro girl named Sarah, aged 13, belonging to an orphan girl named Ann Watson, and having no intention that the said orphan shall be deprived of the said slave, in case of my death, she being entirely ignorant of her right to the same, wherefore may it please Your Excellency to admit testimony that the signature at the Post of Vincennes is that of Antonio Gamelin, Esquire, and that the negro girl was intrusted to me to be delivered to said Ann Watson when she shall come of sufficient age, thereupon to impose your authority and judicial decree declaring the said negro girl is the property of the aforesaid Ann Watson and that a certified transcript of the same be furnished to the petitioner. Valentine Thomas Dalton. // Let the document presented be translated by Don Juan Joseph Duforest by order of His Excellency Don Estevan Miro. 8 June 1790. // [This extends over several pages more. Much repetition.] p. 252. The decree. In pursuance of the foregoing deposition, I therefore declare that the negro woman, named Sarah, is the property of Ann Watson, and in consequence thereof let the petitioner be furnished with the certificate he has required. Miro. // Valentine Thomas Dalton, having instituted sundry proceedings that a certain negro girl is the property of an orphan whom he had under his care since and wishing that the proceeding be finally concluded, prays that Your Excellency will order that the cost be assessed and paid by the said Dalton. // Granted. Miro. New Orleans, 3 May 1797.

p. 253. William Brocus versus Anthony Glass. William Brocus made application for a mare and colt belonging to the late John Sliter, petitioner represents that he received the mare and colt for a beaver trap and other hunting equipage, which he furnished the said Sliter, and is proven by the annexed deposition of Samuel Gibson, Esq., he therefore prays that Your Excellency will refuse the request of said Glass and confirm the property of said mare and colt to petitioner. Natchez. 19 May 1797. For Wm. Brocus. // Having found the proof presented by the petitioner to be sufficient, the mare and yearling colt left in possession by the late John Sliter to be his right and property. Signed: Gayoso. // Let Antonio Glass be notified. // Personally appeared 24 April 1797 at Bayou Pierre before Samuel Gibson, Thomas Evans and made oath that in August last John Sliter was at the house of Isaac Fife, when and where he heard said Sliter say he owed Mr. Brocus as he had furnished him two beaver traps and other necessaries and he told Mr. Brocus to take care of his mare and yearling and if he never returned he should keep them for what he owed him. Signed Samuel Gibson, alcalde. Same date appeared Thomas Harrington and made oath that in Aug. last John Sliter came to his house and told him that Wm. Brocus had let him have two beaver traps and some other necessaries and in consequence of these and what he owed him besides he left a mare and her yearling at his option as to whether he would let him have them again, etc. Samuel Gibson, alcalde. Bayou Pierre, same day, appeared William Tabor who made oath in Aug. last he and John Sliter were at the house of Wm. Brocus, fitting themselves with some necessaries for their hunt up the Mississippi. The said Sliter said to said Brocus that he was in his debt and if he lived to return he would be able to make him satisfaction and if he never returned the mare and yearling he desired Mr. Brocus to take care of would make him satisfaction. Samuel Gibson, alcalde.

p. 254. Edward McCabe versus John Dix. John Dix represents that Capt. McCabe had sued him for the full amount of notes of hand given by petitioner, one for $38 and the other for $32, which were delivered up by said McCabe to Mr. John O'Connor to pay a debt to him. Some time afterwards the petitioner gave to the said McCabe three notes at hand for $15 each which said McCabe promised to deliver to said O'Connor in payment of his two notes but on the contrary he gave one of the notes to Mr. O'Connor on his own account but gave the petitioner no credit for the same; on account of the other note he received $3 and 3 rials which he applied to his own use; the other note he returned but the person who owed it to the petitioner declared that he paid it to the said O'Connor on account of the petitioner. Further Mr. Peter Walker did also pay to O'Connor for the petitioner's account the sum of $14, so instead of being indebted to McCabe to the amount of his note, he only owes him a small balance. 13 March 1795. Signed. // Cause George Wilkinson to appear and depose concerning his own note given to the bearer and said to have been to John O'Connor for the account of John Dix. // George Wilkinson declared that in 1790 he executed a note for $15 to James Watts payable the following December and in February he was called by James Eldergill, clerk to John O'Connor, who had an assignment of this note from Mr. Edward McCabe who told the deponent to receive it from Mr. Richard Harrison, that being thus called on, he discharged him from the note to Mr. Eldergill who could not find the note but gave Wilkinson credit for it in Mr. O'Connor's books and that he should have the note as soon as he laid his hands upon it. Deponent called several times after this but not being able to procure it he demanded a receipt for it from Mr. Patrick Foley who then acted as clerk to Mr. John O'Connor. Mr. Foley after searching for the entry by Mr. Eldergill and satisfying himself that the demand was just, gave him a receipt, of which the following is a true copy: Whereas George Wilkinson says that John Eldergill is possessed of a note of his payable to Mr. Watts which was given to Edward McCabe by Richard Harrison and he has settled his accounts, etc. [Eventually this case was put into the hands of arbitrators, who, having examined the accounts of Dix and McCabe, it appeared to them that a balance of $32 and 2 rials is justly due to Capt. McCabe by said Dix, as the sum of $14 and 3 rials does not appear to be credited to said McCabe on his account current with John O'Connor. Signed: Peter Walker, John Cochran. Jany. 1, 1797. // p. 258. Messrs. John Cochran and John Murdoch were appointed to revise the accounts between Mr. McCabe and John Dix. 8 June 1797.

p. 258. Francis Bailey versus Joseph Vidal. Bailey showeth that his petition of the 25th instant stated that Joseph Vidal was indebted to him for $68. The said Joseph Vidal countered said petition with a certain paper, a compensation for the sum expressed therein, the contents of which were unknown to your petitioner, but which the said Joseph Vidal declared to be a certificate at the Treasury at New Orleans; asks that the said Vidal be made to pay the said debt in Your Excellency's presence. // For the satisfaction of this part, Don Joseph Vidal will pay what he justly owes in my presence. Gayoso. [This also continues for several pages, being a question of the kind of money Bailey should be paid, etc.]

p. 263. William Dunbar versus E. and R. McCabe. William Dunbar, atty. for Daniel Clark, represents that Capt. Edward McCabe is indebted to said Daniel Clark jointly with his wife, Rebbecca, for $500; asks property be seized and sold to satisfy same. Feb. 22, 1797. // Be it notified that Capt. McCabe and wife pay the just debt they owe the petitioner without delay, etc. Signed: Gayoso. // The contents of the above decree communicated to Edward McCabe and his wife and they regretted that they had no money to pay but they intended to sell property for the purpose. // Dunbar petitions for an execution against the property of McCabe. // Natchez, Mch. 1st, 1797. Mr. Jean Girault, the constable of this government, will lay an embargo on the lot and buildings belonging to Capt. McCabe at foot of the hill and will have the same appraised by John Scott and Thomas Thomson, who will be previously sworn before me, and afterwards the said property will be advertised for sale according to law, and proceeds applied to pay the debt of Capt. McCabe. // 4 March 1797 pursuance to the foregoing decree, I have this day levied the execution in the premises mentioned in said decree. J. Girault. Edward McCabe. // 6 March 1797. Appraisers, Scott and Thomson, value property, lot houses and premises, at foot of the hill, belonging to Capt. Edward McCabe, where he now resides. At the request of Rebecca McCabe, have ordered appraisers to value the half of her lot together with the house erected on the southeast corner of said lot, which they valued at $650. Same day, said house and lot exposed to sale for cash, being cried from 10 in the morning to 12, was adjudged to William Dunbar, he being the highest bidder. Cried the second time and adjudged to Wm. Dunbar for $180. Third day, Mr. Ebenezer Rees, who by deed signed in this office became the owner of this debt, has agreed that Mr. McCabe shall make a conveyance of said lot and house mentioned in these proceedings to Thomas Tyler.

p. 265. Ruffin Gray versus Lewis Alston. Whereas a petition has been presented before this tribunal at New Orleans by Ruffin Gray of this post, claiming the property left by his deceased sister, Marian Gray, may be delivered to him, which petition and decree thereon are as follows: Post of Natchez, Ruffin Gray represents that his sister Marian Gray, lawfully married to Lewis Alston, died in 1790 in district aforesaid and at the time of her marriage she was possessed of a negro woman and two children and that she left no heirs but Philip Gray, son of her sister, and petitioner, her brother; that no marriage contract between herself and her said husband relative to her property, nor was any inventory made at the time of her death; and now her said husband represents that all debts outstanding shall be paid out of their joint property which will not appear to Your Excellency as lawful, for the dower of a wife is privileged above all claims and is to be first paid. Signed: Ruffin Gray. // Decree: Let instructions be transmitted to the Governor of Natchez to transmit the inventory taken at the death of Marian Gray, lawful wife of Lewis Alston, and if none was taken at that time, let it now be done in the presence of said Alston and others interested with the usual formalities and transmitted to this tribunal. Signed: El Baron de Carondelet. // Inventory showed 11 negroes, some infants, 400 arpents of land, 3 horses, 35 horned cattle, 35 or 40 hogs, 12 or 15 sheep, some working tools and household furniture. Signed Lewis Alston, Ruffin Gray. There was no inventory taken of the property taken of P. Lewis Alston and his wife, Marianna Gray, the wife of said P. Lewis Alston, at the time of her death which was on 28 Feb. 1790, but Mr. Ruffin Gray, at whose instance the inventory is now called for, declared his belief that the foregoing given by Mr. Philip Lewis Alston is a just and true one. 13 June 1797. Daniel Clark, Alcalde of the Dist. of Buffalo, in the presence of Wm. Miller.

p. 267. Jesse Carter versus Thomas Irwin. Jesse Carter, in 1789, purchased from Mr. Thomas six negroes and gave his bond for same, and on 12 Feb. 1790, he declared to the said Irwin 9 hogshead and 400 carrots of tobacco on his account and on March of the same year he delivered him a flat valued at $100, one half of which was to be passed to the credit of your petitioner; since then the said Mr. Thomas Irwin has negotiated the said bond without giving the necessary credits thereon agreeable to contract, which will appear more fully to Your Excellency by the different vouchers hereunto annexed. Signed. Natchez, 28 April 1797. // Mr. Peter Walker will appear at government house to declare on oath what properties he has in possession belonging to Mr. Thomas Irwin. Signed: Gayoso. In consequence of the above appeared Mr. Peter Walker who declared on oath that John O'Connor, Esq. is atty. for said Irwin and he, being atty. for said O'Connor, he left him with a number of notes belonging to said Irwin, the payment of which he has not yet recovered. 9th July 1797. Signed. [Receipts alluded to in above petition follow.]

p. 268. Rebecca McCabe versus Edward McCabe. Rebecca McCabe represents that her husband has most cruelly and dangerously beat her in such a manner that if it had not been for the interference of some friends her life was endangered; it is needless to repeat the many times and odious manner in which he has displayed his inhumanity to the unhappy petitioner; she prays the necessary process that will establish a permanent and effectual separation between the petitioner and her husband. 11 July 1797. Signed: Rebekah McCabe. // The acts recited in this memorial being notorious to the public, be it notified to Edward McCabe that he may make his reply in continuation hereof. Gayoso. // Edward McCabe, in reply, represents that he can confute the act described in preceding petition; that law cannot dissolve a marriage never lawfully celebrated; his marriage to the woman being performed by a common country constable; she, the said Rebekah has made proposals lately through the medium of Mr. John Scott to pay a certain sum of money to your petitioner and take all the property into her hands lately held jointly, and agreed to discharge all debts; asks that the premises be taken under consideration. July 11, 1797. Signed. // Rebekah McCabe represents that notwithstanding what is said in the foregoing memorial concerning the unlawfulness of her marriage, it was celebrated in as lawful a manner as was then in practice in this country, not by a common country constable as is said but by Mr. Justus King who was then authorized by the government for that purpose and therefore an act of separation duly authorized by government is absolutely necessary for the accomplishment of this business and regularity. With respect to the terms of separating the property, the petitioner is ready to comply with her offer of assuming all debts and keeping the property and paying Mr. McCabe $300 which she offers though it is much more than his part of the estate after liquidation of the debts, which she finds to be more than she, at first expected. Signed. 13 July 1797. [In answer there is a long indenture as to the division of property and signed by both.]

p. 271. John Gayle versus James Nicholson. John Gayle represents that his wife, being the niece of the late Mrs. Nicholson, conceives that she has some claim to inherit a part of her estate. The late Mrs. Nicholson had some property when she married Capt. Nicholson. They had no issue. Mrs. Nicholson has no heirs or descendants. She may have a brother or two in the States but their existence is uncertain. The petitioner's wife is the daughter of Mrs. Nicholson's sister, who is deceased, and has no other heir than the petitioner's wife and another daughter. The petitioner therefore conceives his wife entitled to inherit one-half of the property of Mrs. Nicholson. 28 Jany. 1797. Signed. // James Nicholson represents, in answer to above, Mrs. Gayle, being an orphan and without subsistence, was raised and maintained by Mrs. Nicholson and the petitioner through motives of friendship and Mrs. Gayle might in a kind of pretended gratitude might have called Mrs. Nicholson her aunt but whether she really the legitimate niece or niece of Mrs. Nicholson it rests with her to prove before she can make any claim; therefore your petitioner hopes that Your Excellency will find it just to refuse all claims on her part until she legally establishes her identity. Signed: James Nicholson. 6 Feb. 1797. // Mrs. Nicholson having died without a will, I do hereby commission Mr. William Dunbar Esquire to cause an inventory to be made of the joint estate of her and her husband, in the presence of two witnesses and then require an obligation of Mr. Nicholson in which he shall bind himself not to dispose of said property but to discharge lawful debts of the estate. Be this notified to the parties for their lawful information and compliance. // I do hereby certify that three days before the death of Mrs. Sarah Nicholson, her husband went into the room and asked the deceased how she was and if she stood in the need of anything. Her request was nothing. Her husband said "My dear, if it takes everything, negroes, horses and all I have, it shall be at your service." Her reply was that she was not dangerous and in the time of her sickness she never mentioned any of her nieces. Signed: Wm. Hedger Collins. // I do certify that I have often heard Mrs. Sarah Nicholson who is now deceased say that when she and Capt. Nicholson departed this life that she wished her part of the property should go to Jonas Nicholson, her sister's and Captain Nicholson's brother's son. I do certify that I have often heard Mrs. Nicholson say that as she had no children she wished all that Mr. Nicholson and herself should be worth at their deaths should be left to Jonas Nicholson, her sister Winfred's son, whether he did or not she wished to give her part to him at her death. I heard her say the same thing on the 26th December last, in her own house. Signed

Naomi Nicholson. // I do here certify that on the death bed of Mrs. Sarah Nicholson deceased, the 12 Jany. 1797 that she had a sister married to a brother of James Nicholson in Halifax County, N. C.; that after all their lawful debts were paid, her desire was that if her husband was willing to give their property at his death to the eldest son of Samuel Nicholson and Winifred Jones, now Mrs. Nicholson. On the night before the death of Mrs. Nicholson, her husband told her in my presence that if it took all his property her request should be fulfilled. Signed: Nancy Collins. // Know all men by these presents that I, John Gayle and Martha, my wife, formerly Martha Westcott, do by this present instrument of writing, for divers causes, have constituted and appointed our trusty friend, Ruffin Gray, our lawful attorney to act for us and to settle and receive for us such part of estate of Sarah Nicholson, now deceased, and formerly wife of James Nicholson, due and owing to the afsd. Martha by the laws of this land, and pass receipts, etc. Signed by John Gayle, Martha makes a mark. 2nd Feb. 1797. Before David Brasford and John Barnhill. Wit: Anslem Blanchard. // Inventory and appraisement of the joint estate of Mr. James Nicholson and his late wife, Sarah Jones. Homochitto. 1st June 1797. By command of His Excellency, Don Manuel Gayoso de Lemos, I, William Dunbar proceeded to the plantation of Mr. James Nicholson, accompanied by Messrs. James Prather, Jr., and Robert Davis, as assistant witnesses. Messrs. Patrick Foley and Hugh Davis, as appraisers, and Mr. Ruffin Gray as attorney for John Gayle and his wife and the said Mr. James Nicholson being also present. Inventory and appraisement of the joint estate of said James James Nicholson and his late wife, Sarah Jones, was commenced and carried on, etc. Total $8126. There were 18 slaves. The above an inventory of the visible estate. Signed by all. // 3rd June appeared Mr. James Nicholson and makes bond as required of him not to dispose of any of the said estate until the suit is settled. Before Gayoso. // John Gayle represents that in order to prove his wife's identity as is required by Mr. James Nicholson, it will be necessary to take the evidence of several witnesses many of whom live at a distance and asks that the alcaldes of the districts where the witnesses reside be authorized to take their depositions. Petitioner protesting hereby against Mr. Nicholson for the cost that may attend the business. 13 July 1797. /Alcaldes were instructed to take the depositions mentioned in due form with two assisting witnesses./ // Dist. of Second Cr. Personally appeared before me, Isaac Johnson, one of the alcaldes, etc., Robert Abrams who on oath said that he was formerly well acquainted with a certain William Westcott and his wife; that they lived on Lynch's Creek in South Carolina and they had a daughter, then a baby in their arms and the said William died and his wife removed into this country as he understood in the company of Mr. James Nicholson and his family; that this deponent some years after the removal after the said Nicholson was in Galvestown at the said Nicholson's house and the wife of the said Nicholson pointed to a young girl almost grown up and said that is my sister Westcott's daughter and the young girl to whom she then pointed is now the wife of John Gayle. Signed Robert Abrams. Wit: John Barney and Simon Hook. 14 July 1797. Isaac Johnson. Fee paid by Mr. Gayle 6 rials. // I appoint Ruffin Gray to take such evidence as John Gayle desires, according to the decree of His Excellency. Signed: Isaac Gaillard. July 14, 1797. Government of Natchez, District of Homochitto, before me appeared Pamela McCulloch, who, being duly sworn, declared she is acquainted with Amy Westcott, wife of William Westcott and sister of the late Mrs. Nicholson on Lynch's Creek in South Carolina; that the said Westcott died in that country and the widow removed into this country in company with Mr. James Nicholson and the deponent's father; that soon after her arrival in this country she died, leaving two daughters which Mrs. Nicholson took charge of and they continued with her until they married, the eldest of which is now the wife of John Gayle; the deponent further sayeth that she, herself was married to the brother of the said William Westcott who dying left an only child; that on the death of her child, said Nicholson claimed the property said child died possessed of in behalf of his niece now the wife of said Gayle, alleging she was the lawful heir of her uncle's child. Signed Pamela McCulloch. Wit: Joseph Dove, William Dove. // Personally appeared before me Hugh Davis, who, being duly sworn, declared that he was acquainted with Mr. James Nicholson in 1776 who lived at that time on the river Amite and that he had at that time two small girls who were said to be nieces of Mrs. Nicholson, that they called Mr. Nicholson "uncle" and Mrs. Nicholson "Aunt", nor did he ever hear the smallest insinuation that they were not the nieces of the late Mrs. Nicholson. The eldest of the girls married John Gayle. Signed Hugh Davis. Wit: Eli Spires, Joseph Dove. Sworn before me, Ruffin Gray, 15 July 1797.

p. 277. David Forman versus the estate of Ezekiel Forman. David Forman and the executors of the estate of the late Ezekiel Forman represent that it is being notorious that the whole property and effects enumerated in the inventory of the estate of Ezekiel Forman has appeared by authentic documents, including an instrument by which Margaret Forman, widow of the said Forman, renounces all claim of dower on the estate, does legally belong to the said Forman as his true and actual property. The memorialist prays Your Excellency that you will confirm the surrender now actually made by the executors of all and singular the property and effects of every kind, whether lands, slaves or other effects in favor of David Forman as his absolute property and right and that Your Excellency will be pleased to decree that such instruments in writing may be drawn up if necessary. Signed: Daniel Forman, William Dunbar, Ebenezer Rees, Benajah Osmun. Natchez. 11 March 1797. p. 278. Let the documents referred to be produced for my determination thereon. Signed Gayoso. March 13, 1797. // In pursuit of the will of Ezekiel Forman, in which he gives full power to his executors to settle the business of his estate and it appearing by the accounts presented by David Forman that his brother Ezekiel is indebted to him in the sum of 6813 pounds 7 shillings Pennsylvania currency for the balance of their dealings in this province exclusive of their dealings in the United States, which accounts have been settled and adjusted by Benajah Osmun, executor of said estate, and otherwise confirmed by an instrument executed by Margaret Forman, widow and executrix of the will of her late husband, Ezekiel Forman, stating that she has settled the accounts pending between David Forman and the estate of her late husband and transferring to him the whole of said estate, real and personal in this government of Natchez, and by another instrument executed by the said Margaret Forman renouncing all claims she might have to the said estate of her said husband in favor of the said David Forman. // It is decreed that the said Benajah Osmun, William Dunbar and Ebenezer Rees do confirm the said instruments executed by the said Margaret Forman, executrix of the estate and will of Ezekiel Forman, her husband, by putting David Forman in possession of all of the estate. Signed: Manuel Gayoso de Lemos. [Creditors of the estate of Ezekiel ask that the above transfer be withheld until the creditors have some assurance that they will be paid. 17 April 1797. Signed S. Minor, James Moore for the est. of Alex. Moore, George Cochran for Robt. and Geo. Cochran, Peter Walker, Ferguson and Murdock, Reed and Ford, James Moore for the est. of Robt. Scott. A favorable report on this, the debts of Ezekiel Forman are to be privileged before the said property is disposed of otherwise. Signed Gayoso.] [Several more pages, including an inventory amounting to $17,088.]

p. 285. William Dunbar versus Jaques Rapalie. Your petitioner having made application to the tribunal of Your Excellency for the recovery of the payment of a debt by Garret Rapalje but his son Jacque Rapalje having opposed the delivery of the negro mortgaged for the security of said debt, producing what he alleges to be sufficient proof that the said negro was not the property of his father but his own, the petitioner presents a demand against the said Jacques Rapalje, being his own obligation in favor of Mr. Poydrass for $240 due since January 1790; asks immediate payment with legal interest and in failure thereof that sufficient property may be sold to complete said payment. 14 Jany. 1797. Signed. // Jacques Rapalje to pay without delay the amount of the obligation, etc. [Dunbar petitions again, Rapalje having failed to make payment; asks for an execution against his property, a negro named Joe, and sell the same to pay said debt and cost.] p. 286. Col. Peter Bryan Bruin will cause the negro Joe to be seized and delivered at government house for the purpose that may be required. // Mr. James Harman, constable of this district, will immediately seize the negro Joe, referred to in the above decree, etc. Bayou Pierre. P. Bryan Bruin. // The estate of Garret Rapalje and Jacques Rapalje to Wm. Dunbar. Total: $779. // Natchez 2 March 1797. Tobias Brashears, Esq. is authorized to issue execution on this negro and as much more property as is necessary and send same down to the government house, etc. // Pleasant Hill, Big Black, May 10, 1797. After going myself and examining the property of Mr. Jacques Rapalje I found nothing there except some little cotton about 2000 pounds so I was forced to seize his negro wench Polly as there was no other property there worth sending. Signed Tobias Brashears. [A long petition from Jacques (James) Rapalje.] p. 289. Natchez , 14 Sept. 1797. It is agreed that Mr. Wm. Dunbar will received the two slaves which are at the fort and pay hire of $18 per month and receive an order to take them out of the fort. // Big Black, Aug. 11, 1797. Inventory of the property of the late Jacques Rapalje, deceased, 800 arpents of land, one old negro woman, "Muddy", one negro man, "Joe", crop in the ground, 25 acres in corn and some sweet potatoes, 1200 pounds of cotton of the last crop, farming utensils, household and kitchen furniture, etc. Wit: Tobias Brashears, Isaac Rapalje, Charles Collins, Robert (X) Campbell.

p. 290. John Baker versus John Ellis. John Baker represents that in behalf of Josephus Smith, an orphan, he makes known to Your Excellency that in the lifetime of Josephus Smith, Jr., father to the said orphan, he, the said Smith made a purchase of a negro man named "Ben" from Mr. John Ellis for $400, a part being paid, for which your petitioner has in his possession a receipt from said Ellis, another payment has been made which your petitioner can likewise prove. A short time after the said Josephus Smith died, the said negro was missing and Mr. Ellis came to the widow Smith, the late wife of the said Josephus Smith, and showed signs of sorrow for her misfortune. A few days after the said negro was seen at work in the said Ellis's field. The said negro has been in the possession of the said Ellis for six years or more wherefore your petitioner now begs Your Excellency to cause John Ellis to return the above mentioned negro to your petitioner for the use of the orphan and pay the customary hire for the time he, the said Ellis, has fraudently detained him. Signed: John Baker. 26 ____ 1797. // John Ellis represents that in 1790 he traded with Josephus Smith for of a negro man, the price to be $400. He had the negro man in possession and was to receive title when he completed the payment of the purchase money but the said Smith died before the payment was made and his brother Israel who appeared to have management of his business agreed to give up the negro and allow wages for the time his brother had him and did in consequence deliver him to the petitioner who has had him ever since. It was found that the difference between the payment made and the hire of the negro was about $60 in favor of the estate which said Israel Smith agreed to receive and on account of which he took petitioner's order on Dr. Todd for his bill against the estate paid by the petitioner and amounting to $20 and since the marriage of the widow to John Baker, he applied to the petitioner for payment of the balance to be made in smith work to which the petitioner consented provided it should be agreeable to Israel Smith to whom the petitioner spoke on the matter. 12 Sept. 1797. // By the annexed certificate of Israel Smith, it appears the affair was legally settled according to the established customs of this country and no sale was passed for the negro. The claim of John Baker cannot be admitted. // I do hereby certify that Mr. John Ellis asked me to whom he should apply for the balance due him on the negro man, etc. I acquainted Mr. Cobb of the proposal and as he would not join me in an obligation and my circumstances would not admit my advance of the money, I thought it best for Mr. Ellis to have the negro back.

p. 291. Waterman Crane versus Tomasina Lord. Crane represents that he sold to Richard Lord a yoke of oxen branded in the cushion HCTD, which said yoke was, by your petitioner's obligation 6 Nov. 1790, payable 15 Dec. 1791, to Messrs McNulty and Huling, and by them deposited in the hands of George Cochran, of Natchez. These oxen were expressly sold to said Lord for payment of said obligation and since his departure from this government sold by his attorney and reputed wife, Tomasina Lord. Your petitioner having applied at various periods for payment to the aforesaid Tomsey Lord was told by her that the amount has been settled with the said Cochran who held your petitioner's obligation, which your petitioner finds not to have been done and has reason to believe that she contemplated removal from her present residence on Bayou Pierre, having to that end sold the plantation on which she resided and other effects. He asks an order for immediate payment of said debt to Mr. George Cochran that the petitioner's obligation may be discharged. Signed. Jany. 1st, 1798. // Mrs. Lord will without delay make satisfactory payment. // Appeared at the government house to answer the claim of Waterman Crane, Tomsey Lord. Jany. 17, 1798. Simon Holloway witness. [She claimed that Richard Lord had a settlement with Mr. George Cochran before his departure.] Mr. George Cochran summoned to appear. // George Cochran appeared and made his affidavit that no settlement was made with him by Mr. Lord for the oxen herein mentioned. // As Mrs. Lord knew the conditions under which the bargain for the said oxen was made, she shall pay the amount obligation and I commission the alcalde of the district to compel the said payment. Signed: Stephen Minor. [Details of the settlement follow at much length.]

p. 294. Cato West versus John Smith. To Major Stephen Minor, Governor per interim of Natchez, etc. Sir: Petition of Cato West showeth that some time in 1792, Mr. John Smith cut a quantity of valuable white oak timber on your petitioner's land at the head of the navigation of Cole's Creek, as will be found by the declaration of Messrs. Thomas Calvit, John Vanderwall and Wm. Fairbanks, which timber was cut and carried away contrary to the law and custom of the country, etc. 8 Aug. 1798. Signed: Cato West. Mr. John Smith to Cato West 5 large white oak trees $50. 7 less white oak trees $35. Timber for three saw pits. $15. Total $100. As per certificate and declaration of Thos. Calvit, John Vanderwall and Wm. Fairbanks. // John Ferguson will notify John Smith and if no amicable arrangement can be made respecting the petitioner's demand, Wm. Ferguson, Esq. will transmit the proceedings to me in order that I may reach a final determination of the business. // Natchez, 12 Dec. 1797. (p. 299) Cato West instituted a suit against John Smith for trespass on his land and cutting and carrying away a quantity of timber, etc. I do hereby nominate William Irwin, Thomas Calvit and Justus King to estimate the damage done the said West by the trespass aforesaid. Signed: Stephen Minor. In pursuance of the above order the underwritten have met and proceeded to the business of said directive and after due deliberation do adjudge and assess the damage done by Mr. John Smith the sum of $50. Jany. 24, 1798. Signed by all. // Approved and confirmed and payment of said amount by John Smith and cost of suit. (Cost $35). // (p. 300). Cato West reports that John Smith refuses to make payment to petitioner, for the timber. // [John Smith obtained an appeal. The verdict not given here.]

p. 301. The King versus Miguel Solibellas. Don Juan Ventura de Morales, auditor, etc., acting intendant of the Province of La. and West Fla. for His Majesty to Don Estevan Minor, exercising the functions of Governor at the Post of Natchez, hearing the proceedings against Don Miguel Solibellas, military storekeeper at the Post of Barrancas, for the defalcation of the said Miguel for the sum of $2000, appearing by his accounts to be owing to the said Treasury; it is ordered that the sale of the property of said Solibellas made by the wife of said Solibellas to Don Garcia Texada be annulled as having been made after the discovery of said theft and in violation of the privileged claim of the Treasury on the estate of the debtor. Transcription of the above order having been submitted to Capt. Estevan Minor, etc. with order to proceed in the presence of two witnesses to appraise the property and effects attached by the order of this Tribunal belonging to Don Miguel Solibellas, an account of which will be annexed to the instructions, same being cried out three successive days and adjudged to the highest bidder. (p. 302) By order of His Excellency, Don Juan Ventura Morales, chief auditor, etc. the list of property belonging to said Sollibellas which appears by inventory taken Oct. 26, 1797: a house in the town of Natchez, 50 feet long and 30 feet wide, including galleries, two old chairs, one cypress bedstead, 1 cypress table, 1 small cypress post bed, 1 pair kitchen fire-dogs, etc., belonging to Don Miguel Solibellas which will be cried, etc. 3 Feb. 1798. Signed: Minor. // John Scott and Thomas Thomson, Master Carpenter, appointed to appraise the house, which they valued at $1400 cash. Both sign. The same adjudged (1) to Wm. Gillespie for $600; (2) To Maurice Stacpoole for $750; (3) to Maurice Stacpoole for $940, the same being Square No. 2, Lot No. 3 in the Town of Natchez. 14 Feb. 1798. // 17 Feb. 1798. Daniel Douglass and Samuel Forman appointed appraisers of the effects seized, etc. which they valued as a whole $8. Both signed. Adjudged to Pedro Ancid. Net proceed $933-3 rials.

p. 304. Ebenezer Dayton versus his creditors. At a meeting at the government house 3 Feb. 1798, Messrs Thos. Wilkins, George Cochran, William Dunbar, Ebenezer Rees, trustees, we find that a diminution of his property has taken place without any satisfactory explanation of the same. But notwithstanding engagements made the aforesaid trustees on the 12th January 1798, as appears by his written document, No. 9, to meet the said creditors in a proposed assemble for that purpose, he has in contempt for this engagement, after due notice had been given, refused to attend and to   the authority under which the indulgence was obtained, after the ratification of the treaty with the United States. We have also understood that the said Dayton had absolutely absented himself under pretense of going to Walnut Hills and now without apprehension that his intention may be to remove from this government and he may be attended with injurious consequences. Asks an order of attachment levied on all of the property of said Dayton for the benefit of his creditors and have his books placed in the hands of some person chosen for that purpose. Signed by the above. // Whereas Ebenezer Dayton has not complied with his agreement with his creditors, now attended at government house, etc, I do thereby agree that the trustees appointed by his creditors accompanied by the notary public shall inventory and lay embargo on all the property of the said Dayton for security of his creditors and all books, papers placed in the hands of said trustees. Signed: Stephen Minor. // Let the sequestration of the said Ebenezer Dayton, as ordered on the 7th, be carried fully into effect. // Inv. of effects found on the plantation of Mr. Ebenezer Dayton under the care of Cornelius Seeley. 15 March 1798. [Inventory was largely of house furnishings and kitchen utensils, and a few cattle. Not appraised.] Signed Peter Walker, William Mather, Cornelius Seeley, Thomas Wilkins, Ebenezer Rees, and George Cochran.

p. 307. Bryan Perry versus Stephen Stephenson. A suit pending between these two men was referred to Isaac Johnson, but the said Stephenson had appealed to the government even before the result was given, the proceedings were returned to the Office by Mr. Johnson, but said Stephenson, instead of evading did not appear, therefore your petitioner obtained from Your Excellency an order and asks for judgment. Signed B. Perry. 17 March 1798. // Notified Stephenson a 2nd time. // Second Creek District. Daniel and Bryan Perry appeared before Isaac Johnson.

p. 307. Appeared John Reed, who, on oath, declared that he was present when Bryan Perry did bargain and sell six head of horned cattle which were particularly specified, that is, 4 cows and 2 steers. John (X) Reed. Before Isaac Johnson. (p. 308.) The parties appeared and having examined the proof, it is decided that the cow in dispute was really reserved when the bargain was made in New Orleans, therefore Stephen Stephenson will immediately return the said cow and her increase to said Daniel Perry and pay the cost of the suit. Signed: Vidal.

p. 309. Sarah Scott versus Mary Williams. The subscribers, exrs. of the est. of the late Robert Scott, decd. represent that Mary Williams' people were working on a lot which by legal deed was granted to the deceased, which grant is dated 26 July 1796 and confirmed by el Baron de Carondelet and likewise registered at the Land Office at New Orleans. One of the petitioners did also wait upon Mrs. Mary Williams to know the nature of her claim to which she answered she was possessed of titles to the said lot and that she would persist in improving it. The petitioner being persuaded that the grant issued in favor of the said Robert Scott is legal and valid and that no other grant to the said lot was given prays that Your Excellency order the said Mary Williams to desist in the improvement of the said lot. Natchez. 10 March 1798. Signed: William Moore, James Moore. // Mrs. Mary Williams will on Wed. next at government house produce the titles by which she claims the lot, and it is notified to her that the petitioners' protest is admitted and that she will desist in improving the lot until it is positively proven that it is justly her property. Signed: Minor. // March 14, 1798. On this day appeared the executors of the estate of Robert Scott and the attorney of Mary Williams and produced their respective titles to the lot in question and it appearing that the titles of the said Mary Williams were accompanied by a decree of the 13 Sept. 1795 being much earlier than that obtained by Robert Scott of the date of the 20 July 1796. Ordered that the same be communicated to William Dunbar that he may certify when the decree dated 13 Sept. 1795 was presented to him and the date of the survey made by him by virtue of the said decree. Signed: Vidal. // On the same day of the decree, 13 Sept. 1795, was presented to me on the same day it was signed by His Excellency, Don Carlos de Grand-Pre, acting Governor of Natchez, and in conformity therewith I surveyed in favor of Mary Williams 9 Oct. 1795 two lots, No. 1 and No. 3 of Sq. No. 5 in this town. Natchez, 16 March. Signed: William Dunbar, Dep. Surv. // Natchez 17 March 1798. Let the parties be notified to produce their titles to the lots which they both claim on Monday the 19th in order that authentic copies may be taken thereof. Signed: Vidal. // Mary Williams petitions that wishing to build houses and stores immediately in the new town of Natchez, prays Your Excellency will be pleased to grant her for that purpose Nos. 1 and 3 in Square No. 5 in said town. Signed. 13 Sept. 1795. William Dunbar, Dep-Surv. represents that the said lots were vacant. (p. 311) "I do here certify that I have surveyed for Mary Williams Lots Nos. 1 and 3, Sq. No. 5, etc. 9 Oct. 1795. Signed: William Dunbar, Dep. Surv." // Manuel Gayoso de Lemos, etc. Whereas Mary Williams has promised to fulfil the conditions of this grant, I confirm to her the two lots aforesaid to be held and enjoyed by her as absolute owner thereof, provided that she should contribute to the government of the Town of Natchez as an inhabitant thereof and not to convert the said lots to any other use than which they are now destined, namely to erect houses or stores thereon and not to be left vacant or abandonned. Signed: Manuel Gayoso de Lemos. 2nd Oct. 1795. // Robert Scott, merchant, petitions that he wishes to build a house in this town for his own use asks to be granted lot No. 3, Sq. No. 5, 20 July 1796. Signed: Robert Scott. // Same date, the lot asks for by the petitioner is granted to him by the express condition that he finish the building he has commenced thereon and shall continue to contribute to the expense of the government and the town and William Dunbar will survey the same and make return of same. Manuel Gayoso de Lemos. // I have surveyed for Robert Scott lot No. 3 in square No. 5, for Robert Scott, in this Town, 150 feet square. 25 July 1796. William Dunbar. // Whereas Robert Scott has promised to fulfill the conditions etc. I confirm same to him, etc. Signed Joseph Vidal. 27 July 1796. Confirmed by Baron de Carondelet to Robert Scott. // Examined the results of the whole proceedings and Mary Williams has the first legal possession of Lot No. 3, Square No. 5, which is now claimed by Robert Scott deceased, the pre-occupant cannot be deprived of her right in the lot aforesaid. Therefore let Mary Williams be informed that she is at liberty to continue her improvement on the said lot without being molested. And notify the executors of Robert Scott of this proceeding and the whole to filed in the Archives. // Petition of Sarah Scott, William Moore and James Moore in answer to the above decree. Natchez. 24 March 1798. Asks that the case be submitted to the Superior Tribunal. // Transcriptions of the whole proceedings will be sent to the Superior Tribunal but that is not to prevent Mrs. Mary Williams from proceeding with her improvements on the said lot. Signed: Vidal.

THE END OF BOOK G

I, David Harper, keeper and translator of the Spanish Records for the State of Mississippi, certify that the foregoing contained in 314 pages of faithful translations from the records aforesaid by me carefully collated, compared to agree therewith. In testimony whereof, I hereby set my hand and seal at the Town of Washington, State aforesaid, this 1st day of September, 1818. Signed: D. Harper.

LAND CLAIMS, 1767-1805

WRITTEN EVIDENCES OF LAND TITLES

A FOREWORD

When the United States acquired the Natchez District from Spain, it was agreed that all legal land claims would be recognized. To get this confirmation written proofs of title had to be submitted to the United States Government for consideration.

These abstracts of title are recorded in seven large volumes under the name of WRITTEN EVIDENCES and lettered "A", "B", "C", "D", "E", "F" and "G" and are deposited in the Dept. of Interior, Land Division, National Archives, Washington, D. C. An eighth volume was begun, Book "H", but only a few British land grants were recorded in it. As these particular British grants had been given in the other volumes, they are not included in this collection.

However, one of these grants from Book "H" follows this foreword to give the verbiage of a complete British grant. Following it is a photostat of a Spanish grant, (Claim No. 2, Book "A", page 193) with a translation of same.

The first few pages of Book "A" are instructions from the United States Government to the Register of the Land Office relative to the confirmation of claims, describing the different types and the requirements for each.

The Files

Also available in the same Department of the National Archives are the original files of the claims recorded in the WRITTEN EVIDENCES. There had been in all 2098 files, according to the list at the Archives. They are numbered in the order in which they were registered. Of these, at the time they were examined (July-August 1952), a few more than 361 of the files were missing: 296 of the first 300, which seem to have been definitely gone for some time and so noted; 61 between the numbers 900 and 1000; and 9 from No.1101 to No.1111.

The files give much detailed information that is not included in the Written Evidences. Every file has been examined and is given with the written evidence to which it belongs. Those that were not recorded are given separately. All of the written evidences described above are presented in the following pages.

British Land Grant

West Florida:

George the Third, by the grace of God, of Great Britain, France and Ireland, King, Defender of the faith, and so forth: To all to whom these presents shall come Greeting: Know ye that we of our Special Grace, certain knowledge and mere motion have given and granted, and by these presents for us our heirs and successors Do give and Grant unto David Dickson, Esquire, a reduced Brigade Major his heirs and assigns all that Tract of land situate south westerly about fifteen below White's landing on the North side of Houma Chita Creek at the second high Bluff known by the name of Little's Bluff, butting and bounding north on land of Jacob Winfree's, south westerly on said Creek and on all other sides by vacant land, in our Province of West Florida and having such shape form and marks both natural and artificial as are represented in the plat thereof annexed as drawn by our surveyor General of Lands, which said Tract of land contains one Thousand acres and is bounded, as by the further certificate hereunto likewise annexed under the hand of our said Surveyor General of lands, in our said Province may more fully and at large appear: Together with all woods, underwoods timber and timber trees, lakes, ponds, fishings, waters, water courses, profits, commodities, hereditaments and appurtenances whatsoever thereunto belonging or in any wise appertaining Together also with priviledge of hunting hawking and fowling in and upon same and all mines and minerals; reserving to us our heirs and successors all mines of Gold and Silver. To Have and To Hold the said Tract of land and all and singular the premises hereby granted with the appurtenances unto the said David Dickson his heirs and assigns forever in free and common soccage; yielding and paying to us our heirs and successors or to the Receiver General of our quit Rents for the time being or to such other officer as shall be appointed to receive the same, a quit rent of one half penny sterling per acre at the feast of St. Michael every year, the first payment to commence on the said feast of St. Michael which shall first happen after the Expiration of Ten years from the date hereof or within fourteen days after the said feast annually. Provided always and this grant is upon condition nevertheless that the said David Dickson, his heirs or assigns shall and do within three years after the date hereof for every fifty acres of plantable land hereby granted clear and cultivate three acres at least, in that part thereof which he or they shall judge most convenient and advantageous; or else do clear and drain three acres of swampy or sunken ground; or do drain three acres of Marsh, if any such shall be contained therein, and shall further within the time aforesaid put and keep upon every fifty acres thereof accounted barren three neat cattle, and continue the same thereon until three acres for every fifty be fully cleared and improved and if it shall so happen that there be no part of the said land fit for present cultivation, without manuring and improving the same, if the said David Dickson his heirs or assigns shall within three years from the date hereof erect on some part of the said Tract of land one good dwelling house to contain at least twenty feet in length and sixteen feet in breadth; and put upon his said land the like number of three neat cattle as aforesaid on every fifty acres therein contained or otherwise if any part of the said Tract of land shall be stony or rocky ground not fit for culture or pasture shall and do within three years as aforesaid besides erecting the said house begin to employ thereon and continue to work for three years then next ensuing in digging any stone quarry or mine one good and able hand for every hundred acres thereof it shall be accounted a sufficient cultivation and improvement. Provided also that every three acres which shall be cleared and worked or cleared and drained as aforesaid shall further be accounted a sufficient seating, planting, cultivation and improvement to save forever from forfeiture fifty acres of land in any part of the Tract hereby granted. And the said David Dickson, his heirs and assigns shall be at liberty to withdraw his or their stock or to forbear working in any quarry or mine in proportion to such cultivation and improvements, aforesaid as shall be made upon the plantable lands swamps sunken grounds or marshes therein contained. Provided also that this grant shall be duly Registered in the Registers office of the Province within six months from the date thereof, and also that a docket thereof shall be entered in the Auditor's office within the same time if such establishment shall take place in this Province. Provided always that the said David Dickson his heirs and assigns at any time hereafter having seated, planted, cultivated and improved the said land or any part thereof according to the directions and conditions above mentioned, may make proof of such seating planting cultivation and improvement in the general court or in the court of the county, district or precinct, where the said land lieth; and have such proof certified to the Registry's office and there entered with the Record of this grant, a copy of which duly attested shall be admitted on trial to prove the seating and planting of said land. Provided always nevertheless that if the said David Dickson his heirs and assigns do not in all things fully comply with and fulfil the respective directions and conditions herein above set forth for the proper cultivation of the said land within the time herein above limited for the completion thereof: or if the said David Dickson, his heirs or assigns shall not pay to us, our heirs and successors, or to the Receiver Gen'l of our quit Rents or to the proper officer appointed to receive the same the said quit rent of one half penny Sterling per acre on the said feast of St. Michael or within fourteen days after annually for every acre contained in this grant, that then and in either of these cases respectively this grant shall be void, anything herein contained to the contrary notwithstanding: and the said lands tenements, hereditaments and premises hereby specified and every part or parcel thereof shall revert to us our heirs and successors fully and absolutely as if the same had never been granted. This grant being in pursuance of our Royal Proclamation of the seventh day of October in the Third year of our Reign.

Given under the Great Seal of our Province of West Florida: Witness our trusty and well-beloved Peter Chester, Esquire, our Captain General Governor and Commander in chief in and over our said Province of Pensacola this Twenty seventh day of September in the year of our lord one thousand seven hundred and seventy three and in the thirteenth year of our Reign.

/SEAL/ Peter Chester

1811

D.n Carlos Trudeau Agrimensor Real y Particular desta Provincia de
la Luisiana.

Certifico que ha sido medido a favor de Don Cato West un terreno de sete
cientos arpanes quadrados de superficie medidos con la Percha de la Ciudad de Paris de
dies y ocho pies de Rey de largo segun el uso desta Colonia, Cuyo Terreno situado en
el Distrito de Natchez parage de Coles Creek a como veinte y dos Millas del fuerte
de Natchez, lindando una la parte con Tierra de Mr. Fairbank y el Ramo del Bayou
una la parte del sur con las tierras de Mr. Osborne y parte de terrenos vacantes al
el Oeste con terreno Vacante y al Norte tambien con terreno vacante, los arboles senalados
para linderos, con las explicaciones del plano, estan en el idioma Ingles para la inteligencia
del interesado, el apeo haviendo sido practicado en virtud del decreto de Su Señ.a D.n Estevan
Miro Gov.or Gral &c, con fecha del dia cinco Avril del año pasado de Mil setecientos
Ochenta y cinco, y para que conste doy la presente Certificacion con el plano figurativo que
acompaña armados en conformidad del apeo del dia dose de Septiembre del año
ultimo pasado, y para que conste doy fe Marzo 3 de 1789. = Carlos Trudeau. Rub.ca

D.n Estevan Miro Coronel de los Reales Exercitos, Governador Intend.te de la
Provincia de la Luisiana, Florida Occidental, é Inspector de sus Tropas &c.

Vistas las antecedentes diligencias practicadas por el Agrimensor de esta
provincia D. Carlos Trudeau sobre la posesion que ha dado a D.n Cato West de la
cantidad de setecientos Arpanes de Tierra quadradas, situados en el distrito de
Natchez en el parage llamado vulgarmente Coles Creek lindando de un lado con
Tierras pertenecientes a Mr. Fairbank y a un ramo del dicho Bayou de Coles Creek,
del otro a las de Mr. Osborn y a los demas lados con terrenos vacantes de los dominios
de S. M. como lo demuestra el plano figurativo q.e antecede, y reconociendo estar segun el
estilo de Agrimensura, y a las concesiones de los antedichos circunvecinos sin que a
ellas se les cause perjuicio alguno, ni que lo hayan reclamado y deben consentir
segun justifica su asistencia a dichas operaciones aprobandolas como las aprobamos:
Usando de la facultad q.e el Rey nos tiene concedido, Otorgamos en su Real nombre
al suso Cato West los referidos setecientos Arpanes de Tierra quadradas para que como
suyos propios disponga de ellos y los usufructe arreglandose a las mencionadas diligencias
y observando las condiciones prevenidas en el reglamento del asunto. Damos
el presente firmado de nra mano sellado con el sello de nras Armas y
refrendado por el Infrascripto Secretario por Su Magestad de este Govierno, en
la Nueva Orleans a dies de Marzo de Mil setecientos Ochenta y nueve.

Estevan Miro &c.

L. S.

Por m.do de Su Señ.a

Andres Lopez Armesto

Reg.da

TRANSLATION OF THE PRECEDING LAND GRANT

Don Carlos Trudeau, Royal and Private Surveyor of the Province of Louisiana, certifies that he has surveyed in favor of Don Cato West a tract of seven hundred arpents in area, measured with the Perch of the City of Paris of eighteen Kings' feet in length according to the use of this Colony, which tract is situated in the Natchez District on the waters of Cole's Creek about 22 miles from the Natchez Fort, bounded on one side by land of Mr. Fairbank and a branch of said creek, on the South by land of Mr. Osborne, and on West and North by vacant lands. The designated trees and landmarks for contiguous boundaries, with explanations on the plat, are in the English language for the convenience of any interested party; the survey having been executed by virtue of a decree of His Excellency Don Estevan Miro, Governor General, under date of April 5 of last year (1785), and for which I give my certificate with the figurative plat which accompanies, which is in conformity with a survey made September 12 of the past year.

Given under my hand this March 3, 1789.

Carlos Trudeau, Surveyor

Don Estevan Miro, Colonel of the Royal Armies, Lieutenant Governor of the Province of Louisiana and West Florida, Inspector of the Troops, etc. In view of the foregoing judicial proceedings executed by the Surveyor of this Province, Don Carlos Trudeau, relative to possession which he has given to Don Cato West of a quantity of 700 square arpents of land, situated in the District of Natchez and on the banks of what is commonly called Cole's Creek, bounded on one side by lands belonging to Mr. Fairbank and on a branch of Cole's Creek, on the other side by lands of Mr. Osborne, and on other sides by vacant lands of His Majesty's Realm, all as is shown on the preceding plat and recognizing the survey to be in order with the agreement of the aforesaid surrounding neighbors without causing them any damage; nor have they claimed any, but on the contrary have approved the survey as we approve it; and using the Power vested in us by the King, we grant in His Royal Name to the use of Cato West the referred to 700 arpents for his own proper use, disposal and usufruct, the foregoing proceedings having been executed in due form, we give our hand and seal with our Arms and countersigned by the undersigned secretary for His Majesty's Government in New Orleans, this 10 of March 1789.

Estevan Miro

(Seal) By order of His Excellency,

Andre Lopez Armesto.

Translated by
Campbell J. Miles,
Natchez, Miss.

WRITTEN EVIDENCES

National Archives, Washington, D. C.
Department of Natural Resources. Land Division.

Mississippi Private Grants.
Written Evidences of Claims West of the Pearl River.

BOOK A

p.1. Albert Gallatin, Secretary of the United States, to Edward Turner, Esq., Register of the Land Office established for the disposal of Lands of the United States within the Mississippi Territory, West of the Pearl River. Treasury Dept. July 27, 1804. Sir: The President having appointed you Register of the Land Office established for the disposal of Lands of the United States within the Mississippi Territory, West of the Pearl River, I herewith transmit the forms necessary to be observed in your Office in relation to the proceedings of the Commissioners and which I request may be recorded at large in your books.

Title to land in Mississippi Territory may under the Act of last Session be confirmed either by residence and settlement or by purchase.

I. Residence on the 27th of October 1795 entitles the party to confirmation of

(1) Land held under British and Spanish grants fully executed before that day.

(2) Land inhabited and cultivated on that day by him or for his use and held under British and Spanish warrants or surveys, dated before that date, provided the original grantee was at that date either the head of a family or above 21 years of age.

(3) Land on which settlement was made under the Bourbon Act, namely, between 7 Feb. 1785 and 1 Feb. 1788, on which last day the Act was repealed, provided that the settlement has continued uninterrupted and that the quantity of land claimed by one individual does not exceed the quantity granted by the laws of the State to one person. The articles of agreement with Georgia secured also the claim which might be derived from an actual survey, but a reference to this Act will show that no right can be derived under it with a survey without a settlement.

II. Residence on the evacuation day in 1797 entitles the party to confirmation of land not exceeding 640 acres which on that day he inhabited and cultivated, provided the settler was the head of a family or above 21 years of age, on said day, and does not claim any other tract under the preceding provisions. The looseness of the Bourbon Act induced the insertion of this Donation which will extend to a great many more than were covered by said act and will, it is presumed, prevent the necessity of any application under it.

III. Residence on 3 March 1803 entitles the party to a right of preemption for the tract inhabited and cultivated on that day by him, but the persons of that description must be considered as purchasers.

IV. Spanish grants in favor of persons not residents on 27 Oct. 1795 and Spanish or British warrants or orders of survey in favor of such non-resident persons or for lands not settled on that day are considered as conferring no title; but in favor of persons non-resident on said day who claim under a British grant legally and fully executed, it has been provided (1) that whenever such grant shall interfere with land issued in preceding provisions, altho a certificate will be given by the Commissioners in favor of the resident settler, no patent shall issue unless a judicial decision shall be obtained in his favor and (2) in case where those grants cover land not claimed under the preceding provisions these lands shall not be sold until the end of a year after the report of the amount and the situation shall have been made to Congress by the Commissioners.

V. Lands not granted under the preceding provisions may be purchased either by the highest bidder at public sale or by the first applicant at a private sale.

p.4. Claim No.17. Registered Dec. 19, 1803. British Government to Christopher Gise for 706 acres, 20 miles NE of the Natchez old Fort, b. north by lands of Hon. John Stuart, west Elizabeth Augusta Carrique and George Petries, south by George Petries and William Featherston, east by James Day, in the province of West Florida. (signed) Elihu Hall Bay, Dept. Secy. 11 Nov. 1778. Plat and survey by Elias Durnford, Surv. General. // Lease and Release. 1st Sept. 1784. Christopher Gise and Margaret, his wife, to Johathan Gise, etc. Release. 2 Sept. 1784. Christopher Gise, of Davidson County, N. C.*, and Margaret, his wife, to Jonathan Gise, of same, for Ł10, N. C. money, all that tract of land in West Florida, 20 miles NE of Natchez old fort, 706 acres as granted above. [Signatures not given] // Andrew Erwin in behalf of Francis Prince, Register in County of Davidson, certifies that the above deed, etc. from Christopher Gise and Margaret, his wife, to Johathan Gise is registered in said office. (signed) Andrew Erwin, D. C. [n.d.] [No file.]

*[Now Davidson Co., Tennessee.]

p.8. Claim No.18. Reg. Dec. 12, 1803. Natchez District, Miss. Territory. I, James Cole, of the District, for $100 and six months schooling of five children, have sold all my right to a certain tract whereon I now live, unto Felix Hughes, of sd Dist., which land has been improved upward of ten years. 6 Sept. 1798. (signed) James Cole. Sept. 6, 1798. Then received $50 of the within consideration. (signed) James Cole. [No file.]

p.8. Claim No.19. Reg. Dec. 15, 1803. Br. Government to Wm. Fricker, a Master's mate in our Navy, 2000 acres 13 miles east of Natchez old fort, b. by John Stuart, and Henry Lafleur, in West Florida. (signed) Peter Chester. 8 Nov. 1777. Warrant, Oct. 9, 1777. Surveyed 2000 acres 26 Oct. 1777 by Elias Durnford. // 31 May 1777. William Fricker, Gunner of His Majesty's Sloop of War, the Atlanta, now riding in the harbor of Pensacola, being entitled to 2000 acres in West Florida as a reduced warrant officer, for Ł100 sterling (and the fees for the said 2000 acres), to me in hand paid by Alexander Macullagh and William Wilton, of Pensacola, Esquires, and Thos. Walters and Humphrey Grant, of same, gentlemen, sell the above grant. (signed) Wm. Fricker. Wit: Henry Beaumont, John Sommers. Power of attorney by said Fricker to Edmund Rush Wegg, of Pensacola, Esquire, John Falconer and James Amoss, of same, merchants, to transfer said land. May 3, 1779. // Indentures to each of the said four men and an agreement to division by all four. May 4, 1779. Wit: Jacob Duryee, Henry Beaumont. [No file.]

p.29. Claim No.20. (Also No.119.) Indenture. 3 Aug. 1773. John Southwell, of Pensacola, a reduced staff officer, and Jane, his wife, to Alexander Macullagh, of Pensacola, West Florida, Esq. (lease and release); for 100 Spanish dollars (value Ł23-6-8). 4 Aug. 1773. 1900 acres on east side of Buffalo Cr., b. on NE by Dr. John Sommers, and other sides vacant. (signed) John Southwell. Jane (x) Southwell. Wit: Mary Coltman, Elihu Hall Bay. // p.41. Claim No. 119. British Govt. to John Southwell, a reduced staff officer, 1900 acres on Buffalo Creek, NE from Loftus Cliffs, abt. 8 miles, [and as described above]. 2 Aug. 1773. (signed) Peter Chester. Examined and delivered to Wm. McCaleb, May 2, 1804. [No file.]

pp.34-41. Claim No.21. Reg. Dec. 15, 1803. Br. Govt. to Patrick Kelly, a reduced non-commissioned officer, 200 acres 30 miles NE from Natchez, 4 or 5 miles above land settled on by David Holt on the west side of a small branch that runs into Boyd's Creek*, b. by a small river, and Hannah, William and Jesse Lum, other sides vacant. 2 Sept. 1779. [Patrick Kelly sells right to above land, 18 Nov. 1775, to Alexander Macullagh.] [No file.] *[Became Cole's Creek.]

pp.45-51. Claim No.120. Reg. 12 Jany. 1804. Br. Govt. to William Marshall, 1000 acres on Fairchild's Creek, 12 miles NE from old fort of Natchez, beg. on east line of Capt. Thos. Boyd, bounded by Thomas, Theophilus and Luke Collins, Jr., Elizabeth Augusta Carrique and Mary Ogden. 24 March 1777. (signed) Peter Chester, Our Capt. General, Governor and Commander in Chief in and over our said Province at Pensacola. Warrant, Nov. 15, 1776. Surveyed 28 Dec. 1776. // 27 June 1799. State of S. C. William Marshall, of the City of Charleston, for $1950 to me paid by William McCaleb of Pendleton County, S. C. all that land in West Fla., 950 acres, from Milk Clifts on the Miss. River about 11 miles, b. on the west by a part of 20,000 acres surveyed unto Gov. Brown and on the other sides vacant, granted to Bernard Lintot, 4 Aug. 1777 by Peter Chester then Governor, and conveyed by Bernard Lintot to William Marshall, Esq., father of said Wm. Marshall, party hereunto, 9th and 10th Aug. 1777; also all that other plantation of 600 acres, being a part of grant of 1000 acres, on the south branch of Fairchild's Creek, abt. 12 mi. NE from Natchez [as described above] granted to Wm. Marshall, father of said Wm. Marshall. (signed) W. Marshall. Wit: John Girt, Stephen Lee, Jr.

Prov. by Stephen Lee, Jr., 27 June 1799. Wit: F. Bremar, Certificate of Dom. A. Hall, Justice of the Quoram, that Mrs. Charlotte Marshall renounces all claims of dower. Same date. (p.50.) 29 June 1700. State of S. C., Wm. McCaleb, of Pendleton County, Washington District, S. C., for $775, to Francis Bremar, of Charleston, all that moiety or half part of 950 acres, also all that moiety of 600 acres, as described in foregoing. (signed) Wm. McCaleb. Wit: Ann Elliot. Rec. Bk.Z, No.6, p.54. Daniel Smith, Register. Proved by Artemas B. Darby, 29 June 1799, bef. Daniel James Ravenel, J. P. Charleston District. Register of Mesne Conveyance Office. [No file.]

pp.52-70. Claim No.39. Articles of agreement to convey one-half of 3000 acres to be granted to Amoss Ogden as a reduced Captain.

Whereas Capt. Amoss Ogden, late of the Province of New Jersey, is entitled to 3000 acres under His Majesty's Proclamation at St. James on Oct. 7, 1765 and whereas he hath made application to His Excellency, Gov. Chester, for a grant of same in the Province of West Florida, etc. he agrees to divide the said 3000 acres in two equal halves which shall be ballotted for by the other party, Elihu Hall Bay and Alexander Macullagh, of Pensacola, Province of West Fla., Esquires, and himself, and their part to be deeded to them as soon as the patent has been obtained; for which they will pay Amoss Ogden 1 shilling per acre. Each bound for 500 pounds for the performance of the above agreement. All sign. Wit: James Ferguson, James Murray. 30 Sept. 1773. Prov. by Ferguson Oct. 7, 1773. (p.54) Lease, 9 May 1774; release, 10 May 1774, by Capt. Amoss Ogden. Wit: Wm. Gordon, E. R. Wegg. // pp.61-67. Several agreements on division between Elihu Hall Bay and Alexander Macullagh. The final dated June 27, 1774. Witnesses: H. Beaumont, James Murray. // p.68. Alexander Macullagh, late of the Kingdom of Ireland but now of the City of Charleston in the State of S. C., nephew and heir-at-law of Alexander Macullagh, late of West Florida, deceased, who died intestate; for $750, in hand paid by Elihu Hall Bay, of the city and state aforesaid, all that tract of 750 acres, being the eastern moiety of the 3000 acres within mentioned, the share of Alexander Macullagh. 25 June 1799. Signed. Wit: James Donaldson, A. Henry. Prov. by Jas. Donaldson before Wm. Johnson, Jr. // Certificate of James B. Richardson, Gov. and Commander-in-Chief of the State of S. C., that Wm. Johnson, Jr., Esquire, is one of the associate Judges of the Supreme Courts of Judicature in and for the State of S. C. [No file.]

pp.70-86. Claim No.40. Reg. Dec. 19, 1803. Br. Grant to John Smith for 600 acres, 24 miles NE from Fort Panmure at the Natchez, east 3 miles from the river Mississippi, July 22, 1769. Certificate of survey, pursuant to warrant, Dec. 20, 1768, by Wm. Wilton, Dep. Surv. Gen. June 2, 1769. Plat shows James Watkins on west, Jacob Phillipi on the east, other two sides vacant and an Indian path across the northwest corner. // (p.73.) 23 Feb. 1774. Peter Miller, carpenter, of Pensacola, Prov. of West Fla., to Alexander Macullagh and Elihu Hall Bay, of same, Esquires. Whereas the above John Smith by lease and release, 25th and 26th Sept. 1770 did confirm the said 600 acres to Peter Miller, as recorded in the Secy's and Register's office for sd Prov., he, the sd Miller, for 275 Spanish milled dollars, transfers said land to sd Macullagh and Bay. Wit: James Hamilton, Simon McCormack. // p.79. Partition deed of above 600 acres by Macullagh and Bay, 20 May 1774. Wit: H. Beaumont, James Murray. // p.84. 25 June 1799, Alexander Macullagh, late of the Kingdom of Ireland, etc. [as above] to Elihu Hall Bay, for $300, his share of above tract. Wit: James Donaldson, A. Henry. [No file.]

pp.86-106. Claim No.36. Reg. 19 Dec. 1803. Lease and release of 1050 acres of land by Thaddeus Lyman to Elihu Hall Bay, near Bayou Pierre. Thaddeus Lyman, Esq., of the District of Natchez, to Elihu Hall Bay, of the Town of Pensacola, Esq., 4 Feb. 1775. Whereas His Present Majesty King George III, by a patent under the great seal of West Florida, 2 Feb. 1775, did grant to sd Lyman 20,000 acres, about 15 miles northeasterly from the River Miss. up the Bayou Pierre, butting and bounding northwesterly and southeasterly on said bayou and on all other sides by vacant lands, as in letters patent, plat and certificate by the Surv. Gen.; for $1000 (of value of £233-6-8 sterling), in hand paid sd Lyman, sells every part and parcel of a tract, being part of the said 20,000 acres, beg. SW corner of same, to include 1050 acres. (signed) Thaddeus Lyman. Wit: John T. Lorimer, Samuel Aester. John Lorimer, one of the subscribing witnesses proved the within instrument before me, Alexander Macullagh, deputy surveyor. p.96. Claim No.37. Thaddeus Lyman, of the district of Natchez, to Alexander Macullagh, Esquire, lease for 1050 acres, 3 Feb. 1775. (signed) Thaddeus Lyman. Wit: John Aester and T. Lorimer. p.98. release of the same, 1050 acres near Mississippi and Bayou Pierre, 4 Feb. 1775, for 1000 Spanish milled dollars, etc. in hand paid. (signed) Same witnesses as above. On 14 Feb. 1775, before me, Alexander Macullagh, Esquire, appeared John Lum, one of the subscribing witnesses and certified to same. Alexander Macullagh, dep. surv. p.105. Alexander, Macullagh, late of the Kingdom of Ireland, etc. heir at law of Alexander Macullagh, late of West Fla., deceased, who died intestate, for $1050, to me paid, have granted to Elihu Hall Bay, of Charleston, S. C. 1050 acres mentioned and described in the within deed, being part of 20,000 acres granted to Thaddeus Lyman. (signed) Alexander Macullagh. Wit: James Donaldson, A. Henry. Acknowledged by the above Alexander Macullagh, the nephew and heir at law of the within Alexander Macullagh, before me, Samuel Brooks, J. P. (signed) 15 Dec. 1803. [No file.]

pp.106-117. Claim No.150. Br. grant to John Lum, 350 acres near Boyd's Creek, on south side thereof, b. on east by John Smith and Margaret Baird's land, on NE by James Cole, on south by Benjamin Stanley, on north by Benj. Roberts. Aug. 6, 1778. Warrant, 28 July, 1778. Surveyed Aug. 4, 1778. pp.109-111. Lease. Release, 19 Feb. 1779, John Lum of the district of Natchez to Wm. Ferguson, of same, above tract, for 350 Spanish milled dollars. (signed) John Lum. Margaret (X) Lum. Wit: Wm. Hiorn, Wm. Vousdan. Prov. by Wm. Hiorn, 28 Apr. 1779. // p.457. Wm. Ferguson to James Kirk, 2 acres of land on Cole's Creek, about 7 leagues from the Fort, b. by lands of Thomas Green and those of sd Ferguson which he formerly bought of John Lum, said 2 acres being on the high ground adj. sd Green. // p.114. 3 Dec. 1800. James Kirk and wife, of Adams Co., Miss. Ter., to Thos. Marston Green, of Pickering Co., Miss. Ter., for $10, the two acres in Pickering Co. as above described. Both sign. Wit: Susannah Williams, Abner Green. Proved before John Ellis, J. P., Dec. 3, 1800. // p.456. William Ferguson to Thos. Marston Green, 348 acres on Cole's Creek, b. by lands of John Smith, James Cole, Benj. Stanley, and Benj. Roberts, for $350. 5 Sept. 1790. Wit: Eben Rees, Joseph Vidal. [No file.]

pp.117-139. Claim No.216. Br. grant to James Barbut, 1000 acres, 9 miles east of Fort Natchez, on west side of Second Cr., b. by Michael Hooter, Wm. Alexander, Michael Cradle. Prov. of West Fla. 13 Sept. 1775. Warrant, June 13, 1775. Surv. by Wm. Wilton, dep. surv. 15 July 1775. // p.121. James Barbut, Esq., to Wm. Johnstone, Alexander Macullagh and Elihu Hall Bay, Esquires, 1000 acres [as above], and power of atty. to E. G. Wegg and Thos. Hutchins to convey same. Being entitled to 3000 acres as reduced Captain, said Barbut had received 2000 acres and had applied for remaining 1000 acres near Natchez and received a warrant for same, 14 April 1775. Wit: A. Strother, David Holley. // Leases and releases by attorneys and consent to division. Capt. Wm. Johnstone to have 500 acres and the other two 250 acres each. Oct. 22, 1775. [No file.]

pp.139,146-9. Claim No.139. (Reg. 20 Jany. 1804.) Br. grant to Athanasius Martin, 100 acres 20 miles NE from Natchez Fort, bounded by grants to James Watkins and Jacob Phillipi. Oct. 9, 1777. // p.146. Athanasius Martin to Ann Thompson, both of the Natchez district, West Fla. 10 Feb. 1778. Release: [Top of this missing, including consideration.] Wit: Robt. Collingwood, Thomas Murdock, David Odam. // p.148. Jany. 9, 1783. Wm. Smith and Ann Thompson, his wife, to Thos. Green, for 100 piasters, 100 acres, as above. (See Natchez.) // p.149. May 1790. Thos. Green to his four sons, Henry, Felmer Wells, Abram and Everard Green, slaves, hogs, horses and above 100 acres, adj. John Smith and Bingham. (See Natchez.) [No file.]

pp.150, 154, 458. Claim No.151. (Reg. 13 March 1804.) Br. grant to John Smith, 200 acres on Boyd's Creek, b. by James Cole, Parker Carradine. Boyd's Cr. 26 May 1777. // p.154. Sept. 16, 1777. John Smith and wife, Mary, to Isaac Johnson, all of Natchez Dist. Wit: Dibdal Holt, // p.458. 4 Dec. 1784. Isaac Johnson, a settler of this dist. to Mr. Thos. Green, the son, 200 acres, as above. [No file.]

pp.161-167. Claim No.294. (Reg. 21 Feb. 1804.) Br. grant to John Boles, 150 acres on St. Catherine's Creek, a branch, 1 mile north of tract granted Thomas Gamble, 7 miles east of Natchez Fort. 6 Aug. 1778; warrant 28 July 1778; Survey 4 Aug. 1778 by Elias Durnford, surv. Gen. // p.165. 11 May 1779. John Boles and Marthy, his wife, of Appalusas [Opelousas,] in Prov. of La., Taylor, to William Ferguson, of the Natchez district, the above tract, for 150 Sp. milled dollars. (signed) John Boles. Martha (X) Boles. Wit: Richard Ellis, Jr., Stephen Mayes. // File: Paulina Ferguson, claimant. Wit: James Truly, July 3rd, 1804. Certf. A-403 issued to legal representatives, 5 July 1805. Paulina Ferguson, relict of Wm. Ferguson, late a citizen of Miss. Ter., deceased, claims in behalf of herself and other heirs. She was an actual settler 27 Oct. 1795. Signed by her, 23 Jany. 1804.

pp.168-175. Claim No.295. (Feb. 1804.) Br. grant to James Robertson for 250 acres on St. Catherine's Creek, 12 miles east of Natchez, b. on south by David Waugh, other sides vacant. 19 Nov. 1777. Warrant 15 Oct. 1777; survey 21 Oct. 1777. Plat shows Henry Bradley's improvement on the west. // Release, 18 Apr. 1778, of above 250 acres by James Robertson, carpenter, to William Williams and William Carpenter, for 200 Sp. milled dollars. Signed. Wit: James Murray, Wm. A. Livingston. [No file.]

p.175-179. Claim No.245. (Reg. 17 Feb. 1704.) Br. grant to John Tally, for 300 acres on St. Catherine's Creek, the south fork, 11 miles east of Natchez, b. by Thos. Gamble and vacant lands. 9 Oct. 1777. Warrant 6 Oct. 1777; survey 7 Oct. 1777. Entered at Natchez, Adams Co., Miss., 6 Nov. 1800. John Henderson, recorder. [No file.]

p.180. Claim No.248. (Reg. 22 Feb. 1804.) Bill of sale for house and improvement. Wm. Bovard, of Wilkinson Co., Miss. Ter., 30 Jany. 1804, certifies that he sold James McNeely all his right and claim to a house and improvement on north bank of Buffalo Creek, which land he improved Feb. 1797 and raised two crops and then gave him peaceable possession, which he has cultivated ever since, having received full value. Signed. [No file.]

pp.180-1. Claim No.154. (Reg. 20 Jany. 1804.) Articles of agreement. William Bovard, of Adams County, Miss. Ter. to Wm. Everitt, of Christian Co., State of Kentucky, assigns all his right in a tract of 450 acres, agreeable to a survey made by Wm. Thomas; for $400 and a likely negro man; title to which land Wm. Bovard will defend on penalty of paying $200 for failure and as security for payment by Everitt, April 1802, he pledges 1 horse and 2 mares deposited with Bovard. (n.d.) Both sign. Wit: John Ellis, James McNeely. // p.181. Quit claim by James McNeely to William Everitt to above 450 acres. Nov. 29, 1803. Consideration: $40. Wit: Edward Turner, J. Turner. [No file.]

p.181. No claim number. Article of agreement between Elihu Hall Bay and Alexander Macullagh to keep open a road 100 feet on bank of Miss. river across their two tracts of land above the Three Islands forever. Elihu Hall Bay, of City of Charleston, S. C. and Alexander Macullagh, late of the same place but now in Mississippi Territory, are possessed severally of 1000 acres of land each on the east bank of the Miss. River, about 4 or 5 miles above the Three Islands and a little below the Diamond Island which were purchased from William Grant and whereas it will be difficult to cut a good landing on the lower part of the tract belonging to Macullagh or on the tract of Elihu Bay without going up the low bank near the point of Diamond Island, it is agreed to keep open forever free from all obstructions along the whole breadth of both tracts for the convenience of both parties, a road or space 100 feet back from the margin of the river. Signed by both. 10 Feb. 1804. Wit: David McCaleb, who proves same on same date.

p.183. Claim No.1. (Reg. 15 Nov. 1803.) Spanish grant to Cato West for 800 arpens on Cole's Creek, 20 miles from Fort Panmure, b. by Mr. Stampley, David Holt and Mr. Brezeno. Feb. 23, 1789. [No file.]

p.184. Claim No.278. (Reg. 20 Feb. 1804.) Br. grant to Daniel Perry, 6 May 1776, 250 acres near Cole's Cr., easterly 20 miles from Fort Natchez, southerly 2 miles from the Choctaw Path, bounded on all sides by vacant lands. Plat shows a square. // p.188. Will of Daniel Perry. Feb. 21, 1790. Beloved wife, Magdalen, all estate during her natural life. After her death, eldest son, Barnabas Perry 326 acres on Second Cr., formerly gr. to Edward Mayes, also negroes, etc.; son Daniel 400 acres granted me on east side of tract on which I live, also negro; dau. Ann Perry, the plantation I reside on on Boyd's Creek, 250 acres and negro Dinah, 2 cows and calves; to dau. Lydia Perry negroes and cows; to eldest daughter, Rebecca Perry, negro woman, if said daughter offers for sale the negro I leave her it immediately becomes the property of my son Daniel Perry. The tract left Ann shall not be sold but to remain the property of her and her heirs forever. Wife sole executrix. If wife dies, I appoint my friend, Isaac Johnson, and son Barnabas to take care of property and education of daughter Lydia. Signed with his mark, "D. P." Wit: Jac Funk, Jun., Dennis Collins, John Martin, Stuart Higginson, Sebastian Derr, Andres Scanlan, Isaac Johnson. Filed 6 March 1790. True Copy. John Girault. [No file.]

p.190. Claim No.279. (Reg. 20 Feb. 1804.) Br. grant to Daniel Perry, 21 Sept. 1772, 326 acres in West Florida, 10 miles easterly from Fort Natchez, b. on south by Second Creek, all sides vacant. [No file.]

p.193. Claim No.2. (Reg. 15 Nov. 1803.) Sp. grant to Cato West, 800 arpens on Cole's Creek, b. on one side by land of Mr. Fairbank and a branch of said creek, on the other side by land of Mr. Osborn, others vacant. March 3, 1789. [Note: This included 100 acres adj. Samuel Osborn sold to Cato West by David Smith, 10 Sept. 1784.] [No file.]

p.195. Claim No.4. (Reg. 3 Dec. 1803.) Sp. grant to Maurice Conway for 800 arpens, 14 Dec. 1789. He petitions that he has sufficient number of slaves to cultivate a plantation and asks for a grant of 20 arpens in breadth on Buffalo Creek, b. by land of Mr. Peter Francisco Roze [Rose], and Wm. Conway, 1st Dec. 1788. [No file.]

p.197. Claim No.6. (Reg. 6 Dec. 1803.) Sp. grant to Cadder Rabby for 300 arpens, 10 miles NE from Fort, b. by lands of John Thear, Charles Boardman, Anthony Hoggat and Jayme West. 10 Sept. 1790. // p.198. 12 Sept. 1801. Calder Raby and Elizabeth, his wife, for $1200, sell above tract to Adam Tooley. Wit: Francis Nailor, John Smith. [No file.]

p.200. Claim No.7. (Reg. 6 Dec. 1803.) Sp. grant to James West, for 470 acres, on waters of St. Catherine's Creek, 10 miles east of the Fort, b. on north by Geo. Mars and Charles Boardman, south by Thomas Morgan, east James Oglesby, west by George Killian, 27 Aug. 1797. // p.201. James West and wife, Honor, of Adams Co., Miss. Ter. to Adam Tooley, of same, 300 acres, part of above tract. Both sign with a mark. Wit: ____ Hoggatt, Barton Hannon. 1 Sept. 1801. Ack. by the Wests. [No file.]

p.203. Claim No.11. (Reg. 19 Dec. 1803.) Sp. grant to Mr. David Smith, on waters of St. Catherine's Creek, abt 6 miles northeast from Natchez; b. on one side by Mr. Bonner and Mary Foster, other sides vacant. Plat by Wm. Vousdan. March 3, 1788. // p.205. David Smith, a house-keeper and inhabitant of the district, sells to Mrs. Mary Foster, of the same neighborhood, 500 arpens for $500 in hand paid, b. by lands of Richard Ellis on one side and on other sides by those of John Oxberry, the aforesaid creek and said Mary Foster. Jany. 25, 1785. // p.206. Mary Foster sells to her son, William Foster, on 19 Dec. 1794, land bought from David Smith to whom it was granted in 1788. [No file.]

p.208. Claim No.5. (Reg. 6 Dec. 1803.) Sp. grant to Mary Dewitt, 8 Nov. 1796, 400 arpens in Natchez district, 4 miles east of Fort Panmure, b. by lands of John Stille. [No file.]

p.210. Claim No.12. (Reg. 23 Dec. 1803.) Sp. grant to William Erwin, 14 Feb. 1786, 500 arpens on Cole's Creek, 6 miles NE from Fort Panmure, b. by Isaac Johnson, Jacob Winfree, old disputed grants and lands of His Majesty. [No file.]

p.212. Claim No.16. (Reg. 12 Dec. 1803.) 9 Jany. 1800, John Griffin and Penelope, his wife, of Elliottsville, in the district of Natchez, for $110 in hand paid, sell to George Selser, all claim whatsoever in 10 acres on a branch called the Still House Branch, b. on every side by lands of John and Gabriel Griffing. Both sign. Wit: Mordecai Throckmorton, John Arden. Pickering Co., Miss. Ter. Ack. by John Griffin before Mordecai Throckmorton, J. P. 16 Sept. 1800. [No file.]

p.214. Claim No.23. (Reg. 20 Feb. 1804.) Sp. grant to Joseph Perkins, 23 Feb. 1788, for 177 arpens on St. Catherine's Creek, 5 miles NE of Fort Panmure, b. on north by lands of Anthony Windon, west John Stillee, southeast by sd creek. Plat. [No file.]

p.215. Claim No.24. (Reg. 20 Feb. 1804.) Sp. grant to Robert Carter, 6 Feb. 1789, for 300 arpens on waters of St. Catherine's Creek, 6 miles from Fort Panmure, b. on west by John Stillee and John Hartley, east Charles Adams, other sides vacant. // p.217. 12 March 1799. Robert Carter, of Miss. Ter., to Joseph Perkins, of same, for $305, paid, 140 acres, being the remainder of 300 acres, granted Robt. Carter by Sp. government, the other 160 acres of sd grant were formerly sold to sd Perkins. Carter signed with a mark. Wit: John Girault, Patrick Foley, Mordecai Throckmorton. Proved by Patrick Foley, Adams County Court, 8 Oct. 1802. [No file.]

p.218. Claim No.25. (Reg. 20 Feb. 1804.) Sp. govt. to Thomas Green. [Not filled in.] Petition of Thomas Green, who, having 100 arpens adj. Madame Truly, Mr. Stampley and vacant lands, asks for a grant of 100 arpens more. Warrant for 100 acres. [No file.]

p.219. Claim No.27. (Reg. 20 Feb. 1804.) Sp. government to John Terry. Petition of John Terry, an inhabitant of this district, who has been established here many years on a tract of land; to gain subsistence of my family which contains 14 persons, asks that 700 arpents on Cole's Creek be granted to him, adj. George Stampley and David Odam. 10 Jany. 1791. // Warrant for same, N. O. 29 Dec. 1791. //

Will of John Terry of the district of Villa Gayoso in the Government of Natchez. (See Natchez Records, Bk.C-168.) // p.221. Inv. of est. of John Terry (above), 9 Dec. 1794. Land: 400 acres, 300 acres. [No file.]

p.222. Claim No.41. (Reg. 19 Dec. 1803.) Sp. grant to Daniel Whitaker 400 acres on St. Catherine's Creek, 9 miles east of Fort Panmure, b. by Mr. Richard Carpenter, Mr. Brocus and Joseph Calvet. [No file.]

p.224. Claim No.42. (Reg. 19 Dec. 1803.) Sp. grant to Richard King, 500 acres in the Natchez District, on the north bank of the Big Black River, 45 miles NE from Fort Panmure, b. by Archibald Erwin and vacant lands. Sept. 30, 1793. [No file.]

p.225. Claim No. 43. (Reg. 19 Dec. 1803.) Sp. grant to John Savage, 1000 acres on a branch of Bayou Pierre, called James' Run, 45 miles north of Fort Panmure, b. on east by lands of Patrick Cogan, other sides vacant. 14 Aug. 1794. // p.227. Sale by Richard King and Esther King, his wife, 8 July 1798, to the Rev. Francis Lennan, of the District of Feliciana, Prov. of La., by James White, of Natchez, authorized and acting as attorney in fact, a tract of 800 acres lying in the District of Feliciana, adjoining lands formerly granted to Ruffin Gray, bet. Thompson's Creek and Alexander's Creek, being the same granted by the Sp. Govt. to said Esther King, in exchange for 1000 acres (Paris measure) in the Natchez District on the south fork of James Creek (a branch of Bayou Pierre), adjoining lands granted by Spanish to Melling Woolley, being the same 1000 acres gr. by Spain to John Savage, transferred to Francis Lennan; to the said Esther King and her heirs forever. Signed: James White, for Francis Lennan, Esther King, Richard King. Wit: Christopher Miller, Ebenezer Dayton. Signed and delivered before us: Henry Hogland, Nicholas Jones, Leonard D. Space. Rec. Pickering Co., Feb. 10, 1801. [No file.]

p.229. Claim No. 44. (Reg. 19 Dec. 1803.) Spanish grant to Richard King, 20 June 1795, 1180 arpens in the Natchez Dist. on road to Nogales, 17 miles from Bayou Big Black and 3 miles north of Miss. River, b. by lands of Estevan Minor and vacant lands. [No file.]

p.230. Claim No.48. (Reg. 12 Dec. 1803.) John Watson, of Pickering Co., to Reuben White, a certain improvement 3 miles from Bayou Pierre, 2 miles from Storey's Mill on same creek, for $120, to give possession in Dec. next. 2nd Nov. 1801. Signed. Wit: Eden Brashears, James Gibson, John Foster. [No file.]

p.231. Claim No. 49. (Reg. 19 Dec. 1803.) Robert Cloyd's petition to Spanish Government for land. He is a resident in this district working for the subsistence of his family which consists of 7 persons, white, of which five are men capable of work; asks for 1000 arpens on south branch of Bayou Pierre, b. by lands of Wm. Miller, and Robt. Ashley. 14 March 1794. // I consider this party worthy the Grace he petitions. Manuel Gayoso de Lemos. [No file.]

p.232, p.389. Bk.B. Claim No. 50. (Reg. 19 Dec. 1803.) Spanish Govt. to James McIntyre. Petition of James McIntyre, inhabitant of the Dist. of Natchez, asks for 1000 acres on Fairchild's Cr., b. by Mr. Couperth and vacant lands. // Warrant for the land requested. N. O. 28 July 1787. // Bk.B, p.389. Natchez, 20 Jany. 1795. James McIntyre sells above tract to Samuel Marshall. Bk.B. p.390. At the request of Mr. Samuel Marshall, I have carefully surveyed and traced the original lines, and made some new corner trees where the old ones were down, of a tract of 500 acres formerly granted to James McIntyre by the Sp. Govt., 150 acres of which was sold to Willis Bonner, 350 acres to said Samuel Marshall, situate on waters of Fairchild's Creek, 10 miles east of Town of Natchez. (signed) Wm. Atchinson, surveyor. [The transfer to Willis Bonner is Claim No.52.]

p.233. Claim No.51. (Reg. 19 Dec. 1803.) Sp. grant to Moses Bonner, Dec. 26, 1795. 800 acres 14 miles north of Fort Panmure, b. by James Jones, John Dyson and vacant lands. // p.235. Will of Moses Bonner, 28 Dec. 1800, of Natchez District, sick and weak; wife Elizabeth one-third of my property; son William a horse and bridle when he comes of age; the remaining property to be divided among all my children equally, William receiving his part without counting the horse. Property to be in my wife's hands as long as she remains my widow and if she marrie a person approved of by my exors, property shall still remain in her hands until orphans shall come of age and then be divided, allowing my beloved wife the privilege of any certain creature that her fancy may lead her to. James Bonner, Samuel Marshall and Elizabeth, my wife, to be my lawful executors and James Bonner guardian of my children with a strict charge from a dying man who hopes to meet his fellow creatures in another state that my children shall have the benefit of learning sufficient to answer their ends. (signed) Moses Bonner. Wit: Robt. Turner, Jesse Withers, Manuel Madden. [No file.]

p.236. Claim No.52. (Reg. 22 Dec. 1803.) 8 Nov. 1794. James McIntyre to Willis Bonner 150 acres of land. [No file.]

p.237. Claim No.53. (Reg. 23 Dec. 1803.) Sp. grant to Isaac Fiffe, 300 arpens, on a branch of Bayou Pierre, called Bayou Chubby, 50 miles from Fort of Natchez; all sides vacant. 30 Nov. 1790. Plat. [No file.]

p.239. Claim No.56. (Reg. 24 Dec. 1803.) Sp. grant to Samuel Young, 480 acres in the Natchez District, 35 miles from Natchez, b. west by Bayou Sara, south Reuben Proctor, north Reuben Denham, and east Patrick Foley. 11 April, 1790. [No file.]

p.240. Claim No. 57. (Reg. 24 Dec. 1803.) Pet. to Sp. Govt. for land by Sylvester Stauts, 3 May 1794. Sylvester Stotts, resident in the district, with 8 white persons in his family, asks for land on west side of Wells Creek, a br. of Homochitto River, and bounded by "Dry Bayou" and "Caney Branch". // Warrant for 500 acres granted by Gayoso, 5 May 1794. // 29 Nov. 1799, I assign all my right and title to the within to Lewis Evans, Esq. for 2 reals per acres. (signed) James White. Wit: Chas. F. Todd. Entered at Natchez, 7 Dec. 1799. John Henderson, Recorder. // Bargain and Sale. Sylvester Stauts sells to James White the above tract, May 5, 1794, for $52. Wit: John Murdock, Christopher Miller. Certified by William Dunbar, surveyor of district. (signed) Sylvester Stauts. Ack. by above subscriber who made oath that he cleared 8 atres and made a quantity of rails to fence it in January or February 1795 and at the time he was above 21 years of age and head of a family. 16 Dec. 1803. Signed before Wm. Ogden, J. P. of Wilkinson County, Miss. Ter. // p.242. Bargain and sale. James White to Lewis Evans, both of Natchez, Adams Co., Miss. Ter., for $125 in hand paid, right to above $500 acres. 29 Nov. 1799. Wit: D. Michie, Chas. McKiernan. Prov. by McKiernan, 30 Nov. 1799, before Wm. Kenner, J. P. of Adams County. [No file.]

p.243. Claim No.62. (Reg. 29 Dec. 1803.) Sp. grant to Christopher Guise, 400 acres 26 miles east of the Fort, on a branch of the Homochitto River, b. by Wm. Kennison and vacant lands. 5 March 1795. [No file.]

p.244. Claim No.66. (Reg. Jany. 9, 1804.) Sp. grant to David Holt, for 250 arpens in the Natchez District on Cole's Creek, 20 NE from Fort Panmure, b. by lands of Cato West and vacant lands. March 5, 1789. // p.246. Bargain and sale. David Holt, of Adams Co., to Patsy Westley Moss, dau. of William Moss, of Pickering Co., Miss. Ter., the above tract on the west side of Cole's Cr., b. by Colo. Hutchins's land, now Parker Carradine's, known as Kelly's land, for $700. 21 Jany. 1800. Signed. Wit: Parker Carradine, James Truly, Will. Ferguson. Proved by James Truly before Wm. Thomas, J. P. of Pickering County. // p.247. Release by David Holt and wife, Rebecca, to Patsy Westley Moss, of Jefferson Co., 24 Jany. 1804. Both signed. Wit: Peter Stampley, Elizabeth (X) Holt. Ack. by both before Thos. Rodney, Judge. 28 Jany. 1804. [No file.]

p.250. Claim No.69. (Reg. 24 Feb. 1804.) Sp. grant to John Griffing, 400 arpens in the Natchez District., on Cole's Creek and Fairchild's Cr., 15 miles NE of Fort Panmure, b. by lands of Gabriel Griffing, Marston Green, Jeremiah Coleman and Calvit, Mr. Higdon and vacant lands. Feb. 6, 1789. [No file.]

Bk.B, p.390. Claim No.70. (Reg. 12 May 1804.) Deed of exchange, John Griffing gives 145 arpens of land to brother, Gabriel, in exchange for 345 which he gives me, the sd lands being on Fairchild's creek, wherewith we each acknowledge ourselves satisfied. Natchez, 22 Aug. 1792. [No file.]

Bk.A, p.252. Claim No.71. Bargain and Sale. Gabriel Griffing to George Selser, all my plantation on which I now live together with half of the Horse Mill on the plantation of John Griffing, which half of the mill is my property. 4 July, 1794. Wit: John Arden. [No file.]

p.253. Claim No.76. (Reg. 2 Jany. 1804.) Sp. grant to James Foster, 240 arpens in this district, on waters of St. Catherine's Creek about 5 miles northeast from Fort Panmure, b. on one side by Zachariah Smith and on the other by Mary Foster. March 3, 1788. [No file.]

p.255. Claim No.77. (Reg. 2nd Jany. 1804.) Sp. grant to Zachariah Smith, 240 acres in the District of Natchez, 6 miles NE of Fort Panmure, b. by Richard Harrison and James Foster. 1 July 1790.

// Feb. 18, 1788. Zachariah Smith to James Foster, the above 240 acres on St. Catherine's Creek, b. by Joseph Miller and vacant lands, for $500, $250 of which has been paid. [No file.]

p.257. Claim No.78. (Reg. 2 Jany. 1804.) Bargain and sale. Alexander and John Henderson, brothers and partners and settlers on the coast of the Accadians [Arcadians], sell to James Foster, inhabitant of the Natchez District, tract on St. Catherine's Creek between lands granted Alexander Henderson and those we purchased of Richard Harrison, 100 arpens, for $100, paid in hand. Nov. 25, 1795. Wit: Edw. McCabe, John Girault. [No file.]

p.259. Claim No.79. (Reg. 2 Jany. 1804.) Bargain and sale. 25 Nov. 1786. Richard Harrison to Joseph Miller, 100 square arpens, on St. Catherine's Cr., for $50, paid. (signed) Rd. Harrison, Joseph (J. M.) Miller. // p.260. 20 July 1789. Joseph Miller to Nathaniel Ivy, above 100 sq. arpens, for $200. // p.261. Nathaniel Ivy to James Foster, above land b. on one side by sd Foster, on other by Wm. Gilbert. [No file.]

p.262. Claim No.80. (Reg. 2 Jany. 1804.) Sp. grant to William Gillespie, 263 arpens in the Natchez District on waters of Cole's Cr., 20 miles NE of Fort Panmure, b. by John Holt, Don Estevan De Alva and a branch of said creek. 8 June 1792. // p.264. Deed of exchange. William Gillespie exchanges land in above grant for a tract in the St. Catherine district belonging to John Girault and his wife, Mary Spain. [No file.]

p.265. Claim No.81. (Reg. 2 Jany. 1804.) Sp. grant to Jonathan Guice, for 400 arpens in Dist. of Natchez, 25 miles east of Fort Panmure, all sides vacant. 29 March 1796. [No file.]

p.267. Claim No.82. (Reg. 2 Jany. 1804.) Sp. grant to Abraham Guice, in the Natchez Dist., on a branch of the Homochitto called Morgan's Fork, 20 miles east of the Fort, b. by vacant lands. 24 March 1796. [No file.]

p.268. Claim No.83. (Reg. 2 Jany. 1804.) Sp. grant to Michael Guice, 500 arpens in the Natchez Dist. on Cole's Cr., 18 miles east of Fort Panmure, all sides vacant. 23 Feb. 1788. [No file.]

p.270. Claim No.84. (Reg. 2 Jany. 1804.) Sp. grant to Daniel Grafton, 300 arps. in the Natchez District, east of the Miss. River, 3 miles northeast of Fort Panmure, b. by lands of grantee, John Farquhar, Francis Farrell, Polser Shilling's claim, and vacant land. Surveyed by Wm. Vousdan 27 Nov. 1787. Passed 28 Feb. 1788. [No file.]

p.271. Claim No.85. (Reg. 2 Jany. 1804.) Sp. grant to Daniel Grafton, 160 square arpens in the Natchez Dist., b. by John Farquhar, John Bisland, Stephen Jordan and lands of His Majesty. 1 March 1787. [No file.]

p.273. Claim No.86. (Reg. 2 Jany. 1804.) Sp. grant to Joseph Bonner, 600 arps. in the Dist. of Natchez, 8 miles NE of Fort Panmure, b. by Moses Bonner and James Bonner, both brothers of the grantee, and vacant lands. 25 May 1791. // p.274. Bargain and sale. Natchez, 2 Nov. 1794. Joseph Bonner sells to the heirs of Henry Manadue, for $300 which I received from the aforesaid heirs represented by Mr. Gabriel Benoist, alcalde for the District of Pine Ridge, John Boles and Henry Manadue, Jr., exrs. of the est. of the late Henry Manadue, the above tract of 600 arps. All signed. [No file.]

p.276. Claim No.90. (Reg. 30 Jany. 1804.) Sp. grant to Alexander Montgomery, 500 arps. in the Natchez Dist., on west bank of Bayou Feliciana, 44 miles SE of Fort Panmure, b. by Ezekiel Forman and Daniel Clark. 30 Aug. 1793. // Bargain and sale. Adams Co., Miss. Ter. 5 Feb. 1801. Alexander Montgomery and Catherine, his wife, to Daniel Ogden, for $1000 in hand paid, 500 acres (above) on Thompson's Creek. Wit: Reuben Newman, Prosper King, James N. Chaney. Both Montgomerys sign. Prov. by James Cheney as to Catherine Montgomery, and ack. by Alexander Montgomery. Feb. 14, 1801. [No file.]

p.279. Claim No. 91. (Reg. 30 Jany. 1804.) Sp. grant to Daniel Ogden, 500 arpens in Dist. of Natchez, on Bayou Sara, 54 miles from Fort Panmure, b. by lands of grantee and those of Francisco Poussett. 25 May 1792. [No file.]

p.281. Claim No.92. (Reg. 20 Jany. 1804.) Sp. grant to Daniel Ogden, 500 arpents in Dist. of Natchez, 14 leagues south of Fort Panmure, and 3 leagues east of Miss. River, b. by Francisco Poussett and vacant lands. Apr. 14, 179_. [No file.]

p.282. Claim No.93. (Reg. 30 Jany. 1804.) Sp. grant to William Vousdan, 550 arpens in Dist. of Natchez, on waters of the Homochitto, 3 miles east of Loftus Cliffs, 2 miles from Buffalo Creek and 14 leagues by the Miss. River from Natchez Fort, b. by Alice Blommart, Henry Roach, and Zachariah Smith. 8 Spr. 1788. // p.284. Bargain and sale. Wm. Vousdan and wife, Elizabeth, sell to William Ogden, for $400 in hand paid, the above tract. 28 Jany. 1799. Both sign. Wit: David Jones, Elizabeth Ogden, William (X) Fenner. Prov. by Fenner 23 Dec. 1799 in Adams Co. [No file.]

p.285. Claim No.98. (Reg. 9 Jany. 1804.) Bargain and sale. 21 June 1794. Alexander Henderson to William Foster, 100 arpens on St. Catherine's Creek, for $100. Both sign. (See Natchez Records, Bk.C-136.) // p.286. 6 Nov. 1797. William Foster sells above tract to his brother, Thomas Foster. [No file.]

p.288. Claim No.99. (Reg. 9 Jany. 1804.) Sp. grant to Mrs. Mary Foster, 644 arpens in Dist. of Natchez, on St. Catherine's Cr. b. by James Foster, Moses Bonner and David Smith. Mch. 6, 1788. // Bargain and sale. 7 Nov. 1797. Mary Foster to Thos. Foster, her son, 444 acres on St. Catherines Cr. as granted above. (Natchez Rec. Bk.C-518.) // Natchez, 6 Nov. 1797. Mary Foster to grson, Levi Foster, son of Thos. Foster. 200 acres of above tract. [No file.]

p.292. Claim No.100. (Reg. 9 Jany. 1804.) Sp. grant to Samuel Flowers 95 arpens in Dist of Natchez, 4 miles east of Fort Panmure, b. by Reuben Gibson, Alexander Henderson and the left bank of St. Catherine's Creek. 21 April 1789. [No file.]

p.293. Claim No.101. (Reg. 9 Jany. 1804.) Sp. grant to Moses Bonner, Sr., 310 arpens in Dist. of Natchez, 4 miles N.E. of Fort Panmure, b. on east by Madame Foster, west by Madame Spell, south by right bank of St. Catherine's Cr. 21 April 1789. // Sp. grant to Susannah Spell, 200 arpens in the Dist. of Natchez, 4 miles N.E. of Fort Panmure, b. on east by Dr. Samuel Flower, west by Richard Harrison and Mr. Cochran. 28 Jany. 1789. // p.196. 12 Dec. 1795. Moses Bonner to Samuel Flower, for $400, 310 arpens (as above) (Natchez Rec. Bk.C-366). // p.297. 12 Dec. 1795. Samuel Flower to Thos. Foster settlers, 310 arpens (above) also other land, including part of 200 arpens bou. of Susannah Spell. // p.298. Bargain and sale. Susannah Spell and John Cole sell to Samuel Flower 200 arpens, (above grant), for $200. [No file.]

p.300. Claim No.73. (Reg. 25 Feb. 1804.) James Hyland petition for a grant. A resident of this district before the Spanish accession, and having a large family of 13 whites and six blacks and no concession from this government, asks for land to correspond with size of family, 7 miles NW of Big Black River, adj. lands of Donna Catalina Lintot. Natchez, Feb. 4, 1797. // Warrant for 800 acres of land, by Gayoso. 6 Feb. 1797. [No file.]

p.300. Claim No.74. (Reg. 25 Feb. 1804.) Petition of Jacob Hyland, for grant, 7 miles NW of Big Black River, adj. that petitioned for by James Hyland. 4 Feb. 1797. // Warrant for 700 acres by Gayoso. Feb. 6, 1797. [No file.]

p.305. Claim No. 104. (Reg. 9 Jany. 1804.) Sp. grant to Nathaniel Kennison, 500 acres in Natchez Dist., on a br. of Cole's Cr., 20 miles east of Fort Panmure, b. by Luis Faure and vacant lands. 17 June 1795. [No file.]

p.307. Claim No.105. (Reg. 10 Jany. 1804.) Sp. grant to Peter Miro, 1500 acres in the Dist. of Natchez, on Buffalo Creek, b. by James Smith and William Conway, and by Daniel Clark. 25 Oct. 1790. [No file.]

p.308. Claim No.106. (Reg. 10 Jany. 1804.) Sp. grant to Patrick Foley, 1500 arpents, in the district of Natchez, 33 miles south of Fort Panmure, bounding on north by Don Carlos Percy, south William Vousdan, west Reuben Dunham, Samuel Young and Reuben Proctor, east vacant. 25 June 1791. [No file.]

p.310. Claim No.110. (Reg. 11 Jany. 1804.) Sp. grant to Joseph Bernard, 240 arpens in the Dist. of Natchez, on a br. of Buffalo Cr., 35 miles SE from Fort Panmure, b. by Adam Lenhart, and vacant lands. 7 Dec. 1797. [No file.]

p.311. Claim No.111. (Reg. 11 Jany. 1804.) Sp. grant to Joseph Bernard, 800 arpens in the Natchez Dist., on east bank of Miss. River, 4 miles north of Fort Panmure, b. by Thos. Wilkins, Polser Shilling, and grantee. 10 Apr. 1795. [No file.]

p.313. Claim 112. (Reg. 11 Jany. 1804.) Sp. grant to Stephen Minor, 500 arpens in the Dist. of Natchez, b. by lands of John Farquhar and of His Majesty. 6 May 1786. // p.315. Bargain and sale. 2 Sept. 1786. Stephen Minor to Joseph Bernard, above grant, 500 acres, Both sign. [No file.]

p.317. Claim No.113. (Reg. 11 Jany. 1804.) Sp. grant to Joseph Bernard, 500 arpens in Dist. of Natchez, on waters of Diable, 4 miles north of Fort Panmure, b. by lands of Don Estevan Minor, others vacant. 15 March 1789. [No file.]

p.318. Claim No.117. (Reg. 12 Jany. 1804.) Bargain and sale. 7 Aug. 1782. Isaac Johnson to Nathaniel Tomlinson, 500 arpens on Petit Gulph, land purchased at public auction of confiscated property of the fugitive rebel, John Turner; for $187. Both sign. (Natchez records, Bk.A-109.) // p.319. 25 July 1801. Nathaniel Tomlinson to Joseph Calvit, both of Adams County, Miss. Ter., for $1000 in hand, the above 500 acres. Wit: D. Michie, James Williams. [No file.]

p.321. Claim No.118. (Reg. 12 Jan. 1804.) Sp. grant to Joseph Calvit, 386 arpens in Natchez District on waters of St. Catherine's Cr., 7 miles NE from Fort Panmure, b. by Benj. Belk, Winson Pipes, Daniel Whitaker, Gideon Gibson and Joseph Foster. 12 June 1788. [No file.]

p.322. Claim No.121. (Reg. 2 Jany. 1804.) Petition of Benjamin Dorsey for Spanish grant, 10 May 1795. Wishing to establish himself with his wife and children in this government, asks for grant on Homochitto River, adj. Silvester Stauts, on Dry Bayou, Caney Branch. // Warrant for 500 arpens by Gayoso. 11 May 1795. [No file.]

p.324. Claim No.123. (Reg. 16 Jany. 1804.) Sp. grant to John Lusk, 294 arpens in Dist. of Natchez, b. on lands of John Rault [Row], Benj. Belk, George Rapalje, Saint Germain, interpreter of the Indians. Apr. 20, 1784. // p.325. Bargain and sale. Natchez, 1 March 1788. John Lusk to Richard Carpenter, 294 arpens, for $200. Signed by J. Lusk and heirs and representatives of Richard Carpenter. (Natchez Rec. B-76) p.326. Natchez, 16 August 1788. Petition of Mary Fairchild Carpenter, the widow, Samuel Flower as husband of one of the daughters, Mr. Alexander Moore, representing Mr. Charles Boardman, the husband of another daughter and Messrs. David Williams and Bernard Lintot, guardians and administrators of the property of the minors, requesting public sale by auction which was done. // The plantation of 300 arpens which Richard Carpenter, the deceased, bought of John Lusk, b. by lands of Benj. Belk, Mathew White, Hailer [Isler] and Hartley, was sold to Stephen Minor, the highest bidder on 3rd and last sale, he giving Polser Shilling as security, for $300. 26 Oct. 1788. // p.328. Bargain and sale. 22 Dec. 1788, Stephen Minor sells above tract for $300 to Lt. Col. Charles de Grand-Pre. (Natchez Rec. B-201.) // p.329. Spanish grant to Benj. Belk for 191 arpens in the Dist. of Natchez, b. by lands of George Rapalje and John Lusk. 11 May 1786. // (n.d.) Bargain and sale. Benj. Belk, settler, sells to Charles de Grand-Pre 191 arpens, (above), b. by Adam Bingaman, by purchaser which was John Lusk's, Nathaniel Tomlinson's which was David Mitchell's and Silas Crane and Mathew White, for $400 to be paid Jany. 1791. // p.332. June 1, 1784, William Ferguson to Mathew White 163 arpens on St. Catherine's Cr., one-half league from Fort, which I sell with all the ways, for $300. // p.333. Matthew White sells to Charles de Grand-Pre 52 arpens about a mile from Natchez, adj. on south and west land of purchaser and on east by vendor, $50. 8 Apr. 1790. // p.334. Jonas Oiler [Isler] sells to Chas. de Grand-Pre part of a tract which did belong to John Row afterwards George Furney who sold to my late father, Mark Oiler, and is now my property, for $100. 21 March 1789. // p.336. 28 May 1794. Chas. de Grand-Pre to Ebenezer Rees, 625 arpens, for $2500. Benet Truly on bond for payment. // p.339. 12 Aug. 1800. Ebenezer Rees to Anthony Dogherty, 410 acres (see plat), for $4100 paid. Wit: John Henderson, Wm. N. Galbraith. [No file.]

p.339. Claim No.136. (Reg. 17 Jany. 1804.) Sp. grant to David Henderson, 350 acres in Natchez Dist. on south branch of Cole's Cr., 18 miles east of Fort Panmure, b. by John Fort and vacant lands; surv. by Wm. Dunbar. Dec. 4, 1797, New Orleans. [No file.]

p.341. Claim No.137. (Reg. 19 Jany. 1804.) Sale of land by confiscation, to the last and highest bidder, 10,000 acres on Bayou Pierre, b. on one side by lands of Mr. Philip Barbour and on other sides not granted, in presence of Francis Farrell, Richard Harrison, Isaac Johnson and others assisting, cried in public and adjudged to John Hartley at $501. Witnesses signing with us, the Commandant: Samuel Lewis, Francis Farrell, Silas Crane, James Harman, Richard Harrison, Stephen Minor, William Barland, Cato West, Charles de Grand-Pre. Fort Panmure at Natchez, 30 June 1782. // p.342. Deed of

Gift. John Hartley to Jacob Hartley, for 1000 acres, as above, 11 Aug. 1788. [For this and five other deeds of gift by John Hartley see Natchez Records, Book B, pages 130-133.] // p.343. 10 Oct. 1802. Heirs and exrs. of the last will and testament of John Hartley, decd., to Richard Grimes and Rachel, his wife. Samuel Gibson, Jesse Hamilton, and Christian Harman, exrs., John Hartley and Christiana Wallet, heirs and devisees of said John Hartley, decd., and heirs of Jacob Hartley, late decd., all of Miss. Ter., to Richard Grimes, of said Territory, and his wife, Rachel, for good causes and considerations quit claimed all right, etc., in their own right or otherwise to 1000 acres of land in Claiborne County on the North Fork of Bayou Pierre, devised to Jacob Hartley, deceased, also to all the said Jacob Hartley died possessed of. Signed by Samuel Gibson, John Hartley, Christiana Wallet, Richard Grimes, Rachel Grimes. Wit: E. Hoskinson, Darius Hamilton, who proved above before James Harman, J. P. // Richard and Rachel Grimes relinquished any further claim on estate of John Hartley. [For litigation see Natchez Rec. Bk.] [No file.]

p.345. Claim No.138. (Reg. 18 Jany. 1804.) Petition and Decree. Petition of Salome Lyman that she has learned that the lands of the fugitives must be sold at public auction and my dear father is absent and I, a minor, having no subsistence except that of my grandfather, Mr. Crane [Silas], begs your bounty and to grant her the land that was her father's. Salome Lyman, by Francis Farrell, lawyer. // Natchez, 17 June, 1782. All the land above the 10,000 acres sold and deeded to John Hartley, after the line is drawn from east to west, will remain the property of the daughter of Mr. Lyman, named Salome. [No file.]

p.346. Claim No.139. (Reg. 18 Jany. 1804.) Spanish grant to Thomas Calvit, 800 acres in the Dist. of Natchez, on banks of Miss. River, below Little Gulf, 25 miles NE from Fort Panmure, b. by Peter Belly and Nathaniel Tomlinson, on other by Philip Alston. N. O. 1st Apr. 1795. [No file.]

p.348. Claim No.140. (Reg. 18 Jany. 1804.) Sp. grant to Thomas Calvit, 200 acres in the Dist. of Natchez, on waters of Cole's Cr., 25 miles north of Fort Panmure, b. by land of Mr. Barbour, Richard Deval, the banks of the lake on the west and vacant land. The plan in English for the comprehension of the grantee. N. O. 7 May 1789. [No file.]

p.348. Claim No.141. (Reg. 18 Jany. 1804.) Sp. grant to Thos. Calvet, 200 arpens in the Dist. of Natchez, on waters of Cole's Cr., 25 miles NE from Fort Panmure, b. on all sides by land of His Majesty and not granted. N. O. 27 Feb. 1789. [No file.]

p.351. Claim No.144. (Reg. 19 Jany. 1804.) Sp. grant to Job Routh 400 acres in Dist. of Natchez, on south branch of Cole's Creek, 30 miles NE of Fort Panmure, b. by James Elliot and Wm. Daniel. N. O. 30 May 1793. // Bargain and sale. Oct. 20, 1801. Job Routh and Ann, his wife, and Jeremiah Routh and Anne, his wife, of Adams Co., Miss. Ter., to Capt. Thos. Marston Green, Esq., of Pickering County, for $1000, paid, 400 acres in Pickering Co. (as above). [Job and Jeremiah Routh signed; their wives signed with a mark.] Wit: John Henderson, Joel Bunnell. [No file.]

p.345. Claim No.145. (Reg. 19 Jany. 1804.) Sp. grant to Jesse Smith, 240 arpens in the District of Natchez, on South Fork of Bayou Pierre, 54 miles from Fort Panmure, b. by Abraham Green and vacant lands. N. O. 30 Aug. 1793. // 10 Dec. 1800. Bargain and sale. Jesse Smith and wife, Mary, of Bayou Pierre in Pickering Co. to Thomas Marston Green, for $500, paid, 240 acres, (above). (signed) Jesse Smith, Mary (x) Smith. Wit: Dan'l. James, Daniel Chambers. Proved by Daniel James before Roger Dixon, Esq. in Pickering Co., 20 Jany. 1801. [No file.]

p.357. Claim No.146. (Reg. 19 Jany. 1804.) Sp. grant to David Odam, 375 arpens in the Natchez District, on waters of Cole's Cr., 18 miles NE from Fort Panmure, b. by Jacob Stampley and John Migat. N. O. 24 Dec. 1790. // p.359. 22 July 1800. Bargain and sale. David Odam, of Pickering Co., Miss. Ter., and wife, Fanny, to Abner Pipes, for $100 paid, 375 acres . . . along the line of Roswell Mygatt. (signed) David Odam, Fanny (x) Odam. Wit: Silas Payne, Wm. L. Bevels, Polly (x) Odam. // p.361. Oct. 1, 1801. Fanny Odam, wid. and exor. of David Odam, Sr., of Pickering Co., decd. and Abner Pipes, exor. of said deceased, to Thomas Marston Green, of sd co., for $1000, paid, the above 375 acres. Wit: A. L. Duncan, David (D) Odam. // p.363. 25 Jany. 1802. Abner Pipes, of Pickering Co., Miss. Ter., and Elizabeth, his wife, sell to Thomas Marston Green, of same, for $300 paid, all their claim, etc. in 100 acres on Cole's Creek, being a part of 375 acres granted to David Odam, deceased by Sp. Govt. Signed by both. Wit: A. L. Duncan, David (X) Odam. [No file.]

p.365. Claim No.147. (Reg. 10 Feb. 1804.) Sp. grant to Thos. Marston Green, 800 arpens in Natchez Dist., on waters of Fairchild's Cr., 12 miles NE of Fort Panmure, b. by John Boles, Jeremiah Coleman and lands not granted. N. O. 27 Feb. 1789. [No file.]

p.366. Claim No.148. (Reg. 19 Jany. 1804.) Sp. grant to Thomas Green 200 arpents in Natchez Dist., on waters of the river vulgarly called Cole's Cr., on the south fork, 23 miles NE from Fort Panmure, b. by grantee and William Ferguson. N. O. 12 Feb. 1788. [No file.]

p.368. Claim No.152. (Reg. 28 Jany. 1804.) Sp. grant to Filmer and Abraham Green, 500 arpens in the Dist. of Natchez, on waters of Bayou Pierre, b. on land of Mr. Goodin and of His Majesty. N. O. 10 May 1789. // p.369. 24 Feb. 1801. Will of Filmer Wells Green, of Pickering Co., Miss. Ter. I give and bequeath to my brother, Abraham Green the following negroes (four and names given), one-half of my stock of cattle and all my horses and mares except such as I shall mention hereinafter, also of the share of land, 2000 acres which were granted jointly to my brother and me. My will is that of my part of 1000 acres, my said brother shall have the 500 acres lying on the north side of the south fork of Bayou Pierre. Other legatees: brother Everard Green, sister-in-law, Martha Green, her two sons, Joseph and Filmer, Ann James, and "my father". Bros., Abraham and Thos. Marston, exrs. Wit: Robt. Miller, James Folkes, Chas. Watts, Felix Hughs. Probated 30 March 1801. p.371. Codicil to above. 20 March 1801. Two last witnesses signed. // 20 Aug. 1802. Deed of partition. Martha Green. Division of slaves and land according to above will, between her two sons, Filmer Green and Joseph Green. Filmer to have negroes and Joseph to have the land, 500 acres on Bayou Pierre, adj. the widow Goodwin. (signed) Martha Green. Wit: John Shaw, D. W. B., William West. Joseph to pay his brother $500 if he lives to be of age. // p.374. 27 Aug. 1802. Abraham Green, of Claiborne Co., Miss. Ter., to Joseph Green, of Jefferson Co., sd Ter., relinquishes his right and title to the 500 acres in Claiborne Co. (signed) A. Green. Wit: John Shaw, Samuel Cobun. [No file.]

p.375. Claim No.153. (Reg. 20 Jany. 1804.) Sp. grant to Adam Lenhart, 500 arpens in Dist. of Natchez, on Buffalo Creek, 35 miles SE from the Fort, b. by lands of Mr. Joseph Bernard and vacant lands. 7 Dec. 1797. [No file.]

p.377. Claim No.156. (Reg. 20 Jany. 1804.) Sp. grant to Filmer and Abraham Green, 1000 acres in the Natchez District, on waters of Bayou Pierre, 45 miles by land from the Fort, b. by the branch of sd Bayou and land of James Murray. N. O. 27 Feb. 1789. [No file.]

p.378. Claim No.157. (Reg. 20 Jany. 1804.) Sp. grant to Filmer and Abraham Green, 500 arpens in the Dist. of Natchez, on waters of Bayou Pierre, abt. 45 from Fort Panmure, b. by Moses Armstrong, his mother, sisters and brothers. N. O. 7 March 1788. [No file.]

p.380. Claim No.158. (Reg. 20 Jany. 1804.) Sp. grant to Everard Green, 205 arpens in Dist. of Natchez, on waters of Cole's Creek, 4 miles east of Fort, b. by Mr. Bingaman, Mr. James Elliot, and Mr. David Ross. N. O. 12 Feb. 1788. [No file.]

p.381. Claim No.159. (Reg. 20 Jany. 1804.) Sp. grant to Jacob Stampley, 350 arpens in the Natchez Dist., on waters of Cole's Cr., 25 miles NE of Fort., b. by David Odam and Cato West. N. O. 8 Apr. 1891. [No file.]

p.383. Claim No.160. (Reg. 20 Jany. 1804.) Sp. grant to Everard Green, 337 arpents in the Natchez District, waters of Cole's Creek, 20 miles NE from Fort of Natchez, b. by the left bank of the Miss. River and land of Abner Green. N. O. 12 Feb. 1788. [No file.]

p.384. Claim No.161. (Reg. 20 Jany. 1804.) Sp. grant to Everard Green 650 acres in Dist. of Natchez on Cole's Creek, b. by a survey for James Mather and Richard Deval, by lands of grantee and James Elliot and others not granted. N. O. March 30, 1796. [No file.]

p.386. Claim No.162. (Reg. 20 Jany. 1804.) Sp. grant to Everard Green, 38 arpents in the Dist. of Natchez, on waters of Cole's Cr., 2 miles east of the Miss. River, and 23 miles NE of Fort of Natchez, b. by lands of Mr. Bingaman, Mr. David Ross and a swamp, the sd land being in figure of a triangle. N. O. 12 Feb. 1788. [No file.]

p.387. Claim No.166. (Reg. 24 Jany. 1804.) Sp. grant to Martin Hester 500 arpens in Dist. of Natchez, on North Fork of Cole's Cr., 30 miles NE of Fort, b. on all sides by lands of His Majesty. N. O. 1 Sept. 1795. [No file.]

p.389. Claim No.174. (Reg. 26 Jany. 1804.) Sp. grant to John Bullen. Petition of John Bullen, res. of the district, wishes to establish a residence in this country and work for the subsistence of my wife and five children, asks grant on St. Catherine's creek, adjoining those of Charles Adams and William Selkrig. Natchez, 20 Nov. 1784. // Warrant for 450 acres. Natchez 28 Jany. 1795. // Grant of 450 acres at the place named if it does not interfere with others. (n. d.) [No file.]

p.390. Claim No.179. (Reg. 30 Jany. 1804.) Sp. grant to Josiah Rundle, 240 acres in the Dist. of Natchez, on South Fork of Bayou Pierre, 35 miles NE from Fort Panmure, b. by vacant lands, the domains of His Majesty. [n. d.] // p.392. Bargain and sale. Josiah Rundle assigns right in above grant to Mr. Elisha Flower. Signed. Wit: Hezekiah Harman, James Melwee. // Elisha Flower assigns right in above grant to James Gibson, -- 1800. Same witnesses. // James Gibson assigns same to Randel Gibson, Aug. 19, 1802. (signed) James Gibson. Wit: Gibson Foster, Wm. Johnson, Wm. Talor. [No file.]

p.393. Claim No.186. (Reg. 4 Feb. 1804.) Sp. grant to John Gibson, 700 arpents in Dist. of Natchez, on waters of Bayou Pierre, 45 miles from Fort Panmure, b. on vacant lands. N. O. 8 Jany. 1789. [No file.]

p.394. Claim No.187. (Reg. 4 Feb. 1804.) Sp. grant to Sam'l. Gibson, of 850 acres in Natchez Dist. on Bayou Pierre on South Fork, 40 miles from Fort Panmure, b. by Mr. Murray and vacant lands. Surveyed by Wm. Vousdan, 20 Nov. 1787. N. O. 2 Aug. 1788. [No file.]

p.396. Claim No.188. (Reg. 4 Feb. 1804.) Sp. grant to James Kirk, 800 acres on Tabor's Cr. of Bayou Pierre, 45 miles NE from Fort Panmure, all sides vacant. N.O. 8 April 1789. // Conveyance. 26 June, 1801. James Kirk and Susannah, his wife, of Adams Co., Miss. Ter., to Samuel Gibson, of Pickering Co., sd Ter., for $2000, paid, 800 acres in County of Pickering, as in above grant. Both signed. Wit: William Williams, Richard King. Proved by Richard King, 17 Sept. 1801, before Seth Lewis, J. P. [No file.]

p.399. Sp. grant to Justus King, 500 acres in the Dist. of Natchez, 40 miles NE from Fort Panmure, b. by Jacob Cobun, Prosper King and vacant lands. N. O. 19 Apr. 1793. // p.401. On the plaza of Natchez, the 25th Aug. 1797, before me, Don Estevan Minor, Capt., appeared Justus King who sold to Richard King the above grant, for $300, which he had received. (signed) Justus King. Wit: Estevan Minor. // Indenture. 28 Aug. 1803. Richard King, of Adams County, Miss. Ter. and wife, Esther, to Robert Ashley, of Claiborne Co., same Ter., for $1000, sell above tract. Both signed. Wit: J. Eldergill, John L. Pettit. // p.402. 27 Oct. 1803. Robert Ashley and Sally, his wife, of Claiborne Co., Miss. Ter. to Samuel Gibson, of same, for $1000 to him in hand paid, 500 acres (above described). Both signed. Wit: John Lackey, John Gibson. [No file.]

p.403. Claim No.191. (Reg. 4 Feb. 1804.) Sp. grant to Telfair Monson, 400 acres in Natchez District, between the waters of Bayou Sara, 46 miles south of Fort Panmure, b. by Henry Humter, and Gerard Brandon. Surveyed by Wm. Dunbar. N. O. 10 April 1795. // p.405. 7 Aug. 1801. Daniel Clark, of New Orleans, Esq. by his atty. William Dunbar, Esq. of Adams Co., Miss. Ter. 400 French acres on Bayou Sarah, 46 miles south of the old Fort of Natchez, (same as above.) (signed) Wm. Dunbar for Daniel Clark. Wit: Fred Ward, John Henderson. Proved by Henderson 11 Oct. 1801 before Samuel Hancock, J. P. of Adams Co. [No file.]

p.406. Claim No.197. (Reg. 4 Feb. 1804.) Sp. grant to Daniel Perry, Jr., 733 arpens in Dist. of Natchez, on waters of Cole's Cr. on the South Fork, b. on Daniel Perry, Sr., and the land of Richard Ellis, Sr. N. O. 15 March 1789. [No file.]

p.408. Claim 200. (Reg. 4 Feb. 1804.) Sp. grant to Hezekiah Harman 300 arpents on the south bank of Bayou Pierre 2 leagues from its mouth, 40 miles north of Fort Panmure, b. by lands of His Majesty. N. O. 1 Dec. 1794. [No file.]

p.414. Claim No.206. (Reg. 31 Jany. 1804.) Sp. grant to Gideon Gibson, 335 arpens on waters of St. Catherine's Cr., 7 miles NE from Fort Panmure, b. by Benj. Belk, Doctor McCabe, John Foster, Joseph Calvet, Richard Harrison and Wm. Hayton. N. O. 4 March 1789. // p.416. Gideon Gibson to Randal Gibson, his son, 335 acres, 6 miles from Natchez, (as desc. above). 12 Nov. 1792. (Natchez Rec. Bk.C-45). [No file.]

p.417. Claim No.207. (Reg. 3 Feb. 1804.) Wm. Brocus petition to Sp. Govt. (missing). // p.418. Sp. grant to William Brocus, 600 acres on Muddy Fork of St. Catherine's Cr., 3 leagues NE from Fort Panmure, b. on west by Benj. Belk, other sides vacant. N. O. 29 Feb. 1788.

p.420. Claim No.208. (Reg. 3 Feb. 1804.) Sp. grant to Gerard Brandon, 800 acres in Natchez District, near Loftus Cliffs, 34 miles south from Fort Panmure, b. by David Lejeune and Mr. Ross, and part of land of Mr. Monro. N. O. 12 March 1790. [No file.]

p.421. Claim No.209. Sp. grant to Gerard Brandon. Petition: He desires to establish himself in the Dist. of Bayou Sara; asks for grant to correspond with the number of his family which consists of 15 slaves and ten whites; wishes to have land adj. Wm. Dunbar. Natchez, 20 July 1797. Signed. // Warrant by Manuel Gayoso de Lemos, 21 Jany. 1790. // Grant for 800 arpens where desired, not to interfere with former grants. N. O. 27 Feb. 1797. [No file.]

p.422. Claim No.210. (Reg. 3 Feb. 1804.) Sp. grant to David Monroe, 1000 acres in the Natchez District, 14 miles from the Miss. River, b. by Andrew Hare, David Lejeune and vacant lands. N. O. 20 March 1789. // p.424. 27 Jany. 1794. At public sale of David Munro's estate, plantation adjudged to Gerard Brandon, highest bidder, with Mr. John Bisland surety. Signed by purchaser, surety, executor and witnesses. Receipt of George Fitzgerald, exr. of will of David Munro for full amount paid by Gerard Brandon, 11 March 1801. [No file.]

p.425. Claim No.224. (Reg. 7 Feb. 1804.) Petition, warrant and plat. Petition of Lucius Smith to the Spànish Government for a grant for my subsistence, on Bayou Pierre, adj. Wm. Tabor and James Lobdal. Natchez, 21 July 1789. // Warrant for 240 arpents. Gayoso. 22 July 1789. // Certificate and plat, 29 June 1792. [No file.]

p.426. Claim No.225. (Reg. 7 Feb. 1804.) Sp. grant to William Tabor, for 300 arpens in the Natchez Dist., on a branch of Bayou Pierre, 45 miles NE of Fort Panmure, b. by vacant lands. N. O. Apr. 10, 1795. // 28 March 1799. I do assign within patent to Thos. Harrington. (signed) William Tabor. Wit: Eden Brashears, Wm. Brocus, Jr. [This claim continued Bk.B-109.] [No file.]

p.427. Claim No.226. (Reg. 9 Feb. 1804.) Sp. grant to Manuel Madden, 798 acres in the District of Natchez, bet. St. Catherine and Fairchild's creeks, 8 miles NE from Fort Panmure, b. by Thomas Jordan, James Bonner, Moses Bonner and Jeremiah Bryan. N. O. 15 March 1788. // p.429. 18 Feb. 1802. Manuel Madden, of Adams Co., Miss. Ter., to James Bonner, of same, for $300 paid, 100 acres in Adams Co., the NE part of tract on which sd Manuel Madden now lives, b. by lands of late Charles Boardman, decd., and part of tract on which James Bonner now lives and the tract where Wm. Collins now lives, and the tract on which James Wade now lives, and by a Bayou which divides it from part of the tract on which Manuel Madden now lives. Wit: P. Marshall, Jesse Withers. [No file.]

p.430. Claim No.227. (Reg. 9 Feb. 1804.) Sp. grant to James Bonner, 400 acres in Natchez Dist., on Fairchild's Cr., b. by James McIntyre, Moses Bonner, Jr., Manuel Madden and Thomas Jordan. N. O. 23 March 1790. [No file.]

p.432. Claim No.228. (Reg. 9 Feb. 1804.) Sp. grant to William Daniel, 275 acres in the Natchez Dist., 30 miles from Fort Panmure, b. by Francis Jones and vacant lands. N. O., 4 March 1795. [No file.]

p.433. Claim No.229. (Reg. Feb. 10, 1804.) Sp. grant to Peter Smith, for 400 acres in Natchez Dist. 40 miles south of Fort Panmure, b. by Zachariah Smith, Sr. and Jr., father and brother of grantee, other sides vacant. N. O. 30 March 1793. [No file.]

p.405. Claim No.230. (Reg. 10 Feb. 1804.) Sp. grant to Zachariah Smith, 500 acres in the Natchez Dist., on Buffalo Creek, 6 miles east of Loftus Cliffs, 30 miles from Fort Panmure, b. on all sides by vacant land. Surveyed by Wm. Vousdan. N. O. 30 June 1788. // p.436. 30 Oct. 1800. Zachariah Smith and wife, Frances, to Peter Smith, for divers considerations all the tract on Buffalo Cr., on the south side of Percy's Creek, adj. Zachariah Smith, Jr. Both sign. Wit: Reuben Brasfield, Wm. Ogden. Prov. by Reuben Brasfield. 16 March 1801, before Wm. Miller, Adams Co., Miss. Territory. [No file.]

p.438. Claim No.231. (Reg. 10 Feb. 1804.) Sp. grant to Zachariah Smith, Jr., 500 acres in Natchez Dist., 40 miles south of Fort Panmure, b. by Gilbert Leonard and Thomas Wilkins, and Zachariah and Peter Smith, father and brother of grantee. N. O. 30 March 1793. [No file.]

p.439. Claim No.232. (Reg. 10 Feb. 1804.) Sp. grant to James Smith, for 480 acres in the Natchez Dist., 5 leagues from Fort Panmure, about 20 leagues by water, b. by lands of Don Pedro Miro, decd., and William Conway. N. O. 28 March 1791. [No file.]

p.441. Claim No.233. (Reg. 10 Feb. 1804.) Sp. grant to John Lovelace. [rest of page blank.] p.442. 16 June 1799, John Lovelace, planter, of Miss. Territory, to Thomas Lovelace, of same, for $100 paid, 200 acres on south side of Buffalo Cr., beg. at a corner of 800 acre tract granted said John Lovelace 1788, etc. (signed) John Lovelace, Anne Lovelace. Wit: John Wall, Peter A. Vousdan, Samuel Lightner. Prov. by Vousdan 20 Sept. 1800 before John Ellis, J. P. of Adams Co., Miss. Territory. [No file.]

p.444. Claim No.234. (Reg. 10 Feb. 1804.) Sp. grant to Thomas Cummins, 28- acres in the Natchez District on a br. of the Homochitto River, 17 miles SE from Fort Panmure, b. by Wm. Scott and vacant lands. N. O. 15 March 1789. [No file.]

p.445. Claim No.235. (Reg. 10 Feb. 1804.) Sp. grant to Zachariah Smith, 837 arpents in the Natchez Dist., on one of the west branches of Buffalo Creek, 30 miles from Fort, adj. Wm. Vousdan on two sides, on other, Henry Roach. N. O. 8 Aug. 1797. [No file.]

p.447. Claim No.236. (Reg. 10 Feb. 1804.) Sp. grant to Zachariah Smith, 300 acres in the Natchez District, on a br. of Buffalo Creek, 5 miles east of Loftus Cliffs, 14 leagues from Fort Panmure, adj. Mary Dwyer, Charles Percy and vacant lands. Surveyor: Wm. Vousdan. N. O. 30 June 1788. [No file.]

p.449. Claim No.244. (Reg. 16 Feb. 1804.) Sp. grant to Wm. Kirkwood, 479 acres in the Natchez Dist., 6 miles north of Fort Panmure, adj. Widow Henderson and Benj. Monsanto. N. O., 30 March 1796. [No file.]

p.451. Claim No.251. (Reg. 20 Feb. 1804.) Sp. Govt. to John Barton order of survey. // Petition for 240 acres on waters of St. Catherine's Cr., b. by Christian Harman, George Killian, Thomas Morgan and John Waugh. 23 Jany. 1791. // Warrant, 12 March 1791, by Gayoso. // Patent, 7 April 1791, by Estevan Miro. // p.452. 18 Sept. 1799. John Barton and Margaret, his wife, of Adams Co., Miss. Ter., to Thos Tyler, of same, for $203 paid, tract on Clear fork of St. Catherine's Cr. in afsd Co. and Ter., b. by George Killian, Christian Harman, lands gr. John Waugh and formerly to Melling Wooley, and lands formerly belonging to Thos. Morgan and now to Abram Taylor, a patent (as above.) John Barton, Margaret (X) Barton. Wit: James Ashworth, John Hutton. Prov. by Ashworth before Samuel Hancock, J. P., Adams Co. Aug. 29, 1801. // Indenture. 25 March 1803. Thos. Tyler, of Adams Co., Miss. Ter., to Caleb Perkins, of same, for $500 paid, 240 acres gr. said Barton as above. (signed) Thos. Tyler. Wit: John Elmore, John Henderson. Relinquished by Caty Tyler, 25 March 1803. Wit: John Henderson, John B. Willis. Ack. by both, same date, before John Henderson, J. P., Adams Co., Miss. Ter. [No file.]

pp.456-7. [See p.114.]

p.458. [See p.160.]

p.460. Claim No.253. (Reg. 20 Feb. 1804.) Sp. grant to Martin Owens, 350 acres in the Natchez Dist. on waters of Cole's Creek, called Fairbank's Creek, 15 miles north of the Fort, b. by Melling Wooley, James McIntyre and vacant lands. Survey and certif. by Wm. Dunbar. N. O. 20 June 1795. // p.462. Indenture. 9 July 1802, Martin of Jefferson Co., Miss. Ter., for $300 paid, 150 acres, part of grant to sd Owens in 1795, to be taken off the SE end (metes and bounds). Martin Owens, Mary Owens. Wit: Robt. Turner, Willis (x) Bonner. Ack. by Martin Owens and wife, Mary, before Jesse Withers, J. P., 9 July 1802. [No file.]

p.464. Claim No.259. (Reg. 20, 1804.) Sp. grant to Thomas Foster, 800 acres in the Natchez Dist., on a br. of Buffalo Cr., 25 miles from the Fort, b. on lands of Peter Smith and vacant lands. Surv. by Wm. Dunbar. N. O., 24 Dec. 1797. [No file.]

p.465. Claim No.260. (Reg. 20 Feb. 1904.) Sp. grant to Eustace Humphries, 300 acres in the Natchez Dist., on Fairchild's Cr., 20 miles NE of Fort, b. by lands in the name of Marcus Oliver for Mr. Clark and vacant lands. N. O. 27 Feb. 1788. // p.467. Deed. 18 Apr. 1795. Eustis Humphries to Henry Milburn, 300 acres (as granted above), for $300, paid. // p.468. Deed. 9 Feb. 1797. Henry Milburn to John Courtney, 100 acres of above tract. Ack. 14 Feb. 1798. Wit: John Girault, Isaac Foster, Chas. Surget, before Gayoso.

p.470. Claim No.264. (Reg. 20 Feb. 1804.) Sp. grant to Wm. Bell, 400 acres in the Dist. of Natchez, on waters of Cole's Cr., 18 miles east of Fort Panmure, b. by lands gr. Don Estevan Miro and vacant lands. N. O., 1 Oct. 1794. // Oct. 28, 1797. Wm. Bell, of Dist. of Natchez, and wife, to Wm. Chaney, 120 arpens, part of above grant. // p.473. 6 Jany. 1801. Wm. Bell and Esther, his wife, of Pickering Co., Miss. Ter., to Wm. Chaney, Sr., of same, for $900 paid, 280 acres on waters of Cole's Cr., b. by Jesse Harper, James Jones and vacant lands, patented 1794. Wit: Abel Draughan, Wm. Burch. [No file.]

p.474. Claim No.267. (Reg. 20 Feb. 1804.) Sp. grant to Clement Dyson, 160 acres in the Natchez Dist., on waters of Fairchild's Cr. 20 miles NE of Fort, b. by Daniel Clark, Adam Bingaman and Mr. Humphries. N. O., 26 Nov. 1793. // p.476. 5 Jany. 1798. Clement Dyson to John Courtney, both of Natchez Dist., for $200 paid, 160 acres (above described.) Wit: John Girault, Wm. Owen. [No file.]

p.478. Claim No.268. (Reg. 20 Feb.1804.) 17 Sept. 1796, Parker Carradine, of Natchez Dist. to Peter Hill, of same, 200 arpens on Fairchild's Cr., part of 600 arpens granted to me in 1789, for the consideration that he settled the sd tract and lived thereon 3 years. Wit: Wm. Gillespie. [No file.]

p.479. Claim No.269. (Reg. Feb. 20, 1804.) Sp. grant to Joshua Collins 200 acres in the Natchez District on the waters of Fairchild's Creek, 20 miles distance NE of the Fort, b. by Mr. Rees and Mr. Carradine. N. O., 15 March 1789. // p.481. 19 May 1794. Joshua Collins to Narsworthy Hunter, Capt. of Militia of this dist., 200 acres, as above described, for $200 paid. // p.482. 3 March 1795, Before Don Manuel Gayoso de Lemos, military and political governor of this place, appeared Mr. Narsworthy Hunter and Stephen Scriber who did exchange land, as follows: The sd Hunter delivers to Scriber 200 acres in the dist. of Villa Gayoso, b. by Mr. Ebenezer Rees and Mr. Parker Carradine, which he purchased of Joshua Collins, with six cows in exchange for 350 acres on the north branch of Cole's Cr. b. by lands of James Elliott, which was granted to sd Scriber by the Spanish Govt. as above. Both sign. [No file.]

p.483. Claim No.271. (Reg. 20 Feb. 1804.) Pet. of John Burnet to Sp. Govt. Whereas Your Excellency had long promised him a compensation in lands for various publick services by him rendered and you were pleased lately to direct the petitioner to locate the same and you would order him to be put in possession thereof, the petitioner hath located the same and purchased an improvement thereon, which lies about one-half mile below Grand Gulf on the Miss. River, in which place your petitioner prays ye please, for reasons aforesaid, to grant him 1000 acres. Signed. Natchez. 25 Aug. 1795. // p.484. Gayoso to John Burnet, decree of foregoing petition. Natchez, 27 Aug. 1795. // 8 Feb. 1804. John Burnet, Sr., of Claiborne Co., Miss. Ter., to Gideon Medlock all my right, etc. in following papers and land, to wit: A bill of sale signed by Nelly Price, dated 25 Oct. 1785 and a petition signed by myself and a decree signed by Gayoso, then Gov. of Natchez and a plat of survey dated in 1801, the plat containing 1795 acres on the banks of the Miss. River just below Grand Gulf . . . to Hartley's line . . . for $800 paid. Signed. Wit: Daniel Burnet, James Davenport. [No file.]

p.486. Claim No.272. (Reg. 20 Feb. 1804.) Sp. grant to Joseph Dove, 240 acres in the Natchez District on Bayou aux Boeufs, 21 miles from the Fort, on the east side of Bayou de la Piniera. N. O., 1st Sept. 1795. [No file.]

p.488. Claim No.274. (Reg. 20 Feb. 1804.) Sp. grant to Jeremiah Coleman, 350 acres in the Dist. of Natchez, on Fairchild's Creek, 14 miles NE from Fort, b. by Frederick Calvit and Thos. Marston Green, N. O., 28 Jany. 1789. [No file.]

p.490. Claim No.275. (Reg. 20 Feb. 1804.) Sp. grant to Gabriel Griffin, 200 acres on the south bank of the Big Black River, b. by Daniel Douglas and Gabriel Griffing, 7 miles from its mouth, 30 miles north of Fort. Surv. by Wm. Dunbar. N. O., 10 Jany. 1790. Plat shows land of Wilson Bowles adjoining. [No file.]

p.493. Claim No.276. (Reg. 20 Feb. 1804.) Sp. grant to Ezekiel Newman, 200 acres in the Natchez District, on the south bank of the Big Black River, 45 miles NW from Fort of Natchez, b. by Daniel Douglass and vacant lands. Surveyor, Wm. Dunbar. N. O., 20 July 1793. // p.495. 10 Jany. 1800, Ezekiel Newman to the heirs of Gabriel Griffing, for $22 in hand paid by Cato West in behalf of afsd heirs of Gabriel Griffing, decd, 200 acres on the Big Black River as above. Signed and acknowledged in Pickering Co. Wit: Reuben Newman, Wm. Noble, Henry Noble. // File. Claimants: heirs of Gabriel Griffin, decd. Wit: John Bolls, 21 July 1804. Certif. A-436 issued to legal representatives. 16 July 1805. // Land claimed in Claiborne Co. and claim signed by Cato West, acting executor of the estate and by Jeremiah Coleman, executor. //

p.497. Claim No.277. (Reg. 20 Feb. 1804.) Sp. grant to Daniel Douglass, 200 acres in the Natchez Dist., on the Big Black River, 7 miles from its mouth, 30 miles north of Fort, adj. Gabriel Griffin and Ezekiel Newman. N. O., 10 Jany. 1794. // p.500. 9 Nov. 1797. Daniel Douglass, of Natchez Dist., to heirs of Gabriel Griffin, represented by Cato West and Jeremiah Coleman, of same place, for $25 in hand paid by the late Gabriel Griffin, 200 acres in front by Ezekiel Newman, by Gabriel Griffin, and the River, gr. to Daniel Douglass for military services, 10 Jany. 1794. Ack. by Daniel Douglass, 18 Nov. 1797, before Stephen Minor, Capt., Aid-Major and Governor. [No file.]

p.502. Claim No.280. (Reg. 21 Feb. 1804.) Sp. grant to George Killion, 600 arpens in the Natchez Dist., 9 miles east of Fort Panmure, b. Ferguson, Charles Adams and vacant land. N. O. 15 March 1789. // p.504. Miss. Ter., Adams Co., Jany. 6, 1801. I do certify that I, at the desire and request of George Killion, Joseph Killion and Abraham Galtney, have carefully surveyed for and in the name of Joseph Killion 300 acres, part of 600 acres granted by Sp. Govt. to sd George Killian (as above) on St. Catherine's Creek. (signed) Wm. Atchinson, surveyor. // Indenture. 26 Feb. 1801, George Killion, of Adams Co., Miss. Ter. to Joseph Killian, of same, for nat. love and affection and better maintenance, 300 acres. (signed) George Killian. Wit: John Alston, Wm. Glascock. Ack. 6 July 1801 before Samuel Hancock, J. P. Adams County. // Plat and certificate of other half of above 600 acres to Abraham Galtney, as above, by request of George Killian to measure and lay out for Abraham Galtney, same location. (signed) Wm. Atchinson. Jany. 6, 1801. p.507. 26 Feb. 1801. Deed from George Killian to Abraham Galtney for nat. love and affection and better maintenance, 300 acres, one-half of grant of 600 acres. Ack. 6 July 1801 before Samuel Hancock, J. P. of Adams Co. [No file.]

p.509. Claim No.281. (Reg. 21 Feb. 1804.) Sp. grant to Ithamer Andrews 100 acres in Natchez District, 5 miles from Fort Panmure, b. by Mrs. McIntosh [Eunice, widow of Wm., from the plat.], and by Mr. Adams and vacant lands. N. O. 24 Jany. 1794. // p.511. Deed. 17 Sept. 1794. Ithamar Andrews to Israel Leonard 100 arpents on St. Catherine's Creek, for $280. [No file.]

p.512. Claim No.283. (Reg. 21 Feb. 1804.) Sp. grant to Richard Curtis 200 arpens in Natchez Dist., on Cole's Creek, 15 miles NE of Fort Panmure, b. by Jeptha Higdon, James Cole, Gabriel Griffin, and vacant land. N. O. 25 Mch. 1795. [No file.]

p.513. Claim No.283. (Reg. 21 Feb. 1804.) Sp. grant to Thomas Morgan, 250 arpents in the Natchez Dist., on waters of St. Catherine's Creek and Cole's Creek, 12 miles from Fort Panmure, b. by James Oglesby and vacant lands. N. O. 10 March 1789. // p.515. Conveyance. 30 Jany. 1798. Thomas Morgan to Abram Taylor, 250 arpens as granted above. Both sign with marks. Wit: Estevan Minor, Cato West, John Girault. [No file.]

p.516. Claim No.286. (Reg. 21 Feb. 1804.) Order for survey. Petition of James Clark for lands on Cole's Creek, adj. Richard Curtis, Philip Nevill and Ephraim Coleman. Natchez, 26 Nov. 1794. // Order for survey by Gayoso. 28 Jany. 1794. // Warrant for survey, N. O. Feb. 1795, by Carondelet. [No file.]

p.517. Claim No.287. (Reg. 21 Feb. 1804.) Sp. grant to Abraham Horton, 600 acres in Natchez Dist., 34 miles south of Fort Panmure, on Bayou Sara, b. by lands of Gerard Brandon and Samuel Lewis Wells. N. O. 10 March 1790. [No file.]

p.518. Claim No.288. (Reg. 21 Feb. 1804.) Sp. grant to Samuel Lewis Wells, 400 acres in Dist. of Natchez, on west side of Bayou Sara, 34 miles south of the Fort. N. O. 24 Dec. 1797. // p.520. Power of atty. to sell above from Samuel Lewis Wells to Benjamin Scott. 3 April 1799. Wells of the Dist. of Rapides, Scott of Dist. of Bayou Sara within the American limits. Land sold to Abraham Horton, Sr. Wit: Thos. Thompson, Cesar Archinard, Bernard Despallier. // Deed. Same as above, wit: Samuel Morris, Leonard Shaw. Ack. by Benj. Scott before Judge Peter Brian Bruin, 5 May 1799. [No file.]

p.521. Claim No.292. (Reg. 21 Feb. 1804.) Sp. grant to Wm. Ferguson, 500 arpents in the Natchez District, on Cole's Cr., 20 miles NE of the Fort, b. by Mrs. Truly, Ferguson, and Hannah, Wm., and Jesse Lum. N. O. 15 March 1787. [No file.]

p.523. Claim No.293. Deed. Silas Crane, settler and inhabitant of this district, sells to Mr. Wm. Ferguson 325 arpents of land on Cole's Cr. b. by Hannah Lum, David Odam and Mrs. Sarah Truly. Natchez, 16 June 1784. // William Vousdan, Dep. Surv. certifies that at the request of Mr. Wm. Ferguson and Mr. Waterman Crane, that he laid and surveyed in name of Ferguson 325 acres, being the moiety of 625 acres gr. to Thomas Harman and sold by His Majesty as part of John Blommart's property in 1782. Dec. 2, 1785. [No file.]

p.525. Claim No.296. (Reg. 21 Feb. 1804.) Sp. grant to Samuel Davis 300 arpens in Natchez Dist., on Cole's Cr., 20 miles from the Fort, b. by James Cole, John Stampley and vacant lands. N. O. 24 Dec. 1797. [No file.]

p.527. Claim No.299. (Reg. 21 Feb. 1804.) Petition of Chas. Simmons to Sp. Government, 25 July, 1792, for my family of 8 persons land on Cole's Cr. adj. Curtis. // Order of survey, same date, by Gayoso. // Confirmed by Carondelet at N. O. 2 March 1793. [No file.]

p.527. Claim No.300. (Reg. 21 Feb. 1804.) Sp. grant to Alexander Boyd, 200 acres in Natchez Dist., on a br. of Big Black River, on Bayou Bogasha. N. O. 20 Oct. 1793. // Alexander Boyd transfers his title to Jacob Stampley, of this Govt., for $55, 25 Sept. 1797. [No file.]

p.531. Claim No.301. (Reg. 21 Feb. 1804.) Sp. grant to Jacob Stampley, 250 acres in Natchez Dist., 20 miles east of Fort. N. O., March 1795. File: Claimant, Jacob Stampley. Wit: Thos. M. Green, 22 May 1805. Certf. A231 22 May 1805. For land in Jefferson Co. on waters of Cole's Cr.

p.531. Claim No.302. Deed. 9 May 1799. John Adams to Thomas Rule, both of Adams Co., Miss. Ter. 200 acres on St. Catherine's Cr., b. on all sides by land gr. to Mark Iler [Isler], near a place called the half-way hill, surveyed to sd John Adams by virtue of a warrant to Richard Adams in 1787, by certf. by Wm. Vousdan, Surv., warrants title against himself and against his father and mother, Richard and Elenor Adams. Signed. Wit: John Girault, Joshua Howard, Leonard D. Shaw. Prov. by Shaw 6 Nov. 1800 before Wm. Kenner, J. P. // p.532. Deed. 5 Jany. 1802. Thomas Rule, of Adams Co., Miss. Ter., and wife, Elizabeth, for $100, to William Adams, quit claim all title in 200 acres from John Adams 9 May 1799. Both sign with mark. Wit: Wm. Cooper, Alexander Chambers. File: Claimant: William Adams. Filed 21 Feb. 1804. Wit: William Atchinson, 27 Nov. 1804. Certf. B25, 6 March 1807. Above tract on waters of St. Cath. about 5 miles south of City of Natchez, surveyed by virtue of a warrant issued to Richard Adams for 800 arpens but for want of room was divided into three unequal parts, this tract being one part thereof and was surveyed 17 Jany. 1788 and was improved and occupied ever since 1789. Wm. Atchinson, dep. surveyor to the late Wm. Vousdan, Esq. 7 Jany. 1801.

p.533. Claim No.303. Sp. grant to Jacob Harman, 500 arpents in Natchez Dist. on west side of Wells Cr. 20 miles west of Fort, b. by Chas. Carter and vacant lands. 24 Dec. 1797. File: Claimant Jacob Harman. Reg. 21 Feb. 1804. Rejected 10 June 1807.

p.535. Claim No.304. Sp. grant to John Stampley 200 acres in Natchez Dist., on a br. of Cole's Cr. 18 miles NE of Fort, b. by James Cole and vacant lands. N. O. 20 June 1790. File: Claimant John Stampley. Reg. 21 Feb. 1804. Wit: John Girault, 5 Nov. 1804. Certf. A141 issued to claimant who was an actual settler of the Territory 27 Oct. 1795.

p.537. Claim No.305. I certify that by authority of the Sp. government, I surveyed a tract of land for Solomon Cole, 200 acres on waters of Cole's Cr. and that, to my knowledge Solomon Cole to obtain a patent for same which was lost from the office when Gov. Gayoso had command of the district. (signed) William Thomas. 19 Dec. 1803. File: Claimant, Solomon Cole. Reg. 21 Feb. 1804. Wit: Wm. Thomas, 29 Oct. 1804. Certf. A756 issued 10 Mch. 1806. // May 12, 1804. Wit: Richard King.

p.537. Claim No.307. Sp. grant to Tobias Brashears, 700 acres in the Natchez Dist. on Big Black River, 6 miles from its mouth and 60 miles from Natchez. N. O. 20 March 1795. File: Claimant Tobias Brashears. Reg. 21 Feb. 1804. Wit: Bennet Truly, 6 March 1805. Certf. A142 issued to claimant.

p.539. Claim No.308. Sp. grant Reuben Proctor, 200 arps. in Natchez Dist. on South Fork of Bayou Pierre, 45 miles north of the Fort, b. by John Gibson and vacant lands. N. O. 24 Oct. 1794. File: Claimant: Tobias Brashears. Reg. 21 Feb. 1804. Wit: Catua Wallace, 5 Aug. 1805. Certf. A638 issued to cl. 26 Sept. 1805.

p.541. Claim No.310. Sp. grant to Gideon Gibson, 165 acres in Natchez Dist., on St. Catherine's Cr., 7 miles east of Fort, b. by Joe Harrison and William West. N. O. 10 March 1789. File: Claimant, Joseph Harrison. Reg. 22 Feb. 1804. Wit: John Bullen, Certf. A349 issued 20 June 1805. Gibson transferred to Joe Harrison.

p.542. Claim No.309. I certify that I have surveyed for and in the name of Mr. Joe Harrison 328 acres 5 miles NE of Fort of Natchez. (signed) Wm. Vousdan, Dep. Surv. 13 Nov. 1786. Plat show land adj. Gideon Gibson, Abraham Norton, Alexander Henderson and Dr. McCabe. File. Claimant Joe Harrison. Reg. 22 Feb. 1804. Wit: John Bullen, 2 May 1804. Certf. B-31 issued 10 June 1806. Land on St. Catherine's Cr.

p.542. Claim No.313. Sp. grant to Andrew Hare, 1000 arpens in the Natchez Dist., 14 miles south of the Fort, 3 miles from Miss. River, b. on all sides by Francisco Poussett and vacant lands. N. O. 8 Aug. 1789. // p.544. Power of atty. George Hunter of Philadelphia, Pa., druggist, guardian of John Hare, a minor son and heir of Andrew Hare, decd., appoints Samuel Postlewaite of Town of Natchez, merchant, lawful atty. to lease and to farm let the lands of sd Andrew Hare, decd., in Miss. Territory upon improvement, leases or otherwise as to him shall appear most conducive to the interest of said infant heir for any term not exceeding six years, etc. 6 Nov. 1802. (signed) George Hunter. Personally appeared before me, George Hunter, who ack. the above power of atty. 6 Nov. 1802. Walker Baylor, J. P. Fayette Co. // Fayette Co., St. of Kentucky, as clerk of county afsd I do certify that Walker Baylor, Gent. is J. P. of the Co. and qualified, etc. Nov. 10, 1802. (signed) Levi Todd, C.F.C. // State of Ky., Fayette Co., I, Thos. Lewis, pres. Justice for sd Co. of the Court of Quarter Sessions, do certify that the above attestation of Levi Todd, Clerk of Court, is in due form. 10 Nov. 1802. Thomas Lewis. // Fayette Co. Ky. At a court held for Co. afsd on 12 Oct. 1802, on motion of George Hunter, he is appointed guardian of John Hare, infant orphan of Andrew Hare, deceased; bond for £4000, Security, Frederick Ridgely and Peter January, Sen. In testimony I, Levi Todd, clerk of sd County set my hand, etc. Nov. 16, 1802. Signed. File: Claimant, heir of Andrew Hare. Reg. 23 Feb. 1804. Certf. A717 issued 13 Jany. 1806. Claimant John Hollingsworth Hare, heir and legal representative of Andrew Hare, decd., by Samuel Postlewaite, attorney of George Hunter, guardian of said John, 1000 acres on Bayou Sara. Signed by Postlewaite.

p.545. Claim No.315. Bargain and sale. 24 Oct. 1797. James Montgomery and Tomsey Montgomery, formerly Tomsey Lord, both of the district of Bayou Pierre in the Government of Natchez; for $130 paid, to Robert Ashley all claim to 500 acres whereon we now live, adj. sd Ashley. (signed) James Montgomery, Tomsey (x) Montgomery. Wit: Thos. Ashley. // Robert Ashley, for $150 paid, assigns all my right and claim to the within mentioned land to William Brocus. 25 Oct. 1798. Wit: Thomas Thompson, Walter Hunt, William Brocus, Jr. // William Brocus, Jr. for $500 paid by Thomas Crabbe all right to above land. 18 Feb. 1804. Signed. Wit: James McCobb. File. Claimant Thomas Crabbe. Reg. 24 Feb. 1804. Wit: William Miller, Simeon Holladay, Thomas White. Certf. B.61 issued to claimant by right of occupancy. 8 Sept. 1806. (See No.1359.) Note: The above described 500 acres in Claiborne Co. on the north side of the South or Little Fork of Bayou Pierre, now occupied by Thos. Crabbe, b. by lands of Mr. Samuel Bridgers, Archibald Douglass and Nathaniel Holly. Jan. 23, 1803. (signed) Daniel Burnet.

p.547. Claim No.316. Sp. grant to George Killian, 400 arpents in Natchez Dist. on waters of St. Catherine's Cr. 7 miles from Fort Panmure, b. on north by Charles Adams, west Richard Harris, other sides vacant. N. O. 15 Mch. 1789. Plat No.104. File. Claimant, George Killian. Reg. 24 Feb. 1804. Wit: Christian Harman, 12 June 1804. Certf. A297 issued 10 June 1805.

p.548. Claim No.317. British grant to Sarah Holmes for 200 acres in Natchez Dist. NE of Natchez, on Middle Cr., b. by William Ratcliffe. Pensacola, 21 Sept. 1772, by Peter Chester. File: Claimant, Sarah Holmes. Reg. 24 Feb. 1804. Wit: Joshua Howard, 26 May 1804. Certf. A-4, issued Feb. 27, 1805.

p.553. Claim No.318. Bargain and Sale. John Hamilton, of Claiborne Co., Miss. Territory, sells to Benjamin Beard, of sd co. all title, etc. to a certain tract of land with all improvement thereon, on Big Black River between land known as the block house* land and the land claimed by John Calhoon, in county aforesaid, for which I have received $9. 28 Jany. 1804. John (x) Hamilton. Done before me, James Stanfield, Esq. Receipt of $9, the consideration above mentioned. John (X) Hamilton. Jany. 28, 1804. Wit: James Stanfield. File: Claimant, Benj. Beard. Reg. 24 Feb. 1804. Rejected for want of evidence, Dec. 30, 1806. // Claiborne Co., Miss. Ter., Claim of Benjamin Beard, the right of preference in becoming purchaser from the U. S. of 163 acres in sd Co. on Big Black River, as per within plat, by virtue of having settled on and cultivated by John Hamilton who sold to claimant, 3 Mch. 1803. 24 Feb. 1804. Signed. Note: "Sold to Riley who sold to claimant" was scratched out.

*In file to claim No.409, according to testimony of Anthony Glass, a witness, there was a public Block House on plantation of James Rapalje, brother of Isaac Rapalje, both of whom lived on Big Black River.

p.554. Claim No.326. Sp. grant to Reuben Gibson, 200 acres, on St. Catherine's Cr., 3 miles east of Fort Panmure, b. by Dr. Flower, Mr. Horton and Alexander Henderson. N. O. 4 March 1789. File: Claimant Reuben Gibson. Reg. 24 Feb. 1804. Wit: Thomas Foster, 3 May, 1804. Certf. A-143 issued to claimant.

p.555. Claim No.327. Sp. grant to Henry Richardson, 400 acres in Natchez Dist., bet. Second and Sandy Creeks, 15 miles southeast of Fort, b. by lands of Wm. Reed and Cliff lands, others vacant. N. O. 10 Feb. 1789. // p.557. Exchange of land, 29 Nov. 1794, before Don Manuel Gayoso de Lemos, by Henry Richardson and Joshua Howard. Sd. Richardson to deliver to sd Howard 400 acres on Second Creek, for which he receives a plantation in the district of Homochitto, both plantations as represented in plats and grants which are now reciprocally exchanged. Both sign. // File: Claimant, Joshua Howard. Reg. 24 Feb. 1804. Wit: Isaac Alexander, 12 Apr. 1804. Certf. A144 issued to claimant.

p.558. Claim No.328. Deed. 11 June 1803. Dr. Samuel Flower to Reuben Gibson, of Adams Co., Miss. Ter., for $20, paid in hand, 31 acres on St. Catherine's Cr. adj. Reuben Gibson, Thomas Foster and John Henderson, part of 95 acres gr. by Spain to Samuel Flowers, 5 Apr. 1789. Wit: John Henderson, John B. Willis. Ack. by Dr. Sam'l. Flower before John Henderson, J. P. at Natchez, 23 June 1803. File. Claimant, Reuben Gibson. Reg. 24 Feb. 1804. Wit: Thomas Foster. Certf. A326 issued 17 June 1805. (Also see No.100.)

p.559. Claim No.329. Sp. grant to John Savage, 337 acres in Dist. of Natchez on Fairchild's Cr. 11 miles east from Fort, b. by George Fitzgerald, John Bisland and John and Gabriel Griffin. N. O. 20 Nov. 1793. // p.561. Deed. 28 Feb. 1799. John Savage, of Miss. Ter. to David Ferguson, merchant, of same, for $400 paid, the above tract. Wit: P. Connelly, John Sullivan. // p.563. Deed. 20 June 1800. David Ferguson and Jean, his wife, of the Town of Natchez, Miss. Ter., to Charles McKiernan above tract on Fairchild's Cr. gr. to John Savage by Spain in 1793. David and Jane Ferguson both sign. Wit: P. B. Bruin, T. Hutchins. Ack. before P. B. Bruin, 12 Feb. 1801, one of Judges of Miss. Ter. Receipt of $400 same day as deed. File. Claimant, Charles McKiernan. Reg. 24 Feb. 1804. Wit: John Bolls, 26 July 1804. Certf. A244 issued 24 May 1805. Proved in John Savage.

p.565. Claim No.330. Sp. grant to Richard Harrison, 555 acres in Natchez Dist. 2 miles above Cole's Cr. and 3 miles below Grand Gulf, on a large lake, 25 miles north of Fort Panmure, b. by Alexander McIntosh and vacant lands. N. O. 24 Mch. 1790. // p.566. Deed. 22 Feb. 1790. Richard Harrison to John O'Connor 500 acres as above grant, b. on west by Nathaniel Tomlinson, north by high lands, S. and E. by Miss. River, for $1300 payable in 3 years. Both sign. // p.568. 15 April 1795. John O'Connor to Charles McKiernan 555 arpents as per plan and papers attached, for $346, which tract I purchased of Mr. Richard Harrison, this sum being the price to which same was appraised by appraisers named in the agreement made with said McKiernan in N. O. and which sum I have received. Both sign. File: Claimant, Charles McKiernan. Reg. 24 Feb. 1804. Wit: John Girault, 26 July 1804. Certf. A145 issued to claimant. Translation of the survey by Trudeau, same having been made during the British government, the property of Philip Barbour, the uncle of Richard Harrison.

p.569. Claim No.331. Sp. grant to John Martin, 500 acres in the Natchez District, on Cole's Cr. 18 miles east of the Fort, b. by Daniel Perry and vacant lands. N. O. 25 Feb. 1788. File: Claimant John Martin. Reg. 24 Feb. 1804. Wit: Michael Guice. Certf. A146.

p.571. Claim No.332. Andrew Hare to Archibald Rea. Appeared before Daniel Hickey, J. P. of the district of Baton Rouge, Mr. Andrew Hare, a resident of the Province of Kentucky in North America, who makes a gift deed to Archibald Rea, of the district of Bayou Sara for his sons and heirs in the name of sd Hare 200 arpens, part of 1000 arpens granted to sd Hare by the Gov. Genl. of said Provinces in the district of Bayou Sara, these 200 acres b. by Francis Poussett, John Wall and sd Hare, which donation I make sd Rea, his sons and heirs in consideration of the work he did on said land, clearing, fences, cabins and the care of the highway of said 1000 acres. Baton Rouge, 27 April 1797. Wit: Francis Poussett, Pedro Andrien, Ramon de Cordova. Before Daniel Hickey, Joseph Vahamonde. // Plat of above. // Certificate of survey by Wm. Atchinson, dated 5 July 1796. // p.573. Deed. 8 Jany. 1799. Archibald Ray and wife, Martha, of Natchez District, Miss. Ter. to William Fenner, for $450 paid, 200 acres on Bayou Sara (as above). (signed) Archibald Rea. Martha (X) Rea. Wit: Wm. Ogden, David Jones, Daniel Ogden. Prov. by Daniel Ogden and David Jones before John Collins, J. P. 20 Nov. 1799, Adams Co. // p.575. 12 May 1804. Wm. Fanner to Martha Rea and her dau. Mary, for $700, 200 acres, b. by John Wall, Andrew Hare and Richard Butler and Daniel Ogden. Wm. Fanner and Maser Fanner both sign with a mark. Wit: Wm. Brocus Sr., Joshua Baker, Wm. Newgant. Prov. by Newgent, at Wilkinsburgh, 24 Jany. 1803. // File: Claimants, Martha and Mary Ray. Reg. 24 Feb. 1804. Wit: Patrick Foley, 20 June 1804. Certf. A718 to claimants, 13 Jany. 1806. Claim by Archibald Rea, asking for Martha and Mary Rea.

p.577. Claim No.333. Sp. grant to Jacob Cable, 400 acres in Natchez District, on the waters of Cole's Cr. 25 miles NE. from Fort Panmure, b. by Manuel Texada and Estevan de Alba. N. O. March 10, 1789. File: Claimant, Jacob Cabal. Reg. 24 Feb. 1804. Wit: Francis Nailor, 20 Nov. 1804. Certf. A147 issued to claimant.

p.578. Claim No.334. Sp. grant to David Greenleaf, 500 acres in Dist. of Natchez, on a br. of Cole's Cr., 18 miles NE. of Fort Panmure, b. by William Ferguson, Israel Coleman, Sarah Truly, Edward Paterson. // p.580. Deed. June __, 1802. David Greenleaf, of Adams Co., Miss. Ter., to John Jones of Jefferson Co. afsd Ter., for $750, 500 acres, as above. Signed by David Greenleaf and Phoebe Greenleaf. Wit: Thos. Gibson, John Martin. Ack. in Ct. 12 Nov. 1802. Edwd. Turner. File: John Jones claimant. Reg. 24 Feb. 1804. Wit: Israel Coleman, Alexander Calender, John Bolls, Aug. 12, 1805. Certf. A483, Aug. 12, 1805.

BOOK B

p.1. Claim No.31. (Reg. 19 Dec. 1803.) Br. grant to Elihu Hall Bay, 1100 acres 24 miles northeast of Fort Natchez, 3 miles above the land surveyed for Amos Ogden on north side of Homochitto Creek, b. on west by Thos. Hutchins, south sd creek, others vacant. Pensacola, 27 Sept. 1773. [No file.]

p.4. Claim No.32. (Reg. 19 Dec. 1803.) Br. grant to William Garnier, Esq. 5000 acres, in West Florida, north side of Houma Chito b. on southeast by Messrs. Beard, Wilton, Mongtomery, John Arnot. 28 May 1779. // Warrant certified by Elias Durnford, Sur. Gen. 22 May 1779. // Indenture, (lease and release), 21 March 1783, Wm. Garnier, Esq., Post Capt. in His Majesty's Royal Navy, now residing in parish of Saint Mary le Bon, County of Middlesex, to Andrew Peebles, late of Pensacola, West Fla., now of parish of St. George, Hanover Square, Co. of Middlesex, the above tract, for Ł90 money of Gr. Britain. Signed. Wit: E. R. Wegg, late Atty. Genl. of West Fla., John Stokes. (p.14.) Miss. Territory. Col. Anthony Hutchins personally appeared before me, Samuel Brooks, Esq., 14 Dec. 1803, and identified the writing of E. R. Wegg. Also knew John Stokes and acquainted with his handwriting. (signed) A. Hutchins, Samuel Brooks, J. P. // 20 Dec. 1800, Eleanor Peebles, wid. and executrix of James Peebles, decd., sells to Elihu Hall Bay, above tract, b. on south by land gr. Luke Home, Thos. Hutchins, Elihu Hall Bay, on SE by Messrs. Beard, Wilton, Montgomery and John Arnot, gr. to Wm. Garnier and sold to Andrew Peebles, who soon died without issue and the land desc. to his brother, James Peebles, who d. 15 Dec. 1796, by will authorizing his wife to sell any part of his land for the benefit of herself and children, for $500, the above 5000 acres. (signed) Eleanor Peebles, exr. of James Peebles. Wit: Noah Jones, Joseph Gladding. Proved by Noah Jones before Judge Wm. Johnson, one of the Associate Justices of S. C. // State of S. C. Certificate of Daniel Huger, Secy. of State of S. C. for the Gov. as to the status of Judge Johnson. Aug. 18, 1803. [No file.]

p.17. Claims Nos.33, 34, 35. (Reg. 19 Dec. 1803.) Br. grant of 1000 acres to William Grant, Lt. in our Navy, tract on Miss. River, 2 leagues above Three Islands and above Grand Gulf on the sd River, b. on north by 1000 acres of Wm. Grant, other sides the River and vacant lands, in Prov. of West Fla. // William Grant, Master and Commander of His Majesty's Armed Schooner, the St. John, now riding at harbor of Pensacola. Whereas I am entitled to 3000 acres and have lately applied for a grant of same and have a warrant for the land near Walnut Hills; in consideration for the payment of fees for surveying, etc., and for $428 (Ł100 in money of Gr. Britain) to me actually paid by John Lorimer, Alexander Macullagh and Elihu Hall Bay, all of Pensacola, I assign to them the above grant. 13 Sept. 1775. Wit: Eleazer Davis, H. Beaumont. // Receipt for Ł100 by Wm. Grant same date. // p.27. Indenture. 9 May 1776. Wm. Grant, a Lt. in Navy, by Edmund Rush Wegg, Atty, of Pensacola, to Elihu Hall Bay, 1000 acres of above grant, north of Grand Gulf, above Three Islands, adjoining another grant of 1000 acres on the north to sd Wm. Grant. p.37. Claim No.34. Br. grant to William Grant, 1000 acres at Walnut Hills, 16 leagues above Grand Gulf, Prov. of West Fla. 6 May 1776. p.42. Indenture. 9 May 1776. Wm. Grant, by his attorneys, E. R. Wegg and James Amoss of Pensacola, to John Lorimer, 1000 acres, as above. Wit: Patrick Maxwell, Henry Beaumont. Signatures of attorneys and witnesses proved by John Black, formerly of Pensacola but now of City of Charleston, merchant, before Wm. Johnson, Jr. // Indenture. 10 May 1776. Wm. Grant to Alexander Macullagh, 1000 acres, north of Grand Gulf, [bounded on north and south by other grant of 1000 acres granted to sd Wm. Grant] by his attorneys, E. R. Wegg and James Amoss. // Agreement of division of the 3000 acres, which were granted to Wm. Grant in 3 separate tracts of 1000 acres each. John Lorimer to take the 1000 acres at Walnut Hills; Alexander Macullagh accepted the tract above the Three Islands, and Elihu Hall Bay took the next tract adjoining that of Macullagh on the south.

p.68. Claim No.38. Indenture. 18 Apr. 1774. Capt. Amos Ogden, late of the Province of New Jersey, Esq., to Macullagh and Elihu Hall Bay, of Pensacola, West Fla. Whereas the British Govt. patented to sd Ogden, 27 Oct. 1772, a tract of 25000 acres 21 miles SW. of old Natchez Fort, b. on Homachita Cr., one-fourth mile east of 1000 acres gr. Colin Graham, Esq., one mile from grant to Innis Hooper on Second Creek, other sides vacant. By indenture, 30 Sept. 1773, did grant sd Alexander Macullagh and Elihu Hall Bay 1500 acres, part of sd 25000, according to sd indenture, wherein Ogden promised to give another indenture to insure the proper fixed boundaries, for Ł75. (signed) Amos Ogden. Wit: Wm. Gordon, H. Beaumont. // p.77. Partition deed of 1575 acres by Elihu Hall Bay and Alexander

Macullagh, Esqs. 27 June 1774. Wit: H. Beaumont, James Murray. // p.84. Sale of land of Alexander Macullagh, then decd., 25 June 1799, by his nephew and heir, Alexander Macullagh, late of Ireland, but then of Charleston, S. C. to Elihu Hall Bay. Wit: James Donaldson, A. Henry. [No file.]

p.85. Claim No.149. (Reg. 19 Jany. 1804.) Br. grant to Margaret Stampley* on Boyd's Creek, 30 miles N.E. from Natchez, b. by sd Creek and vacant land. Pensacola, 1 Sept. 1777. By Peter Chester. // p.89. Henry Stampley sells above to Thos. M. Green, Oct. 15, 1785. (signed) Henry Stampley, Margaret (X) Stampley. [No file.] *Note: This land entered in name of Margaret Baird and so designated in plats. W. E. Bk.A 4, 106.

pp.90-1. Blank.

p.92. Claim No.273. Oct. 18, 1803. Benj. Carel, of Wilkinson Co., Miss. Ter., for $1300 paid, to John Nugent, of same, land on Buffalo Cr. on Conner's line. Benja. (X) Carel. Test: Joseph Dove. [No file.]

p.92. Claim No.1008. Ebenezer Fulsom to Moses Foster my right to plantation and house on Homochitto 1 mile below Foster's Cr., also furniture. Signs with a mark. Wit: James (X) Hays, Benjamin (X) Fletcher. [n.d.] // John Foster assigns above rights to John West, May 4, 1795. // John West assigns same to Philip Six, Dec. 28, 1800. John (X) West. Wit: Wm. Calvit. File: Philip Siks claimant. Reg. 23 March 1804. Wit: James Hays, 10 Sept. 1804. Certf. B203 issued Feb. 19, 1807. Philip Siks of Miss. Territory, claims a donation right to above described 640 acres in Adams Co., by a settlement made and continued by Ebenezer Fulsom in 1789, who was, at that time, the head of a family, March 22, 1804. Signed.

p.93. Claim No.48. (Reg. Dec. 21, 1803.) John Watson to Reuben White improvement on Bayou Pierre, 3 miles from Storey's Mill, for $120. 2 Nov. 1801. [No file.]

p.93. Claim No.60. (Reg. Jany. 26, 1804.) 10 Jany. 1802. David Mulkey to Simon Hook 100 acres with improvement adj. John Girault. Signed. Wit: Policarpio Regillo, Robert Moore.

p.94. Claim No. 87. (Reg. 3 Dec. 1803.) 29 Sept. 1803. Benj. Kitchens of Adams Co., Miss. Ter., for divers good causes to Wm. Montgomery, of same, 824 acres in Jefferson Co., Miss. Ter. b. by Caleb Potter, the NE end of Lake Ann, and land of Kitchens. Wit: Ly Harding, Samuel Sidney Mahon. [No file.]

p.95. Claim No.125. (Reg. 16 Jany. 1804.) Thomas Walker, of Claiborne County, Miss. Ter., to Seth Castin, of same, all right of preemption which I am entitled to by law to land where I now live, b. by Fishing Lake, for $78, paid. Dec. 7, 1801. Sealed, signed and delivered 24 Aug. 1803. Wit: Joseph Ferguson, Shelley Booth. [No file.]

p.95. Claim No.132. Reuben Ray to John Armstrong an improvement on a piece of land on waters of Big Black, on a small cr. called Big Sandy, adj. lands improved by Davenport Wiseman, in Claiborne County, for $60 paid. 4 April 1803. Reuben (X) Ray. Wit: Lewellen Price.

p.96. Claim No.165. (Reg. Jany. 24, 1804.) Picron [Pickering] Co. Miss. Ter. Samuel Hackler to William McDonald, tract surveyed to me by William Thomas, 20 July 1797, for $125 paid. Samuel (X) Hackler. Wit: David Davis. [No file.]

p.97. Claim No.171. (Reg. 26 Jany. 1804.) Thos. Vause to Eli Crockett an improvement on Vince's Fork of the Little Bayopier [Bayou Pierre] made by John Pollard, January 1797, for which I bind myself in the penalty of $500, who is to pay me $150 on or before 8 June next, to be paid in 100 pounds of powder and 31 gallons of whisky and $10 cash, to be delivered at Mrs. McCaib's. If sd Crockett fail in payment on the day appointed, this is null and void. 6 May 1803. (signed) Thos. Vause. Wit: Samuel Derosett, Benj. Cooper. Receipt of all of the above payment by Eli Crockett, June 7, 1803. Thos. Vause. Wit: Benj. Cooper. [No file.] 7 June 1803. Eli Crockett assigns right and title above to Samuel Montgomery. Wit: Jesse Griffin. Signed by Eli Crockett. // p.97. Miss. Ter. Jefferson Co. John Pollard came before me, Wm. Rowe, J. P., and made oath that he improved a certain tract on Little Fork of Bayou Pierre, as above, joining land improved by Enoch Birdwell, which land he improved Jany. 1st, 1797 and inhabited and cultivated the same in March. Which land he sold to Thos. Vause with all improvements. Signed. Sworn before me, 28 May 1803. Wm. Row, J. P. [No file.]

p.98. Claim No.173. (Reg. 27 Jany. 1804.) Isaac Erwin to Zadock Barrow, plantation on public road from Natchez to the upper settlement of the Homochitto, 20 miles from Fort, which I warrant, etc. (signed) Isaac Erwin. Wit: Joseph Erwin, John Beckham. // 12 Dec. 1801, Zadock Barrow assigns above to John Chambers. Signed. Wit: Jesse Briant, William Riley. [No file.]

pp.98-9. Claim No.175. (Reg. 26 Jany. 1804.) Robert Ashley, of Claiborne Co., Miss. Ter., agent and attorney of brother, Thomas Ashley, of the Island of Cumberland in the Atlantic Ocean, for $200 paid, to John Burns of Jefferson County, land on which sd Burns now lives. 26 Jany. 1802. Wit: Rd. Claiborne, Edward Turner. [No file.]

p.99. Claim No.182. (Reg. 30 Jany. 1804.) 23 Oct. 1802. Adam Lanehart, of Wilkinson Co., Miss. Ter. to Charles Hamilton, all my right to a piece of land on a small branch of Cole's Cr. which was settled by Mr. James Hayes in 1785 and sold by him to Mr. Chas. King and sold by sd King to Adam Lanehart in 1787. A part of sd land had been in cultivation ever since, b. by Mr. Abram Ellis, Adam Bingaman, Isaac Newman and Jesse Hamilton. Adam (X) Lanehart. Wit: Elias Fisher. [No file.]

p.100. Deed. (Filed 20 Feb. 1804.) 12 Aug. 1802. Francis Odum and Abner Pipes, exors of last will of David Odum, decd., to Drury Breazeale, of Jefferson Co., Miss. Ter. for $30 paid, 3 acres in Jefferson Co. on Platner's fork. Frances (X) Odum, Abner Pipes. Wit: Asahel O'Neal, Leonard Collard. Prov. by O'Neal 12 Nov. 1802. Edwd. Turner, C. J. C. C. [Apparently a misplaced record.]

p.101. Claim No.202. (Reg. 4 Feb. 1804.) 30 Sept. 1803. Thos. Vause of Claiborne Co., Miss. Ter., for $1000 to me paid, to Thomas Ingles of same, a certain improvement which Enoch Bodwell made where I now live and where Benjamin Cooper now lives in sd county on waters of Bayou Pierre. Thos. Vause. Wit: Jesse Griffin, Ann (X) Griffin. [No file.]

p.102. Claim No.133. (Reg. 17 Jany. 1804.) Elizabeth McKim to Capt. Christopher Bingaman, my improvement on Morgan's Fork of the Homochitto, near Hezekiah Williams, for three cows and calves. 20 Dec. 1796. She signed with a mark. Wit: William Cooper. // I endorse my right of this bill of sale to Samuel Ratcliffe, 16 Oct. 1802. (signed) C. Bingaman. Wit: Sarah Pipkin. [No file.]

pp.102-3. Claim No.314. (Reg. 24 Feb. 1804.) Oct. 5, 1802. Constant and Alexander Macgrew, of Miss. Ter., Adams Co., to William Kennison, of same, our right and claim to the land where we now live on east side of Morgan's creek settled under an act of the State of Georgia. [no consideration given.] Wit: Saml. Boyd, Thos. Ford. File: William Kennison, claimant. Wit: Samuel Boyd, 27 Aug. 1804. Certf. B28 Sept. 4, 1806. Kennison claims the right to become the purchaser of 322 acres in Adams Co. by virtue of the said tract having been inhabited and cultivated in Dec. 1801 by Constant and Alexander Macgrew. Petitioner has inhabited and cultivated sd land since his purchase from the above in 1802. William (X) Kennison. Certificate of survey of sd tract by John Dinsmore.

p.103. Claim No.203. 12 Feb. 1801, James Cole, of Cole's Cr., Pickering Co. to James Stansfield, of Township of Big Black, afsd Co. all right and claim to a tract in sd Township bet. lands of Capt. Tobias Brashear and the late Stephen Cole, deceased, James Stansfield to pay all expenses from surveying, obtaining warrant, deed or otherwise, by clearing sd tract at Land Office. Both are bound for penal sum of $1000 each. Both sign. Wit: William (X) Mathews, Mark Cole. // p.104. John Cole, of Cole's Cr., Jefferson Co., for $10 to him paid, to James Stansfield, of Claiborne Co., quit claim to above tract. Signed. Wit: Hezekiah Harman, Elisha Flower. [No file.]

p.104. Claim No.319. Jany. 4, 1804. James Beard, of Claiborne Co., Miss. Ter., to Thos. Beard, of same, my improvement on Gun's Bayou bet. Sam'l. Beard and Wm. Miller, made 15 Feb. 1803. [No consid. given.] Wit: Abel Eastman. // File. Claimant, Thos. Beard, 24 Feb. 1804. Rejected for want of evidence. Claim to become purchaser of 320 acres on Gun's Bayou, a br. of Big Black. Signed.

p.104. Claim No.320. Abraham Guice, of Adams Co., to Thos. Beard, of Claiborne Co. my claim to improvement on Gun's Bayou, for $10, on condition that Abel Eastman hath not made sale of same heretofore. 16 Feb. 1803. // 22 Aug. 1803. Thos. Beard assigns right to above to Wm. Miller, for value recd. Signed. // File. Claimant, Wm. Miller, 24 Feb. 1804. Wit: John Hamilton, 4 Sept. 1804. Certif. D-89, Oct. 29, 1806. Claim south of Thomas Beard's claim, north of Jacob Phillip. Preemption claim. 320 acres.

p.105. Claim No.245. I do hereby certify that I settled and improved the tract whereon John Hopper now lives, in 1796, and that I have sold sd improvement with all privileges to John Hopper, for $125, paid. (signed) Buckner Pittman. 28 May 1801. Wit: Alexr. Montgomery, Prosper King. // John Hopper to Alexander Montgomery, my right and title to above improvement that I now live on and also the improvement I made adjoining this on the road bet. here and Mr. Crane's, for $250. May 28, 1801. (signed) John Hopper. Wit: Prosper King. Reg. 16 Feb. 1804. [No file.]

p.106. Claim No.256. 26 July 1803. James Swain to Jesse Lea, both of Wilkinson Co., Miss. Ter. for $50 paid, tract on Beaver Cr., a br. of River Amite, in sd Co. (signed) James Swain. Wit: McCahger [Micajah] McCulland. [No file.] Reg. 20 Feb. 1804.

p.106. Claim No.258. 21 Mch. 1801. James Haselton, to Jesse Lee, for $30 paid, tract of 300 acres on Beaver Cr. a br. of Amite River, with improvement I made thereon bet. improvements of Leonard Hornsby and James Swain. James (X) Haselton. Wit: John Dinsmore, Isaac Foster. [No file.] Reg. 20 Feb. 1804.

p.107. Claim No.265. Dist. of Natchez, 9 Aug. 1798. Earl Marble, for $100 paid, to William Cole, all my right, etc. to improvement whereon I now dwell, 250 acres b. by John Bowls, John Searcy, Jacob Stampley and Benj. Curtis. (signed) Earle Marble. Wit: Felix Hughes. // Recd. of Wm. Newman $110 for the within plantation, 28 Nov. 1799. (signed) William Cole. Wit: Wm. (X) Mathews. // For $500 paid, I have sold the within premises to Bailey E. Chaney, 19 Dec. 1893. Wm. Newman. [No file.] Reg. 20 Feb. 1804.

p.108. Claim No.297. 4 July 1803. David Odem to Baley E. Chaney, of Jefferson Co., Miss. Ter., for $255, improvement and tract on waters of Cole's Cr., adj. gr. to John Cole, and land of Richard Ellis, which land I settled prior to Oct. 1795. David (X) Odem. Wit: P. Alston, Hoskenson. // For $255, paid, I assign right, etc. to within bill of sale to Prosper King. Signed. 8 July 1803. Wit: Wm. Cole, Alexander Montgomery. [No file.] Reg. 21 Feb. 1804.

p.109. Claim No.225. Spanish gr. to William Tabor, 300 arpens on a br. of Bayou Pierre, 45 mi. NE Fort Panmure, b. by vacant lands. N. O. 10 Apr. 1795. [See Bk.A-426 for transfer to Arrington.] // p.111. 15 Sept. 1800. Thos. Arrington, of Bayou Pierre, Pickering Co., Miss. Ter. and Nannet, his wife, to William Neely, of same, for $600 in hand paid, 300 acres gr. Wm. Tabor, as above, on Tabor's Fork of Bayou Pierre. Signed by both. Wit: Vachel Dillingham, Samuel Gholson. Bayou Pierre, 15 Sep. 1800. Ack. by above the receipt of full sum of $600. Signed. Wit: G. W. Humphreys. // 22 Jany. 1801, before George Wilson Humphreys, one of the Justices of Courts of Quarter Sessions and Common Pleas, for Pickering Co., appeared Thos. and Nannet Harrington who ack. the foregoing deed. (signed) G. W. Humphreys. [No file.] Reg. 7 Feb. 1804.

p.113. Claim No.374. Benj. Butler, of Claiborne Co., for $200 to me paid, to Joseph Aller, one-half of a 300-acre tract of vacant land I have returned to the office of the Clerk of County Court at Warinsville [Warrensville] in my own name on waters of Big Black River. Aller is to have equal division beg. at the creek and running through the center of sd place, reserving to myself the half on which I have begun to improve already. Signed. Wit: John Scarlett. [n.d.] // File. Claimant, George Marshall, 28 Feb. 1804. Wit: Wm. Stephens. Surveyed for George Marshall 100 acres in Claiborne Co. beg. on John Calhoon's upper line. Joseph Aller claims the right of preference to purchase 100 acres. Signed Joseph Aller and George Marshall, the legal rep. of Joseph Aller. Certif. D-93, Oct. 30, 1806.

p.114. Claim No.688. British gr. to Jeremiah Germain, 300 acres on Second Cr., 10 SE. of Fort Natchez, b. by Michael Cradle, Wm. Alexander, Pensacola, 31 Aug. 1775. // p.118. Lease and release, 19 and 20 Nov. 1776. Jeremiah Germain, of Prov. of West Fla., to Oliver Pollock, of the River Miss. in said Province, for $300 (£70 Br. money) paid, the above tract of 300 acres. Signed. Wit: Wm. Henderson, John Henderson. // File. Claimant, Oliver Pollock, 17 Mch. 1804. Reported, 28 Apr. 1807. Miss. Ter., Adams Co. Oliver Pollock claims above 300 acres by virtue by grant and plat by British to Germain and Germain's transfer to the sd Pollock. // Surveyor's Office 11 May 1821. Fractional section No.36 in T6R1W and fractional Sec.27 in T6R2W, and covered by a Reported British claim in name of Oliver Pollock, reg. as No.688, which has been confirmed by an Act of Congress passed 15 July 1812. (signed) Nicholas Gray, Chief Clerk.

p.114. Claim No.375. 22 Nov. 1803. Samuel Marshall to Andrew Bracken improvement made by me January 1803, bet. George Marshall and Jesse Stephens, north of Big Black, which I defend against all claims except those of the United States. Signed. Wit: John Calhoon, W. Reed. // File. Claimant, Andrew Bracken, 28 Feb. 1804. Wit: George Marshall. Notation, Inquire of Major Hicks. D-278. Preemption claim of Andrew Bracken 378 acres by virtue of the tract having been inhabited and cultivated by Samuel B. Marshall on and before 3 Mch. 1804. Signed. Survey and plat by John Cook.

p.123. Claim No.598. British grant to James Hughes, a reduced Lt., all that land situated 4 1/2 miles from Fort of Natchez, b. by Daniel Ward, Wm. McPherson, Richard Carr, James Barbut, Cephas Kennard, John Row and John Jones. Pensacola, 26 Apr. 1779 by Peter Chester. // File. Claimant, James Hughes, 14 March 1804. Reported 28 Apr. 1807. James Hughes, of Montreal in the Province of Canada, by his son and agent, Daniel Hughes, now in the Territory, claims 1000 acres as in above grant. W. B. Shields, atty.

p.128. Claim No.599. British grant to James Hughes, a reduced Lt., 550 acres on the middle fork of Boyd's Cr. 24 mi. from Natchez, 12 mi. NE. from mouth of Boyd's Cr., b. by lands of Peter Walsh and vacant lands. Pensacola, 8 Jany. 1778. // File. Claimant, James Hughes, 14 Mch. 1804. Reported 28 Apr. 1807. James Hughes, of Montreal in the Province of Canada, by his son and agent, Daniel Hughes, now in this territory, claims 550 as in above grant. W. B. Shields, atty.

p.132. Claim No.1486. British grant to Alexander Ross, 1000 acres, 11 mi. NE. of Natchez, b. by Thomas Creek, John Vaughan and General Haldeman. Pensacola, 19 Nov. 1777. // File. Claimant, Alexander Ross, 29 Mch. 1804. Wit: John Ellis, 15 Oct. 1804. Certif. A-167 to claimant. Alexander Ross, a res. of Miss. Ter. on 27 Oct. 1795, claims 1000 acres by virtue of the above grant. Signed.

p.135. Claim No.1488. British grant to Alexander Ross, as a reduced staff officer, 2000 acres, 16 mi. NE of Natchez, b. by lands of Wm. Marshall and those of Hon. John Stewart, Esq. Pensacola, 19 Nov. 1777. // File. Claimant, Alexander Ross, 29 Mch. 1804. Wit: John Ellis, 15 Oct. 1804. Certif. A-168 to claimant. Claimed as above.

p.140. Claim No.1489. British gr. to John Stephenson, Esq., 1200 acres, on the middle fork of Boyd's Cr., 25 mi. from Natchez, 11 mi. south from mouth of sd Cr., bounded by lands of John McDougal and vacant lands. Pensacola, 28 Feb. 1778 by Peter Chester. // File. Claimant, John Stephenson 29 Mch. 1804. Reported, 28 Apr. 1807. Claim as in above grant. Elihu H. Bay for claimant.

p.145. Claim No.1490. British gr. to John Scott, 1000 acres, 18 mi. above Red River on part of Loftus Cliffs, adj. land surv. for Robt. Callendar, Miss. River and vacant lands. Pensacola, 24 July 1772. // File. Claimant, John Stephenson, 29 Mch. 1804. Reported. 28 Apr. 1807. John Stephenson claims 1000 acres, as described in above gr. to John Scott, executor of sd John Scott, in behalf of his heirs and devisees. John Stephenson, by Elihu H. Bay, atty.

p.148. Claim No.335. Spanish grant to James Jones, 400 arpens, on a br. of Cole's Creek, 20 mi. ENE. of Fort, b. by Wm. Bell and Dr. Flower and vacant lands. N. O. 20 June 1795, by Carondelet. // File. Claimant, James Jones, 24 Feb. 1804. Wit: Wm. Thomas, 18 Oct. 1804. Certif. A-81 issued to claimant. Claim as in above grant.

p.150. Claim No.336. Spanish grant to John Griffin, 600 acres in Dist. of Natchez, 20 mi. ENE from Fort, on a br. of Cole's Creek, b. by lands of His Majesty. Pensacola, 30 Sept. 1793, by Carondelet. // File. Claimant, John Griffin, 24 Feb. 1804. Wit: Wm. Thomas, 28 May 1804. Certif. A-82 to claimant. Plat shows Jacob Guice, Esq. with land on one side of sd tract. Miss. Ter. Adams Co. John Griffin claims 600 acres on south fork of Cole's Creek as in above grant. Signed.

p.152. Claim No.338. 12 March 1804. John Keith, for $100 paid, sells to Wm. Noland, of Wilkinson Co. all my preemption right on Thompson's Cr. in sd county, which I cultivated on 3 March 1803. Signs with a mark. Wit: Richard Graves, Moses Starnes. Proved by Starnes before the Board, 22 Mch. 1804. // File. Claimant, Wm. Noland, 22 Mch. 1804. Recorded and examined. Certif. D-250 to claimant, 24 Dec. 1807. Preemption claim by virtue of above assignment. Signed.

p.152. Claim No.340. Spanish gr. to Jeptha Higdon, 400 acres, 18 mi. NE. of Fort, b. lands of Frederick Calvet and those of His Majesty, a league below Petit Gulf. N. O. 20 Nov. 1793, by Carondelet. // File. Claimant, Jeptha Higdon, 25 Feb. 1804. Wit: Wm. Atchinson, 28 Nov. 1804. Certificate 83, issued to Benj. Belk, assignee. Miss. Ter. Jefferson Co., Jeptha Higdon claims 400 acres on the Miss. River in afsd county, by virtue of the above patent. Jeptha (X) Higdon.

p.154. Claim No.342. Petition of James Hyland to the Spanish Govt. for 300 acres on Big Black River, and decree for same by Gayoso. [n.d.] // James Hyland, Jr. petitions for land adjoining his father, James Hyland, 6 miles north of Big Black River. 4 Feb. 1797. // Gov. Gayoso issues decree for 300 acres, 6 mi. north of Big Black River, adj. lands of Mrs. Catherine Smith. Natchez, 4 Feb. 1797. Certif. by Wm. Dunbar. // File. Claimant, James Hyland, Jr., 25 Feb. 1804. Wit: James Barron, March 1, 1805. 200 acres to include his improvement. See No. 534. Certif. D-333 to claimant, Dec. 29, 1806. Claiborne Co., James Hyland, Jr. claims 600 acres in said county, by virtue of the order of survey, at which time he was 21 years of age and inhabited and cultivated the sd tract in 1800. Signed. Note: Mr. Stampley claims the same land under a Spanish order and survey. He was present when J. S. Bannon was examined. T. R. Note: The father of claimant requests that if this claim should not be good under an order of survey the board will grant him 200 acres as a preemption. Survey and plat of 600 acres to James Hyland by John Cook, bet. the Big Black and James Hyland Sr. The same tract of land that is at this time occupied by James Hyland, Jr. beginning at Joseph Pemberton's corner to the edge of the overflow land.

p.155. Claim No.343. Spanish gr. to Benjamin Curtis, 250 acres bet. St. Catherine's Cr. and Cole's Cr., 14 mi. NE. from Fort of Natchez, b. by Richard Bell and James Cole. N. O. Feb. 12, 1788. // p.156. Natchez, 31 Jany. 1797. Benj. Curtis to Daniel and David Douglass, for $400 paid, sells above tract. Signed. Wit: Estevan Minor, Benja. Burnet, before Gayoso. // 2 Feb. 1802. Daniel and Stephen Douglass to Alexander Montgomery, all of Adams Co., Miss. Ter., for $1350 paid, 250 acres, as described above. Both signed. Wit: Johathan Davis, Alexis Fulton. // File. Claimant, Alexander Montgomery, 25 Feb. 1804. Wit: Prosper King, 15 July 1805. Certif. A-506 to claimant. Claim as above.

p.159. Claim No.345. Natchez, 14 May 1795. Petition of Gabriel Griffin to Spanish Govt., desiring a habitation to employ seven negroes at permanent work for the subsistence of my wife and children, asks for a grant on the Big Black River, adj. Don Jacques Rapalje. // Order of survey for 400 arpens, 18 Feb. 1796. // Grant and plat to Alexander Montgomery, executor of Gabriel Griffin, decd., Natchez, 16 Apr. 1796. // File. Claimant, Alexander Montgomery, 25 Feb. 1804. Rejected 10 Apr. 1807. Grant to Gabriel Griffin and sold to Alexander Montgomery by executors of sd Griffin, decd. in 1797.

p.160. Claim No.346. Solomon Whitley petitions the Spanish Govt. for 400 arpens on Bayou Pierre, b. by John Boothe. Natchez, 12 Apr. 1790. // Order by Miro, N. O. 5 May 1790. Certif. and Plat by Wm. Dunbar, 25 Nov. 1797. // File. Claimant, Alexander Montgomery, 10 Mch. 1804. Rejected 10 Apr. 1807. Wit: Prosper King, 15 July 1805. Claims the land by order of survey to Whitley and by Whitley sold to Alex. Montgomery, 1797, land in Adams Co., on Homochitto.

p.161. Claim No.347. Spanish gr. to Alexander Montgomery. 800 arps. on Buffalo Cr., 25 mi. S. of Natchez, b. by William Conway and Daniel Clark, Sr. N. O. 24 Dec. 1797. // File. Claimant, Alexander Montgomery, 25 Feb. 1804. Wit: Prosper King, 15 July 1805. Rejected 10 Apr. 1807. Claim as above.

p.163. Claim No.348. Spanish gr. to Nicholas Rob [Rabb], 500 arps. on Second Cr., 10 mi. from Fort Panmure to the south, b. by Phipp's improvement, and Mr. Hutchins. N. O. 29 Feb. 1788. // File. Claimants, heirs of Nicholas Rob [Rabb], 27 Feb. 1804. Wit: Wm. Clark, 21 Dec. 1804. Certif. A-84, issued to claimants. Miss. Ter., Adams Co. Margaret Rob, John Rob, Peter Rob, and Elizabeth Rob, heirs and legal representatives of Nicholas Rob, decd., claim 500 arpens by virtue of a patent from the Spanish Govt. of La. as above. Sd Rob died intestate. He was an actual settler in sd Ter. on 27 Oct. 1794. (signed) Nicholas Rabb for himself and for the other heirs above-mentioned.

p.164. Claim. No.349. 18 Oct. 1797. George Demange to John Burch, for value recd., all my improvement, six or seven acres, with peach and apple trees, adj. John Holt, Plattner's Cr. and Barney Isenhood. Signed. Wit: James Truly, D. Darden. I do certify that I improved the within tract of land in 1794, which I can prove by responsible evidences. Oct. 20, 1799. (signed) George Demange. // File. Claimant, John Burch, 27 Feb. 1804. Wit: Wm. Donnely, 14 Feb. 1807. See No.1347. Wit: Wm. Thomas and Abner Pipes, 28 Mch. 1806. Certif. C-10, 3 Feb. 1807. Conflicts with No.763. The assignment of George Demange was prov. bef. the Board, 7 Mch. 1805 by James Truly. (signed) R. Claiborne, Clerk of the Board.

p.165. Claim No.350. In consequence of permission by Lt. Col. Chas. de Grand-Pre to Joseph Holden to settle upon ten arpens of land in front by 40 in depth until the grant in due form arrives, I certify that I have this, 7 Jany. 1783, surveyed the aforesaid ten arpens by forty to the foregoing plan, which I certify. (signed) Chas. Trudeau, Sur. Genl. // Received of Joseph Holden $14.00, $8.00 for surveying his land and $6.00 for surveying the lands of his neighbor, John Space. Natchez, 26 Jany. 1783. (signed) Chas. Trudeau. // p.166. Joseph Holden, 14 May 1783, to Mr. Henry Manadue, tract 3 leagues from Fort, 10 acres front by 40 acres deep, joining lands of Mr. St. Germain and those of James Spice and vacant land, for $140 in hand paid and $6.00 to be paid in December next. Joseph (X) Holden, H. Manadue. Wit: James Harman, Estevan Minor, Pedro Piernas. From the within mentioned sum I do assign to be paid to Mr. George Castles the sum of $42, for value recd. from Mr. Castles. Natchez, 24 Oct. 1783. Joseph (X) Holden. // Recd. the sum of $60 in full, 1 Jany. 1784. (signed) Geo. Castles. Wit: Cato West. // p.167. 15 July 1786. James Spice to Henry Manadue, for full and ample satisfaction, 200 acres on Fairchild's Cr. joining land he now lives on as I claim no right or title to the same. I assign it to sd Manadue. James (X) Spice. Wit: Robt. Abrams, John (X) Stowers. // File. Henry Manadue, 27 Feb. 1804, John Wray, 8 Oct. 1804. Wit: Polser Shilling, 23 Aug. 1805. Certif. B-107 issued to legal representatives of Henry Manadue. Claim of Henry Manadue, legal representative of Henry Manadue, his father, claims 800 acres on Fairchild's Cr., 400 acres gr. to Joseph Holden.

p.167. Claim No.351. 16 Apr. 1798. Berry West, of Natchez Prov. of La. to James Bosley, bond for $1000, to relinquish all title to 300 acres now in West's possession and formerly granted to Louis Chachere by the Spanish Govt. Bery (B) West. Wit: John Ferguson, Anthony Hoggat, John Odum. // James Bodley assigns all right in above obligation to Abram Martin. James (B) Bosley. Jany. 1, 1802. Wit: Thos. Bosley, Thos. (B) Beary. // 13 April 1798. Whereas Leonard D. Shaw in co-partnership with James Bosley purchased several tracts now in possession of John Odam, Wm. Baker and Berry West, in the first instance from Louis Chachere and finally from the persons mentioned now. For a good and val. consid. I have sold my equal undivided share to Anthony Hoggatt. (signed) Wit: Leonard D. Shaw. Richard (x) Forguyson, Nathaniel Hoggatt. 4 Feb. 1804. I assign all my right to the annexed conveyance given by Leonard Shaw to myself to Abram Martin. (signed) Anthony Hoggat. Wit: Chas. Bosley, John Hoggatt. // File. Claimant, 27 Feb. 1804, Abraham Martin. Wit: Wm. Thomas. Wit: Anthony Hoggat, 27 Mch. 1806. Certif. B-184, Feb. 13, 1807. Abram Martin claims 640 acres on headwaters of Cole's Cr., Second and Sandy Creeks in Adams Co. originally inhabited and cultivated by John Odam, Berry West and Wm. Baker in 1794, etc. Plat shows land b. by James Hoggat, ______ Tyler, Robt. and James Moore, Wilford Hoggat and Wm. Hoggat.

p.170. Claim No.352. Spanish grant to John Foster, 186 arpens on waters of St. Catherine's Cr., 9 mi. NE. of Fort, b. by Geo. Weigle, Mr. Brocus and Benj. Belk. N. O. 15 Mch. 1789. // p.172. 3 July 1798, John Foster, sells to Wm. Ellis for $100, 186 acres gr. as above. Signed. Wit: Jno. Dick, Thos. Reed. // File. Claimant, Wm. Ellis, 28 Feb. 1804. Wit: Adam Lanehart, 5 Nov. 1804. Certif. A-448 to cl. 18 July 1805.

p.173. Claim No.353. Spanish gr. to Frederick Calvet, 500 acres, 12 mi. from Fort to north, b. by vacant lands. N. O. 15 Mch. 1788. // File. Claimant, heirs of Frederick Calvet, 28 Feb. 1804. Wit: John Bolls, 23 May 1804. Certif. A-85 issued to claimants. Claim of Elizabeth Wells and Levi Wells, Lucretia Stewart and James Stewart, Montford Calvet, Alexander Calvet, Joseph Calvet and Mary Calvet, heirs and legal representatives of Frederick, decd., subscribing claimant was the widow, for 500 acres as above. (signed) Mary Roberts for the sd heirs.

p.175. Claim No.355. Spanish gr. to Polser Shilling, 600 acres, 3 mi. NE. of Fort, b. by Francis Farrell and Daniel Grafton. N. O. 23 Mch. 1790. // File. Claimant, Polser Shilling, 28 Feb. 1804. Wit: Geo. Fitzgerald, 10 Sept. 1804. Certif. A-86 issued. Claim as above.

p.176. Claim No.356. 23 Dec. 1784. The Spanish Govt. instituted a suit agst. Wm. Dueitt [Dewitt] wherein he is accused and convicted of an attempt to abscond from this dist. without a passport with the intention of defrauding his creditors by not paying his lawful debts, by which decree the estate of the said Wm. Dueitt, or so much of it as necessary, be sold at public vendue to the highest bidder, to be put into immediate execution. . . One plantation, 400 arpens on the Miss. River, b. Francis Farrell and Stephen Jordan was sold to Mr. Richard Harrison, the highest bidder, for $209. // Natchez, 15 ___, 1787. Richard Harrison sells to Polser Shilling, the above tract, for $300. Signed by both. Wit: S. Minor, Antonio Soler before Grand-Pre. // p.179. Petition of Polser Shilling to Spanish Govt.,

3 July 1793, that he bought the above described tract from Richard Harrison, asks for grant to same. Order of survey for 400 acres. // File. Claimant, Polser Shilling, 28 Feb. 1804. Wit: John Chonael. Wit: John Bisland. Claim as above.

p.181. Claim No.357. Spanish gr. to Isaac Tabor, 250 acres, 12 mi. N.E. of Fort, b. Thos. Green and Geo. Weigle. N. O. 14 Aug. 1793. // p.183. Natchez, 17 July 1796. Isaac Tabor to Mrs. Sallie West, 75 acres, part of the above grant, for $100. Both sign. Wit: Estevan Minor, Juan Girault. // p.184. 23 Feb. 1801. Isaac Tabor and Elizabeth, his wife, of the 3rd Dist. of New Feliciana, to Wm. Lemon, for $250 in hand paid, 175 acres, the remainder of the above grant. Both sign. Wit: John Habour [Harbour], M. Winn, Jesse (X) Munson. Prov. by Minor Winn and Jesse Munson before Wm. Miller, J. P. of Adams Co. // File. Claimants, William and Sally Lemon, 28 Feb. 1804. Wit: John Bolls, 16 June 1804. Certif. A-87 to claimants. Wm. Lemon and Sallie, his wife, claim 250 arpents, on waters of Fairchild's Cr., pat. to Isaac Tabor who conveyed sd tracts by two conveyances, namely, one to Sallie West, now Sally Lemon for 75 acres, the other to Wm. Lemon. [as above.]

p.185. Claim No.358. Petition, Natchez, 25 Nov. 1785. James Simmons, being a father of a family so large he cannot sustain them except by his work, asks for 400 arpents, square, on Miss. River, 5 leagues from the Fort, b. by lands of Joseph Dyson. (signed) James Simmons. // Natchez, 18 Feb. 1786. Appeared before me, William Curtis, John Courtney and Thomas Dyson, res. of district, and neighbors of the lands asked for and declare that sd lands are vacant and next to theirs and that sd Simmons is an old inhabitant and has a large family. Signed. Wit: Estevan Minor. Before Francisco Bouligny. // Fort of Natchez, 18 Feb. 1786. Order for land for Simmons who has a family of eight children. // N. O. March 7, 1786. Warrant for 400 acres, by Miro. // p.187. Certif. of survey and plat of 400 acres for James Simmons on Miss. River Bluffs 15 mi. n. of Natchez Fort, 2 Nov. 1785. (signed) Wm. Vousdan, Dept. Surveyor. // p.188 5 Sept. 1803. Jacob Simmons and Polly, his wife, of Jefferson Co., Miss. Ter., to Zachariah Kirkland, of same, for $1600 paid, land as above, b. by John Strabraker, Abner Green and Dyson. Wit: D. W. Brazeale, Henry Downs. (signed) Jacob Simmons, Polly (x) Simmons. Ack. 31 Jany. 1804, by Henry Downs before Henry Green and Abner Pipes, two Justices of Peace. Prov. 5 Mch. 1804 by Henry Downs bef. Edm. Hall, J. P. // File. Claimant, Zachariah Kirkland, 28 Feb. 1804. Wit: Abner Green, 23 Dec. 1805. Certif. C-5, 23 Jany. 1807. Conflicting with No.1937. Kirkland claim above 400 arpents of land below mouth of Cole's Cr. gr. to James Simmons, From the death of said James Simmons, it fell into the hands of his son, Jacob Simmons, and by deed from Jacob Simmons to Zachariah Kirkland.

p.191. Claim No.359. Spanish gr. to Stephen Scriber, 350 acres on Cole's Creek, 54 mi. NE. of Fort, b. by Cole's Creek and land of James Elliott. N. O. 26 Nov. 1793, by Carondelet. // p.192. Natchez, 23 March 1795. Norsworth Hunter and Stephen Scriber exchange land. Hunter will cede to sd Scriber 100 arpents bought from Joshua Collins, b. by Ebenezer Rees and Parker Carradine, with six cows in exchange 350 arpents on North Fork of Cole's Cr., b. by land of James Elliot, and gr. to sd Scriber, exchanging grants and plans with permission of His Majesty's Government. (signed) N. Hunter. Stephen Scriber signed in German. Before Don Manuel Gayoso de Lemos. // p.193. 17 Nov. 1800. Norsworthy Hunter, Esq., to Cato West, for $1050 paid, tract on Cole's Cr. as granted to Stephen Scriber. Signed. Wit: A. L. Duncan, Mordecai Throckmorton. // p.195. Deed of Gift. 22 June 1802. Cato West to John A. Davidson, son-in-law of sd Cato West, for affection and better maintenance, etc. the above tract. Signed. Wit: John C. Scott, Andrew K. Bowland. Ack. 13 July 1802, before J. Girault, Clk. of Court. // File. Claimant, John A. Davidson, 28 Feb. 1804. Wit: Wm. Daniel, 25 Sept. 1804. Certif. A-88 to claimant. Claim as above.

p.197. Claim No.360. Natchez, 27 Aug. 1796. James Kelly assigns to John Mitchell for value received, his improvement of a tract of land and houses on said improvement, to be delivered 25 Dec. next. Signed. Wit: James Todd, Robert Hallaway, Morris Custard. // File. Claimant, John Mitchell, 28 Feb. 1804. Wit: Joshua Howard, 15 Oct. 1804. Certif. B-186 issued to Joseph Sessions, assignee, 13 Feb. 1807. Land on Sandy Cr. in Adams Co., Miss. Ter. beg. on line of E. Forman. 640 acres. Mitchell claims a donation right of aforesaid tract.

p.197. Claim No.361. 11 Sept. 1798. Robt. Pendergrass, for $150 in hand paid, to John Bolls, 448 acres with all improvements thereon. (signed) Robert Pendergrass, Jr. Wit: Wm. Erwin, John Callihan. // I assign the within contents to Mr. John James. 15 July 1801. (signed) John Boles. // p.198. 22 March 1804. John Bolls, for $100 paid. to John James, the above tract on Dry Cr., a water of

Homochitto, as tract known as "Pendergrass Place", on which John James now lives with his family. Wit: Edward Turner, J. Turner. // File. Claimant, John James, 22 Mch. 1804. Wit: James Hayes, 10 Sept. 1804. Certif. B-86, 23 Feb. 1807. Claim as above.

p.199. Claim No.362. 12 March 1802. Henry Jacobs to Abner Beckham, a piece of land known by my own improvement, for $200. Henry (X) Jacobs. Wit: J. Stedman, James Howard. // File. Claimant, Abner Beckham, 28 Feb. 1804. Know all men, etc. that I, Abner Beckham have sold, etc. all right to above tract on the Homochitto, near the Ferry, conveyed by Henry Jacobs to me. Wit: Joseph Erwin, Zadock Barrow. Proved by Erwin, Feb. 17, 1806. (signed) T. R.

p.199. Claim No.364. 22 March 1804. John Bolls, for $200 paid, to Elisha Estes, quit claim to 640 acres on Wells Cr., known as "Moses Foster's place", on which Elisha Estes now resides with his family. (signed) John Bolls. Wit: Edward Turner, J. Turner. // p.200. Certificate of Moses Foster that neither he nor his heirs lay claim to above claim on Wells Cr. for he sold his labor to John Bolls in 1796. He settled it in 1791. Mch. 14, 1804. Signed. Wit: Jesse Lea, John Morgan. // File. Claimant, Elisha Estes, 28 Feb. 1804. Wit: William Foster and Samuel Cooper, 20 Aug. 1804. Allowed as a preemption certificate D-305 and issued.

p.200. Claim No.365. Order of survey, Natchez, 3 Mch. 1795, for John Vidal and Sebastian Estader, land fronting on the road, at the landing of the Plaza, 125 ft. on which to build two cabins. // p.202. 13 June 1803. John Vidal and wife, Josepha Vidal, to Charles Forget, for $445 paid, 90 feet of land, square measure, fronting on the road next to the river, 125 ft. depth by 75 feet on upper side and 34 feet on lower, same as granted above. Both sign with mark. Wit: James Wallace, Peter Walker. Ack. and dower relinquished before Samuel Brooks. // File. Claimant, Chas. Forget, 28 Feb. 1804. Rejected, June 10, 1807. Lot at foot of the hill, adj. the bluff.

p.204. Claim No.367. 7 Jany. 1803. Acknowledgment of sale by James Simmons to John Pipes of land adj. Patrick and Thomas Sullivan. Signed. Wit: Robt. McCray. // File. Claimant, John Martin, 28 Feb. 1804. Wit: Joseph Green, Sr., 27 Nov. 1804. Certificate D-5 issued 4 Sept. 1806. Claim of John Martin of 250 acres on Cole's Cr. which tract was inhabited and cultivated before the Spanish troops evacuated said Territory by Mr. James Simmons who sold to Mr. John Pipes and said John Pipes sold to John Martin. (signed) John Martin. Plat shows John Stephens, Joseph Green, J. Pipes, J. Sullivan with lands adj.

p.204. Claim No.368. Petition of David Cory, a res. of Dist. who wishes to work for the livelihood of his father and family, consisting of nine persons, asks for land bet. waters of Sandy Cr. adj. Benj. Holmes. (signed) David Cory. Natchez, 3 Feb. 1794. // Order of survey by Carondelet. N. O. 7 April, 1794, 200 acres where // File. Claimant, David Cory, 27 Feb. 1804. Wit: John McCoy. Rejected 10 Apr. 1807.

p.205. Claim No.369. Spanish grant to Mark Oiler [Isler], for 400 acres on St. Catherine's Creek, 5 mi. east from Fort, b. by lands of Mr. Andrews and Richard Adams, Lewis Bingaman and Peter Surget, on St. Catherine's Cr. (note, this land encircles a tract of 200 acres belonging to John Adams) N. O. 10 Feb. 1789. // p.207. 21 Oct. 1798. Christian Harman, to Thomas Rule, for $300, paid, 400 acres on afsd creek, adj. lands of Mrs. McIntosh, Ithermer Andrews, Richard Adams, William Cobb and Lewis Bingaman, which was gr. to Mark Iler, as above, and sold by his lawful heir to Christian Harman, 22 Feb. 1790. Signed. Wit: Ebenezer Dayton, John Girault. Prov. by Dayton before Wm. Kenner, 6 Nov. 1800, J. P. // File. Claimant, Elizabeth Rule, extrx. of the est. of the late Thos. Rule, for herself and legal representatives. Israel Leonard for Eliz. Rule, Feb. 13, 1804.

p.209. Claim No. 370. 6 Feb. 1804. William Curtis to Thomas Nash, for $100, my claim in Jefferson County now in actual possession of Thomas Nash, adj. lands of John Hamberlin, Robert Dunbar, and the donation right of Hugh Slater, all my right of donation in sd tract. (signed) Wm. Curtis. Wit: John Hamberlin, Wm. McDuggle. Ack. before David Phelps, J. P. of Jefferson Co. // p.210. 7 Feb. 1804. Thos. Nash, for $600 paid, to Joseph Bullen, land as above, settled the last of Dec. 1797 by Wm. Curtis. Thos. (X) Nash. Wit: Armstrong Ellis, Wm. Ferguson. Ack. before Thos. Rodney, Justice of the Sup. Ct. 13 Feb. 1804. // File. Claimant, Joseph Bullen, 28 Feb. 1804. Wit: Abraham Mayes and John Griffin, 10 Mch. 1806. Certificate B-88 issued 3 Feb. 1807. Bullen claims a donation of 640 acres as above.

p.212. Claim No.371. South Carolina, 10 June 1799. William Marshall, of City of Charleston, son and heir of William Marshall, Esq., decd. who d. 13 Sept. 1785, for $1000, to Thos. Wadsworth, merchant of Charleston, 2000 acres on a br. of Boyd's Cr. 21 mi. NE of Natchez, b. by lands of Richard Ellis and vacant lands gr. June 5, 1778 to sd Wm. Marshall by Peter Chester. W. Marshall. Wit: Stephen Lee, John Gist. Charlotte Marshall, wife of Wm. Marshall, Esq. of Charleston, relinq. dower to above before Wm. Turpin, J. Q. 10 June 1799. Prov. in Ct. by Stephen Lee, 24 June 1799. // p.215. 26 June 1797. Thos. Wadsworth, merchant, of Charleston to William McCaleb, planter, of Pendleton Co., S. C. all right to one-half of tract of 2000 acres which is to be equally divided between Wm. McCaleb, Esq. and Thos. Wadsworth, for $1000 to be paid. Signed by Wadsworth. Wit: James Boyle, John Boyle. // Bk.D, p.231. Wm. Caleb, of Miss. Ter., and Wm. Turpin and Benj. Wadsworth, exrs. of Thos. Wadsworth, late of Charleston, S. C., decd. by Elihu Hall Bay, their attorney, agreement. William McCaleb relinquishes all claim to land, having paid nothing and all relinquish all claims to bonds. All sign. Wit: A. Hutchins, John Carter. // File. Claimant, William McCaleb, 28 Feb. 1804. See No.976. Rejected, June 13, 1807. Claim as above, [omitting the quit claim given by sd McCaleb.]

Claim No.372. [Not entered in W.E.] Claimant, John Calhoon, 28 Feb. 1804. Wit: Stephen Marble, 1 Oct. 1804. Wm. Atchison, Abel Eastman, 29 Jany, 1806. Certif. D-276 issued to Moses Floyd, assignee of claimant. Miss. Ter., Claiborne, John Calhoon claims a donation right or right of occupancy lying in said county on the Big Black River, which tract was improved by sd Calhoon by clearing about half an acre, planting some peach trees and by having commenced building a cabin to dwell in in 1797. He intended to inhabit and cultivate the said tract of land at and from that time but was interrupted in his claim by the Choctaw Indians who claimed the said land as being within their boundary line but he continued his claim to the land by working on it from time to time and actually moved on it sometime in 1799 or 1800 and had inhabited and cultivated the same ever since and was the head of a family on the day the final evacuation of the Spanish troops from this territory and claims no other land therein. (signed) John Calhoon. Plat shows John Marshall on one side (east). // Indenture 12 Oct. 1804 between John Calhoon, of Claiborne Co., Miss. Territory, United States of America, and Moses Floyd, of Co. and Ter. afsd, for $400 in hand paid, sd Calhoon sells to sd Floyd all that tract of land on waters of the Big Black River, 320 acres, being all the land claimed by sd John Calhoon, which has been returned in to the Registrar's Office in the Town of Washington and proved agreeable to the Act to Congress, beg. on Big Black River, about 3/4 mile above the old block house and running north (metes and bounds), etc. (signed) John Calhoon. Wit: John Jenkins, James Griffin. Prov. Nov. 8, 1804 by J. Griffin bef. T. R. Note: Be it remembered that James Griffin, one of the subscribing witnesses to the within deed, personally appeared before me and made oath that he saw John Calhoon seal and deliver the within deed, etc. Town of Washington, 8 Nov. 1804. Thomas Rodney, Justice of Sup. Ct.

p.217. Claim No.376. Spanish gr. to Richard Dun, 250 acres on Fairchild's Cr. 8 mi. NE. of Fort Panmure, b. on south by Richard King, on east by Isaac Tabor. N. O. 8 Apr. 1789. // File. Claimant, Richard Dun, 28 Feb. 1804. Wit: Robt. Taylor, 28 Nov. 1804. Certif. A-93 issued to claimant. Claim as above.

p.218. Claim No.379. John Ivers, of this place and a native of Pennsylvania, petitions for 240 acres on Bayou Pierre a league from land of Wm. Brocus on the North Fork of sd Bayou, 30 Sept. 1789. // Natchez, 1 Oct. 1789. The land desired is vacant and order granted by Manuel Gayoso. // Survey and plat certified by Wm. Dunbar, 26 July 1793. // p.219. 23 Nov. 1798, John Ivers to William Brocus, for $300 in hand paid, the above 240 acres. Signed. Wit: Thos. Harrington, Walter Hart. // I assign the within deed to Samuel Bridgers, for value received, 23 June 1807. William (X) Brocus. // p.221. 18 June 1803, Wm. Brocus, Sr., to Samuel Bridgers, both of Claiborne Co., for $700, the above 240 acres on the south branch of Bayou Pierre. Wit: James Shorter, Stephen B. Minor. // File. Claimant, Samuel Bridgers, 29 Feb. 1804. Wit: W. Crane, 19 Nov. 1804. Certif. B-57 issued 8 Sept. 1806. Samuel Bridgers claims 240 arpents on north side of the South Fork of Bayou Pierre by virtue of a warrant of survey to John Ivers who sold the sd tract of Robert Ashley who conveyed it to Wm. Brocus, etc. (signed) Samuel Bridgers. // p.222. 25 Oct. 1798. Robt. Ashley of Bayou Pierre Dist., to Wm. Brocus, for $350, 240 acres gr. to John Ivers. Wit: Thos. Harrington, Walter Hart, William Brocus, Jr.

p.223. Claim No.380. Spanish gr. to John Courtney, 400 arpents, 40 mi. NE. of Natchez, b. by Wm. Curtis and vacant lands. N.O., 7 March 1789. // p.225. 7 Oct. 1795. John Courtney to Jonathan Jones the above 400 acres, in Villa Gayoxo Dist. at "The Bluffs", in exchange for 8 cows with calves which I have recd. and wherewith I am satisfied. (signed) John Courtney, Jonathan Jones. Wit: M. Stacpoole, Ebenezer Rees. // File. Claimant, Jonathan Jones, 27 Feb. 1804. Wit: John Jones, 2 June 1804. Certif. A-94 to cl. Jefferson Co., Miss. Ter., Jonathan Jones claims the above 400 acres on a br. of Fairchild's Cr.

p.226. Claim No.381. Petition of John Holt for 500 arpents near Villa Gayoso, b. by lands of David Odam and Wm. Gillespy. Natchez, 8 Mch. 1793. // Order of survey for same by Carondelet. N. O. 24 Feb. 1795. // p.228. 24 Dec. 1801. John Holt and Chloe, his wife, to Mordecai Throckmorton, for $1000 in hand pd., 500 acres on Plattner's Fork of Cole's Cr., as above. Wit: Edward Robbins, Bernard Isenhoot. Proved by the latter 13 July 1802. // File. Claimant, Mordecai Throckmorton, 29 Feb. 1804. Wit: Thomas Calvet, 8 May 1805. Certif. C-6, 3 Feb. 1807. (Conflicting with No.763.) Claim as above.

p.230. Claim No.382. Petition of Robert Watts that he had come down to this country from the Illinois to establish himself in this dist. with his family, asks for 400 arpents on the north fork of Cole's Cr. by the road to Bayou Pierre. Signed. Natchez, 5 Oct. 1789. // Order for survey, N. O. 17 Dec. 1789 by Estevan Miro. // p.231. 400 arpents surveyed for the heirs of John Watts. [Certif. for 470 acres.] // At the request of Mary Watts, wid. of the late Robert Watts, and of his children as his heirs, I have surveyed same on Cole's Cr., north fork, which land has been since 1789 in peaceable possession of sd widow and ch. who have increased the improvement and are now living on same. Natchez, 10 Aug. 1794. (signed) Ebenezer Dayton. // p.230. 11 June 1789. The land claimed by Mr. Robert Watts, adj. Mr. James Elliott, is not surveyed to any person to best of my knowledge. (signed) Wm. Vousdan, Dep. Surv. // File. Claimant, Mary Watts, Feb. 29, 1804. Wit: John Bolls, 6 June 1804. Certif. B-19, issued to legal representatives of Robt. Watts. Claim of Mary Watts, widow, as legal rep. of Robt. Watts, decd. Signed, Mary Watts by Charles Watts.

p.232. Claim No.383. Petition of John Fenton that he had moved to this Government with family of four and desired land on Second Cr., adj. Wm. Hays, Ephraim Thornhill and John Newton. Natchez, 14 Apr. 1795. // Plat and order of survey of 165 acres to John Fenton on Second Cr. Aug. 5, 1795, by Carondelet. // File. Claimant, John Fenton, 29 Feb. 1804. Wit: Isaac Alexander, 4 Jany. 1806. Certif. B-108 issued 4 Feb. 1807. Claim as above.

p.233. Claim No.384. Spanish gr. George Forman, for 150 acres, 17 mi. east of Natchez, b. by lands of Isaac Johnson. N. O. 4 Mch. 1795. // File. Claimant, George Forman, 29 Feb. 1804. Wit: John Bolls, 23 May 1804. Certif. A-95 to cl.

p.235. Claim No.385. Spanish gr. to George Forman, 200 acres, 16 mi. east of Fort Panmure, b. by William Ervin, Isaac Johnson and Richard Ellis, N. O. 4 Mch. 1795, by Carondelet. // File. Claimant, Geo. Forman, 29 Feb. 1804. Wit: John Bolls, 23 May 1804. Certif. A-96 to cl.

p.236. Claim No.388. Spanish gr. to Thomas Jordan, 600 acres on Fairchild's Cr., 9 mi. NE. of Fort, b. by Jacob Copertwaite and James Conner. Plat certified by Wm. Vousdan, 12 Mch. 1788. New Orleans, 15 Mch. 1788 by Miro. [Plat shows James Bonner on west and James Wade and Copperthwaite on east.] // p.238. Dec. 12, 1797. Thos. Jordan to Wm. Collins and Abner Pipes jointly, 400 acres, southern part of 600 acres gr. as above, for 10,000 pounds of cotton and $221, from Collins, recd., and from Abner Pipes have recd. 2500 pounds of cotton, the remaining 7500 pounds of cotton to be paid in two years. All sign. Wit: Stephen Minor, John Girault, James Spain. // File. Claimant, William Collins, 29 Feb. 1804. Wit: James Bonner, 24 June 1805. Certif. A-499 issued to Wm. Collins and Elijah Cushing, 15 Aug. 1805. Notation: See Nos.1300 and 1339. Claim of Wm. Collins for 600 arpents, as above grant, etc. // Endorsed: Wm. Collins for himself and Elijah Cushing claims 400 acres. Residue of the grant claimed by Jesse Withers and Robt. Turner by above numbers cited.

p.239. Claim No.389. Spanish gr. to Archibald Erwin, for 300 acres on Big Black, 70 mi. from Natchez, b. on vacant lands. [confirmation gives Maurice Joyce with land adj.] N. O. 20 Aug. 1795 by Carondelet. // File. Claimant, Archibald Erwin, 29 Feb. 1804. Wit: John Bolls, 16 June 1804. Certif. A-97 issued to cl. Claim signed by Archibald Erwin.

p.241. Claim No.390. Spanish gr. to Parker Carradine, 600 acres on Fairchild's Cr., b. by lands of Robt. Jones, Mark Olivares, Mr. Justus Humphreys and Joshua Collins. N. O. 15 Mch. 1789. // 9 May 1798, Parker Carradine, Sr., sells to John Joseph Carradine, for a bond of equal date, 500 acres below the American line and 31 degree north latitude, a warrant for which is in the hands of Ebenezer

Rees, as soon as the patent is obtained from the Govt. the sd Parker Carradine transfers sd tract to sd J. J. Carradine, excepting 1/3 to Peter Hill by agreement and 100 acres reserved for himself. The balance, 300 acres, to above John Joseph Carradine. (signed) Parker Carradine, Mary (X) Carradine. Wit: David Carradine, Leonard D. Shaw. Prov. by David Carradine 16 July, 1799 before Roger Dixon, J. P. of Pickering Co. // p.244. 17 Aug. 1803. John J. Carradine, of Jefferson Co., Miss. Ter. and Sarah, his wife, to Richard Carradine, for $1000, the above 300 acres. (signed) John J. Carradine, Sally (X) Carradine. Wit: David Carradine, Daniel Lewis, Parker Carradine, Jr. Prov. by David Carradine, 21 Dec. 1803, before David Phelps, J. P. Jefferson Co. // File. Claimant, Richard Carradine, 29 Feb. 1804. Wit: Parker Carradine, Sr., 6 June 1804. Certif. A-98 to cl. Claim signed by Richard Carradine.

p.246. Claim No.391. Spanish gr. to Anthony Hutchins, 242 acres on Cole's Cr. (Certif. by Charles Trudeau, 30 Mch. 1790.) 30 mi. N.E. of Fort Panmure, b. by vacant lands. N. O. 31 Mch. 1790. // p.247. 1 Jany. 1802. Anthony Hutchins to Parker Carradine, for $5.00 paid, the above land, being the same land I sold sd Carradine, 24 Nov. 1790. Signed. Wit: Benj. Seamans, Ferdinand L. Claiborne. // p.249. 9 May 1798, Parker Carradine, Sr., to Parker Carradine, Jr., for a certain bond of even date tract of land in the Southwest Territory of the United States, commonly called "the Natchez", b. by lands of William Moss and Jesse and Wm. Lum, 242 acres, pat. to Anthony Hutchins and by him conveyed to sd Carradine. (signed) Parker Carradine, Mary (X) Carradine. Wit: David Carradine, Leonard D. Shaw. // p.251. 17 Aug. 1803. Parker Carradine, Jr. of Jefferson Co., Miss. Ter. to John J. Carradine, for $1000 paid, above tract of 242 acres. Signed Parker Carradine, Jr., Leticia Carradine. Wit: Thos. Fenton. // File. Claimant, John J. Carradine, 29 Feb. 1804. Prov. in the actual settlement of Anthony Hutchins, 26 June 1804. Certif. A-99, to claimant.

p.252. Claim No.392. Spanish grant to Parker Carradine, 608 arpents, on Cole's Cr. b. by Francisco Brezina, Wm. Ferguson, and Holt's Fork of Cole's Cr. N. O. 25 Apr. 1793. // p.254. 9 May 1798, Parker Carradine, Sr. to Richard Carradine and G. Rapalje Carradine, land in Villa Gayoso Dist. 508 acres, b. by Wm. Ferguson and land gr. to David Carradine, where he resides at present, being balance of gr. to him in 1793, 100 acres of which he had conveyed to Joshua Collins. Wit: David Carradine, Leonard D. Shaw. Ack. and proved before Roger Dixon, J. P. 16 July 1799. // 18 June 1803. Richard Carradine to Parker Carradine for $1000 with advice and consent of Peninah, his wife, 254 acres, beg. at Truly's fork of Cole's Creek, b. by lands of Rapalje Carradine, John Collins and sd Creek. (signed) Richard Carradine, Peniney (X) Carradine. Wit: Thomas Ritchey, Daniel (X) Lyons, Benj. C. Bartley. Prov. by Bartley. // File. Claimants, P. Carradine and G. R. Carradine, 29 Feb. 1804. Proved in Parker Carradine, 6 June 1804. Certif. A-100 to claimants.

p.258. Claim No.393. British gr. to David Odam, 200 acres on Holt's Fork of Boyd's Cr., 30 mi. from Natchez, b. by vacant lands and creek. Prov. of West Fla. Pensacola, 23 Oct. 1777 by Peter Chester, Gov. etc. // p.263. 2 Jany. 1778. David Odam to Parker Carradine, the above land as in grant, for $500. Signed. Wit: David Holt, Don McPherson. // File. Claimant, Parker Carradine, Sr., 29 Feb. 1804. Wit: David Holt, 4 June 1804. Confirmed, 27 Feb. 1805. Certificate A-5.

p.267. Claim No.394. Spanish gr. to James White, 625 arpents on Wells Cr. 12 mi. east of Fort, b. by vacant lands. N. O. 20 Jany. 1795, by Carondelet. // p.270. 15 Mch. 1799, James White, to Allen Bird Grubb and Abner Lawson Duncan, for $150 paid, the above 625 on Wells Creek as above. Signed. Wit: Lyman Harding, Benj. (X) West. Prov. by Harding 6 May 1800 before Wm. Kenner, J. P. Adams Co. // p.274. 22 May 1799, Abner L. Duncan and Allen Bird Grubb to Nicholas Greenbury Ridgely, now res. in Natchez, Miss. Ter. (Allen Bird Grubb now in N. O. by his atty., A. L. Duncan,) for $390 paid, 525 acres as above. Signed. Wit: George Ruffer, Lyman Harding. Prov. by Harding bef. Wm. Kenner, J. P., Adams Co. // File. Claimant, Nicholas G. Ridgely, 29 Feb. 1804. Wit: William Thomas, 11 June 1806. Disallowed on suspicion of its being antedated, 22 Dec. 1806. Ridgely's claim signed by Henry Turner, his agent.

p.275. Claim No.395. Spanish gr. to Abraham Thickston, 600 acres on Cole's Cr., 25 mi. NE. from Fort, b. by Jacob Crumholt. N. O. 20 Nov. 1793. // p.277. 4 Sept. 1799, Wm. Hutsel, Joseph Hutsel, John Hutsel by sd Wm. Hutsel, his atty., John Swayze and Catherine, his wife, Abraham Oiler, all except John Hutsel of Adams Co., Miss. Ter., to Nicholas Ridgely, of Baltimore, State of Maryland, for $1000, paid, two tracts of land in Pickering Co., 600 acres near Cole's Cr., 25 mi. from Natchez, the above gr., and 400 acres in the same vicinity gr. 28 Feb. 1795, b. by John Stabraker. Wm. (X) Hutsel for self and brother, John, John Swayze, Catherine (X) Swayze, Abraham (X) Oiler. Wit: Alexr. Ross, William Glasscock. // File. Note: It is stated that Thickston married a Mrs. Hootsel, and died under the Spanish Government, without issue, leaving wife, who became entitled to his estate under Spanish law. Mrs. Thickston died leaving several heirs to whom the property descended. Claimant, Nicholas G. Ridgeley, 29 Feb. 1804. Certificate A-700 to claimant, 7 Jany. 1805.

p.279. Claim No.396. Spanish grant to William Curtis, 400 acres in Natchez Dist., 11 mi. north of Natchez, b. by John Strabaker. 28 Feb. 1795. New Orleans. // File. Claimant, N. G. Ridgely, 29 Feb. 1804. Wit: John Jones, 18 Nov. 1805, Roger Dixon, 27 Nov. 1805. Certif. A-699 issued to cl. Claim by Nicholas G. Ridgeley for 400 arpents on the Bluffs near Cole's Cr. gr. by Spanish Govt. to Wm. Curtis, the said tract is claimed by Ridgeley through several intermediate conveyances. (signed) Henry Turner, his agent. Notation on the back: It is further stated that Curtis bargained with Abraham Thickston in his lifetime for the premises but that Thickston died without paying for the land or receiving a title thereto; that, after his death, his widow, Mrs. Thickston, purchased and paid for it and died, being so possessed, and left several heirs who conveyed the premises to the present claimant, by deed dated 4 Sept. 1799. [As above.] // Be it known that I, William Curtis, grant and sell to Jemima Lewis, the plantation on the Miss. Bluff, at Cole's Cr., 394 arpents, b. by John Straybraker, for $500 paid. Natchez, 20 Oct. 1799. (signed) Wm. Curtis, Mimy (X) Lewis. Wit: Stephen Minor, Joseph Vidal before Chas. de Grand-Pre. The foregoing is a faithful translation of the original records in my office. Jean Girault. 10 Sept. 1805. // I, Jemima Lewis, wife of James Lewis, of Dist. of Villa Gayoso, for natural love and affection which I have for my children, to Wit: Wm. Hutsell, John Hutsell, Joseph Hutsell, Catherine Hutsell and Abraham Hyler, etc. gives all her estates of every kind 2 tracts of lands, 600 acres in the forks of Cole's Cr., and 400 acres upon the Bluffs near Villa Gayoso Town, 60 head of cattle, 6 horses, 20 hogs, household furniture, plantation utensils, etc., out of which I give to my son, Abraham Hyler, one bed, bedstead and furniture complete, one mare and colt and one cow and calf, the remainder of all I shall possess at my decease to be equally divided among my five children, named as above, each a one-fifth part, upon the express condition that I reserve to myself the use, etc. during my natural life. Jemima (X) Lewis. Wit: John Bisland, George Overaker. Ack. before Manuel Gayoso de Lemos, Military and Civil Governor of the Dist. of Natchez, by Jemima Lewis, 16 July 1796.

p.281. Claim No.397. Spanish gr. to Samuel Flower, 900 acres on Cole's Cr., the SE fork. N. O. 21 Apr. 1789, by Miro. // File. Claimant, Saml. Flowers, 29 Feb. 1804. Certif. A-602 to cl. 17 Sept. 1805.

p.284. Claim No.398. Spanish gr. to Ebenezer Rees, 1000 acres on Fairchild's Cr., 15 mi. NE. from Natchez. b. by Parker Carradine, Joshua Collins, Mrs. Ramsey, James Fletcher and Robert Jones. N. O. 27 Sept. 1788. // p.286. 12 Aug. 1800, Ebenezer Rees sells to Henry Turner, the above tract of 1000 acres for $3000 paid. Signed. Wit: Daniel Clarke, Bennet Truly. Ack. bef. Judge P. Bryan Bruin, 19 Aug. 1800. // File. Claimant, Henry Turner, 28 Feb. 1804. June 10, 1805. Res. proved in Claim 856. Certif. A-298 to claimant. Claim as above.

p.288. Claim No.405. Petition of Thomas Fortner, wishes to settle in this district, asks for a gr. of 240 acres on the Big Black River b. by Mr. Garret Rapalje and David Roberts. Natchez, 13 Aug. 1789. // N. O. 26 Apr. 1790. Order, warrant and survey of 100 acres, adj. lower side of David Robards survey of 240 acres, John Peter's corner. // File. Claimant, Thomas Fortner, 1 Mch. 1804. Withdrawn as useless.

p.289. Claim No.407. Petition of John Peters for 240 acres on Big Black adj. Wm. Fortner and Mrs. Garet Rapalje. Natchez, 14 Aug. 1789. Order, 19 Aug. 1789 by Gayoso. // Warrant. N. O. 26 Apr. 179_. by Miro. [File too faded to decipher. It was not allowed according to the list of claims.]

p.290. Claim No.408. Spanish gr. to James Rapalje, 890 arpents on Big Black River, 60 mi. north of Fort, b. by Isaac Rapalje, John Peters. N. O. 24 Dec. 1798. // File. Claimants, heirs of James Rapalje, 1 Mch. 1804. Wit: Anthony Glass, 27 July 1804. Certif. B-74 to legal rep. Claiborne Co., Miss. Ter., Isaac Rapalje claims 890 arpens in sd county on Big Black River, by virtue of a pat. by Sp. Govt. to James Rapalje, who died intestate, but who was an actual settler in sd territory on 27 Oct. 1795, leaving no children but the said Isaac, as one of his brothers and heirs, now claims the sd land for the legal representatives of deceased. The land was inhabited and cultivated in 1792 and ever since that time. Signed.

p.292. Claim No.409. Spanish gr. to Isaac Rapalje, 800 acres on west bank of the Big Black, 60 mi. NNE. of Natchez, b. by James Rapalje and John Stowers. N. O. 24 Dec. 1797, by Gayoso. // File. Claimant, Isaac Rapalje, 1 Mch. 1804. Wit: Anthony Glass, 27 July 1804. Certif. B-74 Oct. 26, 1806. Note: Testimony on other side. Claim as above. Land has been inhabited and cultivated in 1792 and ever since. Wit: Anthony Glass, sworn, says that the claimant inhabited and cultivated the premises before the year 1795 and removed from thence on account of danger from the Indians, to his brother's plantation where there was a public block-house, but returned about the year 1796 and has continued to cultivate by himself or by some person for his use ever since. He was of age at the date of the warrant.

Claim No.410. [Not in W. E.] Claimant, Benj. Steel, 2 Mch. 1804. Certif. D-239 issued 22 Dec. 1806. Surveyed 22 Dec. 1803 for Benj. Steel, 55 acres in Claiborne Co., Miss. Ter., on the upper end of an island in the Miss. River, opposite Palmyra Settlement, . . . to Shadrack Haven's corner . . . (signed) John Cook. Steel claims above land by virtue of its being inhabited and cultivated by sd Steel 3 March 1803, he being at that date the head of a family, having a wife with seven children. He asks a right of preference in the purchase of this tract.

Claim No.411. [Not in W. E.] Claimant, John Gaskins, 2 Mch. 1804. Wit: John King. Notation: See No.1984 and No.1739. Claimant suggests that he waives this claim as it interferes with others and has filed a subsequent claim including same improvement. 29 Nov. 1804. (signed) E. Turner. Rejected, May 7, 1807. Claim of land in Jefferson Co. by settlement 1791 being then the head of a family of six.

Claim No.412. [Not in W. E.] Claimant, John King, 2 Mch. 1804. Wit: Abram Clawson, 18 Feb. 1805. Certificate D-166 to David Sims, assignee, 16 Dec. 1806. John King claims a donation right of 640 acres on north fork of Cole's Cr. in Jefferson Co., originally improved by sd King in October 1797 who continued to improve same ever since, being the head of family, etc. [Plat shows Robert Dunbar and John Murdock with land adjoining.] // John King and Ann, his wife, deed tract as above, to David Sims, as a preemption, for $200 in hand paid. (signed) John King, Ann (X) King. Wit: Eli K. Ross, Elizabeth Ross. [n.d.] Proved by Eli K. Ross before Edmund Hall, J. P. Note: The claimant being before the Board, requests that if his claim does not justify a donation that he may receive 100 acres as a preemption including his settlement to be laid off square on the south side, next to Robt. Dunbar. (signed) John King.

p.294. Claim No.413. Spanish gr. to John Bisland, 750 acres 14 mi. east of Natchez, b. by lands of Mr. Chachere and Pierre Camus. N. O. 7 Mch. 1788 by Miro. // John Bisland, for $750 in hand paid, to James Hoggatt, all right in above land without warranting the grant. Signed. Wit: John Girault, Job. Routh. // File. Claimant, James Hoggatt, 2 Mch 1804. Wit: Joshua Howard. Certif. A-184 to claimant. Proved in Bisland.

p.296. Claim No.414. Spanish gr. to Peter Nelson, 300 acres on Sandy Creek, 12 mi. east of Fort, b. by vacant lands. N. O. 15 Mch. 1788 by Miro. // p.298. 12 Apr. 1797. Peter Nelson makes over to James Hoggatt all right in foregoing, conformable to deed signed in Record Office this day. (signed) Peter Nelson. Wit: Stephen Minor, John Girault. // File. Claimant, James Hoggatt, 2 Mch. 1804. Wit: Joshua Howard. Certif. A-185 to claimant. Proven in Nelson.

p.299. Claim No.415. Spanish gr. to John Armstreet, 500 acres 11 mi. east of Fort, b. by John Adams, Peter Nelson, John Waugh, and James Oglesby. New Orleans, 22 Mch. 1795. // p.301. 6 Dec. 1800. John Armstreet and Mary, his wife, to James Hoggatt, for $1000 in hand paid, 500 acres in Dist. of Second Cr., b. by John Odam and Peter Nelson, John Waugh, James Oglesby . . . Wm. Dunbar's corner . . . Anthony Hoggatt . . . James Hoggatt . . . James Bosley . . . Spier's line. Wit: Anthony Hoggatt, Anthony Calvet. Prov. by Hoggatt, 30 Dec. 1800. // File. Claimant, James Hoggatt, 2 Mch. 1804. Wit: Joshua Howard, 22 June 1804. Certif. A-101. Proved in Armstreet.

p.303. Claim No.416. Spanish gr. to Rebecca Dove, 300 acres on Second Cr., 11 mi. east of Natchez, b. by John Tier, George Mars, Patrick Nelson, John Bisland and James Oglesby. N. O. 20 June 1795, by Carondelet. // p.305. Assignment of Rebecca Dove to James Bosley, witnessed by Anthony Hoggatt, Leonard D. Shaw. // p.306. 9 Mch. 1799. Rebecca Dove, widow, of the lower county, Mississippi Territory, to James Bosley, of same, for $300 paid, 300 acres, adj. Anthony Hoggatt, as in above grant. Rebecca (R) Dove. Same wit. as above. Prov. by Anthony Hoggatt, 6 Aug. 1800, before Wm. Kenner, J. P. Adams Co. // p.308. 11 Aug. 1800. James Bosley to James Hoggatt, for $300 paid, 229 acres part of above 300 acres, 71 acres of which were conveyed to Anthony Hoggatt by sd Bosley.

James (B) Bosley. Wit: Anthony Hoggatt, Littlebery (X) West. // File. Claimant, James Hoggatt, 2 Mch. 1804. Wit: Joshua Howard, Certif. A-102 to claimant.

p.310. Claim No.417. Spanish gr. to Frederick Kimble, 1000 acres on Bayou Sara, 40 mi. south of Fort, b. by Levi Wells and Judith Baker, N. O. 1 Sept. 1795 by Carondelet. // p.312. 1st March 1804. Frederick Kimball Sr., of Dist. of New Feliciana, Prov. of Louisiana, to Frederick Kimball, Jr., his son, of same, power of atty. to act for him regarding above land in Wilkinson Co., Miss. Territory, U.S.A. Signed. Wit: Elisha Hunter, Field Pulaski Hunter. Prov. by Elisha Hunter, 1 Mch. 1804, bef. Johathan Davis. // File. Claimant, Frederick Kimball, Sr., 3 Mch. 1804. Wit: Nr. [Norsworthy] Hunter. Certif. A-103 issued to claimant. Claim for 57 acres, the NW. corner of above tract of 1000 acres, it being all that lies above the line of debarkation between the King of Spain's dominion and the United States. By Frederick Kimball, Jr.

p.314. Claim No.418. 28 Feb. 1804. Fred. Gunnell to James McCaleb, both of Claiborne Co., Miss. Ter., for $100 paid, title to improvement on tract adj. John Boothe's land on Boggy Branch, which land sd Gunnell had under cultivation in 1797. Signed. Wit: Daniel Burnet. // File. Claimant, James McCaleb, 3 Mch. 1804. Wit: John Booth. Certif. D-96 issued to cl. 3 Oct. 1806. Proved bef. Board by Daniel Burnet. Claim for 555 acres on Boggy Br. of North Fork of Bayou Pierre, 3 mi. east of Grindstone Ford. Plat shows 513 acres adj. Wm. Kilcrease, John Robinson, Abner Green and the old survey of Catura Proctor.

p.314. Claim No.419. 3 Dec. 1803. I do hereby certify that I was working on a parcel of land in Claiborne Co., adj. land of Abner Green, before and on 3 Mch. 1803 and have a part thereof in cultivation, about 9 acres, I have sold to John Robinson, Senr. all right in afsd work and cultivation and bond myself to deliver same to him Dec. next (the present crop excepted). (signed) Isaac Kemp. Wit: Dancy Kemp, Jonathan Kemp. // File. Claimant, Jno. Robinson, Sr., 3 Mch. 1804. Prov. before Board, 13 March 1804. R. C., clerk. [Richard Claiborne]. Wit: Jonathan Kemp. Certif. D-97, 30 Oct. 1806. Claim for 400 acres on south side of north fork of Bayou Pierre. (signed) Daniel Burnet for Jno. Robinson, Sr. Plat shows land adj. Abner Green, Wm. Kilcrease and Bayou.

p.315. Claim No.421. John Robinson, of Claiborne Co., Miss. Ter., on Little Sand Cr., above upper fork of sd creek before 3 Mch. 1803. I have about 20 acres in cultivation and the sd upper fork is a division bet. me and William Night [Knight] and a ridge the division bet. myself and John Robinson, Jr. I have sold said right to Harwood Jones, 6 Oct. 1803. Signed. Wit: Duncan (X) Cameron. // File. Claimant, Harwood Jones. Wit: William Knight. Certif. D-84, issued 29 Oct. 1806. Claim for 423 acres on Little Sand Cr., a br. of Big Black River, plat showing 20 acres in center of tract not claimed, also lands adj. Duncan Cameron on north and Jno. Robinson on southwest with the Wilderness Road running across the west end, certified by Daniel Burnet, 24 Feb. 1804.

p.316. Claim No.423. Spanish gr. to John Boothe, 600 acres near the north branch of Bayou Pierre, 60 mi. from Fort of Natchez, b. by vacant lands. N. O., 1 Jany. 1793, by Carondelet. Plat certified by Carlos Trudeau, 27 Nov. 1790. // File. Claimant, John Booth, 3 Mch. 1804. Wit: Jesse Smith, 20 Nov. 1804. Certif. A-104 to claimant.

p.318. 11 Nov. 1803. Wilkinson Co., John Nugent sells right to piece of land to Joshua Baker, where I now live, adj. sd Baker and Daniel Ogden, on headwaters of Smith Cr., which was originally settled by William Nugent, in beginning of 1802. (signed) John Nugent. Wit: Edmund Nugent. // File. Claimant, Joshua Baker, 3 Mch. 1804. Wit: Wm. West, Jun. Certif. D-178, 17 Dec. 1806. Claims 320 acres on waters of Buffalo Creek, preemption rights. Plat shows Danl. Ogden, Stephen Ploche and John Wall with land adj.

p.319. Claim No.439. Spanish gr. to Prosper King, 40 mi. N. E. of Fort, b. by John King and Justus King. N. O. 17 Apr. 1793, by Carondelet. Plat certified by Chas. Trudeau, with Bayou Tabor across east side of tract. // File. Claimant, Prosper King, 5 Mch. 1804. Wit: George Selser, 19 May 1804. Certif. A-105 to claimant. Prosper King claims a right to 400 arpents on Tabor's Fork of Bayou Pierre in Claiborne Co., being a tract originally gr. to sd King as above. Signed.

p.321. Claim No.440. Spanish grant to Prosper King, 200 acres on the south bank of Big Black River. 70 mi. NE. of Fort, b. by vacant lands. N. O. 1 Sept. 1793, by Carondelet. // File. Claimant, Prosper King, 5 Mch. 1804. Wit: Geo. Selser, 19 May 1804. Certif. A-106 to cl.

p.323. Claim No. 441. 27 Sept. 1803, Joshua Chandler, of Washington County, Miss. Territory, for $200 paid, to William Cole, of Adams Co., tract in Claiborne Co., adj. Melling Wooley's west line. Joshua (X) Chandler. Wit: Jacob Guice, Esq. // 5 March 1804. For $100 paid. Wm. Cole assigns above right to within bill to Prosper King. Wit: Reuben Morehouse, Patrick Fulham. // File. Claimant, Prosper King, 5 Mch. 1804. Wit: Buckner Pittman, 20 Nov. 1804. Rejected, 7 May 1807. Claim to 640 acres on waters of James Cr. in Claiborne Co., originally settled by Joshua Chandler in 1795, he being at that time the head of a family.

p.324. Claim No.442. Spanish gr. to Prosper King, 800 acres on br. of Homochitto called Morgan's Fork, b. on all sides by vacant lands. N. O. 24 Dec. 1797 by Gayoso. // File. Claimant, Prosper King, 5 Mch. 1804. Wit: Alexander Montgomery, 15 July 1804. Rejected, 10 Apr. 1807.

p.326. Claim No.443. Spanish gr. to Philip Nevil, 300 acres on the waters of Cole's Cr., 15 mi. NE. of Fort Panmure, b. by Ephraim Coleman, Benj. Fletcher, John Stampley, John Clark and William Thomas. N. O. 24 Dec. 1797 by Gayoso. // File. Philip Nevil, claimant, 5 Mch. 1804. Wit: James Clark, 17 Sept. 1804. Certif. B-100, 3 Feb. 1807. Adams Co. Philip Nevil claims 300 arpents on waters of Cole's Cr., as above.

p.328. Claim No.446. Spanish gr. to Anthony Hoggatt, 100 acres 10 mi. NE. of Fort, b. by Carder Rabby, James Oglesby, Madame (widow) Dove and John Thear. N. O. 7 Dec. 1797 by Gayoso. // File. Claimant, Anthony Hoggatt, 5 Mch. 1804. Wit: Thomas Freeman, 30 Apr. 1807. Certif. B-266, 30 Apr. 1807.

p.330. Claim No.447. Spanish grant to John Tear, 700 acres 10 mi. east of Fort, b. by John Bisland, Rebecca Dove, George Mars and Chas. Boardman. N. O. 14 Apr. 1796, by Carondelet. // p.332. John Tear, a res. of the District, sells to William Moore, a neighbor, 700 acres in the district of St. Catherine, as above, for $500 in hand paid. Natchez, 30 Sept. 1797. Both signed. Wit: Estevan Minor, John Girault, George Overaker, John Ferguson. // p.334. 5 Apr. 1802. Robert Moore, for himself, and as atty. for Samuel Philip Moore and James Moore and Anna Maria, his wife, heirs-at-law of their decd. brother, William Moore, all of Miss. Territory, U. S. A. to Anthony Hoggatt, of Adams Co. sd Ter. William Moore died intestate Feb. 1798 and seized of the above tracts of 700 acres, for $2400 in hand paid. Signed by Robert Moore for self and others. Wit: Abijah Hunt, Abner L. Duncan. // File. Claimant, Anthony Hoggatt, 5 Mch. 1804. Wit: Daniel Fowler, 2 Aug. 1804. Certif. C-4 issued 4 June 1806. Notation: Conflicting with D. Waugh's patent, No.1491. Proved in John Tear. Miss. Ter. Adams Co. Anthony Hoggatt claims 700 acres in sd county, as above.

p.336. Claim No.448. Spanish gr. to James Oglesby, 500 arpents on waters of Second and Cole's Creeks, 12 east of Fort, b. by lands of Waugh and Peter Nelson on south, on west by Percy, on other side vacant. N. O., 20 July 1793, by Carondelet. // p.338. 20 May 1798. James Oglesby assigns to Mr. Anthony Hoggatt all right to above grant. James (X) Oglesby. Wit: Nathaniel Hoggatt, Nathaniel Ferguson. Prov. by Nathl. Hoggatt, Nov. 4, 1799, before Wm. Dunbar, J. P., Adams Co. // File. Claimant, Anthony Hoggatt, claimant, 5 Mch. 1804. Wit: Daniel Fowler, proved res. of claimant. Certif. A-186 issued to claimant. Hoggatt claims the above 500 arpents as above.

p.339. Claim No.449. 8 July 1800, James Bosley, of Adams Co., for $100 paid, to Anthony Hoggatt, 71 acres on headwaters of St. Catherine's Cr., adj. lands, of Anthony Hoggat's, formerly that of James Oglesby, Peter Nelson and part of a gr. formerly Rebecca Dove's, containing 300 acres. James (B) Bosley. Wit: Daniel Hawley, Thomas (X) Rule. Proved by Hawley 11 July 1800. // File. Claimant, Anthony Hoggatt, 5 Mch. 1804. Res. of Rebecca Dove proved in 1406, 2 May 1805. Certif. A-107 to claimant. Anthony Hoggatt claims 71 acres, part of 300 acres granted by Sp. Govt. to Rebecca Dove, 20 June 1795, who sold same to James Bosley, etc.

p.340. Claim No.450. Spanish grant to Thomas Reid, 450 acres, on waters of Cole's Cr., 25 mi. from the Fort, b. by vacant lands. N. O., 25 Mch. 1795, by Carondelet. // File. Claimant, heirs of Thomas Reid, 5 Mch. 1804. Wit: John Bolls. Certif. A-108 issued to legal representatives of T. Reid.

p.343. Claim No.452. Spanish gr. to John Rankin Wylie, 400 acres on south branch of Bayou Pierre, 35 mi. NNE. of Fort Panmure, b. by vacant lands. N. O., 30 Aug. 1793, by Carondelet. // p.345. 9 May 1798. John Wylie, of Natchez, to David Ferguson, the above grant for 100 square acres, for $150. (signed) John Wylie, Lowicy Wylie. Wit: Wm. Dunbar, Gabriel Blackburn. // p.346. 6 Jany. 1802. David Ferguson to Antonio Villaverd, for $380, the above tract. Signed by David and Jane

Ferguson. Wit: David Nesbitt. // p.348. 29 Nov. 1801, John Wiley and Louvicy, his wife, for $350, tract of 300 acres on Bayou Pierre, part of 400 acres gr. to John Rankin Wylie by Sp. Govt. Both sign. Wit: Wm. Frisbee, David Ker, William Lemon. Ack. by John Wylie before James Stuart, J. P. of Pickering Co. // Loucy Wylie was ex. by David Ker, a Judge of Sup. Ct. of Miss. Ter. [n.d.] p.350. 14 Jany. 1802. Antonio Villaverd, of Baton Rouge, Prov. of La., but now of Adams Co., Miss. Ter. to John Bolls of sd county and Ter. for $800, the above tract of 400 acres. Signed. Wit: Lyman Harding, Waterman Crane. // File. Claimant, John Bolls, 7 Mch. 1804. Wit: Robert Dunbar. Certif. A-482, 9 Aug. 1805.

p.352. Claim No.453. Spanish gr. to John Boles, 350 arpents on waters of St. Catherine's Cr., 12 mi. NE. of Fort, b. by Luke Collins and vacant lands. N. O. 10 Feb. 1789, by Miro. // File. Claimant, John Boles, 7 Mch. 1804. Wit: Wm. Irwin, 23 May 1804. Certif. A-109.

p.354. Claim No.454. Spanish gr. to John Boles, 400 arpents on waters of Cole's Creek, b. by vacant lands. N. O., 10 Feb. 1789. // File. Claimant, John Boles, 7 Mch. 1804. Wit: Wm. Irwin, 23 May 1804. Certif. A-110 to claimant.

p.356. Claim No.455. Spanish gr. to James Bowles, 200 acres on the south bank of the Big Black, 30 mi. north of Fort, b. by Wilson Bowls and the River. N. O., 15 Jany. 1794, by Carondelet. // File. Claimant, James Bowles, 7 Mch. 1804. Wit: ____, 15 June 1804. Certif. A-111 to claimant.

p.358. Claim No.456. Spanish gr. to Christopher Butler, 240 acres on waters of Cole's Cr., b. by John Boles and vacant land. N. O., 16 Mch. 1789, by Miro. // p.360. Will of Christopher Butler, 8 July, 1791, my lawful debts to be paid out of money due me; if there be any left, I leave it to my friend, James Bolls, with all my personal property, lands, horses, gun and wearing apparel. John Boles to be sole executor. Signed with a mark. Wit: Benj. Newman, Wm. Shaw, Thos. Reid, Robert (X) Carter, Chas. (X) Carter. These witnesses appeared before Don Estevan Minor, 13 Sept. 1797 and made oath, etc. // File. Claimant, James Boles, 7 Mch. 1804. Wit: Wm. Irwin, 23 May 1804. Certif. A-112 to claimant. Dist. of Natchez, 1789, James Boles, a settler in Miss. Ter. 27 Oct. 1795, claims 240 arpents by virtue of the last will and testament of Christopher Butler, decd., as above.

p.361. Claim No.457. Spanish gr. William Vousdan, 1000 acres on Cole's Creek, one mile east of the house of James Cole, and 17 mi. east of Fort Panmûre. N. O. 7 July 1789 by Miro. // p.364. 20 Apr. 1802. William Vousdan and Elizabeth Celeste, his wife, of Adams Co., to James and Wilsòn Bolls, of Jefferson Co., for $2000 paid, the above tract of 1000 acres, b. by Jacob Stampley. Both sign. Wit: Andrew Walker, Thomas Reed. // File. Claimants, Wilson and James Bolls, 7 Mch. 1804. Wit: Robert Dunbar, 21 July 1804. Certif. A-377 to claimants, 26 June 1805. Proved in Vousdan. James and Wilson Bolls, res. of Miss. Ter. claim 1000 arpents, as above. Both signed.

p.366. Claim No.458. Spanish gr. to Wilson Bolls, 240 acres on south bank of Big Black, b. by James Bowles and Gabriel Griffin. N. O. 28 June 1796, by Carondelet. // File. Claimant, Wilson Bolls, 7 Mch. 1804. Wit: Gerard Brandon, 23 May 1804, Adam Rum and John Bolls witness, 29 Oct. 1804, Jeremiah Coleman, 26 June 1806. Certif. B-259 issued 10 Apr. 1807. Claim as above. Claimant at the head of a family at the time the pat. was issued.

p.368. Claim No.459. 4 June 1803, Alexander Callender, of Jefferson Co., Miss. Ter., for good will and regard which I bear to religious and humane institutions in general, to the Presbyterian denomination in particular, also for $6.00 to me in hand paid, I convey all the ground where the Presbyterian meeting house now stands, known by the name of Bethel Meeting House, containing 3 acres of land, to Robt. Miller, Alexr. Montgomery, John Griffin, William Erwin, Jeremiah Coleman and John Boles, trustees for the sd Bethel Congregation. Signed. Wit: Israel Coleman, George Forman, Samuel Davis. Ack. bef. James Stuart, J. P., 12 July 1803. // File. Claimants, trustees of Bethel Congregation, 7 Mch. 1804. Certif. A-245 to trustees of Bethel Congregation, 25 May 1805. Claim signed by all trustees.

p.370. Claim No.462. 27 May 1793. Patrick Sullivan sells to Stephen Miller, 400 acres in Dist. of Villa Gayoso, b. by lands of John Bolls, and lands of His Majesty, for $230 paid in hand. Patrick (X) Sullivan. (No wit.) // Spanish gr. to Patrick Sullivan for 400 acres on Cole's Cr., 24 mi. from Fort, b. by John Cole and Charles Collins. N.O. 5 Feb. 1793, by Carondelet. // File. Claimant, Stephen Miller, 7 Mch. 1804. Wit: Jean Girault, 1 Aug. 1804. Certif. A-113 issued to cl. Miss. Ter., Claiborne Co., Robert Miller, as natural guardian and next friend to his son, Stephen Miller, claims 400 acres, as above.

p.374. Claim No.463. Spanish gr. to Hezekiah Williams, 250 acres fronting on the north bank of Wells Cr., a br. of Homochitto, 24 mi. fr. Fort, b. by vacant lands. N.O., 7 Dec. 1797, by Gayoso. // p.376. 23 Aug. 1799, Hezekiah Williams to Robt. Miller, for $350 paid, 250 acres on Wells Creek as gr. above. (signed) Hezekiah Williams, Rhody (X) Williams. Wit: Abram Martin, Jesse Hooper. Ack. 13 Aug. 1802. // File. Claimant, Robert Miller, 7 Mch. 1804. Wit: John Erwin, 5 June 1804. Certif. B-110 issued, 4 Feb. 1807. Miss. Ter., Adams Co., Robt. Miller claims 250 acres as above.

p.378. Claim No.451. British gr. to Andrew Cypress, 100 acres in West Florida, 10 mi. NE. from Natchez old fort, b. on east by Herbert Minister, west by gr. to Earl of Eglinton, south by John Stephenson. Pensacola, 20 Mch. 1778, by Peter Chester. // p.384. 1 Aug. 1779, Andrew Cypress, by his atty., Donald McPherson, to Luke Collins, Jr. (P.O.A. dated 22 Apr. 1778), for $100 paid 100 acres as gr. above. Wit: William Hiorn, J. Blommart. // p.388. Natchez, 28 Nov. 1784. Luke Collins, the son, resident of Oppelousas, to Mr. John Bolls, of Natchez, 100 acres, adj. the land of Lord Eglinton, as desc. in gr. to Andrew Cypress, for $100 paid. Wit: Stephen Minor, John Ellis. // File. Claimant, John Boles, 7 Mch. 1804. Wit: William Erwin, 23 May 1804. Confirmed Feb. 27, 1805. Certif. A-6. John Boles, a settler in Miss. Ter. on 27 Oct. 1795, claims 100 acres, as above. Plat shows Herbert Munster's land, the Earl of Eglinton and John Stephens.

p.391. Claim No.469. Spanish gr. to Daniel Burnet, 1000 acres on Bayou Pierre, 35 mi. fr. the Fort, b. by vacant lands. N. O., 31 Aug. 1790, by Miro. // File. Claimant, Daniel Burnet, 7 Mch. 1804. Wit: John Booth, 19 Nov. 1804. Certif. A-114 to claimant. Plat shows the above lands on both sides of the north fork of Bayou Pierre and immediately at and around Grindstone Ford. Daniel Burnet was an inhabitant of the now Miss. Territory some before years before and on the 27 Oct. 1795, and had the above land under cultivation before and after that time. Signed.

p.393. Claim No.470. Spanish gr. to James Davenport, 300 acres on north bank of Bayou Pierre, 45 miles from Natchez Fort, b. by lands of _____ Harman, John Burnett, Jesse Hamilton and vacant lands. N. O. 24 Dec. 1797 by Gayoso. // p.395. 5 Feb. 1804, James Davenport to Daniel Burnet, for $2000 paid, 300 acres in above grant on Bayou Pierre. Wit: Prosper King. // File. Claimant, Daniel Burnet, 7 Mch. 1804. Wit: David Phelps, 25 Sept. 1805. Certificate D-209, Dec. 22, 1806. Claim of 300 arpents by virtue of the above patent.

p.395. Claim No.471. Spanish gr. to Mathew C. Tierney, 400 acres on east bank of Bayou Pierre, 50 mi. NNE. of the Fort, b. by John Hartley and vacant lands. N. O. 23 Mch. 1793. Plat to Mathew Conway Terney. // File. Claimant, Mathew C. Tierney, 7 Mch. 1804. Wit: James Truly, 17 June 1805. Certificate A-404, 5 July 1805. Claim as above.

p.397. Claim No.472. Joseph Green assigns to Henry Kiper, tract in above plat, for value recd., 13 Oct. 1803. Signed. Wit: E. Hoskinson. Plat shows: 137 acres surveyed for Joseph Green, June 3, 1802 by David B. Morgan, surv. Land on middle fork of Cole's Cr., b. by John Stephens, John Pipes and George Stampley. // File. Claimant, Henry Kiper, 7 Mch. 1804. Wit: Henry Stampley, 20 June 1804. Certif. B-8, 4 Sept. 1806. Miss. Ter., Jefferson. Henry Kiper claims 137 acres in afsd Ter. and Co. as above.

p.398. Claim No.473. Spanish gr. to Hezekiah Williams, 250 acres, 40 mi. east of Natchez, b. by lands of Joshua Stockstiles and Monsieur Chachere. N. O. 7 Dec. 1797. // p.400. 18 Dec. 1799. Hezekiah Williams to Wilford Hoggatt, above 250 acres for $450, receipt of which ack. Signed. Wit: Joshua Howard, Joseph Sessions. Prov. by Howard, 18 Dec. 1799. // File. Claimant, Wilford Hoggatt, 7 Mch. 1804. Wit: Joshua Howard, 22 June 1804. Certif. B-20 issued June 4, 1806.

p.401. Claim 474. Spanish gr. to John Ratcliff, 400 acres on Sandy Cr., 15 mi. SE. of Fort Panmure. N. O. 10 Feb. 1789 by Miro. // File. Claimant, Wilford Hoggatt, 7 Mch. 1804. Wit: Joshua Howard, 22 June 1804. Certif. A-115. Prov. in Ratcliff. Miss. Ter., Adams Co., Wilford Hoggatt claims 400 acres, as above. Sd. Ratcliff was an actual settler in sd Ter. on 27 Oct. 1795 and he assigned the sd tract to sd Wilford.

p.402. Claim No.475. Spanish gr. to John Jones, for 600 acres on a br. of Fairchild's Cr., 13 mi. NE. fr. Natchez, b. by John Cortney and vacant lands. N. O., 1 Apr. 1795, by Carondelet. // p.404. 9 June 1802, John Jones, of Jefferson Co., to David Greenleaf, of Adams Co., for $900, paid, 600 acres as in above grant. Signed. Wit: Thos. Gibson, John Martin. Ack. in open court, 12 Nov. 1802 by John Jones bef. Edward Turner, Clerk. // p.405. 5 Mch. 1804. David Greenleaf, to Jeremiah Coleman, for $1200, paid, 600 acres as above. (signed) David Greenleaf, Phebe Greenleaf. Wit: James Stuart, John Griffin. Ack. before James Stuart and John Griffin, Justices of Peace, by Phoebe Greenleaf, 5 Mch. 1804, and by David the same date. // File. Claimant, Jeremiah Coleman, 7 Mch. 1804. Wit: John Bolls, 23 July 1804. Certif. A-116. Claims 600 acres in Jefferson Co. as above.

p.406. Claim No.476. Spanish gr. to John Spyres, 300 acres on Second Cr., 13 mi. east of Natchez, b. by Hezekiah Williams and Luis Chachere. N. O. 14 Aug. 1793, by Carondelet. // p.408. 7 Nov. 1800, John Spires and Hetty, his wife, to James Hoggart, for $800 (note in hand), 300 acres in above grant. Both sign with a mark. Wit: Anthony Hoggatt, David Berry. Both ack. 7 Nov. 1800 before Anthony Hoggatt, J. P. // p.410. 5 Feb. 1804. James Hoggatt and Gressilla, his wife, to William Hoggatt, for $1000 paid, 300 acres in foregoing deed. Both sign. Wit: P. Hoggatt, Adam Tooley. // File. Claimant, William Hoggatt, 7 Mch. 1804. Wit: Joshua Howard, 22 June 1804. Certif. A-117 to claimant. Proved in John Spires. Claim as above and signed.

p.411. Claim No.1474. 17 Mch. 1799. John Thompson, of Miss. Territory, Southern County thereof, to William B. Smith, of same, for $300 paid, all of his, John Thompson's, part of a certain tract on St. Catherine's Cr., 3 mi. from the Village of Natchez, 655 acres, b. on all sides by lands of Adam Bingaman. (signed) John Thompson. Wit: David Nesbitt, Isaac Foster, Prov. by Nesbitt, 4 Oct. 1799, before Wm. Kenner, J. P. Adams Co. // p.412. 25 July 1799. Nathan Thompson, of Miss. Ter., Southern Co., to William B. Smith, Jr., for $300, paid, Nathan Thompson's part of a certain tract on St. Catherine's Cr., of which Nathan Thompson's part is a dividend, sd tract containing 655 acres, as above. (signed) Nathan Thompson. Same wit. as above. // p.413. 17 Sept. 1799, Hugh Coyle and Martha, his wife, of Adams Co., Miss. Ter., to William B. Smith, Jr., for $300, all of Hugh Coyle's and Martha's, his wife, part of 655 acres, as described above. Both signed. Wit: Lewis Evans, Thops [Thompson] Clack. Ack. 4 Oct. 1799 before Wm. Kenner, J. P. // p.414. 17 March 1799. Philetus Smith, of Miss. Ter., Southern County, to William B. Smith, of same, for $300 paid, his Philetus Smith's part of a certain tract [samè as in above deeds], Philetus Smith's dividend. Signed. Wit: David Nesbitt, Isaac Foster. Ack. 4 Nov. 1799 before William Kenner, J. P. // p.415. 17 March 1799. Solomon and Sarah Wisdom, of Miss. Territory, Southern County, to William B. Smith, of same, Sarah Wisdom's part of tract of 655 acres, as above. Wit: Same as above. Prov. by David Nesbitt bef. Wm. Kenner, J. P., 4 Oct. 1799. // Book D. p.517. Spanish grant to William Benjamin Smith, 655 acres on St. Catherine's Creek, b. on north and south by Adam Bingaman, east by Lewis Bingaman, and west by Henry Lafleur. // File. Claimant, William B. Smith, Jr., 29 Mch. 1804. Wit: Jeremiah Routh, 8 July 1805. Certif. A-415 to claimant, 9 July 1805. Miss. Ter., Wm. B. Smith, Jr. claims 655 acres in Adams Co. on waters of St. Catherine's Cr. by virtue of a patent to William B. Smith, Sr. and the said Wm. B. Smith, Sr. was an actual settler in that Territory on 27 Oct. 1795 and he sold the said tract of land to William B. Smith, Jr. Signed.

p.416. Claim No. 479. Spanish grant to James Stewart, 280 acres bet. the waters of Second Creek, 10 mi. east of Fort, b. by lands of Joshua Howard, William Alexander and James Perry. N. O. 25 Mch. 1795 by Carondelet. // p.418. 3 Jany. 1801. James Stewart and Sarah, his wife, for $800 paid in hand, to John Callihan, above tract. (signed) James Stewart, Sarah (X) Stewart. Wit: Jesse Ratcliff, Dennis Bradley. Ack. bef. Joshua Howard, J. P. 3 Jany. 1801. // File. Claimant, John Callihan, 31 Jany. 1804. [Jacket of file too faint to make out.]

p.419. Claim No.480. Spanish gr. to Jonas Scoggins, 695 arpents 4 miles north of Fort, b. by lands of Gibson Clarke and Jacob Monsanto. N. O. 3 Apr. 1794, by Carondelet. // File. Claimant, Jonas Scoggins, 8 Mch. 1804. Wit: John Grafton, 27 June 1804. Certif. A-350, 20 June 1805 to claimant.

p.421. Claim No.482. 15 Oct. 1800. Miss. Ter. Adams Co., James Lanier to Joshua Howard, the within mentioned 500 acres, for a valuable consideration. Wit: Simson Holmes, Absalom Griffin. Prov. before the Board by Absalom Griffin, 12 Apr. 1804. R. C., Clerk. // p.421. Petition to Spanish Govt. of Benj. Lanier, res. of this Dist., with a family of nine persons, for land on waters of Second Creek, adj. Ezekiel Forman. Natchez, 18 Mch. 1795. Signed. // Order for same, 18 Mch. 1795, by Gayoso. // File. Claimant, Joshua Howard, 8 Mch. 1804. Wit: Samuel Cooper, 12 Apr. 1804. Certif. B-137, 9 Feb. 1807. Plat show tract on Sandy Cr. beg. at north end of the Ogden Mandamus, surveyed 14 Feb. 1804 by Joseph Sessions, Sr.

p.422. Claim No.483. Spanish gr. to William Cooper, 800 arpents 15 mi. from Fort, b. by lands of James Erwin, George Bailey and Samuel Steady. N. O. 1 Jany. 1793, by Carondelet. // p.424.

22 Feb. 1804. William Cooper of West Florida, sells to Samuel Cooper and Absalom Cooper, of Adams Co., Miss. Terr., for $1200 in hand paid, the above land on Second Cr. (signed) William Cooper, Tarza (x) Cooper. Wit: Benj. Lanier, Jam. Doff, Joseph Thomas Callihan. // File. Claimants, Samuel Cooper and Absalom Griffin, 8 Mch. 1804. Witnesses, Alexander Farar and John Erwin, 8 Mch. 1804. Certif. A-407 to claimants, 9 July 1805. Both claimants settlers on and before 27 October 1795. Both sign.

p.425. Claim No.484. 2 June 1802. Robert Shuffield to Isaac Owen, both of Adams Co., Miss. Ter. a certain improvement made by me in 1794 on the dividing ridge bet. Second and Sandy Creeks, adj. Mr. Wilford Hoggatt, Mr. White, Mr. Morris Custard, Mr. David Ferguson and a tract formerly surveyed by Mr. John Patterson, for $250 paid. He signs with a mark. Wit: Joseph Sessions. // Adams Co. I make over to Richard Sessions my right and title to the above described land. 3 Nov. 1802. (signed) Isaac Owen. Wit: Joshua Howard. // File. Claimant, Richard Sessions, 8 Mch. 1804. Wit: Samuel Cooper, 12 Apr. 1804. Certif. B-190, issued 13 Feb. 1807. Richard Sessions claim 536 acres of land above described by a settlement and improvement thereon made by Robt. Shuffield in 1796, etc. Signed.

p.426. Claim No.486. Spanish gr. to John Farquhar, 360 acres in the Natchez Dist. N. O. 3 Sept. 1784, by Estevan Miro. // Warrant to give possession to John Farquhar 360 acres, 30 Nov. 1782. Plat shows John Bisland and Daniel Grafton with lands adj. // p.428. 27 Apr. 1784. John Farquhar sells to George Fitzgerald, of N. O., merchant, (for 300 acres) 400 acres abt. a league from the Fort, b. by Stephen Minor, John Bisland, as granted to me, for $500 to be paid 1 June 1785. Both signed. Wit: Francis Farrell. // File. Claimant, Geo. Fitzgerald, 360 arpents gr. to John Farquhar, 8 Mch. 1804. Wit: William Barland, 10 Sept. 1804. Certif. A-119 issued.

p.429. Claim No.487. Spanish gr. to James McIntire, 500 acres on waters of Fairchild's Cr., 10 mi. N.E. of Natchez, b. by Mr. Cowperthwait and vacant lands. N. O. 8 Oct. 1787 by Estevan Miro. // p.431. Natchez, 21 Feb. 1790. James McIntire to John Bisland, 500 arpents on Fairchild's Cr., 12 mi. from Natchez, for $500. Both sign before Grand-Pre. // Receipt for payment, 10 Dec. 1794. // File Claimant, Mr. John Bisland for 500 acres gr. to James McIntire, 8 Mch. 1804. Wit: James Barland, 10 Sept. 1804. Certif. A-121 to claimant. Claim signed by Susannah Bisland.

p.432. Claim No.488. Spanish gr. Jeremiah Bryan, 600 arpents on Miss. River and Fairchild's Cr., b. by Mrs. Sarah [Mary] Foster and Mr. Bonner. N. O. 29 Feb. 1788. // p.435. Fort Panmure of Natchez, 14 June 1788. Jeremiah Bryan to Mr. John Bisland, 600 arpents b. by Moses Bonner, Mrs. Vousdan, Mary Foster and Mrs. Madden, which I sell with consent of Mr. John Vauchere to whom it is mortgaged, for $450 to be pd. 1 Jany. 1789. Both sign. Receipt of money, 14 Feb. 1789. // File. Claimant, Mr. Bisland, granted to Jeremiah Bryan, 8 Mch. 1804. Wit: Wm. Barland, 10 Sept. 1804. Certif. A-122 Claim signed by Susanna Bisland.

p.436. Claim No.489. Spanish gr. to John Bisland, 850 acres 8 mi. east of Fort Panmure, b. by vacant lands. N. O. 6 Mch. 1788 by Miro. // File. Claimant, Mr. Bisland's claim for 850 acres, 8 Mch. 1804. Wit: Wm. Barland, 10 Sept. 1804. Certif. A-123. Claim signed by Susanna Bisland.

p.438. Claim No.490. Spanish gr. to John Bisland, 860 acres on waters of Fairchild's Cr., 17 mi. east of Fort, b. by Richard Dun, Isaac Tabor, James McIntire and James Cowpertwet. N. O. 9 Apr. 1790 by Miro. // File. Claimant, John Bisland, for 860 acres, 8 Mch. 1804. Wit: Wm. Barland. Certif. A-124 issued to claimant. Signed by Susanna Bisland.

p.440. Claim No.491. Spanish gr. to William Atchinson, 550 acres 8 mi. east of Fort Panmure, b. by John Bisland, Jeremiah Brian, Richard Harrison, David Smith and Zacariah Smith. N. O. 5 June 1791 by Miro. // p.442. 14 Sept. 1797, Natchez. Wm. Atchinson sells to Charles Dowling, 550 acres on St. Catherine's Cr., b. by lands of David Smith, Jeremiah Bryan, Zachariah Smith and James Foster, according to plat and grant, for $300 in notes. Both signed. Wit: John Girault, Charles King. // p.443. 13 Sept. 1803. Charles Dowling and Milla, his wife, to John Bisland, for $1575, in hand paid, the above tract. (signed) Charles Dowling, Amelia Dowling. Wit: David Nesbitt, Jno. Grafton. Prov. by Grafton before Samuel Brooks, J. P. 14 Sept. 1803. Ack. 13 Sept. 1803 by both. // Claimant, Mr. Bisland, 8 Mch. 1804. Certif. A-125. Signed: Susanna.

p.445. Claim No.492. Spanish gr. to William West, 190 acres 6 mi. from Fort, b. by John Stillee, Doctor McCabe, and St. Catherine's Cr. N. O., 25 May 1792, by Carondelet. Plats also show a Mr. Perkins and Richard Harrison adj. // p.447. 10 Jany. 1798. William West sells to Thos. Hughes, above 190 acres for $500, recd. William (x) West, Thomas Hughes. Wit: Mce. Stacpoole, John Girault, before Stephen Minor. // p.448. Thos. Hughes and wife, Mary, 11 Oct. 1798, sell to John Bisland for $500 paid, above tract on St. Catherine's Cr., as above described. (signed) Thos. Hughes, Mary Hughes. Wit: David Ferguson, John Girault. // File. Claimant, John Bisland for 190 acres gr. Wm. West, 8 Mch. 1804. Wit: Wm. Barland, 10 Sept. 1804. Certif. A-126 to claimant. Claim signed by Susanna Bisland.

p.449. Claim No.493. Spanish gr. to Hugh Coyle, for 240 acres 8 mi. east of Fort, b. by Richard King, Benj. Belk, John Foster and Richard Harrison. N. O. 30 Aug. 1795 by Carondelet. // p.451. [n.d.] Assignment of above grant by Hugh Coyle, for 240 acres, to John Bisland, for value recd. Wit: William Rucker, Thomas Thomson, Hillary Bishop. // File. Claimant, Mr. John Bisland, to whom 240 acres granted to Hugh Coyle, 8 Mch. 1804. Wit: Wm. Barland, 10 Sept. 1804. Certif. A-127 to claimant. Susanna Bisland signs claim.

p.451. Claim No.494. Spanish gr. to Maurice Joyce, 800 acres 7 mi. NNE. from Fort Panmure, b. by Wm. Henderson. N. O. 22 June 1791, by Miro. Plat shows Wm. Henderson's land was bought from Squire Boone, and these lands north of the Big Black. // p.453. New Orleans, 26 Feb. 1802, Charles Norwood, of New Orleans, Prov. of La., executor of Messrs. John Joyce and John Turnbull, deeds to John Bisland, of Natchez Dist., all my right, title etc. to 800 acres at the Big Black gr. to Maurice Joyce, as above. (signed) Charles Norwood. Wit: Daniel Douglass, Joseph McNeil, Oliver Ormsby. Prov. by Douglass, 3 Apr. 1802 before Saml. Brooks, J. P. of Adams Co. // File. Claimant, Mr. John Bisland 800 arpents gr. Maurice Joyce; presented 8 Mch 1804. Wit: John Boles, 10 Sept. 1804. Certif. A-128 to claimant. Claim signed by Susanna Bisland.

p.454. Claim No.495. Spanish gr. to John Joyce, 1000 acres on the Big Black River, 70 mi. NNE from Fort, b. by lands of John Turnbull and the River. N. O. 22 June 1791, by Miro. // File. Claimand, Mr. John Bisland, gr. to John Joyce; presented 8 Mch. 1804. Wit: John Boles, 10 Sept. 1804. Certif. A-129 to claimant. Claim signed by Susanna Bisland.

p.456. Claim No.496. Spanish gr. to John Turnbull, 1000 acres on the Big Black River, 70 mi. NNE from Fort, b. on north land of Hardy Percy and William Henderson, on south by John Joyce, west on River. N. O. 22 June 1791 by Miro. // p.458. New Orleans, 8 May 1802. Charles Norwood, as executor of Messrs. John Joyce and John Turnbull, sells to John Bisland two tracts of 2000 acres at the Big Black, 1000 acres in name of John Joyce and 1000 acres in the name of John Turnbull, for $3000 to be paid in 12 months from date. (signed) Charles Norwood. Wit: A. Brooks, Nathan Thomson, Anthony Glass. Proved by Glass before J. Callender, J. P. Natchez, 18 June 1803. // File. Claimant, Mr. J. Bisland, 1000 arpents gr. to John Turnbull, presented 8 Mch. 1804. Wit: John Boles, 10 Sept. 1804. Certif. A-130. Claim signed by Susanna Bisland.

p.459. Claim No.497. Spanish gr. to James Jones, 500 acres 9 mi. east of Fort, on Fairchild's Cr., b. by Jacob Copperthwait. N. O. 13 Aug. 1787, by Miro. Plat also shows Thomas Jordan with land adj. // p.461. N. O. 9 May 1803. Stephen Jones, a res. and merchant of this City, to William Rucker, of Natchez, present in this city, 500 acres on Fairchild's Cr. as above grant, b. by land of Jacob Copperthwait, which belonged to James Jones, brother to sd Stephen Jones, from whom I have inherited it, for $2000 paid me. (signed) Evan Jones, William Rucker. Certificate from American Consulate. Peter Pedesclaux, Esq., whose name and notarial seal are on the above bill of sale is a Notary Public duly commissioned, etc. (signed) Wm. E. Hulings, 9 May 1803. // 463. 10 June 1803. William Rucker to John Bisland, both of Adams Co., for $2000 in hand paid, 500 acres in Jefferson Co., gr. James Jones and conveyed by Stephen Jones, heir to said James, to Wm. Rucker. Signed. Wit: John Ferral, Daniel McInnis. Signed and ack. before Alexander Sterling, alcalde of the 3rd dist. of New Feliciana, 9 Feb. 1804. Prov. by Daniel McInnis, 13 Feb. 1804, bef. James Stewart, J. P. of Adams Co. Claimant, John Bisland, 500 acres as above, 8 Mch. 1804. Rejected. Claim signed by Susanna. Evan Jones a settler of Prov. of La.

p.464. Claim No.498. Spanish gr. to Alexander Bisland, 192 acres in Natchez Dist., 7 mi. east of Natchez, b. by Richard King, John Bisland, Richard Harrison and Hugh Coile. N. O., 1 June 1795, by Carondelet. // File. Claimant, Alexander Bisland, 8 Mch. 1804. Wit: William Barland, 10 Sept. 1804. Certif. A-193 to claimant. Claim signed by Susanna Bisland.

p.466. Claim No.499. Spanish gr. to Charles Norwood, 400 square acres, 1 1/2 acres from Fort, b. by Richard Harrison, Stephen Minor, John Farquhar, John Bisland and John Lum. N. O., 9 May 1786. // p.468. Baton Rouge, 7 Sept. 1799. Charles Norwood, of New Orleans, Prov. of La., for $1000 paid, to George Fitzgerald, tract in Natchez Dist. gr to him as above, also all the stock thereto belonging. Signed. Wit: Michel Makie, Frans. Poussett, Wm. Rucker. Prov. by oath of Wm. Rucker before Wm. Kenner, J. P. Adams Co., Miss. Ter. 25 Feb. 1800. // File. Claimant, Geo. Fitzgerald, 8 Mch. 1804. Wit: Wm. Barland, 10 Sept. 1804. Certif. A-132 to claimant. Wm. Barland says that Charles Norwood lived in New Orleans but the tract claimed was inhabited and cultivated by his own people for and on his own account and that George Fitzgerald represented him as his agent.

p.469. Claim No.500. Spanish gr. to George Fitzgerald, 1000 acres on Fairchild's Cr., 11 mi. NE. from the Fort, b. by lands of Gabriel Benoist and Mr. Ramsey, James Fletcher and John Reed. N. O. 24 Dec. 1797 by Gayoso. // File. Claimant, Mr. George Fitzgerald, 8 Mch. 1804. Wit: Wm. Barland, 10 Sept. 1804. Certif. D-101, issued 3 Feb. 1807. Claim for 1000 acres as above.

p.471. Claim No.501. British Gr. to John Hostler, 200 acres on waters of Bayou Pierre, b. by lands of John Ross, abt. 3 mi. from mouth of said Bayou. Pensacola, 25 May 1779 by Peter Chester. // p.475. Natchez, West Florida, 20 July 1779. John Hostler and Temperance, his wife, to William Vousdan, of sd dist., Gentleman, for $200 paid, tract of 200 acres as above, John (x) Hostler, Temperance Hostler. Wit: J. Blommart, Richard Harrison, Philip Barbour. // File. Claimants, devisees and legal representatives of William Vousdan, decd. 8 Mch. 1804. Wit: A. Green. Prov. 10 Sept. 1804. Notation: Vousdan's will wanted. Certif. A-134 issued to legal representatives. Miss. Ter., the devisees and legal representatives of William Vousdan, decd., claim 200 acres in Claiborne Co., on waters of Bayou Pierre, by virtue of a Br. pat. to John Hostler, as above, etc. and the sd. William Vousdan willed the sd tract to said devisees and representatives. Signed: Geo. Fitzgerald, exor. to the estate of W m. Vousdan, decd.

p.480. Claim No.502. British gr. to William Vousdan, 200 acres on the Miss. River, at the Three Islands, b. by Thomas James, William Silkredge, the Miss. River and a navigable lake. Pensacola, 15 Sept. 1777, by Peter Chester. Plat, 2 June 1777 by Elias Durnford, Surv. Genl. // File. Claimant, William Vousdan, 8 Mch. 1804. Wit: Abner Green, 2 Aug. 1804. Notation: Vousdan's will wanted. Certif. A-135 issued to legal representatives. Claim signed by Geo. Fitzgerald, exor. of estate of William Vousdan, decd.

p.483. Claim No.503. Lease and release, 31 Aug. 1777, 21 July 1779, Francis Dolony and wife, Lucy, to Wm. Vousdan, for $200 tract of 250 acres on James br. of Bayou Pierre, b. by John Ross, Thos. James and land gr. to Wm. Vousdan, and lands of John Hostler. (signed) Francis Dolony. Lucy (x) Dolony. Wit: Nehemiah Carter, John Bisland, Don McPherson. // File. Claimant, devisees and legal representatives of Wm. Vousdan, decd., 8 Mch. 1804. Wit: Abner Green, 2 Aug. 1804. Rejected June 11, 1807. Claim signed by Geo. Fitzgerald, as above.

p.488. Claim No.504. Spanish gr. to David Lejeune, 400 acres 4 mi. east of the Miss. River, b. by Francis Poussett and David Munro, 14 mi. south of the Fort. N. O. 20 Mch. 1789. // p.489. Bill of Sale. David Lejeune to David Ross. New Orleans, 18 Mch. 1794. The above land grant, for $350. Both sign. Wit: Miguel Gomez. Notary Public, Pedro Pedesclaux, 3 Oct. 1794. // p.491. David Ross to George Fitzgerald, 28 May 1798, for $5000, 1000 acres in the settlement of Bayou Sara, b. by Francis Poussett, David Munro, Cesar Archinard and Charles Percy, desc., patents annexed, one to David Lejeune for 400 acres, one to David Ross for 600 acres. Signed. Wit: Wm. Vousdan, Wm. Barland, James Fitzgerald. Receipt for $5000, same date. Prov. by Wm. Barland and James Fitzgerald, 26 Aug. 1799 before Thos. Wilkins, J. P., Adams Co., Miss. Ter. // p.493. 25 Mch. 1800. George Fitzgerald to Wm. Vousdan, for $5000, the above property. Signed. Wit: Bryan McDermott, J. B. Ragant, John Henderson. Ack. by Geo. Fitzgerald, 25 Mch. 1800, bef. Thos. Wilkins, J. P., Adams Co. // File. Claimant, Wm. Vousdan, 8 Mch. 1804. Wit: Wm. Barland, 10 Sept. 1804. Certif. A-136, to legal representatives. Claim signed by Geo. Fitzgerald, one of the executors of est. of Wm. Vousdan. Note: Wm. Barland says the same of David Ross precisely as of Charles Norwood in Claim No.499.

p.496. Claim No.974. British gr. to William Godley, Esq., 250 acres on the Miss. River, opposite the Three Islands, called the Grand Current, 9 mi. above the cut-off, b. by George Raincock and the river. Pensacola, 21 Oct. 1774, by Peter Chester. Warrant dated 14 Oct. 1771. // File. Claimant, Wm. Godley, 22 Mch. 1804. Reported, 28 Apr. 1807. Claim as above.

p.499. Claim No.976. British gr. to William Marshall, Esq., 2000 acres on a br. of Boyd's Cr. // Pet. 16 June 1777, of Benj. Hickey, late a warrant officer in Our Navy who served in America in last war, asks for 2000 acres, 26 Mch. 1777 on a br. of Boyd's Cr. Marshall purchased tract but Hickey had gone beyond seas and the title could not be perfected. Marshall pet. for tract, which was gr. as above. // p.505. Wm. Marshall, Esq., of Charleston, S. C., son and heir of Wm. Marshall, decd., who died 30 Sept. 1786, to Thos. Wadsworth. 10 June 1799. Wit: Jacob Drayton, Stephen Lee, Jr. // p.507. Charlotte Marshall, wife, sd. William relinq. dower, 15 June 1799 bef. Jacob Drayton, J. Q. // File. Claimant, William Turpin, 22 Mch. 1804. Notation: See No.371. Reported, 3 June 1807. Claim: above tract on a branch of Holt's fork of Boyd's Cr. claimed by Wm. Turpin and Benj. Cudworth, executors of Thos. Wadsworth, decd. on behalf of the heirs and representatives, as above. (signed) E. H. Bay, Atty.

p.508. Claim No.505. Spanish gr. to David Ross, 600 acres 33 mi. south of Fort Panmure, 6 mi. east of River, adj. David Lejeune, Francis Pousset. N. O. 14 April 1790 by Miro. // File. Claimant, W. Vousdan, 8 Mch. 1804. Wit: Wm. Barland, 10 Sept. 1804. Certif. A-137 to legal representatives. Claim signed by Geo. Fitzgerald, one of Exors of Wm. Vousdan. Wm. Barland says the same of David Ross as of Charles Norwood, Cl. No.499.

p.510. Claim No.506. Spanish gr. to Wm. Vousdan, 10 arpens, Natchez, 12 Feb. 1795, by Gayoso. Petition for 10 arps. for family, b. by Francis Lennan and Luis Valeret, and road, 5 Feb. 1795. // File. Claimant, Wm. Vousdan, Esq. 8 Mch. 1804. Wit: Abner Green, 2 Aug. 1804. Certif. A-523 issued to legal representatives, 27 Aug. 1805. Claim signed by Geo. Fitzgerald, one of exors. of Wm. Vousdan's est.

p.512. Claim No.507. Spanish gr. to Wm. Vousdan, 2000 acres on a br. of Bayou Sara, 4 mi. NE of establishment of James Mather and 45 mi. SE. of Fort Panmure. N. O. 30 Aug. 1793, by Carondelet. // File. Claimant, Wm. Vousdan, Esq., 8 Mch. 1804. Wit: Abner Green, 2 Aug. 1804. Wit: Wm. Dunbar, 11 Oct. 1805, Alexander Montgomery, 4 Feb. 1806. Disallowed on suspicion of its being antedated, 22 Dec. 1807. Claim signed by Geo. Fitzgerald, one of exors. of est. of Wm. Vousdan, decd.

p.514. Claim No.508. Spanish gr. to Richard Ellis, 180 acres on Homochitto River, b. by lands of sd Richard Ellis, Dona Celeste Hutchins. N. O. 31 Jany. 1788, by Miro. // p.516. Executors of Richard Ellis, decd., to John Ellis, Sr. of Dist. of St. Catherine, two tracts, 320 arps. and 180 arps, both grants to Richard Ellis, in payment we receive from sd John Ellis 800 arpents which was gr. to him. Signed: John Ellis, Abram Ellis, John Ellis, Jr., Natchez, 22 Feb. 1798. Wit: Wm. Conner, John Blackburn before Estevan Minor. // File. Claimant, John Ellis, Sr., 8 Mch. 1804. Residence prov. before 16 Jany. 1805. Certif. A-148 issued to claimant. Claim as above.

p.518. Claim No.509. Spanish gr. to Moses Bonner, 400 acres 9 mi. NE of Fort, b. by lands of Moses Bonner, Jr., James Bonner and Josh Bonner. N. O. 26 Mch. 1789 by Miro. // p.519. 17 Dec. 1788. Moses Bonner to Melling Wooley, for $1000, on terms, the above tract. Moses (x) Bonner, (signed) Melling Wooley. // p.521. 9 Nov. 1789. Melling Wooley to Wm. Collins and Windsor Pipes, 400 acres on the High Bluff of the Miss. River, 3 leagues from the Fort, as above, for 14,700 lbs. of tobacco. Signed by all three. // p.522. Natchez, 2 Oct. 1791. William Collins to John Stowers, 200 arpents on the Miss. River, other half belongs to Windsor Pipes, for 4000 pounds of tobacco. Both sign. Wit: Fransco. Goday, Joseph Vidal, before Gayoso. // p.525. 8 Dec. 1802. Frances Odem and Abner Pipes, exors of est. of David Odem, to Windsor Pipes, all of Jefferson Co., for $50, a lot in plan of town laid out by Exors. of sd Odem, No.20, 80 sq-ft. Wit: Walter Mackay, Asaph ONeal. (signed) Abner Pipes, Frances (x) Odem. Wit: Walter Mackay, Asaph ONeal. // File. Claimants, John Stowers and Windsor Pipes, 8 Mch. 1804. Wit: David Barry, 8 Jany. 1805. Certif. A-149, to claimants. John Stowers and Winsor Pipes claim 400 acres of land on waters of Fairchild's Cr., each 200 acres, as above.

p.525. Claim No.514. Miss. Ter., Jefferson Co., 18 Feb. 1804. Esther Hackler, agent and atty for Jacob Jrokel, to William Shaw, 475 acres on waters of north fork of Cole's Cr., actually settled and cultivated by sd Jacob Jrokel in 1797, being the tract that William Shaw now lives on, for $50; warrants claim agst Jacob Jrokel, myself and every person. (signed) Esther Hackler. Wit: John Dennis, Conrad Young. Ack. before the Board of Commrs. 13 Apr. 1804. R. C., Clerk. // File. Claimant, Wm. Shaw, 8 May 1804. This claim was rejected 6 May 1806. I do hereby certify that at the request of Mr. Jacob Troxel I have surveyed for him 475 acres [as above] 20 July 1797. (signed) Wm. Thomas.

Wm. Shaw, legal representative of Jacob Jrokel claims donation of above tract in Jefferson Co., purchased by sd Shaw of Easter Hackler, agent and atty. for Jacob Jrokel.

p.526. Claim No.515. 27 Sept. 1798. Stephen Minor, Esq., Commissioner for running the Line of Demarcation on the part of His Majesty, to Solomon Hiram Wisdom, res. of the Southern Dist. of Miss. Ter., for $160, paid, 160 acres on Second Cr. b. by Arthur Cobb, Stephen Minor and David Mitchell, part of a larger tract gr. to sd Minor, Esq. Wit: Arthur Cobb. (signed) Stephen Minor. // p.527. Solomon H. Wisdom, for $650 in hand paid, to Richard Philetus Smith, all right in above described plantation. (signed) Solomon H. Wisdom, Sarah Wisdom. 1 Jany. 1800. Wit: Philander Smith, Courtland Smith, David Nesbitt and John Holliday. // Natchez Dist. 26 Aug. 1792. I do hereby certify that I have carefully surveyed and laid off 160 acres to Solomon Hiram Wisdom, being a part of a tract belonging to Mr. Stephen Minor, and lays on Second Cr., 7 mi. SE. from Natchez Fort. (signed) Wm. Atchinson. David Nesbitt made oath to signing above deed. Dec. 9, 1800 before Wm. Kenner, J. P., Adams Co., Miss. Ter. // File. Claimant, Richard P. Smith, 8 Mch. 1804. Proved in Major Stephen Minor, 1 Oct. 1804. Certif. A-365 issued to claimant, 24 June 1804. Claim signed by Richard Philetus Smith.

p.529. Claim. No.516. Spanish gr. to David Mitchell, 400 acres 10 mi. from Fort Panmure, b. by lands of Don Estevan Minor, a large English concession, Abraham Ellis and Mrs. Smith. N. O. 8 June 1792, by Carondelet. // p.530 Natchez 23 Mch. 1798. David Mitchell sells to Calvin Smith, 400 acres on Second Creek, adj. Philander Smith, Stephen Minor, Abram Ellis and lands of Amos Ogden, for $400 in hand paid. Both sign. Wit: Samuel Hutchins, John Girault. // p.532. 16 Jany. 1798. Joseph Martinez to Luther and Calvin Smith a certain lot of ground near the Town, adj. John Scott's, Job Routh's, the main street leading from John Wilson's, which lot is 100 ft. in front and 125 ft. in depth. Filed 8 April 1799. Signed: John Girault, Keeper of Records. // File. Claimant, Calvin Smith, 8 Mch. 1804. Wit: John Girault, 1 Apr. 1805. Certif. A-150 issued to claimant. Claim of 400 arpents of land on Second Cr. as above. [No reference to a record of the third and last transfer.]

p.532. Claim No.520. Spanish gr. to Ephraim Coleman, 300 acres on Cole's Creek, 20 mi. north from the Fort, b. by Israel Coleman and Samuel Davies. N. O. 11 Apr. 1791 by Miro. // File. Claimants, heirs of E. Coleman, decd., 8 Mch. 1804. Wit: John Jones, 4 June 1804. Certif. A-151 issued to legal representatives. Miss. Ter., Jefferson Co., the heirs of Ephraim Coleman, decd., claim 300 acres on waters of Cole's Cr. granted to sd Coleman as above. Signed: Israel Coleman, acting exr. to estate of E. Coleman, decd.

p.535. Claim No.521. Spanish gr. to Israel Coleman, 300 arpents on Cole's Cr., 20 mi. north from the Fort, b. by Ephraim Coleman and Alexander Callender. N. O. 11 Apr. 1791 by Miro. // File. Claimant, I. Coleman, 8 Mch. 1804. Wit: John Jones, 4 June 1804. Certif. A-152. Miss. Ter., Jefferson Co. Claim as above.

p.537. Claim No.524. Petition of James Mcgill, being married and with four children, bet. the ages of 11 and 16, and desiring to settle in this province with sd family, asks 500 acres south of Bayou Pierre near Robert Cochran. Natchez, 4 Aug. 1789. James McGill. Recommended by Gayoso, 6 Aug. 1789. // Warrant for 400 arpents by Miro. New Orleans, 26 Apr. 1790. // File. Claimant, heirs of James McGill, 9 Mch. 1804. Wit: Buckner Pittman. Certif. D-102 issued, 3 Feb. 1807. Miss. Territory, Claiborne Co. John McGill and James McGill by Mary McGill, their agent, who is the natural guardian of the heirs and legal representatives of James McGill, decd. who died intestate, claim 500 acres on waters of Doud's Creek and the Petit Gulf Creek, by virtue of a Spanish order of survey, as above. James McGill died before the above order was obtained, leaving sd Mary, his widow, and said children, who inhabited and cultivated said land at the date of the afsd order and for a considerable time afterwards and then moved off but resumed habitation and possession in 1797 or 1798. Said tract b. by lands of Robert Cochran and vacant lands.

p.538. Claim No.529. 18 Mch. 1804. Jesse Edwards, of Claiborne Co., to John Stillee, for $300, in hand paid, 640 acres on the Road leading through the Wilderness from the Grindstone Ford at the forks of Big Black and the Wilderness Roads, which land I settled and cultivated in 1797 and am thereby entitled to a donation of 640 acres. Jesse (x) Edwards. Wit: Rd. Claiborne, W. B. Shields. // File. Claimant, John Still Lee, 9 Mch. 1804. Wit: James Holloway, 21 Aug. 1804. Notation: Davenport Wiseman, Thomas F_______, and Sarah Edwards, June 12, 1806. Certif. D-251, issued 8 Apr. 1807.

Miss. Ter., Claiborne Co. The above described 640 acres of land on a branch of Big Black and on the Road through the Wilderness, occupied by sd John Still Lee. Signed: Daniel Burnet. Claim signed by John Still Lee, who was head of a family on the day when the Spanish troops finally evacuated the said territory. Other witnesses, William Miller, John Hamilton, 4 Sept. 1804. Daniel Hoffman.

p.539. Claim No.530. Spanish gr. to Mrs. Margaret Lefleur, 920 acres 17 mi. east of Fort, b. by Robert Dow and Joshua Stockley. N. O. 4 Sept. 1789 by Miro. // File. Claimants, Peter and M. Nelson, 9 Mch. 1804. Wit: Anthony Calvet, 21 Aug. 1804. Certif. A-133, to claimants. Miss. Ter., Adams Co. Peter Nelson and Margaret Nelson, his wife, claim 928 arpents on waters of Cole's Cr. by virtue of a patent by Spanish Govt. to the said M. Nelson, by and in the name of Margaret Lafleur, as above, who was an inhabitant of the said territory 27 Oct. 1795. Peter Nelson and Margaret Nelson. Plat shows Dr. Robert Dow and James Stockstill with lands adj.

p.542. Claim No.531. Spanish gr. to John Ford, 700 arpents 18 mi. east of the Fort, on Cole's Cr., b. by William Calvet and Capt. John B. Perret. N. O. 18 Mch. 1790 by Miro. [File missing.]

p.544. Claim No.533. Spanish gr. to Adam Biclay, 400 arpents on Cole's Cr., 30 mi. NE. from Fort, b. by lands of Thos. Daniel. N. O. 14 Aug. 1794 by Carondelet. // File. Claimant, Jacob Guise, 10 March 1804. Wit: Nathaniel Kennison, 20 June 1804. Certif. A-154 to legal representatives of A. Bickley. Jacob Guise, as administrator of the est. of Adam Bickley, decd., to whom 400 arpents as above were granted, claims the same. Signed. Proved in the claimant and Bickley.

p.545. Claim No.534. Spanish gr. to Hugh Mathews 300 acres near Big Black River, 7 mi. from its mouth at the River Miss., b. by lands of E. Boyd and vacant lands. N. O. 7 Dec. 1797 by Gayoso. // File. Claimant, John Stampley. 10 Mch. 1804. Wit: Adam Lanehart, 5 Nov. 1804. See No.342. Rejected, 10 April 1807. Miss. Ter., Jefferson Co., John Stampley claims the right to tract of land by virtue of a Spanish gr. to Hugh Mathews, as above, and an order of survey, 24 Feb. 1795, 300 arpents on waters of Big Black, the same being conveyed to me by said Mathews. Signed.

p.548. Claim No.535. British gr. to William Alexander, 600 acres 9 mi. east of Miss. River and the Fort at Natchez, b. by Second Cr. and vacant lands, in Prov. of West Florida. Pensacola, 21 Sept. 1772, by Peter Chester. // p.552. 18 Feb. 1774. William Alexander and wife, Mary, of the Natchez settlement, for £20, the above 600 acres to Isaac and Reuben Alexander. (signed) William Alexander, Mary (X) Alexander. Wit: William O'Neal, Robt. Collingwood, Emanuel Madden. Prov. by Wm. O'Neal before Philip Livingstome, Jr. Esq. in Pensacola, 20 Jany. 1777. // File. Claimants, Isaac and Joshua Alexander, 10 Mch. 1804. Wit: Joshua Howard, 12 Apr. 1804. Confirmed 27 Feb. 1805. Certif. A-7 to claimants. Isaac and Joshua Alexander, settlers in the Miss. Ter., at and before 27 Oct. 1795, claim 600 acres on Second Cr. by virtue of a British grant to William Alexander, as above, and by conveyance to said Isaac and Reuben Alexander, decd, of whom the said Joshua is the heir at law.

p.554. Claim No.537. Spanish gr. to Jacob Troop, 127 acres in the Natchez District. // Petition of Jacob Troop who has come from the U. S. to establish himself in this district and had bought a house from Wm. Collins which was built on the land of John Stowers, which I have lost the grant for; asks for grant for enough land to have a plantation for the subsistence of his family of six persons, adj. Chas. Adams, John Bullen, Joseph Perkins, Charles Carter and Wm. West. Natchez, 10 Jany. 1793. // Wm. Dunbar reports that the land requested is vacant. // N. O. 2 Mch. 1793. warrant for 127 acres by Carondelet. // p.555. 2 Jany. 1802. Jacob Troop, Jr. and William Troop to John Perky, for $200 paid, Spanish grant of 127 acres. Both signed. Wit: Wm. Hollingsworth, E. Bradish. // File. Claimant, John Perky, 10 Mch. 1804. Witnesses: John Bullen and Jacob Stroop, Jr. Certif. B-43 issued 29 Aug. 1806. // Miss. Ter. Adams Co., John Perkey, claims 127 acres on St. Catherine's Cr., as above, and by virtue of the gift of the said tract of land to his son-in-law and a release from William and Jacob Stroup to sd John Perkey, who has inhabited and cultivated the same before and ever since Oct. 27, 1795. (signed) John Pirkey. Plat shows land of Edward McCabe adj.

p.555. Claim No.540. Walnut Hills, 9 Dec. 1801. Agreement between Jeremiah Jones and John Summers. Summers obliges himself to settle on a certain improvement and there build and cultivate sd land for 6 years, also to have all he can make on sd land, and at the expiration to deliver sd plantation to Jeremiah Jones with all fences, houses, etc. that Summers may make or cause to be made. Jeremiah Jones to furnish provisions the first year and to assist in building one house and hauling of rails to be got the first year to fence the land. Signed by both. Wit: Joseph Ferguson, Sr., Joseph

Ferguson, Jr. Prov. bef. the Board, 12 Mch. 1804. // File. Claimant, Jeremiah Jones, 12 Mch. 1804. Wit: Joseph Ferguson, Jr. Certif. D-222 issued 22 Dec. 1806. Preemption claim by Jeremiah Jones, 334 acres on Big Fishing Cr.

p.556. Claim No.541. Spanish gr. to William Daniel, 200 acres bet. the waters of Fairchild's Cr., 10 mi. north of the Fort, b. by John Boles, Thomas Green and Wm. Daniel. N. O. 20 Oct. 1793, by Carondelet. // p.558. 7 June 1798. Wm. Daniel to John Wiley, for $30 paid, 200 acres as above granted. Signed. Wit: John Girault, Wm. Dunbar, Jr., to Alex. Ross. // p.559. 4 June 1802. John Wiley and Louvicy, his wife, to Timothy O'Hara, for $410 paid, a certain tract b. by lands of sd John Wiley, John Bolls, 95 acres of sd tract previously sold to David Ferguson, and by Wm. Daniel, Sr.; also another tract of 86 acres, b. by John Boles, Gerard Brandon and Richard Ellis, as by patent for 191 acres. Both signed. Wit: Wm. Lemon, Jonathan C. K. Lyete. // p.561. Natchez, 12 Feb. 1798. John Stampley to Hugh Mathews, 350 acres in Cole's Cr. Dist., b. by Richard Roddy's land and my own, being part of 800 arpents gr. to me, to be taken in the center of grant, leaving 50 acres on east for Richard Roddy, 400 acres to west remaining to me; for $120 and 300 acres of land on Big Black, which I have recd. Both signed. Wit: Isaac Foster, Stephen Minor, Ebenezer Petty. // File. Claimant, Timothy O'Hara, 12 Mch. 1804. Wit: John Boles, 23 May 1805. Certif. A-601 to claimant, 17 Dec. 1805. Miss. Ter., Adams Co. Timothy O'Hara claims 105 arpents of land on waters of Fairchild's and St. Catherine's Creeks, by virtue of a Sp. pat. to Wm. Daniel, as above, for 200 arps. [The deed from Stampley to Hugh Matthews does not seem to belong in this file.]

p.562. Claim No.545. Spanish gr. to Samuel Cobun, 300 arpents on south fork of Bayou Pierre, 45 mi. from the Fort, b. by Elisha Flower and vacant lands. N. O., 9 Apr. 1790 by Miro. // File. Claimant, Samuel Cobun, 12 Mch. 1804. Wit: Caleb King. Certif. A-155 to claimant.

p.564. Claim No.548. Miss. Ter., Claiborne Co., 28 Feb. 1803. Tobias Gibson, for $100, to the heirs of Malachi Gibson, an improvement in Miss. Swamp, below Walnut Hills. Signed. Wit: Seth Caston. Prov. by Caston bef. Board of Commrs. 12 Mch. 1804. // Furney Griffin to Tobias Gibson, 16 Dec. 1803, for $100. [same improvement as above], warranting sd claim agst the claim of Jonathan Dayton, the same lying below the land claimed by Anthony Glass. Prov. bef. Board, 12 Mch. 1804. // File. Claimant, heirs of M. Gibson, 12 Mch. 1804. Wit: Jonas Griffin. Certif. _ 225, issued to claimants. Claim signed by Seth Carton, agent.

p.565. Claim No.550. Spanish gr. to William Owens, 460 arpents bet. waters of Fairchild's Cr. and St. Catherine's, 8 mi. NE from Fort, b. by James Wade, James McIntire, John Bisland and Manuel Madden. N. O. 22 Jany. 1793 by Carondelet. // File. Claimants, heirs of William Owens, 12 Mch. 1804. Wit: Thos. Foster, 16 Sept. 1805. Certif. A-595 issued to legal representatives, 16 Sept. 1805. Claim by virtue of a Spanish gr. as above, which land was settled by William Owens in 1787 and held in peacable possession. Signed: Susannah, guardian for the heirs afsd, namely, Margaret, Martin, Mary, Andrew, David, Alexander, Nancy, William and James Owens, heirs of the sd Wm. Owens, decd.

p.567. Claim No.551. 10 June 1801, Joseph Sessions and Sarah, his wife, to Wm. Nelens, for $700 paid, 200 acres on Sandy Cr., b. by lands of Capt. Benj. Farrar, being part of two tracts of land, gr. to Wm. Ratcliff and Anthony Hoggatt. Both signed. Wit: Richard Sessions, James Howard. Ack. 26 June 1801 before Joshua Howard, J. P. for Adams Co. // File. Claimant, Willian Nealons, 12 Mch. 1804. Certif. A-511 and 512 issued to claimants, 26 Aug. 1805. William Nealons claims 200 acres as above.

p.568. Claim No.555. British gr. to James Perry, 100 acres, 12 mi. SE of Natchez, bet. the lands of Col. Harcourt, James Robertson and Jeremiah Germain. Pensacola. 9 Oct. 1777. // p.571. 5 Mch. 1801. Barnabas Perry, for $300, to Joseph Sessions, 100 acres, b. by lands of Wm. Ratcliff, John Calliham, Isaac Alexander and Joshua Howard, but at time of survey bounded as per British pat. to James Perry, as above. Signed. Ack. 26 Apr. 1801 before Joshua Howard, J. P. Wit: Robert Ford, John Spires. // File. Claimant, Joseph Sessions, 12 Mch. 1804. Wit: Joshua Howard, 26 May 1804. Certif. A-408 issued 9 July 1805. Claims 100 acres on Second Cr. by above British patent.

p.573. Claim No.556. Spanish gr. to Anthony Hoggatt, 768 acres on Second Cr., 10 mi. east of Natchez, b. by Thos. Martin and Wm. Ratcliff. N. O. 14 Aug. 1794, by Carondelet. // p.574. 10 June 1801. Anthony Hoggatt and Sarah, his wife, for $1050 paid, 368 acres in Township of Sandy Cr., beg. at Joshua Howard's corner, the beg. of Peter Vandoran's 400 acres bought by him from sd Anthony

Hoggatt, and was the east end of the same survey with said 386 acres, . . . to James Stewart's and James Perry's lines and Wm. Ratcliff's corner. (signed) Anthony Hoggatt, Sally Hoggatt. Wit: James Howard, Richard Sessions. Ack. 25 June 1801. // File. Claimant, Joseph Sessions, 12 Mch. 1804. Wit: Joshua Howard, 26 May 1804. Certif. A-158, to claimant, for 125 acres. Claim as above.

p.576. Claim No.1176. Agreement. 6 Aug. 1802. J. Pannell promised to transfer all claim to a mill seat on a run issuing from my spring, whereon I have built my house, unto Samuel C. Young, Esq., on Jany. 1st next, in consideration of a purchase agreed on bet. Mr. Young and myself, but it is of no force if that contract should not be perfected. (signed) J. Pannell. By consent of each, the execution of this agreement postponed until 5 Jany. 1803, if not before. Both signed. Wit: Thos. Chapman, Jr., Richard Graham. // File. Claimant, Samuel C. Young, 26 Mch. 1804. Rejected, 12 June 1807. Samuel C. Young claims 300 acres on waters of Buffalo Cr. founded on the 2nd section of the Act of Cong. providing for the disposal of lands of the U. S. south of Tennessee by settlement and cultivation of sd land by Joseph Pannell, since 1796 until 4 Jany. 1803 when he sold it to the present claimant. If, under the Act of Congress cited, the claimant should be precluded from the donation of said land, he prays the preference in becoming the purchaser of so much as may seem mete to the Board, as he has now near 100 negroes and many children on the premises. Signed.

p.576. Claim No.1183. 24 March 1804. John Pollard to James Bownds, an improvement adj. Benj. Capper's line, north of Bayou Pierre, for $20 paid. Signed. Wit: H. Crabb, Ezekial Evans. // File. Claimant, James Bowndes, 20 Mch. 1804. Wit: Martin Cooper. Certif. _ -40, 8 Sept. 1806. James Bounds claims preemption claim of 200 acres of land in Claiborne Co. on Miller's Bayou by virtue of settlement made by John Pollard prior to Mch. 1, 1803 and sold to James Bounds.

p.576. Claim No.1187. 25 March 1800, James Glasscock to Thomas Frazer, for $300 paid, 50 acres, formerly claimed and improved by Harmon Glasscock on St. Catherine's Cr., 3 mi. from Miss. River, b. by lands of Mary Girault and Daniel Myggatt, being part of tract gr. to William Brookes in 1782, containing 208 acres. Signed. Wit: Richard King, Chas. Jones. Prov. by Richard King, 28 July 1801. // File. Claimant, David Lattimore, assignee of Thomas Frazer, 20 Sept. 1805. Thos. H. Williams Register. Claim as above, William Brookes conveying said 50 acres, part of 208 acres granted, to Harmon Glasscock, who conveyed same to sd James Glasscock, who sold to Thos. Frazer. Certif. _ 634 issued to David Lattimore, assignee of claimant.

p.578. Claim No.1188. Spanish gr. to Eunice McIntosh, 566 acres on west bank of St. Catherine's Cr., b. by vacant lands. N. O. 26 Jany. 1787 by Miro. // File. Claimant, Eunice McIntosh, 26 Mch. 1804. Wit: B. Osmun. Certif. A-313 issued to claimant, June 13, 1805. Claimant an actual settler on 27 Oct. 1795, by virtue of above gr.

p.580. Claim No.1189. British gr. to Daniel Clarke, Esq., a reduced Capt. of the Pennsylvania troops, for 3000 acres, 3 mi. south of Fort Panmure, on Miss. River, on St. Catherine's Cr. Pensacola, 15 Jany. 1768, sig. by Montford Brown. // p.584. Lease and release, 10th and 11th Oct. 1776. Daniel Clarke, late a res. of Prov. of West Florida, but now of the Island of New Orleans, Esq. and Jane, his wife, to William Hiorn, of afsd province, Esq., for $2500 Spanish milled dollars, paid, 3000 acres in above grant. Both signed. Wit: Catherine Macnemara, Stephen Watts. Prov. by Stephen Watts 30 Nov. 1776 before John Miller, Esq., Master of Chancery for West Florida. // File. Claimant, James McIntosh, 26 Mch. 1804. Wit: Benajah Osmun. Certif. A-471 issued 1 Aug. 1805. James McIntosh, an actual settler in Miss. Ter. on 27 Oct. 1795, claims 1000 acres, being an undivided part of a tract of 3000 acres orig. gr. to Daniel Clarke, as above, in Adams Co., the sd land having been conveyed by sd Daniel Clarke and his wife to Wm. Hiorn and afterwards, on 31 July, 1790, sold by order of the Spanish Govt. at a public sale and purchased by the claimant, James McIntosh. [Original British grant, 1768, and the Spanish sale of this part of it, in file.]

p.590. Claim No.1190. Spanish gr. to Dona Eunice McIntosh, 800 arpens, on two branches of Bayou Sara, 40 mi. south of Fort, b. by William Dunbar and James McIntosh. N. O. 22 Mch. 1795 by Carondelet. // File. Claimant, Eunice McIntosh, 26 Mch. 1804. Wit: B. Osmun. Certif. A-676, 14 Oct. 1805.

p.592. Claim No.1191. Spanish gr. to James McIntosh, for 800 acres, fronting on the main branch of Bayou Sara, 40 mi. south of Fort, b. by Wm. Dunbar and Eunice McIntosh. N. O. 22 Mch. 1795, by Carondelet. // File. Claimant, James McIntosh, 26 Mch. 1804. Certif. A-675 issued 14 Oct. 1805. Wit: B. Osmun, 28 Nov. 1804.

p.594. Claim No.1192. Petition to Spanish Govt. by Eunice McIntosh for a lot in Natchez on which to build a home, 8 Jany. 1795. Signed. 10 Jany. 1795. Order for same by Gayoso. Warrant for Lot No.3, Sq. No. 6, in City of Natchez, for Mrs. Eunice McIntosh, by Wm. Dunbar. // Ratified, Natchez, 15 Jany. 1795 by Gayoso. [No file.]

p.596. Claim No.1193. Spanish gr. to James McIntosh, 800 acres 6 mi. south of Fort Panmure, b. by David Williams, Wm. Dunbar and Samuel Hutchins. N. O. 12 Feb. 1788, by Miro. // File. Claimant, James McIntosh, 26 Mch. 1804. Wit: Benajah Osmun. Certif. A-315, June 14, 1805. As above.

p.598. Claim No.1197. Spanish gr. to Richard Carpenter, 800 arps. on St. Catherine's Cr., b. by Daniel Whitacre. N. O. 30 June 1788, by Miro. Plat by Wm. Vousdan. // p.599. "First, I give and bequeath a tract of 800 acres gr. me by this govt. (as above) to my son, James Carpenter, and my will and intent further is that a house 35 ft. long by 18 ft. wide be built thereon." The foregoing a true transcript extracted from the last will and testament of the late Richard Carpenter, filed in my office, the same being duly proved and approved. (signed) John Girault, Keeper of Records. // File. Claimant, James Carpenter, 26 Mch. 1804. Wit: Daniel Whitaker, 11 March 1805. Certif. A-314 issued to claimant, 14 June 1805. Prov. in James Carpenter. Claim as above. Williem Lewis, agent for claimant.

p.600. Claim No.1198. Spanish gr. to Daniel Mygatt, 155 acres on St. Catherine's Cr., 4 mi. east of Fort b. by Wm. McIntosh, Richard Adams, Mrs. Mary Girault and Wm. Brown. N. O. 7 Dec. 1797 by Gayoso. // File. Claimants, heirs of Daniel Mygatt, 26 Mch. 1804. Wit: William Atchinson, 2 Jany. 1805. Certif. B-46 issued 29 Aug. 1806. Seth Lewis, agent for the claimants, [not named individually].

p.602. Claim No.1200. Certificate of survey to Elizabeth Tomlinson, 128 acres 2 mi. east of Fort, b. by Daniel Baker, Chas. Truflo and Adam Bingaman. (signed) Carlos Trudeau. // p.603. 20 July 1787. Richard Trevillian, quit claim deed to my old plantation and improvement, adj. Daniel Baker, to Nathaniel Tomlinson. Signed. Wit: James Baker. // p.603. Before Don Francisco Collell, Commandant, etc., appeared Winsor Pipes, a res. of this post, who sells to Mr. Richard Trevilliam, here present and accepting, 150 arpents on St. Catherine's Cr., on which there is a main house, some cabins, a horse-mill, a cow and some pigs; for $675. 6 Aug. 1783. Both signed. Wit: Francis Farrell, Richard Bawn. // p.604. 16 Feb. 1803. Nathaniel Tomlinson and Elizabeth, his wife, and Wm. Daniel Baker, of Adams County, John Baker and Patience, his wife, and Luther Smith and Martha Elizabeth, his wife, of New Feliciana, by said Wm. Daniel Baker, their attorney in fact, (legally constituted in Jany. 1803.), to Samuel C. Young, Esq., of Pointe Coupee, for $6500 in hand paid to Nathaniel Tomlinson and Eliz., his wife and William Daniel Baker, for themselves and the said John Baker and Patience, his wife, and Luther Smith and Martha Eliz., his wife, 3 tracts of land on St. Catherine's Creek, (1) 200 acres gr by Spain to Daniel Baker, 20 Apr. 1784, beg. in a tract formerly belonging to St. Germain, land belonging formerly to David Mitchell and John Coleman; (2) 150 acres, a Sp. gr. to David Mitchell, 20 Apr. 1784, adj. John Coleman, St. Germain and John Lusk; (3) 128 acres, a Sp. gr. to Elizabeth Tomlinson, as above. Signed. Wit: Benj. Frazer, Samuel Tomlinson, Rich. Ray Reeve. // File. Samuel C. Young, claimant, 26 Mch. 1804. Wit: John Ellis, 9 June 1807. Certif. B-281 to claimant, 9 June 1807. Allowed as a donation. Claim founded on a claim of Winsor Pipes, the original grantee by deed of record, for 128 acres to Richard Trevillian, from Trevillian to Tomlinson, etc. The land has been inhabited and cultivated by someone of the above parties since 1783 up to the present time, and for same reason was surveyed to Eliz. Tomlinson by Charles Trudeau. (signed) Samuel C. Young.

p.607. Claim No.1201. Spanish grant to Daniel Baker, 200 acres b. by John Coleman and St. Germain. N. O. 20 Apr. 1784, by Miro. Plat and warrant, 9 Nov. 1782. // File. Claimant, Samuel C. Young, 26 Mch. 1804. Certif. A-622 to claimant, 6 Sept. 1805. Claim founded on above grant and conveyance of same by deed by legal representatives. Signed.

p.609. Claim 1202. Spanish gr. to David Mitchell, 159 acres b. by John Lusk, St. Germain, John Coleman, Daniel Baker and Benj. Belk. N. O. 20 Apr. 1784. Plat and certif. dated 9 Nov. 1782. Signed by Miro. // Jany. 7, 1788. David Mitchell to Nathaniel Tomlinson, the above tract for 400 pesos, paid in hand. // File. Claimant, Samuel C. Young, 26 Mch. 1804. Certif. A-621 issued to claimant, 6 Sept. 1805. Claim founded on the above Spanish patent and the deed of conveyance following.

p.612. Claim No.1203. Spanish gr. to Alexander Pannell, 500 acres on Bayou Sara, 35 mi. SE of Fort, b. by David Pannell, Francis Pousset, and Theophilus Collins. N. O. 7 Dec. 1797 by Gayoso. // p.614. 4 Jany. 1803. Colonel Joseph Pannell and wife, Agnes, of Wilkinson Co., for $30,000 to Samuel C. Young, Esq. of Point Coupee, four tracts of land on the waters of Buffalo Cr., Bayou Sara and the Miss. River, 2700 acres. (1) 100 acres whereon Joseph Pannell lives b. by Daniel Ogden, John Ellis and lands gr. David Pannell and those under claim of occupancy of Joseph B. Pannell; (2) 500 acres on Bayou Sara gr. David Pannell, b. by Joseph Pannell, Wm. Ogden, Alexander Washington Pannell; (3) 500 acres orig. gr. Alex. Washington Pannell; (4) 700 acres part of tract gr. John B. Pannell on Miss. River at Loftus Heights, b. on north by lands of the Garrison, on south by Daniel Clark. (signed) J. Pannell, A. Pannell. Wit: Ebenr. Bradish, Wm. Ogden, David Pannell, Richard Graham. Ack. 7 Dec. 1803 bef. Thos. Rodney, one of the Judges of Sup. Ct. of Miss. Territory. // File. Claimant, Samuel C. Young, 26 Mch. 1804. Rejected. Claims 500 arpents. //

p.616. Claim No.1204. Spanish gr. to David Pannell, 500 acres on Bayou Sara, 35 mi. from Fort, b. by Alexander Pannell, Joseph Pannell and others. N. O. 7 Dec. 1797, by Gayoso. // File. Claimant, Samuel C. Young, 26 March 1804. Rejected, June 12, 1807. Claims 500 acres.

p.618. Claim No.1205. Spanish gr. to Joseph Pannell, 800 arpents on stream called Roche a Davion, b. by Miss. River, John Lovelace, Stephen Plauche and Bartholomy LeBreton. N. O. 20 June 1795. // File. Claimant, Samuel C. Young, 26 Mch. 1804. Rejected June 12, 1807. This claim is founded on the Spanish patent to John Pannell, decd., the infant son of Joseph and Agnes Pannell and a conveyance from sd Joseph and Agnes to claimant. Signed. // On plat to foregoing grant: "In the general map No.5, the land here given to Bartholomy LeBreton, is in the name of Antonio Gras, who sold it to John Bisland, who abandoned it for other land which he asked for on Bayou Sara" signed Carlos Trudeau.

p.620. Claim No.1206. Spanish gr. to Joseph Pannell, 1000 arpents bet. Buffalo and Bayou Sara, 5 mi. east from the Miss. River, b. by Francisco Pousset and Daniel Ogden. N. O. 20 June 1795 by Carondelet. // Adams Co., Miss. Ter., James Moore came personally before me and, being duly sworn, sayeth that he was acquainted with the signature of the Baron de Carondelet and that he really believes the within to be his signature. 1st Apr. 1801. Daniel Tilton. // File. Claimant, Samuel C. Young, 26 Mch. 1804. Rejected, 12 June 1807. Miss. Ter., Samuel C. Young claims 1000 acres founded on the Spanish grant above, and a conveyance of same to claimant.

p.623. Claim No.1213. British govt. to James Simmons a warrant of survey by Peter Chester, Esq., Governor of West Florida and directed to me by Elias Durnford, Esq., Surv. Genl. of West Florida, to survey and lay out in the name of Mr. James Simmons a tract of 550 acres. I hereby certify that in obedience to said warrant, I have surveyed and carefully laid out the afsd land and that the above is a true plat of same. 8 Jany. 1777. Wm. Vousdan, Dep. Surveyor. // p.623. Aug. 2, 1788. Chas. Simmons, makes a quit claim deed of an improvement made by James Simmons, my father, near Bayou Pierre joining an improvement made by Thomas James now in possession of John Burnet, for $200 in note to William Smith. Chas. (X) Simmons. Test H. Manadue. // File. Claimant, William Smith, 26 Mch. 1804. Wit: Thomas Jordan. Certif. B-263 issued Apr. 27, 1807. William Smith, of Claiborne Co., Miss. Ter. claims 550 acres about a mile from the mouth of Bayou Pierre by purchase from Chas. Simmons as above, who held it as heir-at-law to his father, James Simmons, decd., who held it by virtue of a warrant from Peter Chester, Gov. of West Florida, etc. Town of Washington, 26 Mch. 1804. William Smith. The plat shows a lake on one side and opposite the land of Mr. Thos. James, John Ross.

p.624. Claim No.1214. Spanish gr. to William Smith, 800 arpents 2 1/2 mi. from mouth of Bayou Pierre, and 1 mi. south of the Miss. River, b. on one side by Peter Bruin and other sides vacant. N. O. 26 Dec. 1795, by Carondelet. Plat shows Melling Wooley on west across Bayou Cypiera. // File. Claimant, William Smith, 26 Mch. 1804. Wit: Thomas Jordan. Certif. D-336 issued. Miss. Ter. William Smith claims 800 acres of land in the settlement of Bayou Pierre by occupancy from 1792 by improving, building a saw-mill, clearing land and cultivating the same until the present time. He also claims the same 800 acres by virtue of a concession from the Spanish Government by warrant of survey, Dec. 12, 1795 and by letters patent, 26 Dec. 1795, as herewith filed. William Smith. Wm. Smith applies to the Board of Commissioners for leave to amend his claim to 800 arpents near the Miss. River adjoining the land of Judge Bruin so that if he be not entitled to said under the Spanish grant exhibited he may have the said land confirmed to him as a preemption, 21 Oct. 1805. (signed) William Smith. Wit: Thomas Rodney.

p.626. Claim No.1216. Sept. 23, 1802. William Wells to Luke Blunt, improvement on Sandy Cr., adj. John Wells and Vousdan, for $100. Signed. Wit: Alexander McKenzie. Proved bef. the Board, 25 Mch. 1804. // Luke Blunt to Moses Miles, improvement on Sandy adj Absolem Wells, 30 Dec. 1803. Signed. Wit: Thos. Mattingly, Absolem Wells. // File. Claimant, Moses Miles, 26 Mch. 1804. Wit: Absolem Wells. Certif. B-152 issued 16 Dec. 1806.

p.627. Claim No.1217. 30 Dec. 1800. John Richey to Benj. Kitchen, right to an improvement on the Miss River, adj. Geo. Cochran and Randal Graham, for $300. Signed. Wit: P. Connelly, Robt. Barrow. Receipt of $300. Wit: A. Wilkinson. // File. Claimant, Benj. Kitchen, 26 Mch. 1804. Wit: Caleb Potter. Rejected May 12, 1807. Above deed prov. by Patrick Connelly 12 Nov. 1804, before the Board. T. R. Benj. Kitchen gives notice that he claims 640 acres in Jefferson Co. by virtue of occupancy and cultivation of said tract by John Rickey during 1797, he being the head of a family and above the age of 21 years, and by virtue of conveyance of same to claimant, as above.

p.627. Claim No.1218. Spanish Government to John Stampley, 800 arpents on Cole's Cr., 50 mi. NE of Fort Panmure, b. by Richard Ellis, Jesse Hamilton and vacant lands. N. O. 25 Jany. 1794 by Carondelet. // Record Office, 12 Feb. 1798. 350 acres of the within land being in the center of the tract, reserving 50 acres on the east end and 400 acres on the west end, were legally conveyed by John Stampley to Hugh Matthews, by conveyance bearing this date, duly filed in this office. John Girault, Recorder. // For $200, John Stampley to John Minor, 400 acres of land, being part of a concession, said land lying to west of the 50 acres he sold Richard Roddy and 350 acres he sold Hugh Matthews. Feb. 3, 1798. Both signed. Wit: Ebenezer Petty, Josiah Crane, John Girault, before Stephen Minor. // File. Claimant, John Minor, 26 Mch. 1804. Wit: Wm. Barland, 20 Sept. 1804. Certif. A-371 issued to claimant for 400 arpents, 24 June 1805. Proven in John Stampley and Minor. Claim as above.

630. Claim No.1219. Spanish gr. to Isabel Whittle, 800 arpents 45 mi. north of Fort Panmure, b. by Joseph Page and John Minor. N. O. 6 May 1791 by Miro. Plat shows tract on Bayou Pierre. // p.632. Elizabeth Whittle to Estevan Minor 800 arpents on Bayou Pierre, as in above grant, in exchange for 1000 arpents 5 mi. east of Fort, b. by Adam Bingaman, John McIntosh, Wm. Dunbar and Chas. White. 26 Jany. 1793. Both signed. // File. Claimant, Stephen Minor, 26 Mch. 1804. Wit: Wm. Barland, 10 Sept. 1804. Certif. A-609 to claimant, 18 Sept. 1805. Prov. in S. Minor. Claim as above, to Hon. Commrs. Thos. Rodney, Thos. H. Williams and Edward Turner.

p.634. Claim No.1220. Spanish gr to Manuel Gayoso de Lemos, 1000 arps. one-half league NE of Fort, b. by lands of Wm. Barland, Job Routh, Ebenezer Dayton, Swazey, Jos. Duncan, Samuel Gibson, Peter Hutchins and Stephen Jordan. N. O. 10 Sept. 1794 by Carondelet. // Natchez, 12 Feb. 1795 this concession has been transferred to Mrs. Marguerita Watts. (signed) Manuel Gayoso de Lemos. // p.363. New Orleans, 10 Aug. 1799. Margaret Watts Gayoso, widow of His Excellency the late Emanuel Gayoso de Lemos, Gov. of La., for $5000 in hand paid, to Daniel Clark, Jr., Esq. a tract of land known by the name of Concord, one-half league NE from the Fort of Natchez containing 1000 acres. Ack. before Wm. E. Hulings, vice-consul of the U. S. A. at Port of New Orleans. 10 Aug. 1799. // p.637. 15 Aug. 1800, Daniel Clarke to Wm. Lintot, both of Miss. Territory, for $10,000 the above property. Signed. Wit: John Minor, Jas. Campbell. // p.638. William Lintot to Stephen Minor, for $10,000 in hand paid, the above property. 15 Sept. 1800. Signed. Wit: Stephen Minor, Jr., John Minor. // File. Claimant, Stephen Minor, as above.

BOOK C

p.1. Claim No.557. Reg. 12 March 1804. Spanish grant to William Ratcliff for 300 acres on Sandy Creek, 13 mi. east of Natchez, b. on north by James Percy, other sides vacant. N. O. 12 March 1790. // p.2. 10 Apr. 1800. William Ratcliff and Mary, his wife, of Bayou Sarah, to Joseph Sessions, of Adams Co., for $500, the above grant. (signed) William Ratcliff, Mary (X) Ratcliff. Wit: Jesse Ratcliff, Baley E. Chaney. Prov. by Chaney 20 Aug. 1800 before Joshua Howard. File. Claimant, Joseph Sessions. Wit: Joshua Howard, 26 May 1804. Certf. A510, Aug. 26, 1805.

p.4. Claim No.558. Reg. 21 March 1804. Micajah Bennett, of Jefferson County, Miss. Ter., to Andrew K. Bouland, of Claiborne Co., house and improvement I live on in Jefferson Co., for $250, 320 acres adj. Signed. Wit: Samuel McMurtry, Enoch Chamberlin, proved by both before Lewis Moore, J. P., Claiborne Co. 15 Mch. 1804. File. Claimant: Andrew K. Bouland. Wit: Charles Cassna, 25 Sept. 1804.

Certf. D56 issued 11 Sept. 1806. Andrew K. Boland claims a preemption of 179 acres in Jefferson Co. on Fife's Creek, waters of Bayou Pierre, by cultivation and inhabitation in 1802, by Micajah Bennet, who sold same to claimant.

p.5. Claim No.559. 24 Nov. 1802. Aaron Palmer to Henry Butcher, both of Miss. Ter., 225 acres surveyed by Fenton and Morgan, adj. Richard Curtis, Jacob Simmons. Signed. Wit: Thos. Mosely, John M. Alson. [Alston] File: Henry Butcher, claimant, 12 Mch. 1804. Certf. B299 issued 29 Dec. 1806, to T. Mosely, assignee. Henry Butcher claims 225 acres on waters of Cole's Creek, by occupancy. It was inhabited by a Mr. Dyson in 1798, who sold it to Aaron Palmer, who sold it to sd Henry Butcher. Deed from Butcher to Thos. Moseley, tract I live on claimed by me as a donation, adj. a claim by Jacob Simmons, 14 July 1804. Wit: John M. Alston, John Bates.

Claim No.560. [Not recorded in Written Evidences] File. Claimant: John M. Alston. Presented 12 Mch. 1804. Wit: John Roberts. Certf. B49, issued 29 Aug. 1806. Miss. Territory, Jefferson Co., Notice is here given that I, John McCoy Alston, claims a tract of land in afsd county and territory, having purchased the same from Thomas, which tract was settled and cultivated by sd Thomas long before 1797 and has been ever since and now is in actual cultivation. Signed. Plat shows 640 acres to John McCoy Alston, on waters of Cole's Creek, b. by Richard Curtis and vacant lands. [Full name of Thomas not given.]

p.6. Claim No.561. 20 Dec. 1801. John Dyson, of Pickering County, Miss. Ter., to Philip Alston, 320 acres adjoining Mr. Brackston and John Roberts, whereon I now live, binding myself should sd land ever be taken from sd Philip Alston by any prior claim to return to sd Alston $200 and lawful interest which amount was originally given for sd land, 20 Dec. 1801. Signed: Dyson. Wit: Wm. Dadford, E. Hoskinson. // Assignment: Philip Alston to Frankey Dromgoole. I do assign to Mrs. Franky Dromgoole all my right and title to within obligation. (signed) P. Alston. March 12, 1804. File: claimant, Frankey Dromgoole, 12 March 1804. Certf. D-50 issued Aug. 29, 1806. Miss. Ter., Jefferson County,

p.7. Notice is hereby given that I, Frankey Dromgoole, claim the above described tract in Jefferson Co. as legal representative of John Dyson, having purchased the same of Philip Alston, who purchased the same of sd Dyson, who settled and cultivated said land long before 1797, and has been ever since and now is in actual cultivation. Signed: Frankey Dromgoole. Plat shows land on Burrow's Cr. waters of Cole's Creek.

p.7. Claim No.562. Petition of Clement Dyson who wishes to establish himself in the Dist. of Villa Gayoso, northeast of Christian Braxton, for the purpose of making a living for his family which consists of five persons and asks for 400 acres. Natchez, 14 March 1793. Recommended, 19 March 1794, by Gayoso. Warrant for 400 acres by Carondelet, N. O. 28 Mch. 1794. // p.8. 23 May 1798, Clement Dyson, of Villa Gayoso, to Ebenezer Rees, of St. Catherine's, for $300, above tract, b. by Andrew Watkins and vacant land. Clement (X) Dyson. Wit: Chas. T. Todd, George Cramer. Prov. by Todd before Sutton Banks, J. P. Natchez, June 1st, 1798. // p.10. 13 June 1801. Ebenezer Rees, of Adams Co., Miss. Ter. to Ferguson and Woolley, both of Natchez, for $800 paid, 400 acres [above described] and surveyed by Wm. Dunbar, deputy surveyor. Both signed. Wit: Moses Austin, Lyman Harding. p.12. 21 Feb. 1803. David Ferguson for $500, his share in above tract, to Melling Woolley, Signed. Wit: Lyman Harding, Jo Dunbar. Same date, Jane Ferguson, wife of David Ferguson, quit claim to Melling Woolley all claim to above tract. Signed. Wit: J. Dunbar. // p.13. Melling Woolley to John M. Alston, 4 March 1803. for $2000 paid the above 400 acres, [transfers of title given] Signed. Wit: James Carmichael, E. Hoskinson, Edmund Johnson. Prov. by last two wit. 11 July 1803, before Edward Turner, Clerk of Jefferson County Ct. File: John M. Alston, claimant, 12 Mch. 1804. Wit: Bennet Truly, 28 Mch. 1802, and James Truly 29 May 1806. Certf. B42 issued Aug. 29, 1806. Notice is hereby given that I, John McCoy Alston, am claimant to above described land in Jefferson Co., Miss. Ter. [recitation of above transfers of title.] Signed.

p.15. Claim No.563. Spanish grant to James Wade, 400 acres nine miles east of Fort Panmure, b. by Jacob Copperthwaitt and Thomas Jordan. N. O. 15 March 1788 by Estevan Miro. Plat and certf. by Wm. Vousdan, Dep. Surv. File: James Wade, claimant, 12 March 1804. Wit: Manuel Madden, 27 July 1804. Certf. A156 issued to claimant. On waters of Fairchild's Creek.

Claim No.564. [Not recorded in Written Evidences.] File: Claimant, Isma Foreman, 12 March 1804. Wit: William Thomas, 28 May 1804. Certf. B195, Feb. 13, 1807. Miss. Ter., Jefferson Co. Isma Foreman claims a donation right of a tract in afsd county on both sides of a branch of Morgan's Fork of Homochitto, beg. at Alexander Montgomery's corner, being the only claim of land the sd Isma Foreman holds or has held within the Territory which was improved in 1797 and cultivated ever since, Forman being of age at the time of settling and the head of a family of ten.

Claim No.565. File: Heirs of Moses Bonner, claimants. 12 March 1804. Rejected 12 May 1807. Miss. Ter., Jefferson Co., Henry Williams and Anna Williams, his wife; Moses Bonner, James Bonner, Joseph Bonner, John Bonner, and William Bonner, heirs and legal representatives of Moses Bonner, decd., claim 600 acres in afsd county on waters of Fairchild's creek, by right of occupancy, the sd tract having been inhabited and cultivated in 1789 by sd Bonner, deceased, and has been ever since by his widow and heirs. Signed: Grizzell (X) Bonner.

p.16. Claim No.566. Spanish grant to Charles Cason, 300 acres on St. Catherine's and Second Creeks, 9 mi. SE of Fort Panmure, b. by Mr. Robert Ford and vacant land. N. O. 15 March 1789. File: Charles Cason, claimant, 12 March 1804. Wit: Robert Ford, 21 Aug. 1804. Certf. A-157, issued to claimant. Claim as above.

p.18. Claim No.567. Pet. of John Montgomery to the Spanish Govt. A resident of Bayou Pierre, where he is established on lands of His Majesty, not having been able to buy vacant lands on St. Catherine's Creek where he had a concession for 300 acres; he prays that the same 300 acres be granted to him where he now is established, b. by Samuel Gibson and Thomas Hubert, the same being vacant. Natchez, 20 July 1789. Signed. Recommended 20 July 1789 by Gayoso. Warrant by Miro. N. O. 26 Apr. 1790. Description also included lands adj. of Reuben Proctor and Jacob Cobun. File: Alexander Montgomery claimant, 12 March 1804. Wit: Prosper King, 15 July 1805. Rejected. Alexander Montgomery claims 300 acres by virtue of a Sp. grant to John Montgomery, 26 April 1790 and by sd John Montgomery sold to Alexander Montgomery, in Adams Co. on waters of Homochitto. Signed: Alexander Montgomery. Plat by Dunbar.

p.19. Claim No.568. Sp. grant to James Cole, 800 acres 17 miles NE of Fort Panmure, b. by vacant lands. N. O. 8 April 1789. // p.21. 30 March 1802. Richard, William and Henry King, of Adams Co., Miss. Ter., to Alexander Montgomery, of Jefferson Co., for $1600, 400 acres in Adams Co. 17 mi. NE of the Fort, b. by Richard Curtis, Ebenezer Rees, Henry King, Jesse Hamilton, ___ Vousdan, Jeptha Higdon and Alexander Montgomery, being part of a tract gr. to James Cole, as above, and by sd James Cole conveyed to Henry, Wm. and Richard King. Both signed. Wit: Simeon Spring, Esther King. File: Alexander Montgomery and Henry King, claimants, 12 March 1804. Wit: Prosper King, 15 July 1805. Certificate A-507 issued to claimants, 21 Apr. 1805. Claim as above. Grant to Richard, William and Henry King and Richard and Wm. King sold to Alexander Montgomery by deed 30 March 1802.

Claim No.569. (Not in W. E.) File: Levi Lusk, claimant, 12 Marhh 1804. Wit: Samuel Lusk. (See remarks within.) Certf. B-272 issued for 320 acres, May 15, 1807. Notation: This claim and No.570 were made by two brothers who lived together and made a settlement together but, being advised by the surveyor, divided their settlement so as to make two claims of 640 acres each, whereas it seems that they ought to have united in the same claim, being but one family and having but one settlement. Wherefore when these claims are decided it will be better to issue but one certificate so as to include the whole of their improvement. This claim and No.570 will be consolidated and the surveyor will survey 640 acres in the names of the claimants jointly to include their improvement. Signed. T. H. W. [Thos. H. Williams] Claim of Levi Lusk to 640 acres on which he settled in 1794 and he was above the age of 21. File to claim No.570. Jacob Lusk, claimant. Certificate B-273 issued for 320 acres, May 15, 1807. Jacob Lusk claims 640 acres on Homochitto River. He was above 21 years of age when the territory was finally evacuated by the Spanish troops.

p.23. Claim No.571. Sp. grant to Jesse Hamilton for 300 acres on Bayou Pierre, 40 mi. NE of Natchez, b. by John Burnet and vacant lands. N. O. 16 Feb. 1789. On plat east of tract on Bayou Pierre is "original corner of John Terry." File: Jesse Hamilton, original claimant, 12 March 1804. Wit: Hezekiah Harman. Certf. A-425 issued to claimant.

p.25. Claim No.572. Sp. grant to Jesse Hamilton, 800 acres on Cole's Creek, in Dist. of Natchez, b. by sd creek, Richard Ellis and James Coles. N. O. 31 Jany. 1788. File: Jesse Hamilton, claimant, 12 March 1804. Wit: Hezekiah Harman, 18 July 1805. Certf. A-426, July 11, 1805. Claim based on above Spanish grant.

File of Claim No.573. [Not in W. E.] Claimant: Jonathan Kemp, 13 Mch. 1804. Wit: John Robinson. Certf. D-99, Oct. 30, 1806. The above tract of 500 acres is on the north side of the main fork of Bayou Pierre, about 4 miles above the Grindstone Ford in Claiborne County and is occupied by the afsd Jonathan Kemp. (Signed) Daniel Burnet. Kemp claims the right of becoming the purchaser from the U. S. of 500 acres [described as above] by virtue of its having been settled and cultivated by sd Kemp on 3rd March 1803. Bond of Jonathan Kemp to William Brocus, Jr. for $4000, dated 3 Jany. 1805. Condition: Kemp obliges himself to make a complete deed of the above-described rights in land office, to sd Brocus, who is to pay the price for same to the United States in due time and process of law. Wit: R. Ashley, Will. Lindsay. Proved by Lindsay 13 Aug. 1805, before Daniel Burnet and Samuel Cocke, J. P. // Articles of Agreement, 9 April 1805, between William Brocus, Jr. and Dr. Joseph Moore, both of Claiborne County, Miss. Ter. For $2400 in hand paid, William Brocus, Jr. sells to sd Joseph Moore, 500 acres [above described], Brocus binding to make good and sufficient deeds of conveyance, Moore to pay the U. S. the price stipulated for the land. Signed by Brocus. Wit: John L. Reynolds, Alexander Carmichael. Ack. by Brocus before the Justices of Peace, Daniel Burnet, Samuel Cook, 13 Aug. 1805.

p.26. Claim No.574. Petition of Joseph Vidal, Secretary for His Majesty's government, wishes to establish himself near Natchez, adj. lands of Capt. Stephen Minor; asks for 29 or 30 acres, a place to make his residence and employ his slaves, convenient to the city, 15 Oct. 1793. Patent for 29 acres adj. land of Don Estevan Minor. Oct. 25, 1793. Gayoso. // p.28. Oct. 31, 1801. Joseph Vidal, of Natchez, Adams County, Miss. Ter. Esq., to James Campbell, of same, for $4350 sells to sd Campbell tract of 40 acres, near the road that leads to Pine Ridge, adj. Stephen Minor and John Steele. Signed. Wit: Emanuel Garcia de Texada, Stephen Minor. Ack. before William Kenner, 31 Oct. 1801. p.30. 8 Dec. 1802. James Campbell, of Natchez, to James Williams, Esq., of Adams Co., Miss. Ter., for $4000 all the above property. Wit: J. Weir, Sam Postlewait, Jr. // p.31. 3 Sept. 1800, Major Stephen Minor and Catherine, his wife, of Miss. Ter. Southern County, to Capt. Joseph Vidal, for $500, 30 acres, being part of tract granted to Major Stephen Minor 25 Oct. 1793. Both signed. Wit: Edward O. K. Welsh, William Kenner. Ack. 3 Sept. 1801, before Will. Kenner, J. P. // File: James Williams, claimant, 13 March 1804. Certificates A 604-605, issued to claimant. Dec. 18, 1805. James Williams claims 40 acres in the city of Natchez between 29 and 30 acres whereof was granted by patent from the Spanish to Stephen Minor which he conveyed to Joseph Vidal 3 Sept. 1800, the residue of the above 40 acres was granted by the Spanish Govt. to Vidal by patent dated 1793, including other lands now the property of S. Minor. All of above lands of Vidal conveyed to James Campbell and by Campbell to said Williams, 3 Dec. 1802.

p.33. Claim No.575. Spanish grant to Claude Chabot 1600 acres in the Natchez Dist., 12 mi. NE of Loftus Cliffs, b. by Daniel Clark, Jr., Wm. Chabot, lands of Miss Mary Ellis and the left bank of Buffalo Cr. New Orleans, 7 July 1789 by Miro. // p.34. William Collins to Henry Willis 1600 arpents on Buffalo Cr., [bounded as described above,] for 10,000 lbs. of tobacco. 4 Feb. 1792, at Natchez. Both signed. Wit: Joseph Vidal, Valentin Rincon. // South Carolina, Greenville District, Personally appeared Elizabeth Williams, who being duly sworn, maketh oath that Sarah J. Chotard, late Sarah J. Willis, relict of Capt. Henry Willis, decd., was born 1st Jany. 1777 and that she was intermarried with John Chotard Laplace on 25 July 1797. Signed Eliza Williams, before W. Thompson, Justice of Quoram, 5 Sept. 1803. File: James Williams claimant, 13 March 1804. Wit: William McIntosh, 18 June 1804. Certf. A-652 issued to claimant, Oct. 3, 1805. James Williams claims 1600 acres on Buffalo Creek patented to Claude Chabot and sold by Chabot to William Collins by deed recorded in N. O. and conveyed by sd Collins to Henry Willis and devised by sd Willis, 24 Sept. 1794 to his wife, now Sarah F. Chotard and his son Lewis who died in 1794 and by the laws of Spain operating in sd case, the said moiety of sd Lewis is vested in his said mother, now Sarah F. Chotard, who together with her husband, John Chotard Laplace, conveyed the sd land to said Williams, 1 Sept. 1803.

p.35. Claim No.576. Spanish grant to Capt. Lawrence of 1000 acres in Natchez District on Homochitto River, all sides vacant. New Orleans 15 March 1789, by Miro. // p.37. Jason Lawrence to Henry Willis the above land, 1000 acres, gr. as per plat, for 500 pesos, to be paid during four years, 2 May 1791. Both signed. Wit: Miguel Gomez, Antonio Fromentin, James Lemain, before Pedro Padesclaux, notary. File: James Williams, claimant, 13 March 1804. Wit: William McIntosh, 8 June 1804. Certf. A-678, Oct. 19, 1805. James Williams claims the above grant to Jason Lawrence who sold to Henry Willis, and devised by said Willis as related in preceding claim and sold to James Williams.

p.38. Claim No.577. Petition of Henry Willis, res. of the Post of Natchez, wishes to establish a residence and occupation of 100 slaves which he owns; asks for 800 arpents square on Bayou Sarah, 15 miles from its mouth. New Orleans, 16 May 1791. // N. O. 23 May 1791. Order of survey by Estevan Miro. Plat certified by Wm. Dunbar, 21 Dec. 1791, 800 sq. arpents between headwaters of Bayou Sara abt 39 miles from Fort Panmure. Plat shows James Sanders on north. File: Claimant, James Williams, 13 Mch. 1804. Wit: Wm. McIntosh, 18 June 1804. Rejected, June 11, 1807. William's claim the same as in the preceding claims.

p.40. Claim No.578. Petition of James Sanders, resident of the Natchez Dist., wishes to have a habitation in this post; asks for 500 arpens between St. Catherine's and Second Creeks, 2 miles from Fort, b. on lands of Wm. Dunbar. Natchez, 12 June 1787. Signed. // Recommendation for same, by Don Carlos de Grand-Pre. // p.41. Order of survey, N. O. 5 July 1787, by Miro. // I engage to deliver to Mr. William McIntosh a warrant of survey for 500 acres, also to make a deed when land is surveyed. Natchez, 7 March 1791. (signed) James Sanders. Wit: David Mitchell. Witness, William McIntosh, proved before the Board 18 June 1804 that the above signature is the true handwriting of James Sanders and that the subscribing witness is dead and that the above is his handwriting. // p.41. The will of Henry Willis, of the State of Georgia, weak; wife, Sarah S. Willis and my son, Lewis Willis to have all property, equally divided at my death. But if wife should marry, my mulatto man, Lewis, shall be free but to continue as the property of my said wife until such a marriage shall take place. Richard Willis and Nathaniel Willis executors. 25 Sept. 1794. Wit: Wm. Sturgis, Francis Wilson, James Denton. // p.42. Charleston District, S. C. Before Charles Lining, Esq., Ordinary, above will proved by James Denton, 23 Aug. 1803. A true copy from Ordinary's Office, same date. // p.42. Certificate of Governor by Secretary of State, Daniel Huger, that Charles Lining, Esq. is ordinary for the Charleston District, in the State of South Carolina. // p.43. 1 Sept. 1803. John Chotard Laplace and Sarah F. Chotard, his wife, of the State of South Carolina, to James Williams, of Mississippi, for $3000, to them paid, the following tracts of land, 1600 acres in Mississippi Ter. on Buffalo Creek originally gr. to Claude Chabot, adj. Daniel Clark, also 1000 acres on Homochitto River near a place called Carter's Ferry, originally gr. Jason Lawrence, also 800 acres on Bayou Sarah, gr. by Sp. Govt. to Henry Willis, also 500 acres gr. to James Saunders by sd govt. adj. tract of 800 acres. Signed: John Chotard LaPlace, Sarah F. Chotard. Wit: Eliz. Williams, Eliza B. Thompson, Thos B. Williams. State of S. C. Greenville District, proved by Eliza Williams before W. Thompson, Justice of the Quorum, 5 Sept. 1803. Waddy Thompson, one of the Justices of Quorum for and in Greenville Dist. S. C. certifies the acknowledgement of Sarah F. Chotard LaPlace, wife of John Chotard LaPlace, that she willingly signed the above. 5 Sept. 1803. W. Thompson, J. Q. File: James Williams, claimant, 13 March 1804. Wit: William McIntosh, 18 June 1804. Rejected June 11, 1807. James Williams claims 500 arpents of land on Bayou Sarah in virtue of the foregoing instruments.

File: Claim No.579. [Not in W. E.] William Hutcheson, claimant, 13 March 1804. William Downs, witness. Certificate D.-226, 22 Dec. 1806. Miss. Ter., Claiborne Co. William Hutcheson claims the preference in becoming purchaser of 640 acres near the Miss. River, by right of occupancy. This tract of land has been inhabited and cultivated by sd Hutcheson ever since March 1801, and he was above the age of 21 years at the time of the signing of the Acts regulating the sale of lands, etc.

p.44. Claim No.580. British grant to William Hiorn, 500 acres, 18 mi. N.E. from the Natchez, b. by lands surveyed for Hon. John Stuart, Esq. and William Fricker and vacant lands. 19 Nov. 1777. By Peter Chester at Pensacola. [Plat shows tract on southwest fork of Boyd's Creek.] Warrant, Oct. 16, 1777. // p.49. Lease, 23 Dec. 1778. Release, 24 Dec. 1778. William Hiorn to Charles Percy, Esq., for 100 pounds, lawful money of Great Britain, the above tract of 500 acres. Signed. Wit: Ferquard Bethune, Joseph Purcell, Donald McPherson. Proven by McPherson 2 Feb. 1779 before Elihu Hall Bay, Deputy Provincial Secretary. File: John Ellis, claimant, for the heirs of Charles Percy, 13 March 1804. Wit: Alexander Montgomery, 31 Jany. 1805. Certificate A-22. Miss. Territory. John Ellis and Sarah, his wife, formerly Sarah Percy, Thomas G. Percy, Catherine Percy and Ann Percy, the legal representatives of Charles Percy, decd., claim 500 acres on waters of the SW fork of Boyd's Cr., by virtue of a Br. Patent, dated 19 Nov. 1777, to Wm. Hiorn, and a lease and release, dated 23 and 24 Dec. 1778, fr. sd Hiorn to sd Chas. Percy, decd. for the aforsd 500 acres. Signed: George Poindexter for the claimants.

p.53. Claim No.581. Petition of John Conner, late of the Illinnesses [Illinois], wishes to establish residence to support his family which consists of wife and two children, asks for 400 acres on Cole's Creek, adj. lands of Jas. Elliot, Natchez, 12 Sept. 1789. // Recommended by Gayoso, Natchez,

13 Sept. 1789. // N. O. 26 Apr. 1790, Warrant by Miro. Plat. 400 acres b. on east by Robert and John Watts, south by James Elliott. Certified by Wm. Dunbar, 1 Dec. 1796. // Natchez, 23 July 1794. A decree by Gayoso to Peter Presler. In consequence of Peter Presler becoming answerable for debts due by his son-in-law, John O'Conner, he, the sd Presler, is authorized to take into his possession all property of every kind known to be belonging to said John O'Conner. Signed: Gayoso. A true copy of a decree to a petition of Peter Pressler lodged in archives on above date. (signed) John Girault. File: Peter Pressler, claimant, 13 March 1804. Rejected 16 May 1807. Miss. Ter. Peter Presler, a citizen of afsd territory and legal administrator of John Conner, decd., claims 400 arpents in waters of north fork of Cole's Cr. by virtue of a decree of Stephen Miro, Gov. Gen. of Prov. of La., in favor of said John Conner. Signed: W. B. Shields, atty. for the claimant.

p.54. Claim No.582. Charles Marlar, of Wilkinson Co., Miss. Ter., to David Lattimore, of Natchez, for $100, improvement made by Marlar soon after the U. S. obtained possession of Miss. Territory, on Buffalo Cr. [No date.] Wit: Moses Keedsey, George Brown. File: David Lattimore, claimant, 13 March 1804. Rejected for want of evidence, Dec. 30, 1806. David Lattimore, who is legal representative of Charles Marlar, claims 678 acres in Wilkinson Co., Miss. Ter., a mile below Ford's Creek.

Claim No.583. [Not in W. E.] File: Isaac Foster, 5 Nov. 1804. Wit: Chas. Cason, same date, and Mary Mounts, 12 Nov. 1806. Wit. Sam'l. Boyd and Joseph Ford, 5 May 1806. (See No.1650) Rejected 18 Nov. 1806. Evidence insufficient. Isaac Foster claims right of preference in the purchase of the U. S. of 350 acres by virtue of the tract having been improved by Jesse Stockwell in March 1802 and who was actually inhabiting and cultivating the same previous to 1 March 1803. Said Stockwell has since transferred rights and title to the premises to sd Isaac Foster and owns no Br. or Sp. grants in this territory. (Note: The claimant wishes 550 acres granted him agreeable to his notice No.1650.) Jesse Stockwell, in consideration for $1.00 in hand paid by Isaac Foster, all right to an improvement made by me on middle fork of Homochitto River at or near where the Choctaw Indian path crosses said fork. Signed. Wit: Mary Mounts.

p.55. Claim No.584. Rebecca McCabe to Andrew Scandlin, for 300 pesos, paid, a house at the foot of the road which comes down the hill, part of a larger lot. Both signed. Wit: Joseph Vidal, Ebenezer Rees, Chas. Surget. // p.56. Mortgage, Andrew Scandlin to Luther Smith, 28 May 1798. 1st Oct. next, I promise to pay to Mr. Luther Smith or order $100 for a grey horse and to secure same my right and title to a house and lot in Natchez under the hill, adj. the house of Madam McCabe now occupied by Mr. James Stewart. Signed. Wit: David McLelland, Calvin Smith. Proved by Calvin Smith before Philander Smith, 10 May 1800. // p.57. Luther Smith, for $113, assigns to John J. Walton right in above obligation. 30 June 1800. Signed. Wit: Lyman Harding, Wm. Kenner. Ack. by Smith before Wm. Kenner same date. File: John J. Walton, claimant, March 13, 1804. Wit: John Girault, 29 Oct. 1804. Certf. B-1 issued June 2, 1806. John J. Walton, an actual settled in the Territory in 1799, claims a lot at the Natchez landing by virtue of a Sp. Gr. to Rebecca McCabe, and by her sold to Andrew Scandlin, by deed 17 March 1798, and by sd Scandlin mortgaged to Luther Smith [as above].

p.59. Claim No.585. Sp. grant to Joshua Howard, 600 acres on Homochitto River, 30 mi. east of Fort Panmure, b. by vacant lands. N. O. 9 April 1794 by Carondelet. // p.61. Henry Richardson, of this Govt., to Jesse Ratcliff, 600 acres in the Dist. of Homochitto, having received it in exchange for other land from Joshua Howard, as Archives will show; for $100 paid. Natchez, 13 June 1796. Both signed. Wit: Roger Dixon, John Girault. Before Gayoso. // p.62. Jesse Ratcliff to Isaac Tabor, both of the dist., the above 600 arpents gr. to Joshua Howard in 1794, for $150 paid. 17 Aug. 1796. Both sign. Wit: Maurice Stacpoole, John Girault, before Stephen Minor. // p.63. Isaac Tabor to John Foster, both of this govt., same 600 arpents on Homochitto gr. Howard, for $250, Natchez, 23 Sept. 1797. Both sign. Wit: John Girault, Gerard Brandon. File: John Foster, claimant, 3 March 1804. Wit: Peter Smith, 4 June 1804. Certf. A-264 issued to claimant June 3, 1805. John Foster claims 600 acres as above detailed. Proved in Howard by Peter Smith. Original papers in file.

p.64. Claim No.586. Sp. grant to Elias Bonnell, 152 acres in Natchez Dist., 25 east of Fort, on Homochitto River, fronting on land of John Foster. N. O. 7 Dec. 1797 by Gayoso. // p.66. Natchez, 2 Feb. 1798. Elias Bonnell to John Foster for a negress whom I have recd. 400 acres as in above grant and an island in same river as granted Bonnell in plat 284. Elias (X) Bonel, John Foster. Wit: Manuel Garcia de Texada, John Girault, before Esteven Minor. File: John Foster, claimant, 3 March 1804. Wit: Wm. Atchinson, 21 Nov. 1804. Certificate, 8 April 1807.

p.69. Claim No.588. Sp. grant to John Foster, for 214 acres on St. Catherine's Creek, b. by Gideon Gibson, Joe Calvit, Winsor Pipes and Dr. McCabe. N. O. 15 March 1789 by Miro. File: John Foster claimant, 13 March 1804. Wit: Zachariah Smith, Sr., 4 June 1804. Certf. A-164. Claim signed by John Foster.

p.71. Claim No.589. Sp. grant to John Foster, 800 arpents on Homochitto River, 30 miles east of the fort, b. by vacant lands, N. O. 28 March 1793, by Carondelet. File: John Foster claimant, 13 March 1804. Wit: Zachariah Smith, Sr. 4 June 1804. Certf. A-165. [The plat shows the island mentioned in Claim No.586.]

p.73. Claim No.590. 24 Feb. 1804. Ezekiel Dewitt and Mary Dewitt, his wife, to Joseph Pannill, Esq., all of Adams Co., Miss. Ter., for $2000 paid, 400 acres on St. Catherine's Creek in sd Co. adj. John Stilley [Still Lee], a grant to Mary Dewitt by Baron Carondelet, 1789. Both sign with mark. Wit: G. Poindexter, Richard Claiborne. Ack. 23 Feb. 1804 at Town of Washington, Miss. Ter., before Thomas Rodney. File: Joseph Pannill claimant, 29 March 1804. Wit: Jonathan Guice, 28 May 1805. Certf. B-111, 4 Feb. 1807. In claim the grant is dated 14 April 1796.

p.75. Claim No.591. British grant to Thomas James, 200 acres, 20 mi. above Grand Gulf, opposite the uppermost of the Three Islands in the Miss. River. 3 May 1776, at Pensacola by Peter Chester. File: Thos. James claimant, 13 March 1804. Reported 28 April 1807. * Claim as above signed by Ferdinand L. Claiborne, attorney.

p.80. Claim No.592. Br. grant to Susannah Jacobs, 200 acres 25 mi. from the Natchez, on Bayou Pierre. Pensacola, 6 May 1776 by Peter Chester. Plat shows "2 or 3 miles below Bayou Pierre". // p.84. 8 Sept. 1775. Susannah Jacobs, of Prov. of West Fla. to Thomas James, of same, farmer, for $50 paid, above grant. Wit: John Miller, Wm. Swanson. Prov. by Miller before Philip Livingston, Jr., Esq. 30 Aug. 1776. File: Thos. James claimant, 13 March 1804. Reported 28 Apr. 1807. Signed by F. L. Claiborne, atty.

p.89. Claim No.593. Br. grant to Thomas James, 500 acres 3 mi. below Bayou Pierre, b. on north by lands surveyed for Susanna Jacobs. Pensacola, 15 Aug. 1777 by Peter Chester. File: Thomas James claimant, 13 Mch. 1804. Reported, Apr. 28, 1807. Ferdinand L. Claiborne, atty. signed claim.

p.94. Claim No.594. Br. grant to Charles Percy, 600 acres on east branch of Buffalo Creek, 6 mi. from mouth, b. by lands of John Southwell. Pensacola, 23 Sept. 1779, by Peter Chester. File: John Ellis for the heirs of Charles Percy, 13 March 1804. Wit: Alexander Montgomery, 3 Jany. 1805. Certf. A-20, 18 Apr. 1805. Miss. Ter. John Ellis and Sarah, his wife, formerly Sarah Percy, Thos. G. Percy, Catherine Percy and Ann Percy, legal representatives of Charles Percy, decd. claim above grant. Geo. Poindexter, atty. for claimants.

p.99. Claim No.595. Br. grant to James Smith Yarborough, 400 acres, 7 mi. below White Cliffs, south of the Natchez, and one mile from the upper end of an island in the Miss. River, b. on south by a lake. Pensacola, 2 June 1777 by Peter Chester. // p.103. 21 Oct. 1777. James Smith Yarborough of the Natchez in Prov. of West Fla., yeoman, and Mary, his wife, to Charles Percy of same, for $300, 400 acres (as granted above.) Both sign. Wit: Nehemiah Carter, W. P. Williams. File: Alexander Montgomery, 3 Jany. 1805. Certf. A-21, 18 Apr. 1805. Claim signed by Geo. Poindexter, atty. for claimants.

Claim No.596. [Not in W. E.] Claimant: Wm. Downs, 14 Mch. 1804. Wit: Anthony Glass. Certf. D-227, 22 Dec. 1806. Miss. Ter. Claiborne Co., Wm. Downs claims the right of preference in becoming purchaser of U. S. 500 acres on Miss. River in afsd Co. by virtue of having been settled on and cultivated on 3 Mch. 1803. Signed.

Claim No.597. [Not in W. E.] Claimants: Heirs of Sinclair Pruit, 14 March 1804. Wit: Anthony Glass. Certf. D-228, 22 Dec. 1806. Polly and William Pruit, two of the heirs, for themselves, and for the other heirs and legal representatives of Sinclair Pruit, decd. claim the right of becoming the purchasers from the U. S. of 320 acres in Miss. Ter., Claiborne Co. on Big Bayou, by virtue of the sd tract having been inhabited and cultivated by sd heirs on 3rd March 1802 and by sd Sinclair Pruit in 1801 and until he died, and ever since it has been in cultivation. Signed: Anthony Glass, agent for sd heirs. [Plat shows land b. by the heirs of Nathaniel Gibson, other sides vacant.]

p.108. Claim No.600. Petition of Hugh Coyle, who wishes to build a house for his residence and that of his family in the new city of Natchez, asks for a grant of Lot No.2, Square No.8. Natchez, 2 March 1793. Signed. // Recommended by Gayoso same date. // Patent. Since Hugh Coyle has complied with all the conditions of this grant, I ratify same, etc. Signed by Gayoso. Natchez, 12 July 1796. // p.109. 2 Aug. 1799. Hugh Coyle, of Natchez, taylor, to Leonard Pomet, of same, shopkeeper, for $1075, paid, Lot No.2, Sq.8, a certain part of sd lot having been sold to George Furney 3 June 1797. Signed. Wit: Wm. Barland, John Wilson. Prov. by Barland 3 June 1799 before Daniel Clark. [See No.1600 for the part of the above lot sold by Hugh Coyle to George Furney.]

p.111. Claim No.601. Sp. grant to Andrew Gil. Petition of Gill, practitioner of the Royal Hospital, wants to build a house, asks for grant to Lot 2, Sq. No.2, Natchez, 29 May 1793. Signed. // Order by Gayoso same date. // Ratification by Gayoso at Natchez 1795. // p.112. Andrew Gil, of Baton Rouge, by atty in fact, Domingo Lorero, of Natchez, Adams Co., Miss. Ter. to St. James Beauvais and Co, of same, for $900, paid, Lot. No.2, Sq. No.2 in Natchez gr. as above. 12 May 1801. Wit: Joseph Vidal, John Henderson. // p.114. St. James Beauvais, of Natchez, Thomas Prather and James Wiley, of Ky., by their atty-in-fact, St. James Beauvais, to Joseph Newman, for $1500, paid, Lot. No.2, Sq. No.2 (as above). Wit: Lyman Harding, Peter Walker. 26 March 1802. // p.116. 21 July 1803. Joseph Newman, of Adams Co., Miss. Ter. and wife, Dorothy, to Leonard Pomet, of same, for $1800 paid, Lot. No.2, Sq. No.2, (as above). Both sign. Wit: Ezekiel Towson, Lyman Harding. // p.118. William Brooks, of Adams Co., Miss. Ter., for divers good causes, etc., quit claims to Leonard Pomet any claim he may have to above property. 23 July 1803. Signed. Same witnesses as above. Ack. before Sam'l. Brooks, J. P., 25 July 1803.

p.119. Claim No.602. 22 March 1798, William Barland, of St. Catherine's Dist., Government of Natchez, taylor, to Lewis Davis, of Mason County, Ky., for $150 in hand paid, Lot No.1, Sq. No.21 in city of Natchez. Signed. Wit: Simon McKay, Edmund Randolph. // Lewis Davis to Leonard DeK. Lyne Shaw, for value received, 29 March 1798. // Leonard Shaw reassigned all claim to above to Lewis Davis, 9 April 1798. Signed. // p.121. April 30, 1798. Lewis Davis, of Mason Co., Ky. to Bennet Truly, of Dist. of Natchez, Lot No.1, Sq. No.21, in Town of Natchez. Signed. Wit: Anthony (A) Dougherty, Nathaniel (X) Ivy, Silas L. Payne. // p.122. 5 Feb. 1803. Bennet Truly to Peonard Pomet, both of Adams Co., Miss. Ter., for $200 paid, Lot. No.1, Sq. No.21 in Town of Natchez. Wit: Benj. M. Stokes, Darius Moffett. Proved by Moffett before Sam'l. Brooks, J. P. 18 Aug. 1803.

p.123. Claim No.603. Joseph Vidal, Capt. of the Militia and Secy. for His Majesty in the plaza of Natchez, to Antonio Novella, a lot b. by property of Miguel Solivellas and that of Andrew Gil, and the streets at front and side of sd lot, for 100 pesos. Both sign. Wit: John Girault, John Carreras. Before DeGrand-Pre. // p.125. Power of Atty by Antonio Novella to Maria Francesca Boyes, my legitimate wife, to represent me in sale of any of my property. Natchez, 20 Oct. 1790. Signed. Wit: Manuel Garcia de Texada, John Perez. // Maria Francesca Boyes, legitimate wife of Antonio Novellas, by virtue of a power of atty., sells to Domingo Lorero and Pedro Ancid, a house and lot No.1, Sq. 21, in this city, having bought it from Don Joseph Vidal, for $700 paid. 11 Nov. 1797. Signed with a mark. Wit: Wm. Gilespie, John Girault. Before Estevan Minor. // p.126. Will of Peter Ancid. 9 March 1795; 19 Feb. 1799. Legatees: Madame Augustina Solano Cele, 200 pesos for the help and care she gave me during my illness; grand-daughter, Maria Dolores Gonzales; the Church, etc. // p.128. Joseph Vidal, exor. of Domingo Lorero, to Leonard Pomet, 15 Aug. 1802. [Lorero especially designated in will that the above property be sold by exor. Leonard Pomet was the highest bidder, at $3820. Witnesses to transfer, Darius Moffett,, Andrew T. Abrams.]

p.131. Claim No.604. William Barland to Christopher Miller, Lot No.2, Sq. No.21 in the new city of this plaza, being part of the grant to me by Gov. Miro, for $30, 15 April 1794. Both sign. Wit: John Girault, Agapito Corchado. Before Gayoso. // p.132. 22 Apr. 1803. Christopher Miller to Leonard Pomet, both of Natchez, for $200, Lot No.2, Sq.21. Signed. Wit: F. Austie, Sam'l. Brooks. // p.134. Joash Miller, of Adams Co., Miss. Ter., for divers good causes, etc. quit claim to Leonard Pomet Lot No.2, Sq. No.21 (as above). Signed. Witness: Job Routh. Ack, before Samuel Brooks, J. P. 8 Nov. 1803.

Claims 600, 601, 602, 603 and 604, all to Leonard Pomet, are listed in one file, presented 14 March 1804. Witness for all, Manuel Texada. Certificates issued: B-4 for Claim No.600, A-544 for No.601, A-513 for No.602, A-765 for No.603, and A-545 for No.604.

p.135. Claim No.605. William Selkrigs, of Adams Co., Miss. Ter., and Catherine, his wife, to David Eldridge, of same, for $900 in hand pd. 300 acres on St. Catherine's Cr. granted to sd Wm. Selkrigs 3 Jany. 1787. Plat annexed and survey by Wm. Vousdan. Signed by William Selkrigs. Catherine signed with a mark. Wit: A. L. Duncan, James Wilson. // p.137. Petition of Wm. Selkrigs, desiring to establish himself on a tract which is vacant, 3 leagues from Fort Panmure, on St. Catherine's Creek, asks for a grant of 300 arpents adj. Windsor Pipes, Charles Adams, 25 Oct. 1786. // Order for above by De Grand-Pre, 19 Dec. 1786. Warrant by Miro, New Orleans, 3 Jany. 1787. File: David Eldridge, claimant, 14 March 1804. Wit: Ebenezer Rees, 10 June 1805. Certf. B-112, 4 Feb. 1807. David Eldridge claims as above.

p.138. Claim No.606. 17 March 1782. Charles de Grand-Pre, etc., proceeded with sale to the highest bidder of 600 arpents of land confiscated from John Blommart on Bayou Creek, bounded on south by Widow Sarah Truly, on northwest by a man named Lum and Abraham Adams and on vacant lands, which land was adjudged to Mr. Silas Crane at 61 peastres. Witnessed by Richard Devall, Jacques Harman, Francois Farrell and other assistants. Signed by all. // p.139. 20 Oct. 1802. Waterman Crane and Catherine, his wife, of Claiborne Co., Miss. Ter., to Patsy Harrison, of Jefferson, and George Cochran, of same, for $500 in hand paid, 326 acres in Jefferson Co. b. by lands of William Ferguson, decd., and of Richard Harrison, decd. Both sign. Wit: James Truly, Samuel Dunbar, Stephen Bullock. // File: George Cochran and Patsey Harrison claimants, 14 March 1804. Wit: J. Girault, Esq. 26 Nov. 1804. (See claim No.293.) Certificate A-780, 20 Aug. 1806. Note: The land was originally granted by the British Government to Thomas Harman and sold to John Blommart and confiscated as his property and bought by Silas Crane, who sold one-half to Ferguson and the other to the claimant.

p.141. Claim No.607. Spanish grant to Robert Cochran, 412 arpens 14 miles south of the mouth of Bayou Pierre, b. by vacant lands. N. O. 10 Apr. 1795, by Carondelet. // p.142. Deed of release. Whereas the Sp. Government granted Alexander Moore, decd., in his lifetime a tract of 1000 acres on the south side of Bayou Pierre about 3 mi. from its mouth, adj. a tract of 350 acres on N. W. which was granted by the British to John Ross who transferred same to Charles Percy who sold same to Robert Cochran. And whereas, retracing and resurveying the 1000 acres gr. to Alexander Moore as aforesaid, it was found by William Moore, since deceased, who was the legal representative of sd Alexander Moore, decd., to intersect the lines of the original survey made for John Ross so as to include much of sd tract of 350 acres, now the property of Robt. Cochran. And whereas William Moore decd. expressed his disposition to relinquish all claim to any part of the sd tract of 350 acres and with the approbation of the Spanish Govt. altered the lines of his survey to include other land then vacant and thereby complete his tract of 1000 acres without claiming any part of the intervening survey. For $1.00, Samuel P. Moore, James Moore and Robert Moore, heirs of Wm. Moore, decd., quit claim to any part of the 350 acres surveyed for John Ross, to Robt. Cochran. Signed by all. Wit: Sam'l. S. Mahon, D. Michie, J. E. Trask. File: Robert Cochran claimant, 14 Mch. 1804. Wit: John Girault, Esq. 26 Nov. 1804. Certf. A-235, May 23, 1805. From claim of Robert Cochran his land lay on the waters of James Cr., a branch of Bayou Pierre by virtue of a Sp. grant to Robert Cochran, dated N. O. 10 April 1795, and by the above deed of release from Sam'l. P., J. and Robt. Moore, (as above), dated 14 July 1802.

p.145. Claim No.609. Spanish grant to Patrick Cogan, for 400 acres James Run, a branch of Bayou Pierre, 40 mi. north of Fort Panmure, b. by John Savage and vacant lands. N. O. 30 Aug. 1793, by Carondelet. File: Patrick Cogan claimant, 14 Mch. 1804. Wit: Francis Nailor, 20 Nov. 1804. Certf. A-166.

p.147. Claim No.610. Spanish grant to Peter Piernas, tract 92 arpents square, b. by Wm. Barland, Thos. Green and vacant lands. N. O. 24 Feb. 1783, by Miro. // p.149. Don Pedro Piernas, Col. of La. Reg. Inf., sells to Peter Carlos Pierroux the above tract for $700. New Orleans 8 July 1786. Wit: Antonio Rodriguez, Francisco Curasses // p.152. Heirs of P. C. Pieroux to Robert Cochran, for 600 pesos, the above tract. [No file to this claim. It was probably regranted to Robert Cochran in the following grant.]

p.150. Claim No.611. Sp. grant to Robert Cochran for 1000 acres on Cole's Creek, abt. 35 mi. NE of Fort, b. on all sides by vacant lands. N. O. 9 Apr. 1790 by Miro. File: Robert Cochran claimant, 14 March 1804. Wit: John Girault, Esq., 26 Nov. 1805. Certif. A-236, 23 May 1805.

p.153. Claim No.612. Sp. grant to Robert Cochran for 500 arpents, on Homochitto River, 17 mi. SE from Fort, b. on east by Wm. Henderson, other sides vacant lands. N. O. 9 Apr. 1790, by Miro. File: Robert Cochran, claimant, 14 March 1804. Wit: John Girault, Esq., 26 Nov. 1804. Certif. A-237, 23 May 1805.

p.155. Claim No.613. Sp. grant to Waterman Crane for 600 acres on Bayou Pierre b. on south by land of Edward McCabe. New Orleans, 30 Aug. 1793, by Carondelet. // p.157. 14 Aug. 1800, Waterman Crane, of Pickering Co., Miss. Ter., to George Cochran, of Natchez, merchant, for $350 paid, 300 acres in Pickering County afsd, in the Dist. of Bayou Pierre, an undivided half of the above tract, the other half having been formerly conveyed by sd Crane to George Cochran. Signed. Wit: Ebenezer Rees, John Henderson. Wife, Catherine, relinquishes all claim, 26 Dec. 1800, before P. B. Bruin, J. P. // File: George Cochran claimant, 14 March 1804. Wit: J. Girault, Esq., 26 Nov. 1804. Certif. A-238 issued to legal representative, 23 May 1805. Claim signed by Robert Cochran for George Cochran.

p.159. Claim No.614. Petition of Stephen Minor for 12 arpents, as he did not have enough land to grow enough food for use of his house; asks for 12 arpents adj. Joseph Vidal, John Scott and Don Philip Engel, 14 Feb. 1795. // Order for same. Natchez, 16 Feb. 1795. By Gayoso. // Warrant certified by Gayoso, 4 Apr. 1795. // p.161. Stephen Minor to James White, 3 Feb. 1797, 12 acres and 85 perches, adj. the city, for $300 paid, b. by lands of Stephen Minor, John Scott and Philip Engel. Signed. Wit: J. Girault, Francisco Guttierez de Arroyo. Before Gayoso. // p.162. Miss. Territory, 27 Dec. 1798, James White, Esq., to George Cochran, for $257 paid, land on the bluff joining the Town of Natchez, as above. Signed. Wit: P. Bryan Bruin, Melling Wooley. Proved by Wooley before Sam'l. Hancock, J. P., Adams Co., 10 June 1801. // File: George Cochran, 14 March 1804. Proved in Major Minor. Certif. A-524, issued to the legal representatives, Aug. 27, 1805. Claim by Robert Cochran for George Cochran.

p.164. Claim No.615. Spanish gr. to John Perry, 1000 acres on Bayou Pierre, 45 mi. NE of Fort Panmure, b. on high land of Mr. Edward Murray and vacant lands. N. O. 20 Oct. 1788 by Miro. Plat certified by Wm. Vousdan. [Plat shows tract b. on north by South Fork of Bayou Pierre and Murray's land on east.] // p.166. 4 Dec. 1798. John Perry, of Alegany [Allegheny] Co., State of Pa., to George Cochran, of Natchez, Miss. Ter., for $250 paid, above 1000 acres. Signed. Wit: John Girault, Will Ferguson. Ack. before P. Bryan Bruin, 4 Dec. 1798. // File: Claimant, George Cochran, 14 March 1804. Rejected 16 May 1807. Robert Cochran for George Cochran.

p.167. Claim No.616. Spanish gr. to Llewellyn Price, 269 acres in Natchez District, one-half league from Bayou Pierre [South Fork] b. north by Peter Bruin, east Widow Humphreys and William Smith. N. O., 26 Dec. 1795, by Carondelet. // p.169. 1 Jany. 1799. Llewellyn Price, of Pickering Co., Miss. Ter., to George Cochran, of Natchez, for $720 paid, 269 acres on James Cr., adj. Peter B. Bruin and Wm. Smith on the south and land claimed by George Humphreys, gr. as above. Signed. Wit: Bryan Bruin, Waterman Crane. // File: George Cochran, claimant, 14 March 1804. Wit: Waterman Crane, 11 July 1805. Certif. B-113, 4 Feb. 1807. Robert Cochran for George Cochran.

p.171. Claim No.617. Spanish gr. to George Cochran, 640 acres on north fork of Cole's Cr., 6 miles east of the Miss. River and near Petit Gulf, 25 mi. from Fort, b. on John Ross, Llewellyn Price, Mr. William Ritchie and Adam Sidner. N. O. 30 Aug. 1793, by Carondelet. File: George Cochran, claimant, 14 March 1804. Wit: William Thomas. Certif. A-170, issued to legal representatives, claimant being dead, 26 Nov. 1804. For George Cochran by Robert Cochran. [No listing of heirs.]

p.173. Claim No.618. Patent for service. Petition of George Cochran, desiring to build a house near the city and to have a large garden, asks for ten acres near Daniel Douglass and Stephen Minor. Natchez, 9 Feb. 1795. // Order to confirm with dispatch, 10 Feb. 1795, by Gayoso. Plat by Dunbar certified, 20 Feb. 1795. Grant of 10 acres square located as asked. Natchez, 23 Feb. 1795. Gayoso. // File: George Cochran, claimant, 14 March 1804. Wit: William Thomas, 16 Nov. 1804. Certif. A-525 issued to legal representatives, 27 Aug. 1805. Robert Cochran for George Cochran, for services rendered the government.

p.176. Claim No.619. Spanish gr. to George Cochran, for 315 acres on the north fork of Cole's Cr., 5 mi. east of Miss. River, called Little Gulf, 25 mi. north of Fort Panmure, b. by Llewellyn Price, Robert Cochran, Roger Dow and vacant land. N. O., 30 Aug. 1793, by Carondelet. // File: Claimant, George Cochran, 14 March 1804. Wit: W. Thomas. Certif. A-239, issued to legal representatives, 23 May 1805. Robert Cochran for George Cochran.

p.178. Claim No.620. Spanish gr. to Lewellyn Price, 600 arpents on north fork of Cole's Cr., 6 mi. east of Miss. River, called Little Gulf, b. by Wm. Richie, George Cochran and Martin and Ralph Price. N. O., 30 Aug. 1793. By Carondelet. // File: Claimant, George Cochran, 14 March 1804. Wit: Wm. Thomas, 26 Nov. 1804. Certf. A-240, issued to legal representatives, 23 May 1805. Above grant conveyed by Llewellyn Price to George Cochran, 600 acres in Claiborne County. Robert Cochran for George Cochran.

p.180. Claim No.621. Spanish gr. to Adam Sidner, of 600 arpens on north fork of Cole's Cr., 6 miles east of Miss. River, Petit Gulf, 25 mi. north of Fort Panmure, b. by Wm. Moore, Wm. Ritchie, and George Cochran. N. O., 30 Aug. 1793. By Carondelet. // File: Claimant, George Cochran, 14 March 1804. Wit: Caleb Potter, 26 Nov. 1804. Certf. A-449, issued to legal representatives, 22 July, 1805. Geo. Cochran claims 600 acres in Claiborne Co. on waters of Petit Gulf Creek, by virtue of patent to Adam Snider, originally written "Sidner", dated 30 Aug. 1793. For George Cochran by Robt. Cochran.

p.182. Claim No.622. 21 Sept. 1801. Waterman Crane, of Bayou Pierre, Pickering Co., Miss. Ter., and Catherine, his wife, to George Cochran, of Adams Co., afsd Ter., for $250 paid, 100 acres, being part of the tract on which sd Crane resides. beg. corner of Spanish grant of 750 acres to sd Crane. Signed by both. Wit: Wm. Lindsay, Wm. Scott. // p.184. 1st Feb. 1801. Waterman Crane, of Bayou Pierre, and Catherine his wife, to George Cochran (as above), for $250 paid, 200 acres, beg. near bank of Bayou Pierre . . . James Creek Cr. . . . corner tree of tract on which Crane now lives, part of 750 acres gr. by Sp. Govt. 14 Aug. 1794, b. west by lands of George Humphreys, southwest by Colo. Bruin and Joseph Darlington. Signed by both. Wit. as above. // File: Claimant, George Cochran, 14 March 1804. Wit: J. Girault, Esq., 16 Nov. 1804. Certif. A-241, issued to legal representatives, for 300 acres, 23 May 1805. Robert Cochran for George Cochran.

p.187. Claim No.623. Spanish gr to Peter Belly, 630 acres (square) about one-half league below Petit Gulf, 27 mi. north of Fort Panmure, b. north by left bank of Miss. River, south by a large lake, other sides vacant. N. O., 1 June 1792, by Carondelet. // p.189. P. Belly to James McCullough, agreeable to bargain made 21 of last October which remains in my hands this 17 Nov. 1800, transfers the within titles. Wit: Peter Hugh McGee, John McGee. // p.190. 15 Apr. 1803. Peter Belly, of Iberville, Prov. of La., for $100, to James McCullough, of Adams Co., Miss. Ter., 630 acres [as described in above grant]. Signed. Wit: Travis Rivas, Samuel McCulloch, John Wren Scott, Robert Cochran. // p.190. 6 Mch. 1801, James McCulloch, of Pickering Co., Miss. Ter., to George Cochran, of Natchez, for $225 paid, the above tract. Signed. Wit: James Ferrall, William Christy. // File: George Cochran, claimant. 14 March 1804. Rejected May 16, 1807. For George Cochran by Robert Cochran.

p.192. Claim No.624. Petition of Martin Carney, Natchez 9 July 1790. He came down from Kentucky to establish himself in this district and asks for 200 acres on Cole's Cr., adj. Robt. Watt. Order of survey, N. O., 30 Oct. 1790 by Miro. // p.193. Agreement. Natchez, 13 March 1797. Martin Carney to George Cochran, both of Natchez. Whereas Martin Carney had received the above warrant for 240 acres on which he has built a house and made other improvements, and being unable to raise funds for discharging the fees of office, for $75 acknowledged by him, he, the sd Carney, engages to obtain a patent for said land, sd Cochran paying requisite fees, and make over sd patent to sd Cochran. Both signed. Receipt for $75, signed by Carney and wit. by Cornelius Seely. // File: George Cochran, claimant, 14 March 1804. Wit: William Thomas, 1st Oct. 1804. Rejected 16 May 1807. [This land was in Jefferson Co., on waters of Cole's Creek.] Claim for George Cochran by Robert Cochran.

p.195. Claim No.626. Ruffin Gray's plat and certificate of survey for 270 acres in the Natchez Dist., on south fork of the Homochitto, 18 mi. S.E. of Fort, 29th Nov. 1787. Wm. Vousdan, D. Surv. Natchez Dist. // File: Claimants: Heirs of Ruffin Gray, decd., 14 Mch. 1804. Wit: Robert Cochran, 1 Oct. 1804. Same, 26 Mch. 1806. Certif. B-196 issued Feb. 13, 1807. Ruffin Gray and Mary Ann Gray, legitimate children and heirs of Ruffin Gray, decd., claim 270 acres in Wilkinson Co. by virtue of the above survey. For Ruffin Gray and Mary Ann Gray by Robt. Cochran. [Plat shows land of Archibald Palmer, Mr. William Scott and Mr. John Steel.]

p.196. Claim No.631. John Craven, of Adams Co., Miss. Ter., for $400 paid, to Austin Holbrook 300 acres on waters of Sandy Creek, where I now live, being part of the land claimed by me. 24 Sept. 1802. Signed. Wit: Lyman Harding, David Ker. // File: Claimant: Austin Holbrook and David Berry, 15 March 1804. Wit: Peter Nelson, 20 Aug. 1804. Certif. B-33, issued 10 June 1806. Above named claim donation right to 414 acres, by virtue of the same having been improved, cultivated and resided on by John Craven since March 1789 until he sold the same to Austin Holbrook who has since sold one-half share thereof until the sd David Berry. Both sign. Plat and certf. by John Dinsmore. Land adj. Benj. Fletcher, David Howard, Peter Nelson, Edward King and Sam Watson.

p.197. Claim No.632. Spanish gr. to Robert Ford, 500 acres in Natchez Dist., 11 mi. SE of Fort, b. by lands of Daniel Perry, Isaac Johnson, Wm. McIntosh, and Charles Cason. N. O., 10 Feb. 1789. By Miro. // File: Claimant, Robert Ford, 15 March 1804. Wit: Charles Cason, 21 Aug. 1804. Certif. A-171, Miss. Ter., Adams Co. Robert Ford claims the above tract on St. Catherine's and Second Creek.

p.199. Claim No.633. Spanish gr. to Thos. Daniel, 240 acres on a branch of Cole's Cr., 27 mi. NE of Fort. N. O. 24 Dec. 1798 by Gayoso. // File: Claimant, Thos. Daniel, 15 March 1804. Wit: Wm. Daniel, 25 Sept. 1804. Certf. B-114, 4 Feb. 1807.

p.201. Claim No.635. Spanish gr. to Joseph Dyson, 400 acres on Boyd's Cr., 2 mi. south of sd creek, one mile from Miss. River, 20 mi. north of Fort Panmure. N. O. 12 Feb. 1788 by Miro. // p.203. Joseph Dyson, res. of district, to Mr. Abner Green, of same, 400 acres on Cole's Creek, b. by lands of Charles Howard, for $180 paid. 16 Oct. 1784. Joseph (X) Dyson, Abner Green. Wit: E. Minor, Antonio Soler. Before Trevino. // File. Claimant, Abner Green, 15 March 1804. Wit: Anthony Hutchins, 27 July 1804. Certif. A-172.

p.204. Claim No.636. Spanish gr to Abner Green, 665 acres on Bayou Pierre, 45 mi NE of Fort, 28 leagues by water, b. by James Lobdal, Ebenezer Smith, and Daniel Chambers and Samuel Gibson. N. O. 6 March 1789, by Miro. // File. Claimant, Abner Green, 15 March 1804. Wit: Anthony Hutchins, 27 July 1804. Certif. A-173.

p.207. Claim No.637. Spanish gr. to Abner Green, 600 arpens on a bayou of Cole's Cr., 20 mi. NE from Fort of Natchez, b. by the Miss. River and lands of Curtis, Staybraker, Simmons and Dyson. N. O., 12 Feb. 1788 by Miro. // File. Claimant, Abner Green, 15 Mch. 1804. Wit: Anthony Hutchins, 27 July 1804. Certif. A-174.

p.209. Claim No.638. Spanish gr. to Abner Green, 135 acres on St. Catherine's Cr. 8 mi. SE Fort, b. on all sides by John Botler. N. O. 10 March 1789 by Miro. // File. Claimant, Abner Green, 15 Mch. 1804. Wit: Anthony Hutchins. Certif. A-175 to claimant.

p.211. Claim No.639. Spanish gr. to Maria Green 500 acres, 7 mi. SE of Fort, b. by lands of John Row, Richard Ellis, Anthony Hutchins. N. O. 29 Feb. 1788. // File. Claimant, Abner Green and Mary Green, his wife.

p.213. Claim No.640. Spanish gr. to Wm. Bassett, 400 acres on north branch of Bayou Pierre, 65 mi. from Fort Panmure, b. by vacant lands. N. O. 24 Oct. 1794, by Carondelet. // p.215. Wm. Bassett of the northern district of Miss. Territory, for $450 paid, to Abner Green all the above tract. Mch. 5, 1799. Signed at Second Cr. Wit: Wm. Dunbar, D. Dunbar. Prov. before Daniel Clark by Wm. Dunbar. 2 Aug. 1804. Certif. A-177 to claimant.

p.216. Claim No.641. Spanish gr. to Wm. Cunningham, 240 acres on a br. of Buffalo Cr., called Pine Woods Cr., 20 mi. south of the Fort, all sides vacant. N. O. 1 Sept. 1795, by Carondelet. // p.218. 26 May 1798. Wm. Cunningham, of Dist. of Natchez, to Abner Green, of same, above grant. Signed. Wit: J. W. A. Lloyd, John Hutchins, Joseph Stoney [Storey?], Ephraim L. Blackburn. // File. Claimant, Abner Green, 15 March 1804. Certif. A-178 to claimant.

p.219. Claim No.642. Spanish gr. to John Patterson, 350 acres on Second Creek, the south branch of Cole's Cr., b. by Benj. Bullock, William Ratcliff, and vacant lands. N. O. 18 June 1795, by Carondelet. // p.221. 17 Mch. 1799. John Patterson to Abner Green, both of the southern dist. of Miss. Ter., for $350, tract on both sides of main fork of Second Cr. (the above patent). Signed. Wit: James Sanders, John Fenton, A. Hutchins. Prov. by Col. Anthony Hutchins, 13 Sept. 1799, before Wm. Dunbar, J. P., Adams Co. // File. Claimant, Abner Green, 15 March 1804. Wit: Anthony Hoggatt, 2nd Aug. 1804. Certf. A-179.

p.223. Claim No.643. Spanish gr. to Daniel Burnet, 1000 acres in Natchez dist. 70 mi. NE of Fort, b. by Elizabeth Derbin and Bassett. N. O. 20 June 1795, by Carondelet. Plat shows tract to be on south bank of Bayou Pierre. // p.225. 13 May 1801, Daniel Burnet, of Pickering Co., Miss. Ter., and Agnes, his wife, for $500, 1000 acres, as above granted, to Abner Green, on north fork of Bayou Pierre. Signed by both. Wit: A. Green, Jos. White, William Armstrong, Prov. by Abraham Green, before Roger Dixon, J. P. Pickering Co., 19 May 1801. // File. Claimant, Abner Green, 15 Mch. 1804. Wit: John Girault, 2 Aug. 1804. Certf. A-180 to claimant.

p.227. Claim No.644. British grant to Anthony Hutchins, 434 acres of Second Cr., SE 10 miles from Fort Natchez, b. on north by 1000 acres formerly gr. to sd Hutchins. Pensacola, 2 Aug. 1773 by Peter Chester. // p.232. Natchez, 2 March 1791. Anthony Hutchins to Abner Green, 434 acres, as granted above, for $200 paid. Signed. Wit: Stephen Minor, Joseph Vidal. // File. Claimant, Abner Green, 15 Mch. 1803, 434 acres on Second Cr. as above. Wit: Anthony Hutchins, 27 July, 1804. Confirmed Feb. 28, 1805. Certif. A-8.

p.233. Claim No.645. British gr. to John Row, 250 acres, on Second Creek, 14 mi. south of Natchez, b. by Anthony Hutchins and Cephas Kennard. Pensacola, 25 May 1779, by Peter Chester. // p.238. Fort Panmure, at Natchez, 15 Oct. 1785. John Row, 250 acres on Second Cr., to William Vousdan, for $580. // p.239. Dec. 20, 1786. Wm. Vousdan to Abner Green, same land for $600. // File. Claimant, Abner Green, 15 March 1804. Wit: Anthony Hutchins, 27 July 1804. Certif. A-9 issued.

p.240. Claim No.646. 4 June 1803, agreement between Peter Ratcliff, of Wilkinson Co., Miss. Ter. and Abner Green, of Adams Co. afsd Ter. To Abner Green, said Peter Ratcliff sold the improvement whereon he now lives and holds by preemption and occupancy, having settled thereon and improved for more than one year to this day, for $250 which sd Ratcliff acknowledges, sd tract on a branch of the Amite, called Bever Creek, in Wilkinson Co. To complete title, he ack. sd Abner Green to be his true and lawful representative. Signed. Wit: Andrew White, Andrew Kincaid. // File. Claimant, Abner Green, 15 March 1804. Wit: Micajah McCullen, 30 Oct. 1804. Certf. D-118, Dec. 15, 1806. Plat shows Leonard Hornsby, Henry Ratcliffe had land adjoining.

p.241. Claim No.649. Lewis Fullwood, of Natchez, Miss. Ter., sells to James Corbett an improvement made by him in Feb. 1803, on north side of Dowd's Cr., b. by James Norris and vacant lands. 22 Oct. 1803. Signed. Wit: John Hopper. // File. Claimant, James Corbett, 15 Mch. 1804. Wit: Stephen Compton, 19 Oct. 1804. [Certificate number torn.] Miss. Ter., Jefferson Co. James Corbett claims the right to become the purchaser from the U. S. 400 acres, as above. Signed. // Jany. 8, 1806. James Corbett assigns the place he bought from Mr. Lewis M. Fullwood back to sd Fullwood. Same witness.

p.242. Claim No.650. David Roberts, for $24, to Isaac Fife, both of Natchez Dist., claim and improvement on Brocus Fork of Bayou Pierre, adj. lands of sd Isaac Fife, authorizing sd Fife to apply for and receive sd land. 10 Sept. 1797. Signed. Wit: David Chote. // File. Claimant, Isaac Fife, 16 Mch. 1804. Wit: Thomas Vause. Isaac Fife is a Spanish grantee, see C-334 issued to him. Claiborne Co., Isaac Fife claims 640 acres on waters of Bayou Pierre, cultivated and inhabited by David Roberts in 1797. He was at that time above 21 years of age and the head of a family.

p.242. Claim No.656. Wm. Holley, of Claiborne Co., certifies that, as an agent of Thomas White, Esq., he did work and improve a tract on sd Co. on South Fork of Bayou Pierre, the place now occupied by sd White, in November 1797. Signed with X. Wit: Samuel Bridgers. // File. Claimant, Thos. White, 16 Mch. 1804. Wit: Isaac Fife. Certf. B-274 issued, 15 May 1807. Thos. White claims 640 acres.

p.243. Claim No.657. Robert Ashley, of Claiborne, Miss. Ter., in and for a satisfactory consideration, sells to Samuel Bridgers, of same place, my right in a certain improvement and claim on road from James Harman's ferry on Bayou Pierre to Town of Natchez, being previously entered in clerk's office, 4 Apr. 1803. R. Ashley. Wit: Josiah Rundle, M. Armstrong. // File. Claimant, Samuel Bridgers, 16 Mch. 1804. Certif. D-210, issued Dec. 22, 1806. Samuel Bridgers claims 250 acres, as above, on the waters of Storey's Mill Creek, as a donation made by Gibson Clark in 1797, which sd land was in possession of sd Clark until 1801 when it was given by sd Gibson Clark to his son, John Clark, and sold by sd John to Robert Ashley, which was occupied by sd Ashley until Apr. 1803, who sold to sd Bridgers who occupied sd tract to present day. Signed, Samuel Bridgers.

p.243. Claim No.663. 21 May 1803. Samuel Washburn, of Claiborne Co., Miss. Ter., to Reuben Ray, of same, an improvement on waters of Bayou Pierre, adj. lands claims by Mrs. Bryant, widow, and John Rennals, on the big road leading from Grindstone Ford to Cumberland, about one mile from sd road, for $150 in horse flesh, the receipt ack. Signed. Wit: John Reynolds. // 1 Sept. 1803. Reuben Ray confirms all title, etc. to John Murphree for $200. He signs with X. Wit: John L. Reynolds. // File. Claimant, John Murphree, 17 March 1804. Wit: John Reynolds. Certf. D-212, issued 22 Dec. 1806.

p.244. Claim No.673. Spanish gr. to Caleb Weeks, for 400 arpens, 35 mi. south of Fort Panmure, b. by Samuel Young, Christian Bingaman, William Vousdan and Bayou Sara. N. O. 20 June 1795, by Carondelet. // File. Claimant, Richard Graves, 17 March 1804. Wit: Ives, 14 Aug. 1804. Certf. A-655 to claimant, Oct. 3, 1805. Richard Graves, of Wilkinson Co., 28 acres, it being part of a tract of 400 acres granted to Caleb Weeks in 1791, and purchased from sd Weeks by said Graves and improved and settled before 1797, b. by Dr. Camiels's land, lands of Mr. Foley, and of sd Richard Graves. The said tract of 400 acres lies below the line of lattitude between Spain and the United States all except the above 28 acres which lies above the line.

p.249. Claim No.676. Samuel Mason assigns right, etc. to a house and improvement with which I expect to claim 300 acres, the same being known as Poplar Flat, for value received, to William Miller, 13 June 1800. Wit: John Mason. // File. Claimant, Wm. Miller, 17 March 1804. Wit: Robt. Ashley. B-53, issued Aug. 30, 1806. Claiborne Co., Miss. Ter. The above described 400 acres of land is on afsd county on the road leading from Natchez through the Wilderness between the Little or South Fork of Bayou Pierre and Grindstone Ford on the North Fork, which was settled by above Samuel Mason in 1798.

p.249. Claim No.678. Solomon Whitley, of Claiborne Co., Miss. Ter., for $100 paid, to Berryman Watkins, of same, all interest in an improvement of land which I settled and made prior to 1795, on south bank of main Bayou Pierre about 5 miles from Grindstone Ford, adj. John Booth, with power to apply for and receive same. 14 Nov. 1803. Signed. Wit: R. Ashley, Joseph Green. // File. Claimant, Berryman Watkins, 17 March 1804. Rejected, 12 May 1807. Witnesses, Anthony Glass, Wm. Miller. Claimed as a donation by virtue of a settlement before 1798, by Solomon Whitley who was at that time the head of a family and had no other lands, etc. Plat shows the land by Bayou Pierre and Boggy Branch, south of this branch is land of Abijah Hunt and west is Wm. Kilcrease, and south of Kilcrease is John Booth.

p.250. Claim No.680. Spanish gr. to Elizabeth Durben, 283 acres on east branch of Bayou Sara, 40 mi. SE of Fort Panmure, b. by lands of James Mather. N. O. 1 Sept. 1793, by Carondelet. // p.253. Elizabeth Derbin, of Bayou Pierre Dist., to Wm. Bassett, Jr., of same, for the love she bears him, the above land. Natchez 8 Jany. 1798. Before Estevan Minor. Signed: Elizabeth Derbin. Wit: J. Girault, Samuel Cooper, Drury Ledbetter. // File. Claimant, Wm. Bassett, 17 Mch. 1804. Wit: J. Girault, Esq., 26 Nov. 1804. Certif. A-182 to cl. Mrs. Elizabeth Derbin was an actual settler in Miss. Ter. on 27 Oct. 1795 and she conveyed the said tract by deed of gift to sd William Bassett. Note in file: Land Office, Washington, Miss. 29 Nov. 1828. Received of B. L. C. Wailes a Spanish patent in favor of Elizabeth Derbin, reg. No.680, claimed by William Bassett. (signed) George Dougharty.

p.253. Claim No.683. Ambrose Downs, of Claiborne Co., Miss. Ter., having found that I have placed my improvement on a prior claim of Jonathan Dayton, to which I now relinquish all claim of every kind to said Dayton. Walnut Hills, 3 March 1804. (signed) Ambrose Downs. Wit: Joseph Sessions, Anthony Glass. // Agreement bet. Elihu Hall Bay, of Charleston, S. C. and Jonathan Dayton, of Miss. Ter., for $200 to be paid by sd Dayton, will execute deeds for 100 acres of land on the north side of his, the sd Elihu Hall Bay's, 2000 acres on the north part of sd Walnut Hills, agreeable to a survey of said 100 acres made this day by Capt. Joseph Sessions, a copy annexed, and the sd Jonathan Dayton doth relinquish all claim etc. to all other parts of the sd 2000 acres of sd Elihu Hall Bay except the 100 acres to be conveyed to him . . . It is further mutually agreed that Jonathan Dayton, at his own expense is to extinguish and settle all claims of Joseph Ferguson and Jonas Griffin in and to sd 100 acres. 3 Mch. 1804. Signed by both. Wit: Joseph Sessions. The consideration money to be made at one payment in two years. 3 Mch. 1804. E. H. Bay. Same Wit. // File. Claimant, Jonathan Dayton, 17 March 1804. Wit: Anthony Glass. Rejected May 16, 1807. Indenture. Walnut Hills, 19 Mch. 1798. Ebenezer Dayton to Joseph Ferguson. In consideration of repairs, rents and covenants hereinafter reserved, the sd Ebenezer Dayton hath and does lease and farm let to sd Ferguson for two years as much of the lands claimed and owned by sd Ebenezer Dayton at and near the Walnut Hills as he the said Ferguson can and shall fence and plant where it may not interfere with what lands that shall be fenced in and improved by John Ivers, together with the dwelling house and fences belonging to the said Dayton now standing on said land at Walnut Hills, which sd house is out of repair and shall be covered and repaired by said Ferguson, etc. Dayton to have option to take and use said house whenever he may need the same, etc. Fences and cribs to be left on land at end of term. These improvements, with one ear of corn, annually, to be the rent paid by said Ferguson. Both signed. Wit: Jonas Griffen, Joseph Ferguson, Jr. // Jonathan Dayton claims 640 acres, to which the Indian title is extinguished, in Claiborne Co. on the Miss. River, at Walnut Hills, adj. lands of Elihu Hall Bay, Esq.

p.254. Claim No.685. Spanish gr. to Christian Braxton, 260 acres, 22 miles NE of Fort Panmure, b. by Edmund Johnson and Henry Platner. N. O. 30 June 1795, by Carondelet. // File. Claimant, Christian Braxton, 17 March 1804. Wit: William Thomas, 1 Oct. 1804. Certif. A-183, issued to legal representatives. Claimant's death suggested. [Land on Cole's Creek.]

p.256. Claim No.686. James Lobdell's survey of 467 acres on Tabor's Cr., a br. of Bayou Pierre, 50 mi. NE from the Fort. Natchez, July 16, 1792. (signed) William Dunbar. [Plat shows land adj. Abner Green, Ebenezer Smith, Gibson Clark, Wm. Tabor and Lucius Smith.] // 15 Nov. 1799. James Lobdell to John Armstrong, for $500 paid, 400 acres of above tract. Signed. Wit: Thos. Woods, John Ivers, Wm. Brocus, Jr. Ack. 26 Apr. 1800, before G. W. Humphreys, J. Q. Receipt for full payment, 19 Jany. 1802, signed by James Lobdell, Mary Lobdell. Wit: Robt. Trimble. // p.257. 24 Oct. 1801. John Armstrong and Margaret, his wife, to Francis Nailor, for $600 paid, 400 acres, as granted above. John Armstrong, Margaret (X) Armstrong. Wit: Julius Smith, Pliny Smith. // p.259. Ack. before Geo. Wilson Humphreys, Justice of Pickering County, 24 Oct. 1801. // File. Claimant, Francis Nailor, 17 March 1804. Wit: Elisha Flowers, William Atchinson, 19 Nov. 1804. Certif. B-249 issued to Elias Barnes, assignee, 30 March 1807. Francis Nailor, an actual settler, 27 Oct. 1795, claims 467 arpents, as above, warrant of survey, now lost, dated 26 Apr. 1790, to Lobdell who was then a head of a family, etc.

p.260. Claim No.687. Petition of William Cooper to Spanish Govt. He has for two years cultivated 186 acres which were vacant, asks that same be granted to him. Natchez, 19 Feb. 1787. // Order: The land cited has not been claimed and it may be conceded as petitioned. Carlos de Grand-Pre. // Warrant by Estevan Miro, N. O. Oct. 1, 1787. p.261. 26 Aug. 1801. William Cooper to William Wells, for $200 in hand paid, 186 acres on Second Cr. adj. John Hartley, Stephen Stephenson and Reuben Alexander, (as above). Signed. Wit: Absolem Griffin, Samuel Cooper, Jr. // p.262. 12 Sept. 1801. Wm. Wells, of Adams Co., Miss. Ter., to Melling Woolley, for $400 paid, above tract. Signed. Wit: William Kenner, Lyman Harding. // p.264. 13 March 1804, Melling Wooley, of Jefferson Co., Miss. Ter. to Francis Nailor, for $400 paid, the above tract. Wit: H. D. Downs, Bazil Abrams. // File. Claimant, Francis Nailor, 17 March 1804. Wit: Samuel Heady and Samuel Cooper, 20 Aug. 1804. John Still Lee, 20 Nov. 1804. Certif. B-254 issued 30 March 1807. (See Nos. 1665 and 775.)

p.266. Claim No.690. Henry Roach, a survey of 1038 acres on Buffalo Cr. in Wilkinson Co., Miss. Ter., Sept. 22, 1803. (signed) William Atkinson, Dep. Surv. Same surveyed by virtue of an order and grant of Don Manuel Gayoso de Lemos that every person should enjoy the swamp in front of their land which they hold on the east side of Buffalo Creek, dated 1793. A true copy. // File. Claimant, Henry Roach, 18 March 1804. Wit: William Roach, 25 March 1807. Rejected, 16 April 1807. Henry Roach claims 1038 acres of swamp land in the Mississippi swamp on the south side of Buffalo Cr., b. by lands of Daniel Ogden, and Mr. Wall.

p.267. Claim No.691. Spanish grant to Luis Gonzales, who petitioned that he was a carpenter and wished to build a house in the city on Lot No.2, Sq. No.20, which is vacant. He asks a grant of same. Natchez, 1 Aug. 1796. // Warrant, same day. Certif. of survey by Wm. Dunbar, 6 Aug. 1796. Grant by Gayoso, 8 Aug. 1796. // p.268. Luis Gonzales to Daniel Douglass, for $80, above grant. 1 Sept. 1796. Wit: Joseph Vidal, John Girault. // Petition of Stephen Douglas that he wishes to build a house in the city and asks for Lot No.4, Sq. No.20. 12 Nov. 1796. // p.271. 28 June, 1799. Daniel Douglass of Natchez, to Thos. Foster, for $300, two lots in town of Natchez, both in Square No.20, as granted above. Wit: Joshua Howard, John Henderson. [No transfer from Stephen Douglass to Daniel Douglass.] // File. Claimant, Thos. Foster, 19 March 1804. Wit: Philip Engel, 2 Dec. 1805. Certif. B-260 allowed as a Donation, 16 April 1807.

p.272. Claim No.692. 9 Dec. 1799. Anthony Gras and wife, Jenneva Gras, of Natchez, Miss. Ter., to Thos. Foster, of St. Catherine's Cr., for $1500, paid Lot No.2, Sq. No.17, which was conveyed to Wm. Barland, 11 Dec. 1794, and Lot No.4, Sq. No.17, conveyed to Anthony Gras by deed from Luis Delat, 25 Feb. 1797. Signed: Antonio Gras, Genevieve Delatte et Gras, ack. before Wm. Kenner, Wit: P. Connelly, Stephen Douglass. // File. Claimant, Thomas Foster, 19 March 1804. Wit: Reuben Gibson, 3 May 1804. Certif. A-729 issued to claimant.

p.274. Claim No.693. Spanish gr. to William Bishop, 345 acres, 18 mi. NE of Fort Panmure, b. by Richard King, Gerard Brandon, Daniel Whitaker, Richard Carpenter and Charles Boardman. N. O. 10 Feb. 1796 by Carondelet. // 3 Jany. 1803, William Bishop and Mary, his wife, to Wm. Montgomery, for $1325 paid, 345 acres, as above. William (X) Bishop, Mary Bishop. Ack. before Alexander Montgomery, J. P., 3 Jany. 1803. Wit: Josiah Montgomery. // File. Claimant, Wm. Montgomery, 19 March 1804. Wit: John Bolls, 9 June 1804. Certif. B-115, 4 Feb. 1807.

p.278. Claim No.697. Petition to the Spanish Govt. by Jesse Harper, lately arrived in this colony and wishing to establish a plantation in this district to employ six negroes which I own and work for the subsistence of my wife and three children, asks for land adj. Robt. Dow and Mr. Chacharet, on Cole's Cr., Natchez, 8 July 1794. // Order of survey, 28 Jany. 1795, by Gayoso. Warrant, N. O. Feb. 1795, by Carondelet. // File. Claimant, Jesse Harper, 19 March 1804. Wit: James Chaney. Certif. C-7. Marked: conflicting with 976. Claim of 500 arpents on waters of south fork of Cole's Cr. in Adams Co. by virtue of the above. Asks for 140 acres extra as he has a large family.

p.280. Claim No.699. John Stampley to Hugh Matthews, 350 arpents in Dist. of Cole's Creek, adj. Richard Roddy and my own land, part of a gr. of 800 acres in my favor, No.567, for $120 and 300 acres on Big Black River which I have received and ack. Both sign. Wit: John Girault, Isaac Foster, Ebenezer Petty. Before Estevan Minor. p.281. Certificate of survey for Hugh Mathews, 296 acres, being a part of a larger survey granted to John Stampley, as above, adj. Jesse Hamilton and Henry King. March 16, 1804. (signed) John Dinsmore, (Surv.) // File. Claimant, Hugh Matthews, 19 March 1804. Wit: Samuel Davis, 21 June 1804. Certif. A-370 issued to claimant, for 350 arpents. June 24, 1805. Hugh Matthews claims 296 acres, equal to 350 arpents, on Cole's Creek.

p.282. Claim No.700. Spanish grant to Benj. Holmes, on Sandy Creek, 15 miles from Fort, b. by James Erwin and vacant lands. N. O. 6 March 1789 by Miro. // File. Claimant, B. Holmes, 19 March 1804. Wit: John Erwin, 20 Aug. 1804. Certif. A-187 issued to claimant. Claim for 400 arpents by virtue of above grant.

p.286. Claim No.703. Survey of 200 arpents for Anthony Calvit, on east bank of the Miss. River, near Petit Gulf, 30 mi. north of the Fort, as by plat, 2 Nov. 1794. (signed) Wm. Dunbar, Dep. Surv. Plat shows land adj of Jeptha Higdon and Peter Beily. // File. Claimant, A. Calvit, 19 March 1804. Wit: Thomas Calvit, 8 May 1805. Certif. B-279. The said tract was inhabited and cultivated for the benefit of sd Anthony Calvit in 1795.

p.286. Claim No.704. Spanish grant to William Calvit, 800 acres on Sandy Creek, 18 miles east of Fort, all sides vacant. N. O. 15 Mch. 1788 by Miro. Plat and certificate by Wm. Dunbar. // File. Claimant, heirs of William Calvet, decd. Wit: Peter Nelson. Claim signed by Anthony Calvet, one of the said heirs.

p.288. Claim No. 705. Spanish Govt. to Chachere, who petitions for 13 acres front by 40 acres in depth adj Sieur Farkar [Farquhar] and the line made by the English for Lord Eglinton. (signed) Chachere. Natchez, 5 Dec. 1783. // Order for 500 arpents, 3 April 1784 by Trevino. // p.289. Spanish Govt. to Polser Shilling, who petitioned that on 7th Oct. 1784, he bought of Louis Chacheret 500 acres, the titles of which are in possession of the clerk, Mr. John Girault. As a certain Stephen Hayward intends to obtain a grant from the Govt. for the same land, although he, Shilling, has had it surveyed, cleared, improved and built on and has been in possession nine years. He asks a decree that he be left in entire and quiet possession, etc. Signed. Decree as per above request, 2 May 1795 by Carondelet. // p.292. William Vousdan certified that the land abovementioned was unoccupied and claimed only by Marion Yarrow. 30 Jany. 1788. // I do certify that I run for Polser Shilling a tract of 400 acres by order of Mr. William Vousdan, said tract joined Mr. Grafton, Mr. John Farquer, Major Minor, and land of sd Shilling. Mr. Vousdan ordered me to run a part off sd tract for Mr. Joseph Barnard. Feb. 3, 1795. (signed) Wm. Atchinson. // File. Claimant, Polser Shilling, 19 March 1804. Wit: Lawrence Herd, 15 June 1806; George Fitzgerald, 10 Sept. 1804; John Shanauer, 12 Nov. 1804. Certif. D-116 issued to claimant. Occupancy proved in the claimant.

p.293. Claim No.706. Spanish gr. to John Girault, of 361 arpents, 7 miles SE from Fort, b. by Richard Ellis, Mary Green, Philipe Trevino. N. O. 15 March 1789 by Miro. // p.295. 24 Jany. 1794. Christopher Whipple sells to Elias Bonnell, 361 acres on Second Cr., b. by Matthew White, Abner Green, Richard Ellis; for 200 pesos. Signed by both. Wit: Estevan Minor, Ebenezer Dayton. // File. Claimants, heirs of Elias Bonnell, decd., Wit: Simon Presley. Certif. A-625 to legal representatives. Co. of Adams, John Girault conveys to Christopher Whipple the above tract, in 1793, and Whipple conveyed same to Elias Bonnell. Signed: Drucilla Bonnell, widow of Elias Bonnell, decd.

p.297. Claim No.708. Wm. Clark, of Natchez, for $100. sells improvement lying between Alexander Callender and Samuel Davis, John Clark and Ephraim Coleman to Ephraim Coleman, 21 Aug. 1793. Signed. Wit: Elijah Swayze, James Clark. // File. Claimant, heirs of Ephraim Coleman, decd., 19 March 1804. Wit: John Jones, 4 June 1804. Certif. B-91 issued 3 Feb. 1807. Claim for the heirs of Ephraim Coleman, decd., is signed by Israel Coleman, one of the acting exors.

p.296. Claim No.714. British govt. to Nehemiah Carter, order of survey for 1200 acres 3 mi. from Rumsey's land on Boyd's Creek if it does not interfere with Harcourt's Mandamus in West Florida. Pensacola, 21 Nov. 1778 by Peter Chester. // Order for execution of warrant, 24 Nov. 1778, by Elias Durnford, Surv. Gen. // File. Claimant, Nehemiah Carter, 19 March 1804. Wit: John Gaskin, 21 March 1804. Rejected April 27, 1807.

p.297. Claim No.715. Petition of David Lambert that he worked on a piece of land that he found vacant for four years; he asks for 350 acres. Natchez, 2 Feb. 1788. Signed. // New Orleans, 19 March 1789, warrant for land as requested. Miro. // David Lambert to Doctor Debreddy assigns all right to above warrant for 200 acres surveyed in my name, 9 Dec. 1789. Aug. 2, 1799. (signed) David Lambert. Wit: Wm. Dunbar. // p.298. Doctor John D. Brady to Nicholas Rab, his tract on St. Catherine's Creek, adj. Chas. Cason, John Hartley, George Killian, David Lambert, 800 arpents for $800. 18 March 1793. Both sign. Wit: Blas de Bouchet, Valentin Rincon. // File. Claimant, Nicholas Rab, 19 March 1804. Wit: George Killian. Certif. D21 issued June 4, 1807. In claim David Lambert asserts that he was 21 years of age at date of said warrant and lived in Territory 27 Oct. 1795. [Dates conflict.]

p.300. Claim No.717. Spanish grant to James Elliott, 246 acres in Natchez Dist., on Cole's Cr., 25 mi. NE of Fort, adj. Anthony Hutchins and vacant lands. New Orleans, 20 Oct. 1788, by Miro. // p.302. 21 Nov. 1800. Daniel Callaghan, of Opelousas, to David Davis, of Pickering County, Miss. Ter., for $369 paid by John Smith, Esq., of sd Co., in his bond, acknowledged; 246 acres on north fork of Cole's Cr., in sd county, gr. James Elliott, Sr., and by him conveyed to sd Callahan as part of 546 acres, as appears by Peter Padescloe's office in New Orleans. Signed, and ack. same date before Wm. Thomas, J. P. Wit: Jas. Campbell, John Brookes. // File. Claimant, Daniel Callaghan, Mch. 19, 1804.

p.303. Claim No.719. Deed of Gift. Bernard and Lucy Isenhood to their children, Patsey, Catherine and John. To the daughters cattle and furniture, (specified) and to the son more of the same and 60 acres on which they now live, all in Pickering Co., Miss. Ter. 31 Dec. 1799. Wit: John Hopkins, William Smith, John Smith. Prov. 31 Jany. 1800, before John Smith. Bernard Isenhut, Lucy (X) Isenhood. // File. Claimant, John Isenhood, heir and legal representative, 22 March 1804. Claims 342 acres on middle fork of Cole's Creek, by right of occupancy, by virtue of its having been occupied and cultivated ever since 1790 by said Barney, decd. until his death and since by his family. Lucy (X) Isenhood, John Isenhood.

p.304. Claim No.720. Petition of Peter Newman, res. of the district, wishes to establish residence for his family of nine whites, asks for 600 acres on waters of St. Catherine's Cr. adj. Adam Bingaman, James Morrison and Richard Bell. Natchez, Nov. 21, 1791. // Order of survey to Benjamin Newman, 9 Dec. 1791 by Gayoso. // Warrant N. O. 29 Dec. 1791 New Orleans, by Estevan Miro, for 600 acres. // File. Claimant, Benj. Newman, 19 March 1804. Wit: David Gibson, 23 May 1804. Certif. B.81 issued Oct. 30, 1806. Adams Co. Benj. Newman claims 600 arpents on waters of Cole's Creek, by virtue of a warrant of survey of the Spanish Govt. in 1791 to said Benjamin, who was at that date the head of a family and cultivated and inhabited the land Oct. 27, 1795. Plat and survey by Wm. Dunbar, 16 Oct. 1792, for Mr. Benj. Newman, land adj. Dennis Collins, Christian Bingaman, Richard Bell, Benj. Curtis, Jeptha Higdon, James Morrison and Charles Boardman.

p.305. Claim No.721. Spanish grant to James Frazier, for 800 arpents on west bank of Big Black, 55 mi. N.E. from Fort, b. by Richard King and vacant lands. N. O. 1 Sept. 1795, by Carondelet. // p.307. 20 Feb. 1802, James Frazier, by his atty, Melling Woolley, to James Andrews, $1200 paid, the above tract of 800 arpents on Big Black. Signed by Woolley and ack before Thos. Rodney, Judge of Superior Court for Miss. Ter., 12 Dec. 1803. Wit: Edm. Bradish, Arthur Andrews. // File. Claimant, James Andrews, 19 March 1804. Wit: Richard King, 5 April 1806. Certif. A-764 issued Apr. 10, 1806.

p.308. Claim No.728. Spanish gr. to Benajah Osman, 600 acres on the waters of Bayou Sarah, 35 mi. south of the Fort, b. by James Mather and vacant lands. New Orleans, 10 Mch. 1795, by Carondelet. // File. Claimant, Benajah Osman, 19 March 1804. Wit: Robt. Dunbar, 18 May 1804. Certif. A-190 issued to claimant.

p.310. Claim No.729. (No.1) Deed. 14 Apr. 1772, Capt. Amos Ogden, of Sussex Co., Prov. of New Jersey, to Samuel Swayze and Richard Swayze, co. of Morris, Province afsd. Whereas 13 May 1767, the British Govt. granted a patent to Capt. Amos Ogden of 25,000 acres in West Florida to be surveyed in one contiguous tract, the sd Amos Ogden for 900 pounds of proc. Money of New Jersey to him in hand paid, sells to sd Samuel Swayze and Richard Swayze 19,000 acres of afsd 25,000 to be surveyed in any part of West Florida and also 4/5 of another 1000 acres, 500 acres to be divided in small lots for a Town, the remaining 500 acres of the last mentioned 1000 acres to be laid out for parsonages, public buildings, burying grounds and parades. (signed) Amos Ogden. Wit: Joseph King, Justus King. Proved by Joseph King, one of the witnesses, before Samuel Tuthill, Esq., one of the Justices of Morris County, Prov. of New Jersey, 15 Oct. 1774. // p.313. Release of one-half of the above property to Samuel Swayze by Amos Ogden of Rosebury, Morris Co., New Jersey, for $450, 9500 acres in West Fla. on west side of Homochitto River, east of Miss. River. 15 Apr. 1773. Signed by Amos Ogden, Margaret Ogden. Wit: Justus King, Elijah Horton, Stephen Swayze. Prov. by Elijah Horton before Samuel Grandon, Judge of Inferior Court of Morris Co. Oct. 8, 1774. // p.316. Capt. Amos Ogden releases to Richard Swayze, both of Rosebury, Morris Co., Prov. of New Jersey, 9,500 acres (same as above). 15 Apr. 1773. Same wit. Signed by Amos Ogden, Margaret Ogden, Prov. as above. // p.318. Petition of the heirs of Richard and Samuel Swayze, reciting the above deeds of 19,800 from Amos Ogden to Samuel and Richard Swayze, they ask for a grant from Spain for same. Natchez, 21 Nov. 1787. Signed: Sarah Swayze, Samuel Swazey, Nathan Swazey, Elisha Swazey, Obediah Brown, Hannah Curtis, William Wicks, Stephen Swazey, Rachel Swazey, David Lambert, Rhoda Lambert, Richard Swazey, Elisha Swazey, Gabriel Swazey, Sarah King, Lydia Corey and Mary King. Natchez, 21 Nov. 1787. // Natchez, 20 Nov. 1787. Mr. Wm. Vousdan, Dept. Surveyor will make the survey solicited by the parties interested, observing not to include within the survey of the number of acres mentioned in their deeds 4000 acres which they sold about 15 years ago to persons absent from this province ever since that time, which land is to be returned to the domain of His Majesty and subject to be granted to whomsoever may require the same. Etc. Signed: Grand-Pre. // New Orleans, 18 Jany. 1788. I do approve the foregoing decree in all its parts. (signed) Miro. // p.319. Agreement of heirs of Samuel Swazey, decd. to division of lands of sd Samuel Swazey Sr., decd. according to plat and plan annexed. Natchez, 22 Sept. 1795. (signed) Hannah (X) Curtis, Samuel Swazey, Obediah Brown, Nathan Swazey, Rhoda Lambert, Elijah Swazey by written order for Stephen Swazey, Rachel Bell, Elijah Swazey. Wit: Isaac Johnson, Joseph Bernard, Ebenezer Dayton. // p.320. Claim No. 729. (No.2) Spanish gr. to Nathan Swazey, 500 acres 16 mi. south of the Fort, b. by Ceronio and Dayton and Gideon Hopkins. N. O. 21 May 1795, by Miro. // p.322. 12 May 1801. Nathan Swayze, of Adams Co., Miss. Ter. to his son, David, for love and affection and better maintenance, 500 acres as above. Signed: Nathan Swayze. Wit: Caleb King, John Henderson. // File. Claimant, David Swayze, 19 March 1804. Wit: Gideon Hopkins, 2 Aug. 1804. Certif. A-191 issued to claimant.

p.323. Claim No.730. Spanish gr. to Richard Trevillian, 264 acres on Cole's Creek, in Dist. of Natchez, b. by Anthony Hutchins and Gaspar Sinclair. N. O., 17 March 1796, by Carondelet. // p.325. Petition of Manuel Texada, res. of the dist., that Richard Trevillian, an inhabitant, is indebted to him for $303, for hire of negroes, which sum was to have been paid Feb. 1790; asks that he be ordered to pay sum, its tenth and cost. Signed. Natchez, 29 Aug. 1792. // Same date, order that Richard Trevilliam settle at once with Mr. Texada. Gayoso. // Texada petitions that so much of Trevillian's property be executed as will suffice to pay him. Oct. 1, 1792. // Inventory of Trevillain's estate ordered made by Thomas M. Green and Thomas Calvet. // March 9, 1793, the plantation was put up and bid in for $150 by Manuel Texada. // p.328. Deed. Manuel Texada to Cato West, of Villa Gayoso Dist., 264 acres gr. Richard Trevilliam, for $300. 7 March 1798. Both signed. Witness: Ebenezer Rees, Lacy Rumsey. Before Stephen Minor. // File. Claimant, Cato West, 19 March 1804. Wit: James Truly. Certif. C-9, 3 Feb. 1807. (Conflicting with No.763.) Claim as above.

p.330. Claim No.731. Spanish gr. to Reuben Dunham, 500 acres on Bayou Sara, in Natchez Dist., b. by Cesar Archinard, Samuel Young, and vacant lands. N. O., 30 March 1796, by Carondelet. [Plat shows Patrick Foley on one side.] // p.332. Reuben Dunham and Elizabeth, his wife, to Thomas Dawson, all of Bayou Sarah, for $1400, on terms, the 500 acres in above grant. Natchez, 3 Sept. 1797. Both signed with mark. Wit: John Girault, H. Hunter, Alcalde. Before Minor. // File. Claimant, Thos. Dawson, 19 March 1804. Certif. D-117 issued for 398 arpents. Certif. B-18 for 2 arpents. Certif. B-119 for 100 arpents, making in all 500 arpents. (See Nos.1298, 1516 and 1433.) Feb. 4, 1807. Claim as above.

p.333. Claim No.732. Spanish grant to William Smith, 400 acres on waters of Bayou Pierre about one mile from sd Bayou and 15 miles from Miss. River, 41 mi. NE from Fort, b. by Col. Bruin and vacant lands. N. O., 15 Mch. 1788, by Miro. Plat No.107. // File. Claimant, William Smith, 19 March 1804. Certificate A-14 issued to claimant, 18 Sept. 1805. Miss. Territory, William Smith, a citizen of sd Ter., who on 27 Oct. 1795 was an actual settler therein, claims 400 arpents, by above grant. John Girault at the request and in behalf of Wm. Smith. Endorsed: William Smith, Bayou Pierre.

p.335. Claim No.733. Decree of Spanish Govt. to John Girault. Petition that part of the effects mortgaged to him by John Montgomery were sold to Buckner Pittman and others to James Fin and the widow; asks that Mr. George Cochran, of Bayou Pierre, be authorized to claim sd property wheresoever it may be found and that it be estimated at cash price and delivered to sd Mr. Geo. Cochran for acct. of petitioner for payment of his mortgages of $266. (signed) John Girault. Natchez, 16 Oct. 1792. // Decree. Natchez 17 Oct. 1792. To Colo. Bryan Bruin, alcalde for the dist. of Bayou Pierre, order that the plantation be appraised at cash price and delivered to petitioner on acct. of his claim. Gayoso. // 28 Nov. 1792. Melling Wooley and Capt. Richard King apptd appraisers of same, by P. B. Bruin. // p.336. 597 acres on south br. of Bayou Pierre, adj. John Gibson, Fordice, Abner Green, Elijah Smith, Elisha Flowers and Thos. Hubbard, a small house, well, field and orchard, all in bad repair, value $250 cash, from which sum cost of obtaining title is to be deducted. Signed by both. // Natchez 13 Jany. 1793. Possession of property confirmed and mortgage closed in favor of John Girault. Land to be surveyed to him. Gayoso. // File. Claimant, John Girault, 19 March 1804. Wit: Hezekiah Harman, 1 Oct. 1804. Certif. B-238, 30 March 1807. Claim as above. Girault the head of a family January 1793.

p.336. Claim No.734. Natchez, 12 Feb. 1795. Polser Shilling, for myself and in the name of my children, sells to Mr. John Girault 250 acres near the Fort, b. by Job Routh, Ebenezer Rees, John Joseph Rodriguez and Benjamin Montsanto, the property having been purchased of the late John St. Germain; for $150 to be paid in three years. Both signed. Before Gayoso. "A map or plan made by Surveyor Genl. of this district of a grant 10 arpents front by 40 arpents deep of land b. by Chas. Trudeau and Henry Lefleur and others of the demesne of His Majesty, dated 20 Aug. 1782, is marked with the letter K." The foregoing is one of the items in inventory of the estate of late John St. Germain. (signed) J. Girault. // p.337. Agreement. Mr. St. Germain, of Dist., sells to Polser Shilling, of same, 250 arpents in sight of Fort Panmure, for $300 to be paid in merchandize on demand by Mr. Smith who will deliver same. 16 Dec. 1784. Wit: Antonio Soler. Acct. of merchandize delivered $296 and receipt of same in part payment signed by St. Germain, 18 Jany. 1785. // File. Claimant, John Girault, 19 March 1804. Wit: Richard King, 31 May 1804. Claimant appeared before the Board and relinquished the within claim. Signed: Thos. H. Williams. Feb. 25, 1806. Claim for 125 arpents an undivided moiety of the above 250 arpents, claimant having released one-half thereof to said Shilling, 14 Mch. 1797, now claimed by the representative of Chas. Watross, decd.

p.338. Claim No.735. Spanish gr. to Francisco Girault, 395 arps. on the Miss. River, b. by lands of Peyroux, Stampley, Lusk, David Mitchell and Bacon and Lefleur. N. O., 20 June 1795, by Carondelet. // File. Claimant, John Girault in behalf of F. S. Girault, 19 Mch. 1804. Wit: Richard King, 21 May 1804. Certif. A-192, issued to F. S. Girault. John Girault, as next of kin of Francis Spain Girault, both residents and actual settlers, claims as above. Proved in John Girault and F. S. Girault, his son.

p.340. Claim No.376. Spanish gr. to John Girault, 9 arpents and 40 perches, near city, adj. Don Manuel Gayoso de Lemos, Francisco Lennan, Wm. Vousdan, Daniel Douglass and George Cochran. 25 Feb. 1795, by Gayoso. // File. Claimant, John Girault 19 March 1804. Wit: Richard King, 31 May 1804. Certif. A-526, Aug. 27, 1805. Claimed as above.

p.343. Claim No.737. Spanish gr. to Henry Hunter, 2000 acres on Bayou Sara, 40 mi. south of Fort, b. by lands of Frederick Kimble, Lewis Wells, Abraham Horton, Gerard Brandon and David Monroe. N. O., 20 Nov. 1793, by Carondelet. // File. Claimant, Henry Hunter, 19 March 1804. Wit: Gerard Brandon, 20 June 1804. Certif. A-202, May 16, 1805. Claim as above.

p.345. Claim No.738. 19 Nov. 1802. Robert Moore, of Natchez, Adams Co., Miss. Ter., to Thomas Ewing, of Philadelphia, for $1200, Lot No.4, Sq. No.10, in Natchez, gr. Francis Lennan 1794 and conveyed to by him to sd Moore, 29 March 1798. Signed. Ack. before Wm. Darby, J. P. 14 Mch. 1804. Wit: Henry Turner, Wm. Henderson. // File. Claimant, Thomas Ewing, 19 March 1804. Wit: John Henderson, 16 June 1804. Certif. A-549, to claimant. See R. Moore's claim No.1405. Claim signed by John Henderson, and Wm. S. Barr, attys. for Thos. Ewing.

p.346. Claim No.739. Warrant for survey for Wm. Henderson, 1000 acres, 4 mi. NE of fork of Thompson's Creek in West Florida, by Peter Chester, 16 Sept. 1777. Order to Mr. Elsworth, Dep. Surveyor, 30 Sept. 1777 by Elias Durnford, Surv. Genl. [File missing.]

p.346. Claim No.740. Robert Moore, 25 Jany. 1803, to John Henderson, both of Natchez, for $616 in hand paid, Lot No.4 Sq. No.10, 56 feet front. Signed by Moore. Wit: J. Pannell, John B. Willis. //

File. Claimant, John Henderson, 19 March, 1804. Wit: John Bolls, 16 June, 1804. See R. Moore's and Ewing's claims, No.1405 and No.738. Certif. A-550 to claimant, 29 Aug. 1805. Claim for a part of above lot, 56 feet on Main Street, beg. at that part of the lot belonging to Gerraghty and P. Reilly and running up the said street to that part of sd lot belonging to Frederick Ward and from thence back the whole depth of the lot, by virtue of the above sale. Lots 2 and 4 in said Sq.10 were conveyed by Francis Lennan to John Henderson, 29 March 1798.

p.348. Claim No.741. 25 Feb. 1802. Ebenezer Rees, of Adams Co., Miss. Ter. to John Henderson, of Natchez, for $500 paid, 200 acres in Adams Co. on St. Catherine's Cr., part of a tract gr. to Alexander Henderson and conveyed to sd Ebenezer Rees by said John Henderson, as co-partner and atty. for sd Alexander, as records in N. O. and Adams Co. will show. Land adj. Reuben Gibson and Thos. Foster. Wit: James Gormely, W. S. Barr. // File. Claimant, John Henderson, 19 March 1804. Wit: John Bolls, 16 June 1804. Certif. A-342, June 20, 1805. John Henderson claims 200 acres, by virtue of deed of conveyance of Ebenezer Rees, as above, part of 739 arpents, granted to Alexander Henderson, his brother, in 1788. Proved in the settlement of claimant and Alexander Henderson.

p.350. Claim No.742. Spanish gr. to Alexander Henderson, 587 arpents, on Homochitto, b. by Landon Davis and Wm. Gilbert. N. O. March 6, 1788. // p.352. 1 Jany. 1796. Alexander Henderson and Mary, his wife, for $587, to John Henderson above tract. Both signed. Wit: Nathan Thompson, John Bolls. Receipt for $587 (Mexican dollars) by both. Wit: Nathan Thomson, John Bolls. // File. Claimant, John Henderson, 19 March 1804. Wit: John Bolls, 16 June 1804. Certif. A-232 to claimant, 22 May 1805.

p.353. Claim No.743. Spanish gr. to Ebenezer Dayton, 400 arpents on Homochitto River, 16 mi. SE of Fort, b. by lands of Wm. Henderson and Nathan Swazey. N. O. 29 March 1793, by Carondelet. // p.355. 24 Dec. 1799, Ebenezer Dayton, of Adams Co., Miss. Ter., to Robert K. Moore, of Jefferson Co., State of Ky., for $600 paid, two-third undivided part of 400 acres; b. as above. Signed. Wit: Wm. Kenner, John C. Wickoff. Ack. same date, before Wm. Kenner, J. P. // File. Claimants, R. K. Moore and J. C. Wickoff, 19 March 1804. Wit: John Henderson, 16 June 1804. Certificate A-679 issued to Moore, Wickoff and W. G. Garland, 19 Oct. 1805. Robert K. Moore and John C. Wickoff claim 400 arpents of land, as above. John Henderson, atty.

p.356. Claim No.744. Spanish gr. to John B. Perret, 1000 acres on Cole's Cr., Natchez Dist., 19 mi. east of Fort, b. by John Ford and vacant lands. N. O. 12 June 1788 by Miro. // p.358. I, J. B. Perret, declare I have exchanged my concession at the Natchez, of 1000 acres, for a plantation Mr. Boardman has, 15 arpents front, on the river, and the sum of $255. I promise to pay him for the cows at Eveville, 14 Oct. 1789. // File. Claimants, guardians of the orphans of Charles Boardman, decd., 19 March 1804. Wit: John Henderson, 16 June 1804. Certificate A-271 issued to legal representatives, 4 June 1805. Claim as above by John Henderson, guardian.

p.358. Claim No.745. Spanish gr. to Charles Boardman, 1000 acres on waters of St. Catherine's Cr., adj. Mr. Carpenter and Jeremiah Brian. N. O. 6 Mch. 1788 by Miro. // File. Claimants, heirs of C. Boardman, 19 March 1804. Wit: John Henderson, 16 June 1804. Certif. A-203 issued to legal representatives, 16 May 1804. By John Henderson, guardian.

p.361. Claim No.746. Chas. Boardman's survey of 226 acres by Wm. Atchinson, directed by Wm. Dunbar, Esq., surveyor for the Govt. in the vicinity of Pine Ridge, on the east bluffs of the Miss. River, 8 mi. NE from Natchez Fort. Plat shows J. Bonner, Moses Bonner, Sr., and Moses Bonner below the hills to the north; Baptist LaPoint SE.; Richard Goodwin SW. // File. Claimants, heirs of C. Boardman, 19 March 1804. Rejected, 15 Apr. 1807. Also signed by John Henderson, guardian.

p.361. Claim No.747. Charles Boardman's survey of 282 arpents on the mouth of Fairchild's Cr. 6 mi. NNE. of Fort as per plan, by Wm. Dunbar. 2 June 1793. // File. Claimants, heirs of C. Boardman, 19 March 1804. Rejected, 15 Apr. 1807. Claim signed by John Henderson, guardian.

p.362. Claim No.748. Spanish gr. to Chas. Boardman, 900 arpents on south fork of St. Catherine's Cr., 8 mi. east of Fort, b. by own lands. N. O. Apr. 9, 1790, by Miro. // File. Claimants, heirs of C. Boardman, 19 March 1804. Wit: John Henderson, 16 June 1804. Certif. A-204 to legal representatives, 16 May 1805. Claim by John Henderson, guardian.

p.364. Claim No.749. Spanish gr. to Moses Bonner, 600 acres in Natchez Dist., 8 mi NE of Fort Panmure, b. on north by James and Moses Bonner, Senr., brothers, on south by Jeremiah Brian. N. O.

8 Apr. 1789, by Miro. // p.383. Moses Bonner to Charles Boardman, 17 Dec. 1788, for $600, 600 acres adj. my father, Moses Bonner, Manuel Madden and Jeremiah Brian, 3 leagues from Fort. // p.366. 12 Nov. 1799, Abner Pipes, of district of Pine Ridge, to Charles Boardman, Esq., for $750 paid, 112 acres in sd district, being a part of 600 acres gr. Abner Pipes by Spanish Govt, b. by John Bisland, Chas. Boardman, Jonas Scoggins, ____ Kennedy and Benj. Farrarr. Signed. Wit: L. Valcourt, Samuel McElhiney. // File. Claimant, heirs of C. Boardman, 18 March 1804. Wit: John Henderson, 16 June 1804. Certif. A-439 to legal representatives. Claim by John Henderson, guardian of the heirs.

p.367. Claim No.751. Spanish gr. to John Steel, 600 acres on waters of Homochitto in the Natchez Dist., 1788. Plat shows land adj. Wm. Scott, Wm. Mathia and Webb Davis [or Webb and Davis]. File. Claimant, Isaac Gaillard, next friend of James Steel, a minor, 19 March 1804. Certif. A-205 issued to James Steele, 16 May 1805. Isaac Gaillard claimed the above grant was dated 30 June 1788.

p.369. Claim No.752. Spanish gr. to John MaCay, 300 acres on Homochitto, by lands of Ebenezer Dayton, Nathan Swazey and lands abandonned by Stephen Cerenio. N. O., Dec. 7, 1797, by Gayoso. // p.371. Mr. Henderson: Please advertise 300 acres on Homochitto, 1/3 down, 2/3 in 12 months, with approved security. W. Conner for Richard Corey. [n.d.] // 24 Apr. 1802. Richard Cory and Prudence, his wife, to Isaac Gaillard, for $625 paid, 300 acres (as described above.) Both signed. Wit: Abram Ellis, Stephen Colby, James Harwick. // File. Claimant, Isaac Gaillard, 19 March 1804. Wit: Alexander MaCay, 29 March 1805. Rejected June 11, 1807. Isaac Gaillard, legal representative of John McKay.

p.372. Claim No.753. Spanish gr. to Isaac Gaillard, 775 acres on Homochitto River, 15 mi. south of Fort, b. by Stephen Ambrose, Augustine Roddy and vacant lands. N. O., 1 Sept. 1795, by Carondelet. // File. Claimant, Isaac Gaillard, 19 March 1804. Wit: John Girault, 18 Feb. 1805. Certif. A-206 issued to cl., 16 May 1805.

p.374. Claim No.754. Spanish gr. to Jesse Withers, 300 acres in Natchez Dist., 9 miles south of Fort, b. by John Henderson and vacant lands. N. O. 8 May 1793. // p.376. 10 May 1794. Jesse Withers to Isaac Gaillard, 300 acres (above grant) for 400 pesos, paid. Both sign. Before Gayoso. // File. Claimant, Isaac Gaillard, 19 March 1804. Wit: John Girault, 18 Feb. 1805. Certif. A-207, to cl. May 16, 1805.

p.376. Claim No.755. Spanish gr. to John Henderson, 1152 acres b. by Jesse Withers, Donna Rosalie, Nicholas Cobb*, and James Kirk, on waters of Homochitto. N. O., 4 Oct. 1787 by Miro. [*The above may be Nicholas Rabb.] p.378. Natchez, 23 Jany. 1789. John Henderson to Isaac Gaillard 1152 acres, as above, for $1100 paid. Both signed. Before De Grand-Pre. // File. Claimant, Isaac Gaillard, 19 March 1804. Wit: J. Girault, 18 Feb. 1805. Certif. A-208 issued 16 May 1805.

p.380. Claim 757. British gr. to Jacob Paul, 100 acres, 20 miles from Fort Natchez, on Second Cr., b. by lands settled by Jacob Paul, Jr. and that surveyed for Sarah White. Pensacola, 27 March 1776 by Peter Chester. // p.384. British gr. to Jacob Paul, Jr., 100 acres on Second St., b. by lands gr. to Jacob Paul, Sr. Pensacola, 5 Apr. 1777 by Peter Chester. // p.389. Natchez, 25 June, 1783. Jacob Paul to John Lusk, two tracts on Second Creek, the first belongs to be through succession from my father, Jacob Paul, 100 arpents, b. by Mrs. Sarah White; the other, also 100 arpents, a Br. gr. to me also on Second Cr. for $400. Signed. Wit: Samuel Lewis, Francisco Collell, before Estevan Minor. // p.391. Natchez, 16 Jany. 1787. John Lusk to Isaac Gaillard, 650 acres in five grants by British, to John Lusk 150 arps. Sarah Lewis 100 acres, Jacob Paul 100, Jacob Paul, Sr. 100, and Samuel Lewis 200 acres, for $1300, paid. Signed. Before Grand-Pre. // File. Claimant, Isaac Gaillard, 19 March 1804. Certif. A-339, issued to claimant, 19 June 1805. Claim amended. Isaac Gaillard claims 100 acres granted to Jacob Paul, Sr. etc. John Lusk sold to Isaac Gaillard five tracts and they were all presented under Claim No.757 but separate certificates were issued for them.

p.391. Claim No.758. Spanish grant to Thos. Rule, 232 arpents, 9 mi. SE of Natchez, b. by lands of Peter Surget, David Mitchell, John Henderson, Samuel Phipps and Jesse Withers. N. O., 21 Apr. 1790. // p.393. Natchez, 23 March 1793. Thos. Rule to Isaac Gaillard, above 232 acres, for $100 paid. Thomas (X) Rule. Before Gayoso. // File. Claimant, Isaac Gaillard 19 March 1804. Wit: John Girault, 18 Feb. 1805. Certif. A-209, issued to cl. 16 May 1805.

p.394. Claim No.759. British gr. to Sarah Mayes, 100 acres on Homochitto River, b. by sd river, lands of Jacob Paul, Sr. and Wm. Harcourt's land. Pensacola, 23 July 1779, by Peter Chester. //

p.398. Stephen Mayes and Abraham Mayes to John Lusk, 100 arpens on Second Cr. for $200. Natchez, 5 July, 1784. Signed: Stephen Mayes. Wit: Stephen Minor, Antonio Soler. // p.399. John Lusk, to Mrs. Ann Gaillard, 100 acres gr. to Mrs. Sarah Mayes by British Govt., as above, for $231. Natchez, 16 Mch. 1786. Both signed. // p.400. 23 Dec. 1801, Abram Ellis and Margaret, his wife, to Isaac Gaillard, for $1000, 100 acres on Second Creek, gr. to Sarah Mayes, sold to John Lusk, etc. as above. Signed by both. Wit: Nathan Dix, Sr., Wm. Conner. // File. Claimant, Isaac Gaillard, 19 March 1804. Certif. A-423 issued to claimant, 10 July 1805. Claim based on foregoing instruments.

p.401. Claim No.760. Spanish gr. to Isaac Gaillard, 1000 acres on waters of Homochitto, b. by Mr. Maize, Jacob Paul, Sarah White and Madame Savage. N. O. 15 May 1789. // File. Claimant, Isaac Gaillard, 19 March 1804. Wit: John Girault, 18 Feb. 1805. Certif. A-211 to claimant, 17 May 1805. Claim as above, signed by John Girault.

p.403. Claim No.761. British gr. to Augustine Prevost, 1000 acres on middle fork of Boyd's Cr., 25 mi. NE of the Natchez, 11 mi. from mouth of sd Cr., b. by John Stephenson, John Stuart, Esq., and James Hughes. Pensacola, 30 March 1778, by Peter Chester. // File. Claimant, Augustine Prevost, 19 March 1804. Reported, 28 Apr. 1807. John Henderson, Atty.

p.408. Claim No.762. British gr. to Augustine Prevost, 1000 acres 13 mi. SE of the Natchez, b. by David Dickson and Peter Kennedy. Pensacola, 16 Jany. 1778 by Peter Chester. // File. Claimant, Augustine Prevost, 19 March 1804. Reported, 28 Apr. 1807.

p.413. Claim No.763. British gr. to Augustine Prevost, 5000 acres on Boyd's Cr., 30 mi. NE from the Natchez, 1/4 mi. above land grant of James Rumsey, b. by vacant lands. 31 Dec. 1776, Pensacola, by Chester. File. Claimant, Augustine Prevost, 19 March 1804. Reported, Apr. 28, 1807. Claim signed by John Henderson, Atty. [A large, elaborate map.]

p.417. Claim No.764. British grant to Augustine Prevost, a reduced Lt. of 4th Battalion of 60th Reg., 1000 acres, 4 mi. from Miss. River, near Tonica Bayou, b. by Alexander Ross, George Mulcaster and Patrick Stuart. Pensacola, 15 Sept. 1777 by Peter Chester. // File. Claimant, Augustine Prevost, 19 March 1804. Reported, 28 Apr. 1807. Claim also signed by John Henderson, Atty.

p.422. Claim No.765. British gr. to Augustine Prevost, 1000 acres on a br. of Boyd's Cr., 36 mi. NE of the Natchez, b. by lands of Peter Rochat and Col. Wm. Steel. Pensacola, 20 Mch. 1778, by Chester. File. Claimant, Augustine Prevost, 19 March 1804. Reported as above.

p.426. Claim No.766. To Spanish Govt., petition of Garret Rapalje for 1000 acres at Walnut Hills on Miss. River. Natchez, 27 July 1789. // Approved by Gayoso, 28 July 1789. // Warrant by Miro, N. O. 26 Apr. 1790. // File. Claimant, heirs of Garret Rapalje, 20 March 1804. Wit: John Shackler and Anthony Glass. Isaac Rapalje, as one and on behalf of the heirs of Garret Rapalje, decd., claims 1000 acres in Claiborne Co. on the Miss. River, as above. Signed. Note in file: To the Hon. Board of Commissioners, West of the Pearl River. John Girault gives notice that he protests the claim of James Rapalje to a tract of land on a small creek below Walnut Hills, the said Rapalje having extended his survey onto the subscriber's tract, claimed under an older title and surveyed long before Mr. Rapajle surveyed it. Washington [Miss.] 24 May 1805.

p.427. Claim No.773. William Cunningham sells an improvement on Buffalo Cr., adj. Henry Phipps, for $25, to Mr. John Baker. Signed. Wit: Archibald Goldner, Ph. Ryley. Homochitto, 30 Jany. 1797. // John Baker assigns the within sale of improvement on Buffalo Cr. to J. Sanders. 28 Dec. 1797. [No consideration stated.] // James Sanders assigns the above to Hards Ellis for $60 paid. 18 July 1799. (signed) James Sanders. Wit: Wm. Baker, Wm. (X) Collins. // File. Claimant, Hardress Ellis, 20 March 1804. Wit: Mary Donnelly, 2 Aug. 1805. Certif. B-268, issued 11 May 1807. Hardress Elliss claims 234 acres on waters of Buffalo Cr. in Wilkinson Co., as described in plat, by virtue of an improvement and settlement by Wm. Cunningham about 1793 [and above transfers.] To the Hon Board of Commrs., etc. You are requested not to issue a certificate to Hardress Ellis for 234 acres on Pine Creek. The said Ellis claim this as a Donation under Wm. Cunningham, who has had lands granted to him by the Spanish Govt. and further this claim interferes with mine. (signed) John Collins.

p.427. Claim No.774. Miss. Ter., Claiborne Co., 19 June 1803. James Arbuthnot to Eli Crockett improvement where he now lives on Lingon br. of south fork of Bayou Pierre, made 1 May 1798. Signed. Wit: Oliver Blackburn. Ack. 20 Dec. 1803 bef. Edmund Hall, J. P. of Jefferson Co., Miss. Ter. //

In case of my death before my return from the Atlantic States I do make over all my right to the within to Jesse Lum and when I return this assignment to be null and void. 16 Sept. ____. Signed: Eli Crockett. Wit: Stephen Allyn. // File. Claimant, Eli Crockett, 20 March 1804. Wit: Jesse Lamb. 320 acres to include his improvement. Certif. D-172, 16 Dec. 1806. Note: Witness says claimant desires to take only one-half of desired tract as a preemption if it does not prove to be a donation. Claim for 640 acres, 45 mi. from Natchez, by virtue of above records.

p.428. Claim No.775. Lease and release. James Barbut, late of West Florida, by attys, Edmund Rush Wegg and Thos. Hutchins, to Alexander McCullagh, of Pensacola, a British grant to sd Barbut, 2000 acres, part of 3000 acres due him. Oct. 1st and 2nd, 1775. // p.437. Alexander McCullagh to Elihu Hall Bay, the above land, 25 June 1799. Wit: James Donaldson, A. Henry. // p.438. 10 July 1801. Elihu Hall Bay, Esq. of Charleston, S. C., to John Burney, of Adams Co., for $550, 250 acres on Second Creek, the south corner of 1000 acres gr. James Barbut; by Barbut sold to McCullagh, 2 Oct. 1775. Wit: James Scurlock, Darius Moffett. // p.440. Jany. 19, 1804. John Burney, and Lucy, his wife, to Joseph Wm. Albert Lloyd, of Adams Co., for $1600 paid, 250 acres above. Signed. Wit: John Callahan, John B. Mannan. // File. Claimant, Joseph W. A. Lloyd, 20 March 1804. Reported, 28 Apr. 1807. Claim as above records show. Plat gives Michael Hooter and Wm. Johnson with land adj.

p.441. Claim No.776. Petition to Spanish Govt. by Thos. Martin, res. of district, who would like a grant for subsistence of his family, of six white and one negress, on Sandy Cr., adj. John Howard. 20 Oct. 1892. // Same date. Order for 400 acres by Gayoso. // Warrant for same by Carondelet, N. O. March 2, 1793. Plat by Wm. Dunbar shows 600 arpents on Second Cr. b. by Wm. Ratcliffe and Henry Richardson. // p.442. 2 Sept. 1802. Thos. Martin, of Adams Co., Miss. Ter., for $500, sells to Maurice Custard 600 acres on Second Cr., b. by Wm. Ratcliffe, Joshua Howard and Anthony Hoggatt. Signed by James Howard, Atty. for Thos. Martin. Wit: Joshua Howard, Jonathan Kearsley, John Howard. // File. Claimant, Maurice Custard, 20 March 1804. Wit: Joshua Howard, 15 Oct. 1804. Certif. B-120 issued 4 Feb. 1807. Claim for 600 acres as in above records.

p.443. Claim No.777. Spanish Govt. to William Vardeman, plat and certificate of survey by William Dunbar, 500 acres on Wells Cr., a br. of Homochitto River, all sides vacant. N. O. 24 Dec. 1797, by Gayoso. // p.445. 25 Dec. 1798. William Vardeman to Morris Custard, all rights in above 500 acres. Signed. Wit: Joshua Howard, James Howard. // Morris Custard to Joseph W. A. Lloyd and Nathan Dix, assignment of all rights to above tract, April __, 1803. Wit: John C. Wickoff. Ack. before Joseph Sessions, J. P. // File. Claimant, J. W. A. Lloyd and N. Dix, 20 Mch. 1804. Wit: Joshua Howard, 16 Dec. 1805. Rejected, 16 Apr. 1807. Claim based on preceding records.

p.445. Claim No.778. Spanish Govt. to Anthony Calvet. . . . [That is all.] // Anthony Calvet, for a val. consid., to Wm. Vardeman, all right to within 200 acres. (signed) Anthony Calvet. Sept. 1, 1801. Wit: P. Hoggatt, John Smith. Ack, same date, before Anthony Hoggatt, J. P. // p.446. William Vardeman to Joseph W. A. Lloyd, all right to above tract, for value recd., 12 Dec. 1803. Wit: David Nesbitt, John C. Wikoff, John Burney, Calvin Smith. // p.446. Antonio Calvet's survey of 200 acres . . . [Nothing more.] // File. Claimant, Joseph W. A. Lloyd, 20 Mch. 1804. Rejected, 15 Apr. 1807. Joseph Wm. Albert Lloyd, of Miss. Ter. claims 200 acres as shown in above plat, by virtue of a military warrant to Anthony Calvet by Manuel Gayoso de Lemos, Gov. of the Dist. of Natchez, in 1793, for the above-mentioned 200 acres, and [the following assignments.]

p.446. Claim No.781. Samuel Osborne to States Trevillian, for $137.50 in hand paid, 137 1/2 acres adj. Seabud Osborne on Cole's Cr., SE corner of said tract, or 1/4 of whole tract of 550 acres on Boyd's Cr. adj. Augustus Prevost, gr. by British to James Cole, 20 Mch. 1778 and conveyed 9th month of same year by sd James Cole to Isaac Johnson, who transferred to Samuel Osborne 12 Jany. 1796. Signed by Samuel and Jane Osborne, 5 Jany. 1803. Wit: John Hinds, Jr., Andrew Watkins, Wm. Richey, Riel Richey. // File. Claimant, States Trevillian, 20 March 1804. See No.820. Res. proved in claim No.981. Certif. A-671 issued to claimant, 14 Oct. 1805. Claim based on above records.

p.447. Claim No.782. Eustice Humphreys to Henry Milburn, 300 acres b. by Adam Bingaman and Daniel Clark, for $300 paid. 8 April 1795. Both signed. Wit: John Stillee, Juan Carreras, before Grand-Pre. // p.448. 18 Aug. 1796. Henry Milburn to States Trevillian 100 acres, part of a gr. of 300 acres near a br. of Fairchild's Creek, for $80, paid. Signed by Henry Milburn and Richard Trevillian for States Trevillian. Wit: Lewis Throckmorton and John Girault. // File. Claimant, States Trevillian, 20 Mch. 1804. Wit: Wm. Bradstone. In claimant, No.260, 21st Nov. 1804. Certif. A-330 issued to claimant 18 June 1805. Claim based on a patent from the Spanish Govt. to Eustace Humphreys for 300 arpents, of which the said 100 is a part, dated 27 Feb. 1789. And as the above records show.

p.449. Claim No.785. Spanish gr. to Alexander Callender, 300 arps. on Cole's Cr., 20 mi. north of Fort, b. on north by Sarah Truly, east by Joseph Deforest. N. O. 20 Aug. 1794 by Carondelet. // File. Claimant Alexander Callender, 20 Mch. 1804. Wit: John Bolls, 23 May 1805. Certif. A-243, to cl. for 280 arps. May 1805. Claim as above.

p.453. Claim No.787. Spanish Govt. to Thomas Percy, 800 acres, 40 mi. south of the Fort, b. Dona Isabel Hutchins, Wm. Dunbar, Hubert Rowell and Charles Percy, 20 March 1804. Wit: John Collins, 18 July 1805. Rejected 15 April 1807. Thos. Percy claims 800 acres on waters of Bayou Sara, etc. Note: The claimant in this case is still a minor and the land has never been cultivated as being a minor it was not in his power to do it, so says Capt. J. G. [John Girault.] (signed) T. R. [Thomas Rodney.]

p.451. Claim No.786. Spanish gr. to Wm. Kennison, 400 acres on Morgan's Cr., a br. of Homochitto, 20 mi. east of the Fort, all sides vacant. N. O. 20 Aug. 1794, by Carondelet. // File. Claimant, Ezekiel Dewitt, 20 March 1804. Wit: Nathaniel Kennison, 24 Aug. 1804. Certif. A-781, issued to claimant in right of his wife, 20 Aug. 1806. Claims 400 arps. gr. by Sp. Govt. to Wm. Kennison who conveyed the same to Joseph Pannill, who conveyed the same to Mary Dewitt, wife of said Ezekiel by deed of bargain, 4 Jany. 1804. Note: July 1st, 1806. Wm. Kennison, the patentee of this land, ack. before the board that he sold this land to Col. Joseph Pannill who sold same to Ezekiel Dewitt, claimant. (signed) T. R.

p.455. Claim No.788. Spanish gr. to John Ellis, 426 acres on Buffalo Cr., 30 mi. south of the Fort, b. by James Chabot. N. O. 20 June 1793, by Carondelet. [Plat also shows James Smith and Pedro Miro with land adj.] File. Claimant, John Ellis, 20 March 1804. Res. proved before. Certif. A-105, to claimant. Claim as above.

p.457. Claim No.789. Spanish gr. to Jesse Carter, 800 acres near the Homochitto, 18 mi. south of Fort, b. by vacant lands. N. O. 21 May 1791 by Miro. // p.459. 24 May 1800. Jesse Carter, of the Township of Second Creek, Co. of Adams, Miss. Ter., and wife, Sarah, to John Ellis, Major of Militia of sd Township, for $1200 paid, the above 800 acres. Signed by both. Wit: Patrick Foley, J. W. A. Lloyd. Prov. by Lloyd, 10 Sept. 1800 before Wm. Dunbar, J. P. // File. Claimant, John Ellis, 20 March 1804. Wit: Bennet Truly, 15 Oct. 1804. Certif. A-431 issued to claimant, 11 July 1805. Claim as above.

p.460. Claim No.790. Spanish gr. to Theophilus Collins, 800 acres on Bayou Sara, 40 mi. south of the Fort, b. by Donna Isabella Hutchins, Francisco Pousset and vacant lands. N. O. April 1, 1795 by Carondelet. // p.462. 27 Jany. 1804. Theophilus Collins, of Dist. of Opelousas, in late Province of La., to John Ellis, of Wilkinson Co., Miss. Ter., for $1000, above grant of 800 acres, adj. Elizabeth Hutchins. Signed by Collins. Wit: George Poindexter, Wm. L. Collins. Both proved above, same date, before John Collins, J. P. // File. Claimant, John Ellis, 20 Mch. 1804. Wit: John Collins, 2 Sept. 1805. Certif. A-560 issued to claimant in 1805. Claim as above. [*Elizabeth in Spanish is Isabella.]

p.463. Claim No.791. Spanish grant to Francis Pousset, 1000 acres on Bayou Sarah, 40 mi. south of Fort, b. by Dona Isabella Hutchins and Theophilus Collins. N. O. 22 Mch. 1795 by Carondelet. // File. Claimants, representatives of Francis Pousset, 20 Mch. 1804. Certif. A-646, to claimants, 2 Oct. 1805. W. B. Shields, atty. for claimants.

p.465. Claim No.792. Spanish gr. to Lopez Armesto, 800 acres on Buffalo Cr., adj. Gilbert Leonard, Charles Percy and Thomas Wilkins. N. O. 4 May 1787, by Estevan Miro. // p.467. Andrew Lopez Armesto sells to Charles Percy, of the Post of Natchez, 800 acres as in above grant, for $300, paid. New Orleans, 6 April 1791. // File. Claimant, representatives of C. Percy, 20 Mch. 1804. Wit: Alexander Montgomery, 31 Jany. 1805. Certificate A-213 issued to legal representatives, 17 May 1805. John Ellis and Sarah, his wife, formerly Sarah Percy, Thomas G. Percy, Catherine Percy and Ann Percy, legal representatives of Charles Percy, decd. claim as above, on waters of Percy's Creek. G. Poindexter, atty. for the claimants.

p.469. Claim No.794. Spanish gr. to Charles Percy, 1000 acres, 30 miles south of the Fort, b. on lands of Wm. Vousdan, Zachariah Smith, Charles Percy and Thos. Wilkins. N. O. 18 Apr. 1789. // File. Claimant, representatives of Charles Percy, decd., 20 Mch. 1804. Wit: Alexander Montgomery 31 Jany. 1805. Certificate A-214 issued to legal representatives, 1807. Claim naming heirs as in preceding claim.

p.471. Claim No.793. Spanish gr. to Susannah Percy, 800 acres, fronting on a lake called False River, 14 mi. SE of Fort Panmure, b. by Henry Hergeroder and vacant lands. N. O. 20 June 1789 by Estevan Miro. // File. Claimant, legal representatives of Susanna Percy, 20 March 1804. Wit: Alexander Montgomery, 31 Jany. 1805. Certif. A-205, issued to legal representatives, June 1, 1805. Same heirs as above. G. Poindexter, atty.

p.473. Claim No.795. Spanish gr. to Charles Percy, 2400 acres, 54 mi. SE of Fort, b. by David Ross, Cesar Archinard, Francis Pousset and Patrick Foley. N. O. 4 June 1791, by Estevan Miro. [Plat also shows Elizabeth Hutchins with land adj.] File. Claimant, representatives of Charles Percy, decd., 20 Mch. 1804. Wit: Alexander Montgomery, 31 Jany. 1805. Certificate issued. [bottom of the file torn off.]

p.475. Claim No.797. Spanish gr. to John Lusk, 300 acres, 12 leagues south of Fort. All sides vacant. N. O. 29 May 1795, by Carondelet. // [No file.]

p.477. Claim No.798. Spanish gr. to John Lusk, 800 acres on Homochitto River, 15 mi. SE of Fort, b. by Robt. Cochran and grantee. N. O. 24 Dec. 1798 by Gayoso. // File. Claimant, John Lusk, 20 March 1804. Wit: Jacob Lusk, 27 Nov. 1804. Samuel Lusk, 8 Oct. 1805. Certif. B-122, 5 Feb. 1807. For John Lusk by John Girault.

p.479. Claim No.799. Spanish gr. to John Lusk, 800 acres on Homochitto River, 18 mi. SE from Fort, all sides vacant. N. O. 18 Feb. 1790, by Estevan Miro. // File. Claimant, John Lusk, 20 March 1804. Wit: Israel Leonard, 27 Nov. 1804. Certif. A-214, issued 17 May 1805. John Lusk by John Girault.

p.481. Claim No.807. Spanish gr. to Patrick Sullivan, 245 acres, 28 miles NE of Fort, all sides vacant. N. O. 20 Aug. 1796 by Carondelet. p.483. 20 Feb. 1798. Patrick Sullivan, of Villa Gayoso, Govt. of Natchez, to Ebenezer Rees, of Dist. of St. Catherine, for $245 paid, the above grant, on a br. of Cole's Cr. Wit: Isaac Johnson, Edward Randolph, William Collins. The above deed was executed in my presence. (signed) Isaac Johnson. // p.484. 12 May 1801. Ebenezer Rees, of Adams Co., Miss. Ter. to David Ferguson and Melling Wooley,of Natchez, for $735 paid, 245 acres, as above, Signed. Wit: Lym. Harding, Samuel Hancock. Prov. by Harding, 18 May 1801, before Roger Dixon, J. P. // p.485. 23 Dec. 1802. John Pipes, of Jefferson Co., for $800 to Andrew Watkins, of same, 245 acres on Cole's Cr., gr. as above, sold by Ferguson and Wooley to sd John Pipes. Signed. Wit: Daniel James, D. H. Breazeale. Ack. before Abner Pipes, J. P. // File. Claimant, Andrew Watkins, 20 March 1804. Wit: Henry Platner, 15 Nov. 1804. Certif. B-123, Feb. 5, 1807. As above.

p.486. Claim No.808. John Wilson petitions Spanish Govt. for Lots Nos. 3 and 4, Sq. No.11, in Natchez, which sd land he bought from Wm. Barland and built houses on. Jan. 30, 1795. Order and warrant for same. // p.487. 3 Dec. 1801. John Wilson and wife, Charlotte, of Natchez, for $1400 paid, to David and Wm. Lattimore, above lots. (signed) John Wilson. Charlotte (x) Wilson. Ack. before Sam'l. Brooks. Wit: Henry Turner, Samuel Brooks. // File. Claimants, David and Wm. Lattimore, 20 March 1804. Wit: John Ellis, 28 Aug. 1805. See Rabb's claim, No.1827. Certificate _ -537 issued to cl. Aug. 28, 1805. Claim of one-half of above lots, based on grant 6 Feb. 1795 to Wilson, and a conveyance of one-half thereof from sd John Wilson and Charlotte, his wife, to claimants.

p.489. Claim No.809. Spanish gr. to Thomas Green, 800 acres, 35 mi. SE of Fort, b. Francis and Margaret Forman. N. O. 30 March 1797 by Carondelet. // p.491. Feb. 1, 1802. Thomas Green, Esq., of Jefferson Co., for $2000 paid, to John Ellis, Esq., of Adams Co., 800 acres in above grant. Signed. Wit: Alex. Montgomery, John Stampley, Felix Hughes. // File. Claimant, John Ellis, 20 March 1804. Wit: Bennet Truly, 15 Oct. 1804. Wit: F. L. Claiborne, 29 Aug. 1805. Rejected, 15 Apr. 1807. Claim as above.

p.492. Claim No.810. Francis Jones petitions the Spanish Govt. that he had come down from the upper United States and would like a gr. of 400 acres on Cole's Cr., adj. Henry Green. Natchez, 21 May 1790. // N. O. June 6, 1790, order of survey by Miro. // Plat and certif. of survey by Wm. Dunbar, 13 Nov. 1791, on north fork of sd creek. // p.493. 15 Dec. 1800, Francis Jones, of Pickering Co., Miss. Ter., to David Ferguson and Melling Wooley, of Adams Co., the above survey b. by Wm. Daniels and Gabriel Benoist. Signed. Wit: Anthony Hoggatt, Joshua Howard. Prov. by Howard before P. B. Bruin, 12 Nov. 1801. Eliz. Jones relinquishes her dower, 26 Apr. 1802, before Daniel Burnet, J. P. Claiborne Co. // p.494. 12 Nov. 1801, David Ferguson and Jean, his wife, and Melling Woolley, for $600, to Robt. Dunbar, above tract. Signed by the three. Wit: David Nesbitt, Francis Nailor. Receipt by David Ferguson. Wit: James Howard, John Mannan. Ack. by David and Jane Ferguson before Adam Tooley and Joseph

Sessions, two of J. P. of sd county. // File. Claimant, Robert Dunbar, 20 March 1804. Wit: John Roberts, 22 May 1804, and Wm. Thomas, 22 Dec. 1806. Rejected 15 Apr. 1807.

p.495. Claim No.811. Spanish gr. to Richard King, 600 acres 12 mi. NE of Fort, b. by Geo. Weigle and vacant lands. N. O. 8 Apr. 1789 by Miro. // p.497. Richard King to Robt. Dunbar, 600 acres on Bayou St. Catherine. 19 Dec. 1789. Signed before de Grand-Pre. // File. Claimant, Robert Dunbar, 20 Mch. 1804. Wit: Benj. Belk, 9 May 1804. Certif. A-218 to claimant, 17 May 1805. Claims 600 a. on waters of St. Catherine's and Fairchild's Creeks.

p.498. Claim No.812. Spanish gr. to Robert Dunbar, 800 acres on a br. of Cole's Cr., 2 mi. from land of Thomas Arman and 20 mi. north of Fort, b. by lands of Richard Harrison. N. O. 12 June 1788 by Estevan Miro. // File. Claimant, Robert Dunbar, 20 Mch. 1804. Wit: Benj. Belk, 9 May 1804. Certif. A-219, 17 May 1805.

p.500. Claim No.813. Order of survey by British Govt. to Robert Dunbar for 250 acres on Bayou Pierre, 4 mi. from its mouth. Pensacola, 11 Feb. 1778 by Peter Chester. To any lawful deputy surveyor for the Prov. of West Fla. You are hereby directed to execute this warrant, etc. 12 Feb. 1778. (signed) Elias Durnford, Surv. Genl. // File. Claimant, Robert Dunbar, 20 Mch. 1804. Wit: Benj. Belk, 9 May 1804. Rejected 28 Apr. 1807. Robert Dunbar, at date of warrant, was head of a family. Plat shows on south B. Pittman and F. Nailor, east Joseph Newman, north headwaters of Widows Cr. and west vacant.

p.500. Claim No.814. Spanish gr. to Gabriel Benoist, 1000 acres on Fairchild's Cr., 11 mi. NE of Natchez, b. by vacant lands. N. O. 24 Jany. 1788 by Miro. // File. Claimants, E. Benoist et al. 20 March 1804. Wit: Robert Dunbar, 9 May 1804. Certif. A-220, to legal representatives, 21 May 1805. Adams Co., Miss. Ter. Elizabeth Benoist, wid. and devisee of Gabriel Benoist, decd., and Victor and Robert Benoist, heirs and devisees of sd Gabriel Benoist, decd. who devised the above grant to sd claimants.

p.502. Claim No.815. Spanish gr. to Gabriel Benoist, 1000 acres on north br. of Cole's Cr., 35 mi. NE of Fort, b. east John Murdock. N. O. 14 Aug. 1794 by Carondelet. // File. Claimants, legal representatives of Gabriel Benoist, 20 March 1804. Wit: Robt. Dunbar, 9 May 1804. Certif. A-221, to legal rep. 21 May 1805. Claim as above.

p.504. Claim No.816. Spanish gr. to Gabriel Benoist, 600 acres, 11 NE of Fort, b. by James Jones, John Bisland, Jacob Copelthwete and George Fitzgerald. N. O. 1 Jany. 1793 by Carondelet. [Plat shows tract on a br. of Fairchild's Cr.] File. Claimants, E. Benoist et al, 20 Mch. 1804. Wit: Robert Dunbar, 9 May 1804. Certif. A-222 to legal Representatives, May 21, 1805. [Representatives named in claim as in preceding claims.]

p.506. Claim No.817. Spanish gr. to Chas. Fleuriau, 600 acres, 14 mi. NE of Fort, 4 mi. SE of Miss. River, b. by Gabriel, Mr. Rees, Joshua Collins and Stephen Boree. N. O. 1 Jany 1789 by Miro. // p.507. Carlos Fleuriau to Gabriel Benoist, 600 acres in above grant, for $500 paid. N. O. 31 Dec. 1796. // File. Claimants, representatives of G. Benoist, decd., 20 Mch. 1804. Wit: Robt. 9 May 1804. Certif. A-465 to legal representatives. Same devisees as above.

p.508. Claim No.818. Spanish gr. to Estevan Boree, 1050 acres on a br. of Fairchild's Cr., 14 mi. NE of Natchez, b. by James Jones, Melling Woolley, Don Carlos Floriau and Joshua Collins. N. O. 12 May 1789 by Miro. // p.510. Stephen Boree to Gabriel Benoist, 1050 described above, for $1000. N. O. 31 Dec. 1796. // File. Claimant, Elizabeth Benoist, 20 Mch. 1804. Robt. Dunbar, wit., 9 May 1804. Certif. A-466 to legal representatives, 31 July 1805. Same devisees of Gabriel Benoist, decd. as in the previous claims. Land on Fairchild's Creek.

p.511. Claim No.819. Spanish gr. to John Clark, 410 acres on a br. of Cole's Cr., 20 mi. from Fort, b. by Joseph Deforest, Richard Ellis, John Stampley, Samuel Davis and Ephraim Coleman. N. O. 10 Apr. 1795 by Carondelet. // File. Claimant, John Clark, 20 Mch. 1804. Wit: Wm. Clark. Certif. A-233, 22 May 1805. Clark claims 410 arps. in Jefferson Co. based on above patent.

p.513. Claim No.820. British gr. to James Cole, 550 acres on south fork of Cole's Cr., 30 mi. NE of Natchez, 6 mi. east of Miss. River, adj. on northeast Col. Augustus Prevost, north Boyd's Cr. Pensacola, 20 Mch. 1778 by Peter Chester. // p.520. 20 Sept. 1778, James Cole and wife, Mary, to Isaac Johnson, Esq., for $550, the above tract. Wit: J. Blommart, Luke Collins, Jr., Luke Collins, Wm. Collins. // Isaac Johnson to Samuel Osborne, I assign all my right to the within unto Samuel Osborne.

(signed) Isaac Johnson. Cole's Cr., 12 Jany. 1796. Wit: John Johnson, Nathan Mitchell. // File. Claimant, Samuel Osborne, 20 Mch. 1804. See Claim No.781. Certif. A-670 issued to claimant for 412 acres Oct. 18, 1805. Survey of same. West Florida. Pursuant to a warrant from His Excellency, Peter Chester, Capt. General, Governor and Commander-in-Chief, in and over His Majesty's Province, of West Florida, to me directed, bearing the date of 10 Feb. 1778, I have caused to be surveyed, etc.

p.520. Claim No.827. 8 Dec. 1798. John Wilson to John Rabb, for $1100 paid, house and lot in Town of Natchez, on main street leading from river. Wit: Elijah Adams, P. Connelly, Wm. Nicholls. // Claimant, John Rabb, 21 March 1804. Wit: John Ellis, 28 Aug. 1805. See No.808. Certificate A-538, issued 28 Aug. 1805. John Rabb, a citizen, of Natchez, Miss. Ter., claims one-half of Lots 3 and 4, [Sq. No.11], b. on one side by lots of D. and W. Lattimore, on other by those of St. James Beauvais, by virtue of a Sp. gr. to John Wilson who conveyed one-half of said lots to sd John Rabb.

p.521. Claim No.828. Spanish gr. to Stephen Ambrose, 400 acres on waters of Homochitto, 15 mi. S.E. of Fort, b. on vacant lands. N. O. 6 Mch. 1789 by Miro. // File. Claimant, Stephen Ambrose, 21 Mch. 1804. Wit: Philander Smith, 18 July 1805. Certif. A-446, July 1805.

p.523. Claim No.829. Deed. 22 Dec. 1801, Samuel Carnes and Elizabeth, his wife, to David Mitchell, for $800, 240 acres, b. on north by Elijah Swazey, west Wm. Leland, east James Swazey, south Gabriel Swayze, being part of tract gr. to Capt. Amos Ogden by British Govt. and by Ogden to Sam'l. and Richard Swayze. Both signed. Wit: Daniel D. Swayze, John Fry. Ack. before Philander Smith, J. P., Adams Co. // File. Claimant, J. J. and D. D. Mitchell, 21 Mch. 1804. See Swazey's claims. Certif. A-688, to legal representatives, 6 Jany. 1706. John James and David D. Mitchell, heirs of David Mitchell, decd., claim 240 acres in a body of land, called the Ogden Mandamus, granted as above and conveyed to Sam'l. and Richard Swazey, and by them to Samuel Carnes, who conveyed the tract to David Mitchell, Sr., from whom the claimants have heired same.

p.524. Claim No.830. 8 Dec. 1801. Elizah Swazey and Polly, his wife, to David Mitchell, for $1281, 366 acres, b. by Gord. Forman, John Swazey, James Swazey and David Lambert, being part of tract gr. Ogden, as above. Signed by both. Wit: Samuel Carnes, Calvin Smith. Ack. before Philander Smith, J. P. 28 Dec. 1801. // File. Claimants, John J. and D. D. Mitchell, 21 March 1804. Certif. A-555, to legal rep. of David Mitchell, 1 Sept. 1805. Claimed as above by said heirs.

p.525. Claim No.831. Spanish gr. to David Mitchell, 400 acres, 9 mi. SE of Fort, b. by Samuel Phipps and vacant lands. It is the land taken as No.82 by Henry Phipps, who abandonned it in favor of Mitchell. N. O. 3 April 1790 by Estevan Miro. // File. Claimants, John J. and D. D. Mitchell, 21 Mch. 1804. Wit: Benj. Newman, 26 Nov. 1804. Certif. A-234 issued to legal rep. of David Mitchell, decd. Claimed as in preceding.

p.527. Claim No.832. Spanish gr. to Dorothy V. Henderson, widow of William Henderson, 300 acres, 5 mi. NE of Fort, b. by sd Wm. Henderson and Wm. Kirkwood. N. O. 20 Aug. 1794 by Carondelet. // File. Claimants, Heirs of D. Henderson, 21 Mch. 1804. Wit: Bennet Truly, 24 May 1805. Certif. A-453, to legal rep. July 23, 1805. Claim of Sally Henderson, Elizabeth Gibson, William Henderson and Charles Henderson, heirs of Dorothy Henderson, decd., by virtue of the above grant to the sd Dorothy in her lifetime. Signed: Sam Timberlake for said legatees.

p.529. Claim No.833. Spanish gr. to Wm. Cobb and Arthur Cobb, 600 a. near St. Catherine's Cr., 7 mi. ESE of Fort, b. by Monsieur Surget, Adam Bingaman and Daniel Clark. N. O. 7 Dec. 1797, by Gayoso. // p.531. 17 Mch. 1800. William Cobb and wife, Polly, for $1250, paid, to Samuel Timberlake and Samuel Hancock, of Natchez, merchants, 500 acres, part of above grant, b. by Lewis Bingaman, Charles Surget and Thos. Rule. Wit: John Henderson, Thomas Regan, A. Reeder, Thomas Dawson. Wm. and Mary Cobb ack. deed before Wm. Miller, J. P. 19 Apr. 1800. // File. Claimant, Samuel Timberlake, 21 Mch. 1804. Wit: Wm. Adams, 24 May 1805. Certif. B-136, Feb. 9, 1807. Samuel Timberlakd hereby gives notice that he claims 500 acres in Adams Co. by virtue of a Sp. grant including said 500 acres to William Cobb.

p.532. Claim No.837. Spanish grant to Wm. Cocke Ellis, 800 acres on waters of Buffalo Cr., 25 miles SE of Fort, b. by Jesse Carter and John Ellis, Sr. N. O. 16 Feb. 1789. // File. Claimant, John Ellis, representative of Wm. Cocke Ellis, 21 Mch. 1804. Res. proved in Certif. A-337. John Ellis, legal representative of William Cocke Ellis, decd., claims 800 acres in Wilkinson Co., Miss. Ter. on waters of Buffalo River, by virtue of a Spanish gr. to sd Wm. Cocke Ellis, in 1789.

p.534. Claim No.838. Spanish grant to Benj. Curtis, 400 arpens on a br. of Cole's Creek, 20 mi. from Fort, b. by lands of Jacob Stampley and William Irwin. N. O. 28 Feb. 1795, by Carondelet. // p.534. Benj. Curtis to John Ellis, all right as in above grant. 2 Jany. 1801. Signed. Wit: R. Knox, Nath'l. Tomlinson. // File. Claimant, John Ellis, 21 Mch. 1804. Wit: John Stampley, 21 Feb. 1805. Certif. A-193.

p.536. Claim No.839. Spanish gr. to John Ellis, Sr., 800 acres on Homochitto River and Buffalo Cr. N. O. 31 Jany. 1788 by Miro. // File. Claimant, John Ellis, 21 Mch. 1804. Certif. A-194. Claim as above.

p.538. Claim No.853. Spanish gr. to Elizabeth Durbin, 211 acres on waters of Bayou Pierre, b. by Daniel Burnet and vacant lands. N. O. 1 Sept. 1793, by Carondelet. // p.540. Elizabeth Derbin to Sarah Cleveland, her daughter, of same place, a gift of the above lands. Natchez, 8 Jany. 1798. Signed. Wit: Estevan Minor, Drury Ledbetter, Samuel Cooper, John Girault. // File. Claimant, Sarah Cleveland, 21 Mch. 1804. Wit: John Girault, 26 Nov. 1804. Certif. A-195. Claim as above.

p.541. Claim No.854. Spanish gr. to James Elliott, Jr., 1000 acres on waters of Cole's Cr., north fork, 25 mi. NE of Fort, b. on lands of Mr. Elliot, father of grantee. N. O. 20 Oct. 1788. // p.542. Jacque [James] Elliot to Joseph Sorrell . . . [the rest of the page blank]. p.543. Joseph Sorrell, Capt. of militia of Miss., res. of District, power of attorney to Valentine Duforest, to sell 700 acres on northeast fork of Cole's Creek, part of 246 acres to James Elliot, Sr., and 1000 acres to his son, to be laid off at one end of the above lands. 24 Aug. 1799, before Louis Charles DeBlank, Capt. des Armees, etc. // 18 Nov. 1799. Joseph Sorrell, of Attakapas, in Province of La., by his attorney, John Valentine Duforest, to Peter Walker, for $500, 700 acres in Pickering Co. adj. lands of Job Routh and Jacob Scriber, part of tract of 1000 acres gr. to James Elliott, Jr. by Spanish Govt. Ack. by Deforest before Peter Bryan Bruin, June 4, 1800. // p.545. 6 July 1802, Peter Walker and wife, Ann, to John Hopkins, for $2840 in hand paid, 700 acres in above deed. Both sign. Wit: Lacy Rumsey, Thos. Calvet. // p.547. Certificate and plat of the above 700 acres by Wm. Atchinson, surveyor. Natchez, 17 Nov. 1799. // File. Claimant, John Hopkins, 21 March 1804. Certif. A-179 issued to claimant, Jany. 13, 1806. Note: John Griffin, Esq. claims 200 acres out of this same patent in a suit now in Superior Court between these parties, signed T. R. Spanish gr. of 1000 arpents to James Elliot was conveyed by deed, 18 Feb. 1799, to Joseph Sorrell, and conveyed by John Valentine Duforest for sd Sorrell to Walker, and by Walker to claimant.

p.547. Claim No.855. Spanish gr. to Daniel Clark, 565 acres on Second Cr., 2 leagues from Fort. N. O. 6 Feb. 1787 by Miro. // p.549. 12 Oct. 1799, Daniel Clark, Sr., to Jesse Greenfield, above grant, for $1292. Wit: Daniel Clark, Jr., William Dunbar, John Kean. // File. Claimant, Jesse Greenfield, 21 March 1804. Wit: Ebenezer Rees, 11 Apr. 1805. Certif. A-196, to claimant. Claim as above.

p.551. Claim No.1194. Petition of Don Carlos de Grand-Pre to Spanish Govt. for 2847 acres on the Miss. River, b. by Homochitto on one side and on Richard and Samuel Swayze. Natchez, 29 June 1787. Order for same, N. O. 5 July 1787 by Miro. Grant and plat of above. N. O. 13 Aug. 1787. // p.552. Whereas Samuel and Richard Swazey purchased of Amos Ogden 19,000 acres with the allowance of 800 acres more for a town, being part of 25,000 acres gr. Amos Ogden by British Govt. and the land was never divided during the lives of the parties. Now be it known that the heirs of Richard Swazey and Samuel Swazey do agree that William Vousdan, surveyor of the District appointed by Don Chas. Laveau Trudeau, Surveyor of the Province of La., should survey out of the original survey of 25,000 acres, as afsd, 5200 acres, being the residue of sd original survey, leaving us the afsd quantity so purchased, namely 19,800 acres. And we agree that the said 5200 acres may be taken out of said original survey by a line proceeding from the Homochitto and running parralel to the first line of the original survey northerly. May 8, 1787. Signed: Samuel Swazey, Richard Swazey. Wit: Elijah Swazey, Archibald McDuffe. // p.554. Don Carlos de Grand-Pre, of the Post of Baton Rouge, to James McIntosh, of Natchez, 2847 acres, for 5294 pesos, which he has paid me. Baton Rouge, 4 Feb. 1798.

End of Book C

BOOK D

p.1. Claim No.856. Spanish gr. to Ebenezer Rees 700 acres, 40 mi. N. E. of Fort, b. by Isabel Whittle, John Hartley and the Messrs. Green, on north fork of Bayou Pierre. N. O. 17 Aug. 1794 by Carondelet. // p.2. 21 Mch. 1804. Ebenezèr Rees to Jesse Greenfield, for $450, 700 acres as in above grant. Signed. Wit: Daniel Douglass, B. Kitchen. Ack. before Rodney, Town of Washington, 26 Mch. 1804. // File. Claimant, Jesse Greenfield, 21 Mch. 1804. Wit: Moses Armstrong, 11 Apr. 1805. Certif. A-197. Claim as above.

p.3. Claim No.857. Spanish gr. to Jesse Greenfield, 600 acres on Bayou Pierre, b. by vacant lands, 50 mi. N. E. of Fort. N. O. 28 Jany. 1789 by Miro. // File. Claimant, Jesse Greenfield, 21 March 1804. Res. of Jesse Greenfield proved in No.855. Certif. A-198. Land on the north side of the North Fork of Bayou Pierre. // To Mr. Thos. H. Williams. Sir: The tract of land seems to be in dispute with Mr. Geo. Purvis and his relations ought in justice to be the property of the aforenamed George Purvis. Yours with much esteem. John Hutchins. Dec. 28, 1808. [This letter does not seem to belong in this file.]

p.5. Claim No.861. Spanish grant to Gideon Hopkins, 400 acres, 16 mi. south of Fort, b. by Wm. Henderson, Nathan Swayze, and Robert Cochran. N. O. 21 May 1791 by Miro. // File. Claimant, Gideon Hopkins, 21 March 1804. Wit: Nathan Swayze, 2 Aug. 1804. Certif. A-251. Claim on Brooke's Cr. Original Sp. grant and survey, with plat.

p.7. Claim No.862. Spanish gr. to Nathaniel Ivy, 317 acres, 4 mi. east of Fort, adj. John Lum, John Bisland, and Estevan Minor. N. O. 22 March 1795, by Carondelet. // File. Claimant, Nathaniel Ivy, 21 Mch. 1804. Wit: Thomas Wilkins, 15 Oct. 1804. Certif. A-252 to claimant. Land in Adams County, on waters of St. Catherine's Cr.

p.8. Claim No.863. Spanish gr. to Henry Hergeroeder, 800 acres on a lake called False River, 41 mi. S. E. of Fort. N. O. 30 Aug. 1793 by Carondelet. // p.10. 15 Nov. 1797. Henry Hergeroeder, at Opelousas, for 100 piastres, to Madame Susanna Percy, 800 acres in the Natchez Dist. between lands of Madame Percy and those of Theophilus Collins. Wit: Alexander Fulton. // File. Claimant, John Ellis and others, 21 March 1804. Wit: Alexander Montgomery, 31 Jany. 1805. Wit: John Collins, 11 July 1805. Certif. A-427 issued to legal representatives of Mrs. Percy, John Ellis and Sarah, his wife, formerly Sarah Percy, Thomas G. Percy, Catherine Percy and Ann Percy, legal rep. of Susanna Percy, decd. claim 800 acres in Wilkinson Co. on waters of Buffalo Cr. as granted above.

p.11. Claim No.864. Spanish gr. to Benj. Bullock, 300 acres near Sandy Cr. (a br. of Homochitto River), 14 mi. east of Fort, b. by vacant lands. N. O. 7 Dec. 1797 by Gayoso. // p.13. Bond. Caleb and Elizabeth Biggs are bound to Barton Hannon for $500 for value recd. 19 Oct. 1797. Wit: Robt. Ford, Easton Spires. The condition of above that Caleb and Elizabeth Biggs do make or cause to be made to Barton Hannon by the heirs and assigns of Benj. Bullock, decd., a good title to land on the waters of Second Cr. as described in records of the abovenamed Benj. Bullock, then the obligation to be void. // File. Claimant, Barton Hannon, 21 Mch. 1804. Wit: Robt. Ford, 22 Oct. 1804. Certif. B-22, issued June 4, 1806. Barton Hannon claims the 300 arps. in Adams Co. gr. to Benj. Bullock and transferred by Caleb and Elizabeth Biggs, legal rep. of sd Benj. Bullock. Land adj. Wm. Hoggatt, Richard Sessions, John Patterson and Rhoda Stanley.

p.13. Claim No.865. Spanish gr. to William McIntosh 800 acres bet. St. Catherine's and Second Creeks, 6 mi. east of Natchez, b. by Don Stephen Minor and Daniel Perry. N. O. 12 Feb. 1788 by Miro. // File. Claimant, Wm. McIntosh, 21 Mch. 1804. Wit: Benajah Osmun, 18 June 1804. Certif. A-253 to claimant.

p.15. Claim No.866. Spanish grant to Christian Hortsuck, 300 acres on east br. of Bayou Sarah, 35 mi. south of the Fort, b. by William McIntosh and Eunice McIntosh. N. O. 1 Sept. 1795 by Carondelet. // p.17. Christian Hortstruck to William McIntosh, the above 300 acres, for a certain sum to me in hand paid. 21 July 1798. // File 866. Claimant, William McIntosh, 21 Mch. 1804. Wit: Benajah Osmun, 18 June 1804. Certif. A-464 issued to claimant, 30 July 1805. Claim as above.

p.17. Claim No.867. Spanish Govt. to Daniel* Thompson, order of survey. Petition of Daniel Thompson that he had come down from the Illinois and has no land; asks for 240 acres on Wells br. of Homochitto River, adj. Hezekiah Williams. Natchez, 13 Oct. 1789. // Order of survey by Miro, N. O. 18 Nov. 1789. Plat and survey to Mr. Andrew Thompson for 240 acres on sd Wells Cr. 23 mi. SE of Fort, b. by vacant lands. 31 Mch. 1890 by Wm. Dunbar. // File. Claimant, William McIntosh, 21 Mch. 1804. Wit: William Atchinson, 8 June 1804. Certif. B-124 issued 5 Feb. 1807. Claim founded on the above Spanish warrant of survey to Andrew Thompson who has conveyed same to present claimant for a valuable consideration. *[The Spanish wrote the name as it sounded to them, hence the variations.]

p.18. Claim No.868. Spanish gr. to William McIntosh, 800 acres on a br. of Bayou Sarah, 35 mi. south from the Fort of Natchez, b. by lands of Ebenezer Rees and Christian Hortsuck. N. O. 1 Sept. 1795 by Carondelet. // File. Claimant, William McIntosh, 21 Mch. 1804. Wit: Benajah Osmun, 18 June 1804. Certif. A-254 issued 30 May 1805. Claim founded on above patent.

p.20. Claim No.869. Spanish gr. to Joseph Ford, 550 arpents on St. Catherine's Cr., 8 mi. east of Fort, b. by Richard Miller, and Jacob Adams. N. O. 28 Apr. 1790, by Miro. // p.21. 25 Jany. 1803. John King, Sr., sells to Benajah Osmun, for $1200, 370 acres on St. Catherine's Cr., b. by Jacob Adams, James Stoddard, William Ryan, Richard Miller, Benj. Goodwin and John King, being part of 550 acres granted to Joseph Ford as above. (signed) John King, Elizabeth (x) King. Wit: Jno. Wade, Simon Holmes. // File. Claimant, B. Osmun, 21 Mch. 1804. Wit: Wm. McIntosh, 18 June 1804. Certif. A-283 issued to claimant, 6 June 1805. Benajah Osmun claim founded above grant to Joseph Ford who conveyed the same to John King, Sr. and sd John King by deed to claimant, as above.

p.25. Claim No.879. Oliver Walton, of Wilkinson Co., Miss. Ter., to Andrew Richey all claim to a certain tract on the Homochitto adj. Peter McNamee, for $150. Signed. Wit: John Smith, Wm. McNamee. // File. Andrew Richey, 22 Mch. 1804. Wit: John Richey, 4 Mch. 1805. Certif. D-147 to Geo. David, assignee of claimant, 16 Dec. 1806. Andrew Richey claims 531 acres as a preemption right, having inhabited and cultivated same in the latter part of 1798 and ever since by Oliver Walton, who sold it to the sd Andrew. The sd land on the Homochitto River. // A. Richey, for $175 well and truly paid, sells to George David, deputy surv. for and in the said territory, all his right, etc. to the above tract of 531 acres, 4 miles west of Six's Ferry. Wit: Patrick Marrin, Pierson Lewis. Prov. by sd Lewis Mch. 10, 1806. (signed) T. R.

p.22. Claim No.870. Spanish gr. to Richard King, 115 acres 4 mi. SE of Fort, b. by Elisha Flower, Peter Surget, Jonas Oiler, Wm. Atchinson and Thos. King. N. O. 30 Aug. 1794, by Carondelet. // p.24. 3 May 1800. Richard King, for $200 in hand pd., to Benajah Osmun, 115 acres in above grant. Signed. Wit: John C. Wickoff, Wm. Kenner. // File. Claimant, Benajah Osmun, 21 Mch. 1804. Certif. A-210 to cl. May 16, 1805. Claim founded on Sp. pat. to Richard King who conveyed same to present claimant.

p.26. Claim No.880. William Rabb to Michael Crauser, 17 Sept. 1802, a house on the bank of the Miss. River at the Natchez landing, for $100. Signed. Wit: J. Callendar, Florencio Millom. // File. Claimant, Solomon Phelps, Mch. 22, 1804. Rejected for want of evidence, 1806. Solomon Phelps a citizen of Natchez, claims preemption right to one acre in the City of Natchez on the River Miss. founded on the occupation and improvement by William Rabb in 1802 who sold the same to Michael Crauser, now decd. Said Crauser occupied the same until his death, Jany. 1804. Solomon Phelps purchased the premises at a public sale made by William Nichols, Esq. Feb. last, the executor of sd Michael Crauser. // Know all me that I, William Rabb, this day, 17 Sept. 1802, have sold a house at Natchez landing, for $100, same as above.

p.26. Claim No.881. Spanish gr. to Constantine McKenna, 800 acres on north fork of Bayou Pierre, 48 mi. from Fort, b. by John Minor and others. N. O. 9 Apr. 1790. // p.28. Will of Constantine McKenna, curate if the Parish of New Feliciana, a native of the Province of Ultonia, Kingdom of Ireland, legitimate son of Don Michael and Dona Catherine O'Neill, both dead: . . . My 800 acres on Bayou Pierre, mortgaged to Don Carlos Norwood. Father Patrick Walsh, the vicar, to be exor. Some trunks and my personal wearing apparel to be sold and the proceeds to go to Joseph Trotty who served me, also my gun, my bed and furnishing to go to him. Books to be disposed of as Father Walsh wishes. New Orleans, May 10, 1802. // p.30. N. O. 27 Oct. 1802. Power of Atty by John Lind to Joseph Vidal to sell tract to Abner Green. Book D.p.31. John Lind, by Joseph Vidal to Abner Green. Whereas the Reverend Constantine McKenna, late of the Par. of New Feliciana, La., curate, was seized of land in Miss. Territory, U. S. A. by virtue of his last will apptd Rev. Patrick Walsh, of N. O. Presbyter, exor. of his will, so being, to sell tract in Miss., appointed John Lind as atty. to sell land to Abner Green, 27 Oct. 1802, for $1800. Lind appoints Joseph Vidal to act as attorney. (signed) Joseph Vidal. Wit: Samuel Mahon, Wm. T. McCormick, G. Poindexter. 10 Mch. 1800. Prov. by Geo. Poindexter before David Ker, Judge of Sup Ct. of Miss. Territory. // File. Claimant, Abner Green, 22 Mch. 1804. Wit:

Anthony Hutchins, 27 July 1804. Certif. A-566 issued 5 Sept. 1805. Green claims 800 arpents in Claiborne Co. on Bayou Pierre by virtue of Spanish pat. to Constantine McKenna, as above, who died in 1802 leaving a will by which he directed that the sd tract be sold to pay his debts and appointed one Patrick Welsh, who prov. the same. Sd Welsh appointed John Lind as atty., etc. as above. Wit: Anthony Hutchins says that Wm. Vousdan who resided in the Miss. Ter. on 27 Oct. 1795 and he acted as the agent of Constantine McKenna, for the express purpose of securing the afsd tract of land.

p. 33. Claim No.883. Certificate of survey to Mr. John Staybraker, 160 acres on Miss. River Bluffs, 15 miles NE of Natchez. 3 Nov. 1795. William Vousdan, Dep. Surv. Plat shows James Simmons on the north. // File. Claimant, John Stabraker, 22 Mch. 1804. Wit: Thos. M. Green, 22 Feb. 1804, and Abner Green. Certif. C-11, 3 Feb. 1807. Conflicting with No.1937. John Stabraker claims 160 acres on the Bluff of the Miss. River in the neighborhood of Cole's Cr. by a Spanish warrant. He has cultivated this land ever since 1785.

p.34. Claim No.884. William Gardner to Major O'Dair, of Jefferson Co., for $350 in hand paid, plantation, b. on east by Thomas Austie, 1 Jany. 1804. Wit: William Payne, Daniel James. // File. Claimant, Major Adair, 22 Mch. 1804. Wit: Nathan Borden. Certif. D-300, 29 Dec. 1806. Major Adair claim preemption rights to 200 acres in Jefferson Co. on the waters of Cole's Cr., the said Major Adair being the representative of William Gardner, who settled and cultivated said tract before 3 Mch. 1803 and was the head of a family and over 21 years old. Above transfer to Adair from Wm. Gardner. // Transfer from Major Adair to Robert Cocks for $250 in hand paid, a tract of land whereon I now live near James Carmichael's and Company Gin, that is, all my right of occupancy and purchase. 23 June 1804. Wit: Edmund Hall.

p.35. Claim No.885. Spanish gr. to Francis Pousset, 1000 acres on a branch of Bayou Sarah, 54 miles south of Fort, b. by Daniel Ogden and vacant lands. N. O. 20 Aug. 1795 by Carondelet. // p.36. 9 May 1800, Joseph Pannil, Esq., of Adams Co., Miss. Ter., to John Ellis of same, for $3000 in hand paid, 1000 acres in above grant. Signed. Wit: Robt. Simple, John Collins. // File. Claimant, John Ellis, 22 Mch. 1804. Wit: B. Truly, 15 Oct. 1804. Certif. A-304 to claimant. John Ellis claims 1000 arpents as specified in above grant to Francis Pousset, who conveyed the sd tract to Joseph Pannill, 30 Sept. 1796, and sd Pannill conveyed it to John Ellis, as above.

p.37. Claim No.886. British grant to Zaccheus Routh, letters patent to 500 acres 20 mi. NE from Natchez, 2 mi. above the Choctaw Path on the north side of Holt's Fork of Boyd's Creek, b. on all sides by vacant lands. Pensacola. 16 June 1779 by Peter Chester. // File. Claimant, John Ellis, 22 Mch. 1804. Res. proved before. Entered, Jany. 22, 1805. John Ellis claims 400 acres in Jefferson Co., on waters of Holt's fork, as in above British grant, by virtue of sd grant and a deed from sd Routh to said Ellis, 21 Feb. 1784.

p.41. Claim No.1493. British grant to James Marcus Prevost, 1200 acres on Miss. River, about 1/2 mi from the east side of the Great Lake (which runs into the River at Tonica Bayou 4 mi. north of the mouth of the Bayou), b. by Donald McDonald, Wm. McKinnison and vacant lands. Pensacola, 14 July 1778 by Peter Chester. [Plat states that McDonald's land was formerly that of Alexander Ross.] // Lease and Release, 10 and 11 Dec. 1778. Alexander Macullagh, of Pensacola to Elihu Hall Bay, for $750 (value £75)paid, 1500 acres east of the Miss. River. Wit: Jacob Duryee, Henry Beaumont. [In margin: Del. to Elihu Hall Bay, Aug. 10, 1804.]

p.49. Claim No.1491. British gr. to David Waugh, 1000 acres on waters of St. Catherine's Cr., 11 mi. east of Natchez, adj. Francis Hutchinson, Thomas Gamble and Isaac Johnson. Pensacola, 11 Mch. 1777, by Peter Chester. [In margin: Del. to Elihu Hall Bay.]

p.52. Claim No.1492. British gr.to Thos. Hardy, 500 acres 4 mi. below Fort Panmure, b. by Daniel Clarke's south boundary and vacant lands. Pensacola, 4 July 1769, by Montfort Brown. [In margin: Del. to Elihu Hall Bay.]

p.55. Claim No.1494. British gr. to William Bay, 1100 acres near Miss. River, 7 mi. east from River, bet. lands surv. for Gov. Browne and Alexander Callender. Pensacola, 2 Nov. 1776, by Peter Chester. Plat and certificate. // p.57. State of S. C., William Bay, formerly a res. of West Florida but now of the High Hills of Santee in State afsd, for $500 to me paid, to Edward Penman, now of the City of London but formerly of the State of S. C. 1000 acres. 30 April 1803. Signed. Wit: Mary Lick, Anna Waties. Prov. by Mary Lick 30 Apr. 1803 before Thos. Waties, one of the associate judges of

S. C. Thos. Waties certifies that Ann Bay, wife of William, relinquished dower. Same date. // p.58. 6 May 1803. Edward Penman, of London, Kingdom of Great Britain, but formerly of Charleston, S. C. for 5 shillings, sold and released to Robert J. Turnbull and Elihu Hall Bay all that tract in the former Province of West Florida, now known by the name of Mississippi Territory in the U. S. A. (described as above). (signed) Ed Penman. Wit: J. J. Debesse, Noah Jones. Proved by Jones before Wm. Johnston, Jr., one of the Associate Judges of S. C. [In margin: Del. to Elihu Hall Bay.]

p.60. Claim No.975. British gr. to John Firby, 1000 acres on the middle fork of Boyd's Creek, 25 mi. NE of Natchez, b. on north by the southern boundaries of grant to Augustin Prevost and James Hughes. Pensacola, 25 Sept. 1779, by Peter Chester. // File. Claimant, Ann Car, 22 Mch. 1804. Reported, 28 Apr. 1807. To Hon. Commrs, etc. Please to take notice that the following tract of 1000 acres on Boyd's Creek, as in above grant, is claimed by Ann Carr, widow and relict of Richard W. Carr, decd., who was the only child and heiress-at-law of John Firby, decd., by virtue of the grant to her deceased father for said 1000 acres, as above. Original grant registered with the Land Office. E. H. Bay, Atty. for Ann Carr. John Firby died intestate, leaving no other child but Mrs. Carr. Richard W. Carr also died intestate without making any sale of the above land.

p.63. Claim No.977. Captain Amos Ogden to Thomas Willing. Lease and release, 29th and 30th 1774, for £193-6-9. Whereas Amos Ogden was gr. 27 Oct. 1772, 25,000 acres 21 mi. from Natchez, 1/4 mile from 1000-acre grant to Colin Graham, Esq., 1/2 mile from grant to Innes Hooper, to Thomas Willing 1000 acres, part of sd 25,000 acres. Signed: Amos Ogden. Wit: David Hodge, Elihu Hall Bay. // p.67. Thos. Willing and wife, Ann, of Philadelphia, Pa., to James Willing, of sd city, for £163, the above 1000 acres in West Florida, 25 Nov. 1774. Wit: Daniel Longstreet, Cortlan Vanansdol. // p.68. Lease and release, 12 Oct. and 21 Oct. 1776. James Willing, of West Florida, Gentleman, to William Holiday, Esq. of Liverpool, merchant, for £163, same tract as above. Signed. Wit: Philip Francis, Wm. Swanson. // File. Claimant, Samuel Holiday, 22 Mch. 1804. Reported, 13 June 1807. The above tract of land is claimed by Samuel Holiday, it being part of Ogden's Mandamus, 1000 acres about 1/2 mile east of the town laid of by sd Ogden on sd tract, b. on east by 1575 acres gr. by sd Ogden to Macullagh and Bay, and by lease and release, as above, and bargain and sale, above, from Thos. and Ann Willing, as above. E. H. Bay for claimant.

p.73. Claim No.887. Spanish Govt. to Thomas Hutchins, 1000 acres on Second Creek, b. by Anthony Hutchins, Jacob Winfree and Daniel Clarke. N. O. 29 Feb. 1788 by Miro. [No file.]

p.75. Claim No.888. Adam Cloud to George Matthews, 21 Feb. 1803, for $1000, 1000 acres on Bayou Sara, adj. "Miss Hutchins". Signed before W. Stephens, Dist. Judge of Georgia. // File. Claimant, George Matthews, 22 Mch. 1804. Rejected 16 May 1807. // Miss. Ter. Geo. Matthews claims 1000 acres on waters of Bayou Sara, near the boundary line between His Catholic Majesty and the United States by virtue of a Spanish patent to Adam Cloud, who on 21 Feb. 1803 conveyed same to claimant. George Matthews by John Steele, his atty.

p.76. Claim No.889. Spanish gr. to Adam Cloud, who petitions that he has come from the U. S. to establish himself in this district and asks for 500 acres on Cole's Cr., b. by lands of Israel Coleman. 5 Feb. 1790. Order of survey, N. O. 30 March 1790 by Miro. // Feb. 21, 1803. Adams Cloud to George Matthews, of Georgia, for $300 paid, 500 acres in Miss. Ter., as in above survey, adj. Ephraim and Isaac Coleman, Thomas Patterson and Wm. Ferguson, also 130 acres formerly the property of John Cory on St. Catherine's Cr., adj. William Vousdan, also one lot in the Town of Natchez, gr. sd Cloud by Gov. Gayoso. Signed before W. Stephens, Dist. Judge of Georgia. // File. Claimant, Geo. Matthews, 22 Mch. 1804. Wit: John Girault, 27 May 1805. Rejected. Miss. Ter., Geo. Matthews claims 500 acres on Cole's Cr. by purchase as above, from Adam Cloud, gr. him by Spanish Govt. Geo. Matthews by John Steele, his atty.

p.77. Claim No.892. 20 Aug. 1800 Stephen Minor and Catherine, his wife, of Adams Co., Miss. Ter., to Daniel Clark, of same, for $4500, 240 acres comprehending two grants fr. the Spanish Govt. in favor of Stephen Minor, 25 July, 1793 and 6 March 1795, beg. on margin of the Miss. River. Signed by both. Wit: Peter Walker, Wm. Lintot. // p.79. 22 Aug. 1800. Daniel Clark to John Steele for $4500, the above described 240 acres purchased of Stephen and Catherine Minor. Signed. Wit: Wm. Linton, John Minor. // File. Claimant, John Steele, 22 Mch. 1804. Certif. A-608 18 Sept. 1805. John Steele claims 240 acres by virtue of a deed from Daniel Clark, (above), which sd Clark claimed by deed, (above), from Stephen and Catherine Minor, who held the same with other lands by a complete title from the Baron de Carondelet, then Gov. of the Prov. of Louisiana. Stephen Minor holds the orig. Spanish titles for the security of his own lands.

p.81. Claim No.898. Spanish gr. to Charles King, 287 acres, 4 mi. NE of Fort, b. by Ithamar Andrews, Joshua Flowers, and Mary Girault. N. O. May __ 1795, by Carondelet. // File. Claimant, Chas. King, 22 Mch. 1804. Wit: John Girault, 26 July 1804. Certif. A-255 issued to claimant, 5 June 1805. Miss. Ter. Adams Co., Charles King claims 287 acres waters of St. Catherine's Cr., by virtue of a Spanish patent, as above.

p.82. Claim No.899. 8 Feb. 1790. Don Carlos de Grand-Pre to Ebenezer Dayton, 140 acres 2 miles from Natchez, b. by lands of Alexr. Moore, Gabriel Swazey and Samuel Swazey, for $180. Both signed. Wit: Antonio Soler, Christobal Badia, Jose Saint. // p.83. 6 Apr. 1786. Philip Trevino to Charles de Grand-Pre, 140 acres and 15 acres in the swamp, b. by lands of Mrs. Truly, formerly that of Alexander Moore and the Swazeys, for $130. Both signed. Wit: J. Vauchere, Juan Carreras. // p.84. Extracts from public sale of Abraham Mayes and Russell Jones. Mr. Abraham Mayes pet. that he may sell tobacco, corn and a horse-mill and 140 acres, b. by Mrs. Truly, Richard Swazey and Mr. Stowers at public auction to pay creditors for cash, 10 Mch. 1784. At sale 140 acres sold for $71 to Russell Jones, surety Gavin Gowdy. Confiscation of property of Russell Jones, because he attempted to leave Province to evade paying his debts. Above 140 acres b. by Mrs. Truly sold to Mr. Chachere for $120, 23 Dec. 1784. // File. Claimants, heirs of Ebenezer Dayton, Mch. 22, 1804. Wit: Elizabeth Swazey. Certif. B-247, 30 Mch. 1807. Smith Dayton, Phoebe Styles, and Ruth Hickworth, heirs and legal representatives of Ebenezer Dayton, decd., claim with the free consent of their elder brother, (illegible) Dayton, 140 acres in Adams Co., 1 mile from the City, b. by lands of Stephen Minor, Richard King, James Moore and Jeremiah Routh, by virtue of 2nd Sec. of Act. of Congress regulating the grants of lands, etc. The said Ebenezer in his lifetime having, on the day the sd territory was evacuated by the Spanish, actually inhabited and cultivated the said tract, and the same not being claimed by the preceding law or by any British grant. Jonathan Dayton, agent for the above claimants.

p.86. Claim No.900. Spanish Govt. to Josiah Flower, 200 acres 6 mi. east of Fort, b. by John Hartley and Madame Adams. N. O. 10 Feb. 1796 by Carondelet. // p.87. Josiah Flower to Peter Walker, for $200 and other valuable con., all rights to the above land, b. by Charles King and Richard Adams. Wit: Phineas Smith, Ezekiel Flower. Both signed. // p.88. Peter Walker of Natchez to Charles King, of same, the above tract gr. to Josiah Flower, for $369 paid. Wit. James White, John Girault. Before Stephen Minor. 15 Sept. 1797. // File. Claimant, Charles King, 22 Mch. 1804. Wit: John Girault, 6 July 1804. Certif. B-125 issued Feb. 1807. Chas. King claims 200 arpents in Adams Co. on waters of St. Catherine's Cr. as above patent to Josiah Flowers, an actual settler 27 Oct. 1795. Notation: Warrant was granted 21 Jany. 1788.

p.89. Claim No.901. Spanish gr. to Jacob Adams, 313 acres 6 mi. east of Fort, b. by Joshua Flowers and John Hartley. N. O. 4 June 1791, by Miro. // p.91. 11 Oct. 1796. Jacob Adams to William Atchinson, 313 acres, in above grant. Jacob (x) Adams. Wit: Ebenezer Rees, Thos. Withers. [No consideration stated.] // 30 Dec. 1797. Wm. Atchinson to Ephraim Blackburn, 263 acres, part of grant in my favor, of which I have sold 50 acres to Wm. Gillespie. Both signed. Wit: Jno. Girault, Geo. Cochran. // File. Claimant, Ephraim Blackburn, 22 Mch. 1804. Wit: Jno. Girault. Certif. A-462, 24 July 1805. Notation: See Guion's claim. Proved in Jacob Adams. Notation: 50 arpents of the within claimed by Isaac Guion. See. No.1707. (signed) Thos. H. Williams, Register. Ephraim Blackburn claims 313 arpents [the certif. was for only 263 acres,] by virtue of a patent from the Spanish Govt. to Jacob Adams, as above, etc.

p.92. Claim 902. Spanish gr. to Joe Ford, 250 acres on south br. of Cole's Cr., 20 miles east of Fort, all sides vacant. N. O. 28 April 1790 by Miro. [No file.]

p.94. Claim No. 904. Jany. 16, 1804. Stephen Jett to John Gilbert my right of occupancy and preemption in my improvement and labor on Daniel's Cr., a br. of Cole's Cr., 4 miles from Edmond Johnson and Company's Gin, for $100 paid. Stephen (x) Jett. Wit: John Stampley, D. Nance. // p.95. James Cole to John Gilbert, Jany. 21, 1804, his preemption right to land on Daniel's Creek, for $150. Signed. Wit: Thos. Lacey, D. Nance. // File. Claimant, John Gilbert, 22 Mch. 1804. Wit: Wm. Lacey, 15 Oct. 1804. 50 acres to include the improvement. Certif. D-332. Miss. Territory, Jefferson, John Gilbert claims 640 acres, as above described, having purchased the same of Stephen Jett, who settled the same prior to 3 Mch. 1803 and have had same in actual cultivation. Note: The claimant requests 50 acres. Jett of Jefferson and Gilbert of Claiborne Co.

p.95. Claim No.907. British gr. to Alexander Boyd, 250 acres, 15 mi. north of Fort, b. by Miss. River and vacant lands. Pensacola, 15 Dec. 1768 by Montfort Browne. Plat. [No file.]

p.99. Claim No.908. British gr. to John Campbell, 39 mi. above Fort Panmure, at Little Gulf, b. by Alexander McIntosh on south. Pensacola, 11 Feb. 1770 by Chester. Plat. [No file.]

p.103. Claim No.909. British gr. to Thos. Frey, 200 acres, 36 mi. north of Fort Panmure, b. by Miss. River and vacant lands, 1 mile below Petit Gulf. Pensacola, 7 July 1775, by Peter Chester. // p.106. 13 June 1774. Thos. Frey to Philip Barbour, for $250 for a tract he purchased of me below Petit Gulf, 200 acres on the River, including lower end of the bluff. // Philip Barbour to Philip Alston of West Florida, Natchez Dist., 200 acres adj. Little Gulf, formerly the property of Thomas Frey, for $500, for which I guarantee a lawful title. 19 Oct. 1776. // Philip Alston to Philip Alston, Jr. assignment of all my right, etc. in this within bond, 10 Jany. 1800. (signed) Philip Alston. // File. Philip Alston, 22 Mch. 1804. Wit: Bennet Truly, 28 May 1805. Reported, 28 Apr. 1807. Notice is given that I, Philip Alston claim 200 acres at the lower end of the bluff at Petit Gulf as described above, Miss. Territory, Claiborne Co., having purchased same of Philip Alston, decd.; he having purchased the same from Philip Barbour, who bought the same of Thos. Frey, to whom the land was originally gr. by the British Govt.

p.107. Claim No.912. Jacob Hoffman, of Claiborne Co., Miss. Ter., to Anthony Glass, of same, for $300 paid, an improvement and actual settlement made by me, January 1803 on tract 2 miles above Walnut Hills, Jacob (X) Hellmen. Wit: Jeremiah Jones, Henry Eaton. // p.109. Agreement bet. Benj. Steel who has sold to Anthony Glass all his right and title to land he now lives on and also his part in the gin and mill; said Glass to gin all of sd Steel's present crop of cotton, free from toll, finding bagging and cordage and putting it in square bales fit for market, likewise giving Steel a full receipt of all accounts due sd Glass from sd Steel and poll all accounts for meat that was got for the use of the gin and liquor that was got by said Steel and pay Ross for grinding corn. Steel to give Glass a clear receipt. Both signed. Wit: George Marshall, Andrew Glass, John Scarlett. // File. Claimant, Anthony Glass, 22 Mch. 1804. Know all men, etc. that Jacob Hoffman, of Claiborne, Miss. Ter., bargained in consideration of $300 to me in hand paid by Anthony Glass, [same as above, except no agreement.] [No disposition of claim given.]

p.108. Claim No.925. Spanish govt. order of survey. Petition of George Clare for land on Cole's Cr. adj. George Stampley and William Hamberlin, 7 Oct. 1789. // Order of survey for 400 acres. N. O. 25 Nov. 25 Oct. 1789 by Miro. [File missing.]

p.109. Claim No.927. Spanish Govt. to George Robins, 400 acres on Sandy Creek, a br. of Homochitto, 16 mi. ESE of Fort, b. by vacant lands. N. O. 20 Jany. 1793, by Carondelet. [No file.]

p.111. Claim No.931. Spanish govt. to Gibson Clarke, 600 acres on Bayou Pierre, 45 miles NE of Fort, b. by William Brocus and vacant lands. N. O. 10 Feb. 1789 by Miro. Plat shows land in fork of south fork of Bayou Pierre and Wm. Tabor on SW. [No file.]

p.113. Claim No.935. Spanish gr. to James Elliot, 1000 acres 20 mi. NE of Fort, b. by Peter Hawkins, Everard Green, James Smith and Adam Bingaman. N. O. 20 Oct. 1788 by Miro. [No file.]

p.115. Claim No.936. Spanish gr. to William Calvet, 750 acres on Homochitto, 36 mi. SE of Fort. N. O. 27 Feb. 1789, by Miro. Plat shows in Morgan's fork of Homochitto. [No file.]

p.116. Claim No.937. Spanish gr. to Peter Surget, 800 acres on a branch of the Feliciana, 45 miles SSE from Fort, b. by Wm. Dunbar, Charles Surget, Wm. Collins and John Ellis. N. O. 7 Dec. 1797 by Gayoso. // File. Claimant, Catherine Surget, 22 Mch. 1804. Wit: Wm. Atchinson, July 18, 1804. Samuel Stockett, 10 Dec. 1805. Rejected, 21 May 1807. Mrs. Catherine Surget, wid. and extrx. of the late Peter Surget claims for sd estate 800 arps. gr. to him by Spanish warrant, 14 Dec. 1794 and possession 25 Apr. 1795. J. H. White for Catherine Surget.

p.120. Claim No.939. Spanish gr. to Roger Doud, 540 acres on waters of Cole's Cr., 35 mi. NE of Fort, b. by Robert Cochran. N. O. 15 Apr. 1790 by Miro. [No file.]

p.122. Claim No.940. Spanish gr. to Peter Surget, 1000 acres on Second Cr., b. by Mr. Clark, Mr. Cobbs, Mr. Minor and Mr. McIntosh. N. O. 21 June 1788 by Miro. Plat shows Daniel Clark, Estevan Minor and William McIntosh. [No file.]

p.118. Claim No.938. Spanish gr. to Roger Doud, 500 acres between Cole's Cr. and Bayou Pierre, 40 mi. north of Fort, b. on east by Mr. Cochran. N. O. 8 Aug. 1789 by Miro. [No file.]

p.123. Claim No.943. Spanish gr. to Charles White, 400 acres, 7 mi. south of Fort, b. by Adam Bingaman, James McIntosh, David Williams and Estevan Minor. N. O. 16 May 1791 by Miro. Plat also shows Lewis Bingaman to north. Reg. 22 Mch. 1804. [No file.]

p.125. Claim No.941. Spanish gr. to Peter Surget, 3000 acres on Second Cr., b. by Mr. Clark, Mr. Smith, Jesse Withers, Henry Phipps and John Ellis Jr. N. O. 21 June 1788 by Miro. Reg. 20 Mch. 1804. [No file.]

p.127. Claim No.942. Spanish gr. to John Hampton White, 1000 acres 8 mi. SSE of Fort, b. by David Williams, Bernard Lintot, Capt. White, John Girault, Mr. Green, Chas. White, James McIntosh. N. O. 20 Apr. 1791 by Miro. Plat shows Samuel Hutchins by James McIntosh. [No file.]

p.129. Claim No.944. Spanish Govt. to Carlos White, 400 arps, 8 mi. SSE of Fort, b. by Hampton White, Abner Green, Mr. Kennard and Sam'l. Hutchins. N. O. 20 Apr. 1791 by Miro. Reg. 22 Mch. 1804. [No file.]

p.130. Claim No.945. Spanish Govt. to Matthew White, 1150 acres, b. by Philipe Trevino, John Girault, Bernard Lintot and a cypress swamp. N. O. 6 Mch. 1788 by Miro. Plat is to Captain Matthew White. Reg. 22 Mch. 1804. [No file.]

p.132. Claim No.946. Spanish Govt. to Hampton White, 300 acres on the Cypress Creek or Swamp of St. Catherine's Cr., 6 mi. south of Fort, b. by Bernard Lintot, William Dunbar, Matthew White, William Butler and Abner Green. N. O. 7 Dec. 1797 by Gayoso. Reg. 22 Mch. 1804. [No file.]

p.134. Claim No.947. Spanish gr. to Norsworthy Hunter, 1000 acres on the north fork of Cole's Cr., 25 miles NE of Fort, b. by James Todd, Henry Green and Stephen Scriber. N. O. 1 Sept. 1795 by Carondelet. Plat shows William Daniels and Francis Jones on north side of creek, which is the north border of the tract. Reg. 22 Mch. 1804. [No file.]

p.135. Claim No.953. Spanish Govt. to William Brocus, 1000 acres on a branch of Bayou Pierre, 45 mi. NE of Fort, b. by Gibson Clark. N. O. 18 June 1792 by Carondelet. Reg. 22 Mch. 1804. [No file.]

p.137. Claim No.954. Spanish Govt. to Wm. Brocus, 1000 arpents south fork of Bayou Pierre, all sides vacant. N. O. 20 Jany. 1795 by Carondelet. Reg. 3 Mch. 1804. [No file.]

p.139. Claim No.955. Spanish gr. to William Brocus, 400 acres on south fork of Bayou Pierre, 45 mi. NE of Fort, b. by lands of grantee and Thos. Creighton. N. O. 18 July 1795. Reg. 3 Mch. 1804. [No file.]

p.140. Claim No.956. Spanish Govt. to Stephen Minor, 1180 acres on the road leading from Fort Nogales, 80 miles NE of Fort Panmure, 3 mi. north of Miss. River, b. by vacant lands. N. O. 18 June 1795, by Carondelet. [No file.] // p.141. 28th Feb. 1798. Stephen Minor, Capt. of this Plaza and District, transfers to Stephen and William, sons of Nanette Brocus, dau. of William and Lucrecia Brocus, residents of Bayou Pierre in this Dist., the land by which this title was granted him, with the express condition not to mortgage or sell them without my permission; for them and their heirs forever. Signed. Wit: John Girault, Drury Ledbetter, Hugh Mathews, Ebenezer Smith. [No file.]

p.143. Claim No.959. Spanish Govt. to Samuel Hutchins, 200 arps. 6 mi. SE of Fort, b. by Wm. Gorman, Wm. Dunbar and Wm. McIntosh. N. O. 29 ___ 1788 by Miro. // File. Claimant, Samuel Hutchins, 22 Mch. 1804. Wit: Philander Smith, 9 Feb. 1805. Certif. A-39 issued to claimant. Original Spanish grant and survey by Carlos Trudeau in file, the latter in English. Both dated 28 Feb. 1788.

p.144. Claim No.960. Spanish Govt. to Richard Ellis, Sen., 320 arps. bet. Homochitto River and the Miss. River, 12 mi. south of Fort, b. by Mr. Tomlinson, John Ellis, grantee and Dona Celeste Hutchins. N. O. Jany. 1788. [No file.]

p.146. Claim No.3. Spanish gr. to Benj. Bealk, 800 arpents on St. Catherine's Cr., 7 mi. from Fort, b. by Richard Harrison and vacant lands. N. O. 10 Feb. 1789 by Miro. Plat shows land on Muddy Fork of St. Catherine's. [No file.] Reg. 3 Dec. 1803.

p.147. Claim No.961. British gr. to William Gorman, 243 acres 12 mi. SE of Fort, on Second Cr., b. by William Joiner and James Barbut. Pensacola, 12 Sept. 1775, by Peter Chester. Reg. Mch. 22, 1804. [No file.]

p.150. Claim No.962. Spanish gr. to Anthony Hutchins, Esq., 800 acres, 10 mi. south of Fort, b. by Daniel Clark and Dona Celeste Hutchins. N. O. 8 Aug. 1788 by Miro. // File. Claimant, Anthony Hutchins, 22 Mch. 1804. Wit: Philander Smith, 9 Feb. 1805. Certif. A-40 issued to legal representatives of claimant. Certificate of survey for 800 acres at White Cliffs, by Don Carlos Trudeau, Royal Surv. of the Prov. of La. 25 Apr. 1789. Confirmation of same by Estevan Miro, 8 Aug. 1789.

p.152. Claim No.963. Spanish gr. to Dona Celeste Hutchins, 1000 acres, on White Cliffs, 5 mi. from Miss. River, 13 mi. south of Fort, b. on north and west by Anthony Hutchins, south and east by Richard Ellis. N. O. 15 March 1788 by Miro. // File. Claimant, Celeste Hutchins, 22 Mch. 1804. Wit: Philander Smith, 9 Feb. 1805. Certif. A-41 issued to claimant. Copy of plat for 100 acres for Miss Celeste Hutchins, youngest dáughter of Col. Anthony Hutchins, adj. land of her father and Richard Ellis.

p.153. Claim No.964. Spanish Govt. to Anthony Hutchins, 566 acres on White Cliffs, b. by Richard Ellis, Mr. Hughes and the grantee. N. O. 18 Feb. 1790 by Miro. Plat: "laid out for 566 acres but contains only 500." // File, claimant, Anthony Hutchins, 22 Mch. 1804. Wit: Philander Smith, 9 Feb. 1805. Certif. A-42, issued to legal representatives of A. Hutchins. Claim as above.

p.155. Claim No.967. British grant of 2150 acres near Miss. River to Richard Irwin, John Copeland, Robert Russell, Thos. Miller, and George Dewsbery, reduced non-com. officers, John Edwards, James Primrose, Donald McDonald, Kenneth McKoy, John Pikeland, Thomas Appleton, Benj. VanVicten, John Black, John Miller, John Murray, Thos. Neal, John Cooper, George Hayward, John Prior, William Duffy, John Anderson and Richard Meeks, reduced private soldiers, that tract of land on Boyd's Cr., 35 miles NE of Natchez, b. by lands surveyed for Augustin Prevost on south, other sides vacant. Pensacola, 19 Mch. 1777. Plat. // File. Claimant, E. H. Bay, atty. relative to the existence of sundry deeds in favor of Col. Hutchins's claim to 2160 acres of land on the north fork of Cole's Cr. Not to be recorded. Elihu Hall Bay, of Charleston S. C. but now in the Miss. Territory, maketh oath and said in the latter end of year 1775 or beginning of 1776, while the deponent resided in Pensacola, he in conjunction with Alexander Macullagh, of Pensacola, purchased from sundry non-commissioned officers and soldiers 2150 acres of land which were afterwards located on the waters of Boyd's or Cole's Creek, surveyed and carried into a grant under the great seal of West Florida; that the said land, after the passing of said patent was duly conveyed to this deponent and the sd Alexander Macullagh. The deponent has lately seen the original grant for the sd land in the possession of the said Anthony Hutchins, which he knows to the identical abovementioned from the said non-commissioned officers and soldiers, and conveyed to sd Anthony Hutchins as aforesaid, as all the deeds and conveyances were drawn in the deponent's office while residing, as an attorney at Pensacola and passed through his hands. They are all accurate and are of record in the Office of West Florida, which he has no doubt they will be found to have been so recorded upon a reference to the said records wherever they may be found. But deponent knows not what became of the originals, further than that he has heard and believes that in the confusing times which soon afterwards ensued in this part of the world and in the course of the depredations about that time committed, they were lost and destroyed. (signed) E. H. Bay. Sworn, 17 Feb. 1804, before Samuel Brooks, J. P. Sworn to before the Board, 22 Mch. 1804. Original Sp. gr. to Anthony Hutchins for 2146 acres, on north fork of Cole's Cr., lands called "The Soldiers' Right", granted in the time of the English government to a number of soldiers and purchased at the time by Col. Hutchins. N. O. 18 Feb. 1790 by Miro. [The above tract, on partition of sundry lands owned by Elihu Hall Bay and Alexander Macullagh, fell to Macullagh in his share and he sold it to Anthony Hutchins.] [This tract was allowed by the Commrs. to the heirs of Anthony Hutchins.]

p.161. Claim No.969. Spanish Govt. to John Lovelace, 800 arpents on Loftus Cliffs, 40 mi. south of Fort, b. by Robert Johnson and vacant lands. Certificate of survey and plat, only, dated 10 Mch. 1793. [No file.] Reg. 22 Mch. 1804.

p.163. Claim No.987. Spanish Govt. to Madame Jane Rumsey, 2000 acres bet. the Homochitto River and Second Cr., 9 mi. SE of Fort, b. by lands of Mr. Isaac Johnson and gr. to Capt. Amos Ogden. N.O. 8 Oct. 1789 by Miro. // File. Claimant, Lacey Rumsey, 22 Mch. 1804. Wit: John Girault, 27 May 1805. Certif. A-457 to claimant, July 23, 1805. Miss. Ter., Lacey Rumsey a citizen of sd Territory, son and only heir of Jane Rumsey, decd., claims 2000 arpents on waters of Second Cr. as described in above plat, founded on a Spanish patent to sd Jane Rumsey, decd., as above. Rec'd. of B. L. C. Wailes, Reg. of the Land Office at Washington, the original Spanish patent in favor of Madame Jane Rumsey, filed with the Register on 22 Mch. 1804. (signed) Nicholas Gray for J. M. Reynolds. 8 Aug. 1828.

p.165. Claim No.988. Spanish grant to Manuel Texada, 400 acres on north fork of Cole's Cr., 25 mi NE of Fort, b. by Don Estevan de Alvas and vacant land. N. O. 27 Nov. 1788 by Miro. // File. Claimant, William Murray, 22 Mch. 1804. Wit: Benet Truly, 27 May 1805. Certif. A-455 issued to legal representatives, 23 July 1805. William Murray, the legal representative of William Murray, decd., claims 400 arpents on waters of Cole's Cr. founded on a Spanish patent to Manuel Texada, as above, who conveyed the same to the afore-mentioned Wm. Murray, decd., the father of the present claimant, by deed, Jany.__ 1789, which deed also covers the 400 arpents conveyed by Stephen Alva to the afsd Manuel Texada. Copy of the transfer from Stephen Alva to Texada and from Texada to Murray, dated 24 Jany. 1789. These are in Spanish.

p.167. Claim No.989. Spanish gr. to Estevan de Alvas 400 acres on Cole's Cr., 24 mi. from Fort, b. by Manuel Texada and Henry Plattner, and vacant lands. N. O. 27 Nov. 1788 by Miro. Plat gives Plattner's Fork of Cole's Cr. Reg. 22 Mch. 1804. [No file.]

p.169. Claim No.990. Spanish gr. to Samuel Phipps, 440 acres on Second Cr., 9 mi. SE of Fort, b. by David Mitchell, Nicholas Rabb and Philipe Trevino. N. O. 9 Apr. 1790 by Miro. Reg. 22 Mch. 1804. [No file.]

p.171. Claim No.992. Spanish Govt. to Richard Devall, 500 acres, 1 1/2 mile from Cole's Cr. at head of a lake, 24 mi. NE of Fort, b. by Cato West and Mr. Fairbanks. N. O. 24 Dec. 1797. // File. Claimant, (1) Richard Devall, 22 Mch. 1804. Wit: Wm. Atchinson. Rejected. See No.2004. Richard Devall, an inhabitant of Miss. Ter. claims 500 acres in Jefferson Co., by virtue of Spanish patent in 1789 to him, who, residing on the plains near Baton Rouge, presents by Israel Smith, his agent, the grant from Spanish Govt. Claimants (2) Edward and Evan Jones, 22 Mch. 1804. Reported, 11 June 1807. See No.1649 for one-third of this tract. Evan and Edward Jones claim 1000 acres on SW corner of Thaddeus Lyman's Mandamus of 20,000 acres, (said Evan and Edward are survivors of James Jones), under and by virtue of the original Mandamus grant, 22 Feb. 1775, and a deed of conveyance from the said Thaddeus Lyman to claimants and their deceased brother, James Jones, whom they have survived, 10 Feb. 1775, for said 1000 acres which conveyance is filed herewith in the Register's Office. (signed) A. Hutchins, atty. for Evan and Edward Jones. Plat of Lyman Mandamus, showing the land transferred to the Joneses.

p.173. Claim No.993. Spanish gr. to Philetus, Israel and Philander Smith, 500 acres on Second Cr., 8 mi. SE of Fort. N. O. 6 Mch. 1804, by Miro. [No file.]

p.175. Claim No.994. Spanish Govt. to Patrick Foley, who petitions that he has not sufficient land to employ his negroes; asks for 1000 acres more, adj. Wm. Collins. 25 May 1795. 1000 acres grant to him on Buffalo Cr, 26 May 1795 by Carondelet. Reg. 22 Mch. 1804. This was allowed to Throckmorton and Spain. [No file.]

p.176. Claim No.995. Spanish Govt. to Richard Harrison, 661 acres 15 mi. NE of Fort, b. by John Joseph Duforest, Wm. Ferguson and Dona Ellena Truly. N. O. 30 Aug. 1795, by Carondelet. [No file.]

p.178. Claim No.997. British Govt. to John Tally, 300 acres on St. Catherine's Cr., south fork, 11 mi. east of the Natchez, b. by Thos. Gamble and vacant lands. Pensacola, 9 Oct. 1777 by Chester. [No file.]

p.181. Claim No.1000. Spanish Govt. to William Ryan, 200 acres on St. Catherine's and Second Creeks, 8 mi. from Fort, b. by George Killion, Charles Cason and Robert Ford. N. O. 12 May 1789. // I assign my right. Thomas (X) Donaldson. Wit: Wm. Emerson, Rt. Emerson. [n.d.] [No file.]

p.183. Claim No.1001. Spanish Govt. to John Ellis, 800 acres on a branch of the Feliciana, 45 mi. SSE of Fort, b. by Wm. Collins and Geo. Overaker. N. O. 24 Dec. 1797, by Gayoso. // File. Claimant, John Ellis, 23 Mch. 1804. Wit: Wm. Atchinson, 28 Nov. 1804. Rejected, 21 Apr. 1807. John Ellis claims 800 acres on waters of Bayou Sarah, as in above grant, founded on a warrant of survey granted to William Wickoff, 15 April 1789, which was purchased by sd claimant, whereupon the application was made for obtaining regular titles but through the negligence of the government no patent legally and fully executed until 1797. G. Poindexter for claimant. Original warrant for Wm. Wickoff, Jr. A resident of Attakapas, recently arrived with his family from America, wishes to establish a plantation to employ his negroes, petitions for land. 10 Apr. 1789.

p.185. Claim No.1009. Spanish Govt. to David Lejeune, 400 acres. Petition of David Lejeune, wishing more land to employ his negroes, asks for 800 acres on waters of Buffalo Cr. adj. John Lovelace and Henry Roach. Certificate and plat for 400 acres, east of Buffalo Cr. 30 miles south of Fort, adj. Henry

Roach, John Lovelace and Wm. Vousdan. // Feliciana, 19 May 1803. I, David Lejeune, have sold this land. // File. Claimant, Henry Roach, 23 Mch. 1804. Certif. A-749 issued for 100 arpents, 5 Mch. 1806. See No.1013 and No.2074. Roach claims 400 acres founded on the Sp. patent to Lejeune, who conveyed same to Robert Collins by an endorsement on the certificate, and sd Collins conveyed same to sd Roach 18 Jany. 1798.

p.187. Spanish gr. to Wm. Fairbanks 200 acres on south fork of Cole's Cr. 12 league from its mouth at the Miss. River, 20 mi. north of the Fort, b. by James Elliot. N. O. 20 Dec. 1794 by Carondelet. // File. Claimant, Wm. Fairbanks, 23 Mch. 1804. Wit: Caleb Potter, 22 Oct. 1804. Certif. A-280 to claimant, June 1805. Claim as above.

p.189. Claim No.1012. British Govt. to Seth Doud, 113 acres on Second Creek, b. by Samuel Wells, Wm. Joiner and James Barbut. Pensacola, 8 Sept. 1777. // File. Claimant, John Ellis, 23 Mch. 1804. Certif. A-531 to claimant, 28 Aug. 1805. Claim founded on Br. gr. (above) to Seth Doud who conveyed the same to John Blommart, who conveyed the same to Luke Collins, 22 June 1779, and sd Collins to present claimant, sd John Ellis.

p.191. Claim No.1014. Spanish gr. to John Wall, 500 acres 3 mi. fr. the stream called Roche a Davion, 30 mi. south of Fort, b. by Estevan Plauche, Andrew Hare and Daniel Ogden. N. O. June 20, 1795, by Carondelet. // File. Claimant, John Wall, 23 Mch. 1804. Wit: Henry Hunter, 12 Nov. 1804. Certif. A-281, June 5, 1805. John Wall claims 500 acres by virtue of the above Spanish grant.

p.193. Claim No.1015. Spanish gr. to John O'Reilly, 600 acres on Bayou Sara, 35 mi. south of the Fort, b. by Wm. Vousdan. N. O. 30 Mch. 1793 by Carondelet. // File. Claimant, John Wall, 23 Mch. 1804. Wit: John Boles, 15 July 1805. Certif. A-433, to claimant, 16 July 1805. John Wall claims 525 acres in Wilkinson Co., by virtue of the above Spanish patent for 600 acres to John O'Reilly who conveyed the sd tract to David Lejeune, 3 June 1797, and sd Lejeune conveyed the same to present claimant, 10 Dec. 1798, John Wall being an inhabitant of the territory on and prior to Oct. 27, 1795.

p.195. Claim No.1016. Spanish gr. to John Lovelace, 200 acres on Miss. River at Loftus Cliffs, 40 mi. south of the Fort, b. by Antonio Gras. N. O. 23 Mch. 1793 by Miro. // File. Claimant, John Lovelace, 23 Mch. 1804. Wit: John Collins, 9 July 1805. Certif. A-760 issued 27 Mch. 1806. Note: See No. 1297. John Lovelace claims 200 acres founded on a warrant gr. to him by Spanish Govt. 25 Jany, 1788 and a patent as above. John Lovelace inhabited sd tract long prior to and on 27 Oct. 1795, he being at that time at the head of a family. G. Poindexter for the claimant.

p.197. Claim No.1017. Spanish Govt. to John Wall. Petition, that he wants to build a house in Natchez; asks for grant to Lot No.3, Square 14. 8 Jany. 1795. Granted 14 Jany. 1795 by Gayoso. // File. Claimant, John Wall, 23 Mch. 1804. Wit: John Collins, 16 July 1805. Certif. A-542 issued to claimant, Aug. 29, 1805. John Wall claims one lot 150 feet square in the City of Natchez, by virtue of the above patent.

p.198. Claim No.1018. Spanish gr. to John Wall, 400 acres on Buffalo Cr., 16 mi. south of Fort, b. by vacant lands, N. O. 1 Sept. 1795. Plat shows David Lejeune on west. // File. Claimant, John Wall, 23 Mch. 1804. Res. proved in claim No.1014. Certif. A-282 issued, 1805. John Wall claims 400 acres of swamp land on Buffalo cr. by above Spanish grant.

p.200. Claim No.1028. British gr. to Innis Hooper, 250 acres on Second Cr., b. by Samuel Wells. Pensacola, 21 Sept. 1772. // File. Claimants, heirs of Samuel Wells, decd., 23 Mch. 1804. See No. 1029. Confirmed. Samuel Levi Wells, Lewis Wells, Willing Wells and Clemence Wells, for themselves, and Alexander Filton and his wife, Henrietta, in right of sd Henrietta, Richard Edmund Cuny and his wife, Tabitha, in right of said Tabitha, Policarp LaMotte and his wife, Editha, in right the sd Editha, Samuel Morris and his wife, Louisa, in right of sd Louise, William Alston and his wife Amelia, in right of said Amelia, and George Lovelace and his wife, Sophia, in right of the sd Sophia, as heirs and heiresses-at-law of Samuel Wells, decd., claim a tract of land, 250 acres in Adams Co., Miss. Ter. on Second Cr. by virtue of a British grant to Innis Hooper, as above, and by him sold to the said Samuel Wells, decd., [n.d.], the claimants afsd having been settlers in the sd territory on 27 Oct. 1795. (signed) Seth Lewis, agent for the abovenamed claimants.

p.203. Claim No.1029. British grant to Samuel Wells, 1000 acres near the River Miss. 8 mi. SE of Fort, on Second Cr. Pensacola, 21 Sept. 1772. // File. Claimants, heirs of Samuel Wells, 23 Mch. 1804. William Collins, witness, 24 Mch. 1806; George Fitzgerald and Richard King, witnesses, Jany. 13, 1807. Confirmed. Certificate A-807 issued 11 June 1807. Samuel Levi Wells, Lewis Wells,

Willing Wells, and Clemence Wells, one of the daughters and heiresses of deceased, also Alexander Fulton and his wife, Henriette, in right of Henrietta, one of the daughters and heiresses of deceased, also Richard Edmund Cumy and Tabitha, his wife, in right of sd dau. and heiresses of deceased, also Policarp LaMotte, and his wife, Editha, in right of sd Editha, one of the dau. and heiresses of deceased, also Samuel Morris and his wife, Louise, in right of sd Louise, one of the dau. and heiresses of sd deceased, also Amelia Alston who is one of the daughters and heiresses of sd deceased, and George Lovelace and Sophia, his wife, in right of sd Sophia, one of the daus. and heiresses of sd deceased, claim 1000 acres in Adams County, Miss. Ter. by virtue of a British grant to Samuel Wells, decd. as above. Etc. Seth Lewis, agent for the above heirs and heiresses. Take Note: It was also written "also William Alston and his wife Amelia, in right of the said" which was scratched out and left as originally stated.

p.206. Claim No.1031. Spanish gr. to Dona Sarah Lewis, 300 acres on south fork of Cole's Cr., 18 mi. east of Fort, b. on Madame (widow) Cousat, Dona Maria Page and Samuel Flower. N. O. 18 June 1795, by Carondelet. // File. Claimant, Isaac Guion and wife, 23 Mch. 1804. Wit: Ebenezer Rees, 17 July 1805. Certif. A-442, issued to claimant in right of his wife, July 18, 1805. Isaac Guion and Sarah, his wife, the latter of whom was a settler in Miss. Territory on 27 Oct. 1795, claim in right of said Sarah, 300 acres, as in the above grant to said Sarah. The plat is for land of Sarah Lewis alias Sarah Guion. On motion of the agent of the United States resolved that the Board of Commrs. will not consider the patent produced in the above claim as exclusive evidence of the claimant's title but require them to prove when the same issued and at what time and by what authority the land was surveyed because the same does not appear on authenticated abstracts for the Spanish records of grants for the Natchez District. W. B. Shields. Motion sustained and other proof required.

p.208. Claim No.1035. Spanish grant to Andrew Beall, 134 acres on St. Catherine's Creek, b. by Richard Miller, Richard Harrison and John Hartley. N. O. 25 Mch. 1795 by Carondelet. // File. Claimant, heirs of Andrew Beall, 23 Mch. 1804. Wit: John Girault, Esq. 1 Sept. 1804. Certif. A-284 issued to Benajah Osmun, assignee of claimant, 16 June 1805. Miss. Ter., Adams Co. Richard Beall, Peter Brown and Elizabeth Brown, his wife, and Benjamin Brown and Nancy Brown, his wife, heirs and legal representatives of Andrew Beall, decd. claim 134 arpents by virtue of a Spanish patent to said Andrew, decd. as above, who was an actual settler in said county 27 Oct. 1795, and he willed the said tract of land unto the abovementioned heirs.

p.210. Claim No.1036. Spanish grant to John Hartley, 400 acres on St. Catherine's Creek, 6 miles NE of Fort, b. by John Stillee and vacant lands. N. O. 25 Feb. 1788 by Miro. // File. Claimants, heirs of Andrew Beall, 23 Mch. 1804. Wit: John Girault, 1 Sept. 1804. Certif. A-285 issued to Benajah Osmun assignee of claimants, 6 June 1805. Miss. Ter., Adam Co. Richard Beall, Peter Brown and Elizabeth, his wife, Benjamin Brown and Nancy Brown, his wife, heirs and legal representatives of Andrew Beall deceased, claimed 400 arpents of land by virtue of a Spanish grant to John Hartley, as above, who contracted with the said Andrew Beall, decd., for the said tract but the said Hartley died before the deed was executed. The said Andrew Beall then petitioned the government for a title and a decree was granted to said Beall.

p.212. Claim No.1037. Deed of exchange. William Gillespie deeds 300 acres in Dist. of Cole's Cr. b. by John Holt, Estevan de Alva and in exchange John Girault and Mary Spain, his wife, deed a tract on St. Catherine's Cr. adj. John Stillee, John Hartley, Josiah Flower, Carlos King and those of the afsd Mary Spain, according to a plat of said grant. All sign. // File. Claimant, heirs of Andrew Beall, 23 Mch. 1804. Wit: Jean Girault, 1 Sept. 1804. Certif. A-300 issued to B. Osmun, assignee of the heirs of Beall, 11 June 1805. Miss. Ter. The heirs and legal representative of Andrew Beall, decd. claim 100 acres in Adams Co. by virtue of a deed of conveyance from William Gillespie to the said Andrew, decd., 14 Apr. 1800, which sd Gillespie purchased the same of John Girault, as above, and the said Girault claimed it under a patent to him by the Spanish Govt.

p.213. Claim No.1040. Spanish gr. to Daniel Rayner, 260 acres, 10 mi. east of Fort, b. by Antonio Garcia, George Killian, James West and John Ferguson. N. O. March 30, 1795 by Carondelet. [This claim continued on page 271, Book G.]

p.215. Claim No.1041. Spanish gr. to Moses Lewis, 500 acres bet. waters of Bayou Sara, 40 mi. SE of Fort, b. by lands of Wm. Lewis. N. O. 22 Mch. 1795 by Carondelet. Plat shows Silver Creek adj. // Claimant, Moses Lewis, 23 Mch. 1804. Certif. A-287, issued to claimant, 7 June 1805. Wit: Daniel Whittaker, 11 Mch. 1805. Moses Lewis, actually a settler in Miss. Ter. on 20 Oct. 1795 claims 500 acres in Wilkinson Co. as in above grant from Spanish Govt. to him. S. Lewis agent for Moses Lewis.

p.217. Claim No.1042. Spanish grant to Azahel Lewis, 400 acres north of the Fort, b. on lands of Frederick Calvet and Miss. River. N. O. 28 Feb. 1795. // File. Claimants, the heirs of Asahel Lewis. Wit: Ebenezer Rees, 17 July 1805. Certf. A-444, iss. to legal representatives, 18 July 1805. Seth Lewis, one of the heirs at law of Asahel Lewis, decd., Sibyl Nash and Lavinia Lewis, two of the sisters and heiresses of sd deceased, Isaac Guion and his wife, Sarah, in right of the said Sarah, who is also one of the heiresses of the sd deceased, Archibald Lewis, Moses Lewis and William Lewis, nephews and heirs by representation of the said deceased, and Israel Dodge in behalf of his children, by his late wife, Theodotia, who was also one of the sisters and heiresses of sd deceased, claim 400 acres in Jefferson Co., Miss. Ter. 40 mi. above the City of Natchez, b. as in above grant to sd Asahel, decd. prior to 27 Oct. 1795. At the death of sd Asahel said land descended to the claimants afsd, part of whom, to wit, the said Sibyl, Lavinia, Sarah, Archibald, Moses and William were actually residents in the sd Territory on sd 27 Oct. 1795. (signed) Seth Lewis for himself and in behalf of the other claimants.

p.219. Claim No.1043. Spanish Govt. to Antonio Gras, 230 acres on St. Catherine's Creek, b. by Daniel Rayner, John Ferguson and Charles Boardman. N. O. 1 Sept. 1793, by Carondelet. (Cont. on p.276 Book G.)

p.221. Claim No.1045. Spanish grant to William Brown, 350 acres on Bayou Pierre, 40 mi. NE of Fort, b. by vacant lands. N. O. 1 Apr. 1789, by Miro. Plat shows Wm. Vousdan's line. // File. Claimant, Wm. Brown, 24 Mch. 1804. Rejected. (signed) Melling Woolley, agent for Brown.

p.222. Claim No.1044. Melling Woolley petitions Spanish govt. that he has no land in this government and wishes to establish himself; asks for 400 acres near Bayou de las Piedras (Bayou Pierre) with a frontage on the Miss. River, b. by Peter Bryan Bruin. 2 May 1795. Grant, N. O. 2 Aug. 1796, 400 acres, by Carondelet. // File. Claimant, Melling Woolley, 23 Mch. 1804. Rejected 17 May 1807. Miss. Territory, Claiborne Co., Melling Woolley, who was a citizen of sd territory 27 Oct. 1795, claims 400 arpents in sd co. on the Miss. River, by virtue of a Spanish order of survey and grant to him by Gov. Gayoso in 1796, at which time sd Melling was above 21 years of age and inhabited and cultivated sd tract of land. Plat shows Peter B. Bruin on north, William Smith on east, and other sides vacant.

p.223. Claim No.1052. William Williams petitions Spanish Govt. for land with which to occupy my negroes, 800 acres on a br. of Bayou Sara, adj. Mrs. Eunice McIntosh's survey and that of her son, James. 19 Dec. 1794. Above granted, N. O. 20 Aug. 1795 by Carondelet. // File. Claimant, Wm. Williams, 23 Mch. 1804. Wit: James McIntosh. Certif. A-648 to claimant, 2 Oct. 1805. Williams, who was on Oct. 27, 1795 an actual settler, claims 800 acres on a br. of Bayou Sara, adj. Dona Carlotta Trudeau, by virtue of the above grant. S. Lewis, agent for claimant.

p.225. Claim No.1053. Spanish gr. to James Kirk, 1930 acres on waters of the Homochitto, 12 mi. SE of Fort, b. by Isaac Gaillard. N. O. 10 July 1787 by Miro. // File. Claimants, heirs of James Kirk, 23 Mch. 1804. Wit: Ebenezer Rees and Seth Lewis, 17 July 1805. Certf. A-440 to legal representatives, 18 July 1805. John Kirk, one of the heirs, in behalf of himself and other heirs at law and legal representatives of James Kirk, decd., who was an actual settler on Oct. 27, 1795, claims 1930 acres in Adams Co., on Homochitto River, by right of a grant as above, which at the death of the sd James descended to the claimant.

p.227. Claim No.1089. Ebenezer Smith petitions the Spanish Govt. that he desires a grant of 500 acres on a br. of Bayou Pierre (described as Oho Bayou) adj. Daniel Chambers. Natchez, 29 Dec. 1787. // Grant by Miro, at N. O. 15 Feb. 1788. Plat by Vousdan of 500 acres on Tabor's Fork of the South Fork of Bayou Pierre, adj. Chambers. // File. Claimant, Abijah Hunt, 24 Mch. 1804. Wit: John Girault. Certif. B-294 issued 12 June 1807. Abijah Hunt gives notice that he claims 500 acres in Claiborne County, by order of survey from the Spanish Govt., as above, to Ebenezer Smith, who was then above the age of 21 years and the head of a family, etc. Said land was conveyed by sd Ebenezer Smith to Julius Smith by deed, 15 Feb. 1800, and by sd Julius and Pliny Smith to this claimant, 11 Sept. 1802. (signed) Elijah Smith for Abijah Hunt.

p.228. Claim No.1090. Spanish gr. to Richard Devall, 1500 acres on waters of Cole's Cr., 12 leagues from Natchez both by land and by water, b. by James Mather and vacant lands. N. O. 24 Dec. 1797 by Gayoso. Plat shows on east "lands formerly gr. to Alexander Boyd, now in possession of James Mather, Esq., through which Cole's Creek forks from the Mississippi." // Bk. G. p.191. Richard Duvall to

John Turnbull. Charles Norwood, executor of the late John Turnbull to Abijah Hunt and Wm. G. Forman, deed of conveyance, Norwood, of the Town of New Orleans, Prov. of La., by virtue of the last will and testament of said John Turnbull, decd., for $2250 to be paid by Abijah Hunt and William Gordon Forman, both of Miss. Territory, by their notes of this date, have sold, etc. 1500 acres granted to Richard Devall, as above, which same was conveyed by sd Richard Devall to sd John Turnbull 10 Jany. 1799. (signed) Chas. Norwood. 30 May 1802. Wit: John Murdock, Robert Moore. Prov. by Moore same date before Saml. Brooks, J. P. // File. Claimants, Hunt and Forman, 24 Mch. 1804. Rejected, 17 May 1807. Abijah Hunt and Wm. Gordon Forman, give notice that they claim 1500 acres in Jefferson Co., by virtue of a grant, etc. [as above.]

p.230. Claim No.1091. Spanish Grant to Dona Ester Eldridge, 400 acres on a br. of Bayou Sara, 40 mi. south of Fort, b. by David Eldridge and James McIntosh. N. O. 9 Mch. 1797, by Carondelet. // Bk.G. p.195. Deed from Abner Lawson Duncan, of Adams Co. Miss. Ter., and Esther, his wife, to Abijah Hunt, of Natchez, for $900, 400 acres gr. Esther Eldridge, now the wife of Abner L. Duncan. Both signed. 10 Apr. 1801. Wit: Daniel Tilton. // File. Claimant, Abijah Hunt, 24 Mch. 1804. Rejected.

p.233. Claim No.1092. Benj. Montsanto petitions Spanish Govt. that he wishes to build a house in Natchez for the residence of my family; asks for Lot 1, Square 3. 12 Jany. 1793. // Book G., p.198. Dona Clara Montsanto, widow of Benj. Montsanto, decd., petition the Govt. that she be allowed to sell above lot & timber for residence for benefit of estate. (signed) Claire Montsanto. (n.d.) // 5 Nov. 1794. John Scott and Frederick Man appointed to appraise same, by Gayoso. (Same valued at $350). 10 Dec. 1794. Public sale. Timber sold to Antonio Gras for $300. (signed) Antonio Soler, John Girault, John Bisland, J. McIntyre and Antonio Gras. (buyer and witnesses.) // Bk.G, p.200. 13 Oct. 1800. Antonio Gras, of Natchez and wife, Genevieve, to Abijah Hunt, for $3000, Lot 1, Sq. 3, granted to Benj. Montsanto, as above, with houses, outhouses, stables, etc. where Antonio Gras now lives. (signed) Antonio Grasse, Genevieve Grasse. Wit: James Beauvaise, Wm. Kenner. // File. Claimant, Abijah Hunt, 24 Mch. 1804. Wit: Thos. Foster, 26 Aug. 1805. Certif. A-541 to claimant, 26 Aug. 1805. Abijah Hunt hereby gives notice that he claims Lot No.1, Sq. No.3, in City of Natchez, by virtue of a gr. to Benj. Montsanto, 23 Jany. 1793, and sale thereof by Clara Montsanto, etc. as above. (signed) Elijah Smith for Abijah Hunt.

p.234. Claim No.1093. Spanish gr. to David Eldridge, 400 acres on a br. of Bayou Sara, 40 mi. South of Fort, b. by James Mather and Dona Esther Eldridge. N. O. 9 Mch. 1797, by Carondelet. // Bk.G p.204. David Eldridge, of Adams Co., Miss. Ter., to Abijah Hunt, 21 Sept. 1802, for $800, 400 acres, as granted above. Signed. Wit: Abner L. Duncan, John Leybourn. Prov. by Leybourn 25 Jany. 1804, before David Ker, Judge of Miss. Ter. // File. Claimant, Abijah Hunt, 24 Mch. 1804. Rejected. Abijah Hunt gives notice that he claims 400 acres by the above Spanish grant to David Eldridge and conveyance from same to sd Hunt.

p.236. Claim No.1094. Spanish gr. to John Reed, 200 acres on Fairchild's Cr., b. by John and Gabriel Griffin. N. O. 12 June 1788 by Miro. // p.237. John Reed, res. of Natchez, sells to Cornelius Shaw, for 3000 pounds of Agodon, recd., quit claim to above grant. 20 Aug. 1796. Wit: Jos. Vidal, John Girault. Signed. // Bk. G. p.207. 5 Dec. 1798, Cornelius Shaw and wife, Catherine, to Abijah Hunt, for $220 paid, tract, as above. Wit: Saml. L. Crawford, Wm. Stanley, Michael Crousas, J. Elliott. // File. Claimant, Abijah Hunt, 24 Mch. 1804. Wit: John Girault, 7 Dec. 1805. Certif. A-701 issued 7 Jany. 1806. Abijah Hunt gives notice that he claims 200 acres in Jefferson Co. by virtue of a gr. from the Spanish govt. to John Read, as above, and from said Read transferred to Cornelius Shaw, 20 Aug. 1796, and conveyed from Shaw to this claimant. Elijah Smith for Abijah Hunt.

p.238. Claim No.1097. Spanish gr. to James White, 1300 acres on Wells Cr. a br. of Homochitto, 14 mi. east of Fort. N. O. 20 Jany. 1795 by Carondelet. // Bk. G. p.218. 16 Mch. 1799, James White, Esq. of Southern District, Miss. Ter., to Abijah Hunt, for $325, 1300 acres as above. Wit: J. Girault, Wm. Scott. // File. Claimant, Abijah Hunt, 24 Mch. 1804. Wit: Wm. Thomas, 11 June 1806. Disallowed on suspicion of its being antedated, 12 Dec. 1806. Abijah Hunt claims 1300 acres in Adams Co. by virtue of a Spanish gr. to James White as above, and conveyance by White to this claimant. Elijah Smith for Abijah Hunt.

p.239. Claim No.1098. Petition of Hardy Perry to Spanish Govt. that he has a family of five and 10 negroes, asks for 600 arpents on Bayou Pierre and Big Black, b. by lands of William Henderson. 8 Apr. 1789. Grant to same, N. O. 18 Apr. 1789 by Miro. Plat and certificate. 600 acres, 8 miles above

Grindstone Ford, of Bayou Pierre and a small br. of sd creek, including his improvement. // Bk.G. p.222. 31 Jany. 1801. Hardy Perry, of Pickering Co., Miss. Ter. to Abijah Hunt, of Natchez, for $1000 paid, 600 acres, the above grant. Signed and ack. bef. Wm. Kenner, Jany. 31, 1802, Adams Co. Wit: Lyman Harding, James Andrews. // File. Claimant, Abijah Hunt, 24 Mch. 1804. Wit: John Booth. Certif. B-227 issued 6 Mch. 1807. Allowed as a donation. Abijah Hunt claims 600 acres in Claiborne Co. by virtue of a survey from the Spanish Govt. to Hardy Perry as above, who was above the age of 21 years and inhabiting and cultivating said land, and the conveyance from sd Perry to this claimant, 31 Jany. 1801.

p.240. Claim No.1099. Spanish grant to Daniel Chambers, 300 acres on South Fork of Bayou Pierre, 40 mi. NE of Fort, b. by Samuel Gibson. N. O. 30 Aug. 1793, by Carondelet. // Bk.G. p.226. 23 Feb. 1801. Daniel Chambers to Jesse Smith, for $700 paid, 300 acres, as above. Wit: Ebenezer Smith, Larkin White. Ack. before Geo. Wilson Humphreys one of the Justices of Courts of Gen Quarter and Common Pleas of Pickering Co. 23 Feb. 1801. // p.228. 5 Oct. 1801. Jesse Smith and Mary, his wife, to Abijah Hunt, for $1000, paid, 300 acres gr. to Daniel Chambers, as above. (signed) Jesse Smith, Mary (x) Smith. Wit: Daniel Burnet, Henry Hunt, John Gibson. Ack. bef. G. W. H. as above 6 Oct. 1801. // File. Claimant, Abijah Hunt, 24 Mch. 1804. Wit: John Girault. Certif. A-702, issued Aug. 1, 1806. Abijah Hunt claims 300 acres in Claiborne by virtue of a grant from Spanish Govt to Daniel Chambers, as above, etc.

p.242. Claim No.1111. Spanish gr. to William Lewis, 500 acres on waters of Bayou Sara, 40 miles SSE of Fort, b. by Moses Lewis. N. O. 20 Mch. 1795, by Carondelet. // Bk.G. p.244. 26 Jany. 1801. Wm. Lewis sells to Abijah Hunt, for $750, 500 acres gr. sd Lewis, as above. Signed. Wit: Ly Harding, T. Hutchins, Wm. Kenner. Ack. by Lewis bef. Wm. Kenner, 26 Jany. 1801. // File. Claimant, Abijah Hunt, 24 Mch. 1804. Wit: John Girault, 7 Dec. 1805. Wit: Thomas Young, 29 Jany. 1806. Disallowed on suspicion of its being antedated, 22 Dec. 1806. Abijah Hunt gives notice that he claims 500 acres in Wilkinson Co. by virtue of a gr. to William, as above, and his conveyance to sd Hunt.

p.243. Claim No.1113. Spanish gr. to Luis Faure 1000 acres on a br. of Cole's Creek, 12 miles from Fort Panmure, b. by John Fort*, Capt. Perret, Joseph Fort* and Nath'l. Kennison. N. O. 20 July 1796, by Carondelet. // File. Claimants, Thos. Freeman and John McKee, 26 Mch. 1804. Wit: Wm. Kennison, 1 July 1806. Certif. B-276 issued 17 May 1807. Thos. Freeman and John McKey hereby claim 1000 acres by virtue of a grant to Luis Faure from the Spanish Govt., as above, and conveyed by sd Faure to these claimants. // *These names usually spelled Ford.

p.245. Claim No.1114. Spanish gr. to Charles Carter, 450 acres, 24 mi. east of Fort, b. by vacant lands. N. O. 5 Aug. 1796 by Carondelet. Plat shows tract on east br. of Wells Cr. // Bk.G. p.247. 30 Dec. 1800. Chas. Carter and Piercy, his wife, to John Holland and Abijah Hunt, for $300, 290 acres, part of above grant. Both signed with a mark. Wit: Lyman Harding, Wm. Kenner. Ack. before Wm. Kenner, J. P. // p.250. 10 Feb. 1801, Charles Carter and Robert Carter to John Holland and Abijah Hunt, for $200 paid, 160 acres, part of 450 acres granted, as above. // File. Claimants, John Holland and Abijah Hunt, 24 Mch. 1804. Wit: Ezekial Perkins, 24 Aug. 1804. Certif. B-121 issued 4 Feb. 1807. John Holland and Abijah Hunt claim an undivided moiety of 450 acres by virtue of a grant from the Spanish Govt. to Chas. Carter, as above, Carter being then above 21 years of age and residing in the territory, etc. and conveyed from sd Carter to claimants as tenants in common. Elijah Smith for Abijah Hunt.

p.246. Claim No.1117. Spanish gr. to John Girault, 716 acres on Bayou Pierre, on south bank of main fork, b. by Daniel Burnet. N. O. 17 July 1890 by Miro. // Bk.G. p.263. 19 June 1803, John Girault and wife, Mary, for $3250 paid by Abijah Hunt, 716 acres, as in above grant, beginning at corner of tract formerly surveyed to Squire Boon and now in possession of Daniel Burnet. Both signed. Wit: Benj. Osmun, Seth Lewis, Elijah Smith. Ack. before David Ker, Judge. // File. Claimant, Abijah Hunt, 24 Mch. 1804. Certif. A-597 issued to claimant, 16 Sept. 1805. Abijah Hunt hereby gives notice that he claims 716 acres in Claiborne Co. by virtue of a Spanish grant to John Girault, as above, and conveyed by sd Girault to sd Hunt.

p.248. Claim No.1119. Spanish gr. to Caleb Potter, 540 acres 3 leagues from the mouth of Cole's Cr. N. O. 20 Nov. 1793, by Carondelet. // File. Claimant, Caleb Potter, 24 Mch. 1804. Wit: Wm. Fairbanks, 22 Oct. 1804. Certif. A-439 issued 16 July 1805. See Cochran's claims. Miss. Ter., Jefferson Co. Caleb Potter claims 540 acres on Miss. River above the mouth of Cole's Cr., by virtue of a patent by the Spanish Govt. to him, as above. Note: Half of this land sold by Potter to Geo. Cochran, 9 Aug. 1800. Cochran has filed the deed but it is not accompanied by any notice or plat.

p.249. Claim No.1120. Spanish gr. to John Murdock, 250 acres on a br. of Cole's Creek, 25 mi. NE of Fort, b. by lands of Robert Dunbar, John Murdock and Gabriel Benoist. N. O. 25 Mch. 1795 by Carondelet. // File. Claimant, Abijah Hunt and William Gordon Forman 24 Mch. 1804. Certif. A-613 issued 18 Sept. 1805. Abijah Hunt and Wm. Gordon Forman give notice that they claim 250 acres in Jefferson Co. by virtue of a Spanish gr. to John Murdock, as above, and from said Murdock to these claimants, 17 July 1802.

p.252. Claim No.1121. Spanish Govt. to John Murdock, 500 acres on north fork of Cole's Cr., 35 mi. NE of Natchez, b. by lands of Henry Green. N. O. 25 Mch. 1795 by Carondelet. // File. Claimants, Abijah Hunt and Wm. Gordon Forman, 24 Mch. 1804. Certif. A-638 issued to claimants, 25 Sept. 1805. Abijah Hunt and Wm. Gordon Forman claim 500 acres in Jefferson Co. by virtue of a Spanish gr. to John Murdock, as above, and conveyed from sd Murdock to sd claimants 9 July 1802.

p.253. Claim No.1122. Spanish gr. to John Murdoch, 500 acres 30 mi. NE of Fort, b. by Thos. Daniel and John Terry. N. O. 14 Aug. 1794 by Carondelet. // File. Claimants, Hunt and Forman, 24 Mch. 1804. Certif. A-637 issued 25 Sept. 1805. Abijah Hunt and Wm. Gordon Forman claim 500 acres in Jefferson Co., by grant to John Murdoch, as above, and conveyed by sd Murdoch to these claimants, 19 July 1802. Plat shows tract on a br of Cole's Cr.

p.254. Claim No.1123. Spanish gr. to John Murdoch, 400 acres on north fork of Cole's Cr. 30 mi. NE of Fort, b. by lands of Robt. Dunbar, Gabriel Benoist, and vacant lands. // File. Claimants, Hunt and Forman, 24 Mch. 1804. Certif. A-636 issued to claimants, 25 Sept. 1805. Abijah Hunt and Wm. Gordon Forman claim above 400 acres by virtue of sd grant and a conveyance of sd land by grantee to claimants, 19 July 1802. Grant, 14 Aug. 1794.

p.256. Claim No.1124. Spanish grant to John Murdoch, 500 acres on Cole's Cr. 30 mi. NE of Fort, b. by John Terry and David Ferguson. N. O. 14 Aug. 1794, by Carondelet. // Deed, 19 July 1802, John Murdoch, of New Feliciana to Wm. Gordon and Abijah Hunt, of Adams Co. for $2500 paid, the following tracts of land, (1) 500 acres, (2) 250 acres, (3) 500 acres, 400 acres, 500 acres, as in preceding claims. (signed) John Murdoch. Wit: Abner Green, Elijah Smith. // File. Claimants, Wm. Gordon Forman and Abijah Hunt, 24 Mch. 1804. Certif. A-635 issued 25 Sept. 1805. Claim as above.

p.258. Claim No.1125. Spanish gr. to Francisco Pousset, 1000 acres 14 mi. south of the Fort, 3 mi. east of Miss. River, on Bayou Willing. N. O. 12 Nov. 1788 by Miro. // File. Richard Butler, claimant, 24 Mch. 1804. Wit: John Collins. Certif. A-305 issued 12 June 1805. Richard Butler claims 1000 arpents in Wilkinson Co. by virtue of the above grant to Francis Pousset and conveyed by him to John Wall 500 acres thereof, 17 Aug. 1791. Release of mortgage by David Ross to sd Pousset 29 Oct. 1796, and conveyance from sd Wall to Joseph Pannell, of sd 500 acres, 20 Sept. 1796 and release of dower therein from the wife of sd Wall, 21 March 1801, and conveyance from sd Pousset to sd Pannell 1500 acres including the residue of the aforesaid 1000 acres, 20 Sept. 1796, and conveyance from sd Pannell and wife, of 1000 acres to this claimant, 25 Mch. 1801. Richard Butler by Lyman Harding, his attorney.

p.259. Claim No.1126. British Govt. to John Hartley, 200 acres on north fork of Second Creek, b. by lands of Isaac Johnson, William Johnston and James Barbut. Pensacola. 12 Nov. 1778 by Chester. // File. Richard Butler, claimant, 24 Mch. 1804. Wit: Bennet Truly, 8 Apr. 1805. Certif. A-161 issued to claimant. Richard Butler claims 200 acres in Adams Co., by virtue of a British gr. to John Hartley, as above, and conveyance of sd Hartley to Samuel Flowers, 28 Jany. 1789, and from sd Flowers to Chas. Boardman, 5 Apr. 1797, from Boardman to Geo. Cochran 2 Apr. 1799, and from Cochran to this claimant, 10 Nov. 1800, and bonds of indemnity from sd Flowers and Elijah Boardman to sd Cochran, 10 Nov. 1800. Richard Butler by Lyman Harding, his attorney.

p.263. Claim No.1127. Spanish gr. to John Hartley, 800 acres on Second Cr., b. by surveys to Mr. Stephenson, Mr. Cooper's son, Mr. Culberson, Samuel Heady and Mr. Harman. N. O. 25 Feb. 1785 by Miro. // File. Richard Butler, claimant, 24 Mch. 1804. Res. of Samuel Flower proved in No.1126. Certif. A-306 to claimant, 12 June 1805. Richard Butler claims 800 acres in Adams Co. by virtue of the above Spanish gr. to John Hartley and conveyed by sd Hartley to Samuel Flowers, 28 Jany. 1789, from sd Flower to Chas. Boardman, 5 Apr. 1797 and from sd Boardman to Geo. Cochran 2 Apr. 1799, from Cochran to this claimant, 10 Nov. 1800, and bond of indemnity as in preceding.

p.264. Claim No.1128. Spanish Govt. to Ezekiel Forman, 1000 acres, 41 mi. SSE of Fort, b. by Augustine Forman, son of grantee and David Forman. N. O. 30 June 1795, by Carondelet. // File. Richard

Butler, claimant, 24 Mch. 1804. Res. of Ezekiel Forman proved in No.1252. Certif. A-307 issued to claimant. Richard Butler claims 1000 acres in Wilkinson Co. by virtue of the above Spanish gr. to Ezekiel Forman, and conveyed from the executors of sd Ezekiel Forman to David Forman, and from Wm. Gordon Forman, exr. of will of sd David Forman to Joseph Forman, Jr., 30 Oct. 1800 and conveyed from sd Jos. Forman, Jr. to sd Wm. Gordon Forman, 1 Nov. 1800, and conveyance from Wm. Gordon to this claimant, 28 Dec. 1802. Richard Butler by Lyman Harding, his atty.

p.266. Claim No.1129. Spanish Govt. to Joseph Page, 720 acres on waters of Bayou Pierre, 48 mi. north of Fort Panmure, b. by Messrs. Green, John Hartley and Elizabeth Whittle. N. O. 13 Apr. 1790 by Miro. // File. William Morrison, claimant, 24 Mch. 1804. Wit: John Williams, 23 Feb. 1807. Certif. A-788, 4 Mch. 1807. William Morrison claims 720 acres in Claiborne Co. by virtue of a Spanish gr. to Joseph Page, as above, and conveyed by sd Page to Philip Rocheblane, 7 Feb. 1797, and from sd Rocheblane to Don Lafourcade, 8 Feb. 1797, from sd Lafourcade to James Dun, 29 Oct. 1797, and from sd Dun to this claimant, 25 May 1799. William Morrison by Lyman Harding, his atty. Conveyance from James Dun to William Morrison, Esq. is witnessed by J. Edgar and John Rice Jones, and James Dun, of Kaskaskia in the County of Randolph, Territory of the United States Northwest of the Ohio, to William Morrison, of same, for $600, by several conveyances vested in James Dun, having been orig. gr. to Joseph Page. // Transfer of Jean Lafourcade to James Dun, Esq. as above, of lands in Natchez and near Kaskadkia, for $600. Both of Co. of Randolph, Kaskaskia. // Conveyance from Joseph Page to Philip Rocheblade. I, Joseph Page, of Randolph Co., Territory of U. S. A. North of the Ohio, for 300 piastres, paid by Philipe Rocheblave of the village of Kaskaskia, 720 arpents in the Post of Natchez, confirmed to him by the Spanish Govt. Wit: C. W. Carbonneau, Pierre Richard.

p.267. Claim No.1130. Spanish Gr. to David McFarland, 400 acres, 40 mi. north of Fort, b. by Thomas James and William Smith. N. O. 30 Aug. 1795, by Carondelet. // File. David McFarland, claimant, 24 Mch. 1804. Wit: James Truly. 25 Sept. 1805. Certif. A-627 to claimant, 23 Sept. 1805. David McFarland claims 400 acres in Claiborne Co., by virtue of a Spanish gr., as above. By Lyman Harding, his atty.

p.269. Claim No.1131. Reuben Jelks petitions Spanish Govt. that he has no land and asks for a tract to correspond with his family, of three persons, on Bayou Sara, near Thomas Viles. // Grant for 240 acres on west fork of Bayou Sara, b. by Reuben Denham and Thos. Viles. N. O. 28 Mch. 1794. // File. Patrick Foley, claimant, 24 Mch. 1804. Wit: Thomas Viles, 9 Feb. 1805. Certif. B-140 issued 9 Feb. 1807. Patrick Foley claims 240 acres in Wilkinson Co. by order of survey by Spanish Govt. to Reuben Jelks, as above, he being above the age of 21 at the date of the order of survey, etc. and the sd land was transferred from sd Jelks to the claimant, 23 Feb. 1798.

p.270. Claim No.1132. Spanish gr. to Thomas Viles, who petitioned for land to support his family of three, asking for 240 acres on Bayou Sara, adj. Reuben Denham, who has had his land more than three years, desiring the land of Samuel Young who has been absent more than three years. 21 Aug. 1792. // Order of survey by Carondelet, N. O. 2 Mch. 1792. Plat shows 240 acres between Reuben Jelks and Reuben Denham and Patrick Foley. // File. Claimant, John E. Carmichael, 24 Mch. 1804. Wit: Elisha Hunter, 12 Feb. 1805. Certif. B-141, issued 9 Feb. 1807. Conflicting with No.56. John F. Carmichael claims 240 acres in Wilkinson Co., as above grant to Thos. Viles, etc. and conveyed to claimant by sd Thos. Viles and wife, 13 April 1801. By Lyman Harding.

p.272. Claim No.1133. Spanish gr. to Thomas Wilkins, 1000 acres on Buffalo Creek, b. by Wm. Vousdan and Gilbert Leonard. N. O. 22 Jany. 1788 by Miro. // File. Thos. Wilkins, claimant, 24 Mch. 1804. Wit: Nathaniel Ivy, 15 Oct. 1804. Certif. A-308 issued 13 June 1805. Thos. Wilkins claims 1000 acres in Wilkinson Co. by virtue of a Spanish gr. to him, as above. Ly Harding, his atty.

p.273. Claim No.1134. Spanish gr. to Wm. Henderson, 800 acres 6 mi. NE of Fort, b. by Estevan Minor, Charles Harwood. N. O. 12 June 1788 by Miro. Plat shows Cypress Swamp. // File. Claimant, Thos. Wilkins 24 Mch. 1804. Wit: Nath'l Ivy, 12 Oct. 1804; Jean Girault and Stephen Minor, 18 Feb. 1805. Wit: George Fitzgerald 10 Sept. 1805. Certif. A-596 issued to Thos. Wilkins and Stephen Minor, 16 Dec. 1805. Note: The conveyance from Vidal is to Minor and Wilkins jointly. T. H. W. Thomas Wilkins hereby gives notice that he claims 800 acres in Adams Co. by virtue of a Spanish gr. to Wm. Henderson, as above, and a sale thereof by order of the Spanish Govt. to Joseph Vidal and from Joseph Vidal to this claimant, 2 May 1794. Ly Harding, atty.

p.275. Claim No.1135. Spanish Govt. to Thomas Wilkins, 800 acres on Miss. River, b. by Wm. Henderson, 5 mi. NE from Fort. N. O. 1 Sept. 1793, by Carondelet. // File. Claimant, Thos.

Wilkins, 24 Mch. 1804. Wit: Nath'l. Ivy, 15 Oct. 1804. Certif. A-309 issued 13 June 1805. Thos. Wilkins claims 800 acres in Adams Co., by virtue of a Spanish gr. to him, as above. Ly Harding, his atty.

p.276. Claim No.1136. British Govt. to Major Robert Farmer, 3000 acres 12 miles SE of Natchez, adj. Capt. Amos Ogden, other sides vacant. Pensacola, 22 Sept. 1775, by Chester. // File. Claimant, heirs of Robert Farmer, 24 Mch. 1804. Reported, 28 Apr. 1807. Robert A. Farmer, Ann Bishop Barde, Elizabeth Mary Farmer and _____ Barber, children and heirs of Robert Farmer, deceased, claim 3000 acres in Adams Co., by virtue of a British grant to said Robert Farmer in his lifetime. By A. V. Barden/?/ atty. for said heirs. This land, from the plat, adjoins the Ogden Mandamus.

p.280. Claim No.1137. Spanish gr. to Daniel Harrigal; who pet. for land for his family of four on Sandy Creek, adj. William Lee, 20 Feb. 1783. Order of survey, N. O. 10 Mch. 1783, by Estevan Miro. Plat, Dec. 4, 1783 shows Hezekiah Williams, John Ratcliff and Beesley Pruett adj. // File. Lyman Harding, claimant, 24 Mch. 1804. Wit: Ebenezer Rees, 22 Aug. 1805. Certif. B-142 issued 9 Feb. 1807. Lyman Harding claims 300 acres in Adams Co. by virtue of an order of survey from Spanish Govt. to Daniel Harrigal, as above, who was then above the age of 21 years, etc. and conveyed, with wife, same to Littlebury West 4 Nov. 1799, who conveyed same to Abner L. Duncan and this claimant, 30 Nov. 1799 and released from sd Duncan to this claimant, 24 Feb. 1804. Ly Harding. // Indenture from Daniel Harrigal and Isabella, his wife, to Littlebury West, for $100, as above. Wit: James McMullen, A. L. Duncan. Also transfer from West and Tabitha, his wife, to Abner L. Duncan and Lyman Harding, for $150, 300 acres gr. to Harrigal, etc. Wit: Wm. Kenner, Lewis Evans. Ack. and proved.

p.281. Claim No.1139. British Govt. to Thomas Hutchins, Esq., 600 acres on the Homochitto River, 26 mi. NE from Natchez, b. by Luke Holmes. Pensacola, 21 Oct. 1774. // File. Claimant, Rhea and Cochran, 24 Mch. 1804. Order to be surveyed 26 Mch. 1806. Reported 28 Apr. 1807. See No.2627 or 2027. John Rhea and Robert Cochran claim 2/3 part of 600 acres in Adams by virtue of a British grant to Thos. Hutchins, now decd., for 600 acres, as above, conveyed by Thos. Hutchins's son and wife, devisees of sd grantee to the claimants for 2/3 part, 9 Dec. 1802. John Rhea and Robt. Cochran by Lyman Harding.

p.285. Claim No.1140. Thos. Thompson petition to Spanish Govt. that he has six negroes and is Carpenter at the Fort, asks 800 acres. 14 Dec. 1794. Decree for same, N. O. 15 Feb. 1795. Spanish grant to Thos. Thompson for 800 acres facing the first island above the Big Black, all sides vacant. N. O., 2 Dec. 1797, by Gayoso. // File. Claimant, Thos. Thompson, 24 Mch. 1804. Disallowed on suspicion of its being antedated. Dec. 22, 1806. Thomas Thompson claims 800 acres in Jefferson Co. by virtue of a Spanish gr., as above, at which time he was above the age of 21, said land being inhabited and cultivated 27 Oct. 1795 for use of sd Thompson then residing in the Territory. Lyman Harding for Thos. Thompson.

p.288. Claim No.1141. Margaretta Gallagher asks for 1000 acres on Bayou Pierre to employ her slaves. 6 Dec. 1794. Decree by Carondelet for same. [n.d.] // Spanish gr. to Margaretta Gallagher, 1000 acres between the branches of Cole's Cr., 35 mi. NE of Fort, b. by Dona Jacinto Gallagher, Wm. Daniel, Francis Jones and Job Routh. N. O. 2 Dec. 1797, by Gayoso. // File. Claimant, Margarite Thompson, wife of Thomas Thompson, claims 1000 acres in Jefferson Co. by virtue of a Spanish gr. to her, 2 Dec. 1795, when she was above the age of 21 years which was inhabited and cultivated for the use of sd Margaret Thompson. Lyman Harding for Margaret Thompson. Disallowed on suspicion of being antedated. Wit: Wm. Daniel. Survey Feb. 1795.

p.291. Claim No.1142. Petition of Jacinta Gallagher, that she has been in this Province more than 8 years and has 8 slaves she should like to employ; asks for 1000 acres on Cole's Cr. adj. Norsworthy Hunter. 17 Mch. 1794. // Decree by Gayoso, 18 Mch. 1794. // Spanish govt. to Jacinto Gallagher, 1000 acres on north branch of Cole's Creek, 35 miles NE of Fort, b. by Dona Margaret Gallagher. 2 Dec. 1797. // File. Claimants, heirs of Jacintha Vidal; Joseph Vidal, Jacintha Vidal, Daniel Vidal, children and heirs of Jacintha Vidal, claim 1000 acres in Jefferson Co., gr. to Jacintha Gallagher, as above. 2 Dec. 1797, surveyed 25 Mch. 1774, at which time she was above the age of 21 years. Lyman Harding for afsd heirs. Disallowed on suspicion of its being antedated.

p.294. Claim No.1143. Phoebe Calvet petition the Spanish Govt. that she wishes to establish a home for herself and sons; asks for Lot No.3, Sq.No.13, in the City of Natchez. 19 Sept. 1795. // Granted same, 24 Oct. 1795 by De Grand-Pre. // File. Claimant, Phoebe Dayton, 24 Mch. 1804. Wit: Benet Truly, 11 June 1806. Certif. A-782, issued to claimant, 20 Aug. 1806. Phoebe Dayton claims Lot No.3, Sq. No.13 in the City of Natchez by virtue of a grant from Spanish Govt. to this claimant, by the name of Phoebe Calvit, as above. Phoebe Dayton by Lyman Harding, her atty.

p.295. Claim No.1144. Spanish gr. to Patrick Gunnel, 240 acres on waters of St. Catherine's Cr. b. by Alexander McIntosh. N. O. 28 Feb. 1795. // File. Claimant, Patrick Gunnel, 24 Mch. 1804. Certif. A-615 issued to claimant, 18 Sept. 1805. Patrick Gunnel claims 240 acres in Adams Co., by virtue of the above grant to him. Lyman Harding, Atty.

p.297. Claim No.1149. Petition of Louisa Higdon, wife of John Wylie, for Lot No.4, Sq. No.26. Natchez, 24 Aug. 1795. To Spanish Government. // Granted. 3 Oct. 1795, by Grand-Pre. // Deed. 11 Mch. 1801. John Wylie and wife, Lavizay, of Adams Co. to John Stump, of Davidson Co., Tennessee, for $130, Lot No.4, Sq. No.26, gr. to Lavizay Higdon, wife of John Wylie. Ack. before Philander Smith, same date. Wit: J. Henderson, John Bolls. // File. Claimant, John Stump. 24 Mch. 1804. Certif. B-292 issued to claimant.

p.297. Claimant No.1156. British Govt. to John Hocombe, 667 acres on Homochitto Cr., as reduced master's mate in our Navy, 16 mi. south of Fort, b. by David Dickson. May 5, 1775. // p.302. Lease and release, 29th and 30th May 1775. John Hocombe, by Alexander Macullagh, to Richard Ellis, above tract, and another of 1333 acres, for ______. Wit: Samuel Lewis, Thos. Hutchins, Elihu Hall Bay. // File. Heirs of Richard Ellis, claimants. 26 Mch. 1804. Certif. A-405 to A. Ellis, assignee of John Ellis, the legal rep. of Richard Ellis, decd. of Miss. Territory, claim 667 acres in Wilkinson Co., on the Homochitto, founded on a British patent to John Hocombe, who conveyed the afsd tract to the above-named Richard Ellis, as above, the claimant having resided in Miss. Territory from that date to the present time. G. Poindexter for the representatives. Note: This land was devised to John Ellis, in whose name the notice ought to have been originally drawn. John Ellis sold to his brother, Abraham, to whom the certificate has issued. Thos. H. Williams, register. July 5, 1805.

p.299. Claim No.1155. Spanish Govt. to Wm. Chabot, 1600 acres, 12 mi. NE of Loftus Cliffs, adj. John Ellis, Sr. and a br. of Buffalo Creek. N. O. 7 July 1789 by Miro. // File. John Ellis, claimant, 26 Mch. 1804. Wit: John Collins, 11 July 1805. Certif. A-428 issued to claimant. Will of Richard Ellis filed with claim, dated Oct. 17, 1792. John Ellis, a citizen of Miss. Territory, Wilkinson Co., claims 1600 acres on waters of Buffalo, founded on a British patent to William Chabot, whose father, Claudius, as heir to patentee, conveyed the same to Wm. Collins, and sd Collins conveyed the same to Richard Ellis, father of present claimant, sd John Ellis.

p.308. Claim No.1157. Spanish gr. to John Ellis, 1040 acres on waters of the Houmachitto, 12 mi. SE of Fort, b. by John Lusk, Wm. Case, Richard Ellis and the lands on the British General Map as No.89 [Plat shows orig. grantee Jacob Winfree, bou. by Nath. Tomlinson.] N. O. 31 Jany. 1788 by Miro. // File. Claimant, John Ellis, 26 Mch. 1804. Wit: Robert Dunbar, 19 May 1804. Certif. A-312 to Abram Ellis, assignee of John Ellis, 30 June 1805. John Ellis, etc., claims 1040 arpents on the Homochitto, by virtue of a Spanish patent to him, as above.

p.310. Claim No.1158. Spanish gr. to Beesly Pruet, 400 acres on Sandy Creek, 12 mi. east of Fort, b. by Wm. Lee. N. O. 10 Mch. 1789 by Miro. // File. Claimant, David Havard, 26 Mch. 1804. Wit: Anthony Calvet, 27 Nov. 1804. Certif. A-310 to claimant. David Havard, of Adams Co. claims 400 acres by virtue of a Sp. gr., as above, to Beesly Pruett who conveyed same to claimant.

p.311. Claim No.1159. Spanish Govt. to William Tabor, 240 acres on Tabor Fork of Bayou Pierre, 40 mi. NNE of Fort, adj. Waterman Crane. N. O. 6 May 1795 by Carondelet. // File. Lewis Moore, claimant, 26 Mch. 1804. Wit: Ezekiel Harman, 1 Aug. 1804. Certif. A-311 to claimant, 13 June 1805. Lewis Moore claims 240 acres in Jefferson Co. on waters of Cole's Cr. by virtue of a Sp. gr. to William Tabor, which sd Tabor conveyed to present claimant, Lewis Moore.

p.313. Claim No.1221. Spanish gr. to John Minor, 400 acres on Bayou Pierre, 50 mi. north of Fort, adj. Elizabeth Whittle. N. O. 8 June 1792 by Carondelet. // File. John Minor, claimant, 26 Mch. 1804. Wit: Wm. Barland, 10 Sept. 1804. Certif. A-334 to claimant. John Minor claims 400 arpents on waters of Bayou Pierre founded on a Spanish patent, as above, to claimant.

p.314. Claim No.1222. Spanish gr. to Stephen Minor. 260 acres, 4 mi. NE of Fort, b. by Don Manuel Gayoso de Lemos, Samuel Gibson, John Bisland, Daniel Grafton and Polser Shilling. N. O. 6 March 1795. // File. Stephen Minor, claimant, 26 Mch. 1804. Wit: Wm. Barland, 10 Sept. 1804. Certif.

A-722 issued to claimant for 875 acres, 13 Jany. 1806. Stephen Minor claims 1114 arpents on the Miss. River and St. Catherine's Cr. founded on a Spanish patent to him, as above. [no explanation of the extra acreage.]

p.316. Claim No.1223. Petition of Estevan Minor to Spanish Govt. asking for 31 arpents, 63 perches, for garden, near Natchez, on north side of grantee's land and adj. Don Gayoso. N. O. 6 Mch. 1795. File. Claimant, Stephen Minor 26 Mch. 1804. Wit: Wm. Barland. 10 Sept. 1804. Certif. for this land issued to John Steel. See No.608. Rejected, 11 June 1807. Stephen Minor claims 31 arpents as in plat annexed to above petition, founded on a Spanish patent.

p.317. Claim No.1224. Spanish grant to Estevan Minor, following his petition for 12 arpens, 53 perches, 9 Oct. 1794 by Gayoso. // File. Stephen Minor, claimant, 26 Mch. 1804. Wit: Wm. Barland, 10 Sept. 1804. Certif. A-611 to claimant, 18 Sept. 1805. Claim as above plat and grant.

p.319. Claim No.1225. Spanish gr. to Bernard Lintot, 300 acres 5 mi. SE of Fort, adj. lands of grantee. N. O. 6 Mch. 1789 by Miro. File. Claimants, heirs of Bernard Lintot, decd., 26 Mch. 1804. Wit: James McIntosh, 18 June 1805. Certif. A-331 to legal representatives, 18 June 1805. William Lintot and Grace, his wife, Stephen Minor and Catherine, his wife, late Catherine Lintot, Samuel Fulton and Mary Fulton, his wife, late Mary Steer, formerly Mary Lintot, Hubbard Rowell and Sarah Rowell, lately Sarah Lintot, and Catherine Lintot, the legal representatives of Bernard Lintot, decd., claim 300 arpents founded on the above Spanish patent to sd Bernard Lintot, decd. //

p.320. Claim No.1226. Petition of Bernard Lintot to Spanish Govt. A resident of the parish of Manshaque [Manchac], his habitation is insufficient to maintain his numerous family of children, a large part of whom has already come of age of maturity, and to occupy abt. 20 slaves, whom the petitioner would like to use in the culture of tobacco, asks for 1000 acres in the Dist. of Natchez. (n.d.). N. O. 15 Feb. 1786. Order for same by Miro. [The petition in French.] Wm. Pountney and Sutton Banks, nearest residents to tract lately surveyed by Wm. Vousdan, Dep. Surv., testify that sd tract has never to their knowledge been under any degree of cultivation or claims. Natchez, April 1786. // File. Claimants, heirs of Bernard Lintot, 26 Mch. 1804. Wit: James McIntosh, 18 June 1805. Certif. A-332 to legal representatives, 18 June 1805. Same heirs as in preceding claim, claim 1000 arpents as in above, founded on a patent, 5 July 1786, to sd Bernard Lintot, decd., for the sd 1000 arpents. W. B. Shields, atty. for the representatives.

p.323. Claim No.1227. Spanish gr. to John Still Lee, 764 acres, 6 mi. ENE of Fort Panmure, adj. lands of ____ Fuller, Geo. Weigle, John Hartley, Carter Perkins, West Dewitt and ____ Armstrong. N. O. 20 Jany. 1793, by Carondelet. // Bk.G.310. 14 Mch. 1798. John Still Lee and Elizabeth, his wife, of Bayou Pierre, to Ebenezer Rees, for $2000, the 764 acres granted as above. Both signed and ack, 16 Mch. 1798, before Edward Randolph, J. P. Wit: Edward Randolph, Henry Milburn. // p.325. 30 Nov. 1801. Ebenezer Rees and Sarah, his wife to William Kenner, for $3251 paid, 764 acres, as above. Ebenezer Rees, S. Rees. Wit: James Ferrall, A. L. Duncan. // p.326. Quit claim deed, for $600, James McIntosh to William Kenner, to 450 acres on St. Catherine's Creek, conveyed, 22 Dec. 1794, by John Vauchere to Don Carlos de Grand-Pre and by sd Don Carlos de Grand-Pre to sd James McIntosh, 4 Feb. 1798 and for part of a larger tract purchased by sd John Vauchere at public sale of lands of John Still Lee, 20 May 1787. (signed) James McIntosh. Wit: John Minor, Lyman Harding. // File. William Kenner, claimant, 26 Mch. 1804. Wit: Wm. Barland, 10 Sept. 1804. Certif. A-333 to claimant, 18 June 1805. Proved in John Still Lee. William Kenner, a citizen, etc., claims 764 arpens of land on the waters of St. Catherine's Cr., founded on a Spanish patent to John Still Lee, as above, and a conveyance, 14 Mch. 1798, from Lee to Ebenezer Rees, as above, who with wife, Sarah, conveyed same to Wm. Kenner, the present claimant, 30 Nov. 1801. Note: A release from a James McIntosh for what he claims he has a right to, to Wm. Kenner 10 Dec. 1801.

p.328. Claim No.1228. Pet. of Joseph Vidal, Secy. for His Majesty, the Governor, asks for land near the city adj. Stephen Minor. 15 Oct. 1793. // Granted by Gayoso, 29 arpens and 57 perches, 25 Oct. 1793. // 30 Dec. 1797. Joseph Vidal to Stephen Minor the above 29 arpents, for $460. Wit: John Minor, Peter Walker. // File. Stephen Minor, claimant, 26 Mch. 1804. Wit: Wm. Barland, 10 Sept. 1804. Certif. A-606 issued to claimant, for 19 arpents, Sept. 18, 1805. Proved in Joseph Vidal. Stephen Minor claims 29 arpents in City of Natchez, founded on a Spanish patent to Joseph Vidal, as above, who conveyed the same to sd claimant, as above.

p.331. Claim No.1229. Spanish Govt. to Dona Rebecca McCabe, 51 perches under the hill, 2 Aug. 1796 by Gayoso. Assignment: For value recd., to William Lintot, all right, etc. to Lot in the Town of Natchez under the hill, 12 July 1798. Rebecca McCabe. // File. Wm. Lintot, claimant, 26 Mch. 1804. Wit: James McIntosh and Stephen Minor, 25 Nov. 1806. Certif. B-1437, 10 Feb. 1807. William Lintot, a citizen, etc. claims 51 perches in Town of Natchez on the River Miss. founded on a Spanish patent to Rebecca McCabe, as above, and conveyed by her to present claimant.

p.332. Claim No.1230. Spanish gr. to Hubert Rowell, for 850 acres, 54 miles from Fort, adj. Wm. Dunbar. N. O. 16 May 1791 by Miro. // 28 Feb. 1797, Hubert Rowell, of Baton Rouge, to William Lintot, Jr., of Natchez, 850 acres, as above, for $850 received. Signed by both. Wit: John Turnbull, Joseph Vasquez Vahamonde, Francisco Pousset, Peter Andrews. // File. Wm. Lintot, claimant, 26 Mch. 1804. Rejected. Wm. Lintot claims 850 arpents on waters of Bayou Sara, founded on a Spanish patent to Hubbard Rowell who conveyed the same, as above, to present claimant.

p.335. Claim No.1231. British grant to Ephraim Thornell, 100 acres on Second Creek, 10 mi. SE of Fort, adj. lands surveyed for Capt. Barbut. Pensacola, 12 Nov. 1778 by Peter Chester. // p.339. 28 Sept. 1798. Joseph Andrews, of Opelousas, to Elijah Cushing of the Township of Natchez, for $125 in hand paid, as executor of estate of the late Ephraim Thornell, decd., sells the tract above, 100 acres. // File. Elijah Cushing, claimant, 26 Mch. 1804. Wit: Jeremiah Routh, 11 June 1805. Reported 28 Apr. 1807. Notice of claim of Elijah Cushing for 100 acres in Adams, as described in plat and grant above, by purchase as above, from Joseph Andrews, executor and heir to the late Ephraim Thornell, decd.

p.340. Claim No.1232. British gr. to Ithamar Andrews, order of survey for 100 acres on Big Black, adj. lands advised to be granted to Abraham Knapp. Pensacola, 19 Nov. 1778 by Chester. // p.340. 3 Dec. 1798, for $100, Ithamar Andrews to Elijah Cushing the above grant. Wit: Jesse King, Israel Leonard. // File. Elijah Cushing, claimant, 26 Mch. 1804. June 11, 1805, Jeremiah Routh, witness. Rejected 26 April 1807. Elijah Cushing claims 100 acres as described in above grant by purchase from Ithamar Andrews, by whom it was claimed by virtue of a warrant from the British Govt. of West Florida, as above. Sd Andrews was the head of a family and above 21 years of age at the time of the survey, etc.

p.341. Claim No.1233. Petition of John Scott to the Spanish Govt. that he has a family and works as carpenter, asks 9 acres adjoining Joseph Vidal. July 3, 1794. Granted by Gayoso, 16 Feb. 1795. // 2 Nov. 1798. John Scott and Susannah, his wife, sell to Elijah Cushing for $200, lot above Natchez Town, near the River Bluff, 8 acres b. by sd Joseph Vidal and Stephen Minor. Both signed. Wit: John Hinde, Alex. Stacpoole. Receipt in full, same date. Wit: Christopher Miller, Wm. Coleman. // File. Claimant, Elijah Cushing, 26 Mch. 1804. Jeremiah Routh, witness, 11 June 1805. Certif. A-574 issued to claimant, 9 Sept. 1805. Elijah Cushing claims 8 arpents by grant from Spanish Govt. Sd Scott was head of a family and above the age of 21 years when the Spanish troops evacuated the territory.

p.343. Claim No.1236. Spanish Govt. to Richard King, 600 acres on north bank of the Big Black River, 70 mi., following the road, NW of Fort. N. O. 18 Aug. 1795 by Carondelet. // File. Claimant, Richard King, 26 Mch. 1804. Certif. A-138 issued to claimant. Richard King, a citizen of the Territory, etc. claims 600 acres by virtue of the above grant from the Spanish Govt.

p.345. Claim No.1237. Spanish gr. to James Morrison, 400 acres, 12 miles east of Fort, adj. Jeptha Higdon, Frederick Calvet, Benj. Newman, John Bowles and Charles Boardman. N. O. 19 April 1793 by Carondelet. // p.347. Petition of Richard King that he is the bearer of James Morrison's bond for $600 with interest since the time of its coming due and whereas sd James at the time of his departure from this country did have in his possession 400 acres as collateral security for sd debt; he prays that the same be valued and to save expenses, offers to take same in payment of the bond. 25 Aug. 1797. // Messrs John Bowles and Wm. Bishop appointed appraisers. They are neighbors and well acquainted with the land. (signed) Minor. 25 Aug. 1797. // Appraisal $450, 26 Aug. 1797. Wit: Wm. Bryan, Amasa Delano. // p.348. Natchez, 30 Aug. 1797. Capt. Richard King, having presented a legal bond due by James Morrison to sd King for $600 due 1st May 1793, right to the tract of 400 acres is transferred to Capt. King. (signed) Stephen Minor. Wit: Isaac Gaillard, John Girault. // File. Richard King, claimant, 26 Mch. 1804. Wit: John Bolls. Certif. A-335 issued to claimant, 19 June 1805. Richard King, etc. claims 400 acres by virtue of a gr. by Spanish Govt. to James Morrison and adjudged to sd Richard King for a debt to him due by sd James Morrison, as by the legal proceedings of the Government.

p.348. Claim No.1238. Spanish gr. to John Lum, 320 acres, 3 mi. NE of the Fort, adj. Robt. Dunbar, John Bisland, Chas. Boardman and Richard Harrison. N. O. 1 Dec. 1794. // File. Claimant, Richard King, for the heirs of John Lum, decd., 26 Mch. 1804. Wit: Caleb King, 31 May 1804. Certif. A-336 issued to the legal representatives of John Lum, for 180 arpents. Richard King as administrator to the est. of John Lum, decd., in behalf of the legal representatives and heirs claims 320 acres in consequence of a Spanish patent to sd Lum, as above.

p.350. Claim No.1239. Spanish grant to Robert Kidd, 200 acres on north bank of Big Black, 45 miles NE from Fort, adj. Richard King. N. O. 20 Nov. 1793 by Carondelet. // p.351. Petition of Richard King that he has a bond of Robert Kidd for $200 and whereas sd Robert Kidd at his departure from this country left in possession of a patent for 200 acres on the Big Black, as collateral, asks that sd land be appraised, etc. Natchez, 27 Jany. 1798. // Wm. Brocus and John Burnet appointed to appraise said tract. Appraisal $200. 5 Feb. 1798. John Burnet, William (x) Brocus. Right to tract confirmed to Richard King by Estevan Minor, 6 Feb. 1798. // File. Richard King, claimant, 26 Mch. 1804. Wit: Caleb King, 21 May 1804. Certif. A-139 issued to claimant. Richard King, etc. claims 200 acres by virtue of a Spanish grant to Robert Kidd, as above, and adjudged to sd Richard King for a debt to him due by sd Robert Kidd, as appears by the legal proceedings of the Spanish Government.

p.352. Claim No.1240. John Boles petitions that, having material to build a house and no land, he asks for Lot No.4, Sq. No.33. 29 July 1794. Grant of same by Gayoso, 8 Aug. 1796. // p.353. 18 Jany. 1798. John Boles to Richard King, for $50 recd., the land in this grant. (signed) John Bolls. Wit: Ebenezer Dayton, John Roberts before Estevan Minor. // File. Claimant, Richard King, 26 Mch. 1804. Wit: Caleb King, 31 May 1804. Certif. B-8 issued 2 June 1806. Richard King, etc. claims by virtue of a warrant of survey from the Spanish Govt. to John Bolls, as above, who was the head of a family and conveyed the same by deed to sd claimant. Note: There appears to be a mistake in the number of the Square. It should be 33 and not 34.

p.354. Claim No.1241. Petition of Prosper King that he desires to build a house in the New City of Natchez, asks for Lot No.3, Sq. No.33. 20 July 1794. // Granted 21 July 1796 by Gayoso. // 18 Jany. 1798. Prosper King to Richard King, for $50, the land in this grant. Wit: Francis Luse, Samuel Gibson. Before Stephen Minor. // File. Richard King, claimant, 26 Mch. 1804. Wit: P. Connelly, 12 Nov. 1804. Certif. B-9 issued 2nd June 1806. Richard King, by virtue of a warrant of survey to Prosper King, as above, who was on that day above 21 years of age and who conveyed the same to the present claimant by deed, as above.

p.355. Claim No.1242. Petition of Justus King to Spanish Govt. that he desires to build a house in Natchez, asks for Lot No.2, Square No.33. 20 July 1795. Granted, 21 July 1796, by Gayoso. [Grantee called Justus Cobun King in grant.] // File. Claimant, Justus C. King, 26 Mch. 1804. Wit: P. Conelly, 12 Nov. 1804. Certif. B-10 issued 2 June 1806. Miss. Ter. Justus Cobun King claims a lot in the City of Natchez, by virtue of a survey granted to him by the Spanish Govt., as above. He was an actual settler, 27 Oct. 1795 in sd Territory.

p.357. Claim No.1246. Spanish Govt. to Jacob Cobun. Plat and Certif. of survey by Wm. Vousdan, Dep. Surv. I do hereby certify that I have surveyed for Mr. Jacob Cobun 324 acres, 124 of which is the residue of a grant for 600 acres by Gov. Mirp and the 200 acres I have added thereto include Mr. Cobun's Mill, it being of the utmost utility to the inhabitants of Bayou Pierre, on Tabor's Fork, a br. of the South Fork, 40 mi. NE of Fort. 16 Apr. 1788. I sign the within to Elisabeth and Ann Cobun. (signed) Jacob Cobun. // File. Claimants, Elisabeth and Ann Cobun, 26 Mch. 1804. Wit: W. Crane, 19 Nov. 1804. Certif. B-63 issued 10 Sept. 1806. Elisabeth and Ann Cobun claim 324 arpents by virtue of a warrant of survey by Spanish Govt. in favor of Jacob Cobun, as above, and assigned to them, the said Jacob Cobun being at that time the head of a family and the said land was actually inhabited and cultivated on 27 Oct. 1795 for the use of the claimants, who on that day were actual settlers in the Territory.

p.358. Claim No.1247. Petition to the Spanish Govt. by Jacob Cobun of 476 acres. A resident of the Dist. he desires land which he finds vacant about 4 miles from Fort on Bayou Buffalo, 600 arpents. 20 Dec. 1786. // Order of survey, 5 Jany. 1787 by Grand-Pre. // Grant by Miro, N. O. 11 Jany. 1787. // Natchez Dist. Mch. 12, 1788. Finding that Zachariah Smith has an older grant for the above land, I hereby locate this warrant on Tabor's branch, a small fork of South Fork of Bayou Pierre, according to the custom of changing the location when there are two warrants for the same spot of land. Wm. Vousdan, Dep. Surv. of the Natchez District. // File. Claimants, E. and Ann Cobun, 26 Mch. 1804. Wit:

W. Crane, 19 Nov. 1804. Certif. B-64 issued to claimants, 10 Sept. 1806. Elizabeth and Ann Cobun claim 476 arpents by virtue of a warrant of survey in favor of Jacob Cobun, as above, and as in preceding claim.

p.359. Claim No.1248. Spanish gr. to Luis Valleret, 335 acres, 3 mi. east of Fort, b. by Samuel Swazey, Wm. Brocus, Dona Mary Girault, Abraham Mayes and Sarah Truly. N. O. 9 April 1794 by Carondelet. Plat shows St. Catherine's Creek bet. sd land and that of Mary Girault. // Sale. (n.d.) Luis Valleret to Hester Cobun, wife of Richard King, Capt. of the Militia, 350 acres on St. Catherine's Cr. adj. Ebenezer Dayton, James Glasscock, Mr. John Girault and Samuel Swazey. I have recd. at different times cattle and other property belonging to Ester Cobun, I wave and grant a formal receipt. (signed) Louis Valleret, Esther King, Richard King. // File. Claimant, Richard King, 26 Mch. 1804. Certif. A-140 issued to claimant in right of his wife, Esther. Miss. Ter. Richard King, etc. claims 335 acres by virtue of a grant by the Spanish Govt. to Louis Valeret and by sd Valaret conveyed to Hester wife of the present claimant, 3 Mch. 1794.

p.362. Claim No.1249. Spanish grant to Job Cory, 130 acres b. by Obadiah Brown, Ezekiel Dewitt. N. O. 8 June 1792 by Carondelet. // p.363. 23 Jany. 1794. Job Cory transfers above title to Adam Cloud, for which he has paid me. // File. Claimant, Richard King, 26 Mch. 1804. Certif. A-716 issued to claimant, 13 Jany. 1806. Richard King claims 130 arpents by virtue of a Spanish gr. to Job Cory, as above, by him transferred to Adam Cloud, and on 8 Aug. 1795 purchased by the claimant at the public auction thereof made by authority of the Spanish Govt. made by the exrs. of the last will and testament of sd Adam Cloud.

p.363. Claim No.1250. Spanish grant to David Forman, 600 acres, 40 mi. SE of Fort, adj. land of Ezekiel Forman, father of the grantee. N. O. 30 June 1795 by Carondelet. // p.365. Will of David Forman, of Chester Town, Co. of Kent, State of Maryland. To daughter Sarah Marsh Forman all my plate and household furniture, also all my house servants, for and in consideration of the tender care she has shown towards her mother, my beloved wife. The remainder of my estate to be divided into seven equal shares. It has pleased God to deprive my beloved wife, Ann, of her reason, 1/7 to remain in the hands of my exor. for her maintenance. To my son-in-law, William Gordon Forman and Sarah Marsh Forman, his wife, 1/7 of my estate. To my daughters, Ann, Emma, Eliza, Malvina and Elvina, each 1/7, etc. Son-in-law and dau. Sarah, Exrs. 30 Aug. 1796. Prob. Oct. 26, 1797. Wit: Phill Reed, Wm. Burneston, Ben Chambers. // File. Claimant, Wm. G. Forman, 26 Mch. 1804. Nov. 12. 1804, W. G. Forman suggests that he has no claim to this land but that it belongs to D. Forman, Jr. Wit: Nathaniel Ivy, 26 Nov. 1804. Certif. A-378 issued to D. Forman. Wm. Gordon Forman, surviving exr. of David Forman, decd. claims 600 acres in Wilkinson Co. subject to the uses and trusts declared and devised in the last will and testament as above, by favor of a grant from the Spanish Govt. to sd David Forman, decd. By Lyman Harding, his attorney.

p.369. Claim No.1251. Nathan Swazey and wife, Bethia, to William Gordon Forman, of Monmouth Co., N. J. for $1282 paid, 366 acres on Second Creek, part of a British grant to Amos Ogden and designated on plat made by Spanish Govt. b. by lands of the late David Forman, Samuel Swazey, Elijah Swazey and David Lambert. (signed) Nathan Swazey, Bethia (x) Swazey. Wit: Joshua Howard, Elias Fisher. Ack. before Joshua Howard, J. P. // File. Claimant, Wm. G. Forman, 26 Mch. 1804. Wit: Nath'l. Ivy, 26 Nov. 1804. Certif. A-557. Claims 366 acres in Adams Co. founded on a British gr. to Capt. Amos Ogden, etc. [The lower half of the paper torn away.]

p.371. Claim No.1252. Spanish gr. to Ezekiel Forman, 600 acres, 40 mi. SE from Fort, adj. Dona Frances Forman, sister of grantee. N. O. 30 June 1795 by Carondelet. // p.372. Last will of Ezekiel Forman, of Natchez Dist., May 7, 1795. Beloved wife, Margaret Forman, extrx. and friends, Wm. Dunbar, Ebenezer Rees and Benajah Osmun exrs. Joseph Bernard appraiser. Exrs. to be guardians of my dear children, (not named). Sept. 16, 1795. // File. Claimant, Wm. G. Forman for Ezekiel Forman, 26 Mch. 1804. W. G. Forman suggests that this tract of land is still the property of the original claimant. (signed) E. T. Nov. 26, 1804. Wit: Nathaniel Ivy, 26 Nov. 1804. Certif. A-379 issued to legal representatives of Ezekiel Forman, 26 June 1805. [One side of paper torn and parts missing.] Wm. Gordon Forman, executor of the last will and testament of David Forman, decd. hereby gives notice that he claims 600 acres in Wilkinson Co. subject to the uses and trusts expressed in the sd will, 30 Aug. 1796. By virtue of a Spanish grant to Ezekiel Forman now deceased and conveyed by the exrs of the will of sd Ezekiel Forman, decd. to said David Forman in his lifetime. By Lyman Harding, atty.

p.373. Claim No.1253. Spanish grant to James Fletcher, 1000 acres on Fairchild's Creek and Cole's Creek, 15 mi. NE of Fort, adj. Thomas Peterson, Robertson, John Reed and Gabriel Griffin. N. O. 9 Sept. 1788 by Miro. Plat and certif. of survey, 25 May 1796. // p.375. Power of attorney from James Fletcher to John Turnbull. N. O. 17 Dec. 1798. // Charles Norwood, of N. O. exor of the late John Turnbull sells to Abijah Hunt and Wm. G. Forman, for $1600, the above 1000 acres* granted to James Fletcher. May 31, 1802. Signed. Wit: John Murdock, Robert Moore. *This excepts 200 acres James Fletcher granted to have the land improved. // p.377. 10 July 1803. Abijah Hunt to William Gordon Forman, for $500, a quit claim to 800 acres, as above. Wit: Ly Harding, Elijah Smith. // File. Claimant, Wm. G. Forman, 26 Mch. 1804. Wit: James Stewart, 17 Dec. 1805. See No.1062. Certif. A-703 issued to claimant in 1806. William Gordon Forman claims an undivided 800 acres of 1000 acres by virtue of a Spanish grant to James Fletcher, as above, and conveyed from sd Fletcher to John Turnbull, 17 Dec. 1798, and by exr. of Turnbull to this claimant and Abijah Hunt, and released by sd Hunt to claimant.

p.378. Claim No.1254. Spanish grant to Augustina Forman, 600 acres 40 mi. SE of Fort, adj. Ezekiel Forman, father of grantee. N. O. June 30, 1795 by Carondelet. // File. Augustina Forman, claimant, 26 Mch. 1804. Wit: Nathaniel Ivy. Certif. A-380 to Augustina Forman, 26 June 1805. Augustina Forman claims 600 arpents in Wilkinson Co. by virtue of the above Spanish grant. By Lyman Harding.

p.380. Claim No.1255. Spanish gr. to Dona Margarita Forman, 600 acres 40 mi. SE from Fort, adj. Dona Frances Forman, sister of grantee, N. O. 30 June 1795, by Carondelet. // File. Claimant, Margaretta Forman, 26 Mch. 1804. Wit: Nath'l. Ivy, 26 Nov. 1804. Certif. A-380 issued to claimant, 26 June 1805. Margaretta Forman claims 600 acres in Wilkinson Co., by a grant from the Spanish Govt., as above.

p.381. Claim No.1256. Spanish gr. to Francisco (Frances) Forman, 600 acres 40 mi. SE of Fort, b. by Ezekiel Forman and Margarita Forman, brother and sister of the grantee. N. O. 30 June 1795 by Carondelet. Plat shows tracts on Bayou Sara. // File. Frances Forman, claimant, 26 Mch. 1804. Wit: Nath'l. Ivy, 26 Nov. 1804. Certif. A-382 issued to claimant, 26 June 1805. Frances Forman claims 600 arpents in Wilkinson Co., by virtue of a grant from the Spanish Govt. as above.

p.383. Claim No.1257. Jesse Greenfield petitions that he wishes to build a house in the New City and asks for a grant to Lot No.4, Sq. No.7. 3 Apr. 1794. // Grant by Gayoso, 10 Sept. 1796. // Assigns rights to above lot to Mr. Robert Dunbar for $150. 27 Apr. 1799. Signed. Wit: Ebenezer Rees. // File. Claimant, Robert Dunbar, 26 Mch. 1804. Wit: Job Routh, 24 Mch. 1806. The patent being too late, the claimant desires a preemption. Certif. D-45, Sept. 9, 1806. Robert Dunbar claims a lot in the City of Natchez, Lot No.4, Sq. No.7 by virtue of a patent from the Spanish Govt. to Jesse Greenfield, as above, who conveyed same to said Robert Dunbar.

p.384. Claim No.1258. Spanish grant to Ebenezer Rees. Petition and grant. He asks for Lot No.3, Sq. No.7, Apr. 8, 1794. Gr. by Gayoso 28 Apr. 1796. Assigns above to Robt. Dunbar, 28 Apr. 1799. Wit: George Cochran. // File. Claimant, Robert Dunbar, 26 Mch. 1804. Wit: Job Routh, March 24, 1806. The patent being too late, the claimant requests a preemption. Certif. D.46 issued Sept. 9, 1806. Miss. Ter. City of Natchez. Robert Dunbar claims Lot No.3, Sq. No.7 granted by the Spanish Govt. to Ebenezer Rees, as above, who conveyed the same to the sd Robert Dunbar.

p.386. Claim No.1263. Spanish gr. to Henry Green, 600 acres, 30 mi. east of Fort. N. O. 6 Apr. 1791, by Miro. // File. Claimant, Henry Green, 26 Mch. 1804. Wit: Wm. Atchinson, 21 Nov. 1804. Certif. A-283 issued to claimant. Henry Green, citizen etc. claims 600 arpents on north fork of Cole's Cr. in Jefferson Co. by virtue of a Spanish patent, as above.

p.387. Claim No.1264. Spanish gr. to Henry Green, 600 acres, 30 mi. east of Fort, b. by Maria Perkins. N. O. 14 Aug. 1793 by Carondelet. // File. Claimant, Henry Green, 26 Mch. 1804. Wit: Wm. Atchinson, 24 Nov. 1804. Certif. A-384 issued to claimant. Henry Green claims 600 arpents in Jefferson Co. on waters of Cole's Cr. as granted above.

p.389. Claim No.1265. Spanish gr. to Henry Green, 600 acres on north fork of Cole's Cr., 25 mi. NE of Fort. N. O. 1 Sept. 1795 by Carondelet. // File. Claimant, Henry Green, 26 Mch. 1804. Wit: Wm. Atchinson, 21 Nov. 1804. Certif. A-385 to claimant. Henry Green claims 600 arpents in Jefferson Co., Miss. Ter. by virtue of the above grant.

p.390. Claim No.1266. Spanish gr. to John Newton, 200 acres on Sandy Cr., 40 mi. east of Fort. N.O. 22 Mch. 1795 by Carondelet. // p.391. John Newton to Samuel Watson, for $170; the above 200 acres. John (x) Newton, Samuel Watson. Wit: Isaac Alexander, John Burney, Isaac Johnson. // File. Claimant, Samuel Watson, 26 Mch. 1804. Wit: Anthony Calvet. Certif. A-386 issued to claimant. Adams Co. Samuel Watson claims 200 arpents in sd Co. by virtue of a Spanish patent to John Newton and by him conveyed to claimant, as above, 23 Oct. 1797.

p.392. Claim No.1267. Spanish gr. to Benj. Fletcher, 150 acres on Sandy Creek, 18 mi. NE of Fort, b. by lands of Wm. Fletcher and Beesley Pruett. N. O. 24 Dec. 1797 by Gayoso. // Benj. Fletcher, bond for $1000 to be paid William Fletcher, to relinquish all claim to above tract. 26 Dec. 1798. Wit: Anthy. Hoggatt, William Calvit. // File. Claimant, William Fletcher, 26 Mch. 1804. Wit: Anthony Hoggat, 19 June 1805. Certif. B-130 issued to Philip Hoggatt, assignee. William Fletcher, of Adams Co., claims 126 acres on Sandy Cr. by virtue of a Spanish gr. to Benj. Fletcher and by him sold and assigned to sd William Fletcher, as above.

p.394. Claim No.1268. Spanish gr. to Waterman Crane, for 400 acres, 45 mi. NE of Fort, on a br. of Bayou Pierre, b. by Benj. Brashear. N. O. 1st Jany. 1793 by Carondelet. // File. Claimant, Waterman Crane, 26 Mch. 1804. Wit: James Harman, 20 Nov. 1804. Certif. A-387 issued to claimant. Waterman Crane claims 400 acres in Claiborne Co. by a complete Spanish grant to him, as above.

p.396. Claim No.1269. Spanish gr. to Waterman Crane, 750 acres on Bayou Pierre, 40 mi. NNE from Fort, adj. Peter Bruin and Ralph Humphreys. N. O. 14 Aug. 1794 by Carondelet. Plat also shows Darlington on south. // p.397. Proces verbal of sale of two lands of John Alston, confiscated by the King, 17 June 1782. (1) 800 acres on Second Cr. b. by Widow Coleman, Widow Engel and Isaac Johnson, adjudged to Richard Devall for $267. Item (2). Crane land, 500 acres on Bayou Pierre, adj. Thomas James and Mr. Simon, adjudged to Silas Crane, at $30. Buyers, assistants and other witnesses: (signed) Silas Crane, Richard Devall, Francis Farrell, James Harman, Abner Green, Thos. M. Green, John Bay, D. Smith, John Burnet, Cato West, Leson Lurcher and Frs. Germain with De Grand-Pre. // File. Claimant, Waterman Crane, 26 Mch. 1804. Wit: James Harman, 20 Nov. 1804. Certif. A-422, to claimant, for 450 acres, 23 May 1805. Waterman Crane claims 750 acres on waters of Bayou Pierre, by a Spanish grant to him, as above. Notation: 300 acres of the within claim sold to Geo. Cochran to whom a certificate for that property has been issued. See Claim No.622 and Certif.241. Thos. H. Williams, Register. May 23, 1805.

p.399. Claim No.1271. Deed. Oct. 14, 1800. Patrick Connelly and wife, Priscilla, to Benj. Tyree, for $1000. Lot No.3, Sq. No.32, which was granted to John Cammack by Spanish Govt. 3 Aug. 1796; by deed to Thos. Tyler, and by Tyler to Peter Camus, 2 Nov. 1798, by Camus to Patrick Connely, 1 Oct. 1799. P. Connely, Priscilla (x) Connely. Wit: Richard King, James Nicholson. Ack. Before Hugh Davis, J. P. // File. Benj. Tyree, claimant, 26 Mch. 1804. Wit: Thomas Reagan, 26 June 1806. Certif. B-37. 28 Aug. 1806. Benj. Tyree claims above Lot in City of Natchez, by virtue of a Spanish gr. to John Cammack, as above.

p.401. Claim No.1270. Spanish gr. to Gasper Sinclair, 400 acres on Cole's Cr., 25 mi. NE of Fort, adj. Jacob Cable. N. O. 27 ____ 1789 by Miro. // File. Gasper Sinclair, claimant 26 Mch. 1804. Wit: Wm. Atchinson, 27 Nov. 1804. Certif. A-388 to claimant, 26 June 1805. Jefferson Co. Gasper Sinclair claims 400 arpents on Cole's Creek by virtue of a Spanish patent to him as above.

p.402. Claim No.1273. Robert Starke petitions the Spanish Govt. that he was born in Carolina, came to inspect this country, decided to live here; sent for his wife and four children and a large number of slaves; asks for a large place on Bayou Sara, 20 Sept. 1791. N. O. 2000 acres granted, 23 Dec. 1793 by Miro. // File. Claimant, Robert Starke, 26 Mch. 1804. Wit: Moses Johnson, 2nd Jany. 1805. Wit: Matthew Macculloch, 6 Jany. 1806. Rejected. Same land confirmed to James Mather. See No. 1782. April 1807. Miss. Ter. Robert Starke, a citizen of sd territory claims 2000 acres in Wilkinson Co. founded on a Spanish warrant of survey, as above, grant to him, etc. After raising two crops on the land, with five negroes, he was forcibly turned out of the premises by one James Mather, by procurement of Manuel Gayoso.

p.403. Claim No.1274. Deed. 9 April 1801. Job Routh, of Adams Co., Miss. Ter., to Thomas Tyler, for $120, 2 acres adj. the Town of Natchez, part of the plantation of Concord, which was conveyed to Job Routh by Wm. Lintot, the same date as above, adj. Stephen Minor, Job Routh, Wm. Barland and the Town of Natchez. Wit: Melling Woolley, Abner Green. // File. Claimant, Thomas Tyler, 26 Mch. 1804. Wit: John Henderson, 6 Aug. 1805. Certif. A-568 issued to legal representatives, 5 Sept. 1805.

See Nos. 1304 and 1220. Thos. Tyler claims 2 arpents of land adj. the City of Natchez on the Miss. River, founded on a conveyance from Job Routh, as above, being part of a plantation called Concord, containing 1000 arpents which was originally granted by the Spanish Govt. to Manuel Gayoso de Lemos, and which through several conveyances came into the possession of Wm. Lintot who conveyed. 9 April 1801, 244 acres of the 1000 arpents to afsd Job Routh, and out of the 244 acres Job Routh conveyed 2 acres to the claimant, as above.

p.404. Claim No.1275. Spanish gr. to Peter Camus, 800 acres on Cole's Cr., 15 mi. east of the Fort, adj. Robert Dow and John Bisland. N. O. 20 Aug. 1790 by Miro. // p.406. Deed. 2 Nov. 1798, Peter Camus, of Natchez, sells to Thos. Tyler, of same, for $800, 800 acres in above grant. Wit: John Girault, John Carney. // File. Thos. Tyler, claimant, 26 Mch. 1804. Wit: John Henderson, 6 Aug. 1805. Claimant's death suggested. Certif. A-477 issued to legal representatives, 7 Aug. 1805. Thos. Tyler, a cit. of Miss. Ter. claims 800 arpents founded on a Spanish patent to Peter Camus who conveyed same to claimant, as above.

p.407. Claim No.1276. Deed. 13 Oct. 1803. Arthur Cobb and Susanna, his wife, of New Feliciana Dist., Spanish Dominion, by attorney, Wm. Cobb, to Thos. Tyler, of Adams Co., Miss. Ter., for $350, all of Apple Island, lying in the Miss. River, in Adams Co., being the second island above Natchez about 12 miles above sd landing. Wit: Wm. Irwin, John B. Willis. // File. Thos. Tyler, claimant, 26 Mch. 1804. Wit: Geo. Fitzgerald, 6 Aug. 1805. Rejected, 21 Apr. 1807. Miss. Ter., Thomas Tyler claims 2065 acres comprising in the whole an island in the Miss. River commonly known as Apple Island, founded on a purchase made by Arthur Cobb at a public sale of the said island by Charles de Grand-Pre, Spanish Commandant of the District of Natchez, for a valuable consideration, 24 Jany. 1787, and a conveyance from the sd Arthur Cobb and Susan, his wife, of the same to the claimant, as above. Survey and plat of 160 acres made 29 Nov. 1804 on the lower end of Apple Island for the said Thos. Tyler and plotted from notes given to me by him. (signed) Patrick Marrin, teacher of English and Mathematics.

p.408. Claim No.1278. 4 Dec. 1798. Richard Trevillian of the Northern Dist., Miss. Ter. to Bennet Truly of the Southern District, for $168 paid, 336 acres on waters of Bayou Pierre. Signed. Wit: Silas L. Payne, Manuel Texada, States Trevillian. // File. Claimant, Bennet Truly, 26 Mch. 1804. Rejected 21 April 1807. Claiborne Co. Bennet Truly claims 336 arpents on waters of Bayou Pierre, by virtue of a warrant of survey from the Spanish Govt. to Richard Trevillian, who actually lived in sd territory on 27 Oct. 1795, and sold the sd tract to claimant. Land adj. Edward Rose and vacant lands.

p.410. Claim No.1279. Edward Rose petitions the Spanish Govt. that he has a wife and five children and asks for land on north branch of Second Cr. 23 Oct. 1794. N. O. 24 Feb. 1795, 400 acres granted by Carondelet. Plat shows tract on a br. of Bayou Pierre. // Edward Rose and Ann, his wife, sell to Silas L. Payne, 400 acres as in above grant, for $200. 12 May 1798. Wit: Margaret (x) Ganey, Mayry (x) Rose, Hannah Ganey. // p.411. Silas L. Payne, for value received, assigned and transferred to Bennet Truly above land. Signed. 24 Oct. 1798. Wit: Kf. Knox, Wm. Newman. // p.412. Deed. 23 Oct. 1798. Silas L. Payne, of the Southern Dist. of Miss. Territory to Bennet Truly, for $222 in hand paid, 976 acres on a br. of Bayou Pierre, 400 acres as above from Ed. Rose and 336 from Richard Trevillian and 240 acres from Daniel Finan. Silas L. Payne. Wit: Wm. Newman, Polly Truly. // File. Claimant, Bennet Truly, 26 Mch. 1804. Rejected 12 Apr. 1807. Bennet Truly claims 400 acres in Claiborne Co. by virtue of a Spanish warrant of survey, as above, to Mr. Edward Rose, who sold tract to Mr. Payne who sold the same to claimant.

p.413. Claim No.1280. Spanish gr. to John Fowler, 240 acres on St. Catherine's Cr., 12 mi. east of Fort, b. by Dennis Collins. N. O. 28 Feb. 1795 by Carondelet. // File. Claimant, John Fowler, 26 Mch. 1804. Wit: Alexander Montgomery, 21 Aug. 1804. Certif. A-384 issued to legal representatives of John Fowler, 26 June 1805. Daniel Fowler, heir and legal representative of John Fowler, decd., claims 240 acres in Adams County, by virtue of a Spanish grant to sd John Fowler, as above, who died intestate and the said Daniel Fowler, therefore claims as heir and legal representative.

p.414. Claim No.1281. John Read petitions the Spanish Govt. for Lot No.2, Sq. 32. 4 Oct. 1794. // Granted 24 Feb. 1796 by Grand-Pre. // p.415. 26 Mch. 1804. James McGuire to James Gormeley and Edward Paine, for $327, in hand paid, the southern half of Lot No.2, Sq. No.32, granted to John Reed, 24 Feb. 1796 and from John Read to James McGuire, 3 Sept. 1803. Wit: P. Connely, Jno. Cammack. // File. Claimant, Gormeley and Paine, 27 Mch. 1804. Wit: Wm. Barland, 11 June 1806. Certif. B-39 issued 28 Aug. 1806. James Gormeley and Edward Paine claim half of Lot No.2, Sq. 32 in the City of Natchez, by virtue of a Spanish gr. to John Read, and by him to James McGuire, 2 Sept. 1803, and by McGuire by deed to claimants.

p.416. Claim No.1285. Spanish gr. to Jacob Cobb, 350 acres, on branch of Sandy Cr. 18 mi. east of Fort, adj. William Calvet. N. O. 1 April 1795, by Carondelet. // p.418. Jacob Cobb and Rachel, his wife, 3 July 1801, to John Spires, for $900 in hand paid, 350 acres gr. to Cobb, as above. (signed) Jacob Cobb, Rachel (x) Cobb. Wit: Anthony Hoggat, Nathan Hoggatt. [No file.]

p.420. Claim No.1286. Sale. John Tally, Sr., to John Tally, Jr., 640 acres on Morgan's Fork of the Homochitto, Miss. Ter., where I have lately resided, between the claim of Christopher Bingaman and lands gr. to Wm. Kennison. I have recd. full satisfaction for same. John (X) Tally. 16 June 1803. Wit: Wm. Lee, Pearson Wells. p.421. Hezekiah Williams, late of Natchez, to John Tally, Sr. 640 acres, as above, for which I have recd. full satisfaction. (signed) Hezekiah Williams. Wit: David B. Morgan, Hezekiah Williams. // I hereby assign all my right to John Tally, Jr., and have recd. $300 for the land. Same witnesses. // File. Claimant, John Tally, Jr., 27 Mch. 1804. Wit: Thos. Ford. Certif. B-202 issued 13 Feb. 1807. John Tally, Jr. claims a donation of 640 acres on waters of the Homochitto, as above, founded on the habitation and cultivation of the premises claimed by Hezekiah Williams or some person for his use, from 1794 until 18 June 1803, when he sold the same to his son, John Tally, Jr. in 1803, who has occupied the land ever since.

p.421. Claim No.1287. Agreement. William Smith and John Burns. 30 Nov. 1803. William Smith assigns 640 acres on North Fork of Cole's Creek adj. Christopher Harkless and the place whereon William Smith now lives. The condition is that if sd John Burns does not pay to Smith within six months from date $30, then the above obligation is void. Wm. (L) Smith, John Burns. // File. Claimant, John Burns, 27 Mch. 1804. Rejected for want of evidence. John Burns claims preemption on 100 acres in Jefferson Co. which he purchased of William Smith who inhabited and cultivated in November 1802.

p.422. Claim No.1289. Spanish gr. to Mordecai Richards, 600 acres on Crooked Creek, a br. of the Homochitto, adj. Nathan Swazey. N. O., 24 Dec. 1797, by Gayoso. [No file.]

p.423. Claim No.1290. Spanish gr. to William Vardaman, 300 acres, on north br. of the Homochitto, 28 mi. east of Fort, b. by William Calvet and Monsieur Vaucheret. N. O. 24 Dec. 1797 by Gayoso. // File. Claimant, Stephen Henderson, 27 Mch. 1804. Rejected, 21 April 1807. Stephen Henderson claims 300 arpents by virtue of a warrant of survey from the Spanish Govt. as above, to Wm. Vardaman who was head of a family and settled and cultivated the sd tract before 27 Oct. 1795, and conveyed it to Ebenezer Rees, 7 Feb. 1797, and by sd Rees to Ferguson and Woolley 8 Sept. 1801, who conveyed it to James Ferrall, 1 Oct. 1802, who conveyed it to the claimant, 14 Feb. 1803. Arthur Andrews for Stephen Henderson.

p.425. Claim No.1291. James Wiley petitions to the Spanish Govt. that he wishes to establish himself and family in the New City and asks for lot. 19 July 1793. // Certificate of survey of Lot No.1, Sq. No.32, 10th ______ 1794 by Wm. Dunbar. // p.425. 15 May 1799. James Wiley and his wife, Eleanor, of Natchez, for $400 paid, to John Holland, Lot No.1, 150 ft square in Sq. No.32 on Main St. from Church to St. Catherine's. Jas. Wiley, Eleanor (X) Wiley. Wit: J. Elliott, John Wells, Hardy Ellis, P. Connely. // p.426. 10 Feb. 1803. Whereas John Wells, Sr., complained on oath to Samuel Brooks, one of the Justices of Adams Co. on 10 May 1802 that John Holland, an absconded debtor, was justly indebted to him in sum of $211.25, with legal interest, the sd John Wells having given bond, the sheriff attached the estate of John Holland and found that he had one lot with two houses on it, Lot No.1, Sq. No.32 on Main St., which was advertised according to law and sold to the highest bidders, Stephen Henderson and Arthur Andrews for $470. The sheriff herewith confirms the transfer to the above lot and houses. (signed) William Brooks. Wit: Peter Walker, Jr. Lyman Harding. // File. Claimants, Henderson and Andrews, 27 Mch. 1804. Wit: Nathan Dix, 12 June 1806. Certif. B-38 issued 28 Aug. 1806. Stephen Henderson and Arthur Andrews claim a lot in the City of Natchez, Lot No.1, Sq. No.32, claimed by James Wiley by virtue of a settlement thereon by the building thereon by sd James Wiley and conveyed by him and his wife to John Holland and to the sd Stephen Henderson and Arthur Andrews by William Brooks, Esq. as sheriff of Adams Co., as above, being the highest bidders at public sale of sd lot.

p.428. Claim No.1292. Samuel Heady petitions the Spanish Govt. that, in 1779, he bought from an Englishman who was living in this country 250 acres with the English title which was lost in the revolution of this government, since which Gov. Miro granted me 400 acres on Sandy Cr. and having discovered vacant land near this tract, he begs for a title of 650 acres to cultivate . . . and horses that I have. This land is on Second Cr. adj. Melling Woolley, Samuel Flower and Robert Abrams. 5 Sept. 1793. //

Grant by Carondelet, 15 Sept. 1793. // File. Claimant, Samuel Heady, 27 Mch. 1804. Wit: Joshua Howard, 2 Sept. 1806. Certif. B-131, 1st Feb. 1807. Samuel Heady claims 600 acres under a Spanish warrant of survey and improvement made 25 years ago, the land adj. Wm. Dunbar, first gr. to Isaac Johnson, Richard Butler, first gr. to John Hartley, and Wm. Dunbar, Jr., first gr. to Peter Camus.

p.429. Claim No.1293. Spanish gr. to John Calvet, 550 acres on the waters of the Homochitto, 20 mi. SE of Fort. N. O. 27 Feb. 1789 by Miro. // File. John Armstreet, claimant, 27 Mch. 1804. Wit: Anthony Calvet, 5 Nov. 1804. Certif. A-418, 9 July 1805. John Armstreet claims 350 arpents by virtue of a conveyance 6 Dec. 1800 from John Calvet, to whom the same was gr. by the Spanish Govt. as above. Both have been settler in this territory for more than ten years past.

p.430. Claim No.1296. Miguel Solibellas petitions the Spanish Govt. He is 1st Sergeant of the 1st Co. of Grenadiers of La. Reg. of Inf., and with his family, he needs a house in the villa. 13 Feb. 1793. // Grant of Lot No.3, Sq. No.1 (or 7), 6 May 1793. // File. Manuel G. de Texada, claimant, 27 Mch. 1804. Wit: Peter Walker and Anthony Calvet, 8 July 1805. Certif. A-682 issued 19 Oct. 1805. City of Natchez, Manuel Garcia de Texada claims Lot No.3, Square No.2, b. by Second South St. and on north by Geo. Overaker, and Leonard Pomet on west, by virtue of a Spanish patent to Solibellas, as above, and by sale of same to Maurice Stacpoole, made by the Govt. to satisfy the debts of said Solibellas, who sold the sd lot to this claimant.

p.431. Claim No.1297. Deed. 25 Sept. 1802. Francis Jones, of Wilkinsburgh, Wilkinson Co., to John Wall, for $102, in hand paid, Lot No.5, in town of Wilkinsburgh, joining Lot No.4 and the cross street and fronting on Main St. Signed. Wit: Gabriel Bailey, Will Jones. // p.433. 27 Sept. 1802. Francis Jones to John Wall, for $150, Lot No.7, in Wilkinsburgh, adj. Lot 8 and side street. Same wit. // File. John Wall, claimant, 27 Mch. 1804. Rejected, 12 June 1807. John Wall claims two lots in the town of Wilkinsburgh, Wilkinson Co. by virtue of two deeds of conveyance made as above.

p.434. Claim No.1298. 10 Mch. 1801. Thos. Dawson and Elizabeth, his wife, to John Wall, for $25, lot in town of Pinckneyville, Nos. 34 and 36. Both signed. Wit: Wm. Miller, John Kean. // p.435. Receipt for $255 for above lots, same date and witnesses. Signed. // p.436. Same date, for $25, Thos. Dawson and wife, Eliz. to John Wall, lot No.40 in Pinckneyville. Signed. // File. John Wall, claimant, 27 Mch. 1804. Certif. B-118, Feb. 4, 1805. See No.731. John Wall, etc. claims two acres of land in the town of Pinckneyville, Wilkinson Co. by virtue of three deeds, as above.

p.439. Claim No.1303. Spanish gr. to John Stampley. 27 Jany. 1783. In virtue of a mandate from Gov. Miro, Col. of Reg. of La., etc. we have gr. to John Stampley 158 acres adj. Peter Pearnas, His Majesty's lands of Fort Panmure, Francis Spain, John Rawls and San Germain, interpreter for the Indians. N. O. 4 June 1785 by Miro. // File. Job Routh, claimant, 27 Mch. 1804. Wit: John Girault, May 13, 1805. Certif. A-265 issued 5 Sept. 1805. Miss. Ter. Job Routh claims 158 arpents near the City of Natchez, founded on a Spanish patent to John Stampley, as above, who conveyed to the present claimant by deed dated 6 Sept. 1794. Signed.

p.439. Claim No.1306. Spanish gr. to John Rault (Routh), for 170 acres, adj. John Stampley, John Lusk, George Rapalje and Frank Spain. N. O. 15 May 1795, by Carondelet. // File. Job Routh and Jeremiah Routh, claimants, 27 Mch. 1804. Certif. A-651 issued to claimants for 83 arpents, Oct. 2, 1805. Miss. Ter. Job Routh claims 170 arpents on waters of St. Catherine Cr., founded on a Spanish gr. to John Routh after his death but the warrant of survey was made between the years 1780 and 1790 and in his lifetime he sold the said tract for a valuable consideration to John Fourney, who took possession of the same and in a short time sold it to Mark Iler, who inhabited and cultivated it for several years, about until 1789, when and where he died and then Jonas Iler, the legal representative of sd Mark, with the consent of all parties concerned, herein named, sold the land, now claimed to the present claimant, in June 1793. The conveyance of the same tract was made by Margaret Coleman, formerly Margaret Routh, the widow and relict of the said John Routh, and the patent was delivered in conformity of the parties afsd. The present claimant has inhabited and cultivated the said tract ever since the year 1793. // *Miss. Ter. Job and Jeremiah Routh, citizens of the sd Territory, claim 170 arpents in Adams Co. founded on a Spanish patent to John Routh, 15 May 1795, and the said John Routh having departed this life, the above-mentioned tract was conveyed to the present claimants by Margaret Coleman, formerly Margaret Routh, wid. and relict of the sd John, and extx. of his will and testament by and with the knowledge and consent of John Routh, heir-at-law of John Rault, decd. 23 Oct. 1797.
*Job Routh's notice amended by order of the Board.

p.440. Claim No.1307. Spanish gr. to Adam Bingaman, 1040 acres on Bayou Sara, 35 mi. south of Fort, adj. John O'Reilly and Wm. Dunbar, (500 acres of Martin Smith, 240 arpents of Jacob Jarrey and 300 acres to grantee, 13 Apr. 1791.) N. O. 3 Sept. 1793, by Carondelet. // File. Claimant, Adam Bingaman, 27 Mch. 1804. Wit: Wm. Atchinson, 25 Sept. 1804. Certif. A-317 issued 17 June 1805. Adam Bingaman claims 1040 acres grant to him by the Spanish Govt., as above, improved previous to year 1795.

p.442. Claim No.1308. Spanish gr. to Adam Bingaman, 500 acres 4 mi. SSE of Fort, b. by David Williams, Lewis Bingaman, Richard Thompson and Daniel Clark by virtue of . . . in favor of grantee . . . Henry LaFleur who had the said land of the British Government. May 15, 1789, N. O. by Miro. Plat, Apr. 25, 1789, shows land gr. to Richard Thompson now in possession of William Smith, gr. to Daniel Clarke, Esq. sold to Mr. Hiorn and Noble Taylor. // File. Claimant, Adam Bingaman, 27 Mch. 1804. Certif. A-318 to cl. Adam Bingaman claims 500 acres granted to him as above.

p.443. Claim No.1309. Sale. 6 Mch. 1780. Jacob Harman to Silas Crane, the right to a plantation called the Fort land and now in my actual possession. Wit: John Shunk, John Lovelace. // p.444. 24 Feb. 1790. Waterman Crane to Wm. Groden, 110 acres with house (old) adj. Mrs. McIntosh, Mr. Bingaman and Matthew White, for $100 paid. Groding signs in German, Waterman Crane. Wit: Antonio Soler, John Carreras before Grand-Pre. // 9 Mch. 1791. Deed. William Grodin to Adam Bingaman 96 acres. Both signed. Joseph Vidal, Valentin Rincon. // File. Claimant, Adam Bingaman, 27 Mch. 1804. Certif. Adam Bingaman claims 96 arps. Original Claimant, Jacob Harmon, by him to Silas Crane, 6 Mch. 1780; by Waterman Crane, heir of sd Silas to William Grodinger, as above, and sd Grodinger to sd Bingaman, 3 miles east of Natchez.

p.445. Claim No.1312. Spanish gr. to Adam Bingaman, 858 acres on waters of St. Catherine's Cr., adj. Benj. Mark Oiler, Lewis Bingaman, grantee, Michael, Baker and Coleman. N. O. 15 May 1787 by Miro. Plat shows "the corner of 500 acres formerly gr. to Mr. Alexander McIntosh," also 500 acres in the name of Richard Thompson. // File. Claimant, Adam Bingaman, 27 Mch. 1804. Wit: Wm. Atchinson, 25 Sept. 1804. Certif. A-319 issued June 17, 1805. Res. proved 25 Sept. 1804. Adam Bingaman claims 858 arpents of land originally in five different tracts afterwards connected into one granted to him by a Spanish patent, as above. (1) 325 acres from Alexander McIntosh, (2) 190 surveyed for Alexander McIntosh, (3) 83 acres surveyed for Alexander McIntosh, (4) originally surveyed for S. Minor, 165 acres, (5) 95 acres originally surveyed for J. Coleman.

p.448. Claim No.1313. Spanish gr. to Lewis Bingaman, 500 acres 6 mi. SE of Fort, adj. Adam Bingaman. N. O. May 15, 1787 by Miro. // File. Claimant, Lewis Bingaman, 27 Mch. 1804. Wit: Wm. Atchinson, 25 Sept. 1804. Certif. A-320 issued 17 June 1805. Lewis Bingaman claims 200 arpents granted to him as above.

p.448. Claim No.1314. Spanish gr. to Mark Oiler, 101 arps. 3 mi. east of Natchez, adj. Silas Crane, Stephen Minor and Adam Bingaman. N. O. 13 Feb. 1797 by Miro. // p.450. Jonas Oiler to Wm. Groding, 100 acres adj. Adam Bingaman and Mrs. McIntosh, for $200. Natchez 1789. Wit: Lewis Bingaman, Thos. Irwin. // William Groding to Adam Bingaman right to the above land. Natchez, 8 Feb. 1791. Wit: Thos. Irwin. // File. Claimant, Adam Bingaman, 27 Mch. 1804. Wit: Wm. Atchinson. Cert. A-490 to cl. Adam Bingaman claims 110 arps gr. to Mark Oiler, as above, by Jonas Oiler to Wm. Groding, by him to sd claimant.

p.450. Claim No.1315. Daniel Clark to George Denshire Banks, 25 Aug. 1800, for respect, love and affection and $5.00, 500 acres in Adams Co., Miss. Ter., 2 1/2 mi. below the town of Natchez granted to Colo. Daniel Clark by British Govt. Signed. Wit: William Cook, William Dunbar. // File. Claimant, Geo. D. Banks, 27 Mch. 1804. Wit: Wm. Atchinson, 25 Sept. 1804. Certif. A-770 issued 15 May 1806. George D. Banks claims 500 arpents gr. to Col. Daniel Clark by the British Govt. and conveyed by Danl. Clark Jr. to sd Banks, as above.

p.452. Claim No.1316. Spanish gr. to Adam Bingaman, 80 ft. by 120 ft, 16 perches west from Fort. N. O. 15 May 1789 by Miro. // File. Claimant, Adam Bingaman, 27 Mch. 1804. Wit: Wm. Atchinson, 25 Sept. 1804. Certif. A-321 issued for 9600 ft, 17 June 1805. Adam Bingaman claims a lot 80 ft front by 150 ft deep between the old Fort of Natchez and the landing granted to him as above.

p.453. Claim No.1317. Spanish gr. to Adam Bingaman 1000 arpents on St. Catherine's Cr. 5 mi. SE of Natchez, b. by Alex. McIntosh, Richard Thomson and Henry Lafleur. N. O. 8 Mch. 1788 by Miro. // File. Claimant, Adam Bingaman, 27 Mch. 1804. Wit: Wm. Atchinson, 25 Sept. 1804. Certif. A-322 issued 17 June 1805. Adam Bingaman claims 1000 arpents granted to him by the Spanish Govt. as above.

p.454. Claim No.1318. Spanish gr. to Christian Bingaman, 450 acres on waters of St. Catherine's Cr. 4 mi. SE of Fort, b. by lands of Hiorn & Taylor, David Williams and Mr. Bingaman. N. O. 8 Mch. 1788 by Miro. // File. Claimant, Adam Bingaman, 27 Mch. 1804. Wit: Wm. Atchinson, 25 Sept. 1804. Certif. A-631 issued 24 Sept. 1805. Adam Bingaman claims 450 arps. granted to Christian Bingaman, Sr., as above, and purchased of the sd C. Bingaman for a val. consideration by claimant.

p.456. Claim No.1380. Spanish gr. to Stephen Cole, 300 acres, 18 mi. NE of Fort on SE fork of Cole's Cr. N. O. 8 Mch. 1792, by Carondelet. // File. Claimant, William Thomas, 28 Mch. 1804. Certif. A-616 issued 18 Sept. 1805. William Thomas claims 300 arpents by virtue of a grant to Stephen Cole and by him conveyed, 12 Feb. 1798 to Solomon Cole and by sd Solomon Cole to present claimant, 14 March 1798.

p.457. Claim No.1381. Spanish gr. to Jacob Silling (Shilling), 500 acres on Cole's Cr. 20 ESE of Fort, adj. Wm. Bell. N. O. 24 Dec. 1797 by Gayoso. // File. Claimant, Jesse Harper, 28 Mch. 1804. Wit: Wm. Thomas, 2 July 1805. Certif. C-8, 3 Feb. 1807. Conflicting with No.900 and No.976.

p.459. Claim No.1383. Deed. 20 Jany. 1804. William Nicholson, of Wilkinson Co., to Henry Phipps, for $50 paid, tract of vacant land settled and claimed by Nicholson, b. by gr. to Matthew McCulloch. Wit: Hugh Davis, Mathew McCulloch, D. R. Crosby. // File. Claimant, Henry Phipps, 28 Mch. 1804. Certif. B-210 issued 19 Feb. 1807. Henry Phipps claims 640 acres on Dry Cr. waters of Buffalo, by virtue of a settlement begun and continued from 1795 to present date by William Nicholson and held to sd Henry Phipps to be confirmed by sd Nicholson, as above.

p.459. Claim No.1385. Spanish gr. to Stephen Stephenson, 300 acres, 9 miles east of Fort, adj. Chas. Cason, Isaac Johnson, Reuben Alexander, William Cooper and Mr. John Hartley. N. O. 15 Mch. 1789. // File. Stephen Stephenson, claimant, 28 Mch. 1804. Wit: John Girault, 5 Nov. 1804. Certif. A-353 issued 21 June 1805. Stephen Stephenson claims 300 arpents of land by virtue of the above grant from the Spanish Govt.

p.461. Claim No.1388. Spanish gr. to James Burnet, 1180 acres on the road from the Fort to Nogales, 16 miles from the Big Black, adj. lands of Richard King. Certificate of survey by Carlos Trudeau, 23 Mch. 1795. // File. James Burnett, claimant, 28 Mch. 1804. Rejected, 13 June 1807. Claiborne Co., Miss. Territory, James Burnett claims 1180 arpents about ten miles below the Walnut Hills by virtue of a Spanish order of survey to him, as above. He was a cit. of the Territory in 1795 and above 21 years of age.

p.463. Claim No.1390. British gr. to John Boles, 100 acres on Second Creek, bet. the lands of Wm. Johnston and Wm. Joiner. Pensacola, 26 May 1777 by Chester. // p.466. 30 Oct. 1777. John Bolls, taylor, of Natchez, and his wife, Martha, to Robert Collingwood, for $100 the above tract. (signed) John Bolls, Martha (x) Bolls. Wit: Nehemiah Carter, Wm. Williams. File. Claimant, Jesse Carter, 28 Mch. 1804. Wit: Philander Smith, 9 Feb. 1805. Certif. A-355 issued to claimant. Jesse Carter, who was an actual settler in Miss. Ter. 27 Oct. 1795, claims 600 acres in Adams Co. by virtue of two grants, (1) for 100 acres gr. by the British Govt. to John Bolls and by him conveyed to Robert Collingwood, and by him to Nehemiah Carter 27 Nov. 1777, being part of the land hereby claimed and the other was granted by the Spanish Govt. to Rachel Carter on 16 May 1791, both of which tracts are joined, and were conveyed by the said Nehemiah Carter and Rachel, his wife, to the claimant 26 March 1804. 27 Nov. 1777. Robert Collinwood to Nehemiah Carter, lease and release, for $300, 100 acres gr. to John Boles, as above. Signed. Wit: Thos. Beriwck, Isaac Mitchell. Manchac Dist. proved by Thomas Berwick before Stephen Watts, 20 Dec. 1777. // Deed. 26 Mch. 1804, Nehemiah Carter and wife, Rachel, to Jesse Carter, for $350 paid, the above tract, abt. 7 miles south of Natchez, adj. Henry Phipps, Samuel Phipps, John Ellis, Osborne Sprigg and Second Creek. (signed) N. Carter, Rachel Carter. Wit: John Ellis, Hugh Davis, William Brown.

p.477. Claim No.1391. Spanish gr. to Mrs. Sarah Kenner, 250 acres on Second Creek, 9 mi. SE of Fort, b. by Samuel Hutchins, John White, Abner Green. N. O. 21 May 1791 by Miro. // File. Claimant, Sarah Carter. 28 Nov. 1804. Wit: Philander Smith. Certif. A-354 issued 21 June 1805. Sarah Carter, late Kenner, wife of Jesse Carter, claims 250 arps. on Second Cr. by virtue of a complete Spanish patent, as above, Plat shows tract almost triangular in form, Abner Green, John Hampton White, and Samuel Hutchins, having lands adjoining. This claim signed: Washington, 19 Mch. 1804, by Jesse Carter for Sarah Carter. The original Spanish grant in the file is made out to Madame Sarah Kenner, as was the plat.

p.479. Claim No.1392. Spanish gr. to Madame Sarah Carter, 500 acres 7 mi. south of Fort, b. by the grantee, Osborn Sprigg, Samuel and Henry Phipps. N. O. 16 May 1791 by Miro. [No file.]

p.480. Claim No.1395. Spanish gr. to George Rapalje, 231 acres, adj. Frank Spain, John Rawls, John Lusk, Wm. Ferguson, Stephen Mayes and James Cabel. N. O. 11 Mch. 1788 by Miro. Plat dated 12 Dec. 1782. // File Robert Moore, claimant, 28 Nov. 1804. Certif. A-666. Robert Moore claims 231 acres 2 miles from Natchez, bounded as above grant describes, founded on sd grant to George Rapalje who sold it to Matthew White, by said White to Alexander Moore, who gave the same by his last will to his children who by their deed of partition, 18 July 1803, allotted and conveyed same to claimant. Signed.

p.482. Claim No.1396. Spanish survey to Jacob Cable, 76 acres, by Carlos Trudeau, 10 Dec. 1782, on St. Catherine's Cr., adj. George Rapalie, Stephen Mayes, and Wm. Ferguson. // File. Claimant, Robert Moore, 28 Mch. 1804. Wit: Ebenezer Rees, 22 Aug. 1805, Jacob Cable, 28 Nov. 1805. Certif. B-245 issued 30 Mch. 1807. Robert Moore, who on 27 Oct. 1795 was a settler in Miss. Ter. claims 74 arpents in Adams Co. 2 1/2 mi. from Natchez, by virtue of the first Sec. of the Act of Congress, etc. being the legal representative of Jacob Cable who in 1782 obtained from the Spanish Govt. an order of survey, for this land, being then full of age, and sold it to Polser Shilling and said Shilling sold same to Matthew White, who sold it to Alexander Moore, decd. who gave it to his children in his last will who by deed of partition conveyed same to the claimant.

p.482. Claim No.1397. Spanish warrant of survey to Wm. Ferguson, 163 acres on St. Catherine's Cr., adj. Benj. Belk, Jacob Cable, George Rapalje and Silas Crane. // File. Claimant, Robert Moore, 28 Mch. 1804. Wit: Ebenezer Rees, 22 Aug. 1805. A. Daugherty claims 52 arpents of the within. See Certif. B-147. Certif. B-146 issued for 111 arpents, 10 Feb. 1807. Robert Moore, legal representative of Wm. Ferguson, claims 163 acres in Adams Co. about 2 mi. from Natchez, by virtue of the afsd Act of Congress, Wm. Ferguson having prior to sd 27 Oct. 1795, claimed from the Spanish Govt. for a warrant of survey, dated 1782, he being above the age of 21 and afterwards sold the same to Matthew White, who conveyed the same to Alexander Moore, who gave the same by his will to his children, etc. as before.

p.483. Claim No.1399. Spanish gr. to John Joseph Duforest, 1000 acres on Cole's Cr., 15 mi. NE of Fort, adj. Madame Truly, Richard Harrison, Alexander Callender and Richard Ellis, Mch. 24, 1794. Certf. by Trudeau. // File. Robert Moore, claimant, 28 Mch. 1804. Wit: James Spain, 21 Aug. 1805. Certif. A-745 issued 4 Feb. 1806. See No.996. Robert Moore claims 400 acres in Jefferson Co. 15 mi. NE from Natchez, being part of a tract of 1000 acres originally gr. to John Joseph Duforest by Spanish patent, as above, and by him to James Moore 29 May 1797, and by him to said claimant, 18 July 1803.

p.484. Claim No.1400. Spanish gr. to Robert Moore 1000 acres on a br. of Bayou Sara, 3 mi. NE of James Mather, 40 mi. SE of Fort. N. O. 26 Dec. 1795, by Carondelet. // File. Claimant, Robt. Moore, 28 Mch. 1804. Wit: on the part of the U. S. Alexander Montgomery, 31 July 1805. Disallowed on suspicion of its being antedated, 22 Dec. 1806. Robert claims 1000 arps. by virtue of a Spanish grant, as above.

p.486. Claim No.1401. Spanish grant to Ebenezer Rees, 320 acres on St. Catherine's Creek, 3 mi. ESE of Fort, b. by Wm. Brocus, Sarah Truly, Geo. Rapalje, Jacob Cable, and John Stampley. N. O. 20 June 1795 by Carondelet. // File. Claimant, Robert Moore, 28 Mch. 1804. Wit: June 10, 1805, Moses Armstrong. In Claim No.856. Certif. A-75_ issued 1805. Robert Moore claims 320 acres by virtue of a Spanish grant to Ebenezer Rees, as above, 27 March 1801 to James Moore, and 18 July 1803 James Moore conveyed same to claimant. Letter of protest from Polser Shilling.

p.487. Claim No.1402. Spanish gr. to Alexander Moore, 1000 acres on waters of Bayou Pierre, 30 mi. NE from Fort, 1 mi. east of River Miss. 4 mi. from mouth of Bayou Pierre. Survey by Wm. Vousdan, Certif. by Carlos Trudeau. Plat shows English grant to John Ross, now in possession of Robt. Cochran. // File. Claimant, Robert Moore, 28 Mch. 1804. Wit: Ebenezer Rees, 22 Aug. 1805. Certif. A-598 issued to claimant. Robt. Moore, etc., claims 1000 arpents by virtue of a Spanish grant to Alexander Moore, as above, which land was willed by him to son, William Moore, and from the said William the said land, at his death, descended to his brothers, Samuel P. Moore, James Moore and Robert Moore and his sister Sarah Scott, and the said Sarah Scott being since dead, her part therein hath descended to said brothers above, who by their deed of partition have allotted and conveyed this tract to the claimant.

p.487. Claim No.1403. Spanish gr. to Nicholas Kimplin, 400 acres on Bayou Sara, adj. Robert Moore. N. O. 22 Mch. 1795 by Carondelet. // File. Claimant, Nicholas Kimplin, 28 Mch. 1804. Disallowed on suspicion of its being antedated, 22 Dec. 1806. Nicholas Kimplin, who was an actual settler in the Miss. Territory 27 Oct. 1795, claims 400 acres in Wilkinson Co., on Bayou Sara, by virtue of a grant to him by the Spanish Govt. Nicholas Kimplin by J. Dunlap. Note in file: Nicholas Kimplin. Let no certificate issue in this case until a witness in behalf of the U. S. has been summoned. (signed) W. B. Shields, U. S. A.

p.488. Claim No.1434. Spanish gr. to Gilbert Leonard, 1600 acres, 3 leagues from Miss. River on Buffalo Cr., 6 mi. north of Loftus Cliffs, adj. Wm. Vousdan. N. O. 26 May 1787 by Miro. // File. Claimant, Daniel Clark, 28 Mch. 1804. Certif. A-706 issued to legal representatives, for 600 arpents, 7 Jany. 1806. The heirs of the late Daniel Clark, Sen., claim 1600 arpents by virtue of a Spanish gr. in favor of Gilbert Leonard, as above and conveyed by him, 18 June 1787, to sd Daniel Clark, Sen., etc. Daniel Clark, agent for the heirs. This is on Cypress Swamp, of Buffalo Creek.

p.490. Claim No.1435. Spanish gr. to Ceasar Archinard, 800 acres 33 miles south of the Fort, 6 mi. east of River Miss., adj. David Ross and Gerard Brandon. N. O. 29 March 1794 by Carondelet. // File. Daniel Clark, claimant, 28 Mch. 1804. Proof in Claim No.1081. Certif. A-472 issued 1 Aug. 1805. 800 arpents of land claimed by Daniel Clark, by virtue of a complete Spanish grant to Caesar Archinard, as above, and sold and conveyed by him, 4 Apr. 1794 to Daniel Clark, Sr. and sold by Daniel Clark Sr. to the claimant, 10 Oct. 1799.

p.491. Claim No.1436. Spanish Govt. to Dona Rosalia, 1153 acres, on the Homochitto, 12 mi. SE of Fort, b. by lands of Don Carlos de Grand-Pre by Miro. N. O. 13 Aug. 1787. // File. Daniel Clark, claimant, 28 Mch. 1804. Certif. A-707 issued in 1806. Daniel Clark, late Consul for the U. S. at New Orleans, claims 1153 acres by virtue of a Spanish grant in favor of Rosalia de la Grand-Pre, a free mulatress, sold and conveyed by the said Rosalia and her husband, Joseph Garcia Capetillo to Don Francisco de Riano, 25 June 1789, and by said Francisco to the claimant, 20 Aug. 1798.

p.493. Claim No.1437. Spanish gr. to Peter Francis Rose, 1600 acres, 3 leagues from the River Miss., on Buffalo Creek, 7 mi. NE from Loftus Cliffs, adj. Gilbert Leonard. N. O. 26 May 1787 by Miro. // File. Claimant, Daniel Clark, Sen., 28 Mch. 1804. Certif. A-708 issued to claimant, 7 Mch. 1806. The heirs of the late Daniel Clark, Sen. claim 1600 arpents by virtue of a complete grant from the Spanish Govt. to Francis Rose, as above, sold and conveyed by him to sd Daniel Clark, Sen. 18 June 1787. Daniel Clark, agent for the heirs.

p.495. Claim No.1438. Spanish gr. to Mark Olivares, 1000 acres on Cole's Cr., adj. Mr. Bingaman. N. O. 26 May 1787 by Miro. // File. Daniel Clark, claimant, 28 Mch. 1804. Certif. A-437 issued 1 Aug. 1805. Daniel Clark claims 1000 acres of land founded on a Spanish patent to Marcus Olivares, as above, and sold and conveyed by same to Daniel Clark, Sr. uncle to the claimant, and finally sold and conveyed by sd Daniel Clark, Sen. to Daniel Clark, the claimant, 10 Oct. 1799. Daniel Clark by his attorney.

p.496. Claim No.1439. Spanish gr. to Bartholomew LeBreton, 800 acres at El Penasco a Davion, Loftus Cliffs, 2 mi. SE of mouth of Buffalo Cr., b. by 1023 arpents gr. to Daniel Clark, N. O. 14 June 1787 by Miro. // File. Claimant, Daniel Clark, 28 Mch. 1804. Certif. A-474 issued 1st Aug. 1805. 800 arpents of land claimed by Daniel Clark by virtue of a Spanish patent to Bartholomew LeBreton as above, sold to Daniel Clark, Sen., 17 Nov. 1790, and finally sold by sd Daniel Clark, Sen. and to Daniel Clark, the claimant, 10 Oct. 1799.

p.498. Claim No.1440. Spanish gr. to Mr. Clark, 1000 acres, near el Penasco a Davion, 14 leagues south of Fort. N. O. 28 Jany. 1789. // File. Claimant, Daniel Clark, 28 Mch. 1804. Certif. A-475 to claimant, Aug. 1805. The above is a plat of 1000 arpents, claimed by Daniel Clark, by virtue of a Spanish patent to Daniel Clark, Sen., as above, and conveyed from sd Daniel Clark Sen., to the claimant, 10 Oct. 1799.

p.499. Claim No.1441. Spanish gr. to Daniel Clark, 5800 acres on a br. of Feliciana Bayou, 45 mi. SE of Fort. N. O. 9 April 1794, by Carondelet. // File. Claimant, Daniel Clark, 28 Mch. 1804. Certif. A-476 issued 1 Aug. 1805. The above a plat of 5800 arpents claimed by Daniel Clark by virtue of a Spanish patent to Daniel Clark, Sen., uncle to the claimant, and sold by sd Daniel Clark Sen., to claimant, 10 Oct. 1799. The sd Daniel Clark, Sen., having been a resident in the Miss. Territory 27 Oct. 1795. Daniel Clark, by his atty., William Dunbar. This is on a br. of Thompson's Cr.

p.501. Claim No.1442. Spanish gr. to Daniel Clark, 800 acres on Miss. River, adj. Thos. Burling and James Kennedy. N. O. 30 Sept. 1793 by Carondelet. // File. Claimant, Daniel Clark, 28 Mch. 1804. Certif. A-647 issued 2 Oct. 1805. Plat of 600 arpents claims by Daniel Clark by virtue of a Spanish gr. to Daniel Clark, Sen., as above, who sold to said claimant, Daniel Clark, 10 Oct. 1799.

p.502. Claim No.1443. Spanish gr. to Daniel Clark, 1023 arpents on Penasco a Davion, Loftus Cliffs, on Miss. River, 2 mi. from mouth of Buffalo Cr. N. O. 6 Feb. 1797. // File. Claimant, Daniel Clark, 28 Mch. 1804. Certif. A-632 to claimant. Plat of 1023 arpents claimed by Daniel Clark by virtue of the above Spanish gr. to Danl. Clark, Sen. and sold to claimant.

p.504. Claim No.1446. George Cochran petitions that he wants to build a house in Natchez, asks for lot No.4, Sq. No.9, 14 July 1797. // Granted by Carondelet 3 Mch 1797. // File. Claimant, Andrew Marschalk, 29 Mch. 1804. Allowed under Barland's patent, No.1468. Claim confirmed and Certif. A-108 issued 12 June 1807. Andrew Marschalk claims Lot No.4, 130 ft front, Sq. No.9, founded on a grant to George Cochran, and conveyance from sd Cochran by deed, 16 Sept. 1802, to present claimant.

p.505. Claim No.1449. Petition of William Scott to the Spanish Govt. asking for 400 acres which are vacant on the Bayou of Homochitto. 26 Apr. 1787. Warrant by Miro, 21 May 1787. Plat and certificate of survey by William Vousdan, 23 Nov. 1787. // File. Claimants, heirs of William Scott, 28 Mch. 1804. Rejected, May 19, 1807. Wilkinson Co. James Bolls, and Elizabeth, his wife, formerly Elizabeth Scott, William, Gabriel, and Thomas Scott, heirs and legal representatives of William Scott, decd., claim 400 arpents on the Homochitto by an order of survey by the Spanish Govt. to said Wm. Scott in his lifetime, as above, at which time he was the head of a family and inhabited and cultivated said land and died intestate. Land adj. those of Thos. Cummings.

p.506. Claim No.1451. Spanish gr. to Christian Harman, 132 acres on St. Catherine's Cr., 7 mi. SE of Fort, adj. Geo. Killiam, Charles Adams, David Lambert. [n.d.] // File. Claimant, Christian Harman, 29 Mch. 1804. Wit: George Killian, 12 June 1804. Certif. B-23 issued 4 June 1806. Christian Harman claims 132 acres in Adams Co. by virtue of a Spanish order of survey to him, as above, in January 1795.

p.506. Claim No.1452. Spanish gr. to Carlos Adams, 425 acres on waters of St. Catherine's Cr., 9 mi. NE from Natchez, adj. lands of George Killian, Richard Harris and Robert Carter. N. O. 15 Mch. 1789 by Miro. // p.508. 13 Mch. 1799, Chas. Adams to Christian Harman, for $280 paid, the above grant for 425 acres. Signed. Wit: John Girault. Prov. by John Girault before John Smith, J. P. of Pickering Co., Miss. Ter. // File. Claimant, Christian Harman, 29 Mch. 1804. Wit: Geo. Killian, 12 June 1804. Certif. A-590 issued 16 Sept. 1805. Adams Co. Christian Harman claims 200 arpents of land part of a tract of 425 arpents in sd county, granted by the Spanish Govt. as above to Chas. Adams who conveyed the said 200 arpents to said Christian, 13 Mch. 1799, taken off the east end of sd tract.

p.509. Claim No.1453. Spanish survey to Christian Harman, 368 acres on a br. of Sandy Creek, 13 mi. SE of Fort, adj. James Erwin. Plat and certificate of survey by Charles Trudeau, 28 Mch. 1797. // p.510. 25 Feb. 1804. Christian Harman and Martha, his wife, to Richard Miller, for $550, the above 386 acres. (signed) Christian Harman, Martha (x) Harman. Wit: Elijah Lloyd, Joseph Killian, George Killian. // File. Claimant, Richard Miller, 29 Mch. 1804. Wit: George Killian, 12 June 1804. Certif. B-148 issued 10 Feb. 1807. Adams Co. Richard Miller claims 368 arpents in sd co. by virtue of an order of survey by the Spanish Govt. to Christian Harman, Jany. 1795, at which time he was the head of a family, etc., and of a survey made under the sd government and of a sale from sd Harman, of sd land, to the claimant. In the Spanish, the name is spelled Arman.

p.511. Claim No.1454. Spanish gr. to Richard Miller, 200 acres, 8 mi. east of Fort, adj. Robt. Harris, George Killian, Wm. Ryan and Joe Fort (Ford). N. O. 15 Mch. 1789. // File. Claimant, Richard Miller, 29 Mch. 1804. Wit: Geo. Killian, 12 June 1804. Certif. A-617, 18 Sept. 1805. Richard Miller, of Adams Co. claims 200 arps on St. Catherine's Cr. by virtue of the above Spanish grant to him.

p.513. Claim No.1461. Petition of James Stoddard for 1000 acres bet. lands of Robert Ford and Joseph Ford, near a place called Half-Way Hill, which are vacant. // File. Hooks and James, claimants, 29 Mch. 1804. Wit: Robert Wood. Certif. B-277 issued May 26, 1807. Simon Hook and Bartholomew James claim each an undivided moiety in 200 arpents of land in Adams Co. on a br. of St. Catherine's Cr. by virtue of a warrant of survey to James Stoddard, as above, who was the head of a family at that date, etc. The sd Stoddard conveyed one undivided moiety of the sd tract to John Girault and he to Policarpo Regillo who conveyed the same to sd Bartholomew James, another 100 acres, an undivided moiety, was debt assigned to John Girault by the Spanish Govt. and by Girault sold to sd Simon Hook.

p.514. Claim No.1462. Lewis Davis petitions the Spanish Govt. that he has from the succession of his father 4 slaves and a number of horses and other cattle and he asks for 800 acres bet. the waters of Buffalo Cr. and Thomson's Cr. adj. Ezekiel Forman. 8 Jany. 1795. // Confirmed by Gayoso, 9 Jany. 1795. // 28 Sept. 1801. Lewis Davis, a subject of His Catholic Majesty to John McCulloch, land south of the Homochitto, 25 mi. from Natchez, adj. Mordecai Richards, which at this time is in possession of John Richey, having a clearing of 12 acres. Lewis Davis, ack. before Saml. Hancock, J. P. of Adams Co. Wit: Hugh Davis, Leonard D. Shaw. // File. Claimant, John McCulloch, 29 Mch. 1804. Wit: Landon Davis, 5 Sept. 1804. 600 acres only to be surveyed. Certif. B-216 for 600 acres, 4 Mch. 1807. John McCulloch claims a donation of 640 acres, comprised of 800 acres in Wilkinson Co. in plat, founded on the above petition of Lewis Davis for same. No warrant of survey so far as claimant knows was ever issued but the sd Davis took possession of the sd land in 1795 and continued to inhabit and cultivate the same until after the evacuation of the Spanish troops, making considerable improvements on the premises and by deed, 21 Sept. 1801, conveyed sd 800 acres to present claimant. As the claimant may not be able to claim the whole 800 acres under the Act of Congress, etc., he prays a certificate for 640 acres.

p.515. Claim No.1467. Spanish Govt. to Josiah Smith 240 acres. Plat No.445. [Nothing more.] // File. Claimant, Abner Wilkinson, 29 Mch. 1804. Wit: Simeon Halliday, 26 Nov. 1804. Certif. B-65 issued 10 Sept. 1806. Abner Wilkinson claims 240 acres of land in Claiborne Co. on the waters of Tabor's Cr., a water of Bayou Pierre, by virtue of a patent to Josiah Smith from Spanish Govt. on 7 Sept. 1797, who transferred all his right, etc. to sd Wilkinson, 10 Mch. 1803. Plat shows James Lobdell, Lucius Smith with land adjoining, also Samuel Cobun, Elijah Smith and land patented for Josiah Smith. // Saml. Reed and John Fry witnesses to transfer to Wilkinson.

p.516. Claim No.1468. Spanish gr. to Wm. Barland, 105 acres, adj. Richard Harrison and Don Pedro Piernas. N. O. 8 May 1786. Plat dated 21 Aug. 1782. // File. Claimant, Wm. Barland, 29 Mch. 1804. Wit: George Fitzgerald, 10 Sept. 1804. Certif. A-356 issued 21 June 1805. William Barland claims 105 arpents by virtue of the above grant to claimant.

p.517. Claim No.1474. Spanish gr. to William Benjamin Smith, 655 acres on St. Catherine's Cr. b. north and south by Adam Bingaman, east by Lewis Bingaman, west by Henry Lafleur. [n.d.] // File. William B. Smith, Jr., 29 Mch. 1804. Wit: Jeremiah Routh, 8 July 1805. Certif. A-415, 9 July 1805. Claim based on above patent by Spanish Govt. to Wm. B. Smith, Sr., who sold land to claimant. [See same claim W. E. Bk.B-411.]

p.519. Claim No.1469. Spanish gr. to John Bisland 525 acres adj. John Farquhar, Daniel Grafton, Stephen Jordan and Stephen Minor. N. O. 3 Sept. 1784 by Miro. Certif. of survey, 28 Nov. 1782. // File. Claimant, Mr. Barland, 29 Mch. 1804. Wit: Geo. Fitzgerald. Certif. A-357 issued to claimant, 1805. William Barland claims 527 arpents by virtue of the above Spanish gr. to John Bisland and by him conveyed to John Farquhar and the claimant, jointly, on 19 July, 1786 and by John Farquhar, his part, to the present claimant, 21 Dec. 1787.

p.520. Claim No.1475. Spanish gr. to Landon Davis, 800 acres on a br. of Homochitto River, 15 mi. south of Fort. N. O. 12 Feb. 1788 by Miro. Plat and certif. 11 Feb. 1788. Plat shows Francisco Brezino adj. // p.521. 28 Mch. 1804. Landon Davis to Hugh Davis, for $3500, the 800 acres as above granted. Signed. Wit: David R. Crosby, John McCulloch. // File. Hugh Davis, 29 Mch. 1804. Wit: Mathew McCulloch, 5 Sept. 1804. Certif. A-35 issued, 21 June 1805. Hugh Davis claims 800 arpents by virtue of a Spanish gr. to Landon Davis, as above, and by him to the present claimant.

p.523. Claim No.1476. Spanish gr. to Martha Davis, 600 arpens on waters of Homochitto, 17 mi. SE of Fort, adj. Wm. Scott and Rocky Stone Spring br. N. O. 12 Feb. 1788 by Miro. // File. Claimants, heirs of Martha Davis, 29 Mch. 1804. Wit: Mathew McCulloch, 5 Sept. 1804. Certif. A-359 issued to legal representatives, 21 June 1805. Prov. in Martha Davis. The heirs of Martha Davis claim 600 acres by the above Spanish gr. to sd Martha Davis. (signed) Lewis Davis.

p.525. Claim No.1477. Spanish gr. to Archibald Palmer, 800 acres on South Fork of the Homochitto, 17 mi. south of Fort, adj. Jesse Carter. N. O. 15 Mch. 1789 by Miro. // p.526. 27 Mch. 1801. Archibald Palmer and wife, Hannah, to Hugh Davis, for $1500 paid, the above grant of 800 acres. Both sign. Wit: William Dunbar, Dinah Dunbar. // p.528. 28 Mch. 1804. Hugh Davis, of Wilkinson Co. to Landon Davis, of same, for $3500 paid, the above grant, 800 acres. Signed. Wit: David R. Crosby, John McCulloch. // File. Landon Davis, claimant, 29 Mch. 1804. Wit: Mathew McCulloch, 5 Sept.

1804. Certif. A-360 issued 21 June 1805. Prov. in Palmer. Landon Davis claims 800 acres by virtue of a grant by the Spanish Govt. as above, to Archibald Palmer, by him to Hugh Davis and by Hugh Davis to claimant.

p.530. Claim No.1480. Petition of James Nicholson, Capt. of Militia in Dist. of Galvez Town, wishes to employ negroes I have; asks for lands adj. Wm. Webb and Landon Davis, 10 Jany. 1788. // Spanish Govt. grants order of survey, 11 Jany. 1788. Miro. // Certif. of survey, 600 acres on Bayou aux Boeufs, 20 mi. south of Fort, adj. John Steel, Arch. Palmer and Jesse Carter. // File. Heirs of James Nicholson, claimants, 29 Mch. 1804. Wit: Mathew McCulloch, 5 Sept. 1804. Certif. B-149 issued 10 Feb. 1807. Hugh Davis, Abram Ellis and Benj. Farrar, executors in behalf of the legal representatives of James Nicholson, decd., claim 600 arpents by virtue of a warrant of survey from the Spanish Govt. to sd deceased, who was then the head of a family.

p.531. Claim No.1481. Spanish gr. to William Webb, 600 acres on south fork of the Homochitto, adj. Martha Davis. 12 Feb. 1788 by Miro. // p.532. 9 Mch. 1804. William Webb, heir and devisee of Wm. Webb, decd. to William Nicholson, Watkins Nicholson, James Nicholson, Mary Davis, wife of Robert Davis, Samuel Nicholson, Pamilia Nicholson, and Henry Nicholson, Jr., children of Henry Nicholson and devisees of James Nicholson, decd. William Webb in his lifetime did bargain and sell to James Nicholson, now deceased, 600 acres granted to Wm. Webb, as above, and James Nicholson died and in his will devised all his real estate to the afsd children of Henry Nicholson, for $450 in hand paid by the afsd executors of will of James Nicholson. (signed) Wm. Webb. Wit: Mathew McCulloch, Michael Walsh, John Sullivan. // File. Heirs of James Nicholson, claimants, 29 Mch. 1804. Wit: Landon Davis, 5 Sept. 1804, 12 July 1805. Certif. A-454 issued to legal representatives, 23 July 1805. The Executors of the will of James Nicholson, as above, claim 600 arpents by virtue of a grant by Spain to Wm. Webb and by Wm. Webb, heir and devisee to the grantee, to sd claimants, as above.

p.533. Claim No.1482. Spanish gr. to Stephen Minor, 1015 acres, the sd land being in possession of sd Stephen Minor, to whom it was sold by Richard Devall who had it from the auction of the property of John Alston, the fugitive rebel. This land is on Second Creek, 7 mi. south of the Fort, adj. Mrs. Sarah Holmes, Daniel Perry, Mr. Mayes's British grant, now gr. to William McIntosh, and land of Mr. Hogue [?] N. O. 15 Aug. 1787 by Miro. // File. Alexander Ross, claimant, 29 Mch. 1804. Wit: John Ellis, 5 Oct. 1804. Certif. A-351 issued 21 June 1805. See No.575. Alexander Ross claims 855 acres by virtue of a Spanish gr. to Stephen Minor which was sold to the claimant, 22 Aug. 1795.

p.535. Claim No.1485. Spanish gr. to Jacob Earhart, by Grand-Pre, Dec. 1, 1796, following Earhart's petition for Lot No.1, Sq. No.33, May 9, 1795, as he wished to build a house in the New City. // File. Jacob Earhart, claimant, 29 Mch. 1804. Wit: Bennet Truly, 13 Jany. 1807. Certif. B-196 issued 13 June 1807. Jacob Earhart claims Lot No.1, Sq. No.33 in the City of Natchez by virtue of the above grant.

p.536. Claim No.1495. British gr. to Jacob Phillippi, 600 acres, warrant of survey, 4 Jany. 1769, NE 24 mi. fr. Fort Panmure, east 4 mi. from Miss. River, b. by John Smith. Pensacola. 22 July 1769, by Montford Brown. Survey and Certif. by Wm. Wilton, Dep. Surv. Genl. // p.539. Jacob Phillipi and Catherine, his wife, to David Ross, lease and release, 6th and 7th Aug. 1772, for $60, the above tract granted. Signed by both grantors in German. Wit: Alexander Solomon, Ja. Ferguson. // File. John Smith, claimant, 29 Mch. 1804. Wit: John Brooks, 8 Oct. 1804. Certif. A-534, issued to claimant, 28 Aug. 1805. John Smith claims 600 acres on the bluff of the Mississippi River, granted by the British Govt. of West Florida to Jacob Phillippi, by patent as above, who conveyed the same to David Ross, of New Orleans, and sd David Ross conveyed the same to John Smith, 10 Mch. 1789. (signed) John Smith.

p.544. Claim No.1497. Spanish gr. to John Smith, 450 acres, 5 leagues north of Fort by Miss. River, adj. Joe. Dyson and David Ross. N. O. 6 March 1789 by Miro. // File. Claimant, John Smith, 29 Mch. 1804. Wit: John Brooks, 8 Oct. 1804. Confirmed. Certif. A-366, June 24, 1805. John Smith claims 450 arpents on the Bluff in Miss. Ter., 25 mi. NE fr. the Natchez Fort, by patent to him from the Spanish Govt. as above.

p.545. Claim No.1498. Spanish gr. to Frederick Metzo, 300 acres on South Fork of Cole's Cr., 20 mi. NE of Fort, adj. Eliz. Douglas. N. O. 30 Sept. 1793 by Carondelet. // p.546. 16 Sept. 1800. Frederick Metzo to John Smith, both of Pickering Co., Miss. Ter., for $200 paid, the above land, as granted. Metzo signed with a mark. Wit: Jno. Girault, Wm. Newman. // File. John Smith, claimant, 29 Mch. 1804. Wit: Raleigh Hogan, 8 Oct. 1804. Certif. A-367, issued to claimant, 24 June 1805. John Smith claims 300 arpents on waters of Cole's Cr. by a Spanish patent to Frederick Medsco, as above, and conveyed by him to John Smith, the claimant.

p.548. Claim No.1499. Spanish gr. to John Smith, 142 acres on waters of Fairchild's Cr. 20 Mi. NE of Fort, adj. James Elliot, Mr. Green, David Ross and Mr. Bingaman. Plat 5 Sept. 1788. N. O. 6 Mch. 1789 by Miro. // File. Claimant, John Smith, 29 Mch. 1804. Wit: John Brooks, 8 Oct. 1804. Certif. A-368 issued to claimant, 24 June 1805. John Smith claims 142 arpents in Miss. Territory 1 mile from the bluff, by a Spanish grant to him as above.

p.549. Claim No.1500. Petition to the Spanish Govt. by Mark Cole for 187 acres, now vacant, adj. Joe Dyson, Clement Dyson, David Ross and Adam Bingaman, 21 Jany. 1789. // Order of survey by Miro, N. O. 14 Feb. 1789. Plat and certif. by Wm. Vousdan, 5 Sept. 1788. // p.550. 25 July 1789. Mark Cole and Hannah, his wife, of Jefferson Co. to John Smith, of same, for $1000, the above 187 acres on waters of Fairchild's Cr. Both sign. Wit: John Hopkins, Richard Burney. // File. John Smith claimant, 29 Mch. 1804. Wit: John Brooks, 8 Oct. 1804. Certif. B-150 issued 10 Feb. 1807. John Smith claims 187 acres by a patent from the Spanish Govt. to Mark Cole, as above and conveyed by sd Cole to claimant, John Smith.

p.551. Claim No.1501. Spanish gr. to Richard Wynne, 240 acres 2 mi. south of the main fork of Bayou Pierre, 60 miles NE of Fort, b. by Wm. Bassett. 14 Jany. 1790. // File. John Smith claimant, 29 Mch. 1804. Said land was granted to Richard Wynne, who died and the land was ordered for sale by the Spanish Govt. to pay Wynne's debts and sd Smith purchased sd land and holds the same by the Spanish Governor's order. Rejected.

p.552. Claim No.1506. Petition of Thos. Sullivan, who came from Kentucky to settle in this district, asks for 240 acres on Cole's Cr. adj. Hugh Logan. 3 Feb. 1791. Order of survey by Gayoso, 12 Mch. 1791. Grant, Apr. 7, 1791 by Estevan Miro. // File. Thos. Sullivan, claimant, 29 Mch. 1804. Wit: Joseph Green, 21 Aug. 1804. Certif. B-157, issued Feb. 1st, 1807. Thos. Sullivan claims 240 acres in Jefferson Co. founded on a warrant of survey by the Spanish Govt. to said Sullivan. Signed G. Poindexter, atty. for the claimant.

p.552. Claim No.1514. Spanish gr. to John Smith, 230 arpents on Fairchilds Cr., 20 mi. NE of Natchez, adj. Adam Bingaman, Thos. Erwin and Philip Arman (Harman). N. O. 23 Mch. 1790 by Miro. // File. Claimant, John Smith, 29 Mch. 1804. Wit: John Brooks, 8 Oct. 1804. Certif. A-369 issued 24 June 1805. John Brooks for John Smith claims 230 arpents 2 mi. from the Bluffs on Fairchild's Cr. as patented above.

p.554. Claim No.1524. Petition of James Dealy, of the American Nation, United States, with two sons, asks for vacant land adj. Julian Bracier and Michael Mecho. // Galveztown, 13 Jany. 1790. Marcus Devilliers depones as to lands being vacant. // Plat and certif. of survey by Christopher Bolling, Dep. Surv. for 320 acres 9 leagues from Willings Bayou on the Miss. on headwaters of Bayou Sarah, 29 Oct. 1794. Plat shows land of Daniel Douglass and James Carroll adj. // Book G. p.291. 10 Aug. 1794. James Dealy to Christopher Bolling, bill of sale of the above warrant for 320 acres. Signed. Wit: David Walsh. // p.292. 25 Apr. 1798, Christopher Bolling, of Feliciana, Govt. of Louisiana, to Ebenezer Rees, of Dist. of St. Catherine, for $160 the 320 acres in above gr. Signed. Wit: John Rogers, Samuel Burch. I hereby promise to obtain from my wife, Catherine Bolling, her relinquishment. Apr. 25, 1798. Christopher Bolling. // p.295. Oct. 3, 1801. Ebenezer Rees, of Adams Co., to David Ferguson and Melling Woolley for $1200, two tracts, -- 320 acres as above, and 280 acres surveyed for James Carroll. Eben Rees. // p.298. 25 Feb. 1803. Melling Woolley for $3000 to David Ferguson, several tracts, including the above 320 acres. Signed. Wit: Lyman Harding, Jas. Brandt, Jos. Dunbar. // File. David Ferguson, claimant, 29 Mch. 1804. Rejected, 12 June 1807.

p.555. Claim No.1525. Spanish gr. to Lacy Rumsey, 500 acres, on a br. of Fairchild's Cr., 15 mi. NE of Fort, b. by George Fitzgerald, Ebenezer Rees and Gabriel Benoist. N. O. 15 Sept. 1792 by Carondelet. // Book G. p.302. Lacy Rumsey to Eben Rees, 7 Mch. 1798. Lacy Rumsey of Villa Gayoso, for $400 paid, the above land in the Dist. of Pine Ridge. Signed. Wit: Chas. F. Todd, Peter Walker, George Cochran. // p.305. 12 May 1801, Ebenezer Rees, of Adams Co., Miss. Ter., merchant to David Ferguson and Melling Woolley, merchants, for $1500, the above tract. Signed. Wit: Lyman Harding, Samuel Hancock. // File. David Ferguson, claimant, 29 Mch. 1804. Certif. A-162, issued 18 Sept. 1805. Claim as above.

p.556. Claim No.1526. Spanish to John Sullivan, 400 acres, 30 mi. NE of Fort, adj. Thomas Sullivan. N. O. 20 June 1795 by Carondelet. // File. John Sullivan, claimant, 29 Mch. 1804. Wit: Benajah

Osmun, 16 Jan. 1806. John Sullivan claims 400 acres on Cole's Cr. in Jefferson Co. by virtue of the above grant. Certif. A-737 issued to David Ferguson, assignee.

p.557. Claim No.1527. Petition of Chas. Howard to the Spanish Govt. that he has a wife and five children, and asks land on Fairchild's Cr., adj. John Jones, 28 Aug. 1794. // Order of survey by Gayoso, Natchez, 18 Jany. 1795. Warrant by Carondelet, N. O. 24 Feb. 1795. // File. Claimant, Ebenezer Rees, 29 Mch. 1804. Wit: Henry Manadue. Certif. B-229 issued to D. Ferguson, assignee, 6 Mch. 1806. Ebenezer Rees claims 400 acres as granted above to Chas. Howard, which his widow, Lydia Howard, with permission of the Spanish Government, conveyed to sd Rees. J. Dunlop for E. Rees.

p.558. Claim No.1528. Spanish gr. to William Thomas, 600 acres on a br. of Chubby Fork of Bayou Pierre, 45 mi. north of the Fort. N. O. 7 Dec. 1797 by Gayoso. // File. Claimant, William Thomas, 29 Mch. 1804. Wit: James Truly, 28 May 1804. Rejected 12 June 1807. Wm. Thomas claims 600 acres in Jefferson Co. by virtue of a warrant of survey from the Spanish Govt. as above.

p.560. Claim No.1529. Spanish gr. to Jacob Crumholt, 600 acres on north fork of Cole's Cr. 25 mi. NE of Fort, adj. Henry Platner, Edward Johnson and Abraham Stickston [Hickston]. N. O. 24 Dec. 1797 by Gayoso. // File. Claimant, Jacob Crumholt, 29 Mch. 1804. Wit: Robert Dunbar, 1 Apr. 1806. Claim based on above grant, thewarrant of survey being gr. in 1790.

p.561. Claim No.1530. Spanish gr. to John Newton for 200 acres on Second Cr. 12 mi. east of Fort, adj. Peter Camus, and Isaac Alexander. N. O. 2 Mch. 1795 by Carondelet. // File. Claimant, Joshua Howard, 29 Mch. 1804. Certif. A-618 issued 18 Dec. 1805. Above claim by Howard founded on the Spanish patent to John Newton and the intervening conveyances herewith submitted. [These conveyances not in the file.]

p.562. Claim No.1531. Petition of James Carroll, of Ireland, for land on Bayou Sara. [n.d.] Galveztown, 22 Sept. 1791. Report of Marcos de Villiers. // Grant, 19 Dec. 1793, 280 acres by Carondelet. // Certif. and plat by Christopher Bolling, 24 Oct. 1794. Land 8 leagues from Willing's Bayou on the head br. of Bayou Sara. // Bk.G. p.307. 25 Apr. 1798, Christopher Bolling, of New Feliciana, for $1401, to Ebenezer Rees, 280 acres b. by James Dealy. Signed. Wit: John Rogers, Samuel Burch. // Assignment of warrant for above by James Carrell to Christopher Bolling, 17 Feb. 1795. // Christopher Bolling promises to have wife, Catherine, relinq. her dower. 25 Apr. 1798. // File. Claimant, David Ferguson, 29 Mch. 1804. Rejected, 12 June 1807. David Ferguson claims 280 acres by above warrant by Spanish Govt. to James Carroll and by certain intermediate conveyances. J. Dunlap for David Ferguson.

p.563. Claim No.1538. Petition of George Cochran for Lot No.2, Sq. No.9 in Natchez, 25 Aug. 1794. // Order of survey by Gayoso, 5 Aug. 1794. // Gr. by Carondelet. N. O. 3 Mch. 1797. // File. George Cochran, claimant, 29 Mch. 1804. Wit: Lewis Evans, 26 Mch. 1804. Certif. B-6, issued 6 June 1806. George Cochran claims above by virtue of the above patent. Robert Cochran for George Cochran.

p.564. Claim No.1543. George Cochran petitions the Spanish Govt. for Lot No.1, Sq. No.20 in City of Natchez, 10 Jany. 1795. // Granted by Carondelet, 20 June 1795. // File. Claimant; George Cochran, 29 Mch. 1804. Wit: W. Thomas, 26 Nov. 1804. Certif. A-684, issued to legal representatives. Above claim founded on the Spanish patent.

p.565. Claim No.1544. Spanish gr. to Patrick Foley, 500 acres, 25 mi. SE of Fort, on Buffalo Cr., adj. Wm. Cock Ellis and Miss Mary Ellis. N. O. 12 Apr. 1790 by Miro. // File. Patrick Foley, claimant, 29 Mch. 1804. Certif. A-739 issued 16 Jan. 1806. Claim founded on above patent.

p.567. Claim No.1545. Petition of William Conway to the Spanish Govt. for 800 acres on Buffalo Cr., 3 leagues from the Miss. River, 3 leagues from Loftus Cliffs, adj. lands of Maurice Conway, grandfather of the grantee, Peter Miro, and James Smith. N. O. 14 June 1787 by Miro. // File. Claimant, Wm. Conway, 29 Mch. 1804. Rejected, 12 June 1807.

p.569. Claim No.1546. Spanish Govt. to Peter Brian Bruin, 1800 acres on the Miss. River and Bayou Pierre, 40 mi. north of Fort, adj. on east Llewellyn Price and William Smith, and on SW by Wm. Smith, at mouth of Bayou Pierre. N. O. 20 July, 1796 by Carondelet. // File. Claimant, P. Bruin, 29 Mch. 1804. Wit: Buckner Pittmen, 21 Nov. 1804. Notation: 640 acres confirmed as a Donation. Certif. B-295. The residue, 1160 arpents confirmed as a preemption, Certif. D-342, issued 13 Jan. 1807. Claim from Spanish patent above.

BOOK E

p.1. Claim No.978. British gr. to Michael Hooter, 450 acres, 10 mi. east of Fort, adj Daniel Perry, on Second Cr. Pensacola, 21 Sept. 1772. Peter Chester. // p.97. Lease and release, 7th and 8th March 1776, Michael Hooter, of the Dist. of West Florida, and Mary, his wife, to Isaac Johnson, 450 acres, as above, for $130. Both sign with a mark. Wit: Anthony Hutchins, Luke Collins, Donald McPherson. [No file.]

p.6. Claim No.979. British gr. to Evan Cameron, 150 acres on Second Creek, 9 mi. east from Natchez, adj. Edward Mayes, Michael Hooter and William Johnston. Pensacola, 22 July 1776. // p.105. Lease and release, 12th and 13th Sept. 1777. Evan Cameron sells to Isaac Johnson, for $300, 150 acres on Second Cr., as above. Evan (x) Cameron. Wit: John Smith, Samuel Heady. // p.113. Isaac Johnson, Alcalde for the Dist. of Second Creek, to Benj. Farrar, 1400 acres on sd creek, (1) 450 acres bought from Michael Hooter, 8 Mch. 1776, (2) 150 acres from Evan Cameron, and (3) 800 acres granted to Isaac Johnson, for $4200. Signed. Wit: Stephen Minor, John Minor, Peter Walker. // File. Claimant, Benj. Farrar, 22 Mch. 1804. Wit: Wm. Glasscock. Claims 150 acres in Adams Co. on Second by virtue of a British gr. to Evan Cameron, as above, and by Cameron conveyed to Isaac Johnson and by sd Isaac Johnson to sd Benjamin Farrar. [No record of the disposition of this claim.]

p.11. Claim No. 980. British gr. to Richard Ellis, 1000 acres between Second Cr and the White Cliffs below St. Catherine's Cr. on the River Miss., adj. Anthony Hutchins land. Pensacola, 16 June 1779, by Peter Chester. // p.155. Agreement of division between Mrs. Mary Ellis, wid. of Richard Ellis, Esq., decd. and the heirs of sd Richard, decd. [File missing.]

p.17. Claim No.981. British gr. to Isaac Johnson, 800 acres on Second Cr., 8 mi. SE of the Fort, adj. lands of Mr. Alexander and Mr. Montsanto. N.O. 26 Mch. 1789. [File missing.] See Claim No. 979.

p.21. Claim No.982. Spanish gr. to Richard Ellis, 150 acres on White Cliffs, 5 leagues from Natchez, adj. lands of Daniel Clark, Anthony Hutchins, the grantee and Col. Philippe Trevino. N.O. 31 Jany. 1788 by Miro. // p.24. Will of Richard Ellis. [See Natchez Records, Book C, page 200.] // B. Farrar and wife, claimants. Cert. A-27 issued.

p.25. Claim No.983. Spanish gr, to Isaac Johnson, 1100 acres, as petitioned in 1790, adjoining the plantation he had, and lands of . . . Andres de Armesto and William Savage. // Warrant N.O. 20 Sept. 1793 // Grant, 9 Dec. 1797, adj. Wm. Alexander, Jane Rumsey, Wm. Ratcliff and Jane Rapallie. // p.19. Dec. 2, 1800. Isaac and Mary Johnson for $3300, to Benj. Farrar, of the Township of Second Cr., 1100 acres bounded as above, the plantation of Jane Rumsey having been granted by Spain to Ezekiel Forman, and the grantee's land purchased by sd Benj. Farrar, 28 Mch. 1794. Signed. Wit: William Thomas, Wm. Dunbar. [File missing.] Claim reg. 22 Mch. 1804.

p.31. Claim No.984. Spanish gr. to Miguel Fortier, 2650 acres on the Bluffs, adj. Benj. Ward, Thos. Hutchins, Jacob Winfree, Thomas Hutchins, Jr., and Anthony Hutchins. N.O. 26 Jany. 1787 by Miro. // p.33. New Orleans, 6 Feb. 1787. Miguel Fortier to Daniel Clark, 2650 acres as in above grant, for $400 paid. // p.123. 13 Oct. 1802. Daniel Clark, Jr., exor. of the will of Daniel Clark, Sr, decd., by atty. Wm. Dunbar, to Benj. Farrar 2419 acres adj. Anthony Hutchins which he purchased of Michael Fortier, of New Orleans, orig. grantee. Wit: Jesse Carter, Israel Smith. [File missing.] Reg. 22 Mch. 1804.

p.35. Claim No.985. Spanish gr. to William Butler, 600 acres on St. Catherine's Cr. 8 mi. south of Fort, adj. Abner Green. N.O. 16 Feb. 1789 by Miro. [Plat shows the land at the mouth of St. Catherine's creek below Natchez.] Reg. 22 Mch. 1804. [No file.]

p.37. Claim No. 1358. Spanish gr. to Elizabeth McKimm, 600 acres, 9 mi. north of Big Black. N.O. 24 Dec. 1797 by Gayoso. // Reg. Mch. 22, 1804. Claimant, Maurice Custard. Wit: Jeptha Higdon, 16 Aug. 1805. Rejected 22 April 1907. Maurice Custard claims 600 arpents founded on the above Spanish patent to Elizabeth McKimm and by her conveyed to present claimant, 4 Aug. 1798. Witness to bill of sale, James White, Benj. Fletcher and he signed as Morris Custard.

p.39. Claim No.986. British gr. to James Ferguson, 600 acres, 9 mi. east from Natchez, adj. lands surveyed for Wm. Alexander and Second Cr. Pensacola, 21 Sept. 1772 by Peter Chester. // File. James Ferguson, claimant, 22 Mch. 1804. Reported, 11 June 1807. James Ferguson claims for the use of Benjamin Farrar and his wife, Mary, 600 acres in Adams Co. on Second Creek, by virtue of the above British grant thereof to sd Ferguson. S. Lewis agent for claimant.

p.44. Claim No.1054. Spanish gr. to Robert Casbole, 650 acrès on the Homochitto, 9 mi. SE of Fort, adj. lands of Samuel Phipps, Nicholas Rabb, Messrs Kirk and Henderson and Mrs. Savage, Mr. Lusk, Thos. Hutchins and Anthony Hutchins. N.O. 15 Mch. 1789 by Miro. // File. The heirs of James Kirk, claimants, 23 Mch. 1804. Wit: Ebenezer Rees, July 7th, 1805. Certif. A-441 issued to legal representatives, 18 July 1805. John Kirk, one of the heirs of James Kirk, decd., for himself and the other heirs of sd deceased, claims 650 acres in Adams Co. near the Homochitto, by virtue of the above Spanish gr. to Robert Casbole, as above, by whom the sd tract was conveyed to sd James Kirk, decd. 6 Oct. 1790, from whom it descended to the claimants.

p.48. Claim No.1055. Spanish gr, to Daniel Hickey, 1200 acres on Sandy Cr. 3 mi. SE of Fort, adj the Swazey brothers on three sides. N.O. 10 Mch. 1789 by Miro. Plat shows heirs of Samuel Swazey, Richard Swayze, and Samuel Swazey. // File. Daniel Hickey, claimant, 23 Mch. 1804. Wit: Samuel Swazey, 7 Feb. 1806. Wit: Samuel P. and James Moore, 11 June 1806. Rejected 12 June 1807. Daniel Hickey claims 1200 acres in Adams Co. by virtue of a patent by the Spanish Govt. to sd claimant. Seth Lewis, agent for Daniel Hickey.

p.52. Claim No.1056. Spanish gr. of 675 acres to Maria Spain, wife of Don John Girault, one league east of Fort, adj. lands of John Stillee, Ezekiel Dewitt, John Hartley, Richard Adams, Daniel Mygatt, Wm. Brocus and Job Cory. N.O. 17 July 1790 by Miro. // p.54. 7 Oct. 1799. John Girault and Mary, his wife, of Pickering Co., Miss. Ter., for $2000 in hand pd. to Seth Lewis, of Davidson Co., State of Tennessee, as in grant above. Both signed. Wit: Sam. L. Crawford, Wm. Lewis. // File. Seth Lewis, claimant, 23 Mch. 1804. Certif. A-299 issued to claimant, 11 June 1805. Res. of John Girault proved. Seth Lewis claims 540 acres in Adams Co. by virtue of a Spanish gr. to John Girault, and by deed to claimant.

p.56. Claim No.1063. Spanish Govt. to David Greenleaf, 200 acres, 6 mi. from mouth of Big Black. N.O. 20 Feb. 1793 by Carondelet. // File. David Greenleaf, claimant, 24 Mch. 1804. Wit: James Stewart, 5 Mch. 1805. Certif. A-301 issued 11 June 1805. David Greenleaf claims 200 acres in Claiborne Co. on waters of the Big Black, 70 miles from Natchez, by grant from the Spanish Govt. to sd Greenleaf, as above.

p.60. Claim No. 1064. Spanish gr. to Daniel Perry, 400 acres on a br. of Cole's Cr., 18 mi. ENE of Fort. N.O. 25 Feb. 1788 by Miro. // p.62. I do assign all my right to the within to David Greenleaf, for value received. 19 Jany. 1801 Signed: Daniel Perry. // File. David Greenleaf, claimant, 24 Mch. 1804. Wit: James Stewart, 5 Mch. 1805. Certif. A-489 to claimant. David Greenleaf claims 400 acres in Adams Co. by Spanish gr. to Daniel Perry, as above, and by sd Perry conveyed to claimant.

p.63. Claim No.1065. Certificate of survey of 300 acres from the Spanish Govt. to Frederick Calvet, on Miss. River, facing the island below Little Gulf, 30 mi. NNE of the Fort. Natchez, 26 July 1792. (signed) William Dunbar. Plat shows Jeptha Higdon on one side. // File. Claimant, heirs of Frederick Calvet, 24 Mch. 1804. Wit: Wm. Atchinson, 20 July 1804. Certif. B-241 issued 30 Mch. 1807. Levi Well, Elizabeth Wells, James Stewart, Lucretia Stewart, Montfort Calvet, Alexander Calvet, Joseph Calvet and Mary Calvet, the legal heirs of Frederick Calvet, decd., claim 300 acres in Jefferson Co. on the Miss. River, it being part of a tract gr. to Frederick Calvet by an order of survey by the Spanish Govt. By Mary Roberts, for the heirs afsd.

p.64. Claim No.1071. Spanish gr. to Nancy Gilbert, 1000 acres on the Homochitto, 16 mi. SE of Natchez, adj. lands of Wm. West, and John Steel. N.O. 20 Jany. 1788. // File. Claimant, Nancy Gilbert, 24 Mch. 1804. Wit: Alexander Callender, 16 June 1804. Certif. A-302 issued to legal representatives of W. Gilbert, 11 June 1805. Nancy Gilbert, widow and executive of William Gilbert, decd. claims 1000 arpents by virtue of a Spanish gr. as above. William Foster, for heirs. Proved in the deceased and heirs.

p.68. Claim No.1077. Spanish gr. to Henry Phipps, 500 acres on Buffalo Cr., 20 mi. south of Natchez, adj. Joseph Dove. N.O. 30 Aug. 1793 by Carondelet. // p.71. 16 Jany. 1801. Henry Phipps, for $400 to him paid, to Isaac Gaillard, the tract in the above grant. Henry (X) Phipps, Phoebe (x) Phipps, who renounced dower. Wit: Abram Ellis, Wm. Conner. // p.127. 16 Jany. 1801. Isaac Gaillard to John Collins, for $1000, 500 acres on Buffalo Cr. Signed. Wit: Wm. Conner, Abram Ellis. // File. John Collins, claimant, 24 Mch. 1804. Wit: John Ellis, 3 Aug. 1804. Certif. A-303 issued to claimant, 11 June 1805. Proved in Henry Phipps. John Collins claims 500 acres in Wilkinson Co. by virtue of a Spanish grant to Henry Phipps, as above, and conveyance from sd Phipps to Isaac Gaillard and from sd Gailliard to this claimant.

p.72. Claim No.1078. British gr. to William Collins, 200 acres 15 mi. NE from the Natchez, adj. Alexander Ross, Archibald Dalziel and John Collins. Pensacola, 20 Mch. 1778 by Peter Chester. // File. Wm. Collins, claimant, 24 Mch. 1804. Reported, 28 April 1807. William Collins claims 200 acres by virtue of a gr. from the British Govt. of West Florida, as above. John Collins for Wm. Collins.

p.77. Claim No.1080. British gr. to Jno. Collins, 200 acres NE of the Natchez, adj. Wm. Hiorn and Archibald Dalziel. Pensacola, 20 Mch. 1778 by Peter Chester. // File. John Collins, claimant, 24 Mch. 1804. Wit: John Ellis, 6 Aug. 1804. Confirmed 12 Mch. 1805. Certif. A-11. John Collins claims 200 acres in Jefferson, by virtue of a gr. from the British Govt. of West Fla. to this claimant, as above.

p.83. Claim No.1320. British Gr. to Christian Bingaman, 600 acres on south fork of Boyd's Cr. 14 mi. East of the Natchez, adj. James Lovell, Patrick Stuart, Alexander McIntosh, Daniel [Donald] McPherson, Daniel Perry and Richard Ellis. Pensacola, 11 Oct. 1777 by Peter Chester. // p.88. Lease and release, 17th and 18th Nov. 1777. Christian Bingaman and Charity, his wife, for $1000, to Alexander McIntosh, 600 acres, as in above grant. C. Bingaman, Charity (x) Bingaman. Wit: Wm. Vousdan, Luke Collins, Jr., Donald McPherson. // File. Adam Bingaman, claimant, 27 Mch. 1804. Wit: Wm. Atchinson, 25 Sept. 1804. Certif. A-223 issued 22 May 1805. Adam Bingaman claims 600 acres gr. to Christian Bingaman by an English patent, as above, and conveyed to Alexander McIntosh and it became the property of sd Adam Bingaman by the last will and testament of Ann Bingaman, the wife of the said Adam, formerly Ann McIntosh.

p.125. Claim No.1070. 26 Aug. 1788. Richard Harrison to William Gilbert, 390 acres on St. Catherine's Cr. adj. Wm. Lum, Benj. Belk, a br. of Sandy Fork and Muddy Cr. for $398. Both signed. Wit: Juan Carreras, Antonio Soler, before Grand-Pre. // File. Claimants, heirs of William Gilbert, decd. 24 Mch. 1804. Wit: Alexander Callender, 16 June, 1804. Certif. A-345 issued to legal representatives. Claim of heirs to 390 acres gr. by Spanish Govt. to Richard Harrison and by him conveyed, as above, to William Gilbert, decd. By William Foster, exor.

p.130. Claim No.1079. Lease and release, 1st and 2nd Aug. 1779. Archibald Dalziel, of the Parish of Kingston, Island of Jamaica, gentleman, by Wm. Hiorn, Esq. of Natchez Dist., 300 acres on Boyd's Cr. to Luke Collins, Sr., for £100. Signed by Hiorn. Wit: J. Blommart, Donald McPherson. Large plat showing Luke Collins, Sr. with 2 tracts, adjoining, of 300 acres each; Theophilus Collins 300 acres, Luke, Jr. 300 acres, William Collins 200 acres and John Collins, 300 acres, with Sarah Truly, Wm. Hiorn, Esq. and Alex. Ross adjoining. // File. Claimants, Luke Collins and others, 24 Mch. 1804. Rejected, 12 June 1807. Luke Collins, Theophilus Collins, John Collins and Wm. Collins, children and heirs of Luke Collins, decd. claim 300 acres gr. to Archibald Dalziel in 1778, which sd gr. is lost, and conveyed to sd Luke Collins in his lifetime, as above. John Collins for Theophilus Collins.

p.137. Claim No. 1081. 15 Aug. 1800. Daniel Clark to John Collins, for $100, 1000 acres, part of 1600 acres gr by Spanish Govt. to Gilbert Leonard, 26 May 1787, and conveyed to sd Clark. (signed) Daniel Clark. Wit: John Henderson, Henry Turner. Plat shows tract on Buffalo Cr. adj. Mrs. Percy and Daniel Clark. // File. Claimant, John Collins, 24 Mch. 1804. Wit: John Ellis, 14 Aug. 1804. Certif. A-705 issued 7 Jany. 1806. See No.1434. Prov. in Daniel Clark, Sr. John Collins claims 1000 acres in Wilkinson Co. by virtue of a Spanish gr. to Gilbert Leonard, including sd 1000 acres and conveyed by sd Leonard to Daniel Clark, 18 June 1787, and sd Clark to this claimant, 15 Aug. 1800.

p.140. Claim No.1084. Wilkinson Co., Miss. Ter., surveyed for ________ 600 acres on Big Pine Woods Cr., waters of Buffalo, adj. Henry Phipps, 25 Jany. 1804. (signed) Elijah Pope. // p.140. Marian Sanders sold her right to the land to Rebecca Greaton, 5 Dec. 1798. She signed with a mark. Wit: Arthur Conway. // File. Rebecca Graton, claimant, 24 Mch. 1804. Wit: Hugh Davis, 5 Sept. 1804. Plat for 640 acres surveyed for ____ (not filled in) , as above. The within instrument of writing and plat admitted of record.

p.141. Claim No.1085. Lease and release, 1st and 2nd Aug. 1779, [as in No.1079, above] to Luke Collins, Jr. 300 acres 15 mi. NE of the Natchez, same lands adj. for £100. Signed by Hiorn. Wit: J. Blommart, Donald McPherson. // File. Claimant, Luke Collins, 24 Mch. 1804. Rejected 12 June 1807. Luke Collins, Jr. claims 300 acres by virtue from British Govt. to Archibald Dalziel, etc. as in above claim. John Collins for Luke, Jr.

p.147. Claim No.1086. Archibald Dalziel to Theophilus Collins, 1st and 2nd Aug. 1779, 300 acres, for £100, adj. Wm. Hiorn and Richard Ellis. same wit. as above. // File. Claimant, Theophilus Collins, 24 Mch. 1804. Rejected, 12 June 1807. Claim as above. John Collins for Theop.

p.153. Claim No.1087. Lease and release from Dalziel to Luke Collins 300 acres on Boyd's Cr. adj. John Stuart, for £ 100, same date, witnesses, etc. as in preceding instruments. // File. Claimant, heirs of Luke Collins 24 Mch. 1804. Rejected 12 June 1807.

p.175. Claim No.1321. British gr. to Alexander McIntosh, 500 acres adj. Thos. Taylor Byrd, Henry Fairchild and on west Richard Thompson. Pensacola, 19 Arp. 1773 by Chester. // File. Claimant, Adam Bingaman, 27 Mch. 1804. Wit: Wm. Atchinson, 25 Sept. 1804. Certif. A-224 issued 22 May 1805. Adam Bingaman claims 500 acres gr. to Alex. McIntosh, as above, and became the property of sd Adam Bingaman by last will of Ann Bingaman, wife of sd Adam, formerly Ann McIntosh.

p.180. Claim No.1322. British gr. to Alexander McIntosh, 400 acres 25 mi. from Natchez, adj. John Smith. Pensacola, 5 May 1777 by Chester. // File. Claimant, Adam Bingaman, 27 Mch. 1804. Wit: Wm. Atchinson. Certif. A-225 issued May 1805. Adam Bingaman claims 400 acres gr. by the British Govt. to Alex. McIntosh and became property of sd Bingaman by will of Ann Bingaman, his wife, formerly Ann McIntosh. Land near Fairchild's Cr.

p.186. Claim No.1323. British gr. to Daniel McGillivray, 300 arpents, 14 mi. NE from Natchez, adj. Richard Ellis and Christian Bingaman. Pensacola, 25 May 1779 by Chester. // File. Claimant, Adam Bingaman for Daniel McGillivray, 27 Mch. 1804. Wit: Wm. Atchinson. Confirmed. Certif. A-536, issued Aug. 28, 1805. Adam Bingaman, as atty. for Daniel McGillivray, claims in his behalf 300 acres gr. to him by the British Govt., as above.

p.160. Claim No.1324. British gr. to John Bentley, 200 acres, 2 mi. NW of the Natchez, adj. lands of Jacob Phillippi and Alexander McIntosh, Pensacola, 21 July 1777. // Lease and release, 3rd and 4th Aug. 1777. John Bentley, schoolmaster, to Alexander McIntosh, 200 acres on waters of Fairchild's Cr. adj. Jacob Phillippi, John Smith and Alex. McIntosh for $60. Wit: Richard Ellis, Patrick Foley, Samuel Gibson. // File. Adam Bingaman, claimant, 27 Mch. 1804. Wit: Wm. Atchinson. Certif. A-226. Adam Bingaman claims 200 acres gr. by British Govt. to John Bentley and conveyed by him to Alexander McIntosh, as above, and by will of Ann Bingaman, wife of sd Adam, formerly Ann McIntosh, became the property of said Adam.

p.192. Claim No.1325. British gr. to William Brown, 150 acres, 12 mi. east of Natchez, b. by James Robertson and David Waugh. Pensacola, 21 July 1777 by Chester. // p.198. Lease and release, 1st and 2nd Nov. 1777, William Brown and wife, Mary, of West Florida, to Alexander McIntosh, 150 acres granted as above, for 100. Wit: Wm. Swanson, Patrick Foley. // File. Claimant, Adam Bingaman, 27 Mch. 1804. Wit: Wm. Atchinson. Certif. A-227, issued 22 May 1805. Adam Bingaman claims 150 acres gr. and conveyed as above, as legatee of his wife, formerly Ann McIntosh.

p.205. Claim No.1326. British gr. to Philip Harman, 150 acres, 20 mi. NE of the Natchez, adj. John Bentley and Alexander Boyd. Pensacola, 21 July 1777 by Chester. Plat shows land on north fork of Fairchild's Cr. // p.220. Lease and release, 9th and 10th Nov. 1777. Philip Harman to Alexander McIntosh, the above gr. for 150 acres, for $100. Wit: Patrick Foley, William Smith. Harman signed with a mark. [File missing.]

p.220. Claim No.1327. British gr. to Alexander McIntosh, 200 acres on a br. of Boyd's Cr., 12 mi. NE of the Natchez, adj. Patrick Stuart. Pensacola, 9th Nov. 1777. // File. Claimant, Adam Bingaman, 27 Mch. 1804. Witness: Wm. Atchinson. Certif. A-229 issued to claimant. Adam claims above gr. of 200 acres by virtue of the Br. gr. above and the will of his wife, Ann Bingaman, formerly Ann McIntosh, wid. of sd Alexander.

p.226. Claim No.1328. British gr. to Samuel Gibson, 100 acres, 12 mi. east of the Natchez, adj. David Waugh and Wm. Brown. Pensacola, 9 Oct. 1777. Lease and release, 17th and 18th Nov. 1777. Samuel Gibson to Alexander McIntosh the above tract. Wit: Patrick Foley and Will Eason. // File. Adam Bingaman, claimant, 27 Mch. 1804. Wit: Wm. Atchinson. Certif. A-230 issued to claimant. Claim founded on above grant and transfer and will of Ann Bingaman, wife of sd Bingaman, and formerly wid. of Alex. McIntosh.

p.246. Claim No.1329. Lease and release, 1st and 2nd March 1776. John Watkins to Alexander McIntosh, 500 acres 4 mi. NE of Fort, 3 mi. from River Miss. granted to James Watkins who died intestate, and land descended to his oldest son, as John Watkins; for $530. Wit: Anthony Hutchins, Donald McPherson. // File. Claimant, Adam Bingaman, 27 Mch. 1804. Wit: William Atchinson, 24 Sept. 1804. Certif. A-53 issued to claimant. [Adam Bingaman's claim founded on the above release and his inheritance of the land from his wife, who was the widow of sd McIntosh.] The original grant was burned when Watkins' house was consumed by fire.

p.250. Claim No.1330. Spanish gr. to William Norris, who had completed six months service in the Mounted Volunteers under Capt. Richard King, for which he was granted 200 acres. 18 Jany. 1793. // File. William Norris, claimant, 27 Mch. 1804. Wit: John Searcy, 5 Nov. 1804. Rejected. Wm. Norris claims a right to 200 acres on the Homochitto by virtue of a warrant of survey, for services rendered as above.

p.250. Claim No.1333. Spanish gr. to David Waltman, order of survey. N.O. 26 Apr. 1790 by Miro. // His petition for land on Homochitto, 9 Aug. 1789. // p.251. Benjamin Kitchen assigns a certain improvement on the Homochitto that he purchased from Mordecai Richards and give over all papers to John Richey, for $500. (n.d.) Wit: P. Connelly, Robert Barrow, A. Wilkinson. // File. John Richey claimant, 28 Mch. 1804. Mathew McCulloch, witness, 4 Mch. 1805. Certif. B-270 issued for 240 arpents under the warrant of survey, 11 May 1807. John Richey claims a Donation of 640 acres as described in plat, founded on a Sp. warrant of survey to David Waltman for 240 acres, who verbally transferred this to Mordecai Richards, who made improvements on the 240 acres and extended the same on the remaining 400 acres. He then sold verbally the premises with his improvements to Benjamin Kitchens, who cleared 25 acres and built five or six houses thereon, and sold his right to the present claimant, in October 1800, who immediately took possession and greatly improved the 240 acres. The claimant has resided 18 years in the Territory and has a wife and 8 children.

p.252. Claim No.1334. Spanish gr. to Elizabeth Maria Celeste Hutchins, 800 acres, 40 mi. south of Fort, on a br. of Bayou Sarah, adj. Wm. Dunbar, N.O. 25 May 1791 by Miro. // File. Claimants, W. Brooks and wife. Wit: Abner Green, 2 Aug. 1804. Certif. A-396 issued to W. Brooks in right of his wife. William Brooks and Elizabeth Maria Celeste, his wife, formerly Elizabeth Maria Celeste Hutchins, claims 800 acres in Wilkinson, as granted to her above.

p.255. Claim No.1335. Spanish gr. to William Wicks [Weeks], 277 acres one league NE of Fort, adj. Wm. Vousdan, Abraham Horton, Ezekiel Horton, and Gideon Gibson. N.O. 3 Apr. 1790. // Wicks to Vousdan, above tract, for $250 paid. 7 Dec. 1794. Maria Wicks, Wm. Wicks. Before Gayoso. // File. Claimant, Wm. Brooks, 28 Mch. 1804. Wit: Abner Green, 2 Aug. 1804. Certif. A-397 issued to Brooks in right of his wife, 2 July 1805. William Vousdan, legal representative of William Vousdan, decd. claim 277 acres in Adams Co. founded on a Spanish gr. to William Weeks who conveyed the same to William Vousdan, afsd., as above. G. Poindexter for the claimant.

p.259. Claim No.1336. Spanish gr. to Samuel Gibson, 380 acres on St. Catherine's Cr., adj. Joseph Forster, N.O. 16 Jany. 1784 by Miro. // File. Claimant, William Brooks and wife, 28 Mch. 1804. Wit: Abner Green, 2 Aug. 1804. Res. of Thomas Foster proved in claim No.100. Certif. A-401 issued to Brooks in right of his wife, 5 July 1805. William Brooks and Elizabeth Maria Celeste, his wife, formerly Elizabeth Maria Celeste Vousdan, legal representatives of William Vousdan, claim 380 acres in Adams Co. by virtue of a Spanish gr. to Samuel Gibson who conveyed the same to Henry Stephens. Said Stephens conveyed the same to sd Wm. Vousdan, 13 Jany. 1798. G. Poindexter atty. for the claimants. Notation: Gibson conveyed to Patten, he to Williams, he to Calvet, he to Foster, he to Flowers, he to Stephens, and Stephens to Vousdan. (signed) T.R.

p.262. Claim No.1337. Spanish gr. to Samuel Gibson, 150 acres on St. Catherine's Cr., 3 mi. east of Fort, adj. lands of Wm. Vousdan and Obediah Brown. N.O. 8 April, 1789 by Miro. // File. Claimant, William Brooks and wife, 28 Mch. 1804. Wit: Abner Green, 2 Aug. 1804. Certif. A-398 issued to W. Brooks in right of his wife. William Brooks and Elizabeth Maria Celeste, his wife, formerly Elizabeth Maria Celeste Vousdan, representatives of Wm. Vousdan, claim 150 acres in Adams Co., founded on Spanish patent to Samuel Gibson who conveyed the same to sd Vousdan, 3 Nov. 1792. G. Poindexter for claimant.

p.266. Claim No.1338. Spanish gr. to David Ferguson, 87 arpents on St. Catherine's Cr., 3 mi. east of the Fort, adj. Samuel Swazey, Samuel Gibson and Don Manuel Gayoso de Lemos. N.O. 14 Aug. 1794 by Carondelet. // File. Claimant, William Brooks, 28 Mch. 1804. Wit: Abner Green. Certif. A-432 to claimant. William Brooks claims 87 acres by virtue of a Spanish patent to David Ferguson, who conveyed the same to the present claimant.

p.269. Claim No.1339. When the affairs of this country are settled so that business can be done in a regular manner, Thomas Jordan will make to Robert Turner a right to 100 acres, part of a tract belonging to Thos. Jordan and sold to him by Thomas Jordan. Natchez, 24 July 1795. Both signed. Wit: Jesse Withers. // File. Robert Turner, claimant, 28 Mch. 1804. Wit: Randal Gibson, 23 June 1805. Certif. A-502 issued 1805. Robert Turner claims 100 acres of land in Jefferson Co. on Fairchild's Cr. founded on a Spanish pat. to Thomas Jordan, 15 March 1788, for 600 acres, who conveyed the said 100 acres to present claimant, being a part of the 600 acres.

p.269. Claim No.1340. Spanish gr. to Wm. Vousdan, 140 acres on St. Catherine's Cr., 3 mi. east of Natchez, adj. Wm. Weeks, Samuel Gibson and Ezekiel Dewitt. N.O. 8 June 1792 by Carondelet. // File. Claimant, William Brooks and wife, 28 Mch. 1804. Abner Green, witness. Certif. A-399 issued to W. Brooks in right of his wife, July 1805. William Brooks and Elizabeth Maria Celeste, his wife, formerly Elizabeth Maria Celeste Vousdan, rep. of William Vousdan, decd., claim 140 acres in Adams Co., founded on a Spanish patent to sd Vousdan, of whom the claimants are the legal representatives. G. Poindexter, atty.

p.272. Claim No.1341. Spanish gr. to William Vousdan, 71 arpens, 4 mi. NE of the Fort, b. by Samuel Gibson and Job Cory. N.O. 29 May 1795 by Carondelet. // File. Claimants, W. Brooks and his wife, 28 Mch. 1804. Wit: Abner Green. Certif. A-400 issued to W. Brooks in right of his wife, 2 July 1805.

p.274. No.1346. 17 June 1782. Sale of land, part of confiscated property of Jacob Winfree, on Second Cr. and the Homochitto, 1000 acres b. by Thos. Hutchins, Richard Harrison, Samuel Lewis, Mr. Dickson, and Richard Ellis sold to Nathaniel Tomlinson for $324, signed by the Commandant, witnesses and assistants: Silas Crane, St.Germain, Nath'l Tomlinson, Francis Farrell, James Harman, Staphen Mayes, Francis Spain, David Smith and Samuel Gibson before Chas. DeGrand-Pre. // File. Claimant, Nathaniel Tomlinson, 28 Mch. 1804. Wit: Philetus Smith, 1 Oct. 1804. Certif. A-779 issued 27 May 1806. Nathaniel Tomlinson claims 1000 acres on Second Cr. by virtue of a sale by the Spanish Government to the sd Tomlinson 17 June 1782, the 1000 acres being confiscated and returned to the King of Spain's domain.

p.276. No.1350. British gr. to Wm. Vousdan, 500 acres on Bayou Pierre, b. SW by Thomas James, NW by John Alston. Pensacola 19 Mch. 1779, by Peter Chester. No plat. // William Vousdan to Joseph Darlington, 500 acre tract above. Signed by both before GrandPre. // p.280. Power of Atty. Joseph Darlington to Peter Brian Bruin, of Adams Co., Miss. Ter. (signed) Joseph Darlington, at Chillicothe, Ross Co., Territory Northwest of the Ohio, 5 Nov. 1800. // 5 Sept. 1801. Joseph Darlington, of Ter. NW of the Ohio to George Wilson Humphreys, of Pickering Co., Miss. Ter. for $825 in hand paid, 500 acres above granted to Wm. Vousdan. Signed by P. B. Bruin. Wit: Wm. Scott, Wm. Atchinson, Bryan Bruin. [No file.]

p.285. Claim No.1352. Spanish gr. to John Pickens, 240 acres on a br. of the North Fork of Cole's Cr., adj. lands of Henry Green. N.O. 1 Jany. 1793 by Carondelet. // [The file is a claim for an altogether different tract of land. It was apparently numbered wrong.]

p.287. Claim No.1355. Petition of Sarah Smith, wife of George Humphreys, and Mary Smith, her sister, that being established on a tract of land in His Majesty's Government, on which their father, David Smith, lived, but having no grant whatever and being absent from their father, they ask a piece of land in this location be given them adjoining those of John Hartley. Natchez, 14 March 1794. Sarah Smith and Mary Smith. // Recommendation of Gayoso that they be granted 480 acres to be divided equally between the two. Natchez, 28 Jany. 1795. (signed) Manuel Gayoso de Lemos. // N.O. 24 Feb. 1795. Grant for 480 acres. El Baron de Carondelet. // File. Claimant, George W. Humphreys, 28 Mch. 1804. Wit: William Smith, 15 Dec. 1807. Certif. B-145, 10 Feb. 1807. Miss. Territory, Claiborne Co. George W. Humphreys, Sarah Humphreys, his wife, and Maria Dillingham claim 480 acres in sd Co. on the North Fork of Bayou Pierre, by virtue of a warrant of survey by the Spanish Government, 24 Feb. 1795, to the said Sarah Humphreys and Maria Dillingham, in the name of Maria and Sara Smith. altho the said Sarah was, at the date of the said warrant, the wife of said Humphreys. G. W. Humphreys for Sarah and Mary Smith. Certificate of survey by Wm. Dunbar that he had measured for Sarah and Mary Smith 48- acres on the north bank of Bayou Pierre bounded by lands of His Majesty. Natchez, 24 Mch. 1795.

p.293. Claim No.1360. British gr. to Josiah Flower, 400 acres south of land granted the late Phineas Lyman, Esq. on Bayou Pierre. Pensacola, 4 Aug. 1779. [File missing.]

p.293. Claim No.1361. Spanish gr. to Henry Platner, 200 arps. on waters of Cole's Cr. 16 mi. NE of Fort. [n.d.] File. Claimant, Henry Platner, 28 Mch. 1804. Wit: Andrew Watkins, 5 Nov. 1804. Cert. B-133 issued Feb. 5, 1807. Henry Platner claims 200 acres in Jefferson Co. founded on a Spanish patent, 24 Dec. 1797 to sd Henry, as above.

p.297. Claim No.1362. Spanish gr. to Henry Platner, 240 acres on a br. of Cole's Cr., 18 mi. NE of Fort, adj. Christian Braxton. N.O. 24 Dec. 1797, by Gayoso. // File. Claimant, Henry Platner, 28 Mch. 1804. Wit: Andrew Watkins, 5 Nov. 1804. Cert. B-2 issued 1807. Henry Platner claims 240 acres founded on the above Spanish patent.

p.299. Claim No.1363. John Keese, a notary public of and for the State of New York, certified the following deposition by John Blague, of New York City, merchant, stating that he was well-acquainted with Amos Ogden, who was Capt. of a Company of Rangers in His Brittanic Majesty's service and was employed in such service in America during the War between Great Britain and France in the Expedition against Canada. Amos Ogden died during the year 1775, leaving two sons, the eldest named John. The sd Amos Ogden sometime previous to his death received a grant or grants from the King of Great Britain for lands in West Florida and was residing there until shortly before he died, that after his death the deponent was possessed of some of his papers relative to his lands in West Florida. Amongst which as nearly as the deponent recollects was a patent for a part of sd lands and that during the late war with America whilst the papers were in his possession, some of them, and particular the sd patent, was destroyed or taken away by a party of British troops. N. Y. July 3, 1799. (signed) J. Blagge. // File. Claimant, John Ogden, 28 Mch. 1804. Wit: Nehemiah Carter, 8 Oct. 1804. Reported, 12 June 1807. John Ogden, a citizen of Miss. Territory, heir at law of Amos Ogden, decd., claims 25,000 acres on the Homochitto River by virtue of a mandamus granted to sd Amos Ogden, father of claimant, by Great Britain, about 1772 but which is now lost by time and accident. Claimant asks an amendment to claim of only the residue after several sales made by his father, about 4500 acres.

p.301. Claim No.1364. British gr. to Amos Ogden, 3000 acres, 20 mi. SE of the Natchez Fort, 14 mi. below White's landing on Homochitto creek 1 mile east from a lake on sd creek near the cow ford on a branch of Buffalo Cr. Pensacola, 6 May 1774, by Peter Chester. A two-page plat. // File. Claimant, John Ogden, 28 Mch. 1804. Wit: Nehemiah Carter, 8 Oct. 1804. Reported 28 Apr. 1807. Miss. Ter., Wilkinson Co., John Ogden, a citizen of New York, heir-at-law of Amos Ogden, claims 3000 acres in Wilkinson Co. on waters of Buffalo Cr. by virtue of a patent from the British Govt. to sd Amos Ogden, as above. Note: The claimant applies to the Board for a leave to alter his claim for only one moiety of the land, the other moiety being conveyed away by his father, which is granted by the Board. Signed: T. R. and E. T., Commrs.

p.310. Claim No.1366. British gr. to Hannah Lum, William Lum and Jesse Lum, 300 acres, 30 mi. NE of Fort, on Boyd's Creek. Pensacola, 14 Nov. 1776 by Chester. Plat and certif. show tract about 4 mi. above lands of Dibdy Holt and adj. on NW by Patrick Foley. // File. Claimants, heirs of Hannah, William and Jesse Lum, 28 Mch. 1804. Wit: Alexander Callender, 16 June 1804. [No report as to confirmation.] The legal representatives of Hannah, William and Jesse Lum claim 300 acres by virtue of a British patent to them executed as above. G. Poindexter, atty for claimants.

p.315. Claim No.1367. Spanish gr. to Hyram Sweazy, for having served six months in the company of Mounted Volunteers of Mr. Richard King, 200 acres, 18 Jany. 1793, by Gayoso. // File. Heirs of Hiram Swazey, claimants, 28 Mch. 1804. Wit: Richard King, 31 July 1805. Prosper King, 2 Aug. 1805. [No report as to confirmation.] The heirs and legal rep. of Hiram Swazey, decd., claim 164 arpents in Adams Co. about 1 mile east from the Fort by virtue of a Spanish order of survey. The sd Hiram Swazey died intestate, 24 Dec. 1793, leaving sundry heirs. By Richard Swazey.

p.309. Claim No.1365. Spanish gr. to Daniel McCoy, 300 acres on the Homochitto, 15 mi. SE of Fort, adj. Landon Davis and Estevan Ambrose. N.O. 10 Mch. 1789 by Miro. // File. Heirs of D. McCoy, claimants, 28 Mch. 1804. W. Atchinson, Wit. Certif. A-417 to legal representatives, 9 July 1805. Legal representatives of Daniel McCoy, decd. claim 300 acres in Wilkinson Co. as above, pat. to sd D. McCoy, decd.

p.315. Claim No.1368. Spanish gr. to Sarah Moore, widow Scott, 1000 acres on Bayou de la Feliciana, 40 mi. SSE of Fort, adj. William Moore, James Moore and Wm. Dunbar. N.O. 2 Mch. 1795, by Carondelet. // File. Samuel P. Moore and others, claimants, 28 Mch. 1804. Wit: (on the part of the U.S.) Alexander Montgomery. Wit: Ebenezer Rees,, 22 Aug. 1805. Disallowed on suspicion of its being antedated, 22 Dec. 1806. Samuel P. Moore, James Moore and Robert Moore, heirs at law of Sarah Moore, alias Sarah Scott, alias Sarah Zerbin, dec., claim 1000 acres on west br. of Bayou Sara by virtue of the above grant.

p.316. Claim No.1369. Spanish gr. to John Tier. His petition, as a carpenter and res. of this City, asks for Lot. No.3, Sq. 20 in sd city, on which he wishes to build a house. 10 Jany. 1795. Granted, 15 Jany. 1795, by Gayoso. // File. Claimants, Samuel, James and R. Moore, 28 Mch. 1804. Res. of John Tier proved in Claim No.447. Claim Lot. 1[1], Sq. 20. Claim confirmed. Certif. B-290, issued June 1, 1807. Samuel P. Moore, James Moore and Robert Moore, legal rep. of William Moore, decd., claim above lot by virtue of a gr. by Spanish Govt. to John Tier, as above, and sold by sd Tier to sd William in 1797 and from whom, the said lot, at his death, descended to sd claimants and Sarah Moore, alias Scott, alias Zerbin since deceased. Said Sarah's part at her death being descended to the claimants, as her heirs.

p.317. Claim No.1370. Spanish gr. to William Moore, 1000 acres on a br. of Bayou de la Feliciana, 49 mi. SSE of Fort, adj. James Moore, Mrs. Sarah Scott and William Scott. N.O. 22 Mch. 1795, by Carondelet. // File. Claimants, Samuel P. Moore and others, 28 Mch. 1804. Wit: on part of U.S., Alexander Montgomery, 31 July 1805. Wit: Ebenezer Rees, 22 Aug. 1805. Disallowed on suspicion of being antedated, 22 Dec. 1807. Samuel P. Moore, James Moore and Robert, legal rep of William Moore, decd., claim 1000 acres in Wilkinson Co. by virtue of a Spanish patent to sd William Moore, as above, from whom, at his death, the land descended to sd claimants and Sarah Moore, alias Sarah Scott, alias Sarah Zerbin, since decd.

p.320. Claim No.1371. Spanish survey to Arthur Cobb, 100 acres, part of a warrant for 500 acres, surveyed in a tract of 400 acres granted to William Cobb, making 600 acres and now there is 500 acres left. Having sold land to Mr. Chas. Surgett and the sd 100 acres was surveyed by desire and consent of both parties between St. Catherine's and Second Creeks, 6 mi. SE of Fort. The said 600 acres was surveyed for Wm. and Arthur Cobb, 29 Aug. 1788. // File. Claimant, Chas. Surget 28 Mch. 1804. Wit: Wm. Atchinson, 18 July 1804. Certif. B-134 issued in 1807. Proved in Arthur Cobb. Chas. Surget claims 100 arpents by virtue of a warrant of survey by the Spanish Govt. granted, July 1787 to William Cobb, as above, etc., 100 acres being gr. to Arthur Cobb which he sold to the claimant, 17 Nov. 1797. Plat and survey by Wm. Atchinson.

p.321. Claim No.1372. Spanish gr. to Chas. Surget, 500 acres on a br of Feliciana Bayou, 45 mi. SSE of the Fort, adj. Peter Surget and John Ellis. N.O. 7 Dec. 1797, by Gayoso. // File. Chas. Surget, claimant, 28 Mch. 1804. Wit: Wm. Atchinson, 18 July 1804; Samuel Stockett, 10 Dec. 1804. Rejected 21 May 1805. See No.1564. Chas. Surget claims 500 arps. by virtue of a warrant of survey by Sp. Govt. to alaimant; surv. April 1795, and gr. as above.

p.324. Claim No.1373. Spanish gr. to Arthur Cobb, 400 acres on Second Creek, 9 mi. SE of Fort, adj. Stephen Minor, Peter Surget and Daniel Clark. N.O. 7 Dec. 1797, by Gayoso. // File. Claimant, Chas. Surget, 28 Mch. 1804. Wit: Wm. Atchinson. Certif. B-135, 5 Feb. 1807. Proved in Arthur Cobb. Chas. Surget claims 400 arpents by virtue of a Spanish warrant to Arthur Cobb, 16 April 1787, and issued by Gov. Gayoso, as above, on which land was established a plantation and considerable improvements long before the date of the U.S. Treaty with Spain.

p.327. Claim No.1374. British Gr. to William, Walter and Alexander Moore, a tract 62 miles below Natchez, 13 miles above Red River on the Miss., b. on north by lands of Francis Poussett. Pensacola, 28 Nov. 1768, by Montfort Brown. A large plat. // File. S. P. Moore and others, claimants, 28 Mch. 1804. Wit: John Girault, 5 Aug. 1805. Certif. A-509 issued to claimants. Samuel P. Moore, James Moore and Robert Moore claim a tract of 1500 acres in Wilkinson Co. on the Miss. River by virtue of a British grant in 1768 unto William Moore, Walter Moore and Alexander Moore, of whom the said Walter died and his share thereof came by survivorship came to sd William and Alexander, and afterwards the said Alexander died and by the Spanish laws then in force, his share of the said land descended unto his father, Alexander, decd. who gave the same by last will and testament to the claimants, who were also heirs-at-law of the last original claimant, William.

p.332. Claim No.1379. Spanish gr. to Richard Curtis, 400 acres on Cole's Cr., 26 mi. NE of Fort. N.O. 25 Jany. 1795, by Carondelet. // File. Claimant, Richard Curtis, 28 Mch. 1804. Wit: James Truly, 5 Mch. 1804. Certif. A-352 to claimant, 21 June 1805. Richard Curtis claims 400 acres by virtue of the above grant.

p.335. Claim No.1892. British gr. to John Blommart, 2000 acres on waters of Fairchild's Cr., 18 mi. from Fort; adj. gr. to Philip Harman. Pensacola, 29 Apr. 1777, by Peter Chester. // File. Heirs of Thomas Durham, claimants, 5 Apr. 1804. Reported, 28 Apr. 1807. The heirs and legal representatives of Thos. Durham, decd., claim 2000 acres by virtue of British patent to John Blommart, as above, and a conveyance of the sd tract by sd Blommart to sd Thos. Durham, 29th and 30th April 1777, and of their being the heirs of the sd Thomas Durham.

p.338. Claim No.1891. Spanish gr. to Robert Dunbar, 200 acres on the north fork of Cole's Creek, 26 mi. NE of Fort, adj. Wm. Dunbar and John Murdoch. N.O. 14 Aug. 1794, by Carondelet. // File. Robert Dunbar, claimant, 9 May 1804. Confirmed. Certif. A-500, 15 Aug. 1805. Adams Co., Robert Dunbar claims 200 acres by virtue of the above Spanish grant.

p.343. Claim No.1895. Warrant of survey for 400 acres from the British Govt. to Sarah, Coleby, Jonathan, Susanna, Catherine, George and William Rucker, on south side of Bayou Pierre to cover the improvement made by Sarah Rucker. Pensacola, 11 Feb. 1778, by Peter Chester. // File. Sarah Davis and others claimants, 21 Mch. 1804. Rejected 27 April 1807. Sarah Davis, formerly Sarah Rucker, Coleby, Jonathan, Susanna, Catherine, George and William Rucker claim 400 acres in Claiborne Co. on south side of Bayou Pierre above the mouth of a small cr. called the Widow's Cr., 10 mi. up Bayou Pierre from where it empties into the Miss. River, by virtue of a British order of survey granted to them, as above. Sarah Davis for herself and other claimants.

p.344. Claim No.1896. British gr. to Richard Barry, 50 acres, 24 mi. NE from Fort, adj. Simon McCormack, 3 mi. east from River Miss. on Boyd's Cr. Pensacola, 22 July 1769, by Montfort Brown. // File. Claimant, Richard Barry, 7 July 1804. Reported 28 April 1807. Richard Barry claims 50 acres on Boyd's or Cole's Cr. by virtue of a British patent as above. Signed Thos. Durnford, agent for Richard Barry.

p.348. Claim No.1897. British gr. to William Mills, 50 acres 24 mi. NE from Fort, adj. survey to Samuel Osburn, 3 mi. east of River Miss. Pensacola, 22 July 1769 by Montfort Brown. Plat. // File. Claimant, William Mills, 7 July 1804. Reported, 28 April 1807. William Mills claims 50 acres by virtue of a British grant to him, as above. Thos. Durnford, agent for Wm. Mills.

p.353. Claim No.1898. British gr. to James Rumsey, 1000 acres, 26 mi. NE of Fort, east 2 mi. from River Miss. NE 2 mi. from survey of Richard Barry, adj. Richard Pearnes east boundary, on Boyd's Cr. Pensacola, 26 Mch. 1774. // File. David Hodge, claimant, 7 July 1804. Reported, 28 Apr. 1807. The heirs of the late David Hodge claim 1000 acres by virtue a British title granted James Rumsey, as above, and sold and conveyed by sd James Rumsey and Jane, his wife, to sd David Hodge, 23 July 1774 and 6 Dec. 1776; the two releases for which are herewith presented. Thos. Durnford, exor of the last will and testament of David Hodge.

p.358. Claim No.1899. British gr. to James Amoss, 600 acres, 19 mi. north of Red River and part on high bluff of Loftus Cliffs. Pensacola 24 July 1772. // File. James Amoss claims 600 acres, Loftus Cliffs, 7 July 1804. Reported 28 April 1807. James Amoss claims 600 acres by virtue of a British gr., as above. James Amoss by his agent, Thos. Durnford.

p.364. Claim No.1548. Spanish gr. to Squire Boone, 200 acres on Bayou Pierre, 55 mi. NE of Fort, on the Big Black. N.O. 18 Oct. 1788 by Miro. // File. Claimant, Squire Boone, 29 Mch. 1804. Wit: Richard King, 21 Nov. 1805. Certif. A-711 issued to legal representatives of William Henderson, 8 Jany. 1806. Squire Boone claims 200 arpents on Big Black by virtue of the above Spanish patent. (See Claim No.1553.)

p.367. Claim No.1549. Spanish gr. to William Brocus, 240 acres, on Bayou Chubby, a br. of Bayou Pierre, 35 mi. NNE of Fort. N.O. 30 May 1793, by Carondelet. // File. Claimant, Wm. Brocus, 29 Mar. 1804. Wit: William James, 29 Oct. 1804. Certif. A-374, issued 25 June 1805. Claim founded on Spanish gr. above.

p.370. Claim No.1550. Spanish gr. to John O'Connor, 330 acres on Buffalo Cr. 14 mi. SE of Fort, adj. William Conway. N.O. 30 Aug. 1793, by Carondelet. // File. Claimant, John O'Conner, 29 Mch. 1804. Certif. A-169, 18 Sept. 1805. Claim based on above Spanish grant. O'Conner an actual settler, 27 Oct. 1795.

p.375. Claim No.1552. Spanish gr. to Squire Boone, 250 acres on Big Black River. N.O. 22 Mch. 1795, by Carondelet. // File. Squire Boone claimant, 29 Mch. 1804. Wit: Richard King, 21 Nov. 1805. Certif. A-712, to legal rep. of Wm. Henderson, 8 Jan. 1806. Claim founded on above patent. (See Note in No.1553.)

p.389. Claim No.1553. Spanish gr. to Squire Boone, 250 acres on Bayou Pierre, 55 mi. NE of Fort. N.O. 18 Oct. 1788, by Miro. Plat. // File. Claimant, Squire Boone, 29 Mch. 1804. Wit: Richard King, 21 Nov. 1805. Certif. A-713, to legal rep of Wm. Henderson, 8 Jany. 1806. Claim founded on above Spanish gr. Note: The claim should have been drawn in the name of the heirs of William Henderson who, previous to his death, purchased of the patentee. (signed) T.H.W.

p.381. Claim No.1554. Spanish gr. to William Henderson, 500 acres on Homochitto on the new road from Natchez to N.O., 18 mi. from Fort. N.O. 10 Feb. 1787, by Miro. Plat. // File. Claimant, William Henderson, 29 Mch. 1804. Wit: Richard King, 21 Nov. 1805. Certif. A-695, to legal rep. 6 Jany. 1806. Claim founded on above Spanish gr.

p.384. Claim No.1559. Spanish gr. to Widow Armstrong. Decree, Natchez, 13 Sept. 1794. . In consequence of representations made me by Widow Armstrong, I do hereby authorize her to take possession of the plantation lately abandonned by her son, Moses Armstrong, to hold the same for her use and that of her children until further orders. // Josiah Stansbery who has lately petitioned for said plantation will appear at Government house to have his location altered. Signed: Manuel Gayoso de Lemos. // File. Claimant, Thomas White, 30 Mar. 1804. Wit: Gibson Clark, 20 Nov. 1804. Certif. B-153 issued 10 Feb. 1804. Thomas White claims 400 acres, by order of survey from Spanish Govt. to Sarah Armstrong, as above and by conveyance from her to claimant, tract on Bayou Pierre, adj. lands of Abraham Green, now Claiborne Co. // Deed, the heirs of Armstrong to Thomas White. 17 Aug. 1798, Moses, Sarah, Robert, Felix, Elizabeth, and Polly Armstrong, of the Dist. of Bayou Pierre, Govt. of Natchez, to Thos. White, of same, for $300 in hand paid, 400 acres, adj. on NE Filmer and Abraham Green, other sides vacant at time of survey. Signed by all. Wit: Ebenezer Smith, Joseph White, John Pollard.

p.384. Claim No.1561. Spanish gr. to Richard Bell, 500 acres on Cole's Cr., 15 mi. NE of Fort, adj. Adam Bingaman, James Coles and Benjamin Curtis. N.O. 29 Feb. 1788. // File. Claimant, Peter A. Vandorn, 30 Mch. 1804. Wit: Alexander Montgomery, 18 Mch. 1805. Certif. A-792, 18 Mch. 1807. Peter A. Vandorn claims 500 acres founded on the above Spanish patent to Richard Bell who conveyed same to Robert and Mordecai Throckmorton who conveyed same to present claimant. Original patent, survey and plat in file. The conveyance from Bell lost. Deed, ____ 1802. Robert Throckmorton, Mordecai Throckmorton and Patsy, his wife, all of Jefferson Co. to Peter A. Vandorn, of Adams Co. for $3000, in hand paid, the 500 acres afsd on Cole's Cr. All three signed. Wit: Abijah Hunt, A. L. Duncan. Ack. by each before Henry Green, J. P.

p.388. Claim No.1566. Lease and release, 1st and 2nd Oct. 1778, James Marcus Prevost, Major 2nd Battalion of His Majesty's 60th Reg. of Foot, now stationed at St. Augustine, East Fla., by Edmund Rush Wegg and Elihu Hall Bay of Pensacola and James Amoss, merchant, of same, to Alexander Macullagh, one-half part of two tract, 3000 acres as reduced Major and 3000 acres as reduced Captain, sd Macullagh to pay fees. // File. Claimant, Alexander McCullagh, 30 Mch. 1804. (See No.1493 for the residue of the patent.) Reported 28 Apr. 1807. . . . the southerly half of the above tract of 1500 acres, say 750 acres, on the east side of the Miss. near the great lake above the mouth of Tonica Bayou, adj. lands of Donald McDonald, Wm. McKennon and Alexander McCullagh, by virtue of a gr. to James Marcus Prevost, 14 July 1778 and indentures from Prevost's attorneys to claimant. John McCaleb, atty. for Alexander McCullagh.

p.404. Claim No.1568. Petition of Thomas Smith to the Spanish Govt. for 140 arps on Bayou Pierre adj. _____ Slater. 29 Dec. 1789. // Warrant by Miro, 9 Feb. 1790. // p.405. Plat to foregoing by Wm. Thomas, D. S. 10 Feb. 1795. Land on North fork of Bayou Pierre. // File. Claimant, Daniel Burnet, 30 Mch. 1804. Wit: Richard King, 9 June 1807. Rejected. See No.1030. Daniel Burnet claims 240 acres on waters of Bayou Pierre in Claiborne Co. by virtue of a warrant of survey from Spanish Govt. to Thomas Smith, and by him conveyed to Stephen Douglass and by Douglass to claimant, 2 Jany. 1795. The said claimant settled and improved and held in continual possession until the present time. Signed. Note on reverse: The claimant says this tract is included in the survey of Donation claim, No.1030 of 500 acres, 23 Apr. 1805. Signed: T. R.

p.406. Claim No.1571. Petition to the Spanish Govt. of Bridget Roberts that she is a widow with two sons and a negro, asks for a grant near Natchez. 2 April 1792. Certif. for Lot No.3, Sq.No.4, 8 Jany. 1793. Grant 7 June 1796 by Gayoso. // File. Claimant, Juliana Stacpoole, 30 Mch. 1804. Wit: Bennet Truly, 2 Nov. 1805. Certif. B-7, issued 2 June 1806. Juliana Stacpoole, heiress and devisee of Joseph Murray, late of this territory, decd., claims a lot in the City of Natchez by virtue of a grant to Bridget

Roberts from the Sp. Govt. and by her conveyed to Joseph Murry, decd., and by the sd Murray devised to the claimant by his last will, filed in the proper office of New Orleans. The sd lot is No. 3, Sq.No.4. In the file the original warrant, survey and patent, on the back of the last is written Bridget Robert's assignment of house and lot to Joseph Murray for $160. Wit: George Overaker.

p.408. Claim No.1574. British gr. to Daniel Mygat, order of survey for 100 acres on Bayou Pierre, 5 mi. from mouth. Pensacola, 19 Nov. 1779. // File. Claimants, heirs of Daniel Mygatt, 30 Mch. 1804. Rejected. Apr. 27, 1807.

p.409. Claim No.1576. Spanish gr. to Richard Goodwin, 600 acres. [Nothing more but plat showing St. Germain on NE, Cypress Swamp and a lake on NW, the lake extending into the 600-acre tract.] // File. Claimants, heirs of Asahel Lewis. [Details missing here.] Seth Lewis in behalf of himself and other heirs of Asahel Lewis, decd., claim 600 acres granted by the Spanish Govt. to Richard Goodwin, 10 July 1787; by Goodwin's representative to Henry Manadue, by sd Manadue to Bennet Truly, by Truly to Asahel Lewis, decd. and Charles Boardman, and sd Boardman's part conveyed by him to Asahel Lewis, decd., from whom the same descended to the claimants. Seth Lewis for self and other claimants.

p.412. Claim No.1578. Reg. 30 Mch. 1804. Spanish warrant of survey for 1000 arpents to Edward Murray, on south fork of Bayou Pierre, 45 miles NE of Fort Panmure, adj. John Terry, Samuel Gibson and Filmer and Abraham Green. Aug. 18, 1795. Carlos Trudeau. Grant for the same, 20 Aug. 1795 by Carondelet. // File. Edward Murray, Certif. granted, 19 May 1807, to Edward Murray for the use of William Scott. Seth Lewis for claimant.

p.415. Claim No.1579. Spanish Govt. to William Scott, warrant for 1000 acres, 24 Feb. 1795. Signed by Trudeau. Grant for tract 45 mi. SSE of the Fort, adj. Ezekiel Forman and James Moore. 22 Mch. 1795 by Carondelet. // File. Claimant, William Scott, 30 Mch. 1804. Wit: Ebenezer Rees, 7 July 1805. Disallowed on suspicion of its being antedated, 22 Dec. 1807. Claim founded on the above grant.

p.418. Claim No.1580. Spanish Govt. fr William Scott, petition for 2 lots, Nos. 2 and 4 in Sq. No.27 of the city, Natchez, 8 Jany. 1795. Grant to same, by Gayoso. Jany. 10, 1795. Certif. of survey by Dunbar, 15 Jany. 1795. // File. Claimant, William Scott, 30 Mch. 1804. Proved in 1759. Certif. __-683 issued 19 Oct. 1805. S. Lewis, agent for claimant.

p.420. Claim No.1581. Spanish gr. to Fusilier de la Clare, 1100 acres 13 mi. SE of Fort Panmure, on the Homochitto River, adj. the lands of Don Carlos de Grand-Pre and a man named Swazey, 8 Aug. 1789 by Estevan Miro, at N.O. // File. Claimant, Fusilier de la Clare, 30 Mch. 1804. Rejected 12 June 1807. S. Lewis for claimant.

p.423. Claim No.1583. Spanish Govt. to Louis Charbonneau, warrant and patent for 500 acres adj. lands of Bacon, Peter Nelson, and a British concession, warrant 22 Dec. 1772, grant by Estevan Miro, 31 Mch. 1786. File. Claimant, George Rapalje, 30 Mch. 1804. Wit: Ebenezer Rees, 17 July 1805. See Nos. 1398 and 1637. Rejected, 16 May 1806. See Moore's claim. George Rapalje claims 500 acres by virtue of the above Spanish gr to Louis Charbono, who conveyed the land to the claimant. Deed: Louis Charbono to George Rapalje, 100 arpents for 400 bu. of corn in the grain, which he will deliver Oct. 1783. Dated 3 July 1783. Signed by both before Francisco Collell.

p.426. Claim No.1591. Warrant and patent for 600 arpents from the Spanish Govt. to George Rapalje; warrant signed 20 June 1783 by Carlos Trudeau; the patent by Miro, 31 Mch. 1787. The tract on east bank of the Miss. River, adj. Louis Charbono. // File. George Rapalje claimant, 30 Mch. 1804. See Nos. 1398 and 1637. Rejected 16 May 1806. Claim founded on the above grant.

p.429. Claim No.1592. Spanish Govt. to Jane Rapalje, certificate of survey, 11 Feb. 1789, by Carlos Trudeau; patent, N.O. 17 Feb. 1789, by Estevan Miro, for 1000 arpents on Second Cr., 10 mi. SE of Fort Panmure, adj. lands of Isaac Johnson, Esq. and Mr. Monsanto on north, on east by lands of Mrs. Jane Rumsey, on west by Abraham Ellis, and on south by an English concession, called the Mandamus line. // File. George Rapalje, in right of his wife, Jane Rapalje, 30 Mch. 1804. Certif. A-656 issued 3 Oct. 1805. George Rapalje and Jane, his wife, claim 1000 acres by virtue of the above Spanish patent, made prior to Oct. 27, 1795. Geo. Rapalje for Jane and Geo. Rapalje.

p.432. Claim No.1595. Spanish Govt. to Solomon Swazey. Petition of Solomon Swazey, a res. of this district, wishing to build a house in the New City of Natchez, asks for Lot.No.1, Sq.No.18, it being vacant. Natchez, 5 June 1795. Warrant for same, 6 June 1795 by Grand-Pre. Certif. of survey by Wm. Dunbar, 15 Oct. 1795. Patent for same to Solomon Swazey by Manuel Gayoso de Lemos, 5 Oct.

1795. File. Claimant, Patrick Connelly, 30 Mch. 1804. Wit: Bennet Truly, 18 June 1806. Certif. A-785, to legal rep., 30 Aug. 1806. Patrick Connelly claims above lot by virtue of the above grant to Solomon Swazey, by whom the same was conveyed to William Scott, who conveyed the same to claimant.

p.434. Claim No.1596. Petition of John Scott to the Spanish Govt. Having built a house on Lot No.4, Sq.No.1, in the city and having no title, he asks for grant to same. 20 July 1796. Certificate that the above lot has not been granted, by Dunbar, same date. // Grant for the above lot to sd John Scott, 20 July 1796, by Gayoso. // File. Claimant, Susanna Scott, 30 Mch. 1804. Wit: Bennet Truly, 5 June 1806. Certif. D-48, issued 7 Sept. 1806. Susanna, admx. and wid. of John Scott claims above lot by virtue of the Spanish grant of same to John Scott, her late husband, 22 July 1796.

p.436. Claim No.1596. Petition to the Spanish Govt. by George Cochran, who desires to locate in this district and asks for 300 arpents on Fairchild's Cr. adj. lands of Moses Bonner and Mr. Stampley, in consideration of a family which consists of his mother and brother, who have not received any grant from the Government. Natchez, 16 Oct. 1791. // Warrant for the land and location desired unless it is already taken up. Estevan Miro. N.O. 29 Dec. 1791. [File is missing.]

p.439. Claim No.1599. Certificate that Lot No.3, Sq.26 is vacant, Natchez, 27 Aug. 1795. (signed) William Dunbar. // File. Claimant, John Williams, 30 Mch. 1804. Wit: Neil McCane. Confirmed. Certif. B-283 issued 9 June 1807. John Williams, a citizen of Miss. Territory, who on 27 Oct. 1795, was an actual settler therein, claims Lot No.3, Sq.No.26 in the City of Natchez, by virtue of inhabiting and cultivating the sd ground before the day the Spanish troops evacuated the territory, at which time he was the head of a family. // Miss. Ter., Adams Co., 28 Mch. 1804. Personally appeared before me, William Darby, J. P. of sd county, William Barland and Neil McCane who made oath that the within John Williams did improve the sd lot by building a house upon it in 1796. William Barland, Neil (X) McCane.

p.440. Claim No.1603. Spanish Govt. to Daniel Miller, survey and patent for 300 acres, survey dated 10 Sept. 1793, patent by the Baron de Carondelet at New Orleans, 30 Sept. 1793. Tract on Tabor's fork of Bayou Pierre, adj. lands of Jacob Cobun, Justus and Prosper King and Waterman Crane. // File. Claimant, James Gibson, 30 Mch. 1804. Wit: David Gibson, 23 May 1804. Certif. A-649 issued 2 Oct. 1805. Claim by virtue of above grant to Daniel Miller who conveyed the same to Wm. Brocus, 3 June 1798, who conveyed to present claimant, 24 Jan. 1804. David Gibson for James Gibson.

p.443. Claim No.1608. Petition of Philip Engel to the Spanish Govt. wishing to establish a store, asks for a grant to land near the City of Natchez, adj. land of Joseph Vidal and Francisco Lennan. Natchez, 4 Feb. 1795. // Warrant for same 5 Feb. 1795, by Gayoso. // Certif. of survey by Wm. Dunbar, 8 Feb. 1795. // Patent for same by Gayoso de Lemos, 19 Feb. 1795. // File. Claimant, Polser Shilling, 30 Mch. 1804. Wit: John Shannauer, 12 Nov. 1804. Wit: Bennet Truly, 25 Feb. 1805. Certif. A-527 issued 27 Aug. 1805. Polser Shilling claims 10 arpents in the City of Natchez, by virtue of a Spanish grant to Philip Engle, as above, who conveyed the same to the claimant, 24 Jan. 1801.

p.446. Claim No.1612. Petition of Maria Gertrudis Solibellas to Spanish Govt. for a lot in the City on which to build a house. Natchez, 22 Jany. 1793. // Warrant for the above by Gayoso, 13 Feb. 1793. // Survey of Lot No.4, Sq.No.2 in the city for Maria Gertrudis Solibellas by Wm. Dunbar, 3 Feb. 1793. // Grant for same to same by Carlos de Grand-Pre, 24 Feb. 1796. // File. George Overaker, claimant, 30 Mch. 1804. Wit: Polser Shilling. Certif. B-13, issued 2 June 1806. George Overaker claims the above lot by virtue of a sale by Gertrude Solibellas to him of same which was granted to sd Solibellas in 1793 and improved and built on by the claimant in 1795.

p.448. Claim No.1614. Petition of George Overaker, an inhabitant of the City. to the Spanish Govt. for Lot No.4, Sq. No.14, in order to build a house thereon. 10 Jany. 1795. // Warrant for same to same by Gayoso, 10 Jany. 1795. // Certif. of survey by Wm. Dunbar, 12 Jany. 1795. // Grant from Gayoso, 15 Jany. 1795. // File. George Overaker, claimant, 30 Mch. 1804. Wit: Joshua Howard, 29 Aug. 1805. Certif. A-541, 29th Aug. 1805. Claim by virtue of the above Spanish grant.

p.450. Claim No.1615. Order of survey from Spanish Govt. to George Overaker for 1000 acres on River Feliciana, 46 mi. SSE from Fort Panmure, adj. land of John Ellis, by Carlos Trudeau, Surv. Genl. 2 Aug. 1797. // Grant to same for above tract by Manuel Gayoso de Lemos, 24 Dec. 1797. // File. George Overaker, claimant, 30 Mch. 1804. Rejected, 19 May 1807. // George Overaker claims 846 acres by virtue of the above Spanish gr to him, being that part of 1000 acres in said patent now found above the line of division between the Territory of the United States and the Dominion of His Catholic Majesty. Claimant explains that this land was thought to be in Spanish Territory when surveyed and he had spent much on improvements of same.

p.453. Claim No.1622. Spanish Govt. to Josiah Flower, survey of 100 acres, by Trudeau, 1 April 1795. // Grant to same of 100 acres on Tabor's Fork of Bayou Pierre, 50 mi. NE of Fort, by Carondelet. N.O. 10 April 1795. // File. Josiah Flower, claimant, 30 Mch. 1804. Certif. A-620, issued 8 Sept. 1805. Claim founded on the above Spanish grant. P. Walker for Josiah Flower.

p.456. Claim No.1623. Petition of Peter Walker to the Spanish Govt., being established a long distance from the Plaza and desiring to be nearer to the City to attend to his business and at the same time to have comfortable quarters for his family, asks land near Natchez. 3 Feb. 1795. // Warrant for same, by Gayoso, 4 Feb. 1795. // Survey of 10 acres near the City, adj. Joseph Vidal and Estevan Minor on north and northwest, by Mrs. Ann Dunbar on south, on NE by land of Louis Valeret, by Wm. Dunbar, 7 Feb. 1795. // A grant of the same to sd Peter Walker by Gayoso, 10 Feb. 1795. // File. Peter Walker, claimant, 30 Mch. 1804. Wit: Wm. Atchinson. Certif. A-528 issued 27 Aug. 1805. Peter Walker claims the above 10 acres by virtue of the above grant. [Plat shows the land of Louis Valeret belonging to Peter Walker and William Vousdan.]

p.459. Claim No.1624. Louis Valaret, res. of this City, petitions the Spanish Govt. that, desiring to establish a brick-kiln for the use of the city, asks for a gr. of 4 arpents of land near to Natchez, adj. Joseph Vidal. 6 Jany. 1795. // Warrant for same to same by Gayoso, 8 Jany. 1795. // Certif. of survey for Luis Vilaret of 4 arpents near the city, adj. NE Joseph Vidal, by Wm. Dunbar, 4 Feb. 1795. // Patent for afsd acres to Vilaret by Gayoso, 5 Feb. 1795. // Power of atty. from my mother and father, I, Abraham Vilaret, sell and transfer to Lewis Evans the land in this concession. 21 Mch. 1797. Wit: Joseph Vidal, Domo. Bouligny before Gayoso. // File. Peter Walker, claimant, 30 Mch. 1804. Wit: Wm. Atchinson, 25 Sept. 1804. Certif. A-529 issued 27 Aug. 1805. Peter Walker claims 4 acres, an outlot of the City, b. by the Public Jail, a lot of sd Peter Walker and a lot of Wm. Vousdan, Esq., being all that lot gr. by Spanish Govt. to Louis Villaret, as above, and conveyed by Abram Villaret, atty-in-fact for sd Louis, to Lewis Evans and by sd Evans and his wife to sd Peter Walker, 26 June 1801.

p.462. Claim No.1625. The Spanish Govt. to Robert Jones, 1000 acres on Fairchild's Cr, adj. lands of Thomas and Edward Patterson and part of a tract belonging to Marcus Olivares. N.O. 17 Jany. 1788 by Miro. // File. Claimant, Robert Jones, 30 Mch. 1804. Wit: Wm. Atchinson, 25 Sept. 1804. Non-residence is proved. Wit: Lyman Harding, 5 Mch. 1806. Certif. A-758 issued 10 Mch. 1806. Claim by Robert Jones for 1000 acres is founded on the above Spanish grant to him. Peter Walker, his atty.

p.465. Claim No.1626. The Spanish Govt. to Peter Cabanee, order of survey, 11 Dec. 1788, and grant, 14 June 1796, 400 acres in Adams Co., 1 mi. from the Homochitto and 18 mi. south of Fort Panmure, adj. Alexander Boulle, John Vauchere and Samuel Swazey. // File. Claimants, John Walker and Andrew Augustus Ellicot, 30 Mch. 1804. Rejected, 12 June 1807. Witness: Peter Walker, 13 June 1804. Claim confirmed. Certif. B- issued. Claim founded on above grant to Peter Cabanee from Spanish Govt. and by him conveyed to Peter Camus, 26 July 1796, and by Camus to claimants, 19 Mch. 1798.

p.468. Claim No.1627. Petition of Peter Nelson to the Spanish Govt. that he has not enough land to cultivate and being established by warrant of the Commandant, Don Carlos de Grand-Pre, on a tract 5 acres front by 40 depth, bounded by lands of Henry Lefleur and Luis Charbono, asks that he be granted said land and that the surveyor general establish its limits. Natchez, 19 July 1782. // Order by Miro that the land be so surveyed. Certificate of survey by Carlos Trudeau, Surv. Genl., 24 Aug. 1782. Grant to Pedro Nelson, land 5 arpents front by 40 arpents, b. by English concessions on north, east by Lefleur, west Luis Charbono, by Andres Lopez Armesto. N.O., 12 Oct. 1797. // File. William Scott, claimant, 30 Mch. 1804. Wit: Stephen Minor, 11 Nov. 1805. Certif. B-25 issued 4 June 1806. William Scott claims 200 arpents by virtue of warrant of survey, etc. as above, to Peter Nelson and by him sold to Francis Basso, decd., and by Sebastian Bosque, exor. of sd Basso, sold to Antonio Gras, and by sd Gras to present claimant, the 8th instant [March 1804.]

p.472. Claim No.1629. Henry Lafleur petitions the Spanish Govt., being established on a tract of land 10 arpents front by 40 arpents depth, which he asked of the Commandant, Don Carlos de Grand-Pre, who consented that he establish himself there until a grant came from the Superior Govt., now begs that the Surveyor General fix its limits and that he gets a patent for same. 19 July 1782. // Order for survey as requested. Miro. Fort Panmure, 20 Aug. 1782. Certif. of survey of 400 arpents to Henry Lafleur by Carlos Trudeau. 24 Aug. 1782. // Patent to same for the above tract adj. Peter Nelson, (signed) Estevan Miro. 1 March 1787. // File. Claimant, William Scott, 30 Mch. 1804. Wit: Stephen Minor, 11 Nov. 1805. Certif. A-789, to claimant in right of his wife, Clara, 4 Mar. 1807. Wm. Scott claims

400 acres by virtue of the above Spanish patent to Henry Lafleur, who by deed conveyed the same to Jacob Monsanto, 18 June 1787, and at the final adjustment of accounts of sd Jacob and his brother, Benjamin, was allotted to Mrs. Clara Monsanto, the wife of the present claimant. // Margarita Lafleur sells to Jacob Monsanto, represented by Estevan Minor, by a power of attorney, a tract of land, 10 arpents front by 40 arpents depth, [as granted above to Henry Lafleur,] and with the consent of Peter Nelson, tutor of the minor heirs of Lafleur, for 400 pesos, at Fort Panmure, Natchez, 18 June 1787. Margarita signed with a mark, not being able to write. Also signing: Peter Nelson, Estevan Minor. Carlos de Grand-Pre. [The plat also shows adj. land of J. St. Germain.]

p.476. Claim No.1630. Patent for 100 arpents to Carlos Truflo by Spanish Govt. near St. Catherine's Creek, 2 mi SE of Fort Panmure, adj. the lands of St. Germain, Lafleur and vacant lands. By Estevan Miro. N.O. 12 Mch. 1788. // File. Wm. Scott, claimant, 30 Mch. 1804. Wit: Stephen Minor, 11 Nov. 1805. Certif. A-740 issued to claimant in right of his wife, Clara. The claim founded on above Spanish patent to Carlos Truflo for 100 arpents and by him conveyed to Jacob Monsanto. 15 Mch. 1788, and in the final adjustment of accounts between Jacob Monsanto and his brother, Benjamin, was allotted to Clara Monsanto, relict of Benjamin Monsanto and now wife of the claimant. She was an actual resident on the said premises on 27 Oct. 1795.

p.479. Claim No.1635. Patent from Spanish Govt. to Ellena Truly, wife of Francis Spain. Certif. of survey to Mrs. Ellena Truly, wife of Francis Spain. In her presence and in the presence of Mr. Richard Harrison, surveyed 100 arpents in the Dist. of Natchez, on St. Catherine's Cr., 15 mi NE of Fort Panmure, bounded on three sides by land of Richard Harrison, and on the north by land of Francis Spain, being made to form a division of land by Mrs. Sarah Truly in favor of Mrs. Elena Truly and Mr. Richard Harrison, the daughter and son-in-law of said widow, Sarah Truly, according to a written agreement made by them 2 June of this year. Natchez, 29 Aug. 1795. Signed by Carlos Trudeau. // Grant to the above land by the Spanish Govt. to Mrs. Helena Truly, wife of Francis Spain, 180 arpents, as described above. By Carondelet. N.O. 30 Aug. 1795. // File. Claimants, James Spain and John Girault. 30 Mch. 1804. Wit: Richard King, 30 May 1804. Certif. A-375 issued, 3/4 to Girault and 1/4 to Spain, 25 June 1805. James Spain and John Girault, claim jointly as tenants in common but not as joint tenants, to wit: the said James Spain one undivided fourth and the sd John Girault three undivided fourths of 180 arpents by virtue of a Spanish gr. to Helena Spain, decd, 30 Aug. 1795, as above, and at the division of the est. of the sd Helena, one half was allotted to sd John Girault in behalf of his wife, Mary, and the other half to Stephen and Tabitha Mayes, daughter of sd Helena, and by sd Stephen and Tabitha Mayes was conveyed to the claimants, 14 Jan. 1802. For James Spain and self, John Girault.

p.482. Claim No.1638. Spanish Govt. to Maria Page 800 arpents on Cole's Creek, certificate of survey, 13 Aug. 1789, by Carlos Trudeau. Patent of same to Mrs. Francisco Paget, widow of the decd. Alexander Cousso, Capt. of the Grenadiers of Infantry of this Province, tract bounded by lands of Seth Lewis. N.O. July 7, 1789, by Estevan Miro. // File. Maria Page, claimant, 30 Mch. 1804. Wit: John Girault, 11 Oct. 1805. Certif. A-673 issued 14 Oct. 1805. For Miss Maria Page by John Girault.

p.485. Claim No.1639. Spanish Govt. to Christian Harman a survey for 600 arpents 10 mi. east of Fort Panmure, adj. John Hartley. N.O. 3 Mch. 1788, by Carlos Trudeau. // Patent for same. N.O. 6 Mch. 1788, by Estevan Miro. // File. Claimant, Nicholas Rabb, 30 Mar. 1804. Wit: George Killian. Certif. A-600 issued 16 Sept. 1805. Nicholas Rabb claim 600 acres in Adams Co. on St. Catherine's Creek by virtue of the above Spanish grant to Christian Harman, who conveyed the same to the sd Nicholas Rabb by deed, 30 Mch. 1804.

p.488. Claim No.1642. Order of survey for 1400 acres by British Govt. to Benjamin Day. // Warrant to Elias Durnford, Surv. Genl. You are hereby directed and required to measure and lay out to Benjamin Day a tract of land of 1400 acres about 18 mi. up the Big Black on the north side thereon, in West Florida. Pensacola, 19 Nov. 1779, by Peter Chester. // To any lawful Deputy Surveyor of the Province of West Florida, you are hereby directed to execute this warrant and return the same with plat annexed unto my office within the time prescribed. Aug. 4, 1779, by Elias Durnford, Surveyor General. // File. Henry Day, claimant, 30 Mch. 1804. Henry Day, of West Springfield, in the State of Massachusetts, the legal rep. of Benjamin Day, hereby gives notice that he claims 1400 acres in Claiborne Co. in the Miss. Territory by virtue of the above order of survey from the Govt. of West Florida to sd Benjamin Day, as above, at which time he was upward of 21 years of age. Claim rejected, 28 Apr. 1807.

p.489. Claim No.1643. Order of survey for 1100 acres by British Govt. of West Florida to Henry Dwight. To Elias Durnford, Surv. Genl. You are hereby directed and required to measure or cause to be admeasured and laid out unto Henry Dwight, 110 acres 24 miles up the Big Black on the south side thereof in West Florida. Pensacola, 19 Nov. 1778, by Peter Chester. // To any lawful Dep. Surv. for the Prov. of West Fla., you are hereby directed to execute this warrant according to the tenor thereof and your instructions, and return the same with plat annexed into my office, etc., 4. Aug. 1779. By J. Gannaway, for Elias Durnford. // File. Claimant, Henry Day, 30 Mch. 1804. Henry Day, of West Springfield, in the State of Massachusetts, legal rep. of Henry Dwight claims 1100 acres, as above, in Miss. Territory, by virtue of the above order of survey, at which time he was upward of 21 years of age. Claim rejected, 27 April, 1807.

p.491. Claim No.1644. Patent to J. Eldergill by Spanish Govt. Petition of John Eldergill, a res. of this Government, wishing to build a house in the new City of Natchez, asks for Lot.No.2, Sq.18 in this City. 12 Jany. 1795. // Warrant for same by Manuel Gayoso de Lemos, 13 Jany. 1795. // Certif. of survey by Wm. Dunbar, 15 Jany. 1795. // Patent for the said lot asked for to John Eldergill. 14 Jany. 1795. Manuel Gayoso. // File. John Eldergill claimant, 30 Mch. 1804. Lot patented as above. Wit: John Williams. Certif. A-685 to claimant, 26 Oct. 1805.

p.493. Claim No.1645. Petition of Charles Jones to the Spanish Govt. that he desires to build a house in the New City of Natchez, asks for Lot No.1, Sq. No.34. 24 Aug. 1795. // Warrant for same, 29 Aug. 1795, by Grand-Pre. // Certif. of Survey by Wm. Dunbar, 1 Oct. 1795. // File. Claimant, John Eldergill, 30 Mch. 1804. Wit: John Williams, John Eldergill, claims above lot in the City of Natchez, which was granted to Charles Jones from the Spanish Govt. and by said Jones transferred to me, 27 Sept. 1727. Certif. B-11 issued to claimant, June 2, 1806.

p.494. Claim No.1646. Petition of John Eldergill, of this Dist., wishing to establish himself in the City, and not having land on which to do so, asks for Lot No.3, Sq. No.25. 19 Sept. 1795. // Warrant for same, 19 Sept. 1795, by Grand-Pre. // Certif. of survey by Wm. Dunbar, 25 Sept. 1795. // Patent to John Eldergill, Sept. 1, 1796. by Gayoso. // File. Claimant, John Eldergill, 30 Mch. 1804. Claim founded on above patent. Certif. B-12 issued June 2, 1806.

p.496. Claim No.1652. Certificate of survey for 600 arpents by Spanish Govt. to Daniel Douglass, by Carlos Trudeau, 10 Mch. 1796. // Patent for same in the Dist. of Natchez, 27 mi. NE of Miss. River on a br. of Bayou Sara. Manuel Gayoso de Lemos, at New Orleans, 24 Dec. 1797. // File. Claimant, Daniel Douglass, 30 Mch. 1804. Wit: Richard King, 22 May 1804. Daniel Douglass claims 600 acres in Wilkinson Co. by virtue of the above patent. Rejected, 22 April 1807.

p.499. Claim No.1653. Patent for 200 acres by Spanish Govt. to David Douglass. Certif. of survey signed 18 July 1793 by Carlos Trudeau, surv. // Patent to David Douglass for 200 acres in the Dist. of Natchez, on the Miss. River 36 mi. north of the Fort, adj. the land of the widow Calvet. N.O. 20 July 1793, by Carondelet. // File. Claimant, David Douglass, 30 Mch. 1804. Claim by virtue of the above patent. Certif. A-484 issued 15 Aug. 1805.

p.502. Claim No.1654. Spanish Govt. to David Douglass, certf. of survey for 1200 arpents by Carlos Trudeau, Dep. Surv. 10 Mch. 1796. // Grant for same 1200 arpents in the Dist. of Natchez, fronting on the Big Black River, 75 mi. NE of the Fort, 12 mi. from the banks of the River Miss. N.O., 24 Dec. 1797, by Gayoso. // File. Claimant, Daniel Douglass, 30 Mch. 1804. Rejected 22 April 1807.

p.505. Claim No.1655. Spanish Govt. to Daniel Douglass. Petition by Daniel Douglas, a res. and merchant of this City, desiring to build a house in the environs of this City with the convenience of a large garden and other plantings that he may be able to support his family, asks for a gr. of ten acres a little distance from the city and adj. the lands of Wm. Vousdan. 7 Feb. 1795. // Warrant for the above by Gayoso, 8 Feb. 1795. // Certif. of survey of ten acres in the environs of this City, b. on NE by lands of Wm. Vousdan. 19 Feb. 1795. by Wm. Dunbar. // Patent to Daniel Douglass for above land by Gayoso, Natchez, 20 Feb. 1795. // File. Claimant, Daniel Douglass, 30 Mch. 1804. Claims 10 arps. of land in the City of Natchez by virtue of the above patent from the Spanish Govt. Certif. A-530 issued 23 Aug. 1805.

p.508. Claim No.1656. Petition of Maurice Stacpoole who wishes to build a nice house in the New City, asks for Lot No.1, Sq. No.9, and he will conform with the established rules. Natchez. 26 Nov. 1794. // Warrant for same, same date, by Gayoso. // Certificate of survey by Wm. Dunbar, 30 Jany. 1795. // Patent for Maurice Stackpoole the above lot by Gayoso, 4 Feb. 1795. // Sale by Maurice Stacpoole to

Daniel Douglass the above lot for 550 pesos, 2 July 1796. Wit: Ebenezer Rees, J. Girault. // File. Claimant, Daniel Douglass, 30 Mch. 1804. Certif. A-698 issued to claimant, 7 Jany. 1806.

p.511. Claim No.1657. Patent for 280 arpents by Spanish Govt. to James White. Certif. of survey with plat by Carlos Trudeau, 12 Jany. 1795. // Patent of same in the Dist. of Natchez on Sandy Cr. a br. of the Homochitto River, 12 mi. east of the Fort, adj. Henry Cooper, to James White. N.O. 20 Jany. 1795, by Carondelet. // File. Claimant, Edward Evans, of Adams Co., Miss. Ter., by virtue of the above patent to James White who on 6 Mch. 1799 sold sd land to sd Edward Evans. Note: Let no certif. issue on this claim until the testimony of Samuel Cooper, Wilford Hoggatt and others can be had on behalf of the United States. (signed) W. B. Shields, agent, etc. 27 Aug. 1805. Disallowed on suspicion of its being antedated, 22 Dec. 1807.

p.513. Claim No.1658. James Cole petitions the Spanish Govt. that he is a carpenter and desires to build a house in the New City of Natchez so that he may have his residence there; asks for Lot No.4, Sq. No.12. 5 June 1795. // Certificate by Wm. Dunbar, that sd lot is vacant, same date. // Warrant for same by Grand-Pre Natchez, 6 June 1795. // Certificate of survey for sd lot. Wm. Dunbar, 3 Oct. 1795. // File. Claimant, James Cole, 30 Mch. 1804. Witness, Thomas Regan, 26 Jany. 1806. Rejected, 13 June 1807. See claim No.1873.

p.515. Claim No.1659. Petition of Richard King to the Spanish Govt. He, Capt. of the Militia in this Govt., wishing to build a house in this city, asks for Lot No.4, Sq. No.32, promising to conform to the rules of sd grant. Feb. 16, 1795. // Warrant for same by Gayoso, same date. // Certif. of survey by Wm. Dunbar, 2 Mch. 1795. // Patent to Richard King sd lot, by Gayoso, 12 Mch. 1795. // File. Claimant, Patrick Connelly, 30 Mch. 1804. Claim founded on above grant to Richard King from the Spanish Govt. as above who by deed, 3 Feb. 1800, conveyed to sd Connelly, which said transfer is recorded in Register's Office of Adams District. Confirmed. Certif. A-686 issued to legal representatives, 25 Oct. 1805.

p.518. Claim No.1660. Certificate of survey for 179 arpents from Spanish Govt. to Abraham Horton by Carlos Trudeau, surv., 3 Mch. 1789. // Patent for sd land in Dist. of Natchez on a br. of St. Catherine's Cr., adj. the lands of residents names Wm. Weeks, Wm. Hayton and Company and Mr. Gibson, by Estevan Miro, N.O. 3 Mch. 1789. // File. Claimant, Patrick Connelly, 30 Mch. 1804. By conveyance from sd Abraham Horton to him, 29 Jany. 1800. Certif. A-459 issued to J. F. Claiborne, assignee of claimant, 24 July 1805.

p.521. Claim No.1661. Spanish Govt. to Dennis Collins, 248 arpents near Cole's Cr. 12 mi. east of Fort Panmure, adj. lands of Benjamin Newman and Christian Bingaman on north, Alexander McIntosh on east, John Fowler on south, by Carlos Trudeau, 29 Aug. 1795. // A patent for sd lands for Dennis Collins as per certificate and plat by Carondelet. N.O. 1 Sept. 1795. // File. Patrick Connelly, claimant, 30 Mch. 1804. Claim for 248 acres of land gr. by Spanish Govt. to Dennis Collins, as above, and conveyed by him to Philip McHugh, 18 Nov. 1797, and by McHugh to sd claimant, 9 Feb. 1801. Witness to claim, Stephen Minor, 9 July 1805. (Claimant's death suggested.) Certif. A-463 issued to legal representatives, 25 July 1805.

p.524. Claim No.1678. Certificate of survey to Richard Harrison by the Spanish Govt. 300 arpents in the Dist. of Natchez, adj. land of the Fort, land gr. to William Barton, being included in this grant all the land below which are not considered useful, and by lands of His Majesty on NE. (signed) Carlos Trudeau, surv., 22 Mch. 1798. // File. Claimant, Stephen Minor, 30 Mch. 1804. The subscribers of land within the City of Natchez claim the land expressed in the above plat by virtue of a grant executed 20 Oct. 1795, by the Govt. of Spain to Richard Harrison, by him conveyed to Stephen Minor who sold so much thereof as is contained within the above-described lines, for the purpose of erecting thereon the City, the original grant being lost, a transcript of the original records herewith presented. 29 Mch. 1804. Stephen Minor, John Minor. Note: The various lots in the City are claimed by the individuals to whom they were granted. Rejected, 16 May 1806.

p.526. Claim No.1679. Petition of Rebecca McCabe to the Spanish Govt. Mrs. Rebecca McCabe asks that she be given a lot at the landing, situated at the foot of the new road which runs from the barracks and that Wm. Dunbar be empowered at once to put her in possession of sd lot. Natchez, 2 May 1795. // Warrant to William Dunbar to place Edward McCabe in possession of a lot at the landing near the new road. (signed) Grand-Pre. This grant was due to have been made in the name of his wife. // I hereby assign to William Lintot, for value recd. all my right, etc. to the lot decreed to me upon the within petition. (signed) Rebecca McCabe. 12 July 1798. Wit: William Conner. // For value received in settlement of accounts with B. Lintot, I make over all my right to the within unto the said B. Lintot. (signed) W. Lintot, June 1802. // File. Heirs of Bernard Lintot, claimants, 30 Mch. 1804. Exrs. of the will of Bernard Lintot claim for the estate one lot under the hill at the Natchez landing, by virtue of a grant by the Spanish Govt. of Natchez to Rebecca McCabe, as above, upon which a dwelling house was erected and afterwards sold by sd Rebecca McCabe to Wm. Lintot, and by him sold to sd Bernard Lintot, decd. John Minor for the exors of Bernard Lintot. Certif. B-2 issued to claimants, June 2, 1806.

p.527. Claim No.1681. Petition of Wm. Lintot that he wishes to build two houses in the New City of the Govt. and asks for Lots Nos. 1 and 2 in Sq. No.7. Natchez 27 July 1796. // Certificate that the lots desired are vacant. Wm. Dunbar, 29 July 1796. // Patent for above named lots to William Lintot. Natchez, 30 July 1796. // File. Claimant, Wm. Lintot, 30 Mch. 1804. Wit: Wm. Scott, 9 June 1807. Certif. B-282 issued 9 June 1807. Allowed as a Donation.

p.530. Claim No.1682. Petition of John Minor, a res. of this Govt. wishes to build some houses in the New City of Natchez, having material ready to build two, asks for lots Nos. 1 and 2, Block No.6. 2 Dec. 1794. Warrant for two lots to be surveyed, by Gayoso. Natchez, 22 Dec. 1794. // Certificate of survey for same by Wm. Dunbar, 28 Dec. 1794. // Patent for sd lots to John Minor, by Gayoso, 2 Jany. 1795. // File. Claimant, John Minor, 30 Mch. 1804. Wit: Wm. Barland, 10 Sept. 1804. Claim by virtue of afsd patent. Certif. A-515 to claimant, 26 Aug. 1805.

p.534. Claim No.1690. Spanish Govt. to Justus Andrews. [Nothing but the plat, showing 592 acres on Buffalo Cr. adj. Joseph Dove, Capt. James Nicholson and Joseph Miller.] File. Claimant, Justus Andrews, 30 Mch. 1804. Claims 592 acres of land upon which the claimant established his residence and cultivated the same on and before 27 Oct. 1795, which said lands were surveyed and put into the possession of the claimant, 24 Jany. 1795, by virtue of a Spanish warrant of possession, gr. in 1794. Samuel Lusk, witness, 28 Nov. 1804. Certif. B-221 issued 4 Mch. 1807. Claimant has 13 in his family.

p.535. Claim No.1691. Spanish Govt. to Joseph Miller. [Nothing but the plat recorded.] Plat shows survey for 350 arpents to Joseph Miller, adj. lands of Justus Andrews, Buffalo River, Jesse Carter and William Cock Ellis. // File. Claimant, admr. of the est. of Joseph Miller, decd. 30 Mch. 1804. Samuel C. Lusk, witness, 28 Nov. 1804. Notice: The administrator of the est. of Joseph Miller claims 350 arps. on Buffalo River by residence and cultivation on 27 Oct. 1795, which was surveyed 14 Jany. 1795, etc. Justus Andrews. Certificate of survey and plat by Wm. Dunbar, the tract 25 mi. south of the Fort. Certif. B-220 issued 4 Mch. 1807.

p.538. Claim No.1692. Spanish Govt. to Wm. Dunbar, patent for 800 arpents. // Cert. of survey by Carlos Trudeau, N.O. 26 May 1787. // Patent for 800 arpents in Dist. of Natchez, 2 leagues SE fr. Fort, adj. lands John Ellis, Samuel Hutchins. N.O. 26 May 1787, by Estevan Miro. // File. Claimant, William Dunbar, 30 Mch. 1804. Wit: Wm. Atchinson, 8 July 1804. Wm. Dunbar claims 800 arpents by virtue of a complete Spanish title in his favor, as above. Certif. A-409 issued 9 May 1805.

p.541. Claim No.1693. Spanish Govt. to Wm. Dunbar for 150 arpents. Certif. of survey by Carlos Trudeau, Surv. Gen., 12 Jany. 1795. // Patent for same to Wm. Dunbar 150 arps. at White Cliffs 3 leagues from Fort Panmure, adj. Philipe Trevino, Richard Ellis, William Butler and Chas. Wheet. N.O. 13 Jany. 1795, by Carondelet. // File. Claimant, Wm. Dunbar, 30 Mch. 1804. Wit: Wm. Atchinson, 18 July 1804. Claim above by virtue of a complete Spanish title, as above. Certif. A-410 issued 9 July 1805.

p.544. Claim No.1694. Spanish Govt. to Wm. Dunbar 800 arpents. Certif. of survey by Carlos Trudeau, Surv. Gen. 14 May 1791. // Patent to Wm. Dunbar 800 arpents, in Dist. of Natchez, 55 mi. fr. Fort Panmure, adj. lands of Hubert Rowel and Elizabeth Hutchins. N.O. 17 May 1791, by Estevan Miro. // File. Claimant, Wm. Dunbar, 30 Mch. 1804. Wit: Wm. Atchinson, 18 July 1804. Claim for 800 arpents of land by virtue of the above patent. Certif. A-411 issued 9 July 1805.

p.547. Claim No.1695. Spanish Govt. to Wm. Dunbar 1400 arpents. Certif. of survey by Carlos Trudeau, Surv. Gen. 14 May 1791. // Patent to Wm. Dunbar 1400 arps. in Dist. of Natchez, 54 mi. SE of Fort Panmure, adj. lands of Hubert Rowell, Charles Percy and Patrick Foley. N.O. 16 May 1791 by Estevan Miro. // File. Claimant, Wm. Dunbar, 30 Mch. 1804. Wit: Wm. Atchinson. Claim founded on above grant. Cert. A-412, 9 July 1805.

p.550. Claim No.1696. Spanish Govt. to Wm. Dunbar 800 arpents. // Certif. of survey by Carlos Trudeau, Surv. Gen., 23 Apr. 1794. // Patent to Wm. Dunbar 800 arpents in Dist. of Natchez, 40 mi. south of Fort Panmure, bounded on south by two br. of Bayou Sara, N.O., 5 May 1794, by Carondelet. // File. Claimant, Wm. Dunbar, 30 Mch. 1804. Wit: Wm. Atchinson, 18 July 1804. Claim as above. Certif. A-413 issued 9 July 1805.

BOOK F

p.1. Claim No.1405. Petition to the Spanish Govt. of Francis Lennan, who wishes to cultivate a garden and build some houses for his better comfort, asks for Lots Nos. 2 and 4, Sq. No.10. Natchez, 1 Dec. 1794. Patent and certif. of survey to Don Francisco Lennan, curate of this Parish of San Salvador, the above lots. Natchez, Dec. 6, 1794. // File. Claimant, Robert Moore, 28 Mch. 1804. Wit: Ebenezer Rees, 22 Aug. 1805. Certif. A-557 to claimant for part of Lot 2 and part of Lot 4, Aug. 1805. Robert Moore claims two lots in City of Natchez, No.2 and No.4 of Sq.10 by virtue of a Spanish gr. to Francis Lennan and by him conveyed to claimant, 29 Mch. 1798.

p.2. Claim No.1406. Petition of Robert Moore to the Spanish Govt. desiring to build some houses, asks for Lots 3 and 4, Sq.13. // Patent 18 Jany. 1795, by Gayoso. // File. Claimant, Robert Moore, 28 Mch. 1804. Claims sd lots by virtue of the above patent. Eben. Rees, 22 Aug. 1805. Certif. A-731 issued 15 Jany. 1806.

p.4. Claim No.1407. David Michie petitions the Spanish Govt. that wishing to establish himself in the City, asks for Lot 2 Sq.26, 10 Dec. 1796. // Patent for same, Natchez, 17 Dec. 1796, by Gayoso. // File. David Michie, claimant, 28 Mch. 1804. Rejected, 12 June 1807. David Michie claims the above lot by virtue of a Spanish grant to same.

p.5. Claim No.1408. Petition of William Moore to Spanish Govt. desiring to build two houses in Natchez asks for Lots 1 and 3 in Sq.27. Natchez, 8 Jany. 1795. // Patent for same, 15 Jany. 1785 by Gayoso. // File. Claimants, S. P. Moore and others, 28 Mch. 1804. Wit: Ebenezer Rees, 22 Aug. 1805. Certif. A-694 issued to legal rep. 6 Jany. 1806. Samuel P. Moore, James Moore and Robert Moore, legal rep. of Wm. Moore, decd., claim the above two lots in the City of Natchez, the same having been granted to sd Wm. Moore, as above.

p.7. Claim No.1409. Petition of Robert Scott, who wishes to build a house in City, asks for Lot 3, Sq.5. Natchez, 20 July 1796. // Patent for same. N.O. 23 Sept. 1796, by Carondelet. // File. Claimants, Samuel P. Moore and others, 28 Mch. 1804. Rejected, 15 June 1807. Samuel P. Moore, James Moore and Robt. Moore, claims above lot in City by virtue of a Spanish gr. to Robert Scott, who by his will devised the same to his wife, Sarah Scott, alias Zerbin, now deceased, and sd lot descended to claimants, being heirs at law.

p.10. Claim No.1411. Petition of James Moore, res. and merchant of Natchez, wishes to build some houses, asks Lots 1 and 2, Sq.13. 8 Jany. 1795. Granted 18 July 1795, by Gayoso. // File. Claimant, James Moore, Mch. 28, 1804. Wit: John Girault, 5 Aug. 1805. Certif. A-730 issued to claimant. Claims above-named lots by virtue of a grant from Spanish Govt.

p.11. Claim No.1412. James Moore petitions the Spanish Govt. that having bought from the agent of Mr. Adam Cloud some improvements which he had made on a certain lot, conceded verbally but having no title in form, asks for a grant to Lot 1, Sq.12 in this city. 10 Jany. 1795. // Order, survey and grant, 15 Jany. 1795, by Gayoso. // File. James Moore, claimant, 28 Mch. 1804. Wit: John Girault, 5 Aug. 1805. Certif. A-629 issued to claimant for part of Lot 1, Sq.12. Claim by virtue of the above Spanish gr.

p.13. Claim No.1413. Luis Faure petitions the Spanish Govt. wishing to build house in the New City, asks for Lot 1, Sq.4 in this city. 29 Mch. 1794. // Order and gr. for same by Gayoso, 30 Jany. 1795. // File. Claimant, James Moore, 28 Mch. 1804. Wit: Stephen Minor, 11 Nov. 1805. Certif. A-692 issued 6 Jany. 1806. James Moore claims above lot on Main Street by virtue of above gr. to Luis Faure and by him sold to Francisco Guitterez de Arroyo and by Arroyo sold to Samuel P. Moore and by sd Samuel conveyed to claimant, 18 July 1803.

p.15. Claim No.1414. Petition of Edward McCabe, wishes to build in New City, asks for one of the lots that are vacant. June 14, 1793. // Order and patent to Edward McCabe for Lot 4, Sq.3, 15 July 1794. Gayoso. // File. Claimant, James Moore, 28 Mch. 1804. Wit: John Girault, 5 Aug. 1805. Certif. A-548 issued 29 Aug. 1805. See Claim No.1319. James Moore claims lot on Main Street by virtue of the above grant to Edward McCabe and by him conveyed to Rebecca McCabe, 15 July 1797, and by sd Rebecca sold to Benjamin Kitchin, 14 Mch. 1799, and by sd Kitchin to Robert Moore, 2 Oct. 1799, and by sd Robert to claimant, 18 July 1803.

p.17. Claim No.1415. Petition of Jeremiah Routh to Spanish Govt. desiring to build a house in the City, asks gr. of Lot 2, Sq.12, 12 June 1795. // Order and grant by Gayoso, 15 June 1795. // File. James Moore, claimant, 28 Mch. 1804. Wit: John Girault, 5 Aug. 1805. Certif. A-518 issued 27 Aug. 1805. James Moore claims above lot by virtue of a grant to Jeremiah Routh and by him conveyed to claimant, 23 Nov. 1803.

p.19. Claim No.1416. Petition of Frances Assheton Watts that she wants to build a house in the New City and asks for Lot 2, Sq.5. 1 Jany. 1795. Order and grant, 21 Jany. 1795, by Gayoso. // 12 Sept. 1797. Frances Asheton Watts sells to James Moore, res. and merchant of this Dist., the grant to Lot 2, Sq.5 in this City, for $120. Signed. Wit: Estevan Minor, Eben. Rees, John Girault. // File. James Moore, claimant, 28 Mch. 1804. Wit: John Girault. Certif. A-546 issued to claimant. James Moore claims above lot by virtue of a gr to Frances Asheton Watts and by sd Frances conveyed to claimant, as above.

p.21. Claim No.1417. Cader Raby pétitions that for many years he has been living on rented land which causes much hardship to my family, which consists of seven grown persons; asks for land on Sandy Cr. which is vacant. 31 Jany. 1795. // Grant for 400 acres. N.O. 24 Feb. 1795, by Carondelet. // File. James Moore, claimant, 28 Mch. 1804. Wit: Christian Harman, 1 Dec. 1806. Certif. B-127 issued 5 Feb. 1807. James Moore, legal rep. of Cader Rabey, claims 400 acres of land in Claiborne Co. on waters of Sandy Creek by virtue of the 1st sect. of act of Congress, 3 Mch. 1803, etc. Cader Rabey sold the said land, 23 Dec. 1800, to sd claimant, he being above 21 years at the time of obtaining the warrant, and the Indian title to said land having been extinguished.

p.22. Claim No.1418. Thomas Hubberd petitions the Spanish Govt. that he has established a plantation on Bayou Pierre for the support of his family but he has no title of ownership, asks for a grant on waters of Bayou Pierre, adj. Jacob Cobun, 12 Aug. 1789. // N.O. 28 Apr. 1790, grant to Thos. Hubberd by Estevan Miro. Plat shows land b. by Elijah Flower, Tabor's Cr. and Jacob Cobun. Certif. by Dunbar, 28 June 1792. // File. Claimant, James Moore, 28 Mch. 1804. Wit: Gibson Clark, 27 Nov. 1806. Certif. B-128, issued 5 Feb. 1807. James Moore claims 400 acres in Claiborne Co. on waters of Bayou Pierre, 50 mi. from City of Natchez, by virtue of the Act of Congress regulating the Grant of Lands, etc. and he being a legal rep. of Thomas Hubbard who had before Oct. 27, 1795 obtained a Spanish warranty of survey for sd lands, and afterwards, 13 Nov. 1800, sold the sd tract to sd claimant.

p.24. Claim No.1419. Thomas Wells petitions the Spanish Govt. for 240 acres, 27 June 1794. Grant by Carondelet at N.O. Feb. 1795. Plat shows tract on waters of Homochitto, 20 mi. east of Fort, and certified by Wm. Dunbar, 30 Mch. 1795. // File. Claimant, James Moore, 28 Mch. 1804. Wit: Christian Harman, 1 Dec. 1806. Certif. B-129 issued 5 Feb. 1807. James Moore claims 240 acres in Wilkinson Co. by virtue the Act of Congress, 3 Mch. 1803, etc., he being the legal rep. of Thomas Wells who had obtained from the Spanish Govt. a warrant of survey for sd land, and sold 23 Mch. 1803 the sd tract to claimant.

p.25. Claim No.1420. Spanish Govt. to James Moore 1000 acres on east branch of Bayou de la Feliciana, adj. Wm. Moore, Wm. Scott, Wm. Dunbar, Ezekiel Forman and Robt. Scott. N.O. 26 Dec. 1795, by Carondelet. // File. Claimant, James Moore, 28 Mch. 1804. Wit: on the part of the U.S., Alexander Montgomery, 31 July, 1805. Disallowed on suspicion of being antedated, 22 Dec. 1806. James Moore claims 1000 arpents of land by virtue of the above grant from the Spanish Govt.

p.28. Claim No.1421. Spanish Govt. to Joshua Stockstill, 500 acres on waters of Cole's Cr. 16 mi. east of Fort, adj. Madame Lafleur, Mr. Chachere and Beasly Pruet. N.O. 15 Mch. 1790, by Miro. // File. Claimant, James Moore, 28 Mch. 1804. Wit: Stephen Minor, 11 Nov. 1805. Certif. A-691 to claimant, 6 Jany. 1806. James Moore claims 500 arps. by virtue of a Spanish gr. to Joshua Stockstill and by him sold to Joshua Howard, 9 Apr. 1796, and by the sd Joshua Howard to claimant, by deed, 28 Feb. 1797.

p.30. Claim No.1422. Spanish Govt. to Edward McCabe, 500 acres, 40 miles NE of Fort, N. O., 4 Mch. 1795, by Carondelet. Plat shows Chubby Creek and the Choctaw Path. // File, Claimant, James Moore, 28 Mch. 1804. Res. proved in claim No.1414. Certif. A-561 issued 4 Sept. 1805. James Moore claims 500 acres by virtue of a Spanish gr. to Edward McCabe and by him conveyed to the claimant, 25 Apr. 1797, situated on Bayou Pierre.

p.33. Claim No.1423. Spanish Govt. to Abraham Taylor, 250 acres on a br. of Homochitto River called Well's Cr., 23 mi. east of Fort. N.O. 20 Dec. 1794, by Carondelet. // File. Claimant, James Moore, 28 Mch. 1804. Wit: Ebenezer Rees, 22 Aug. 1805. Certif. A-554 issued 1805. James Moore claims 250 acres by virtue of a Spanish gr. to Abraham Taylor and by him sold to Thomas Morgan and by sd Morgan conveyed to the claimant, the land being in Adams Co.

p.35. Claim No.1424. Spanish Govt. to William Ryan, 160 acres 9 mi. east of Fort, adj. Stephen Stephenson, Chas. Cason, Christian Harman and John Hartley. N.O. 10 Mch. 1789, by Miro. // File. Claimant, James Moore, 28 Mch. 1804. Certif. A-562 issued 5 Sept. 1805. James Moore claims 160 arpents by virtue of Spanish gr. to Wm. Ryan and by him sold to Alexander Moore, decd., 10 Aug. 1790, and by sd Alexander, decd., devised to his children by whom the same was allotted to the claimant, 18 July 1803.

p.38. Claim No.1425. Spanish Govt. to Maria Whittle, 700 acres on east br. of Bayou Sara, 45 mi. SSE of Fort, adj. Thos. Burling and Thomas Green. N.O., 18 June 1795, by Carondelet. // File. Claimants, James Moore and wife, 28 Mch. 1804. Wit: John Girault, 5 Aug. 1805. Alexander Montgomery witness for the U.S. Disallowed on suspicion of its being antedated, 22 Dec. 1806. James Moore and Maria Moore, his wife, claim 700 arpents by virtue of sd Maria Whittle. Signed James Moore and A. M. Moore.

p.40. Claim No.1426. Spanish Govt. to Mrs. Sarah Truly, 161 acres adj. Abraham Mayes, William Halbert, William Silkrist, Francis Spain and John Stampley. N.O. 31 Jany. 1785, by Miro. Plat dated: Luisiana ano de 1782, Distrito del fuerte Panmure de Natches. // File. Claimant, James Moore, 28 Mch. 1804. Certif. A-563 issued 5 Sept. 1805. James Moore claims 160 arpents by virtue of a grant to Mrs. Truly, widow, and by her sold to Alexander Moore, 20 Oct. 1784, and by him devised to his children, by whom it was allotted and conveyed.

p.42. Claim No.1427. Spanish Govt. to Alexander de Bouille, 1000 acres on the waters of Sandy Creek, 18 mi. SE of Fort, adj. Mr. Vaughns, Richard Swazey, and Samuel Swazey. N.O. 30 May 1789 by Miro. // File. Claimant, James Moore, 28 Mch. 1804. Wit: Robt. Moore, 15 June 1807. Certif. A-811, 15 June 1807. James Moore claims 1000 arpents of land by virtue of a gr. to Alexander de Bouille near the Homochitto River and was sold by order of the Spanish Govt. after the death of de Bouille and purchased by Alexander Moore who gave it by his will to his children.

p.45. Claim No.1428. Spanish Govt. to William Fletcher, 300 acres on waters of Sandy Creek, 18 mi. SE of Fort, adj. Wm. Calvet. N.O. 12 June 1788, by Miro. // File. Claimant, James Moore, 28 Mch. 1804. Wit: Ebenezer Rees, 22 Aug. 1805. Certif. A-555 issued 3 Sept. 1805. James Moore claims 300 acres by virtue of a gr. to Wm. Fletcher and by him conveyed to the claimant, 3 Feb. 1801.

p.48. Claim No.1429. Spanish Govt. to Alexander Moore 2364 acres, 75 mi. NNE from Fort, on the Miss. River. N.O., 22 June 1791, by Miro. Footnote: Land Office, Washington, Miss. This claim confirmed to James Moore has been relinquished to the U.S. by act of Congress, 13 July 1834, for relief of Nathaniel A. Ware on instruction from Elijah Haywood, Commissioner of General Land Office, 19 Feb. 1834. // File. James Moore, claimant, 28 Mch. 1804. Certif. A-564 issued 5 Sept. 1805. James Moore claims 2364 arpents by virtue of a grant to Alexander Moore by the Spanish Govt. which land is in Claiborne Co., Miss. Ter. on the Miss. River 65 mi. above the City of Natchez, and was devised by the sd Alexander Moore in his will to his children, by whom partition has been made and said tract was allotted to said claimant.

p.51. Claim No.1430. Spanish Govt. to George Profit, 800 acres on waters of Sandy Cr., 18 mi. east of Fort. N.O. 15 Mch. 1789, by Miro. // File. James Moore, claimant, 28 Mch. 1804. Rejected, 12 June 1807. James Moore claims 800 acres by virtue of a grant to George Profit and by his exors conveyed to the claimant, 2 Nov. 1800.

p.53. Claim No.1431. Spanish Govt. to John Burnet, Jr., 170 acres, 45 mi. north of Fort and 18 miles by river, adj. Jesse Hamilton and Bayou Pierre. N.O. 14 April 1796, by Carondelet. // File. Francis Nailor, claimant, 28 Mch. 1804. Wit: William Howe, 29 Nov. 1804. Certif. B-261 issued as a Donation,

22 April 1807. Francis Nailor claims 170 arpents of land in Claiborne Co. by virtue by Spanish Govt. to John Burnet, Jr. as above, who 21 Mch. 1804. sold said tract to claimant. Indenture from John Burnet, Jr. to Francis Nailor, for $900, 170 acres north side of Bayou Pierre 7 mi. from the mouth. Wit: Wm. Scott, Vance Scott. Ack. by John Burnet, Jr. before Brian Bruin.

p.56. Claim No.1697. British Govt. to Isaac Johnson, 1000 acres on NE fork of Second Cr., 8 mi. SE of Fort, adj. lands of William Johnston and Francis Hutchinson. Pensacola, 1 Sept. 1777, by Peter Chester. // File. Claimant, Wm. Dunbar, 30 Mch. 1803. Wit: Wm. Atchinson, 18 July 1804. Certif. A-13 issued 16 Apr. 1805. Proved in Melling Woolley. Wm. Dunbar, a res. etc., claims 1000 acres by virtue of a British patent to Isaac Johnson, which he sold to Melling Woolley 10 Jany. 1789, and conveyed by said Woolley to claimant, 23 Jany. 1800, and ratified and confirmed by the trustees of the estate of sd Woolley, 7 June 1805. Isaac Johnson having remained an inhabitant of the Natchez District, West Florida, after the peace of 1783, this tract has always been held by him or his representatives free from all interfering claims. (signed) Wm. Dunbar.

p.63. Claim No.1698. Spanish Govt. to William Brown, 450 acres on a br. of Bayou Pierre called James Creek, 50 mi. north of Fort, adj. lands of Wm. Vousdan and Thomas James. N.O. 8 Aug. 1789, by Miro. // File. Claimant, Wm. Dunbar, 30 Mch. 1804. Wit: Wm. Atchinson. Certif. A-488 issued 15 Aug. 1805. William Dunbar claims 450 acres by virtue of a Spanish gr. to Wm. Brown and conveyed by sd Brown to Melling Woolley 20 Dec. 1789, and by said Woolley to claimant, 23 Jany. 1800. The afsd tract of 450 acres was the customary residence of the sd Melling Woolley on and before 27 Oct. 1795. Plat shows this land on James Creek.

p.66. Claim No.1699. Spanish Govt. to James McCulloch. Alexander McCullagh, a res. of this Dist. desired to establish himself and family in this Dist., asks for 500 acres near to Buffalo Cr., 11 miles from River Homochitto. Has a family of six persons. Signed: James McCulloch. Gr. N.O., 25 Nov. 1789, by Estevan Miro. Plat shows land adj. Henry Nicholson and William Gilbert, 17 mi. south of Fort. // File. Claimant, Wm. Dunbar, 30 Mch. 1804. Wit: Wm. Atchinson. Certif. B-154, issued 10 Feb. 1807. Proved in Matthew McCulloch. Wm. Dunbar claims 500 arps. of land by virtue of a Spanish warrant of survey in favor of Alexander McCulloch, which sd 500 arpents were inhabited and cultivated on 27th Oct. 1795 by Matthew McCulloch, brother and partner to said Alexander, and afterwards sold by Matthew McCulloch to Ebenezer Rees, 28 Jany. 1798, and by sd Rees to David Ferguson and Melling Woolley, 15 June 1801, and the sd 500 arpents were sold by sd David Ferguson and Melling Woolley to the claimant, 1 July 1805.

p.68. Claim No.1700. Spanish Govt. to Henry Nicholson, 400 acres. Petitioner desires to settle with family in this Dist. wishes land on waters of Homochitto River, 700 acres adj. Landon Davis and _____ McCoy. Natchez 2 Jany. 1788. // Grant for 400 acres by Miro, N. O. 16 Jany. 1789. Plat shows land adj. Eli Ambrose, D. McCoy, L. Davis, Alex. Henderson, G. Gilbert, bet. the Homochitto and Buffalo, 20 mi. south of Fort. 27 Nov. 1789, by Wm. Dunbar. // File. Claimant, Wm. Dunbar, 30 Mch. 1804. Wit: Wm. Atchinson, 18 July 1804. Certif. B-155 issued 10 Feb. 1807. Proved in Henry Nicholson. William Dunbar claims 400 arpents of land by virtue of a warrant of possession to Henry Nicholson which said tract became the residence of the family of Nicholson considerable improvements having been made thereon before Oct. 27, 1795, etc. and was sold to the claimant, 30 Mch. 1801. Plat shows land adj. Wm. Gilbert, Alex. Henderson, D. McCoy, Stephen Ambrose.

p.70. Claim No.1701. Spanish Govt. to Policarpo Regillo, who petitioned that he wished to establish himself and family of three grown white persons on Buffalo Creek adj. James Sanders and Elijah Phipps, Natchez, 24 Nov. 1793. Grant of 300 acres by Carondelet, N.O., 28 Mch. 1794. Plat shows land b. by Buffalo and Piney Woods Creeks, across from the latter James Sanders, and on north Wm. Cunningham. // Assignment of above 300-acre grant for $50, to Wm. Dunbar, April 25, 1798. Signed. Wit: George Rapalje, Patrick Tegart. // File. Claimant, Wm. Dunbar, 30 Mch. 1804. Wit: Wm. Atchinson, 18 July 1804. Certif. B-240 issued to claimant. Wm. Dunbar claims 300 arpents by virtue of a warrant of possession to Policarpo Regillo, which were sold to the claimant by the proprietor, 23 Apr. 1798. The said 300 arpents are claimed under a perfect title although not accompanied by what is generally called a patent, it being notorious that 9/10 of the land held under the Govt. of Louisiana was not confirmed by any stronger form of title, the English and Americans who composed the mass of the population of the District of Natchez, having been accustomed under their own government to consider patents as indispensable to the completion of their titles naturally demanded of the Spanish Government a similar instrument of writing, otherwise it was not probable that the Commissioners would have found one title in ten within the Mississippi Territory furnished with that additional proof of its validity. A

Spanish warrant or decree annexed to the petition of the party is properly a warrant of possession, ordering the surveyors to give the petitioners possession of soil. The moment this is done, he has always been considered (under the Spanish Government) as absolute master or proprietor of the land and very few French and Spanish inhabitants have ever suspected that any further of their titles was necessary. The claimant, having purchased of a Spaniard whose mind was impressed with those ideas, no doubt was entertained by either seller or purchaser of the perfect form of the title, the claimant therefore prays the Commissioners to confirm his claim upon the principle that it was founded upon a title which under the then existing government was admitted to be perfect and complete. Under the chancery jurisdiction with which the Commissioners are invested, the claimant has no doubt of obtaining their justice, to which his equitable demand is entitled. (signed) William Dunbar.

p.72. Claim No.1702. Spanish Govt. to Richard Harrison, 450 acres, on St. Catherine's Cr., adj. Don Estevan Minor. N.O. 20 Apr. 1784, by Miro. // Warrant, 15 July 1783. // File. Claimant, William G. Forman, 30 Mch. 1804. Wit: Nathaniel Ivy, 26 Nov. 1804. Certif. A-391, 1 July 1805. Wm. Gordon Forman claims 450 acres in Adams Co. by virtue of a Spanish gr. to Richard Harrison, as above, and conveyed from sd Harrison to Ezekiel Forman, and from exrs. of the will of sd Ezekiel Forman to David Forman and from exrs. of sd David Forman to Joseph Forman, Jr. and from said Joseph to this claimant. W. G. Forman by Ly Harding, his atty.

p.75. Claim No.1703. Natchez, 8 Aug. 1796. John Lum sells to Gen. David Forman, 133 acres on St. Catherine's Cr. gr. to him Dec. 1794, for $183. Both signed. Wit: Wm. Dunbar, Benajah Osmun. // p.77. Deed 13 Oct. 1800, William G. Forman, surviving exor of will of Gen. David Forman, decd., to Joseph Forman, Jr. (Will, 13 Aug. 1796, by wh. Wm. G. Forman and Sarah M. Forman, since dead, exrs. empowered to sell estate.) W. G. Forman adv. for sale certain lands on 22 Sept. last, at auction, to highest bidder. Joseph Forman, Jr., being the same, the following tracts, containing in the whole 1000 acres, was struck off to him for $3600, sd tract being known as the Wilderness Plantation and containing, (1) 450 acres, gr. to Richard Harrison, 1784; (2) 225 acres, gr. to Ezekiel Forman, 28 Feb. 1795; (3) 133 acres bou. from John Lum, (above); (4) land bought by Ezekiel Forman from Samuel Flower, 4 Feb. 1795. Wit: John C. Wikoff, Bryan Bruin. // p. 80. Joseph Forman, Jr., of Baltimore, Maryland, to William Gordon Forman, of Monmouth, New Jersey, for $3600, paid, the above desc. lands in Adams Co., Miss. Territory. Wit: Bryan Bruin, Seth Lewis. // File. Claimant, Wm. G. Forman, 30 Mch. 1804. Wit: Nathaniel Ivy, 26 Nov. 1805. Certif. A-393 issued 1 July 1805. Wm. Gordon Forman claims 133 acres in Adams Co. by virtue of a Spanish gr. to John Lum, from the said Lum to David Forman, now decd., and conveyed by exrs. of will of sd David Forman to Joseph Forman, Jr., and from sd Joseph to the claimant, all as above.

p.83. Claim No.1706. Spanish gr. to Ezekiel Forman, 225 acres 4 mi. east of Fort, b. by lands of Madame (widow) Spell, Moses Bonner, Mary Foster, Richard Harrison and Charles Norwood. N.O., 28 Feb. 1791. // File. Claimant, Wm. G. Forman, 30 Mch. 1804. Wit: Nathaniel Ivy. Certif. A-406, 5 July 1805. Wm. Gordon Forman claims 225 arpents of land in Adams Co. by virtue of a Spanish gr. to Ezekiel Forman, now decd., and conveyed by exrs of the last will of sd Ezekiel to David Forman, now decd., and from exrs. of the last will of sd David Forman to Joseph Forman, Jr. and from sd Joseph to claimant.

p.86. Claim No.1708. Spanish Govt. to Domingo Lorero, who petitions for Lots Nos. 3 and 4, Sq. No.34 in Natchez, 4 Jany. 1795, grant by Gayoso, 10 Jany. 1795. // File. Claimant, John Minor, 30 Mch. 1804. Wit: Wm. Barland, 10 Sept. 1804. Certif. A-735 issued 16 Jany. 1806. John Minor claims lots 3 and 4, Sq.34 in the City of Natchez by virtue of the above Spanish gr. to Domingo Lorero and conveyed by sd Domingo to the claimant, 8 Nov. 1797. John Minor by Ly Harding, atty.

p.88. Claim No.1711. British gr. to Thomas Hutchins 1000 acres on Second Cr. 13 mi. SE from old Natchez Fort, adj. on north 1000 acres gr. to Anthony Hutchins. Pensacola, 12 May, 1773, by Peter Chester. // File. Thos. Hutchins, Jr., claimant, 30 Mch. 1804. Wit: Stephen Minor, 29 July, 1805. Wit: Eben. Rees, 2 Apr. 1806. Rejected. Land confirmed to A. Hutchins. See No.1887, April 8, 1807. Thos. Hutchins claims 1000 acres in Adams Co. by virtue of a Spanish gr. to this claimant, 29 Feb. 1788, and a British gr. to Thos. Hutchins, now decd., whose son and heir this claimant is, said tract having been confirmed to this claimant by two lawful verdicts and judicial decisions. Thos. Hutchins by Ly Harding, atty.

p.95. Claim No.1712. Spanish Govt. to Abraham Ellis, 1000 acres on waters of Second Cr. 10 miles SE from Fort, adj. Estevan Minor, Senores Monsanto, David Mitchell, Madam Jane Rapalje and the Mandamus line. N.O. 16 Feb. 1789, by Miro. // File. Claimant, Abraham Ellis, 30 Mch. 1804. Wit: John McCulloch, 4 Mch. 1805. Certif. A-419 issued 9 July 1805. Abram Ellis claims 1000 arpents of land by virtue of a Spanish gr. to him as above. For Abraham Ellis and at his request. John Girault.

p.98. Claim No.1714. Spanish Govt. to John Murray, 349 acres 12 mi. south of Fort, adj. Landon Davis and the Homochitto River. N.O. 16 May 1791, by Miro. Plat shows Daniel McCoy on east. // File. Abraham Ellis, claimant, 30 Mch. 1804. Wit: John McCulloch, 4 Mch. 1805. Certif. A-422 issued 10 July 1805. Abram Ellis claims 340 arpents by Spanish grant to Thomas Murray and by Oliver and Alice Walton, legal rep. of the sd Thos. Murray, conveyed to the present claimant, 4 March 1803. John Girault for Abram Ellis and at his request.

p.101. Claim No.1715. British gr. to William Case, 300 acres 20 mi. south of Fort, on Second Cr., adj. lands of Samuel Lusk and Major Dixon. Pensacola, 9 Oct. 1777, by Chester. / Plat shows tract begins where Second Cr. comes out of Homochitto River. / File. Claimant, Abram Ellis in right of his wife, 30 Mch. 1804. Gaillard's res. proved in his claim No.751. Certif. A-91 issued to claimants. Abram Ellis claims 300 acres by virtue of a British gr., as above, to Wm. Case and by him sold to Isaac Gaillard, 24 Mch. 1787, and by the sd Gaillard conveyed to Margaret, the wife of the claimant, by deed 23 Dec. 1801. For Abram Ellis at his request, John Girault.

p.108. Claim No.1716. British Govt. to John Lusk, 150 acres on Second Cr. adj. Samuel Lewis, about 1 mile from Juncture of sd creek with Homochitto River. Pensacola, 11 Oct. 1777, by Peter Chester. // File. Claimant, Abraham Ellis in right of his wife, 30 Mch. 1804. Certif. A-18 issued to claimants. Abram Ellis claims 150 acres by virtue of a British gr. to John Lusk and by him sold to Isaac Gaillard, 16 Jany. 1787, and by him conveyed to Margaret, the wife of the claimant by deed, 23 Dec. 1801. For A. Ellis at his request, John Girault.

p.115. Claim No.1717. British Govt. to Richard Ellis, 1850 acres on waters of Boyd's Cr. 18 mi. from Fort, b. by land of Daniel Perry on south. Pensacola, 16 June 1779 by Peter Chester. // File. Abraham Ellis, claimant, 30 Mch. 1804. Res. of claimant prov. in his claim No.1712. Certif. A-19 issued 17 April 1805. Abram Ellis claims 1850 acres by virtue of a British gr. as above, to Richard Ellis, Sr., late of this Territory, decd., and by him devised to the present claimant by will, dated 17 Oct. 1792. For Abram Ellis by his request by John Girault.

p.122. Claim No.1718. British Govt. to Nathan Swazey 250 acres on Homochitto, adj. Wm. Case and Col. Dixon. Pensacola, 13 Oct. 1777, by Peter Chester. // File. Claimant, Abraham Ellis in behalf of his wife, 30 Mch. 1804. Res. of claimant proved in No.1712. Certif. A-17 issued 18 Apr. 1805. Abraham Ellis claims, in behalf of his wife, 250 acres by virtue of a British gr. to Nathan Swazey, as above, and by him sold to John Lusk, 3 Nov. 1784, and by sd Lusk to Anne Gaillard, late of this Territory, decd., by deed, 16 Mch. 1786, and by sd Anne Gaillard in her will, 3 Nov. 1788, devised to her daughter, Margaret, wife of the present claimant. John Girault for and at the request of Abram Ellis.

p.129. Claim No.1725. Spanish gr. to William Dunbar, 26 acres, (Petition for above for work he has done the Govt.), land adj. Stephen Minor, and a street of the city. Natchez, 19 April 1797. Gayoso. // File. Claimant, William Dunbar, 30 Mch. 1804. Wit: John Henderson, 29 Dec. 1806. Rejected 9 Apr. 1807. Wm. Dunbar claims 26 arpents in the vicinity of Natchez by virtue of a Spanish patent to Richard Harrison, for more than 300 arpents which were cultivated and improved and afterwards sold by sd Harrison to Major Stephen Minor, 300 acres of this land was again sold, by the sd Minor to the King of Spain, on which the City of Natchez was afterwards laid out under the direction of Gov. Gayoso, who as the agent and representative of the sd King, granted to individual subjects lots both within and without the limits of the said city, at his discretion; and, lastly, the said lot was granted and laid out by the sd Gov. Gayoso to the claimant, as above. The original patent to said Richard Harrison and his conveyance to Minor, etc., not being in the claimant's power to produce he prays to avail himself of such other evidence thereof as may be in his power and of the patent and conveyances, if they should be shown to the Commrs. by other persons interested therein. And as the grant to the claimant is similar to the generality of other Spanish titles existing in this territory, he takes leave to present thereof the following explanation. After the treaty between the United States and Spain was known in this territory, the claimant applied to sd Gov. Gayoso for compensation for various unsatisfied services and the lot now claimed upon which sd Governor as early as sometime in 1790 had caused to be erected a private building, with the approbation of the Governor of Louisiana to appropriate certain lots to his own private use, was offered to be conveyed to the claimant in satisfaction of his demand by His Excellency in his double capacity as Governor and private proprietor, as will more fully appear by the inspection of the Spanish title herewith presented. The claimant accepted the position, believing the preferred titles to be legal and valid for the following reasons, (1) first because the land made no part of the said King's public domain but was a portion of an improved tract of land devised to him from an ancient patent and conveyed to him from a private subject, etc., (2) because the said land as purchased by the King being a private not public property, the claimant was and yet is persuaded that it was disposable by the laws of the Treaty, etc. [He gives examples, etc.]

p.134. Claim No.1726. Spanish Govt. to William Dunbar, who petitions for Lots 1 and 2 Sq.14, 10 Jany. 1795, granted by Gayoso, 15 Jany. 1795. // File. Claimant, Wm. Dunbar, 31 Mch. 1804. Wit: Wm. Atchinson, 18 July 1804. Certif. A-543 to claimant. William Dunbar claims two lots, Nos. 1 and 2 in Sq. No.14 in City of Natchez, by virtue of a Spanish patent to this claimant by the Gov. of Natchez. Plat shows Pope's Hill.

p.136. Claim No.1727. Spanish Govt. to Wm. Dunbar who petitions for Lot 1, Sq.10, 1 March 1795, granted 12 Mch. 1795 by Gayoso. // File. Wm. Dunbar, claimant, 30 Nov. 1804. Wm. Atchinson, witness. Certif. A-748, issued 26 Feb. 1806. Wm. Dunbar claims above lot by virtue of a patent, 12 Mch. 1795.

p.138. Claim No.1728. Spanish Govt. to Wm. Dunbar, who petitions for Lot 3, Sq.26, 1 Dec. 1794, granted by Gayoso, 5 Dec. 1794. // File. Wm. Dunbar, claimant, 31 Mch. 1804. Wit: Wm. Atchinson. Disallowed on suspicion of its being antedated. Wm. Dunbar claims Lot 3, Square 26, in Natchez by virtue of a Spanish patent by the Governor under the Spanish Administration. Caveat: Let no certif. issue to Wm. Dunbar for Lot 3, Square 26, in City of Natchez, because the same is claimed by John Williams under a warrant of survey from the Spanish Govt. through their deputy surveyor, to wit: said Wm. Dunbar, and the same actually surveyed and actually inhabited and cultivated for the use of John Williams prior to and on 27 Oct. 1795; and because the patent of sd Dunbar to said lot is antedated. (signed) G. Poindexter, atty. for Williams.

p.140. Claim No.1729. Spanish Govt. to Wm. Dunbar, who petitions for Lot No.2, Square 3, 15 Oct. 1793, granted by Gayoso, 25 Oct. 1793. // File. Claimant, Wm. Dunbar, 31 Mch. 1804. Wit: Wm. Atchinson. Certif. A-547 issued 1805. Wm. Dunbar claims Lot 2, Sq.3 by virtue of a Spanish grant to this claimant, as above.

p.142. Claim No.1730. Wm. Dunbar, petitions the Spanish Govt. for Lot 4, Sq.6, 6 Dec. 1794. Grant of same 15 Dec. 1794 by Gayoso. // File. Wm. Dunbar, claimant, 31 Mch. 1804. Wm. Atchinson, witness. Certif. A-517 issued Aug. 1805. Claim of above by above patent.

p.144. Claim No.1731. Spanish Govt. to Dona Anna Dunbar, 1000 acres on west brach of Bayou Feliciana, 45 mi. adj. lands of Wm. Dunbar. N.O. 20 Nov. 1793, by Carondelet. // File. Claimant, Anne Dunbar, 31 Mch. 1804. Wit: Wm. Atchinson, 1804. Certif. A-420 to claimant, 9 July 1805. Anne Dunbar claims 1000 arpents by complete Spanish title, as above, tract on Thompson's Creek.

p.147. Claim No.1732. Spanish Govt. to Anna Dunbar, who petitions for 10 acres for house and garden, 20 Aug. 1794. // Grant to same adj. Manuel Gayoso de Lemos and Stephen Minor, Sept. 4, 1794, by Gayoso. // File. Anne Dunbar, claimant, 31 Mch. 1804. Wit: Wm. Atchinson. Certif. A-540, 28 Aug. 1805. Anne Dunbar claims 10 acres at the town of Natchez by virtue of a complete title from the Spanish Govt., as above. Bounded by Concord Plantation.

p.150. Claim No.1733. Spanish Govt. to William Dunbar, Jr., 1000 acres on Bayou Feliciana, adj. lands of Ana Dunbar. N.O. 29 Nov. 1793, by Carondelet. // File. Claimant, Wm. Dunbar, Jr., 31 Mch. 1804. Wm. Atchinson, witness. Certif. A-421 issued 9 July 1805. Wm. Dunbar, Jr. claims 1000 arpents of land by virtue of the complete title from the Spanish Govt., as above. On west branch of Thompson's Cr.

p.153. Claim No.1734. Spanish Govt. to Carlos Trudeau, 1180 acres, 18 mi. north of Big Black River, on road from Nogales to a place called Dayton's Cowpens, between Big Bayou and Middle Bayou, 3 mi. east of Miss. River. N.O. 20 Oct. 1794 by Carondelet. // File. Claimant, Charles Trudeau, 31 Mch. 1804. Wit: Wm. Atchinson, 18 July 1804. Wit: Stephen Minor, 25 Nov. 1806. Certif. A-796 issued 9 June 1807. Charles Trudeau, late Surveyor General of the Province of Louisiana and West Florida, claims 1180 arpents by virtue of a complete Spanish title in favor of claimant, as above. The claimant has been informed that the regulations of the United States require as a qualification of persons claiming land that they should have been residents in the Miss. Territory on 27 Oct. 1795. He has therefore to urge upon that point in support of his claim that his occupation of surveyor called him to all parts of the two provinces and in passing from one to the other he was frequently a resident in one as well as in the other and this being the sole claim he makes upon the Mississippi Territory, he flatters himself that the equality and legality of his demand will be confirmed by the Honorable Board of Commissioners. The claimant forwarded some years ago his original patent to the late Wm. Vousdan who was his attorney but since the death of that gentleman the patent cannot be found and it remains doubtful whether it ever camé into his hands, as the claimant never received any answer to his letter enclosing the patent, which happened but a short time before the death of Mr. Vousdan, the claimant therefore thought it advisable to extract a copy of his patent from the Intendant's Office, certified by that office, which is herewith presented. Charles Trudeau, by his atty. Wm. Dunbar.

p.155. Claim No.1735. Spanish Govt. to Robert Dow, 1000 acres on waters of Cole's Cr., 16 mi. east of Fort, adj. Madame Lafleur, Peter Camus, Michael Guiche [Guice] and John Martin. N.O. 16 May, 1791, by Miro. // File. Claimant, Robert Dow, 30 Mch. 1804. Wit: Wm. Dunbar, 25 Nov. 1806. Rejected, 21 May 1807. Robert Dow claims 1000 arpents by virtue of a complete title from the Spanish Govt., as above. Robt. Dow, by his agent, Wm. Dunbar.

p.159. Claim No.1736. Spanish Govt. to Don Fergus Allard Duplantier 1740 acres, 50 miles NNE from Fort, 6 mi. from mouth of Big Black to the north. N.O. 18 June 1795, by Carondelet. // File. Fergus Allard Duplantier, claimant, 31 Mch. 1804. Certif. A-797 issued 9 June 1807. Fergus Allard Duplantier claims 1740 arpents of land by virtue of a complete title from the Spanish Govt., as above. Wm. Dunbar, agent.

p.162. Claim No.1737. Spanish Govt. to Henry Garvey, 200 acres on a br. of Homochitto called Pretty Creek, 21 mi. from Fort. N.O. 25 Jany. 1795, by Carondelet. // File. Claimant, Henry Garvey, 31 Mch. 1804. Wit: William Thomas, 11 June 1806. Disallowed on suspicion of its being antedated, 22 Dec. 1807. Henry Garvey claims 200 acres by virtue of a complete Spanish title in his favor, as above.

p.168. Claim No.1739. Petition of John Gaskins that he lives in a house with wife and four children on land that is not his; asks for 350 acres on the Bayou of Cole's Cr., adj. Charles Collins. 29 Aug. 1789. // Order of survey by Gayoso, Aug. 30, 1789. // Grant. N.O. April 1790, by Miro. // File. Claimant, John Gaskins, 31 Mch. 1804. See Nos. 411 and 1984. Certif. B-228 issued 6 Mch. 1807. John Gaskins claims 350 acres by virtue of a warrant of possession in his favor and with survey of land, 10 Mch. 1796. Sd land was inhabited and cultivated by claimant on 27 October 1795. Tract is on Tabor's Cr. adj. William Thomas.

p.165. Claim No.1738. Spanish Govt. to Henry Garvey, 330 acres on Wells Cr. a br. of the Homochitto, 20 mi. from Fort, adj. Robt. Miller. N.O. 25 Jany. 1795, by Carondelet. // File. Henry Garvey, claimant, 31 Mch. 1804. Wit: Wm. Thomas. Disallowed on suspicion of its being antedated, 1807. Henry Garvey claims 330 acres by complete Spanish title, as above.

p.170. Claim No.1740. Petition to Spanish Govt. of Leonard Kipley, with wife and two children, asks for land on the Big Black in front of those of John Turnbull. 11 July 1794. Signed. // Grant of 350 acres 8 miles from the mouth of the Big Black. N.O. 24 Feb. 1795. // File. Claimant, Leonard Kipley, 31 Mch. 1804. Wm. Thomas, wit. 14 Mch. 1805. Certif. B-75 issued 28 Oct. 1806. Leonard Kipley claims 350 acres of land by virtue of a warrant of survey and possession, as above. This land, on the Big Black, was inhabited and cultivated 27 Oct. 1795.

p.172. Claim No.1741. British Govt. to Wm. Dunbar, order of survey, 1200 acres on west branch of Thompson's Cr., adj. lands of Stephen Watts. Pensacola, 30 Sept. 1777. File. Claimant, Wm. Dunbar, 31 Mch. 1804. Rejected 27 April 1807. William Dunbar claims 1200 acres of land by virtue of a British warrant of survey, issued from the Government of West Florida in favor of the claimant, as above, which was prevented from being executed from the troubles of the country, (1) by the invasion of an American detachment and finally by the conquest of West Florida by the Spanish arms, etc.

p.174. Claim No.1742. Petition of David Roberts for 240 arpents on the Big Black River, adj. Mr. Garet Rapalje. 11 Aug. 1789. // Order of survey by Gayoso, 14 Aug. 1789. // Grant by Miro, N.O. 26 Apr. 1790. // Plat and certificate by Dunbar, 21 Sept. 1790. // File. Claimant, David Roberts, 31 Mch. 1804. Rejected, 22 Apr. 1807. David Roberts claims 240 acres on the Big Black by warrant of possession, as above. Wm. Dunbar for David Roberts.

p.175. Claim No.1745. Spanish Govt. to Martin and Ralph Price, 500 acres on waters of North Fork of Cole's Cr., 25 mi. north of Fort, adj. William Richey, Roger Dove and Llewellyn Price. N.O. 30 Aug. 1793, by Carondelet. // File. Claimants, Martin and Ralph Price, 31 Mch. 1804. Wit: P. B. Bruin, 23 Nov. 1805. Certif. A-697 issued 6 Jany. 1806. Martin and Ralph Price claim 500 acres on waters of Bayou Pierre in Claiborne Co. by a complete Spanish grant as above.

p.178. Claim No.1746. Spanish Govt. to Elizabeth Lyman. [Nothing but plat and certificate of survey, which show 1000 acres on west waters of Tabor's Creek, a south branch of Bayou Pierre, 40 mi. NE from Natchez Fort. adj. Justus King and Prosper King adj. on south.] File. Claimant, Elizabeth Lyman, 31 Mch. 1804. Relinquished by the claimant's attorney, S. Bullock. Rejected 12 June 1807. Title papers withdrawn by S. Bullock for the claimant. Elizabeth Lyman claims 1000 acres on Tabor's Cr. in Claiborne Co. by a fully executed grant.

p.181. Claim No.1751. Petition of Edmund Johnson, for 100 acres on waters of Cole's Cr. near Chas. Collins. 16 Aug. 1790. // Granted by Miro, N.O. 30 Oct. 1790. // Plat and certif. by Dunbar, 8 June 1792. Land on north fork of Cole's Cr., 25 mi. NE of Fort, adj. Henry Green. // File. Claimant, Edmund Johnson, 31 Mch. 1804. Wit: Henry Patton, 8 Dec. 1806. Certif. B-161 issued 10 Feb. 1807. Edmund Johnson claims 600 acres in Jefferson Co., near Huntstown, by virtue of a Spanish warrant of survey and patent as above. J. Dunlap for Edmund Johnson.

p.183. Claim No.1752. 20 Mch. 1804. Sarah Waddle to Abijah Hunt, for $100 in hand paid, all claim to tract and improvement made by my husband, John Waddle, decd., adj. lands sd Abijah Hunt purchased of Hardy Perry on waters of Bayou Pierre. (signed) Sarah Waddle. Wit: John Moore. // File. Claimant, Abijah Hunt, 30 Mch. 1804. Wit: William McCaleb, 30 Aug. 1806. Certif. D-322, issued 29 Dec. 1806. Abijah Hunt claims 640 acres in Claiborne Co. which was inhabited and cultivated 3 Mch. 1803 by Sarah Waddle, the head of a family and above the age of 21 years, and previous to that time by John Waddle, her husband, now decd., and conveyed to the claimant by the sd Sarah 20 Mch. 1804. The tract is on Bayou Pierre.

p.184. Claim No.1753. Spanish Govt. to Thos. Burling, 1000 acres on east branch of Bayou Sara, 45 mi. SE of Fort, adj. Mary Whittle, Thomas Green and Daniel Clark. N.O., 18 June 1795, by Carondelet. // File. Thomas Burling, claimant, 30 Mch. 1804. Alexander Montgomery wit. for the U.S., 13 Sept. 1805. Disallowed on suspicion of its being antedated, 22 Dec. 1807. Thos. Burling claims above tract by virtue of a Spanish grant executed prior to 27 Oct. 1795.

p.187. Claim No.1754. Spanish Govt. to Thos. Burling, 1000 acres on Penasco a Davion, adj. lands of Daniel Clark. N.O., 3 Dec. 1787, by Miro. // File. Claimant, Thos. Burling, 30 Mch. 1804. Wit: Henry Roach, 15 Aug. 1805. Confirmed. Certif. A-485. 15 Aug. 1805. Thos. Burling claims 1000 acres on the Miss. River in Adams Co. by virtue of the above grant. Thos. Burling by J. Dunlap.

p.190. Claim No.1755. British Govt. to Robert Callender 2000 acres 60 miles below the Natchez, at the great cliffs, adj. Silvester and James Fanning. Pensacola, 2 Aug. 1768, by Montfort Browne. // File. Heirs of Robert Callender, claimants, 30 Mch. 1804. Reported, 28 Apr. 1807. Claim as above of 2000 acres in Wilkinson Co. and by the will of said Robert Callender. J. Dunlap, atty. for legal representatives.

p.196. Claim No.1756. Wm. Dunbar, 1000 acres on North Fork of Cole's Creek, 35 mi. NE of Fort, adj. lands of grantee. N.O., 14 Aug. 1794. // File. Claimant, Wm. Dunbar, Jr., 30 Mch. 1804. Res. proved No. 1733. Certif. A-57 issued to claimant, 5 Sept. 1805. Wm. Dunbar, Jr. claims 1000 acres in Jefferson Co. by virtue of the above Spanish patent, as above. J. Dunlap for claimant.

p.199. Claim No.1757. Spanish Govt. to Don Pedro Camus, 200 arps. on Second Creek, 10 mi. east of Fort, adj. John Newton, Isaac Alexander and John Hartley. N.O. (n.d.) by Carondelet. Certif. June 2, 1795. [File missing.]

p.202. Claim No.1758. Spanish Govt. to Samuel Cooper 400 acres 15 mi. SE of Natchez, adj. George Bayley and Henry Cason. N.O., 26 Dec. 1795, by Carondelet. // p.204. Natchez, 4th July 1797, before Gayoso. Samuel Cooper sells to James Moore, the tract in above grant for $400 in hand paid. (signed) John Cooper, executor for the est. of my father. Wit: Sutton Banks, Wm. McIntosh. // File. Claimant, Walter Burling, 30 Mch. 1804. Wit: Ebenezer Rees, 22 Aug. 1805. Certif. B-156 issued 10 Feb. 1807. Walter Burling claims 400 arpents on Sandy Creek in Adams County by virtue of a Spanish patent Dec. 1795, sd claimant having been in actual possession for many years by virtue of a conveyance from said Cooper to James Moore who on the 13 January ____ conveyed it to this claimant. Walter Burling by J. Dunlap, atty.

p.205. Claim No.1759. Spanish Govt. to Don Estevan Minor, 1000 acres 5 miles from Fort on SE, adj. John McIntosh, Wm. Dunbar, Charles White, Wm. Cobbs, Adam Bingaman and Peter Surget. N.O., 25 May 1792, by Carondelet. // File. Walter Burling, claimant, 30 Mch. 1804. Certif. A-571 issued 5 Sept. 1805. Wit: John Ellis, 5 Sept. 1805. Walter Burling claims 1000 acres on Second Cr. in Adams Co. by virtue of the above grant to Stephen Minor and by him conveyed to Elizabeth Whittle in Aug. 1793, part of which land was exchanged by the sd E. Whittle with _____ as appears from a deed of exchange hereto annexed and by a conveyance from sd Elizabeth Whittle to Walter Burling. By J. Dunlap.

p.208. Claim No.1760. Spanish Govt. to John Burnet, Jr. 130 acres on Bayou Pierre. N.O., 14 Apr. 1796. // File. Claimant, John Burnet, Jr., 30 Mch. 1804. Rejected for want of evidence, 10 June 1807. Claim of 130 acres in Claiborne by virtue of a Spanish warrant of survey before 1795, etc.

p.211. Claim No.1761. Daniel Douglass, wishing to establish himself in the City of Natchez, asks for one of the vacant lands, adj. that of John Wilson, 8 July 1793. // Order July 1794, and grant 3 March 1795, by Gayoso. // File. Claimant, Daniel Douglass, 30 Mch. 1804. Certif. A-643 issued 27 Sept. 1805. Notation: No.642 issued to Christopher Miller for part of Lot No.2, Sq. No.11. Daniel Douglass claims two lots in the Town of Natchez, Nos. 1 and 2, Sq. No.11, by virtue of the above grant.

p.213. Claim No.1762. Spanish Govt. to John Cammock, 400 acres on a br. of Bayou Sarah, 45 mi. SSE of the Fort, adj. Thos. Lilly White and Daniel Clark. N.O., 7 Dec. 1797, by Carondelet. // File. Claimants, Nevill and Beauvais, 30 Mch. 1804. Rejected 3 June 1807. Samuel Nevill and James Beauvais claim 400 acres of land in Wilkinson Co., as above, and the intermediate conveyances annexed. (signed) Neill and Beauvais.

p.216. Claim No.1764. Spanish Govt. to William Collins 500 acres on a br. of Bayou de la Feliciana, adj. Wm. Dunbar. Dist. of Natchez, 1795. // File. Claimant, Neill and Beauvais, 30 Nov. 1804. Rejected 13 June 1807. Samuel Neill and St. James Beauvais claim 500 arpents as above granted to Wm. Collins, a res. etc. and by the intermediate conveyances.

p.219. Claim No.1744. Spanish Govt. to Benjamin Brashears 400 arps. on waters of Bayou Pierre, 45 mi. east of Fort. N.O., 20 March 1795, by Carondelet. // File. Claimant, Benj. Brashears, 30 Mch. 1804. Wit: James Harman, 20 Nov. 1804. A-424 issued 10 July 1805. Claim as above in Claiborne Co.

p.224. Claim No.1747. Spanish Govt. to James Allen Mathews 400 acres on main branch of Bayou Pierre, adj. Jesse Greenfield, other sides vacant. N.O., 1 Jany. 1793, by Carondelet. // p.227. James Allen Mathews to James White 400 acres on Bayou Pierre granted as above, for $300 in hand paid. 15 Dec. 1796. Signed. Wit: Lewis Evans. Prov. by Evans before Seth Lewis Ch. Justice of Miss. Territory. // p.228. 9 Mch. 1799, James White, Esq. to Edward Evans, Esq., for $400 paid, the above described tract. Wit: Lewis Evans. // p.230. 12 Dec. 1801. Edward Evans by James Truly and Daniel Douglass, his attorneys, to Wm. Lindsay, for $600. (Edward Evans, formerly a res. of Natchez, Miss. Ter.), the above tract. // p.233. 1 Aug. 1803. Wm. Lindsay, of Claiborne Co., Miss. Ter., to Stephen Bullock, of same, for $1200 paid, 400 acres on Bayou Pierre, as above. (signed) Will Lindsay. No. witnesses. // File. Claimant, Stephen Bullock, 30 Mch. 1804. Wit: John Girault, 2 Aug. 1804. Certif. A-503 issued 19 Aug. 1805. Stephen Bullock claims founded on above grant and conveyances.

p.220. Claim No.1766. Spanish Govt. to Don Luis Faure, 14 acres adj. Estevan Minor and Philip Engle. // File. Claimant, David Ferguson, 30 Mch. 1804. Wit: B. Truly. Certif. A-768 issued 15 May 1806. David Ferguson claims 14 arpents in the City of Natchez by virtue of a patent to Don Luis Faure, as above, and Faure sold same to Ferguson.

p.236. Claim No.1767. Spanish Govt. to David Ferguson 1000 acres on North Fork of Cole's Cr. 30 mi. ENE of Fort, adj. John Murdock. N.O., 14 Aug. 1793, by Carondelet. [Plat shows a br. called Sharp's Fork.] // File. Claimant, David Ferguson, 30 Mch. 1804. Certif. A-681 issued Oct. 1805. David Ferguson claims 1000 arps. in Jefferson Co. as above.

p.239. Claim No.1768. Petition of Francisco Lennan for a large garden of 10 acres adj. those of Joseph Vidal and Anna Dunbar. // Grant for same 10 Jany. 1795. Plat shows two tracts of five acres each, one adj. Joseph Vidal and the other across a road from Anna Dunbar, for Francisco Lennan, curate of this parish, 4 Feb. 1795. // File. Claimant, David Ferguson, 30 Mch. 1804. Certif. A-769 issued 15 May 1806. David Ferguson claims 5 arpents in the City of Natchez by virtue of above patent to Francis Lennan, as above, who sold the sd 5 arps to David Ferguson.

p.255. Claim No.1769. 9 April 1777. William Hays and Sarah, his wife, to William Ratcliff, for £40 sterling, paid, 200 acres, 10 miles north[?] of Natchez on Second Cr., patented to sd Hays 14 Nov. 1776, adj. Jeremiah Germain. (signed) William Hays, Sarah (x) Hays. Wit: A. B. Llewelin. // p.258. 12 June 1798. Reuben Baxter, of Dist. of Natchez in U.S. to Wilford Hoggat, of same, for $300 paid, 200 acres adj. Wm. Ratcliffe, which sd land was conveyed to Reuben Baxter by William Hayes, 6 Nov. 1797. Signed. Wit: Joshua Howard, James Howard, John Girault. // File. Claimant, David Ferguson, 30 Mch. 1804. Certif. A-772 issued 15 May 1806. David Ferguson claims 400 acres in Adams Co. on Second Cr. by virtue of a British patent to Wm. Hays, who sold 200 acres of grant of 400 acres to Wm. Ratcliff and 200 acres to Reuben Baxter, and the said Ratcliff conveyed his 200 acres to James McMullen and McMullen conveyed the same to James Hoggat and James Hoggat conveyed same unto David Ferguson, and the remaining 200 acres were conveyed by Reuben Baxter, to whom the said Hays sold it, unto Wilford Hoggat who sold the same unto David Ferguson.

p.272. Claim No.1770. British Govt. to Emanuel Madden warrant of survey for 100 acres, 25 Sept. 1777. Grant of same on south fork of Second Cr. 10 miles east the Natchez, b. on SW by Wm. Hays. Pensacola, 16 Feb. 1779, by Peter Chester. // p.279. 26 Feb. 1801, James McMullens and Lucy, his wife, to James Hoggat, $650 paid, two tracts containing 300 acres; (1) 200 acres being upper half of 400 acres gr. Wm. Hays by British, 14 Nov. 1776, adj. Joshua Howard and Emanuel Madden, and (2) 100 acres adj. afsd tract on east, gr. to Emanuel Madden 16 Feb. 1778. (signed) James McMullens, Lucy (x) McMullens. Wit: Wilford Hoggatt, James Howard. // p.282. James Hoggatt and wife, Grisélla, of Adams Co., Miss. Territory, to David Ferguson, 1 Mch. 1804, for $650 paid, 300 acres in two tracts, as described above. Both sign. Wit: P. Hoggatt, Adam Tooley. // File. Claimant, David Ferguson, 30 Mch. 1804. Certif. A-771 issued 15 May 1806. Claim as above, of 100 acres gr. by British Govt. of West Florida to Emanuel Madden, who sold to Wm. Ratcliff who sold it to James McMullens who sold to James Hoggatt.

p.242. Claim No.1775. British Govt. to Silas Crane, order of survey for 300 acres on waters of Homochitto. Pensacola, 19 Nov. 1778, by Peter Chester. Directive to any lawful surveyor of the Prov. of West Fla. to lay out same. D. Gannaway, Sur. Genl. // File. Claimants, heirs of Silas Crane, 31 Mch. 1804. Wit: Richard King, 29 Nov. 1804. Rejected 27 April 1807. The legal representatives of Silas Crane, decd., claim 300 acres of land in Adams Co. on the Homochitto by virtue of the above warrant of survey to Silas Crane from the British Govt. G. Poindexter, atty of the rep.

p.243. Claim No.1778. Spanish Govt. to Francisco Bazo and Antonio Gras for 800 acres on waters of what is called "la Roche a Davion", 4 leagues south of Fort Panmure, adj. Bartholomew LeBreton, John Lovelace and Stephen Ploche. N.O., 16 Nov. 1792. // File. Francisco Bazo and Antonio Gras, claimants, 30 Mch. 1804. Certif. A-801 issued 9 June 1807. Francison Bazo and Antonio Gras claim 800 acres in Wilkinson Co. on the Miss. River by virtue of the above Spanish grant.

p.246. Claim No.1781. Spanish Govt. to Jacob Copelthwait 1000 acres on a br. of Fairchild's Cr. 9 mi. NE of Fort, adj. James McIntire, William Owen, John Bisland, Joshenoul (?) Dugens de Livaudais, James Jones, Thos. Jordan, and James Wade. N.O., 8 Oct. 1787, by Miro. // File. Claimants, heirs of Jacob Copelthwait, 31 Mch. 1804. Certif. A-654 issued to legal rep. for 800 arpents, 18 Oct. 1805. Heirs and legal rep. of Jacob Coplethwait, decd., claim 1000 arps. by virtue of the above patent. Note: 200 arpents of the 1000 arps were conveyed to Taylor and the remainder is only 800. Certif. A-653 is issued to Robert and Isaac Taylor, for 200 arps, part of the within. See No.1618.

p.249. Claim No.1782. Spanish Govt. to James Mather 2000 acres 40 mi. south of Fort, adj. Ezekiel Forman. N.O., 3 April 1794, by Carondelet. // p.252. 26 April 1803. James Mather, a native subject of the King of Great Britain but now residing in the Prov. of Louisiana, to George Mather, brother of the afsd James, for $10000 to him paid, 2000 acres in above grant. (signed) James Mather. Wit: Chas Surget, Nathan Meriam. Prov. by Surget in Wilkinson Co., Miss. Ter., before Hugh Davis, J. P. // File. Claimant, George Mather, 31 Mch. 1804. Wit: Wm. Atchinson, 18 July 1804. Wit: John Wall, 31 Jany. 1806. Certif. A-763 issued 10 Apr. 1806. George Mather claims 2000 arpents by virtue of a complete title granted by the Spanish Govt. to James Mather, as above, and sold by sd James Mather to claimant. A plantation has been established and cultivated on said tract by the proprietor since the time of its having been granted, being the same land which was intended by the Spanish Govt. for Col. Robert Stark and granted to James Mather when the sd Col. Stark declared his intention to abandon the then Spanish District of Natchez, upon the subject of which interfering claim a judicial decision has already been had in favor of the claimant before the Superior Tribunal of this Territory. (signed) George Mather.

p.285. Claim No.1783. Spanish Govt. to Richard Deval 800 acres on waters of Boyd's Creek, b. on east by David Wanderward, north by a large lake. N.O., 16 July 1787, by Miro. Plat shows Alexander Boyd on south and the location of the mill of Richard Deval. // File. Claimant, James Mather, 31 Mch. 1804. Wit: Ebenezer Rees, 2 Oct. 1806. See No.907. Certif. A-603 issued for 800 arpents, 9 June 1804. James Mather claims 1050 arpents at the mouth of Cole's Creek, an original grant to Richard Deval. This claim was by a Judicial Sale made at public vendue of the said land, the property of Richard Deval, purchased for the claimant by his agent, Bernard Lintot, the said Richard Devall received a grant from the Spanish Govt. for 800 arpents and remaining 250 arpents was obtained by purchase at a public sale ordered by the Spanish Govt. of certain confiscated properties, the evidences of which the claimant has been unable to get but in due time they will be produced. A valuable saw mill was built on the lesser tract.

p.289. Claim No.1784. Spanish Govt. to Charles King, 375 acres on a branch of Cole's Creek, adj. James Cole and Richard Bell. N.O., 8 Apr. 1795, by Miro. File. Claimant, Isaac Newman, 31 Mch. 1804. Wit: Daniel Whitaker, 8 Oct. 1804. Certif. A-491 issued 15 Aug. 1805. Isaac Newman claims 375 acres by virtue of a Spanish patent to Chas. King, as above, who conveyed the same to this claimant by sale 29 Nov. 1794.

p.293. Claim No.1785. Spanish Govt. to William Curtis, 200 acres on a br. of Cole's Cr. 20 mi. NNE of Fort, adj. Chas. Simmons. [n.d.] The branch called Platner's Fork. // p.294. George Cochran, a res. of Natchez, says that he has bought from Wm. Curtis the land in the above warrant. // Grant of same to William Curtis. N.O., 20 Jany. 1790, by Carondelet. // File. George Cochran, claimant, 31 Mch. 1804. Wit: Henry Platner, 8 Dec. 1806. Certif. A-791 issued 4 Mch. 1807. Geo. Cochran claims 200 acres on Platner's Fork of Cole's Cr. by virtue of Spanish patent to William Curtis who conveyed the said tract to this claimant, but the conveyance has been lost and proof of its existence will be referred to this Board. (signed) George Cochran.

p.339. Claim No.1786. Lewis Evans petitions the Spanish Govt. for Lot 2, Sq.19 in Natchez, 9 Jany. 1795. Order by Gayoso. Grant, 20 June 1795, by Carondelet. // File. Claimant, George Cochran, 31 Mch. 1804. Certif. A-628 to claimant 23 Sept. 1805. Claim of above by virtue of the Spanish patent to Lewis Evans and conveyed to sd Cochran in Feb. 1798. Signed Robt. Cochran.

p.297. Claim No.1789. Spanish Govt. to Joseph Deas, 12,800 feet 50 toises, NE of Fort Panmure, adj. Mr. Duon. N.O., 10 July 1788, by Miro. // File. Claimant, Christopher Lee, 31 Mch. 1804. Wit: Peter Walker, 13 June 1807. Certif. A-809 issued. Christopher Lee, as legal representative of Joshua Dias claims 13,800 ft of land in the City of Natchez by virtue of a Spanish patent to sd Josh Dias who conveyed the sd lot to Catherine Lambert who conveyed it together with other lands to James Barr, who conveyed it to this claimant.

p.299. Claim No.1790. Spanish Govt. to Alonzo Segovio 9600 ft. 40 toises, west of Fort Panmure, adj. Mr. Adam Bingaman and the King's Garden. N.O., 12 June 1788, by Miro. In plat also adj. Wm. Vousdan and Carlos de Grand-Pre. // File. Claimant, Christopher Lee 31 Mch. 1804. Wit: Peter Walker, 13 June 1807. Confirmed. Certif. A-810. Christopher Lee, as legal rep. of Alonzo Segovia, claims 9600 ft. of land in the City of Natchez by virtue of a Spanish patent to sd Alonzo, as above, and was conveyed by Catherine Lambert to James Barr, 14 Dec. 1800. He conveyed the same together with another lot to sd claimant.

p.306. Claim No.1791. Spanish Govt. to Richard King 86 acres, 9 mi. east of Fort, adj. David Williams, Gerard Brandon, John Rawls and John Foster. N.O., 20 Aug. 1794, by Carondelet. // File. Claimant, John R. Wiley, 31 Mch. 1804. See No.1720 and No.541. Rejected 16 May 1806. John R. Wiley claims, as legal rep. of Richard King 86 arpents in Adams Co. on waters of St. Catherine's Cr. by virtue of a Spanish gr. to sd Richard King who sold the same to this claimant.

p.310. Claim No.1792. Spanish Govt. to Page V. Cussett, widow of Capt. Cussett, 800 acres on waters of Cole's Cr., 16 mi. east of Fort, adj. Seth Lewis and Samuel Flowers. N.O., 7 July 1789. // File. Claimant, Ebenezer Rees, 31 Mch. 1804. Res. of Ebenezer Rees proved in Claim No.856. Certif. A-492 issued to claimant, 15 Aug. 1805. Ebenezer Rees claims 800 acres on Cole's Cr. by virtue of a Spanish patent to Madam Coussot who conveyed the same by deed, 13 Oct. 1794, to the claimant.

p.315. Claim No.1793. Petition of Elizabeth Douglass, widow, for herself and her three children, Lott Douglass, Eve Douglass and Elizabeth Douglass, for 400 acres on which they are living and have cultivated on a br. of Cole's Cr. called Lick Branch, adj. Cato West. Certificate of survey by Wm. Vousdan, surveyor, 22 Nov. 1788, warrant and grant by Miro. N.O., 16 Jany. 1789. // Petition of Elizabeth Douglass, that on 16 Jany. 1793, she did obtain from His Excellency, Gov. Miro, 400 acres for herself and three children, Lott, Eve and Elizabeth, which land she now holds but she finds it difficult to support said children, and asks a decree authorizing her to sell said tract to enable her to school and support her afsd children. Elizabeth (X) Douglass, now Elizabeth Leightliter. Natchez, 16 Mch. 1798. Wit: Cato West. Petition granted, Mch. 1798, by Vidal. // p.318. Deed. 16 Mch. 1798. Elizabeth Douglass, of the Dist. of Villa Gayoso to Ebenezer Rees, for $400 paid, the above grant. Wit: Edward Randolph, Nathaniel Brown, Cato West. // p.320. Release by Philip Leighliter, 16 Mch. 1798. Wit: Cato West. // File. Claimant, Ebenezer Rees, 31 Mch. 1804. Wit: Wm. Thompson. Certif. B-793. Claim of Ebenezer Rees for 400 acres in Dist. of Villa Gayoso by warrant from Spanish Govt. to Eliz. Douglas who conveyed same to claimant.

p.321. Claim No.1794. Spanish Govt. to Frederick Mann, 500 acres on a br. of Bayou Feliciana, adj. Daniel Clark. 31 Jany. 1795. Pet. of Fred. Mann, a carpenter, same date. // Plat shows the tract on east fork of Bayou Sarah adj. Ebenezer Rees and William McIntosh. // File. Claimant, Frederick Mann, 31 Mch. 1804. Rejected 23 Apr. 1807. Ebenezer Rees, legal rep. of Frederick Mann claims 500 arpents by virtue of a Spanish order of survey, at which time sd Mann was at the head of a family, etc. (No decree from the Gov. General.)

p.322. Claim No.1795. Wilkinson Co., Miss. Ter., Mch. 24, 1804. Sylvester Stouts came before me, one of the Justices of sd Co., and declared that in 1795 William Bovard did actually settle and occupy a tract in Adams Co. on Dry Bayou near Sandy Creek which land sd Bovard sold to John Lockhart and Lockhart to Dr. James White. Signed by Sylvester Stouts and by William Ogden, J. P. // p.322. Deed. James White to Ebenezer Rees, a tract on Dry Bayou, waters of Caney br. of Well's Creek purchased by me from Lockhart and by him from William Bovard, 640 acres, adj. land taken up by Sylvester Stouts. Full consideration recd. (signed) James White. Wit: Jacob Stroop, Thos. (x) Due // File. Claimant, Ebenezer Rees, 31 Mch. 1804. Rejected, 15 May 1807. Ebenezer Rees claims 640 acres, as above, by virtue of its being inhabited and cultivated in 1795.

p.323. Claim No.1796. 3 Feb. 1799, James White, for $800 ($200, $90 by a horse and bond for $510) 400 acres on Sandy Cr. granted by Spanish Govt. to Henry Cason Cooper and surveyed 18 Aug. 1787, to James Griffin. Signed. Wit: Joshua Howard, Morris Custard. // p.325. James Griffin and Elizabeth, his wife, to Eben Rees, for $1500 in hand paid, all that land granted to Henry Cooper and by him conveyed to Doctor James White, as above. (signed) James Griffin, Elizabeth (x) Griffin. Wit: James Bossley, John Reating, Vines L. Collier. // File. Claimant, Ebenezer Rees, 31 Mch. 1804. Wit: Samuel Cooper, 16 Apr. 1805. Allowed as a Donation. Certif. B-299, issued 13 June 1807. Ebenezer Rees claims 400 acres by virtue of an order of survey to Henry Cooper, as above, who conveyed it to Doctor James White, who sold it to James Griffin and sd Griffin conveyed sd land 6 Oct. 1803, to present claimant.

p.326. Claim No.1797. Deed. 10 Dec. 1798, James McGill and Ann, his wife, of Baton Rouge, to Ebenezer Rees, of Miss. Territory, Southern part, for $250 paid, 500 acres in northern part of sd Territory on Chubby's Fork of Bayou Pierre. Both signed. Wit: Chas. Bakler, Patrick Lynch, Philip Fields, Silas L. Payne. // File. Claimant, Ebenezer Rees, 31 Mch. 1804. Rejected, 13 June 1807. Ebenezer Rees claims 500 acres of waters of Bayou Pierre by an order of survey to James McGill and from McGill to sd claimant. Caveat versus Ebenezer Rees: The Board of Commrs. West of the Pearl River will not grant a certificate confirming Ebenezer Rees's claim of 500 acres on warrant of survey to James McGill because the same tract of land lies within the tract by complete grant to Thaddeus Lyman who leaving this country by order of the Spanish Govt., one moiety of the land in which lies the claim of Ebenezer Rees was confirmed and granted to Salome Lyman, dau. of the sd Thaddeus, who since marrying John Ellison, the same is claimed by said Ellison for his wife. Duly entered before this board. By S. Bullock, their atty.

p.332. Claim No.1798. Deed Pierre Roque to Ebenezer Rees. (nothing more) // File. Claimant, Ebenezer Rees, 31 Mch. 1804. Certif. A-576 issued 15 Jany. 1806. Ebenezer claims Lot 3, Sq.8, in City of Natchez by virtue of a patent of the Spanish Govt. to William Barland who conveyed it to Francis Caudle, who conveyed it to Pierre Rogue who conveyed it to the claimant, 17 June 1799.

p.333. Claim No.1799. Petition of Ezina Barker, having a large family, 7 sons and 4 daughters, of whom one half are men capable of working to earn their living, asks for lands which are abandoned, adj. lands of Daniel Clark. Natchez, 28 Dec. 1794. // Grant for 500 acres on the middle br. of the Homochitto, adj. Jacob Stampley and Winsor Pipes, 25 mi. east of Fort. N.O., 24 Feb. 1795, by Carondelet. // Natchez, 15 Feb. 1795. Know all men that I give my land warrant to my eldest son. (Not signed). Wit: Asnak Barker, Ethered Barker, Lyda Barker, William Barker, Burwil Barker. // I do hereby make over my right in a warrant of 500 acres, now in the hands of William Dunbar, Esq., to Mr. Ebenezer Rees for value recd. 22 Dec. 1795. Burwell Barker. Wit: Robert Moore, Parker Carradine. // p.336. Miss. Ter. Co. of Pickering, 13 April 1801. John Girault and wife, Mary, to Melling Woolley, Esq. for $80 a lot of land adj. Wm. Barland, in form of a triangle. Both signed. Wit: Wm. B. Cotten, A. McKinnan. // File. Claimant, Ebenezer Rees, 31 Mch. 1804. Rejected 23 Apr. 1807. Ebenezer Rees claims 500 acres on waters of the Homochitto by virtue of an order of survey to Encina Barker, who gave it to her eldest son, Burrell Barker, and he conveyed to present claimant. [The deed from John Girault and wife to Melling Woolley was apparently a stray document in the wrong file.]

p.342. Claim No.1800. Petition of Joseph King to the Spanish Govt. for 240 acres on Bayou Pierre. 10 Sept. 1789. // Order of survey. Grant N.O., 25 Apr. 1790. Certif. of survey and plat by Dunbar, 8 Mch. 1795. // Plat shows south fork of Bayou Pierre, adj. Jeremiah Bryan and Edward Rose. // File. Claimant, Silas L. Payne, 31 Mch. 1804. Rejected 23 Apr. 1807. Ebenezer Rees of Silas L. Payne claims 240 acres on Bayou Pierre by virtue of a Spanish survey to Joseph King, as above, who conveyed the same to Silas L. Payne, 20 May 1798.

p.345. Claim No.1801. Spanish Govt. to William Richie, 400 acres on North Fork of Cole's Cr. 6 mi. east of Miss. River, called Petit Gulf, 25 mi. north of Fort, adj. Adam Sidney, Martin and Ralph Price, George Cochran. N.O. 30 Aug. 1793 by Carondelet. // File. Claimant, Hoggatt and Bell, 31 Mch. 1804. Wit: Bennet Truly, 6 Mch. 1805. Certif. A-493 issued 15 Aug. 1805. Proved in Richie. James Hoggatt and John Bell claim 500 acres on waters of Bayou Pierre by virtue of a patent to William Richie who sold to Ebenezer Rees who sold the same to the claimants.

p.348. Claim No.1802. Spanish Govt. to John Adams 500 acres of Chubby's Creek, a south br. of Bayou Pierre, 45 mi. NE of Fort. // Petition that he has a family of four whites and one negro; asks for grant on Sandy Creek, adj. John Bisland and John Nelson, 20 Dec. 1792. Signed, John Odam. // p.351. 3 Jany. 1799. John Odam and Elizabeth, his wife, sell to Ebenezer Rees for $250, 500 acres on waters of Bayou Pierre. Both sign with a mark. Wit: Catherine (x) White, Peggy (x) White, Silas L. Payne, Steven Henderson. // p.353. John Still Lee relinquishes all right to above tract with all improvements thereon to Ebenezer Rees. Signed. Wit: Bryan Bruin. // File. Claimant, Ebenezer Rees, 31 Mch. 1804. Wit: Bennet Truly, 16 Dec. 1805. Certif. B-262 issued 23 Apr. 1807. Ebenezer Rees claims 500 acres on waters of Bayou Pierre by virtue of a Spanish order of survey to John Odam, who conveyed by deed to present claimant.

p.354. Claim No.1803. Petition of Richard and George Rapalje Carradine, sons of Parker Carradine, having six slaves they wish a plantation to cultivate, asks for a grant. 20 Mch. 1797. // Spanish Government to Richard and George Carradine 1000 acres on Bayou de la Feliciana, 50 mi. ESE of the Fort. Plat showing land adj. those of John Joseph Carradine, Mr. Surgett and William Dunbar. // File. Claimants, Richard and George Carradine, 31 Mch. 1804. Rejected, 23 Apr. 1807. Ebenezer Rees, legal rep. of Richard and George Carradine claim 1000 arpents as above.

p.356. Claim No.1804. Spanish Govt. to William Thomas 400 acres on a br. of Cole's Cr. 4 mi. NE of Fort, b. on south by Richard King, SE Richard Curtis, and west by George Selser. N.O., 20 June 1795, by Carondelet. // p.359. 16 July 1798. William Thomas and Henrietta, his wife, of Villa Gayoso, to Ebenezer Rees, for $300 paid, 380 acres as in the above grant. Both signed. Wit: R. Knox, John Barclay. // File. Claimant, Ebenezer, 31 Mch. 1804. Res. of Wm. Thomas proved in claim 1528. Certif. A-494 issued 15 Aug. 1805. Ebenezer Rees claims 400 acres by virtue of a patent to William Thomas, as above, who conveyed same to present claimant.

p.362. Claim No.1805. Spanish Govt. to Daniel Finnan 240 arps on the South Fork of Bayou Pierre, 45 mi. NE from Fort, b. by lands of Mr. Rout(h). N.O., 26 Apr. 1790. // File. Daniel Finnan, claimant, 31 Mch. 1804. Rejected 23 Apr. 1807. Ebenezer Rees, legal rep. of Daniel Finnan, claims 240 arpents by virtue of a Spanish order of survey as above.

p.364. Claim 1806. Jacob Stampley, having served 6 months in company of mounted volunteers of Natchez in command of Don Richard King, receives an order of survey for 200 acres, 18 Jany. 1792. Certificate of survey and plat by Wm. Dunbar, 10 May 1795. Plat shows land adj. Abner Pipes and

Encina Barker. // File. Claimant, Jacob Stampley, 31 Mch. 1804. Rejected 23 April 1807. Ebenezer Rees, legal rep. of Jacob Stampley, claims 200 acres of land by virtue of an order of survey, etc.

p.366. Claim No.1807. Petition of Robert Davis to the Spanish Govt. that he holds as succession of my father, 4 slaves and considerable horses and other cattle, asks for 800 arpents bet. Buffalo and Thompson's Creeks, adj. Mr. Ezekiel Forman. 8 Jany. 1795. // Order of survey. // Plat and certificate for 800 acres on east br. of Bayou Sarah, 40 mi. SSE of Fort, by Dunbar. // Assignment of right, etc. to within warrant to Wm. Collins for value received. 27 Oct. 1797. (signed) Robert David. Wit: Robert M. Causland. // File. Ebenezer Rees, claimant, 31 Mch. 1804. Rejected 23 Apr. 1807. Ebenezer Rees claims 800 arpents of land by virtue of a warrant of survey to Robert Davis who sold it to Wm. Collins, who sold it to sd Rees. Note: No decree by Gov. Genl.

p.368. Claim No.1808. Spanish Govt. to Jesse Lum, order of survey of 200 acres for service in mounted volunteers of Natchez, commanded by Don Richard King. 18 Jany. 1793, by Gayoso. // Assignment of right to Ebenezer Rees by Jesse and Lovicy (x) Lum, 31 Mch. 1798. Wit: Silas L. Payne. Plat shows tract on south fork of Bayou Pierre. // File. Claimant, Ebenezer Rees, 31 Mch. 1804. Rejected 23 Apr. 1807. Claim 200 arpents on Bayou Pierre by virtue of the above order of survey.

p.371. Claim No.1809. Petition of Parker Carradine that his family consists of five sons, the youngest is fifteen and some of them have served in the militia and others in the cavalry for the protection of this district. I have 21 slaves; asks for more land. 19 Feb. 1797. Grant of 600 acres on Mill Cr. a br. of Feliciana, 50 mi. from Natchez. N.O. 28 Feb. 1795. Plat and cert. by Dunbar, 9 Oct. 1797. // File. Claimant, Parker Carradine, 31 Mch. 1804. Rejected, 23 Apr. 1807. Claim as above.

p.374. Claim No.1810. Petition of Joseph Striker for land bet those of Thomas Rule and Michael Mecho, to Spanish Govt. // Grant of 400 arpents on Willing's br. of the Miss. River, head branch of Bayou Sarah, 16 Sept. 1794. Surveyed by Christopher Bolling, D. S. // p.376. Conveyance of Joseph Striker to Christopher Bolling the above warrant. Wit: John Scott, James Kelly, 7 Apr. 1794. // File. Claimant, Ebenezer Rees, 31 Mch. 1804. Rejected, 23 Apr. 1807. Ebenezer Rees claims 400 arpents on waters of Bayou Sarah by virtue of a warrant of survey from the Spanish Govt. to Joseph Striker who sold same to Christopher Bolling who sold it to the claimant. // Deed. 25 Apr. 1798. Christopher Bolling of the Dist. of Feliciana, to Ebenezer Rees, for $200, 400 acres on Bayou Sarah. Signed. Wit: John Rogers, Samuel Burch.

p.379. Claim No.1811. Petition of Parker Carradine, Jr. who has 4 slaves and requests a grant. 20 March 1797. Order of survey, certificate and plat (by Dunbar), 8 Oct. 1797, for 500 acres on Bayou de la Feliciana, 50 mi. ESE of the Fort. // File. Claimant, Ebenezer Rees, 31 Mch. 1804. Rejected 23 Apr. 1807. Claims 500 arpents by virtue of warrant of survey, as above, to Parker Carradine who sold the same to Ebenezer Rees. Remarks: Local Governor's recommendation, District Surveyor's Certificate of survey, but no decree from the Governor General.

p.381. Claim No.1812. Spanish Govt. to James Spain for 200 acres on Cole's Cr. 20 mi. north of Fort, adj. Wm. Burch. N.O., 10 Jany. 1794, by Carondelet. // p.384. 28 May 1798. James Spain to Doctor Chas. F. Todd, for $140, the above grant of 200 acres. Signed. Wit: John McKee, Eben Rees. // File. Claimant, Ebenezer Rees for Chas. F. Todd, 31 Mch. 1804. Wit: Bennet Truly 16 Apr. 1805. Certif. A-495 issued to Chas. F. Todd, 15 Aug. 1805. Chas. F. Todd claims 200 arpents by virtue of a Spanish patent to James Spain, as above, who sold the same to Chas. F. Todd.

p.386. Claim No.1813. Spanish Govt. to William Burch, 200 acres on Cole's Cr. 20 mi. north of Fort, adj. James Spain and Thos. Calvit. N.O. 10 Jany. 1794 by Carondelet. // File. Ebenezer Rees, claimant, 31 Mch. 1804. Wit: Moses Armstrong, 11 Apr. 1805. Certif. A-496 issued to claimant, 15 Aug. 1805. Proved in Wm. Birch. Ebenezer Rees claims 200 arpents by virtue of a Spanish patent to Wm. Burch, as above, who sold to sd Rees, 28 Nov. 1797.

p.390. Claim No.1814. Petition to the Spanish Govt. of John Joseph Carradine, that he has a wife, two children and two negroes and asks for a grant of land. 16 Feb. 1797. Certificate and plat by Dunbar for 500 acres adj. Parker Carradine and Richard and George Carradine on Bayou de la Feliciana. 7 Oct. 1797. // File. Ebenezer Rees, claimant, 31 Mch. 1804. Rejected 23 Apr. 1807. Claim as above, and Carradine sold the same to sd Rees. Remarks: Claimant's petition, local Governor's recommendation, district surveyor's certificate, but no decree by the Governor General.

p.394. Claim No.1815. Spanish Govt. to Ephraim Bates for 400 acres on Sandy Creek. 15 mi. SE of Fort, adj. Mr. Cooper. N.O. 24 Mch. 1790 by Miro. // p.397. 10 Mch. 1798. Ephraim Bates and Sarah, his wife, to Ebenezer Rees, for $425, 400 acres in above grant. (signed) Ephraim Bates, Sarah (x) Bates. Wit: Benj. Lanier, William Lee, // File. Ebenezer Rees, claimant, 31 Mch. 1804. Wit: Samuel Cooper, 16 Apr. 1805. Certif. A-497, 15 Aug. 1805. Ebenezer Rees claims 400 acres by virtue of the above Spanish patent and conveyance.

p.399. Claim No.1816. Petition of Ebenezer Rees to Spanish Govt. desiring to establish himself and family, which consists of 12 slaves, in this Govt. asks for land on Bayou Sarah. 10 Jany. 1795. // Order for survey of 1000 acres, 20 Jany. 1795, by Gayoso. // Plat and certificate of survey by Dunbar, 24 Oct. 1796. [Plat shows tract on east fork of Bayou Sarah, adj. James Mather.] // File. Claimant, Ebenezer Rees, 31 Mch. 1804. Rejected 23 Apr. 1807. Claims 1000 arps. by virtue of the above warrant of survey. [No decree from Gov. Genl.]

p.401. Claim No.1817. Spanish Govt. to William Lee, 400 acres on Sandy Creek, 14 mi. south of Fort, adj. Ephraim Bates. N.O., 15 Mch. 1788, by Miro. // p.404. 2 Jany. 1802. William Lee and Susannah, his wife, for $800, to Ebenezer Rees 400 acres in the above grant. (signed) William Lee, Susannah (x) Lee. Wit: Anthony Hoggatt, P. Hoggatt. // File. Claimant, Ebenezer Rees, 31 Mch. 1804. Wit: Samuel Cooper, 16 Apr. 1805. Certif. A-498, 15 Aug. 1805. Claim by virtue of the above patent and conveyance.

p.406. Claim No.1818. Spanish Govt. to Alexander Henderson 723 acres on waters of St. Catherine's Cr. 4 mi. NE of Fort, adj. Richard Harrison, William Vousdan, Gideon Gibson, Mr. McCabe, Mr. Flower and Reuben Gibson. N.O., 6 Mch. 1788, by Miro. // File. Claimant, Ebenezer Rees, 31 Mch. 1804. Certif. A-343 issued to claimant for 423 arpents, 20 June 1805. Conveyance to Rees filed in No.1299. Note: 100 arpents of the within claimed by Thomas Foster to whom Certif. No.341 issued; 200 arpents also claimed by John Henderson to whom a certif. has issued this day. (signed) Thos. H. Williams, Reg. Claim for 723 acres by virtue of the above Spanish patent to Alex. Henderson who sold the same to Ebenezer Rees 8 Nov. 1799.

p.409. Claim No.1819. Petition of Jeremiah Bryan to Spanish Govt. asking for a gr. of 800 acres on Bayou de los Buyes, 30 or 40 mi. from the Homochitto where I would erect buildings for the convenience of travellers and the maintenance of horses and other animals. 5 Nov. 1788. // Order by Miro, N.O. 8 Nov. 1788. Plat and certificate of survey, 20 Aug. 1794, of 800 acres on Buffalo Cr. 45 mi. NE [?] of Fort, by Dunbar. // File. Claimant, Jeremiah Bryan, 31 Mch. 1804. Rejected 31 Apr. 1807. Claim by virtue of the above warrant of survey, and Jeremiah Bryan was the head of a family at the date of the warrant.

p.411. Claim No.1820. Petition of Abner Pipes, who has a family of 8 persons, all white, and asks for gr. on Fairchild's Cr. adj. Moses Bonner and Jeremiah Bryan. 17 Jany. 1793. // Certificate that lands desired are vacant. 17 Jany. 1793. Wm. Dunbar, D.S. // Order of survey by Gayoso, same date. // Grant by Carondelet 2 Feb. 1793. Plat shows land on Homochitto adj. Jacob Stampley and Encina Barker. // File. Claimant, Ebenezer Rees, 31 Mch. 1804. Wit: Wm. Collins, 14 Dec. 1805. Rejected. See No.689. March 30 1807. Ebenezer Rees, legal rep. of Abner Pipes, claims 480 acres by virtue of the above warrant of survey to sd Pipes, who sold the sd land to sd Rees.

p.413. Claim No.1821. Deed. 16 Oct. 1798. Jacob Krumbholt, of Cole's Creek, to Ebenezer Rees, for $100, 600 acres adj. Chas. Simmons, Wm. Curtis and Wm. Hamberlin. Signed. Wit: Chas. F. Todd, Jacob Krumbholt, Jr. // File. Ebenezer Rees, claimant, 31 Mch. 1804. Rejected 15 May 1805. Ebenezer Rees, as the legal rep. of John Roberts, Anthony Hamberlin and Jacob Krumbholt claims 600 acres in Jefferson Co. by virtue of said tract of land having been inhabited and cultivated by sd John Roberts and Anthony Hamberlin in and before 1797, and by virtue of sd land by sd Hamberlin to sd Roberts who conveyed the same to sd Krumbholt who conveyed the same to claimant. Certificate of survey Wm. Thomas, 5 April 1795, shows tract to be on Platner's Fork of Cole's Cr.

p.416. Claim No.1822. Natchez, 6 Nov. 1797. I certify at the request of Thomas Robertson that in or about the fall of 1791, I wrote a petition for a tract of land for him, which petition I saw his wife deliver to Colonel de Grand-Pre, who promised her the land and wrote permission for sd Robertson and family to settle upon it unmolested; I believe he promised them 600 acres on the waters of Cole's Creek. (signed) John Girault. // Assignment of claim to above-mentioned tract where he had resided six years, for $150. Thos. (x) Robertson. Wit: Wm. McIntosh, John Burch. // Certificate by William

Thomas, Nov. 10, 1794, shows tract adj. E. Johnson, Clement Dyson, Mr. John Murdoch and John Levy on a br. of north fork of Cole's Cr. // File. Claimants, Ebenezer Rees and C. F. Todd, 31 Mch. 1804. Wit: Wm. Thomas, 16 Apr. 1805. Rejected 13 June 1807. Ebenezer Rees and Chas. F. Todd claim 600 acres in Jefferson Co. by virtue of sd tract having been inhabited and cultivated by Thomas Robertson in 1792, at which time he was the head of a large family and until 4 Nov. 1797 when he sold the sd land and all rights to the said Ebenezer Rees and C. F. Todd.

p.419. Claim No.1829. Petition of Thomas Tyler to the Spanish Govt., a merchant and res. of Natchez, for 1000 acres on Bayou Pierre, adj. Wm. Brown. 7 Apr. 1795. // Order for same. Certificate that land wanted was vacant by Dunbar, 7 Apr. 1795. // File. Thos. Tyler, claimant, 31 Mch. 1804. Rejected 15 May 1807. Thomas Tyler claims 1000 acres by virtue of a decree of Manuel Gayoso de Lemos for the same. (BUT no decree from the Governor General.)

p.420. Claim No.1835. Spanish Govt. to William O'Connor for 200 acres on Cole's Cr. 17 mi. NE of Fort, adj. Patrick Gunnel and John Bisland. N.O., 3 May 1795, by Carondelet. // File. Claimant, James Wallace, 31 Mch. 1804. Wit: James Stewart, 24 July 1805. Certif. A-458 issued to F. L. Claiborne and E. Wooldridge, assignees of claimant, 24 Mch. 1805. James Wallace claims 300 arpents by virtue of the above grant to Wm. O'Connor who sold the same to Walter Cummins, 24 Apr. 1798, and sd Cummins deeded sd land to Patrick Conelly, 13 Nov. 1798 who conveyed sd land to sd James Wallace 2 Aug. 1803.

p.423. Spanish Govt. to Landon Davis, 800 arpents on south fork of Homochitto, called Beaver Dam Cr., 25 mi. SE of Natchez, adj. John McCay (or McCoy), Nathan Swazey and Hugh Davis, N.O., 4 Dec. 1797, by Gayoso. // File. Claimant, Landon Davis, 31 Mch. 1804. Wit: Mathew McCulloch, 5 Sept. 1804. 640 acres to be surveyed so as to include his improvement. Certif. B-224 issued 4 Mch. 1807. Landon Davis claims 800 arpents in Wilkinson Co. founded on the above Spanish patent to claimant, which the claimant did inhabit and cultivate before 27 Oct. 1795, and to the present day. G. Poindexter for the claimant. Note: The patent and survey, in this instance, being dated in 1797, the claimant in the premises desires that the claim be granted as a Donation. 5 Sept. 1804. (signed) T.R.

p.426. Claim No.1849. Petition of Andrew Beall for Lot 2, Sq.1 in the city. 20 July 1796. // Granted by Gayoso, 22 July 1796. // File. Claimant, heirs of A. Beall, 31 Mch. 1804. Wit: Christopher Miller, 5 June 1806. Certif. B-49, 9 Sept. 1806. Heirs of Andrew Beall, decd., claim Lot 2, Sq.1 in the City of Natchez, by virtue of above grant. Richard Beall, exor.

p.427. Claim No.1850. British Govt. to Daniel Clark, 3000 acres on Miss. River at St. Catherine's Cr. Pensacola, 15 Jany. 1768. // p.436. Daniel Clark and Jane, his wife, to James Dallas, late of the Island of Jamaica, now of Pensacola, and John Noble Taylor, late of the Island of Bermuda but now of the Kingdom of Great Britain, Esq., for $4680 paid. // File. Claimant, John Noble Taylor, 31 Mch. 1804. Witness, Wm. Atchinson, 27 Nov. 1804. Certif. A-471 issued to Taylor and the legal representatives of James Dallas, 1 Aug. 1805. John Noble Taylor in behalf of himself and the heirs of James Dallas, decd. who were actual settlers in the Miss. Territory on the 27 Oct. 1795, claim 2000 acres in Adams Co. 3 miles south of the City on the Mississippi River at a place known as St. Catherine's being part of a tract by virtue of a British grant to Daniel Clark as above, by whom the same was conveyed to sd John Noble Taylor and James Dallas, 10 Feb. 1780. At the death of the sd James the same has descended through his heirs. [This paper is badly torn.]

p.445. Claim No.1851. Spanish Govt. to Hugh Davis 800 acres on south fork of River Homochitto called Beaver Dam Cr. adj. Landon Davis. N.O., 24 Dec. 1797, by Gayoso. // File. Claimant, Hugh Davis, 31 Mch. 1804. Wit: Landon Davis, 2 Oct. 1805. Certif. D-341 issued 12 June 1807. Hugh Davis claims 800 acres in Wilkinson Co. founded on the above Spanish patent, etc. G. Poindexter, atty. for claimant.

p.447. Claim No.1853. Spanish gr. to Bertrand Favreau for Lot 2, Sq.25. Natchez, 8 Aug. 1796, by Gayoso. // File. Claimant, Joseph Vidal 31 Mch. 1804. Wit: James Moore, 7 June 1807. Certif. B-288 issued to claimant. Joseph Vidal, exor of the will of Domingo Lorero, decd., claims Lot 2, Sq.25, in the City of Natchez by virtue of a Spanish patent to Bertrand Favreau who conveyed the same to sd Domingo Lorero, 14 Jany. 1801. Joseph Vidal, exr. of Domingo Lorero.

p.449. Claim No.1855. Petition of Hugh Logan to Spanish Govt. for land on Cole's Cr. adj. Jacob Stephens. 3 Feb. 1791. // Order by Gayoso, 12 Mch. 1791. // Grant for 240 acres by Miro at N.O., 7 April 1791. // p.450. Deed. 21 Jany. 1799. Hugh Logan to Bennet Truly, for $120, the above 240 acres. Hugh (x) Logan. Wit: Ambrose Foster, Eli Gibson. [File missing.]

p.452. Claim No.1856. Petition of Bennet Truly to Spanish Govt. 200 acres on St. Catherine's Cr. adj. Messrs. Harrison, Flowers and Foster. 20 Nov. 1786. // Grant by Miro, 3 Jany. 1787. // File. Claimant, Bennet Truly, 31 Mch. 1804. Rejected 24 April 1807. Bennet Truly claims 200 arps. in Wilkinson Co., by virtue of a warrant of survey by Spanish Govt. Plat shows the tract on the east branch of Bayou Pierre adj. Anna Maria Whittle.

p.454. [The following petition and confirmation recorded here, under Claim No.1856 appear to be misplaced but are given.] Petition of William Ferguson to be Spanish Govt. that he bought on Feb. 23, 1778 from William Williams 500 acres on a branch of Boyd's Creek, bounded on the east by Richard Ellis, about a mile from Mr. Hiorn, 12 Jany. 1786. // Confirmation of sale made 23 Feb. 1778 by Mr. Wm. Williams to Wm. Ferguson for 500 acres. (signed) Miro. N.O. 20 April 1786.

p.456. Claim No.1860. Spanish Govt. to William Brocus 208 acres on St. Catherine's Creek, adj. Stephen Mayes. N.O., 20 July 1786, by Miro. // File. Claimant, Thomas Tyler, 31 Mch. 1804. Wit: John Henderson, 6 Aug. 1805. Rejected, 16 May 1806. Certif. A-33 issued to Elizabeth Whittle to whom the land was sold by Tyler, 28 May 1804. See Nos. 1592 and 1187. Thos. Tyler claims 208 arps by virtue of a Spanish patent to William Brocus who conveyed the same to James Glasscock who conveyed it to the present claimant. Plat shows land adj. Halbert Silkrist and Francisco Spain, as well as Mayes.

p.459. Claim No.1862. Spanish Govt. to Richard Bacon 250 acres adj. Luis Charbono, George Rapalje, Peter Nelson, Ben Monsanto, St. Germain and John Girault. // File. Claimant, Thos. Tyler, 31 Mch. 1804. Wit: George Fitzgerald, 6 Aug. 1805. Claimant's death suggested. Certif. A-478 issued to legal rep. 7 Aug. 1805. See No.1832. Thomas Tyler claims 131 acres founded on a Spanish patent to Richard Bacon for 250 acres who by several deeds, to wit, (1) 12 Aug. 1788 (2) 10 Nov. 1788 conveyed 150 acres to present claimant, the difference in the quantity conveyed and in the quantity claimed is the difference in the measure.

p.460. Claim No.1863. Petition of Ann Savage to Spanish Govt. // p.461. Spanish Govt. to Anne Savage 1000 acres on Second Cr., 10 mi. from Fort, adj. John Lusk and Sarah White. N.O. 15 Mch. 1789, by Miro. // p.463. I certify that Mrs. Savage has purchased of William Case 100 acres which lies on the south side of Second Creek and seemingly within the boundaries of her tract of 1000 acres. N.O. 10 Apr. 1792. // File. Claimants Wm. Conner and Mary, his wife, late Mary Savage, 31 Mch. 1804. Wit: Benjamin Farrar. Certif. A-450 issued to Conner in right of his wife, 22 July 1805. Wm. Conner and Mary, his wife, the legal representatives of Anne Savage claim 1100 acres of land on Second Creek by virtue of Spanish patent to Ann Savage, as above, for 1000 acres and 100 acres which are laid down in the plat book originally granted to Francis Fisher and through several intermediate conveyances came to the said Anne Savage. The whole of the 1100 acres have been inhabited and cultivated by Ann Savage and her heirs before and since 1789.

p.464. Claim No.1864. British Govt. to Robert Robinson, 100 acres 15 mi. south of Natchez, on Second Cr., adj. Thomas Hutchins and Mr. Wm. Harcourt. Pensacola, 14 Nov. 1776, by Peter Chester. // File. Claimant, Wm. Conner and others, 31 Mch. 1804. Wit: Benj. Farrar. Confirmed. Certif. A-532 issued to claimant, 28 Aug. 1805. William Conner and Mary, his wife, late Mary Savage, legal rep. of Anne Savage, decd., claim 100 acres on waters of Second Cr. founded on a British patent to Robert Robinson, then a res. who conveyed the 100 acres to Wm. Coleman, 18 Oct. 1779, and through several intermediate conveyances, from the sd Coleman, the land came into the possession of the said Anne Savage, decd., who devised the same to the said Mary Conner, late Mary Savage. William Conner in right of his wife.

p.470. Claim No.1865. British Govt. to Samuel Lewis 200 acres on Second Creek, 20 mi. from Fort, adj. Jacob Winfree, Sr. and David Dickson. Pensacola, 27 March 1776, by Peter Chester. // File. Claimant, William Conner, 31 Mch. 1804. Wit: Benj. Farrar. Certif. A-480 issued 8 Aug. 1805. William Conner claims 200 acres on Second Cr. founded on a British patent to Samuel Lewis from sd Lewis through several conveyances came to Isaac Gaillard who by deed, 23 Dec. 1801, conveyed the same to said claimant.

p.477. Claim No.1866. British Govt. to Sarah Lewis, late Sarah White, 1000 acres on Second Creek. Pensacola, 27 Mch. 1776, by Peter Chester. [File missing.]

p.484. Claim No.1867. Spanish Govt. to Maria Savage 1000 acres fronting on Buffalo Cr. 20 miles south of Fort. N.O., 30 Mch. 1796, by Carondelet. // File. Claimants, William Conner and others, 31 Mch. 1804. Wit: Elijah Phipps, 30 July 1805. Certif. B-160 issued 10 Feb. 1807. William Conner and Mary, his wife, late Mary Savage, claim 1000 arpents on Buffalo founded on a Spanish patent, as above, to afsd Mary Savage.

p.487. Claim 1868. Spanish Govt. to John Burnet. // File. Claimant, Peter B. Bruin, 31 Mch. 1804. Certif. A-709 issued 7 Jany. 1806. Peter Brian Bruin claims 500 acres founded on a Spanish grant to John Burnet for the afsd 500 acres who by his assignment, 20 Dec. 1789, transferred the same to the present claimant. By an accident a part of the patent was torn or destroyed but sufficient remains to evidence fully the claimant's title. Allowed.

p.488. Claim No.1869. Spanish Govt. to Peter Brian Bruin, 500 acres . . . [only the plat which shows Bayou Pierre on south, a lake on north and vacant lands on east and west.] // File. Claimant, Peter B. Bruin, 3 Mch. 1804. Rejected 13 June 1807. Peter Bryan Bruin claims 500 acres on waters of Bayou Pierre by virtue of a Spanish grant to him.

p.493. Claim No.1871. Spanish Govt. to Robert Scott, grant of Lot 2, Square 4. Natchez, 27 Sept. 1794, by Gayoso. // Petition of Scott for same, 12 Apr. 1794. // File. Claimant, Frederick Zerban, 31 Mch. 1804. Wit: Richard King, 9 June 1807. Certif. A-800 issued to legal rep. of Robert Scott. Natchez, Frederick Zerban, the legal representative and tenant, by courtesy, of the real estate late in the seizin of his wife Sarah Zerban, decd., who was an actual settler in the Miss. Territory in 1795, claims a lot in the City of Natchez, No.2, Square 4, by virtue of a Spanish grant to Robert Scott, 27 Sept. 1794. who by his will devised the same to the sd Sarah, at whose death, the said claimant became tenant as aforesaid with reversion in fee to Samuel P. Moore, James Moore and Robert Moore.

p.491. Claim No.1870. Spanish Govt. to Joseph Vidal, Lot No.4, Sq.5, by Gayoso. Natchez, 11 Apr. 1795. // Petition of Vidal for same, 9 Apr. 1795. [File missing.]

p.495. Claim No.1874. Petition of Andrew Scantling, [Scandlan] for Lot 1, Sq.26 in Natchez, 25 Aug. 1796. Granted by Gayoso. Natchez, 10 Sept. 1796. // File. James Moore, claimant. Robt. Moore, wit. Certif. B-289.

p.497. Claim No.1876. British Government to Anthony Hutchins 1000 acres on Second Creek, 10 miles SE of Fort. Pensacola, 21 Sept. 1772, by Peter Chester. // File. Claimant, John Hutchins, 31 Mch. 1804. Wit: Philander Smith, 9 Feb. 1805. Assignment to Ann Hutchins, 18 Apr. 1805. White Apple Village. The above tract of 1000 acres on both sides of Second Creek whereon Anthony Hutchins has resided since 1772 is claimed by John Hutchins under survival of his brother, Thomas Hutchins, under letters patent from the Government of West Florida to his father, the said Anthony Hutchins, and by virtue of a deed of gift from the said father, Anthony, to him, the claimant, and his deceased brother, the said Thomas Hutchins, as joint tenants, whom he, the claimant, hath survived.

p.504. Claim No.1877. British Govt. to John Alston 450 acres 5 mi. south of the Natchez, b. by Edward Mayes, Mrs. Haigh, Absalom Hooper, Wm. Ratcliff and Mrs. Holmes. Pensacola, 16 June 1777, by Peter Chester. // File. Claimant, Solomon Alston, 31 Mch. 1804. Wit: Bennet Truly, 28 May 1805. Reported. I, Solomon Alston, claim the above tract of land, as heir and representative of John Alston, decd. the same being granted to said John by George III, 6 June 1777. Plat also included Enoch Horton, Rickey with land adj.

p.511. Claim No.1878. British Govt. to Thomas Comstock 150 acres 13 miles from the Natchez, adj. Herbert Munster, John Bowls and Benj. Gower. Pensacola, 6 Aug. 1778, by Chester. // File. Claimants, heirs of Wm. Ferguson, 31 Mch. 1804. Wit: James Truly, 18 July 1805. Certif. A-447 issued 18 July 1805. The heirs of Wm. Ferguson, decd. claim 150 acres of land by virtue of a British Patent to Thomas Comstock which is found among the papers of the said William, decd. The heirs being young when their father died they were not informed by him in what manner the said William, decd., came in possession of the patent and have not yet discovered any conveyance from the said Comstock to sd William. Finding this patent in the papers of said William, decd., they are confident that it must have been the property of the said William, of whom they are the legal representatives and heirs. Therefore they pray for a confirmation of the afsd claim in their favor. Paulina Ferguson. Note: July 17, 1805, Amended to the notice by leave of the Board of Commrs. and by virtue of the sale by the sd Thomas Comstock to the sd Wm. Ferguson, 15 June 1782. See the back of patent.

p.518. Claim No.1879. British Govt. to Absalom Hooper 250 acres on Second Cr. Pensacola, 1 Sept. 1772, by Peter Chester. // File. Claimant, Absalom Hooper, 31 Mch. 1804. Wit: Bennet Truly, 28 May 1805. Reported 28 Apr. 1807. Absalom Hooper claims 250 acres being unto me granted as above. Plat shows Indian Old Fields.

p.525. Claim No.1880. British Govt. to Wm. Ratcliff 150 acres on Second Cr. adj. Absalom Hooper. Pensacola, 21 Sept. 1772, by Chester. File. Claimant, William Ratcliff, 31 Mch. 1804. Wit: Bennet Truly. Certif. A-461 issued 24 July 1805. Claim based on above British grant.

p.532. Claim No.1882. British Govt. to Enoch Horton 200 acres 9 mi. NE of Fort, on Second Creek, adj. Daniel Perry and Sarah Holmes. Pensacola, 4 May 1775, by Peter Chester. // File. Claimant, Hore Browse Trist, 31 Mch. 1804. Wit: Wm. Dunbar, 12 Oct. 1805. Certif. A-802 issued 9 Jany. 1807. Hore Browse Trist, legal rep. of Nicholas Trist, decd., claims 200 acres by virtue of a British grant to Enoch Horton who conveyed same to Elihu ______ who by lease and release conveyed same to present claimant. G. Poindexter, atty.

p.541. Claim No.1883. Spanish Govt. to Robert Smith 200 acres for having served 6 months in company of mounted volunteers under command of Richard King, 18 Jany. 1793. // File. Claimant, Robt. Smith, 31 Mch. 1804. Rejected 1807. Claim as above.

p.542. Claim No.1884. Spanish Govt. to Maria McIntosh, widow of William, 2690 acres on Miss. River, 7 mi. from Fort, adj. the estate of Williams (David), N.O., 4 Apr. 1795, by Carondelet. // File. Claimant, Winthrop Sargent, 31 Mch. 1804. Wit: Philander Smith, in claim No.1886. Certif. A-451 issued to Sargent in right of his wife, 22 July 1805. Winthrop Sargent in right of his wife, Maria, claims 2690 arpents in Adams Co. on the Miss. River, adj. the Grove plantation, by virtue of a patent from the Spanish Government, as above.

p.545. Claim No.1885. Spanish Govt. to Mary Williams who has petitioned for Lot No.1 Sq. No.5 in Natchez, 30 Sept. 1795, same being granted to her Sept. 1796, by Gayoso. File for above claim No. 1885. Claimant, Winthrop Sargent, 31 Mch. 1804. See No.1416. Rejected, 13 June 1807. Claim for above lots by virtue of a patent from the Spanish Government.

BOOK G

p.1. Claim No.1886. British Grant to John, Cadwallader, William, Mary and Ann Williams, 1000 acres on Daniel Clark's south line, six miles south of Fort Panmure, adj. Daniel Clark, Richard Carr and William MacPherson. Pensacola, 20 Feb. 1776, by Peter Chester. // File. Claimant, Winthrop Sargent, trustee, etc., 31 Mch. 1804. Wit: Philander Smith, Seth Lewis, Ebenezer Rees, 17 July 1805. Certif. A-445, issued to the legal representatives of David Williams. Winthrop Sargent, as trustee and executor in behalf of the heirs of David Williams, decd. claims 1000 acres known as Grove plantation, by virtue of British patent to John, Cadwallader, William, Mary and Ann Williams, as above, and by virtue of the said tract of land having legally descended to the heirs and rep. afsd.

p.10. Claim No.1887. Spanish grant to David Williams, 1000 acres, 5 miles south of Fort, adj. William Williams, brother of the grantee, on south by Bernard Lintot. N.O., 23 May 1787, by Miro. // File. Heirs of David Williams, claimants, 31 Mch. 1804. Wit: Philander Smith, in claim No.1886. Confirmed. Certif. A-452, issued to legal rep. July 22, 1805. Winthrop Sargent, in behalf of the heirs and legal rep. of David Williams, decd., claims 1000 acres on St. Catherine's Cr. in Adams Co., adj. the Grove plantation, by virtue of a Spanish patent to sd David Williams, 23 May 1787.

p.13. Claim No.1900. British Govt. to Sylvester and James Fanning. Plat. [Does not give acreage.] [In margin: This grant is not recorded. The parchment on which it was written in some way, before it was filed in this office, got wet.] // File. The heirs of Sylvester and James Fanning claim 2000 acres on Loftus Cliffs, 7 July 1804. Reported, 28 Apr. 1807. The heirs of Sylvester and James Fanning claim 2000 acres by virtue of a complete British title in favor of sd Sylvester and James Fanning, 15 Dec. 1768. Thos. Durnford, agent of the heirs of Sylvester and James Fanning. (pp.15-21 blank.)

p.22. Claim 1901. British grant to John Sommers 2000 acres, he a reduced staff officer, 8 mi. NE of Loftus Cliffs, on Buffalo Cr. Pensacola, 2 Aug. 1773, by Peter Chester. // File. Heirs of David Hodge, claimants, 4 July 1804. Reported, 28 Apr. 1807. The heirs of David Hodge claim 2000 acres on Buffalo Cr. by virtue of a British grant to John Sommers, sold and conveyed to David Hodge, 20 Jany. 1778, by lease and release here presented. Thos. Durnford, exor. of will of David Hodge.

p.31. Claim No.1902. British grant to Andrew Rainsford, Esq., 1250 acres on the Miss. River, adj. tract surveyed for Jonathan Ogden and a 500-acres grant to Frederick Haldemand. Pensacola, 12 May 1773, by Peter Chester. // File. Claimant, heirs of the late David Hodge, 7 July 1804. Reported, 28 Apr. 1807. The heirs of the late David Hodge claim 1250 acres by virtue of a British patent to Andrew Rainsford and sold by sd Rainsford to David Hodge, 13 May 1773. (signed) Thos. Durnford, exor. of will of David Hodge, decd.

p.39. Claim No.1903. British grant to Richard Freeman Pearnes 50 acres, 26 mi. NE of Fort Panmure, 2 mi. east of River Miss., adj. John Hayton and Boyd's Creek. Pensacola, 22 July 1769, by Montford Brown. // File. Claimant, Richard Freeman Pearnes, 7 July 1804. Reported 28 Apr. 1807. The above claim of 50 acres is by virtue of a complete British title, as above. Thos. Durnford, agent for Richard Freeman Pearnes.

p.47. Claim No.1904. British grant to Frederick Haldemand 2000 acres, 40 mi. above Mobile, 4 mi. above the entrance of the Tensas River, b. on west by John Miller and Peter Swanson and west by Mobile River. Pensacola, 17 Jany. 1770, by Elias Durnford, Lt. Gov. and Commander-in-Chief. Signed in Council. Francisco Poussett, D.C.C. // Claimants, heirs of David Hodge, 7 July 1804. Claim for 2000 acres by virtue of a British patent, as above, and conveyed to David Hodge 19 April ____ by lease and release, herewith annexed.

p.56. Claim No.1906. British grant to Alexander McIntosh 500 acres 30 mi. above Fort Natchez, ½ mile from River Miss. Pensacola, 8 Mch. 1770, by Durnford. // File. Edward Todd, claimant, presented by Col. Girault, 24 July 1804. See No.117. Reported 28 Apr. 1807. Edward Todd, the legal rep. of John Turner, decd., claims 500 acres near Petit Gulf, granted to Alexander McIntosh by a British patent, as above, and by sd McIntosh conveyed to sd Turner, decd. Signed: John Girault, atty. for claimant.

p.64. Claim No.1910. Spanish Govt. to Philip Engle 16 acres on Miss. River, adj. Stephen Minor and Mrs. Rebecca McCabe. [n.d.] // File. Isaac Locke, claimant, 31 Aug. 1804. Certif. A-575 issued 9 Sept. 1805. City of Natchez. Isaac Lockes claims a lot in said city on the Miss. River, about 7 arpents, being part of 16 arpents granted by the Spanish Govt. to Philip Engle, as above, who conveyed the said lot of 7 arps. to Thos. Tyler, 1 Aug. 1798, who conveyed the same to the present claimant, 1 Sept. 1801. The sd Philip Engle was an actual settler in the territory on 27 Oct. 1795.

p.68. Claim No.1915. British grant to Jacob Winfree 1000 acres on Second Creek, adj. Thos. Hutchins, 14 miles from Natchez. Pensacola, 7 July 1773, by Chester. // File. Claimant, Jacob Winfree, 27 Sept. 1804. Wit: A. Hutchins, 5 Oct. 1804. Reported, 28 Apr. 1807. Jacob Winfree claims 1000 acres of land by virtue of a British patent granted in favor of Jacob Winfree, decd., as above, who died leaving the present claimant his heir-at-law. Jacob Winfree by his agent, Wm. Winfree.

p.77. Claim No.1916. Spanish grant to Thomas Lilly White 500 acres in the Dist. of Natchez, Prov. of Louisiana, adj. Daniel Clarke. N.O. 1794. // File. Claimants, the heirs of Thos. L. White, 27 Sept. 1804. Wit: Wm. Atchinson, 3 Mch. 1807. Certif. B-231 issued 6 Mch. 1807. The heirs of Thos. Lilly White claim 500 acres bet. the waters of Bayou Sarah and Thompson's Cr. by virtue of a Spanish gr. to sd Thos. L. White, as above, dated 24 May 1796, which was cultivated in 1795, of which one-half may lie to the north of the line of demarcation and the other half to the south thereof. Daniel Clarke for the heirs of Thomas Lilly White.

p.80. Claim No.1918. Spanish Govt. to Margaretta Williams patent for Lot 4, Sq.25 in Natchez. [n.d.] [Small plat showing North St. on one side with Fifth St. at right angles to it.] // File. Anne Martin, claimant, 4 Oct. 1804. Wit: John Williams, 28 Aug. 1805. Certif. A-533 issued 28 Aug. 1805. Adams Co. Anne Martin claims Lot 4, Sq.25 in City of Natchez by virtue of a Spanish patent to Margaretta Williams in Sept. 1795, who conveyed the same to Thomas Martin, decd., who conveyed the same to this claimant by deed 6 June 1801.

p.82. Claim No.1926. Spanish Govt. to Patrick McDermott 440 acres in Dist. of Natches, ___ 1797. Plat only. // File. Patrick McDermott, claimant, 15 Mch. 1804. Wit: N. Hunter and Polser Shilling. Wit: Patrick Foley, 22 July 1805. Rejected 13 June 1807. Patrick McDermott claims 440 arpents of land by virtue of a Spanish patent in his favor, 24 Dec. 1797, in consequence of warrants of survey 5 May 1790 and 18 Jany. 1793, he, the claimant, being then above the age of 21 years of age. The said land is in the settlement of Bayou Tonica, etc.

p.85. Claim No.1936. British gr. to William Joiner 500 acres on Second Cr., 10 mi. NE from the Natchez. Pensacola, 21 Sept. 1772, by Chester. // File. Claimant, John Ellis, 22 Oct. 1804. Res. of claimant proved before, 1 Jany. 1805. By assignment, see No.1881. John Ellis claims 500 acres in Adams Co. near the Miss. River by virtue of a British patent to William Joiner, as above, and by him conveyed, 2 Apr. 1775.

p.93. Claim No.1939. Spanish Govt. to Pedro de Miro. petition, etc. (blank). Plat for 1600 acres on Buffalo Cr. adj. Daniel Clarke, James Smith and Wm. Conway. // File. Claimant, James Kennedy, 24 Oct. 1804. Rejected 13 June 1807. See Nos. 105 and 1450. Note: This land regranted to Patrick Foley, 25 Oct. 1790, who sold 400 arpents to the Marbles who are confirmed in their title. June 24, 1805. Thos. Rodney. James Kennedy claims 1600 arpents by virtue of a Spanish grant to Don Pedro de Miro, 9 June 1787.

p.98. Claim No.1951. Spanish Govt. to James Kennedy 1000 acres on waters of Penasco a Davion, adj. Thos. Burling, in Dist. of Natchez. 1787. // File. Claimant, James Kennedy, 3 Nov. 1804. Rejected, 13 June 1807. James Kennedy claims 1000 arps. in Wilkinson Co. near Loftus Heights, by virtue of a Spanish grant to him 4 Dec. 1787. S. Lewis, agent for the claimant.

p.102. Claim No.1953. British grant to Daniel Ward, Esq., 1500 acres 12 mi. below Fort Panmure on the Miss. River. Pensacola, 24 Nov. 1768, by Montfort Browne. [Plat shows tract at the mouth of St. Catherine's Cr.] // File. Claimants, heirs of Daniel Ward, 5 Nov. 1804. Reported, 28 Apr. 1807. The heirs and legal representatives of Daniel Ward, late of the Miss. Territory, decd., claim by James Kennedy, their atty., 1500 acres of land on the River Miss. and St. Catherine's Creek in Adams Co. by virtue of a British patent to sd Daniel Ward, as above, who resided in the sd territory until he departed this life.

p.111. Claim No.1959. British Govt. to Wm. Hulburd order of survey for 100 acres on Bayou Pierre, 11 miles from its mouth. Pensacola, 19 Nov. 1779, by Peter Chester. // File. Samuel Brooks, claimant, 17 Mch. 1804. Wit: James Harman and William Selkrig, 19 Nov. 1804. Rejected, 27 Apr. 1807. Samuel Brooks claims 100 acres on a br. of Bayou Pierre in Claiborne Co. by virtue of a warrant from the British Govt. to William Hulburd, which was sold to William Selkrig [spelled Silkrag] and from him to Samuel Brooks. Plat and survey by Daniel Burnet.

p.112. Claim No.1962. Spanish Govt. to Thos. Berry 500 acres adj. Benjamin Holmes, ____ 1792. // File. Joshua Howard, claimant, 21 Nov. 1804. John Erwin, wit. 28 Nov. 1804, June 9, 1806. Certif. D-159 issued 10 Feb. 1807. Joshua Howard claims 500 arpents on the dividing ridge between Sandy and Wells Creeks by patent from the Spanish Govt. to Thos. Berry, 7 Dec. 1797, and by the sd Thomas Berry conveyed to present claimant, 19 Nov. 1804.

p.115. Claim No.1966. Spanish Govt. to Estevan Ploche, 1600 acres on waters of Mr. Clarke's Creek, adj. Mr. LeBreton, Daniel Clarke, and Mr. Andrew Hare. // File. Claimant, Stephen Ploche, 24 Nov. 1804. Rejected 13 June 1807. Stephen Ploche claims 1600 arpents in Wilkinson Co. by virtue of a Spanish patent to the claimant 3 Mch. 1789. Stephen Plauche by Andre Plauche.

p.118. Claim No.1967. British gr. to Joshua Ward 600 acres 16 miles south of Fort, on Miss. River, adj. John Ward. Pensacola, 24 Nov. 1768, by Montfort Brown. // File. Claimant, Joshua Ward, 24 Nov. 1804. Reported 28 Apr. 1807. Joshua Ward claims 600 acres founded on a British patent to sd claimant as above.

p.126. Claim No.1986. Spanish Govt. to Cornelius McKain Lot 2, Sq.32 in City of Natchez, 6 Apr. 1795. // File. Claimant, William Murray, 26 Nov. 1804. Certif. A-773 issued 16 May 1806. William Murray claims one-half of Lot 2, Sq.32 in City by virtue of a Spanish grant for same to Cornelius McCan and by deed the 17th instant, to claimant. John Girault at the request of William Murray

p.129. Claim No.1988. Spanish Govt. to Juan St. Germain, petition, etc. // File. Claimant, John Girault, 26 Nov. 1804. Rejected 24 Apr. 1807. John Girault claims 1000 acres near the Three Island that are at or near the mouth of the Yazoo River, which were granted to John St. Germain by the Spanish Govt. 15 Dec. 1785, he being then 21 years of age, the same having been inherited by his daughter Louisa, wife of Joseph Laforce, and by sd Joseph and Louise Laforce conveyed under sanction of the Spanish Govt. to the present claimant, 26 Mch. 1793. (signed) John Girault.

p.131. Claim No.1989. Spanish Govt. to Chas. Henry Barchellot, petition, etc. // File. Claimant, John Girault, 26 Nov. 1804. Rejected, 24 April 1807. John Girault claims 600 arpents about 2 mi. below the Walnut Hills, for which Henry Barchellot obtained a warrant from the Govt. of Spain 22 Mch. 1785, he being then above 21 years of age and on the 23 Sept. of same year made over his right thereto to Miss Louisa St. Germain who afterwards married Joseph Laforce and on 26 March 1793, the sd Joseph and Louisa with the sanction of the Spanish Government conveyed the same to the present claimant.

p.134. Claim No.1010. Spanish Govt. to Claudio Bougaud 1000 acres on Penasco a Davion, 35 mi. from Fort, 2½ mi. from establishment of John Alston and 6 miles from Penasco a Davion called Loftus Cliffs, adj. Christian Bingaman. N.O., 6 March 1789, by Miro. // File. Claimant, Claudio Bougaud, 30 Nov. 1804. Deposition of Joseph Bonneville, 20 March 1806. Rejected 12 June 1807. Don Claudio Bougaud claims 1000 arpents by virtue of a Spanish patent, as above.

p.137. Claim No.2013. Spanish Govt. to Solomon Hiram Wisdom, petition, etc. // File. H. Wisdom, claimant, 30 Nov. 1804. Wit: John Girault, 11 Oct. 1805. This lot confirmed to James Moore. See No.1411. Rejected 24 Apr. 1807. Solomon Hiram Wisdom claims a lot Lot 2, Sq.13 in Natchez, Oct. 2, 1795. Signed by W. B. Smith, Sr.

p.138. Claim No.2014. Spanish Govt. to Claudio Bougaud, 1034 acres between the Cypress Swamp north of Lake LaCroix and the hills, adj. land of the grantee, 40 mi. south of the Fort. N.O. 30 Aug. 1794, by Carondelet. // File. Claimant, Don Claudio Bougaud, 30 Nov. 1804. Wit: Joseph Bonneville, 20 Mch. 1806. Rejected 12 June 1807. Claim to 1034 arpents by virtue of the above Spanish grant to claimant.

p.141. Claim No.2021. Spanish patent to George Overaker for a lot. // p.143. 25 April 1804. Francis Jones to John Wilkins, Jr. of Pittsburg, Pa., for $3000 in hand paid. Lot No.3, Sq. No.3, gr. by Spanish Govt. to Geo. Overaker, 19 July 1796 and conveyed to Stephen Henderson, Oct. 1796, and sd Henderson conveyed same to Francis Jones, 2 Dec. 1799, said lot b. on south by South St., on east by Second St. and westward by lot belonging to Abijah Hunt. (signed) Francis Jones. Wit: J. Dunlap, Wm. Scott. // File. Claimant, John Wilkins, Jr., 30 Nov. 1804. Certif. D-50 issued 9 Sept. 1806. John Wilkins, Jr. claims above lot in the City of Natchez by virtue of a Spanish patent of same to George Overaker and conveyed as above. Said Overaker lived in the Miss. Territory, 27 Oct. 1795, and inhabited and cultivated the lot at that time and ever since. John Wilkins, Jr., by Francis Boardman.

p.146. Claim No.2028. Deed. 1 Nov. 1800. Elijah Bunch to Peter Walker, both of Adams Co., Miss. Ter., for $260 paid, 800 acres b. by Joseph Walker, Beaver Cr. a br. of Buffalo, and the land of the estate of Henry Willis. Wit: Joseph Dove, Peter Walker, Jr. // File. Claimant, heirs of Peter Walker, 30 Nov. 1804. Wit: Wm. Atchinson, 2 Jany. 1805. Rejected 15 June 1807. The heirs of Peter Walker, decd., claim 800 arps. in Wilkinson Co. on waters of Buffalo Creek patented by the Elijah Bunch in 1799 and conveyed from sd Elijah to Peter Walker, 1 Nov. 1800. Lyman Harding, atty. for sd heirs.

p.149. Claim No.2035. Petition of William Foster to the Spanish Govt. that he had come from the American settlements and wishing to establish himself in this district, asks for 240 arpents which are said to be vacant on the Homochitto River between the Sandy Cr. and Petty Creek. Natchez, 22 Mch. 1790. // These papers are certified by John Girault, translator. This claim was presented by William Foster, 30 Nov. 1804. Rejected Apr. 24, 1807.

p.150. Claim No.2036. Petition of Francis Erwin to Spanish Govt. wishing to establish himself in this dist. asks for 240 arpents on the Homochitto, adj. the land of Mr. Dayton. // Warrant for same, 26 Apr. 1797, by Estevan Miro // This claim rejected, 24 Apr. 1807.

p.152. Claim No.2037. Petition of James Stoddard for 400 arpents as he wishes to establish himself, with his family which is composed of five persons, in this district. 7 Aug. 1789. // Warrant for same signed by Miro. 26 Apr. 1790. // This claim was rejected, 24 April 1807.

p.153. Claim No.2038. Petition of Isaac Lothrop, 17 Aug. 1789, wishing to settle and establish himself in this district, asks for 240 arpents on the waters of the Homochitto. // Warrant, 26 Apr. 1790 for same by Miro. // Claimant, Isaac Lothrop, 30 Nov. 1804. This claim rejected 24 Apr. 1807.

p.155. Claim No.2039. Petition of Peter Martin, wishing to have a plantation to cultivate on the waters of Cole's Creek, asks for 240 arpents adj. Joel Byrd, 21 July 1789. // Warrant for claim, 26 Apr. 1790, by Estevan Miro. // This claim was rejected, 24 Apr. 1807.

p.156. Claim No.2040. Petition of Jacob Stephen to Spanish Govt. for 240 acres on Coles Cr.. adj. Stephen DeAlba and George Stampley, 21 July 1789. // Warrant for same, 26 Apr. 1790, by Miro. // Claimant, Jacob Stephen, 30 Nov. 1804. Rejected, 24 Apr. 1807.

p.158. Claim No.2041. Petition of John Sinclair to Spanish Govt., 27 July 1789, for 240 arpents on Cole's Creek, adj. Mr. Collins. // Warrant for same, 26 Apr. 1790, by Estevan Miro. // Claimant, John Sinclair for 240 acres. Rejected 24 Apr. 1807.

p.159. Claim No.2042. Petition of Henry Quirk to Spanish Govt. that he had come to this district with his wife to settle and asks, 5 Aug. 1789, for 240 arpents on Bayou Pierre adj. the lands of Filmer and Abraham Green. // Warrant, 26 Apr. 1790, for same by Miro. // Claimant, Henry Quirk, 30 Nov. 1804. This claim rejected, 24 Apr. 1807.

p.161. Claim No.2043. Petition of William Ivers to Spanish Govt. for 240 arpents on Bayou Pierre, 30 Sept. 1789. // Warrant 26 Apr. ____ for the same. // William Ivers, claimant. Rejected, 24 Apr. 1807.

p.162. Claim No.2044. Petition of William Estill to Spanish Govt. for 240 arpents, 30 Sept. 1784, on Bayou Pierre, adj. Wm. Brocus. // Warrant 26 Apr. 1790, by Estevan Miro. // Claimant, Wm. Estill, 30 Nov. 1804. Rejected 24 Apr. 1807.

p.164. Claim No.2045. Petition of Lambert de Selle to Spanish Govt. for 300 arpents, 29 Sept. 1789, on Homochitto River. // Warrant 25 Nov. 1789, for same by Miro. // Claimant, Lambert de Selle, 29 Nov. 1804. Rejected.

p.166. Claim No.2046. Petition of Patrick Quin to Spanish Govt., 27 July 1789, for 340 acres on Bayou Pierre adj. Mr. Miller. // Warrant, 26 Apr. 1790, for same by Miro. Claimant, Patrick Quin, Nov. 30, 1804. Rejected, 24 Apr. 1807.

p.168. Claim No.2047. Petition of Ephraim Story to Spanish Govt., for 400 arpents on the first bluff on the south side of Big Black River, 15 Nov. 1789. // Warrant for 300 arpents only, 8 Dec. 1789. // Claimant, Ephraim Story, 30 Nov. 1804. Rejected 24 Apr. 1807.

p.170. Claim No.2048. Petition of Jacob Paul to Spanish Govt. for 240 arpents on James' Run of Bayou Pierre, adj. Wm. Brown and James White, 31 Oct. 1789. // Warrant, 24 Nov. 1789, for same by Miro. // Claimant, Jacob Paul, 30 Nov. 1804. Rejected, 24 Apr. 1807.

p.172. Claim No.2049. Petition of Edmund Folson to Spanish Govt., in behalf of himself and his two sisters, Sarah and Abigail, for 300 arpents on Buffalo Creek, adj. Jeremiah Bryan. // Warrant for same, 17 June 1789. // Claimant, Edmund Folsom, 30 Nov. 1804. Rejected, 24 Apr. 1807.

p.174. Claim No.2050. Petition of Samuel Porter to Spanish Govt. who had come to this district from Kentucky two months before, asks for 240 arpents of land on Cole's Creek, adj. George Jones, Charles Collins and Chas. Simmons, 14 Feb. 1791. // Warrant for same, 7 Apr. 1791, by Miro. // Claimant, Samuel Porter, 30 Nov. 1804. Rejected 24 Apr. 1807.

p.176. Claim No.2051. Petition of Adam Pickle to Spanish Govt. desiring to have a plantation as a home and for support of my family, which consists of six persons, asks for land on the waters of Cole's Creek, adj. Thomas Daniel, 25 Nov. 1792. // Warrant for 400 arpents, 24 Mch. 1793, by Carondelet. // Claimant, Adam Pickles, 30 Nov. 1804. This claim rejected, 24 Apr. 1807.

p.178. Claim No.2052. Petition of Hezekiah Harman to Spanish Govt. for 300 arpents on Bayou Pierre, opposite a tract granted to James Harman, 18 Nov. 1788. // Warrant, 16 Jany. 1789. // I acknowledge to have sold my right of property in 300 arpents granted me by the General Government for $30, cash in hand, Natchez, 14 May 1792. Signed. // Claimant, Hezekiah Harman, 30 Nov. 1804. This claim rejected, 24 Apr. 1807.

p.180. Claim No.2053. Petition of Gabriel Fusilier to Spanish Govt. for 800 arpents on Homochitto River, adj. lands of Col. Charles de Grand-Pre, Caleb King and the family of Swazey, 8 Nov. 1780. // Warrant for 400 arpents thereof, 6 Jany. 1789, by Miro. // Petition states that Fusilier came to the district from Illinois. // Claimant, Gabriel Fusilier, 30 Nov. 1804. Rejected, 24 Apr. 1807.

p.182. Claim No.2054. Petition of Chas. Henry Barchelot des Hubles to Spanish Govt. for Apple Island, 3 Aug. 1786. // Recommended, 22 Nov. 1786. // Warrant, 1 Dec. 1786, by Miro. // Claimant, Chas. Henry Bachelot. Rejected. Notation: This land claimed by Thomas Tyler. See No.1276.

p.184. Claim No.2055. Petition of Samuel Young to Spanish Govt. for 240 arpents on Willing's Bayou. // Warrant for same, 25 Nov. 1787, By Miro. // Claimant, Samuel Young, 30 Nov. 1804. // Rejected, 24 Apr. 1807.

p.186. Claim No.2056. Petition of Pierre Bissardon to Spanish Govt. for a lot in the flat before the Fort, adj. Mr. Duon's lot, 7 Jany. 1787. // Warrant directing the Commandant of Natchez to put the petitioner in possession of a lot containing so many feet in width and depth as he may think proper. 2 Feb. 1787. Miro. // Claimant, Pierre Bissardon, 30 Nov. 1804. Rejected, 24 Apr. 1807.

p.188. Claim No.2057. Peter Chas. Peyroux to Spanish Govt. for 1600 arps. at the confluence of the Homochitto with the River Miss., 20 arps. front on the Miss. on each side of the Homochitto by 40 deep, 14 June 1786. // Warrant for same by Miro, same day. // Claimant, Peter Charles Peyroux. Rejected.

p.190. Claim No.1088. Deed. 22 Dec. 1797. George Bailey to James White, for $100 paid, 640 acres on Wells Cr. adj. James Oglesby, with house and improvements. George (X) Bailey. Wit: John Sheppard. Ack. Oct. 15, 1804 before T.R. // File. Abijah Hunt, claimant, 30 Mch. 1804. Certificate of survey and plat for 640 acres to Abijah Hunt, 2 Mch. 1804. (signed) Joseph Sessions. Claim by virtue of the land having been inhabited and cultivated by sd Geo. Bailey with his family on and before 13 Mch. 1798, etc. and conveyance from Bailey to James White, and from sd White to claimant, 6 Dec. 1799. Certif. B-255 issued 9 Apr. 1807.

p.193. Claim No.1090. (continued from Bk. D, p. 230) Charles Norwood, exor. of the late John Turnbull, to Abijah Hunt and Wm. G. Forman deed. Norwood of the Town of New Orleans, Prov. of La., as exor of Turnbull, for $2250 to be paid by Abijah Hunt and William Gordon Forman, both of the Miss. Territory by their notes of this date, sells, etc. a tract of land 12 leagues from Natchez, granted by Gov. Gayoso, 24 Dec. 1797 to Richard Devall, bounded on south by the Miss. River, east by lands of Mr. Mather, being the same conveyed by Richard Devall to sd John Turnbull, 10 Jany. 1799, containing 1500 acres. (signed) Charles Norwood. 31 May 1802. Wit: John Murdoch, Robert Moore. Prov. by Moore same date before Samuel Brooks, J.P. // File. Claimants, Hunt and Forman, 24 Mch. 1804. Rejected, 17 May 1807. Claim of Hunt and Forman dof 1500 acres in Jefferson Co. by virtue of a grant to Richard Devall, as above, and order of survey dated 1788 and made 2 Jany. 1789, etc. Elijah Smith for Hunt and Forman.

p.210. Claim No.1095. See in Unrecorded Claims.

p.214. Claim No.1096. See in Unrecorded Claims.

p.232. Claim No.1100. Deed. David Odam and Frances, his wife, of Pickering Co., to John Hinds, merchant, of same, for $400, paid, 111 acres in sd county whereon sd Hinds is now erecting a cotton gin, on the waters of Platner's Fork of Cole's Cr., beg. at John Terry's corner. (signed) David Odam, Frances (x) Odam. Wit: William Thomas, James Truly, Edward Gallagher. 10 Oct. 1799. Ack. by Odam and wife, Frances, 20 Sept. 1800 before William Thomas, J.P. of sd county. // p.235. John Hinds to Abijah Hunt, 23 June 1800, for $1000, 111 Franch acres, as described in the preceding deed. (signed) John Hinds. Wit: John Holland and C. B. Howell. Ack. by John Hinds before George Cochran, J.P. 25 June 1801, in Adams Co. and in Jefferson Co. before David Phelps, of Jefferson Co., 2 Jany. 1804. // 16 April 1803, Frances Odam and Abner Pipes, extrx and exor of the will of David Odam, decd. the residue of the entire tract of 620 acres to Abijah Hunt. // For file see Unrecorded Claims.

p.255. Claim No.1115. Abijah Hunt, claimant, 24 Mch. 1804. Wit: Joshua Howard. Certif. B-265 issued 9 Apr. 1807. Abijah claims an undivided 525 acres in Adams Co. by grant to James Irwin before 1795 and sold thereof at public auction after the decease of grantee, by order of the Spanish Govt., to James White, 18 Feb. 1797, and conveyed from sd White to Lewis Evans, 29 Nov. 1799, and from sd Evans to William Kenner, 10 Apr. 1800 and from Kenner to claimant, 11 Nov. 1801.

No. 306. Claimant, Ezekiel DeWitt, presented 21 Feb. 1804. Wit: [David or Daniel] Whitacre. Certif. B-179 issued Feb. 11, 1807. [Part of claim torn away.] . . . William West for whom said tract was surveyed . . . . sold the land to Dewitt about 1789 who was the head of a family on the day the Spanish troops evacuated the Mississippi Territory. Ezekiel (E.D.) Dewitt. Plat and certificate of survey by William Vousdan, Dep. Surv., 3 Nov. 1786, show Joe Harrison, Mr. Dewitt and Mr. Still Lee with land adjoining.

No. 311. Claimant, Samuel Stockett, 21 Feb. 1804. Certif. D-176 issued 17 Dec. 1806 . . . . acres in Wilkinson County on waters of Buffalo Creek. Samuel Stockett.

No. 312. Claimants, heirs of William Dillahunter, 23 Feb. 1804. Certif. D-177 issued 1 Dec. 1806. The heirs of William Dillahunter, deceased, claim the right to become purchasers of 100 acres on the waters of Buffalo Creek by virtue of the said tract having been inhabited and cultivated on 3rd of March 1803 by said William Dillahunter, deceased. (signed) Isaac Johnson, the next friend of Isaac, John and Mary Dillahunter, heirs and legal representatives of William Dillahunter, deceased.

No. 321. Jacob Phillips, claimant, 24 Feb. 1804. Certif. B-90 issued 29 Oct. 1806. Miss. Ter. Claiborne Co. Jacob Phillips claims the right of preference in becoming the purchaser from the U.S. of 320 acres on the waters of Big Black, by virtue of having settled on and cultivated the same on 3 Mch. 1803.

No. 323. Elijah Phipps, claimant, 24 Feb. 1804. See No. 1171 and No. 1858. Certif B-180 issued to Israel Smith, assignee, 11 Feb. 1807. Elijah Phipps claims 640 acres in Wilkinson Co. on Big Pine Woods Creek which empties into the Buffalo, which was actually inhabited and cultivated by sd Phipps prior to and at the time the Miss. Territory was finally evacuated by the Spanish troops, he being at that time above the age of 21 and the head of a family, having a wife and several children. Elijah Phipps prays a Donation of the afsd tract. Proved before the Board by William Allen Lusk, 25 Feb. 1804. Richard Claiborne, Clk.

No. 324. Wm. A. Lusk, claimant, 24 Feb. 1804. Certif. B-181 issued 11 Feb. 1807. William A. Lusk claims 640 acres in Wilkinson Co. on Buffalo Creek which land was inhabited and cultivated by sd William A. Lusk at the time the territory was evacuated, etc., he being over 21. He asks for a Donation of said tract. Proved before the Board, 25 Feb. 1804 by Elijah Phipps. Richard Claiborne, Clk.

No. 322. Abel Eastman, claimant, 24 Feb. 1804. Certif. B-76 issued 28 Oct. 1807. Claiborne Co. Abel Eastman claims 640 acres in sd county on Gun's Bayou, a br. of Big Black, by right of occupancy, having inhabited and cultivated sd tract on and before the territory was evacuated, etc. and sd Abel at that time, 7 March 1798, at the head of a family. [Plat shows John Griffin on other side of Gun's Bayou.]

No. 325. Abraham Clawson, claimant, 24 Feb. 1804. Wit: John King, 18 Feb. 1805. Uriah Dudley, 3 Mch. 1806. Certif. B-186 issued 13 Feb. 1807. Abraham Clawson claims 637 acres in Jefferson Co. on North Fork of Cole's Cr. founded on a transfer of sd tract by Thomas Splane to sd Clawson which sd Splane actually inhabited and cultivated prior to and on 7 March 1798, etc. Transfer from Splane to Clawson, 12 Jany. 1802. Wit: William Dadford.

No. 337. Parciés Noland, claimant, 24 Feb. 1804. Written in "Peirsion Noland" Wit: John Nugent. Certif. D-249, issued 24 Dec. 1806. Peirson Noland claims 200 acres on Thompson's Cr. joining the line of latitude on 20-mile post on improvement made by sd Noland before and on 3 Mch. 1803.

No. 339. Job Corey, claimant. 25 Feb. 1804. Wit: W. Crane, 19 Nov. 1804. Rejected 27 April, 1807. Job Corey claims 400 acres in Jefferson county on the waters of Cole's Creek by order of survey from the British Govt. to sd Job, abt 1776, at which time he was 21 years old. The said warrant, as was customary was sent to the Town of Pensacola to obtain a patent from sd Govt. but shortly after this the Spanish took this country which prevented sd Job from obtaining a patent, or even getting his warrant or order of survey from thence. Notation: This land regranted by the Spanish Govt. to Jacob Stampley.

No. 341. Jeptha Higdon, claimant, 25 Feb. 1804. Wit: Wm. Atchinson, 28 Nov. 1804. Certif. B-278 issued 3 June 1807. Jeptha Higdon claims a right to 718 acres on St. Catherine's Cr. in Adams Co. by virtue of a warrant of survey granted to him by the Spanish Govt. 1787. Certificate of survey and plat by Wm. Atchinson.

No. 344. David Carradine, claimant, 25 Feb. 1804. Wit: Bennet Truly, 27 Feb. 1804. Certif. B-86, issued Feb. 3, 1807.

No. 363. Caleb Worley, claimant, 28 Feb. 1804. Wit: Elisha Eastes, 20 Aug. 1804. Certif. D-143 issued 15 Dec. 1806. Caleb Worley claims preemption rights of 238 acres in Wilkinson Co. The said tract was inhabited and cultivated by the said Caleb 3 Mch. 1803, at which time he was the head of a family of a wife and one child.

No. 366. John Parker, claimant, 28 Feb. 1804. Wit: Chas. Melkohn, 5 Nov. 1804. Rejected 7 May 1807. Miss. Ter. Jefferson Co. John Parker claims 600 acres in sd county on Fairchild's Cr. by right of occupancy. The land was improved by Willis Bonner in 1794 and ever since by the said Willis who sold sd land unto sd John Parker who was then the head of a family.

No. 372. John Calhoun, claimant, 28 Feb. 1804. Wit: Stephen Marble, 1 Oct. 1804. Wm. Atchinson and Abel Eastman, 29 Jany. 1806. Certif. D-276 issued to Moses Floyd, assignee of claimant, 24 Dec. 1806. John Calhoun claims a Donation right or right of occupancy for 320 acres in Claiborne Co. on the Big Black River which tract of land was improved by said Calhoon by clearing about one-half an acre, planting some peach trees and having commenced building a cabin to dwell in 1797 and he intended to inhabit and cultivate the said tract at and from that time but was interrupted in his claim by the Choctaw Indians who claimed the said land as being within their boundaries but he continued his claim to this land by working on it from time to time and actually moved on it in 1799 and has inhabited and cultivated the same ever since and was the head of a family on the evacuation of the Territory. // Transfer of land from John Calhoun to Moses Floyd. Indenture, 20 Oct. 1804. John Calhoun of Claiborne Co., Miss. Ter. U.S.A. to Moses Floyd, of same, for $400, to him in hand paid, by sd Floyd, he does sell, etc. all that tract of land on the waters of the Big Black River in sd county 320 acres claimed by sd John Calhoun, etc. and returned to the Register's Office in the Town of Washington. Wit: John Jenkins, James Griffin. Prov. 9 Nov. 1804 by J. Griffin, before T.R. Tract on Big Black River about three-quarters of a mile above the old blockhouse.

No. 373. George Marshall, claimant, 28 Feb. 1804. Wit: Wm. Stephens. Certif. D-277 issued to B. Hicks, assignee, 24 Dec. 1806. George Marshall claims preemption rights in 351 acres in Claiborne Co., Miss. Ter., on Marshall's Lake, by virtue of his having settled on and cultivated the said tract on 3 Mch. 1803. Surveyed by John Cook, with plat, Dec. 28, 1803. This land on the north side of the Big Black adjoining a lake and including the house and plantation where the said George Marshall now liveth. Andrew Bracken's corner on the Big Black swamp. // Geo. Marshall sells the above claim to John Cochran, of said county, all right, etc. containing 351 acres, for which I have recd. from said John Cochran $200. (signed) George Marshall. Wit: Isaac Rapalje, H. Jones. // Rec'd, 3 Jany. 1806 the sum of $200 in full consideration for the preemption right, etc. I do hereby transfer to B. Hicks. (signed) John Cochran. Wit: Isaac Rapalje, James Sinclair. Prov. by Isaac Rapalje bef. Arthur B. Ross, J.P. of Claiborne Co.

No. 377. John McCaleb, claimant, 29 Feb. 1804. Wit: Capt. Thomas White and Henry Milburn. Certif. D-94 issued 30 Oct. 1806. John McCaleb claims preemption rights on 365 acres of land in Claiborne Co., on north fork of Bayou Pierre, by virtue of his having inhabited and cultivated it on 3 Mch. 1803. William McCaleb for John McCaleb. Plat shows the tract 8 miles above Grindstone Ford, adj. Samuel McCaleb and Henry Milburn, and about 3 miles below the Indian boundary line.

No. 378. Samuel McCaleb, claimant, 29 Feb. 1804. Wit: Capt. Thomas White and Henry Milburn. Certif. D-160 issued 16 Dec. 1806. Samuel McCaleb claims preemption right on 350 acres in Claiborne Co. on the north fork of Bayou Pierre, by virtue of having inhabited and cultivated it on 3 Mch. 1803. William McCaleb for Samuel McCaleb.

No. 386. Abraham Mayes, claimant, 29 Feb. 1804. Wit: Peter Stampley. Certif. B-48 issued 29 Aug. 1806. Abraham Mayes claims 640 acres in Jefferson Co. on waters of Cole's Creek, by right of occupancy, which said tract was inhabited and cultivated by sd Mayes in 1796 who also inhabited and cultivated it when the Spanish troops evacuated the Territory and was at that time the head of a family.

Petition: To His Excellency, Robert Williams, Esq., Governor of the Miss. Territory and one of the Commissioners, etc., and to the Honorable other Commrs. Abraham Mayes petitions that your petitioner, for nearly thirty years a resident in this country, and has never asked or obtained any grant of land from either the British or Spanish Governments, being by habit living not by man's declarations but by the sweat of his brow, that about 12 years hence finding his family and expenses increased, he moved into a piece of vacant land where he now lives; that his is the oldest Donation claim in this vicinity, that he bounded his land on Robert Dunbar's east line and when John Hamberlin came to settle the land adjoining your petitioner, your petitioner procured a surveyor and chainman to run a line to be a boundary between your petitioner and said Hamberlin, that your petitioner has continued to cultivate and improve said land ever since and that about 5 years since your petitioner was informed that, on giving in a plat and notice to the Commrs. of the land that would be granted to him accordingly, that being no scholar or surveyor himself, he procured Daniel James to make out a plat agreeable to his survey which he supposed correct and included all his improvements, but when Isaac Selser came on the 11th, instant, to run out your petitioner's land, he refused to begin at his corner and follow said old line but ran an entire new line which has left out of your petitioner's claim a considerable part of his improvement and has otherwise much injured the claim, and your petitioner begs leave to represent to Your Honor that he is old and has a numerous sickly family, etc. and that he may hold onto his northwest line according to his old survey, which your petitioner is able to prove was made in 1797.

No. 387. David Hunt, claimant, 29 Feb. 1804. Wit: Theophilus Marble, 1 Oct. 1804. Certif. D-6 issued 4 Sept. 1806. David Hunt claims the preemption right to 260 acres on waters of Cole's Cr. in Jefferson County, improved cultivated and actually inhabited by him since the Spring of 1800.

No. 399. Claimant, Thomas Hubbard, 1 Mch. 1804. Wit: Joshua Rundle. Certif. D-248 issued Dec. 22, 1806. Thomas Hubbard claims 524 acres under the 3rd Sec. of the Act of Congress, etc. in consequence of his having actually settled on the premises and had part of the same in cultivation on and before 3 Mch. 1803. Land is in the county of Claiborne, beg. on the banks of the Miss. River, corner of James Lobdal's land.

No. 400. Claimant, Joshua Rundle, 1 Mch. 1804. Wit: Seth Rundell. Certif. D-51 issued 11 Sept. 1806. Joshua Rundell claims the preemption right to 100 acres inhabited and cultivated in Feb. 1802 by him who was at the head of a family at that time.

No. 401. Claimant, Henry Gibson, 1 Mch. 1804. Wit: Joshua Rundell. Rejected for want of sufficient evidence, 30 Dec. 1806. Henry Gibson claims preemption right to 100 acres of land, improved by Asahel Jacoway, ever since last of Feb. 1803, at which time he was 21 years old and sold sd improvement to sd Henry Gibson, August 1803. Tract was on the headwaters of Widdow's Creek.

No. 402. Claimant, Eleazer Tharp, 1 Mch. 1804. Wit: Joshua Rundell. Certif. D-197 issued 17 Dec. 1806. Eleazer Tharp claims preemption right to 60 acres, improved and cultivated ever since 1802 by James Macklewee, who was the head of a family on 3 Mch. 1803 and conveyed the premises to one English who sold to said Tharp, the present claimant. John Rundell for Eleazer Tharp. On Clark's Cr., waters of Bayou Pierre, Claiborne Co., beg. on Seth Rundell's line.

No. 403. Claimant, John Ragsdale, 1 Mch. 1804. Wit: Duncan Cameron, Certif. D-83 issued 29 Oct. 1806. The above survey of 400 acres in Claiborne Co. is the place that John Ragsdale now lives on, on a br. of Big Black. John Ragsdale claims preemption right to 405 acres, having been settled and cultivated on 1st Nov. 1801 and ever since.

No. 404. Claimants, heirs of Zaccheus Tharp, 1 Mch. 1804. Wit: Seth Rundell. Certif. D-165 issued 16 Dec. 1806. Katy Tharp, widow and her younger children, to wit, Katy, Ezekiel, Jesse and Nathan Tharp, heirs and legal rep. of Zaccheus Tharp, decd. claim preemption right to 50 acres in Claiborne Co. on the waters of Bayou Pierre, it having been inhabited and cultivated ever since 1802 by Zaccheus Tharp until the month of January 1804 when he, the said Zaccheus, died. Joshua Rundell for the said heirs.

No. 406. Claimant, Thomas Fortner, 1 Mch. 1804. Withdrawn by the claimant. Thos. Fortner claims 140 acres on Beaver Creek, a water of Big Black River, being part of 240 acres for which he obtained an order of survey from the Spanish Govt. 26 Apr. 1790 but there not being vacant land enough in the place the order called for, the claimant surveyed the 140 acres, being the residue of the said 240 acres, which he has not improved but now he is the head of a family and 31 years of age.

No. 407. Claimant, Alexander McKenzie, 7 Mch. 1804. Rejected, 16 May 1807. Alexander McKenzie certifies that the tract of land containing 148 acres was settled and cultivated by Luke Blunt on 1 Jany. 1800 and assigned to him, sd McKenzie, Jany. 1802, ever since which time he has resided on and cultivated the same. This is on the north side of Sandy Cr. in Adams Co.

No. 424. Claimant, Charles Marler, of donation of 640 acres, presented 3 Mch. 1804. Wit: Barnabus Donally. Certif. B-187 issued to David Lattimore, assignee, 13 Feb. 1807. Claim for 640 acres in Wilkinson Co. on Buffalo Cr. He was of age and the head of a family when the Spanish troops evacuated the Miss. Territory. He inhabited and cultivated said land the 3rd March 1803 for his own use, the same being unclaimed by any British grant or articles of cession between the United States and the State of Georgia, etc. By A. Lattimore, agent for Chas. Marler.

No. 426. Claimant, William Ogden, 5 Mch. 1804. Wit: Wm. Farmer [or Fanner], 12 Nov. 1804. Certif. B-188, issued, Feb. 13, 1807. Wilkinson Co., Miss. Ter., William Ogden claims 605 acres on waters of Buffalo and Bayou Sarah, by right of occupancy, it having been inhabited and cultivated in 1797 by said Wm. Ogden, who was, at that time, the head of a family. Signed. // Survey with plat, ... beg. at Mr. Samuel Young's corner . . . Dunbar's Fork of Bayou Sarah . . . Mr. Young's line. Feb. 2, 1804. (signed) Wm. Brown, surv.

No. 427. Claimant, John Babcock, 5 Mch. 1804. Wit: Elijah Thearel. Certificate D-179, 17 Dec. 1806. Wilkinson Co., Miss. Ter., John Babcock claims preemption right to 150 acres in sd county on waters of Buffalo Cr. and Bayou Sarah, by virtue of having inhabited and cultivated it in 1800 and ever since. John (X) Babcock. Survey: 150 acres on Dunbar's Fork, beg. at Terrill's corner, on Jones's line, to Forman's, to Staut's line. Feb. 8, 1804. (signed) Wm. Brown, surv.

No. 428. Claimant, William Jones, 5 Mch. 1804. Witnesses: John Babcock and Elijah Terrill. Certif. D-180, 17 Dec. 1806. William Jones claims the right to become purchaser of 190 acres in Wilkinson Co., Miss. Ter., on waters of Buffalo and Bayou Sarah, by virtue of having inhabited and cultivated in 1802 and ever since. Signed. // Survey: Beg. at Wm. Ogden's line, Forman's N.W. corner. Feb. 9, 1804. Wm. Brown.

No. 429. Claimant, Sylvester Stauts, 5 Mch. 1804. Wit: Elijah Thearel and Wm. Jones. Certif. D-181, 17 Dec. 1806. Wilkinson County, Miss. Ter. Sylvester Stauts claims preemption rights 105 acres on waters of Buffalo Creek, by virtue of having inhabited and cultivated the land in 1802 and ever since. Elijah (X) Thearel for Sylvester Stauts. Survey: beg. near Stauts' house . . . with Terrill's and Cox's line, Feb. 15, 1804. Wm. Brown // Conveyance from S. Staut to I. Johnson, Sen., Sylvester Stout to Isaac Johnson, Sen., for $390, my preemption claim to a tract of land where I, the said Stout live, which entry is now in the Office of the Commrs. Wit: James Collinsworth, William Brown. Prov. by Collingsworth before T.R. [Thomas Rodney], 18 Oct. 1804. // Isaac Johnson, Sen. for $400 paid, to Joseph Johnson, all that tract of land conveyed by Sylvester Stouts to me, being 105 acres. The Board of Commrs. are hereby requested to issue certificate in name of Joseph Johnson. (signed) Isaac Johnson. Wit: Isaac Williams, Samuel Stockett.

No. 430. Claimant, Daniel Leatherman, 5 March 1804. Wit: Elijah Thearel. Certif. D-182, issued, 17 Dec. 1806, to cl. Wilkinson Co., Miss. Ter., Daniel Leatherman claims right of preference in becoming purchaser of the U.S. of 124 acres, on waters of Bayou Sarah by virtue of his having inhabited and cultivated it in the Fall of 1802 and ever since. Elijah (X) Thearal for Daniel Leatherman. Survey by Wm. Brown, Feb. 22, 1804. Beg. on Dunbar's NE corner.

No. 431. Claimant, Elijah Thearal, 5 Mch. 1804. Rejected for want of evidence, 30 Dec. 1806. Wilkinson Co., Miss. Ter., Elijah Thearel claims 200 acres in sd county on waters of Thompson's Cr., by virtue of having cultivated it in Sept. 1802 and it was under cultivation 3 Mch 1803. Survey by William Brown: Beg. at Wm. Moore's line . . . 27 Feb. 1804.

No. 432. Claimant, Elijah Thearal, 5 Mch. 1804. Wit: John Babcock. Certif. D-183 issued 17 Dec. 1806. Miss. Ter., Wilkinson Co., Elijah Thearal claims the right to become the purchaser of the U.S. of 390 acres in sd co. on Buffalo and Bayou Sarah waters, by virtue of his having inhabited and cultivated sd tract in 1799 and ever since. Survey for Mr. Elijah Therrill by William Brown: Beg. at Stout's corner on a br. of Dunbar's Fork of Bayou Sarah, 20 Feb. 1804.

No. 433. Claimant, James Milligan, 5 Mch. 1804. Wit: Wm. Daniel, 25 Sept. 1804. Certif. D-7, 4 Sept. 1806. Miss. Ter., Jefferson Co., James Milligan claims a preemption of 438 English acres on Tabor's Fork, improved in Aug. 1801 and settled personally in following Oct. Signed.

No. 434. Claimant, William Fanner, 5 Mch. 1804. Wit: Wm. Ogden, 12 Nov. 1804. Certif B-189, issued Feb. 1807. Wm. Fanner claims 500 acres in Wilkinson Co., on Bayou Sarah. Wm. (X) Fanner.

No. 435. Claimant, Robert Glass, 5 Mch. 1804. Wit: Chas. Cassna, 25 Sept. 1804. Rejected for want of sufficient evidence, 30 Dec. 1806. Jefferson Co., Miss. Ter., Robert Glass claims a preemption of 202 Eng. acres of land in afsd county, on waters of Bayou Pierre, known as Tabor's Fork, improved in May 1802 and cultivated. Signed. Plat shows Bowling on one side, and Aaron Neil opposite. Survey, 9 Jany. 1804, by Joseph D. Lewis.

No. 436. Claimant, Gideon Foster, 5 Mch. 1804. Wit: John Still Lee, 27 Nov. 1804. Josiah Flower, a Spanish patentee. See No. 1622. Rejected, May 7, 1807. Miss. Ter., Claiborne Co., Gibeon [or Gibson] Foster claims 640 acres in said county on Bayou Pierre, by right of occupancy. The land was improved in 1796 by Josiah Flower, who cultivated it until he sold same to Gideon Foster who has continued to cultivate it ever since.

No. 437. Claimant, Isaac Corey, 5 Mch. 1804. Wit: Prosper King, 12 May 1804. Certif. D-144, 16 Dec. 1806. Isaac Cory claims a preemption right to 200 acres on the middle fork of the Homochitto River improved by him in 1803 and cultivated ever since. Signed.

No. 438. Claimant, William Cole, 5 Mch. 1804. Wit: Richard King, 12 May 1804. Certif. A-755 issued 10 Mch. 1806. William Cole claims preemption rights to 200 acres on middle fork of the Homochitto, it being a survey of land granted to the said Cole by the Spanish Govt. in 1793, for services rendered sd Govt. in Capt. Richard King's company of rangers. Said Cole did obtain a patent for same which was lost from the Office of Gov. Gayoso, when he had command of the Natchez District. Signed.

No. 444. Claimant, Jonathan Mackey, 5 Mch. 1804. Wit: Joseph Montgomery, 9 June 1804. Certif. D-290, 29 Dec. 1806. Jonathan Mackey claims a preemption right to 341 acres by virtue of a settlement and residence made on and prior to Mch. 3 last past, land in Claiborne Co., on waters of Bayou Pierre, adj. lands of Waterman Crane, George Humphreys, Alexander Montgomery and others. Plat also shows Pittman and Thomas Green. // Indenture. Alexander Montgomery to Jonathan Mackey, on or abt. 1st of 1802, sold the above tract of land and the small improvement thereon .... [the rest is faded.] Wit: R. Claiborne, W. B. Shields.

No. 445. Claimant, John Hannah, 5 Mch. 1804. Wit: Ezekiel Flowers. Certif. D-198, 17 Dec. 1806. Miss. Ter., Claiborne Co., John Hannah claims preemption right to 50 acres in sd county on Bayou Pierre by virtue of his having inhabited and cultivated it in 1802 and ever since. Signed.

No. 460. Claimant, Asa Watkins, 8 Mch. 1804. Rejected for want of evidence, 30 Dec. 1806. Miss. Ter., Jefferson, Asa Watkins claims a preemption of 200 acres on north fork of Cole's Cr. by an improvement made in 1802, and personally in Jany 1804. Plat shows land adj. by Willis McDonald.

No. 461. Claimant, John Watts, 8 Mch. 1804. Wit: Wm. Sherburt, 8 Oct. 1804; Mary Watts, 25 Feb. 1806. Certif. B-71 issued 26 Sept. 1806. Claimant says that if his claim does not amount to a Donation, asks that 180 acres be granted as a preemption to include his improvement. John Watts claims a donation of 380 acres in Jefferson Co. on Cole's Creek by an improvement and cultivation which he made thereon in Aug. 1797 and ever since. Land adj. James Hyman, Wm. Shaw, Peter Pressley and Mary Watts.

No. 464. Claimant, William Kilcrease, 7 Mch. 1804. Wit: John Booth, 19 Nov. 1804, Berryman Watkins. Certif. D-328, 29 Dec. 1806, to James McCaleb, assignee. Miss. Ter., Claiborne Co., Miss. Ter., Wm. Kilcrease claims 390 acres in sd county on Bayou Pierre, by right of occupancy. Said tract was inhabited and cultivated in 1797 and ever since by sd William, who was the head of a family on the day when the Spanish troops finally evacuated the Territory, etc. Signed. Plat shows Boggy Branch and John Booth's land adj. Certified by Daniel Burnet. // Miss. Ter., Claiborne County, 24 Nov. 1804. for $100 paid, William Brocus, Jr. buys fr. Wm. Kilcrease, 360 acres claimed as a preemption right adj. John Boothe on the east and James McCaleb on south, John Robinson on west. // Endorsed: This is to certify that Wm. Brocus doth give unto James McCaleb peaceable possession of the within mentioned tract of 390 acres, etc. Signed. Wit: John Boothe. 20 Apr. 1806.

No. 465. Claimant, Andrew Mundell, 7 Mch. 1804. Wit: Daniel Burnet, 23 Apr. 1805. Certif. D-279, 24 Dec. 1806. Miss. Ter., Claiborne Co., Andrew Mundell, citizen of sd Ter. and Co., claim preference of becoming purchaser of 410 acres, by virtue of his settlement made thereon in 1800, on the waters of Bayou Pierre. Signed.

No. 466. Claimant, Barnabas Perry, 7 Mch. 1804. Rejected, 7 May 1807. Barnabas Perry claims a donation right of 213 acres on the waters of Second Cr. in Adams Co., same being cultivated and improved in 1796. Plat shows McIntosh and Robert Ford.

No. 467. Claimant, Catura Proctor, 7 Mch. 1804. Wit: Gibson Clarke, 19 Nov. 1804. Certif. B-80 issued 30 Oct. 1806. Miss. Ter., Claiborne Co. Claim for 640 acres on a br. of north fork of Bayou Pierre and is the place now occupied by claimant, who claims it by the right of settlement. She settled there in 1797 and has lived there ever since. The land is adj. that of John Booth and John Clark.

No. 468. Claimant, Daniel Burnet, 7 Mch. 1804. Wit: Stephen Minor and Richard King, 25 Nov. 1806. Rejected, 8 Apr. 1807. Confirmed by the Register and Receiver under Act of Congress, 11 April 1818 by Certificate No. 33 to Daniel Burnet, dated 9 June 1818. Certificate of survey in Spanish by Wm. Dunbar. I have surveyed unto James Stuart two hundred arpents of land on the north branch of Bayou Pierre, 70 mi. from the fort of Natchez, b. as shown in the annexed plat. Natchez, 16 Nov. 1794. Land b. by Daniel Burnet and John Girault and vacant lands. Claiborne Co., Daniel Burnet claim 200 arpents in sd county, on waters of Bayou Pierre by virtue of a warrant from the Spanish Government to James Stuart, who was 21 years of age and an actual settler 27 Oct. 1795. The sd James Stuart sold the sd tract unto sd Daniel Burnet.

No. 481. Claimant, John Clark, 8 Mch. 1804. Wit: Gibson Clark, 20 Nov. 1804. Certif. B-267 issued 7 May 1807. Miss. Ter., Claiborne Co., John Clark claims 640 acres on waters of Bayou Pierre by right of occupancy. The said John inhabited and cultivated sd tract in 1797 and ever since and he was at the time of settling it the head of a family. Land adj. John Booth.

No. 485. Claimant, John Erwin, 8 Mch. 1804. Certif. B-191 issued Feb. 13, 1807. John Erwin, settler in Miss. Ter., claims 636 acres on the dividing ridge between Sandy and Wells Creeks, by virtue of settlement and improvement made in 1792 and continued upon ever since.

No. 510. Claimant, William Boyd, 8 Mch. 1804. Wit: John Burns, Certif. D-213 issued to J. Bedsell, assignee, for 250 acres, 22 Dec. 1806. Miss. Ter., Jefferson Co. William Boyd claims a preemption of 640 acres on headwaters of the north fork of Cole's Cr. and south fork of Bayou Pierre, by improvement and inhabiting in Aug. 1801. // This is to certify that James Bedsel and Wm. Boyd bargained for an improvement, that is sd Boyd has sold said improvement and half of the tract to sd Bedsell. 13 Oct. 1806. (signed) William Boyd. James Bedsell, assignee of claimant, wishes 250 acres granted.

No. 511. Claimant, Sam Boyd, 8 Mch. 1804. Wit: Thos. Morgan, 27 Aug. 1804. Certif. D-13 issued 14 Sept. 1806. Samuel Boyd claims a preemption right to 458 acres on both sides of Morgan's Fork of Homochitto in Adams Co., settled by him in 1801, he being at that time the head of a family. He has continued to live on and cultivate said land ever since. Signed. Plat shows lands of Wm. Kennison and Thos. Ford adj.

No. 512. Claimant, James Vincent, 8 Mch. 1804. Wit: Samuel Boyd, 27 Aug. 1804. Certif. D-14, issued 4 Sept. 1806. James Vincent claims a preemption right to 200 acres on Morgan's Fork of the Homochitto, settled by him in 1802, he being at that time the head of a family and he has lived on and cultivated the same land ever since. Signed.

No. 513. Claimant, Thos. Morgan, 8 Mch. 1804. Wit: Samuel Boyd, 27 Aug. 1804. Certif. D-15, issued 4 Sept. 1806. Thomas Morgan claims a preemption right to 210 acres on Morgan's Fork of Homochitto River, in Adams Co., settled by him in 1801 and he has continued to live on and cultivate the same ever since, he being at the time of settling said claim the head of a family. Signed. Lands adj. claims of Wm. Kennison and Joseph Ford.

No. 517. Claimant, Francis Baldridge, 8 Mch. 1804. Wit: Thomas Lacey, 15 Oct. 1804. Certif. D-16 issued 4 Sept. 1806. Miss. Ter. Francis Baldridge claims a preemption right to 640 acres on waters of north fork of Cole's Cr., settled by Benajah Spell in 1802 for him, the said Baldridge, who now lives on and cultivates the same. Signed.

No. 518. Claimant, Thos. Lacey, 8 Mch. 1804. Wit: Francis Baldridge, 15 Oct. 1804. Certif. D-17 issued 4 Sept. 1806. Miss. Territory, Thos. Lacey claims a preemption right to 320 acres on both sides of a branch of the north fork of Cole's Creek, improved by him in 1802 and inhabited and cultivated ever since, he being at that time the head of a family. Signed. Plat shows John Gilbert's claim and William Lacey's.

No. 519. Claimant, William Lacey, 8 Mch. 1804. Wit: Francis Baldridge, 15 Oct. 1804. Certif. D-18, issued 4 Sept. 1806. Miss. Ter., Wm. Lacey claims 320 acres of land by preemption and settlement in 1802 by claimant, on north fork of Cole's Cr. in Jefferson County. Plat shows claim of Thomas Lacey adj.

No. 522. Claimant, Stephen Richards, 9 Mch. 1804. Certif. B-252 issued 9 Apr. 1807. Miss. Ter., Claiborne Co. Stephen Richards claims 640 acres on Bayou Pierre by right of occupancy, he having inhabited and cultivated the said tract in Oct. 1797 and before and ever since that time, being the head of a family. Plat shows tract b. on north by Bayou Pierre, on west by Goodwin's and Green's, south by Patterson and Ezekiel Flowers.

No. 523. Claimant, heirs of Richard Goodwin, 9 Mch. 1804. Wit: William Smith, 26 Mch. 1804. Certif. B-192 issued to Phoebe Goodwin, 13 Feb. 1807. Miss. Territory, Claiborne Co., Samuel, William, Sarah and Elizabeth Goodwin, heirs and legal representatives of Richard Goodwin, decd., claim 300 arpents on the south side of Bayou Pierre, by right of occupancy, said tract of land having been inhabited and cultivated in 1786 by Mr. John Terry who sold it in the said year to said Richard Goodwin, decd. and his family have inhabited and cultivated it ever since. (signed) Samuel Goodwin, one of the sd heirs, for himself and the others. b. on north by Bayou Pierre; west by Green's land, south by Stephen Richard. // Know all men that I have bargained and sold unto Richard Goodwin a certain improvement made by me on the south side of Bayou Pierre, which I give and grant with all my good will, 14 Jany. 1786. John (X) Terry. Wit: Thos. Jordan. Proved before the Board, 25 Mch. 1804. R.C.

No. 525. Claimant, Buckner Pittman, 9 Mch. 1804. Wit: Stephen Richards. Rejected 9 April 1807. Miss. Ter., Buckner Pittman claims by virtue of his own habitation and cultivation 640 acres on the waters of Bayou Pierre, which sd Buckner inhabited and cultivated Feb. 1797 and ever since. He therefore claims the sd land by right of occupancy, having been the head of a family at that time. // Indenture by Buckner Pittman to Francis Nailor, for $1000 paid, sells all claim, etc. to a right of donation of 640 acres on which he now lives on the waters of James Cr., etc. Wit: Stephen Richards, Isaac Hayes. Prov. by Hayes 14 Dec. 1805, before J. Moore, J. P. of Claiborne Co.

No. 526. Claimant, Ezra McCall, 9 Mch. 1804. Wit: Buckner Pittman. Certif. B-89, 3 Feb. 1807. Miss. Ter., Claiborne Co. Ezra McCall claims 640 acres on waters of Bayou Pierre by right of occupancy, having by his legal representatives inhabited and cultivated the sd tract in Feb. 1797 for the use of the said Ezra who was then the head of a family.

No. 528. Claimant, Abram Frisbee, 9 Mch. 1804. Wit: James Milligan, 25 Sept. 1804. Rejected for want of sufficient evidence, 30 Dec. 1806. Miss. Ter., Jefferson Co. Abraham Frisbee claims 200 acres on Cole's Cr. by improving and inhabiting in Aug. 1801.

No. 532. Claimant, John Searcy, 10 Mch. 1804. Wit: Baley Chaney, 12 May 1805. Certif. B-193, issued 13 Feb. 1807. Miss. Ter., Jefferson Co. John Searcy claims a donation right to 640 acres on south fork of Coles Cr. originally improved by him in 1797 and inhabited and cultivated ever since, he being at that time the head of a family. N.B. The aforesaid Searcy has a wife and 8 children. Signed: J. Searcy. Plat shows lands of Earl Marble, John Bolls and Robert Miller, adjoining, and James Bolls' claim.

No. 536. Claimant, James Norris, 10 Mch. 1804. Wit: Stephen Compton, 9 Oct. 1804. Certif. D-167 issued 6 Dec. 1806. Miss. Ter., Jefferson Co. James Norris claims preemption right to 400 acres on Dowd's Cr. by virtue of having inhabited and cultivated same in Feb. 1802 and ever since.

No. 538. Claimant, Ambrose McDonald, 12 Mch. 1804. Wit: Jonas Griffin. See No. 1262. Certificate D-223 issued to Jonas Griffin, assignee of claimant, Jan. 22, 1806. Plat of 371 acres 11 mi. below Walnut Hills, joining the Miss. Swamp in Claiborne Co., beg. on Jonas Griffin's line. [Surveyor's name not given.] // Ambrose McDonald for and in consideration of $100 paid to Jonas Griffin all right, etc. to preemption or any other claim I have to 371 acres where I now reside. Signed. Ambrose McDaniel. Wit: Joseph Ferguson, Joseph Ferguson, Sr.

No. 539. Claimant, Edmund Hall, 20 Mch. 1804. Certif. D-32, issued to J. B. Ferry, assignee of claimant, 10 June 1806. Miss. Ter., Adams Co. Edmund Hall claims 640 acres in Jefferson Co. on south fork of Bayou Pierre by right of occupancy. // Tract of land surveyed for Edmund Hall, the legal representative of Henry Milburn, b. Joseph D. Lewis. Note: Milburn who sold this tract to Hall claimed a preemption right to another tract. T. R. Hall claims that Milburn conveyed the sd tract to

Hall by deed, 9 Dec. 1801.

No. 542. Claimant, William Lawrence, 12 Mch. 1804. Wit: Thos. Beckham. Certif. D-110 issued 15 Dec. 1806. Miss. Ter., Wilkinson Co. Wm. Lawrence claims 237 acres on the west prong of the River Amite by improvement previous to and on 3 Mch. 1803 by sd Lawrence, b. by lands of Robt. Montgomery, Edmund Andrews and vacant lands. Survey of 237 acres as above by Robt. Griffin, 9 Mch. 1804. Note: six mi. above the line and 50 mi. from Miss. River.

No. 543. Claimant, Jacob Curry, 12 Mch. 1804. Wit: Wm. Lawrence. Certif. D-111 issued Dec. 15, 1806. The said 500 acres in plat above surveyed for Jacob Curry in Wilkinson Co., on west fork of the Amite River. (signed) Robert Griffin. Claim by virtue of improvement made previous and on 3 Mch. 1803 by sd Curry.

No. 544. Claimant, Thomas Arrandes, 12 Mch. 1804. Wit: Jonas Griffin. Certif. D-224 issued 22 Dec. 1806. Thomas Arrandes, of Claiborne Co., Miss. Ter., claims preemption right to 640 acres in sd county on the Miss. River, by virtue of his having inhabited and cultivated it on Feb. 10, 1802. Survey by Samuel Cook.

No. 546. Claimant, Moses Foster, 12 Mch. 1804. Wit: Henry Johnson and John Morgan. Certif. B-112 issued 15 Dec. 1806. Preemption claim for 320 acres on the waters of Beaver Cr. which he actually inhabited and cultivated on and before 3 Mch. 1803, and was at that time the head of a family. Geo. Poindexter, atty. for claimant.

No. 547. Claimant, Edmund Andrews, 12 Mch. 1804. Wit: Wm. Lawrence. Certif. B-113 issued 15 Dec. 1806. Preemption claim for 300 acres on River Amite, by his having inhabited and cultivated same in Jany. 1803 and ever since. Survey by Robt. Griffin.

No. 549. Claimant, John Gibson, 12 Mch. 1804. Wit: James Ashworth. Certif. D-168 issued 16 Dec. 1806. Miss. Ter., Claiborne Co., John Gibson claims preemption right for 246 acres on north fork of Bayou Pierre, by virtue of having inhabited and cultivated the same, by another person, for the use of sd claimant in June 1802 and ever since, and sd claimant was 21 years of age on 3 Mch. 1803. N. B. Claimant says he claims another tract of 700 acres by a Spanish grant. T.R.

No. 552. Claimant, James Howard, 12 Mch. 1804. Certif. A-159 to claimant for 166 acres. See No. 556. James Howard, settler in Miss. Ter. at and before 27 Oct. 1795, claims 166 acres on waters of Sandy Cr. by deed from Joseph Sessions, 5 May 1803. Signed.

No. 553. Claimant, James Howard, 12 Mch. 1804. Wit: John Mitchell, 22 June 1804. Certif. B-194, issued 13 Feb. 1807. Adams Co. James Howard claims 502 acres by virtue of an improvement made and occupied by Sarah Kelly in 1797 and by her conveyed to present claimant, 30 May 1801. The above notice is amended by leave of the Board of Commrs. as follows: [to the above is added that sd Sarah Kelly was upward of 21 years of age when the Spanish troops evacuated this territory, 30 March 1798.] E. Turner, atty. for the claimant, May 23, 1803.

No. 554. Claimant, Kinchen Suffield, 12 Mch. 1804. Rejected 15 May 1807. Know all men, etc. that I, Zadoc Barrow, of Adams Co., Miss. Ter. for $500 paid, to James Howard, of same, all my right, etc. in a certain improvement and occupancy of a tract of land on the south side of the Homochitto, being the land whereon I lived in 1798 and 1799. (signed) Zadoc (B) Barrow, 2 Apr. 1804. Wit: Wm. Erwin. Ack. Nov. 26, 1804, before T.R. Amended by leave of the Board, as follows: Claims 640 acres of land, as above, by his having inhabited and cultivated the land and being upward of 21 years 30 Mch. 1798, and of a conveyance to Kinchen Shuffield, 14 Feb. 1798, of an improvement made on sd tract in 1793, etc. // Kinchen Shuffield, settler in Miss. Ter., at and before 27 Oct. 1795, claims 640 acres of land, as above.

No. 478. George Ellis, claimant, 7 Mch. 1804. Wit: John Berry, 5 Oct. 1804. Certif. D-269 issued 24 Dec. 1806. George Ellis claims the preemption right to 640 acres on Beaver Cr. by improvement made before and on 3 Mch. 1803 by said Ellis.

No. 608. Claimant, William Howey, 14 Mch. 1804. Wit: B. Pittman, 20 Nov. 1804. Certif. B-90 issued 3 Feb. 1807. William Howey claims 640 acres on James Run of Bayou Pierre, by occupancy, he having settled, improved and cultivated the same in 1797 when the Spanish troops evacuated the territory, he being at that time at the head of a family and above the age of 21. Robert Cochran for Wm. Howey. [Plat shows lands of Pittman and Melling Woolley adj.]

No. 627. Claimant, Robert Trentham, 15 Mch. 1804. Wit: James Burney. Certif. D-114, issued 15 Dec. 1806. Miss. Ter., Wilkinson Co. Robert Trentham claims 425 acres on the west prong of River Amite, by an improvement made Oct. 1802 and continued 3 Mch. 1803 by said Trentham. Tract adj. Robt. Montgomery.

No. 628. Claimant, James Burney, 15 Mch. 1804. Wit: Robert Trentham. Certif. D-115 issued to M. Tool, assignee, 15 Dec. 1806. James Burney claims 320 acres on west br. of the Amite River, by improvement made before 3 Mch. 1803 by sd Burney. // For value recd, I, James Burney have sold to Mathew Tool all my preemption claim on the Amite whereon I now live, containing 320 acres. Mathew Tool to pay all lawful claims in obtaining the title to same and the Commrs. are requested to issue the certificate in his name. (signed) James Burney. Wit: Jo. Johnson, Thomas Batchelor.

No. 629. Claimant, William Lea, 15 Mch. 1804. Wit: James Burney. Certif. D-116 issued 15 Dec. 1806. William Lea claims 261 acres in Wilkinson Co. on the east side of the Amite River, by improvement made on 3 Mch. 1803 and before that in 1802, by William Furlow, whose right to the land sd Lea has obtained. Plat and survey by Robert Griffin.

No. 630. Claimant, Thomas Daniel, 15 Mch. 1804. Wit: Jno. A. Davidson, 25 Sept. 1804. Certif. D-291, issued 29 Dec. 1806. Thomas Daniel claims preemption right to 320 acres in Jefferson Co. on waters of Cole's Cr.

No. 634. Claimant, Henry Ratcliff, 15 Mch. 1804. Wit: Peter Ratcliff, 29 Oct. 1804. Certif. D-117, issued 15 Dec. 1806. Henry Ratcliff gives notice that he claims preemption right to 170 acres on headwaters of Beaver Cr., a br. of Amite River in Wilkinson Co, by having inhabited and cultivated sd tract on and before 3 Mch. 1803, he being upward of 21 yrs. of age. Plat shows the "road from New Orleans to Natchez."

No. 647. Claimant, Ben Goodall, 15 Mch. 1804. Wit: John Hopper, 12 Nov. 1804. Certif. B-272, issued 24 Dec. 1806. Benjamin Goodall claims preemption right to 100 acres on the waters of Petty Gulf Cr. by virtue of having inhabited and cultivated the same in 1802 and ever since.

No. 648. Claimant, Samuel Goodall (or Goodail), 15 Mch. 1804. Wit: John Hopper, 12 Nov. 1806. Certif. D-165, issued 16 Dec. 1806. Samuel Goodall claims preemption right to 200 acres in Jefferson Co. on the waters of Doud's Cr by having inhabited and cultivated this tract in 1801 and ever since.

No. 651. Claimant, Jesse Griffin, 16 Mch. 1804. Wit: Thomas Evans. Certif. D-199 issued 17 Dec. 1806. // Miss. Ter., Claiborne Co. I have admeasured and laid out to Jesse Griffin, Esq., 320 acres on the north side of the south fork of Bayou Pierre, 9 Mch. 1804. (signed) Ezekiel Evans. // Jesse Griffin claims 320 acres above the mouth of Burton's Fork, by occupancy.

No. 652. Claimant, Ezekiel Evans, 16 Mch. 1804. Wit: Thomas Evans. Certif. D-42. Ezekiel Evans claims a preemption right to a tract on south fork of Bayou Pierre in Claiborne Co., having settled and occupied sd tract 7 April 1802. [No acreage given.]

No. 653. Claimant, Thomas Evans, 16 Mch. 1804. Wit: Samuel Bridges. Certif. D-19, issued 4 Sept. 1806. Thomas Evans claims preemption right to 500 acres in Claiborne Co. on south fork of Bayou Pierre, by virtue of settlement on sd land 5 Apr. 1802. Plat shows land adj. that of Saml. Holley, Thomas English and Ezekiel Evans.

No. 654. Claimant, Lewis Coursey, 16 Mch. 1804. Wit: Thos. Evans. Certif. B-200, issued 17 Dec. 1806. Lewis Coursey claims preemption right to 272 acres in Claiborne on south side of the south fork of Bayou Pierre by virtue of settlement made on sd land by him on and before 1 March 1803. // For $600 to me in hand paid, I sell to Westly W. Nealey 272 acres in Claiborne Co, being my preemption right to same. 16 Dec. 1805. Lewis Coursey. Ack. before J. Moore, J. P. Wit: J. Moore, James Harris.

No. 655. Claimant, Stephen Lee, 16 Mch. 1804. Wit: Moses Lee, 10 Nov. 1804, John Hopper and Stephen Compton, 7 Nov. 1806. Rejected for lack of evidence, 29 Dec. 1806. // Receipt for $50 for improvements made by me on a certain tract in Claiborne Co. on Doud's Cr. and hereby convey my right in sd improvements to Stephen Lee, 25 July 1802. Jas. Glasscock. Ack. before the Board, 20 Nov. 1804. Wit: Moses Lee. Stephen Lee claims preemption right to 300 acres, by virtue of its having been cultivated in 1802 as above.

No. 658. Claimant, Ephraim Story, 17 Mch. 1804. Wit: Isaac Fife. Certif. D-197, issued 13 Feb.

1807. Ephraim Story claims 640 acres in Claiborne Co., on waters of Bayou Pierre by right of occupancy, this tract having been inhabited and cultivated by sd Story ever since 1794 and he was of age and the head of a family when the Spanish troops evacuated the territory.

No. 659. Claimant, John Reynolds, 17 Mch. 1804. Wit: Reuben Gray. Certif. D-86, issued 29 Oct. 1806. John Reynolds claims preemption right to 120 acres in Claiborne Co. on a br. of the Big Black, 3 mi. above Grindstone Ford, by virtue of the settlement on said tract by John Miller before 1 Mch. 1803 and transferred to said Reynolds, 6 Aug. 1803. // Indenture: John Miller hath sold to John Reynolds a certain parcel of land and improvement where sd Miller now lives in Claiborne Co, on waters of Big Black. John Miller, ack. before the Board, 17 Mch. 1804. Wit: Reuben Gray, Reuben Reynolds.

No. 660. Claimant, John Reynolds, 17 Mch. 1804. Wit: John Murphree. Certif. B-101 issued 30 Oct. 1806. John Reynolds claims preemption right to 26 acres in Claiborne Co. on the Road leading through the Wilderness and a br. of Bayou Pierre 2 miles from Grindstone Ford, by virtue of the settlement thereof in 1802. Note: This is the same person that also claimed a preemption right by purchase from John Miller. (signed) T.R. [Judge Thomas Rodney, one of the Commissioners.]

No. 661. Claimant, Samuel Dearmond, 17 Mch. 1804. Wit: John Reynolds and Thomas Vause. Certif. D-102, issued 30 Oct. 1806. Samuel Dearmond claims 640 acres on south fork of Bayou Pierre in Claiborne Co. under the 3rd Sec. of the Act. of Congress, etc.

No. 662. Claimant, Simeon Holliday, 17 Mch. 1804. Wit: Wm. Pippin, 26 Nov. 1804. Certif. B-54, issued 11 Sept. 1806. Simeon Holliday claims preemption rights to 170 acres in Claiborne Co. settled by sd Holliday in 1801, adj. lands of John Gibson and Seth Rundell.

No. 664. Claimant, Joseph Dunham, 17 Mch. 1804. Wit: Reuben Dunham, 16 Nov. 1806. Certif. D-251, issued 24 Nov. 1806. Joseph Dunham claims 692 acres on Thompson's Cr. in Wilkinson Co., by virtue of an improvement by sd Dunham previous to and on 3 Mch. 1803, adj. John Graves and Reuben Dunham.

No. 665. Claimant, William Dunham, 17 Mch. 1804. Wit: Reuben Dunham. Evidence incomplete. Rejected. William Dunham claims 820 acres in Wilkinson Co. on Thompson's Cr. by improvement made by sd William Dunham before and on the 3 Mch. 1803.

No. 666. Claimant, Reuben Dunham, 17 Mch. 1804. Wit: John Graves. Certif. D-252, issued 24 Dec. 1806, to William Cane, assignee. Reuben Dunham claims 400 acres in Wilkinson Co. on Thompson's Cr. adj. Joseph Dunham. // Reuben Dunham, for $550 to him paid, to William Cane, all right in preemption land, 409 acres. Reuben (X) Dunham. Wit: J. Graves. 21 Oct. 1806.

No. 667. Claimant, Reuben Ray, 17 Mch. 1804. Wit: John Reynolds. Certif. D-100 issued 30 Oct. 1806. Reuben Ray claims preemption right to 100 acres in Claiborne Co. on north side of the north fork of Bayou Pierre, a mile above Grindstone Ford, by virtue of settlement and improvement on premises before March 1, 1803 by John Murphree as will appear by sale, 24 Jany. 1803 to sd Murphree and then 1 Sept. 1803 by sd Murphree to sd Ray. Plat shows tract bounded on west by D. Burnet.

No. 670. Claimant, Henry Roach, 17 Mch. 1804. Withdrawn by claimant. Henry Roach claims 359 acres in Wilkinson Co, by virtue of an improvement made by sd Roach before 3 Mch. 1803, adj. John Graves and Robert Sims.

No. 671. Claimant, Christopher Nelson, 17 Mch. 1804. Wit: John Graves. Certif. D-120 issued 18 Nov. 1806. Christopher Nelson claims 610 acres by improvement made previous and on 3 Mch. 1803 by sd Christopher.

No. 672. Claimant, Samuel Harper, 17 Mch. 1804. Wit: John Graves. Certif. B-121 issued to Samuel Lacy, assignee, 15 Dec. 1806. Samuel Harper claims 224 acres on the Comite by improvement made by him before and on 3 Mch. 1803, adj. Richard Graves and _____Baker. // Samuel Harper of Wilkinson Co. for $50 paid in hand, to Samuel Lacy my preemption right to 275 acres on the Comite, adj. Richard Graves, being the tract on which sd Lacy is now settled. Signed. Wit: Richard Graves, Robert Sims.

No. 674. Claimant, Anthony Crockett, 17 Mch. 1804. Wit: Thomas Newman, 20 Feb. 1805. Certif. B-240 issued 22 Dec. 1806. Note: By order of the Board, this claim is amended from Anthony Crocket to Simeon Holiday, 24 Feb. 1804. Anthony Crockett claims 640 acres on southeast side of the Miss. River, at the lower end of Palmyra settlement, which land he settled in 1800 under the 3rd Sec. of Laws, etc. Leave is given the Board to strike out the name of Anthony Crockett and insert the name of Simeon

Holiday in the above notice, he being the actual claimant. (signed) Richard Claiborne, Clk.

No. 675. Claimant, Thomas Vause, 17 Mch. 1804. Original patent [Spanish], 20 June 1795 to Thomas Vause, 200 arpents on a br. of Bayou Pierre, called Chubby's Cr., adj. Isaac Fyffe and William Brocus. Warrant dated 20 June 1789, certified 29 Nov. 1789. (signed) John Girault, Translator. Certif. A-181 issued to claimant.

No. 677. Claimant, Joseph White, 17 Mch. 1804. Wit: Robert Ashley, 9 Feb. 1805. Certif. B-198 issued 13 Feb. 1807. Plat by Ezekiel Evans shows land on Chubby Creek [Claiborne Co.] which was settled Feb. 1798 and improved under the Spanish government and now claimed under the Act of the Disposal of Lands, etc. [No acreage given.]

No. 679. Claimant, Wm. H. Wooldridge, 17 Mch. 1804. Wit: Robert Ashley, George W. Humphreys, Joseph White and William Brocus, 5 Aug. 1805. Certif. D-293 issued 9 Dec. 1806. This land was inhabited by Patrick Forbush in 179- under the Spanish government, by virtue of which, sd Wooldridge claims this land under the law for the disposal of lands in the Miss. Territory. The claimant, being before the Board, requests if the proof does not amount to a Donation, that a preemption be allowed. Note: The claim conflicts with that of Daniel Burnet, No. 1030.

No. 681. Claimant, Thos. Waggoner, 17 Mch. 1804. Rejected for want of evidence. Thos. Waggoner claims preemption right to 325 acres in Claiborne Co. adj. Anthony Glass on the westerly side of his survey on the road leading from Big Black to Walnut Hills, 4 miles from Walnut Hills, by virtue of an improvement and actual cultivation.

No. 684. Claimant, John Nailor, 19 Mch. 1804. Wit: Capt. Burnet. John Nailor claims preemption rights to 313 acres in Claiborne Co. on the Miss. River below Grand Gulf and above the mouth of Bayou Pierre, adj. on east Killian Medlock, by virtue of John Nailor inhabiting the premises before 1st Mch. 1803.

No. 698. Claimants, heirs of Abner Pipes, Mch. 1804. Wit: John Stylus, April 1804. Certif. B-235. (See Nos. 1820 and 1907). Joseph, Philip, Ann, Abraham, Mary, Abner and John Pipes, heirs and representatives of Abner Pipes, decd., claim 600 arpents in Adams Co. on the high ground of Miss. River, 2 miles from sd river. Abner Pipes was the head of a family and had a Spanish warrant for sd land, Feb. 2, 1793. Mary Pipes, mother of the above heirs and acting guardian.

No. 694. Claimant, Henry Milburn, 19 Mch. 1804. Wit: Wm. McCaleb. Certif. D-95 issued 30 Oct. 1806. Henry Milburn claims the preemption right to 640 acres on the north side of Bayou Pierre in Claiborne Co. for actually settling on sd land before 3 Mch. 1803 at which time he was the head of a family. Plat marked "Capt. Henry Milburn's plat," 640 acres.

No. 695. Claimant, Shadrick Chaven, 19 Mch. 1804. Wit: Benj. Steel, 6 Aug. 1805. Certif. D-229 issued 22 Dec. 1806. Shadrick Chaven claims preemption right to 135 acres in Claiborne Co. on an island called "the upper of the Three Islands", on the upper part of same, by virtue of settling and cultivating same ever since the spring of 1802.

No. 696. Claimant, Buckner Darden, 19 Mch. 1804. Wit: James Chaney. Certif. D-171 issued 16 Dec. 1806. Buckner Darden claims a preemption right to 300 acres in Jefferson Co. on both sides of Irwin's Fork of Cole's Cr., settled by him in 1801 and inhabited and cultivated by him ever since, being at the time of settling said land the head of a family.

No. 698. Claimant, James Chaney, 19 Mch. 1804. Wit: Buckner Darden. Certif. D-2 issued 29 Dec. 1806. (Conflicting with Nos. 975 and 761.) James Chaney claims preemption right to 196 acres in Jefferson Co. on Platner's Fork of Cole's Cr. settled by him in 1802 and he has continued to cultivate and improve same ever since, he being at that time the head of a family. Plat shows land adj. John Gaskins, David Darden, and Daniel Harrigil.

No. 702. Claimant, Edward King, 19 Mch. 1804. Wit: Anthony Calvit. Certif. B-55 issued 4 Sept. 1806. Miss. Ter., Adams Co. 6 Feb. 1802. John Calvit, for $500 in hand paid, to Edward King my Spanish grant, right, title and improvement to 300 acres now occupied by me, 16 miles east of Natchez, adj. Joe Ford, Peter Nelson and Daniel Hawley. Signed. Wit: John Mayes, D. Hawley. Prov. by D. Hawley, Oct. 20, 1804 before T.R. // Edward King claims a Donation right to 310 acres cultivated and inhabited by John Calvit in 1792 and ever since, bought by King who continues to live on it, the land lying on the ridge between the headwaters of Cole's and Sandy Creeks, in Adams Co.

No. 707. Claimant, James King, 19 Mch. 1804. Wit: John Callihan, 22 Mch. 1804. Certif. D-62 issued 26 Sept. 1806. James King claims preemption right to 225 acres on the Homochitto River by virtue of having inhabited and cultivated said land on and before 3 Mch. 1803 and ever since. On that date he was 35 years of age. Note in file: May it please Your Honors, I wish to inform you that I was present when Mr. John Callihan was examined on oath respecting a claim of land for Mr. James King on the Homochitto improvement sold by me to said Mr. King which is not so. I never saw Mr. Callihan before yesterday to my knowledge and I thought I ought to have spoke at the time but am ready to come forward with three of my neighbors and give satisfactory information connecting the same. (signed) James Sanders. Oct. 23, 1804.

No. 709. Claimant, Joseph Bullen, 19 Mch. 1804. Wit: Abram Mayes. Certif. D-294 issued 29 Dec. 1806. Joseph Bullen claims preemption right to 640 acres on waters of Cole's Cr. sold to me by Betsey Nash on 6 Feb. 1804. This tract the said Betsey did actually inhabit and cultivate on 3rd Mch. 1803 and was then the head of a family and more than 21 years of age. By plat Hugh Slayter and sd Joseph Bullen have adj. lands. // Betsey Nash, for $30 paid me, to Joseph Bullen, now living in Jefferson Co., all my right, etc. to the preemption right to the improvements on the land on which he now lives in sd County, about 2 miles southeast of the Courthouse, supposed to contain 600 acres. Feb. 4, 1804. Wit: John Hamberlin, William MacDuggle.

No. 710. Claimant, Rachel Sloan, 19 Mch. 1804. Wit: Jesse Lum. Certif. D-9 issued to A.B. Ross, assignee, 4 Sept. 1806. Land claimed by Mr. Cessna for the heirs of John Sloan. Jefferson Co., Rachel Sloan claims a donation of 640 arpents on waters of Bayou Pierre for her children, Lemuel, Thomas, Hiram, Mary and [two others. Paper torn.] six in all. Memorandum: Agreement 18 Dec. —— bet. Stephen Allen and Arthur Brown Ross. Allen sells to Ross all preemption rights to tract on Lum's Cr. of Bayou Pierre, for $200 to be paid on time, $50 now, etc. Wit: Elizabeth Ross, Isaac A.B. Ross who proved above before the Board, 27 Mch. 1806. (signed) T.R.

No. 711. Claimants, Prosper and Richard King, 11 Mch. 1804. Wit: Caleb King, Nathan Swayze. Rejected. Adams Co., Prosper and Richard King claim 500 acres in Adams Co. by virtue of a warrant from the British Govt. to their father, Justus King, and legally surveyed 1778, tract on main branch of the Homochitto River bet. Hooper's Cr. and Morgan's Fork. Both signed. Note: Heirs of Justus King, to wit: Richard King, Prosper King, Henry King, Elizabeth Moorehouse, Catherine Montgomery, children and descendants. (signed) T.R.

No. 712. Claimant, Stephen Swayze, 19 Mch. 1804. Rejected, 27 Apr. 1807. Stephen Swayze claims 500 acres in Adams Co. by virtue of a warrant from the British Government to his father, Samuel Swayze, and legally surveyed in 1778.

No. 713. Claimant, Nathan Swayze, 19 Mch. 1804. Nathan Swayze claims 500 acres in Adams by virtue of a warrant from the British Govt. to his father, Samuel Swayze, and surveyed in 1778. Rejected, 27 Apr. 1807. Nathan Swayze signed as exor of Samuel Swayze.

No. 716. Claimant, Alexander McKay, 19 Mch. 1804. Wit: John McKay. Certif. D-122 issued 15 Dec. 1806. Alexander McKay claims preemption right to 84 acres in Wilkinson Co. which he did actually inhabit and cultivate on 3 March and before, he being at that time the head of a family and above the age of 21. Plat shows land on Little Beaver Cr., a south branch of Buffalo, adj. Capt. Willis' line.

No. 718. Claimant, Thomas Jones, 19 Mch. 1804. Rejected for want of evidence as a Donation, 30 Dec. 1806. Thomas Jones claims 640 acres in Claiborne Co. by virtue of having inhabited and cultivated same prior to and on the day the Miss. Territory was evacuated by the Spanish troops, he being at that time the head of a family and above the age of 21 years.

No. 722. Claimant, John Woods, 19 Mch. 1804. Wit: Jesse Lum. Certif. D-25 issued 4 Sept. 1806. Jesse Lum claims preemption right to 250 acres in Jefferson Co. on Milburn's Cr., waters of Bayou Pierre, which he inhabited 10 Dec. 1801.

No. 724. Claimant, David Sims, Mch. 19, 1804. Wit: John Hill, 27 Nov. 1804. Certif. D-202 issued 17 Dec. 1806. David Sims claims 640 acres in Jefferson Co. on south fork of Bayou Pierre and north fork of Cole's Cr. by an improvement in Dec. 1802 and a crop in Feb. 1803. (the claimant suggests his inability to pay for the whole tract and asks for 200 acres to be laid off the west end. 18 Dec. 1805. T.H.W.) [Thomas H. Williams, one of the Commissioners.] Marked on jacket. "Survey of 200 acres on west end."

No. 723. Claimant, E. K. Ross, 19 Mch. 1804. Wit: John Hill, 27 Nov. 1804. Certif. D-201 issued 17 Dec. 1806. Eli K. Ross claims preemption right to 640 acres on south fork of Bayou Pierre and north fork of Cole's Cr. in Jefferson Co. by an improvement Dec. 1802 and he moved permanently to live on it in Feb. 1803.

No. 725. Claimant, Gideon Lowry, 19 Mch. 1804. Wit: John Hill. Certif. D-54 issued 11 Sept. 1806. Gideon Lowry claims a preemption to 320 acres in Jefferson Co. on south fork of Bayou Pierre by an improvement made in Sept. 1802 and he moved there in October following.

No. 726. Claimant, Robert Hill, 19 Mch. 1804. Wit: John Hill, 27 Nov. 1806. Certif. D-56 issued 11 Sept. 1806. Robert Hill claims a preemption right to 320 acres in Jefferson Co. on south fork of Bayou Pierre by an improvement in Sept 1802 and moving on the tract in Oct. following. Eli K. Ross for Robert Hill. Plat shows land adj. Gideon Lowry and the claim of William Tabor.

No. 727. Claimant, Jesse Lum, 19 Mch. 1804. Wit: Henry Milburn. Certif. B-92 issued 1 Feb. 1807 to Asahel Gardner. Jesse Lum claims a Donation of 640 acres in Jefferson Co. on south fork of Bayou Pierre which he improved in Aug. 1797 and moved personally to the tract in Oct. following. He inhabited and cultivated sd tract on and before the Miss. Ter. was evacuated by the Spanish troops and at that time had a wife and two children. // Natchez, 12 Sept. 1797. Surveyed to Henry Milburn 840 acres on south fork of Bayou Pierre and received payment at the same time. William and Jesse Lum, chain carriers. (signed) Silas L. Payne. [This is also marked No. 727. The plat is the same as that made for Jesse Lum but is simply marked: "Filed Aug. 26, 1807. Thos. H. Williams, Register." and on the back "Henry Milburn's place, 640 acres." No transfer recorded.]

No. 750. Claimant, Thomas Calvit, 19 Mch. 1804. Wit: Wm. Atchinson, 16 June 1804. The claimant appeared before the Board and relinquished the within claim. (signed) Thos. H. Williams, Register. 24 Feb. 1806. (See No. 140.) Thomas Calvit claims 300 acres of land in Jefferson Co. being a part of a warrant of survey for 500 acres issued in 1788 or 1789 by the Surveyor Genl. of the Prov. of Louisiana in his favor. The warrant of survey was returned to the Spanish Govt. in N.O. and a copy of which, the claimant, if possible will obtain, etc.

No. 767. Claimant, Joshua Matthews, 20 Mch. 1804. Wit: Reuben White, 5 Feb. 1805. Certif. D-203 issued 17 Dec. 1806. Joshua Matthews claims preemption right to 250 acres, improved and cultivated ever since 1st Mch. 1801 by sd Mathews and surveyed 21 Dec. 1803 by Ezekiel Evans, land adj. Reuben White, Mr. Bridgers and Wm. Pope, on the waters of Story's Mill Cr., waters of Bayou Pierre. [Claiborne Co.]

No. 768. Claimant, William Pope, 20 Mch. 1804. Wit: Reuben White, 5 Feb. 1805. Certif. D-204 issued 17 Dec. 1806. William Pope claims a preemption right to 100 acres improved and cultivated ever since 1802 by sd Pope, surveyed on the waters of Widows Cr, a water of Bayou Pierre, in Claiborne Co.

No. 769. Claimant, Edward Turner, 20 Mch. 1804. Wit: W. E. Brazeal 29 Apr. 1805. Certif. D-3 issued 22 Dec. 1806. (Conflicting with No. 763.) Edward Turner claims preemption right in 320 acres on the middle fork of Cole's Cr. in Jefferson County, the same is included in a donation claim of John Burch for 640 acres. G. Poindexter for claimant. Description: 160 acres, an oblong square, with the improvement in the center, b. on south by D. Odum's patent. (signed) E. Turner. [Register. Later a Commissioner.]

No. 770. Claimant, E. K. Ross, 20 Mch. 1804. Witness, John Hill, 27 Nov. 1804. 100 acres to include the improvement. Certif. D-295 issued 29 Dec. 1806. Eli K. Ross claims a preemption of 640 acres in Jefferson Co. on the north fork of Cole's Cr. and the south fork of Bayou Pierre, by an improvement and settlement of Samuel Jackson in April 1802 and transferred to Robert Hill by bill of sale and transferred to Ross as assignee of the said Jackson. The claimant wishes the claim to be reduced to 400 acres, 7 Nov. 1806. (signed) T.H.W. // Bill of sale from Hill to Ross of land improved by Jackson. Wit: John I. Ross, John Craven. 27 Mch. 1806. // This is to certify that a certain claim of land on waters of Bayou Pierre and Cole's Cr. formerly improved by Samuel Jackson and entered in the name of Nancy Jackson, his wife, since transferred to me, [Robert Hill] and now entered in the Land office by Eli K. Ross, as assignee, now transferred to Isaac A.B. Ross, said transfer having gotten burnt, I do transfer all my claims. (signed) Robert Hill. 6 Jany. 1806. Wit: John J. Ross, John Craven. Prov. by Ross Mch. 27, 1806. (signed) T.R.

No. 771. Claimant, Joseph Montgomery, 20 Mch. 1804. Wit: Prosper King, 18 Mch. 1805. Certif. D-146 issued 16 Dec. 1806. Joseph Montgomery claims preemption right to 350 acres in Jefferson Co. by improvement and residence by sd Montgomery on and before 3 Mch. 1803. Land joining Isaac Corey.

No. 772. Claimant, William Taylor, 20 Mch. 1804. Wit: Joseph Bradley, 5 Aug. 1806. Rejected 12 May 1807. Wm. Taylor claims a Donation right to 330 acres inhabited and improved in 1796 by sd Taylor on Buffalo Cr. in Wilkinson Co.

No. 779. Claimant, Charles Cessna, 20 Mch. 1804. Wit: James Milligan 25 Sept. 1804. Certif. D-10 issued 4 Sept. 1806. Chas. Cessna claims a preemption 271 acres in Jefferson Co. on waters of Bayou Pierre, improved by sd Charles in Sept. 1802 and settled personally the Oct. following.

No. 780. Claimant, Aaron Neel, 20 Mch. 1804. Wit: James Milligan, 25 Sept. 1804. Certif. D-11 issued 4 Sept. 1806. Aaron Neel claims the preemption of 300 acres in Jefferson Co. on waters of Tabor's Cr. of Bayou Pierre by cultivation and habitation by sd Neel.

No. 783. Claimant, Martha Trevilion and the heirs of Richard Trevilion, 20 Mch. 1804. Richard Trevilion is a Spanish patentee. (See No. 730.) Rejected 11 June 1807. Martha Trevilion in behalf of the heirs of Richard Trevilion, decd., claims 640 acres on waters of Fairchild's Creek, by virtue of his having inhabited and cultivated sd tract in Jany. 1795, at which time he was the head of a family, till his death in 1800 and by his heirs ever since. Martha Trevilion, wid. of Richard Trevilion, decd., for the heirs of sd Richard. // We, Anthony Nicholas and Mahala Nicholas, formerly Mahala Trevillian, dau. of Richard Trevillian, relinquish all right, etc. in a certain tract of land, claimed by Martha Trevillian, wid. of sd Richard, in behalf of the heirs of sd Richard Trevillian, 640 acres registered No. 783 in Land Office. July 30, 1804. Wit: Gideon Fitz. Ack. before the Board. above date. (signed) Edward Turner. (Commissioner).

No. 784. Claimant, John Hill, 20 Mch. 1804. Wit: Chas. Cessna, 25 Sept. 1806. John Hill claims preemption of 196 acres in Jefferson Co. on waters of Bayou Pierre, by his cultivating and inhabiting in Jany. 1803. Plat shows lands adj. of ______ Bowland, Mr. Cessna and Jesse Lum.

No. 800. Claimant, James Patton, 20 Mch. 1804. Wit: Wm. Collins. Certif. B-199, 13 Feb. 1807. Note: See No. 2028. James Patton claims 640 acres on Buffalo Creek by inhabitation and cultivation in Oct. 1797 by Edward Bunch who continued to do so until he sold it to Patton who was the head of a family and had no other land. Plat shows land on Little Beaver Creek a branch of Buffalo adj. land of Alexander McKay and Peter Walker, also Mr. Willis. // Bill of sale from Elijah Bunch to James Patton, 6 Sept. 1803 and proved before the Board by William Collins. (signed) T.R.

No. 801. Claimant, William B. Cotton, 20 Mch. 1804. Rejected 12 May 1807. William B. Cotton claims 340 acres in Jefferson Co., as legal rep. of actual settlers long before the year 1797 who were heads of families and above the age of 21 years and continued down to the present time, asks for a donation. Survey shows tract adj. Michael Fake, M. Throckmorton, B. Shipp, J. Strickling and ______ Blundell.

No. 802. Claimant, Bartlett Shipp, 20 Mch. 1804. Wit: Drury W. Brazeale, June 3, 1805. Certif. D-296 issued 29 Dec. 1806. Bartlett Shipp claims preemption right of 120 acres in Jefferson Co. on waters of Cole's Cr. // Deed. 22 Nov. 1804. Bartlett Shipp to A. Parrot, for $100 to him in hand paid, transfers right, title, etc. to land near Huntston now in possession and occupation of sd Bartlett. Wit: Beverly P. Grayson, Henry D. Downs.

No. 803. Claimant, Asahel O'Neal, Abijah Hunt, assignee, 15 July 1806. Wit: Edmund Hall, 16 Mch. 1805. Certif. D-203 issued 1st Dec. 1806. Asahel O'Neal claims preemption to 403 acres in Jefferson Co, being the legal rep. of Thomas H. Woods who on and before 3 Mch. 1803 was in actual possession, occupation and cultivation of sd tract, on Lick Fork of Bayou Pierre. // Indenture. 19 Feb. 1805. Sebal O'Neal, admx. of the estate of Asahel O'Neal who was a legal representative of Thomas H. Woods, to Abijah Hunt, for $400 to her in hand paid, transfers to him all that tract of land in Jefferson Co. on Lick Fork of Bayou Pierre, on Edward Hall's line. Sebal (x) O'Neal. Wit: Robert McCray, David Hunt. Ack. by Sebal O'Neal before E.H. Hale, J.P. and Abner Pipes, J.P. 19 Feb. 1805.

No. 804. Claimant, James Lewis, 20 Mch. 1804. Wit: Henry Green, 23 Jany. 1805. Certif. C-396. Rejected, June 11, 1807. James Lewis claims 640 acres in Jefferson Co. by virtue of an actual settlement long before 1797 and continued to the present time by sd Lewis, etc. Plat: ——— Crumholt, Johnson, Henry Green, Thos. Daniel and Thomas Sullivant had lands adjoining. // Note: Let no Certificate issue to James Lewis on his claim No. 804. for 640 acres in Jefferson Co. as Nicholas G.

Ridgeley claims same land by virtue of a patent from the Spanish Govt. to Abraham Brixton and conveyed to sd Ridgeley, No. 395. E. Turner, attorney for sd Ridgeley. To the Board of Commissioners, West of the Pearl River.

No. 805. Claimant, Moses Armstrong, 20 Mar. 1804, donation claim for 640 acres. Witness: R. Ashley, 6 Jan. 1806. Rejected. Evidence insufficient as a donation. An allowance as an exemption. Wit: Thomas White. Rejected, 9 April 1807. Moses Armstrong claims 640 acres in Claiborne Co. on waters of Bayou Pierre, sd Armstrong having inhabited and cultivated tract before the Miss. Ter. was evacuated, at which time he was above 21 years of age and the head of a family.

No. 806. Claimant, Rebecca Dove, 20 Mch. 1804. Wit: James Patton. Certif. D-184 issued 17 Dec. 1806. Rebecca Dove, claims preemption right to 30 acres of land in Wilkinson Co. on Buffalo Cr. by virtue of its having been inhabited and cultivated in Aug. 1802 by sd Rebecca. For Rebecca Dove, James (x) Patton.

No. 821. Claimant, William Smith, 21 Mch. 1804. Wit: Davenport Wiseman. Certif. B-263 issued 24 Dec. 1806. William Smith, a citizen of Mississippi Territory, claims the preference in becoming the purchaser of the United States of a tract of land containing 427 acres on a branch of Big Black known as Commissioners Creek by virtue of his settling it on 5th February 1803 at the head of a family, and remaining on same and cultivating and improving it ever since. (signed) William Smith. Miss. Territory, Claiborne Co. The above plat describes a tract of 427 acres adjoining the Indian boundary line and on the road leading from Natchez through the Wilderness in Claiborne Co. afsd. It is the place where the said William Smith now lives and occupies. Surveyed 23 Feb. 1804 by Daniel Burnet.

No. 822. Claimant, Wm. Cooper, ... [Nothing as to confirmation and issuance of a certificate.] . . 216 acres on a branch of Big Black called Little Sandy about one mile from Rocky Springs on the road leading through the Wilderness, the sd Cooper having settled and cultivated sd land in 1802 and continued on it ever since. Plat by Burnet also shows Wilderness Road.

No. 823. Claimant, Davenport Wiseman . . . . [No details.] Davenport Wiseman, the head of a family, claims preemption of 298 acres in Claiborne Co. on Big Sandy Creek on the Wilderness Road, having settled and occupied sd premises in January 1802 and ever since. Survey by Daniel Burnet shows "the road from this Territory to Tennesse State where the Road crosses Big Sandy."

No. 824. Claimants, Robert and Felix Armstrong, 31 Mch. 1804. Rejected for want of evidence, 30 Dec. 1806. Robert and Felix Armstrong claim preemption of 200 acres in Claiborne Co. on Big Sandy a branch of Big Black between the place where the Wilderness Road crosses the creek and its juncture with the Big Black, by right of settlement on the premises before 3 Mch. 1803.

No. 825. Claimant, Stephen Ambrose, 20 Mch. 1804. Wit: Nehemiah Carter. Certif, B-200 issued 14 Feb. 1807. Stephen Ambrose claims 640 acres in Wilkinson Co. on waters of the Homochitto River by virtue of sd land having been inhabited and cultivated in 1790 by Augustus Roddy who was the head of a family and sold his claim to James Wood who sold same to sd Ambrose. // 6 Aug. 1803. James Wood ack. to have received $450 from Stephen Ambrose, it being in full for my right and title to that tract of land which I, the said James Wood, purchased of Augustus Roddy, adj. land surveyed for Isaac Gaillard and the lines of a survey for Stephen Ambrose. (signed) James Wood. Wit: Hugh Davis.

No. 836. Claimants, heirs of Joseph Box, 21 Mch. 1804. Wit: Joseph Bullard. Certif. D-75 issued 29 Oct. 1806. Sally, Keziah, Fanny, Polly and Jennie, heirs and legal representatives of Joseph Box, decd. claim preemption of 162 acres in Claiborne Co. on a branch of the Big Black about 3 miles from Grindstone Ford, b. on NW by John Reynolds, east by Francis Jones, by virtue of an improvement made before 21 Oct. 1802 by Silas Marsh and sold to Joseph Box, decd., and the sd premises were inhabited and and cultivated on and before 3 Mch. 1803 for the use of the said heirs of sd Box. (signed) Mary Box for the heirs afsd. Plat shows "Mary Box 162 acres".

No. 874. Claimant, Benj. Rogers, Sr., 22 Mch. 1804. Wit: Henry Quine. Certif. D-186 issued 17 Dec. 1806. Benj. Rogers, Sr., who on the 3rd Mch. 1803 was the head of a family, claims a tract of 134 acres in Wilkinson Co., on forks of Percy's Cr., a br. of Buffalo, b. by lands of Thomas Foster, by virtue of his having actually inhabited and cultivated said land on the sd 3rd of Mch. 1803.

No. 875. Claimant, Robert Quine, 22 Mch. 1804. Wit: Benj. Rogers, Sr. Certif. D-187 issued 17 Dec. 1806. Robert Quine claims preemption right to 128 acres in Wilkinson Co., on Percy's Cr., by virtue of sd tract being inhabited and cultivated in 1802 by Mr. William West who sold it to John McCullagh who died intestate and his admr. Reuben Jackson, sold it to the present claimant. Survey of same shows land adj. that of Herring and Jones, Henry Quine and Benj. Rogers, Sr.

No. 876. Claimant, Mathew Cole, 22 Mch. 1804. Wit: Henry Quine. Certif. D-188 issued 17 Dec. 1806. Mathew Cole claims preemption right to 61 acres in Wilkinson Co., on Percy's Cr. by virtue of his having inhabited and cultivated sd land 3 Mch. 1803, when he was the head of a family, and before and since that time.

No. 826. Claimant, Littleton Sanders, 21 Mch. 1804. Wit: Waddle Saunders. Certif. D-63 issued 26 Sept. 1806, to H. Ford, assignee. Miss. Ter. Littleton Sanders claims preemption right to 414 acres, improved and cultivated in Feb. 1803, and he has continued to live on the tract ever since, which lies on the Homochitto River in Adams Co. // Littleton Sanders, for $200, to me paid, hereby sell to Hezekiah Ford all my preemption right to 514 acres on the Homochitto, beg. at James Owens' corner. (signed) Littleton Sanders and ack. Aug. 1806 before T.R. Wit: Parke Walton. // Agreement between Ford and Saunders, Aug. 20, 1806. Whereas Saunders has made over to Ford a tract of 514 acres, the said Ford agrees to deed back to Saunders 100 acres on the north end at $2.00 per acre, on time. Both signed and ack. before Thomas Rodney, Commissioner.

No. 834. Claimant, John Robinson, Jr., 21 Mch. 1804. Wit: Raymond Robinson. Certif. D-73, 29 Oct. 1806. Miss. Ter. Claiborne Co., John Robinson, Jr. claims preemption rights to 152 acres on waters of Big Black by virtue of having inhabited and cultivated the sd tract since Feb. 1803 at which time he was the head of a family, etc. // Said land surveyed by Daniel Burnet, and situated on a branch of Big Sandy Cr. in Claiborne Co., on the road leading from Natchez through the Wilderness.

No. 835. Claimant, Joseph Bullard, 21 Mch. 1804. Wit: Davenport Wiseman. Certif. D-74 issued 29 Oct. 1806. Joseph Bullard claims the right of becoming the purchaser of the United States of 200 acres in Claiborne Co., on the south side of Big Sandy Creek, a br. of Big Black, one-half mile above the place where the Wilderness Road crosses said Creek. Joseph Bullard was above the age of 21 years on 3rd Mch. 1803 and before and after that time was inhabiting and cultivating this land and is now the head of a family and continues to occupy the premises. Survey of tract by Daniel Burnet.

No. 877. Claimant, Henry Quine, 22 Mch. 1804. Wit: Benj. Rogers, Sr. Certif. D-189, issued 17 Dec. 1806. Henry Quine claims preemption right to 130 acres in Wilkinson Co., on waters of Buffalo Cr., by virtue of his having inhabited and cultivated the same 3 Mch. 1803, when he was the head of a family.

No. 878. Claimant, John Smith, 22 Mch. 1804. Wit: Thomas Vause. Certif. D-201 issued 13 Feb. 1807. John Smith claims 640 acres in Claiborne Co. on south fork of Bayou Pierre by right of occupancy. The sd tract was inhabited and cultivated in 1797 by sd John Smith, who at that time was the head of a family and he claims no other land in sd Territory. Survey by Ezekiel Evans, 10 Feb. 1804, shows William Brown's land adjoining.

No. 796. Claimant: Charles Trefore, Mar. 20, 1804. Witness: Robt. White, Dec. 19, 1806. Survey of 100 acres to include the improvements. Certificate D-298, Dec. 29, 1806. Miss. Ter., Jefferson Co., Charles Trefore claims the right of preference of becoming the purchaser of the United States of 320 acres in Jefferson County on the waters of Cole's Creek by virtue of his inhabiting and cultivating it in March 1803 and ever since.

No. 842. Claimant: George Sorrell, Mar. 21, 1804. Witness: Duncan Cameron. Certificate D-76, Oct. 29, 1806. Miss. Ter., Claiborne Co., George Sorrell, the head of a family in afsd county, claims the preference of becoming the purchaser of the United States of 204 acres of land in sd county on Little Sandy, a branch of Big Black. He claims his preference from his actual settlement and cultivation of said land on and before the 3rd of March 1803 and has continued on the premises ever since. Plat by Daniel Burnet shows William Cooper on one side, other side's vacant.

No. 843. Claimant: Raymond Robinson, Mar. 21, 1804. Wit: Joseph Bullard. Certificate D-77, Oct. 29, 1806. Miss. Ter., Claiborne Co., Raymond Robinson, a citizen of afsd county, claims the preference of becoming a purchaser of the United States of 350 acres in Claiborne County at the juncture of the Big Black and Big Sandy Creek, by virtue of a deed of conveyance given to him by William Dempsey who lived on and cultivated the premises on and before the 3rd March 1803 and Dempsey was at that time and is now the head of a family. And the said Robinson is above the age of twenty-one years. Plat by Daniel Burnet shows Duncan Cameron adj. on one side. // Deed from William Dempsey to Raymond Robinson. Duncan Cameron witness. (Note: Proved before the Board by subscribing witness,

Duncan Cameron, (signed) Robt. Claiborne, Clk.)

No. 844. Claimant: Duncan Cameron, Mar. 21, 1804. Witnesses: John Robinson, Jr. and Joseph Bullard. Certificate D-78, Oct. 29, 1806. Miss. Ter., Claiborne Co., Duncan Cameron, a citizen of the county aforesaid, and head of a family, claims the preference of becoming the purchaser of the United States of 365 acres in sd county on Big Sandy and Little Sandy Creeks, branches of Big Black River, about three miles from the Rocky Spring and one mile from Big Black, by virtue of an improvement and cultivating and inhabiting the premises, on and before the 3rd of March 1803 by Raymond Robinson and Jeptha Dempsey, who were both 21 years of age. Duncan Cameron derived his right by actual purchase from the aforesaid Dempsey and Robinson. Plat by Daniel Burnet.

No. 845. Claimant: Duncan Cameron, Mar. 21, 1804. Witness: Joseph Bullard. Certificate D-79, issued to Hezekiah Wright, assignee, Oct. 29, 1806. Miss. Ter., Claiborne Co., Duncan Cameron claims the right of preference to become the purchaser of the United States of 126 acres of land in sd county on the waters of the Big Black by virtue of his inhabiting and cultivating the same in January 1803 and ever since. The above tract was situated in Claiborne County at a place known as Rocky Springs, ten miles from the Grindstone Ford, and on the road leading from Natchez to Tennessee State, and is the place that the abovenamed Duncan Cameron now lives on. Survey dated Dec. 14 1803, and signed by Daniel Burnet.

No. 846. Claimant: Duncan Cameron, Mar. 21, 1804. Witness: Raymond Robinson. Certificate D-80, Oct. 29, 1806. Miss. Ter. Duncan Cameron claims the right of preference of becoming purchaser of the United States of 211 acres in Claiborne County on the waters of Big Black by virtue of it having been inhabited and cultivated by William Knight in February 1803 and he continued it until he sold it to sd Duncan. // The above described 211 acres is in Claiborne County on a small creek known as Little Sand, and on all sides vacant land. From survey signed by Daniel Burnet. // Miss. Territory, 3 Oct. 1803, Claiborne Co., this will certify that I, William Knight, have sold to D. Cameron an improvement made and cultivated by me on Little Sand Creek, also my preemption right on said place and all other rights. (signed) Wm. Wright. Wit: Joseph Bullard. Proved before the Board, R.C., Clk.

No. 847. Claimant: Mary Box, Mar. 21, 1804. Witness: Joseph Bullard. Certificate D-81, to the heirs of Joseph Box, Oct. 29, 1806. (Note: The claimant claims for herself and the heirs of Joseph Box, her deceased husband. (signed T.R.) Miss. Ter., Claiborne Co., Mary Box, widow, of the county afsd. for herself and the heirs of her late husband, Joseph Box, the preference in becoming the purchaser of the United States of 120 acres on Big Sandy, a branch of Big Black, and on the Wilderness Road, as represented by the annexed plat. Mary Box and Joseph Box, aforesaid, actually living and cultivating the above premises in January 1802 and ever since by Mary Box and her children. Plat by Daniel Burnet showing Davenport Wiseman on one side and the Wilderness Road going through the edge of it.

No. 848. Claimant: Gustavus Campbell, a claim of 200 acres, Mar. 21, 1804. Witness: Roger Dixon, 20 Nov. 1804. Certificate D-297, issued Dec. 29, 1806. (Note: The claimant wishes this claim to be reduced to 100 acres to avoid interfering with other claims.) Miss. Ter. Jefferson Co., Gustavus Campbell, a citizen of Miss. Ter. and the Co. of Jefferson, claims the right of preference in the purchase of 200 acres of land in sd. county on waters of Cole's Creek. The above named Gustavus Campbell did actually inhabit and cultivate the aforesaid tract prior to and on the 3rd March 1803, he being at that time above the age of 21 years, and the head of a family. Plat shows land adjoining owned by ______ Kelly and W. Murray, David [Davis?] and Ruth [Routh].

No. 849. Claimant: Heir of Samuel Lyon, decd., Mar. 21, 1804. Wit: Davenport Wiseman. Certificate D-82, issued to heirs of S. Lyon. Oct. 29, 1806. Miss. Ter., Claiborne Co., Peter Lyon, heir of Samuel Lyon, deceased, claims the right of becoming the purchaser of the United States of 200 acres in sd county on Big Sandy Creek, a watercourse of Black River, by virtue of the said tract of land having been inhabited and cultivated by the said Sam'l Lyon in his lifetime, namely on the 30th January 1803 and ever since that time, and by virtue of the Third Act of Congress, etc.

No. 850. Claimant: Thomas Cogan, March 21, 1804. Witness: B. Pitman, 20 Nov. 1804. Rejected May 12, 1807. Thomas Cogan claims 400 acres of land in consequence of having improved the same prior to the year 1795, and ever since has labored thereon to the present time. Evidence: Patrick Cogan. Survey and plat by William Atchinson shows that James Creek runs through the northern part of tract and that ______ Lynn sold adjoining land to Patrick Cogan.

No. 851. Claimant: Joseph Newman, Mar. 21, 1804. Rejected for want of evidence, Nov. 30, 1806.

Miss. Ter. Joseph Newman, of the city of Natchez, aforesaid Territory, claims the preference of becoming the purchaser of the U.S. of 640 acres on waters of Bayou Pierre, surveyed for claimant in August 1802. Claimant never inhabited the said tract of land but had some cane cleared off with the express purpose of settling upon it. Plat by Fenton and Morgan, surveyors.

No. 852. Claimant: John Callender, Mar. 21, 1804. Rejected for want of evidence, Dec. 30, 1806. Miss. Ter. John Callender, a citizen of Natchez, in the afsd. Territory, claims preference to purchase 102 perches of land lying in said city on the River Mississippi, by virtue of having inhabited and cultivated the same on and before the 3rd of March, 1803. In the plat William Rabb's land is on one side, and Daniel Barney on another.

No. 858. Claimant: Elijah Loyd, Mar. 21, 1804. Rejected for want of evidence, Dec. 30, 1806. Miss. Territory, County of Adams, Elijah Loyd claims 28 perches of land in right of preemption, by virtue of an actual settlement made thereon by the sd Elijah before 3 March 1803, the same being built on and occupied by and at this time in the possession of said Elijah, being situate in the City of Natchez, in the lower part of said city near the Mississippi River. The plat shows land adj. owned by John Walton and C. Forgatt.

No. 859. Claimant: Daniel Barney, Mar. 21, 1804. Rejected for want of evidence. Dec. 30, 1806. Miss. Ter., County of Adams, Daniel Barney claims 38 square perches of land in right of preemption, by virtue of an actual settlement made thereon by the said Daniel before the 3rd of March 1803, the same being built on and occupied at that time and now in the occupancy of him, being situate in the City of Natchez, in the lower part thereof near the Mississippi River. Plat shows John Callender on two sides and the river on another.

No. 860. Claimant: Thomas Donaldson, Mar. 21, 1804. Rejected for want of evidence, Dec. 30, 1806. Adams County, Miss. Ter. I do hereby certify that the annexed plat is a true representation of 320 acres situated on the waters of Dry Bayou, beginning on John Erwin's east line, which I have been in possession of and an actual settler thereon since the 14 day of January 1803. (signed) Thomas Donaldson.

No. 871. Claimant: Alexander Armstrong, Mar. 22, 1804. Witness: John Armstrong. Certificate D-206, issued 17 Dec. 1806. Feb. 28, 1804. Surveyed for Alexander Armstrong 100 acres of land in Claiborne County, Miss. Ter., on the waters of Bayou Pierre, including the houses and improvements where the said Alexander Armstrong now lives, to which land the said Alexander claims a preemption right, agreeable to an Act of Congress, having cultivated the same on and before the 3rd of March 1803. (signed) John Cook for Alexander Armstrong.

No. 872. Claimant: John Armstrong, March 22, 1804. Witness: Alexander Armstrong. Certificate D 207, issued 17 Dec. 1806. Miss. Ter., Claiborne County, John Armstrong claims the right of preference of becoming a purchaser of the United States of 100 acres of land in Claiborne Co. on the waters of Bayou Pierre, by right of occupancy, which tract of land has been inhabited and cultivated by the said John Armstrong ever since the year 1801 and he was the head of a family at the passing of the Act regulating the grants of land, etc. and he claims no other land therein. // Survey and plat by John Cook, showing the tract of 100 acres adj. the land of Tobias Brashears.

No. 873. Claimant: Benjamin Rogers, Jr., Mar. 22, 1804. Witness: Benjamin Rogers, Sr. Certificate D 185, Dec. 17, 1806. Benjamin Rogers, Jr., who on the 3rd March 1803 was above the age of 21 years, claims 84 acres in Wilkinson County, Miss. Territory, on the Dry Fork of Percy's Creek, a branch of Buffalo, joining the land of Thomas Foster on the south, which land he claims by virtue of the Third Section of the Act of Congress of 3rd March 1803, having actually inhabited and cultivated the said land not being claimed by virtue of any other section of said Act or by a British concession, or by agreement of the United States and the State of Georgia, and the Indian title having been extinguished. Benjamin (x) Rogers, Sr. for Benjamin Rogers, Jr.

No. 882. Claimant: John Crunkleton, Mar. 22, 1804. Witnesses: Patrick Cogan, Col. Zacheriah Kirkland, March 22, 1804. Joseph Dyson, Oct. 1, 1804. Rejected April 22, 1807. Miss. Ter., Jefferson Co. Personally appeared before me Mary Lewis and made oath that in the year 1779 that James Crunkleton, father of John Crunkleton, was then in actual possession of a certain tract on James Creek on the south side of Bayou Pierre. Said tract was granted to her husband, James Crunkleton, by the British Government the same year previous to the date mentioned above. The said Crunkleton cultivated and lived on the land three years then moved to the United States, from thence he returned with an intention to settle on said tract but immediately upon his arrival he died. In consequence of his death, the family was in such distress they were not able to settle said tract until John, the only surviving child, came of age. The deponent says that John Crunkleton is the only heir of his father, James, that she, the mother, declares that she has no other tract of land whatever and that the right lies in him, the said John. Mary (x) Lewis. Ack. Mch. 19, 1804 before Henry Green, J.P. Miss. Ter., Claiborne Co., John Crunkleton, the heir and representative of James Crunkleton, deceased, claims 640 acres in Claiborne County on the waters of Bayou Pierre, by virtue of a warrant of survey from the British Government of West Florida to the said James Crunkleton in his lifetime, which sd warrant is since lost, and by virtue of an actual settlement and cultivation of the same by the said James Crunkleton in his life, and on which said tract of land the said John Crunkleton now resides and cultivates. // Miss. Ter., Jefferson Co., before Zacheriah Kirkland, Esq., one of the Justices of Peace, personally came John Stabraker, Sr., and on oath said that to his certain knowledge James Crunkleton, deceased, was an actual settler on James Creek in the year 1779 or 1780 and to the best of his knowledge the same place the said John Crunkleton is now in possession of is the identical place on which the said James Crunkleton, deceased, did settle on the above date. Sworn to 21 March. (signed) John Stabraker.

No. 890. Claimant: George Matthews, Mar. 22, 1804. Witness: John Girault, 27 May 1805. Rejected May 16, 1806. (The Patent to Cory is filed in R. King's claim, No. 1249. This land has been adjudged to Richard King. See Certificate No. 716.) George Matthews claims 130 acres by purchase and deed of conveyance, dated Feb. 3, 1803, from Adam Cloud, who held it by an instrument of transfer on the letters patent of J. Cory and dated Jan. 24, 1794, which letters patent from the Spanish Government to the said Job Cory were dated June 8, 1792. Geo. Matthews by his atty. John Steel. // A letter enclosed addressed to Mr. John Bowles, St. Catherine's, Natchez, kindness of Mr. Walker. Dear Sir: Mr. Walker, the gentleman who hands you this, is from the State of Georgia. My particular acquaintance with his brother induced me to recommend him to your notice. Any favors shown him will be a favor to myself. I have been very unfortunate in my family since I came hither. In the three years I have lost three children, my two eldest and the youngest I had when I left Natchez. The country is very sickly. I have in contemplation to move to Natchez as soon as the time may appear settled. I intended to have set out next summer but the news of a French party at Natchez causes me to hesitate. I fear the settlement may be injured if the people should oppose the government of the United States. Our Executive is now determined upon defensive measures. The people are unanimous for the defense of government, one that is at sea and . . . . . .(not clear). . . . . . Take my advice: Let it be. Be true to the government that protects you. I have been anxious to hear from you and have not had a line from any person in Natchez since I came to the States nor ever received a six-pence of my property. I will thank you to send me the best account in your power how my business has been conducted and who you may have reason to think has it in possession. I expect Col. Forman's executors the person. If so try to find out what measures they have taken and by what authority, whether by an order of government or only by Col. Forman's executors. At the same time, keep the matter a secret. You can find out the affair without their knowing and give me an answer by Mr. Walker. Direct to Newport, Liberty County, Georgia. My respect to all your family and neighbors. Expect me as soon as the time will admit. Your humble servant. (signed) Adam Cloud. // Notation on outside of the above: The handwriting of Adam Cloud to the within letter proven by J. Bowles. May 27, 1805. (signed) T.R.

No. 891. Claimant: George Matthews, Mar. 22, 1804. Witness: John Girault, May 27, 1805. Rejected May 16, 1807. Miss. Ter. George Matthews claims a lot in the City of Natchez, No. ——, by deed of conveyance from Adam Cloud who held the same by concession from the Spanish Government and by occupancy and improving it and building on it between the years 1792 and 1795. George Matthews by John Steel, his attorney.

No. 893. Claimant John Anderton, Mar. 22, 1804. Witness: John Allison. Certificate B 78, issued Oct. 28, 1806. (See claim No. 1956 interference) Miss. Ter., Claiborne Co., John Anderson claims 640 acres in said county on Big Black River by right of occupancy, which tract of land has been inhabited and cultivated by the said John Anderton ever since the year 1794 and he was the head of a family when the Spanish troops evacuated this territory. (signed) John Anderton.

No. 894. Claimant: Ezekiel Henry, Mar. 22, 1804. Witness: John Anderton. Rejected for want of sufficient evidence, Dec. 30, 1806. Miss. Ter., Claiborne Co., Ezekiel Henry claims 640 acres in said county, by right of preemption, which tract the said Ezekiel Hanry has inhabited and cultivated ever since October 1801 and was the head of a family on the 3rd of March 1803.

No. 895. Claimants: Heirs of Stephen Cole, deceased, Mar. 22, 1804. Witness: John Allison. (Stephen Cole is a Spanish grantee. See No. 1380). Rejected May 16, 1807. // John Cole, guardian and friend of his nephews and nieces, John Cole, James Cole, William Cole, Sarah Cole, Jennie Cole and Mary Cole, orphans and heirs of Stephen Cole, deceased, claim 640 acres on the Big Black River in Claiborne County, originally improved, inhabited and actually cultivated in 1795 by him, the said Stephen, and continued to be so until the day of his death, which took place in 1798, and which tract of land has been ever since actually inhabited and cultivated under the direction and management of the said guardian for the sole use and benefit of the said orphans. John Cole for the within named heirs of Stephen Cole.

No. 896. Claimant: Thomas Shropshire, Mar. 22, 1804. Witness: William Hickman, 22 Oct. 1804. 100 acres to be surveyed. Certificate D 123, Dec. 15, 1806. Miss. Ter. Wilkinson Co., Thomas Shropshire claims 120 acres on Beaver Creek, by improvement made previous to the 3rd March 1803 by sd Shropshire. (The claimant requests that his claim be reduced to 100 acres agreeable to annexed plat for that quantity. Granted. Signed E.T.)

No. 897. Claimant: William Hickman, Mar. 22, 1804. Witness: Thomas Shropshire, 22 October 1804. Certificate D 124, issued Dec. 15, 1806. Miss. Ter. Wilkinson Co., William Hickman claims 150 acres on Second Creek, by improvement made previous and on the 3rd March 1803 by the said William Hickman. Plat.

No. 905. Claimant: John Gilbert, Mar. 22, 1804. "D 33" marked on jacket. Jany. 21, 1804. This is to certify that I, James Cole, of the county of Jefferson, Miss. Ter., have bargained and sold to John Gilbert, of Claiborne Co., aforesaid Territory, my right of occupancy in my improvement, it being on Daniel's Creek, a branch of Cole's, about a mile from Edmund Johnson and Company's Gin, for which improvement I have received in hand $150, it being for the value of my labor and work on said improvement, which I transfer to said Gilbert. James Cole. Wit: Thos. Leacy. Prov. before the Board, 15 Nov. 1804 by Thos. Leacy.

No. 906. Claimant: James Findley, Mar. 22, 1804. Rejected May 12, 1807. James Findley claims a tract of land in Miss. Ter., Jefferson Co., in consequence of having purchased the same from John Roberts, he having improved the premises in 1797. It is now in actual cultivation. // Plat shows all sides vacant land except one inhabited by Henry Green, and is on the waters of Cole's Creek, 10 miles from Huntston.

No. 924. Claimant: William Clare, Mar. 22, 1804. Witness: Henry Stampley, 3 Sept. 1805. Rejected April 15, 1807. William Clare claims 240 acres on the waters of Platner's Fork of Cole's Creek in Jefferson County, surveyed Feb. 20, 1795 in consequence of a warrant of survey from the Surveyor General's Office at New Orleans, and improved and cultivated ever since. Note: Mr. Thomas will please survey for Mr. William Clare 240 acres of land adjoining his father's plantation and covering his own improvement. Feb. 13, 1795. (signed) W. Dunbar.

No. 929. Claimant: Anthony Glass, Mar. 22, 1804. Rejected for want of evidence Dec. 30, 1806. Miss. Ter., Claiborne Co., Anthony Glass, a citizen of the sd Territory for many years and the head of a family, claims the preference of becoming the purchaser of the United States of 640 acres in the aforesaid county on the Mississippi River Swamp above the mouth of the Big Black River about 12 miles, and on the Middle Bayou, by virtue of its having been inhabited and cultivated by one William Hutcheson who was above the age of 21 years on the 3rd March 1803 and claims no other land in said Territory and for his use ever since March 1801, who conveyed the said tract of land to the said Anthony Glass by deed, dated 6 January 1804. // Plat shows King's land and Mr. Wm. Lewis.

No. 930. Claimant: Gibson Clarke, Jr., Mar. 22, 1804. Relinquished Nov. 20, 1804. (Note: The claimant appeared before the Board and relinquished the claim in favor of David Burney who claims the said land. Washington. Nov. 19, 1804.) Miss. Ter., Claiborne Co., Gibson Clarke claims 640 acres in said county on south fork of Bayou Pierre, by virtue of said tract having been inhabited and cultivated by one Davenport Wiseman on and before the last day of March 1798 who was then the head of a family of wife and one child, who sold the same to Samuel Mason who conveyed it to the said Gibson Clark on 7th Nov. 1800.

No. 932. Claimant: Gibson Clark, Mar. 22, 1804. Witness: Gibson Clark, 28 Nov. 1804. Rejected for want of sufficient evidence, Dec. 30, 1806. Miss. Ter., Claiborne Co., Gibson Clarke, Jr. claims the preference to become the purchaser of the United States of 350 acres in sd county on the waters of

Bayou Pierre, by virtue of its having been inhabited and cultivated on and before the 3rd March 1803 for the use of the said Gibson Clarke, Jr., by John Joiner. Survey and plat by Ezekiel Evans dated 6 March 1804, shows the land on Coursey's Fork of Bayou Pierre.

No. 934. Claimant: John Hopper, Mar. 22, 1804. Witness: Stephen Compton, 12 Nov. 1804. Rejected for want of sufficient evidence, Dec. 30, 1806. Miss. Ter. John Hopper claims the right of becoming the purchaser of the United States of a tract of land 100 acres in Claiborne Co. on the waters of Dowd's Creek, by virtue of his settling and improving it on and before 11 March 1803 and remaining on it ever since.

No. 948. Claimant: Thomas Viles, Mar. 22, 1804. Rejected May 1806. To the Commissioners of Land Grants, Gentlemen: The claim that I have to the land that I am now living on is that in the year 1799 Thomas Daniels settled it and lived on it two years and then I bought his improvement and have occupied it ever since. (signed) Thomas Viles.

No. 949. Claimant: William Miller, Mar. 22, 1804. Rejected 12 May 1807. William Miller, a citizen of Miss. Ter., county of Claiborne, claims 640 acres in said county on the waters of Bayou Pierre, who did actually inhabit and cultivate the aforesaid tract prior to and on the day the Mississippi Territory was finally evacuated by the Spanish troops, he being at that time above the age of 21 years and the head of a family.

No. 950. Claimant: Sarah Cleveland, Mar. 22, 1804. Donation claim for 640 acres. Rejected May 12, 1807. Sarah Cleveland, a resident of the Miss. Ter. and Co. of Claiborne, claims 640 acres in said county on the waters of Bayou Pierre. Susannah Cleveland, or some person to her use, did actually inhabit and cultivate the aforesaid land prior to and when the Miss. Territory was evacuated by the Spanish troops, she being at that time above the age of 21 years and the head of a family.

No. 952. Claimant: Thomas M. Green, Mar. 22, 1804. (Note: See Nos. 1919, 1920, 1921, 1922 and 1923.) Thomas M. Green, a citizen of the Miss. Ter., County of Jefferson, claims 1222 acres in said county on the waters of Cole's Creek. The above claim is founded on respective titles following, to wit: 250 acres, a part of the aforesaid tract, was originally granted by a warrant of survey by the British Government of West Florida to a certain Roberts long since deceased who took possession and occupied the same and from the said Roberts the possession and occupancy of the aforesaid tract was transferred to James Cole, which said James Cole transferred the same to Richard Bacon by writing, 6 March 1784, which said Richard Bacon conveyed the same, 23 Jan. 1786 to James Elliot, the said James Elliot, by Daniel Clark, his attorney in fact, transferred the same to the said Thomas Green, by deed dated 4 Oct. 1799. The aforesaid 250 acres of land has been actually inhabited and cultivated since the original order of survey, which was about 30 years past. Unknown to the present claimant the said warrant has been lost; 600 acres, another portion of the aforesaid 1222 acres, was conveyed to same James Elliot by Peter Hawkins by deed May 3, 1788 which said Hawkins claimed the same in the following manner: 200 acres sold to sd Hawkins by Henry Roach which said Roach had previously obtained by order of survey of the Spanish Government of West Florida, which survey has been casually lost or destroyed, and 400 acres was originally granted to a certain Joseph Dawes by the British Government of West Florida, who who has long since departed this life and the grant lost and destroyed but Dawes, previous to his death transferred the sd 400 acres to Peter Hawkins and the said Peter Hawkins by deed conveyed the same to James Elliot; also 200 acres, a part of the 1222 acres, which was originally granted to Ebenezer Gossett by the British Government of West Florida which grant cannot be procured, and sold by him to Peter Hawkins and by the said Hawkins conveyed to John Girault by deed, dated 3 May 1788, and the said John Girault conveyed the same to James Eliott 5 Jan. 1789, which several tracts of land, making the quantity of 800 acres was conveyed by Daniel Clark, attorney in fact for the said James Elliot, to the said Thomas M. Green, by deed Oct. 4, 1799; and also 122 acres conveyed by Jeremiah Bryan to James Elliot, 10th Jan. 1785, which said Bryan became entitled to the same as set forth in a deed, which the said James Elliot, by Daniel Clark, his attorney in fact, conveyed to sd Thomas M. Green, as above; which several parcels of land making the whole one entire tract of 1222 acres which have been actually inhabited and cultivated by the persons hereinbefore mentioned for above the space of 30 years and in the actual possession of the said Thomas M. Green since the year 1799 until the present time. By plat the land adjoins Samuel Osborn, Adam Bingaman, James Elliot, ______ Ferguson, John Lum, James Cole and Cole's Creek.

No. 957. Claimant: Rebecca McCabe, Mar. 22, 1804. Rejected for want of evidence, Dec. 30, 1806. Miss. Ter. Claiborne Co. Rebecca McCabe claims 200 acres in said county on the south fork of Bayou

Pierre, by virtue of her having inhabited and cultivated the same by another person for her use on and before 3 March 1803. (signed) Stephen B. Minor for Rebecca McCabe. The plat by Fenton and Morgan, dated March 2, 1803, shows the tract bounded on two sides by William Brocus, on one side vacant, and on the other by the South Fork of Bayou Pierre, with the road to Natchez crossing it.

No. 958. Claimant: Ann Brashier, Mar. 22, 1804. Witness: William Thomas, 29 Oct. 1804, and Major Estevan Minor, 5 Nov. 1804. Rejected May 12, 1807. Miss. Ter. Claiborne Co. Ann Brashier claims 300 arpents of land in said county on Bayou Pierre, by virtue of an order of survey from the Spanish Government to her, dated 1788, at which time she was the head of a family and above 21 years of age, and inhabited and cultivated the said land on 27 Oct. 1795. Stephen B. Minor for Ann Brashiers. Plat and certificate of survey of 300 acres laid out for Madame Ann Brashiers by William Vousdan, dep. surv. 29 Sept. 1788. // Marked on back of plat and survey; "Lyman Mandamus". // Another paper: 18 April 1789, "Benjamin Foy 320 arpents at Bayou Pierre, bounded northwardly by Madame Brashier and John Burnet". The foregoing is true translation of an entry made in a book wherein the Spanish Commandant entered the warrants of survey that was sent up to their care from the Superior Government at New Orleans. Certified under my hand and seal as Keeper of the Spanish Records at Natchez, the 27 of October, 1804. (signed) John Girault, with seal.

No. 965. Claimant: Isaac Johnson, Mar. 22, 1804. Witness: Robert Miller, 2 Jany. 1805. Rejected. The within tract of 300 acres is claimed by Isaac Johnson by virtue of an order of survey from the British Government to Jemima Morgan and conveyed from the said Jemima Morgan by Anthony Hutchins, her attorney, to Isaac Johnson for the same. (signed) A. Hutchins, Atty. for Isaac Johnson. // Plat, 350 acres claimed by Isaac Johnson on Holt's Fork of Boyd Creek, 20 April 1779, then surveyed for Jemima Morgan, about 20 miles northeast from Natchez, bounded on south by northern line of land surveyed for Benjamin Hickey and George Alexander; east by west line of sd Alexander and a branch of Holt's Fork of Boyd's Cr.; northwest by William Williams' and Jacob Winfree's southeast lines. "I certify the above plat to be a true duplicate of the original in my hand and agreeable to the plat which I returned to the office of the Honorable Elias Durnford, Esq., Surveyor General of West Florida, in virtue of a precept from him to me directed. Given at the Opelousas, 28 Jan. 1801." (signed) Luke Collins, Jr.

No. 966. Claimant: Evan Jones, Mar. 22, 1804. Order to be surveyed by Lyman Harding, 5 March 1806. Rejected June 11, 1807. The Commissioners of Land Claims in Mississippi Territory will be pleased to take notice that the western moiety or half part of the 1000 acres of land is claimed by Evans Jones, of the City of New Orleans, survivor of Evans and James Jones, under and by virtue of a grant to Thomas Gamble, made 13 June 1774, and indentures of lease and release from the sd Thomas Gamble to claimant and his brother, James Jones, who he had survived, dated 7 Dec. 1774, which conveyances are lodged with the Register of Lands to be recorded agreeable to law, and to which he begs leave to refer. A. Hutchins, atty. for Evans Jones. // Copy of plat of 1000 acres of land on the Homochitto, granted to Thomas Gamble by letters patent under the seal of West Florida, 13 June 1774. (This shows vacant lands south of the above tract and Amos Ogden's Mandamus eastern boundary, a 25,000 acre tract, adjoining and 500 acres sold to Messrs. Jones and now claimed by Evan and Edward Jones, survivors of Evans, James and Edward Jones.)

No. 971. Claimant: Love Baker, Mar. 22, 1804. (See No. 1044) Rejected June 11, 1807. Miss. Ter. Love Baker claims as legal representative of Melling Woolley 400 acres in Claiborne County, adjoining Peter Bryan Bruin, Esq. and fronting on the Mississippi, which land was granted to sd. Melling Woolley by Baron Carondelet on 24 July 1796 and by the said Melling Woolley to the said Baker on 12 Jany. 1803, the patent and other papers being lost or mislaid.

No. 972. Claimant: John Holt, Mar. 22, 1804. Rejected June 11, 1807. John Holt, legal representative of Joseph Sharp, who claimed under a Spanish order of survey in 1795, 640 acres in Jefferson County on the waters of Cole's Creek, which said Sharp at the time of said warrant issuing was head of a family and above the age of 21 years, and immediately settled and improved the said land. (Signed) John Holt.

No. 1002. Claimant: Samuel Phipps, Mar. 23, 1804. Witness: Col. Nehemiah Carter. Certificate B 242, issued Mar. 30, 1807. Samuel Phipps, a citizen of Miss. Ter., county of Adams, claims 370 acres in sd county, on the waters of Second Creek, founded on a warrant or order of survey granted to claimant by the Spanish Government the 24 Sept. 1793 by virtue of which he took possession of sd tract and continued to occupy, cultivate and improve same from the date of said warrant to the present time, during which time the said claimant had been the head of a family, having a wife with .... (torn) .. children. Plat shows Jesse Carter, Col. Hutchins and Christy Gilbert with lands adjoining. // Mr. Phipps requests the Board not to issue a certificate to Mr. Davidson. (signed) Thos. H. Williams. // Know all men by these presents that I, Samuel Phipps, of Adams Co., Miss. Ter., being entitled to a Donation of 640 acres, if so much may be found vacant, for $500 to me in hand paid, I do convey title and tract to Thomas I. Davidson, be it understood that the above-named Davidson is to deliver to said Phipps one likely negro boy 14 years of age, healthy and sensible, on demand and pay in the Land Offices all expenses of the tract. 23 Nov. 1804. Witness: Israel Smith.

No. 1003. Claimant: William B. Elam's Donation Claim, 640 acres, Mar. 23, 1804. Witness: William Stevens, 1 Oct. 1804. Certificate D 88, issued Oct. 29, 1806. Miss. Ter. Claiborne Co. William B. Elam, a citizen of Claiborne County, claims 640 acres in sd county on the waters of the Big Black River, the aforesaid tract having been actually inhabited and cultivated for Jesse Stevens by some person to his use prior to and on the day the Mississippi Territory was finally evacuated by the Spanish troops, he being at that time the head of a family and above the age of 21 years, which said Jesse Stevens transferred his right in the aforesaid tract to Ezra McCall by deed 2 Sept. 1803 and the same was transferred by assignment from the said Ezra McCall to the present claimant on 15 March 1804. Note: The claimant being advised that he cannot obtain a Donation desires to order his claim to a preemption and to take but 200 acres of the land described in his plat, including his improvement. (signed) T.R. // Jesse Stevens, of the county of Claiborne, Miss. Ter., for and in consideration of $200 in hand paid, sold to Ezra McCall all my right, etc. in said tract on the Big Black Bayou two miles above the Block House and southwest of the said Bayou on Ragdail's Creek, which improvement was made in 1797 by John Calhoun and legally conveyed by him to me, the said Stevens, all of which I legally transferred to said Ezra McCall. 2 Sept. 1803. Witness: R. Ashley, John Saxon. (signed) Jesse Stevens.

No. 1004. Claimant: Micajah Frazier, Mar. 23, 1804. Witness: William Brown. Certificate D-258, issued Dec. 24, 1806. Miss. Ter., Wilkinson Co. Micajah Frazier claims preemption right to 640 acres in said county on the headwaters of Bayou Sara, by virtue of said tract having been inhabited and cultivated January 1802 by said Micajah Frazier and ever since that time. // Plat and certificate of survey by William Brown: I have laid off the above tract for Micajah Frazier on the headwaters of Bayou Sara known as Big Beaver Creek and Ford's Creek, bounded by Rawling's survey and part of Robert Moore's 1000 acre tract and by Brown's survey. March 20, 1804.

No. 1005. Claimant: William Bovard, Mar. 23, 1804. Witness: Micajah Frazier. Certificate D-248, issued Dec. 22, 1806. Miss. Ter. Wilkinson Co. William Bovard claims the preemption right to 170 acres in said county on the headwaters of Bayou Sara, by virtue of said tract having been inhabited and cultivated by said Wm. Bovard in April 1802 and ever since.

No. 1006. Claimant: William Walker, Mar. 23, 1804. Wit: Micajah Frazer. Certificate D-259, issued Dec. 24 1806. Miss. Ter. Wilkinson County. William Walker claims the preemption right to 640 acres in sd county on Bayou Sara, by virtue of said tract having been inhabited and cultivated January 1802 by sd Wm. Walker and ever since.

No. 1007. Claimant: Zach. Walker, Mar. 23, 1804. Wit: William Brown. Certificate D-247 issued Dec. 22, 1806. Miss. Ter. Wilkinson Co. Zacheriah Walker, assignee of David Lewis, claims the preference to become the purchaser of the United States of 200 acres in said county on Bayou Sara, by virtue of same having been inhabited and cultivated in December 1802 by said David Lewis and ever since that time. // Transfer of Lewis to Walker: David Lewis has bargained and sold his right and title of preemption to Zacheriah Walker for $100 in hand paid, the land lying on Bayou Sara, joining lands with Ousbon, Leatherman and others, settled 5 October 1802. 21 Mar. 1804. (signed) David Lewis. Wit: Wm. Brown.

No. 1011. Claimant: William Fairbanks, Mar. 23, 1804. Rejected May 12, 1807. William Fairbanks claims 300 acres in said county on Cole's Creek, which tract he did actually inhabit and cultivate in 1786 and has continued to do so or some person to his use until the present day. Plat showing land adjoining Cato West and vacant lands.

No. 1013. Claimant: John Wall, Mar. 23, 1804. Wit: John Collins, July 10, 1805. Certificate A-594, issued Sept. 16, 1805. (See No. 1009.) John Wall, a resident of Miss. Ter. on the 27 Oct. 1795, claims 200 acres in Wilkinson County on waters of Buffalo Creek, by virtue of a deed of conveyance from Henry Roach to claimant, 8 Aug. 1803, being a part of 400 acres originally granted to David Lejeune by the

Spanish Government in 1789 and conveyed by said David Lejeune to Robert Collins and by said Robert Collins to Henry Roach and by said Henry Roach to claimant aforesaid. Plat shows land adjoining owned by Daniel Douglass, Henry Roach, and Swamp of Buffalo Creek.

No. 1019. Claimant: John Wall, Mar. 23, 1804. Wit: John Collins, July 10, 1805. Certificate A-593 issued to claimant Sept. 16, 1805. (See No. 969.) John Wall, a res. of Miss. Ter. on 25 Oct. 1795, claims 440 acres by deed from John Lovelace, dated 6 Dec. 1798, being a part of 800 acres granted to said John Lovelace by Spanish Government in 1788.

No. 1020. Claimant: Elizabeth Swayze, Mar. 23, 1804. Witness: Richard King. Certificate B-204, issued Feb. 19, 1807. Elizabeth Swayze, who has been an inhabitant of Miss. Territory for more than 20 years, claims 102 acres in Adams County, on St. Catherine's Creek, by virtue of having inhabited and cultivated in the year 1775 and ever since and she claims no other land, by either British or Spanish titles in said Territory. The said land was inhabited at the time the Spanish troops finally evacuated the country. Elizabeth (X) Swayze. // Paper: I certify that Samuel Swayze claimed of the Spanish Government a warrant of survey of 100 arpents of land in or before 1793. This land was surveyed and returned on 21 August 1793. Not a warrant or plat which accompanied it still remain in my possession. 25 Sept. 1804. (signed) William Dunbar at Second Creek. The original certificate of survey and plat by William Dunbar shows Luis Valeret, Joseph Duncan and John Girault as having lands adjoining.

No. 1021. Claimant: John Burnet, Mar. 23, 1804. July 18, 1805 relinquished by the claimant. Note: The claimant, John Burnet, being before the Board, says that having sold the land before the year 1798 to Judge Bruin, he now relinquishes all claim to it. July 18, 1805. Witness: T.R. (signed) John Burnet. Miss. Ter. Claiborne County. John Burnet of the county aforesaid claims 500 acres in sd county on James Creek, a branch of Bayou Pierre, and known by the name of Thomas James' Mound Place, by virtue of a certificate of a public sale thereof by the Spanish Government to the said Burnet, dated 2 Nov. 1784 and signed by Carlos De GrandPre, and by virtue of a settlement thereon soon after the date of said writing, the said Burnet at that time was the head of a family and was in this country in October 1795. (signed) John Burnet. // Translation of the sale of the above land by De GrandPre, representing the Spanish Government, to John Burnet. Don Charles De GrandPre, Lieutenant Colonel Graduated and Captain of the Grenadiers in the Stationary Regiment of this place, I certify that Mr. John Burnet, resident of the District of Natchez, is in possession of a plantation of 500 acres of land on Bayou Pierre, the same which was the property of the fugitive, Thomas James, which was confiscated and sold at public auction where it was purchased by the said John Burnet, who is proprietor of the said estate, which I do certify, I having been the Judge of the said proceedings, being at that time Political and Military Commandant in this District and that the same may appear, I give the present in New Orleans. 2 Nov. 1784. (signed) Charles De GrandPre. A faithful translation by John Girault, Translator.

No. 1022. Claimant: Walter and Ben Rawlins, Mar. 23, 1804. Witness: William Brown. Certificate D-248, issued Dec. 22, 1806, to Ben Rawlins and I. D. Wiles, assignee of Walter Rawlins. Miss. Ter. Wilkinson Co. Walter and Benjamin Rawlins, sons of Benjamin Rawlins, deceased, claim a preference to become the purchasers of the United States of 200 acres in said county on the headwaters of Bayou Sara, by virtue of the said tract having been cultivated and inhabited by said Benjamin Rawlins in April 1801 and by him and his children ever since. The certificate of survey shows the land adjoined that of Robt. Moore, and Micajah Frazier, also William Bovard, Mar. 6, 1804, Wm. Brown, Surveyor.

No. 1023. Claimant: James Collingsworth and Co., Mar. 23, 1804. Witness: Micajah Frazier. Certificate D-206 issued Dec. 24, 1806. Miss. Ter. Wilkinson Co. James Collinsworth, William and George Brown claim the preference to become the purchasers of the United States of 1600 acres in said county on the headwaters of Bayou Sara, by virtue of the said tract having been inhabited and cultivated February 1803 by the said J. Collinsworth, William and George Brown and ever since. (signed) Wm. Brown for the others. // George Brown, of the County of Wilkinson, Miss. Ter., for $500 to me in hand paid, have sole, etc. to William Brown all my claim and title, an undivided one-third part of a preemption claim containing 1600 acres surveyed and registered in the names of James Collinworth, William and George Brown, in Wilkinson Co. Mar. 5, 1800. Wit: Micajah Frazier, Alexander Jordan. (signed) George Brown.

No. 1024. Claimant: Daniel Hughes, Mar. 23, 1804. Reported, June 11, 1807. Miss. Ter. Daniel Hughes, now in the Territory, agent for the legal representatives of Col. William Johnston, of the Kingdom of Great Britain, deceased, and formerly a Captain of the Royal British Artillery in His British Majesty's Province of West Florida, claims 500 acres of land on Second Creek. The above claim is founded on a patent, dated 13 Sept. 1775, to James Barbut for 1000 acres, and on 15 April 1775, the said patent then being in expectancy, conveyed to the aforesaid Colonel, then Captain, William Johnston, Alexander McCullagh and Elihu Hall Bay. . . . (paper torn here) . . . . . . And in deed partition between . . . . dated the 2nd Oct. 1775, the benefits of the said 500 acres were assigned to William Johnston. Wm. B. Shields, atty.

No. 1025. Claimant: Francis Nailor, Mar. 23, 1804. Witness: Buckner Pittman, 20 Nov. 1806. Rejected 12 May 1807. Francis Nailor, of the county of Claiborne, claims a Donation from the United States of 640 acres in sd county on the west fork of James Creek, a branch of Bayou Pierre, by virtue of his settlement and cultivating the above premises in 1794 and by permission of the then Governor Gayoso to commence a settlement of the premises, 19, Oct. 1794. Francis Nailor was, on Oct. 27, 1795, an inhabitant of this county and at that time 21 years of age. // Natchez 29 Oct. 1794. Permission is granted to Francis Nailor to construct a mill and other buildings upon the land he has now petitioned for. (signed) Gayoso.

No. 1026. Claimant: John Kneelan, Mar. 23, 1804. Witness: John Berry. Certificate D-126 issued Dec. 15, 1806. Certificate of survey and plat. Surveyed for John Kneelan in Wilkinson County on the waters of the Amite River. 31 Jan. 1804. (signed) Robin Griffin.

No. 1027. Claimant: Robert Farlow, Mar. 23, 1804. Witness: John Berry. Certificate D-127, Dec. 15, 1806. Miss. Ter. Wilkinson Co. Robert Ferlow claims a preemption of 100 acres on the waters of the River Amite, he having improved and cultivated the same prior to and on 3rd March 1803. // For value received I have sold unto Matthew Tool all my right to 100 acres with all my improvements belonging thereto, the said land lying on Kneeland's Creek, bounded on the south by John Kneeland, which I warrant and defend. 3 Oct. 1805. (signed) R. Ferlow. Wit: Thomas Batchelor.

No. 1032. Claimant: John Wray, 23 Mar. 1804. Entered Sept. 11, 1805. Certificate A-579 issued to claimant 11 Sept. 1805. Miss. Ter. John Wray, a citizen of said territory, claims 37 acres in Adams County on Fairchild's Creek, by virtue of a Spanish patent to Martin Owen for 350 acres, of which he conveyed 37 acres by deed, 16 Dec. 1801 to the present claimant. // Deed of conveyance fr. Martin Owen to John Wray. Original Indenture. 15 Sept. 1801, Martin Owens, of the township of Fairchild's Creek, County of Pickering, Miss. Ter., to John Wray, of same, for and in consideration of $130 to him in hand paid, Martin Owen tranfers and sells to the said John Wray 37 acres in sd township being a part of that tract on which the said Martin Owen now lives, bounded by Willis Bonner, John Wray. (signed) Martin Owens, Mary Owens. Wit: James Bonner, Manuel Madden, Gavin C . . . . . age.

No. 1033. Claimant: Charles Mulholland, 23 Mar. 1804. Witness: John Pipes, 15 Jan. 1805. Certificate A-578, issued Sept. 11, 1805. Charles Mulholland, a citizen of Miss. Ter., claims 150 acres, part of a tract of 350 acres granted to Martin Owen by the Spanish Government, 20 June 1795, and by deed, July 1802, conveyed to said Mulholland, the said 150 acres, lying and being in Jefferson County on the waters of Fairchild's Cr. Plat shows land adj. owned by Melling Wooley and J. McIntyre. // July 1802, Martin Owen, of Jefferson Co. to Charles Mulholland, of same, for $300 to him in hand paid, 150 acres on the waters of Fairchild's Cr. in sd county, being a part of 350 acres gr. to said Martin Owen by the Baron De Carondelet in 1795. Wit: Willis (X) Bonner. (signed) Martin Owens, Mary Owens. Ack. before Jesse Withers, J.P., Jefferson Co.

No. 1034. Claimant: William Mackey, 23 Mar. 1804. Wit: Levi Fletcher, 12 Nov. 1804. Certificate D-70 issued Sept. 26, 1806. William Mackey claims 640 acres in Jefferson County on the Mississippi River, about 30 miles above Natchez, by residence and occupancy made thereon by the said Mackey in and prior to 3rd March 1803. Plat shows tract adj. land grant to Douglass.

No. 1030. Claimant: Daniel Burnet, Mar. 23, 1804. Wit: Elizabeth Cloyd, 23 April 1805, and John Burnet, 21 July 1805, also Patrick Gunnel, 12 July 1806. Rejected May 12, 1805 [?]. See Nos. 1568 and 679. // W. H. Wooldridge claims by the above donation, May 25, 1804. (signed) T.S. // Daniel Burnet, a citizen of Claiborne County, Miss. Ter., claims a Donation from the United States of 500 acres in said county on the north side of Grindstone Ford, on the Wilderness Road, which said land the said Burnet had surveyed by a surveyor from the state of Georgia in 1787 under the Bourbon Act, and in the year 1797 Patrick Forbes settled on the premises and the said Burnet bought all his settlement by a sale, dated 23 Jan. 1799. Patrick Forbes was the head of a family.

No. 1038. Claimant: John J. Walton, 23 Mar. 1804. Certificate A-76 issued to claimant Jan. 15, 1806. (See Girault's Claim.) Miss. Ter., City of Natchez. John J. Walton claims a lot of ground in the City of Natchez, by virtue of a grant by the Spanish Government to Catherine Caudle, who on 18 July 1801 together with her husband, Francis Caudle, by their attorney, Manuel Lopez, conveyed the said lot to the said John J. Walton. // Miss. Ter. City of Natchez. John J. Walton claims a lot in the City of Natchez containing 26250 superficial feet, by grant by Spanish Government to William Barland prior to 27 Oct. 1795, for 105 arpents. Said Barland on 27 Sept. 1788 sold 11 acres thereof to John Girault out of which the said John Girault sold to Simon de Arze all within his lines and said Simon did afterwards sell the same to Catherine Caudle who by her attorney, Manuel Lopez, did convey the said lot to the present claimant. The said Catherine was a resident of this territory on 27 Oct. 1795.

No. 1039. Claimant: John J. Walton, 23 Mar. 1804. Witness: J. Girault, 29th Oct. 1804. Certificate D-3 issued June 2, 1806. Miss. Ter., City of Natchez. John J. Walton gives notice that he claims a lot of ground under the hill at the Natchez landing, by virtue of a grant from Spain to Charles Ureco Maltez, dated 1793, a conveyance thereof from him to Telso Del Mexo, dated 10 May 1798, and a transfer from Domingo Lorero to Joseph Tegles, 29 April 1799, and a transfer from him to Andrew Carragill, dated 29 April 1799, a conveyance thereof by Edward and Sarah Durgin, formerly Sarah Carragill, to John Courtney, dated 2 March 1801, and from said Courtney to present claimant, 14 May 1801. // Original indenture: 14 May 1801, John Courtney, of the State of Pennsylvania, County of Westmoreland, to John Walton, Miss. Ter., County of Adams, for and in consideration of $150 in hand well paid, to John Walton, a certain lot of ground at the foot of the Natchez hill, formerly occupied by Andrew Carragill and afterward by Edward Durgin and now the said John Courtney, with dwelling house and everything pertaining thereto, adjoining to John, a Frenchman, and down the square from public buildings. (signed) John Courtney. Wit: Jacob Oliver, Caleb Burns. Indenture (in Spanish) from Carlos Uresco Maltez a grant by Don Manuel Gayoso de Lemos, for 70 pesos, a lot at the landing to Terso del Mexo. 10 May 1798. Wit: John Girault, Lewis Shelton and Isaac Foster.

No. 1046. Claimant: Christopher Miller, 23 Mar. 1804. See J. Moore's claim. Certificate A-519, issued to claimant Aug. 27, 1805. Christopher Miller claims a part of Lot No. 1, Square No. 2 in the City of Natchez, by virtue of conveyance from James Moore and Maria, his wife, dated 23 Nov. 1803, east of Thomas Hardesty's line, on the First North Street. (signed) Christopher Miller.

No. 1047. Claimant: Christopher Miller, 23 Mar. 1804. Certificate A-642, issued Sept. 27, 1805. See Douglass' claim, No. 1761. Christopher Miller claims a part of Lot No. 2, Square No. 11 in the City of Natchez, 150 feet fronting the River and 98 feet on the side back toward the Church, by virtue of a grant from the Spanish Government to Daniel Douglass, dated 3rd March 1795, and which part of lot was afterwards conveyed by the said Daniel Douglass, by deed 16 Aug. 1794, to David Ferguson and by the said David Ferguson and Jane, his wife, by deed 20 Dec. 1801, conveyed to the said Christopher Miller, together with dwelling, outhouse, kitchen, stable, improvements, etc. (signed) Christopher Miller.

No. 1048. Claimant: B. Farar and wife, 23 Mar. 1804. Witness: William Glasscock, March 15, 1805. Certificate A-289 issued to B. Farar, in right of his wife, June 7, 1805. Benjamin Farar and Mary, his wife, who were settlers in the Mississippi Territory on the 27th day of Oct. 1795, claim a tract of 600 acres in Wilkinson County, on Buffalo Creek, joining lands granted to William Cocke Ellis, which land is claimed in right of the said Mary by virtue of a grant thereof by the Spanish Government to her the 16 Feb. 1789. (signed) Benjamin Farar.

No. 1049. Claimant: Heirs of David Kennedy, deceased, 23 Mar. 1804. Witness: James Bonner, Aug. 19, 1805. Certificate B-239, issued Mar. 30, 1807. Miss. Ter., Adams Co. Jesse Withers, for the heirs of David Kennedy, claims 500 arpents of land in said county on the Mississippi River, by virtue of an order of survey from the Spanish Government to Benjamin Montsanto and surveyed for him by the Spanish Surveyor in 1788 and of a conveyance of said land by said Montsanto to David Kennedy, now deceased. The said land has been inhabited and cultivated by the above claimants ever since the year 1795. Jesse Withers for Addison, Sarah and David M. Kennedy, heirs of David Kennedy, decd. // I certify that a conveyance from Benjamin Monsanto to David Kennedy, dated 23 Oct. 1793, for a plantation in the swamp, about 6 miles from the Fort, and also a conveyance, dated 12 Feb. 1795, from John Scoggins to David Kennedy for a tract in the swamp aforesaid, containing 4 arpens in front by 40 arpens in depth, bounded by the lands of said Kennedy and Gibson Clarke, both of which conveyances are legally executed according to the laws of Spain and filed in my office, 16 Feb. 1804. (signed) J. Girault, with seal. Keeper of Records.

No. 1050. Claimant: Heirs of David Kennedy, 23 Mar. 1804. Witness: Robert Turner, 25 Mar. 1805.

Certificate A-501 issued to legal representatives, Aug. 19, 1805. Miss. Ter. Adams Co. Addison, Sarah and David Kennedy, heirs of David Kennedy, deceased, claim 160 arpents of land in said county, on the Mississippi River, by virtue of a patent by the Spanish Government to Jonas Scoggins for 695 arpens, of which the above 160 arpens is a part, who conveyed the said 160 arpens to the said Kennedy in his lifetime, on 12 Feb. 1795. (signed) Jesse Withers. Plat shows bounded on the north by Gibson Clarke; on the south side by Jacob Monsanto.

No. 1051. Claimant: John B. Walback, 23 Mar. 1804. Witness: Davenport Wiseman, June 12, 1804. Certificate D-337. John B. Walback, who is the legal representative of Joseph White, claims 214 acres in Claiborne County on the Main Fork of Bayou Pierre, bounded on the west by Captain Sparks, by virtue of the Third Section of the Act of Congress of the United States, 3 March 1803, etc., the same tract of land having been actually inhabited and cultivated by the said Joseph White who was then above the age of 21 and not being claimed by either of the three sections of the said Act or any British grant, etc. (signed) S. Lewis, agent for the claimant. // Conveyance of land purchased of Joseph White, Bayou Pierre, by Lieut. Walback. I, Joseph White, of Claiborne County, Miss. Ter., in consideration of $375, in hand paid, have this day bargained and sold to John B. Walback, serving in the Army of the United States, as Aide to Gen. James Wilkerson, all right etc. in my improvements and preemption right to 642 acres in Claiborne County on Bayou Pierre near a place in the Creek called Grindstone Ford and which improvement and right thereto lies between the land claimed by Elizabeth Bryan and now occupied by the said Elizabeth and the land of Col. Daniel Burnet, and the land of Capt. Richard Sparks and the North Fork of Bayou Pierre. (signed) Joseph White. Wit: Wm. H. Woolridge, George T. Ross, Daniel Burnet, John Linton, Jr. // Receipt of $375 pd. by Lt. John B. Walback signed by Joseph White. Wit: Daniel Burnet.

No. 1057. Claimant: Vincent Fortner's Preemption Claim of 240 acres, March 23, 1804. Witness: Thomas Fortner. Certificate D-87, issued Oct. 29, 1806. Vincent Fortner, a citizen of Miss. Ter., Claiborne Co., claims the right of preference in the purchase of 240 acres in said county on the waters of Big Black. The abovenamed Vincent Fortner did actually inhabit and cultivate the aforesaid tract prior to and on the 3rd March 1803, he being at that time above the age of 21 years. Plat shows the land originally granted to John Peters and bounded on land of James Rapalje.

No. 1058. Claimant: George Hayes, 24 Mar. 1804. Witness: John Berry. Evidence insufficient. Rejected Dec. 24, 1806. See No. 478. Miss. Ter. Wilkinson Co., George Hayes, a citizen of sd Territory and county, who was the head of a family on the 3rd March 1803, claims the right of preference in becoming a purchaser of the United States of 640 acres in said county on Beaver Creek, a branch of Amite River, by virtue of his having inhabited and cultivated same by his negroes and others for the use of the claimant on and before the day and year abovementioned and by virtue of the Third Section of the Act of Congress Regulating the grants of Land, etc. (signed) George Hayes.

No. 1059. Claimant: Amos Donelly, 24 Mar. 1804. Wit: John Flanagan, Sept. 10, 1805. Evidence incomplete. Rejected Dec. 24, 1806. Amos Donelly, a citizen of Miss. Ter., Wilkinson County, claims 196 acres in said county, founded on a settlement on said tract by the said Amos Donelly on and before March 3rd 1803 did inhabit and cultivate the same, he being at that time the head of a family. // Fieldnote: Wilkinson Co. Personally appeared before me, William Lee, one of the Justices of the aforesaid county, Amos Donelly and made oath that he settled on the Tickfaw where William Flanagan now lives in October 1803 and transferred his right to the said Flanagan October 1804 and he believeth that he was the first that ever settled and cultivated said tract. 13 June 1806. William Lee, J.P.

No. 1060. Claimant: Mathew Robertson, 24 Mar. 1804. Wit: William Flanagan, 10 May 1805. 437 acres to be surveyed according to plat within provided it includes the improvement. Certificate B-270, issued to T. Holden, assignee, Dec. 24, 1806. Mathew Robertson, a citizen of Miss. Ter. Wilkinson Co., claims 992 acres in said county, founded on settlement made on said tract by said Mathew Robertson who did the 3rd March 1803 actually inhabit and cultivate the same. Mathew (X) Robertson. // I, Mathew Robertson, of Wilkinson County, Miss. Ter., for value received, have sold all my right, title and interest to an improvement on the waters of the Tickfaw to Thomas Holden, Sr., which improvement is returned in my name to the Board of Commissioners. 26 April 1805. Wit: John Holden. Miss. Ter. Wilkinson Co., Personally appeared before me, William Lee, one of the Justices of Peace for said county, Mathew Robertson and made oath that he settled on the land on the Tickfaw River that Thomas Holden now lives on 4th April 1803 and left it Dec. 1804. To the best of his knowledge, he was, he believes, the first that ever settled on aforesaid tract of land as he never saw any improvement whatsoever but what he made himself. 8 June 1806. William Lee, J.P.

No. 1061. Claimant: Robert Childress, 24 Mar. 1804. Rejected May 12, 1807. Robert Childress, a citizen of the Miss. Ter., Adams Co., legal representative of Thomas Ash, claims 160 acres in said county, on the waters of Sandy Creek, by virtue of the said tract having been inhabited and cultivated by the said Thomas Ash in the month of October 1794, who was then the head of a family and continued in his possession until he conveyed the premises to Wilford Hoggatt, who sold the same to this claimant. The said land has been inhabited and cultivated ever since the year 1794 and is now claimed under section of the Act of Congress Regulating the Grants of Land.

No. 1062. Claimant: David Greenleaf, 24 Mar. 1804. Certificate A-804 issued to claimant, Jan. 7, 1806. See No. 1253. David Greenleaf claims 200 arpens in Jefferson County on the waters of Fairchild's Creek about 14 miles from Natchez, it being part of a tract of 1000 acres granted by the Spanish Government to James Fletcher, and said 200 acres was by the said Fletcher transferred to Samuel Chidester and by Samuel Chidester to David Greenleaf, 21 Feb. 1798. (signed) David Greenleaf.

No. 1066. Claimant: Thomas Hill, 24 Mar. 1804. Rejected May 12, 1807. The annexed plat represents a tract made for Thomas Hill March 12, 1804, in Adams County, Miss. Ter. on the Homochitto River, 640 acres. The above land was cultivated and improved in 1792 and 1794 and again by the claimant in 1802. First by Thomas Morgan who transferred it to Thomas Ford, who transferred it to the claimant, who now claims by virtue of occupancy. (signed) T. B. Hill.

No. 1067. Claimant: Ritchey and Temple, 23 Mar. 1804. Witness: John Berry. Evidence incomplete. Rejected Dec. 24, 1806. See No. 478. Miss. Ter. Wilkinson Co., Thomas Richey and William Temple, citizens of the said Territory, who were the heads of families on 3rd March 1803, claim the right of preference in becoming the purchasers of the United States of 640 acres in county aforesaid on Beaver Creek, a branch of the Amite River, by virtue of inhabiting and cultivating the said tract by themselves and others for the use of these claimants on and before the year abovementioned and by virtue of the Third Section of the Act of Congress, etc. Signed by both.

No. 1068. Claimant: Thomas Newman, 24 Mar. 1804. Witness: John Cocke, or Cook. Certificate D-230, Dec. 22, 1806. Thomas Newman claims the right of preference to 237 acres in consequence of being settled on the premises on and before the 3rd March 1803 and having improved and cultivated the same as the Act of Congress directs for Regulating the Grants of Lands in the Miss. Ter., the tract lying in the County of Claiborne and bounded by Cheliab Smith, on the bank of the Mississippi River. (signed) Thomas Newman.

No. 1069. Claimant: Richard Carradine, 24 Mar. 1804. Witness: William Bradstone. Residence of Henry Milburn proved in claim No. 260, Nov. 14, 1804. Certificate A-754 issued March 10, 1806. Miss. Ter., Jefferson Co., Richard Carradine claims 100 acres in said county on the waters of Fairchild's Creek, by virtue of a patent by the Spanish Government to Eustis Humphreys for 300 arpens of which the above 100 acres is a part, who conveyed the same 300 arpens to Henry Milburn, who conveyed the same to John Dyson who conveyed the same to Andrew Watkins, who conveyed the same to the present claimant. // Plat shows the tract in the name of John Dyson, 100 acres, bounded on one side by Henry Milburn. "I do certify that at the request of John Dyson and Henry Milburn I have surveyed in the name of the former 100 acres, part of said Milburn's tract, which was formerly surveyed in the name of Eustis Humphreys, on the waters of Fairchild's Creek." // Deed of Andrew Watkins, of Miss. Ter., County of Jefferson, for and in consideration of $500 in hand paid by Richard Carradine, of same, transfers said tract of land, bounded on the south by land of States Trevillian and on the north by John Courtney, on the west and east by Daniel Clark. (signed) Andrew Watkins. Ack. before David Phelps, J.P. Wit: John Brooks. // Indenture, 23 Jany. 1801, between John Dyson and Andrew Watkins, also given. This is witnessed by Daniel Swetland and Stephen Terry, and acknowledged by John Dyson before Mordecai Throckmorton, J.P.

No. 1072. Claimant: Wylie Atkins, 24 Mar. 1804. Witness: Hugh Nelson. Certificate D-149, Dec. 16, 1806. Wylie Atkins claims preemption rights of the tract of land, 100 acres, by virtue of having improved the same in March 1801 and of having settled on it in January 1803, ever since which period he has resided on and cultivated same, and he claims no other land in this Territory. (signed) Wylie Atkins. // Plat and certificate of survey by John Dinsmore, dated Jany. 31, 1804. "Surveyed for Wylie Atkins 100 acres on the waters of Dry Bayou Fork of Wells' Creek in Adams County, Miss. Ter. including his improvement."

No. 1073. Claimant: John Robinett, 24 Mar. 1804. Wit: William Cisnea. Certificate D-36 issued Sept. 5, 1806. Miss. Ter. John Robinett claims the preemption right to 280 acres settled by him in

1802 and having continued to live on and cultivate the same ever since, on Morgan's Fork of the Homochitto in Adams Co.

No. 1074. Claimant: John Reed, 24 March 1804. Witness: William Cisnea. Certificate D-31, issued Sept. 4, 1806. Miss. Ter. John Reed claims the preemption right to 210 acres improved and cultivated in January 1803 and he has continued to live on it ever since, lying in the middle fork of Homochitto in Adams County.

No. 1075. Claimant: John Delany, 24 Mar. 1804. Wit: William Cisnea. Certificate D-27, issued to Reuben Mayfield, assignee of claimant, Sept. 4, 1806. Miss. Ter. John Delany claims a preemption right to 242 acres, settled and cultivated Feb. 9, 1803. He is living on it, situated on the Middle Fork of Homochitto River, Adams County. Enclosure: I relinquish my right, title and claim to 242 acres on the Middle Fork of the Homochitto, the same being a preemption right, whereon I now live, together with the improvements thereunto belonging, to Reuben Mayfield, for $200 to me in hand paid, possession of the land to be given Oct. 1, 1805. Dated Sept. 24, 1805. (signed) John Delany. Ack. July 26, 1806 before T. R. Wit: Hiram Downs.

No. 1076. Claimant: William Cisna, 24 Mar. 1804. Wit: John Delany. Certificate D-35, issued Sept. 4, 1806. William Cisna claims a preemption right to 320 acres on the Middle Fork of Homochitto River in Adams County, settled by him in 1802, he being the head of a family and has lived on and cultivated the said claim ever since. // Plat shows Joseph Galbreath and John Robinett as having land adjoining.

No. 1082. Claimant: John Berry, 24 Mar. 1804. Wit: John Nelin. Certificate D-128, issued Dec. 15, 1806. Miss. Ter. Wilkinson Co., John Berry claims a preemption of 534 acres on the waters of Amite River, he having improved and cultivated the same prior to and on the 3rd March 1803. // "For a valuable consideration to be paid, I assign all my right, title and interest of the within preemption claim of 534 acres of land to Isaac Jackson and William Temple, 13 Dec. 1806." Wit: Parke Walton. (signed) John Berry.

No. 1095. Claimant: Abijah Hunt, 24 Mar. 1804. Wit: Charles Carter, 24 Aug. 1804. Certificate B-269 issued May 12, 1807. Abijah Hunt hereby gives notice that he claims 640 acres of land in Adams County by virtue of an improvement made thereon by Skipith Durbin previous to 1797, which said land was inhabited and cultivated by said Durbin in whole of said year, he then being above the age of 21 years. Conveyance from said Durbin to James White, dated the 10th June 1798, and conveyance from said White to said claimant, Dec. 6, 1799. Elijah Smith for Abijah Hunt. // Filed with notice No. 1095: A plat and certificate of survey for 640 acres to Abijah Hunt made by Joseph Sessions, surveyor, Mar. 20, 1804, on the east side of Well's Creek.

No. 1096. Claimant: John Holland and Abijah Hunt, 24 Mar. 1804. Witness: Charles Carter, 24 Aug. 1804. Certificate B-206, Feb. 19, 1807. To the Register of the Land Office West of the Pearl River: John Holland and Abijah Hunt hereby give notice that they claim 640 acres in Adams County, by virtue of an improvement made thereon by James Hayes before the year 1797, which said land was inhabited and cultivated by the said James Hayes during the whole of that year, he then being above the age of 21 years and the head of a family, tenants in common, 30 Dec. 1800. Elijah Smith for Abijah Hunt. Certificate of survey and plat for Abijah Hunt by Joseph Sessions, dated 20 March 1804.

No. 1100. Claimant: Abijah Hunt, 24 Mar. 1804. Wit: Robert Throchmorton, April 29, 1805. See No. 207. Certificate A-581, issued to claimant Sept. 11, 1805. Abijah Hunt hereby gives notice that he claims 195 acres of land in Jefferson County, by virtue of a grant, including the land, from the Spanish Government to David Odum, now deceased, fully executed previous to the 27th October 1795, and conveyance of 100 acres of said grant from said Odum to John Hinds, dated the 20 Oct. 1799; and conveyance thereof from said Hinds to this claimant, dated June 3, 1801; and conveyance of 84 acres, the residue, of said 195 acres from Frances Odum and Abner Pipes, executors of the will of said deceased, dated 16 April 1803, to this claimant; also three square lots in the town of Huntston, in the county aforesaid, Nos. 15, 16, and 17, by virtue of the aforesaid grant to said Odum and conveyed from said Odum to the said Hinds, and said conveyance from said Hinds to this claimant. Elijah Smith for Abijah Hunt.

No. 1101. Claimant: John Ellis, 24 Mar. 1804. Wit: John Ellis, Esq. 31 Jan. 1806. Certificate D-280 issued Dec. 24, 1806. John Ellis, Sr. claims a preemption right to 500 acres of land which he has possessed and cultivated upward of 20 years and would therefore be entitled to a grant under the Act of Congress were he not excluded from the higher privilege by the possession of a grant of land held under a patent. The following is a plat of the said 500 arpents of land. (signed) John Ellis. // This is bounded by Mathew White, Abner Green, Richard Ellis and William Dunbar, near the Mississippi River.

No. 1112. Claimant: Samuel Osborn, 24 Mar. 1804. Wit: Caleb Potter. Certificate D-20 issued Sept. 14, 1806. Samuel Osborn, a citizen of the Miss. Ter., Jefferson Co., claims the right of preference in the purchase of 67 acres of land in said county, on the Mississippi River. The abovenamed Samuel Osborn did actually inhabit and cultivate the aforesaid tract prior to and on the 3rd March 1803, he being at that time above the age of 21 years and the head of a family. (signed) Samuel Osborn.

No. 1116. Claimant: Henry Platner, 24 Mar. 1804. Wit: Samuel Osborn. Certificate D-309, issued Dec. 29, 1806, to W. Barland, assignee. Henry Platner, a citizen of the Miss. Ter. Jefferson Co., claims the right of preference in the purchase of 640 acres in said county on the Mississippi River. The above claim is founded on the transfer from John Maylone to the claimant, dated 8 Oct. 1803, which said Malone had previously purchased the right of settlement to the aforesaid tract from Jesse Edwards and John Holden, which said Edwards and Holden did actually inhabit and cultivate the same on and prior to 3 March 1803, they being at that time above the age of 21 years and the heads of families. (signed) Henry Platner. // Deed: Malone to Platner: John Malone, of Jefferson County, Miss. Ter., hath bargained and sold unto Henry Platner a certain improvement, settled by Jesse Edwards and John Holden, on the Mississippi River, against the middle of Cole's Creek, inland 6 miles above the mouth, for the sum of $180. (signed) John Maylone. Wit: Abraham Clawson, Edmund Johnson. // "For value received of William Barland, I have this day assigned all my right, title, claim and interest in this within mentioned tract of land unto to him, the said William Barland, being a preemption claim of 640 acres, on the River Mississippi. 9th Dec. 1806. For the sum of $200. (signed) Henry Platner. Wit: Parke Walton.

No. 1118. Claimant: Caleb Potter, 24 Mar. 1804. Wit: Samuel Osborn. This claim interferes with No. 87. Certificate D-243, issued Dec. 22, 1806. The certificate rescinded by the Board on 24 Dec. following. Caleb Potter claims 100 acres in Jefferson County, Miss. Territory, on the Mississippi River above the mouth of Cole's Creek, by virtue of his having inhabited and cultivated the same ever since 1797. He claims the right of preference in becoming the purchaser thereof from the United States.

No. 1138. Claimant: George Cochran, 24 Mar. 1804. Wit: James Truly, 23 Sept. 1805. Certificate A-757 issued to legal representatives March 10, 1806. George Cochran hereby gives notice that he claims 240 arpents of land in Jefferson County, by virtue of a grant from the Spanish Government to James Todd, dated 1 June 1793, which said grant is lost or mislaid, and conveyance from said Todd to said claimant is dated 16 Aug. 1802. George Cochran by Ly Harding, his atty.

No. 1145. Claimant: George Aldridge, 24 Mar. 1804. No evidence adduced. Rejected Dec. 24, 1806. Miss. Ter. Adams County. George Aldridge claims 640 acres in said county on Homochitto River, by virtue of said tract of land having been settled on 1799 by ______ who sold the same to Elijah Polk who sold the same to this claimant and by virtue of the Second Section of the Act of Congress regulating the Grants of Land, etc. (signed) George Aldridge. // Plat shows: Richardson Cr and Homochitto River, with J. Bass's Ferry. Surveyed by Elijah Polk, 23 Mar. 1804.

No. 1146. Claimant: Robert Ford, 24 Mar. 1804. Witness: Adam Lanehart. Rejected for want of evidence, Dec. 30, 1806. Miss. Ter., Wilkinson Co. Robert Ford claims 354 acres of land in right of preemption, on Buffalo Creek in county aforesaid, by virtue of a settlement made by another person for the use of the said Robert in 1796 and continued to occupy the same until 1800 and has ever since held and claimed the same. // Deed from Ford to Lattimore: Indenture made 12 Nov. 1804 Robert Ford of the County of Adams, Miss. Ter. to David Lattimore, of same, for $150 to him in hand paid, quit claims to said David the above tract of land on Buffalo Creek. (signed) Robt. Ford. Wit: Seth Lewis.

No. 1147. Claimant: John Caston, 24 Mar. 1804. Witness: Joseph Sanders, 2 Oct. 1804. Certificate D-150 issued Dec. 16, 1806. Miss. Ter. Wilkinson Co. John Caston claims 250 acres on the Homochitto River in said county, in right of preemption by virtue of an actual settlement made on said land by said Caston 8 Nov. 1802, said Caston has ever since that day occupied and cultivated the said tract of land. // "For and in consideration of the sum of $50 to me in hand paid, by William R. Caston, a citizen of the Miss. Ter., I have sold all my right of preference to 250 acres, lying on the east side of the Homochitto." (signed) John Caston. 20 May 1806. Wit: Samuel W. Caston, Charlotte Caston.

No. 1148. Claimant: John R. Wylie, 24 Mar. 1804. Certificate A-316, issued to legal representatives of Wylie, June 17, 1805. Proved in Thomas M. Green, No. 147, April 26, 1805. "I do hereby certify that at desire and request of Thomas M. Green and John R. Wylie, I carefully surveyed and admeasured for and in the name of John R. Wylie 100 acres, it being a part of 800 acres granted by the Spanish Government to said Thos. M. Green, on the headwaters of Fairchild's Creek, about 10 miles east from the town of Natchez. Jan. 31, 1801." (signed) William Atchinson. // On plat: Lands adjoining owned by Thos. M. Green, Richard King, John Bowls, William Daniels. // Miss. Ter. John Wylie claims 100 acres of land in Adams County, on headwaters of Fairchild's Creek, by virtue of a patent from the Spanish Government for 800 acres to Thomas M. Green, 27 Feb. 1789, and the sd Green conveyed 100 acres to present claimant. (signed) John R. Wylie. // Thos. M. Green to Louisa Wylie 100 arpents of land. Deed in Spanish. Deed of 100 arpens of land from Thomas Marston Green to Louisa Wylie, being part of a grant to him of 800 arpens and to be taken from the south side thereof, running four arpens on the west line 9 March 1796, for the price of 100 pesos. [Louisa Wylie was the daughter of John and Louisa (Higdon) Wylie.]

No. 1150. Claimant: Joseph Irwin, 26 Mar. 1804. Wit: Abner Beckham, 10 Sept. 1804. Certificate D-157 issued Dec. 16, 1806. Miss. Ter. Adams Co. Joseph Irwin, holding 165 acres on the Homochitto at the mouth of Dry Creek, adjoining the land of Abner Beckham, the said improvement was made by John House February 1803 and purchased by said Joseph Irwin from said House, holding the same in actual cultivation and peaceable possession until the present day. (signed) Joseph Irwin. // Conveyance from John House, Miss. Ter., Adams County, to Joseph Irwin, of same, all my labor and good will made and done on a certain tract on the Homochitto (described as above). John (x) House. Wit: Abner Beckham, Joseph House. //

No. 1151. Claimant: Zadock Barrow, 26 Mar. 1804. Wit: William Irwin, 10 Sept. 1804. Rejected May 12, 1807. Miss. Ter., Wilkinson Co. Zadock Barrow, holding by occupancy 648 acres on the south side of the Homochitto, joining the lands of Henry Richardson, said improvement made in 1791 by Thomas Lloyd and transferred from said Lloyd to said Barrow in 1798, and he continues to hold the same until this present date in peaceable possession. (signed) Zadock Barrow.

No. 1152. Claimant: Elias Fisher, 26 Mar. 1804. Wit: Adam Lanehart. Withdrawn by the claimant. Rejected for want of sufficient evidence, Dec. 30, 1806. Elias Fisher, an inhabitant of Miss. Ter., claims a preemption right to 640 acres on Buffalo Creek in Wilkerson County, by virtue of an improvement made in 1802 in the month of August. (signed) Elias Fisher. // Plat shows the tract bounded by: D. R. Crosby.

No. 1153. Claimant: Elias Fisher, 26 Mar. 1804. Wit: Adam Lanehart, 26 Mar. 1804. This notice must be altered according to title. Wit: James McNulty, 5 July, 1806. Rejected 12 May 1807. Elias Fisher, an inhabitant of Miss. Ter., claims a donation right of 640 acres on Buffalo Creek in Wilkerson County, by virtue of an improvement made in 1797 previous to the Spanish troops leaving the Natchez, and agreeable to an Act passed the 3rd March 1803, which land said Fisher now lives on and cultivates and has no claim to any other land in said Territory. Petition for 400 acres on north fork of Buffalo Creek, by Adam Lanehart, 30 Jan. 1797, a certificate of the same date by Mr. Dunbar that the land is vacant; 31 Jan. 1797, Governor Gayoso recommended that the grant be made.

No. 1154. Claimant: William Fairbanks, 26 Mar. 1804. Wit: Caleb Potter, 22 Oct. 1804. Certificate D-110, issued Dec. 29, 1806. William Fairbanks, of Miss. Ter., Jefferson Co., claims the right of preference in the purchase of 200 acres of land in said county on the waters of the Mississippi River. Said William Fairbanks did actually inhabit and cultivate the aforesaid tract, long prior to and on the 3rd March 1803, he being at that time above the age of 21 and the head of a family. Plat shows: James White and Henry Platner having land adjoining.

No. 1160. Claimant: John Francis, 26 Mar. 1804. Wit: William Curtis. Certificate D-129, issued Dec. 15, 1806. Miss. Ter., Wilkinson Co., John Francis claims 176 acres in said county on Berry's Creek joining Beaver Creek Swamp, by improvement made previous to and on the 3rd Mar. 1803 by said John Francis, bounded on northeast by Mark Cole's land.

No. 1161. Claimant: William Curtis, 26 Mar. 1804. Wit: John Courtney. Certificate D-130 issued Dec. 15, 1806. Miss. Ter., Wilkinson Co., William Curtis claims 382 acres on Beaver Creek by improvement made previous to and on 3rd March 1803 by the said William Curtis, bounded on the northeast by Thomas Courtney.

No. 1162. Claimant: William Burd, 26 Mar. 1804. Wit: William Curtis. Certificate D-131, issued Dec. 15, 1806. Miss. Ter., Wilkinson Co., William Burd claims 320 acres on Beaver Creek by improvement made previous to and on the 3rd March 1803 by said William Burd, bounded on southwest by Peter Haines, on the northeast by Thomas Courtney.

No. 1163. Claimant: Richard Curtis, 26 Mar. 1804. Wit: John Berry, 15 Oct. 1804. Rejected for want of sufficient evidence, Dec. 30, 1806. Richard Curtis claims the right of becoming the purchaser of the United States of 640 acres, bought by said Curtis from Mark Cole Dec. 1803. This land was improved in Feb. 1803 by Benjamin Richey and by him sold to said Cole, said land lying in the county of Wilkinson on Beaver Creek, waters of the Amite, surveyed March 19, 1804. (signed) Richard Curtis.

No. 1164. Claimant: John Dennis, 26 Mar. 1804. Wit: Thos. Dering, 10 Feb. 1806. Certificate D-57, issued Sept. 11, 1806. Miss. Ter., Jefferson Co., John Dennis, a citizen of said Territory on 3rd March 1803, claims the right of preference in becoming the purchaser of the United States of 300 acres in said county on Tabor's Fork of Bayou Pierre by virtue of said land having been inhabited and cultivated by him on above date and ever since.

No. 1165. Claimant: Joseph D. Lewis, 26 Mar. 1804. Wit: William Shaw, Nov. 29, 1804. Certificate D-56 issued Sept. 5, 1806. Miss. Ter., Jefferson Co., Joseph D. Lewis claims 196 acres on the waters of the North Fork of Cole's Creek in said county, improved and cultivated 1st Jan. 1798 and settled personally October 1802.

No. 1166. Claimant: John Courtney, 26 Mar. 1804. Wit: William Curtis. Certificate D-132 issued Dec. 15, 1806. Miss. Ter. Wilkinson Co., John Courtney claims 590 acres in said county on Beaver Creek by improvement made previous to and on 3 March 1803 by said John Courtney, bounded on northeast by Mark Cole.

No. 1167. Claimant: Mark Cole, 26 Mar. 1804. Wit: John Courtney. Certificate D-133 issued Dec. 15, 1806. Miss. Ter. Wilkinson Co., Mark Cole claims 360 acres in said county by improvement made previous to and on 3 March 1803 by said Mark Cole, bounded by John Courtney and John Francis and Beaver Creek.

No. 1168. Claimant: Peter Bumbard, plat and notice, 26 Mar. 1804. Rejected for want of evidence. (Note in file: This land claimed by Peter Bombard is within the lines of a patent granted to Francis S. Girault, for which a certificate is issued, therefore the undersigned prays to give this notice to the Honorable Board of Commissioners, 17 Aug. 1806. (signed) John Girault.) // The Claim of Bombard: Miss. Ter., Adams Co., Peter Bombard claims 1224 feet of land in City of Natchez, county aforesaid, and the right of preemption, by virtue of an actual settlement and building made on the said lot by the said Peter Bombard on 1 Dec. 1802 and he has continued in possession and occupancy of the same. (signed) Peter Bombard.

No. 1169. Claimant: John Morrison's plat and notice, 26 Mar. 1804. Rejected for want of evidence. Miss. Ter., Adams Co., John Morrison claims 4082 feet of land in the right of preemption, situate in the City of Natchez, county aforesaid, by virtue of settlement made on said lot by William McKee about 25 Dec. 1802, who continued to occupy and build on the said lot until 26 Nov. 1803, on which day the said William McKee did sell and transfer the said lot and building thereon to said John Morrison.

No. 1170. Claimant: Matthew Tardae's plat and notice, 26 Mar. 1804. Rejected for want of evidence, Dec. 30, 1806. Miss. Ter., Adams Co., Matthew Tardae claims 7752 feet of land in right of preemption in the City of Natchez, county aforesaid, by virtue of an actual settlement made thereon by said Matthew 1 Feb. 1803, who continued to occupy said lot.

No. 1171. Claimant: William Baker, 26 Mar. 1804. Witnesses: William Phipps, 26 Nov. 1804, and James Sanders, 23 Nov. 1805. Elijah Phipps, who owned this land 1 March 1798, claims a donation in his own name. See No. 323. Rejected, May 12, 1807. Miss. Ter., Wilkinson Co., William D. Baker claims 640 acres on Pine Creek in said county as a Donation by virtue of an actual settlement made on this land by Elijah Phipps in 1796 and he continued to occupy the said land until 1 March 1797, on which date the said Elijah Phipps did, for a valuable consideration, sell and transfer the said improvement and right. (signed) William Baker. // Paper: Phipps Sale: I, Elijah Phipps acknowledge to have received $130 in money and other property from William Baker for an improvement on land on Buffalo Creek, it being the place and improvement whereon said Phipps has lately lived and occupied, also another improvement near thereto, which said Phipps bought of Cunningham, the weaver, both of which improvements I, Phipps, have sold to said Baker and do hereby deliver the possession thereof, with all my right and title. 1 March 1797. (signed) Elijah Phipps. Wit: William Dunbar. // Another paper: John Collins vs Baker. Caveat. To the Honourable Board of Commissioners, Settling the questions of

Lands West of the Pearl River: Gentlemen: You are requested not to issue certificate to William Baker for 640 acres of land on Big Pine Creek because he claims under E. Phipps, who before selling this claim to Baker, did claim under Cunningham, who had land granted to him by the Spanish Government and who has also conveyed another donation claim to Hardress Ellis, and this claim interfers with John Collins. // Paper: Oct. 17, 1795. Received of Elijah Phipps one cow and yearling and 12 heads of hogs, valued by James Nicholson and Ruffin Gray at $50, being in full for an improvement which I promised to give said Phipps possession of on the last of November next, as per agreement. (signed) William Cunningham, in the presence of R. Gray and James Nicholson.

No. 1172. Claimant: Stephen Douglass, 26 Mar. 1804. Witnesses: Samuel Goodwin, Hezekiah Harman and Stephen Richards, 8 Feb. 1805. Rejected May 12, 1807. Miss. Ter. Claiborne Co. Stephen Douglass claims 640 acres on waters of Bayou Pierre by virtue of an actual settlement made thereon by Mordecai Throckmorton in 1789 and the said Mordecai Throckmorton did on the 9 Oct. 1802 bargain and sell unto the said Stephen Douglass all his right and claim to said land and improvement. // Note: Patterson, Mackey and Montgomery interfere with this claim. Patterson and Mackey present at the examination of above witnesses for Douglass. (signed) T.R. // Plat shows George Humphreys, Waterman Crane, ______ Thompson, Filmer Green and Stephen Richards as having lands adjoining. // Conveyance of headright of land from Mordecai Throckmorton to Stephen Douglass, the 29 Oct. 1802. "I, this day, have sold to Stephen Douglass my claim to land on Bayou Pierre joining the lands of Phoebe Goodwin, Filmer Green and Abraham Green, which said land I settled on and improved 1789, cleared one acre and dug a well, 106 ft. deep, and planted some fruit trees, which claim of land I have sold this 9 Oct. 1802. The above said land I claim as my headright, having five in family at that time." (signed) Mordecai Throckmorton. Wit: David Nesbit, Joseph Graham, Prov. by J. Graham Feb. 18, 1805 before the Board. Signed T. R.

No. 1173. Claimant: Stephen Douglass, 26 Mar. 1804. Witness: Hezekiah Harman, 18 Feb. 1805. Witness: James Harman, 28 May 1806. Certificate B-207, issued Feb. 19, 1807. Miss. Ter. Jefferson Co., Stephen Douglass claims 500 acres of land on Bayou Pierre in Claiborne County, by virtue of an actual settlement made thereon in 1792 by John Hambleton who occupied and cultivated the said land until 3 Feb. 1798 on which day the said Hambleton sold to said Stephen Douglass all right and claim to said 500 acres and improvement. (signed) Stephen Douglass. // Plat marked: "Surveyed for John Hamilton 500 acres, bounded by John Davenport, the heirs of John Hartley and Bayou Pierre".

No. 1175. Claimant: Martin Cooper, 26 Mar. 1804. Wit: David Lum. Certificate D-21 issued Sept. 4, 1806. Miss. Ter. Claiborne Co., "I have admeasured and laid out to Martin Cooper a plantation of 200 acres of land on the headwaters of Burnet Mill Creek, waters of the North Fork of Bayou Pierre." (signed) E. Evans. Miss. Ter. Claiborne Co., Martin Cooper claims the right of preference in becoming the purchaser of the United States of 200 acres in said county, by virtue of having settled on and cultivated same 3 March 1803.

No. 1177. Claimant: Jeremiah Robinett, 26 Mar. 1804. No evidence adduced. Rejected Dec. 24, 1806. Miss. Ter. Jeremiah Robinett claims a preemption right to 200 acres on Middle Fork of Homochitto, improved in 1802 and cultivated by him ever since. // Plat shows Abram Taylor and Joseph Galbreath with land adjoining.

No. 1178. Claimant: Joseph Ford, Jr., 26 Mar. 1804. Witness: Samuel Boyd, 27 Aug. 1804. Certificate D-29, issued Sept. 4, 1806. Miss. Ter. Joseph Ford, Jr. claims preemption right to 304 acres on both sides of Morgan's Fork of Homochitto, settled by him in 1802 and he has continued to live on and cultivate the same ever since. Plat shows: Thomas Morgan adjoining and the county of Wilkinson.

No. 1179. Claimant: Hugh Nelson, 26 Mar. 1804. Witness: James Crow, 21 July. See No. 286. Certificate B-237 issued to James Clark, assignee, Mar. 30, 1807. Miss. Ter. Adams Co. Hugh Nelson claims 114 acres in said county on the waters of Wells Creek, by virtue of a warrant of survey to James Clark by the Spanish Government, dated 1794, and said Clark was 21 years at that time, and inhabited and cultivated the said tract on 27 October 1795 and he sold the said 114 acres, part of the aforesaid warrant to said Nelson. (signed) Hugh Nelson. Certificate of Survey and Plat by John Dinsmore: "Surveyed for Hugh Nelson 114 acres on Wells Creek called the Dry Bayou in Adams Co., Miss. Ter".

No. 1180. Claimant: Samuel Lum, Sr., 26 Mar. 1804. Witness: Martin Cooper. Certificate D-39, issued Sept. 8, 1806. Miss. Ter. Claiborne Co. Samuel Lum, Sr. claims preference of becoming the purchaser of the United States of 400 acres in said county on a branch of South Fork of Bayou Pierre between that and the North Fork on the main road leading from the Wilderness and passing the Grindstone Ford. Samuel Lum, as the head of a family, settled on and cultivated the above premises on June 1802 and claims his preference from the settlement aforesaid. Samuel Lum, Sr. Plat by Daniel Burnet shows all sides vacant and two houses on the land described.

No. 1181. Claimant: Samuel Lum, Jr., 26 Mar. 1804. Witness: David Lum, brother to claimant. Miss. Ter. Claiborne Co. The above 200 acres of land is situated on Widows Creek, a branch that empties into the North Fork of Bayou Pierre on the south side, and surveyed for Samuel Lum, Jr. 27 Jan. 1804, which land was occupied by the said Samuel Lum Jr. before March last. (signed) Daniel Burnet. [n.d.] Miss. Ter. Samuel Lum Jr. claims the preference of becoming the purchaser of the United States of the above described 200 acres about two miles from Grindstone Ford, from his settlement on the premises in June 1802 and is at the head of a family.

No. 1182. Claimant: Benjamin Cooper, 26 Mar. 1804. Witness: Martin Cooper, son of claimant. Evidence incomplete. Rejected Dec. 24, 1806. Benjamin Cooper claims a right of preference in becoming the purchaser of the United States of 200 acres in Claiborne County on Miller's Bayou, water of South Fork of Bayou Pierre, by virtue of a settlement made and occupied by me, the said Cooper, prior to the 1 March 1803.

No. 1184. Claimant: David Drennan, 26 Mar. 1804. Witness: Peter Haines. Certificate D-134, issued Dec. 15, 1806. Miss. Ter. Wilkinson Co. David Drennan claims 124 acres on west prong of River Amite in said county by improvement made previous and on 3rd March 1803 by Dave Drennan. Plat and survey by Robert Griffin, 13 March 1804.

No. 1185. Claimant: Peter Haines, 26 March 1804. Witness: David Drennan. Certificate D-135, issued Dec. 15, 1806. Miss. Ter. Wilkinson Co. Peter Haines claims 260 acres in said county on the West prong of the River Amite, by improvement on 3 March 1803 by said Peter Haines, bounded by William Burd and the Spanish line.

No. 1186. Claimant: William Collins, 26 Mar. 1804. Witness: Henry Phipps, June 10, 1806. Rejected May 12, 1807. Miss. Ter. Wilkinson Co. William Collins claims 640 acres on the waters of Pine Woods Creek in said county as a Donation, by virtue of an actual settlement made on said land by Peter Padeth in 1797 who occupied and cultivated the said land when the Spanish troops evacuated the Territory and in 1798 did sell all his right and improvement to said William Collins.

No. 1195. Claimant: George Bailey, 26 Mar. 1804. Witness; John Armstreet, 15 Apr. 1804. Rejected. The same land granted to Abijah Hunt. See 1088. April 9, 1807. George Bailey claims 640 acres on waters of Wells Creek, four miles from the Homochitto, by virtue of a deed of conveyance from Moses Foster, dated 1796. Plat shows: E. H. Bay, J. Oglesby and E. Estes with land adjoining. // Transfer from Moses Foster: Natchez, Sandy Creek District. This is to certify that I have sold my rights of two improvements on the west side of Wells Creek for $60, $50 paid me in hand and the other $10 to be paid next fall, to George Bailey. 29 Sept. 1796. Witness by me, William Cooper. Signed Moses Foster. // I do assign the within right to this improvement to John Smith and his heirs, in the consideration of $200 in hand paid, 23 Jany. 1804. (signed) George (B) Bailey. Wit: Wm. Smith. [The following papers in this file do not seem to properly belong here.] Know all men by these present that we, George Bailey and Jemima Bailey of Miss. Ter., Adams Co. do sell and deliver unto Barton Hannon, of the same, our improvement on the waters of Second Creek, adjoining John Armstreet, John Spires and said Hannon. 29 Oct. 1800. Wit: John Spires, Estes Spires. // On back: I assign all my rights to within bill of sale to Joseph Stanley, 4 Feb. 1802. (signed) Barton Hannon. Wit: John Mayes. I assign my right to within bill of sale to David Ellison for value received. Nov. 23, 1805. (signed) Rhoda Stanley. Wit: Andrew Forsythe.

No. 1212. Claimant, Jacob Jones, 26 Mch. 1804. Wit: Stephen Jackson. Certif. D-192, issued 17 Sept. 1806. Miss. Ter., Wilkinson Co. Jacob Jones claims preemption rights to 500 acres on br. of Buffalo Cr. called Percy's Cr., having improved and cultivated the same prior to and on 3 Mch. 1803. Signed. Personally appeared before the undersigned, one of the Justices of the Peace for Adams Co., Jacob Jones and made oath that by a resurvey of land, a part of his improvement is left out and that the same can be taken in by extending his line, without interfering with the claim of any individual. 23 Nov. 1808. John Henderson, J.P.

No. 1215. Claimant, David Christian, 26 Mch. 1804. Wit: Thomas Jordan. Rejected for want of sufficient evidence, 30 Dec. 1806. Miss. Ter., Claiborne County. David Christian claims preemption rights to 330 acres on waters of Alston's Creek in Claiborne Co. by right of occupancy, which tract he has inhabited and cultivated ever since 1802 and he was the head of a family at the time of the passing of the act on the grant of lands, etc. Signed. Plat shows Thos. Jordan, George Cochran with land adj.

No. 1243. Claimant, David Pickens, 26 Mch. 1804. Chas. Carter, 1805. Rejected. David Pickens claims 640 arpents on Wells Creek, adj. the part surveyed for Charles Carter, which sd Pickens purchased from Thos. Jones, who made an actual settlement prior to 1795. Sd Pickens claims a donation for same. Richard King, atty for David Pickens.

No. 1502. Claimant, John Smith, 29 Mch. 1804. Wit: John Brooks, 8 Oct. 1804. Certif. A-557 issued to claimant, 3 Sept. 1805. Notation See No. 935. John Smith claims 200 arpents of land, part of a tract of 1000 arpents 20 mi. NE of Natchez Fort, 1 1/4 mi. from the Bluff, as part of a Spanish patent to James Elliott, Sr. for 1000 arpents and by him to John Smith the date whereof not exactly remembered, the deed being in the office in New Orleans. Plat shows lands of Surgett on two sides and Adam Bingaman on another and John Brooks on the south.

No. 1152. Claimant, Richard Butler, 24 Mch. 1804. Wit: John Collins. Certif. A-305 issued 12 June 1805. Richard Butler claims 1000 arps. in Wilkinson Co. by virtue of Spanish grant to Francis Pousset, 12 Nov. 1788, and conveyed by sd Pousset to John Wall 500 acres thereof, 17 Dec. 1791, and release of mortgage by David Ross to sd Pousset, 29 Oct. 1796, and conveyance from sd Wall to Joseph Pannell of said 500 acres, 20 Sept. 1796 and the release of dower therein from the wife of sd Wall to said Pannell, 21 Mch. 1801, and conveyance from sd Pousset to sd Pannell for 1500 acres including the residue of the afsd 1000 acres, 20 Sept. 1796, and conveyance from said Pannell and wife for 1000 acres to this claimant, 25 Mch. 1801. Richard Butler by Lyman Harding.

No. 1207. Claimant, Wm. Berry, assignee of Thomas Herrin, 2 Aug. 1805. Thos. H. Williams, Register. Miss. Territory, Wilkinson Co. Know all men, etc., that I, Thomas Herrin, am firmly bound to Wm. Berry for $1000 to be paid to said Berry, etc. 23 June 1805. The condition, to relinquish to sd William Berry all claim, etc. and right of preemption 500 acres on Percy's Creek, b. by Jacob Jones, Foster's land, which when done the above obligation will be null and void. (signed) Thos. Herrin. Delivered in presence of Isaac and Reuben Jackson. Thomas Herrin claims preemption right to 500 acres inhabited and cultivated in 1802 on Percy's Creek. Wit: Jacob Jones. Notation: sold to Wm. Berry. Certif. D-190, issued to Berry, as assignee of claimant, Dec. 17, 1806.

No. 1208. Claimant, Reuben Jackson, 26 Mch. 1804. Wit: Jacob Jones. Certif. D-191 issued Dec. 17, 1806. Miss. Ter., Wilkinson Co. Reuben Jackson claims the preemption right for 226 acres on Percy's Cr., by virtue of his having inhabited and cultivated the same in Sept. 1802, at which time he was the head of a family, and ever since that time.

No. 1209. Claimant, Bryan Wheeler, 26 Mch. 1804. Wit: Louis Coursey, 26 Mch. 1804. Certif. D-312, issued Dec. 29, 1806. Know all men, etc., that I, Bryan Wheeler, of Claiborne Co., Miss. Ter. have, for a satisfactory consideration to me in hand paid, by Major Wm. Coursey, sold all my preemption right to a certain improvement whereon I now live which I settled and improved in Feb. 1803. Wit: Thos. Lewis. Bryan Wheeler gives power of atty also to Major Wm. Coursey to act for and in my name with the Board of Commissioners to secure the right to this land, on the little fork of Bayou Pierre. // Miss. Ter., Claiborne Co. I have measured and laid out unto Arthur Patton 640 acres on south fork of Bayou Pierre. Arthur Patton claims the preemption right to the said land by virtue of a settlement made by Wheeler whose sold his right to Arthur Patton.

No. 1210. Claimant, William Devine, 26 Mch. 1804. Wit: Louis Coursey, 26 Mch. 1804. Certif. D-313 issued to Samuel Gibson, assignee, 29 Dec. 1806. William Devine claims a preemption right to 320 acres in Claiborne Co., on the north side of the south fork of Bayou Pierre, in the Act. of Congress for the disposal of lands south of Tennessee, by settlement made and occupied by him prior to March 1, 1803. Signed. Claiborne Co. Know all men, etc. that I, Wm. Devine hath this day bargained and sold to Wm. Coursey all my rights, etc. to place I now live on for $100 in hand paid, etc. 320 acres which I have entered with the Commrs. for the purpose. 25 Oct. 1804. // Wm. Coursey hath this day bargained and sold and delivered to Samuel Gibson all his right unto the place Wm. Devine formerly lived on, for $150 in hand paid, etc. 3 Dec. 1804. Wit: Louis Coursey.

No. 1211. Claimant, William Coursey, 26 Mch. 1804. Wit: Louis Coursey. Certif. D-314 issued 29 Dec. 1806 to W. Brocus, assignee. Claiborne Co. Wm. Coursey claims 640 acres on both sides of the south fork of Bayou Pierre, by preemption, which land was settled by Coursey and family in Dec. 1802 and inhabited and cultivated until the present date. // Wm. Coursey for and in consideration of $400 in hand paid, to William Brocus, Sen., all my preemption right to the place where I now live as described above, and direct that the title be issued in the name of sd Wm. Brocus, Sen. 14 Feb. 1805. Wit: W. B. Elam, J. Loring.

No. 1196. Claimant: Vincent Carter, 26 Mar. 1804. Witness: George Bailey, 28 March 1806. Certificate B-08 issued 19 Feb. 1807. Vincent Carter claims 640 acres in Adams County, Miss. Territory, on both sides of Wells Creek, a branch of the Homochitto, joining lands settled and improved by Moses Foster, by virtue of the Second Section of the Act of Congress 3 March 1803. He, the said Vincent, actually inhabited and cultivated the said land on the day the Spanish troops evacuated the Territory, he being then above the age of 21 years and claiming no other land in the territory. S. Lewis, agent for said claimant.

No. 1199. Claimant: Richard Singleton, 26 Mar. 1804. Witness: George Humphreys, Esq. Rejected for want of sufficient evidence, Dec. 30, 1806. Miss. Ter. Claiborne Co. Richard Singleton claims 640 acres in said county on the North Fork of Bayou Pierre, by preemption, which tract was improved by said Singleton in the Spring 1802 and been cultivated by him to the present date. // Plat shows land adjoining Stephen Minor and Ebenezer Rees. // The Board of Commissioners will not grant to Richard Singleton the certificate for 640 acres of land claimed by him as the right of preemption from the State because the said claimed tract lies within the boundaries of a tract belonging to Salome Lyman, heir and child of Thaddeus Lyman, who holds the said land by virtue of a British grant from the British Government of West Florida and who, leaving this country by order of the Spanish Government, the moiety of said land, within which lies the claim of Richard Singleton, was granted and confirmed by said Spanish Government to the above Salome Lyman, who since married John Ellison, who has entered the said claim and now claims the land in the name of himself and wife. John Ellison and wife by S. Bullock, their attorney.

No. 1234. Claimant: Absolem Wells, 26 Mar. 1804. Witness: John Wells, 31 Aug. 1804. Certificate D-153 issued Dec. 16, 1806. Absolem Wells, who was the head of a family 3 March 1803, claims a preemption right of 178 acres by virtue of having improved the same February 1802 and having settled thereon February 1803, ever since which period he has resided on and cultivated the same. He owns no other land in this Territory. // Survey and plat by John Dinsmore, dated Feb. 3, 1804: "Surveyed for Absolem Wells 178 acres on a branch of Sandy Creek, called Bates Creek, in Adams County, Miss. Ter. . . . . . Vousdan's land . . . . . Moses Miles."

No. 1235. Claimant: Francis Ballard, 26 Mar. 1804. Witness: Absolem Wells, 31 Aug. 1804. Certificate D-154, issued Dec. 16, 1806. Miss. Ter. Adams Co. Francis Ballard claims right to become the purchaser from the United States of 102 acres in said county on the waters of Sandy Creek, by virtue of its having been inhabited and cultivated in 1801 by Robert Hollaway, who sold it unto Daniel McNeeley and Daniel McNeeley sold it to said Francis Ballard. The said tract was also inhabited and cultivated by this claimant on 3 Mar. 1803. At this time he was the head of a family.

No. 1244. Claimant: Heirs of Joseph King, deceased, 26 Mar. 1804. Witness: Alexander Montgomery and Caleb King, 3 Sept. 1804. Rejected June 12, 1807. Miss. Ter. Adams Co. Constant Rufus King, George King and other heirs of Joseph King, claim 1000 acres of land, being an undivided part of 25,000 acres granted to Amos Ogden by the British Government, who conveyed to Richard Swayze, deceased, 9,500 acres being an undivided part of said 25,000, who conveyed to said Joseph King an undivided part or share of 1000 of the 9,500 acres by conveyance dated the 18 Nov. 1774. (signed) Constant Rufus King and George King. // To Samuel L. Winston, Register, West of Pearl River. Sir: Sections number 12 in township 5 range 1 west and section Number 3 in township 6 range 1 west are covered by a Reported British Claim in the name of the legal representatives of Joseph King, Register No. 1244. Surveyor's Office, Jany. 5, 1820. (signed) Thomas Freeman.

No. 1245. Claimants: Richard and Prosper King, 26 Mar. 1804. Witness: Caleb King, 3 Sept. 1804. Rejected April 27, 1807. Miss. Ter. Adams Co. Richard and Prosper King claim 100 acres by virtue of a warrant by the British Government to their father, Justus King, surveyed in 1776, bounded by lands of Caleb King, in the county aforesaid, on a branch of the Homochitto. (signed) Richard King, Prosper King, executors. // This claim is in behalf of heirs of Justus King, to wit. Richard King, Prosper King, Henry King, Elizabeth Morehouse and Catherine Montgomery's children, descendants of Justus King. (signed) T. R.

No. 1259. Claimant: Ambrose Crawford, 26 Mar. 1804. Rejected for want of evidence, Dec. 30, 1806.

Miss. Ter. Wilkinson Co. Ambrose Crawford hereby gives notice that he claims the right of preference in becoming the purchaser of the United States of 632 acres in said county on the Comite River by virtue of his having inhabited and cultivated the said tract on 3 Mar. 1803, at which time he was of great age and the head of a family and by virtue of the Third Act of Congress. James Hyland for Ambrose Crawford. Plat by Robert Griffin, 8 Jan. 1804.

No. 1260. Claimant: Mark Waters, 26 Mar. 1804. Witness: Charles Gwynne, 26 Nov. 1804. Certificate D-232 issued Dec. 22, 1806. Miss. Ter. Claiborne Co. Mark Waters hereby gives notice that he claims the right of preference in becoming the purchaser of the United States of 320 acres in said county on the waters of Bayou Pierre, by virtue of his having inhabited and cultivated the same 3 March 1803, at which time he was above 21 years of age. Plat shows land of Patrick Cogan adjoining.

No. 1261. Claimant: Mark Waters, 26 Mar. 1804. No evidence adduced. Rejected Dec. 24, 1806. Miss. Ter. Claiborne Co. Mark Waters claims 640 acres in said co. on Clark's Lake, by virtue of John Woods having inhabited and cultivated same Oct. 8, 1802, being at that time above the age of 21 yrs. 29 Aug. 1803, he transferred all his right and title to said Mark Waters who now claims the same.

No. 1272. Claimant: Levi Norrell, 26 Mar. 1804. Witness: Charles Gwynne, 26 Nov. 1804. Certificate D-233 issued Dec. 22, 1806. Miss. Ter. Claiborne Co. Levi Norrell claims the preference to become the purchaser of the United States of 500 acres in said county on waters of Bayou Pierre, by virtue of its being inhabited and cultivated January 1803 by the said Norrell who was the head of a family at that time. He inhabited and cultivated it on 3 March 1803.

No. 1277. Claimant: Mary Oliver, 22 Mar. 1804. Witness: Hardy Ellis, 6 June 1804. Certificate A-690 issued to T. Calvit, assignee, Jan. 6, 1806. Miss. Ter. Jefferson Co. Mary Oliver claims 150 acres in said county on the waters of Cole's Creek about 3 miles from Petit Gulf, by virtue of its having been inhabited and cultivated previous to 27 Oct. 1795 for her use and benefit. The claimant was at that time at the head of a family and had been an inhabitant of the territory for about 20 years. [No paper showing transfer to Calvit.]

No. 1282. Claimant: John Carcourt, 27 Oct. 1804. Witness: Stephen Middleton. Certificate D-64 issued Sept. 26, 1806. Miss. Ter. John Carcourt claims a preemption right to 320 acres improved and cultivated in 1802 by Darius Anderson who holds no other claim in this Territory and now bought by John Carcourt, on the Homochitto in Adams County. // Transfer from Darius Anderson: I, Darius Anderson do bargain and sell to John Carcourt all my right to that improvement whereon he now lives on the main Homochitto River, adjoining John Callagan and James Owens. This improvement I made in May 1802. Darius Anderson. Wit: James Owens. Washington, Miss. Ter. The foregoing instrument acknowledged by Darius Anderson before the Board, Oct. 22, 1804.

No. 1283. Claimant: James Owens, 27 Mar. 1804. Witness: Stephen Middleton. Certificate D-65 issued Sept. 26, 1806. Miss. Ter. James Owens claims a preemption right to 946 acres cultivated and improved 2 March 1803. He has continued to live on it ever since, in Adams County on the Homochitto River. (signed) James Owens. Plat: Land adjoined Littleton Sanders.

No. 1284. Claimant: Stephen Middleton, 27 Mar. 1804. Witness: Joseph Bradley. Certificate D-66 issued Sept. 26, 1806. Miss. Ter. Stephen Middleton claims a preemption right to 155 acres, improved and cultivated in 1803. He has lived on it ever since, on the main fork of Homochitto, in Adams County.

No. 1288. Claimant: Caleb Biggs, 27 Mar. 1804. Witness: John Armstreet, 16 Jan. 1806. Witness: John Keath, 13 Mar. 1806. Certificate B-209 issued Feb. 19, 1807. Miss. Ter. Wilkinson Co. Caleb Biggs claims 640 arpents in said county on the waters of Weeks Creek by right of occupancy. Said tract was inhabited and cultivated in 1795 by said Biggs who was at that time at the head of a family and it has been inhabited and cultivated ever since by him or for his use.

No. 1294. Claimant: James McIntosh, 27 Mar. 1804. See No. 1684. Rejected 10 June 1807. James McIntosh claims 244 acres in Jefferson County, Miss. Territory on Cole's Creek, adjoining Adam Bingaman, Thomas Irwin and James Elliot, by virtue of a grant to said James Elliot from the Spanish Government, the said James Elliot having conveyed same to Don Carlos De GrandPre on 27 Feb. 1790 and said Don Carlos, who was an inhabitant of said territory on 27 October 1795, conveyed the said land to the claimant 4 Feb. 1798. (signed) James McIntosh.

No. 1295. Claimant: James McIntosh, 27 Mar. 1804. Rejected June 15, 1807. James McIntosh, an inhabitant of Miss. Ter. on 27 Oct. 1795, claims 800 acres in Jefferson County, Ter. aforesaid, on

Cole's Creek, 400 acres part thereof having been recently granted to Joseph Dawes and the said Dawes conveyed to Peter Hawkins and said Hawkins to James Elliot and by said Elliot to Don Carlos De GrandPre, 13 Feb. 1789; the other 400 acres being part of a 1000-acre grant James Elliot conveyed to Don Carlos De GrandPre 13 Feb. 1789, the whole of which said 800 acres were on the 4 Feb. 1798 conveyed by the said Don Carlos to the claimant and said Don Carlos was an inhabitant on the 27 Oct. 1795 of said territory. (signed) James McIntosh.

No. 1299. Claimant: Aseneth Willis, 27 Mar. 1804. Note: Residence of Henderson proved in Claim No. 741. Certificate A-347 issued June 20, 1805. Miss. Ter. Adams Co. Aseneth Willis hereby gives notice that she claims 219 arpents in said county on St. Catherine's Creek by deed to her from Ebenezer Rees, by virtue of a patent by the Spanish Government to Richard Harrison for 1200 arpents 15 Feb. 1787, who conveyed 602 arpents of said tract to John and Alexander Henderson who conveyed the same to Ebenezer Rees, who conveyed the said 219 arpents, part and parcel thereof, to this claimant. (signed) Aseneth Willis.

No. 1300. Claimant, Jesse Withers, 27 Mar. 1804. Witness: Robert Turner, 25 Mar. 1805. Certificate A-373 issued June 25, 1805. See Nos. 388 and 1339. Miss. Ter. Jesse Withers hereby gives notice that he claims 100 arpents in said county on the waters of Fairchild's Creek, by virtue of a patent from the Spanish Government in favor of Thomas Jordan for 600 arpents including the said arpents, dated 15 Mar. 1788, and of a conveyance from said Jordan to said Withers for said 100 arpents, 9 July 179_ (torn) (signed) Jesse Withers. // "I, Jean Girault, Keeper of the Spanish Records, do certify that filed in my Office is a conveyance from Thomas Jordan to Jesse Withers, dated 9 July 1794, for 100 arpents of land, being part of a grant of 600 arpents gr. to sd Jordan, bounded by the lands of James Bonner, James McIntire and others . . . . Certified 20 Mar. 1804." (signed) John Girault, with his seal.

No. 1301. Claimant: John Callihan, 27 Mar. 1804. Witness: Joseph Gilbreath, 30 Apr. 1804. Certificate D-155 issued Dec. 16, 1806. Miss. Ter. John Callihan, a citizen of said territory, claims a preemption right of 640 acres on Homochitto River in Adams County, settled by him in 1802 and he has continued to live on and cultivate the same ever since, he being at that time a head of a family, that is he had a wife and eight children.

No. 1302. Claimant: Joseph Galbreath, 24 Mar. 1804. Witness: John Bullen, 30 Apr. 1804. Certificate D-37 issued Sept. 5, 1806. Miss. Ter. Joseph Galbreath claims 455 acres by preemption right on the Middle Fork of Homochitto River in Adams County, settled by him, the said Galbreath, in 1802, he being the head of a family at that time, and has continued to live on and cultivate the same ever since.

No. 1303. Claimant: Job Ruth, 27 Mar. 1804. Witness: John Girault May 13, 1805. Certificate A-265 issued Sept. 5, 1805. Miss. Ter. Job Routh, a citizen of this Territory, claims 158 arpents lying near the City of Natchez, founded on a Spanish patent to John Stampley, dated 4 June 1785, who conveyed to the present claimant by deed dated 16 Sept. 1794. (signed) Job Routh.

No. 1304. Claimant: Job Routh, 27 Mar. 1804. Witness: John Girault, May 13, 1805. Certificate A-569 issued for 242 arpents 5 Sept. 1805. See Nos. 1274 and 1220. Miss. Ter. Job Routh, a citizen of said Territory, claims 244 arpents lying near the City of Natchez, founded on a conveyance of William Lintot by deed, dated 19 Apr. 1801, to present claimant. The abovedescribed 244 arpents was part of the plantation called "Concord", originally granted to Manuel Gayoso and through several conveyances from him came to the said William Lintot. (signed) Job Routh. // Notation on back: Certificate A-568 issued to the heirs of Thomas Tyler for 2 arpents, part of this claim.

No. 1305. Claimant: Job and Jeremiah Routh, 27 Mar. 1804. Wit: Bennet Truly, 24 Mar. 1806. Certificate B-265 issued to Mr. Stiller, assignee, 28 Apr. 1807. Miss. Ter. Job Routh and Jeremiah Routh, as tenants in common, citizens of the Territory aforesaid, claim 550 acres on Cole's Creek, founded on a purchase made by the claimants at the King's Sale, made by Charles De GrandPre, His Spanish Majesty's Commandant of the District of Natchez. (signed) Job Routh and Jeremiah Routh. Plat shows the North Fork of Cole's Creek running through the edge of the tract, Hodges' line and Jacob Cable's line on two sides and on the side of Cole's Creek William Murray.

No. 1310. Claimant: Chileab Smith, 27 Mar. 1804. Witness: John Cook. Certificate D-31 issued Dec. 22, 1806. Miss. Ter. Claiborne Co. Chileab Smith claims the preference of becoming a purchaser of the United States of 115 acres in said county on the Mississippi River, opposite the Upper Island of the Three Islands in Palmyra Settlement, which land has been inhabited and cultivated by the said Chileab Smith ever since March 1802.

No. 1311. Claimant: Lucius Smith, 27 Mar. 1804. Witness: John Cook. See No. 1838. Miss. Ter. Claiborne Co. Lucius Smith claims the right of preference in becoming the purchaser of the United States of 214 acres in said county on the Mississippi River, adjoining the upper side of James Lobdell's plantation in the Palmyra settlement, opposite the Upper Island of the Three Islands, which land has been cultivated and inhabited by the said Lucius Smith since November 1801 and he was the head of a family on 3 Mar. 1803.

No. 1319. Claimants: Henry Turner and others, 27 Mar. 1804. Certificate A-672 issued Oct. 14, 1805. Miss. Ter. City of Natchez. Henry Turner and Company claim a lot in the City of Natchez, being part of Lot No. 4, Square No. 3, by virtue of a patent from the Spanish Government to Edward McCabe, a conveyance from Rebecca McCabe, widow of said Edward, to Christopher Miller, 2 Aug. 1797, who conveyed the said parcel to the present claimants, 4 Nov. 1801.

No. 1331. Claimants: Augustus Roddy, 28 Mar. 1804. Witness: James Wood. Certificate D-193 issued Dec. 17, 1806. Augustus Roddy, of Miss. Ter., claims 90 acres on a branch of Hutchins Creek in Wilkinson County, by right of purchase from an actual improvement made before 3 Mar. 1803 and continued to the present.

No. 1332. Claimant: Stephen Middleton, 28 Mar. 1804. Witness: Reuben Mayfield. Certificate D-67, issued 26 Sept. 1806. Miss. Ter. Stephen Middleton claims the right to become the purchaser of the United States of 112 acres on the south side of the Homochitto, by virtue of its having been inhabited and cultivated in 1802 by Joseph Bradley, who was at that time the head of a family, and inhabited and cultivated the same on 3 Mar. 1803, and the said Joseph Bradley sold the tract to said Stephen Middleton.

No. 1342. Claimant: John Newel's plat and notice, 28 Mar. 1804. Witness: George W. Humphreys. Note: Lies within Lyman Mandamus. Rejected Dec. 30, 1806. Miss. Ter. Claiborne Co. John Newel claims the right of becoming the purchaser of the United States of 300 acres in said county on Bayou Pierre, by virtue of his having inhabited and cultivated it in 1801 and ever since, and the said Newel, on the 3 Mar. 1803, the head of a family. // Caveat against John Newel for 300 acres on Bayou Pierre by John Ellison and wife, Salome, formerly Salome Lyman, same as in Claim No. 1199.

No. 1343. Claimant: Archibald Lewis, 28 Mar. 1804. Rejected 12 June, 1807. Archibald Lewis, heir at law of Daniel Lewis, claims 500 acres in Claiborne County, Miss. Ter., on the Big Black River, above its confluence with the Mississippi, on the south side and on a small branch thereof, which said Archibald claims by virtue of a grant by the British Government of West Florida to the said Daniel Lewis, deceased, prior to 27 Oct. 1795, which is now lost by accident, the said Daniel having departed this life prior to 1795 and the said Archibald having on the last date been resident of this territory. (signed) A. Lewis.

No. 1344. Claimant: F. L. Claiborne, 28 Mar. 1804. Witness: William Barland, 19 Feb. 1805. Certificate D-47, issued 9 Sept. 1806. Miss. Ter. F. L. Claiborne, a citizen of said Territory, on 3 March 1803 did occupy a lot in the City of Natchez, of 9,800 French feet, one-third whereof is ungranted, he being the head of a family, claims the right of preference to become a purchaser of said one-third of a lot. (signed) Ferdinand Claiborne.

No. 1353. Claimant: Joseph W. A. Loyd, 28 Mar. 1804. Witness: John Vardiman, 6 Dec. 1805. Certificate 315 issued Dec. 29, 1806. [The top of this claim is badly torn.] Miss. Ter. Joseph Will . . . . , citizen of the territory afsd. claims . . . . becoming the purchaser of the United States of . . . . . . acres of land, on the waters of . . . . by virtue of the same being inhabited and cultivated before and on 3 Mar. 1803 and a transfer of said Harrington's improvement . . . . to the present claimant, on . . . . present year. (signed) Joseph W . . . . // Transfer from Harrington to Loyd: For and in consideration of the sum of $100 to me paid by Joseph W. Loyd I make over for myself and heirs 320 acres, which land I actually cultivated from Jan. 15, 1802 with the view of obtaining a preemption from the United States. Thomas (X) Harrington. Wit: Wm. Glasscock, John B. Mannon.

No. 1354. Claimant: Caleb King, 28 Mar. 1804. Witness: Nathan Swayze, 3 Sept. 1804. Rejected 27 Apr. 1807. Miss. Ter. Adams Co. Caleb King claims by virtue of a warrant from the British Government and legally surveyed in 1776 a tract of 300 acres in said county on a branch of the Homochitto, adjoining Ogden's Mandamus, the sd. Caleb being the head of a family at the date of the said warrant, and inhabited and cultivated the said land on 27 Oct. 1795.

No. 1355. Claimant: George W. Humphreys, 28 Mar. 1804. Witness: William Smith, 15 Dec. 1804. Certificate B-145, issued Feb. 10, 1807. Miss. Territory, Claiborne Co. George W. Humphreys, Sarah Humphreys his wife, and Maria Dillingham claim 480 arpents of land in said county and on the North Fork of Bayou Pierre, represented by the annexed plat, by virtue of a warrant of survey by the Spanish Government of Louisiana, dated 24 Feb. 1795, to the said Sarah Humphreys and Maria Dillingham, in the name of Maria and Sarah Smith, although the said Sarah Humphreys was at the date of the said warrant the wife of the said Humphreys but for causes which will be made to appear to the satisfaction of the Honourable Commissioners it was granted in aforesaid name Smith and they inhabited and cultivated the said tract of land from the 27 day of October 1795. (signed) G. W. Humphreys for Sarah and Mary Smith. District of Natchez: Sarah and Maria Smith. Certificate of survey in Spanish and plat, by William Dunbar. 24 Mar. 1795.

No. 1345. Claimant: Nathaniel and Elizabeth Tomlinson, 28 Mar. 1804. Witness: Benjamin Newman, 26 Nov. 1804. Rejected April 21, 1807. Miss. Ter. Adams Co. Nathaniel Tomlinson and Elizabeth, his wife, formerly Elizabeth Baker, claim 800 arpents on the waters of Second Creek in Adams County, by virtue of order of survey from the Spanish Governor, Don Estevan Miro, dated 27 Apr. 1790, to Elizabeth Baker, and by a final decree of the Baron De Carondelet, Governor General of the Province of Louisiana, 21 Mar. 1795.

No. 1347. Claimant: John Holt, 28 Mar. 1804. Witness: A. Watkins, 5 Nov. 1804. See No. 381 and No. 347. Rejected 12 May 1807. Jefferson County. John Holt claims a Donation of 640 acres in said county on the waters of Cole's Creek, by virtue of a settlement and actual cultivation and improvement long prior to 1797 and continued down to the present by himself and others for his use, the said Holt having been during the whole time a resident of this territory, above the age of 21 years and head of a family. J. A. Parrot, atty. for John Holt.

No. 1348. Claimant: Peter McNama, 28 Mar. 1804. Witness: John Ritchey, 4 Mar. 1804. Evidence insufficient. Rejected 24 Dec. 1806. Miss. Ter. Peter McNama, a citizen of the Territory afsd., claims the preference of becoming the purchaser of 446 acres on the waters of Homochitto, by virtue of it having been cultivated in Spring of 1802 by William Ritchey who verbally conveyed the same to the present claimant in June last, who has inhabited and cultivated the same ever since, and the said Ritchey was 21 years of age 3 March 1803.

No. 1349. Claimant: George W. Humphreys, 28 Mar. 1804. Certificate A-687 issued 28 Oct. 1805. Miss. Ter. Claiborne Co. George W. Humphreys claims 500 acres in said county and territory on the waters of Bayou Pierre, by virtue of a patent of the British Government of West Florida, 19 March 1779, to William Vousdan who was a settler in this territory on 27 Oct. 1795, and the said Vousdan sold the said tract unto Joseph Darlington, 4 Feb. 1789, and said Darlington conveyed by his attorney, Peter B. Bruin, Esq. the said tract to the said George W. Humphreys, by deed 25 Sept. 1801. (signed) G. W. Humphreys. Notation: By the testamony of Judge Bruin, it appears that Col. Humphreys, the father of the claimant was bound jointly with Darlington to Mr. Vousdan for the purchase money, that he held the land for his indemnification in case he, Darlington, should fail to make payment, that he did fail to do so and the claimant, after the death of his father, paid the money, whereupon a title in form was executed by Darlington to the claimant. (signed) Thomas H. W.

No. 1356. Claimant: George W. Humphreys, 28 Mar. 1804. Witness: William Smith, 15 Dec. 1804. (Lies within the Lyman Mandamus.) Rejected 30 Dec. 1806. On back: Mr. George Wilson Humphreys, his claim and plat. 164 acres. // To the Commissioners appointed to adjust the claims to lands West of of Pearl River: take notice that George W. Humphreys claims 164 acres by virtue of that Section of the Act of Congress which entitles the party to a preemption right, the said land lies on the north side of the Main Fork of Bayou Pierre. (signed) G. W. Humphreys. Plat shows land on one side of the tract "Sarah Smith" and on the other "John Hartley".

No. 1359. Claimant: Richard Lord, 28 Mar. 1804. Witness: Stephen Richards, 16 Oct. 1804. See No. 315. Rejected 17 May 1807. Notice: The Honourable Commissioners of the Land Office are hereby notified that Richard Lord claims 640 acres in Claiborne County, not claimed by any British grant or order of survey, by his improvement on it by actual habitation and cultivation in 1797, and the said Richard Lord was the head of a family and more than 21 years of age at the time of making the sd improvement, and has been an inhabitant of this territory since 1787 and when the Spanish troops evacuated said territory, and claims no other tract of land. Note: The claimant suggests that this land is claimed by Thomas Crabb under several intermediate claimants from Robert Ashley. (signed) E.

Turner. This claim rejected and Crabb's confirmed, Sept. 6, 1806. (signed) T.R. and T.H.W.

No. 1375. Claimant: Reuben Mayfield, 28 Mar. 1804. Witness: Stephen Middleton. Certificate D-68, issued to J. Scarlet, assignee of claimant, 26 Sept. 1806. Miss. Ter. Reuben Mayfield claims a preemption right to 620 acres improved and cultivated in Feb. 1803, on the main fork of Homochitto River in Adams County.

No. 1376. Claimant: John Burch, 28 Mar. 1804. Rejected for want of evidence, 30 Dec. 1806. Miss. Ter. John Burch, a citizen of sd. Ter., claims a preemption right to 172 acres on Irwin's Fork of Cole's Creek in Jefferson County, settled by claimant in 1802, who has continued to improve and cultivate the same ever since. // Plat shows land adjoining: Jacob Shilling, James Jones, John Cole and Jesse Harper.

No. 1377. Claimant: Joseph Slocumbe, 28 Mar. 1804. Witness: Samuel Ratcliff, 7 Sept. 1804. Certificate D-32, issued Sept. 4, 1806. Miss. Ter. Joseph Slocumbe claims a preemption right to 227 acres on a branch of Morgan's Fork of Homochitto in Adams County, settled by him in 1802 and lived on and cultivated ever since, the said Slocumbe having no other claim of land within the territory.

No. 1378. Claimant: Baptiste Moncla, 28 Mar. 1804. Rejected for want of evidence, 30 Dec. 1806. Baptiste Moncla claims the right of preference in becoming the purchaser of the United States of a lot in the City of Natchez, by virtue of its having been inhabited and cultivated on and previous to 3 Mar. 1803 by Peter La Bombarde who conveyed the same to present claimant 11 Jan. 1804.

No. 1382. Claimant: Anthony Villaverde, 28 Mar. 1804. Witness: John Shackler. Rejected. Evidence insufficient, Feb. 19, 1807. Miss. Ter. Anthony Villaverde, a citizen of sd. Territory, who on the 27 Oct. 1795, was an actual settler therein, above the age of 21 years, and did on the day when the Mississippi Territory was finally evacuated by the Spanish troops and also on the 30th Mar. 1797 inhabited and cultivated land in sd Territory and he claims no other land in same, except this Donation of 640 acres. Plat shows lands adjoining: E. Beauregarde, Mr. Stockman, and Jonathan Dayton.

No. 1384. Claimant: Simon Pressley, 28 Mar. 1804. Witness: William Barker, 20 Aug. 1804. Certificate D-254, issued Apr. 9, 1807. Miss. Ter. Simon Pressler, a citizen of sd territory, claims 640 acres in Adams County on Old River, by virtue of his having inhabited and cultivating it in 1794 and ever since, and he was above the age of 21 at the time of settling it and he claims no other land by either Spanish or British titles.

No. 1386. Claimant: Nehemiah Carter, 28 Mar. 1804. Witness: Elijah Phipps, 21 Feb. 1807. Rejected 12 May 1807. Nehemiah Carter of Miss. Ter. claims 640 acres on the north branch of the south fork of Buffalo Creek, Wilkinson County, by virtue of settlement made by Daniel Walton prior to the year 1797, from the said Daniel Walton conveyed to Barnaby Donley and from the said B. Donley conveyed to me. // I, Barney Donelly, have bargained and sold unto Nehemiah Carter a tract of land on Buffalo near Bullard's Springs, which was improved, inhabited and cultivated by Daniel Waltman previous to 1797; was signed over by said Waltman to me and I assign over to said Nehemiah Carter. 24 Feb. 1804. (signed) B. Donelly. Wit: Edward Hackett.

No. 1387. Claimant: Edward Hackett, 28 Mar. 1804. Witness: Hugh Davis. Certificate D. 156, issued 16 Dec. 1806. Edward Hacket, an inhabitant of Miss. Territory, claims 200 acres on Hutchins Creek, Wilkinson County, by virtue of a settlement made by James Knowles previous to 1795, for which he, the said James Knowles had a certificate from the Surveyor General of the Province. (signed) Edward Hackett. A rough plat shows: Gaillard's, Lyon's and Hutchin's Creek.

No. 1389. Claimant: Heirs of Christian Braxton, 28 Mar. 1804. Witness: Elisha Flower, 1 Oct. 1804. Note: Braxton is a Spanish grantee. See 685. 100 acres to include the improvement. Certificate D-22, issued to legal representatives for 100 acres, 4 Sept. 1806. Claiborne Co., Miss. Ter. The heirs of Christian Braxton claim 222 acres by settlement in 1797 by Christian Braxton, decd. (signed) Hezekiah Harman, administrator for the heirs.

No. 1393. Claimant: Parsons Carter, 28 Mar. 1804. Witness: Nehemiah Carter, 6 Dec. 1806. Rejected 12 May 1807. Parsons Carter, a citizen of Miss. Territory, Adams County, claims 640 acres in Wilkinson County on the waters of Buffalo Creek. The abovenamed Parsons Carter or some persons to his use did actually inhabit and cultivate said tract on the day the Miss. Territory was finally evacuated by the Spanish troops, he being at that time above the age of 21 years, wherefore the said Parson Carter prays a Donation for said tract. (signed) G. Poindexter, Atty. for claimant.

No. 1394. Claimant: Jesse Carter, 28 Mar. 1804. Witness: Nehemiah Carter 6 Dec. 1806. Rejected 12 May 1807. Miss. Ter. Jesse Carter, Parsons Carter and Isaac Carter, legal representatives of Nehemiah Carter, decd., claim 640 acres in Wilkinson County on Buffalo Creek. The abovementioned tract was actually inhabited and cultivated by the said Nehemiah Carter, deceased, prior to and on the day the Miss. Territory was finally evacuated by the Spanish troops, he being at that time above the age of 21, wherefore the present claimants ask a donation as legal representatives. G. Poindexter for claimants.

No. 1398. Claimant: Robert Moore, 28 Mar. 1804. Witness: Ebenezer Rees, 22 Aug. 1805. Certificate A-352, issued 16 Jan. 1806. Robert Moore, who was a settler in the Miss. Territory on 27 Oct. 1795, claims 700 acres in Adams County on the Miss. River, being part of 1100 acres contained in two grants by the Spanish Government, one to George Rapalje for 600 acres, dated 1780, and the other to Louis Charbonneau of 500 acres, (dated not filled out), by Charbono conveyed to said Rapalje, 3 July 1783, and afterwards, on the 1 Sept. 1787, 700 acres, part of the 1100 acres, was sold at Public Sale by order of the Government and purchased by Alexander Moore, deceased, who gave the same by his last will to his children, who by their deed of partition conveyed the same to the said claimant. The said two original tracts of land adjoining each other. Notation: See patent to Rapalje, Folio in No. 1591 and No. 1583. (signed) B.L.C.W. // Note: On the side of the plat: "The 500 arpents granted to Charbono were sold to Rapalje by two deeds, one 100 arpents 3 July 1783 for a certain sum and 400 arpents remaining by deed of exchange on said date." [No signature.]

No. 1404. Claimant: Robert Moore, 28 Mar. 1804. Residence of Henderson proved in claim No. 741. Certificate A-348, issued to claimant, 20 June 1805. Miss. Ter. Robert Moore, a citizen of the Territory, claims 345 acres by virtue of a grant to Richard Harrison for 602 acres by him conveyed to John and Alexander Henderson and by them conveyed to Ebenezer Rees, who 27 Oct. 1795 was a settler in the Territory afsd. The above tract of 345 acres being part of the abovedescribed grant, conveyed by said Ebenezer Rees to Abner L. Duncan, 13 Nov. 1801, and by said Duncan conveyed to claimant, 16 Feb. 1804. (signed) Robert Moore. The plat shows: Gideon Gibson, Ebenezer Rees and T. Foster with land adjoining.

No. 1410. Claimant: Margaret Ury, 28 Mar. 1804. Certificate A-767 issued 10 Apr. 1806. Margaret Ury claims a lot in the City of Natchez, No. 3, Square 12, by virtue of a Spanish grant, she having actually inhabited and improved the said lot on 3 March 1803 and many years prior to that date, namely from 1796 and 7, and being above the age of 21 years. (signed) James Moore agent for Margaret Ury.

No. 1431. Claimant: Francis Nailor, 28 Mar. 1804. Witness: William Howe, 29 Nov. 1804. Certificate B-261 issued as a Donation, 22 Apr. 1807. Miss. Ter. Claiborne Co. Francis Nailor hereby gives notice that he claims 170 arpents of land in said county on Bayou Pierre by virtue of a patent from the Spanish Government to John Burnet Jr., dated 14 Apr. 1796, granted in pursuance of an order of survey by the said government, 9 July 1782, who on 21 Mar. 1804 sold the said tract to this claimant. (signed) Francis Nailor. Plat shows: Jesse Hamilton with land adjoining. // Deed 21 Mar. 1804. John Burnet, of Claiborne Co., Miss. Ter. to Francis Nailor, of same, for $900 in hand paid, 170 acres on the north side of Bayou Pierre about 7 miles from the mouth, in Claiborne County. (signed) John Burnet. Wit: Vance Scott, William Scott. // Receipt for $900 for above described land, Mch. 23, 1804. John Burnet ack. within before Bryan Bruin, J.P.

No. 1432. Claimant: Stephen Marble, 28 Mar. 1804. Witness: David Hunt, 1 Oct. 1804. Certificate D-316 issued Dec. 29, 1806. Miss. Ter. Jefferson Co. Stephen Marble claims the preemption right to 112 acres on the waters of Cole's Creek in Jefferson County, improved, cultivated and actually inhabited by him since Feb. 1802.

No. 1444. Claimant: Moses Jones, 29 Mar. 1804. Witness: Elisha Flowers, 1 Nov. 1804. Certificate D-236, issued 22 Dec. 1806. The above plat describes Moses Jones' claim of 105 acres in Claiborne County on the waters of Bayou Pierre settled by John Roden in 1802 for a preemption right. John Roden sold it to John Thompson and Thompson sold to present claimant. // Indenture from Roden, 8 Nov. 1802, sold to John Thompson a tract on Widows Creek. John (x) Roden. Wit: Moses Jones, Ezekiel Flowers. // "I, John Thompson, of Miss. Territory, Claiborne County, for $40 to me in hand paid by Moses Jones, the receipt of which is hereby acknowledged, all my right title in a tract on waters of Widows Creek. (signed) John Thompson. Wit: Ezekiel Flowers, Joab Thompson. Proved before the Board, 21 Nov. 1804. T.R.

No. 1445. Claimant: Elisha Flowers, 29 Mar. 1804. Witness: Ezekiel Flowers, 21 Nov. 1804. Certificate D-125, Dec. 22, 1806. Elisha Flowers claims 240 acres by a right of preference that the land was settled in 1800 by a small cabin and clearing in Claiborne County. Plat shows that the land was on branch of Tabor's Creek and next to Gibson's line. // John Flanagan of the Miss. Ter., Claiborne Co. in consideration of $30 to me paid by Elisha Flowers, of same, do assign forever the improvement that I am now living on and since 1802, being on the waters of Clark's Creek, bounded by Richard King. 13 May 1805. (signed) Joseph Flannagan. Wit: John A. Gibson, Gadi Gibson.

No. 1446. Claimant: Andrew Marshalk, 29 Mar. 1804. Allowed under patent No. 1468, Barland's, June 16, 1807. Confirmed. Certificate A-108, issued Feb. 12, 1807. Miss. Territory. Andrew Marchalk, a citizen of Natchez, claims a lot in the City of Natchez, containing 130 feet front, bounded on a Spanish grant to George Cochran of sundry lots in said city, and a conveyance from said Cochran to Lot No. 4, Square 9, to the present claimant, 16 Sept. 1802. Plat shows lot on the South First Street 130 feet, John Cochran on side and Luke Whitney on rear.

No. 1447. Claimant: Thomas Hardesty, 29 Nov. 1804. Certificate A-520 issued to claimant 27 Aug. 1805. Thomas Hardesty claims a part of Lot 1, Square 12 in the City of Natchez, beginning on the eastern side of John Perkins' line, on First North Street, by virtue of a grant from the Spanish Government to James Moore and of a conveyance from said James Moore and Anna Maria, his wife, 1 Oct. 1803, to him the said Thomas Hardesty.

No. 1448. Claimant: Frederick Mayers, 29 Mar. 1804. Witness: Isaac Rapalje, 28 Nov. 1804. See No. 1740. Rejected 19 May 1807. Frederick Mayers claims a Donation of 490 acres in Claiborne Co. for his settlement and cultivation of the premises on 1792 and continuing thereon until compelled to leave the premises by the repeated assaults of the Indians. Then the said Mayers again took possession of the place in October 1795 and continued there three years after the expiration of which time the Indians again forced him to leave the premises and the said Mayers has no claim to other land in the Territory in his own name. At the time of his first settlement on the premises he was the head of a family. (signed) Frederick Meiers.

No. 1450. Claimant: E., A. and E. Marble, 29 Mar. 1804. Certificate A-364 issued 24 June 1805. Miss. Ter. Wilkinson Co. Ezra, Ambrose, and Earl Marble hereby give notice that they claim 400 arpens in said county on Buffalo Creek on the east side of P. Foley's 1264-arpens tract, by virtue of a Spanish grant to said Patrick Foley, 25 Oct. 1790, who conveyed the said 400 arpens to Ezra, Abner, Ambrose and Theophilus Marble, 1 June 1799, and the said Abner and Theophilus gave their part to the said Earl Marble 4 Jan. 1804. (signed) Theophilus Marble. // Plat shows land adjoining owned by: James Smith, Col. John Ellis and Patrick Foley.

No. 1455. Claimant: G. W. Humphreys, 29 Mar. 1804. See No. 282. Rejected 12 May 1807. (James Davenport says that this claim is adverse to his, No. 282, and that his is the best title.) Miss. Ter. Claiborne Co. George W. Humphreys, heir and legal representative of Ralph Humphreys, deceased, claims 250 acres in said county on the Mississippi River, by right of occupancy. The said tract was improved for the use of the said George W. Humphreys in 1797 and the same improvement is still on the said land. The said tract was vacant in time of the Spanish Government and the Surveyor of said government placed the said Ralph, deceased, on the said tract of land, as he claimed no other land in said territory either by Spanish or British patents, or warrant of survey. (signed) G. W. Humphreys. // "Mr. William Vousdan, Deputy Surveyor of this District, will have Mr. Ralph Humphreys put in possession of 600 acres of land on Bayou Pierre, bounded by the lands granted to Henry Green and vacant lands. This will serve said Mr. Humphreys for title until he presents his petition for others to His Excellency. Natchez, 29 Jan. 1789." (signed) GrandPre. // "Laid off 220 acres, three or four miles above the mouth of Bayou Pierre, Finney's old place, 200 acres, adjoining Henry Green and said Humphreys' lines, the residue joining Llewellyn Price and the said Humphreys, 1 Aug. 1789". (signed) Bryan Bruin. On the reverse: "Came before me Dempsey White and being duly sworn sayeth that he saw Samuel Davenport sign and deliver the within and himself and John Burnet signed as witnesses, before me 2 Sept. 1802." (signed) James Harman, Justice of the Peace. "I have sold the within land to William Thompson, Dec. 1, 1797, (signed) James Davenport. Wit: John Burnet, Dempsey White. By order of the Court the within is permitted to be recorded this 1st day of December, 1802. Mathew Tierney, Clk.

No. 1456. Claimant: Stephen Stephenson, 29 Mar. 1804. No evidence adduced. Rejected 24 Dec. 1806. Miss. Ter. Stephen Stephenson, a citizen of the territory afsd., claims the preference of becoming a purchaser of the United States of 500 acres on the Mississippi River, about 4 miles about the Homochitto, by virtue of having inhabited and cultivated the same before and on 3 March 1803, and continuing to do so ever since. The claimant was the head of a family at that time.

No. 1457. Claimant: Asher Perkins, 29 Mar. 1804. Witness: Joseph Slocumb, 12 Nov. 1804. Certificate D-38 issued 5 Sept. 1807. Asher Perkins claims a preemption of 169 acres by settlement in March 1802 and cultivating the same ever since, lying in Adams County, Miss. Ter. on a small branch of Morgan's Fork of Homochitto. The claimant was the head of a family when he settled the afsd. land.

No. 1458. Claimant: James White, 29 Mar. 1804. Wit: John Maylone, 24 Nov. 1804. Certificate D-26 issued to Thomas Thompkins, assignee, 4 Sept. 1806. Miss. Ter. James White claims the preference to become the purchaser of the United States of 100 acres on the Mississippi in Jefferson Co., by virtue of its having been inhabited and cultivated in 1801 by Henry Kyper who sold it to the said James in 1802 and the said James has inhabited and cultivated the said tract ever since. // I, Henry Kyper, have bargained and sold to James White my improvement and labor and right of land lying between Asa Gober's and William Fairbank's, 15 May 1802. (signed) Henry Kyper. Wit: Sam'l. Osborn, Joseph Jackson. James White, of Jefferson Co., Miss. Ter., hath bargained and sold to Thomas Thompkins, of same, 100 acres on Miss. River, about a mile below Smith's Mill, improved by Curtis Borer and made over by him to Henry Kyper and by him to the said James White. And know ye that I, for the sum of $300, have sold all my title and claim of and into the same to Thomas Thompkins. 15 July 1804. (signed) Jas. White.

No. 1459. Claimant: Thomas Essex, 29 Mar. 1804. Wit: Caleb Potter, 27 Nov. 1804. Certificate D-273, 24 Dec. 1806. Miss. Ter. Thomas Essex, a citizen of said territory, claims the right of preference of becoming the purchaser of the United States of 300 acres on the Mississippi River by virtue of its having been inhabited and cultivated in 1801 by John Maylone who sold it to said Essex 17 June 1802, and it has been inhabited and cultivated by him ever since. // John Maylone, of Pickering County, Miss. Ter., has bargained and sold to Thos. Essex an improvement on the Mississippi against the lower end of Cole's Creek 17 June 1802. Ack. before R. C. Claiborne, Clk. // Thos. Essex, of Jefferson Co., to Thos. Thompkins, of same, 320 acres improved in 1802 by John Maylone and made over to Thos. Essex 27 Oct. 1804. John Maylone, Washington King, and Thomas Essex. Proved before the Board by John Maylone, 27 Nov. 1804. E.T.

No. 1460. Claimant: Thomas McCrora, 29 Mar. 1804. Wit: Landon Davis, 29 Mar. 1804. Wit: John Bullen, 24 Nov. 1804. Certificate B-211, issued Feb. 19, 1807. Miss. Ter. Thomas McCrora, the legal representative of Thomas Lanphier, claims a Donation of 640 acres. The said Thomas Lanphier did, on the day the Spanish troops evacuated the said territory, actually inhabit and cultivate the said tract, he being then the head of a family and claiming no land by British or Spanish survey in said territory. (signed) Thomas McCrory. // Paper: I, Thomas Lanphier bargain and sell an improvement with 4 acres of corn to Mordecai Richards of the Homochitto for $25 to be paid in cotton delivered at Natchez, this improvement being vacant land above Hugh Davis on the Homochitto, 11 Oct. 1798. Wit: James Smith, Charles Adams. (signed) Thomas Lanphier. // In fine handwriting on the side: "On 8 Nov. 1804, personally and voluntarily appeared before the subscriber, alcalde of the 2nd division of New Feliciana, in Province of West Florida, and in the presence of two assisting witnesses, Thomas Lanphier, the within grantee [?] and being duly sworn, deposes that the within signature of Thomas Lanphier is his own proper handwriting and acknowledges this to be his voluntary act. (signed) William Gildart, John Mears, Isaac Johnson. // The reverse of the paper: "Mordecai Richards obligates myself to make over to John Bullen Thomas Lanphier's right to an improvement on the Homochitto above Hugh Davis', 29 Nov. 1798." Mordecai Richards. Wit: Henry Gary. // I do hereby transfer the within right to Thomas McCrory, 21 Feb. 1804. Wit: David Eldridge. (signed) John Bullen. Ack. the above bef. Board, 12 Nov. 1804.

No. 1463. Claimant: David R. Crosby, 29 Mar. 1804. Witness: Matthew McCulloch. Certificate D-317 issued Dec. 29, 1806. David R. Crosby, a citizen of Miss. Ter., Wilkinson Co., claims the right of preference in purchase of 640 acres in said county on the waters of Buffalo Cr. The abovenamed David R. Crosby did actually inhabit and cultivate the abovementioned tract prior to and on 3 Mar. 1803 and at that time was above the age of 21 years and the head of a family.

No. 1464. Claimant: Watkins Nicholson, 29 Mar. 1804. Witness: Matthew McCulloch. Rejected for want of sufficient evidence, 30 Dec. 1806. Watkins Nicholson, a citizen of Miss. Ter. Co. of Wilkinson, claims 640 acres in said county on waters of Homochitto. The above Watkins Nicholson did actually inhabit and cultivate the afsd. tract on and prior to the Mississippi Territory was finally evacuated by the Spanish troops, he beiug at that time above the age of 21 and the head of a family.

No. 1465. Claimant: Thomas Owens, 29 Mar. 1804. Wit: Theophilus Marble, 1 Oct. 1804. Jonathan Curtis, 3 March 1806. Francis Baldridge, 11 March 1806. Certificate D-318 issued Dec. 29, 1806. Thomas Owens claims a preemption right to 200 acres on waters of Cole's Creek in Jefferson County, settled in 1802 by claimant, who still lives on and cultivates the same, having no other claim within the territory. // Know all men, etc: I, Thomas Owens, of Jefferson County, has sold unto James Nelson, of Adams County, all my right to 200 acres in Jefferson County on Cole's Cr., which I claim as a preemption, in virtue of settlement of Jonathan Curtis, and in consideration of James Nelson having paid me $350, the receipt of which I do hereby acknowledge. 12 Feb. 1806. (signed) Thomas Owens. Wit: Thomas Baldridge, Isaac Caldwell.

No. 1466. Claimant: John Kennison, 29 Mar. 1804. Rejected 19 May 1807. John Kennison, a citizen of Miss. Ter., claims the right of preference in becoming purchaser of 200 acres in Adams County on the waters of the South Fork of Cole's Creek, by virtue of its having been inhabited and cultivated by him and for his use in 1802 and ever since. // Surveyed and laid out for John Kennison a tract of land in Miss. Ter. on South Fork of Cole's Creek near a tract of Jacob Guise, Esq., 200 acres. 31 Dec. 1803. (signed) John Dinsmore.

No. 1470. Claimant: James Howard, 29 Mar. 1804. Rejected 19 May 1807. James Howard claims 148 acres in Adams County on Wells Creek, by virtue of said tract having been inhabited and cultivated by Charles Carter and by his legal representatives who were upward of 21 years of age on the day that the Spanish troops evacuated the Miss. Ter. and of a conveyance of said land by said Carter to this claimant. E. Turner for the claimant. // Transfer of Charles Carter of Adams Co., Miss. Ter. to James Howard of same 148 acres on Wells Cr. adj. lands of Holland and Hunt, and Benj. Carter. 6 Jan. 1804. John (X) Carter. Wit: Simon Carter.

No. 1471. Claimant: Joshua Howard, 29 Mar. 1804. Wit: Henry Phipps, 2 Sept. 1806. Rejected 27 Apr. 1807. Miss. Ter. Adams Co. Joshua Howard, a settler in the Territory before and on 27 Oct. 1795, claims 200 acres on south fork of Second Creek by virtue of an order of survey from the British Government of West Florida to said Joshua Howard, dated 1776, which land was settled upon by the claimant and improved. Plat shows: Manuel Madden and John Small with land adjoining.

No. 1472. Claimant: John Howard, 29 Mar. 1804. Rejected, 12 May 1807. Miss. Ter. Adams Co. John Howard claims a preference to become the purchaser of 165 acres on south fork of Second Creek by an improvement made in 1798 and claims no other land in the territory. Plat shows: Joshua Howard, David Ferguson and R. Sessions with lands adjoining.

No. 1473. Claimant: Martin Owens, 29 Mar. 1804. Rejected 12 May 1807. Miss. Ter. Martin Owens, an actual settler of sd. territory, claims a donation right of 300 arpens on Fairchild's Cr. in Jefferson Co., it being a tract surveyed for sd Owens by virtue of a grant from His Excellency Gov. Gayoso in 1794, for going on an expedition to the Walnut Hills. Said claim he has cultivated and improved, being the head of a family, to wit: a wife and four children and two slaves. Plat shows land adjoining: Melling Woolley, Willis Bonner and Jno. Dyson. Coles Creek, 7 Jan. 1805. I certify that I surveyed 300 acres for Martin Owens by virtue of his . . (torn) . . . . adj. 11 Apr. 1795. (signed) William Thomas.

No. 1474. Claimant: William B. Smith, Jr., 29 Mar. 1804. Witness: Jeremiah Routh, 8 July 1805. Certificate A-415 issued 9 July 1805. William B. Smith Jr. claims 655 arpents in Adams on waters of St. Catherine's Cr. by virtue of a patent to William B. Smith Sr. by the Spanish Government of Louisiana on 5 May 1794. Said William B. Smith Sr. was an actual settler in said Territory 27 Oct. 1795 and he sold the said tract of land to said Wm. B. Smith Jr.

No. 1478. Claimant: John Maylone, 29 March 1804. Witness: Samuel Osborn 10 June 1804. Certificate D-23 issued 4 Sept. 1806. Miss. Ter. Jefferson Co. John Maylone claims the right of preference of becoming the preference of the United States of 200 acres in said county and territory on the Miss. River abt. 12 miles above the mouth of Coles Creek, by virtue of an improvement made John Young in 1797 who sold the same to Caleb Potter in 1798 who sold it to John Maylone in June 1799, who sold it to Daniel Johnson in March 1801, who sold it to Amos Hubbard in said year who sold it to Curtis Voris, 26 Jan. 1804, who sold and conveyed the same to present claimant 17 Feb. 1804. But unfortunately all of the said sales except one from Amos Hubbard to Curtis Voris and from Curtis Voris to the claimant were consumed in the claimant's house which was burned Dec. 1801. The said tract has been cultivated and inhabited by and for the use of the claimant ever since the year 1799. // Transfer from

Curtis Voris (marked on back "not to be recorded at request of claimant" signed E.T.) same as above, consideration $200, near a saw mill, the claim of Hubbard. 17 Feb. 1804. Witness; Samuel Osborn. signed Curtis Voris. // Amos Hubbard to Curtis Voris, same as above, reciting each transfer, for $200 in merchandise, Jan. 26, 1804. signed Amos Hubbard. // I do assign my right to within to John Maylone for value rec'd. 17 Feb. 1804. Curtis Voris. Wit: Samuel Osborn.

No. 1479. Claimant: Daniel McNeely, 29 Mar. 1804. Wit: Abraham Wells, 29 Oct. 1804. Certificate D-319, issued Dec. 29, 1806. Daniel McNeely claims preemption right of 105 acres, settled Lank Stuart, December 1801, who resided on and cultivated the same about 1 Oct. 1803 until he sold his title therein to Daniel McNeely. The said Stuart never had any lands granted to him either by the British or Spanish Government. (signed) Daniel McNeely. // Survey: 105 acres on Bates Fork of Sandy Creek, a branch of the Homochitto, Adams Co., Miss. Ter. John Dinsmore.

No. 1483. Claimant: Jesse Bryant, 29 Mar. 1804. Witness: George Bailey, 15 Oct. 1804. Certificate D-157, issued 16 Dec. 1806. Miss. Ter., Adams Co. Jesse Bryant, a resident of said territory, claims a preemption right of 160 acres in said county on Dry Bayou by a settlement made and continued by Joseph Irwin in 1801 and conveyed by said Irwin to present claimant by bill of sale 21 Jan. 1804. (signed) Jesse Bryant. // Bill of sale by Irwin. His labor and good will. Signed. Wit: Henry Moore.

No. 1484. Claimant: Philip Leaflighter, by James Spain, his representative, 29 Mar. 1804. Rejected 12 May 1807. Miss. Ter. Philip Leaplighter, the head of a family a wife and five children, did on the day the Spanish troops finally evacuated the said territory and also on 30 Mar. 1797 actually inhabit and cultivate 200 acres and claims no other land in said territory, and claims a donation of the said 200 acres, on the waters of Cole's Creek. (signed) James Spain.

No. 1487. Claimant: Jeremiah Bass, 29 Mar. 1804. Wit: John Stapler. Certificate D-158 issued 16 Dec. 1806. Miss. Ter. Jeremiah Bass claims 184 acres in Adams County on the Homochitto River by virtue of his having inhabited and cultivated it in 1801 and ever since and therefore claims the right of preference in becoming the purchaser of the United States of said tract. Plat by Elijah Pope.

No. 1496. Claimant: John Smith, 29 Mar. 1804. Duplicate of No. 1830. Rejected 19 May 1807. John Smith claims 300 acres on North Fork of Cole's Cr. part of 1000 acres gr. to James Elliot by the Spanish Govt. 20 Oct. 1788, conveyed by sd Elliot to Daniel Callahan and by sd Callahan to John Smith 21 Nov. 1800. (signed) John Smith.

No. 1497. Claimant: John Smith, 29 Mar. 1804. Wit: John Brooks, 8 Oct. 1804. Confirmed. Certificate A-366, June 24, 1805. John Smith claims 450 arpents on the Bluff in Miss. Ter. about 25 miles northeast of Natchez Fort by patent fr. the Spanish Government, 6 Mar. 1789. (signed) John Smith.

No. 1503. Claimant: John Williams, 29 Mar. 1804. Wit: Gaspar Sinclair, 21 Nov. 1804. Rejected for want of sufficient evidence, 30 Dec. 1806. Miss. Ter. John Williams claims the right to become the purchaser of the United States of 640 acres on Cole's Cr. by virtue of his having inhabited and cultivated it in 1802 and ever since. The said John was at the time of the first settlement the head of a family. Plat by Joseph Session dated 20 Apr. 1803, showing Col. Hutchins' land on one side.

No. 1504. Claimant: Robert Throckmorton, 29 Mar. 1804. Witness: Adam Snider, 29 Apr. 1805. Certificate B-852 to W. Brooks, assignee, 29 Aug. 1806. Robert Throckmorton claims by right of occupancy 600 acres in Jefferson Co. by virtue of settlement and improvement and cultivation thereon in 1797 made by Simon Grimlier, who was then the head of a family and conveyed his right to same in 1804 to present claimant. Said Grimlier having cultivated the land ever since 1797. // Indenture 19 Mar. 1806 Robert Throckmorton and Sally, his wife, of Jefferson Co., Miss. Ter. to William Brooks, of Adams Co., in consideration of $1000 to them paid grant and sell all tract on North Fork of Cole's Cr., bounded on the west by land now claimed by the heirs of Anthony Hutchins, 600 acres, settled by Simon Grimlier. Robert (X) Throckmorton. Wit: Wm. Snodgrass. Ack. by Robt. Throckmorton and Mrs. Sarah Throckmorton before Edw. Haile, J.P. 9 March 1800. Indenture 23 Jan. 1804. Simon Grimlier, of Jefferson Co., to Robt. Throckmorton, of same, for $10, paid, to land adjoining J. Hutchins on west, Christian Hackler on northeast. (signed) Simon Grimlier. Wit: Joe A. Parrott.

No. 1505. Claimant: Anthony Nicholas, 29 Mar. 1804. Wit: Henry Manadue, 11 June 1804. Certificate B-94 issued Feb 1807. Miss. Ter. Anthony Nicholas, a citizen of Ter. afsd., claims a Donation of 204 acres on the waters of Fairchild's Cr., bounded by the habitation and cultivation of the premises now claimed by John Carrel before the 29 Mar. 1798, who was at that time the head of a family and who by a verbal transfer conveyed the same to said Anthony Nicholas. The claimant has also obtained a conveyance from Mary Carrel, the wife of said John Carrel, now deceased, of her right to the same. 28 Dec. 1803. Plat: Land adjoining: Joseph Bonner, Willis Bonner and Margaret Vaucherey. // Conveyance from Mary Carrel to Anthony Nicholas, consideration $77. 28 Dec. 1801. Wit: William Dailey. (signed) Mary Carrel. // Indenture, 4 Feb. 1806, Anthony Nicholas to Anthony Vaucherey, for $500 in hand paid, 204 acres, joining the Pine Ridge, abt. 12 miles above Natchez. Anthony (X) Nicholas. Ack. 29 Oct. 1806. T.R. Wit: Margaret Vaucherey.

No. 1506. Claimant: Thomas Sullivan, 29 Mar. 1804. Wit: Joseph Green, 21 Aug. 1804. Certificate B-151 issued Feb. 10, 1807. Thomas Sullivan, a citizen of the Miss. Ter. Jefferson Co., claims 240 acres in sd county on Cole's Cr. founded on a warrant of survey gr. by the Spanish Government to sd Thomas Sullivan, who did actually inhabit and cultivate the sd tract prior and on 27 Oct. 1795, he being at that time the age of 21 years and the head of a family. G. Poindexter, atty for claimant.

No. 1507. Claimant: Moses Moore, 29 Mar. 1804. Rejected for want of evidence, 30 Dec. 1806. Miss. Ter. Moses Moore, by virtue of an improvement made prior to 3 Mar. 1803, claims 640 acres, beginning at a high bluff on the south side of Buffalo Creek.

No. 1508. Claimant: John Moore, 29 Mar. 1804. Rejected for want of evidence, 30 Dec. 1806. Miss. Ter. John Moore claims a tract of land by virtue of an improvement made prior to 3 Mar. 1803. (No acreage given.)

No. 1509. Claimant: Thomas J. Donaldson, preemption claim of 108 acres, 29 Mar. 1804. Rejected for want of evidence, 30 Dec. 1806. Thomas Donaldson, a citizen of Miss. Ter. Adams Co., claims a right of preference in the purchase of 108 acres in sd county on Dry Bayou, founded on the transfer of afsd. tract from Isaac Irwin to Jesse Bryant who conveyed the same to George Bailey and the sd Bailey to the present claimant. The sd Irwin or some person to his use did actually inhabit and cultivate the afsd. land prior to the 3 Mar. 1803, he being at that time above the age of 21 yrs, and the head of a family. G. Poindexter, atty for the claimant.

No. 1510. Claimant: Roger Dickson, 29 Mar. 1804. Rejected, 12 May 1807. Roger Dickson claims 1526 acres on south fork of Bayou Pierre, the said land having been surveyed and improved by sd Dickson 1 Sept. 1797, on a location made by John Smith in and before 1787 and surrendered to said Dickson. Plat shows land of John Smith on one side and that of John Brooks on the other.

No. 1511. Claimant: William Nolen, 29 Mar. 1804. Rejected 12 May 1807. William Nolen, by his representative, Roger Dickson, claims 640 acres on James's Run, bounded on west by land of William Dunbar, purchased of Melling Woolley, on east Patrick Cogan, on south by Richard King. (signed) R. Dickson.

No. 1512. Claimant: Roger Dickson, 29 Mar. 1804. Rejected 12 May 1807. Roger Dickson claims 800 acres on Platner Fork of Cole's Cr., adj. the land of John Terry, deceased above him, and John Holt below, on part of which tract sd Roger Dickson lived and improved and cultivated in 1790, and part of the same further improved in 1796.

No. 1513. Claimant: John Brooks, 29 Mar. 1804. Wit: Raleigh Hogan, 8 Oct. 1804. Certificate B-95 issued Feb. 3, 1807. Miss. Ter. Jefferson Co. John Brooks hereby gives notice that he claims 640 acres in sd county on waters of Cole's and Fairchild's Creeks, by virtue of his having inhabited and cultivated the same, with his family, consisting of a wife and six children and nine negroes ever since the year of 1794, and claims no other land in sd. territory. (signed) John Brooks. Plat shows land adjoining: Thomas Irwin, Adam Bingaman, John Smith and ______ Surget.

No. 1514. Claimant: John Smith, 29 Mar. 1804. Wit: John Brooks, 8 Oct. 1804. Certificate A-369 issued June 24, 1805. John Brooks for John Smith claims 230 arpents about 20 miles from Natchez Fort and 2 miles from the Bluff on the waters of the Mississippi and Fairchild's Cr. by patent of the Spanish Government to John Smith, 23 Mar. 1790. John Smith by John Brooks.

No. 1515. Claimant: John Burnet, Sr., 29 Mar. 1804. Wit: B. Pitman, 20 Nov. 1804. Same land sold to F. Nailor. See No. 1431. John Burnet is a grantee. Rejected 22 Apr. 1807. Miss. Ter. Claiborne Co. John Burnet claims 170 arpents in sd. county on Bayou Pierre, by virtue of having inhabited and cultivated the same ever since 1784, being the head of a family during the whole of the time.

No. 1516. Claimant: William Mofford, 29 Mar. 1804. Rejected 12 June 1807. Miss. Ter. Town of Pinckneyville. William Mofford hereby give notice that he claims two lots in town of Pinckneyville Nos.

46 and 48, lying opposite to each other, one-half acre each, by virtue of a Spanish patent to Thomas Dawson who conveyed the said two lots to William Miller, who conveyed them to this claimant by deed 1 Oct. 1803. (signed) William Morford. // Conveyance from William and Ursula Miller to William Morford, (William Miller, and Ursula, his wife, of the Province of La.), for $1000 in hand paid. (signed) William Miller, Ursula Miller. Wit: Levi Wells, Ennemonde Meullion. Prov. by Levi Wells before John Wall, J.P. of Adams Co. 17 Nov. 1803.

No. 1517. Claimant: Robert Griffin, 29 Mar. 1804. Fanny Griffin, witness, 28 Nov. 1804. Certificate D-174, issued 24 Dec. 1806. Miss. Ter. Claiborne Co. Robert Griffin claims 320 acres on and adjoining the Miss. Swamp about 5 miles below Walnut Hills by improvement made previous to and on 3 Mar. 1803 by sd Griffin.

No. 1518. Claimant: William Barnes, 29 Mar. 1804. [No details.] William Barnes, of Miss. Ter., claims 210 acres on west prong of the River Amite by improvement made before and on 3 Mar. 1803, by William Lorimer, whose right the sd Barnes has obtained as part of sd Lorimer's preemption. // Certificate of survey and plat by Robert Griffin, 13 Mar. 1804.

No. 1519. Claimant: James Truly, 29 Mar. 1804. Wit: Wm. Thomas, 28 May 1804. Certificate B-212 issued Feb. 19, 1807. Miss. Ter. James Truly claims 355 acres as a Donation on the south fork of Cole's Cr. sometimes called Holt's Fork in Jefferson Co., the same being improved by him in 1795. He has continued to cultivate same ever since. Plat shows land adjoining John Hamberlin, David Carradine and Robert Dunbar and Mayes.

No. 1520. Claimant: Washington Burch, 29 Mar. 1804. Wit: John Burch, 14 Feb. 1805. B-7, 29 Dec. 1807. (Note: Conflicting with Nos. 973, and 761.) Miss. Ter. Washington Burch claims a preemption right of 600 acres on the waters of Platner's Fork of Cole's Cr. in Jefferson County, improved by him in 1802 and cultivated ever since he being the head of a family to wit a wife and two children and claiming no other land in this territory. The Plat shows land adjoining: Daniel Harrigil, William Chaney and John Gaskin.

No. 1521. Claimant: Jacob Stroope, 29 Mar. 1804. (Notation: See No. 1452.) [Claim is torn.] Plat shows the land is bounded by Andrew Bell and George Killian, David Burney and Joseph Perkins, and surveyed by Charles De France, 27 Mar. 1804. On reverse is the end of the claim which was for 81 acres by virtue of a Spanish grant to Charles Adams, being a part of 400 acres so granted, which was sold to Julian Thomas and sd Thomas conveys the said land to present claimant, 27 Feb. 1801. Jacob Stroope by Ezekiel Perkins, his attorney.

No. 1522. Claimant: Heirs of Jacob Vaucherie, 29 Mar. 1804. Rejected 12 June 1807. The legal representatives of Jacob Vaucherie, deceased, claim 600 acres on Homochitto River, founded on a Spanish patent . . . . (torn) . . . . . . Plat shows Mr. Vaughan's land on one side, Samuel Swayze's heirs and vacant lands.

No. 1523. Claimant: Jacob Cable, 29 Mar. 1804. Wit: Roger Dickson, 20 Nov. 1804. Rejected 14 May 1807. Miss. Ter., Jacob Cable claims 1620 acres on the waters of Bayou Pierre, which was petitioned for by Elizabeth Stoope from the British Government of West Florida. The said Elizabeth inhabited and cultivated the tract in 1774 and continued to do so until compelled to leave by the many outrages committed upon her family by the Indians. She continued to live in this territory until she died. The said Jacob Cable bought the sd tract from the sd Elizabeth and he has been an actual settler in sd territory since 1773. He signs with a mark. Plat shows Thomas Woods and Roger Dickson with land adjoining.

No. 1531. Claimant: David Ferguson, 29 Mar. 1804. Rejected 12 June, 1807. David Ferguson, a resident within the Miss. Ter. on and prior to 27 Oct. 1795, claims 280 acres in Wilkinson Co. by virtue of a warrant from the Spanish Government to James Carrol, dated 22 Sept. 1791, and an improvement prior to 1798 and by virtue of certain intermediate conveyances. David Ferguson by J. Dunlap.

No. 1532. Claimant: Heirs of John Vauchere, 29 Mar. 1804. Witness: Anthony Nicholas, 27 Oct. 1806. Certificate B-243 issued 30 Mar. 1807. Miss. Ter. the legal representatives of John Vauchere, deceased, claim 1000 acres, except as hereinafter excepted, on Miss. River, about 5 leagues from Fort Natchez, founded on a purchase of sd tract by Anthony Gras at public sale of same as the property of San Germain made by the Spanish Government when the same was regularly and fairly struck off to the sd Anthony Gras who by deed 4 Jan. 1787 for a valuable consideration made over the same to John Vauchere, now deceased. Said John by his last will and testament, dated 7 Sept. 1797, and written in the French language, exhibited herewith, devised the moiety of sd 1000 acres to his spouse and wife,

Margaret L'Estage, who by her deed conveyed her half to John Wilson whose representative by their lawyers claim the same. The Honourable Board of Commrs. will consider from a fair investigation of the will of John Vauchere whether his widow, Margaret L'Estage, was entitled to take the one-half of the aforementioned tract. W. B. Shields, atty. for the claimant. Commissioners; Robert Williams, Thomas Rodney, Edward Turner. Miss. Ter. County of Adams, 16 Mar. 1801: I certify that at the request of Mrs. Vauchere, widow, having extended the lines containing 1000 acres formerly granted Mr. St. Germain and by him sold to the late Mr. Vauchere, decd., the front of said tract having been formerly run by Mr. Charles Laveau Trudeau, and the plat thereof being burnt by the first fire of New Orleans. The said tract is on the east side of Miss. River, adjoining the swamp, about 7 miles northeast from the town of Natchez. (signed) Wm. Atchinson. [No will in the file.]

No. 1533. Claimant: John Perkins, 29 Mar. 1804. Certificate A-522, issued 27 Aug. 1805. John Perkins claims a part of Lot No. 1, Sq. No. 12, in City of Natchez, by virtue of a grant from the Spanish Government to James Moore, 15 Jan. 1795, and the conveyance from sd. Moore and Anna Maria, his wife, 1 Sept. 1803, to sd John Perkins.

No. 1534. Claimant: Joseph and George Newman, 29 Mar. 1804. Certificate A-573 issued 9 Sept. 1805. Joseph and George Newman claim a part of Lot No. 2, Sq. No. 10 in the City of Natchez by virtue of a Spanish grant to Francis Lennan, 6 Dec. 1794, and by him conveyed, 29 Mar. 1798, to Robert Moore and by sd Robert Moore, 16 Sept. 1802, to sd Joseph and George Newman.

No. 1535. Claimant: Thomas Bills, 29 Mar. 1804. Wit: Bennet Truly. Certificate A-766 issued 10 Apr. 1806. Thomas claims half of Lot. No. 3, Sq. No. 12 in the City of Natchez by virtue of a conveyance, 27 Mar. 1804, from Margaret Urie, by Nancy Bradston, her atty-in-fact, to sd Thomas Bills, which premises were granted to sd Margaret Urie by the Spanish Government. Thomas Bills signs with a mark.

No. 1536. Claimant: George Cochran, 29 Mar. 1804. Wit: Hezekiah Harman, 1 Oct. 1804. Certificate D-234, issued 22 Dec. 1806. George Cochran claims the right to become the purchaser of the United States of 172 acres on Bayou Pierre. Said land was inhabited and cultivated in 1802 to the use of said George and ever since. Plat shows: Hezekiah Harman, Christopher Braxton and Dempsey White as having land adjoining, also a gin and a store on the property.

No. 1537. Claimant: George Cochran, 29 Mar. 1804. Wit: William Smith, 19 Dec. 1804. Rejected 14 May 1807. Miss. Ter. Claiborne, George Cochran claims 169 arpents in sd county on the waters of Bayou Pierre. He purchased the sd tract from George W. Humphreys, heir and legal representative of Ralph Humphreys, decd., which sd Ralph Humphreys obtained permission from the Spanish Government to take possession of sd land and also ordered a survey of same. This 169 acres is only part of the land that he had permission to improve. Robert Cochran for George Cochran. // Certificate and plat by Wm. Atchinson, Surveyor, 20 Sept. 1801. Miss. Ter., Pickering County. I do certify that at the request of Mr. George Cochran and Mr. George Humphreys that I have surveyed and made out in the name of Mr. Cochran 169 acres sold to him by the sd Mr. Humphreys on Bayou Pierre about 45 miles northeast of Natchez. Shows adj. lands of George Cochran lately owned by R. Humphreys and purchased of Waterman Crane, of Cochran bought of Llewelyn Price. // Transfer from G. W. Humphreys and Sarah Humphreys, both of whom signed, 16 July 1797, to George Cochran, for $50, land on James Cr ..... (torn) . . . part of a grant to Ralph Humphreys, decd. Wit: Waterman Crane, Llewellyn Price. Receipt of fifty Mexican dollars, payment in full, acknowledged, before Bryan Bruin, J.P.

No. 1538. Claimant: George Cochran, 9 Mar. 1804. Residence of claimant proved. Wit: Lewis Evans 26 Mar. 1804. Certificate B-6 issued 2 June 1806. Miss. Ter. George Cochran claims Lot No. 2 Square No. 9 by virtue of a patent by Spanish Government 20 July 1796 to sd George Cochran who was an actual settler in sd Ter. 27 Oct. 1795. Robert Cochran for George Cochran.

No. 1539. Claimant: George Murray, 29 Mar. 1804. Rejected 14 May 1807. Miss. Ter. George Murray claims 640 acres on Miss. River by right of occupancy. The sd. tract has been inhabited and cultivated ever since 1789 by sd Murray or to his use and the sd Murray was the head of a family on the day the Spanish troops evacuated the territory and claims no other land.

No. 1540. Claimant: Peter B. Bruin, 29 Mar. 1804. Rejected 13 June 1807. Miss. Ter. Claiborne Co. Peter Bryan Bruin claims 800 arpents in sd county on Miss. River by virtue of his having inhabited and cultivated the same ever since 1789. He was at that time 21 years of age and claims sd tract from a certificate of survey from the Spanish Government.

No. 1541. Claimant: William Lindsay and Co., 9 Mar. 1804. Certificate A-599, issued 16 Sept. 1805. Miss. Ter. Claiborne Co., William Lindsay and Company claim all that land in sd county called Gibson Port by plat Lot 1 in Sq. No. 2 by virtue of a patent by Spanish Government to Samuel Gibson, an actual settler in sd territory 27 Oct. 1795, and he, the sd Gibson, and wife, sold the sd lot to sd William Lindsay and Co.

No. 1542. Claimant: Robert and George Cochran, 29 Mar. 1804. Certificate A-724, issued 15 Jan. 1806. Miss. Ter. Robert and George Cochran claim all that undivided moiety of land in Adams County joining the City of Natchez by virtue of Spanish patent, dated 1782, to Mr. William Barland and by sd Barland conveyed to John Girault and by John Girault conveyed to Simon Arze and by sd Arze to Francis Caudel and by the sd Francis Caudel sold to Melling Woolley and by sd Woolley conveyed to sd Robert and George Cochran.

No. 1545. Claimant: William Conway, 29 Mar. 1804. Rejected 12 June 1807. Miss. Ter. William Conway claims 800 acres on Buffalo Cr. by patent to William Conway by Spanish Government. William Conway was an actual settler 27 Oct. 1795. Plat shows Maurice Conway, James Smith and Peter Miro adjoining.

No. 1547. Claimant: Squire Boone, 29 Mar. 1804. Wit: Richard King 28 Nov. 1805. Certificate A-710 issued to legal representatives of William Henderson 8 Jan. 1806. Miss. Ter. Squire Boone claims 100 arpents on Bayou Pierre by virtue of a patent from the Spanish Government 8 Oct. 1798. (See remark in No. 1553).

No. 1551. Claimant: P. Bruin, 29 Mar. 1804. Notation: See No. 1021 and No. 1868. Rejected 13 June 1803. Miss. Ter. Peter B. Bruin claims 500 arpents on waters of Bayou Pierre by virtue of a sale by the Lt. Gov. of Louisiana of land formerly belonging to Thomas James, at which sale John Burnet became purchaser and said John Burnet sold the same unto Peter B. Bruin. By this sale now claims the said tract of land. Proceeding of this sale filed in Register's Office. Confiscation Sale of James's land to Burnet and by Burnet to Judge Bruin in No. 1668.

No. 1555. Claimant: Thomas Courtney, 30 Mar. 1804. Wit: John Francis, 3 Nov. 1806. Certificate B-136 issued Dec. 15, 1806. Miss. Ter. Wilkinson Co. Thomas Courtney claims 320 acres on Beaver Cr. by improvement made previous to and on 3 Mar. 1803, by the sd Thomas Courtney, adjoining lands of William Bird and William Curtis.

No. 1556. Claimant: John Hooser, 30 Mar. 1804. Wit: Samuel Lusk. Certificate D-159, issued 16 Dec. 1806. Miss. Ter. Wilkinson Co. John Hooser claims the right of preference in the purchase of 600 acres in sd county on the Homochitto River. The abovenamed John Hooser or some person to his use has actually inhabited and cultivated the sd land prior to and on 3 Mar. 1803, he being at that time above the age of 21 years and the head of a family. Signed G. Poindexter, atty. for claimant. Plat shows land adjoining owned by Jeremiah Bass.

No. 1557. Claimant: Adam Beard, 30 Mar. 1804. Rejected 30 Dec. 1806. Miss. Ter. Adam Beard claims a preemption of 420 acres in Jefferson County on Cole's Cr. improved July 1801 and personally settled in January following and actually inhabited and cultivated by him to this day. On 3 Mar. 1803 he was above the age of 21 yrs.

No. 1558. Claimant: Thomas Cammock, 30 Mar. 1804. See No. 865. Certificate A-559 issued 3 Sept. 1805. Miss. Ter. John Cammock claims 100 acres in Adams County on St. Catherine and Second Creeks by virtue of a Spanish patent for 800 arpents to William McIntosh who conveyed the sd 100 acres by deed 14 Feb. 1798. // Bill of sale: William McIntosh 100 acres of land to John Cammack. Wit: Estevan Minor, Ebenezer Rees.

No. 1560. Claimant: Peter A. Vandorn, 30 Mar. 1804. Patent to Hoggatt, filed with No. 556. Deed from Anthony Hoggatt to Peter A. Vandorn, 26 May 1801. Hoggatt of Adams Co., Miss. Ter. and Peter A. Vandorn of Town of Natchez, for $6100, to him in hand paid, 400 acres, part of 768 acres granted to sd Anthony Hoggatt by Carondelet, 14 Aug. 1794, in the Dist. of Second Creek, bounded by Thomas Martin and William Ratcliff, signed Anthony Hoggatt. Wit: John Wilson and John Henderson. Ack. before George Cochran, J.P.

No. 1562. Claimant: Joseph Johnson, 30 Mar. 1804. Wit: Samuel Stockett, 17 May 1805. Certificate D-137, issued 15 Dec. 1806. Joseph Johnson, a citizen of Miss. Ter., Wilkinson Co., claims the right of preference in the purchase of 325 acres in sd county, on the waters of Amite. Joseph Johnson did actually inhabit and cultivate the sd tract prior to and on 3 Feb. 1803, he being at that time above the age of 21 years and head of a family.

No. 1563. Claimant: Ephraim Bates, 30 Mar. 1804. Wit: William Lee, 3 Sept. 1805. Survey of 400 acres to include the improvements as a preemption. Bates is a Spanish patentee. Certificate D-138 issued to Turner Linton and Co., assignees, 15 Dec. 1806. Ephraim Bates, a citizen of Miss. Ter. Wilkinson Co., claims a right of Donation to 640 acres in sd county on the waters of River Amite. He did actually inhabit and cultivate the afsd. land on and prior to the day the territory was evacuated by the Spanish troops, he being at that time above the age of 21 years and the head of a family, having a wife with five children. G. Poindexter atty. for claimant. // Conveyance from Ephraim Bates, for value received, to Joseph Johnson, tract abovedescribed. Wit: Isaac Williams, Jesse Lee. Prov. by Williams bef. Sam Brooks, J.P. // Transfer from Joseph Johnson, for value received, to Messrs Linton and Co. Natchez 18 Oct. 1806.

No. 1564. Claimant: William Pharr, 30 Mar. 1804. Wit: Joseph Johnson, 1 Apr. 1805. Certificate D-261 issued 24 Dec. 1806. See No. 1372. William Pharr, a citizen of Miss. Ter. Wilkinson Co., claims a preference in the purchase of 1150 acres in sd county on waters of Thompson's Creek. William Pharr did actually inhabit and cultivate the afsd. tract prior and on the 3 Mar. 1803, he being at that time above the age of 21 years and the head of a family. G. Poindexter, atty.

No. 1565. Claimant: Hugh Denham, 30 May 1804. Wit: Samuel Stockett, 8 Feb. 1805. Certificate D-262 issued to Henry Johnson, assignee, 24 Dec. 1806. Hugh Denham, a citizen of Miss. Ter. Wilkinson Co., claims the right of preference in the purchase of 570 acres in Wilkinson Co. on Thompson's Creek. The abovenamed Hugh Denham did actually inhabit and cultivate the sd land prior to and on 3 Mar. 1803, being at that time above the age of 21 years and the head of a family. George Poindexter, atty for claimant. // Conveyance of Hugh Denham to Henry Johnson, for $80 in hand paid, quit claim for above described land, 567 acres, signed Hugh Denham. Wit: Sam'l. Stockett who prov. same before the Board 17 May 1805. R. Claiborne, Clk.

No. 1567. Claimant: Thomas Parks, 30 Mar. 1804. Wit: Thomas White, 20 Nov. 1804. Certificate D-173, issued 16 Dec. 1806. Thomas Parks claims 200 acres by virtue of a preemption, settled Feb. 1803 on south side of Rapalje's Cr. 2 miles from Grindstone Ford, in Claiborne County, all sides vacant.

No. 1569. Claimant: Peter Lyon, 30 Mar. 1804. Wit: Thomas White, 20 Nov. 1804. Rejected for want of sufficient evidence, 30 Dec. 1806. Miss. Ter. Claiborne Co. Peter Lyon claims preference of becoming the purchaser from the United States of 261 acres on Bayou Pierre, the North Fork, by his actual settlement on and cultivating the premises in April 1798 and continuing the same ever since. He was the head of a family at and before his settlement afsd. Plat shows land adjoining Peter Greenfield and Llewellyn Price. Notice to the Board of Commrs. not to grant Peter Lyon his claim for 261 acres because the land lies within the tract belonging to Salome Lyman, etc. S. Bullock for John Ellison and his wife, Salome.

No. 1570. Claimant: David Burney, 30 Mar. 1804. Wit: Wm. Brocus, 16 Feb. 1805. Rejected 14 May 1807. Miss. Ter. Jefferson Co., David Burney claims 640 acres in sd county on a branch of Bayou Pierre, known as Lick Creek, he having improved it while under the British Government and in conformity with the then existing regulations.

No. 1572. Claimant: Roswell Mygat, 30 Mar. 1804. Rejected 14 May 1807. Roswell Mygat claims 150 acres in Jefferson County, Miss. Ter., on the South Fork of Cole's Cr. bounded by the lands of Thomas M. Green and David Odum, he having actually inhabited and cultivated the said land on the day the Miss. Territory was finally evacuated by the Spanish troops, being then above the age of 21 yrs. S. Lewis for the claimant.

No. 1573. Claimant: Heirs of D. Mygat, 30 Mar. 1804. Wit: William Atkinson 2 Jan. 1805. Certificate B-66, issued 10 Sept. 1806. Margaret Barton, for and in behalf of her children, Rebecca Frazier, Elizabeth Mygat, and Webster Mygatt, who are the heirs at law and representatives of Daniel Mygatt, decd., who in his lifetime was an actual settler of the Miss. Ter. where he died before the 27 Oct. 1795, leaving the said claimants his children and heirs who have ever since continued to reside on and claim a tract of land of 345 acres on Tabor's branch of Bayou Pierre. Said Daniel having in his lifetime obtained from the Spanish Government a warrant of survey for 500 acres, of which the land claimed is a part, being at the time he obtained the warrant above the age of 21 years, the Indian title to the said land being extinguished. S. Lewis, agent for the claimants.

No. 1575. Claimant: Benjamin Farrar, 30 Mar. 1804. See No. 45. Witnesses: Stephen Minor and Francis Nailor, 12 June 1806. Willis Bonner and James Bonner, 26 June 1806. Rejected 30 Mar. 1807. Benjamin Farrar who resided in Miss. Ter. 27 March 1795 claims 600 acres in Adams County near the Miss. River, bounded by lands of Baptiste LaPoint . . . . which land he claims as legal representative, purchaser, under Gibson Clark who obtained from the Spanish Government a warrant of survey prior to 27 Oct. 1795, being above the age of 21 years, and afterwards the sd Clark sold the sd land to Henry Manadue who sold the same to Benjamin Farrar, Sr., decd, who gave by his last will and testament the same to the claimant who is his son and one of the heirs. The same land having also been inhabited and cultivated. S. Lewis for the claimant.

No. 1577. Claimant: Uriah Vining, 30 Mar. 1804. Wit: Jesse Vining. Certificate D-286 issued 29 Dec. 1806. The above plat represents a tract of land in Wilkinson Co., Miss. Ter. was in actual cultivation in 1799 by Uriah Vining. [No acreage given.]

No. 1578. Claimant: Edward Murray, 30 Mar. 1804. Certificate A-795 issued 19 May 1807. Edward Murray who was a settler in the Miss. Territory 27 Oct. 1795, claims for the use of William Scott 1000 acres by virtue of a grant from the Spanish Government to him on 20 Aug. 1795. Seth Lewis for claimant.

No. 1582. Claimant: Thomas Harrington, 30 Mar. 1804. Wit: Buckner Pittman, 15 Jan. 1805. Mitchell Ward, 4 May 1806. Rejected. Evidence insufficient. Apr. 9, 1807. Thomas Harrington, a citizen of the sd Territory, who on the day the Spanish troops did finally evacuate the Territory did inhabit and cultivate 640 acres on James' Run, a branch of Bayou Pierre, under the Second Section of the Act of Congress, etc. Seth Lewis, agent. Miss. Ter. Claiborne Co. Personally appeared before me, Jesse Griffin, one of the Justices of the Peace for sd county, William Brocus, who being duly sworn, said that in 1795 Thomas Harrington had 800 acres surveyed for him on James's Cr. and in 1798 early spring the sd Harrington made a settlement on sd land and made a crop of corn thereon and the deponent recollects to have assisted the sd Harrington with the work of a negro in making his settlement on sd land and the sd Thomas as, at the time of making his settlement and had been for some years past the head of a family. He also knew the land to be free of any claim but that of the sd. Thomas. William Brocus signs with a mark.

No. 1584. Claimant: Joel Humphreys, 30 Mar. 1804. Wit: Eustis Humphreys. Certificate D-303 issued Dec. 29, 1806. Miss. Ter. Joel Humphreys, a citizen of sd ter., claims a preemption right to a tract on Cole's Cr. in Jefferson Co., settled by sd claimant in January 1803 and cultivated ever since. Plat shows land adj. James Cole and Thomas Reed. [No acreage given.]

No. 1585. Claimant: George Cathey, 30 Mar. 1804. Rejected for want of evidence, 30 Dec. 1806. Miss. Ter. George Cathey claims a preemption right to 640 acres on the Middle Fork of the Homochitto in Jefferson Co. improved by him, the sd Cathey, in 1802 and cultivated ever since.

No. 1586. Claimant: George Rapalje, 30 Mar. 1804. See No. 1921. Rejected, being confirmed to Thomas M. Green. 10 June 1807. George Rapalje, who was a settler of the territory 27 Oct. 1795, in behalf of Garret Rapalje, claims 200 acres in Jefferson Co. about 4 miles from the mouth of Cole's Cr. His claim being founded on a British grant to Peter Hawkins and by sd Hawkins conveyed to the claimant for the use of the sd Garret Rapalje, 8 Jan. 1785. // Peter Hawkins, an inhabitant of the Dist. of Natchez, 8 Jan. 1785, assigns all interest in above tract to George Rapalje, for Garret Rapalje, which was granted to Jacob Paul, and 200 acres granted to Ebenezer Gossett, for $300, now recd. Witnesses: Parker Carradine and William Gilbert.

No. 1587. Claimant: John Thompson, 30 Mar. 1804. See No. 163. Rejected 16 May 1806. John Thompson, heir at law of Richard Thompson, decd., and legal representative of Anathasius Martin, claims 100 acres in Jefferson Co. commonly called and known as Villa Gayoso, which he claims by virtue of a grant by the British Govt. to Anathasius Martin, by whom the same was conveyed to sd Richard Thompson, decd. at wnose death it descended to sd claimant as heir, the sd claimant having been an actual settler in the Ter. on 27 Oct. 1795. Signed John Thompson.

No. 1588. Claimant: George Rapalje, 30 Mar. 1804. Rejected, the same land being confirmed to Zachariah Smith, Sr., see No. 235. June 7, 1807. George Rapalje, who was a settler of Miss. Ter. on 27 Oct. 1795, claims 1837 acres in Wilkinson Co. on a branch of Buffalo Cr. adjoining land of William Vousdan, by virtue of a Spanish grant 27 Oct. 1795. S. Lewis for claimant.

No. 1589. Claimant: Jane Rapalje, 30 Mar. 1804. See No. 1012. Rejected 15 May 1806. John Ellis, for the use of Jane Rapalje, who was an actual settler of Miss. Ter. on 27 Oct. 1795, claims in right of sd Jane, 113 acres in Adams Co. on Second Cr., by virtue of a British grant to Seth Dowd and by him conveyed to sd claimant. S. Lewis for claimant. Notation: George Rapalje and wife claim land of 113 acres. Another paper: John Ellis to Jane Rapalje: Obligation. "I hereby promise to give all right and title I have to two tracts of land on Second Cr., one granted to Wm. Joiner by English Government of 500 acres and the other 113 acres granted to Seth Dowd unto Mrs. Jane Rapalje, being in and to be considered in consequence of a final judgment of all affairs and accounts relating to the estate of the late Richard Ellis, Esq., which being terminated I agreed to perform when I receive her powers to invest me with 800 acres she was entitled to by the will of her late father, of which I acknowledge to be in full possession by her receipt of this date. Signed John Ellis, Abram Ellis and Benj. Farrar. Certified as a true copy by Manuel de Lemos. John Girault, Keeper of the Spanish Records, also certified the same.

No. 1590. Claimant: Jane Rapalje, 30 Mar. 1804. See No. 1881 and No. 1936. Rejected, 16 May 1806. John Ellis, for the use of Jane Rapalje, who was an actual of this Ter. on 27 Oct. 1795, claims in right of sd Jane, 500 acres in Adams on Second Cr., which land she claims by virtue of a British grant to William Joiner, by whom the same was conveyed to John Ellis and by him sold to claimant, Jane. Seth Lewis for the claimant.

No. 1593. Claimant: Susanna Scott, 30 Mar. 1804. Rejected 13 June 1807. Susanna Scott, admx. to the estate of John Scott, decd., claims Lot No. 6, Square No. 17 in the town of Bruinsburg on the Miss. River, by virtue of a deed from Peter Bryan Bruin and Elizabeth, his wife, 4 Jan. 1801, to afsd. John Scott.

No. 1594. Claimant: Susanna Scott, 30 Mar. 1804. Rejected 13 June 1807. Susanna Scott, admx. of the estate of John Scott, decd., claims Lot No. 1, Square No. 12 in the town of Bruinsburg on the Miss. River, by virtue of a deed from Peter Bryan Bruin and Elizabeth, his wife, 4 Jan. 1801, to afsd. John Scott.

No. 1598. Claimant: Philip Briscoe, 30 Mar. 1804. Rejected for want of evidence 30 Dec. 1806. Miss. Ter. Philip Briscoe claims a preemption right to 100 acres on waters of James' Cr. in Claiborne, improved by him in 1802 and ever since.

No. 1600. Claimant: William Price, 30 Mar. 1804. See No. 600. Certificate B-5, issued 2 June 1806. Certificate of survey and plat. Natchez, 24 Mar. 1804. I certify that I measured for and in the name of William Price Lot No. 2, Square No. 8, granted by Spanish Government to Hugh Coyle and sold by sd Coyle to George Furney and by sd Furney to William Price. Signed William Atchinson, Surveyor.

No. 1601. Claimant: Daniel Hughes, 30 Mar. 1804. Rejected 12 June 1807. Miss. Ter. Adams Co. Daniel Hughes, legal representative of Angelique Brodaque Johnstone, decd., claims 1000 acres in sd county near the White Cliffs, by virtue of a British patent to sd Angelique dated 15 Aug. 1777, who gave and bequeathed the same to him, the sd Daniel Hughes, who now claims the said land. The plat shows land adjoining that of Richard Ellis and Daniel Ward.

No. 1602. Claimant: William Mackey, 30 Mar. 1804. See No. 443. Part of this claim. Wit: Patrick Cogan 20 Oct. 1806. Certificate B-246, issued 30 Mar. 1807. Miss. Ter. William Mackey, a citizen of sd territory, claims 100 acres in Claiborne Co. on James's Cr., by virtue of an order of survey for same to James Nevill, 24 Feb. 1791, by the Spanish Government, who sold it to Alexander Callender and sd Callender sold it to present claimant. The sd land has been inhabited and cultivated ever since 1795. Alexander Callender, atty. for the claimant.

No. 1604. Claimant: William Newman, 30 Mar. 1804. Wit: William Cole, 29 Apr. 1805. Certificate D-320 issued 29 Dec. 1806, to R. Darden, assignee. Miss. Ter. William Newman claims a right of preemption to 400 acres on Irwin's Fork of Cole's Cr. in Jefferson Co., settled by Stephen Jett in 1802 and conveyed by him to the present claimant, 23 Dec. 1803. Richard Darden prays that a certificate for this claim issue to him, he having a conveyance from Wm. Newman.

No. 1605. Claimant: Joseph Ford, 31 Mar. 1804. Wit: John Tally, 6 Aug. 1805. Certificate B-219 issued 4 Mar. 1807, to Richard King, assignee. Survey and plat by Charles Defrance, a plot in Adams Co., adjoining John Brophy and Adam Guise, 640 acres on Morgan's Fork of the Homochitto, for Joseph Ford, 24 Mar. 1804. Note: This plot being filed without a regular notice, the Board proceeds to take testimony, reserving a decision of the propriety of admitting this as a claim until a future date. Aug.

6, 1805. Signed T.R.

No. 1606. Claimant: Ann Martin, 30 Mar. 1804. Wit: Joshua Harrison and John Girault, 14 Jan. 1805. Certificate B-35 issued 11 June 1806. Miss. Ter. Adams County. Ann Martin claims 152 arpents on waters of St. Catherine's Cr. in sd county, by virtue of a settlement and improvement made thereon in 1785 by Edward McCabe who was then the head of a family and inhabited and cultivated this land, of a mortgage thereof to Alexander Moore and the sale thereof made by the Spanish Government to David Ferguson to satisfy the sd mortgage and of a sale thereof by sd Ferguson to Thomas Martin, decd., and by sale thereof to this claimant, by deed, dated 6 June 1801. The said tract has been actually inhabited and cultivated by the said Edward McCabe and by his sd legal representatives ever since 1785, the claimants being above the age of 21 years. Survey and plat by William Atchinson, 6 Aug. 1803. Said tract adjoining the Town of Washington and about 6 miles northeast of the City of Natchez.

No. 1607. Claimant: Amos Hubbard, 30 Mar. 1804. Wit: Orren Smith. 12 Nov. 1804. Rejected for want of sufficient evidence, 30 Dec. 1806. Amos Hubbard, a citizen of Miss. Ter., claims a preference in becoming the purchaser of one-half of 600 acres on the Mississippi in Jefferson Co., a correct plat of which hath been exhibited to the Register of the Land Office by Phineas Smith. The above claim is founded on a purchase made by the claimant of Phineas Smith of the said 300 acres for a valuable consideration. Said Smith inhabited and cultivated the same on and before 3 Mar. 1803 and sd Phineas Smith and Amos Hubbard occupied and improved the whole 600 acres, as tenants in common from Feb. 1801 to Nov. 1802 during which time this claimant had erected a mill thereon at a considerable expense, by an agreement made by sd Phineas Smith and Hubbard. Conveyance of 300 acres by Smith to Hubbard 14 Nov. 1802. Phineas Smith conveyed his 300 acres to Ebenezer Smith. A suit in courts by parties.

No. 1609. Claimant: Polser Shilling, 30 Mar. 1804. See No. 1608 and No. 1678. Certificate A-776 issued 15 May 1806. Miss. Ter., City of Natchez. Polser Shilling gives notice that he claims 13 acres in afsd. city by virtue of a Spanish grant to Philip Barbour who conveyed the same to Stephen Minor who sold the sd quantity of land first mentioned to Philip Engle 12 July 1797 who conveyed the same to claimant. Note: The notice is erroneous. The patent issued to Harrison and not to Barbour. See No. 1676 and 1678. T.H.W.

No. 1610. Claimant: Polser Shilling, 30 Mar. 1804. Wit: John Girault, 12 Nov. 1804 and James Glasscock on 20 Nov. and William Atchinson 21 Nov. and William Dunbar 11 Oct. 1805. Rejected. See Nos. 1396, 1401. Notice: Polser Shilling hereby claims 437 acres by virtue of three purchases: one from Francis Spain for 235 acres, dated 30 Jan. 1786, one other from Stephen Mayes of 128 acres, dated 13 Jan. 1784, and one other from Jacob Cable for 74 acres, dated 27 Sept. 1784, all of which are severally described in the annexed plat. A grant for the whole of the land wrote in my name by William Dunbar 30 July 1793 which grant was confirmed by the Gov. Genl. of La. in New Orleans.

No. 1611. Claimant: Polser Shilling, 30 Mar. 1804. Rejected 14 May 1807. Miss. Ter. City of Natchez. Polser Shilling hereby gives notice that as legal representative of St. Germain he claims 130 acres about a mile south of Natchez Fort on the ridge between the waters of St. Catherine's Cr. and the Miss. River, founded on an improvement, settlement and cultivation made on sd land in 1783 by St. Germain and for his use, who was the head of a family and sold the sd premises to sd Shilling abt 1786, who has continued to inhabit and cultivate the same.

No. 1613. Claimant: George Overaker, 30 Mar. 1804. Rejected. George Overaker gives notice that by virtue of a deed from Richard Bacon, he claims 100 acres in town of Natchez. Also a plat.

No. 1616. Claimant: William Brocus, 30 Mar. 1804. Rejected 19 May 1807. Miss. Ter. Claiborne Co. William Brocus gives notice that he claims 500 arpents in sd county on Bayou Pierre, by virtue of an order of survey from Spanish Government which is now lost by time and accident, dated 1788, at which time the sd William was the head of a family and the sd tract has been inhabited and cultivated before the year 1795. Stephen B. Minor for William Brocus. Plat and certificate of Survey dated Feb. 5, 1784, signed Stephen B. Minor.

No. 1617. Claimant: Robert Moore, 30 Mar. 1804. Rejected for want of evidence, 30 Dec. 1806. Miss. Ter. Robert Moore claims 163 arpents on St. Catherine's Cr. by having actually inhabited and improved the said land on 3 Mar. 1803 and being then above the age of 21 years. Plat shows adj. lands: Silas Crane, Benjamin Belk, George Rapale and ______ Cable.

No. 1618. Claimant: Robert Taylor, 30 Mar. 1804. Wit: Richard Deen, 28 Nov. 1804. Certificate A-

653, issued to Robert and Isaac Taylor, 3 Oct. 1805. Miss. Ter., Robert Taylor claims 200 arpents of land in Jefferson Co. on Fairchild's Cr. by virtue of a Spanish grant to Jacob Cowperthwait, who was an actual settler of the territory 27 Oct. 1795 and sold the sd tract 200 arpents, part of 1000 arpents granted, to said Robert Taylor. Certificate of Survey by William Thomas: At the request of Mr. Ebenezer Rees, atty. for Jacob Cowperthwait, and ______ Taylor, I have surveyed in the name of Taylor 200 acres, 5 Apr. 1797. Plat shows land adj: Cowperthwait, James Wade and James McIntyre.

No. 1619. Claimant: Joseph Walker, 30 Mar. 1804. Wit: William Atchinson, 25 Sept. 1804. Rejected 22 Apr. 1807. Joseph Walker hereby gives notice that he claims 500 arpents in Wilkinson Co. on Beaver Creek, by virtue of a Spanish order of survey 30 Jan. 1795, and an actual survey 20 March 1795. The order of survey having been mislaid by accident, it cannot be produced. Certificate of survey and plat by William Atchinson, Natchez Government, 20 March 1795, about 26 miles south of Natchez, bounded by Peter Celestino, William Collins and Peter Walker, Esq.

No. 1620. Claimant: John Walker, 30 Mar. 1804. Wit: Wm. Atchinson, 25 Sept. 1804. Rejected 22 Apr. 1807. John Walker hereby gives notice that he claims 500 arpents in Wilkinson Co. on south branch of Buffalo, called Beaver Cr. by virtue of a Spanish order of survey, dated 30 Jan. 1795, and actual survey 23 March. Certificate of survey and plat by William Atchinson, bounded by Peter Celestino Walker's land.

No. 1621. Claimant: Peter Walker, Jr., 30 Mar. 1804. Wit: William Atchinson, 25 Sept. 1804. Rejected 22 Apr. 1807. Peter Walker, Jr. hereby gives notice that he claims 500 arpents in Wilkinson Co. on Beaver Cr. by Spanish order of survey 30 Jan. 1895 and actual survey 21 Mar. 1795.

No. 1625. Claimant: Robert Jones, 30 Mar. 1804. Wit: Wm. Atchinson, 25 Sept. 1804. Non-Residence is proved. Wit: Lyman Harding, 5 Mar. 1806. Certificate A-758 issued 10 Mar. 1806. Robert Jones hereby gives notice that he claims 1000 acres in Jefferson Co. on Fairchild's Cr. bounded by lands of Thomas and Edward Patterson on north, by part of a tract belonging to Marcus Olivares on ......, being all that tract granted to Robert Jones by the Spanish Government, dated 17 Jan. 1788. Robert Jones by P. Walker, his atty.

No. 1626. Claimant: J. Walker and A. A. Ellicot, 30 Mar. 1804. Rejected 12 June 1807. Witness: Peter Walker, 13 June 1807. Claim confirmed. Certificate B ___ issued ____. Andrew Augustus Ellicot and John Walker hereby give notice that they claim 400 acres in Adams County about one mile from the Homochitto and 18 miles south of Fort Panmure bounded Alexander Boulle, John Vauchere and Samuel Swayze, by virtue of a Spanish patent to Peter Cabanee, dated 14 June 1796, and by an order of survey dated 11 Dec. 1788, and an actual survey made 18 June 1797, which land was conveyed by sd Peter Cabanee to Peter Camus and by deed 26 July 1796 by sd Camus to sd Andrew Augustus Ellicot and John Walker, 19 March 1798.

No. 1627. Claimant: William Scott, 30 Mar. 1804. Wit: Stephen Minor, 11 Nov. 1805. Certificate B 25 issued 4 June 1806. William Scott, a citizen of Miss. Ter. and legal representative of Antonio Gras, who on the 27 Oct. 1795 was an actual settler therein, claims 200 arpents by virtue of a legal warrant by Spain 20 Aug. 1782 to Peter Nelson and by him sold to Francis Basso, decd., and by the exor. of sd Basso, Sebastian Bosque, sold to Antonio Gras, and by sd Antonio Gras conveyed to present claimant, by deed, 8 inst. Same is near the City of Natchez and bounded as by plat. The land has been cultivated many years, the sd Peter Nelson being above 21 years of age when he obtained the said warrant.

No. 1628. Claimant: William Scott, 30 Mar. 1804. Wit: John Girault, 12 June 1807. Certificate D 293 issued 12 Jan. 1807. William Scott, the legal representative of John Joseph Rodriguez, who on 27 Oct. 1795 was an actual settler in this territory, claims 150 acres by virtue of a Spanish grant 1785 to John St. Germain for 400 acres, the above 150 acres whereof were bought by John Joseph Rodriquez at the public sale of the estate of sd St. Germain, made by the Spanish Government 26 May 1786 and by sd Rodriguez conveyed to the claimant, 22 Jan. 1798.

No. 1629. Claimant: William Scott, 30 Mar. 1804. Wit: Stephen Minor, 11 Nov. 1805. Certificate A 789 issued to claimant, in right of his wife, Clara, 4 Mar. 1807. Miss. Ter. William Scott, a legal representative of the late Henry Lafleur, claims 400 arpents by virtue of a Spanish grant to the said LaFleur, prior to 1795, who by deed conveyed the same to Jacob Monsanto, 18 June 1787, and at the final adjustment of accounts of sd Jacob and his brother, Benjamin, was allotted to Mrs. Clara Monsanto, the wife of the present claimant.

No. 1630. Claimant: William Scott, 30 Mar. 1804. Wit: Stephen Minor, 11 Nov. 1805. Certificate A-740, issued to claimant in right of his wife, Clara, 4 Mar. 1807. William Scott, a citizen of Miss. Ter. and legal representative of Charles Truflo, claims 100 arpents by virtue of Spanish grant prior to 27 Oct. 1795 to sd Truflo and by him conveyed to Jacob Monsanto and his brother, Benjamin, was allotted to Clara Monsanto, relict of Benjamin Monsanto, and now wife of the claimant. She was an actual resident of the premises 27 Oct. 1795.

No. 1631. Claimant: William Scott, 30 Mar. 1804. Rejected 12 June, 1807. Miss. Ter. William Scott, a citizen of the afsd. Ter., claims a lot under the bluff at the Natchez landing, being the same whereon a battery was erected by the government of Spain and sold at public auction by order of the United States and purchased by the claimant. "To Captain William Scott 1800; to John Wilkins, Jr. one bake house sold to you in Natchez $131; and one small house under the hill $10. Received payment in full for the account, 1 July, 1801."

No. 1632. Claimant: John Girault, 30 Mar. 1804. Wit: Richard King, 31 May 1804. Certificate A-728, issued 15 Jan. 1806. Miss. Ter. John Girault, a citizen of sd Territory, who on the 27 Oct. 1795 was an actual settler therein, claims 11 acres by virtue of a grant, 8 May 1786, to William Barland for 105 arpents, of which sd grantee, on 17 Sept. 1788, conveyed to sd claimant 11 acres. Plat shows, William Barland, City of Natchez, and land granted to Mr. Piernas as adjoining.

No. 1633. Claimant: John Girault, 30 Mar. 1804. Wit: Richard King, 31 May 1804. Certificate 582 issued 11 Sept. 1805. Jean Girault, a citizen of sd Ter. who, on 27 Oct. 1795, was an actual settler therein, claims Lot No. 19 in the town of Wormsville, alias Huntston, alias Greensburg, by virtue of a Spanish grant to David Odum, prior to above date, conveyed to sd claimant by the executors of the sd Odum, decd, by deed 14 July 1802.

No. 1634. Claimant: Jean Girault, 30 Mar. 1804. Jean Girault, a citizen of this territory who, at the time of the passing of an Act entitled For the Regulation of Land Grants, was the head of a family and did inhabit and cultivate a tract within the territory, claims the preference of becoming a purchaser of the United States of same by virtue of the Third Section of said act.

No. 1636. Claimant: Augustina Solano, 30 Mar. 1804. Rejected 12 June 1807. Mrs. Augustina Solano, who on 27 Oct. 1795 was an actual settler in this territory, claims by virtue of a Spanish grant prior to that date to Peter Camus who by deed 15 Dec. 1788 conveyed the same to claimant, a lot situate between the Natchez landing and the old Fort on the Half-Way Hill along the old road from said landing. For Augustina Solano signed Miguel Solibellas.

No. 1637. Claimant: John Joseph Rodriguez, 30 Mar. 1804. Wit: Job Routh, 16 Jan. 1806. Certificate A-733 issued 16 Jan. 1806. John Joseph Rodriguez, who on 27 Oct. 1795 was an actual settler in this territory claims 400 arpents by virtue of Spanish grants issued prior to that date; one to George Rapalje for 600 arpents; and the other to Louis Charbonneau for 500 arpents, which was conveyed by grantee to George Rapalje, 3 July 1784, the 400 arpents now claimed being part of both grants, sold at public auction for the payment of the said Rapalje's debts and purchased by the claimant. For John Joseph Rodriguez signed Miguel Solibellas.

No. 1640. Claimant: Edward Turner, 30 Mar. 1804. Residence proved in Journal. Certificate A-583 issued 11 Sept. 1805. Edward Turner hereby gives notice that he claims 15 acres by virtue of a Spanish patent to David Odum in 1790, who afterwards died, leaving a will with Abner Pipes and Fanny Odum his exors. and by sd will authorized sd exrs. to sell sd tract to pay his just debts, who conveyed the sd land by two deeds, 13 Jan. and 23 Feb. 1803 to said Edward Turner, being that tract of land in Jefferson County on the Middle Fork of Cole's Creek adjoining the town of Greenville, on the west side thereof, beginning at Dr. Shaw's corner, the dividing land between the land of the legal representatives of sd Odum decd. and Mordecai Throckmorton.

No. 1641. Claimant: Thomas Carter, 30 Mar. 1804. Rejected 27 Apr. 1807. Henry Day, of West Springfield, Massachusetts, legal representative of Thomas Carter, gives notice that he claims a tract in Jefferson County in Miss. Territory on waters of Cole's Creek formerly called Boyd's, bounded by John Stampley and Isaac Johnson by virtue of a survey by the British Survey of West Florida previous to 27 Oct. 1795.

No. 1647. Claimant: John Dix, 30 Mar. 1804. Rejected 12 June 1807. John Dix claims Lot 4 Square 18 in the City of Natchez.

No. 1648. Claimant: Mayor and others of the City of Natchez, 30 Mar. 1804. Witnesses: 20 Nov. 1805, Lewis Evans, Job Routh, Polser Shilling, John Girault, Richard King, E. Rees and Manuel de Texada. Rejected 9 Apr. 1807. To the Register of the Land Office, West of the Pearl River: The Mayor, aldermen and assistants of the City of Natchez hereby give notice that they claim for and behalf of the corporation of the said city, for the public use, benefit and behalf of all the inhabitants thereof the lots of ground in said city marked No. 1 and No. 3 and Square No. 10 and about 30 acres of land commons of the same, lying between that part of the city laid out in lots and the river bluff, said lots and commons are included in the grant of a tract of land from the Spanish Government to Richard Harrison, in or about the year 1784 and then included in a conveyance of sd tract from Richard Harrison to Stephen Minor and then in a conveyance of the principal part of said tract from Stephen Minor to the said Government in 1789, for the sole purpose of creating and establishing the town of Natchez on the said tract of land, granted as aforesaid. Said grant and conveyances are lost by time and accident or are among the archives of the Province of Louisiana. From the derangement of the records of said province consequent on change of government in that province your claimants after having procured diligent search to be made have not been able to find a proved copy of same. They further give notice that the said lots were reserved by the Spanish Government at the time of the laying out of the town of Natchez in 1789, now incorporated with city privileges for the use and benefit of the said town and from that time have been occupied, inhabited and improved as such. By the order of the Mayor, Aldermen, and Assistants of the City of Natchez. Samuel Brooks, Mayor, and Charles B. Green, Recorder. Arguments for this claim follow.

No. 1649. Claimant: Tench Coxe, 30 Mar. 1804. Reported 12 June 1807. Notation: 333 acres. See No. 992. Tench Coxe hereby gives notice that he claims one full, equal, undivided one-third part of 1000 acres in Claiborne Co. Miss. Ter. on Bayou Pierre, by virtue of British patent to ______ Lyman for __000 acres including the sd 1000 acres and conveyed by Thaddeus Lyman, son and heir of sd Lyman, decd. to Evans Jones, James Jones and Edward Jones, and the sd Edward Jones conveyed the sd undivided third part to this claimant by deed, 20 Sept. 1790.

No. 1650. Claimant: Isaac Foster, 13 Mar. 1804. Notation: see No. 583, same tract enlarged by this. Rejected 18 Nov. 1806. Evidence insufficient. The above plat of land of 555 acres claimed by Isaac Foster, on the Middle Fork of the Homochitto River, Adams County, Miss. Territory, includes an improvement made by Jesse Stockwell.

No. 1651. Claimant: Bernard Bowdes, 30 Mar. 1804. Rejected. Bernard Bowdes hereby gives notice that he claims in the City of Natchez 100 square perches adjoining a lot belonging to John Rodriguez below the Fort usually called Fort Panmure, which lot was granted to Peter Camus in 1785 or 6 and conveyed by him to Leonard Pomet and by the said Pomet to Blas Ramirez by bill of sale 13 Jan. 1799, and by the sd Blas to Domingo Lorero and by sd Lorero to Joseph Mendoza, 15 June 1801, and by the sd Mendoza to aforesaid Bernard Bowdes by bill of sale 10 Aug. 1802.

No. 1662. Claimant: Stephen Douglass. 30 Mar. 1804. Rejected 15 May 1807. Miss. Ter. Claiborne Co. Stephen Douglass claims 132 acres on Bayou Pierre, by virtue of an actual settlement made on sd land by sd Stephen Douglass about 1 Dec. 1797. He continued to occupy and cultivate the same until the Spanish troops evacuated this territory. Plat by Fenton and Morgan shows Elisha Flowers, and ______ Richards, and Widow's Creek.

No. 1663. Claimant: William Oglesby, 30 Mar. 1804. Wit: George Bailey, 15 Oct. 1804. Certificate B-98 issued 3 Feb. 1807. William Oglesby claims 640 acres on Wells Creek in Adams Co. as a Donation by virtue of an actual settlement made by Benjamin Fletcher on or about 1 Feb. 1798, who continued to cultivate and occupy the said land until 23 July 1798, on which date the sd Benjamin Fletcher did sell to James Oglesby all his claim to same and the said James Oglesby did on 24 July assign all his right to sd William Oglesby, who has ever since been in possession and has cultivated the sd land.

No. 1664. Claimant: Francis Rogers, 30 Mar. 1804. Wit: John Armstreet, 15 Oct. 1804. Notation: James Oglesby was a Spanish grantee. See No. 448. Rejected 12 June 1807. Francis Rogers claims 640 acres on waters of Wells Cr. Adams Co. by virtue of actual settlement made by John West in 1794 and continued until 1 Mar. 1795. The sd West sold the land and improvement to Moses Foster who in 1796 sold the same to George Bailey who in 1796 sold it to James Oglesby, who occupied and cultivated the same until 25 July 1803, on which day transferred the land to the sd Francis Rogers. Notation on the back: The party appeared afterwards and requested that this Board not allow this as a preemption.

No. 1665. Claimant: Heirs of Robert Abrams, 30 Mar. 1804. Witness: Anthony Calvet, 6 Dec. 1805. William Dunbar. 25 Nov. 1806. Certificate A-793 issued for 262 arpents 30 Mar. 1807. See No. 687 and No. 775. Miss. Ter. Adams Co. Lydia Abrams, widow and relict of Robert Abrams, decd. and Amelia, daughter and heiress of sd Robert, now the wife of John Carton, claim 640 acres on Second Cr. in Adams Co. by virtue of an actual settlement thereon in 1777 by Reuben Alexander who in that year sold the said land to sd Robert Abrams, who occupied and cultivated the same until his death in 1800.

No. 1666. Claimant: Joseph Strickland, 30 Mar. 1804. Rejected for want of evidence, 30 Dec. 1806. Miss. Ter., Adams Co. Joseph Strickland claims 400 acres by right of preemption in the City of Natchez, by virtue of actual settlement made on sd lot by sd Joseph Strickland previous to the 3 Mar. 1803, who continued to occupy and build on the sd lot to the present day.

No. 1667. Claimant: James Wallace, 30 Mar. 1804. Rejected for want of evidence, 30 Dec. 1806. Miss. Ter., Adams Co. James Wallace claims 7140 Sq. ft. by right of preemption in the City of Natchez, by virtue of an actual settlement made on sd lot by William Rabb before March 1803, who continued to occupy same till March 1804 when the sd William Rabb sold his right to sd lot and building to sd James Wallace. Notice to the Commissioners that the within claim lies within the lines of a claim confirmed by sd Commrs. to Francis S. Girault. Signed Jean Girault. Washington, 15 Aug. 1806.

No. 1668. Claimant: James Griffin, 30 Mar. 1804. Rejected for want of evidence, 30 Dec. 1806. Miss. Ter., Adams Co. James Griffin claims 3000 sq. ft. in right of preemption in City of Natchez by virtue of actual settlement made on sd lot before 3 Mar. 1803 and he has continued to occupy and improve the same to this day.

No. 1669. Claimant: Stephen Douglass, 30 Mar. 1804. Wit: Robert Ashley, 18 Feb. 1805. Certificate B-58 issued 8 Sept. 1806. Miss. Ter., Claiborne Co. Stephen Douglass claims 640 acres on waters of Bayou Pierre in sd county by virtue of an actual settlement made on the sd land by William Miller in 1792 who continued to occupy and cultivate the same until the 15 Nov. 1798 when he sold his right to same to sd Stephen Douglass. The plat shows the Wilderness Road going through the west corner of tract and the land to southwest was formerly owned by Robert Ashley but then owned by Thomas Crabbe, to the south ______ Budwell owned land formerly but now Thomas Vause held it.

No. 1670. Claimant: Robert McCausland, 30 Mar. 1804. Rejected for want of evidence, 30 Dec. 1806. Miss. Ter., Wilkinson Co. Robert McCausland, heir at law of Mark McCausland, decd., claims 640 acres in right of preemption on waters of Beaver Creek in county, by virtue of an actual settlement made thereon by sd Mark McCausland before 3 Mar. 1803, who continued to occupy and cultivate the same until Nov. of that year.

No. 1671. Claimant: John Armstrong, 30 Mar. 1804. Rejected, 15 May 1807. Miss. Ter., Clabiborne Co. John Armstrong claims 640 acres on waters of Bayou Pierre in sd county by virtue of an actual settlement made on sd land by sd Armstrong 1 Jan. 1798, who continued to occupy and cultivate same long after the Spanish troops evacuated the territory.

No. 1672. Claimant: Peter Presler, 30 Mar. 1804. Rejected 15 May 1807. Miss. Ter., Adams Co. Peter Presler hereby gives notice that he claims 640 acres in sd county on Miss. River at the foot of the White Cliffs, by virtue of his having inhabited and cultivated sd land before 1797 when the Spanish troops finally evacuated the territory, being the head of a family of a wife and eight children and eight negroes. Signed Peter Presler. By plat land adjoining: Benj. Farrar and Col. Hutchins. Note: Col. Hutchins has suggested that this claim interferes with one of his, by virtue of a Spanish patent.

No. 1673. Claimant: Robert Simmons, 30 Mar. 1804. Wit: John Searcy, 30 Jan. 1805. Certificate D-304 issued to Lewis Humphreys, 29 Dec. 1806. Miss. Ter. Robert Simmons claims a preemption right to 155 acres including his improvement made in 1802 and cultivated ever since, on waters of Cole's Cr. in Jefferson Co. // Transfer from Robert Simmons of Jefferson Co., for $80 in hand paid, all claim to above to William Kennedy on 7 Jan. 1806. Wit: Felix Hughes and Nathaniel Johnston. Prov. by Hughes 5 Mar. 1806 bef. the Board. Signed T.R. // Transfer from William Kennedy, of Jefferson Co., for $300 in hand paid, to Jonathan Curtis all claim to above land on which he resided and which he purchased of Robert Simmons, late of this county. Wit: Felix Hughes. // Jefferson Co., Miss. Ter. Jonathan Curtis, for $300, in hand paid, conveyed to Lewis Humphreys of same, 155 acres whereon he now lives, 27 Dec. 1806. Wit: Felix Hughes.

No. 1674. Claimant: Charles Peak, 30 Mar. 1804. No report (on back). Miss. Ter. Charles Peak, who on 27 Oct. 1795 was an actual settler therein, claims 350 arpents by virtue of a Spanish grant to

Leonard Keply and by sd Keply sold to claimant by deed 28 Sept. 1795.

No. 1675. Claimant: Samuel Hubbard, 30 Mar. 1804. Wit: Amos Hubbard, 12 Nov. 1804. Certificate 275 issued 24 Dec. 1804. Miss. Ter. Lemuel (?) Hubbard, a citizen of territory afsd., claims the right of preference in becoming a purchaser of 300 acres on the Miss. River, by virtue of the same having been inhabited and occupied by William Smith before and on 3 Mar. 1803, which sd Smith conveyed to Amos Hubbard who conveyed to present claimant, and the said Smith was above the age of 21 years and the head of a family before 3 Mar. 1803. Wm. B. Shields, atty. for claimant. Notice: Same claim by Emanuel Hubbard.

No. 1676. Claimant: Stephen Minor, 30 Mar. 1804. See No. 1109. Certificate A-775 issued 15 May 1806. Stephen Minor, a resident of Miss. Territory 27 Oct. 1795, claims 359 arpents by virtue of a Spanish grant in favor of Richard Harrison in March 1783. Patent is lost or mislaid but a copy will be obtained as soon as the Office at New Orleans shall be opened and an officer appointed to give certified copies of original patents. Said land was afterwards sold and conveyed to Minor, the claimant, by sd Richard Harrison, 16 Mar. 1788. John Minor for Stephen Minor. Plat shows land adj. land of Col. John Steele.

No. 1677. Claimant: Stephen Minor. Wit: William Barland. Note: This land is included with the patent, claim 1222. Rejected. Stephen Minor claims land granted to Peter Hawkins by British Government and by him sold at public sale and purchased by Michael Esclava who sold the same to Phillipe Trevino and sd Trevino sold to present claimant in 1786. John Minor for Stephen Minor.

No. 1680. Claimant: William Lintot, 30 Mar. 1804. Certificate A-576 issued 9 Sept. 1805. Note: See No. 1910. William Lintot, a resident in the territory on 27 Oct. 1795, claims a lot under the hill at Natchez by virtue of a Spanish grant to Philip Engle and sold by sd Philip Engle to Bernard Lintot, 25 Mar. 1797, and finally sold by sd Bernard Lintot to claimant. For William Lintot by John Minor.

No. 1683. Claimant: James McIntosh, 30 Mar. 1804. Rejected 15 June 1807. James McIntosh, who was a settler in this territory 27 Oct. 1795, claims 800 acres on Cole's Creek in Jefferson County, by virtue of two patents, one to James Elliot prior to 27 Oct. 1795, 1400 acres, part of which land claimed was conveyed by Elliot to Carlos de GrandPre, and another a grant also from the British Government for 400 acres to ______ Dawze, which he conveyed to Peter Hawkins who conveyed the same to Don Carlos who conveyed the 780 acres to claimant. Seth Lewis for the claimant.

No. 1684. Claimant: James McIntosh, 30 Mar. 1804. Wit: Col. Osmun, 29 Nov. 1804. Duplicate of No. 1294. Rejected 10 June 1807. James McIntosh, an inhabitant of Miss. Ter. on 27 Oct. 1795, claims 250 arpents on Cole's Creek in Jefferson Co. by virtue of a Spanish grant to James Elliot prior to 27 Oct. 1795 and by sd Elliot conveyed to Don Carlos de GrandPre by whom the same was conveyed to the claimant. S. Lewis for claimant. Notation: Washington, Miss. Ter., 4 Sept. 1805. No. 1294. Deed 800 arpents Elliot to GrandPre, 7 Feb. 1789, 400 of which is said to be part of pat. to Elliot for 1000 arpents and other 400 arpents a grant to Dauze who sold it to Hawkins and he to Elliot. GrandPre sells the same to claimant, James McIntosh. No. 1683 claims the same land. Last mentioned grant is, of course, the same as 1294. See also No. 224, also 2025, 2026. Note: The within claim comprehends 200 arpents said to have been granted to Hawkins, 200 said to have been granted to Gossett, and 400 arpents said to have been granted to Daws, also 200 arpents out of Elliot's own patent for 1000 arpents. John Smith is entitled to 200 arpents out of the above 1000 and the remaining 800 was sold lately to Catherine Surget but the sale to GrandPre being part of the 1000 was in 1789. Also 257 acres said to be part of the grant to Elliot of 500 arpents but there is no grant produced as evidence of these claims but the patent to Elliot for 1000 arpents, and only 400 arpents claimed by McIntosh above lie within this patent and is the only quantum that can be entitled to a certificate. And these claims covering this are doubtful as Mrs. Surget purchased the remainder of the said patent after deducting Smith's 200 arpents. The sale from GrandPre may have been a continuance when he was going away but if good Mrs. Surget takes out 400 instead of 800 arpents in this case. Signed T.R. The sales of 400 arpents of Elliot pat. to GrandPre in 1789 must be considered good. The only question is whether the sale to McIntosh is good.

No. 1685. Claimant: Richard King. 30 Mar. 1804. Wit: John Tally, 6 Aug. 1805. Certificate B-271 issued 14 May 1807. Richard King, a citizen of Miss. Ter., Co. of Adams, claims 640 acres in sd county on Homochitto, founded on transfer of sd tract from William Cason to Austin Holbrook, which sd Holbrook conveyed to John Ferguson who conveyed the same to John Calvit on 4 Jan. 1802 and sd Calvit conveyed the same to the present claimant. The abovenamed William Cason actually inhabited and cultivated the aforesaid tract prior to the day Spanish troops evacuated the territory, he being at that time the head of a family and above 21 years of age. Plat shows: Joseph Ford and Christopher Guice with lands adjoining.

No. 1686. Claimant: Richard King, 31 Mar. 1804. Rejected 15 May 1807. Richard King, a citizen of Miss. Ter. Adams Co., claims 640 acres in sd county on the waters of Homochitto, founded on a transfer of sd tract by Hezekiah Williams to John Ferguson, the said Ferguson conveyed to John Calvit and the sd Calvit conveyed to present claimant. The afsd. tract was actually inhabited and cultivated by sd Hezekiah Harman prior to and on the day the Miss. Ter. was finally evacuated by the Spanish troops, he being at that time above the age of twenty-one years and the head of a family.

No. 1687. Claimant: Joshua Presler, 30 March 1804. Rejected for want of evidence, 30 Dec. 1806. Miss. Ter., Adams Co., Joshua Presler hereby gives notice that he claims 640 acres in sd county about 4 miles above the mouth of Old River on the Miss. River, by virtue of his having settled and improved the sd tract on and before 3 Mar. 1803. He therefore claims the right of preference in becoming the purchaser of the United States of sd tract of land.

No. 1688. Claimant: Justus Andrus, 30 Mar. 1804. Wit: Samuel Lusk, 28 Nov. 1804. Certificate D-221 issued 4 Mar. 1807. Justus Andrus claims 592 arpents upon which the claimant established his residence and cultivated on and before 27 Oct. 1795, which sd land was surveyed and put into the possession of the claimant 14 Feb. 1795, by virtue of a Spanish warrant of possession, granted in 1794. Plat: bounded by Joseph Dove, Joseph Miller and James Nicholson.

No. 1689. Claimant: Justus Andrus, 30 Mar. 1804. Rejected for want of evidence, 30 Dec. 1806. Justus Andrews claims the preference to become purchaser from the United States of 250 acres in Wilkinson County on Buffalo Cr. by virtue of his having improved and cultivated the sd tract in 1795 and it has been improved by him or for his use at different times ever since.

No. 1704. Claimant: William G. Forman, 30 Mar. 1804. Wit: Nathaniel Ivy, 26 Nov. 1804. Certificate A-392, issued 1 July, 1805. See No. 101. William Gordon Forman hereby gives notice that he claims 95 acres in Adams Co. by virtue of a Spanish grant to Susanna Spell, 28 Jan. 1789, and conveyed from sd Flower to Ezekiel Forman, 14 Feb. 1795, and from the exr. of sd Ezekiel's last will and testament to David Forman, now deceased, and from exr. of David Forman to Joseph Forman and from Joseph Forman, Jr. to this claimant. By Lyman Harding, Atty. Amendment to No. 1704: Susanna Spell, grantee of 95 acres on St. Catherine's Creek, Adams Co., conveyed same to Samuel Flower, 5 Nov. 1794, and sd Flower conveyed to Ezekiel Forman. Done by order of the Board. Thomas H. Williams, Register. 1 July 1805. Note: the plat of land exhibited on the deed from Flower to Ezekiel Forman.

No. 1705. Claimant: William G. Forman, 30 Mar. 1804. Witness: Nathaniel Ivy, 26 Nov. 1804. Certificate A-747 issued to legal representatives of David Forman, 27 Feb. 1806. William Gordon Forman, surviving executor of the last will and testament of David Forman, decd., hereby gives notice that he claims 2000 acres in Adams County, by virtue of a Spanish grant to Ezekiel Forman, now deceased, 1 June 1792, and conveyed by the executors of his last will to sd David in his lifetime. W. G. Forman by Ly Harding, Atty.

No. 1707. Claimant: Isaac Guion, 30 Mar. 1804. Certificate A-734 issued 16 Jan. 1806. See No. 901. Isaac Guion, whole legal representative, was actually settled in the Miss. Territory prior to the 24 Oct. 1795 and claims 50 acres under a title by the Spanish Government to Jacob Adams, which being in the possession of Charles King is believed to be already entered. The following is the claim of title which is in the hands of the Keeper of the Spanish Records, (the originals of) which have been lost by time and accident and cannot be .... at present, namely: Conveyance from Jacob Adams to William Atchinson, from William Atchinson to William Gillespie, from William Gillespie to Joseph Vidal. The other conveyances I have and herewith present: the conveyance from Joseph Vidal to David Johnston and his conveyance to me.

No. 1709. Claimant: Samuel S. Mahan, 30 Mar. 1804. Certificate A-736 issued 16 Jan. 1806. Samuel Sidney Mahan, a citizen of Miss. Ter., whole legal representative, and an actual resident in this territory on 22 Oct. 1795, claims Lot No. 3 in Square No. 34 in the City of Natchez, by virtue of a Spanish grant. grant.

No. 1710. Claimant: Frederick Zerban, 30 Mar. 1804. Rejected 12 June 1807. See Nos. 1581 and 2003. Frederick Zerban hereby gives notice that he claims 1100 acres in Adams Co. on the Homochitto, by virtue of a Spanish Government to Samuel Philip Moore, granted before 27 Oct. 1795 and conveyed by sd Moore to Helen Soileau and by her to sd Frederick Zerban, 17 Mar. 1802.

No. 1713. Claimant: Abram Ellis, 30 Mar. 1804. Wit: John McCulloch, 4 Mar. 1805. Rejected. Miss. Ter. Abram Ellis, a citizen of Miss. Ter., on 27 Oct. 1795 was an actual settler therein and claims Lot No. 5 in Square No. 2 in the Town of Bruinsburg, by virtue of a Spanish grant to Peter Bryan Bruin, who conveyed the same to the claimant, 4 Jan. 1801. For Abram Ellis at his request, John Girault.

No. 1719. Claimant: Jonathan Jones, 30 Mar. 1804. Rejected 15 May 1807. Miss. Ter., Claiborne Co. Jonathan Jones claims 640 acres in sd county on the south fork of Bayou Pierre by right of occupancy. The sd tract was first inhabited and cultivated in 1796 by Mr. William Lum, who was at that time the head of a family and inhabited and cultivated the sd tract on the day when the Spanish troops finally evacuated the sd territory. He died leaving William Foster his executor, who sold the sd land unto the sd Jonathan Jones. Plat and certificate of survey, dated 12 Sept. 1797, by Silas L. Payne. Witnesses: Jesse Lum and Henry Milburn, chain carriers.

No. 1720. Claimant: Timothy O'Hara, 30 Mar. 1804. Note: See Nos. 541 and 1791. Certificate A-746 issued 24 Feb. 1806. Note: Patent filed in No. 1791. Miss. Ter. Adams Co. Timothy O'Hara claims 86 acres, part of a tract granted William Daniel Jr. who conveyed the same to John Wiley who conveyed it to sd Timothy O'Hara. Note: The patent was issued to Richard King who sold it to J. R. Wiley who sold it to claimant. Deposition of Richard King who acknowledged to have sold a tract adjoining Gerard Brandon to John R. Wiley which is said to be now the property of Timothy O'Hara. 6 Feb. 1806. Richard King. Wit: Edward Turner.

No. 1721. Claimants: Heirs of C. Watrous, 30 Mar. 1804. Certificate A-539 issued to legal representatives, 28 Aug. 1805. Miss. Ter. The legal representatives of Charles Watrous, late of this territory, deceased, claims 5 arpents in the City of Natchez, by virtue of a grant before 27 Oct. 1795 to Francisco Lennan, who was an actual settler in sd territory on that date, and by him conveyed to Charles Watrous, deceased, 9 May 1797.

No. 1722. Claimants: Heirs of C. Watrous, 30 Mar. 1804. Col. Girault, the agent of the claimants appeared before the board and relinquished the within claim. Signed Thomas H. Williams, Register. 25 Feb. 1806. Miss. Ter. the legal representatives of Charles Watrous, late of this territory, one undivided moiety of 250 acres by virtue of a warrant for 300 arpents from the Spanish Government August 1782 by John St. Germain, he being then the head of a family, who on 16 Dec. 1784 sold 250 arpents as above claimed to Polser Shilling. Polser Shilling on 27 Feb. 1795 conveyed to John Girault who on 27 Oct. 1795 was an actual settler in the territory, and on that day actually inhabited and cultivated the same. The sd Girault, on 4 March 1797, did release one half of the 250 arpents to said Polser Shilling, the said half the sd Shilling on 13 June 1797 sold to Charles Watrous, deceased.

No. 1723. Claimants: Heirs of N. Hunter, 30 Mar. 1804. Certificate A-508 issued to legal representatives, 21 Aug. 1805. The heirs and legal representatives of Narsworthy Hunter, decd., claim 150 acres in Wilkinson County on the waters of Bayou Sarah, being part of 2000 acres granted by the Spanish Government to Henry Hunter, Sr. by virtue of sd patent and conveyance of sd 150 acres from sd Henry to sd Narsworthy, 20 Sept. 1801.

No. 1724. Claimants: Heirs of M. Hackler, 30 Mar. 1804. Witness: William Dunlee and Henry Fortner. Certificate D-36 issued June 1806. Miss. Ter., Jefferson Co. Charlotte, Mary, Samuel, Anna Maria, Jacob, and Esther Hackler, legal heirs and representatives of Martin Hackler, lately deceased, claim 640 acres on Cole's Cr. by virtue of the land having been settled by the sd Hackler in his lifetime in 1797 and cultivated ever since by him. Esther Hackler, natural guardian of the heirs aforesaid.

No. 1743. Claimant: Catherine Harman, 30 Mar. 1804. Note: This land is included in the general certificate issued to the heirs of John Hartley. See No. 137. May 16, 1806. Take notice that Catherine Harman claims 1000 acres of land as laid out in the division of 10,000 acres, which she claims by conveyance of His Excellency, Don Carlos De GrandPre, then Governor of the District of Natchez and it has been regularly settled and occupied since the grant.

No. 1748. Claimant: Philip Barbour, 30 Mar. 1804. Rejected 15 May 1807. To the Commissioners: Take notice that Philip Barbour, son and heir of Philip Barbour, decd., claims 250 acres on Roper Creek, purchased by Philip Barbour, decd., from Archibald McDuffy, who lived on and cultivated it for some time previous to the Spaniards' evacuation of this country. Philip Barbour, the father of the present claimant, is deceased, his papers left in much confusion and many of them lost. It is more than probable that the foregoing land was carried into a complete grant. The plat shows the land to be in Claiborne County south of Bayou Pierre but not adjoining it, near the lands of Thomas James, James Simmons and John Sims. Enclosed also is a plat by William Vousdan for "Captain Philip Barbour" for 250 acres in Jefferson County on Boyd's Creek.

No. 1749. Claimant: Phil Barbour, 30 Mar. 1804. Rejected June 1807. To the Commrs, etc. Take notice that Philip Barbour, son and heir of Captain Philip Barbour, decd., claims 1500 acres at Grand Gulf in Claiborne Co. granted by the British Government of West Florida to sd Capt. Philip Barbour and he resided on and cultivated the land for many years. After the Spaniards had taken possession of the country, the sd Capt. Philip Barbour left and his relative and friend, Capt. Richard Harrison, generously interposed and saved the said land, as appeared by the Spanish grant hereunto annexed by His Excellency Don Carlos de GrandPre. By the sudden death of Captain Philip Barbour most of his valuable papers were lost. But many letters and papers are appended which will show the land laid out and surveyed for the sd Philip Barbour. Plat and certificate of survey by William Vousdan, dep. surveyor of the Natchez Dist., dated 17 Jan. 1789, that he had surveyed and laid out for and in the name of Capt. Richard Harrison all that tract of land called "Barbour's Grand Gulf" containing 1500 English acres, originally granted by His Brittanic Majesty to Capt. Richard Barbour, uncle to the sd Harrison, 8 leagues above the Fort of Natchez. By plat the beginning is at a tree up the Big Black River but the tract runs down the sd River to the Mississippi and then into the curve that makes Grand Gulf.

No. 1750. Claimant: Philip Barbour, 30 Mar. 1804. Rejected. To the Commrs, etc: Take notice that Philip Barbour, son and heir of Capt. Philip Barbour, decd., claims 500 acres at or near the Petit Gulf in Jefferson Co., which was granted by British Government of West Florida to Capt. Philip Barbour and was cultivated and improved by him and for his use and was resurveyed under the Spanish Government by William Vousdan. Said son and heir now a minor. (Note by M. W. McB. This is the same plat as that made out to Richard Harrison in Claim No. 330.)

No. 1763. Claimants: Neill and Beauvais, 30 Mar. 1804. Rejected. Neill and Beauvais claim 4 acres in Town of Natchez, by virtue of a Spanish patent in name of Baptiste Trenier prior to 27 Oct. 1795, and an improvement made sd Trenier in 1797, while an actual settler of the Territory. Plat shows lots adjoining those of George Cochran, John Girault and S. Minor.

No. 1765. Claimant: David Ferguson, 30 Mar. 1804. Certificate A-777, issued 16 May 1806. Miss. Ter. David Ferguson claims 2 arpents of land in Natchez by virtue of a Spanish patent to Mr. Minor who was an actual settler in sd territory on 27 Oct. 1795, and he sold the said 2 arpents to Mr. L. Faure, who sold it to David Ferguson.

No. 1771. Claimant: Zadock Barrow, 31 Mar. 1804. Wit: George Bailey. Certificate B-222 issued to James Howard, assignee, Mar. 4, 1807. (Claim badly torn.) Zadock Barrow, a citizen of Miss. Ter., ... 31st Mar. 1790 .... in Wilkinson County, on Homochitto, at which time he was 21 years of age and had a family with wife and two or three children. G. Poindexter for claimant. Plat shows land of John Hooser, adjoining.

No. 1772. Claimant: Thomas Sullivan, 31 Mar. 1804. Wit: Joseph Green, 21 Aug. 1804. William Dunbar, 11 Oct. 1805. Rejected 13 June 1807. Thomas Sullivan, a citizen of Miss. Ter. Jefferson Co., claims 400 acres in sd county on waters of Cole's Creek, founded on a Spanish patent to present claimant, who was a resident of the territory prior to 1795 and to the present day. G. Poindexter for claimant.

No. 1773. Claimants: Hoskinson and Carmichael, 31 Mar. 1804. Rejected. Ezekiel Hoskinson and James Carmichael, citizens of Miss. Ter. Jefferson County, claim 370 acres in Claiborne Co. on the waters of Bayou Pierre, by virtue of a deed of conveyance from Richard Graham and Rachel Graham to Melling Woolley for afsd tract, which sd Woolley conveyed to present claimants.

No. 1774. Claimant: Thomas Donaldson, 31 Mar. 1804. Wit: Samuel Cooper, 5 Nov. 1804. Notation: Certificate No. 257 issued to him in right of his wife, Winifred, for 500 acres to be surveyed conformably to No. 121, April 10, 1807. Thomas Donaldson, of Miss. Ter., Adams Co., asks for 640 acres in sd county on waters of Dry Bayou. The conveyance from Benjamin Dorsey to Winifred Ryan, now the wife of the claimant. The sd Dorsey did actually inhabit and cultivate the afsd. tract prior to and on the day the Miss. Territory was finally evacuated by the Spanish, he being at that time above the age of 21 years and the head of a family. George Poindexter, atty. for claimant.

No. 1776. Claimant: William Pharr, 31 Mar. 1804. Rejected. (In the claim he is called Pharis and in the plat Pharris.) William Pharris, of Miss. Ter. Wilkinson Co. claims 640 acres in sd county on the waters of Buffalo Cr., founded on the actual settlement and cultivation by sd William Pharris prior to and on the day the Miss. Territory was evacuated by the Spanish troops, being at that time above the age of 21 years and the head of a family.

No. 1777. Claimants: Moses Bonner's heirs, 31 Mar. 1804. See No. 51. Claim relinquished. Legal representatives of Moses Bonner, Sr. decd., inhabitants of the Miss. Territory, claim 800 acres in Jefferson County on waters of Cole's Creek, by virtue of a Spanish patent . . . (date torn away) . . . . Notation: This land is claimed by the heirs of Moses Bonner in Claim No. 51 and Willis Bonner, in behalf of sd heirs, directs that this notice shall be considered as relinquished. Thos. Williams, Register.

No. 1779. Claimant: Melling Woolley, 31 Mar. 1804. Certificate A-723 issued 15 Jan. 1806. Melling Woolley gives notice that as a legal representative of John Girault, Esq., he claims a tract by virtue of a Spanish patent to John Girault who conveyed the same by deed 23 April 1801 to sd Melling Woolley. Plat shows it near Natchez and bounded by land of Mr. Cochran, surveyed for Col. Piernas, by William Barland and land sold to S. Arze, beyond which is "the street from the church".

No. 1780. Claimant: Francis Brezino, 31 Mar. 1804. Rejected. Francis Brezina, a resident of the Miss. Territory, claims 2000 acres on an island of the Homochitto River commonly called Cypress Island, by virtue of an order of survey of the Spanish Government to him, which was lost in the conflagration in New Orleans, but which the claimant can prove.

No. 1787. Claimant: George Cochran, 31 Mar. 1804. Rejected. George Cochran claims the right of preference in becoming the purchaser from the United States of 150 acres in Claiborne County on Bayou Pierre, including his gin, beginning on the north side of sd creek, above the said gin, by virtue of his having inhabited and cultivated the sd land on 3rd Mar. 1803.

No. 1788. Claimant: Thomas Tyler, 31 Mar. 1804. Rejected. Thomas Tyler, as legal representative of James Glasscock, claims 48 acres near Natchez, by virtue of its having been inhabited and cultivated by the sd Glasscock who was the head of a large family on and long before and since 1797, and sold by him to the sd Tyler. Certificate of survey by Atchinson shows sd tract was part of land granted to William Brocus by Spanish Government, adj. St. Catherine's Cr. (Not dated.)

No. 1823. Claimant: Patrick Conelly, 31 Mar. 1804. Certificate A-804 issued 9 June 1807. Patrick Conelly claims 90 acres in Adams Co. on St. Catherine, part of Spanish grant to John Girault, who conveyed the same to Thomas Gillespie and sd Gillespie conveyed it to James White, who conveyed it to the present claimant, by deed, dated 4 Dec. 1799.

No. 1824. Claimant: William Atchinson, 31 Mar. 1804. Wit: Isaac Fortner, 24 Mar. 1806. Certificate D-321 issued 29 Dec. 1806. Miss. Ter., Adams Co. Mar. 26, 1804. William Atchinson, a resident of afsd. territory, gives notice that he claims the right of preference in becoming the purchaser of 130 acres on waters of St. Catherine's Creek, by virtue of having inhabited and cultivated the same on and before 3 Mar. 1803. Certificate and plat of same by himself shows the location "a place known as the Half-Way Hill" on eastern waters of above creek, 6 miles southeast from Natchez, which was claimed by Jacob Adams and purchased by Vousdan along with 313 arpents. "There was some improvement in 1781 and since I had a cabin built and land cleared." Plat show Col. Benajah Osmun, Ephraim Blackburn, Major John Guion, William McIntosh and Mr. Peter Surget with lands adjoining.

No. 1825. Claimants: Trustees of Jefferson College, 31 Mar. 1804. See No. 118. Rejected 13 June 1807. Miss. Ter. The trustees of Jefferson College claim 12 acres and 58 perches square on the waters of St. Catherine's Creek in Adams County, founded on a British patent to John Foster who conveyed a part thereof to his brother, James Foster, which said James Foster and Elizabeth, his wife, out of the part conveyed to sd James by the sd John, conveyed the abovementioned 12 acres and 58 perches to said trustees and their successors to and for the use and purpose of erecting said college thereon and to and for the use of the same for a public school and for no other purpose whatsoever, by their deed, dated 31 Mar. 1804. W. B. Shields, atty for the Trustees.

No. 1826. Claimants: Trustees of Jefferson College, 31 Mar. 1804. See No. 118. Rejected 13 June 1807. Miss. Ter. The trustees of Jefferson College claim 19 acres and 121 square perches of land on the waters of St. Catherine's Creek in Adams County, founded on a Spanish patent to John Foster and a conveyance from sd John Foster and Mary, his wife, of the abovementioned 19 acres and 121 square perches out of sd patented tract, to the trustees and their successors to and for the purpose of erecting sd college thereon and to and for the use of same for a public school and for no other purpose whatsoever, by their deed, 31 May 1804. W. B. Shields, atty. for the Trustees.

No. 1827. Claimant: Isaac Johnston, 31 Mar. 1804. Rejected for want of evidence, 30 Dec. 1806. Isaac Johnston, a citizen of Miss. Ter. and Wilkinson Co., claims 326 acres in sd county on the waters of Thompson's Cr. which he inhabited and cultivated on and prior to 3 Mar. 1803 and was at that time the head of a family. Therefore he wishes to become the purchaser of same under the 3rd Section of the Act of Congress.

No. 1828. Claimant: Peter B. Bruin, 31 Mar. 1804. Rejected for want of evidence. Miss. Ter. Peter Bryan Bruin, a citizen of the territory, claims the preference of becoming the purchaser of 200 acres by virtue of having inhabited and cultivated the same on and before 3 Mar. 1803, or some person doing so for his use. The plat is marked "Susan Ann Mary 200 acres", nothing else but the measurements.

No. 1830. Claimant: John Smith, 31 Mar. 1804. Certificate A-721 issued to J. Hopkins, assignee of claimant, 13 Jan. 1806. Miss. Ter. John Smith claims 300 acres in Jefferson County, on the north fork of Cole's Cr., a part of 1256 arpents, a Spanish patent to James Elliot, Jr. who conveyed the sd 300 arpents by deed 3 Dec. 1798 to Daniel Callaghn who conveyed the same to the present claimant, 21 Nov. 1800. W. Murray for John Smith. Note: The patent cites that the grant was for 1000 arpents. T. R.

No. 1831. Claimant: Benjamin Carrol, 31 Mar. 1804. Wit: Martin Owens, 15 Jan. 1805. Notation: Sold by the claimant to John Nugent. See No. 273. Rejected 15 May 1807. Benjamin Carrol, a citizen of Miss. Ter. Wilkinson Co., claims 640 acres in sd county on the waters of Buffalo Cr. which was actually inhabited and cultivated by Benjamin Carrol or some person for him prior to and on the day the Spanish Troops finally evacuated the territory, he being at that time above the age of 21 years and the head of a family. G. Poindexter, Atty. for claimant. From plat, the tract was bounded on one side by Mrs. Savage.

No. 1832. Claimant: George Overaker, 31 Mar. 1804. Certificate A-479 issued 7 Aug. 1805. George Overaker, a citizen of Miss. Ter., claims 100 acres on the Miss. River bounded on a Spanish patent lately executed to Richard Bacon for 250 acres, who conveyed the above 100 acres to sd George Overaker, which appears in deed to Thomas Tyler from sd Bacon. The small plat shows St. Germain, Benjamin Monsanto, Thomas Tyler and John Girault as having lands adjoining.

No. 1833. Claimant: Baley E. Chaney, 31 Mar. 1804. Wit: John Searcy, 12 May 1804. Rejected. Miss. Ter., at the request of Bailey E. Chaney, Esq., I have admeasured and laid off to him 300 acres on Cole's Creek in Jefferson County, Grimball Robert, surveyor. This shows James and Wilson Boles and Buckner Darden with lands adjoining. The petition of Bailey Chaney sheweth that he claimed 300 acres, first settled 1794 by Martin Hackler and by him sold to Thomas Splane who also occupied and conveyed sd premises to Thomas Owen, of whom the petitioner purchased the same.

No. 1834. Claimant: Patrick Foley, 31 Mar. 1804. Same land claimed by J. F. Carmichael to whom a certificate has been issued. Apr. 24, 1807. Miss. Ter., Wilkinson Co. Patrick Foley claims 240 acres on waters of Bayou Sara in sd county, by virtue of a Spanish order of survey, 1 Mar. 1794, to Reuben Jelks, who settled and cultivated the said land before that time and was an actual settler in the territory and sold the same land to Foley about Dec. 1795. This land bounded by Reuben Dunham, John F. Carmichael and Patrick Foley.

No. 1836. Claimant: Alexander Montgomery, 31 Mar. 1804. Rejected, 1807. Alexander Montgomery claims 500 acres by virtue of a Spanish grant to James McGill, dated 1794, and sd McGill sold to Alexander Montgomery, in Jefferson County on the north fork of Cole's Creek about 36 miles from Natchez.

No. 1837. Claimant: Sheliab Smith, 31 Mar. 1804. No evidence. Rejected Dec. 1806. Sheliab Smith, a citizen of Miss. Ter., Claiborne Co., claims the right of preference in the purchase of 74 acres in sd county on the River Miss. He did actually inhabit and cultivate the afsd. tract prior to the 3 March 1803, he being at that time above the age of 21 years and the head of a family. G. Poindexter, atty. for claimant. Certificate of Survey, in Claiborne Co. for Sheliab Smith, in Palmyra settlement, opposite the upper island, beg on River at Ezra Marble's corner ..... Thomas Newman's lower line. James Cook, surveyor. Dec. 6, 1803.

No. 1838. Claimant: Lucius Smith, 31 Mar. 1804. Wit: Jesse Smith, 21 Nov. 1804. Notation: See No. 1311. Certificate D-242 issued 22 Dec. 1806. Lucius Smith, a citizen of Miss. Ter., Claiborne Co., claims a right of preference in the purchase of 177 acres in sd county on the Miss. River, which he did actually inhabit and cultivate on and before the 3 Mar. 1803, he being at that time above the age of 21 years and the head of a family. G. Poindexter, atty for claimant.

No. 1839. Claimant: Pliny Smith, 31 Mar. 1804. Wit: Caleb Potter, 22 Oct. 1804. Certificate D-24 issued 24 Sept. 1806. Pliny Smith, a citizen of Miss. Ter., Claiborne Co., claims 640 acres in sd county on the waters of the Miss. founded on a transfer of the sd land from John Young to Caleb Potter who conveyed the same to Phineas Smith who conveyed same to Pliny Smith. The afsd John Young or some person under him did actually inhabit and cultivate the said tract prior to and on the day this territory was finally evacuated by the Spaniards, he being at that time above the age of 21 years and the head of a family. G. Poindexter for claimant.

No. 1840. Claimant: Peter Neilson, 31 Mar. 1804. Witnesses: Anthony Calvit and Austin Holbrook, 21 Aug. 1804. Rejected May 1807. Miss. Ter. Peter Neilson claims a donation right to 640 acres cultivated and improved in 1795, on Wells Creek in Adams County.

No. 1841. Claimant: Tench Coxe, 31 Mar. 1804. Notation: See No. 1649. Rejected 13 June 1807. Tench Coxe, a citizen of Philadelphia, claims 1500 acres, founded on a conveyance to sd Tench Coxe from Edward Jones by deed, 20 Sept. 1790, the sd 1500 acres claimed part of General Lyman's Mandamus for 20,000 acres, the plat of which has been entered with the Register of this Land Office. Thaddeus, son and heir of Gen. Lyman, of the City of New York, conveyed part of the afsd 20,000 acres to Evans Jones, James Jones and the sd Edward Jones, of West Florida, which sd Edward Jones, by his deed, conveyed his full and equal undivided one-third to the present claimant. The parties are not certain whether the tract contained 1000 or 1500 acres. William B. Shields, atty. for the claimant.

No. 1842. Claimant: William Chaney, 31 Mar. 1804. Wit: Bailey E. Chaney, Sept. 1806. Rejected May 1807. William Chaney claims 200 acres by virtue of a settlement, residence and cultivation on sd land on and prior to 1797, when the Spanish troops finally evacuated the territory, in county of Adams, about 20 miles from Natchez, on the waters of Cole's Creek, adj. William Bell.

No. 1844. Claimant: John Armstreet, 31 Mar. 1804. See No. 34. Reported 13 June 1807. John Armstreet, a resident of the Miss. Ter. claims 200 acres on the Homochitto River in Adams Co., part of 500 acres granted to William Garnier by the Spanish Government, 28 May 1779, and by sundry conveyances to Elihu H. Bay and by sd Bay to the present claimant, by deed, 7 July 1801.

No. 1845. Claimant: Littleberry West, 31 Mar. 1804. Wit: Peter Nelson, 25 Mar. 1805. Certificate B-223 issued 4 Mar. 1807. Miss. Ter. Jefferson County. Littleberry West claims 290 arpents in sd county on Cole's Creek by right of occupancy, the said land having been inhabited and cultivated in 1795 by Thomas Nichols who was the head of a family and sold the sd tract to sd West 26 Dec. 1798. Plat shows Peter Camus, Robert Dow, Peter Neilson, Joshua Stockstill and Capt. Bozley with land adjoining. // Deed from Thomas Nichols, of Adams Co., to Littleberry West for value recd., tract and improvement adjoining the above named and Mr. Martin. Thomas Nichols signs with a mark. Wit: William Noland, William West. Prov. by William West, who signs with an X, Dec. 18, 1804, before T. R.

No. 1846. Claimant: John Vardiman, 31 Mar. 1804. Miss. Ter., Adams County, John Vardiman claims the preference of becoming the purchaser of 390 acres on north side of the Homochitto in sd county, by virtue of its having been inhabited and cultivated in April 1803 by sd John who was at that time the head of a family, and cultivated it the same year on March 3 and ever since.

No. 1847. Claimants: The heirs of Andrew Beall, 31 Mar. 1804. Wit: William Atchison, 3 Sept. 1804. Certificate A-286 issued to Benajah Osmun, assignee of claimant, 6 June 1805. Miss. Ter. The heirs and legal representatives of Andrew Beall, deceased, claim 100 arpents in Adams County on St. Catherine's Creek, which is a part of 555 arpents granted by the Spanish Government to Joseph Ford, 28 April 1790, and sd Ford sold the 555 acres to John King who sold the afsd. 100 arpents to Andrew Beall, deceased. Richard Beall, executor.

No. 1848. Claimants: Heirs of A. Beall, 31 Mar. 1804. Witness: John Girault, 1 Sept. 1804. Certificate A-811 issued to Benajah Osmun, assignee, 13 June 1807. The heirs of Andrew Beall claim 240 acres in Adams Co. on waters of St. Catherine's Cr. by virtue of a Spanish patent to John White who sold sd land to Caleb Owens and Richard Harris as joint tenants by deed, 11 Feb. 1785, and sd Owens who survived the sd Harris, by John Girault, his attorney, sold the tract to sd Andrew Beall, decd., by deed, 20 April 1795. Richard Beall, executor.

No. 1852. Claimants: John Furney and Co., 31 Mar. 1804. Certificate A-725 issued 15 Jan. 1805. See Girault's claim. George Furney and Charles McBride claim Lot No. 1, Sq. ——, in the City of Natchez, by conveyance __ June 1796 from John Girault to Simon De Arze who conveyed the sd lot to Luther Smith who conveyed the same to Courtland Smith, 19 Apr. 1799, who conveyed sd lot to George Furney and Charles McBride, by deed, 18 May 1801. The Notice Amended: George Furney, a citizen of the Miss. Territory, claims a lot of land by virtue of a Spanish grant, before 27 Oct. 1795, to William Barland for 105 arpents, out of which he sold 11 acres to John Girault, 20 Sept. 1788, who sometime in 1795 or thereabouts sold the sd lot to Simon De Arze, and 15 June 1796 the sd De Arze sold same to Luther Smith who by deed, 19 Apr. 1799, conveyed same to Courtland Smith and he on 18 May 1801, by deed, sold the same to Charles McBride and George Furney, and sd Charles McBride, 15 Apr. 1805 conveyed all his share to George Furney, the present claimant. The sd Simon De Arze and John Girault were both residents in said territory on 27 Oct. 1795.

No. 1854. Claimants: Heirs of John Wilson, 31 Mar. 1804. See No. 1532. Rejected June 1807. Miss. Ter., Jefferson County, James Wallace and Margaret, his wife, John Wilson and Joseph Wilson, heirs and legatees of John Wilson, deceased, claim 400 arpents, being an undivided part or share of 1000 acres situated in sd county, by virtue of a conveyance from Margaret L'Estage, alias Vauchere, dated 29 Oct. 1801. Signed: James Wallace, Margaret Wallace, John Wilson and Joseph Wilson, by their attorney. The plat is of 1000 acres granted to St. Germain, of which this claim was a part, with Richard Goodwin on one side, and Joseph Bonner and Henry Manadue on other sides.

No. 1857. Claimants: Heirs of William Ferguson, 31 Mar. 1804. Note: See No. 12. Rejected 13 June 1807. Miss. Ter., Jefferson County, the heirs and legal representatives of William Ferguson deceased, claim 500 acres in sd county on the waters of Cole's Creek by virtue of a British patent to William Williams who, by will, gave the same to William Ferguson, deceased, for a confirmation of which sd Ferguson applied to the Spanish Government and received a grant of same. Plat shows: Isaac Johnston and Jacob Winfree with land adjoining.

No. 1858. Claimant: Elijah Pope, 31 Mar. 1804. Wit: Nehemiah Carter, 1 Apr. 1806. Note: See No. 323. Rejected for want of sufficient evidence, 30 Dec. 1806. Elijah Pope, an inhabitant of the Miss. Ter., claims 200 acres in Wilkinson Co. on the waters of Buffalo, asking the preference of purchase by virtue of an improvement begun and continued before and after 3 March 1803, by John Moore, to me conveyed 26 Dec. 1803.

No. 1859. Claimant: David Lum, 31 Mar. 1804. Wit: Lewis Coursey, 1 Dec. 1804. Certificate D-41 issued 8 Sept. 1806, to S. Dearmond, assignee of claimant. Miss. Ter., Claiborne Co. David Lum claims preference for becoming the purchaser of 150 acres on waters of the south fork of Bayou Pierre about 4 and one-half miles southeast of Grindstone Ford, for his purchase of the premises from Robert Thompson, by deed, 29 March 1804. The sd Thompson inhabited and cultivated the place 3 March 1803 and was on that day and before the head of a family. Transfer from David Lum to Samuel Dearmond, 2 Apr. 1804. Wit: Samuel McMurtry. Prov. before the Board, 1 Dec. 1804. Signed T. R.

No. 1861. Claimant: Thomas Tyler, 31 Mar. 1804. Certificate A-693 issued to legal representatives, 6 Jan. 1806. Notation: See No. 1468. Miss. Ter. Thomas Tyler, a citizen of the territory afsd, claims a lot in the vicinity of Natchez, of 16500 feet by virtue of a conveyance from William Barland to him for the same, dated 30 June 1801, part of a tract of 100 acres granted sd Barland by the Spanish Government.

No. 1872. Claimant: Robert Moore, 30 March 1804. Notation: See No. 103. Rejected June 1807. The above plat is of 12 acres near Washington, purchased by Robert Moore of John Bullen and surveyed 25 Apr. 1803. Signed Fenton and Morgan. Plat shows a triangle bounded by John Bullen and David Eldridge.

No. 1873. Claimant: Samuel P. Moore, 31 Mar. 1804. Wit: James Moore, 11 Jan. 1807. Certificate B-291 issued. Samuel P. Moore, a citizen of Miss. Ter. who on 27 Oct. 1795 was an actual settler therein, claims Lot No. 4, Square No. 12, in City of Natchez, by virtue of a Spanish grant to Jane Rose, who was likewise a settler in the territory the aforesaid date, and said lot actually improved prior to that date by said Rose, who conveyed the same to claimant, 19 Mar. 1799. Samuel P. Moore by his agent, James Moore.

No. 1875. Claimant: Robert Moore, 31 Mar. 1804. Wit: John Girault and Thomas Philips, 15 Jan. 1807. Rejected 15 June 1807. Robert Moore who was an actual settler in the territory on 27 Oct. 1795, claims a tract of 200 acres in Jefferson County on Cole's Creek by virtue of a Spanish grant to John Stampley and by Stampley conveyed to Stephen Minor and by sd Minor to Richard Roddy, and by sd Roddy to John Arden and by sd Arden to the claimant by deed 29 Dec. 1800. Signed Robert Moore. Plat shows John Stampley and Hugh Matthews as adjoining.

No. 1881. Claimant: William Joiner, 31 Mar. 1804. Transferred to John Ellis. See No. 1936. signed T. H. W. William Joiner, a citizen of the Miss. Territory, claims 500 acres in Adams County near the Miss. River, by virtue of a British patent, 21 Sept. 1772.

No. 1888. Claimant: Zachariah Kirkland, 31 Mar. 1804. Witness: John Staybraker, Jr., 1 Oct. 1804. Certificate B-15, 29 Dec. 806. Conflicting with Rodney's survey. Zachariah Kirkland hereby gives notice that he claims the right of preference of becoming the purchaser from the United States of 640 acres in Jefferson Co. on the Miss. River, about 13 miles above Natchez, by virtue of his having improved and settled the sd land in 1800. The plat shows: John and Thomas Neeley's land adjoining.

No. 1889. Claimant: Polser Shilling, 31 Mar. 1804. Wit: John Stowers, 23 Aug. 1804. Rejected May 1807. Miss. Territory, Adams Co. Polser Shilling gives notice that as legal representative of John Stowers, Sr., he claims 640 acres on Fairchild's Cr. founded on a settlement, cultivation and improvement by the said Stowers in 1784, at which time he was the head of a family, and continued thereon some years and sold the said tract to sd Polser Shilling in 1786, since when it has been in cultivation and continually claimed by the sd Shilling.

No. 1890. Claimant: Polser Shilling, 31 Mar. 1806. Wit: Henry Manadue, 23 Aug. 1805. Rejected May 1807. Miss. Territory, Adams Co. Polser Shilling hereby gives notice that he claims 400 acres in county afsd on south side of Fairchild's Creek, by virtue of the tract having been inhabited and cultivated by Charles Howard in 1785 who sold the same to James Brown who inhabited it until 1786 or 7 when the sd Brown departed this life, and by virtue of a sale of sd land made to this claimant, 20 May 1787, by Spanish to pay the debts of the sd deceased. The tract was inhabited and cultivated until 1795 and all the aforesaid claimants were above the age of 21 years, and Howard and Shilling were the heads of families.

No. 1893. Claimants: Gabriel H. Ford and others, 26 Apr. 1804. See No. 79. Rejected June 1807. Gabriel H. Ford gives notice that George III, King of Great Britain, by Letters Patent, dated 1763 and 1772, did grant to Amos Ogden and his heirs 25,000 acres of land to be taken up within the Province of West Florida, the said patentee being a native of the Co. of Morris in New Jersey, who was known as Captain Amos Ogden who claimed the grant as reward for distinguished services in behalf of this country in the French War, so-called, preceding the peace of 1753. It is said that the said patent was recorded in the Land Office at Pensacola, West Florida. In virtue of the said Letters Patent, 25,000 acres were laid out and surveyed for the said Amos Ogden on the northwesterly side of the Homochitto River, about 10 miles from Natchez on the banks of the Miss. River in the sd Province of West Florida . . . . . I do hereby give notice that a part of the lands within the said survey, supposed to be a tract of about 10,000 acres, which from the time of the survey and unto now has been known and called by the name of "Ford's Tract", by deed of conveyance from said Amos Ogden was given and granted to Col. Jacob Ford, Jr., my father, his heirs and assigns, a native inhabitant of the County of Morris, aforesaid, who in 1777 during the Revolutionary War was in the services of his country, which deed by accident and time was lost but is recorded in the Land Office at Pensacola; and I do further give notice that the right of Col. Jacob Ford, Jr., decd. by virtue of his last will and testament is vested in his four children: Timothy, Gabriel H., Elizabeth who is since intermarried with Henry William DeSaussure, Esq. and Jacob and their heirs as tenants in common . . . . I do therefore, living in Morristown, New Jersey, ask for Timothy Ford, Esq., Jacob Ford, Esq. and Henry William Desaussure, Esq. and Elizabeth, his wife, all of Charleston, South Carolina.

No. 1894. Claimant: Michael Hackler, 27 Apr. 1804. Rejected for want of evidence, 3 Dec. 1806. Miss. Ter. Jefferson County, Michael Hackler claims a preemption of 50 acres in sd county on the waters of the North Fork of Cole's Creek, by an improvement made in 1800 and continued cultivation, bounded by Esther Hackler and Christian Hackler.

No. 1905. Claimants: Thomas Fenton and David B. Morgan, 21 July 1804. Rejected 1807. Miss. Ter., Jefferson County, Thomas Fenton and David B. Morgan claim a Donation of 640 acres in sd county on waters of Cole's Creek about 2 miles southeast from the Town of Greenville, by virtue of its having been inhabited and cultivated in 1798 by ______ Pendleton who sold it to John Strickling (Strickland) by deed, who conveyed the same to the present claimant, 8 Aug. 1802. Signed by Thomas Fenton.

No. 1907. Claimants: Heirs of C. Boardman, decd., 31 July 1804. Wit: John Henderson, 7 Sept. 1804. Notation: See Nos. 689 and 1825. Certificate B-271 issued 6 Mar. 1807. The guardians of the orphans and heirs of Charles Boardman, deceased, claim in their name 112 arpents in the District of Pine Ridge, which sd tract is part of 600 arpents granted to Abner Pipes from the Spanish Government, 22 Feb. 1793, which said grantee, as also the said Charles Boardman, were heads of families and actually cultivated the said tract on 27 Oct. 1795. Signed John Henderson, guardian. Plat shows Abner Pipes, John Bisland and Pine Ridge adjoining.

No. 1908. Claimant: Charles McCollister, Aug, 23, 1804. Witness: Joseph Bradley, 22 Oct. 1804. Roan Godbolt, 19 Jan. 1805. Rejected for want of sufficient evidence, 30 Dec. 1806. Miss. Ter., Wilkinson Co. Charles McCollister claims the right of preference in becoming the purchaser of 150 acres in sd county on the Homochitto including the Blue Springs, which tract was inhabited and cultivated 3 Mar. 1803 by Abraham Guice who relinquished his right to the present claimant, 15 Oct. 1804. Signed Charles McAllister.

No. 1909. Claimant: John Wells, 31 Aug. 1804. Wit: Darling Bradley, 31 Aug. 1804. Certificate D-160 issued 16 Dec. 1806. Miss. Ter. John Wells, who was the head of a family on 3 Mar. 1803, claims a donation right of 640 acres cultivated and settled before 1795. He has been living on it ever since, situated on the headwaters of Sandy Creek in Adams Co.

No. 1911. Claimant: Samuel May, 30 Aug. 1804. Rejected for want of evidence, 30 Dec. 1806. Samuel May, being of full age, claims 500 acres in Claiborne Co., Miss. Territory, on waters of Bayou Pierre, by virtue of 3rd Section of the Act of Congress.

No. 1912. Claimant: John Grafton, 17 Sept. 1804. Residence proved in Claim No. 491. Certificate A-429 issued 11 July 1802. John Grafton claims 200 acres in Adams Co., Miss. Territory, on St. Catherine's Creek, part of 555 acres granted by the Spanish Government to William Atchinson who conveyed the same to Charles Dowling, who, with his wife, conveyed same to the present claimant, 25 Feb. 1802.

No. 1913. Claimant: Abner Green, 24 Sept. 1804. Certificate A-644 issued to David Lattimore, assignee, 27 Sept. 1805. Abner Green claims Lots No. 2 and 4, Square No. 15 in the City of Natchez, by virtue of a Spanish patent to William Barland for 100 arpents which forms a part of City of Natchez, who conveyed 8 arpents of same to David Ferguson, by deed, 13 Jan. 1793, and sd Ferguson and Murdoch conveyed the same to claimant, 1 Apr. 1796.

No. 1914. Claimant: Lancelot Porter, 24 Sept. 1804. Witness: Reuben Mayfield, 22 Jan. 1805. Certificate D-161 issued 16 Dec. 1806. Miss. Ter., Adams Co. Homochitto River. Purchased from Thomas Aldridge the right of preference as claim by sd Aldridge in Feb. 1803, when he cleared a parcel of land, made a brush fence and planted corn, also peach trees and in 1804 Lancelot Porter settled sd place and cleared 3 acres and is now living on it. Miss. Ter., Adams Co. // Thos. Aldridge, of sd county, for $500 in hand paid by Lancelot Porter, of sd county, sells all right of occupancy on land on south side of Homochitto River, June 1804. Wit: Hiram Downs, John Scarlett and Shad Porter. Proved before the Board, 10 Sept. 1805.

No. 1917. Claimant: Thomas Fortner, 1 Oct. 1804. Wit: Vincent Fortner, 19 Nov. 1804. Rejected June 1807. Miss. Ter., Claiborne Co. Thomas Fortner claims 240 acres by virtue of petition to the Spanish Government in 1789 and granted to me by sd Government at New Orleans April 1796 and by me cultivated May 1, 1799. Plat: Land near the Big Black. Note: The claimant being present before the Board, desires that if the testimony in this case is not sufficient for a donation that the land may be granted to him as a preemption by virtue of an improvement.

No. 1919. Claimant: Thomas M. Green, 8 Oct. 1804. Wit: William Fairbanks, 28 Jan. 1805. Certificate B-284 issued 10 June 1807. Miss. Ter. Jefferson County. Thomas M. Green, who was an actual settler of sd territory on 27 Oct. 1795, claims 200 acres on Cole's Creek in sd county, by virtue of a British patent to Ebenezer Gossett, in 1777, who sold the same to Peter Hawkins who sold the same to John Girault, by deed, 3 May 1788, who sold the same to James Elliott, 31 Jan. 1789, who, by Daniel Clark, his attorney, conveyed the same by deed, 4 Oct. 1799, to the present claimant. It has been cultivated for many years by the said Gossett and his legal representatives afsd.

No. 1920. Claimant: T. M. Green, 8 Oct. 1804. Wit: Thomas Calvit, John Staybraker, 28 Jan. 1805.

Certificate B-285, issued 10 June 1807. Thomas M. Green, an actual settler in this territory on 27 Oct. 1795, claims 350 acres on Cole's Creek in sd county, by virtue of a warrant from British Government of West Florida to Benjamin Roberts on 1775, who was then above 21 years of age and took possession of and inhabited and cultivated the same, and is long since deceased. The sd Roberts transferred by delivery to James Cole, who transferred the same to Richard Bacon by writing, 16 March 1784, who conveyed the same to James Elliott by deed, 23 Jan. 1786, who, by Daniel Clark, his atty., conveyed the same to the present claimant, 4 Oct. 1799, which land has been actually inhabited and cultivated by the sd parties and their legal representatives from the date of the original warrant to the present day, they having been respectively inhabitants of this territory and above the age of 21 years.

No. 1921. Claimant: T. M. Green, 8 Oct. 1804. Wit: William Fairbanks, 28 Jan. 1805. Certificate B-286 issued 1807. Thomas M. Green, of Jefferson Co., Miss. Ter., who was an actual settler the 27 Oct. 1795, claims 200 acres on Cole's Cr. by virtue of a British Warrant to Henry Roach, dated about 1776 who conveyed the same to Peter Hawkins who sold the same to James Elliot, 3 May 1788, who by Daniel Clark, his atty., conveyed the same to the claimant.

No. 1922. Claimant: Thomas M. Green, 8 Oct. 1804. See No. 1683. Wit: William Fairbanks, 13 June 1807. Certificate B-297. Miss. Ter. Thomas M. Green, who was an actual settler in this territory on 27 Oct. 1795, claims 400 acres on Cole's Creek, in sd county, by virtue of an order of survey granted by the former British Government of West Florida to Joseph Daws, now deceased, about 1775, who transferred the same to Peter Hawkins who conveyed the same to James Elliott by writing, 3 May 1788, who by Daniel Clark, his atty., conveyed sd land to this claimant, 4 Oct. 1799. The sd Dawes was at the date of the sd warrant above the age of 21 years and the said land by his legal representatives inhabited and cultivated ever since.

No. 1923. Claimant: Thomas M. Green, 8 Oct. 1804. Wit: William Fairbanks, 28 Jan. 1805. Certificate B-287 issued 10 June 1807. Miss. Ter. Jefferson Co. Thomas M. Green, who was an actual settler in this territory 27 Oct. 1795, claims 122 acres on Cole's Creek in sd county, by virtue of a British order of survey to Alexander Boyd, now deceased, about 1773, who was then above 21 yrs. of age, for 250 acres. 72 acres, part of the sd 250 acres was sold by the Spanish Government by public sale for the benefit of the children of the sd Alexander Boyd, whereupon Jeremiah Bryan became the purchaser thereof and also of 50 acres of the balance, making 122 acres of the grant to the sd Boyd, and the sd Bryan conveyed the said 122 acres, among other things, by deed, 10 Jan. 1785, to Capt. James Elliott, who by Daniel Clark, his atty., conveyed the same among others, 4 Oct. 1799 to present claimant. This tract was inhabited and cultivated on 27 Oct. 1795 and before and since that time, 1st by the said Boyd and since by the legal representatives of the said Boyd.

No. 1924. Claimant: Jonathan Jones, 15 Oct. 1804. Wit: John Atkinson, 12 Nov. 1804. Certificate D-305 issued 29 Dec. 1806. Miss. Ter. Jefferson Co., Jonathan Jones claims the right of preference in becoming the purchaser of 100 acres in sd county on the North Fork of Cole's Creek, by virtue of its having been inhabited and cultivated on and before 3 March 1803 by this claimant.

No. 1925. Claimant: Samuel Brooks, 15 Oct. 1804. Wit: Anthony Hutchins, John Girault and William Selkrig, 19 Nov. 1804. Rejected 27 April 1807. Adams Co. Samuel Brooks, a resident of the Miss. Territory, claims 200 acres on the Miss. River in Claiborne County, opposite the Three Islands or a little above them, which land was surveyed by William Vousdan, Dep. Surveyor, appointed by the British Government. This survey was made in the name of Wm. Selkrig, 21 Apr. 1777, in pursuance of an order of survey granted to sd Selkrig previous to that time. Several acres of the sd land were cleared by sd Selkrig but he was driven off during the American Revolution and on his return has been driven from the same by Indians, and the order of survey lost which caused the sd Selkrig to apply to the above Vousdan for the above certificate, which was given on 12th Feb. 1801. This land sd Selkrig sold to Samuel Brooks the present claimant, 2 June 1804. From the plat: the location on the Miss. River, with William Vousdan adjoining on the east and adjoining Vousdan, Thomas James.

No. 1927. Claimant: John Cheat, 16 Oct. 1804. Rejected 27 Apr. 1807. Miss. Ter., Adams Co. John Cheat, a resident of the Spanish Province of Louisiana on 27 Oct. 1795, long before and since that time, claims 100 acres in sd county on the south side of Second Creek, by virtue of an order of survey from the British Government of West Florida granted to the claimant about 1776, and a survey made in pursuance thereof by the Dep. Surveyor. He was the head of a family at the date of said order of survey and inhabited and cultivated the sd tract for two years about that time and on the 27 Oct. 1795. Signed John Cheate.

No. 1928. Claimant: John Choat, 16 Oct. 1804. Rejected 27 Apr. 1807. Miss. Ter., Adams Co. John Choate, a resident of the Spanish Province of Louisiana on 27 Oct. 1795 and before and since, claims 100 acres in sd county on the upper side of Second Creek, on the waters thereof, by virtue of an order of survey from the British Government of West Florida, granted this claimant in 1777, a survey thereof made by the Dep. Surveyor in 1778, who was the head of a family at the date of the warrant and inhabited and cultivated the sd tract at that time and on the day and year first abovementioned. Signed John Choate.

No. 1929. Claimant: Sarah Choat, 16 Oct. 1804. Rejected 24 Apr. 1807. Miss. Ter., Adams Co. Sarah Choat, a resident of the Spanish Province of Louisiana on 27 Oct. 1795 and long before and since that time, by John Choate, her husband, claims 500 arpents in sd county on south side of Clear Fork of St. Catherine's Cr. by virtue of an order of survey by the Spanish Government granted to sd Sarah Choate, by the name of Sarah Holstein, in 1782, at which time she was the head of a family and with her husband and family inhabited and cultivated the said land in 1783 and 4 and on the 24 Oct. 1795.

No. 1930. Claimant: James Land, 18 Oct. 1804. Wit: James Collingsworth, 22 Oct. 1804. Certificate C-194 issued 17 Dec. 1806. Miss. Ter., Wilkinson Co. James Land hereby gives notice that he claims the right of becoming the purchaser of 57 acres in afsd. county on Percy's Cr. by virtue of his having inhabited and cultivated the sd tract on 3 March 1803 by his legal representative, at which time this claimant was the head of a family. James Collingsworth for James Land.

No. 1931. Claimant: Darius Anderson, 20 Oct. 1804. Wit: Jacob Guice and Christopher Guice, 22 Oct. 1804. Certificate D-223 issued 29 Dec. 1806, to W. H. Morrow, assignee. Miss. Ter., Adams Co. Darius Anderson hereby gives notice that he claims the right of preference in becoming the purchaser of 100 acres on the waters of Morgan's Fork of Homochitto in Adams Co. by virtue of his having located, settled and improved the premises in 1801, being above the age of 21 years at that time, and having cultivated the same on 3 Mar. 1803. // Wilkinson Co., Miss. Ter. Assignment by Darius Anderson to Robert H. Morrow, all claim to above improvement on 100 acres. (No consideration given). Witness: Harmanus Taulman. Ack. by Darius Anderson 13 Mar. 1806. Signed T.R.

No. 1932. Claimant: Terrence Smith, 22 Oct. 1804. Rejected for want of evidence, 30 Dec. 1806. Miss. Ter. Terrence Smith claims the preemption rights to 100 acres improved by Thomas Herod in 1801 and gifted to aforesaid T. Smith, on the waters of Morgan's Fork of the Homochitto.

No. 1933. Claimant: Henry Manadue, 20 Oct. 1804. Wit: John McGill, 22 Oct. 1804. Certificate B-96 issued 3 Feb. 1807. Miss. Ter., Jefferson Co. Henry Manadue, head of a family and 21 years of age and a resident of this territory 27 Oct. 1797, claims 640 acres in sd county on Fairchild's Creek. The said land was settled, cultivated and improved on and before the above date by sd Manadue or his legal representatives for his use to the present period.

No. 1934. Claimant: Henry Manadue, 22 Oct. 1804. Wit: John McGill, 29 Oct. 1804. Anthony Nichols, 8 Apr. 1806. Certificate B-97 issued 3 Feb. 1807.

No. 1937. Claimants: Heirs of G. B. Rodney, decd., 23 Oct. 1804. Rejected 28 April 1807. Notice is hereby given that undersigned, as friend and agent, claims in behalf of the lawful heirs of Sir George Bridges Rodney, late Lord Rodney of the Kingdom of Great Britain, 5000 acres in the territory West of the Pearl River on the east side of the Miss. River near Apple Island, which said tract of land was granted and surveyed for the said George Bridges Rodney by the Government of West Florida, as a reduced Naval Post Captain in virtue of the Great King of Britain's Proclomation of 1763, by warrant and survey, dated 13 June 1774, and patented to sd George Bridges Rodney 13 Oct. 1775. Signed Anthony Hutchins. [The original is written by Thomas Rodney.] Note: A survey and plat, also a plat of the Miss. River showing the location of the land; a certificate of the Sec'y. of State of the U.S. annexed to the Minutes of the Government and Council of West Florida showing the dates of the warrants, survey and patent, all filed with this claim. A. Hutchins. [The plat is most elaborate showing the types of land within the survey and what would grow on it.]

No. 1938. Claimant: William Hootsel, 23 Oct. 1804. Wit: Robert Ford, 23 Oct. 1804, but minuted "the 22 Oct. 1804". Certificate D-141, issued 16 Dec. 1806. William Hootsel, a citizen of Miss. Ter., claims the right of preference of purchase of 390 acres in Adams County on Second Creek, which the sd William Hootsel did actually inhabit and cultivate long prior to and on 3 March 1803, being on that day above the age of 21 yrs. and the head of a family.

No. 1940. Claimant: William Vardiman, 29 Oct. 1804. Wit: Joshua Kelly, 12 Nov. 1804. Certificate D-163 issued 16 Dec. 1806. William Vardiman, a citizen of Miss. Territory, claims the right of preference in the purchase of 320 acres in Wilkinson Co. on the waters of the Amite River, founded on a transfer of afsd tract to the claimant by John Morgan by writing, 15 Sept. 1804. The sd. John Morgan did actually inhabit and cultivate the same prior to and on 3 March 1803, he being at that time above the age of 21 years and the head of a family.

No. 1941. Claimant: Anthony Dougherty, 29 Oct. 1804. Witness: Col. John Girault, 29 Oct. 1804. Certificate B-147 issued 10 Feb. 1807. Anthony Dougherty, a resident of Miss. Territory, claims under Ebenezer Rees, an actual settler of sd territory on 27 Oct. 1795, 52 arpents near the City of Natchez, part of larger Spanish grant to William Ferguson, 7 Sept. 1782 and by sd Ferguson conveyed to Matthew White, 1 June 1784, who conveyed 52 arpents thereof to Charles de GrandPre, 8 Apr. 1790, and the same together with other parcels of land, forming together 625 arpents were conveyed by sd Grandpre to Ebenezer Rees, 28 May 1794, out of which the sd Rees by deed, 12 Aug. 1800, conveyed 410 arpents, including 52 arpents here claimed. Plat shows: John Lusk's grant, Benjamin Balk, George Rapalje and Hiler's grant. This last is Isler.

No. 1942. Claimant: Anthony Dougherty, 29 Oct. 1804. Residence of E. Rees proved, 29 Oct. 1804. Certificate A-650, issued 2 Oct. 1805. Anthony Dougherty claims through Ebenezer Rees, who on the 27 Oct. 1795, was an actual settler in this territory, 87 arpents of land near the City of Natchez, part of a larger Spanish grant, 15 May 1795, to John Rowe and by him conveyed to George Furney, who on 10 Oct. 1787 conveyed the same to Mark Oiler (Isler) and on 21 Mar. 1789 Jonas Oiler, sole heir of Mark, conveyed to Charles de Grandpre the 87 arpents thereof now claimed and the same with other parcels thereunto adjoining were conveyed by the said Grandpre to Ebenezer Rees, 28 May 1794, out of which the sd Rees by deed 12 Aug. 1800 did convey to the present claimant 410 arpents wherein the present claim is included.

No. 1945. Claimant: Jonathan Curtis, 19 Oct. 1804. Rejected for want of evidence, Dec. 1806. Miss. Ter., Jefferson County. Jonathan Curtis claims a preemption right to 100 acres on the waters of Platner's Creek in county afsd., originally improved and inhabited by him in Feb. 1803. By plat, Theophilus Marble, Daniel Harrigil and David Hunt had land adjoining.

No. 1946. Claimant: Owen Ellis, 29 Oct. 1804. Wit: George Ellis, 20 Nov. 1804. Certificate D-139 issued 15 Dec. 1806. Owen Ellis claims 187 acres on the waters of Beaver Creek on the east side thereof, by improvement made previous to and on 3 Mar. 1803, by sd Owen Ellis.

No. 1947. Claimant: Benjamin Ratcliff, 30 Oct. 1804. Wit: Peter Ratcliff, 30 Oct. 1804. Rejected for want of evidence. 30 Dec. 1806. Benjamin Ratcliff claims the right of preference in becoming the purchaser of 222 acres on the waters of Beaver Cr. Wilkinson County, by virtue of his having inhabited and cultivated sd tract on and before 3 Mar. 1803, at which time he was upward of 21 years of age and by virtue of the 3rd Sec. of the Act of Congress. Peter Ratcliff for Benjamin Ratcliff.

No. 1948. Claimant: William Collins, 30 Oct. 1804. Wit: Peter Pait, 3 Oct. 1804. Rejected June 9, 1807. Miss. Ter., Adams County. William Collins claims 640 acres in sd county on the waters of Buffalo Cr. The above land was inhabited, cultivated and improved on and before 27 Oct. 1795 by William Berry then the head of a family who continued thereon until about 1797 or 8; then sold to James Knoles about that time, who continued on the premises until 1798 and sold the same to present claimant, 10 Oct. 1798. Paper in file: Nos. 1948 and 1949, William Collins, Donation. In the two claims depositions of witnesses have been taken and returned to the Board, etc. Signed William B. Shields.

No. 1949. Claimant: William Collins, 30 Oct. 1804. Wit: Peter Pagit. Rejected 9 June 1807. Miss. Ter., Adams Co. William Collins claims 640 acres on Buffalo, improved by James Knoles, the head of a family on and before 27 Oct. 1795, and Knowles sold to present claimant, 6 June 1798.

No. 1950. Claimant: Richard Nye, 30 Oct. 1804. Rejected May 1807. Richard Nye claims 100 acres as a donation right, it having been inhabited and cultivated by sd Nye at the time required by the Act of Congress. From plat and survey, this is on Bayou Pierre in Claiborne Co., adjoining land commonly called Lyman Mandamus, belonging to the heirs of John Hartley.

No. 1952. Claimant: Stephen Dunn, 5 Nov. 1804. Wit: James Crow, 5 Nov. 1804. Samuel Watkins 27 Nov. 1804. Rejected May 1807. Stephen Dunn, a resident in the Miss. Territory, claims a donation right of 597 acres by virtue of the same having been improved, settled and cultivated by William Lucas in 1794 and who has had it cultivated and resided on by himself or some other person ever since until he assigned his right therein unto the abovenamed Stephen Dunn, by bill of sale 30 Oct. 1804. Stephen Dunn never had any land granted to him either by the British or the Spanish in this territory. Certificate of survey and plat by John Dinsmore, Oct. 11, 1804., shows location on Sandy Creek in Adams Co., adjoining David Howard.

No. 1954. Claimants: Heirs of D. Ward, 5 Nov. 1804. Patent file in Claim No. 19. Reported. 25 April 1807. The heirs and legal representatives of Daniel Ward, late of the Miss. Territory, by James Kennedy, their attorney, give notice that they claim 500 acres in Adams Co. on Cole's Cr. formerly Boyd's, and designated as Lot No. 3 or Humphrey Grant's-500 acres, by virtue of a British patent to William Fricker, 8 Nov. 1777, for 2000 acres, including the above 500, and of a conveyance of sd 500 acres from sd Wm. Fricker, by E. R. Wegg, J. Falconer and James Amoss, his attorneys, to Humphrey Grant, 10 and 11 May 1779, and of a conveyance thereof from the said Humphrey Grant to said Daniel Ward, 8 and 9 of June 1779, and by virtue of a confirmation thereof by the Spanish Government 6 March 1783 to the then claimant.

No. 1955. Claimant: Daniel Johnson, 10 Nov. 1804. Rejected May 1807. Miss. Ter., Jefferson Co. Daniel Johnson, a resident of the sd territory, claims 640 acres in sd county on Miss. River which was settled, cultivated and improved in 1801 by John Malone who was prior to that date 21 years of age and sold the same to the present claimant, for a valuable consideration, on or before 3 March 1803, and the land has been cultivated ever since by the present claimant, or some person for him.

No. 1956. Claimant: Patsey W. Moss, 17 Nov. 1804. Wit: Vincent Fortner, 19 Nov. 1804. Theophilus Marble, 17 June 1805. Rejected 15 May 1807. See Claim No. 839 for interference. Miss. Ter., Claiborne Co. Patsey W. Morse, as heir-at-law and legal representative of William Moss, decd., by Drucilla Moss, her natural guardian, claims 640 acres on Moss's Bayou just below the Big Black River adjoining the Miss. River Swamp in sd county by virtue of the said tract having been inhabited and cultivated by the said William Moss who was the head of a family in his lifetime before and at the time the said territory was finally evacuated by the Spanish troops. Drucilla Moss, guardian of Patsey W. Moss.

No. 1957. Claimant: Benjamin Watkins, 19 Nov. 1804. Rejected for want of evidence, 30 Dec. 1806. Miss. Ter., Claiborne Co. Berryman Watkins, the head of a family in county afsd., claims the preference of becoming the purchaser of 239 acres in sd county, on a branch of the North Fork of Bayou Pierre, about 2 miles above or east of the Grindstone Ford, and bounded by Abner Green, by virtue of his settlement on and cultivation of the premises on and before 3 Mar. 1803 and his continuance thereon at this date.

No. 1958. Claimant: Samuel Lum, Jr., 21 Nov. 1804. Wit: David Lum, 21 Nov. 1804. Rejected for want of sufficient evidence, 30 Dec. 1806. Miss. Ter., Claiborne Co. Samuel Lum, Jr., a citizen and head of a family of sd county, claims the preference in becoming the purchaser of 400 acres in sd county on the north side of the South or Little Fork of Bayou Pierre, on White's Branch, by virtue of the settlement and cultivation of the premises by Richard Parish on and before 3 Mar. 1803 and said Parish's sale to said Lum of the land, 10 Nov. 1804.

No. 1960. Claimant: John Ebby, 21 Nov. 1804. Wit: James Quine, 10 Nov. 1804. Rejected for want of sufficient evidence, 30 Dec. 1806. Miss. Ter., Wilkinson Co. John Ebby, a resident of sd Territory, claims the right of preference of becoming purchaser of 100 acres in sd county on waters of Percy's Cr., which was settled, cultivated and improved in 1801 by William Hodges who has since left the territory and since sold to the present claimant by Elizabeth Hodges, wife of said William Hodges, for a valuable consideration, by bill of sale, 19 Sept. 1804. Said land was cultivated on 3 Mar. 1803 to the present time by present claimant.

No. 1961. Claimant: Joseph Strong, 20 Nov. 1804. Wit: Samuel McCarly and Samuel Cooper, 20 Nov. 1804. Joseph Erwin, 17 Feb. 1806. Note: See No. 1483. Rejected for want of sufficient evidence, 30 Dec. 1806. Joseph Strong, a citizen of the Miss. Territory, Adams County, claims 250 acres in sd county on Dry Bayou, founded on a transfer of the afsd. land from Jesse Bryant, to Thomas J. Donelson, which sd Thos. J. Donelson conveyed the same to the claimant by deed, 16 Nov. 1804. The sd Jesse Briant did actually inhabit and cultivate the sd tract prior to and on the day the Mississippi Territory was evacuated by the Spanish troops, he being at that time above the age of 21 years and the head of a family.

No. 1963. Claimants: Heirs of Sutton Banks, 21 Nov. 1804. Witness: William Atchinson, 28 Nov.

1804. Rejected May 15, 1807. Miss. Ter., Adams Co. Sarah Banks, in behalf of the heirs of Sutton Banks, a resident of the territory and head of a family, claims the right of donation in 400 acres in Adams Co. on the Miss. River, by virtue of her not having received any grants from the Spanish Government in her own name nor in the name of her husband, in his life, also by virtue of the 2nd Sec. of the Act of Congress, etc. This tract was inhabited, cultivated and improved prior to 27 Oct. 1797. Sarah Banks, signed by William Atchinson, at her request. Plat shows: George D. Banks as having land adj.

No. 1964. Claimant: Lewis Bingaman, 21 Nov. 1804. Wit: Wm. Atchinson, 28 Nov. 1804. Rejected for want of sufficient evidence, 30 Dec. 1806. Miss. Ter., Adams Co. Lewis Bingaman, a resident of this Territory, claims the right of preference in becoming the purchaser from the United States of 300 acres in sd county on the Miss. River, by virtue of having cultivated and improved the same on 3 Mar. 1803 to the present time. By John Todd Taylor, by request.

No. 1965. Claimant: Thomas Tyler, 23 Nov. 1804. Wit: William Kirkwood, 21 July 1806. Rejected for want of sufficient evidence, 30 Dec. 1806. Miss. Ter., Adams Co. Thomas Tyler gives notice that he claims 103 acres on the Miss. River in sd county, by virtue of his having inhabited and cultivated it, being the head of a family, on and before 3 Mar. 1803, and by virtue of the 3rd Sect. of the Act of Cong. etc. Certificate of survey and plat by Patrick Marrin, Teacher of English, Grammar and Mathematics, Natchez. Plat shows: Col. Girault, Overaker, and Mr. Rapalje with land adjoining.

No. 1968. Claimant: R. S. Blackburn, 26 Nov. 1804. Rejected Apr. 24, 1807. R. S. Blackburn claims 3000 arpents on the Miss. River in Claiborne County by virtue of a warrant executed before 25 Oct. 1795. By his attorney J. Dunlap. Title papers not filed.

No. 1969. Claimant: John Lewis, 26 Nov. 1804. Rejected 24 Apr. 1807. John Lewis claims 2000 acres in Claiborne County by virtue of a Spanish warrant of survey about 1789 and located before 25 Oct. 1795. By Dunlop, his attorney. Notation: Title papers not filed.

No. 1970. Claimant: John Lewis, 26 Nov. 1804. Rejected 24 Apr. 1807. John Lewis claims 1000 acres on the Miss. River in Claiborne County, by virtue of a Spanish warrant and located before 25 Oct. 1795. By Dunlap, his attorney. Title papers not filed.

No. 1971. Claimant: Athanasius Martin, 26 Nov. 1804. Rejected 24 Apr. 1807. Athanasius Martin claims 613 acres in Adams County adjoining Ogden's Mandamus by virtue of a patent from the Spanish Government before 25 Oct. 1795. By Dunlap, his attorney. Title papers not filed.

No. 1972. Claimant: R. S. Blackburn, 26 Nov. 1804. Rejected 24 Apr. 1807. R. S. Blackburn claims 3000 acres on the Miss. River within Claiborne Co. by virtue of a Spanish warrant of survey issued and located previous to 25 Oct. 1795. By Dunlap, his attorney. Title papers not filed.

No. 1973. Claimant: John J. Walton, 26 Nov. 1804. Rejected 13 June 1807. John J. Walton who was an actual settler in the Miss. Ter. 27 Oct. 1795 claims Lot No. 3, Square No. 11 in Bruinsburg by virtue of Spanish patent to Peter Bryan Bruin, who deeded the sd lot to the present claimant 4 Jan. 1801.

No. 1974. Claimant: John J. Walton, 26 Nov. 1804. Rejected 13 June 1807. John J. Walton, an actual settler in Miss. Ter. 27 Oct. 1795, claims Lot No 1, Square No. 9 in Town of Bruinsburg, which was conveyed to present claimant from Peter Bryan Bruin, 4 Jan. 1801.

No. 1975. Claimant: John J. Walton. John J. Walton, of Claiborne Co. claims Lot 4, Square 11 in town of Bruinsburg, which was conveyed to him by Peter Bryan Bruin, 4 Jan. 1801.

No. 1976. Claimant: John J. Walton, 26 Nov. 1804. Rejected June 1807. John J. Walton claims Lot No. 1, Square 11 in Bruinsburg, by virtue of a Spanish patent to Peter Bryan Bruin who conveyed the sd lot to the present claimant, 4 Jan. 1801.

No. 1977. Claimant: John J. Walton, 26 Nov. 1804. Certificate A-774 issued 16 May 1806. John J. Walton, who on 27 Oct. 1795 was an actual settler in the territory claims a lot at the Natchez landing, immediately at the foot of the hill to the left of the old road, which was a Spanish grant to Richard Harrison at an early date in their administration. The said Harrison sold it to Polser Shilling under the sanction of the Spanish Government, 16 Apr. 1785, and by the sd Shilling sold under the sanction of the Spanish Government to Francis Arroyo, 2 Oct. 1792, ... by Anthony Marmillion to Manuel Lopez, 14 Mar. 1795, and the sd Lopez sold to the present claimant. Signed John Girault, at the request of J. J. Walton. By the plat, the lot is bounded on one side by the road and the street; and on another by the hill and next to the hill, opposite to the street, Basso and Gras, and on the other side

Richard Carpenter, afterwards Edward McCabe's.

No. 1978. Claimant: Arthur Patterson, 26 Nov. 1804. Wit: Samuel Goodwin, 18 Feb. 1805. Rejected for want of sufficient evidence, 30 Dec. 1807. Miss. Ter., Claiborne Co. Arthur Patterson, a resident of the Territory, claims the right of becoming the purchaser of 413 acres in sd county on waters of Bayou Pierre by virtue of having inhabited, cultivated and improved the same on and before 3 Mar. 1803 to the present time. The plat shows: G. W. Humphreys on west, and W. Crane, and William Thompson.

No. 1979. Claimant: Simpson Holmes, 26 Nov. 1804. Certificate B-239 issued 6 Mar. 1807. Simpson Holmes, a citizen of Miss. Terrtiory, claims 640 acres in Adams County on the headwaters of Beaver Creek founded on a verbal transfer of said land from William Joiner to sd Simpson Holmes, which said William Joiner did actually inhabit and cultivate on and prior to the day the territory was finally evacuated by the Spanish troops, he being at that time above the age of 21 years and the head of a family. Transfer from Simpson Holmes, 22 May 1805, all claim to above land. Ack. 23 May 1805 before T. R. [Apparently a suit pending with Joiner.]

No. 1980. Claimant: Vincent Fortner, 26 Nov. 1804. Rejected for want of evidence. Miss. Ter., Claiborne Co. Vincent Fortner claims preference in becoming the purchaser of 200 acres in sd county on the Miss. River, which had been inhabited and cultivated since 20 Aug. 1801. Survey and plat by John Cook, 26 Dec. 1803, nearly opposite the Big Black Island, known as John Allison's improvement.

No. 1981. Claimant: Thomas J. Donelson, 26 Nov. 1804. Wit: Jesse Bryant, 26 Nov. 1804. Certificate D-326 issued 1806. Thomas J. Donelson, of Miss. Ter., Adams Co., claims the right of preference of becoming the purchaser of 183 acres in sd county on Dry Bayou. He was an actual inhabitant the 3 Mar. 1803 and above the age of 21 years and the head of a family.

No. 1982. Claimant: George Cochran, 26 Nov. 1804. Wit: Caleb Potter, 15 May 1806. Rejected 15 May 1807. Miss. Ter., Claiborne Co. George Cochran, by Robert Cochran, his legal representative, who was 21 years old and a resident of this territory 27 Oct. 1797, claims a right of donation in 640 acres in sd county on the Miss. River, which was inhabited, cultivated and improved on and before the above date by George Murray, who conveyed the same to Adam Sneider and Sneider conveyed to George Cochran, all of which conveyances are now lost.

No. 1984. Claimant: John Gaskins, 26 Nov. 1804. Wit: Daniel Harrigil, 12 Feb. 1806. See No. 1739. Rejected 7 May 1807. John Gaskins, a citizen of the Miss. Territory, Jefferson Co., claims 640 acres in said county on the waters of Cole's Cr. which was inhabited and cultivated by sd Gaskins prior to and on the day this territory was finally evacuated by the Spanish. He was at that time above the age of 21 years and the head of a family.

No. 1985. Claimant: William Roach, 26 Nov. 1804. Wit: John Graves, 27 Nov. 1804. Certificate D-271 issued to M. Davis, assignee, for 320 acres, 24 Dec. 1806. Miss. Ter., Wilkinson Co. William Roach claims 540 acres on Beaver Cr. in sd county, by virtue of an improvement made previous to and on 3 Mar. 1803 by sd William Roach. Enclosed evidence: To the Commrs. etc. Enclosed evidence to which John Graves, Esq. will qualify in favor of William Roach's claim for 640 acres. The enclosed testimony is certainly much stronger than your record which I acknowledge to be too slight to obtain a legal equitable decision in Roach's favor, nevertheless when the circumstances under which he labored are understood it is not thought to be strange that he made no crop nor resided on the premises, namely his residence 30 miles distance and his wife going into a situation not to be left alone without danger of suffering. Strong evidences present themselves to me that he intended to reside on the premises, to wit: several acres of land are cleared, potato hills are made, a log house is built with a wooden floor about halfway laid and part of the walls are ceiled with boards, and from the whole view of the case and the strong view of the neighborhood that his claim is just and lawful gave me entire satisfaction in his title to the land, whereon I became the purchaser of one-half and having no doubt respecting the issue paid him the cash for the same, whereupon I immediately began a plantation, a little after the beginning of the year and now have about 20 acres growing in corn. Having travelled from the City of Richmond, Virginia, a distance upward of 1150 miles, with the view to be well suited in a land to bring a large family to, to be in jeopardy of being without a home will be more than an ordinary disappointment to me. . . . . asking your indulgence to alter the lines so as to accommodate to suit my plantation, having cleared some for building. Signed Micajah Davis. "Please to transfer to Micajah Davis one-half of my claim of land on Beaver Creek, called Dawson's, beg. at the lower end and include my house and improvement made thereon. Signed William Roach. Wit: John

Grandos, Wilkinson Co. June 28, 1806.

No. 1987. Claimant: Abram Ellis, 26 Nov. 1804. Wit: Jesse Hamilton, 29 Dec. 1806. Certificate D-335 issued. Miss. Ter. Abram Ellis, a resident therein, who on the 27 Oct. 1795 was an actual settler in this territory, claims 200 acres formerly granted by the Spanish Government to Stephen Jordan, late of the territory, and by him sold to John Terry, 7 Jan. 1786, who on 5 Jan. 1787 assigned the same to the late Richard Ellis, deceased, and the sd Richard by will, dated 17 Oct. 1799, devised the same to the present claimant. Natchez. Signed John Girault at the request of Abram Ellis.

No. 1990. Claimant: John Girault, 26 Nov. 1804. Same land claimed by Bennet Truly. See No. 1855. Rejected 24 Apr. 1807. Miss. Ter. John Girault, a citizen of sd territory who on 27 Oct. 1795 was an actual settler therein, and a legal representative of Hugh Logan, claims 240 acres on waters of Cole's Cr., for which the sd Logan obtained a Spanish warrant, he being then above the age of 21 years, and which he sold to the claimant by deed, 7 Oct. 1791.

No. 1991. Claimant: Charles Allen, 26 Nov. 1804. Wit: Bennet Truly. Rejected 27 Apr. 1807. Miss. Ter., Adams Co. Charles Allen by George M. Falls, agent, claims 450 acres in sd county on waters of St. Catherine's Cr. about one mile above the town of Washington, by virtue of a British order of survey to the sd Charles Allen, in 1775. A survey thereof made a little after the sd year. And also by virtue of a British order of survey to the sd Charles Allen, in 1775. A survey thereof made a little after the sd year. And also by virtue of the sd Allen having inhabited and cultivated the sd tract with his family at the time aforesaid and on 27 Oct. 1795. The plat shows land on St. Catherine's Creek made out to Stephen Holstein, 450 acres.

No. 1992. Claimants: The heirs of Robert Gibson, 26 Nov. 1804. Rejected 15 May 1807. Miss. Ter. The heirs of Robert Gibson, decd., claim a donation right of 640 acres in Jefferson County on the north side of Cole's Creek, as represented by the annexed plat, by virtue of a purchase made by sd Robert Gibson from John Kincaid, 4 July 1786, and the said Kincaid had about ten acres cleared and under cultivation, and the death of said Robert Gibson prevented the continuation of same. Signed Richard Gibson and William Gibson, heirs.

No. 1993. Claimant: Zadock Barrow, 27 Nov. 1804. Rejected 15 May 1807. Miss. Ter., Adams Co. Zadock Barrow, a resident of this territory, gives notice that he claims the right of preference in becoming the purchaser from the United States of 180 acres on the Homochitto River, by virtue of having inhabited, cultivated and improved the same on and before the 3 Mar. 1803 to the present time.

No. 1994. Claimant: Luke Carol, 27 Nov. 1804. Rejected for want of evidence 30 Dec. 1806. Miss. Ter., Jefferson Co. Luke Carol, a resident of the territory afsd., gives notice that he claims the right of preference in becoming the purchaser of 90 acres by virtue of having cultivated, inhabited and improved the same on and before 3 Mar. 1803.

No. 1995. Claimant: William Patterson, 27 Nov. 1804. Wit: Adam Bingaman, 15 June 1807. Certificate A-812 issued. Miss. Ter., Jefferson Co. William Patterson, by William Gordon Forman, his lawful atty., gives notice that he claims 800 arpents in county and territory afsd. between Fairchild's and Cole's Creeks, adjoining lands of Robert Jones and Don Marcus Olivares, at the time of the survey, by virtue of a Spanish patent to Edward Patterson, 20 Mar. 1789, and conveyed by him to the present claimant, for a valuable consideration, by deed, the sd claimant being then the head of a family and 21 years of age. The sd land was cultivated, inhabited and improved on and before 27 Oct. 1795 by the sd claimant or his legal representatives for him. Patent and deed furnished.

No. 1996. Claimant: William Patterson, 27 Nov. 1804. Wit: Adam Bingaman, 13 June 1807. Certificate A-813 issued. Miss. Ter., Jefferson Co. William Patterson, by William Gordon Forman, his lawful atty., gives notice that he claims 800 arpents in sd county between Fairbanks and Cole's Creeks, adjoining the land of Robert Jones and Don Marcus Olivares at the time of the survey, by virtue of a Spanish patent to Thomas Irwin, 20 Mar. 1789, and conveyed to present claimant for a valuable consideration, the claimant being the head of a family and above the age of 21 years and the sd land having been inhabited, cultivated and improved on and before 27 Oct. 1795 by the sd claimant or his legal representatives for him. Patent and deed furnished.

No. 1997. Claimant: William Patterson, 27 Nov. 1804. Wit: Adam Bingaman, June 1807. Certificate A-814 issued. Miss. Ter., Jefferson Co. William Patterson, by William Gordon Forman, his lawful atty., gives notice that he claims 800 acres in sd county between Fairchild's and Cole's Creeks, adjoining Robert Jones and Don Marcus Olivares, by virtue of a Spanish grant to Thomas Patterson, 20 Mar. 1789, and by him conveyed for a valuable consideration to the present claimant.

No. 1998. Claimant: John Burnet, Sr., 27 Nov. 1804. Rejected 22 Apr. 1807. Sold by the claimant to F. Nailor. See No. 1431. Note: This is a claim of John Burnet, Jr., not Sr. as acknowledged by John B. Sr., 18 July 1805. Miss. Ter. Claiborne Co. John Burnet, Sr. gives notice that he claims 170 arpents, part of 300 arpents granted him by Spanish order of survey in 1782, which was surveyed in two separate tracts for want of vacant land in this place. The sd 170 arpents is on Bayou Pierre in Claiborne County. He was head of a family at the date of the warrant and inhabited and cultivated the land 27 Oct. 1795.

No. 1999. Claimant: John Burnet, Sr., 27 Nov. 1804. Rejected June 10, 1807. Notation: This is the claim of John Burnet, Jr. and not of Sr. as acknowledged by the latter 18 July 1805. See No. 1760.

No. 2000. Claimant: John Burnet, Sr., 27 Nov. 1804. Wit: William Barland, 18 July, 1805. See No. 1431. John Burnet is a Spanish grantee. See No. 1868. Rejected 10 June 1807. Miss. Ter. Claiborne Co. John Burnet, Sr., who was the head of a family and 21 years of age on 27 Oct. 1797, gives notice that he claims the right of donation of 640 acres in afsd county on the Big Black by virtue of having inhabited, cultivated and improved the said tract from the above date to the present time.

No. 2001. Claimant: Sarah Ross, 27 Nov. 1804. Wit: Isaac Rapalje, 24 Nov. 1804. Rejected. See No. 249. Certificate B-83, Oct. 30, 1806. Sarah Ross claims 200 acres on the waters of the Big Black in Claiborne County, adjoining Isaac Rapalje, by right of occupancy. The said claimant was in actual possession and cultivated the land before and at and after the Spanish troops evacuated this country, and was at that time the head of a family, and above the age of 21 years and claimed no other lands in this territory.

No. 2002. Claimant: Daniel McCaleb, 27 Nov. 1804. Wit: William Shaw, 9 July 1805. Certificate D-285 issued 29 Dec. 1806. Miss. Ter., Jefferson Co. Daniel McCaleb claims a preemption of 157 acres in sd county on the North Fork of Cole's Creek, by inhabiting and occupying in June 1801.

No. 2003. Claimant: George Pollock, 28 Nov. 1804. Rejected 12 June 1807. See No. 1581 and No. 1710. George Pollock, as mortagee of Frederick Zerban, claims 1100 arpents in Adams County on the Homochitto River, by virtue of a Spanish grant to Don Fusilier de la Clair, prior to 27 Oct. 1795, and by him conveyed to sd Frederick Zerban, who mortgaged the same to Samuel Wilson who assigned the said mortgage to the claimant, those who make the claim having been inhabitants of the territory on 27 Oct. 1795. S. Lewis, agent for the claimant. All the papers are in Spanish and in this file. One is from Samuel Philip Moore to Eleanor Soileau, widow of Gabriel Fusilier de la Clair, for 1100 acres in the Natchez District, 3 miles south of Fort Panmure on the right bank of the Homochitto River. Eleanor Soileau sells the same to Frederick Zerban. She also mortgages the land to S. P. Moore.

No. 2004. Claimant: Thomas Calvet, 29 Nov. 1804. Wit: William Atchinson, 29 Nov. 1804. William Fairbanks 28 Jan. 1805. Certificate B-244, issued 4 Mar. 1807. Miss. Ter., Jefferson Co. Thomas Calvet, a resident of the territory afsd., claims 500 arpents in sd county on Cole's Cr., by virtue of a Spanish order of survey to Richard Duvall, 23 Feb. 1789, and patented to him 24 Dec. 1797, who was at the date of the warrant the head of a family, and 21 years of age. He conveyed it to the present claimant, 1 June 1792. Said tract has been inhabited, cultivated and improved on and before 27 Oct. 1795 by sd Thomas Calvet to the present time.

No. 2005. Claimants: Heirs of Joe Miller, 29 Nov. 1804. Rejected, 24 Apr. 1807. See No. 1690. The heirs and legal representatives of Joseph Miller, decd., by Justus Andrews, their agent, gives notice that they claim 350 arpents in Adams Co. on Buffalo River by virtue of a Spanish order of survey to sd Joseph Miller, dated about 1794, he being at the date of the warrant above the age of 21 years and the head of a family and inhabited and cultivated the land on 27 Oct. 1795. Plat: Justis Andrews, James Nicholson, Jesse Carter and William Cocke Ellis adjoining.

No. 2006. Claimant: Roger Dixon, 29 Nov. 1804. Rejected 15 May 1807. Roger Dixon claims 640 acres adjoining a small tract he had purchased of David Odum and settled himself before the year 1797, on the waters of Platner's Fork of Cole's Creek, to the eastward and southward of afsd tract, and west of John Terry's heirs. He located the same 7 April 1796, running his back line as by agreement with his neighbor, John Holt, having lived on and cultivated it for several years, removed a few miles from it in 1797 making a small improvement further out and leaving it in care of a neighbor.

No. 2007. Claimant: Roger Dixon, 29 Nov. 1804. Rejected 5 May 1807. Roger Dixon claims 640 acres on James' Run of Bayou Pierre, having purchased a donation right of William Nolin, by deed, 26 July 1803. The said Nolin settled this land with his family in 1781, lived on and cultivated the same until the Indians being troublesome, he removed to Cole's Creek, visiting his place frequently since and having a tenant on it part of the time. He has continued a resident in the territory until the present year, 1804. // Indenture, 26 July 1803, William Nolin of Bayou Pierre, Miss. Ter., to Roger Dixon, of Cole's Cr., for $120 in hand paid, land whereon the sd William Nolin settled in 1781 and has since cultivated, (described above). Plat: William Dunbar, of Second Creek, purchased of Melling Woolley, Patrick Cogan, and Richard King lands adjoining. Witness: William B. Cotten and Charles Hopkins.

No. 2008. Claimant: James Frazier, 30 Nov. 1804. Rejected 24 Apr. 1807. Title papers not filed. Miss. Ter. James Frazier, now a resident in the Chickasaw Nation, by his atty., Joseph Bullen, claims 600 acres on the west side of the Tombigbee River, in the County of Washington, granted to him, the said Frazier, by order of the Spanish Government, dated July 1788, which is lost, and which tract was actually inhabited, improved and cultivated by him on 27 Oct. 1795 and for several years afterwards. For James Frazier, by James Bullen. Plat: The tract of 600 acres on the Tombigbee River is bounded by John Baker and vacant lands.

No. 2009. Claimant: John Dixon, 29 Nov. 1804. Rejected 15 June 1807. Title papers not filed. John Dixon claims 600 acres near St. Catherine's Cr. about 4 miles from Natchez, bounded by Thompson,* Alexander McIntosh, Henry Fairchilds and LaFleur, the same being granted, 1 Sept. 1772, to Thomas Taylor Byrd, a British patent issued to Philip Livingston and conveyed by Livingston to sd Byrd and from Byrd to Robert Page and by Robert Page to said Dixon. Roger Dixon for John Dixon.

No. 2011. Claimant: P. Shilling, 30 Nov. 1804. Rejected for want of sufficient evidence, 30 Dec. 1806. Polser Shilling claims the preference of purchasing from the United States 2040 acres in Adams County on the waters of St. Catherine's Cr. adjoining Stephen Jordan, Daniel Grafton and the sd Polser Shilling, said tract being surveyed in 1782 for Francis Ferrall by the Spanish Government.

No. 2012. Claimant: William Mann, 30 Nov. 1804. Rejected for want of evidence, 3 Dec. 1806. Miss. Ter. William Mann, a settler in the said territory at and before 1795, claims 25 acres in same by right of preference and wishes to become the purchaser of the United States. Plat: land adjoining B. Farrell, William Nyland and ______ Mitchell.

No. 2015. Claimant: John Erwin, 30 Nov. 1804. Wit: Benjamin Holmes, 28 Jan. 1805. See No. 485. Rejected 15 May 1807. John Erwin, a citizen of the Miss. Ter., Adams Co., claims 480 acres in sd county on the waters of Sandy and Wells Creeks, by virtue of actually inhabiting and cultivating the aforesaid long prior to and on the day this territory was evacuated by the Spanish troops, he being at that time above the age of 21 years and the head of a family, having a wife and four children. A donation claim filed heretofore by the claimant is withdrawn.

No. 2016. Claimant: Lewis Dunn, 30 Nov. 1804. Rejected for want of evidence, 30 Dec. 1806. Miss. Ter., Adams Co. Lewis Dunn, a resident of Miss. Ter., gives notice that he claims the right of preference in becoming the purchaser of 50 acres in sd county on Bates Creek, by virtue of having inhabited, cultivated and improved the same on and before 3 Mar. 1803 to this present time.

No. 2017. Claimants: Heirs of P. Hawkins, decd., 30 Nov. 1804. Rejected 15 June 1807. Miss. Ter., Jefferson Co. The heirs and legal representatives of Peter Hawkins, decd., by Abram Mayes, their agent, give notice that they claim 400 acres in sd county, about 3 miles above the mouth of Cole's Creek, adjoining lands of Ebenezer Gossett, James Elliott and others at the time of the survey, by virtue of a British patent to ______ Daws in 1775 and the sd Daws in his lifetime devised the sd land to Peter Hawkins who died and his heirs on 27 Oct. 1795 were residents in this territory, and the land was inhabited and cultivated for their use on that day and year, and improved. Signed Abraham Mayes, agent for the heirs of Peter Hawkins. Will of Joseph Daws, of the Natchez District: "I, Joseph Daws, being now on journey to Pensacola with intent to become a British subject and many difficulties and uncertainties lying in my journey, well know life to be transitory, I therefore ..... (torn) ..... all my personal and real estate I bequeath to Peter Hawkins, my true and worthy friend, he paying all my just and legal debts. I leave and bequeath to the Worshipful and Honorable Lodge of Free Masons of St. Andrew's Lodge, of Edinborough, that the same may be distributed to all the poor, distressed and indigent brothers of that or any other lodge of accepted Masons in the world, at the will and discretion of

* Richard Thompson. See claim No. 1317, W. E. Bk. D 453-4.

the Master Warden (Deacon) of said Lodge .... Witness my hand this 19 Jan. 1780, in the presence of George Boles, John Harvey and MacPherson. Signed Joseph Daws. [Legacy bequeathed to the Free Masons was torn off.] Codocil to will of Joseph Daws: "I leave and constitute and appoint William Ferguson and John Bisland, of the within District, Gentlemen, my true and lawful executors, appointed by me to execute the within will. [Part is torn.] (signed) Joseph Daws." Same witnesses. (Richard King being sworn say that he believes the name (of witness) "D. MacPherson" is in his own handwriting. Signed T.R.)

No. 2018. Claimants: Heirs of P. Hawkins, decd., 30 Nov. 1804. Wit: Richard King, 2 Sept. 1805. See 1921. Rejected. Same is confirmed to Thomas M. Green. Miss. Ter., Jefferson Co. The heirs and legal representatives of Peter Hawkins, deceased, by Abraham Mayes, their agent, claim 200 acres in sd county on Cole's Creek by virtue of a British patent to Peter Hawkins, which was inhabited, cultivated and improved by the sd Hawkins or his legal representatives for him on and before 27 Oct. 1795.

No. 2019. Claimant: John Lusk, 30 Nov. 1804. Rejected 15 May 1807. Miss. Ter. Adams Co. John Lusk gives notice that he claims 640 acres in sd county, by virtue of its having been inhabited, cultivated and improved before 3 Mar. 1798 by Asà Barrow who was then the head of a family and above 21 years of age, and who conveyed it to the present claimant by deed, in 1795, and it has been cultivated by this claimant to the present time. Signed Samuel Lusk.

No. 2020. Claimant: John Lusk, 30 Nov. 1804. Rejected 15 May 1807. Miss. Ter. Adams Co. John Lusk give notice that he claims the right of donation for 640 acres in sd county on the Homochitto River by virtue of its having been inhabited, cultivated and improved before 30 Mar. 1798, by Zadock Barrow, who was then the head of a family and of 21 years of age, and who conveyed same to present claimant by deed, 1795, and it has been cultivated ever since by him. Signed Samuel C. Lusk. Enclosed paper: "First I bought these two plantations about 1795 of Ace [?] Brashears and got a bill of sale for both, which is lost but I can prove the bill of sale by two or three evidences, if required. Zadie Barrow lived on land that Mr. Barrow rented of me at that time. The articles of agreement were left with Gabriel Swayze and can be proved. I paid 20 bu. of corn to William Joiner, Esq. Howard's father-in-law, in 1800 for cutting a road from Samuel Lusk's down to Alexander Becton's on the lake. That can be proved. Fourth, in 1801, I paid Moses Foster for building a cabin on the plantation and have his receipt for it."

No. 2022. Claimant: Christopher Connelly, 30 Nov. 1804. See No. 1727. This lot confirmed to William Dunbar in 1787. Rejected 24 Apr. 1807. Miss. Ter. Adams Co. Christopher Connelly and Thomasina Connelly, formerly known by the name of Thomasina Lord, claim a Lot No. 1, Square No. 19 in the City of Natchez, by virtue of a warrant of survey in 1795 in favor of Thomasina, wife of sd Christopher Connelly, the said warrant and certificate being lost, the claimant intending to prove the same by parole evidence.

No. 2023. Claimant: Robert Page, 30 Nov. 1804. Rejected June 1807. Robert Page, a citizen of the State of Virginia, claiming 300 acres in Miss. Territory, by virtue of a British patent to Thomas Taylor Byrd, 1 Sept. 1772, for 600 acres, of which the above 300 acres is a moiety, and by the sd Byrd the afsd. 600 acres were conveyed to Philip Livingston who, 10 May 1779, reconveyed the above 300 acres to sd Thomas Taylor Byrd who conveyed the same to claimant by deed, 31 Jan. 1797. G. Poindexter, atty. for claimant.

No. 2024. Claimant: James McIntosh, 30 Nov. 1804. Rejected June 15, 1807. James McIntosh, an inhabitant of the Miss. Territory 27 Oct. 1795, claims 400 acres in Jefferson County. Comment: Having been granted by the British Government to Joseph Daws and by said Daws conveyed to Peter Hawkins and by sd Hawkins to James Elliot and by sd Elliot to Don Carlos de Grandpre 19 Feb. 1789, and on 4 Feb. 1789 conveyed by Don Carlos to the claimant. Don Carlos de Grandpre was an inhabitant of sd territory in 1795.

No. 2025. Claimant: James McIntosh, 30 Nov. 1804. Rejected the same land being confirmed to Thomas M. Green. See No. 1919. June 10, 1807. James McIntosh, an inhabitant of Miss. Territory on 27 Oct. 1795, claims 200 acres in Jefferson County on Cole's Creek by virtue of Spanish grant to James Elliot or to Gossett prior to above date and conveyed by James Elliot to Don Carlos de Grandpre, 13 Feb. 1789, and by Don Carlos to claimant, 4 Feb. 1798.

No. 2026. Claimant: James McIntosh, 30 Nov. 1804. See No. 1921. Rejected, the same land being confirmed to Thomas M. Green. 10 June 1807. (Data on this in File No. 1921)

No. 2027. Claimant: Thomas Hutchins, Jr., 30 Nov. 1804. Reported, 200 acres, 15 Jan. 1807. See No. 1139. Miss. Ter., Adams Co. Thomas Hutchins, Jr., claims 600 acres in sd county on Homochitto by virtue of a British patent to Thomas Hutchins, Sr., 21 Oct. 1774, who devised by his will same to the present claimant.

No. 2029. Claimant: Thomas Smith, 30 Nov. 1804. Rejected 15 June, 1807. Thomas Smith claims 5000 acres northeastward from Milk Cliff about 5 miles, by virtue of a British patent to sd Smith. Signed Richard Claiborne for Thomas Smith. [From the plat it looks as if this land did not lie West of the Pearl River.]

No. 2030. Claimant: Edmund Rush Wegg, 30 Nov. 1804. Rejected 15 June 1807. Miss. Ter. The heirs and legal representatives of Edmund R. Wegg claim 2000 acres on a branch of Fairchild's Creek about 14 miles northeast from the Natchez, by virtue of a British patent to sd Edmund R. Wegg. Richard Claiborne for the heirs.

No. 2031. Claimant: Edmund Rush Wegg, 30 Nov. 1804. Rejected 15 June 1807. Miss. Ter. Heirs of Edmund Rush Wegg claim 1000 acres on the south Fork of Bayou Pierre by virtue of a British patent to sd Edmund. Richard Claiborne for the heirs. West Florida. Pursuant to a warrant from His Excellency, Captain, General, Governor and Chief in and over His Majesty's Province of West Florida to me directed, dated 31 July 1778, I have caused to be surveyed and laid out unto Edmund Rush Wegg 1000 acres on the South Fork of Bayou Pierre bounded on the northwest by lands surveyed for John Christie, southwest by Bayou Pierre and on the other two sides by vacant lands, about 34 miles distant from the Natchez, 15 Aug. 1778. Signed Elias Durnford, Surveyor General.

No. 2032. Claimant: William Jud, 30 Nov. 1804. Rejected 15 June 1807. Miss. Ter. William Jud claims 1000 acres southerly about 30 miles from Fort Natchez on the south side of Buffalo Cr. by virtue of a British patent to sd William Jud. Richard Claiborne for William Jud. Warrant of survey, 25 May 1775. Certificate of survey, 27 May 1775, by William Wilton, Dep. Surveyor General.

No. 2033. Claimant: Lorenzo Dow, 30 Nov. 1804. Reported 15 June 1807. Lorenzo Dow claims 100 acres on west side of Briar Creek, abt. 70 miles from Pensacola*, by virtue of a British patent to Joseph Jackson, 21 July 1778, and by sd Jackson assigned to Lorenzo Dow, 10 Dec. 1803.

No. 2034. Claimant: Lorenzo Dow, 30 Nov. 1804. Reported 15 June 1807. Lorenzo Dow claims 500 acres on east side of Briar Creek, 70 miles from Pensacola*, by virtue of a British patent to Joseph Jackson, 21 July 1778, and by sd Jackson assigned to Lorenzo Dow, 10 Dec. 1803.

No. 2058. Claimant: James E. Matthews, in right of his wife, Elizabeth, for 10 arpents. The title papers filed 27 March 1804. The patent filed in Gibson's claim No. 205. Notice dispensed with by the Board, 19 Aug. 1805. Thomas H. Williams, Register. Certificate A-504 issued 19 Aug. 1805.

No. 2059. Claimant: James E. Matthews, 27 acres. The title papers were with the Register in Claim No. 205, 31 Mar. 1804. Notice dispensed with by the Board, 19 Aug. 1805. Thomas H. Williams, Register. Certificate A-505 issued 19 Aug. 1805.

No. 2060. Claimant: Nathan Swayze, one of the heirs of S. Swayze, 660 acres, part of the Ogden Mandamus. See No. 729. Certificate A 657 issued 12 Oct. 1805.

No. 2061. Claimant: Samuel Swayze, one of the heirs of S. Swayze, 786 acres, part of Ogden's Mandamus. See No. 729. Certificate A 658 issued 12 Oct. 1805.

No. 2062. Claimant: Elijah Swayze, one of the heirs of S. Swayze, 660 acres, part of Ogden's Mandamus. See No. 729. Cert. A-659, 12 Oct. 1805.

No. 2063. Claimants: The legal representatives of Obadiah Brown, in right of his wife, Penelope, one of the heirs of Samuel Swayze, 1276 acres, part of the Ogden Mandamus. See No. 729. Certificate A-660, issued 12 Oct. 1805.

No. 2064. Claimant: Hannah Curtis, one of the heirs of Samuel Swayze, 1026 acres, part of Ogden's Mandamus. See No. 729. Certificate A-661 issued 12 Oct. 1805.

No. 2065. Claimant: Rhoda Lambert, one of the heirs of Samuel Swayze, 1026 acres, part of Ogden's Mandamus. See No. 729. Certificate A-662, issued 12 Oct. 1805.

* Not West of the Pearl River.

No. 2066. Claimants: the legal representatives of Stephen Swayze, one of the heirs of Samuel Swayze, 1026 acres, part of the Ogden Mandamus. See No. 729. Certificate A-663 issued 12 Oct. 1805.

No. 2067. Claimants: the legal representatives of Samuel Swayze, decd., 464 acres, part of Ogden's Mandamus. See No. 729. Certificate A-664 issued 12 Oct. 1805.

No. 2068. Claimant: Gabriel Swayze, one of the heirs of Richard Swayze, 3057 acres, part of Ogden's Mandamus. See No. 729. Certificate A-665 issued 12 Oct. 1805.

No. 2069. Claimant: Richard Swayze, one of the heirs of Richard Swayze, decd., 1528 acres, part of the Ogden Mandamus. See No. 729. Certificate A-666 issued 12 Oct. 1805.

No. 2070. Claimant: Caleb King, in right of his wife, Mary, one of the heirs of Richard Swayze, 828 acres, part of the Ogden Mandamus. See No. 729. Certificate A-667 issued 12 Oct. 1805.

No. 2071. Claimant: Sarah Swayze, wife of Richard Swayze, decd., 1028 acres, part of the Ogden Mandamus. See No. 729. Certificate A-668 issued 12 Oct. 1805.

No. 2072. Claimant: Job Cory in right of his wife, Lydia, one of the heirs of Richard Swayze, 728 acres, part of the Ogden Mandamus. See No. 729. Certificate A-669, issued 12 Oct. 1805.

No. 2073. Claimants: Richard King and other children of Sarah King, one of the legal representatives of Richard Swayze, 728 acres, part of Ogden's Mandamus. See No. 729. Certificate A-689 issued 6 Jan. 1806.

No. 2074. Connected with No. 1009. Claimants: James Sterrett and Nathaniel Evans, 100 arpents, part of a Spanish patent to David Lejeune for 400 arpents. Certificate A-750 issued 5 Mar. 1806.

No. 2075. Claimants: James Sterrett and Nathaniel Evans, 350 arpents, part of a Spanish grant to Henry Roach for 600 acres, 23 June 1788. See No. 1009. Certificate A-751 issued 5 Mar. 1806.

No. 2076. Claimant: Daniel Ogden, 250 arpents, part of a Spanish patent to Henry Roach for 600 arpents, 23 June 1788. See No. 2075 and No. 1009. Certificate A-752 issued 5 Mar. 1806.

No. 2078. Connected with No. 1943. Claimant: George Overaker, 157 arpents, part of a Spanish patent to John Lusk for 294 arpents. Certificate A 761 issued 4 Apr. 1806. In this file: Indenture, 24 Jan. 1803, Lewis Evans, of Adams Co. and Sarah, his wife, to George Overaker, of same, for $3500, in hand paid, convey one-half of 240 acres in sd county, beginning on the bayou which divides the land of Anthony Dougherty from the afsd tract, being the land conveyed to sd Lewis Evans by Daniel Clark and Jane, his wife, 25 Mar. 1800. Signed Lewis Evans, Sarah Evans. Wit: Lyman Harding, Jacob Hyland. Ack. before James Ferral, J.P. 14 Mar. 1804.

No. 2079. Connected with No. 1944. Claimant: George Overaker, 57 arpents, part of a Spanish grant to Benjamin Belk for 191 arpents, 6 May 1806. Certificate A-762 issued 4 Apr. 1806. Conveyance of Daniel Clark to Lewis Evans, dated 1800 also filed, signed by Daniel and Jane Clark, witnessed by William Kenner and John Keane, being for 240 acres conveyed to sd Clark by Ebenezer Rees, 14 Jan. 1800. Also deed from Rees to Clark for $4000. Wit: A. L. Duncan and Lyman Harding.

No. 2080. Claimant: Richard Sparks. Certificate A-786 issued 20 Aug. 1806.

No. 2081. Claimant: Richard King, 400 arpents . . . . . . J. B. LaPoint. Connected with No. 45. Certificate B-234 issued 30 Mar. 1807.

No. 2082. Claimant: William Kirkwood, 71 acres, Spanish order of survey, 20 Mar. 1794. Connected with No. 244. Certificate B-236 issued 30 Mar. 1807.

No. 2083. Claimant: Thomas Davey, 1000 acres on South Fork of Bayou Pierre. Presented: 29 Sept. 1805. A plat of 2000 acres, one-half of which is claimed by Davey by virtue of British grant to Weston Barlow and by sd Barlow conveyed to claimant, 27 Feb. 1779. William Dunbar, agent for Thomas Davey.

No. 2084. Claimant: Thomas Davey, 1000 acres on South Fork of Bayou Pierre, 29 Sept. 1805. Plat of same: Claim by virtue of a British patent in favor of Weston Barlow, by Barlow to claimant in 1779. William Dunbar, agent for Thomas Davey.

No. 2085. Claimant: Thomas Davey, 500 acres on South Fork of Bayou Pierre, 29 Feb. 1807. Plat of same: 1000 acres British grant to Weston Barlow, one-half of which conveyed by Barlow to sd Davey, 27 Feb. 1779. William Dunbar, agent for Davey.

No. 2086. Claimant: Thomas Davey, 100 acres on Homochitto River 29 Sept. 1805. Plat of 1000 acres claimed by Thomas Davey by virtue of a British patent to David Dixon, 27 Sept. 1773, and by sd Dixon to claimant, 8 Oct. 1776. William Dunbar, agent for Thomas Davey. On plat Jacob Winfree had land adjoining.

No. 2087. Claimant: William Wilton, 500 acres, 1 Nov. 1805. William Wilton claims 500 acres in Adams County, Miss. Ter. by virtue of a British grant to him, 17 Oct. 1774, on the Homochitto River.

No. 2088. Claimant: William Wilton, 1 Nov. 1805. William Wilton claims 400 acres on south side of Fairchild's Creek, about 12 miles north of Fort Natchez, bounded on east by lands gr. to Capt. Thomas Boyd, north by Thomas, Theophilus and Luke Collins, Jr., by a British grant to William Marshall of 1000 acres, of which the above is a part, dated 24 March 1777, and afterwards conveyed by sd Marshall to claimant, 30 and 31 Aug. 1777.

No. 2089. Claimant: William Wilton, 1 Nov. 1805. William Wilton claims 200 acres on west side of Second Cr. in Adams Co., Miss. Ter. by virtue of a British grant to James Barbut for 1000 acres, of which the above 200 acres was conveyed by Barbut to William Johnstone, 1 and 2 Oct. 1775, and by sd Johnstone and Angelica, his wife, to claimant, 3 and 4 Oct. 1775. S. Lewis, agent.

No. 2090. Claimant: William Wilton, 1 Nov. 1805. William Wilton claims 500 acres about 13 miles east of Natchez Fort, by virtue of a British grant to William Fricker, 8 Nov. 1777, and conveyed by him to the claimant, 10 and 11 May 1779. S. Lewis, agent.

No. 2091. Claimants: the legal representatives of William Clark, 400 acres, 25 Nov. 1805. The legal representatives of William Clark, decd., the sd William Collins, being a resident in the territory 27 Oct. 1795, claims 400 acres on Briar Cr. in Washington County*, patented by the British Government to Daniel Ryan, 23 Apr. 1779, and by him conveyed to afsd. William Clark. Signed William Collins, attorney.

No. 2092. Claimants: the legal representatives of William Clark, 25 Nov. 1805. The legal representatives of William Clark, decd. claim 576 acres on the Alabama, in Washington County*, patented by the British Government to sd Clark, 22 Oct. 1779.

No. 2093. Claimants: the legal representatives of William Clark, 25 Nov. 1805. William Clark claims 500 acres on the Pascogoula* granted, 29 Dec. 1778, to James Peterson and by him conveyed to afsd. Clark.

No. 2094. Claimant: A. F. Haldeman, 17 May 1805. To the Board of Commissioners West of the Pearl River: Notice hereby given that Anthony Francis Haldeman claims 500 acres in Adams County, by virtue of a British patent to Frederick Haldemand for said 500 acres. Order of survey, 21 July 1772. Signed by Evans Jones, attorney for Anthony Francis Haldemand. Certificate of survey shows the land near the Natchez Fort bounded on west by lands of Henry Fairchild, on north by Edward Mease.

No. 2095. Claimant: A. F. Haldemand, 17 May 1805. Notice of claim.

No. 2096. Claimant: A. F. Haldemand, 17 May 1805. Notice of claim. Land also west of Henry Fairchild's tract.

No. 2097. Claimant: John Peck, 18 Nov. 1805. Claim for 6500 acres. [Nothing more.]

No. 2098. Claimants: the legal representatives of the Earl of Eglinton, 20,000 acres, 19 Nov. 1805. Certificate by James Madison, Secretary of State of the United States, showing an extract from the statement of lands granted in West Florida, same having been received from the British Government among the records of that Province and now remaining in the Office of this Department: "Granted, 1 Jan. 1760, to the Earl of Eglinton, 20,000 acres, north of Fort Panmure at the Natchez on the River Mississippi, at the distance of one league, bounded on west by the Miss. River, and other three sides by vacant lands."

* Not West of the Pearl River.

NOTES

ALSTON. In his account of the heart-breaking voyage with his family from New England, Captain Mathew Phelps tells of having to take his wife ashore after passing the Natchez landing on their way to Bayou Pierre, because of her illness, and that she died at the house of Philip Alston near Petit Gulf, 14 Oct. 1776. (Cl 110) This place, 200 acres, below Petit Gulf, Philip Alston had bought from Philip Barbour on Oct. 19, 1776. (Nat. Rec.) On 6 Nov. of that year, both Philip Alston and his brother, John, with a long list of others, petitioned the West Florida Council for lands, Philip asking for 1100 acres and John for 850 acres. Both received warrants as requested but no locations were designated. (E (24) W Fla) However, a British grant was issued to John Alston for 450 acres southeast of Natchez, 16 June 1777, which was surveyed in January of that year, and may have been part of the above warrant. (MPA-ED 218) Philip Alston is said to have moved from Wake Co., N.C. to the Natchez District about 1772. (Finley 20) On July 10, 1771, there was filed for record in the Court of Anson Co., N.C. the transfer by Philip Alston and Mildred, his wife, of their interest in lands in that county inherited from her father, John McCoy. (McB 60,69.) The records do not show that Philip Alston ever lived in Anson County, but it is not improbable that he came to the Natchez District with Anthony Hutchins from that section. John and Philip Alston were among the Loyalists who participated in the Natchez insurrection early in 1781. Goodspeed also included another brother, George Alston, a confirmation of which may be in the following excerpt from the Miss. Prov. Arch., Spanish Dominion, "Blommart and Farmer stayed at the house of John Alston, John Alston and his brothers being accomplices" (in the insurrection). After the rebellion, George Alston, with others was sent in irons to New Orleans, John Alston took refuge in the Chittimache Nation of Indians in southern Louisiana where he was later captured, and Philip Alston escaped to the Cumberland settlement around Nashville. (Gd I 71,75) Philip Aston's family soon joined him, as shown by the records of the Mero District, Mildred Alston, Frankey and James Drumgoole being witnesses in a case against Joshua Howard, also from the Natchez District, 3 Oct. 1786, and John McCoy Alston receiving land grants in that section. (Min. BkA 131,165; Land Rec. 106, Davidson Co. Mero Dist.) Philip Alston and his family lived in Tennessee and the adjoining Kentucky counties for nearly twenty years, returning to the Natchez District about 1799 or 1800. He was living in 1804. He had three sons, John McCoy, Philip and Peter, and two daughters, Frankey who married James Drumgoole, and Elizabeth who married (1) John Gilbert (see) and (2) Edmund Duggan, of Claiborne Co., Miss. (Finley 24-5; Nat. Rec.)

ASHLEY. Robert Ashley, from South Carolina to the Natchez District, in a suit over a runaway slave before Judge Peter Bryan Bruin of Bayou Pierre District, 24 Jany. 1795, stated that General Elijah Clark, of Georgia, was his uncle by marriage. (Cl. 152) General Elijah Clark's wife was Hannah Harrington, of Halifax Co., North Carolina. (Hays 14,226)

BAIRD. Margaret Baird, (see Stampley)

BINGAMAN. John Bingeman and his family were early settlers in the Shenandoah Valley on North River, (the north fork of the Shenandoah River), in what was then almost limitless Augusta County, Virginia. On 3 July 1755, their home near the "Fairfax Line", which now separates Shenandoah and Rockingham Counties, was raided by Indians. John Bingeman and his wife were killed, as was Adam Bingaman who was probably their son. (Chalk. II 507-510, Preston Papers, Wis. Hist. Soc.) At this same period, a little farther up the river, the house of another member of this family was attacked, near the site of New Market, Shenandoah Co., Va., Bingeman, the father of the family, defending his household and killing two of the Indians. However, his wife, a son and a daughter were wounded and his nephew, Lewis Bingeman, was carried off a captive and spent the rest of his life with the Indians. (Chalk. II 510, Shen. Way 68) This last undoubtedly was Christian Bingaman and the skirmish with the Indians may have grown, as Dr. Sydnor declares, with frequent recountings by the time the Bingamans had reached the Natchez District, but the two accounts above verify the episode and its main features. (Sydnor 45) In Augusta County Court, 19 May 1756, John Bingeman was appointed the admr. of the estate of his father, John Bingeman, with Jacob Nicholas and Henry Seller as bondsmen. On 16 February 1763, John Bingeman presented to the court an account of the settlement of his father's estate, having made payments to Mathias Carsh (Kersh), Wm. Leppard, Nicholas Keys, Conrad Bloss, and Henry and Christian Bingaman.

All of these may have been heirs. On August 19, 1756, Christian, John and Henry Bingaman had been added to the tithables. By March 28, 1770, Christian Bingaman may have been on the long journey to the banks of the Mississippi in West Florida for as defendant in a suit by John Anderson, he is reported as being "no inhabitant" of Augusta County. (Chalk. I 74,160; III 42,76.) Christian Bingaman petitions and receives a warrant for 600 acres in the Natchez District, 6 Nov. 1776, and on Oct. 11, 1777 he pays the fees for his grant. (E (24) W. Fla.) This land was on the south fork of Boyd's Cr., 14 miles east of Natchez. (MPA-ED 245)

BRADLEY. At a meeting of the Council of West Florida, at Pensacola, 18 Dec. 1767, the petition of John Bradley was presented, asking for a grant of 1000 acres on the Mississippi where vacant. This was granted with the location unspecified. The next petition was that of David Williams for 1000 acres on the Mississippi adjoining lands of John Bradley, and was also granted. Bradley's tract was surveyed 5 Feb. 1768 as being 4½ miles south of Fort Panmure and 4 miles from the River, bounded by Daniel Clark on the west and Servil Lafleur on the east. The patent was issued 22 July 1769 and signed by Gov. Montfort Browne. (Howard 85; MPA-ED 90)

Estate of John Bradley, decd., by Nathan H. Luce, executor. Heirs: Synthia Bradley, born May 25, 1781, Amelia Bradley, born 23 Dec. 1782, Harriet Bradley, 25 Aug. 1784, Rachel Bradley born 6 July 1786, Calvin Bradley, born 17 Jany. 1789, Luther Bradley, born 20 Nov. 1890, Archibald Bradley, born 27 Jany. 1793, Bradford Bradley, born 24 Nov. 1794, Bailey Bradley, born 2 July 1797, Levinia Bradley, born 3 Feby. 1799, Warren Bradley, born 15 Sept. 1800. Receipts of all of the above heirs except Warren "who was not of age." 3 Oct. 1821. Calvin Bradley, living in New Orleans on 25 Feb. 1810, by letter requests that his part of his father's estate be paid to "Mr. Henry". Synthia Bradley married James Cole, Amelia Bradley married Wm. Henry, Harriet Bradley married (1) Jeremiah Cory, (2) Elijah Swazey (his 2nd wife), son of Samuel, the pioneer, Rachel Bradley married Nathan Luse, son of Israel Luse and his wife, Deborah, daughter of Richard Swazey, the pioneer, Calvin Bradley married June 1823 Lydia Swazey, widow of Gabriel Swazey, Sr., Archibald Bradley married Phoebe, dau. of Samuel Swazey, the pioneer. (Prob. File No. 2, Adams Co., Miss., Eaton 21,22,24, Hendrix 63,66)

Benjamin, Joseph, Harry, Catherine and Sarah Bradley, whose petition for 5000 acres on River Mississippi where vacant was presented the Council at Pensacola, 16 Aug. 1768, were no doubt the "heirs of John Bradley" who received a grant of 4,140 acres near Natchez, but these claimants were classed as non-residents, against whom the case was decided in favor of the settlers who had inhabited, cultivated and improved the land, when all such claims came up before the U.S. Congress for consideration. (ASP-PL II 893.)

A Thaddeus Bradley had a militia donation in St. Clair County, Northwest Territory, now Illinois, by an Act of 3rd March 1791. This and two other tracts were claimed by his heirs through Susannah Bradley. He may well have been the Thaddeus Bradley who came to the Natchez District with the Lymans in 1773. There was much intercourse between the people of "the Illinois" and those of "the Natchez". (Howard 92, ASP-PL II 235-7.)

BRANDON. Gerard C. Brandon II. Nelson Co., Ky. (Bardstown) Deed Bk. 13-495. Geo. W. Chambers for himself and Maria Chambers, Peggy Brandon, formerly Peggy Chambers, Stephen O. Chambers and Benj. S. Chambers, heirs of the estate of Dr. James Chambers, decd., to John Caldwell certain property. Mention of the widow. March 22, 1817. Wit: Walter Brashear, Jno. Smelley. Deed Bk. 14-291. Quit claim deed from Amelia Chambers, Maria Chambers, Gerard C. Brandon and Margaret, his wife, late Margaret Chambers, and Stephen O. Chambers, widow and heirs of the late Dr. James Chambers, to property sold by James Chambers in 1800 to John Caldwell. All signed Aug. 3, 1819 in Wilkinson Co., Miss. and acknowledged same before Judge Edward Randolph and Isaac Dillahunty, clerk.

BURNET. Daniel Burnet, son of John Burnet, m. (1) _______ and had a daughter who m. _______ Patterson; (2) Agnes (Wilson) Humphreys, widow of Col. Ralph Humphreys, between 1794 and 1800. Daniel Burnet's will: Claiborne Co., Miss. 28 Dec. 1826. My grandchildren, Daniel Burnet Patterson, Wm. Lindsay Patterson, Mary Jane Patterson and James Patterson all my estate except special bequests. To George Wilson Humphreys slaves (named) being the remainder of the increase of slaves I got with my late wife at our marriage, except Peter, whom I retain for special favors done Humphreys; my sister Jane Bonner; brother-in-law, Dr. Thomas Anderson, my portrait in the gilt frame; my nephews, Samuel and John B. Cobun and my niece Kitty Cobun. Exrs; brothers, David and John Burnet. (signed). Wit: James B. Robinson, Josiah B. Sugg, Augustus W. Robinson, John Robinson. Probated 15 May 1827.

CALVIT. (See Wells Family.)

CALVIT. Frederick Calvit was shot and scalped near Rice's Mill [Washington County, Tenn.], April 1777 but lived. (Draper MSS LXX2)

CARRADINE. Parker Carradine, [Jr.] married Lettice Thornton in Jefferson County, Tenn. Bond dated 1 Dec. 1800, with Thomas Thornton surety. Division of estate of Charles Thornton, deceased. Heirs: Thos. Thornton, Lettice Thornton and children of Charlotte Curtis, decd. June Court 1796. Fauquier Co., Va. Wills, Bk. 3-50. (Courtesy of Geo. W. Glass.)

CARRIQUE. Richard Carrique's marriage license, March 25, 1776. (E (25) W. Fla.)

CHANEY. About 1790, Bailey and William Chaney came to the Natchez District from South Carolina. Bailey Chaney, a Baptist preacher, is said to have been the first to preach a sermon in Mississippi under the American flag. A large arbor was erected soon after the Spanish evacuated the Fort on 30 March 1798 and Bailey Chaney preached there to a great gathering. He died in 1816. (Miss. Bpts. 12,131)

CHOAT. Petition of John Choat for 100 acres on Second Creek, presented by Thomas Hutchins. Warrant for same, Jany. 3, 1776. (E (25) W. Fla.) Certif. of survey by Luke Collins, 26 June 1776 by order of Elias Durnford, Surv. Genl. of W. Fla. (AST-PL I 622)

CLARK. Gibson Clark, Sr. STATE OF GEORGIA, WILKES COUNTY. This is to certify that Gibson Clark, Citizen, hath steadfastly done his Duty from the Time of Passing an Act at Augusta to-wit on 10th of August 1781 until the Total exption [expulsion] of the British from this State and the said Gibson Clark cannot be to our knowledge and belief convicted for Plundering or Distressing said County and is therefore under said Act Intitled to a Bounty of Two Hundred and fifty acres of land. Given under my hand this 8th March 1784.
Pr order Thos. McCall. E. Clarke Col.
On Reverse of the order. 179 Gibson Clark
Gibson Clarke Pet. dismissed he being on the Mississipi (sic).

Gibson Clark received a Bounty Grant of 287½ acres in Washington Co., Ga. Book "GGG", Register of Grants, 1785. (Originals of both documents in Ga. State Archives. Courtesy of Mr. Milton Harper.)

Gibson Clark, born in 1760, seems to have been a brother of Gen'l. Elijah Clark although the General was 27 years older. (Nat. Rec.) Gibson Clark married Susannah Phillips in Georgia. They came to the Natchez District about 1783. He died in Claiborne Co., Miss. in January 1822, naming in his will his wife, Susannah, daughters, Nancy Clark Headrick [Hedrick], wife of John A. Hedrick, Mary Clark Stiller (or Stillee), deceased; sons, John Clark, deceased, Elijah L. Clark, Gibson Clark William Clark, grandchildren Susannah Piety Rosannah Gibson Clark, daughter of Gibson Clark, Gibson Clark, Elijah Clark, Gibson Clark Hedrick, Elizabeth Susannah Piety Stiller, Sarah Stiller, daughters of Mary Clark Stiller, deceased; Elizabeth Minor Clark, Susannah Gibson Clark, daughters of John Clark, deceased. Executors: Sons, Gibson Clark, Elijah L. Clark and John Headrick. Gibson (x) Clark. Wit: Julius Bettys, Reuben Spear, James Perry, Daniel Burnett.

CLOUD. One of the protestant ministers in the Natchez District during the Spanish rule was Rev. Adam Cloud, an Episcopalian who apparently preached rather openly. Gov. Gayoso, after attending a service by Cloud, remarked that personally he was in favor of religious tolerance but that he had "a master". The next day Cloud was notified not to preach again. But he continued to do so and was soon arrested and sent out of the country. He lived in Georgia many years before returning to the District to spend the remainder of his days. Records at Christ Church show his long service at Spring Hill in Jefferson County. (Cl. 528)

COMSTOCK. Thomas Comstock came to the Natchez District with the Lymans in 1773. The Comstock family had been in Connecticut more than one hundred years. (Cl. 108; Savage I 439)

COYLE. Hugh Coyle. (See Richard Thompson.)

CRANE. Capt. Silas Crane, from New England, with the Lymans in 1773. (Cl. 108)

CURTIS. When Richard Curtis, Sr., came from South Carolina to the Natchez District early in 1780, with him was a large contingent of relatives. Besides his own immediate family were the families of his step-son, John Jones, his sons, William, Benjamin and Richard, Jr., and his sons-in-law, John Courtney and John Stampley. They were all Baptists, Richard Jr., born in 1755, being a licensed preacher, the first Baptist preacher to live in Mississippi. Richard Curtis, Sr. had married a young Widow Jones in Dinwiddie County, Va., about 1748. In 1775 they were living on the Great Peedee in

South Carolina, whence they made the perilous journey, by water, to "New Spain", landing near the mouth of Cole's Creek, in which neighborhood they took up residence. Soon they were holding religious meetings in the private dwellings, public Protestant services being unlawful in that Catholic country. Neighbours soon joined and among the converts were Stephen de Alva, a Spaniard, and William Hamberlin who became ardent co-workers with Richard Curtis. This conversion of a Spaniard followed by Curtis performing the marriage ceremony uniting David Greenleaf and a daughter of John Jones, a rite heretofore performed only by a priest, led to the expulsion of the three men from the country. Threatened with being arrested and sent to work in the silver mines in Mexico, they made their escape in August 1795, going to South Carolina. There they lived until the evacuation of the territory by the Spaniards in March 1798. On learning this good news the three men immediately return to join their families after a separation of nearly three years. (Miss. Bpts. 7,8,9,176-182)

DEVALL. Richard Devall came to British West Florida about 1776 with a party of young men from Liverpool. He settled in the Natchez Country, acquiring much land between Little Gulf and the mouth of Cole's Creek. He was twice married. His first wife, Elizabeth, was living 26 Oct. 1786. By her he had two sons. Before 1800, he married Edith, daughter of Elnathan Smith (q.v.) and widow of John Buhler, of Baton Rouge. Moving to Baton Rouge, he became a large landholder there, the central part of the city being, at one time, called "Devall Town". He died in 1823. His widow died Feb. 26, 1826. By this 2nd marriage there were 6 sons and 2 daughters. (Natchez Rec.; La. 29-289)

DICKSON. Gen. David Dickson, from Georgia. (Cl. 357)

DINSMORE. Silas Dinsmore, a surveyor and U. S. Agent to Choctaw Indians, was from New Hampshire. His homely humor made him many friends. (Sydnor 54-55,125)

DIXON. Roger Dixon, son of Roger and Lucy (Rootes) Dixon, b. 1763 in Fredericksburg, Va., d. 2 July 1833 in Fayette [Jefferson] Co., Miss; came to the Natchez District in the 1790's; m. Mildred _______, who d. in Fayette [Jefferson] Co., Miss. 30 Dec. 1849. Nine ch: Thos. (1795-1855), Philip, William, Robert, Lucy, Eliza, Priscilla, Mary and Nancy. (Va. 19-286)

GIBSON. Gideon Gibson, born in England, came to America with his mother, his step-father, Geo. Saunders, and his four brothers, Jordan, David, Stephen and Roger. He married in Virginia; came down to the Natchez District, [apparently during the Spanish regime,] and lived on St. Catherine's Creek. They had six daughters and three sons: Sarah, 2nd wife of John Foster, and m. (2) _______ Ferguson, Elizabeth m. Daniel Whitaker, Edna m. John Bullen, Mary m. Joseph Harrison, Rachel m. John Foster, his 1st wife, Cynthia m. G. Holstein, David, b. 1761, m. (1) Frances McKinley, (2) Mary (Smith) Mundell, [(3) Sarah _______ (1783-1861)], Randal, b. 1766, m. Harriet McKinley, Reuben m. Mildred Dolan. (This material compiled by the dau. of Tobias Gibson, son of Randal Gibson, furnished by Mrs. Hugh Rush, who had it from Mrs. Mary F. H. Rodes, of Lexington, Ky., also a desc. of Randal Gibson.) Tobias Gibson, the Methodist minister, died unmarried in Claiborne Co., Miss. in 1804. He was the son of Jordan and Mary (Middleton) Gibson, of Darlington Dist., S. C. Jordan was the brother of Gideon Gibson, above. His children were Tobias, Nathaniel, Stephen, John, Malachi and one daughter, Rhoda, all of whom came to the Mississippi Territory.

GILBERT. John Gilbert married Elizabeth, daughter of Philip and Mildred (McCoy) Alston. (See ALSTON) State of Tennessee, Mero District. (Nashville) Court of Equity. May Term 1809. John Howard, admr. vs. Alexander M. Gilbert and John Gilbert, heirs of William Gilbert, decd. John Gilbert was dead at the time of the filing of said bill and Milly Gilbert, Sally Gilbert, Frankey Gilbert, Philip Gilbert, William Gilbert and John Gilbert, his heirs-at-law, are ordered to be added as party defendants. William Gilbert owed Henry Giles (in N. C.). Gilbert died and James Holland was appointed admr. Giles sued him in Morganton, Morgan Dist., N. C. Judgment for 300 pounds, 1 Mch. 1801. Holland had only 184 pounds which he paid. Giles recovered from Alexander M. and John Gilbert, as heirs of William, their ancestor, 12 Sept. 1805, a writ of execution to Rutherford County where the lands they inherited were located and no lands were found there. Alexander M. Gilbert resides in the Miss. Territory where the said John Gilbert resided but they own 5000 acres in Mero Dist., Maury County, which descended to them from their ancestor, William Gilbert.

GIRAULT. Jean Girault was born in London Feb. 1755, of Huguenot parents; came to America with his brother. They contracted smallpox on boat coming over from which the brother died. Jean Girault went to the Illinois and two days after Gen. George Rogers Clark captured the island of Kaskaskia he offered his services and was accepted as interpreter. That was July 4, 1778. Jean Girault had a classic education. He served five years, part of the time as State's Attorney in Illinois under Todd. He also served in the militia and was honorably discharged in 1783. Then he moved to New Orleans where he studied Spanish and from there went to the Natchez District in 1786 or later. (Ill Hist. Soc. 8-636-657) Col. John Girault died 28 May 1813, leaving two sons, Francis S. and James A. He was Keeper of Records during the Spanish regime. (Row. Enc. I 790)

GRAY. May 19, 1781. Examination of Mayo Gray, an inhabitant of Galveztown. In March, convalescing from a long illness and gaining strength slowly he had come, with his wife and son, to Natchez in search of health, staying with his brother-in-law, Jacob Winfree. Don Francisco Collell, Commandant of Galvestown, had given a passport. His brother-in-law had taken part in the insurrection and under pretext of going to look for some horses, he, Jacob Winfree, had left home. (MPA-SD III 426) Gray a native of Va. (MPA-SD I 817) A survey of 1000 acres for Joseph Blackwell, 16 Oct. 1775, on east side of Amit River, 3 mi. from river on a "creek called Mayo Gray's Creek", shows an earlier settlement by Gray. Jacob Winfree's first grant was dated 7 July 1773. (MPA-ED 119,167) Marriage bonds in Goochland Co., Va. July 3, 1743, Edmund Gray to Mary Mayo, Geo. Dabbs bondsman, H. Wood wit. Consent from William Mayo. (W (1) 7 99). Philip Poindexter gr 400 acres in Goochland Co. adj. lands of Jacob Winfrey, March 5, 1747. (Va. 19 326).

GREENLEAF. David Greenleaf was born March 9, 1763, in Worcester, Mass. (Cl. 143)

GRUBB. Nicholas and Benjamin Grubb were witnesses to the codocil to the will of Col. Ralph Humphreys on March 29th, 1790, at his home at Grindstone Ford on Bayou Pierre. They were step-brothers or half-brothers of Col. Ralph Humphreys, their father, Benjamin Grubb having, in Frederick Co., Va., between 1751 and 1756, married Hannah Humphreys, admx of Ralph Humphreys, decd. who was father of Col. Humphreys. (Order Bks. 3 453 and 7 112, Fred. Co. Va.) Both Ralph Humphreys (II) and Benjamin Grubb moved to South Carolina before the Revolution. Benjamin Grubb died there, in Craven County, Camden Dist. before 2 Feb. 1776 when Nicholas, his eldest son and heir-at-law, appoints Bryan Bruin, of Frederick Co., Va., his attorney to collect what is due him in Virginia and elsewhere, and to dispose of his property for him. Ralph Humphreys was one of the witnesses to this instrument and, at the same time, sold two tracts of land in Hampshire Co., Va. to Bryan Bruin, of Frederick Co. (Fred. Co., Va. Deed Bk. 17 72,73) On Feb. 23, 1790, Benjamin Grubb, with his wife, a daughter, six negroes and one negress, arrived in the Natchez District overland from South Carolina. (Kin. II 300). Nicholas Grubb settled west of the Mississippi in the Rapides country on Red River, receiving a certificate of survey by Wm. Cook, a surveyor under the Spanish Govt., dated 7 Nov. 1791. (ASP-PL III 160). However, Benjamin Grubb worked the Humphreys plantation on Bayou Pierre for two years after the death of Col. Humphreys, (ASP-PL I 620) but was established in Rapides in 1794, petitioning to be allowed to take up lands on Catahoula Lake which had been denied the settlers and in 1795 is listed as having "persisted in settling over the Catahoula". (Kin. III 333) Nicholas also moved to Catahoula. He died before 1811 when his claims for land were issued to his widow and heirs. (ASP-PL II 829) The paternal ancestor of Nicholas and Benjamin Grubb was Emanuel Grubb, who as of Brandywine Hundred, New Castle, Delaware, on 11 Feb. 1746, deeded land in Frederick Co., Va. to Benjamin Grubb. (Fred. Co. Va. Deed Bk. 1 389) His will, New Castle Co., Province of Delaware, May 5, 1764; Aug. 19, 1767, named his wife, Anne; heirs of son Joseph, decd.; son Thomas; heirs of son Nicholas; heirs of son John; son Benjamin; heirs of son Peter; dau. Edith Thacker, dau. Ann Black, son Emanuel, who was named executor. (Del. Wills. New Castle County. 65.)

HICKEY. Daniel Hickey petitioned the British Govt. of West Florida, on Feb. 3rd, 1768, for 500 acres near Natchez, which was granted him, as was a grant of 50 acres on Dec. 18, 1767. (How 84,87) The next record of him is an entry on Apr. 3rd, 1776, in the Secy's Book, of the fees for his marriage license and bond. These were for 2 pounds 5 sh. for the Secy. and 4 pounds for the Gov. (E (25) W. Fla) Daniel Hickey is said, by Arthur, to have been born in Ennis, County of Clare, Ireland and to have married Martha Scrivner, of Worcestershire, England, also to have been one of the six young men who came together to America from Liverpool, settling in West Fla. about 1775. If this be true, he returned to the British Isles after receiving the above grants. The tract on Second Cr. he sold William G. Forman and was Alcalde of the district of Baton Rouge in 1797. His only child, born 17 June 1778, married Ann, a dau. of James Mather, one of the men who came with Daniel Hickey, Isaac Johnson and three other companions. (Arthur 33; Nat. Rec.)

HOLSTEIN. Stephen Holstein (Holston) petitioned the British Govt. of West Florida for 700 acres on 6 Nov. 1776 and received a warrant for same. (E (24) W. Fla.) Holstein and his family had come to the Natchez Country from Ninety-Six Dist. of S. C. His son, John Holstein, and Absolem Hooper testified in Davidson Co., Mero Dist. N. C. (now Tennessee) in December 1783 that Daniel Oglesby, son of

Elisha Oglesby, decd., of Ninety-Six Dist., S. C. had been brought up from childhood by Capt. Stephen Holstein after the death of Oglesby's parents and he was taken by Capt. Holstein with his family to Natchez on the Mississippi. This testimony had been given to prove Oglesby's right to the property of his father in S. C. (Dav. Co. Will Bk. 1 3-5) It also upholds the supposition that this Stephen of the Natchez Dist. was the son of the Stephen Holstein for whom the Holstein River was named. In a spirit of adventure, he, too, after exploring the river on which he had built his cabin and which thereafter bore his name, with a few companions went down the Tennessee, Ohio and Mississippi Rivers as far as Natchez. On their return, a rumor of a planned Indian raid led Holstein to move to upper South Carolina. But he did not escape the Indians. In 1753, while he was in Charleston on business, his wife, who was Lucy Jane Looney, with their young infant in her arms, jumped out of a window and escaped through the woods to a neighbor's house, 3 miles away. (E.T. 8 28-9) Most of the descendants of Stephen Holstein of the Natchez District moved to the Rapides country in Louisiana, settling on the Red River and Chatahoula Lake. (ASP-PL II passim)

HOLT. For Holt see TRULY.

HOWARD. Joshua Howard, also, was among those who petitioned the British Govt. of West Florida for land on 6 Nov. 1776. He was given a warrant for 200 acres on Second Creek in the Natchez District and the receipt for surveying fees was dated Jany. 22, 1777. But after the Spaniards took possession of that territory, Howard left the District. (ASP-PL I 260) 24 Oct. 1781, the appraisers of the estate of John Holloway, decd., listed the plantation he lived on as belonging to Joshua Howard who was absent from the country. Joshua Howard went from the Natchez District to the Cumberland settlement in what is now Middle Tennessee, returning to Natchez in 1789 (Min. Dav. Co. Ct. 1783-1791) A certificate as to the above from Anthony Hutchins reads "I hereby certify that Mr. Joshua Howard some time after his marriage left this country and did return hither in the year 1789 where he has lived ever since and hath supported the character of an honest peasable man and a good neighbor A Hutchins Natchez, 15 Sept. 1797." (Gov. Winthrop Sargent Papers.)

HUNTER. Norsworthy Hunter was born in Fairfax Co., Va., moved in his youth to Kentucky, coming to Miss., not in 1801, as Claiborne says, but when it was still Spanish territory. He was captain of the militia of the District of Natchez in May 1794, owning land there before that date. In 1795 he received a grant of 1000 acres and his kinsman, Henry Hunter, was granted 2000 acres by the Spanish in 1793. (Cl. 229; ASP-PL I 867,873; Nat. Rec.)

HUTCHINS. Anthony Hutchins came to the Natchez District, West Fla. from Anson County, N. C. where he is of record as early as April 1750. His intention of leaving the province is recorded 12 July 1771 and Ann, his wife, relinquishes dower to land there Oct. 11, 1771. As "of the Province of West Florida" he gives power of attorney to Samuel Spencer, 18 Oct. 1772 to attend to his affairs in the Carolinas. (McB 118,70,72,53)

ILER (Isler, Ailer, Oiler, Hailer). Augusta Co., Va. Court Judgments. Apr. 1799. Halker vs Parsons. Bill filed 12 May 1798. Marcus Isler (Ailer) sold Adam Halker land in Dunmore County in 1773. Marcus left this country and died, leaving Adolphus (Jonas) Isler, his own son, who is living in New Spain. Isaac Ruddle answers in Bourbon County, Ky. 21 June 1800. He sold the land to Iler in 1768. (Chalk. II 67) Dunmore Co., Va. Court Minutes, Aug. 27, 1776. Land transfers: Mark Iler and wife to Henry Fravell. (Shen. Way. 114) (Note: Shenandoah County was first named Dunmore County. The name was changed in 1778.)

JOHNSON. Isaac Johnson, with five other young men, left his home in England to settle in West Florida about 1775, he having been sent to America by a mercantile firm. The other five adventurers were Richard Duvall, another Englishman; James Mather, a merchant from England; an Irishman named Rickey; and two Scots, named Nicholson and Dunbar. Isaac Johnson was the son of Rev. John Johnson, an Episcopal minister and writer, of Liverpool, and his mother was Margaret Hunter. ("Spanish Records", Baton Rouge, East Baton Rouge Parish, La. "These notes were adapted from 'Old Louisiana Families' by Arthur and deVernion".) Soon after his arival in the Natchez District, Isaac Johnson married Mary Routh, daughter of Jeremiah Routh and wife Margaret, who with their large family had settled on Cole's Creek. (Nat. Rec.) On 11 Aug. 1777 Isaac Johnson received a British grant for 1000 acres about 8 miles southeast of the old Natchez Fort, on a fork of Second Cr. (MPA-ED 228) However, he bought land also on Cole's Creek and below Petit Gulf near the Rouths. He was well-educated and energetic and after the Spanish took the territory from the British he was one of the first inhabitants to be made an alcalde of the district in which he lived. He held that office until, persuaded by his son-in-law, John Mills, he moved to the Feliciana section, (now Louisiana). There he bought a large plantation near St. Francisville, which town John Mills founded, and called his place Troy Plantation. He died June 22, 1805. Isaac and Mary (Routh) Johnson had twelve children, ten of whom lived to maturity: John Hunter Johnson m. Thenia Munson; Ann Waugh Johnson m. (1) John H. Mills, (2) Moses Sample; Isaac Johnson m. Melissa _______; Mary Johnson m. Aaron Gorham from Conn.; Charles Grandpre Johnson m. Ann Dawson; Caroline Matilda Johnson m. Benjamin Collins; Joseph Eugenius Johnson m. Martha Lane; William Gayoso Johnson m. Eliza Collins Johnson (no kin); Elizabeth Johnson m. Dr. Thos. Withers Chinn; Martha Johnson m. Dr. Nathaniel Wells Pope. (Reminiscences of the Routh and Johnson Families, by Mrs. Pope, the youngest dau. of Isaac Johnson and his wife, Mary Routh. (MS) Courtesy of Mr. J. H. Percy, of Baton Rouge, La.)

KILLION. Washington Co., N. C. (now Tenn.) Court Minutes, May 26, 1779. Ordered that a dedimus issue to take deposition of George Killion in the County of Burke on behalf of John Nave, plaintiff in suit with James Greenlee, defendant. George Killion, Sen. and Joseph Killion bought tracts of land in St. Helena Parish, La. in 1803-4, and in 1806 George Killion received a grant in the same parish for 2000 acres and Joseph a grant for 1000 acres. George Killion, Jr. settled in Feliciana Parish, La. (ASP-PL III 66,446,448)

McBEE. Silas E. McBee, in the Natchez District for a short time only, went on to the Baton Rouge section where he settled permanently. (ASP-PL III 387,499; East Baton Rouge Par. records.) Note: He was not the Silas McBee, a first settler of Lowndes Co. Miss., who was quoted by Draper in his "Men of King's Mountain", although they may have stemmed from the same ancestor.

MINOR. Since much has been written of Stephen Minor, the "Don Estevan Minor" of the Natchez District, these notes will be concerning his brothers and sister who also came to that section. Stephen Minor was the eldest son of William Minor, of Greene Co., Pa.; William Minor, his father was son of Stephen Minor, born at Lyme, Conn. Apr. 9, 1706; Stephen, his grandfather, was the son of William Minor, born Nov. 6, 1670; this William, his gr-grandfather, was the son of Clement Minor, born 1638. William Minor, father of Stephen, the last Governor under the Spanish rule in the District of Natchez, had nine children, eight sons and one daughter, namely: Stephen, born Feb. 8, 1760; William, born Jany. 27, 1766; John, born Feb. 26, 1768; Theophilus, born May 26, 1770; Philip, born June 26, 1771; Frances, born Feb. 26, 1774; Joseph, born Dec. 10, 1775; Samuel, born June 26, 1777; Noah, born Nov. 12. 1779. Of these, William, the second son, died before April 28, 1803, the date of his father's will. He married Elinor Phillips, who married (2) Theophilus Minor, his brother. (The above by courtesy of Mr. Frank M. Brand, Morgantown, W. Va.) William Minor named all of his children in his will which was probated 24 Oct. 1804, except William who was dead, and to whom he had evidently given his share of his estate. To Stephen, John, Philip, Fanny, Samuel and Noah, to whom he had apparently also given property, he bequeathed each five pounds and an equal share in the one-third of his real estate which he had bequeathed to his wife, Hannah, for life or widowhood. It is not known whether Hannah was the mother of the above children. (Will Bk. 1, page 45, Greene Co. Pa.) Noah and Samuel Minor remained in Pa. where they now have many descendants. (Mr. Brand) John Minor joined his brother Stephen in Natchez before 1790 when he is recorded as having land adjoining a survey on Bayou Pierre, the patent for which he received in 1792. (ASP-PL I 868; Nat. Rec.) In 1811, John and Joseph Minor had land grants in Concordia Parish, La., which is across the Mississippi River from Natchez. John's land was on the river and Joseph's was on Concordia Lake. (ASP-PL II 812) However, John appears often in the Natchez records and, after the death of his brother Stephen, late in 1815, he seems to have been the head of Stephen's family and living with them. In July 1816, Joseph Minor wrote his brother John that he was leaving for Oak Hill, Illinois, apparently to settle there (Letters. Minor Coll.) John Minor bought land in Ascension Parish, La., on the Miss. River, near two tracts purchased, jointly, by William Kenner and Philip Minor. This was prior to 1823 when the claims were presented Congress for confirmation. (ASP-PL III 520) John Minor may have died in this section. There is no record of his having married. William Kenner was the son-in-law of Stephen Minor, having married his daughter, Mary, whose mother was Martha Ellis. (Nat. Rec.) Mary (Minor) Kenner died before Dec. 8, 1814. (Letter from Gen. J. A. Wilkinson to Major Stephen Minor. Minor Coll.) Theophilus Minor, who died Dec. 13, 1817, and is buried in the cemetery at "Linwood", the Minor plantation in Ascension Parish, (Marchand 46) was evidently one of the seven brothers of Major Stephen. He may have been owner of that large plantation at that time but the palatial mansion built there, now in ruins, was of a later period. His brother, Philip Minor, is said to have built the house, as he owned the place when he made his will July 11, 1836, naming Theophilus P. Minor his executor. (Marchand 126) This Theophilus Phillips Minor, nephew of Philip and Theophilus Minor, of Ascension Parish, and step-son of the latter, married in Nashville, Tenn. Myra Eakin. (Mr. Brand.)

Their eldest daughter, Ellen Frances Minor, b. June 7, 1826, d. Nov. 21, 1846, was also buried at Linwood, as were other members of the family. (Marchand 126,149) Frances (Fanny), the only daughter of William Minor, married Andrew Mundell in Greene Co., Pa. and their son, Joseph M. Mundell was born in 1798 and a daughter, Frances, was born in 1801. (Prob. File M-17, Claiborne Co. Miss.) Frances (Minor) Mundell had died before 1806 when Andrew Mundell married (2) Mary (Smith) Dillingham, a daughter of Major David Smith, then of Ky., whose husband, Vachel Dillingham, Jr., had died in Ky. in 1803, leaving her a son, A. D. S. Dillingham, born Dec. 1799 and a daughter, Margaret Esther Dillingham, born before June 1803. (Will Bk. A 13, Ch. Co., Ky.) Mary Smith Dillingham had come down to Claiborne Co., Miss. Territory, with her two small children about 1804/5 to visit her sister, Sarah, wife of George Wilson Humphreys. She had one son by Andrew Mundell, named Abijah Hunt Mundell. Andrew Mundell died Jany. 22, 1817. To his son, Joseph, he left his gun and to daughter Frances a Bible and to them together "the property secured to them by a deed of gift by their uncle, Stephen Minor". (Will Bk. A, p. 69, Claib. Co., Miss.) In the settlement of his father's estate, Joseph Mundell states that he and his sister were entitled to nine slaves "by deed of gift from Stephen Minor" to his mother (Prob. File M-17, Claib. Co., Miss.) Joseph Mundell died unmarried on his plantation in Concordia Parish, La. in Dec. 1829. (Adams Co. Will Bk. 1, p. 487) Frances Mundell m. Dennis Burns, Jany. 6, 1825, in Claiborne Co., Miss. (Mar. Rec. Bk. B, p. 180)

MULKEY. Philip and David Mulkey were sons of the Rev. Philip Mulkey and his wife, Ann Ellis, of Fairforest Church in upper South Carolina. (S. C. Bpts. 125.) Philip, like his father, was evidently a Loyalist as he was in the Natchez District before 1781 when he was an instigator in the insurrection against the Spanish. After he escaped to South Carolina repeated threats of his contemplated return with troops were reported. (Kin II 12,16,17) David Mulkey came to the district later and was mentioned as Rev. Mulkey. He was in the 1792 Spanish Census. His descendants remained in the deep South for a period, an Ellis Mulkey having land in the Felicianas in 1806. (Nat. Rec.; ASP-PL III 56).

NELSON. Peter Nelson and his wife, Margaret, formerly the widow of Henry Lafleur, both made their wills on 19 Dec. 1812. These wills were very nearly the same, except for one item in which Peter Nelson willed to his wife, Margaret, one-half of his whole estate, real and personal. The other half he willed to their three children, Marson, Peter, Jr., and Catherine. Whereas Margaret left to their three children all of her estate except $5.00 to each of her five daughters by her first marriage, to whom Peter Nelson had also left the same amount. They had apparently received the property due to them from their father's estate. Peter Nelson's will was probated Apr. 8, 1817; Margaret Nelson's at the Nov. Term of Court, 1820. A lawsuit in 1830 indicates that Magdeline Lafleur m. Austin Holbrook, Margaret m. Lewis Sharberson, Mary m. John Craven, Ann m. James Tyler and Sarah m. James Clark. (Hen. 91, 330,332.)

RABB. John Nicholas Rabb was born in Wurtenberg, Germany. In 1776, after the death of his wife, he left that country with his four-year-old son, John, and his brother-in-law, George Fite, landing at Philadelphia. Later he removed to the Natchez District, where he lived [on Second Creek] until his death, leaving three sons, John, Nicholas and Peter. John, born in Germany, March 7, 1762, m. Cecelia Clark in 1797. Their children were: Elizabeth, Peter, Nicholas, John, William, Joseph, George A., Gabriel W., Francis B. and Mary Ann. (Above data from the Rabb Family Bible of Avaline Cecilia (Rabb) Whitaker (Mrs. Aquilla Whitaker), dau. of the above John, son of John, and gr-granddaughter of John Nicholas Rabb, copied in 1930 for Mrs. Hattie (Rabb) Blanchard, of Greenwood, Miss., a niece of Mrs. Whitaker.)

SMITH. After the Revolution, in which he fought in the militia for two years, David Smith and his little family, with his younger brother, William, set out for the Cumberland settlement from Montgomery Co., N. C. (estab. from Anson Co. in 1779), David in charge of the military guard for a large group of other settlers. (N. C. Rev. Sol. 486; Pension W24,006) Like many others, they landed in the Natchez District because they were unable to navigate their frail crafts against the swift current of the Ohio and perforce had to go downstream with it. (Kin II, 17.) David Smith's wife, formerly Margaret Terry of Anson Co., N. C., (McB. 116) died early in 1790 and a few months later he went to the Cumberland settlement (Nashville) with Andrew Jackson who was returning there to attend court. David Smith served as Captain under General Jackson both on the Natchez campaign and in the war against the Creeks. (Jack. Pap.) Sarah, his elder daughter, by his first marriage, married George Wilson Humphreys, and the younger dau., Mary (Polly) m. (1) Vachel Dillingham, of Ky., (2) Andrew Mundell, (3) David Gibson, both of Claiborne Co., Miss. (Gov. Hum.)

SMITH. Elnathan Smith, brother of Rev. Jedediah Smith (q.v.) In 1773, times being hard in Granville, Conn., where he and his wife, Hannah Bates, lived, Elnathan Smith joined an expedition to the Natchez District, West Florida, under the leadership of Gen. Phineas Lyman, leaving his wife and two small daughters with his brother. Lyman had recruited fifty adventurous followers to colonize a large grant of land he had secured from the British government in what is now Claiborne Co., Miss. But after their long and hazardous voyage, Elnathan acquired a desirable tract of land for himself in this new country. He prospered and wrote home urging his brother Jedediah to join him. Elnathan, however, died before Jedediah reached the District in 1776, bringing with him his wife and children as well as Elnathan's wife and two daughters. The daughters, Edith, b. 1767, m. (1) John Christian Buhler, of Baton Rouge, (2) Richard Devall, and Eunice, b. 1769, m. William Lilley. (La. 29 277-295).

SMITH. Rev. Jedediah Smith, brother of Elnathan (above) was born at Suffield, Conn., Jany. 1726; received a B. A. at Yale in 1750 and an M. A. degree in 1754. He was also ordained as a Presbyterian minister in 1754 and called to a church in Granville, Mass. the next year. He served this charge 21 years, at the end of which time his being a Loyalist estranged him from his congregation and he resigned the charge. Deciding to join his brother, Elnathan, in the British possessions on the Miss. River, with his wife and eleven of their twelve children and his brother, Elnathan's, wife and two daughters, they left Conn. about the middle of May 1776. The voyage was unspeakably rough and perilous but in about three months they reached New Orleans, only to be held in quarantine for a time and not allowed to land because of an epidemic of small-pox in that city. Eventually securing a small craft they began their journey up the river to Natchez. This trip was fraught with more trials and hardships. A clergyman with a wife and family was questioned sharply at each Spanish post. Knowing nothing of the Spanish language itself, Rev. Jedediah's knowledge of Latin had enabled him to converse in that ancient language, which however did not remove the stigma placed on him and family as heretics. At Loftus Heights, later Fort Adams, 38 miles below Natchez, Jedediah Smith learned of his brother's death. Overcome with grief, exposure and fatigue, he developed a fever. On 2 Sept. 1776, a week after the party landed at Natchez, this first Protestant minister to come to the Natchez District died and was buried on the high bluff overlooking the river. Sara (Cook) Smith, his widow survived the rough voyage, dying at Natchez in the 1790's. Their eldest son, Jedediah, remained in Mass. and one named Ebenezer died young. All the others married in the Natchez District and have many descendants in Louisiana and Mississippi. William m. Mrs. Nettles, no ch; Sarah, b. 1756, m. Joshua Alexander; Josephus, b. 1758, m. Patience Cobb; Richard Philetus, b. 1760, m. Mary Thompson, dau. of Richard Thompson (q.v.); Israel, b. 1763, m. (1) Sallie Cobb, (2) Jane Lorenza Doane; Philander, b. 1765, m. (1) Esther Brashiers, (2) Susannah (Miller) Scott; Philomena, b. June 4, 1766, m. David Mitchell; Calvin, b. 1768, m. (1) Patsy Baker, (2) Ann Eliza Davis, sister of Jefferson Davis, the Confederate president; Courtland, b. 1772, m. (1) Narcisse Boone, (2) Jane Boone. (La. 29 277-295.)

SMITH. Having heard of the fine lands in West Florida, John Smith came down from Pennsylvania in the fall of 1768 to have a look at them. Much pleased, on Dec. 8th, he petitions for 600 acres on the Mississippi River or wherever vacant, proposing to bring down his wife and family of five in the spring. The land was granted to him under the usual conditions, that is, his taking out the grant in 7 months and giving bond to settle in two years. (How. 97.) Since the above land grant identifies this John Smith as one who was prominent in the Villa Gayoso District [now in Jefferson Co., Miss.] (Nat. Rec.), the natural supposition that his "family of five" were his children is apparently erroneous. They might have been his parents and brothers and sisters, or his wife's. The seven children who survived him seem to have been born between 1775-1800. (Gentry Papers.) Also, in a deed, 26 Sept. 1770, in which he sold the above land grant, he was "now of Pensacola". (MPA-ED 49) This suggests that his wife might have died and he had fled the loneliness of the undeveloped plantation 24 miles from the old Natchez Fort. In 1776-7, there were, in the Province of West Florida, William Smith, Thomas Smith, Henry Smith, Sarah Smith and the above John Smith. Each of them petitioned for a land grant in the above years but no connection, one with another, is shown. (E (24) W. Fla.) On 26 May 1777, John Smith was granted 200 acres on the south branch of Boyd's Creek (later called Cole's Creek.) (MPA-ED 213.) In the insurrection of April 1781, John Smith was one of the leaders in an attempt to overthrow the Spanish rule and reestablish the British Government. For this, he was imprisoned in New Orleans for two years and then pardoned and allowed to return to his family and plantation. John Smith was successful in his undertakings, constantly adding to his holdings, both real and personal. He was held in high esteem not only by the community in which he lived but also by the Spanish officials at Natchez who appointed him alcalde of the Villa Gayoso District, deputizing him repeatedly to examine principals and witnesses. (Nat. Rec.) He died in 1804 and the division of his estate showed about 2000 acres, many slaves, cattle, etc. His wife was named Mary and his children were: Mary (Polly), wife of John Brooks, William who died soon after his father's death, Thomas, James, Anna Maria, who m. Thomas Lovell, Roxanna, who m. Pleasant Elam and John Poor Smith. The last four were minors in 1804. John Poor Smith m. (1) Frances ______, probably from Rutherford County, Tenn. as they lived there many years; (2) Sarah Wood, in Natchez, May 11, 1833. He died in Adams Co., Miss. in 1840, leaving his widow and the following children, James, Frances, Olivia, Roxanna and a posthumous child named J. Pinkney Smith. (Gentry Papers.)

STAMPLEY. Margaret Stampley, later recorded as the wife of Henry Stampley, (Nat. Rec.), on her petition, received a warrant for 100 acres from the British Govt., followed by a grant Sept. 1, 1777. (E (24) W. Fla.) However, she apparently applied for the grant in the name of Margaret Baird and it was so entered in the Surveyor General's Book, for the plats of both John Lum and John Smith, who received grants in 1778 and 1777 to land adjoining, show "Margaret Baird" as owning the tract which Henry Stampley and wife, Margaret, later sold to Thomas Green. Lum's grant lists the lands of John Smith and Margaret Baird as adjoining his tract. (MPA-ED 377). A James Baird, in 1776, received a warrant for 10,000 acres. (E (24) W. Fla.) He may have been the father of Margaret. Apparently the 2nd wife of Henry Stampley, she seemed to have property of her own as Stampley, in his will made no provision for her except that she might live on his plantation so long as she desired. (Nat. Rec.) It is recorded in the original minutes of the first Baptist church in the State of Mississippi that "at the request of Rev. Richard Curtis and William Thomas, the Baptists in the vicinity of Natchez, in October 1791, met at the house of Sister Stampley on Cole's Creek and formed into a body. Seven men and two women weht into the organization." The two women were Margaret Stampley and Ealiff Lanier. (Row. Hist. II 593) John Stampley, a son-in-law of Richard Curtis, Sr., came to the Natchez Dist. in 1780 with the Curtis family and their connections, all Baptists from S. C. (Miss. Bpts. 8) Henry Stampley was in this section by 1777 for the land grant to Margaret Stampley was issued Sept. 1st of that year.

THOMPSON. At a meeting of the Council of the Province of West Florida, 18 Dec. 1767, Richard Thompson's petition for 500 acres of land near Natchez was presented and he was granted 300 acres. (How. 84). However, on 25 Aug. 1770, he was issued a grant of 500 acres 4 miles southeast of Fort Panmure, 4 miles from the Mississippi River and bounded on all sides by vacant lands. (MPA-ED 106). On 6 Nov. 1776, again he petitioned for 300 acres and received a warrant for same. But he apparently did not live to get full possession of this tract. Letters of Admr. on the estate of Richard Thompson were issued to Philip Barbour on Feb. 11, 1778. The fees for this were 8 pounds, 5 shilling to the Gov. and 9 pounds 4 shillings to the Secy. (E (24) W. Fla.) On 16 Nov. 1778 William B. Smith married Ann, widow of Richard Thompson, after which he obtained letters of admr. on Thompson's estate, with Wm. Heson and Capt. Philip Barbour his sureties. Inv. and appraisal were taken Dec. 12, 1781 in the Natchez district. The heirs, children of Richard Thompson and wife, Ann: Mary 16, John 14, Sarah 12, Nathan 10, Thomas 8, Martha 6, Richard 4. In 1799, William Smith settled with all of the above heirs except Thomas and Richard, who may have died before that time. Mary had married Richard Philetus Smith, Sarah had married Solomon H. Wisdom, and Martha had married Hugh Coyle. (Nat. Rec.) It may be interesting to note that one of the papers in the settlement of the Richard Thompson estate was witnessed by Thompson Clack whose grandfather, Thomas Thomson, of Louisa Co., Va., in his will, 22 Apr. 1774 - 10 Oct. 1774, specified that should his son, Richard, or his heirs, not return in ten years to claim the land he left him that it was to go to other heirs. (Louisa Co. Will Bk. 2, pp. 202-204.) Thomson Clack and Jane Frazier, both of the Miss. Territory, were married 18 Sept. 1800 by Philander Smith, J. P. (Adams County Deed Bk. "B" p. 87)

THROCKMORTON. Robert Throckmorton m. June 16, 175_, Lucy ______. Children: (1) Robert, b. 175_, (2) Mary, b. Mar. 12, 1760, (3) Mordecai, b. Feb. 2, 1761, (4) Frances, b. Feb. 24, 1765, (5) Lucy, b. Jan. 15, 1767, (6) Elizabeth, b. Apr. 6, 1769, m. Ebenezer Potter, (7) Lewis Read, b. May 14, 1773. Ebenezer Potter and wife, Elizabeth Throckmorton, had dau. Lucy Throckmorton Potter, b. at Natchez, La. [now Mississippi] Jan. 10, 1793, d. at Leesburg, Va. 1870. She m. Dr. Charles Burgess Ball, who died 2 July 1823. (Hayden 134)

TRULY-HOLT. In the Virginia Gazette of Sept. 5, 1771, Robert Montford, David Holt and Debdal Holt announced their intention of leaving the country for a few months. Debdal Holt, having been sent by a number of people in Virginia to inspect the lands on the Mississippi, was evidently accompanied to West Florida by the other two men. They liked the country and were promised a large slice of land on the river. (Johnson 139) In 1773 the party came to the Natchez District to settle. (Carter V 115) With Debdal Holt and his family were David Holt and their sister, Sarah Truly, and her family, including her son-in-law, Francis Spain, his wife and young children. Hector Truly, Sarah's husband, had died in

Amelia County, Va., in 1761, leaving, besides his wife, formerly Sarah Holt, three sons, John, James and Bennet and four daughters, Ellinah [Eleanor], Sarah, Judith and Patsy [Martha]. Of these, John remained in Virginia. Eleanor had married, in Amelia County, May 28, 1761, Francis Spain. (W (1) 17 37) Sarah Truly was a rather remarkable woman, remaining the real head of her family until her death in 1792/3. Her will was dated March 15, 1792 and an agreement on the division of her estate, 7 May 1793. (Nat. Rec.) On April 5, 1776, Sarah Truly petitioned the British Govt. of West Florida for 500 acres and received a warrant for the same. On Nov. 6th of that year, Dibdell Holt petitioned for 1000 acres, also receiving a warrant. Both of these warrants were renewed Oct. 11, 1777, which was often done in lieu of paying the larger fees for a grant at that time. However there is no record of British grants being issued for the lands for which the above warrants had been given. (E (24) W. Fla.) Doubtless the expulsion of the British from the Natchez District by the Spanish intervened. The 600-acre Spanish grant to Debdal Holt and the 225 acres granted Sarah Truly probably covered parts of the same tracts. (Nat. Rec.) Sarah Truly, the second daughter of Hector and Sarah Truly, married Richard Harrison, the first record of whom, in West Florida, is in April 1778 when he was a Lieutenant under Capt. James Willing's command and "on duty up the River". (Kin. I 264) On July 7th of that year, Richard Harrison was in New Orleans writing to Oliver Pollock, Esq. as "Agent of the Continental Congress of America, in whose service I have the honor to be", concerning his uncle, Capt. Phillip Barbour, who had been in prison at Pensacola since June 11th, "betrayed into the hands of the enemy by Morgan and Mather." (Kin. I 294-5) Phillip Barbour was released but just when is not stated. He and Richard Harrison witnessed a deed in Natchez on July 20, 1779. In the meanwhile, at New Orleans, Aug. 18, 1778, Capt. Robert George and Lieut. R. G. Harrison write to Governor Galvez, acknowledging his permission to march their party of men through the Spanish Territories, on condition that they should not attack any part of the British Dominions or their subjects or property en route. (Kin. I 303-4) Before leaving New Orleans, they were given a letter from Capt. James Willing to Col. George Rogers Clark, saying: "This will be handed you by Capt. Robert George and Lieut. Richard Harrison to whom I have given command of a party of Continental troops to pass through the Spanish Country unto the Kaskaskias where I understand you have the Honor to Command and there join you untill further orders from Congress or Genl. Hand." (Ill. 8 Va. Ser. III. George Roger Clark Papers, 1771-1786. p. 66). A list of the officers of the "Illinois Regiment of Volunteers" under command of Col. George Rogers Clark shows "Richard Harrison, Captain, for bounty as Lieutenant and Captain for 3 years, received 2666 acres, April 1784." (Ill. 8 p. 106). Richard Harrison died Dec. 29, 1799 and his children were: Philip B. Harrison, Richard Harrison, Hay Battaile Harrison, Mabella Harrison, wife of James Dunbar, Caroline Harrison, who married _______ Dougherty and had one child, Philip B. Dougherty. (Brum. Va. 594) After the death of Sarah, his first wife, Richard Harrison married her youngest sister, Martha (Patsy) Truly. (Nat. Rec.) James Truly married Elizabeth, widow of Samuel Burch. It is said that James Truly went back to Virginia and served with the State troops in the Revolution. No record is available on this but that his sympathies were with the American troops is shown in an account of his having led a detachment of Willing's soldiers to the house of Alexander McIntosh in February 1778. (Ellicott's Journal 130) Bennet Truly married Mary Lum and Judith Truly married one of the sons of Stephen Holstein. (The above largely by courtesy of Mrs. Adlai Morgan.)

WEST. Cato West, a native of Fairfax County, Va., was son-in-law of Thomas Green, the elder, emigrating with him to Georgia (Cl. 212) and then to South Carolina where they lived on the Wateree before going to the Natchez District. (Nat. Rec.) Here, with 32 other men, Cato West volunteered in writing, addressed to "Mr. Robert Ellison, between the Wateree and Congaree Rivers on Simpson's Creek" "to make up a company to march to any part of the Province to defend it against the enemies of its liberty", dated 2nd Sept. 1775. A list of officers and men follow, with Robert Ellison captain. (S. C. I 195-6).

WISDOM. Solomon Hiram Wisdom married before 1799 Sarah, daughter of Richard and Ann Thompson. (See Richard Thompson.) Will of William Cook, Sept. 10, 1798. Legatees: Solomon H. Wisdom 500 acres on Bayou Sara, "bequeathed to me by John Mathews, whose will is on record in Westmoreland County, Pa."; John Jackson also a legatee. (King. Adams Co. Will Bk. 1) On 11 Nov. 1818, John Smith and wife, Margaret (Wisdom) Smith, sell to John Harbour 300 acres on Thompson Cr. in West Feliciana Par., La. adj. lands of Joseph Robinson, Mrs. C. Turnbull, John Harbour and part of the original tract gr. to William Cook by the Spanish Govt. in April 1797. Later Margaret Wisdom Smith confirms the 200 acres remaining in the tract to Mary (Dalton) Harbour, widow of John Harbour, for $500. Wm. Wisdom was one of the witnesses. (W. Fel. Par. Deed Bks. B p. 10, C p. 36.)

WILLIS. Henry Willis, son of Col. Lewis Willis, of Spottsylvania Co., Va., and his 1st wife, Mary Champe, m. before 1791 Anne Savage, of the Natchez District. (W (1) 6 209) She was the daughter of

John Savage, deceased, and his wife, Anne Gaillard. The Gaillards, formerly of South Carolina, had large holdings there and in the Natchez District. Anne Willis died in 1791, her husband inheriting her property. (Nat. Rec.) Henry Willis m. (2) Sarah ______ and died in Georgia a few years later. By his will he left his property to his wife and their infant son, Lewis Willis, to be divided equally. After his death, his wife gave birth to a posthumous daughter, Anna S. Willis, and after her birth, their son, Lewis Willis died, an infant intestate. Henry Willis died in 1794 and Sarah, his widow, in 1797 married John Chotard. Sarah F. Chotard, whose husband, John Chotard, was dead, filed a bill in Circuit Court of Tuscaloosa, Alabama, charging that Henry Willis, her 1st husband, was entitled to certain lands on Bayou Sara [Natchez Dist.] which were sold by the United States Government. Anna S. Willis m. Josiah M. McComas. (Gandrud III 81 Alabama Reports I 421.) This case not dated but the claim was presented to the House of Representatives at the 2nd Session of the 15th Congress on Jany. 18, 1819 with the recommendation that the petition be not granted. However, at the first session of the next Congress, on Feb. 7, 1820, it was decided that the petitioners were entitled to relief, not confirmation of the title to the lands claimed but to a substitutation in the same district. (ASP-PL IV 362,373.)

BIBLIOGRAPHY

Unpublished Source Materials.

Official Documents, National, State, County and Miscellaneous.

Written Evidences of Land Claims in the Mississippi Territory West of the Pearl River. National Archives, Interior Dept., Washington, D. C.

Revolutionary Pension Papers. Pension Bureau. National Archives, Washington, D. C.

(MPA-ED) Mississippi Provincial Archives, English Dominion, 1765-1783. Dept. of Archives and History, Jackson, Miss.

(MPA-SD) Mississippi Provincial Archives, Spanish Dominion, Vols. I, III. Dept. of Archives and History, Jackson, Miss.

(MTA-I-A) Mississippi Territorial Archives. Series A, Vol. 1. Winthrop Sargent Papers. Dept. of Archives and History, Jackson, Miss.

Georgia Revolutionary Grants. Dept. of Archives and History, Atlanta, Ga.

County Court Records of:

Christian County, Kentucky, at Hopkinsville.

Nelson County, Kentucky, at Bardstown.

East Baton Rouge Parish, Louisiana, at Baton Rouge.

West Feliciana Parish, Louisiana, at St. Francisville.

Adams County, Mississippi, at Natchez.

Claiborne County, Mississippi, at Port Gibson.

Wilkinson County, Mississippi, at Woodville.

Davidson County, N. C. (Tenn.), at Nashville. (microfilm)

Washington County, N. C. (Tenn.), at Jonesboro. (microfilm)

Fauquier County, Virginia, at Warrenton.

Frederick County, Virginia, at Winchester.

Louisa County, Virginia, at Louisa.

(E (24) W Fla) Provincial Records of British West Florida, Manuscript Division, Library of Congress, Washington, D. C.

Jackson Papers, Manuscript Division, Library of Congress, Washington, D. C.

The Minor Collection, Louisiana Archives, Louisiana State University, Baton Rouge, La.

The Autobiography of Governor Benjamin G. Humphreys of Mississippi. Privately owned.

The Gentry Papers, Jefferson County, Miss. Court Records of the Smith, Brooks and Foster families. Mr. F. M. Gentry, Manhasset, New York.

Published Source Materials.

(ASP-PL) American State Papers. Public Lands, Vols. I, II, III and IV.

(Carter) Territorial Papers of the United States. Mississippi Vol. V. Edited by C. E. Carter.

(How.) The British Development of West Florida, 1763-1769, by Clinton H. Howard.

(Johnson) British West Florida, 1763-1783, by Cecil Johnson.
Spain in the Mississippi Valley, 1765-1794, by Lawrence Kinniard.
The Journal of Andrew Ellicott, Late Commissioner on Behalf of the United States during part of 1796.
(Brum.) Revolutionary War Records. Vol. 1. Va. By G. M. Brumbaugh.
(Chalk.) Records of Augusta County, Virginia. 3 volumes. By Lyman Chalkley.
(Del.) Calendar of Delaware Wills, New Castle County. By Colonial Dames of Delaware.
(Hen.) Mississippi Court Records, 1799-1859, by Louise Hendrix.
(King.) Mississippi Court Records, by Estelle Stewart King.
(McB.) Anson County, North Carolina. Abstracts of Early Records. Compiler, May Wilson McBee.

Other published materials.

(Cl.) Mississippi as a Province, Territory and State, by Claiborne.
History of Mississippi, 2 vols. by Dunbar Rowland.
Mississippi Cyclopedia, 2 vols. by Dunbar Rowland.
(E.T. 8) East Tennessee Historical Society's Publications, No. 8.
(Ill.) Illinois Historical Library Publication Vol. VIII.
Illinois Historical Library Collections. Va. Series Vol. III.
(La.) Louisiana Historical Quarterly.
(S.C.) South Carolina Historical Magazine.
(Va.) The Virginia Magazine.
(W(1)) William and Mary Quarterly, first Series.
(Shen. Way.) History of Shenandoah County, Va., by Wayland.
A Gentleman of the Old Natchez Region, Benj. L. C. Wailes, by Charles S. Sydnor.
South Carolina Baptists, by Leah Townsend.
North Carolina Revolutionary Soldiers.
(Marchand) The Flight of a Century, by Sidney A. Marchand.
(Hays) Hero of Hornet's Nest, a Biography of General Elijah Clarke, by Louise F. Hays.
Memoirs of Mississippi by Goodspeed. 2 volumes.
Mississippi Baptists, by L. S. Foster.
The West Florida Rebellion, by Stanley C. Arthur.
Jersey Settlers, by Henry B. Eaton.
History of Russellville and Logan County, Kentucky, by Alexander F. Finley.
Savage's Genealogical Dictionary of New England.
Hayden's Virginia Genealogies.

INDEX

The names of the functionaries of the Spanish Government in the Natchez District are not given in the index. So many were present at the court hearings before the Commandant a listing would be repetitious and of no special value. As the NOTES were not ready in time to be indexed the families included therein are listed alphabetically and the material may be easily scanned for desired information.

Abbreviations: b., brother; d., deceased; da., daughter; est., estate; f., father; h., husband; m., mother; m.c., marriage contract; s., sister; w., wife; wid., widow.

****

****

****

****

****

****

****

Places

www.ingramcontent.com/pod-product-compliance
Ingram Content Group UK Ltd.
Pitfield, Milton Keynes, MK11 3LW, UK
UKHW020122290926
15471UKWH00003B/226

9 780806 314525